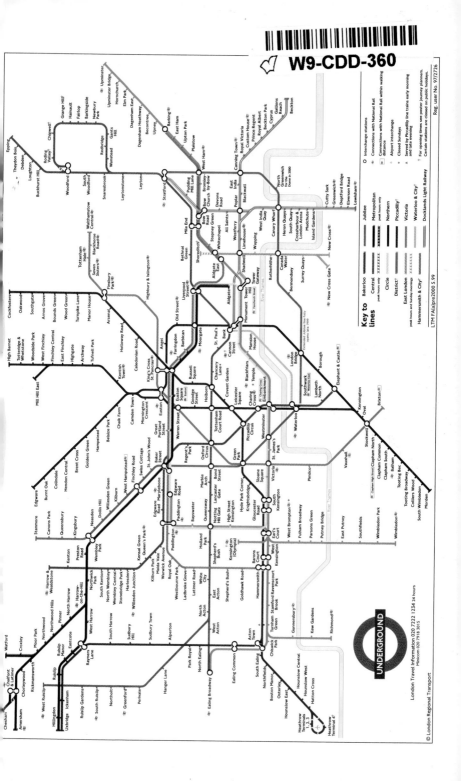

W9-CDD-360

Reg. user No. 97/2726

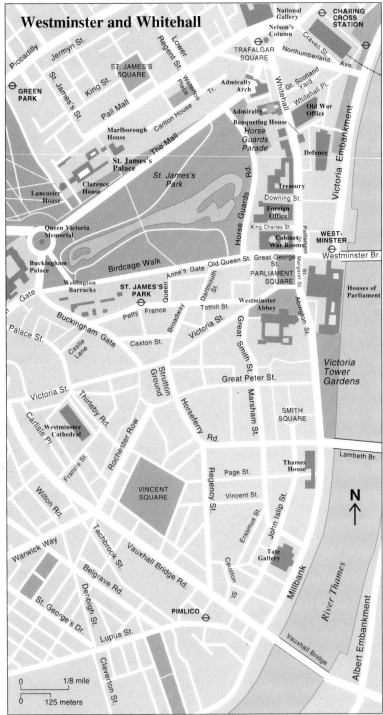

Westminster and Whitehall

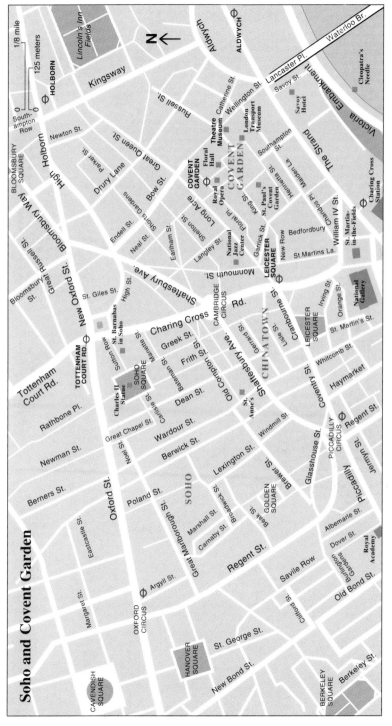

Soho and Covent Garden

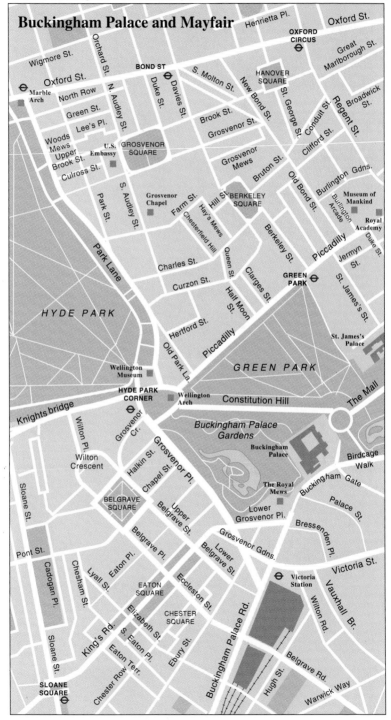

Buckingham Palace and Mayfair

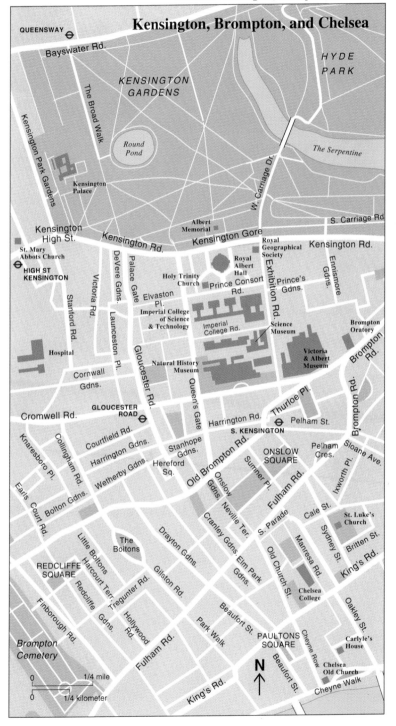

Kensington, Brompton, and Chelsea

QUEENSWAY

Bayswater Rd.

HYDE PARK

KENSINGTON GARDENS

The Broad Walk

Kensington Park Gardens

Round Pond

Kensington Palace

The Serpentine

W. Carriage Dr.

S. Carriage Rd.

Kensington High St.

Kensington Rd.

Albert Memorial

Kensington Gore

Royal Geographical Society

Kensington Rd.

St. Mary Abbots Church

HIGH ST KENSINGTON

DeVere Gdns.

Palace Gate

Royal Albert Hall

Ennismore Gdns.

Victoria Rd.

Holy Trinity Church

Prince Consort Rd.

Prince's Gdns.

Stanford Rd.

Launceston Pl.

Elvaston Pl.

Imperial College of Science & Technology

Imperial College Rd.

Science Museum

Exhibition Rd.

Brompton Oratory

Hospital

Gloucester Rd.

Natural History Museum

Victoria & Albert Museum

Brompton Rd.

Cornwall Gdns.

Queen's Gate

Thurloe Pl.

Cromwell Rd.

GLOUCESTER ROAD

Harrington Rd.

Pelham St.

Knaresboro Pl.

Collingham Rd.

Courtfield Rd.

S. KENSINGTON

Harrington Gdns.

Stanhope Gdns.

Old Brompton Rd.

ONSLOW SQUARE

Pelham Cres.

Sloane Ave.

Earls Court Rd.

Harrington Gdns.

Wetherby Gdns.

Hereford Sq.

Summer Pl.

Fulham Rd.

Ixworth Pl.

Bolton Gdns.

Onslow Gdns.

Neville Ter.

S. Parade

Cale St.

Sydney St.

St. Luke's Church

Britten St.

Little Boltons

The Boltons

Drayton Gdns.

Cranley Gdns.

Elm Park Gdns.

Old Church St.

Manresa Rd.

King's Rd.

REDCLIFFE SQUARE

Harcourt Terr.

Tregunter Rd.

Gilston Rd.

Redcliffe Gdns.

Hollywood Rd.

Chelsea College

Oakley St.

Finborough Rd.

Park Walk

Beaufort St.

PAULTONS SQUARE

Cheyne Row

Carlyle's House

Brompton Cemetery

Fulham Rd.

King's Rd.

Beaufort St.

Chelsea Old Church

Cheyne Walk

N

0   1/4 mile

0   1/4 kilometer

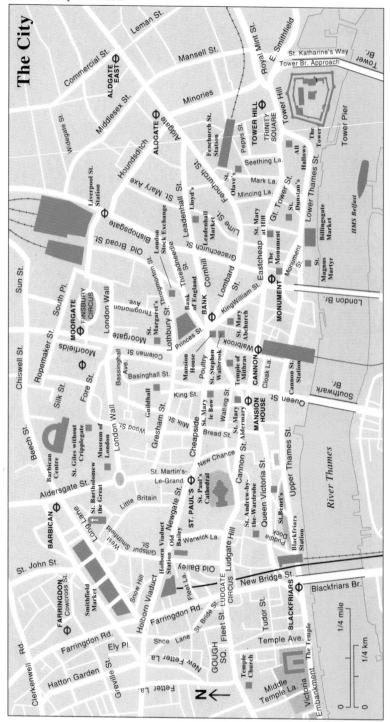

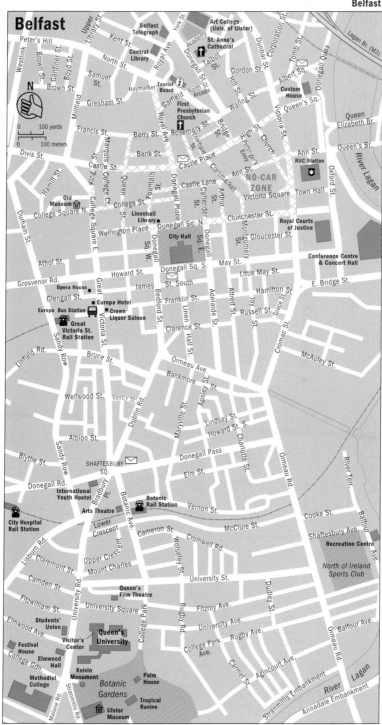

Belfast

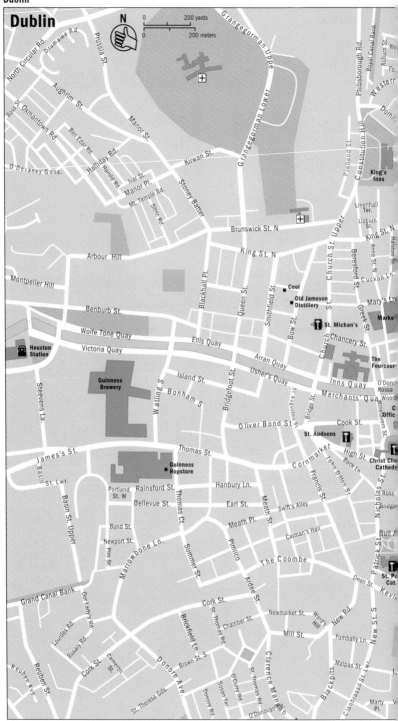

Cork and Galway

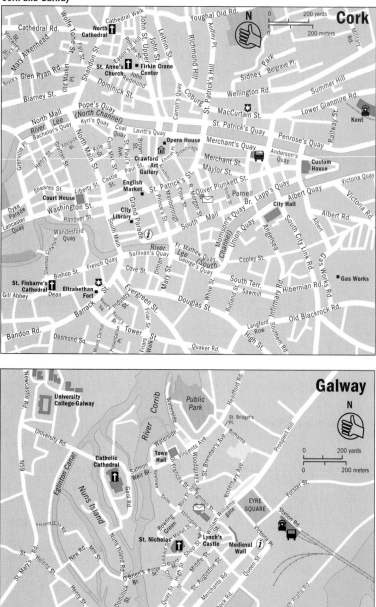

Cork

Galway

Let's Go writers travel on your budget.

"Guides that penetrate the veneer of the holiday brochures and mine the grit of real life."

—The Economist

"The writers seem to have experienced every rooster-packed bus and lunar-surfaced mattress about which they write."

—The New York Times

"All the dirt, dirt cheap."

—People

Great for independent travelers.

"The guides are aimed not only at young budget travelers but at the independent traveler; a sort of streetwise cookbook for traveling alone."

—The New York Times

"A guide should tell you what to expect from a destination. Here *Let's Go* shines."
—The Chicago Tribune

"An indispensible resource, *Let's Go*'s practical information can be used by every traveler."

—The Chattanooga Free Press

Let's Go is completely revised each year.

"A publishing phenomenon...the only major guidebook series updated annually. *Let's Go* is the big kahuna."

—The Boston Globe

"Unbeatable: good sight-seeing advice; up-to-date info on restaurants, hotels, and inns; a commitment to money-saving travel; and a wry style that brightens nearly every page."

—The Washington Post

All the important information you need.

"*Let's Go* authors provide a comedic element while still providing concise information and thorough coverage of the country. Anything you need to know about budget traveling is detailed in this book."

—The Chicago Sun-Times

"*Let's Go* guidebooks take night life seriously."

—The Chicago Tribune

Let's Go Publications

Let's Go: Alaska & the Pacific Northwest 2002
Let's Go: Amsterdam 2002 **New Title!**
Let's Go: Australia 2002
Let's Go: Austria & Switzerland 2002
Let's Go: Barcelona 2002 **New Title!**
Let's Go: Boston 2002
Let's Go: Britain & Ireland 2002
Let's Go: California 2002
Let's Go: Central America 2002
Let's Go: China 2002
Let's Go: Eastern Europe 2002
Let's Go: Egypt 2002 **New Title!**
Let's Go: Europe 2002
Let's Go: France 2002
Let's Go: Germany 2002
Let's Go: Greece 2002
Let's Go: India & Nepal 2002
Let's Go: Ireland 2002
Let's Go: Israel 2002
Let's Go: Italy 2002
Let's Go: London 2002
Let's Go: Mexico 2002
Let's Go: Middle East 2002
Let's Go: New York City 2002
Let's Go: New Zealand 2002
Let's Go: Paris 2002
Let's Go: Peru, Ecuador & Bolivia 2002
Let's Go: Rome 2002
Let's Go: San Francisco 2002
Let's Go: South Africa with Southern Africa 2002
Let's Go: Southeast Asia 2002
Let's Go: Southwest USA 2002 **New Title!**
Let's Go: Spain & Portugal 2002
Let's Go: Turkey 2002
Let's Go: USA 2002
Let's Go: Washington, D.C. 2002
Let's Go: Western Europe 2002

Let's Go *Map Guides*

Amsterdam	New Orleans
Berlin	New York City
Boston	Paris
Chicago	Prague
Dublin	Rome
Florence	San Francisco
Hong Kong	Seattle
London	Sydney
Los Angeles	Venice
Madrid	Washington, D.C.

BRITAIN & IRELAND

2002

Matthew B. Sussman editor
Kate D. Nesin associate editor

researcher-writers
Matthew D. Firestone
Nathaniel D. Myers
Jennifer O'Brien
A. Morgan Rodman
Robert Willison

Julia Stephens map editor
Brian R. Walsh managing editor

St. Martin's Press ✼ New York

HELPING LET'S GO If you want to share your discoveries, suggestions, or corrections, please drop us a line. We read every piece of correspondence, whether a postcard, a 10-page email, or a coconut. Please note that mail received after May 2002 may be too late for the 2003 book, but will be kept for future editions. **Address mail to:**

> **Let's Go: Britain & Ireland**
> **67 Mount Auburn Street**
> **Cambridge, MA 02138**
> **USA**

Visit Let's Go at **http://www.letsgo.com,** or send email to:

> **feedback@letsgo.com**
> **Subject: "Let's Go: Britain & Ireland"**

In addition to the invaluable travel advice our readers share with us, many are kind enough to offer their services as researchers or editors. Unfortunately, our charter enables us to employ only currently enrolled Harvard students.

HOW TO USE THIS BOOK

"Goddag! Erik Bloodaxe the Norseman here. Some Viking mates of mine and I set sail on the North Sea for a little cruise a while back, and before we knew it we were here in Britannia, so we figured we might as well loot and pillage a bit, to prove we'd actually been somewhere on our vacation rather than just sailing the high seas aimlessly, drinking mead and mucking about. (You know how it is—the folks back home always demand souvenirs and mementos, plundered gold, charred wood from torched cottages, that sort of thing.) Turns out we liked this Britannia tolerably well, and thought we'd stay a while.

"Once you get here, so should you! Just look at what you're holding—this, my friends, is a copy of *Let's Go: Britain and Ireland 2002*, the most comprehensive budget travel guide ever written about these isles. I wish I'd had one of these when I arrived. All my mates and I had were longswords and a boat. We didn't know how to greet the natives, so we burned their towns! You, on the other hand, are armed with a handy-dandy yellow book, so you shouldn't make our mistake. The first chapter, **Discover Britain and Ireland,** provides you with an overview of these rain-driven plots o' land, including **Suggested Itineraries.** The **Essentials** section is full of vital information about where to get the leak in your ship mended and how to spend your gold effectively. If my comrades Olaf and Thorleifur could read, I'd make them read it! Learn something about this strange and sheep-strewn land and its strange and sheep-strewn people in the next section, **England,** featuring Vikings and all our historical friends (not to mention some enemies), as well as news of what verses the bards have been reciting lately. Introductory chapters specific to **Wales, Scotland, Northern Ireland,** and the **Republic of Ireland** follow later.

"The remainder of the book is divided into places that we Vikings have raided and settled in, and places that we haven't. Well, actually, there aren't any that we haven't raided, but we didn't settle in Wales. For instance, **England,** land of lush valleys, adorable little villages, and monasteries ripe for the taking, we sacked. **Wales,** home to bright, windy beaches, we looted, but not for long. **Scotland,** birthplace of haggis, we also looted, and for considerably longer. **Northern Ireland** we plundered. The **Republic of Ireland** we robbed of everything we could find, then we settled in Dublin. The **black tabs** in the margins will help you to navigate between chapters quickly and easily, while the **Appendix** contains useful **conversions** and a **glossary** of handy phrases in the many semi-intelligible languages these barbarians speak.

"My Viking friends and I have arranged all the information about towns in an elegant, easy-to-plunder manner for your gold-seeking pleasure. In each section (accommodations, food, sights, entertainment, and so on), we list sleeping barns, meadhouses, forts, and minstrel fairs in order from best to not-quite-as-super. Our absolute favorites are so denoted by the highest honor given out, the *Let's Go* thumbs-up (◙). I would have preferred a two-horned helmet in miniature, but there you have it. The **phone code** for each region, city, or town appears opposite the name and is denoted by the ☎ icon. **Phone numbers** in text are also usually preceded by the ☎ icon. **Grayboxes** at times provide wonderful cultural insight, at times simply crude humor. (We Vikings like crude humor. We're so crude we drink mead out of skulls! But I digress.) **Whiteboxes,** on the other hand, provide important practical information, such as warnings (⚠) and helpful hints and further resources (◧). I think that's about it for now. Happy looting and pillaging!"

......in Central London

WESTPOINT HOTEL
170-172 Sussex Gardens
Hyde Park London W2 1TP
Tel: (020) 7402 0281
Fax: (020) 7224 9114
www.westpointhotel.com
e-mail info@westpointhotel.com

- ☑ Pleasant central location
- ☑ Convenient for all major sights, museums & theatres
- ☑ Close to all shopping districts, Oxford Street & Piccadilly Circus
- ☑ Clean, comfortable, well-decorated rooms
- ☑ All rooms with ensuite shower, toilet, colour TV & radio
- ☑ Lift to all floors, free daytime luggage room facility
- ☑ 2 minutes from Paddington station & Heathrow Express
- ☑ 4 minutes from Lancaster Court tube station & Airbus

ABBEY COURT HOTEL
174 Sussex Gardens
Hyde Park London W2 1TP
Tel: (020) 7402 0704
Fax: (020) 7262 2055
www.abbeycourt.com
e-mail info@abbeycourt.com

- ☑ Convenient location 2 minutes from Paddington station & Heathrow Express, & 4 minutes from Airbus
- ☑ Easy access to all London's important tourist sights, shopping districts and theatres
- ☑ Ensuite shower and w.c. in all rooms
- ☑ Lift to all floors
- ☑ Each room with colour TV, radio & intercom
- ☑ Car parking by arrangement

SASS HOTEL
11 Craven Terrace
Hyde Park London W2 3QD
Tel: (020) 7262 2325
Fax: (020) 7262 0889
www.sasshotel.com
e-mail info@sasshotel.com

Sass Hotel offers superb value for money accommodations in a convenient, quiet location, just 3 minutes walk from Hyde Park, Lancaster Gate tube station with Heathrow Express is just 5 minutes away. Easy access to all London's famous sights and entertainment.

- ☑ All rooms with ensuite shower, toilet & colour TV
- ☑ Friendly personal service
- ☑ Car parking by arrangement

RATES Per Person per night	Low Season	High season
Singles	from £48	from £56
Doubles	from £32	from £37
Triples	from £26	from £28
Family Room	from £22	from £24

FROM £22

RATES Per Person per night	Low Season	High season
Singles	from £48	from £56
Doubles	from £32	from £37
Triples	from £26	from £28
Family Room	from £22	from £24

FROM £22

RATES Per Person per night	Low Season	High season
Singles	from £35	from £48
Doubles	from £24	from £28
Triples	from £23	from £26
Family Room	from £21	from £24

FROM £21

ALL PRICES INCLUDE COMPLIMENTARY CONTINENTAL BREAKFAST, SERVICE CHARGE & ALL TAXES

CONTENTS

MAPS

Britain & Ireland: Regional

✚ Hospital	✈ Airport	🏛 Museum	▲ Mountain
🚨 Police	🚌 Bus Station	🛏 Hotel/Hostel	
✉ Post Office	🚂 Train Station	⛺ Camping	⬜ Park
ⓘ Tourist Office	Ⓜ METRO STATION	🍎 Food & Drink	
💲 Bank	⚓ Ferry Landing	🛍 Shopping	⬜ Beach
🏛 Embassy/Consulate	⛪ Church	♪ Club or Music Venue	
▪ Site or Point of Interest	✡ Synagogue	🍺 Pub	⬜ Water
☎ Telephone Office	🕌 Mosque	💻 Internet Café	
🎭 Theater	♖ Castle	⋯ Pedestrian Zone	The Let's Go thumb always points NORTH.

ABOUT LET'S GO

FORTY-TWO YEARS OF WISDOM

For over four decades, travelers crisscrossing the continents have relied on *Let's Go* for inside information on the hippest backstreet cafes, the most pristine secluded beaches, and the best routes from border to border. *Let's Go: Europe*, now in its 42nd edition and translated into seven languages, reigns as the world's bestselling international travel guide. In the last 20 years, our rugged researchers have stretched the frontiers of backpacking and expanded our coverage into the Americas, Australia, Asia, and Africa (including the new *Let's Go: Egypt* and the more comprehensive, multi-country jaunt through *Let's Go: South Africa & Southern Africa*). Our new-and-improved City Guide series continues to grow with new guides to perennial European favorites Amsterdam and Barcelona. This year we are also unveiling *Let's Go: Southwest USA*, the flagship of our new outdoor Adventure Guide series, which is complete with special roadtripping tips and itineraries, more coverage of adventure activities like hiking and mountain biking, and first-person accounts of life on the road.

It all started in 1960 when a handful of well-traveled students at Harvard University handed out a 20-page mimeographed pamphlet offering a collection of their tips on budget travel to passengers on student charter flights to Europe. The following year, in response to the instant popularity of the first volume, students traveling to Europe researched the first full-fledged edition of *Let's Go: Europe*. Throughout the 60s and 70s, our guides reflected the times—in 1969, for example, we taught you how to get from Paris to Prague on "no dollars a day" by singing in the street. In the 90s we focused in on the world's most exciting urban areas to produce in-depth, fold-out map guides, now with 20 titles (from Hong Kong to Chicago) and counting. Our new guides bring the total number of titles to 57, each infused with the spirit of adventure and voice of opinion that travelers around the world have come to count on. But some things never change: our guides are still researched, written, and produced entirely by students who know first-hand how to see the world on the cheap.

HOW WE DO IT

Each guide is completely revised and thoroughly updated every year by a well-traveled set of nearly 300 students. Every spring, we recruit over 200 researchers and 90 editors to overhaul every book. After several months of training, researcher-writers hit the road for seven weeks of exploration, from Anchorage to Adelaide, Estonia to El Salvador, Iceland to Indonesia. Hired for their rare combination of budget travel sense, writing ability, stamina, and courage, these adventurous travelers know that train strikes, stolen luggage, food poisoning, and marriage proposals are all part of a day's work. Back at our offices, editors work from spring to fall, massaging copy written on Himalayan bus rides into witty, informative prose. A student staff of typesetters, cartographers, publicists, and managers keeps our lively team together. In September, the collected efforts of the summer are delivered to our printer, who turns them into books in record time, so that you have the most up-to-date information available for your vacation. Even as you read this, work on next year's editions is well underway.

WHY WE DO IT

We don't think of budget travel as the last recourse of the destitute; we believe that it's the only way to travel. Our books will ease your anxieties and answer your questions about the basics—so you can get off the beaten track and explore. Once you learn the ropes, we encourage you to put *Let's Go* down and strike out on your own. You know as well as we that the best discoveries are often those you make yourself. When you find something worth sharing, please drop us a line. We're Let's Go Publications, 67 Mount Auburn St., Cambridge, MA 02138, USA (feedback@letsgo.com). For more info, visit our website, www.letsgo.com.

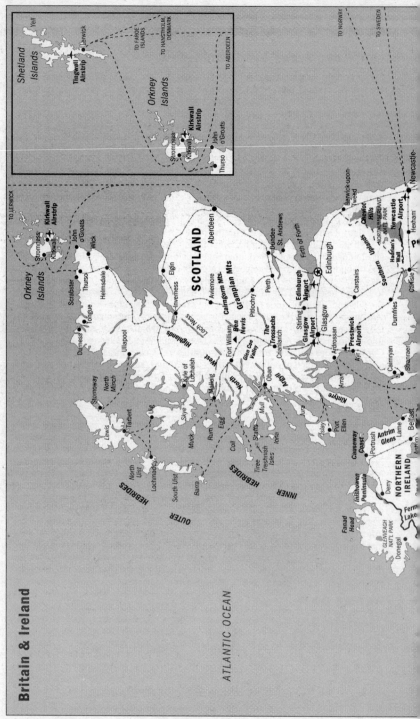

Britain & Ireland

ATLANTIC OCEAN

SCOTLAND

Shetland Islands

Yell
Lerwick
Tingwall Airstrip

TO FAROE ISLANDS
TO HANSTHOLM, DENMARK
TO ABERDEEN

Orkney Islands

Kirkwall Airstrip
Stromness
Kirkwall
John o'Groats
Thurso

TO NORWAY
TO SWEDEN

TO LERWICK

Orkney Islands

Kirkwall Airstrip
Stromness
Kirkwall
John o'Groats
Wick

Scrabster
Durness
Thurso
Tongue
Helmsdale

Ullapool

Stornoway
Lewis
North Minch

Tarbert
Uig

North Uist
Lochmaddy
South Uist
Barra

HEBRIDES
OUTER
HEBRIDES
INNER

Coll
Tiree
Treshnish Isles
Iona
Staffa
Mull
Muck
Eigg
Rum
Skye
Kyle of Lochalsh

Highlands
Loch Ness
Inverness
Elgin

Aviemore
Cairngorm Mts
Grampian Mts

Aberdeen
Dundee
St. Andrews
Firth of Forth

Fort William
Ben Nevis
West
Glen Coe Valley
The Trossachs
Crianlarich
Oban
Mallaig
North
A&Sul

Pitlochry
Perth
Stirling
Edinburgh Airport
Edinburgh
Glasgow Airport
Glasgow
Carstairs

Jura
Islay
Port Ellen
Kintyre
Arran
Ardrossan
Prestwick Airport
Ayr

Carnlough
Stranraer
Dumfries
Southern Uplands
Carlisle
Hadrian's Wall
Hexham
NORTHUMBERLAND NAT'L PARK
Cheviot Hills
Newcastle Airport
Newcastle

Berwick-upon-Tweed

Causeway Coast
Portrush
Antrim Glens
Larne
Belfast

Inishowen Peninsula
Fanad Head
Derry
Donegal
GLENVEAGH NAT'L PARK
Fermanagh Lakes
Antrim

NORTHERN IRELAND

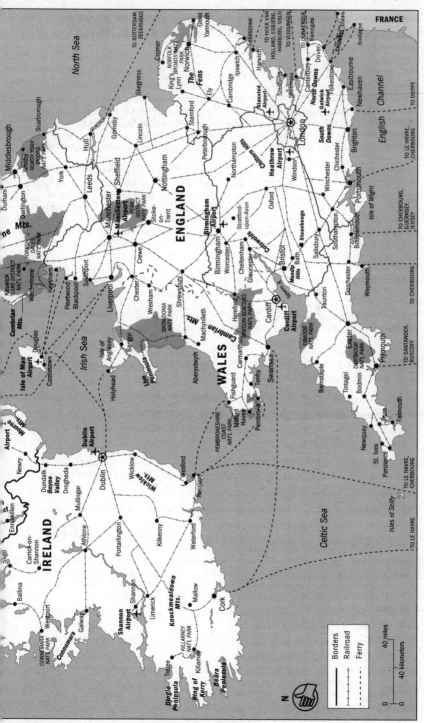

RESEARCHER-WRITERS

Matthew D. Firestone   *Northeast and Northwest England, Southern and Central Scotland*

If anyone was born to work for *Let's Go*, it's Matt: we've never seen such unbridled enthusiasm at the sight of livestock pyres and mint bars. Boundlessly energetic, this insatiable travel-lover hopped fences and broke quarantine to do the most thorough research imaginable, dashing off grayboxes like so many Cumbrian lakes. We thought he'd hit fever pitch in Newcastle, conquering the city with a pro's finesse and marginalia that flowed like the Wear. Little did we know he'd become an Edinburgh celebrity, deservedly worshiped as a *Let's Go* prophet and beloved in whatever circles he moved.

Nathaniel D. Myers   *Wales, Midlands, Northwest England*

Dylan Thomas, step aside: is that a hurricane siren we hear? With the worldly insight of a professional traveler, Nat soared through Wales like a pack of air-mailed pretzels, seasoned with elegant turns of phrase yet threatening to break under so much beauty. From the hippest hostel to the best Caernarfon curry, all competed gamely for his coveted *Let's Go* thumb, dispensed with formidable profundity and care. The only things more reliable than Nat's rock-solid copy were his terrific sense of humor and unflagging appreciation for accuracy.

Jennifer O'Brien   *South and Northeast England, Heart of England, East Anglia, Midlands*

Beleaguered by warring schoolchildren, tyrannical B&B owners, and the imperialist fantasies of the Royal Navy, Jenn attacked England with the heady enthusiasm of a new recruit and the unwavering discipline of an experienced soldier. For this veteran of *Let's Go: Eastern Europe 2001*, no hedge-maze was left unsolved and no secret passageway unexplored, as her reams of meticulous copy and beyond-bionic maps made us the envy of the office. Jenn's flare for the historical detail and knack for the quirky fact proved her the ideal travel companion, even from halfway 'round the globe. Our only regret: Sandwich.

A. Morgan Rodman   *Southwest and Northern England, Heart of England, Midlands*

A city-savvy veteran of *Let's Go: Washington, D.C. 2001*, Morgan charmed his way from Leeds to Land's End, mining the grit of industrial England for its bohemian hotspots and techno-gems. Manna-like, his nightlife coverage fell from the skies in little packets of perfection, replete with phrases so fluid and metaphors so mouth-watering, we inevitably thirsted for more. When this Tulsa-born jet setter landed beyond city limits, the same artistry distinguished his work, leaving us convinced that there's no landscape for which Morgan can't find the words.

Robert Willison   *Glasgow, Central Scotland, Highlands and Islands*

Though Scotland's black-cloud conspiracy rarely broke for Rob, this indefatigable road-warrior weathered every storm with grace. His copy was a constant joy; witty, candid, and refreshingly frank, Rob effortlessly rewrote and expanded coverage to ensure that no loch, cliff, or pressurized shower went unnoticed. Though harrowed by demented seagulls and snoring bunkmates indifferent to pelted pence, his keen eye and easy voice rewarded the good and annihilated the bad in one deadly keystroke, serving readers above and beyond the call.

Daryush Jonathan Dawid	*Editor, London*
Daniel L. Wagner	*Editor, Ireland*
Sonja Nikkila	*Associate Editor, Ireland*
Sheila A. Baynes	*Republic of Ireland*
Melissa Johnson	*Republic of Ireland*
Michael Liam O'Byrne	*Northern Ireland, Republic of Ireland*
Jacob Rubin	*Northern Ireland, Republic of Ireland*

ACKNOWLEDGMENTS

The Let's Go 2002 series is dedicated to the memory of Haley Surti

TEAM B&I THANKS: Matt, Nat, Jenn, Morgan, and Rob, the best team in B&I history, for unrivaled devotion and spirit: it was an absolute pleasure from Day 1. B[Har]ri[s]an, for eagle-eyed edits and encouragement to the last. Julie, our incomparable mapper, always here and always smiling. Smoove K, for endless SparkTests and Song of the Day. Nathaniel, for diversity *and* distinction. Emily and Andrea, for sharing their focus and humor. Dan and Sonja, for having a "funnier" book than ours. Jonathan, for more than enough impeccable prose. And everyone who's called *Let's Go* home this summer, for making us feel like we peaked at 20.

MATTHEW THANKS: Kate, Kate, and Kate again, for infallible editing, unfailing commitment, and unsurpassed loveliness. The RWs, not only great researchers, but great people. Brian, for arbitrating way back when. The pod, for first-rate banter and other "cosmic connections." Bruegger's, for some fine tuna salad. Johs, for the mother of all final reports. Alex Leichtman, for babying me when I needed it most. Diana, for sustaining conversation. Thalia, my closest companion just a ytalk away, for clever headers, the entire popular music section, and more love than I ever deserve. Bubbie, Mokey, Poppy, Jilli, and Dad, for everything plus and then a thousand times more. And above all Mom, for helping me find this path and to whom my gratitude can only be more than words.

KATE THANKS: Matthew, for letting me in on this extraordinary project, for sharing his remarkable and hysterical "world of words." Our researchers, who have been one big grin from start to finish. The Germany/B&I/2-marvey-MEs pod, for creating such a lighthearted work space; I've laughed my summer away, and I can't imagine how better to do away with anything. Mom, Dad, Gracie, for—oh; wow; for everything always; I wouldn't know where to begin. My dear friends blocks, cities, states, continents away, for remembering me and for letting me remember them. Sarah S. and Cali for making possible so much of this summer's peace and quiet.

Editor
Matthew B. Sussman
Associate Editor
Kate D. Nesin
Managing Editor
Brian R. Walsh
Map Editor
Julia A. Stephens

Publishing Director
Sarah P. Rotman
Editor-in-Chief
Ankur N. Ghosh
Production Manager
Jen Taylor
Cartography Manager
Dan Barnes
Design & Photo Manager
Vanessa Bertozzi
Editorial Managers
Amélie Cherlin, Naz F. Firoz, Matthew Gibson, Sharmi Surianarain, Brian R. Walsh
Financial Manager
Rebecca L. Schoff
Marketing & Publicity Managers
Brady R. Dewar, Katharine Douglas, Marly Ohlsson
New Media Manager
Kevin H. Yip
Online Manager
Alex Lloyd
Personnel Manager
Nathaniel Popper
Production Associates
Steven Aponte, Chris Clayton, Caleb S. Epps, Eduardo Montoya, Melissa Rudolph
Some Design
Melissa Rudolph
Office Coordinators
Efrat Kussell, Peter Richards

Director of Advertising Sales
Adam M. Grant
Senior Advertising Associates
Ariel Shwayder, Kennedy Thorwarth
Advertising Associate
Jennie Timoney
Advertising Artwork Editor
Peter Henderson

President
Cindy L. Rodriguez
General Manager
Robert B. Rombauer
Assistant General Manager
Anne E. Chisholm

DISCOVER BRITAIN AND IRELAND

In which the Reader is invited to Explore the Isles of Great Britain, and all the Pleasures promised therein.

Having spearheaded the Industrial Revolution, colonized two fifths of the globe, and won every foreign war in its history but two, Britain seems intent on making the world forget its tiny size. But this small island nation is just that: small. The rolling farms of the south and the rugged cliffs of the north are only a day's train ride apart, and peoples as diverse as London clubbers, Cornish miners, Welsh students, and Gaelic monks all occupy a land area half the size of Spain. It's perhaps because its residents keep such close quarters that Britain has been rocked by a political history bloodier and more thrilling than most, a past whose defiant fortresses, subterranean dungeons, imposing castles, and expansive battlefields still account for much of the island's appeal. But beyond the stereotypical snapshots of of Merry Olde England—gabled cottages with herbaceous borders, tweed-clad farmers shepherding their flocks—Britain today is a cosmopolitan destination driven by international energy. Though the British Empire may have ended with a whimper, its legacy survives in multicultural urban centers and a dynamic arts and theater scene—the most accessible in the world, as long as English remains the planet's most widespread language. Brits eat kebab as often as they do lemon curd and scones, and five-story dance clubs in post-industrial settings draw as much attention as fairy-tale country homes with picturesque views.

Travelers who come to Ireland with images from poetry or film in mind will not be disappointed: spectacular, windswept scenery wraps the coast, mist cloaks dramatic mountain peaks, and the dazzling greens of Ireland's hills and vales prove the moniker "Emerald Isle" no exaggeration. Traditional music and pub culture thrive in village and city alike, and despite the pervasive influences of globalization on one of Europe's fastest-growing economies, the voices—literary, mythical, wise-cracking—of an older Ireland still sound out loud and strong.

FACTS AND FIGURES

CAPITALS London (UK and England), Cardiff (Wales), Edinburgh (Scotland), Belfast (Northern Ireland), Dublin (Republic of Ireland).

LANDS England and Scotland are kingdoms, Wales a principality, and Northern Ireland a constituent part of the United Kingdom. Ireland is a republic. Together they comprise the British Isles.

LAND AREA Great Britain 94,251 sq. mi. (244,110 sq. km). Northern Ireland 5,452 sq. mi. (14,120 sq. km). Ireland 27,137 sq. mi. (70,285 sq. km).

POPULATIONS England 49.1 million, Wales 2.9 million, Scotland 5.1 million, Northern Ireland 1.6 million, Republic of Ireland 3.8 million.

1

WHEN TO GO

The popularity of Britain and Ireland as tourist destinations makes it wise to plan around the multitudes that smother the Isles in high season. While the weather is most hospitable from June to August, hostels, B&Bs, and sights will be packed. Spring or autumn (Apr.-May and Sept.-Oct.) are more appealing times to visit; the weather is still reasonable and flights less expensive. If you intend to visit large cities and linger indoors at museums and theaters, traveling during the off season (Nov.-Mar., excluding holidays), when airfares and rooms are cheapest, is most economical. Keep in mind, however, that sights, accommodations (particularly hostels), and tourist information centres often run reduced hours or even close, especially in rural regions.

WEATHER. In Britain, the nursery rhyme "Rain, Rain, Go Away" is less a hopeful plea than a pitiful exercise in futility. Regardless of when you choose to go, it *will* rain. Scotland, Wales, and Ireland are especially soggy; be prepared with warm, waterproof clothing at all times. Relatively speaking, April is the driest month in Ireland (though in England it's the cruellest), especially on the east coast near Dublin. Aside from the heavenly drool, the weather in Britain and Ireland is subject to frequent changes but few extremes. Excluding high altitudes and northern Scotland, temperatures average in the mid-60°s Fahrenheit (15-20°C) in summer and the low 40°s Fahrenheit (5-7°C) during winter. In general, southern England is pleasant and dry May through September. For a temperature chart, see **Climate,** p. 750. Another factor to consider is hours of **daylight,** particularly if you're going to Scotland—Edinburgh, after all, is on the same line of latitude as northern Labrador. In winter, the sun sets around 4pm, depending on how far north you are. Those planning outdoor activities will enjoy the best conditions in summer.

THINGS TO DO

With Manchester's clubs only an hour by train from the Lake District fells, Britain and Ireland provide unparalleled opportunities within an amazingly compact space. For more specific regional attractions, see the **Highlights** box at the beginning of each chapter.

DOING IT NATURAL

> *In which the Reader is Called upon to Take the Waters, and Air his Lungs.*

Forget the satanic mills: the diversity of Britain and Ireland's 16 national parks is worthy of a small continent. Discover the romantic (or the Romantic) in you in the surprisingly peaceful **Lake District** (p. 361). Its gnarled crags and crystalline waters have been lauded as the best in English scenery ever since they induced Elizabeth's raptures in *Pride and Prejudice.* With seasprayed bravura, Wales meets the Atlantic Ocean at **Pembrokeshire Coast National Park** (p. 453), where sandy beaches—some of the island's finest—are fringed with lofty cliffs and idyllic harbors. Scotland lacks official parks, but the whole country might as well be designated an area of outstanding natural beauty. A wonder of human engineering, the **West Highland Railway** slices through the lochs and moors of Scotland's Highlands from Glasgow to Fort William, steps away from big guy **Ben Nevis** (p. 595). Farther up, the amethyst sea and misty peaks of the **Northwest Highlands** (p. 618) look like they just jumped off your postcard home. In Northern Ireland, the honeycomb columns of the basaltic **Giant's Causeway** (p. 658) resemble a geological freak-out in the middle of Antrim's rocky outcrops and pristine white beaches. Southwest in the Republic, the **Ring of Kerry** (p. 715) encircles a peninsula speckled with mountains, waterfalls, and cliffs, best concentrated in **Killarney National Park** (p. 719).

HISTORY, PRE-1066

> *Concerning Events of no small Importance to these great Isles.*

Well, how far back do you want to go? Britain and Ireland had been one of Europe's hotspots long before the arrival of William. **Stonehenge** (p. 198) is the most famous of the Stone Age sites, though next-door neighbor **Avebury** (p. 199) is an entire village made of 40-ton rocks. In Ireland's Co. Meath, the underground passages of the **Boyne Valley** (p. 699) still stump engineers; their 5000-year-old patterns and designs represent the bulk of Western Europe's neolithic art. On Scotland's Isle of Lewis, the **Callanish Stones** (p. 611) reveal ancient knowledge of astronomy and math. On the other hand, the Neolithic burial tomb of Wales's **Bryn Celli Ddu** (p. 483) pops up in the middle of a modern farm. Before they declined and fell, the Romans certainly had an orgiastic time in old Britannia. Fabulous mosaics and a theater have been excavated at **St. Albans** (p. 249), once a raging capital second only to London. After a trip to the vomitorium, a dip in the baths at **Bath** (p. 200) cleaned things right up. On the border with Scotland, **Hadrian's Wall** (p. 415), a marvel of ancient ingenuity, marks a Roman emperor's frustration with his pesky neighbors to the north. Finding the light in the Dark Ages, early Christianity got its start in Canterbury, where the **Church of St. Martin** (p. 155) is the country's oldest house of worship. But a new era of British history was soon to be inaugurated in that fateful year when the Conqueror trounced the Saxons at **Hastings** (p. 163).

CHURCH AND STATE

> *In which the Reader is requested to Emulate his Betters, and Be upright in his Ways.*

The abundance of defensive and religious sites throughout Britain and Ireland makes for a wild game of connect-the-dots. Wherever a castle or cathedral could be imposingly built, it was; wherever one could be defiantly razed, it was too. Edward I of England had a rough time containing the Welsh; his massive castles in Wales—**Beaumaris** (p. 484), **Caernarfon** (p. 478), **Conwy** (p. 485), and **Harlech** (p. 466)—are lined like spectacular soldiers along the northwestern coast. Two castles, equally grand, top extinct volcanoes in Scotland, one in **Edinburgh** (p. 513), the other, ringed with gargoyles, in **Stirling** (p. 562). Outside of Stratford, **Warwick Castle** (p. 282) impresses with its castellated gatehouses and stately apartments; but only heads-of-state get to stay at glorious **Windsor Castle** (p. 282), the largest inhabited castle in the world. You can play the lord or lady at hilltop **Durham Castle** (p. 404), which lets out its rooms to travelers, as does 15th-century **St. Briavel's Castle** (p. 437), once King John's hunting lodge and now a hostel near Tintern. Not strictly castles, the sumptuous mansions of **Castle Howard** (p. 394) and **Blenheim Palace** (p. 263) give a heady taste of how the other 0.001% still lives, their elegant rooms and landscaped grounds surpassing even the most royal of residences.

In northeast England, **York Minster** (p. 392), the country's largest Gothic cathedral, jockeys with **Durham Cathedral** (p. 404) in competition for most awe-inspired pilgrims, while **Salisbury Cathedral** (p. 197) sets a record of its own with England's tallest spire. In London, thousands flock to **Westminster Abbey** (p. 114) and to **St. Paul's Cathedral** (p. 112), where Poets' Corner and the Whispering Gallery take their breath away. Across the Irish Sea, Dublin's **Christ Church Cathedral** (p. 684) is a medieval masterpiece; the quiet interior belies its contested history.

LITERARY LANDMARKS

> *In which the gentle Reader Shall Discover the Origins of these Textboxes.*

Even if you've never been to Britain or Ireland, their landscapes should look familiar if you've done your English homework. **Virginia Woolf** drew inspiration for her novel *To the Lighthouse* from St. Ives (p. 241). **Jane Austen** grew up in Winchester (p. 187), wrote in Bath (p. 200), took the odd trip to the Cobb in Lyme Regis (p. 217), and immortalized all the areas in her novels. **Sir Arthur Conan Doyle** set Sherlock Holmes's house on 221b Baker St. in London (p. 135), but sent the sleuth to Dartmoor (p. 225) to find the Hound of the Baskervilles. **Thomas Hardy** was a Dorchester (p. 215) man, whose fictional county of Wessex mirrored southwest England perfectly. Stratford-upon-Avon (p. 264) has never forgotten **William Shakespeare,** long after he shuffled off this mortal coil. Farther north, the **Brontës**—Charlotte, Emily, and Anne—lived in the parsonage in Haworth (p. 379), and vividly captured the wildness of Yorkshire's moors (p. 394). **Wordsworth** and **Coleridge** grew up in the Lake District (p. 361), and much of their poetry was compelled by walks near its waters and along its mountain ridges. The Welsh **Dylan Thomas** was born in Swansea (p. 446), moved to Laugharne (p. 453), and always looked longingly to his homeland. Scotland's national poet is **Robbie Burns,** and every town in Dumfries and Galloway (p. 529) pays tribute to him. **James Joyce** is the most famous of the Dubliners (p. 687). **W.B. Yeats** scattered his poetic settings throughout Ireland, but chose Co. Sligo (p. 740) for his gravesite. Oh, and **Salman Rushdie** has come out of hiding, but we're not sure where he is. London, probably.

A SPORTS FAN'S PARADISE

> *In which the Reader Demonstrates athletic Prowess, winning Honors and Admirers.*

Football (soccer, if you must) fanaticism is unavoidable: the Queen Mum is an Arsenal fan, and the police run a National Hooligan Hotline. At the **football grounds** of London, become a gunner for a day at Highbury, chant for the Spurs at White Hart Lane, or don the Chelsea blue. Then head up to **Old Trafford** (p. 338), Manchester United's grounds on Sir Matt Busby Way (named for their legendary manager), or move west to the grounds of bitter rivals **Everton** and **Liverpool** (p. 336). **Rugby** scrums are held in gaping **Millennium Stadium**, Cardiff (p. 434). Discouraged by the terrace yobs and the mud? Tree-trunk throwers and other **highland games** devotees reach their own rowdy heights annually at **Braemar** (p. 584). **Cricket** is altogether more refined; watch the men in white at London's **Lords** grounds. **Golf** draws sedate but driven followers to the historic coastal courses of **St. Andrews** (p. 568). **Tennis**, too, demands genteel conduct, and the strawberries and cream at **Wimbledon** are a perfect accompaniment.

But you want to join in, eh? The surf is up along the Atlantic coast at alternative **Newquay** (p. 244), artsy **St. Ives** (p. 241), and hardcore **Lewis** (p. 610). Go canyoning or whitewater rafting at **Fort William** (p. 595), or try the more tranquil punting at **Oxford** (p. 253) or **Cambridge** (p. 302). **Snowdonia National Park** (p. 472) challenges hikers, while every park has plenty of cycling trails. And, of course, any town worth its boots will offer spontaneous kickabouts: go forth and seek your game.

FEELING FESTIVE?

> *In which the Reader is requested to Eat, Drink, and Be merry.*

It's difficult to travel in Britain without bumping into some kind of festival. Every town seems to celebrate its right to, well, celebrate. The **Edinburgh Inter-**

national Festival and its **Fringe** (p. 521) take over Scotland's capital with a head-spinning program of experimental performances by professional troupes and poor-but-passionate amateurs. In Manchester's Gay Village, **Mardi Gras** (p. 343) is the wildest of street parties, while the **Glastonbury Festival** (p. 212) is Britain's biggest homage to rock—if you can get tickets and don't mind mud. The **International Musical Eisteddfod** is Wales's version of the mega-fest, annually swelling modest Llangollen (p. 492). In London, things turn fiery during the **Chinese New Year Festival.**

In the warmer months, virtually all of Ireland's villages find reason to gather their sheep for show and tune their fiddles. Joycean scholars join an 18hr. ramble through Dublin's streets on June 16, **Bloomsday** (p. 692). Around August, every set in Ireland tunes in to the nationally televised **Rose of Tralee Festival and Pageant** (p. 722), a personality contest of epic proportions.

◳ LET'S GO PICKS

BEST SUNSETS. The walled Welsh city of **Caernarfon** (p. 478) sits on the water, facing the western horizon full on. In Ireland, Yeats still can't get enough of the views from **Drumcliff** (p. 742) toward Benbulben. The extreme northern location of the **Shetlands** (p. 630) makes for breathtaking skies, while **Arthur's Seat** (p. 517) grants 360° views of shimmering Edinburgh.

BEST PUB CRAWLS. Tradition mandates a pub crawl in **Edinburgh** (p. 505): troop down the **Royal Mile,** or muster stamina for the **Rose St.** stumble. If the blonde in the black skirt is your drink of choice, the pubs of **Dublin's Grafton St.** (p. 688)—not to mention the rest of Ireland—serve up copious pints of Guinness.

BEST PLACE TO CATCH A WAVE. Bleach-blond surfers hang loose at **Newquay** (p. 244) on the dazzling Cornwall coast, while 20 ft. rollers at **Lewis** (p. 610) scare off even the biggest Kahunas. Britain's pebbly shores got you down? Unspoiled sands stretch near **Tenby** (p. 450) and on the colorful **Isle of Wight** (p. 184)—though **Tongue** (p. 623) has got them both licked.

BEST NIGHTLIFE SCENES. The Beatles' hometown, **Liverpool** (p. 332) comes together every night, especially at top club Cream. Students command most of **Newcastle** (p. 407)—must be something in the ale. Manchester's **Gay Village** (p. 344) is a hip place for all orientations. Oh, and **London** (p. 146) has the odd club, too.

BEST WATER PRESSURE. The **Wester Caputh Independent Hostel** (p. 559) has the best showers in the Highlands, though the top floor of the **St. Andrews Tourist Hostel** (p. 553) is a close runner-up. **British weather** also manages to keep travelers perpetually drenched.

BEST FEATHERS. As cocky as their predecessor, but not quite as handsome, a flock of peacocks patrols **Newstead Abbey** (p. 294), former home of Lord Byron. In the Shetlands, over 50,000 puffins overwhelm northerly **Unst** (p. 634). Birdwatchers spot everything from graceful heron to gabbing grebes on East Anglia's delicate **Norfolk Coast** (p. 316).

BEST FLIPPERS. Swim with the sleekest at the **Blakeney Point Nature Reserve** (p. 316), the only permanent seal colony in Britain. Or zip up your wetsuit and take a dip with Fungi the dolphin, **Dingle's** resident orca (p. 720).

BEST JEWELRY. The **Dog Collar Museum** in Leeds Castle (p. 157) puts all other neckwear collections to shame.

BEST EXCUSE FOR BAD BRITISH. TEETH Sets of antique dentures glint at **Old Bridge House Museum,** Dumfries (p. 530), where unwieldy old appliances give new credence to dentophobes.

BEST COCONUTS. It's hard to believe, but up in the Highlands, tiny **Plockton** (p. 619) is graced by warm currents and slender palms. On the "English Riviera," the tropical gardens of **Lyme Regis** (p. 217) are a dose of the Mediterranean in Dorset.

SUGGESTED ITINERARIES

THE BEST OF BRITAIN AND IRELAND

(1 day; p. 642). Then back across the Irish Sea to Stranraer (p. 534), where a train leads to hip **Glasgow** (1 day; p. 535) and nearby **Loch Lomond** (p. 566). The **Isle of Mull** (1 day; p. 573) offers the serene beauty of the Hebrides, and you'll need the rest before you enter exuberant **Edinburgh** (3 days; p. 505). The standout views of the **Lake District** (2 days; p. 361) never cease to inspire. Pass through historic **York** (1 day; p. 388) and **Cambridge** (1 day; p. 302) to complete the south-bound journey with a bit of culture—just in case you haven't had your fill.

THE BEST OF BRITAIN AND IRELAND (1 MONTH)

Start in swinging **London** (4 days; p. 91) for the world's best in museums, shopping, theater, and night-life. Then sample the waters in picture-perfect **Bath** (1 day; p. 200), the 18th century's answer to Aspen. **Oxford** (2 days; p. 253) beckons with its univer-sity and Blenheim Palace, while **Strat-ford-upon-Avon** (1 day; p. 264) is a year-round celebration of Shakespeare. On to **Liverpool** (2 days; p. 332), the Beatles' hometown. Nearby, **Caernar-fon** (1 day; p. 478) sports a world-famous castle and good proximity to **Mt. Snowdon** (1 day; p. 472), Wales's loftiest peak. From the ferry port of Holy-head (p. 485), cross to **Dublin** (2 days; p. 672), home to Joyce and Guinness. Don't forget a daytrip to the heather-topped **Wicklow Mountains** (p. 697). A trendy university town, **Cork** (1 day; p. 708) is close to the stunning **Dingle Peninsula** (p. 720), rural Ireland at its greenest. Next, **Galway** (2 days; p. 730) is a center of Irish culture near the **Cliffs of Moher** and the moon-like **Bur-ren** (p. 726). **Donegal** (2 days; p. 742) serves as a base to see Slieve League, Europe's highest sea cliffs. From there, enter Northern Ireland through boister-ous **Derry** (1 day; p. 658), enjoy the gorgeous scenery of **Giant's Causeway** and the **Antrim Coast** (1 day; p. 658), and head for politically-divided **Belfast**

THE BEST OF ENGLAND

ENGLAND (3 WEEKS)

All-encompass-ing England—from pastoral plains to cut-ting edge clubs—offers highlight after highlight. Start in **London** (4 days; p. 91), the cosmopolitan center of every-thing in England and arguably the world—culture, nightlife, this city has it all. For an infamously "dirty weekend," head south to **Brighton** (2 days; p. 167), stopping to admire the fairy-tale castle at **Arundel** (p. 174) on your way to **Salisbury** (1 day; p. 194), famous for steak and stakes (its cathedral has the tallest spire in Britain). Take a day to study the stone circles at **Stonehenge** (p. 198) and **Avebury** (p. 199), before heading west to **Dartmoor** (1 day; p. 225), countryside long immortalized in literature. **Newquay** (1 day; p. 244) offers an incongruous slice of surfer culture, while stunning **Bath** (2 days; p. 200) was Georgian England's most fashionable watering hole. It doesn't get prettier than the villages in the **Cotswolds** (1 day; p. 275), close to the medieval university and sumptuous Blenheim Palace of **Oxford** (2 days; p. 253). Next, catch a play at **Stratford-upon-Avon** (1 day; p. 264), Shakespeare's hometown, and make sure to save time for a daytrip to breathtaking **Warwick Castle** (1 day; p. 282). The northern cities have their charms, too. **Manchester** (1 day; p. 338) sets the standard for post-industrial clubbing, and **Liverpool** (2 days; p. 332) has Beatles sites and exuberant nightlife. Partied too hard? Go north to the **Lake District** (2 days; p. 361), which admittedly is where all tourists go. Hey, if Wordsworth liked it, why shouldn't you? Continue northeast to **Hadrian's Wall** (p. 415) before making your way back south to **York** (1 day; p. 388), ready-made for history buffs with its preserved city walls and England's largest Gothic cathedral. Finish off your trip with a punt by the University of **Cambridge** (2 days; p. 302), topped off with a quick train ride back to London.

SCOTLAND (2 WEEKS) Not just men in kilts, Scotland balances remote romantic glens and islands with lively cities. **Edinburgh** (4 days; p. 505) has an amazing Festival in August, and it's festive year-round, with the historic Royal Mile and unbeatable pubs. Then westward ho to its rival, **Glasgow** (2 days; p. 535), a city of art, culture, hip nightlife, and a daytrip to the bonnie banks of **Loch Lomond** (p. 566). The scenery only gets better as you head up to **Fort William** and scale Scotland's tallest peak, **Ben Nevis** (1 day; p. 595). From there, hiking in the calendar-worthy **Isle of Skye** (2 days; p. 602) is worth the effort for dramatic views of the Cuillins. After taking in a Hebride or two (**Lewis, Uist,** or **Barra**), continue north to the remote and beautiful Highlands via the spectacularly scenic villages of **Durness,** with its beaches and caves, and **Tongue,** source of endless photo-ops (1 day; p. 623). **Inverness** (1 day; p. 590) is more transport hub than destination, but it's a good base for seeing **Loch Ness** (p. 594)—and maybe even Nessie. Next, hit up **Aberdeen** (1 day; p. 580), a masterpiece in granite, before dropping by **Dunkeld** and **Birnam** (1 day; p. 558), whose unique musical community is best experienced by a stay at the local hostel. With its beautiful castle and innumerable references to William "Braveheart" Wallace, **Stirling** (1 day; p. 562) rounds off the tour before heading back to Edinburgh for a wee dram.

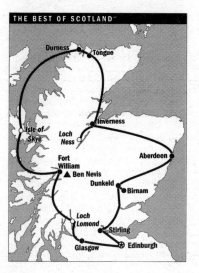

THE BEST OF SCOTLAND

WALES (10 DAYS) With thousands of acres of undisturbed country, Wales may be Britain's last undiscovered realm. **Cardiff** (2 days; p. 428), capital of the resurgent nation, has impressive castles nearby. From picturesque **Chepstow** (1 day; p. 436), it's only a quick jaunt to haunting **Tintern Abbey** (p. 437), which still inspires Wordsworthian paeans to beauty. Then catch some rays at **Tenby,** beach resort town with flair (1 day; p. 450). Magical **St. David's** (1 day; p. 457), Britain's smallest city, has a disproportionately majestic cathedral; it's also in the scenic **Pembrokeshire Coast National Park** (p. 453). Farther north, kick back on the seaside promenade of the university town of **Aberystwyth** (1

DISCOVER

day; p. 461). Tiny **Harlech** (1 day; p. 466) boasts panoramic views of sea, sand, and summits, not to mention Wales's most dramatic fortress. Contained within the city walls of **Caernarfon** (1 day; p. 478) is a Byzantine castle and Roman fort. **Llanberis** (1 day; p. 475) lets you ascend lofty **Mt. Snowdon,** whether you choose to do it by foot or by train. Finally, **Conwy** (1 day; p. 485) delights with a bevy of curious attractions flanking a turquoise harbor. From here, let your wanderlust be your guide: east to **Liverpool** (p. 332), in England, or west to **Holyhead** (p. 485), where you can take the ferry to Dublin.

THE BEST OF WALES

Conwy
Caernarfon
Llanberis
Mt. Snowdon
Harlech
Aberystwyth
St. David's
PEMBROKESHIRE COAST NAT'L PARK
Tenby
Tintern
Chepstow
Cardiff

ESSENTIALS

DOCUMENTS AND FORMALITIES

CONSULAR SERVICES

ENTRANCE REQUIREMENTS
Passport (p. 11). All foreign nationals need a passport to travel into Britain or Ireland, though EU citizens may not have them checked.
Visa (p. 12). Citizens of Australia, Canada, New Zealand, South Africa, the US, and many other western countries do not need visas to enter Britain or Ireland. If you are unsure, call your local embassy or complete an online enquiry form at www.fco.gov.uk/ukvisas.
Inoculations: No inoculations are necessary for visiting Britain or Ireland.
Work and Study Permits (p. 12). Work or study permits are required for all non-EU citizens planning to work or study in either Britain or Ireland.
Driving Permit (p. 44). A valid foreign driver's license or an International Driving Permit is required for all those planning to drive.

UK EMBASSIES AND CONSULATES ABROAD

For addresses of British embassies in countries not listed here, call the **Foreign and Commonwealth Office** (☎(020) 7270 1500; www.fco.gov.uk/directory/posts.asp), or consult your local telephone directory. Some large cities (e.g., New York) have a local British consulate that can handle most of the same functions as an embassy.

Australia: British High Commission, Commonwealth Ave., Yarralumla, Canberra, ACT 2600 (☎(02) 6270 6666; www.uk.emb.gov.au). Consulate-General, Level 10, SAP House, Canberra Centre, Canberra, ACT 2601 (☎(19) 0294 1555). Consulates-General in Brisbane, Melbourne, Perth, and Sydney; Consulate in Adelaide.

Canada: British High Commission, 80 Elgin St., Ottawa, K1P 5K7 (☎(613) 237-1530; www.britain-in-canada.org). British Consulate-General, 777 Bay St., Suite 2800, Toronto, ON M5G 2G2 (☎(416) 593-1290). Consulates-General also in Montreal and Vancouver; Consulates in Halifax, St. John's, Quebec City, and Winnipeg.

France: British Embassy, 35 Rue du Faubourg-St-Honoré, 75383 Paris CEDEX 08 (☎01 44 51 31 00; www.amb-grandebretagne.fr); British Consulate-General, 18 bis rue d'Anjou, 75008 Paris (☎01 44 51 31 00). Consulates-General also in Bordeaux, Lille, Lyon, and Marseille.

Ireland: British Embassy, 29 Merrion Rd., Ballsbridge, Dublin 4 (☎(01) 205 3700; www.britishembassy.ie).

New Zealand: British High Commission, 44 Hill St., Thorndon, Wellington 1 (☎(04) 472 6049; www.britain.org.nz); mail to P.O. Box 1812, Wellington. Consulate-General, 17th floor, NZI House, 151 Queen St., Auckland 1 (☎(09) 303 2973); mail to Private Bag 92014, Auckland 1.

South Africa: British High Commission, 91 Parliament St., Cape Town 8001 (☎(021) 461 7220); also at 255 Hill St., Arcadia 0002, Pretoria (☎(012) 483 1200; www.britain.org.za). Consulates-General in Johannesburg and Cape Town; Consulates in Port Elizabeth and Durban.

US: British Embassy, 3100 Massachusetts Ave. NW, Washington, D.C. 20008 (☎(202) 588-6500; www.britainusa.com). Consulate-General, 845 3rd Ave., New York, NY 10022 (☎(212) 745-0200). Other Consulates-General in Atlanta, Boston, Chicago,

Houston, Los Angeles, and San Francisco. Consulates in Anchorage, Dallas, Kansas City, Miami, Minneapolis, Nashville, New Orleans, Phoenix, Pittsburgh, Portland, Salt Lake City, San Diego, Seattle, St. Louis, and Puerto Rico.

IRISH EMBASSIES AND CONSULATES ABROAD

Australia: Irish Embassy, 20 Arkana St., Yarralumla, Canberra ACT 2615 (☎(02) 6273 3022).

Canada: Irish Embassy, 130 Albert St., Ottawa, ON K1P 5G4 (☎(613) 233-6281).

France: Irish Embassy, 4 rue Rude, Paris 75116 (☎01 44 17 67 00).

New Zealand: Irish Consulate, Dingwall Bldg., 2nd fl., 87 Queen St., P.O. Box 279, Auckland 1 (☎(09) 302 2867).

South Africa: Embassy of Ireland, Delheim Suite, Tulbach Center, 1234 Church St., 0083 Colbyn, Pretoria (☎(012) 342 5062).

UK: 17 Grosvenor Pl., London SW1X 7HR (☎(020) 7235 2171). Consulates in Edinburgh and Cardiff.

US: Irish Embassy, 2234 Massachusetts Ave. NW, Washington, D.C. 20008 (☎(202) 462-3939; www.irelandemb.org). Consulate, 345 Park Ave., 17th fl., New York, NY 10154 (☎(212) 319-2555). Other Consulates in Chicago, San Francisco, and Boston.

EMBASSIES AND CONSULATES IN THE UK

Australia: Australian High Commission, Australia House, The Strand, London WC2B 4LA (☎(020) 7379 4334; www.australia.org.uk).

Canada: Canadian High Commission, 1 Grosvenor Sq., London W1K 4AB (☎(020) 7258 6600; www.dfait-maeci.gc.ca/london).

France: French Embassy, 58 Knightsbridge, London SW1X 7JT (☎(020) 7201 1000; www.ambafrance.org.uk); Consulate-General, 21 Cromwell Rd., London SW7 2EN (☎(020) 7838 2000).

Ireland: See **Irish Embassies and Consulates Abroad,** above.

New Zealand: New Zealand High Commission (consular section), New Zealand House, 80 Haymarket, London SW1Y 4TQ (☎(0171) 930 8422; www.nzembassy.com/britain).

South Africa: South African High Commission (consular section), 15 Whitehall, London SW1A 2DD (☎(020) 7925 8900; www.southafricahouse.com); mail to South Africa House, Trafalgar Sq., London WC2N 5DP.

US: American Embassy, 24 Grosvenor Sq., London W1A 1AE (☎(020) 7499 9000; www.usembassy.org.uk). Consulates in **Scotland** at 3 Regent Terrace, Edinburgh EH7 5BW (☎(0131) 556 8315), and in **Northern Ireland** at Queen's House, 14 Queen St., Belfast BT1 6EQ (☎(028) 9032 8239).

EMBASSIES AND CONSULATES IN IRELAND

Australia: Australian Embassy, Fitzwilton House, 2nd fl., Wilton Terr., Dublin 2 (☎(01) 676 1517).

Canada: Canadian Embassy, Canada House, 65/68 St. Stephen's Green, Dublin 2 (☎(01) 478 1988).

France: French Embassy, 36 Ailesbury Rd., Dublin 4 (☎(01) 260 1666).

New Zealand: Consulate-General, 37 Leeson Park, Dublin 6 (☎(01) 660 4233).

South Africa: South African Embassy, Alexandra House, 2nd fl., Earlsfort Terr., Dublin 2 (☎(01) 661 5553).

UK: See **UK Embassies and Consulates Abroad,** above.

US: American Embassy, 42 Elgin Rd., Ballsbridge, Dublin 4 (☎(01) 668 7122; after-hours ☎(01) 668 9612).

PASSPORTS

REQUIREMENTS. Citizens of all countries need valid passports to enter Britain and/or Ireland and to re-enter their own country. EU citizens (including Irish visitors to Britain and vice versa) should carry their passports, even though they will probably not be checked upon entry. Depending on your nationality, you may be prevented from entering either country if you have less than six months left before your passport expires; check with your local consulate or embassy. Arriving home with an expired passport is always illegal, and may result in a fine.

PHOTOCOPIES. Be sure to photocopy the page of your passport with your photo, passport number, and other identifying information, as well as any visas, travel insurance policies, plane tickets, or traveler's check serial numbers. Carry one set of copies in a safe place, apart from the originals, and leave another set at home. Consulates also recommend that you carry an expired passport or an official copy of your birth certificate in a part of your baggage separate from other documents.

LOST PASSPORTS. If you lose your passport, immediately notify the local police and the nearest embassy or consulate of your home government. To expedite its replacement, you will need to know all information previously recorded and show identification and proof of citizenship. In some cases, a replacement may take weeks to process, and may be valid only for a limited time. Any visas stamped in your old passport will be irretrievably lost. In an emergency, ask your embassy for immediate temporary traveling papers that will permit you to re-enter your home country. Your passport is a public document belonging to your nation's government. You may have to surrender it to a foreign government official, but if you don't get it back in a reasonable amount of time, inform the nearest mission of your home country.

NEW PASSPORTS. File any new passport or renewal applications well in advance of your departure date. Most passport offices offer rush services for a steep fee. Citizens living abroad who need a passport or renewal should contact the nearest consular service of their home country.

Australia: Info ☎ 13 12 32; www.passports.gov.au. Apply for a passport at a post office, passport office (in Adelaide, Brisbane, Canberra, Darwin, Hobart, Melbourne, Newcastle, Perth, or Sydney), or overseas diplomatic mission. Passports AUS$132 (36-page) or AUS$198 (64-page); valid for 10 years. Children AUS$66 (36-page) or AUS$99 (64-page); valid for 5 years.

Canada: Canadian Passport Office, Department of Foreign Affairs and International Trade, Ottawa K1A 0G3 (☎(613) 994-3500 or (800) 567-6868; www.dfait-maeci.gc.ca/passport). Applications available at passport offices, Canadian missions, post offices, and online. Passports CDN$60; valid for 5 years.

Ireland: Pick up an application at a *Garda* station, post office, or ask at a passport office. Then apply by mail to the Department of Foreign Affairs, Passport Office, Molesworth St., Dublin 2 (☎(01) 671 1633; www.irlgov.ie/iveagh), or the Passport Office, Irish Life Building, 1A South Mall, Cork (☎(021) 272525). Passports IR£45/€57.14; valid for 10 years. Under 16 or over 65 IR£10/€12.70; valid for 3 years.

New Zealand: Send applications to the Passport Office, Department of Internal Affairs, P.O. Box 10-526, Wellington, New Zealand (☎(0800) 225 050; www.passports.govt.nz). Standard processing time is 10 working days. Passports NZ$80; valid for 10 years. Children NZ$40; valid for 5 years. 3-day "urgent service" NZ$160; children NZ$120.

South Africa: Department of Home Affairs. Passports are issued only in Pretoria, but all applications must still be submitted or forwarded to the nearest South African consulate. Processing time is 4 months or more. Passports around ZAR192; valid for 10 years. Under 16 around ZAR136; valid for 5 years. For more information, check out http://usaembassy.southafrica.net/VisaForms/Passport/Passport2000.html.

UK: Info ☎(0870) 521 0410; www.ukpa.gov.uk. Get an application from a passport office, main post office, travel agent, or online (for UK residents only) at www.ukpa.gov.uk/forms/f_app_pack.htm. Then apply by mail or in person at one of the passport offices, located in London, Liverpool, Newport, Peterborough, Glasgow, or Belfast. Passports UK£28; valid for 10 years. Under 15 UK£14.80; valid for 5 years. The process takes about 4 weeks; faster service (by personal visit to the offices listed above) costs an additional £12.

US: Info ☎(900) 225-5674 or (888) 362-8668 for credit card users; www.travel.state.gov/passport_services.html. Apply at any federal or state courthouse, authorized post office, or US Passport Agency (in most major cities); see the "US Government, State Department" section of the telephone book or a post office for addresses. Processing takes 3-4 weeks. New passports US$60; valid for 10 years. Under 16 US$40; valid for 5 years. Passports may be renewed by mail or in person for US$40. Add US$35 for 3-day expedited service.

ONE EUROPE. The idea of European unity has come a long way since 1958, when the European Economic Community (EEC) was created to promote solidarity between its six founding states. Since then, the EEC has become the European Union (EU), with political, legal, and economic institutions spanning 15 member nations: Austria, Belgium, Denmark, Finland, France, Germany, Greece, Ireland, Italy, Luxembourg, the Netherlands, Portugal, Spain, Sweden, and the UK.

What does this have to do with the average non-EU tourist? In 1999 the EU established **freedom of movement** across 14 European countries—the entire EU minus Denmark, Ireland, and the UK, but plus Iceland and Norway. This means that border controls between participating countries have been abolished, and visa policies harmonized. While you're still required to carry a passport (or government-issued ID card for EU citizens) when crossing an internal border, once you've been admitted into one country, you're free to travel to all participating states. Britain and Ireland have also formed a **common travel area,** abolishing passport controls between the UK and the Republic of Ireland. This means that the only times you'll see a border guard within the EU are traveling between the British Isles and the Continent and in and out of Denmark.

For more important consequences of the EU for travelers, see **European Customs** (p. 16) and **The Euro** (p. 18).

VISAS AND PERMITS

VISAS. EU citizens do not need a visa to enter Britain or Ireland. For visits of fewer than six months, citizens of Australia, Canada, New Zealand, South Africa, and the US do not need a visa; neither do citizens of Iceland, Israel, Japan, Malaysia, Mexico, Norway, Singapore, Switzerland, and some Eastern European, Caribbean, and Pacific countries. Citizens of most other countries need a visa to enter Britain and Ireland. Tourist visas cost £33 for a one-time pass and allow you to spend up to six months in the UK. Visas can be purchased from your nearest British consulate (listed under **Embassies & Consulates Abroad,** on p. 9). US citizens can take advantage of the **Center for International Business and Travel** (CIBT; ☎(800) 925-2428; www.cibt.com), which secures visas for travel to almost all countries for a variable service charge. If you need a **visa extension** while in the UK, contact the Home Office, Immigration and Nationality Department (☎(020) 8686 0688; www.ind.homeoffice.gov.uk).

WORK PERMITS. Admission as a visitor does not include the right to work, which is authorized only by a work permit. Entering Britain or Ireland to study requires a special visa. For more information, see **Alternatives to Tourism,** p. 63.

IDENTIFICATION

When you travel, always carry two or more forms of identification on your person, including at least one photo ID; a passport combined with a driver's license or birth certificate is usually adequate. Many establishments, especially banks, may require several IDs in order to cash traveler's checks. Never carry all your forms of ID together; split them up in case of theft or loss. It is useful to bring extra passport-size photos to affix to the various IDs or passes you may acquire along the way. Most central London Tube stations have photo booths (£2.50 for four photos).

STUDENT AND TEACHER IDENTIFICATION. The **International Student Identity Card (ISIC),** the most widely accepted form of student ID, provides discounts at select sights, clubs, accommodations, restaurants, and transport ticket agents. ISIC cards are preferable to institution-specific cards (such as a University ID) because tourism personnel in Britain and Ireland are instructed to recognize the former. All cardholders have access to a 24hr. emergency helpline for medical, legal, and financial emergencies (in the UK, call collect (020) 8762 8110), and holders of US-issued cards are also eligible for insurance benefits (see **Insurance,** p. 28). Many student travel agencies issue ISICs, including Campus Travel and STA Travel in the UK and usit in the Republic of Ireland and Northern Ireland; they are also issued on the web (www.counciltravel.com/idcards). The card is valid from September of one year to December of the following year and costs £5, AUS$15, CDN$15, or US$22. Applicants must be degree-seeking students of a secondary or post-secondary school and must be of at least 12 years of age. Because of the proliferation of fake ISICs, some services (particularly airlines) require additional proof of student identity, such as a school ID or a letter attesting to your student status, signed by your registrar and stamped with your school seal. The **International Teacher Identity Card (ITIC)** offers the same insurance coverage and similar but limited discounts. The fee is £5, AUS$13, or US$22. For more info on both cards, contact the **International Student Travel Confederation (ISTC),** Herengracht 479, 1017 BS Amsterdam, Netherlands (☎ +31 (20) 421 28 00; www.istc.org).

YOUTH IDENTIFICATION. The International Student Travel Confederation also issues a discount card to travelers who are 26 or under, but are not students. This one-year **International Youth Travel Card (IYTC;** formerly the **GO 25** Card) offers many of the same benefits as the ISIC. Most organizations that sell the ISIC also sell the IYTC (US$22).

ISICONNECT SERVICE. If you are an ISIC card carrier and want to avoid buying individual calling cards or wish to consolidate all your means of communication during your trip, you can activate your ISIC's ISIConnect service, a powerful integrated communications service (powered by eKit.com). With ISIConnect, one toll-free access number (☎ (0800) 376 2366 in the UK, ☎ (1800) 555180 in Ireland) gives you access to several different methods of keeping in touch via the phone and Internet, including: a reduced-rate international calling plan that treats your ISIC card as a universal calling card; a personalized voicemail box accessible from payphones anywhere in the world or for free over the Internet; faxmail service for sending and receiving faxes via email, fax machines, or pay phones; various email capabilities, including a service that reads your email to you over the phone; an online "travel safe" for storing (and faxing) important documents and numbers; and a 24hr. emergency help line (via phone or email at ISIConnect@ekit.com) offering assistance and medical and legal referrals. To activate your ISIConnect account, visit the service's web site (www.isiconnect.ekit.com) or call the customer service number of your home country (which is also your home country's access number): in Australia (1800) 114 478; in Canada (877) 635-3575; in Ireland (1800) 555180 or (1800) 577980; in New Zealand (0800) 114 478; in the UK (0800) 376 2366 or (0800) 169 8646; in the US (800) 706-1333; and in South Africa (0800) 992921 or (0800) 997 285.

TOURIST SERVICES

ABOUT BRITAIN

BRITISH TOURIST AUTHORITY (BTA). The BTA (www.visitbritain.com) is an umbrella organization coordinating the activities of the four separate UK tourist boards outside the UK; it also sells the **Great British Heritage Pass** (p. 15). In addition to those listed below, the BTA has many branches in Western Europe and throughout the rest of the world.

Australia: Level 16, Gateway, 1 Macquarie Pl., Circular Quay, Sydney NSW 2000 (☎(02) 9377 4400; www.visitbritain.com/au).

Canada: Air Transit Bldg., 5915 Airport Rd., Suite 120, Mississauga, ON L4V 1T1 (☎(888) 847-4885 or (905) 405-1840; www.visitbritain.com/ca).

Ireland: 18-19 College Green, Dublin 2 (☎(01) 670 8000).

New Zealand: 151 Queen St., 17th Fl., Auckland 1 (☎(09) 303 1446).

South Africa: Lancaster Gate, Hyde Park Ln., Hyde Park, Sandton 2196 (☎(011) 325 0343); mail to P.O. Box 41896, Craighall 2024.

US: 551 Fifth Ave. #701, New York, NY 10176 (☎(800) 462-2748 or (212) 986-2200; www.btausa.com).

WITHIN THE UK. The Scottish, Welsh, Northern Irish, and Irish tourist boards all have additional locations at the Britain Visitor Centre (see English Board below).

English Tourist Board, Britain Visitor Centre, 1 Lower Regent St., London SW1Y 4NX (www.travelengland.org.uk); walk-in enquiries only.

Scottish Tourist Board, 23 Ravelston Terr., Edinburgh EH4 3EU (☎(0131) 332 2433; www.visitscotland.com).

Welsh Tourist Board, Brunel House, 2 Fitzalan Rd., Cardiff CF24 0UY (☎(029) 2049 9909; www.visitwales.com).

Northern Ireland Tourist Board, 59 North St., Belfast BT1 1NB (☎(028) 9023 1221; www.ni-tourism.com).

ABOUT IRELAND

IRISH TOURIST BOARD (BORD FÁILTE). Bord Fáilte (bored FAHL-tshah; ☎(01) 666 1258; www.ireland.travel.ie). The head office is at Baggot St. Bridge, Dublin 2 (☎(01) 850 230 330 or (01) 602 4000).

Australia: Level 5, 36 Carrington St., Sydney NSW 2000 (☎(02) 9299 6177).

Canada: 120 Eglinton Ave. E., Ste. 500, Toronto, ON M4P 1E2 (☎(800) 223-6470).

New Zealand: Dingwall Bldg., 87 Queen St., Auckland (☎(00649) 379 8720).

South Africa: Everite House, 20 De Korte St., 2001 Braamfontein, Johannesburg (☎(002711) 339 4865).

UK: 150 New Bond St., London W1Y 0AQ (☎(020) 7493 3201).

US: 345 Park Ave., New York, NY 10154 (☎(800) 223-6470; www.irelandvacations.com).

SIGHTS

Most sights in Britain and Ireland list **concession** prices among their admission prices; these are usually the prices for students, seniors (called Old Age Pensioners, "OAPs"), the disabled, and children (although children often have an even lower rate). *Let's Go* lists "concessions" when visitors in all those categories are charged the same reduced price. The last admission into many sights is 30 minutes before the listed closing time; *Let's Go* notes unusually early last admissions. Sites listing "summer" hours are usually referring to tourist **high season,** roughly from Easter to September or October, though these date ranges can vary, especially in small towns. The organizations listed below run many of the major historical sights in Britain and Ireland; most sell **special passes** that save those intending to sight-hop a fair bit of money.

Cadw, Welsh Historic Monuments, National Assembly for Wales, Cathays Park, Cardiff CF10 3NQ (main switchboard ☎(029) 2050 0200; www.cadw.wales.gov.uk). Runs many Welsh sights, including most of Edward I's grand castles. Yearly "Heritage in Wales" membership £24, seniors £16, youth (16-20) £15, under 16 £12, adult couple £40, family £42.

English Heritage, Membership Department, P.O. Box 569, Swindon, SN2 2YP. (☎(0870) 333 1181; www.english-heritage.org.uk). Sells an **Overseas Visitor Pass,** which lets you into any English Heritage sight (including Stonehenge). 7-day pass £13, 2 adults £25, families £29; 14-day pass £17, 2 adults £32, families £37.

The Great British Heritage Pass gains you access and/or discounts into over 500 National Trust, English Heritage, Historic Scotland, and Cadw properties throughout Britain. Purchase it at any British Tourist Authority office, at the Britain Visitor Centre (p. 14), or online from North and Central America at www.raileurope.com/us/rail/passes/british_heritage_pass.htm. 7-day £32, US$54; 15-day £45, $75; 1-month £60, $102.

Historic Scotland, Longmore House, Salisbury Pl., Edinburgh EH9 1SH (☎(0131) 668 8600; www.historic-scotland.gov.uk) runs many sights in Scotland. The **Scottish Short Break** and **Explorer** tickets, available at any of their sights or at Scottish tourist information centres, give access to all their attractions. 3-day ticket £10, seniors and children £7.50, families £20; 7-day £15, £11, £30; 14-day £20, £14, £40.

The National Trust, National Trust Membership Department, P.O. Box 39, Bromley, Kent BR1 3XL (☎(0870) 458 4000; www.nationaltrust.org.uk). Dedicated to preserving the countryside and historic homes in England, Wales, and Northern Ireland. The **National Trust for Scotland,** 28 Charlotte Sq., Edinburgh EH2 4ET (☎(0131) 243 9300; www.nts.org.uk) maintains the countryside and properties north of the border. Members of either receive free entry to over 300 Trust sites. (Membership £31, ages 13-25 £15, families £44-58.) US and Canadian residents contact **The Royal Oak Foundation,** 285 West Broadway #400, New York, NY 10013 (☎(800) 913-6565 or (212) 966-6565; www.royal-oak.org; membership US$50, families US$75), the National Trust's North American membership branch. Memberships can be purchased through their web site.

CUSTOMS

ENTERING BRITAIN AND IRELAND

Upon entering Britain or Ireland, you must declare certain items from abroad and pay a duty on the value of those articles that exceed the allowance established by Her Majesty's Customs or by the Irish authorities. It is wise to make a list, including serial numbers, of any valuables that you carry with you from home; if you register this list with customs before your departure and have an official stamp it, you will avoid import duty charges and ensure an easy passage upon your return. Be especially careful to document items manufactured abroad. **Do not bring dogs, cats, or other pets into the United Kingdom or Ireland.** Strict anti-rabies laws mean that Fido will be kept in quarantine for six months. If you and your pet arrive in Britain from a western European nation, or by air from certain "long haul" countries (not including North America), you can avoid the quarantine by participating in the **PETS** "pet passport" scheme. Provisions for the scheme include having your pooch or feline friend microchipped, vaccinated, bloodtested, and certified against tapeworm and ticks six months before entering the UK. Consult www.defra.gov.uk/animalh/quarantine for a thorough presentation of requirements.

EUROPEAN CUSTOMS Though travelers in the United Kingdom and Ireland only experience freedom of movement between Britain and the Republic, there are no customs controls regulating the **freedom of goods** at *any* of the European Union's internal borders. When crossing the Channel Tunnel or arriving at British and Irish airports from another EU country (take the blue customs channel), travelers are thus free to transport whatever legal substances they like as long as it is for their own personal (non-commercial) use—up to 800 cigarettes, 10L of spirits, 90L of wine (60L of sparkling wine), and 110L of beer. Note that **duty-free** was abolished for travel between EU member states on June 30, 1999; however, travelers between the EU and the rest of the world still get a duty-free allowance when passing through customs.

LEAVING BRITAIN AND IRELAND

If you're leaving for a non-EU country, you can claim back any **Value Added Tax** paid (see p. 22). Keeping receipts for purchases made abroad will help establish values when you return. Upon returning home, you must declare all articles acquired abroad and pay a **duty** on the value of articles that exceed the allowance established by your country's customs service. Goods and gifts purchased at **duty-free** shops abroad are not exempt from duty or sales tax at your point of return; you must declare these items as well. "Duty-free" merely means that you need not pay a tax in the country of purchase. For more specific information on customs requirements, contact the following information centers:

Australia: Australian Customs National Information Line (in Australia call (01) 300 363 263, from elsewhere call +61 (2) 6275 6666; www.customs.gov.au).

Canada: Canadian Customs, 2265 St. Laurent Blvd., Ottawa K1G 4K3 (in Canada call 24hr. (800) 461-9999, from elsewhere call (204) 983-3500; www.ccra-adrc.gc.ca).

Ireland: Customs Information Office, Irish Life Centre, Lower Abbey St., Dublin 1 (☎(01) 878 8811; www.revenue.ie).

New Zealand: The Customhouse, 17-21 Whitmore St., Box 2218, Wellington (☎(04) 473 6099; General Enquiries ☎(0800) 428 786; www.customs.govt.nz).

South Africa: Commissioner for Customs and Excise, Department of Finance, Private Bag X47, Pretoria 0001 (☎(012) 314 9911; www.gov.za).

UK: Her Majesty's Customs and Excise, Passenger Enquiry Team, Wayfarer House, Great South West Rd., Feltham, Middlesex TW14 8NP (☎(020) 8910 3744; National Advice Service ☎(0845) 010 9000; www.hmce.gov.uk).

US: US Customs Service, 1330 Pennsylvania Ave. NW, Washington, D.C. 20229 (☎(202) 354-1000; www.customs.gov).

MONEY

Britain is expensive. Even if you stay in hostels and prepare your own food, you can still expect to spend anywhere from £15-30 per person per day, depending on where you choose to visit. Accommodations start at about £6 a night for a bed in a hostel in rural areas, or £14-15 per night in a B&B, while a basic sit-down meal at a pub costs about £5. London is a particular budget-buster, with £25-35 a day being the bare minimum for accommodations, food, and transport, without including the costs of visiting sights or going out at night. Don't let that daunt you, however. Bargains exist—top-quality theater, for example, is fairly inexpensive. In Ireland you can expect to spend about IR£20-30 a day.

CURRENCY AND EXCHANGE

Carrying **cash** with you is risky, even in a money belt, but necessary; foreign personal checks are never accepted, and even traveler's checks may not be accepted in some locations. The **Pound Sterling** is the main unit of currency in the **United Kingdom,** including Northern Ireland. It is divided into 100 pence, issued in standard denominations of 1p, 2p, 5p, 10p, 20p, 50p, and £1 in coins, and £5, £10, £20, and £50 in notes. (Scotland uses a £1 note, and throughout the UK you may still see the odd £2 coin now and again.) Northern Ireland and Scotland have their own bank notes, which can be used interchangeably with English currency, though you may have occasional difficulty using Scottish £1 notes outside Scotland, and Northern Irish notes are not generally accepted outside Northern Ireland. In the **Republic of Ireland,** the monetary unit is the **Irish pound** or "punt," which may share a similar name with its British counterpart but is not interchangeable. Residents of both nations refer to pounds as "bob" or "quid," as in "ten quid" (never "quids").

The currency chart below is based on August 2001 exchange rates between local currency and Australian dollars (AUS$), Canadian dollars (CDN$), Irish pounds (IR£), New Zealand dollars (NZ$), South African Rand (ZAR), British pounds (UK£), US dollars (US$), and European Union euros (EUR€). Check the currency converter on the *Let's Go* homepage (www.letsgo.com/Thumb) or a large newspaper for the latest exchange rates..

THE BRITISH POUND	£1 =
AUS$1 = £0.37	= AUS$2.73
CDN$1 = £0.45	= CDN$2.23
IR£1 = £0.80	= IR£1.25
NZ$1 = £0.30	= NZ$3.29
ZAR1 = £0.08	= ZAR12.16
US$1 = £0.69	= US$1.45
EUR€1 = £0.63	= EUR€1.59

THE IRISH POUND	IR£1 =
AUS$1 = £0.46	= AUS$2.19
CDN$1 = £0.56	= CDN$1.79
NZ$1 = £0.38	= NZ$2.64
ZAR1 = £0.10	= ZAR9.73
UK£1 = £1.25	= UK£0.80
US$1 = £0.86	= US$1.16
EUR€1 = £0.79	= EUR€1.27

As a rule, it's cheaper to convert money in Britain or Ireland than at home. However, you should bring enough foreign currency to last the first 24 to 72 hours of a trip to avoid being penniless should you arrive after bank hours or on a holiday.

When changing money abroad, try to go only to banks or bureaux de change that have at most a 5% margin between their buy and sell prices. Since you lose money with every transaction, convert as much as you think prudence allows.

If you use traveler's checks or bills, carry some in small denominations (the equivalent of US$50 or less) for times when you are forced to exchange money at disadvantageous rates, but bring a range of denominations since charges may be levied per check cashed. Store your money in a variety of forms; ideally, you will at any given time be carrying cash, traveler's checks, and a cash and/or credit card.

TRAVELER'S CHECKS

THE EURO. Since January 2001, the official currency of 12 members of the European Union—Austria, Belgium, Finland, France, Germany, Greece, Ireland, Italy, Luxembourg, the Netherlands, Portugal, and Spain—has been the euro. Actual euro banknotes and coins will be available beginning January 1, 2002; but don't throw out your francs, pesetas, and Deutschmarks just yet. The old national currencies remain legal tender through July 1, 2002, after which it's all euros, all the time. Where helpful, *Let's Go: Britain & Ireland* lists prices in both denominations, euro (€) and pound (£), based on actual figures or fixed conversion rates. The currency has some important—and positive—consequences for travelers hitting more than one euro-zone country. For one, money-changers across the euro-zone are obliged to exchange money at the official, fixed rate (see below), and at no commission (though they may still charge a small service fee). So now you can change your guilders into escudos and your escudos into lire without losing fistfuls of money on every transaction. Second, euro-denominated traveler's checks allow you to pay for goods and services across the euro-zone, again at the official rate and commission-free.

The exchange rate between euro-zone currencies was permanently fixed on January 1, 1999 at 1 EUR = 40.3399 BEF (Belgian francs) = 1.95583 DM (German marks) = 166.386 ESP (Spanish *pesetas*) = 6.55957 FRF (French francs) = 0.787564 IER (Irish pounds) = 1936.27 ITL (Italian *lire*) = 40.3399 LUF (Luxembourg francs) = 2.20371 NLG (Dutch guilders) = 13.7603 ATS (Austrian schillings) = 200.482 PTE (Portuguese *escudos*) = 5.94573 FIM (Finnish *markka*). For more info, see www.europa.eu.int.

Traveler's checks (**American Express, Thomas Cook,** and **Visa** are the most recognized) are one of the safest and least troublesome means of carrying funds. Several agencies and banks sell them for a small commission, though members of the American Automobile Association, and some banks and credit unions, can get American Express checks commission-free (see p. 44). Each agency provides refunds if your checks are lost or stolen, and many provide additional services, such as toll-free refund hotlines abroad, emergency messages, and stolen credit card assistance.

While traveling, keep check receipts and a record of which checks you've cashed separate from the checks themselves. Also leave a list of check numbers with someone at home. Never countersign checks until you're ready to cash them, and always bring your passport with you to cash them. If your checks are lost or stolen, immediately contact a refund center (of the company that issued your checks) to be reimbursed; they may require a police report verifying the loss or theft. Ask about toll-free refund hotlines and the location of refund centers when purchasing checks, and always carry emergency cash.

American Express: Call (800) 251 902 in Australia; in Ireland (01) 679 9000 or (01) 605 7709; in New Zealand (0800) 441 068; in the UK (0800) 521313; in the US and Canada (800) 221-7282; elsewhere call US collect +1 (801) 964-6665; www.aexp.com. Traveler's checks are available in British pounds as well as US dollars at 1-4% commission at AmEx offices and banks, commission-free at AAA offices (see p. 18). *Cheques for Two* can be signed by either of 2 people traveling together.

Citicorp: In the US and Canada call (800) 645-6556; in Europe, the Middle East, or Africa call the UK +44 (20) 7508 7007; elsewhere call US collect +1 (813) 623-1709. Traveler's checks (available only in US dollars, British pounds, and German marks) at 1-2% commission. Call 24hr.

Thomas Cook MasterCard: In the US and Canada call (800) 223-7373; in the UK call (0800) 622101; elsewhere call UK collect +44 (1733) 318950. Checks available in 13 currencies at 2% commission. Thomas Cook offices cash checks commission-free.

Visa: In the US call (800) 227-6811; in the UK call (0800) 895078; elsewhere call UK collect +44 (20) 7937 8091. Call for the location of their nearest office.

CREDIT CARDS

Credit cards are accepted by many businesses in Britain and Ireland. However, small establishments—including many B&Bs—will often either not accept them or add a surcharge. Where they are accepted, credit cards offer superior exchange rates. Particular cards may also offer services such as insurance or emergency help, and card numbers are sometimes required to reserve accommodations or rental cars. **MasterCard** (a.k.a. **Access** in Britain) and **Visa** (a.k.a. **Barclaycard**) are widely accepted. **American Express** cards work at some cash machines and at AmEx offices and major airports, but their surcharges annoy B&B proprietors.

Credit cards are also useful for **cash advances,** which allow you to withdraw pounds from associated banks and cash machines throughout Britain and Ireland instantly. However, transaction fees for all credit card advances (up to US$10 per advance, plus 2-3% extra on foreign transactions after conversion) tend to make credit cards a more costly way of withdrawing cash than cash cards or traveler's checks. In an emergency, however, the transaction fee may prove worth the cost. To be eligible for an advance, you'll need to get a four-digit **Personal Identification Number (PIN)** from your credit card company (see **Cash Cards,** below). If you already have a PIN, check with the company to make sure it will work in Britain and/or Ireland; also ask about any foreign transaction fees that they may charge.

CREDIT CARD COMPANIES. Visa (US ☎ (800) 336-8472; for lost cards, call (0800) 891725 in Britain or (1800) 558002 in Ireland) and **MasterCard** (US ☎ (800) 307-7309; for lost cards, call (0800) 964767 in Britain or (1800) 557378 in Ireland) are issued in cooperation with banks and other organizations. **American Express** (UK ☎ (01273) 620555; US ☎ (800) 843-2273) has an annual fee of up to US$55. AmEx cardholders may cash personal checks at AmEx offices abroad, access an emergency medical and legal assistance hotline (24hr.; UK ☎ (012) 226 6555; from Ireland call the UK at +00 44 12 2266 5555; in North America call (800) 554-2639; elsewhere call US collect +1 (715) 343-7977), and enjoy American Express Travel Service benefits (including plane, hotel, and car rental reservation changes; baggage loss and flight insurance; mailgram and international cable services; and held mail). The **Discover Card** (in US call (800) 347-2683, elsewhere call US +1 (801) 902-3100) offers cashback bonuses on most purchases, but is less widely accepted.

CASH CARDS

Cash cards—called ATM cards in the USA—are widespread in both Britain and Ireland, and you can assume that all banks listed in *Let's Go* have 24hr. cash machines (sometimes called "cashpoints") outside unless otherwise stated. Depending on the system that your home bank uses, you can probably access your personal bank account from abroad. Cash machines get the same wholesale exchange rate as credit cards, but there is often a limit on the amount of money you can withdraw per day (around US$500), and computer networks sometimes fail. There is typically also a surcharge of US$1-5 per withdrawal. Be sure to memorize your PIN code in numeric form since machines elsewhere often don't have letters on their keys (see "Please Sir, May I Have Some More?" below). Also, if your PIN is longer than four digits, ask your bank whether you need a new number.

The two major international money networks are **Cirrus** (US ☎ (800) 424-7787) and **PLUS** (US ☎ (800) 843-7587). The cash machines of all major British and Irish banks (including Barclays, HSBC, Lloyds TSB, National Westminster, Royal Bank of Scotland, Bank of Scotland, Allied Ireland Bank (AIB), and Ulster Bank) usually accept both networks. To locate cash machines in Britain and Ireland, call the above numbers, or consult www.visa.com/pd/atm or www.mastercard.com/atm.

Visa TravelMoney (for customer assistance call (0800) 963833 in Britain; (1800) 559345 in Ireland; www.visa.com/pd/trav/main.html) is a system allowing you to access money from any Visa cash machine. You deposit an amount before you travel (plus a small administration fee), and you can withdraw up to that sum. The cards, which give you the same favorable exchange rate for withdrawals as a regular Visa, are especially useful if you plan to travel through multiple countries. Obtain a card by either visiting a nearby Thomas Cook or Citicorp office, calling toll-free in the US (877) 394-2247, or checking with your local bank to see if it issues TravelMoney cards. **Road Cash** (US ☎ (877) 762-3227; www.roadcash.com) issues cards in the US with a minimum US$300 deposit.

> **PLEASE SIR, MAY I HAVE SOME MORE?** To use a cash or credit card to withdraw money from a cash machine in Europe, you must have a four-digit **Personal Identification Number (PIN)**. If your PIN is longer than four digits, ask your bank whether you can simply use the first four, or whether you'll need a new one. **Credit cards** in North America don't usually come with PINs, so if you intend to hit up cash machines in Europe with a credit card to get cash advances, call your credit card company before leaving to request one. People with alphabetic, rather than numerical, PINs may also be thrown off by the lack of letters on European cash-machine keypads. The following handy chart gives the corresponding numbers to use: 1=QZ; 2=ABC; 3=DEF; 4=GHI; 5=JKL; 6=MNO; 7=PRS; 8=TUV; and 9= WXY. Note that if you mistakenly punch the wrong code into the machine three times, it will swallow your card for good.

GETTING MONEY FROM HOME

AMERICAN EXPRESS. Cardholders can withdraw cash from their checking accounts at any of AmEx's major offices and many representative offices (up to US$1000 every 21 days; no service charge, no interest). AmEx "Express Cash" withdrawals from any AmEx ATM in Britain and Ireland are automatically debited from the cardholder's checking account or line of credit. Green-card holders may withdraw up to US$1000 in any seven-day period (2% transaction fee; minimum US$2.50, maximum US$20). To enroll in Express Cash, cardmembers may call (800) 227-4669 in the US. To contact AmEx from the UK and Ireland, call collect +1 (336) 393-1111.

WESTERN UNION. Travelers from the US, Canada, and the UK can wire money abroad through Western Union's international money transfer services. In the US, call (800) 325-6000; in Canada, (800) 235-0000; in Ireland, (0800) 395395; in the UK, (0800) 833833. The rates for sending cash are generally US$10-11 cheaper than with a credit card, and the money is usually available at its destination within an hour. To locate the nearest Western Union location, see www.westernunion.com.

US STATE DEPARTMENT (US CITIZENS ONLY). In dire emergencies only, the US State Department will forward money within hours to the nearest consular office, which will then disburse it according to instructions for a US$15 fee. If you wish to use this service, contact the Overseas Citizens Service division of the US State Department (☎ (202) 647-5225; nights, Sundays, and holidays ☎ (202) 647-4000).

TIPPING AND BARGAINING

Tips in restaurants are usually included in the bill (sometimes as a "service charge"); if gratuity is not included, you should tip 10-15%. Tipping the barman in pubs is not at all expected and almost never done, though a waiter or waitress should be tipped. Tour guides and theater ushers are rarely tipped. Taxi drivers should receive a 10% tip, and bellhops and chambermaids usually expect somewhere between £1 and £3.

Money From Home In Minutes.

If you're stuck for cash on your travels, don't panic. Millions of people trust Western Union to transfer money in minutes to over 185 countries and over 95,000 locations worldwide. Our record of safety and reliability is second to none. You can even send money by phone without leaving home by using a credit card. For more information, call Western Union: USA 1-800-325-6000, Canada 1-800-235-0000.

www.westernunion.com

WESTERN UNION | MONEY TRANSFER

The fastest way to send money worldwide.

If you're at an outdoor market, bargaining is sometimes acceptable. A general rule is that if there is a price tag, don't bargain, but if there is no indication of price then bartering is fair game. Don't expect to barter anywhere else.

TAXES

Both Britain and Ireland have a 17.5% **Value Added Tax (VAT)**, a sales tax applied to everything but food, books, medicine, and children's clothing. The tax is **included** within the price indicated on the price tag—no extra expenses should be added at the register. The prices stated in *Let's Go* include VAT unless otherwise specified. Non-EU citizens can reclaim VAT through the **Retail Export Scheme** upon exiting Britain, though this is a complex procedure only worthwhile for large purchases. Not all shops participate in the scheme, and of those that do, many have a purchase minimum of £50 before they offer refunds. An administrative fee is often deducted from your refund. Shops that do give refunds fill out a form, which must be presented with the goods and receipts to customs upon departure (look for the TaxFree Refund desk at the airport). At peak hours, this additional process can take as long as an hour, so plan accordingly. Once you have checked in and passed security, you may receive your refund directly. To obtain the refund by check or credit card, send the form (stamped by customs) back in the envelope provided; the shopkeeper will then credit your refund. You must leave the country within three months of your purchase in order to claim a VAT refund, but you cannot receive a refund unless you apply for it before leaving the UK. You cannot receive a refund on accommodations and meals.

SAFETY AND SECURITY
PERSONAL SAFETY

> **!** The **national emergency number** in both Britain and Ireland for police, ambulance, fire, and (in appropriate areas) coastguard and mountain rescue services is **999**. The **112** EU-wide number will also work.

EXPLORING. If you keep your wits about you, traveling in Britain and Ireland is relatively safe. Be alert about your belongings, surroundings, and companions, and exercise caution in larger cities. Both **muggers** and **pickpockets** are present in big-city transport systems and packed streets and markets. To avoid unwanted attention, try to blend in as much as possible. The gawking camera-toter is a more obvious target than the low-profile traveler. Wearing a backpack on both shoulders, a baseball cap, or a hip pack (always called a bum-bag in Britain; see **Language,** p. 751) immediately marks you as a foreigner. Familiarize yourself with your surroundings before setting out, and carry yourself with confidence; if you must check a map on the street, duck into a shop rather than stopping in the middle of the sidewalk. If you are traveling alone, be sure someone at home knows your itinerary, and never admit that you're on your own.

SELF DEFENSE. There is no sure-fire way to avoid all the threatening situations you might encounter when you travel, but a good self-defense course will give you concrete ways to react to unwanted advances. **Impact, Prepare, and Model Mugging** can refer you to local self-defense courses in the US (☎ (800) 345-5425). Visit the web site at www.impactsafety.org/chapters for a list of nearby chapters. Workshops (2-3hr.) start at US$50; full courses run US$350-500.

DRIVING. Driving in Britain and Ireland is considered relatively safe, and the roads and motorways are for the most part in excellent condition. Britons and the Irish drive on the left—if you come from a country that drives on the right then expect to spend at least a few hours becoming accustomed to driving on the other side of the road and to having the steering wheel on the right side of the car.

You must wear a **seatbelt** in the front of the car, and in the back provided the car has them fitted. The driver is responsible for ensuring that all passengers under age 18 are wearing seatbelts. Children under 40lbs. should ride only in a specially designed carseat, available for a small fee from most car rental agencies. Study route maps before you hit the road, especially in Northern Scotland, where shoulders, motorways, and gas stations are rare. For long drives in desolate areas, invest in a cellular phone and a **roadside assistance program** such as the RAC or the AA (see p. 43). **Sleeping in your car** is one of the most dangerous (and often illegal) ways to get your rest. If your car breaks down on a motorway, call 999 and wait for the police to assist you. For more information, see **By Car,** p. 43.

CYCLING. If you're cycling, wear reflective clothing, drink plenty of water (even if you're not thirsty), and ride on the same side as the traffic. Learn the international signals for turns, and use them. Know how to fix a modern derailleur-equipped chain mount and change a tire, and practice on your own bike; a few simple tools and a good bike manual will be invaluable. Cycling on a motorway is illegal and highly dangerous.

PUBLIC TRANSPORT. Britain's system of public transport is well developed and reasonably safe. Avoid getting into train or Underground carriages by yourself late at night, and stick to the more populated parts of the platform when waiting for a train. **Night buses** are a reliable if unsavory way of traveling around big cities; you may be accompanied by drunken revelers, but drivers are well aware of potential problems and usually throw troublemakers off the bus before problems start. Taxis fall into two groups—government-licensed **taxis** and freelance **minicabs.** The former is usually the safer option: while there are some reputable minicab firms that *Let's Go* lists, others may not be reliable and may compromise your safety.

Let's Go does not recommend **hitchhiking** under any circumstances, particularly for women—see **Getting Around** (p. 36) for more information.

TERRORISM. Terrorist groups in Northern Ireland have attacked cities throughout Britain over the past several decades. It is obviously difficult to predict where or when these attacks will occur. Most Irish terrorist organizations set out to cause maximum monetary damage but minimum casualty. Britain deals with terrorism by asking the population to stay alert—if you see **unattended packages** on public transport, notify the driver or a guard immediately. "Travel Advisories" offers a list of informative government offices. Check for updates on the situation at www.state.gov or www.visitbritain.com.

TRAVEL ADVISORIES. The following government offices provide travel information and advisories by telephone, by fax, or via the web:

Australian Department of Foreign Affairs and Trade: ☎ (02) 6261 1111; www.dfat.gov.au.

Canadian Department of Foreign Affairs and International Trade (DFAIT): In Canada call (800) 267-8316, elsewhere call +1 (613) 944-4000; www.dfait-maeci.gc.ca.

New Zealand Ministry of Foreign Affairs: ☎ (04) 494 8500; www.mft.govt.nz/trav.html.

United Kingdom Foreign and Commonwealth Office: ☎ (020) 7008 0232; www.fco.gov.uk.

US Department of State: ☎ (202) 647-5225; http://travel.state.gov. For *A Safe Trip Abroad,* call (202) 512-1800.

FINANCIAL SECURITY

PROTECTING YOUR VALUABLES. Theft in Britain and Ireland is not exceptionally common, but this does not mean you should let your guard down. Hostels, train stations, and tourist sights are some of the most common areas for petty theft. There are a few steps you can take to minimize the financial risk associated with traveling. First, bring as little with you as possible. Leave expensive watches, jewelry, cameras, and electronic equipment at home; chances are you'd break them, lose them, or get sick of lugging them around anyway. Second, buy a few combination **padlocks** to secure your belongings either in your pack—which you should **never leave unattended**—or in a hostel or train station locker. **Don't put a wallet in your back pocket, or in the back of your backpack,** and never count your money in public. Third, **carry as little cash as possible;** instead carry traveler's checks and cash/credit cards, keeping them in a money belt—not a "fanny pack"—along with your passport and ID cards. Fourth, **keep a small cash reserve separate from your primary stash.** This should entail about US$50 sewn into or stored in the depths of your pack, along with your traveler's check numbers and important photocopies.

CON ARTISTS AND PICKPOCKETS. Among the more colorful aspects of large cities are **con artists.** They often work in groups, and children are some of the most effective. They possess an innumerable range of ruses. Beware of certain classics: sob stories that require money, rolls of bills "found" on the street, mustard spilled (or saliva spit) onto your shoulder to distract you while they snatch your bag. Don't ever hand over your passport to someone whose authority you question (ask to accompany them to a police station if they insist), and **don't ever let your passport out of your sight.** Similarly, don't let your bag out of sight; never trust a "station-porter" who insists on carrying your bag or stowing it in the baggage compartment or a "new friend" who offers to guard your bag while you buy a train ticket or use the restroom. Beware of **pickpockets** in city crowds, especially on public transportation. Take care between 8-10am and 4-6pm—rush hour is no excuse for strangers to press up against you on the Tube or on buses. Also, be alert in public telephone booths. If you must say your calling card number, do so very quietly; if you punch it in, make sure no one can look over your shoulder.

ACCOMMODATIONS AND TRANSPORTATION. Never leave your belongings unattended; crime occurs in even the most demure-looking hostel or hotel. Bring your own **padlock** for hostel lockers, and don't ever store valuables in any locker.

Be particularly careful on **buses** and **trains;** horror stories abound about determined thieves who wait for travelers to fall asleep. Carry your backpack in front of you where you can see it. When traveling with others, sleep in alternate shifts. When alone, use good judgement in selecting a train compartment: never stay in an empty one, and use a lock to secure your pack to the luggage rack. Try to sleep on top bunks with your luggage stored above you (if not in bed with you), and keep important documents and other valuables on your person.

If traveling by **car,** don't leave valuables (such as radios or luggage) in it while you are away. If your tape deck or radio is removable, hide it in the trunk or take it with you. If it isn't, at least conceal it. Similarly, hide baggage in the trunk—though savvy thieves can tell if a car is heavily loaded by the way it sits on its tires.

DRUGS AND ALCOHOL

A meek "I didn't know it was illegal" will not suffice. Remember that you are subject to the laws of the country in which you travel, and it's your responsibility to familiarize yourself with these laws before you go. If you carry insulin, syringes, or any other **prescription drugs** while you travel, it is vital to have a copy of the prescriptions themselves and a note from your doctor. The Brits and the Irish certainly love their drink, and the pub scene in Britain and Ireland is one of unavoidable vibrance. **Public drunkenness,** on the other hand, *is* to be avoided; it can jeopardize your safety. The drinking age in Britain and Ireland is 18.

Needless to say, **illegal drugs** are best avoided altogether; the average sentence for possession in the United Kingdom is around two years. One of the worst things you can do is carry drugs across an international border: not only could you end up in prison, you could be blessed with a "Drug Trafficker" stamp on your passport for the rest of your life. If arrested, call your country's consulate, as embassies may not be willing to help those arrested on drug charges. Refuse to carry anyone's excess luggage onto a plane; it's not chivalrous, we know, but neither will you risk winding up in jail for possession of a controlled substance.

HEALTH

BEFORE YOU GO
Preparation can help minimize the likelihood of contracting a disease and maximize the chances of receiving effective health care in the event of an emergency. For tips on packing a basic **first-aid kit** and other health essentials, see p. 22.

In your passport, write the names of people you wish to be contacted in case of a medical emergency, and also list any allergies or medical conditions of which you would want doctors to be aware. Matching a prescription to its British or Irish equivalent is not always easy, safe, or possible. Carry up-to-date, legible prescriptions or a statement from your doctor stating the medication's trade name, manufacturer, chemical name, and dosage. While traveling, be sure to keep all medication with you in your carry-on luggage.

IMMUNIZATIONS AND PRECAUTIONS
Travelers over two years old should be sure that the following vaccines are up-to-date: MMR (for measles, mumps, and rubella); DTaP or Td (for diptheria, tetanus, and pertussis); OPV (for polio); HbCV (for haemophilus influenza B); and HBV (for hepatitis B). For recommendations on immunizations and prophylaxis, consult the CDC (see below) in the US or the equivalent in your home country, and check with a doctor for guidance. No injections are specifically required for entry into the UK, though protection against hepatitis B and tetanus is highly recommended. Your home country may require further vaccinations for re-entry.

USEFUL ORGANIZATIONS AND PUBLICATIONS
The US **Centers for Disease Control and Prevention (CDC; ☎** (877) FYI-TRIP (394-8747); www.cdc.gov/travel) maintain an international fax information service and an international traveler's hotline (☎ (404) 332-4559). The CDC's comprehensive booklet *Health Information for International Travel*, an annual rundown of disease, immunization, and general health advice, is free online or US$25 via the Public Health Foundation (☎ (877) 252-1200). Consult the appropriate government agency of your home country for consular information sheets on health, entry requirements, and other issues for your country or countries of destination (see the listings in the box on **Travel Advisories,** p. 23). For quick information on health and other travel warnings, call the **Overseas Citizens Services** (☎ (202) 647-5225; after-hours ☎ (202) 647-4000), or contact a passport agency, embassy, or consulate abroad. US citizens can send a self-addressed, stamped envelope to the Overseas Citizens Services, Bureau of Consular Affairs, #4811, US Department of State, Washington, D.C. 20520. For information on medical evacuation services and travel insurance firms, see the US government's web site at http://travel.state.gov/medical.html or the **British Foreign and Commonwealth Office** (www.fco.gov.uk).

MEDICAL ASSISTANCE ON THE ROAD
In both Britain and Ireland, medical aid is readily available and of the quality you would expect in major Western countries. For minor ailments, **chemists** (drugstores) are plentiful. Individual chemists often hang green, symmetrical crosses outside their stores, whereas the **Boots** chain has a blue logo and can be found in almost every town. **Late night pharmacies** are rare, even in big cities. If you are in

need of more serious attention, most major hospitals have **24hr. emergency rooms** (called "casualty departments" or "A&E," short for Accident and Emergency). Call the numbers listed in the box below for assistance.

> **!** Call the local police station for the nearest doctor or hospital casualty department. In England and Wales you can also call **NHS Direct**, a 24hr. advice service staffed by nurses (☎ 0845 4647). In Scotland, the NHS **Helpline** (☎ (0800) 224488) offers information on health services. In more serious emergencies, the emergency number for ambulance assistance is ☎ **999** in both Britain and Ireland, and the EU-wide ☎ **112** works as well.

In Britain, the state-run **National Health Service (NHS)** encompasses the majority of health-care centers. There are a few private hospitals in larger cities, but these cater to the wealthy and are not often equipped with full surgical staff or complete casualty units. Citizens of EU countries and certain Commonwealth countries are entitled to free medical care in the UK at any NHS hospital or clinic. EU nationals also receive free medical care in Ireland. **Health insurance** is a must for all others visiting either Britain or Ireland, who will be charged for all medical services. If you are working or studying legally in the UK, however, NHS tax is deducted from your wages, and care is free. Most travel insurance covers health care, while most American health-insurance plans (except Medicare) cover members' medical emergencies during trips abroad; check with your insurance carrier to be sure. For more information, see **Insurance**, p. 28.

Those with medical conditions (diabetes, allergies to antibiotics, epilepsy, heart conditions) may want to obtain a stainless-steel **Medic Alert** ID tag (first year US$35, annually thereafter US$20), which identifies the condition and gives a 24hr. collect-call number. Contact the Medic Alert Foundation, 2323 Colorado Ave, Turlock, CA 95382, USA (☎ (888) 633-4298; www.medicalert.org).

ONCE IN BRITAIN AND IRELAND

ENVIRONMENTAL HAZARDS
While the local weather has a reputation for overcast skies, there always remains the possibility of **sunburn:** the sun can be fierce even through the clouds. Apply sunscreen liberally and often. If you get sunburned despite safety measures, drink more fluids than usual and apply calamine or an aloe-based lotion.

Travelers to the Scottish Highlands during the winter, and anyone attempting to climb mountains, should take precautions against the cold. A rapid drop in body temperature is the clearest warning sign of **hypothermia.** Victims may also shiver, feel exhausted, have poor coordination or slurred speech, hallucinate, or suffer amnesia. Seek medical help, and *do not let hypothermia victims fall asleep*—their body temperature will continue to drop and they may die. To avoid hypothermia, keep dry, wear layers, and stay out of the wind. In wet weather, **wool** and **synthetics** such as pile retain heat. Most other fabrics, especially cotton, will make you colder. If a region of skin turns white, waxy, and cold, do not rub the area; it may be a sign of **frostbite.** Drink warm beverages, get dry, and slowly warm the area with dry fabric or steady body contact until a doctor can be found.

The common European **stinging nettle** is an annoyance rather than a serious health risk. The nettles are found from early spring to late autumn almost everywhere that plants can grow, and are distinguished by their serrated leaves. Getting caught in a patch of nettles results in a stinging feeling followed by small reddish swellings and possible numbness.

INSECTS AND TICK-BORNE DISEASES
Be aware of insects—particularly fleas and lice—in wet or forested areas. Vitamin B-12 and garlic pills, taken regularly, act as natural repellents. Calamine lotion or topical cortisones (like Cortaid) stop bites from itching, as can a bath with half a cup of baking soda.

Ticks can be particularly dangerous in rural and forested regions. Pause periodically while walking to brush off ticks using a fine-toothed comb on your neck, scalp, and legs. **Lyme disease,** carried by ticks, is a bacterial infection marked by a circular bull's-eye rash of two inches or more that appears around the bite. Later symptoms include fever, headache, fatigue, and aches. Antibiotics are effective if administered early. Left untreated, it can cause problems in joints, the heart, and the nervous system. If you find a tick attached to your skin, grasp its head parts with tweezers as close to your skin as possible and apply slow, steady traction. Do not remove ticks by burning them or coating them with nail polish remover or petroleum jelly. Removing a tick within 24hr. greatly reduces the risk of infection.

FOOD- AND WATER-BORNE DISEASES

Two recent diseases originating in British livestock have made international headlines, and rightly given travelers pause. Bovine spongiform encephalopathy (BSE), better known as **Mad Cow Disease,** is a chronic degenerative disease affecting the central nervous system of cattle. The human variant is called Cruetzfeldt-Jakob disease (nvCJD), and both forms of the disease involve invariably fatal brain damage. Information on nvCJD is not conclusive, but the disease is thought to be caused by consuming infected beef; however, the risk is extremely small (around 1 case per 10 billion meat servings). Scientists believe that consuming milk and milk products does not pose a risk. **Foot and Mouth Disease (FMD)** experienced one of its worst outbreaks in 2001, largely in the UK and other countries in Western Europe. FMD is easily transmissible between cloven-hoofed animals (cows, pigs, sheep, goats, and deer), but does not pose a health threat to humans, causing mild symptoms if any. As of publication, the UK and Ireland have restricted travel to farms and other rural areas, but the majority of both countries remain accessible to visitors, and the epidemic is expected to subside by 2002. FMD is believed to be killed by heat, making cooked meats safe for consumption; fish, poultry, fruits, and vegetables pose no FMD risk.

Parasites such as microbes and tapeworms hide in unsafe water and food. **Giardiasis,** for example, is acquired by drinking untreated water from streams or lakes. Symptoms of parasitic infections include swollen glands or lymph nodes, fever, rashes or itchiness, digestive problems, eye problems, and anemia. Tap water throughout Britain and Ireland is safe, but when **camping,** boil your water or treat it with **iodine tablets** (available at any camping goods store), wear shoes, and eat only cooked food.

AIDS, HIV, AND STDS

For detailed information on **Acquired Immune Deficiency Syndrome (AIDS)** in Britain and Ireland, call the **US Centers for Disease Control's** 24hr. hotline at (800) 342-2437, or contact the **Joint United Nations Programme on HIV/AIDS (UNAIDS),** 20, av. Appia, CH-1211 Geneva 27, Switzerland (☎ +41 (22) 791 36 66). The Council on International Educational Exchange's pamphlet, *Travel Safe: AIDS and International Travel*, is posted on their web site (www.ciee.org/Isp/safety/travelsafe.htm), along with links to other online and phone resources. Currently the UK has slight restrictions on **HIV-positive travelers;** if you appear unwell you may be tested on entrance, and a positive result may block your entrance to Britain. Contact your local British consulate or embassy (see p. 9) for details.

Sexually transmitted diseases (STDs) such as gonorrhea, chlamydia, genital warts, syphilis, and herpes are easier to catch than HIV and can be as deadly. **Hepatitis B** and **C** are also serious STDs. Though condoms (such as the common British brands Durex and Mates) may protect you from some STDs, oral or even tactile contact can allow transmission. Warning signs include swelling, sores, bumps, or blisters on sex organs, the rectum, or the mouth; burning and pain during urination and bowel movements; genital itching; swelling or redness of the throat; and flu-like symptoms. If these symptoms develop, see a doctor immediately.

WOMEN'S HEALTH

Women traveling are vulnerable to **urinary tract** and **bladder infections,** which can cause a burning sensation and painful and frequent urination. To avoid these, drink plenty of vitamin C-rich juice and clean water, and urinate frequently, especially right after intercourse. Women are also susceptible to **vaginal yeast infections,** which are likely to flare up in hot and humid weather; wearing loose-fitting clothes and cotton underwear will help, as will over-the-counter remedies like Monistat or Gynelotrimin. **Tampons** and **pads** are easily available, and reliable **contraceptive devices** are also relatively easy to find. Women on the Pill should bring enough supplies to allow for possible loss, or should bring their prescription. Women who need an **abortion** while in the UK should contact the **United Kingdom Family Planning Association,** 2-12 Pentonville Rd., London N1 9PF (☎(0171) 837 5432), for more information. Abortions are illegal in Ireland; call the London office if you need help. For **further information,** consult the *Handbook for Women Travellers*, by Maggie and Gemma Moss (Piatkus Books, £8 or US$15).

INSURANCE

Travel insurance generally covers four areas: medical/health problems, property loss, trip cancellation/interruption, and emergency evacuation. Although your regular insurance policies may extend to travel-related accidents, you might consider purchasing travel insurance if the cost of potential trip cancellation/interruption is greater than you can absorb. Prices for travel insurance purchased separately generally run about US$50 per week for full coverage, while trip cancellation/interruption may be purchased separately for about US$5.50 per US$100 of coverage.

Medical insurance (especially university policies) often covers costs incurred abroad; check with your provider. **US Medicare** does not cover foreign travel. **Canadians** are protected by their home province's health insurance plan for up to 90 days after leaving the country; check with the provincial Ministry of Health or Health Plan Headquarters for details. **Australians** traveling in the UK are entitled to many of the services that they would receive at home as part of the Reciprocal Health Care Agreement. **Homeowners' insurance** (or your family's coverage) often covers theft during travel and loss of travel documents (passport, plane ticket, railpass, etc.) up to US$500.

ISIC and **ITIC** (see p. 13) provide basic insurance benefits, including US$100 per day of in-hospital sickness for up to 60 days, US$3000 of accident-related medical reimbursement, and US$25,000 for emergency medical transport. Cardholders have access to a toll-free 24hr. helpline (run by the insurance provider TravelGuard) for medical, legal, and financial emergencies overseas (UK ☎(020) 8762 8110; US and Canada ☎(877) 370-4742; or call US collect +1 (715) 345-0505). **American Express** (UK ☎(012) 226 6555; US ☎(800) 528-4800) grants most cardholders automatic rental car insurance (collision and theft, but not liability) and ground-travel accident coverage of US$100,000 on flights purchased with the card.

INSURANCE PROVIDERS. Council and **STA** (see p. 30) offer a range of plans that can supplement your basic coverage. Other private insurance providers in the US and Canada include: **Access America** (☎(800) 284-8300); **Berkely Group/Carefree Travel Insurance** (☎(800) 323-3149; www.berkely.com); **Globalcare Travel Insurance** (☎(800) 821-2488; www.globalcare-cocco.com); and **Travel Assistance International** (☎(800) 821-2828; www.worldwide-assistance.com). Providers in the **UK** include **Campus Travel** (☎(01865) 258000) and **Columbus Travel Insurance** (☎(020) 7375 0011). In **Australia,** try **CIC Insurance** (☎9202 8000).

PACKING

You should be able to purchase most things you need in Britain and in Ireland, so **pack lightly:** a good rule is to lay out only what you absolutely need, then take half the clothes and twice the money. The less you have, the less you have to lose, store, or carry, plus you'll have space for the souvenirs you pick up along the way. If you plan to do a lot of hiking, see the section on **Camping & the Outdoors,** p. 52.

LUGGAGE. If you plan to cover most of your itinerary by foot, a sturdy **frame backpack** is unbeatable. (For the basics on buying a pack, see p. 53.) Before you leave, pack your bag, strap it on, and imagine yourself walking uphill on hot asphalt for three hours: this should give you a sense of how important it is to pack lightly. Toting a **suitcase** or **trunk** is fine if you plan to live in one or two cities and explore from there, but a very bad idea if you're going to be moving around. In addition to your main piece of luggage, a **daypack** (a small backpack or courier bag) is a must.

CLOTHING. While temperatures in Britain and Ireland never reach arctic levels, it's still a good idea to bring a **warm jacket** or wool sweater. No matter when you're traveling, bring a **rain jacket,** sturdy shoes, and thick socks. Remember that wool will keep you warm even when soaked through, whereas wet cotton is colder than wearing nothing at all. **Flip-flops** or waterproof sandals are must-haves for grubby hostel showers. Those intending to go out at night should also include a **dressier outfit** (and a nicer pair of shoes if space permits) in case dress codes are in place.

SLEEPSACK. Some hostels require that you provide your own linen or rent sheets from them. Save cash by making your own sleepsack (fold a full-size sheet in half the long way, then sew it closed along the long side and one of the short sides), or buy one at a camping store.

CONVERTERS AND ADAPTERS. In both Britain and Ireland, electricity is **240 volts AC,** enough to fry any 110V North American appliance; most European 220V appliances are fine. Visit a hardware store for an adapter (which changes the shape of the plug to the three-square-pin kind used in the UK) and a transformer (which changes the voltage).

TOILETRIES. Toothbrushes, towels, cold-water soap, talcum powder (to keep feet dry), deodorant, razors, tampons, and condoms are readily available in Britain and Ireland at chemists such as the Boots chain. **Contact lenses,** on the other hand, may be expensive and more complicated to find, so bring an extra pair, solution, your glasses, and a copy of your contact prescription. If you use heat-disinfection, either switch temporarily to a chemical disinfection system (check first to make sure it's safe with your brand of lenses), or buy a converter to 220/240V.

FIRST-AID KIT. For a basic first-aid kit, pack: bandages, pain reliever, antibiotic cream, a thermometer, a Swiss Army knife, tweezers, moleskin, decongestant, motion-sickness remedy, diarrhea or upset-stomach medication (Pepto Bismol or Immodium AD), an antihistamine, sunscreen, insect repellent, and burn ointment.

FILM. Film in Britain generally costs £4 for a roll of 24 color exposures; film in Ireland costs around IR£4. Developing film in the UK usually costs about half of what it does in the US. Since you're likely to get overcast conditions, you should use film marked ISO 200 or higher. Less serious photographers might consider bringing a **disposable camera** or two rather than an expensive permanent one. Despite disclaimers, airport security X-rays *can* fog film, so either buy a lead-lined pouch, sold at camera stores, or ask the security to hand inspect it. Always pack film in your carry-on luggage, since higher-intensity X-rays are used on checked luggage.

OTHER USEFUL ITEMS. For safety purposes, you should bring a **money belt** and small **padlock.** Basic **outdoors equipment** (plastic water bottle, compass, waterproof matches, pocketknife, sunglasses, sunscreen, hat) may also prove useful. **Quick**

repairs of torn garments can be done on the road with a needle and thread; also consider bringing electrical tape for patching tears. **Other things** you're liable to forget: an umbrella; sealable plastic bags (for damp clothes, soap, food, shampoo, and other spillables); an alarm clock; safety pins; rubber bands; a flashlight; earplugs; garbage bags; laundry detergent and a makeshift clothesline for doing laundry by hand; and a small calculator.

IMPORTANT DOCUMENTS. Don't forget your passport, traveler's checks, credit and/or cash cards, and adequate ID (see p. 13). Also check that you have any of the following that might apply to you: an ISIC or ITIC card (see p. 12); a hosteling membership card (see p. 47); your driver's license (see p. 13); travel insurance forms; and/or rail or bus passes (see p. 38).

GETTING THERE

BY PLANE

When it comes to airfare, a little effort can save you a bundle. If your plans are flexible enough to deal with the restrictions, courier fares are the cheapest. Tickets bought from consolidators and standby seating are also good deals, but last-minute specials, airfare wars, and charter flights often beat these fares. The key is to hunt around, to be flexible, and to ask persistently about discounts. Students, seniors, and those under 26 should never pay full price for a ticket.

AIRFARES

Airfares to Britain and Ireland peak between June and September; holidays (such as Christmas and Easter) are also expensive. The cheapest flights tend to arrive very early in the morning, local time. Midweek (M-Th morning) round-trip flights run US$40-50 cheaper than weekend flights, but they are generally more crowded and less likely to permit frequent-flier upgrades. Traveling with an "open return" ticket can be pricier than fixing a return date when buying the ticket. Round-trip flights are by far the cheapest; "open-jaw" (arriving in and departing from different cities) tickets tend to be pricier. Patching one-way flights together is the most expensive way to travel. Most long-haul flights into Britain land at one of the two major London airports, Heathrow or Gatwick. Some fly directly to regional airports such as Manchester, Glasgow, or Edinburgh. Flights to Ireland usually land in Dublin or Shannon.

If Britain or Ireland is only one stop on a more extensive globe-hop, consider a round-the-world (RTW) ticket. Tickets usually include at least 5 stops and are valid for about a year; prices range US$1200-5000. Try **Northwest Airlines/KLM** (US ☎(800) 447-4747; www.nwa.com) or **Star Alliance,** a consortium of 22 airlines including United Airlines (US ☎(800) 241-6522; www.star-alliance.com).

Fares for roundtrip flights to London from the US or Canada range from US$160-350 (during the off season) to US$200-600 (during the summer).

BUDGET AND STUDENT TRAVEL AGENCIES

While knowledgeable agents specializing in flights to Britain and Ireland can make your life easy and help you save, they may not spend the time to find you the lowest possible fare—they get paid on commission. Travelers holding **ISIC** and **IYTC cards** (see p. 13) qualify for big discounts from student travel agencies. Most flights from budget agencies are on major airlines, but in peak season some may sell seats on less reliable chartered aircraft.

> **usit world** (www.usitworld.com). Over 50 **usit campus** branches in the UK (www.usitcampus.co.uk), including 52 Grosvenor Gardens, **London** SW1W 0AG (☎(0870) 240 1010); **Manchester** (☎(0161) 273 1880); and **Edinburgh** (☎(0131) 668 3303). Nearly 20 **usit NOW** offices in Ireland, including 19-21 Aston Quay, O'Connell Bridge, **Dublin** 2 (☎(01) 602 1600; www.usitnow.ie), and **Belfast** (☎(02) 890 327 111; www.usitnow.com). Offices also in Athens, Auckland, Brussels, Frankfurt, Johannesburg, Lisbon, Luxembourg, Madrid, Paris, Sofia, and Warsaw.

Council Travel (www.counciltravel.com). Countless US offices, including branches in Atlanta, Boston, Chicago, L.A., New York, San Francisco, Seattle, and Washington, D.C. Check the web site or call (800) 2-COUNCIL (226-8624) for the office nearest you.

CTS Travel, 44 Goodge St., **London** W1T 2AD (☎(0207) 636 0031; ctsinfo@ctstravel.co.uk).

STA Travel, 7890 S. Hardy Dr., Ste. 110, Tempe AZ 85284 (24hr. reservations and info ☎(800) 777-0112; www.statravel.com). A student and youth travel organization with countless offices worldwide (check their web site for a listing of all their offices), including US offices in Boston, Chicago, L.A., New York, San Francisco, Seattle, and Washington, D.C. Ticket booking, travel insurance, railpasses, and more. In the UK, walk-in office 11 Goodge St., **London** W1T 2PF or call (0870) 160 6070. In New Zealand, 10 High St., **Auckland** (☎(09) 309 0458). In Australia, 366 Lygon St., **Melbourne** Vic 3053 (☎(03) 9349 4344).

StudentUniverse, 545 Fifth Ave., Suite 640, New York, NY 10017 (toll-free customer service ☎(800) 272-9676, outside the US (212) 986-8420; help@studentuniverse.com; www.studentuniverse.com), is an online student travel service offering discount ticket booking, travel insurance, destination guides, and much more. Customer service line open M-F 9am-8pm and Sa noon-5pm EST.

Travel CUTS (Canadian Universities Travel Services Limited), 187 College St., **Toronto,** ON M5T 1P7 (☎(416) 979-2406; www.travelcuts.com). 60 offices across Canada. Also in the UK, 295-A Regent St., **London** W1R 7YA (☎(0207) 255 1944).

Wasteels, Skoubogade 6, 1158 Copenhagen K. (☎3314 4633; www.wasteels.dk/uk). A huge chain with 165 locations across Europe. Sells Wasteels BIJ tickets discounted 30-45% off regular fare, 2nd-class international point-to-point train tickets with unlimited stopovers for those under 26 (sold only in Europe).

✈ **FLIGHT PLANNING ON THE INTERNET.** The Internet is without a doubt one of the best places to look for travel bargains—it's fast and convenient, and you can spend as long as you like exploring options without driving your travel agent insane.

Many airline sites offer special last-minute deals on the Web. The following airlines fly frequently to Britain and Ireland and have useful reservation services and search engines at their web sites: **Air New Zealand** (www.airnz.com); **American Airlines** (www.americanair.com); **British Airways** (www.british-airways.com); **Qantas** (www.qantas.com.au); **Singapore Airlines** (www.singaporeair.com); **United Airlines** (www.ual.com); **Virgin Atlantic** (www.fly.virgin.com). Other sites do the legwork and compile the deals for you—try www.bestfares.com, www.onetravel.com, www.lowestfare.com, and www.travelzoo.com.

 Student-Universe (www.studentuniverse.com), **Council** (www.counciltravel.com), and **STA** (www.sta-travel.com) provide quotes on student tickets, while **Expedia** (msn.expedia.com) and **Travelocity** (www.travelocity.com) offer full travel services. **Priceline** (www.priceline.com) allows you to specify a price, and obligates you to buy any ticket that meets or beats it; be prepared for antisocial hours and odd routes. **Skyauction** (www.skyauction.com) allows you to bid on both last-minute and advance-purchase tickets.

COMMERCIAL AIRLINES

The commercial airlines' lowest regular offer is the **APEX** (Advance Purchase Excursion) fare, which provides confirmed reservations and allows "open-jaw" tickets. Generally, reservations must be made seven to 21 days ahead of departure, with seven- to 14-day minimum-stay and up to 90-day maximum-stay restrictions. These fares carry hefty cancellation and change penalties (fees rise in summer). Book peak-season APEX fares early; by May you will have a hard time getting your desired departure date. Use **Microsoft Expedia** (msn.expedia.com) or **Travelocity** (www.travelocity.com) to get an idea of the lowest published fares, then use the resources outlined here to try and beat those fares. Low-season fares should be appreciably cheaper than the high-season (mid-June to Aug.) ones listed here.

TRAVELING FROM NORTH AMERICA
Basic round-trip fares to London range US$200-600. Standard commercial carriers like American (☎(800) 433-7300; www.aa.com) and United (☎(800) 241-6522; www.ual.com) will probably offer the most convenient flights, but they may not be the cheapest, unless you manage to grab a special promotion or airfare war ticket. You might find flying one of the following airlines a better deal, if any of their limited departure points is convenient for you.

Icelandair: ☎(800) 223-5500; www.icelandair.com. Stopovers in Iceland for no extra cost on most transatlantic flights. New York to London May-Sept. US$450-800; Oct.-May US$390-$500. For last-minute offers, subscribe to their email Lucky Fares.

Finnair: ☎(800) 950-5000; www.us.finnair.com. Cheap round-trips from San Francisco, New York, and Toronto to London; connections throughout Europe.

TRAVELING FROM AUSTRALIA AND NEW ZEALAND
Air New Zealand: New Zealand ☎(0800) 35 22 66; www.airnz.co.nz. Auckland to London.

Qantas Air: Australia ☎13 13 13, New Zealand ☎(0800) 808 767; www.qantas.com.au. Flights from Australia and New Zealand to London for around AUS$2400.

Singapore Air: Australia ☎13 10 11, New Zealand ☎(0800) 808 909; www.singaporeair.com. Flies from Auckland, Sydney, Melbourne, and Perth to western Europe.

Thai Airways: Australia ☎(1300) 65 19 60, New Zealand ☎(09) 377 3886; www.thaiair.com. Auckland, Sydney, and Melbourne to London.

TRAVELING FROM SOUTH AFRICA
Air France: ☎(011) 880 80 40; www.airfrance.com. Johannesburg to Paris; connections throughout Europe.

British Airways: ☎(0860) 011747; www.british-airways.com/regional/sa. Cape Town and Johannesburg to the UK and the rest of Europe from ZAR3400.

Lufthansa: ☎(011) 484 4711; www.lufthansa.co.za. From Cape Town, Durban, and Johannesburg to the UK through Germany.

Virgin Atlantic: ☎(011) 340 3400; www.virgin-atlantic.co.za. Flies to London from both Cape Town and Johannesburg.

AIR COURIER FLIGHTS
Those who travel light should consider courier flights. Couriers help transport cargo on international flights by using their checked luggage space for freight. Generally, couriers must travel with carry-ons only and deal with complex flight restrictions. Most flights are round-trip only, with short fixed-length stays (usually one week). In addition, most of these flights only operate out of major gateway cities, primarily in North America. Round-trip courier fares from the US to Britain and Ireland run about US$150-350. Most flights leave from New York, Los Angeles, San Francisco, or Miami in the US; and from Montreal, Toronto, or Vancouver in Canada. Generally, you must be over 21 (in some cases 18). In summer, popular destinations like London tend to require an advance reservation of about two weeks, though you can often book up to two months ahead. Super-discounted fares are common for "last-minute" flights (three to 14 days ahead).

TRAVELING FROM NORTH AMERICA
The first four organizations below provide their members with lists of opportunities and courier brokers worldwide for an annual fee (typically US$50-60). Alternatively, you can contact a courier broker (such as the last three listings) directly; most charge registration fees, but a few don't. Prices quoted below are round-trip.

Air Courier Association, 15000 W. 6th Ave. #203, Golden, CO 80401 (☎(800) 282-1202; elsewhere call US +1 (303) 215-9000; www.aircourier.org). Ten departure cities throughout the US and Canada to London and throughout western Europe (high-season US$150-360). 1-year US$64.

International Association of Air Travel Couriers (IAATC), 220 South Dixie Highway #3, P.O. Box 1349, Lake Worth, FL 33460 (☎(561) 582-8320; fax 582-1581; www.courier.org). From 9 North American cities to western European cities, including London. 1-year US$45-50.

Global Courier Travel, PO Box 3051, Nederland, CO 80466 (www.globalcouriertravel.com). Searchable online database. 6 departure points in the US and Canada to London, among other western European cities. 1-year US$40, 2 people US$55.

NOW Voyager, 74 Varick St. #307, New York, NY 10013 (☎(212) 431-1616; www.nowvoyagertravel.com). To Dublin and London (US$499-699). Usually 1-week maximum stay. 1-year US$50. Non-courier discount fares also available.

Worldwide Courier Association (☎(800) 780-4359, ext. 441; www.massiveweb.com). From New York, San Francisco, Los Angeles, and Chicago to western Europe, including London (US$259-299). 1-year US$58.

FROM AUSTRALIA AND NEW ZEALAND

Although the courier industry is most developed from North America, there are limited courier flights in other areas. From **Australia** and **New Zealand, Global Courier Travel** (see above) often has listings from Sydney and Auckland to London and occasionally Frankfurt.

STANDBY FLIGHTS

Traveling standby requires considerable flexibility in arrival and departure dates and cities. Companies dealing in standby flights sell vouchers rather than tickets, along with the promise to get you to your destination (or nearby) within a certain window of time (typically 1-5 days). You call in before your specific window to hear your flight options and the probability that you will be able to board each flight. You can then decide which flights you want to try to make, show up at the appropriate airport at the appropriate time, present your voucher, and board if space is available. Vouchers can usually be bought for both one-way and round-trip travel. You may receive a monetary refund only if every available flight within your date range is full; if you opt not to take an available (but perhaps less convenient) flight, you can only get credit toward future travel. Carefully read agreements with any company offering standby flights, as tricky fine print can leave you in the lurch. To check on a company's service record in the US, call the Better Business Bureau (☎212 533-6200). It is difficult to receive refunds, and clients' vouchers will not be honored when an airline fails to receive payment in time. One established standby company in the US is Whole Earth Travel, 325 W. 38th St., New York, NY 10018 (☎(800) 326-2009; www.4standby.com) and Los Angeles, CA (☎(888) 247-4482), which offers one-way flights to Europe from the Northeast (US$169), West Coast and Northwest (US$249), Midwest (US$219), and Southeast (US$199).

TICKET CONSOLIDATORS

Ticket consolidators, or **"bucket shops,"** buy unsold tickets in bulk from commercial airlines and sell them at discounted rates. The best place to look is in the Sunday travel section of any major newspaper (such as *The New York Times*), where many bucket shops place tiny ads. Always insist on a receipt that gives full details of restrictions, refunds, and tickets, and pay by credit card (in spite of the 2-5% fee) so you can stop payment if you never receive your tickets. For more info, see www.travel-library.com/air-travel/consolidators.html. In London, the **Air Travel Advisory Bureau** (☎(0207) 636 5000; www.atab.co.uk) can provide names of reliable consolidators and discount flight specialists.

CHARTER FLIGHTS

Charters are flights a tour operator contracts with an airline to fly extra loads of passengers during peak season. Schedules can change or be cancelled at the last moment (as late as 48hr. before the trip, and without a full refund), and check-in, boarding, and baggage claim are often slow, yet the flights tend to be cheaper.

Discount clubs and **fare brokers** offer members savings on last-minute charter and tour deals. Study contracts closely; you don't want to end up with an undesirable overnight layover. **Travelers Advantage,** Trumbull, CT, USA (☎ (203) 365-2000; www.travelersadvantage.com; US$60 annual fee includes discounts and cheap flight directories) specializes in European travel and tour packages.

BY CHANNEL TUNNEL

In 1994, the **Channel Tunnel** (Chunnel) was completed, physically connecting England and France. With a wry wink, the primary British terminus of the **Eurostar** cross-channel train is London's **Waterloo Station.** Napoleon is not amused. Traversing 27 mi. under the sea, the Chunnel is undoubtedly the fastest, most convenient, and least scenic route from England to France and back again.

BY TRAIN. Eurostar, Eurostar House, Waterloo Station, London SE1 8SE (UK ☎ (0990) 186186; US ☎ (800) 387-6782; elsewhere call UK +44 (1233) 617575; www.eurostar.com; www.raileurope.com) runs a frequent train service between London and the continent. Ten to 28 trains per day run to **Paris** (3hr., US$75-159, 2nd class) and **Brussels** (3hr., US$75-159, 2nd class). Routes include stops at Ashford International in Kent, England, and Calais and Lille in France. Eurostar ticketing operates like an airline, with similar discounts, reservations, and restrictions. While BritRail passes, Eurail passes, and such do not include free Eurostar travel, they do garner discounts, as does being under 26. Book at major rail stations in the UK, at the office above, by phone, or on the web.

BY BUS. Both **Eurolines** and **Eurobus** provide bus-ferry combinations (see below).

BY CAR. If you're traveling by car, **Eurotunnel** (UK ☎ (08000) 969992; www.eurotunnel.co.uk) shuttles cars and passengers between Kent and Nord-Pas-de-Calais. Return fares for vehicle and all passengers range from UK£219-299 with car, UK£259-598 with campervan, and UK£119-299 for a trailer/caravan supplement. Same-day return costs UK£110-150, five-day return UK£139-195. Book online or by phone. Travelers with cars can also look into sea crossings by ferry (see below).

BY FERRY

Ferry travel is dependable, inexpensive, and slow. Most European ferries are comfortable and well equipped; the cheapest fare class often includes a reclining chair or couchette where you can sleep. Almost all sailings in June, July, and August are **controlled sailings,** which means that you must book the crossing at least a day in advance. If you're traveling with a **car** in July or August, reserve through a ferry office or travel agency. Advance planning and reserved ticket purchases through a travel agency can spare you days of waiting in dreary ports for the next sailing. Ask ahead where to board the ferry, arrive at the port an hour in advance, and remember your passport. Unlike train or air travel, ferries lack the convenience of location; you often land in odd parts of the country, and must then arrange connections to larger cities at additional cost.

Prices vary greatly by ports, season, and length of stay. In the summer expect to pay at least £25 per person to cross from France and £60 from Belgium and the Netherlands. Limited-day returns (usually 5-10 nights including travel) are generally not much more expensive than the single fare. Ask for **discounts; ISIC** holders can sometimes get student fares, and **Eurail pass-holders** can get many reductions and free trips (check the brochure that comes with your railpass). Children under 4 often travel free, and bicycles can be carried for a small fee, if any. Some travelers ask car drivers to let them travel as one of the four or five free passengers allotted to a car. This can reduce costs considerably, but consider the risks before getting into a stranger's car. The main ferry companies operating between Britain and France or Northern Europe are listed below; call or write for brochures with complete listings of routes and fares.

The following fares listed are **one-way** for adult foot passengers unless otherwise noted. Though standard return fares are in most cases simply twice the one-way fare, **fixed-period returns** (usually within five days) are almost invariably cheaper. Ferries run **year-round** unless otherwise noted. **Bikes** are usually free, although you may have to pay up to UK£10 in high-season. For a **camper/trailer** supplement, you will have to add anywhere from UK£20-140 to the "with car" fare. If more than one price is quoted, the quote in UK£ is valid for departures from the UK, etc. A directory of ferries can be found at www.seaview.co.uk/ferries.html.

Brittany Ferries: France ☎(08) 25 82 88 28; UK ☎(0870) 901 2400; www.brittany-ferries.com. **Plymouth** from **Roscoff, France** (6hr.; in summer 1-3 per day, off season 1 per week; UK£20-58) and **Santander, Spain** (24-30hr., 1-2 per week, return UK£80-145). **Portsmouth** from **St-Malo** (8¾hr., 1-2 per day, 150-320F/€22.87-48.78) and **Caen** (6hr., 1-3 per day, 140-290F/€21.34-44.21), **France. Poole** from **Cherbourg, France** (4¼hr., 1-2 per day, 140-290F/€21.34-44.21). **Cork** from **Roscoff** (13½hr., Apr.-Sept. 1 per week, 340-650F/€51.83-99.10).

DFDS Seaways: UK ☎(08705) 333000; www.scansea.com. **Harwich** from **Hamburg** (20hr.) and **Esbjerg, Denmark** (19hr.). **Newcastle** from **Amsterdam** (14hr.), **Kristiansand, Norway** (19hr.), and **Gothenburg, Sweden** (22hr.).

Fjord Line: www.fjordline.no. Norway ☎(55) 54 88 00; UK ☎(0191) 296 1313. **Newcastle, England,** from **Stavanger** (19hr.) and **Bergen** (26hr.), **Norway.** Also between **Bergen** and **Egersund, Norway,** and **Hanstholm, Denmark**.

Hoverspeed: France ☎(03) 21 46 14 54; UK ☎(08702) 408070; www.hoverspeed.co.uk. **Dover** from **Calais** (35-55min., every hr., UK£24) and **Ostend, Belgium** (2hr., 5-7 per day, UK£28). **Folkestone** from **Boulogne, France** (55min., 3-4 per day, UK£24). **Newhaven** from **Dieppe, France** (2¼-4¼hr., 1-3 per day, UK£28).

Irish Ferries: France ☎(01) 44 94 20 40; Ireland ☎(1890) 313131; UK ☎(08705) 171717; www.irishferries.ie. **Rosslare** from **Cherbourg** (18hr., IR£57-82/€72.38-104.12), **Roscoff** (17hr., Apr.-Sept. 1-9 per week, 470-680F/€71.65-103.67), and **Pembroke, England** (3¾hr.). **Dublin** from **Holyhead, England** (2-3hr., return IR£20-60/€25.39-76.18).

P&O North Sea Ferries: UK ☎(0870) 129 6002; www.ponsf.com. Daily ferries to **Hull** from **Rotterdam, Netherlands** (13½hr.) and **Zeebrugge, Belgium** (14hr.). Both UK£38-48, students UK£24-31, cars UK£63-78. Online bookings.

P&O Stena Line: UK ☎(08706) 000611; from Europe ☎+44 (13) 0486 4003; www.posl.com. **Dover** from **Calais** (1¼hr., 1-2 per hr., UK£24).

SeaFrance: France ☎(03) 21 46 80 00; UK ☎(08705) 711711; www.seafrance.co.uk. **Dover** from **Calais** (1½hr., 15 per day, UK£15).

Stena Line: UK ☎(1233) 646826; from Europe +44; www.stenaline.co.uk. **Harwich, England** from **Hook of Holland** (5hr., UK£25). **Fishguard** from **Rosslare** (1-3½hr., UK£22-30). **Holyhead, Wales,** from **Dublin** (4hr., UK£18-20) and **Dún Laoghaire** (1-3½hr., UK£20-28). **Stranraer** from **Belfast** (1¾-3¼hr., Mar.-Jan., UK£18-24).

Swansea-Cork Ferries: UK ☎(01792) 456116; Ireland ☎(021) 271166; www.swansea-cork.ie. **Swansea, Wales,** from **Ringaskiddy, Co. Cork** (10hr., UK£24-34).

GETTING AROUND

Fares on all modes of transportation are either **single** (one-way) or **return** (round-trip). "Period returns" require you to return within a specific number of days; "day return" means you must return on the same day. Unless stated otherwise, *Let's Go* always lists single fares. Return fares on trains and buses in Britain and Ireland are often less than double the one-way fare.

BY PLANE

Though flying is almost invariably more expensive than traveling by train, it works for those short on time (or flush with cash). Student travel agencies sell cheap tickets, and budget fares are frequently available in the spring and summer on high-volume routes. The Irish and British national carriers, **Aer Lingus** (Ireland ☎(01) 886 8888; UK ☎(08459) 737747; www.aerlingus.ie) and **British Airways** (☎(0845) 722 2111; www.british-airways.com), fly regularly between London and Dublin; fares start from £81 (Aer Lingus 1½hr., every hr. 7:40am-10:45pm; BA 1½hr., 6 flights per day). If you plan to go to the **Shetland Islands** (see p. 630) or the **Isle of Man** (see p. 347), the time saved may be worth the extra cost of flying.

If you can book in advance and/or travel at odd hours, the newly popular discount airlines (see listings below) may be another high-speed option for travel within the British Isles, as well as a way of making cheap, quick jaunts from Britain and Ireland to the continent. A good source of offers are the travel supplements of newspapers or the classifieds in *Time Out*; many of the airlines will also advertise fares (and sell tickets) online.

British Midland (London ☎(08706) 070555; Dublin ☎(01) 283 0700; Belfast ☎(02132) 241188; US ☎(800) 788-0555; www.britishmidland.com). Service between Aberdeen, Belfast, Dublin, Edinburgh, Glasgow, Leeds, London Heathrow, Manchester, and Teesside (Newcastle).

Debonair (UK ☎(0541) 500300) offers budget flights between Britain and Ireland, as well as France, Germany, Spain, and Italy.

easyJet (UK ☎(0870) 600 0000; www.easyjet.com). Luton to Aberdeen, Edinburgh, and Glasgow; Belfast to Luton and Liverpool; and to Britain from many European cities.

Go (UK ☎(0845) 605 4321; from abroad ☎+44 (1279) 666388; www.go-fly.com). Stansted (3-7 flights a day) to Edinburgh, Denmark, Italy, and Portugal, to name a few.

Ryanair (UK ☎(0541) 569569; www.ryanair.ie) flies from Luton and Stansted to Cork, Dublin, Kerry, Knock, and Glasgow, as well as European destinations.

Virgin Express (UK ☎(020) 7744 0004; Ireland ☎(061) 704470; www.virgin-express.com). To Shannon and the continent from Heathrow, Gatwick, and Stansted.

BY TRAIN

BRITAIN

Britain's train network is extremely well-developed, criss-crossing the length and breadth of the island. Privatization of British Rail, which occurred in 1995, seems only to have brought confusion and delays: Deputy Prime Minister John Prescott has called privatized trains "a national disgrace." In cities which have more than one train station, the city name is given first, followed by the station name (for example, "Manchester Piccadilly" and "Manchester Victoria" are the two major stations in Manchester). In general, traveling by train costs more than by coach or bus. *Let's Go* quotes one-way prices for standard (also known as 2nd-class) seats, unless specified otherwise. Railpasses covering specific regions are sometimes available from local train stations; these may include travel on bus and ferry routes. *Let's Go* lists available passes where appropriate. Prices and schedules often change; find up-to-date information from **National Rail Inquiries** (☎(08457) 484950), or online at **Railtrack** (www.railtrack.co.uk; schedules only). For information on using the **London Underground**, see p. 95.

TICKET TYPES

The array of available tickets on British trains is bewildering, and prices aren't always set logically—it's entirely possible that buying an unlimited day pass to the region will cost you less than buying a one-way ticket. Instead of just stating a destination, which will get you a single, you might want to ask what the cheapest ticket to the destination is. **Single** or **one-way** tickets are valid for just one trip.

There are two types of return (round-trip) tickets: **day return** tickets, which allow a return trip only on the same day and usually cost only slightly more than a single, and **open return** (also known as **period return**) tickets, which allow a return within 30 days but are usually pricier than day returns. Prices for many fares rise on Friday and Saturday; prices before 9:30am are often more expensive. **Always keep your ticket with you,** as it will sometimes be inspected on the journey or collected at the station when you arrive. Tickets should be purchased before boarding, except at unstaffed train stations, in which case tickets are bought on the train.

There are five major **discount ticket** types. **APEX** (Advance Purchase Excursion) tickets must be bought at least seven days in advance; **SuperAPEX** tickets are similar but must be bought at least 14 (sometimes 21) days in advance. **Saver** tickets are valid any time except before 9:30am; **SuperSaver** ones are not valid before 9:30am or on Fridays and most Saturdays; and **SuperAdvance** tickets are similar to SuperSavers, but you must buy them before 2pm on the day before you travel.

BRITRAIL PASSES

If you plan to travel a great deal on trains within Britain, the **BritRail Pass** can be a good buy. Eurail passes are *not* valid in Britain, but there is often a discount on BritRail passes if you purchase the two simultaneously. BritRail passes are only available outside Britain; **you must buy them before traveling to Britain.** They allow unlimited train travel in England, Wales, and Scotland, regardless of which company is operating the trains, but they do not allow free travel in Northern Ireland or on Eurostar. BritRail pass prices are listed below. **Youth** passes are for travelers under 26, while **senior** ones are for travelers over 60. One child aged 5-15 can travel free with each adult pass, as long as you ask for the **Family Pass** (free). Additional children pay half the standard adult fare, while children under 5 travel free. In deciding which pass to buy, consider what kinds of train journeys you will be making, since first-class seats are not available on short routes. Other varieties of passes (e.g., passes for rail travel including Eurostar) are also available; contact the distributors listed below for more details.

1st-class Classic: Consecutive days travel: 8 days US$399, 15 days US$599, 22 days US$759, 1 month US$899.

Standard-class Classic: Consecutive days travel: 8 days US$265, 15 days US$399, 22 days US$499, 1 month US$599.

Youth Classic: Standard-class only; consecutive days travel: 8 days US$215, 15 days US$279, 22 days US$355, 1 month US$419.

Senior Classic: 1st-class only; consecutive days travel: 8 days US$339, 15 days US$509, 22 days US$639, 1 month US$759.

Flexipass: Travel within a 2-month period: any 4 days (1st-class US$349, 2nd-class US$235), any 8 days (US$509/US$339), any 15 days (US$769/US$515).

Youth Flexipasses: 2nd-class only; travel within a two-month period: 4 days US$185, 8 days US$239, 15 days US$359.

Senior Flexipasses: 1st-class only; travel within a two-month period: 4 days US$299, 8 days US$435, 15 days US$655.

Britrail Pass Plus Ireland: Travel for a limited number of days within a month on all British and Irish (both Northern Ireland and the Republic of Ireland) trains, plus a round-trip crossing on Stena Ferries: any 5 days (1st-class US$529, 2nd-class US$399), any 10 days (1st-class US$749, 2nd-class US$569).

Freedom of Scotland Travelpass: Standard-class travel on all trains within Scotland, the Glasgow Underground, and selected ferry routes to the islands. 4 out of 8 days US$134, 8 out of 15 days US$168, 12 out of 20 days US$219.

Freedom of Wales Flexipass: A brand-new, standard-class only pass, valid for travel on any 4 days out of 8 by rail with daily bus travel (adult US$85, child US$56), or any 8 days out of 15 by rail with daily bus travel (adult US$159, child US$105). Includes discounts on sights, YHA hostels, and the Welsh system of historic private railways.

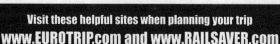
ESSENTIALS

BRITRAIL DISTRIBUTORS

Passes and additional details on discounts are available from most travel agents (see p. 30). The distributors listed below will either sell you passes directly, or tell you the nearest place to buy passes.

Australia: Rail Plus, Level 3, 459 Little Collins St., Melbourne, Victoria 3000 (☎(09) 9642 8644; www.railplus.com.au). **Concorde International Travel** (Rail Tickets), Level 9, 310 King St., Melbourne Victoria 3000 (☎(03) 9920 3833; www.concorde.com.au).

Canada and the US: Rail Europe, 226 Westchester Ave., White Plains, NY 10604 (Canada ☎(800) 361-7245, US ☎(800) 456-7245; www.raileurope.com), is the North American distributor of BritRail products. Or try **Rail Pass Express** (☎(800) 722-7151; www.railpass.com).

Ireland: BritRail Ireland, 123 Lower Baggot St., Dublin 2 (☎(01) 661 2866).

New Zealand: Holiday Shoppe, (☎(0800) 729 435, www.holidayshoppe.co.nz). **Budget Travel,** (☎(0800) 808 040; www.budgettravel.co.nz).

South Africa: World Travel Agency, Liberty Life Centre, 7th fl., 22 Long St., P.O. box 2889, Cape Town 8000 (☎(021) 4252470; www.world-travel.co.za)

RAIL DISCOUNT CARDS

Unlike the passes above, these can be purchased in Britain. The **Young Person's Railcard** (£18, valid for 1 year; www.youngpersons-railcard.co.uk) offers 33% off most fares and discounts on Holyman Sally Ferries. Buy it at Travel Centres in train stations in the UK. You must prove you're either between 16 and 25 (with a passport or other form of ID), or a full-time student over 25 at a "recognized educational establishment," and submit a passport-sized photo. Those 60 and over can purchase a **Senior Railcard** (£18; www.senior-railcard.co.uk) from Travel Centres, also taking up to 33% off most fares. There are also Family Railcards and Railcards for travelers in wheelchairs.

IRELAND

Iarnród Éireann (Irish Rail) is useful only for travel to urban areas, from which you'll need to find another form of transportation to reach Ireland's picturesque villages and wilds. Trains from Dublin's Heuston Station chug toward Cork, Tralee, Limerick, Ennis, Galway, Westport, Ballina, and Waterford; others leave from Dublin's Connolly Station to head for Belfast, Sligo, Wexford, and Rosslare. Trains also make various connections between these cities. For schedule information, pick up an *InterCity Rail Traveller's Guide* (50p/€.63), available at most train stations. The **TravelSave** stamp, available for £8 at any **usit** agency with an ISIC card, cuts fares by 30-50% on national rail. (It also provides 30% discounts on bus fares above £1/€1.27.) A **Faircard** (£8/€10.16) can get anyone aged 16 to 26 up to 50% off the price of any intercity trip. Those over 26 can get the less potent **Weekender card** (£5/ €6.35; up to 33% off, valid F-Tu only). Both are valid through the end of the year. The **Rambler** allows unlimited train travel on five days within a 15-day travel period (£90/€114.28). Information is available from Irish Rail, 35 Lower Abbey St., Dublin (☎(01) 836 3333; www.irishrail.ie). Unlike bus tickets, train tickets sometimes allow travelers to break a journey into stages yet still pay the price of a single-phase trip. Bikes may be carried on most trains for a fee of £2-6/€2.54-7.62, depending on weight; check at the station for the restrictions of specific trains.

While the **Eurailpass** is not accepted in Northern Ireland, it *is* accepted on trains (but not buses) in the Republic. A range of youth and family passes are also available, but Eurailpasses are generally cost-effective only if you plan to travel to the Continent as well. The BritRail pass does not cover travel in Northern Ireland, but the month-long **BritRail Plus Ireland** works in both the North and the Republic with rail options and round-trip ferry service between Britain and Ireland (US$399-569). Great value resides in the youth passes for individuals under 26. You'll find it easiest to buy a Eurailpass before you arrive in Europe; contact Council Travel (p. 30), or any of many other travel agents. **Rail Europe** (☎(800) 438-7245; www.raileurope.com) also sells point-to-point tickets.

Northern Ireland Railways (☎ (028) 9033 3000; www.nirailways.co.uk) is not extensive but covers the northeastern coastal region well. A valid **Northern Ireland Travelsave** stamp (UK£7, affixed to back of ISIC) will get you up to 33% off all trains and 15% discounts on bus fares over UK£1.45 within Northern Ireland. The **Freedom of Northern Ireland** ticket allows unlimited travel by train and Ulsterbus and can be purchased for seven consecutive days (UK£40), three consecutive days (£27.50), or a single day (£11).

BY BUS AND COACH

The British and the Irish distinguish between **buses** that cover short local routes, and **coaches** that cover long distances. For practical purposes, *Let's Go* usually uses the term "buses" to refer to both. Regional bus/coach **passes** offer unlimited travel on buses within a certain area for a certain number of days; these are often called **Rovers, Ramblers,** and **Explorers;** *Let's Go* lists these where available.

BUSES IN BRITAIN

Long-distance coach travel is more extensive in Britain than most of Europe, and is the cheapest option. **National Express** (☎ (08705) 808080; www.gobycoach.co.uk) is the principal operator of long-distance coach services in Britain, although **Scottish Citylink** (☎ (08705) 505050) has extensive coverage in Scotland. National Express tickets can usually be purchased at the bus station; otherwise, *Let's Go* lists a ticket agent in the town. **Discount Coachcards** are available for seniors (over 50), students, and young persons (ages 16-25) for £9 (valid for 1 year) and reduce fares on National Express by about 30%. For those planning a lot of coach travel, the **Tourist Trail Pass** offers unlimited travel for a number of days within a given period. (2 days out of 3 £49, concessions £39; 5 out of 10 £85, £69; 7 out of 21 £120, £94; 14 out of 30 £187, £143.) Tourist information centres often carry timetables for the buses in their regions and will help befuddled travelers decipher them. Most National Express buses from **London** leave from **Victoria Coach Station** (p. 94).

BUSES IN IRELAND

Ireland's national bus company, **Bus Éireann** (☎ (01) 836 6111; www.buseireann.ie), operates both long-distance **Expressway** buses, which link larger cities, and **Local** buses, which serve the countryside and smaller towns. Find timetables for bus services by visiting local bus stations, or Bus Éireann's web site. The invaluable bus timetable book (IR£1/€1.27) should be available for purchase at Busáras Station in Dublin and the occasional tourist information centre. Expressway buses allow passengers to store luggage under the bus, or carry hand-luggage on board. Bicycles may be stored for a IR£5/€6.35 fee in the undercarriage, provided there's room. A myriad of **private bus services** are faster and cheaper than Bus Éireann. *Let's Go* lists these private companies in areas they service.

Return tickets are always a great value. For students, purchasing a **TravelSave** stamp (see **Trains in Ireland,** p. 41) along with your ISIC affords huge discounts on bus travel. Bus Éireann's discount **Rambler** tickets, offering unlimited bus travel within Ireland (3 days in 8 IR£32/€40.63; 8 days in 15 £73/€92.70; 15 days in 30 £105/€133.32; children half-price) aren't usually worth buying; individual tickets often provide better value. A combined **Irish Explorer Rail/Bus** ticket allows unlimited travel on eight in 15 consecutive days on train and bus lines (IR£124/€157.44, children £62/€78.72). Purchase these tickets from Bus Éireann at their main bus station on Store St. in **Dublin** (☎ (01) 836 6111), or at their Travel Centres in **Cork** (☎ (021) 450 8188), **Waterford** (☎ (051) 879000), **Galway** (☎ (091) 562000), **Limerick** (☎ (061) 313333), and other transportation hubs.

Ulsterbus, Laganside, Belfast (☎ (028) 9033 3000; www.ulsterbus.co.uk), runs throughout Northern Ireland, where there are no private bus services. Coverage expands in summer, when several buses run a purely coastal route, and full- and half-day tours leave for key tourist spots from Belfast. Pick up a free regional timetable at any station. Again, the bus discount passes won't save you much money: a **Freedom of Northern Ireland** bus and rail pass offers unlimited travel for one day (UK£10), or several consecutive days (3-day pass UK£25; 7-day £38).

The **Irish Rover** pass covers Bus Éireann and Ulsterbus services. It sounds ideal for visitors intending to travel in both the Republic and Northern Ireland, but unless you'll be taking lots of bus trips, its true value is debatable. (Unlimited travel on 3 in 8 days IR£42/€53.34, children £21/€26.67; 8 in 15 days £93/€118.11, £47/€59.69; 15 in 30 £145/€184.15, £73/€92.71.) The **Emerald Card** offers unlimited travel on Ulsterbus; Northern Ireland Railways; Bus Éireann Expressway, Local, and City services in Dublin, Cork, Limerick, Galway, and Waterford; and intercity, DART, and suburban rail Iarnród Éireann services. (8 days in 15 IR£124/€157.48, children £62/€78.74; 15 days in 30 days £214/€271.78, £107/€135.89.)

BUS TOURS

Staffed by young and energetic guides, these tours cater to backpackers, with minibuses stopping right at the doors of hostels. They are a good way to meet other people traveling independently and to get to places that public transport doesn't reach. Some tours are "hop-on, hop-off," which means you can stay for as long as you like at any of the stops. Accommodations are not included in the price, although the companies will usually book beds in hostels.

Britain: Stray Travel, 171 Earl's Court Rd., London SW5 9RF (☎(020) 7373 7737; www.straytravel.com), sends 3 coaches a week on a clockwise circuit of London, Bath, Llangollen, the Lake District, Edinburgh, and York, arriving at the doors of hostels and stopping at all major sights and towns along the way, including Stratford and Oxford. £139 buys a ticket, good for 4 months, so travelers can move at any rate they wish. Also offers other shorter routes.

Wales: Hairy Hog, The Magic Tour Company, Lauderdale House, 11 Gower St., Bloomsbury, London WC1E 6HB (☎(0207) 636 7555; www.magictours.co.uk). Regular horseback-riding weekend tours in Wales for £99. Also offers a number of other trips within England; all trips leave from London.

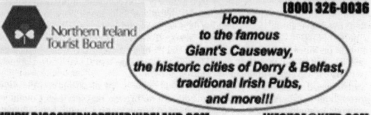

Scotland: HAGGiS, 60 High St., Edinburgh EH1 1TB (☎(0131) 557 9393; www.radical-travel.com), runs excellent hop-on, hop-off flexitours from Edinburgh through major sights of Scotland (from £85). They also conduct day trips for £18 and 3- to 6-day tours for £79-139, plus tours of **Britain** (£129) and fully Irish-staffed tours of **Ireland** (3 days UK£69, 6 days UK£119). Lodgings prices not included.

Scotland: MacBackpackers, 105 High St., Edinburgh EH1 1SG (☎(0131) 558 9900; www.macbackpackers.com), runs terrific tours of Scotland, focusing on Skye, the West Coast, and the Highlands (3-7 days £39-129), as well as £15 day trips from Edinburgh and £55 hop-on, hop-off flexitours. Lodgings prices not included.

Ireland: Stray Travel, 6 William St. S., Dublin (☎(01) 679 2684; www.straytravel.com), runs 3 coaches a week between Dublin, Cork, Schull, Killarney, Galway, and Donegal, stopping at major sights along the way. UK£129 buys a hop-on/hop-off ticket good for 4 months. Shorter routes also available.

BY CAR

Cars offer speed, freedom, access to the countryside, and an escape from the town-to-town mentality of trains. Unfortunately, they insulate you from the *esprit de corps* of rail travel, and introduce the hassle of driving and parking in large cities and the high cost of petrol (gasoline). Although a single traveler won't save by renting a car, four usually will. If you can't decide between train and car travel, you may benefit from a combination of the two; combination rail-and-drive packages can be bought from BritRail pass distributors (p. 40). Remember you may not be used to **driving on the left,** or driving a **manual transmission** ("stick-shift"; far more common than automatic transmissions in cheap rental cars). Be particularly cautious at **roundabouts** (rotary interchanges), and remember to give way to traffic from the right. Road atlases for the UK are available in any travel bookshop and from many tourist information centres. Petrol is sold by the liter, not the gallon; there are about four liters to the gallon (see **Measurements,** p. 751). For an informal primer on European road signs and conventions, check out www.travlang.com/signs. Additionally, the **Association for Safe International Road Travel (ASIRT),** 11769 Gainsborough Rd., Potomac, MD 20854 (US ☎(301) 983-5252; www.asirt.org), can provide more specific information about road conditions.

DRIVING IN BRITAIN

You must be 17 and have a license to drive in Britain. The country is covered by a high-speed system of **motorways** ("M-roads") that connect London with major cities around the country. These are supplemented by a tight web of "A-roads" and "B-roads" that connect towns: A-roads are the main routes between towns, while B-roads are narrower but often more scenic. **Distances** on road signs are in miles (1mi.=1.6km). **Speed limits** are 70mph (113km/h) on motorways (highways) and dual carriageways (divided highways), 60mph (97km/h) on single carriageways (non-divided highways), and usually 30mph (48km/h) in urban areas. Speed limits are always marked at the beginning of town areas; upon leaving, you'll see a circular sign with a slash through it, signaling the end of the restriction. The law requires drivers and front-seat passengers to wear **seat belts,** and rear-seat passengers are also required to buckle up when belts are provided. Driving in **London** is a nightmare superseded only by parking in London—to maintain sanity, stick to public transport. Copies of the **Highway Code,** which details Britain's driving regulations, can be purchased at most large bookstores or newsagents.

In the event of a breakdown in Britain, contact the **Automobile Association** (☎(0800) 887766), **Green Flag** (☎(0800) 400600), or the **Royal Automobile Club** (☎(0800) 828282). All three are open 24hr., though you may have to be a member to receive breakdown assistance (see below). Membership is sometimes available on the spot. Call **999** in an emergency.

DRIVING IN IRELAND

In the Republic, roads between towns are designated as "N" and "R" roads, though locals refer to them by destination ("the Kerry Road"). Roads numbered below N50 are primary routes that connect all major towns; roads numbered N50 and above are secondary routes, similar to Britain's A-roads; regional R-roads are comparable to Britain's B-roads. Most of these are two-lane. The general **speed limit** is 55mph (90km/h) on the open road and either 30mph (50km/h) or 40mph (65km/h) in town. Signs on roadways are usually in both English and Irish; destinations are sometimes listed only in Irish. Old black-and-white road signs give distances in miles; new green and white signs are in kilometers. Speed limits are signed in miles. For breakdown service, call the **Irish AA** (toll-free ☎(0800) 667788).

INTERNATIONAL DRIVING PERMIT (IDP)

If you plan to drive a car while in Britain or Ireland, you *must* have **a valid foreign driver's license.** An International Driving Permit (IDP) is also advisable. Valid for one year, an IDP must be issued in your own country before you depart. An application for an IDP includes two passport-sized photos, a current local license, an additional form of identification, and a fee. You must be 18 years old to receive the IDP. EU license-holders do not need an IDP to drive in Britain or Ireland.

Australia: Contact your local Royal Automobile Club (RAC) or the National Royal Motorist Association (NRMA) if in NSW or the ACT (☎(08) 9421 4298; www.rac.com.au/travel). Permits AUS$15.

Canada: Contact any Canadian Automobile Association (CAA) branch office in Canada, or write to CAA, 1145 Hunt Club Rd., Suite 200, Ottawa K1V 0Y3 (☎(613) 247-0117; www.caa.ca/CAAInternet/travelservices). Permits CDN$10.

New Zealand: Contact your local Automobile Association or their main office at Auckland Central, 99 Albert St. (☎(09) 377 4660; www.nzaa.co.nz). Permits NZ$8.

South Africa: Contact your local Automobile Association of South Africa office or the head office at P.O. Box 596, Johannesburg 2000 (☎(011) 799 1000; www.aa.co.za). Permits ZAR28.50.

US: To buy an IDP, visit any American Automobile Association (AAA) office or write to AAA Travel Related Services, 1000 AAA Drive (mail stop 100), Heathrow, FL 32746 (☎(407) 444-7000; www.aaa.com); you do not have to be a AAA member. Offers travel services and auto insurance. Permits US$10.

CAR INSURANCE

Most credit cards cover standard insurance. If you rent, lease, or borrow a car, you will need a **green card,** or **International Insurance Certificate,** to certify that you have liability insurance and that it applies abroad. Green cards can be obtained at car rental agencies, car dealers (for those leasing cars), some travel agents, and some border crossings. Rental agencies may require you to purchase theft insurance in countries that they consider to have a high risk of auto theft.

RENTING A CAR

You can rent a car from a US-based firm (Alamo, Avis, Budget, or Hertz) with European offices, from a European-based company with local representatives (Europcar, Renault Eurodrive), or from a tour operator (Auto Europe, Europe By Car, and Kemwel Holiday Autos) that will arrange a rental for you from a European company at its own rates. Multinationals offer greater flexibility, but tour operators often strike better deals. Rentals vary by company, season, and pickup point. Expect to pay UK£130 or IR£100-300/€126.97-380.92 per week for a small car. Automatics are generally more expensive than manuals (stick-shifts). If possible, reserve well before leaving for Britain or Ireland and pay in advance. It is significantly less expensive to reserve a car from the US than from Europe. Always check if prices quoted include tax and collision insurance; some credit card companies cover the deductible on collision insurance, allowing their customers to decline the collision damage waiver. Ask about discounts and check the terms of insurance, particularly the size of the deductible; the UK tends to offer some of the lowest rates. Ask airlines about special fly-and-drive packages, as you may get up to a week of free or discounted rental. A special BritRail **Pass 'N' Drive** pass combines rail travel and car rental. At most agencies, all that's needed to rent a car is a driver's license and proof that you've had the license for a year; some will ask for an additional ID confirming your home address. For insurance reasons, renters in Britain must be over 21; those 18-21 should consider leasing. In Ireland, those under 23 generally cannot rent. You can rent cars from the following agencies:

Auto Europe, 39 Commercial St., P.O. Box 7006, Portland, ME 04112 (US and Canada ☎(888) 223-5555 or ☎(207) 842-2000; www.autoeurope.com).

Avis (UK ☎(0990) 900500; Australia ☎(800) 22 55 33; New Zealand ☎(0800) 65 51 11; US and Canada ☎(800) 331-1084; www.avis.com).

Budget (UK Help Desk ☎+44 (1442) 280181; US and Canada ☎(800) 527-0700; www.budgetrentacar.com).

Europe by Car, One Rockefeller Plaza, New York, NY 10020 (US ☎(800) 223-1516 or (212) 581-3040; www.europebycar.com).

Europcar, 145 av. Malekoff, 75016 Paris (☎(01) 45 00 08 06); Canada ☎(800) 227-7368; UK ☎(01923) 811000; US ☎(800) 227-3876; www.europcar.com).

Hertz (Australia ☎9698 2555; UK ☎(0990) 996699; US ☎(800) 654-3001; Canada ☎(800) 263-0600; www.hertz.com).

Kemwel Holiday Autos (US ☎(800) 576-1590; www.kemwel.com).

Renault Eurodrive, 6 E. 46th St., New York, NY 10017 (US ☎(800) 221-1052; www.renaultusa.com).

LEASING A CAR

For longer than 17 days, leasing can be cheaper than renting; it tends to be the only option for those aged 18 to 21. The cheapest leases are agreements to buy the car and then sell it back to the manufacturer at a prearranged price. As far as the buyer's concerned, though, it's a lease and doesn't entail enormous financial transactions. Leases generally include insurance coverage and are not taxed. Expect to pay around US$1100-1800 (depending on size of car) for 60 days. Contact **Europe by Car, Kemwel Holiday Autos,** or **Renault Eurodrive** (see above) before you go.

BY FERRY

Ferry services connecting ports in England, Scotland, Wales, and Ireland are inexpensive and usually the cheapest way of crossing the Irish Sea. Ferry companies advertise special low rates for day returns in local papers; otherwise, expect to pay £20-30 depending on route, season, and length of stay. Ferry companies often offer special discounts in conjunction with bus or train companies. A little advance research can save you and your wallet much angst.

Caledonian MacBrayne, The Ferry Terminal, Gourock, Renfrewshire PA19 1QP (☎(01475) 650100; www.calmac.co.uk). CalMac's the daddy of Scottish ferries, with routes in the Hebrides and the west coast of Scotland.

Irish Ferries, 2-4 Merrion Row, Dublin 2 (in Ireland ☎(1890) 313131; in Northern Ireland ☎(0800) 018 2211; www.irishferries.ie) and Corn Exchange Building, Brunswick St., Liverpool L2 7TP (☎(08705) 171717). **Dublin, Ireland,** to **Holyhead, Wales** (2hr.; return £35-60, students and seniors £28-48); **Rosslare, Ireland,** to **Pembroke, Wales** (4hr.; return £35, students and seniors £28).

Isle of Man Steam Packet Company serves the Isle of Man; see p. 347 for details.

P&O Scottish Ferries, P.O. Box 5, P&O Ferries Terminal, Jamieson's Quay, Aberdeen AB11 5NP (☎(01224) 589111 or 572615; www.poscottishferries.co.uk). Sails between **Aberdeen, Lerwick, Stromness,** and **Scrabster.**

SeaCat Scotland, 34 Charlotte St., Stranraer, Wigtownshire DG9 7EF (UK ☎ (08705) 523523; Ireland ☎ (1800) 551743; www.seacat.co.uk). **Belfast, Northern Ireland,** to **Stranraer, Scotland.**

Stena Line, Charter House, Park St., Ashford, Kent TN24 8EX (24hr. enquiries in UK ☎ (08705) 707070; outside UK +44 (1232) 647022; www.stenaline.co.uk), and Dún Laoghaire Travel Centre (☎ (01) 204 7777). **Dún Laoghaire** (near Dublin), **Ireland,** to **Holyhead, Wales** (£22-35, students and seniors £18-28); **Belfast, Northern Ireland,** to **Stranraer, Scotland** (£22-42, day return £18, students and seniors £18-32); **Rosslare, Ireland,** to **Fishguard, Wales** (£18-41, students and seniors £14-40).

Swansea-Cork Ferries: UK ☎ (01792) 456116; Ireland ☎ (021) 271166; www.swansea-cork.ie. **Swansea, Wales,** from **Ringaskiddy, Co. Cork** (10hr., UK£24-34).

BY BICYCLE

Biking is one of the key elements of the classic budget voyage. Much of the British and Irish countryside is well-suited for cycling, as many roads are not heavily traveled. Consult tourist offices for local touring routes, and always bring along the appropriate **Ordnance Survey maps.** Keep safety in mind—even well-traveled routes often cover highly uneven terrain.

GETTING OR TRANSPORTING A BIKE. Many airlines will count a bike as part of your luggage, although a few charge an extra US$60-110 each way. If you plan to explore several widely separated regions, you can combine cycling with train travel. In addition, bikes often ride free on ferries leaving Britain and Ireland. A better option for some is to buy a bike in Britain and Ireland and sell it before leaving. A bike bought new overseas is subject to customs duties if brought home; used bikes, however, are not taxed. **Renting** (or **hiring**) a bike is preferable to bringing your own if your touring will be confined to a few regions. *Let's Go* lists bike rental stores in many towns. Those who need more details on cycling in Britain should consult the free British Tourist Authority pamphlet *Britain for Cyclists*.

BICYCLE EQUIPMENT. Riding a bike with a frame pack strapped to it or your back is about as safe as pedaling blindfolded over a sheet of ice; panniers are essential. A suitable **bike helmet** (US$25-50) is a must. U-shaped **Citadel** or **Kryptonite locks** are expensive (from US$30), but the companies insure their locks against theft of your bike for one to two years. According to British law, your bike must carry a white light at the front and a red light and red reflector at the back.

USEFUL ORGANIZATIONS. The **Cyclists' Touring Club,** 69 Meadrow, Godalming, Surrey GU7 3HS (☎ (01483) 417217; www.ctc.org.uk), is a treasure trove of route maps and books. Membership costs £25 (under 26 or over 65 £15, families £40), and includes free touring advice and a bi-monthly magazine.

If you're nervous about striking out on your own, **CBT Tours,** 2506 N. Clark St. #150, Chicago, IL 60614 (☎ (800) 736-2453; www.cbttours.com), offers seven- to 12-day biking, mountain-biking, and hiking tours (around US$100 per day).

BY THUMB

> ▌**!** *Let's Go* strongly urges you to consider seriously the risks before you choose to hitch. We do not recommend hitching as a safe means of transportation, and none of the information presented here is intended to do so.

No one should hitchhike without careful consideration of the risks involved. Not everyone can be an airplane pilot, but any bozo can drive a car. Hitching means entrusting your life to a random person who happens to stop beside you on the road and risking theft, assault, sexual harassment, and unsafe driving. Nonetheless, there are gains to hitching. It can allow you to meet local people and get where you're going, especially in rural parts of Scotland, Wales, and Ireland, where public transportation is sketchy. The choice, however, remains yours. Depending on the circumstances, men and women traveling in groups and men traveling alone might consider hitching beyond the range of bus or train routes. If you're a woman traveling alone, don't hitch—it's just too dangerous. A man and a woman are a safer combination, two men will have a hard time, and three will go nowhere.

Where one stands is vital. Experienced hitchers pick a spot outside built-up areas, where drivers can stop, return to the road without causing an accident, and have time to look over potential passengers as they approach. Hitching or even standing on motorways (any road labelled "M," such as the M1) is illegal. Success also depends on what one looks like. Successful hitchers travel light and stack their belongings in a compact but visible cluster. Drivers prefer hitchers who are neat and wholesome. No one stops for anyone wearing sunglasses.

Safety issues are always imperative, even for those not hitching alone. Safety-minded hitchers will not get into a car that they can't get out of again in a hurry (especially the back seat of a two-door car) and never let go of their backpacks. If they feel threatened, they insist on being let off, regardless of where they are. Acting as if they are going to open the car door or vomit on the upholstery usually gets a driver to stop. Hitching at night can be particularly dangerous and difficult; experienced hitchers stand in well-lit places, and expect drivers to be leery.

BY FOOT

BRITAIN. An extensive system of well-marked and well-maintained long-distance paths cover Britain, ranging from the gently rolling paths of the **South Downs Way** (p. 164) to the rugged mountain trails of the **Pennine Way** (p. 373). The Ordnance Survey 1:25,000 maps mark almost every house, barn, standing stone, graveyard, and pub. Less ambitious hikers will want the 1:50,000 scale maps. Representatives at tourist information centres, hostel owners, and fellow travelers are all fine sources of footpath recommendations. The **Ramblers' Association,** Camelford House, 2nd Fl., 87-90 Arnold Embankment, London SE1 7TW (☎(020) 7339 8500; www.ramblers.org.uk), publishes a *Yearbook* on walking and places to stay, as well as free newsletters and magazines. Their web site is chock full of helpful details. (Membership £22, students and seniors £11, couples and families £26.)

IRELAND. There are many long-distance rural paths in the Republic, though they lack the sophisticated infrastructure of England's. **Wicklow Way** (p. 697), a popular trail through mountainous County Wicklow, is an exception, with hostels within a day's walk of each other. Bord Fáilte publishes numerous brochures describing the trails. The best hill-walking maps are the Ordnance Survey series, which cost IR£4.20 each. The **Ulster Way** encircles **Northern Ireland** with 560 mi. of marked trail. For detailed leaflets on various trails, contact **Sports Council for Northern Ireland,** House of Sport, Upper Malone Rd., Belfast BT9 5LA (☎(028) 9038 1222).

ACCOMMODATIONS

HOSTELS

A HOSTELER'S BILL OF RIGHTS. There are certain standard features that we do not include in our hostel listings. Unless we state otherwise, you can expect that every hostel has: no lockout, no curfew, a kitchen, free hot showers, secure luggage storage, and no key deposit.

Hostels generally provide dorm-style accommodations, usually in large single-sex rooms with bunks, although some have private rooms for families and couples. They offer a chance to meet others, and often have kitchens for your use, bike rentals, storage areas, and laundry facilities. There are drawbacks: some hostels (particularly YHA hostels in rural areas) close during daytime "lockout" hours, have a curfew, impose a maximum stay, or, less frequently, require you to do chores. In Britain, a hostel bed will cost around £6 in rural areas, £12 in larger cities, and £13-20 in London; in Ireland, around IR£6/€7.62 (IR£10/€12.70 in Dublin).

Youth hostels in the UK and Ireland are run by the **Youth Hostels Association (YHA) of England and Wales,** the **Scottish Youth Hostels Association (SYHA), Hostelling International Northern Ireland (HINI),** and **An Óige** (an OYJ) in the Republic of Ireland. All four are affiliated with **Hostelling International (HI),** and in most cases you must be a member of an HI-affiliated association (see below for a partial listing) to stay in any of their hostels. Many HI hotels accept reservations via the **International Booking Network** (Australia ☎(02) 9261 1111; Canada ☎(800) 663-5777; England and Wales ☎(01629) 581418; Northern Ireland ☎(01232) 324733; Republic of Ireland ☎(01) 830 1766; New Zealand ☎(03) 379 9808; Scotland ☎(08701) 553255; US ☎(800) 909-4776; www.hostelbooking.com). HI's umbrella organization's web page (www.iyhf.org), which lists the web addresses and phone numbers of all national associations, can be a great place to begin researching hostelling in a specific region. Other comprehensive hostelling web sites include **Hostels.com** (www.hostels.com) and **Eurotrip** (www.eurotrip.com/accommodation).

Unless noted as "self-catering," the YHA hostels listed in *Let's Go* offer cooked meals at roughly standard rates—breakfast £3.20, small/standard packed lunch £2.80/£3.65, evening meal £4.15 (£4.80 for a three-course meal in some hostels), and children's meals (breakfast £1.75, lunch or dinner £2.70).

Most HI hostels also honor **guest memberships**—you'll get a blank card with space for six validation stamps. Each night you'll pay a nonmember supplement (one-sixth the membership fee) and earn one guest stamp; get six stamps, and you're a member. Most student travel agencies (see p. 30) sell HI cards, as do all of the national hosteling organizations listed below. All prices listed below are valid for a **one-year membership** unless otherwise noted.

Australian Youth Hostels Association (AYHA), Level 3, 10 Mallett St., Camperdown NSW 2050 (☎(02) 9565 1699; www.yha.org.au). AUS$52, under 18 AUS$16.

Hostelling International-Canada (HI-C), 400-205 Catherine St., Ottawa K2P 1C3 (☎(800) 663-5777 or (613) 237-7884; www.hostellingintl.ca). CDN$35, under 18 free.

An Óige (Irish Youth Hostel Association), 61 Mountjoy St., Dublin 7 (☎(01) 830 4555; www.irelandyha.org). IR£10/€12.70, under 18 IR£4/€5.10.

Youth Hostels Association of New Zealand (YHANZ), P.O. Box 436, 193 Cashel St., 3rd Fl. Union House, Christchurch 1 (☎(03) 379 9970; www.yha.org.nz). NZ$40, under 17 free.

Hostels Association of South Africa, 3rd fl. 73 St. George's St. Mall, P.O. Box 4402, Cape Town 8000 (☎(021) 424 2511; www.hisa.org.za). ZAR45.

Scottish Youth Hostels Association (SYHA), 7 Glebe Crescent, Stirling FK8 2JA (☎(01786) 891400; www.syha.org.uk). UK£6.

Youth Hostels Association (England and Wales) Ltd., Trevelyan House, 8 St. Stephen's Hill, St. Albans, Hertfordshire AL1 2DY (☎(0870) 870 8808; www.yha.org.uk). UK£12.50, under 18 UK£6.25, families UK£25.

Hostelling International Northern Ireland (HINI), 22-32 Donegall Rd., Belfast BT12 5JN (☎(02890) 315435; www.hini.org.uk). UK£10, under 18 UK£6.

Hostelling International-American Youth Hostels (HI-AYH), 733 15th St. NW, #840, Washington, D.C. 20005 (☎(202) 783-6161; www.hiayh.org). US$25, under 18 free.

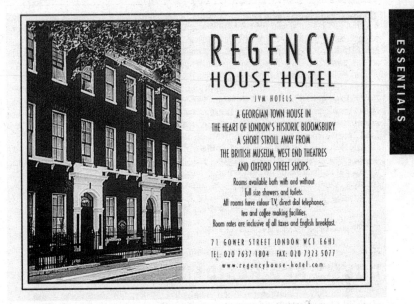
Independent hostels tend to attract younger crowds, be closer to city centers, and be much more relaxed about lockouts or curfews than their YHA or An Óige counterparts. On the other hand, they may not have single-sex rooms, nor be as family-oriented. One useful web site for hostel listings throughout the UK is www.backpackers.co.uk. **Backpackers Britain** (www.backpack.co.uk) also operates a web site listing their network of good independent hostels in England and Wales. A number of hostels in Ireland belong to the **IHH (Independent Holiday Hostels)** organization. IHH hostels require no membership card, accept all ages, and usually have no lockout or curfew; all are Bord Fáilte-approved. For a free booklet with complete descriptions of IHH hostels, contact the IHH office at 57 Lower Gardiner St., Dublin (☎(01) 836 4700; www.hostels-ireland.com). For an extensive list of independent hostels in Britain and Ireland, see *The Independent Hostel Guide: Britain & Europe* (The Backpackers Press, £4.95).

BED AND BREAKFASTS

For a cozier alternative to impersonal hotel rooms, B&Bs and guest houses (often private homes with rooms available to travelers) range from the acceptable to the sublime. The "breakfast" that's included in the price is usually a **full cooked breakfast** (bacon, eggs, sausages, and more), but vegetarian alternatives are sometimes available. A **continental breakfast** is just juice and tea or coffee with cereal, pastries, and bread with jam. B&B owners will sometimes go out of their way to be accommodating, giving personalized tours or offering home-cooked meals. On the other hand, some B&Bs do not provide private bathrooms (rooms with private bathrooms are referred to as **ensuite** rooms; *Let's Go* uses the phrase "with bath"), and most do not provide phones. The cheapest rooms in British B&Bs cost £12-20 for a single—not always easy to find—and £20-40 for a double. London, as always, boasts a stratospheric price range all its own. In Ireland, expect to pay IR£14-18/€15-23 for a single and IR£20-36/€25-46 for a double. A "double" room is one with a large bed for two people; a "twin" room is one with two separate beds; *Let's Go* lists B&B prices by room type (not per person) unless otherwise stated.

You can book B&Bs by calling directly, or by asking the local **tourist information centre** (TIC) to help you find accommodations; most can also book B&Bs in other towns. TICs usually charge a 10% deposit on the first night's or the entire stay's price, deductible from the amount you pay the B&B proprietor. Often a flat fee of £1-3 is added on. In Wales, a £1 fee is always added to the 10%.

The British tourist boards operate a B&B **rating system,** using a scale of one to five diamonds (in England) or stars (in Scotland and Wales). Rated accommodations get to be part of the tourist board's booking system, but don't treat these ratings as the final word. It costs money to be rated; some perfectly good small B&Bs choose not to participate in ratings. Approval by the **Northern Ireland Tourist Board** is legally required of all Northern Ireland accommodations. In the Republic of Ireland, **Bord Fáilte** approves accommodations, symbolized by a green shamrock. Bord Fáilte's standards are very specific and, in some cases, far higher than budget travelers expect or require. Most official TICs in Ireland will refer *only* to approved accommodations; some may not tell you how to get to an unapproved hostel, B&B, or campground.

For more info on B&Bs, see **Bed & Breakfast Inns Online,** P.O. Box 829, Madison, TN 37116 (☎(615) 868-1946; www.bbonline.com), **InnFinder,** 6200 Gisholt Dr. #105, Madison, WI 53713 (☎(608) 285-6600; www.inncrawler.com), or **InnSite** (www.innsite.com).

DORMS AND RESIDENCE HALLS

Many universities open their residence halls to travelers when school is not in session (mid-June to mid-October, and sometimes for the Christmas and Easter holidays); some do so even during term-time. These dorms offer the privacy of personal space, are often close to student areas, and are usually clean, though many do not offer private bathrooms. Getting a room may take a couple of phone calls and require advanced planning, but rates tend to be low. *Let's Go* lists dorm rooms where available, and **Venuemasters,** The Workstation, Paternoster Row, Sheffield S1 2BX (☎(0114) 249 3090; www.venuemasters.co.uk), has a list of rates and schedules on their web site.

YMCAS AND YWCAS

Not all **Young Men's/Women's Christian Association** (YMCA/YWCA) locations offer lodging; those that do are often located in urban downtowns, which can be convenient but gritty. In Britain and Ireland, many YMCAs (www.ymca.org.uk) cater more to long-term residents, though they accept short-term stays. Rates are usually lower than a hotel's but higher than a hostel's and may include daily housekeeping and 24hr. security. Many YMCAs accept women, while most YWCAs are women-only. Some will not lodge people under 18 without parental permission.

Y's Way International, 224 E. 47th St., New York, NY 10017 (☎(212) 308-2899). For a small fee ($3 in North America, $5 elsewhere), this "booking service" makes reservations for the YMCAs in Britain and Ireland.

World Alliance of YMCAs, 12 Clos Belmont, 1208 Geneva, Switzerland (☎(022) 849 5100; www.ymca.int).

CAMPING AND THE OUTDOORS

Britain and Ireland have quite a number of campsites, which sadly tend to be a long hike away from many of the popular sights and cities. Campsites are often privately owned, with basic sites costing £3 per person, and posh ones costing up to £10 per person. **It is illegal to camp in national parks,** since much of their land is privately farmed. Don't camp without permission; not only is it against the law, but you could receive a midnight visit from cows or sheep.

USEFUL PUBLICATIONS & RESOURCES

A variety of publishing companies offer hiking guidebooks to meet the educational needs of novice or expert. An excellent general resource for travelers planning on camping or spending time in the outdoors is the **Great Outdoor Recreation Pages** (www.gorp.com). For more information about camping, hiking, and biking, write or call the publishers listed below to receive a free catalog. Campers heading to Europe should consider buying an International Camping Carnet. Similar to a hostel membership card, it's required at a few campgrounds and provides discounts at others. It is available in North America from the Family Campers and RVers Association and in the UK from The Caravan Club (see below). See also Alan Rogers' *Good Camps Guide: Britain and Ireland* (Deneway Guides and Travel, £8).

Automobile Association, A.A. Publishing. Orders and enquiries to TBS Frating Distribution Centre, Colchester, Essex CO7 7DW, UK (☎(01206) 255678; www.theaa.co.uk). Publishes *Camping and Caravanning: Europe* (UK£9) and *Britain & Ireland* (UK£8).

The Caravan Club, East Grinstead House, East Grinstead, West Sussex RH19 1UA, UK (☎(01342) 326944; www.caravanclub.co.uk). For UK£27.50, members receive equipment discounts, a 700-page directory and handbook, and a monthly magazine.

Ordnance Survey (☎(08456) 050505; worldwide helpline ☎+44 (23) 8079 2912; www.ordsvy.gov.uk). Britain's national mapping agency (also known as OS) publishes topographical maps of the country, available at tourist and park information centres and many bookstores. Their excellent *Outdoor Leisure* (£6.50), *Explorer* (£5.50), and *Pathfinder* (£4.50) map series covers the whole of Britain in detailed 1:25,000 scale.

CAMPING AND HIKING EQUIPMENT

WHAT TO BUY...

Good camping equipment is both sturdy and light. Camping equipment is generally more expensive in Britain and Ireland than in North America.

Sleeping Bag: Most sleeping bags are rated by season ("summer" means 30-40°F at night; "four-season" or "winter" often means below 0°F). They are made either of **down** (warmer and lighter, but more expensive, and miserable when wet) or of **synthetic** material (heavier, more durable, and warmer when wet). Prices range from US$80-210 for a summer synthetic to US$250-300 for a good down winter bag. **Sleeping bag pads** include foam pads (US$10-20), air mattresses (US$15-50), and Therm-A-Rest self-inflating pads (US$45-80). Bring a **stuff sack** to store your bag and keep it dry.

Tent: The best tents are free-standing (with their own frames and suspension systems), set up quickly, and only require staking in high winds. Low-profile dome tents are the best all-around. Good 2-person tents start at US$90, 4-person at US$300. Seal the seams of your tent with waterproofer, and make sure it has a rain fly. Other tent accessories include a **battery-operated lantern**, a **plastic groundcloth**, and a **nylon tarp**.

Backpack: Internal-frame packs mold better to your back, keep a lower center of gravity, and flex adequately to allow you to hike difficult trails. **External-frame packs** are more comfortable for long hikes over even terrain, as they keep weight higher and distribute it more evenly. Make sure your pack has a strong, padded hip-belt to transfer weight to your legs. Any serious backpacking requires a pack of at least 4000 in^3 (16,000cc), plus 500 in^3 for sleeping bags in internal-frame packs. Sturdy backpacks cost anywhere from US$125-420—this is one area in which it doesn't pay to economize. Fill up any pack with something heavy and walk around the store with it to get a sense of how it distributes weight before buying it. Either buy a **waterproof backpack cover,** or store all of your belongings in plastic bags inside your pack.

Boots: Be sure to wear hiking boots with good **ankle support.** They should fit snugly and comfortably over 1-2 pairs of wool socks and thin liner socks. Break in boots over several weeks first in order to spare yourself painful and debilitating blisters.

Other Necessities: Synthetic layers, like those made of polypropylene, and a **pile jacket** will keep you warm even when wet. A **"space blanket"** will help you to retain your body heat and doubles as a groundcloth (US$5-15). Plastic **water bottles** are virtually shatter- and leak-proof. Bring **water-purification tablets** for when you can't boil water. Although most campgrounds provide campfire sites, you may want to bring a small **metal grate** or grill of your own. For those places that forbid fires or the gathering of firewood, which includes most British and Irish campsites, you'll need a **camp stove (the classic Coleman starts at US$40)** and a propane-filled **fuel bottle** to operate it. Also don't forget a **first-aid kit, pocketknife, insect repellent, calamine lotion,** and **waterproof matches** or a **lighter.**

...AND WHERE TO BUY IT

The mail-order/online companies listed below offer lower prices than many retail stores, but a visit to a local camping or outdoors store will give you a good sense of the look and weight of certain items.

Campmor, 28 Parkway, P.O. Box 700, Upper Saddle River, NJ 07458 (US ☎(888) 226-7667; elsewhere call US +1 (201) 825-8300; www.campmor.com).

Discount Camping, 880 Main North Rd., Pooraka, South Australia 5095 (☎(08) 8262 3399; www.discountcamping.com.au).

L.L. Bean, Freeport, ME 04033 (UK ☎(0800) 891297; US and Canada ☎(800) 441-5713; elsewhere call US +1 (207) 552-3028; www.llbean.com).

Mountain Designs, P.O. Box 1472, Fortitude Valley, Queensland 4006 (☎(07) 3252 8894; www.mountaindesign.com.au).

Recreational Equipment, Inc. (REI), Sumner, WA 98352 (☎(800) 426-4840 or (253) 891-2500; www.rei.com).

YHA Adventure Shop, 14 Southampton St., London, WC2E 7HA (☎(020) 7836 8541). The main branch of one of Britain's largest outdoor equipment suppliers.

CAMPERS, RVS, AND CARAVANS

Renting a camper van (RV in the US) is always more expensive than tenting or hosteling, but the costs compare favorably with the price of staying in hotels and renting a car. Rates vary widely by region, season (July and August are the most expensive months), and type of van; contact several companies to compare vehicles and prices. **Auto Europe** (☎(0800) 899893; US ☎(800) 223-5555) rents caravans in London (4-passenger caravan for a week $1300). For further information, consult publications from the A.A. and the Caravan Club (see **Useful Resources,** p. 53).

WILDERNESS SAFETY

Stay warm, stay dry, and stay hydrated. The vast majority of life-threatening wilderness situations can be avoided by following this simple advice. On any hike, however brief, you should pack enough equipment to keep you alive should disaster strike. This includes **raingear, hat, mittens, first-aid kit, reflector, whistle, high energy food,** and extra **water.** Dress in warm layers of **synthetic materials** designed for the outdoors, or **wool.** Pile fleece jackets and Gore-Tex raingear are excellent choices. Never rely on cotton for warmth, as it is absolutely useless when wet. Check all equipment for any defects before setting out.

Check **weather forecasts** and pay attention to the skies when hiking. Weather patterns can change suddenly. Always let someone know when and where you are going hiking, either a friend, your hostel, a park ranger, or a local hiking organization. Do not attempt a hike beyond your ability—you may be endangering your life. See **Health,** p. 25, for information about outdoor ailments such as heatstroke and hypothermia, as well as basic medical concerns and first-aid. The **emergency number**—for police, ambulance, and, in some areas, mountain rescue—is ☎999.

For more information, consult *How to Stay Alive in the Woods,* by Bradford Angier (Macmillan Press, $5.95, US$8).

ESSENTIALS

KEEPING IN TOUCH

BY MAIL

SENDING MAIL FROM BRITAIN AND IRELAND

Airmail is the best way to send mail home from Britain and Ireland. **Aerogrammes,** printed sheets that fold into envelopes and travel via airmail, are available at post offices. It helps to mark "airmail" if possible, though "par avion" is universally understood. Most post offices will charge exorbitant fees or simply refuse to send aerogrammes with enclosures. **Surface mail** is by far the cheapest and slowest way to send mail. It takes one to three months to cross the Atlantic and two to four to cross the Pacific—good for items you won't need to see for a while, such as souvenirs or other articles you've acquired along the way that are weighing down your pack. British stamps are indicated by a profile of the Queen's head, and are the only stamps in the world without the country's name on them; this privilege stems from being the first country in the world to issue prepaid postage stamps, in 1840.

These are standard rates for mail from Britain and Ireland to:

Australia: Allow 4 days for regular airmail home. Postcards/aerogrammes cost 40p. Letters up to 20g cost 65p; packages up to 0.5kg £4.95, up to 2kg £19.20.

Canada: Allow 4 days for regular airmail home. Postcards/aerogrammes cost 40p. Letters up to 20g cost 65p; packages up to 0.5kg £4.55, up to 2kg £17.30.

Ireland: Allow 2 days for regular airmail home. Postcards/aerogrammes cost 37p. Letters up to 20g cost 37p; packages up to 0.5kg £2.73, up to 2kg £9.60.

New Zealand: Allow 4 days for regular airmail home. Postcards/aerogrammes cost 40p. Letters up to 20g cost 65p; packages up to 0.5kg £4.95, up to 2kg £19.20.

The UK: Allow 2-5 days for 2nd class mail within the UK. Postcards/aerogrammes cost 19p. Letters up to 60g cost 19p; packages up to 0.5kg £1.30, up to 2kg £6.56.

The US: Allow 4 days for regular airmail home. Postcards/aerogrammes cost 40p. Letters up to 20g cost 65p; packages up to 0.5kg £4.55, up to 2kg £17.30.

SENDING MAIL TO BRITAIN AND IRELAND

Mark envelopes "air mail" or "par avion" or your letter or postcard will never arrive. In addition to the standard postage system whose rates are listed below, **Federal Express** (Australia ☎ 13 26 10; US and Canada ☎ (800) 247-4747; New Zealand ☎ (0800) 73 33 39; UK ☎ (0800) 123800) handles express mail services from most home countries to Britain and Ireland; for example, they can get a letter from New York to Britain and Ireland in two days for US$26.50.

Australia: Allow 4-5 days for regular airmail to Britain and Ireland. Postcards and letters up to 50g cost AUS$1-1.50; packages up to 0.5kg AUS$13, up to 2kg AUS$46. **EMS** can get a letter to Britain or Ireland in 3-4 days for AUS$32. www.auspost.com.au/pac.

Canada: Allow 2-4 weeks for regular airmail to Britain and Ireland. Postcards and letters up to 20g cost CDN$1.05; packages up to 0.5kg CDN$10, up to 2kg CDN$34.

New Zealand: Allow 4-5 days for regular airmail to Britain and Ireland. Postcards NZ$1.50. Letters up to 20g cost NZ$3; small parcels up to 0.5kg NZ$6, up to 2kg NZ$52. www.nzpost.co.nz/nzpost/inrates.

US: Allow 4-7 days for regular airmail to Britain and Ireland. Postcards/aerogrammes cost US$0.70; letters under 1 oz. US$.80. Packages under 1 lb. cost US$8.70; larger packages cost a variable amount (around US$15). Global Express Mail takes 2-3 days and costs US$20/25 (0.5/1 lb.). US Global Priority Mail delivers small/large flat-rate envelopes to Britain and Ireland in 3-5 days for US$5/9. http://ircalc.usps.gov.

RECEIVING MAIL IN BRITAIN AND IRELAND

There are several ways to arrange pickup of letters sent to you by friends and relatives while you are abroad. Mail can be sent via **Poste Restante** (the international phrase for **General Delivery**) to almost any city or town in Britain and Ireland with a post office. Address *Poste Restante* letters like so: David BECKHAM, Poste Restante, 26 Spring Gdns., Manchester M2 2AA, UK. The mail will go to a special desk in the central post office, unless you specify a post office by street address or postal code, as in the example above. It's best to use the largest post office, since mail may be sent there regardless. When possible, it is usually safer and quicker to send mail express or registered. However, post offices often will *not* accept FedEx and other non-postal service deliveries. When picking up your mail, bring a form of photo ID, preferably a passport. There is generally no charge, unless the sender has not paid enough postage. If the clerks insist that there is nothing for you, have them check under your first name as well. Post offices usually hold Poste Restante mail for a month. *Let's Go* lists post offices and their postal codes in the **Practical Information** section of our listings.

American Express's travel offices throughout the world offer a free **Client Letter Service** (mail held up to 30 days and forwarded upon request) for cardholders who contact them in advance. Address the letter in the same way shown above. Some offices offer these services to non-cardholders (especially AmEx Travelers Cheque holders), but call ahead to make sure. *Let's Go* lists AmEx office locations for most large cities in **Practical Information** sections; for a complete, free list, call (800) 528-4800.

BY TELEPHONE

CALLING HOME FROM BRITAIN AND IRELAND

A **calling card** is probably your cheapest bet. Calls are billed collect or to your account. You can usually call collect without even possessing a company's calling card just by calling their access number and following the instructions. **To obtain a calling card** before leaving home, contact your national telecommunications service using the numbers listed below in the first column. **To call home with a calling card,** contact the operator for your service provider in Britain and Ireland by dialing the appropriate toll-free access number, listed below in the second column.

COMPANY	TO OBTAIN A CARD, DIAL:	TO CALL ABROAD, DIAL:
AT&T (US)	(1800) 222-0300	UK (0800) 013 0011. Ireland (1800) 550000.
British Telecom Direct	(0800) 345144	Ireland (0800) 550144.
Canada Direct	(1800) 668-6878	UK (1800) 890016. Ireland (1800) 555001.
Ireland Direct	(1800) 400000	UK (0800) 890353.
MCI (US)	(1800) 444-3333	UK (0800) 890222. Ireland (1800) 551001.
New Zealand Direct	(0800) 00 00 00	UK (0800) 890064. Ireland (1800) 550064.
Sprint (US)	(1800) 877-4646	UK (0800) 890877. Ireland (1800) 552001.
Telkom South Africa	10 219	UK (0800) 890027. Ireland (1800) 550027.
Telstra Australia	13 22 00	UK (0800) 890061. Ireland (1800) 550061.

Many newsagents in the UK sell **prepaid international phonecards,** such as those offered by Swiftcall. These cards are usually the cheapest way to make long international phone calls, but sometimes carry a minimum charge per call, which make quick calls less cost-effective. Stores such as **Call Shop** offer cheap international calls from their booths, and can be found in parts of cities with large numbers of tourists and/or immigrants.

Calling cards are the next best option for making international phone calls, as international rates are often exorbitant. You can make direct international calls from **payphones,** but if you aren't using a calling card you may need to drop your coins as quickly as your words. **BT phonecards** and occasionally major credit cards can also be used for direct international calls, but they are still less cost-efficient. Although incredibly convenient, in-room **hotel calls** invariably include an arbitrary, sky-high surcharge (as much as £6). The rare B&B in-room phones tend to be less expensive than those in hotels, but they are still more costly than calling cards.

If you do **dial direct,** you must first insert the appropriate amount of money or a phonecard (*not* a calling card), then dial 00 (the international access code in both Britain and Ireland), and then the country code followed by the local number (see box below). Phone rates tend to be highest in the morning, lower in the evening, and lowest on Sunday and late at night. Many BT phone booths have country codes listed inside.

The expensive alternative to dialing direct or using a calling card is using an international operator to place a **collect call.** The **international operator** in Britain can be reached by dialing 155. Alternatively, dialing the appropriate service provider listed above will connect you to an operator from your home nation, who will usually place a collect call even if you don't possess one of their calling cards.

PLACING INTERNATIONAL CALLS. To call Britain and Ireland from home or to call home from Britain and Ireland, dial:

1. The **international dialing prefix.** To dial out of **Australia,** dial 0011; **Canada** or the **US,** 011; the **Republic of Ireland, New Zealand,** or the **UK,** 00; **South Africa,** 09.
2. The **country code** of the country you want to call. To call **Australia,** dial 61; **Canada** or the **US,** 1; the **Republic of Ireland,** 353; **New Zealand,** 64; **South Africa,** 27; the **UK,** 44.
3. The **city/area code.** *Let's Go* lists the city/area codes for cities and towns in Britain and Ireland opposite the city or town name, next to a ☎. If the first digit is a zero (e.g., 020 for London), omit the zero when calling from abroad (e.g., dial 011 44 20 from Canada to reach London).
4. The **local number.**

CALLING WITHIN BRITAIN AND IRELAND

To make a call within a city or town, just dial the number; from outside the region, dial the phone code and the number. For **directory inquiries,** which are free from payphones, call 192 in the UK or 1190 in Ireland. *Let's Go* lists phone codes opposite the city or town name next to the ☎ symbol, and all phone numbers in that town use that phone code unless specified otherwise. To call Britain from Ireland, or vice versa, you will have to make an international call; dial 00 44 followed by the British phone number, or 00 353 followed by the Irish one; remember to drop the initial 0 of the city code. Northern Ireland is part of the UK phone network, and calls there should be treated like calls to any other part of the UK.

PHONE CODES. Recent changes to British phone codes have produced a system in which the first three numbers of the phone code identify the type of number being called. **Premium rate calls,** costing about 50p per minute, can be identified by their 090x phone code, while **freephone** (toll-free) numbers have a 080x code. Numbers with the 084x code incur the **local call rate,** while calling the 087x code incurs the **national call rate** (the two aren't significantly different for short calls). Your British friends might give you their **mobile phone** (cellphone) number; note that calling a mobile is more expensive than a regular phone call. All mobile phone numbers carry 077, 078, or 079 codes, and pager numbers begin with 076.

ESSENTIALS

Note that several regions underwent recent phone code changes. London (020), Cardiff (029), Coventry (024), Portsmouth and Southampton (023), and Northern Ireland (028) began using their new codes in April 2000. *Let's Go* lists all new area codes, but you might see old codes listed in brochures and advertising. For more information on these changes, or to check the status of a number, call the toll-free number change helpline at (0808) 224 2000 or check www.numberchange.org.

PUBLIC PHONES IN BRITAIN. Public payphones in Britain are mostly run by **British Telecom (BT)**, recognizable by the ubiquitous piper logo, although in larger cities you may find some run by upstart competitors such as Mercury. Many public phones in the UK now only accept **phonecards** or credit cards. The BT phonecard, available in denominations from £2-20, is probably a useful purchase, since BT phones tend to be omnipresent. Still, it's a good idea to carry some change in addition to a BT phonecard, since non-BT phones will not accept the phonecards.

Public phones charge a minimum of 10p for calls, and don't accept 1p, 2p, or 5p coins. The dial tone is a continuous purring sound; a repeated double-bell means the line is ringing. A series of harsh beeps will warn you to insert more money when your time is up. For the rest of the call, the digital display ticks off your credit in suspenseful 1p increments. You may use remaining credit on a second call by pressing the "follow on call" button (often marked "FC"). Otherwise, once you hang up, your remaining phonecard credit is rounded down to the nearest 10p, or unused coins are returned. Pay phones do *not* give change—if you use 22p out of a 50p coin, the remaining 28p is gone once you put the receiver down.

PUBLIC PHONES IN IRELAND. Most people in Ireland use **callcards;** they're essential for international calls. When the unit number on the digital display starts flashing, you may push the eject button on the card phone; you can then pull out your expired card and replace it with a fresh one (don't wait for the units to fall to zero or you'll be disconnected). Public coin phones will sometimes make change, but private payphones in hotels and restaurants do not. In any payphone, do not insert money until you are asked to, or until your call goes through. The frightening "pip-pip" noise that the phone makes before it starts ringing is normal and can last up to 10 seconds. Local calls cost 20p/€.25 for 4min. on standard phones.

EMAIL AND INTERNET

Britain is one of the world's most online countries, and cyber cafes or public terminals can be found in all larger cities (*Let's Go* lists them under **Internet Access** in the **Practical Information** section of cities and towns). They tend to cost £4-6 an hour, but often you pay only for time used, not for the whole hour. Cyber cafes can also be found in the larger cities of Ireland, and cost IR£3-5 per hour. Online guides to cyber cafes in Britain and Ireland that are updated daily include **The Cybercafe Search Engine** (www.cybercaptive.com) and **Cybercafes.com** (www.cybercafes.com). Many hostels are also starting to offer email services to their residents, charging about the same rates. **Libraries** in Britain usually have Internet access, often at lower rates than cyber cafes; the downside is that you might have to wait, or even make an advance reservation, to use their computers.

Though in some places it's possible to forge a remote link with your home server, in most cases this is a much slower (and thus more expensive) option than taking advantage of free **web-based email accounts** (e.g., www.hotmail.com and www.yahoo.com). Travelers with laptops can call an Internet service provider via a **modem.** Long-distance phone cards specifically intended for such calls can defray normally high phone charges; check with your long-distance phone provider to see if it offers this option.

SPECIFIC CONCERNS

> **!** If you need to talk confidentially about emotional problems, the **Samaritans** number in the UK is ☎(08457) 909090; in Ireland call (1850) 609090. Both are open 24hr., and can also refer you to the appropriate sources.

WOMEN TRAVELERS

From the Suffragettes on, British and Irish women have fought long and hard to bring about improvements in women's status; Britain and Ireland can now be counted among the world's best destinations for women travelers. Of course, women exploring the two countries on their own inevitably face some additional safety concerns, particularly in larger cities such as London or Dublin. The following suggestions shouldn't discourage women from traveling alone—it's easy to keep your sense of adventure without taking undue risks.

Stick to **centrally located accommodations** and avoid solitary late-night treks or metro/Tube rides. You might consider staying in places that offer single rooms that lock from the inside. Some hostels offer safer communal showers than others; check them before settling in. If catching a bus at night, wait at a well-populated stop. Choose train or Tube compartments occupied by other women or couples. When traveling, always carry extra money for a phone call, bus, or taxi. **Hitchhiking** is never safe for lone women, or even for two women traveling together.

Carry a **whistle** on your keychain or a **rape alarm** (£9.95 from John Lewis or other department stores), and don't hesitate to use them in an emergency. Mace and pepper sprays are illegal in Britain. The national **emergency** number is ☎999. The number for the **London Rape Crisis Centre** is ☎ (020) 7837 1600; the **Dublin Rape Crisis Centre** is ☎(1800) 778888. *Let's Go* lists other hotlines in the **Practical Information** section of our city write-ups. An **IMPACT Model Mugging** self-defense course can prepare you for a potential attack, as well as raise your level of awareness of your surroundings and your confidence (see **Self Defense**, p. 22). Women also face some specific health concerns when traveling (see **Women's Health**, p. 28).

TRAVELING ALONE

There are many benefits to traveling alone, among them greater independence and more interactions with local residents. Freed from hangers-on, you too can write a great travelogue in the tradition of Samuel Johnson, Jonathan Swift, and Joseph Conrad. On the other hand, any solo traveler is a more vulnerable target of harassment and street theft. Lone travelers need to look confident at all times. Try not to stand out as a tourist. If questioned, **never admit that you are traveling alone.** Maintain regular contact with someone at home who knows your itinerary.

For the socially-inclined, backpacker bus tours (see p. 42) are a good way for solo travelers to meet people. **Connecting: Solo Travel Network,** 689 Park Road, Unit 6, Gibsons, BC V0N 1V7, Canada (☎(604) 886-9099; www.cstn.org; membership US$28) has a bimonthly newsletter featuring going solo tips, single-friendly tips, and travel companion ads; its annual directory lists holiday suppliers that avoid supplemental charges. **Travel Companion Exchange,** P.O. Box 833, Amityville, NY 11701, USA (☎(631) 454-0880 or ☎(800) 392-1256; www.whytravelalone.com) publishes *Travel Companions*, a bimonthly newsletter for travelers seeking a travel partner (subscription US$48). For **further information,** pick up *The Single Traveler Newsletter*, P.O. Box 682, Ross, CA 94957 (☎(415) 389-0227; 6 issues US$29).

OLDER TRAVELERS

Senior citizens are often eligible for a wide range of discounts on transportation, museums, movies, theaters, restaurants, and accommodations. Discount prices are sometimes listed under "concessions" or "OAPs" (Old Age Pensioners). If you don't see a senior-citizen price listed, ask, and you may be delightfully surprised.

A useful resource while traveling in Britain is the information line of the national pressure group **Age Concern** (☎ (020) 8765 7200). Two British magazines targeted to the growing older population are *Yours*, a nostalgic, middle-of-the-road publication, and Richard Ingrams's hilariously dour *The Oldie*. Agencies for senior group travel are growing in enrollment and popularity. These are only a few:

ElderTreks, 597 Markham St., Toronto, ON M6G 2L7 (☎ (800) 741-7956; www.elder-treks.com). Adventure travel programs for travelers 50+.

Elderhostel, 11 Ave. de Lafayette, Boston, MA 02111 (☎ (877) 426-8056; www.elder-hostel.org). Programs at colleges, universities, and other learning centers in Britain and Ireland on varied subjects, as well as walking or bus tours, lasting 1-4 weeks for those 55+ (spouse can be of any age).

The Mature Traveler, P.O. Box 15791, Sacramento, CA 95852 (☎ (800) 460-6676). Deals, discounts, and travel packages for travelers 50+. Subscription US$30.

Walking the World, P.O. Box 1186, Fort Collins, CO 80522 (☎ (800) 340-9255; www.walkingtheworld.com). Runs 2-week trips to Britain and Ireland for travelers 50+ (US$2000-2500).

BISEXUAL, GAY, AND LESBIAN TRAVELERS

Britain, the land of W.H. Auden, Noel Coward, Boy George, and Virginia Woolf, has long had an open and accepting gay scene, but even this is far from perfect. As is true elsewhere, people in rural areas of Britain and Ireland may not be as accepting of gay travelers as those in big cities. Public displays of affection in Ireland and most of Britain may bring you verbal harassment. The legal age of consent for homosexual and heterosexual sex is 16 in the UK, and 17 in Ireland.

Large cities, notably London, Dublin, Manchester, and Brighton, are far more open to gay culture than rural Britain, though evidence of bigotry and violence remains. On one hand, the visibility of gay culture is evident in the Gay Listings section of *Time Out* magazine; on the other, queer bashings do occur.

With so many bisexual-, gay-, and lesbian-specific periodicals, it's easy to educate yourself of the current concerns of Britain's gay community. *Capital Gay* (free) mostly caters to men in London and the surroundings. The *Pink Paper* (free) is available from newsagents in larger cities, covering stories of interest to the pink community. Its bimonthly sister publication, *Shebang*, covers all aspects of lesbian life. *Gay Times* (£3) covers political issues; *Diva* (£2.50) is a monthly lesbian lifestyle magazine with an excellent mix of features and good listings.

Listed below are contact organizations, mail-order bookstores, and publishers which offer materials addressing some specific concerns.

The British Tourist Authority (US ☎ (877) 857-2462) publishes a gay guide to British cities called *You Don't Know The Half Of It!* Call the number above, contact the BTA (p. 14), or visit www.usagateway.visitbritain.com and click on the gay and lesbian link.

Gay's the Word, 66 Marchmont St., London WC1N 1AB (☎ (020) 7278 7654; www.gay-stheword.co.uk). The largest gay and lesbian bookshop in the UK. Mail-order service available. No catalog of listings, but they will provide a list of titles on a given subject.

Ireland's Pink Pages (www.pink-pages.org). Ireland's web-based bisexual, gay, and lesbian directory. Extensive urban and regional info for both the Republic and the North.

International Gay and Lesbian Travel Association, 52 W. Oakland Park Blvd. #237, Wilton Manors, FL 33311 (☎(954) 776-2626 or (800) 448-8550; www.iglta.com). An organization of over 1350 companies serving gay and lesbian travelers worldwide. Call for lists of travel agents, accommodations, and events.

London Lesbian and Gay Switchboard (☎(020) 7837 7324; www.llgs.org.uk). Confidential advice, information, and referrals. Open 24hr.

TRAVELERS WITH DISABILITIES

Many transportation companies in Britain are very conscientious about providing facilities and services to meet the needs of travelers with disabilities. It is strongly recommended that you notify a bus or coach company of your plans ahead of time so that they will have staff ready to assist you; trains also require advance notice especially by those using wheelchairs. There's also a discounted railcard for disabled British citizens, with up to 50% discount on train tickets. Not all stations are accessible, though; write for the pamphlet *British Rail and Disabled Travelers.* For travel on the London **Underground,** pick up the free booklet *Access to the Underground* from Tourist Information Centres and London Transport Information Centres, or from the Unit for Disabled Passengers, London Transport, 172 Buckingham Palace Rd., London SW1W 9TN (☎(020) 7918 3312). Several **car rental agencies,** such as Wheelchair Travel in Surrey (☎(01483) 233640) can provide and deliver hand-controlled cars, but at a hefty price.

The British Tourist Boards have begun rating accommodations and attractions using the **National Accessible Scheme** (NAS), which designates three categories of accessibility. Look for the NAS symbols in Tourist Board guidebooks, or ask a site directly for their ranking. Many **theaters** and performance venues have space for wheelchairs; some larger theatrical performances include special facilities for the hearing-impaired. Guide dogs (called "seeing-eye dogs" in the US) fall under the new PETS regulations (see p. 15) concerning bringing animals to the UK; guide dogs coming from EU countries need to be microchipped, vaccinated, blood-tested, and certified against tapeworm and ticks before entering the UK. The same conditions apply to canines from long-haul countries such as Australia and New Zealand except these animals may only enter Britain by air. Guide dogs from elsewhere need to be quarantined for six months. Call the PETS helpline at (087) 0241 1710 or consult www.maff.gov.uk/animalh/quarantine for details.

The following organizations provide information that might be of assistance, or arrange tours or trips for disabled travelers:

Directions Unlimited, 123 Green Ln., Bedford Hills, NY 10507 (☎(800) 533-5343; www.travel-cruises.com). Specializes in arranging individual and group vacations, tours, and cruises for the physically disabled.

The Guided Tour Inc., 7900 Old York Rd., Suite 114B, Elkins Park, PA 19027, USA (☎(800) 783-5841; www.guidedtour.com). Organizes travel programs for persons with developmental and physical challenges around London and Ireland.

Holiday Care Service, 2nd fl., Imperial Bldg., Victoria Rd., Horley RH6 7PZ (☎(01293) 774535; reservation service ☎(01293) 773716); fax ☎(01293) 784647. Info on site accessibility and books accommodations around the UK for travelers with disabilities.

Society for the Advancement of Travel for the Handicapped (SATH), 347 Fifth Ave., #610, New York, NY 10016 (☎(212) 447-7284; www.sath.org). An advocacy group that publishes the quarterly travel magazine *Open World* (free for members, US$13 for nonmembers). Also publishes a wide range of info sheets on disability travel facilitation and destinations. Annual membership US$45, students and seniors US$30.

Tripscope, The Courtyard, Evelyn Rd., London W4 5JL (☎(08457) 585641; outside UK ☎+44 (20) 8580 7021). Provides information for the elderly and disabled on traveling by public transport in London, the UK, and Europe. Helpline open M-F 9am-4:45pm.

For **further information,** consult **Global Access** (www.geocities.com/Paris/1502/disabilitylinks.html) for links to resources for disabled travelers in Britain, or contact the British Tourist Authority for free handbooks and access guides. The **Green Book** (http://members.nbci.com/thegreenbook/home.html) has a partial listing of disabled-access accommodations and sights in Britain and Ireland, while *Access in London,* by Gordon Couch (Quiller Press, £8; or Cimino Publishing Group, US$12), details wheelchair-accessible locations in the Greater London area.

MINORITY TRAVELERS

In the 1991 census, roughly 5.5% of the British population chose not to categorize themselves as white. The majority of Britain's ethnic communities are centered around London or other English cities. Ireland is only beginning to experience racial diversity, while rural Scotland and Wales remain predominantly white. Minority travelers should steel themselves for reduced anonymity in the latter regions, but onlookers are usually motivated by curiosity rather than ill will, and should not cause you to alter your travel plans. It's hard to look like a minority in London, Manchester, Bradford, and other large English cities. This is not to say that these cities do not have problems with racism, only that as a traveler you will probably not feel their effects. There are few resources specifically oriented toward minority travelers in Britain; in cases of harassment or assault, contact the police or the **Commission for Racial Equality,** Elliot House, 10-12 Allington St., London SW1E 5EH (☎ (020) 7828 7022; www.cre.gov.uk).

TRAVELERS WITH CHILDREN

Family vacations usually require that you slow your pace, and always require that you plan ahead. If you pick a B&B or a small hotel, call to make sure it allows children. If you rent a car, make sure the company provides a car seat for younger children. Be sure as well that your child carries some sort of ID in case of an emergency or in case he or she gets lost. Many restaurants in Britain and Ireland have children's menus, and almost all tourist attractions have a children's rate, applicable to those under 16 (those under 5 often get in free). Children under 2 generally fly for 10% of the adult fare, though this does not necessarily include a seat. International fares can be discounted 25% for children aged 2-11.

DIETARY CONCERNS

Vegetarians should have no problem finding exciting cuisine, with the abundance of ethnic food and the increasing apprehension to meat that followed the BSE crisis. Joy of joys, you can now get a vegetarian fried breakfast (complete with veggie sausage) in most cafes and some B&Bs. Virtually all restaurants have vegetarian selections on their menus, and many cater specifically to vegetarians. *Let's Go* notes restaurants with good vegetarian selections. For more information about vegetarian travel, contact **The Vegetarian Society of the UK** (☎ (0161) 925 2000; www.vegsoc.org) or the **North American Vegetarian Society** (☎ (518) 568-7970; www.navs-online.org).

Travelers who keep **kosher** should contact synagogues in larger cities for information; your own synagogue or college Hillel should have access to lists of Jewish institutions across Britain and Ireland. The significant Orthodox community in North London (in neighborhoods such as **Golders Green** or **Stamford Hill**), Leeds, and Manchester provide a market for kosher restaurants and grocers. Kosher options decrease in rural areas, but most restaurants and B&Bs will be open to your concerns and will try to accommodate them. **The Jewish Travel Guide** lists synagogues, kosher restaurants, and Jewish institutions in over 100 countries including Britain and Ireland. (Vallentine-Mitchell Publishers, £12.50; in the US, check larger bookstores or order from ISBS at (800) 944-6190, $16.95 plus shipping).

ALTERNATIVES TO TOURISM

Studying or working in Britain or Ireland gives you a chance to experience culture in a way that tourists never do. For an extremely useful guide to making the transition to life in Britain, read *Living and Working in Britain: A Survival Handbook*, by David Hampshire (Survival Books, £12.95, US$21.95). A more general guide to possible options is *The Alternative Travel Directory* (US$19.95), available from **Transitions Abroad** (www.transabroad.com), which publishes a bimonthly online newsletter for work, study, and specialized travel abroad.

STUDY

Britain has a history of welcoming foreign students—education, in fact, is a good source of foreign revenue for the country. Studying abroad in Britain, whether for a summer, a year, or even for the entire period of your undergraduate career, is thus relatively easy, administratively speaking. Space permits us to list only a few of the myriad study abroad programs available; research other programs at your own colleges, or at your local British Council.

Short **study-abroad** programs (less than a year) in Britain often do not require much paperwork. You won't need a visa if you're from the EU, or from most Western countries. Rules, however, often change, and it's a good idea to check at your local embassy. Enrolling as a **full-time student** requires non-EU citizens to get a student visa from your local embassy. If you encounter any troubles while you're in Britain, contact the **UK Council for Overseas Student Affairs,** 9-17 St. Alban's Pl., London N1 0NX (☎(020) 7226 3762), an organization dedicated to meeting the needs of international students in the country.

THE BRITISH COUNCIL

The British Council is the arm of the government charged with promoting educational opportunities in Britain, among other responsibilities. Its offices are an invaluable source of information for those intending to study in Britain at a secondary or university level, or for those enrolling in language classes in Britain. For their numerous branches in countries not listed here, call the London office or check out their web site at www.britishcouncil.org.

London Office: 10 Spring Gdns., London SW1A 2BN (☎(020) 7930 8466).

Australia: Suite 401, Level 4, Edgecliff Centre, 203-233 New South Head Rd. (P.O. Box 88), Edgecliff, Sydney NSW 2027 (☎016 301 204 in Australia; www.britishcouncil.org.au).

Canada: 80 Elgin St., Ottawa K1P 5K7 (☎(613) 237-1530; www.britcoun-canada.org).

Ireland: Newmount House, 22/24 Lower Mount St., Dublin 2 (☎(01) 676 4088).

New Zealand: 44 Hill St., P.O. Box 1812, Wellington 6001 (☎(04) 495 0898; www.britishcouncil.org.nz).

South Africa: 76 Juta St. (P.O. Box 30637), Braamfontein 2017, Johannesburg (☎(011) 403 3316).

United States: British Embassy, 3100 Massachusetts Ave., Washington, D.C. 20008-3600 (☎(202) 588-6500; www.britishcouncil-usa.org).

UNIVERSITIES IN BRITAIN

The British higher-education system is almost a thousand years old, and many universities offer study abroad programs. Most American undergrads enroll in programs sponsored by US universities. Though receiving academic credit for them may involve more administrative hassle, UK university programs can be cheaper than American ones and allow more interaction with locals. Some organizations that offer study abroad programs in the UK are listed below. Those who wish to undertake a full degree course in Britain should apply through the Universities and

Colleges Admissions Service (UCAS), Rosehill, New Barn Ln., Cheltenham, Gloucestershire GL52 3LZ (☎(01242) 222444; www.ucas.ac.uk); non-EU residents pay full tuition, while EU residents pay the same (minimal) rates as UK students. Further information can be found at your local British Council (see above).

American University Programs:

The American Institute for Foreign Study, College Division, River Plaza, 9 West Broad St., Stamford, CT 06902 (☎(800) 727-2437 ext. 5163; www.aifsabroad.com) organizes summer-, semester-, and year-long programs for high school and college students in Britain and Ireland.

Arcadia University for Education Abroad, 450 S. Easton Rd., Glenside, PA 19038 (☎(866) 927-2234; www.arcadia.edu/cea), conducts summer, semester, and year-long programs and internships in Britain and Ireland, from US$2400 for a summer to $20,000 for a year.

Central College Abroad, Office of International Education, 812 University, Pella, IA 50219 (☎(800) 831-3629; www.studyabroad.com/central), has semester- and year-long study abroad programs in London, Colchester, and Carmarthen. US$25 application fee.

Association of Commonwealth Universities, John Foster House, 36 Gordon Sq., London WC1H OPF (☎(020) 7380 6700; www.acu.ac.uk). Administers scholarship programs and publishes information about Commonwealth universities.

Council on International Educational Exchange (CIEE), 633 3rd Ave. 20th fl., New York, NY 10017-6706 (☎(888) 268-6245 or (800) 407-8839; www.ciee.org/study); also at 91 York St., Level 3, Sydney NSW 2000, Australia (☎(02) 8235 7000; www.ciee.org.au). Sponsors work, volunteer, academic, internship, and professional study abroad programs in Britain and Ireland.

University College London, International Office, UCL, Gower St., London WC1E 6BT (☎(020) 7679 2000; www.ucl.ac.uk). Offers a Junior Year Abroad program, and treats students on study abroad programs like regular students for better cultural exchange.

Queen's University Belfast, International Liaison Office, Queen's University Belfast, Belfast BT7 1NN (☎(028) 9033 5415). Has semester- and year-long study abroad programs, and a new 4-week "Introduction to Northern Ireland" program in January that studies the political, social, and economic questions unique to the North.

UNIVERSITIES IN IRELAND

Irish universities are also open to foreigners; non-EU residents pay full tuition (EU students pay the same rates as Irish students), though places can be limited.

Irish Studies Summer School, usit NOW, 19-21 Aston Quay, Dublin 2 (☎(01) 602 1600; www.usitnow.ie). From North America, contact Irish Studies Summer School, usit, New York Student Centre, 891 Amsterdam Ave., New York, NY 10025 (☎(212) 663-5435). A 7-week program held at Trinity College Dublin in Irish culture and history. Also administers **Ireland in Europe,** 2 weeks of summer courses about Irish civilization.

Trinity College Dublin, The Office of International Student Affairs, Arts and Social Sciences Bldg., Trinity College, Dublin 2 (☎(01) 608 2011). Runs a 1-year program of high-quality courses for visiting undergraduates. Graduates can also register as one-year students not reading for a degree.

University College Galway, International Office, National University of Ireland, Galway (☎(091) 750304). Semester- and year-abroad opportunities for junior-year students who meet the college's entry requirements. **Summer school** courses July-Aug. include Irish studies, education, and creative writing.

LANGUAGE STUDY

Many come to Britain and Ireland to improve their English; others to study the various Celtic languages—Irish, Welsh, and Scottish Gaelic—of the Isles. The British Council has a special web site dedicated to English language education; check out www.englishinbritain.co.uk. **Oideas Gael,** Glencolmcille, Co. Donegal, Ireland (☎(073) 30248; www.oideas-gael.com). conducts week-long Irish-language and culture courses from Easter until August in various activities including hill walking, dancing, archaeology, and weaving.

WORK

Unless you're an EU citizen, you need a **work permit** to work legally in Britain and Ireland. **EU citizens** can work in both Britain and Ireland, and if your parents were born in an EU country, you may be able to claim dual citizenship or at least the right to a work permit. If your parents were born in Britain, you may be eligible for a British passport, which allows unrestricted employment. If your grandparents are British, you can apply for a Right of Abode visa (£50), which allows you to stay and work for up to four years in Britain without a permit. Citizens of certain **Commonwealth countries** (including Australia, Canada, New Zealand, and South Africa) between 17-27 years old can apply for a **working holiday visa** at their local British embassy (£33). This allows you to work in Britain during a visit of up to two years if the employment you take is "incidental to your holiday." **American citizens** who are full-time students at American universities and are older than 18 can apply for a **Blue Card Permit** from BUNAC (see **Work/Travel Programs,** below), which allows them to work for up to six months. Non-EU students who are full-time students in the UK may work up to 20 hours per week on their student visas.

Temporary jobs are rarely glamorous or well paid. Still, they're a good way of finding out more about Britain or Ireland beyond the tourist view. Prepare a **C.V.** (curriculum vitae), bring along proof of your qualifications, and prepare references. Backpacker magazines such as *TNT* or *Southern Cross* often list classifieds looking for part-time workers. Those intending to work **full-time** in Britain should be sponsored by a UK employer.

JOBS: AU-PAIR AND AGRICULTURE

InterExchange, 161 Sixth Ave., New York, NY 10013 (☎(212) 924-0446); www.interexchange.org) provides information on international work and au-pair programs in both Britain and Ireland.

Childcare International, Ltd., Trafalgar House, Grenville Pl., London NW7 3SA (☎(020) 8906 3116; www.childint.co.uk) offers au-pair positions in the UK. Provides info on qualifications required and local language schools. £100 application fee.

Willing Workers on Organic Farms (WWOOF), P.O. Box 2675, Lewes, East Sussex BN7 1RB (www.phdcc.com/sites/wwoof). Membership (£15) allows you to receive room and board at organic farms throughout Britain and Ireland in exchange for help on the farm. However, unless you're an EU citizen, you'll need to get a valid work visa first.

WORK/TRAVEL PROGRAMS

British Universities North America Club (BUNAC), P.O. Box 430, Southbury, CT 06488 (US ☎(800) 462-8622; UK ☎(020) 7251 3472; www.bunac.org.uk), procures 3-6 month work permits for US college students.

International Exchange Programs (IEP), 196 Albert Rd., South Melbourne, Victoria 3205, Australia (☎(03) 9690 5890), and P.O. Box 1786, Shortland St., Auckland, New Zealand (☎(09) 366 6255; www.iepnz.co.nz). Runs work/travel programs in Britain for citizens of Australia and New Zealand.

South Africa Student Travel Services, 11 Bree St., Box 1381, Cape Town 8000 (☎(021) 418 3794; www.sasts.org.za). Their "Work and Travel Britain" program helps South Africans on two-year working holiday visas find jobs and meet other participants.

VOLUNTEERING

Volunteer jobs are fairly easy to secure. However, if you receive room and board in exchange for your labor, you are considered a worker and have to get a work visa. You can sometimes avoid the high application fees charged by the organizations that arrange placement by contacting the individual workcamps directly. **Volunteers for Peace,** 1034 Tiffany Rd., Belmont, VT 057302 (☎(802) 259-2759; www.vfp.org), is a non-profit organization that arranges placement in 2- to 3-week workcamps in Britain and Ireland comprising 10-15 people (registration fee US$200). For more information, see the *International Directory of Voluntary Work*, by Victoria Pybus (Vacation Work Publications, £10.99 or US$20).

THE WORLD WIDE WEB

Almost every aspect of budget travel (the most notable exception, of course, being experience) is accessible via the web. Even if you don't have Internet access at home, seeking it out at a public library or at work is well worth it; within 10 minutes, you can make a reservation at a hostel, get advice on travel hotspots or experiences from other travelers who have just returned from the British Isles, or find out exactly how much a train from Nether Wallop to Shellow Bowells costs.

Listed here are some budget travel sites to start off your surfing; other relevant web sites are listed throughout the book. Because web site turnover is high, use search engines (such as **www.google.com**) to strike out on your own. But in doing so, keep in mind that most travel web sites simply exist to get your money.

▩ OUR PERSONAL FAVORITE...

Let's Go: www.letsgo.com. Our constantly expanding web site features photos and streaming video, online ordering of all our titles, info about our books, a travel forum buzzing with tips and stories, and links to help you find everything you'd ever want to know about Britain and Ireland.

LEARNING THE ART OF BUDGET TRAVEL

How to See the World: www.artoftravel.com. A compendium of great travel tips, from cheap flights to self defense to interacting with local culture.

Rec. Travel Library: www.travel-library.com. A set of fantastic links to general information and personal travelogues.

Backpacker's Ultimate Guide: www.bugeurope.com. Tips on packing, transportation, and where to go. Also travel information for European destinations.

INFORMATION ON BRITAIN AND IRELAND

CIA World Factbook: www.odci.gov/cia/publications/factbook/index.html. Tons of vital statistics on Britain and Ireland's geography, government, economy, and people.

MyTravelGuide: www.mytravelguide.com. Country overviews, with everything from history to transportation to live web cam coverage of Britain and Ireland.

Geographia: www.geographia.com. Describes the highlights, culture, and people of Britain and Ireland.

Atevo Travel: www.atevo.com/guides/destinations. Detailed introductions, travel tips, and suggested itineraries.

TravelPage: www.travelpage.com. Links to official tourist information sites throughout Britain and Ireland.

ENGLAND

While the terms "Great Britain" and "England" may seem interchangeable, England is in fact only one part—along with Scotland and Wales—of the island of Great Britain, the largest of the British Isles, which together with Northern Ireland forms Her Majesty's United Kingdom of Great Britain and Northern Ireland. Never refer to the Scots or the Welsh as "English"; besides being incorrect, you may make some life-long enemies. United as a kingdom in the 9th century, England had by the 17th century conquered Wales and Ireland and united with Scotland in 1707. Ireland won independence in 1921, and while Scotland and Wales have for centuries been part of a United Kingdom administered primarily from London, they are, like Ireland, separate and distinct lands, with their own languages, cultures, and customs. The following pages focus primarily on the history, literature, and culture of England; Scotland (p. 495) and Wales (p. 420) are treated separately, as are Northern Ireland (p. 636) and the Republic of Ireland (p. 663).

LIFE AND TIMES

History will be kind to me, for I intend to write it.
  —Winston Churchill

AN ISLAND TO CALL THEIR OWN

Once connected to the European continent by a land bridge, Britain had been inhabited for nearly half a million years before Captain Matthew Webb swam the Channel in 1875. While little may be known about the island's prehistoric residents, the stone circles left behind at **Stonehenge** (p. 198) and **Avebury** (p. 199) prove they were anything but Neanderthals. Erected between 3200 and 1400 BC, Stonehenge's 50-ton megaliths align perfectly with the midsummer sun, suggesting that the site was as much an astronomical calculator as a religious shrine, though its true purpose remains a mystery. Seeking shelter on Britain's isolated shores, **Celts** and nature-loving **Druids** emigrated from the continent in the first millenium BC, only to submit to the carnage-loving armies of Emperor Claudius in AD 43. By the end of the first century, the Romans held all of "Britannia" (England and Wales), their northernmost colony, and had established major cities at **Londinium** (London) and **Verulamium** (St. Albans, p. 249). Expansion farther north was to prove more difficult. Scared spearless by the fiercely resistant Picts, the Romans constructed **Hadrian's Wall** (p. 415) to keep out unfriendly neighbors—at 73 mi. long and 12 ft. high, it made Britain the ancient world's largest gated community.

The 4th century saw the decline of the Roman Empire, leaving Britannia vulnerable to raids. Angles and Saxons—Germanic tribes from Denmark and northern Germany—established settlements and kingdoms in the south, pushing the Celts into Wales, Cornwall, and Scotland. The name "England" in fact derives from "Anglaland," land of the Angles.

CHRISTIANS AND VIKINGS AND NORMANS, OH MY!

Christianity, which had fallen out of favor with the Romans, returned for good in AD 597 when hotshot missionary **Augustine** converted King Æthelbert of Kent and founded England's first papal church at **Canterbury** (p. 154). The **Venerable Bede** (p. 404) immortalized the conversion of the pagan Anglo-Saxons to the new religion in his *Ecclesiastical History of the English People* of 731, becoming the first historian to perceive of an English nation. From the 8th to the 10th century, Norsemen like Eric Bloodaxe sacked Scotland, Ireland, and the north in search of booty (see **How to Use this Book,** p. v), while Danish Vikings raided England's east coast. Better known as the backdrop to Thomas Hardy's novels, **Wessex** (now Dorset, Hampshire, Wiltshire, and Somerset) was one of England's few remaining kingdoms, ruled by the legendary

Alfred the Great. In 878, Alfred defeated the Danes at Edington, successfully seizing London in 896. As English power grew, the Vikings were circumscribed by the **Danelaw,** an autonomous area running roughly from modern Durham to the Thames estuary; by the mid-11th century, looting and pillaging was a thing of the past.

Better known for his piety, Edward the Confessor was the last Anglo-Saxon king, having promised the throne in 1051 to William I of Normandy. Better known as **The Conqueror,** William invaded in 1066, won the pivotal **Battle of Hastings** (p. 163), slaughtered his rival Harold II—and for good measure, his two brothers—and promptly set about cataloguing his new English acquisitions in the epic **Domesday Book** (p. 182). Completed in 1088, this landmark survey of all landholders and their possessions was meant to facilitate taxing (hence its ominous name); since then it has been the starting point for the written history of most English towns. Painfully remembered as the "Norman Yoke," William introduced **feudalism** to Britain, doling out vast tracts of land to the king's cronies and subjugating English tenants to French lords. Norman French became the language of the educated and elite, and English was marginalized, developing within 14 dialects; Henry IV, crowned in 1399, was the next king whose mother tongue was English.

WAR AND MORE WAR; ALSO, WAR

The Middle Ages in England were a time of bloody conquest and infighting. Henry Plantagenet, Duke of Normandy, ascended the throne as Henry II in 1154 and initiated the conquest of Ireland, proclaiming himself its overlord in 1171. His son **Richard the Lionheart** was more interested in taxing nobles to finance the Crusades than in the well-being of his subjects, and spent only six months of his ten-year reign on the island. Tired of such royal pains, noblemen forced his hapless brother and successor, King John, to sign the **Magna Carta** in 1215 (see Salisbury Cathedral, p. 197), which greatly restricted royal prerogative. The document, often seen as a battle cry against oppression, also laid the groundwork for modern English democracy—the first **Parliament** convened only 50 years later. In 1284, Edward I absorbed Wales under the English crown, a move that still rankles in Wales today. But while English kings expanded the nation's territory, the **Black Death** ravaged its population, killing more than one-third of all Britons between 1348 and 1361. Many more fell in the **Hundred Years' War** (or the 116 Years' War, to be precise), which started with Edward III's 1337 invasion of France in response to the French invasion of English-ruled Aquitaine; Edward's claim to the French throne had prompted the maneuver by his rival, King Philip VI.

While King Richard II was on an Irish holiday in 1399, his cousin Henry Bolingbroke invaded Britain and usurped the throne, demonstrating the fragility of the medieval monarchy. This bold move put the Lancasters in control and gave Shakespeare something decent to write about. More Shakespearian subject matter was created when **Henry V** defeated the French in the **Battle of Agincourt** (1415), a legendary victory for the British underdogs that rendered the young prince heir to the French throne. But the next Henry blew it when, failing to stave off French resistance under Joan of Arc, he lost almost all English land in France. Henry's losing streak continued when he suffered two bouts of insanity that precipitated the **Wars of the Roses** (1455-85). This lengthy crisis of royal succession between the houses of Lancaster and York (whose respective emblems were a red and a white rose) culminated in the suspicious disappearance of the boy-king Edward V from the Tower of London. His uncle Richard had placed him there for "safe-keeping"; with Edward out of the way, Richard III himself became king.

THE 3 R'S: REFORMATION, RENAISSANCE, AND REVOLUTION

The Lancasters claimed final victory in the Wars of the Roses, when the last of their line, Henry VII, won the throne in 1485 and inaugurated the rule of the **House of Tudor.** His successor, **Henry VIII,** reinforced England's control over the Irish, proclaiming himself their king in 1542. However, Henry may be better known for his failure to produce a male heir. In his infamous battle with the Pope over divorce, the King converted Britain from Roman Catholicism to Protestantism, establishing the **Anglican Church** and placing himself at its head—which is ironic, considering most of his wives lost theirs.

Henry wasn't much of a religious man, but his advisor **Thomas Cromwell** destroyed monasteries and trashed churches until he was executed himself in 1540 for persuading the King to marry Anne of Cleves, whom he found unattractive. Henry's own death in 1547 did not help the Protestant cause, as the blandness of his first successor, the nine-year-old Edward VI, was matched only by the fiery personality of his second successor and staunch Catholic **Bloody Mary,** who earned her gory nickname for the mass burnings of Protestants. In a nice spate of sibling rivalry, **Elizabeth I** reversed the religious convictions imposed by her sister and cemented the success of the Reformation—under her reign the English defeated the **Spanish Armada** in 1588, **Sir Francis Drake** circumnavigated the globe, and Britain became the leading Protestant power in Europe. Henry VII's great-granddaughter, the Catholic claimant **Mary, Queen of Scots,** briefly threatened the stability of the throne in this age of unparalleled splendor. Her implication in a plot on the Queen's life led to 20 years in prison and a comparably swift execution (see **Squabbles with England,** p. 499).

The union of England, Wales, and Scotland effectively took place in 1603, when **James VI** of Scotland, Mary's son, ascended to the throne as **James I** of England. But controversy was brewing as James and his successor, **Charles I,** began to irk a largely Puritan parliament with their Catholic sympathies, extravagant spending, and firm belief in a "divine right" of kings. After Charles ruled without parliament for 11 years, tensions erupted in the **English Civil Wars** (1642-51). The Parliamentarians were nicknamed **Roundheads** for their short haircuts, which defied the long-locked tradition of the Court, while Charles's supporters called themselves **Cavaliers.** The monarchy was abolished when Parliament saw to it that Charles I and his head parted ways, and the first British Commonwealth was founded in 1649.

TWO MORE R'S: REPUBLICANISM AND RESTORATION

Oliver Cromwell emerged as the charismatic military leader of the new Commonwealth, but frequent purges revealed his despotic tendencies. Cromwell's conquest of Ireland led to the death of nearly half its indigenous population. At home, oppressive measures such as the outlaw of swearing and theater betrayed a deeper religious fanaticism. Much to the relief of the masses, the Republic collapsed under the lackluster leadership of Cromwell's son Richard. As the philosopher **Thomas Hobbes** had observed in his 1651 treatise **Leviathan,** life was "poor, nasty, brutish, and short" in the absence of an absolute sovereign: **Charles II** returned to power unconditionally in 1660. Yet even the Restoration did not end England's troubles; although Charles was pliant enough to suit Parliament, debate raged over whether to exclude Charles's fervently Catholic brother **James II** from the succession. Side-taking during the Exclusion Crisis established England's first political parties: the **Whigs,** who insisted on exclusion, and the **Tories,** who supported hereditary succession.

KEEPING UP WITH THE GEORGES

James II took the throne in 1685, but his inclusion of Catholics in the government infuriated his Protestant peers. At the invitation of several prominent Englishman, James's son-in-law, Dutch Protestant **William of Orange,** marched on London in 1688 in a bloodless military coup which the winners called the **Glorious Revolution.** After James fled to France, William accepted the throne, and he and his wife Mary wrote the **Bill of Rights** to ensure the Protestantism of future kings. Supporters of James II (called **Jacobites**) remained a distant threat and became only less so in 1745 when James II's grandson, **Bonnie Prince Charlie,** failed in his attempt to invade and recapture the throne.

The ascension of **William and Mary** marked the end of a century of upheaval and the debut of a more liberal age in which Britain rose to economic and political superstardom. England's nationally-funded debt enhanced participation in foreign politics; by the end of the **Seven Years' War** (1756-1763), Britain controlled Canada, the 13 American colonies, and much of the Caribbean, fulfilling the prophecy of James Thomson's 1740 anthem "Rule Britannia." Meanwhile, as the head of the Royal Society since 1707, **Sir Isaac Newton** had theorized the laws of gravity and

ENGLAND

invented calculus on the side, while **John Locke** cleared the slate by developing his philosophy of **empiricism**. In his *Essay Concerning Human Understanding* (1697), Locke claimed that ideas enter through the senses, defying the orthodox doctrine that knowledge of God is innate. Such increased secularism was countered mid-century by a wave of religious fervor, when bible-thumping **Methodists** preached to outdoor crowds, anticipating modern evangelists.

Politically, Parliament's role in the Glorious Revolution had worked a quiet revolution of its own, and under the ineffectual leadership of the Hanoverian kings, **Georges I, II, and III,** the office of Prime Minister eclipsed the monarchy as the seat of power. The first prime minister, master negotiator **Robert Walpole** maintained a Whig hegemony in the century's early decades, while fiery orators like **William Pitt the Elder** galvanized enthusiasm for overseas wars. Although his son **Pitt the Younger** encouraged Catholic emancipation in Ireland and helped defeat Napoleon, he may be best remembered for levying the first **income tax** in 1799.

EMPIRE AND INDUSTRY

During the 18th and 19th centuries, Britain came to rule more than one quarter of the world's population and two-fifths of its land. Originally, such domination stemmed from private companies working in overseas trade—control of the Cape of Good Hope secured shipping routes to the Far East, while colonies in the New World produced lucrative staples like sugar and rum. During the Napoleonic Wars, Britain acquired Ceylon (Sri Lanka) and South Africa, and followed up by establishing bases on islands as disparate as Hong Kong and the Falklands. Parliament soon joined in, acquiring all of Australia and New Zealand by 1840 and throwing in the Western Pacific Islands in 1877. Finally, India—the jewel of the imperial crown—was under full Parliamentary control by 1858. **Imperialism** headlined the economic and moral agenda, as Englishmen considered it their duty to "civilize" the non-Christian world. Despite the loss of the American colonies in 1776, it could rightfully be said in the mid-1800s that "the sun never set on the British Empire."

The **Industrial Revolution** gave Britain the economic power needed for colonization. With the perfection of the steam engine by **James Watt** in 1765 and the mechanization of the textile industry, England soared ahead in machine-driven production, building roads and canals to transport raw materials like iron and coal. Massive portions of the rural populace, pushed off the land and lured by rapidly growing opportunities in industrial employment, migrated to towns like **Manchester** (p. 338) and **Leeds** (p. 381). The age-old gulf between workers and landowners was replaced by a wider gap between factory owners and their laborers. As German visitor **Frederick Engels** wrote in 1845 in his *Condition of the Working Class in Britain,* "What is true of London is true of all great towns. Everywhere barbarous indifference, hard egotism on one hand, and nameless misery on the other." The **Gold Standard,** which Britain adopted in 1821, ensured the pound's value with gold and by 1870 had become an international financial system, securing Britain's economic supremacy. The first hundred years of industrialization irreversibly altered the social texture of Britain and her colonies around the globe.

VICTORIA'S SECRET

The stable rule of **Queen Victoria** (1837-1901) dominated the 19th century in foreign and domestic politics and even stylistic mores. Spurred by civil unrest and harrowing workplace conditions, her Parliament saw the passage of numerous bills promoting industrial regulation. A series of **Factory Acts** throughout the century limited child labor and the average workday. Prime Minister **Robert Peel** restored order by establishing the London police force in 1829: the term "bobbie" stems from his name. As free trade directed economic policy, the **Reform Act** of 1832 made sweeping changes in voting rights, expanding the franchise by 50% for middle-class men. Workers were less successful: the **Chartist Movement,** generated by underclass resentment, demanded universal male suffrage but floundered in the 1850s when it received little response.

The high point of the era was unquestionably Prince Albert's 1851 **Great Exhibition,** in which over 10,000 consumer goods from Britain's far-flung realms were assembled in London's Crystal Palace (p. 80), a pre-modern shopping mall. Yet while commercial self-interest defined middle-class conservatism, not everyone approved. In *Utilitarianism* (1863), **John Stuart Mill** claimed citizens must do the greatest good for the greatest number of people. Similar crowd-pleasing jingos were taken up by the **Fabian Society** in 1884, a socialist organization whose members included George Bernard Shaw and H.G. Wells.

By the end of the century, trade unionism strengthened, encouraged by the 1889 London dock strikes and finding a political voice in the **Labour Party** in 1906. Yet pressures to alter the position of other marginalized groups proved ineffectual, as the rich and bohemian embraced fin-de-siecle decadence. Increasing troubles with Ireland had plagued the nation for half a century, but Prime Minister **William Gladstone**'s attempts in 1886 and 1892 to introduce a Home Rule Bill splintered the Liberal Party and ended in defeat. Meanwhile, the **Suffragettes,** led by **Emmeline Pankhurst,** fought for female voting rights by disrupting Parliament and staging hunger strikes, but their measures alienated support. Women would only receive the vote after the trauma of **World War I.**

HAVE WE MENTIONED WAR?

The **Great War,** as WWI was known until 1939, brought British military action back to the European stage, scarred the British spirit with the loss of a generation of young men, and dashed Victorian dreams of a peaceful, progressive society. The technological explosion of the 19th century was manifested in new weaponry, as gas attacks, machine guns, and tanks caused unprecedented casualties on both sides. The war demoralized the nation: in a conflict that was expected to last for four months and dragged on for four years, almost a million British men died and twice as many were wounded. The scars of the Great War left Britons determined never to repeat large-scale involvement in international conflict, explaining their reluctant entry into World War II just twenty years later.

With the end of WWI, England's hope for a new beginning faltered—though women gained suffrage at this time—as a sense of aimlessness overtook the nation's politics. The 1930s brought **depression** and mass unemployment; in a 1936 publication, social economist **John Maynard Keynes** argued with prescience that German war reparations would come to no good. That same year, King Edward VIII shocked the world and shamed the Windsor family with the announcement of his **abdication** of kingship, prompted by his desire to marry Wallace Simpson, a twice-divorced Baltimore socialite, to leave the throne to his brother George. Meanwhile, tensions in Europe were once again escalating with the German reoccupation of the Rhineland. The Prime Minister, **Neville** "Peace in Our Time" **Chamberlain,** pushed through a controversial appeasement agreement with Hitler.

Appeasement lasted only so long: in response to the German invasion of Poland, Britain declared war on Germany on September 3, 1939, precipitating the outbreak of **World War II.** The previous Great War, with its trench warfare in continental Europe, failed to prepare the British Isles for the utter devastation of concerted military attacks. German air raids started as early as the summer of 1940, when the prolonged **Battle of Britain** began. London, Coventry, and other English cities were further demolished by the thunderous **"Blitzkriegs"** of the early 40s, which destroyed military factories and left scores of Britons without homes. As soon as war broke out, the majority of city children were evacuated to host families in the countryside, leaving them orphans when they returned to bombed-out homes. The near-immediate fall of France in 1940 precipitated the end of the Chamberlain government and the creation of a war cabinet led by the determined and eloquent **Winston Churchill.** British invasion of Europe commenced only with the 1944 **D-Day Invasion** of Normandy, augmented by American forces; the move swung the tide of the war and eventually produced peace in Europe in May 1945.

ENGLAND

THE POST-WAR YEARS

With increasing immigration from former colonies and a growing rift between the rich and poor, post-war Britain faced economic and cultural problems that still rankle today. Left-wing politics enjoyed a boost when in 1946 the institution of the **National Health Service** guaranteed government-funded medical care to all Brits, a radical experiment in socialist medicine. In keeping with the spirit of the 60s, Harold Wilson's Labour government relaxed divorce and homosexuality laws and abolished capital punishment. Under Wilson's successor, Edward Heath, Britain joined the **European Community** in 1971, a move that received a rocky welcome from many British MPs and citizens and continues to inflame passions today. Britain's new economic liberalism, however, was unable to counter losses incurred by the decline of its colonial empire, which began in earnest after WWII. Conservative and Labour governments alike floundered in attempts to curtail unemployment while maintaining a base level of social welfare benefits, and economic unrest culminated in a series of public service strikes in 1979's **"Winter of Discontent."**

It was against this backdrop that Britain grasped for change, electing the Tory **Margaret Thatcher** ("The Iron Lady") as Prime Minister, putting faith in her nationalism, Victorian values, and world-famous helmet-hair. Thatcher's term seemed hexed by painful economic recession, but by 1983 British victory against Argentina in the dispute for the **Falkland Islands** and embarrassing disarray in the Labour Party clinched her second term. Thatcher turned from the war in the Falklands to the state of the British Isles, denationalizing and dismantling the welfare state with quips like "there is no such thing as society." Unlike her post-war predecessors, Thatcher rejected low unemployment as a policy goal and focused on economic growth. Her policies brought dramatic prosperity to many but sharpened the divide between the haves and have-nots. Thatcher prided herself on "politics of conviction," but her stubbornness was her undoing, as she clung to the unpopular **poll tax** and resisted the European Community. Though still divided on Europe, the Conservative Party conducted a vote of no confidence that led to Thatcher's 1990 resignation and the intraparty election of **John Major** as Prime Minister.

In 1993, the Major government suffered its first embarrassment when the British pound toppled out of the EC's monetary regulation system. In August of the same year, Britain ratified the Maastricht Treaty on a closer **European Union (EU),** but only after severe division between Major and anti-treaty rebels within the Conservative Party. Despite these Conservative debacles and a string of scandals, the Tories won the April 1992 election, mostly due to Labour's failure to shed its 1970s image of ineffectiveness. Yet Major remained unpopular, and by 1995 his ratings were so low that he resigned as Party leader to force a leadership election. Major won the election, but the Conservatives had lost parliamentary seats and continued to languish in the polls.

BRITAIN TODAY

The Labour Party, under the leadership of charismatic **Tony Blair,** reduced ties with the labor unions, refashioned itself into the alternative for discontented voters, and finally began to rise in popularity. The "new" Labour Party won a clear victory under Blair in 1997, earning the biggest Labour majority to date, and garnered a second landslide victory in June 2001. Once elected, Blair nurtured closer relations with the EU, maintained a moderate economic and social position, and was named one of *People Magazine*'s "50 Most Beautiful People." All in all, not a bad year for Tony. 1999 was more turbulent, with Britain's stance on the Kosovo crisis gaining Blair the title of "little Clinton" for his blind conformance to American foreign policy. Under Blair, Britain has held fast to its refusal to adopt the euro—a single European currency that went into operation in January 1999—but as the value of the pound dropped in 2001, many predict that eventual British participation in the unified currency is inevitable.

The Labour government has also tackled various constitutional reforms promised in its platform, beginning with domestic **devolution** in Scotland and Wales. The Scots voted in a 1997 referendum to have their own Parliament, which opened in 1999, paving the way for greater independence (p. 499), and the Welsh opened the first session of their National Assembly in 1999 (p. 425). Progress has been more halting in the latest attempts at **Northern Irish autonomy;** the British government suspended the Stormont Assembly for several months in 2000 after debilitating squabbles over the decommissioning of weapons, but restored its powers again after the Irish Republican Army promised to begin disarming. Still, the movement for modernization continued when the Labour government sent over 600 hereditary peers scuttling home from the House of Lords in November 1999. A Royal Commission in 2000 unveiled further reform proposals for the Lords, including the introduction of elected peers, but Blair has put further action on hold.

A ROYAL MESS?

The royal family has had its share of troubles in recent years. In 1992, over a hundred rooms in Windsor Castle burned on Queen Elizabeth II's wedding anniversary, and in 1993 she started paying income tax. The spectacle of royal life took a tragic turn in 1997 as **Princess Diana** died in a car crash in a Paris tunnel. The subsequent outpouring of grief has now calmed, but tourists still mourn at the Diana memorial at Althorp. The immediate fate of the royals will depend on whether the monarchy embraces Diana's fervent populism or retreats with traditional aloofness to the private realm. Royal-watchers are hoping that the 1999 marriage of the youngest royal brother, **Edward,** to Sophie Rhys-Jones will fare better than those of his three divorced siblings. True to their usual form, bookies are offering 5:1 odds that the royal couple will stay married for 20 years. However, it is clearly the young **Prince William** on whom the spotlight shines. After Wills finished his studies at Eton, speculation on his university of choice (he now attends St. Andrews in Scotland) and revelations of a pen-pal correspondence with American popstar Britney Spears consumed his adoring, often pre-pubescent, public. Whether "His Royal Sighness" will gracefully survive his trip to adulthood under the paparazzi's unforgiving lens remains to be seen.

GOVERNMENT

Despite being one of the world's most stable constitutional monarchies, Britain has no written constitution. A combination of parliamentary legislation, common law, and convention create the flexible system that runs the British government. While kings once ruled, since the 1700s the monarch has served in a purely symbolic role, leaving real political power to **Parliament.** Consisting of the **House of Commons,** with its elected Members of Parliament (MPs), and the **House of Lords,** most of whom are government-appointed Life Peers, Parliament holds supreme legislative power and may change and even directly contradict its previous laws (flexible, isn't it?). Of Parliament's two houses, power has shifted from the Lords to the Commons over the course of the centuries, and Blair's latest move to abolish hereditary peerage is just one step in this process. All members of the executive, which includes the **Prime Minister** and the **Cabinet,** are also MPs; this fusing of legislative and executive functions, called the "efficient secret" of the British government, ensures the quick passage of the majority party's programs into bills. The Prime Minister is generally the head of the majority party, and he (or she) chooses the members of the Cabinet, who serve as heads of the government's departments. British politics is a group effort; the Cabinet may bicker over policy in private, but their sense of collective responsibility ensures that they present a cohesive program to the public. Political parties also keep their MPs in line on most votes in Parliament and provide a pool of talent and support for the smooth functioning of the executive. The two main parties in UK politics are **Labour** and the **Conservatives,** representing roughly the left and the right respectively; a smaller third party, the **Liberal Democrats,** tries its best to be the fulcrum on which power balances shift.

LANGUAGE AND LITERATURE

Outdone worldwide only by Mandarin Chinese in sheer number of speakers, the English language reflects in its history the diversity of the hundreds of millions who use it today. Originally a minor Germanic dialect, English was enriched by words and phrases from Danish, French, and Latin, thus giving even its earliest speakers, poets, and wordsmiths a supple and vast vocabulary rivalled by few world languages. In the last few centuries, with English spread to the corners of the world by British colonialism, the language has endlessly borrowed from other tongues and serves as the voice literary and popular of people far removed from the British Isles, from Chinua Achebe in Nigeria to Derek Walcott in the Caribbean. A well-chosen novel or collection of poems will illuminate any sojourn in Britain, and the following survey hopes to give an idea of the range of choices available. Welsh (p. 425) and Scottish (p. 501) literature are treated separately.

YE BARDS OF OLDE

Most of the earliest poetry in English was part of an oral tradition of which little survives. The finest piece of Anglo-Saxon (Old English) poetry for which record does exist is *Beowulf*. Dated tenuously at the first half of the 7th century, the anonymously authored poem details the Scandinavian prince Beowulf's struggle against the monster Grendel. **Geoffrey Chaucer,** writing centuries later, tapped into the spirited side of Middle English; his *Canterbury Tales* (c. 1387) remain some of the funniest—and sauciest—stories in the English canon. The anonymously authored *Sir Gawain and the Green Knight*, another Middle English masterwork (c. 1375), is a romance of chivalry in a mysterious, magical landscape. A more meditative masterpiece is **William Langland**'s *Piers Plowman* (c. 1367), which turns the theme of pilgrimage into an intense, tortured allegory.

The need to adapt religious material into a form understood by the masses led **John Wycliffe** to make the first translation of the Bible into English in the 1380s, thus enhancing the English language's prestige at a time when French was the language at court. English translations, however, soon fell out of style with Catholic authorities, who sought to be the only link between worshipers and God. Persecuted for his efforts, the Biblical translator **William Tyndale** fled to the Continent in 1524 but was martyred there by ecclesiastical foes. His work became the model for the **King James Version,** an English edition of the Word of God that Protestant King James could tolerate. Completed in 1611 by 47 translators, the enduring tome rumbles with magnificent pace and rhetoric.

THE ENGLISH RENAISSANCE

English literature flourished under the reign of Elizabeth I. **Sir Philip Sidney** wrote glittering sonnet sequences, **Edmund Spenser** composed moral allegories like *The Faerie Queene*, and **John Donne,** the Dean of London's St. Paul's Cathedral, wrote introspective devotional poetry and penned erotic verse on the side. The era's greatest contributions were dramatic, with the appearance of the first professional playwrights. As *Shakespeare in Love* movie-goers know, **Christopher Marlowe** lost his life to a dagger in a pub brawl, fortunately not before he guided *Tamburlaine* (c. 1587) and *Dr. Faustus* (c. 1588) into the world of English letters. Meanwhile, **Ben Jonson,** when he wasn't languishing in jail (for acts as varied as insulting Scotland and killing an actor in a sword-fight), redefined satiric comedy in *Volpone* (1606) and *Bartholemew Fair* (1614). The giant of the day, and still the figure against whom all things literary are measured, was **William Shakespeare,** who mixed high and low to create some of the finest comedies, histories, and tragedies ever to grace the world. Those who equate the Bard with a schoolroom avalanche of "whithers" and "wherefores" should know that he held one of the filthiest feathers ever to scrawl the English language, and that Shakespeare invented (or used for the first time) a staggering number of words now in everyday use, among them "arouse," "laughable," and "scuffle," as well as such common phrases as "tower of strength," "sleep not one wink," "dead as a doornail," and "foregone conclusion." An entire town bustles year-round in tribute to the man (see Stratford-upon-Avon, p. 264), but his plays, from *Hamlet* and *King Lear* to *The Tempest*, remain the truest monuments to his genius.

SHAKESPEARE MADE EASY

To have great sex.	"Put a ducat in her clack-dish" (*Measure for Measure*)
This guy from Iceland's a moron, and I hate him.	"Pish for thee, Iceland dog! Thou prick-ear'd cur of Iceland!" (*Henry V*)
Some guy in a bar is annoying you.	"Thou art a boil, a plague-sore, or embossed carbuncle, in my corrupted blood" (*King Lear*)
You kicked his butt and want to tell your friends.	"I took by the throat the circumcised dog, and smote him, thus." (*Othello*)
Dude, you suck.	"Methink'st thou art a general offense and every man should beat thee." (*All's Well That Ends Well*)
You are the worst human being ever to walk on the planet.	You are "a base, proud, shallow, beggarly, three-suited, hundred-pound, filthy worsted-stocking knave; a lily-livered, action-taking, whoreson, glass-glazing, super-serviceable, finical rogue." (*King Lear*)

GODS AND MEN

The British Puritans of the late 16th and early 17th centuries produced a huge volume of obsessive and beautiful literature. In *Paradise Lost* (1667), the epic poem to end all epic poems, the blind **John Milton** gave Satan, Adam, and Eve a complexity the Bible did not grant them. Another Puritan vision came from **John Bunyan,** a self-taught nonconformist pastor whose *Pilgrim's Progress* (1678) charts the Christian's quest for redemption in a world awaiting the apocalypse. The mood at the royal court was rather less pious: as Charles II earned a reputation for debauchery, playwrights like **George Etherege** and **William Wycherley** dramatized country girls and coxcombs, littering the stage with curse words. **John Dryden** set a more conservative tone for the 18th century, spearheading a Neoclassical revival with translations of Ovid, while **Alexander Pope** continued the trend with his keen satires of English social and political life. **Dr. Samuel Johnson** was the major literary figure and critic of the late 18th century. His greatest achievement was spending nine years in Gough Square in London (p. 119) writing the first definitive (and lovably idiosyncratic) English **dictionary.**

HOW NOVEL!

In 1719, **Daniel Defoe** inaugurated the era of the English novel with his popular island-bound *Robinson Crusoe*. Explorations of the new form continued with **Samuel Richardson**'s moralizing *Pamela* (1740) and **Henry Fielding**'s picaresque *Tom Jones* (1749), an "epic in prose" which shows that traveling was far more dangerous in those pre-*Let's Go* times. **Jane Austen** perfected narrative techniques from her cottage near Winchester (p. 187), slyly criticizing self-importance in *Pride and Prejudice* (1813) and *Emma* (1815). In the Victorian period, poverty and social change spawned the classic novels of **Charles Dickens;** his sentimental stories *Oliver Twist* (1838) and *A Christmas Carol* (1843) draw on the bleakness of his childhood (see Portsmouth, p. 179) and the severe destitution of the English poor. From their Haworth home (p. 379), the **Brontë sisters** turned to the English landscape for inspiration. In *Wuthering Heights* (1847), Emily Brontë contrasts the limp Edgar Linton with the ferocious Heathcliff and the intensity of the North York Moors. Not to be surpassed, her sister Charlotte invented madwoman Bertha in *Jane Eyre*. Around mid-century, **George Eliot** (Mary Ann Evans) suffered a crisis of religious faith, seeking refuge in the security of traditional village life. Weighing in at over 800 pages, her *Middlemarch*

(1871), which depicts the entangled lives of an entire town, is majestic in scope and monumental in stature. **Thomas Hardy** brought the Victorian age to an end on a dark note in the fate-ridden Wessex landscapes of *Tess of the d'Urbervilles* (1891) and *Jude the Obscure* (1895). It is easy to recognize similarities to real locales in southwest England—"Casterbridge" is Dorchester (p. 215), for instance, while "Melchester" is Salisbury (p. 194).

ROMANTICISM AND THE 19TH CENTURY

Partly in reaction to the rationalism of the preceding century, the Romantic movement of the early 1800s found its greatest expression in poetry. Painter-poet **William Blake**'s *Songs of Innocence and Experience* (1794) was a precursor to the movement in its antimaterialist spirit, but the watershed event launching Romanticism in Britain was the joint publication of *Lyrical Ballads* in 1798 by **William Wordsworth** and **Samuel Taylor Coleridge,** which included such classics as "Lines Composed a Few Miles above Tintern Abbey" (p. 437) and "The Rime of the Ancient Mariner." The Romantic poets celebrated the transcendent beauty of nature and the power of the imagination to a degree never before seen in English letters; many of their revolutionary ideas—such as the profound influence of childhood experiences on adulthood—are accepted as common sense today. Wordsworth's immense blank-verse poem *The Prelude* (1805 and 1850), in which he remembers childhood "spots in time," cemented his reputation as Romantic icon, but early deaths did not prevent his younger colleagues from achieving fame. The great **John Keats** died of tuberculosis at 26—just in time to have penned the maxim "beauty is truth, truth beauty" and odes full of the richest language since Shakespeare. **Percy Bysshe Shelley** drowned off the Tuscan coast at 29. **Lord Byron**'s *Don Juan* (1819-24) established him as the heartthrob of the age before the 36-year-old was killed in the Greek War of Independence.

The poetry of the Victorian age struggled with the impact of societal changes and religious skepticism. **Lord Alfred Tennyson** spun gorgeous verse about faith and doubt for over a half-century. His Arthurian idylls, like "The Lady of Shalott" (1842), inspired a medievalist revival. Combining skepticism and the grotesque, **Robert Browning** composed piercing dramatic monologues. **Matthew Arnold** began as an introspective lyricist but rebelled against the industrialization of literature and the anarchy of mass rule; he abandoned poetry in 1867 to became the greatest cultural critic of the day. Educated at Oxford, Jesuit priest **Gerard Manley Hopkins** penned tortuous verse that remained virtually unknown to his contemporaries. His verbal technopyrics and unique "sprung rhythm" made him the chief forerunner of poetic modernism.

THE MODERN AGE

Willing or not, English audiences experienced the poignant outrage of war poets like **Siegfried Sassoon** and **Wilfred Owen.** After WWI, London was the home of artistic movements such as the **Bloomsbury Group,** whose bohemian intellectuals valued free love over fidelity. **Virginia Woolf,** a key group member, explored the private yearnings of the individual mind in *To the Lighthouse* (1927), revolutionizing the novel form. **T.S. Eliot** grew up a Missouri boy but became the "Pope of Russell Square" (p. 135); *The Waste Land* (1922), one of this century's most important poems, portrays London as a fragmented and barren desert awaiting redemption. **D.H. Lawrence** explored tensions in the British working-class family in *Sons and Lovers* (1913) before traveling the other way across the Atlantic. Although he spoke only a few words of English when he arrived in the country at 21, **Joseph Conrad** became a master of the language in *Heart of Darkness* (1902). Disillusionment also pervades **E.M. Forster**'s half-modern, half-romantic novels such as *A Passage to India* (1924), which connects repression and class hypocrisy. Authors in the 1930s captured the tumult and depression of the decade: **Evelyn Waugh** turned a satirical eye on society in *Vile Bodies* (1930), while **Graham Greene** studied moral ambiguity in *Brighton Rock* (1938). More optimistic poets such as **W.H. Auden** saw in Freud and socialism hope for a better future.

LATE 20TH-CENTURY LITERATURE

Fascism and the horrors of WWII led to **William Golding**'s and **Muriel Spark**'s musings on the nature of evil, while in **George Orwell**'s *1984* (1949), a ravenous totalitarian state strives to strip the world of memory and words of meaning. Later, the end of Empire and rising affluence splintered British literature in a thousand directions. Nostalgia pervades the poems of **Philip Larkin** and **John Betjeman**, which, in contrast to the vigorous poems of the Yorkshire-raised **Ted Hughes** and **Tony Harrison,** search for beauty amid knowledge of mortality. Post-colonial voices have also become an important literary force in an increasingly multicultural country. **Timothy Mo** examines British rule in East Asia in *An Insular Possession* (1986), while Nigerian-born-and-educated **Ben Okri** draws on the myths of Africa and Europe. The South Asian writing contingent, including **Hanif Kureishi** and **Vikram Seth,** has been especially strong—**Salman Rushdie**'s *Midnight's Children* (1981) is a spellbinding amalgam of Indian myth and modern culture. Closer to home, **A.S. Byatt** captivated poet-detectives everywhere with her story of academic fortune-finding, *Possession* (1990). The grittier tales of **Martin Amis** are ruthlessly satirical. British playwrights, as always, continue to innovate. **John Osborne** looked back in anger at the Establishment, **Harold Pinter** infused living rooms with horrifying silences, and **Tom Stoppard** challenged everything you thought you knew about theater in plays like *Rosencrantz and Guildenstern are Dead* (1967).

OUTSIDE THE CLASSROOM

Away from the ivory tower, English literature rollicks with irreverence and wit. The elegant mysteries of **Dorothy L. Sayers** and **Agatha Christie** are known the world over. The espionage novels of **John le Carré** and **Ian Fleming**—whose James Bond seduced women on and off the page—provide thrills of another sort. **P.G. Wodehouse** (featuring Bertie Wooster and his butler Jeeves) hilariously satirizes the idle aristocrat. **James Herriot** (Alf Wight), author of *All Creatures Great and Small* (1972), faced a backlash when a flock of steadfastly unanthropomorphized sheep broke his leg. Until his death in 2001, **Douglas Adams** parodied sci-fi in his hilarious series *Hitchhiker's Guide to the Galaxy.*

Britain has also produced volumes of children's literature. **Lewis Carroll**'s *Alice's Adventures in Wonderland* (1865) and **C.S. Lewis**'s *Chronicles of Narnia* continue to enchant generations, and the stories of **Enid Blyton** remain vastly popular despite allegations of stereotyped characters. **Roald Dahl** spun tales of chocolate fantasy for children (and tales of other types of fantasy for adults). Adolescence in Thatcherite Britain found its voice in **Sue Townsend**'s *Adrian Mole* series, while contemporary twentysomethings identify with **Helen Fielding**'s hapless Bridget Jones. Recently, **J.K. Rowling** has swept the world with her tale of juvenile wizardry in the blockbuster *Harry Potter* series. But staples like **Richard Adams**'s *Watership Down* and **J.R.R. Tolkien**'s *The Hobbit* (1937) prove that old classics die hard.

> **ROAD BOOKS** Besides the works listed above, these books are our picks for futher glimpses into British life—and for sheer reading entertainment.
>
> **Julian Barnes,** *England, England*: One visionary mogul seeks to create an all-things-England theme park for the discerning tourist on the Isle of Wight.
>
> **Bill Bryson,** *Notes from a Small Island*: An American expatriate's acute (and acutely funny) observations about Britain.
>
> **Nick Hornby,** *Fever Pitch*: If you've ever been a fan of any sport, you'll appreciate this fine novel about the Arsenal Football Club and obsessive fanship.
>
> **Zadie Smith,** *White Teeth*: A grubby North London neighborhood and its residents are inventively rendered in this affecting epic.

ART AND ARCHITECTURE

EARLY DAYS: ROMAN AND ANGLO-SAXON

British art has long been bolstered by patronage and dominated by influences from abroad, and the many cathedrals and castles of England's skyline trace a history of foreign conquests and invasions. Pre-Christian builders of the Bronze Age marked southern England with the famed rock ring of **Stonehenge** (p. 198), as early domestic architecture echoed the henge's curves with round, thatched huts of timber or stone. The Romans brought civic architecture to England on a grand scale, with their forts along **Hadrian's Wall** (p. 415) and the military outpost of **Deva** (now Chester, p. 327). The remnants of the spa at **Bath** (p. 200) testify to the less soldierly engineering savvy of England's ancient conquerors.

When the Romans scuttled south again, Anglo-Saxon art flourished under the new grasp of church patronage, particularly in the form of **illuminated manuscripts**, religious texts elaborately decorated with colored inks and gold leaf. By the 10th century, the first sturdy stone churches of the Dark Ages, such as **St. Martin's Chapel** in Canterbury (p. 155), gave way to increasingly intricate structures with towers and sculptured ornamentation, as at **Winchester Cathedral** (p. 187).

THE MIDDLE AGES: NORMAN AND GOTHIC

After the Norman Conquest in 1066 (p. 67), royal patronage replaced the earlier role of the church. Manuscripts and religious wall painting remained primary modes of expression, and the Normans introduced the **Romanesque** style of architecture, seen in the rounded arches of thick-walled, cruciform churches (see Durham Cathedral, p. 404), and an intense program of castle-building. Within a century, the landscape was defined by the commanding volumes of cathedrals and the squat, square towers of its first stone castles (see the Tower of London, p. 113).

Gothic architecture, too, may have originated in France, but the English, obsessed with surface pattern and busy ornamentation, made it their own in three distinct and ever-more elegant stages: **Early English, Decorated,** and **Perpendicular.** In addition to the pointed arches and ribbed stone vaulting common to Gothic architecture, 13th-century **Wells Cathedral** (p. 210) has the lancet windows of the Early English stage. Decorated period buildings like the 1334 **Salisbury Cathedral** (p. 197) boast densely carved window tracery, and the 80 ft. **King's College Chapel** in Cambridge (p. 307), completed in 1547, has the long, lean windows and powerful vertical lines characteristic of the Perpendicular. Homes in this period acquired more rooms and floors, some roofed with fantastically detailed woodwork. Domestic functions soon outstripped military ones, and the late-13th-century castles built by Edward I in northern Wales form a jewel-like chain of the ultimate in fortified residences (see Harlech, p. 467; Caernarfon, p. 478; and Beaumaris, p. 484).

GET THEE TO A NUNNERY Residents of early England may have kept their glossary of cathedral terminology up-to-date, but we modern types are not always so capable. Read on for a demystification of common terms.

Buttress: a spidery, external support that absorbs stress and weight

Clerestory: the uppermost part of a cathedral wall whose windows welcome light and lessen the weight of the structure's soaring heights

Cruciform: the cross-shaped floor-plan of many Norman churches

Nave: the central aisle of a church leading from its entrance to the altar

Tracery: carved stonework such as lacy Gothic windows

Transept: the transverse part of a church with a cruciform floor plan

Vaulting: a lofty, arched structure supported by columns or a wall that serves as a roof or as further support for upper storeys

. . . and, because we're looking out for you

Reredorter: a monastic toilet

POST-REFORMATION: CITY, COUNTRY, AND COURT

Once the Reformation (p. 68) brought the medieval tradition of religious art to a close, a string of secular portraitists from across the Channel dominated the court-sponsored art scene of the 16th and 17th centuries. The subtly illusionistic skills of Swiss painter **Hans Holbein** the Younger (1497-1543) granted him a celebrated home in the palace of Henry VIII. **Charles I** (1600-1649) ranked among the leading patrons and collectors of art in 17th-century Europe. Indulging an early preference for Venetian painting, Charles dropped small fortunes on block purchases of Italian collections until inviting Flemish painter **Peter Paul Rubens** (1577-1640) to exercise his easel at court. A true Renaissance man, Rubens was knighted for his role in peace talks between England and Spain, while lending visual expression to Charles's "divine right" of kings. **Anthony van Dyck** (1599-1641), a one-time pupil of Rubens, was Charles's court painter for nearly a decade, and his glamorous full-length portraits are as aristocratically imposing now as then. Even the works of acclaimed British-born artists of the time, Elizabethan court painter **Nicholas Hilliard** (1547-1619) and Baroque decorative artist **Sir James Thornhill** (1675-1734; see the Royal Naval College in Greenwich, p. 131), exhibit continental influences.

The post-Reformation also saw a shift to secular building projects, such as the palaces of Henry VIII, including the sumptuous **Hampton Court** (p. 129). More attention was paid to the country and town homes of courtiers and other gentry, many of which display the **half-timbering** and gabling stereotypical of the Elizabethan and Jacobean ages (see Shrewsbury, p. 289). The age of the architect dawned with **Inigo Jones** (1573-1652), whose admiration for Italian design is visible in the symmetry and grace of his **Queen's House** in Greenwich (p. 130) and the **Covent Garden piazza** in London (p. 117). When the **Great Fire** of London destroyed most of the city in 1666, amateur architect **Sir Christopher Wren** (1632-1723) rebuilt 53 churches, including **St. Paul's Cathedral** (p. 112).

THE EIGHTEENTH CENTURY: AN AGE OF ELEGANCE

The Glorious Revolution (p. 68) freed British artists from the constraints of the court, making way for **William Hogarth** (1697-1764) and his narrative engravings of distinctly "modern" and "moral" English subject matter in *A Rake's Progress*. Portraiture continued to flourish at the dignified studio of **Sir Joshua Reynolds** (1723-92), the founder of the Royal Academy of Art, whose lofty and dramatic work often incorporated elements of history painting. The softer, elegant brush of his contemporary **Thomas Gainsborough** (1727-88) produced portraits and, later, movingly rendered classical British landscapes.

The influences of Wren and imported knowledge of French architecture helped develop a heady style of **English Baroque,** dazzlingly seen in **Castle Howard** (p. 394), designed by **John Vanbrugh** in 1692. It was, on the other hand, a posthumous appreciation for the classicism of Inigo Jones that sparked a rage for **Palladianism** in the early 18th century, its severe, stream-lined symmetry perfectly in tune with the practical aesthetic of the Whigs. **Houghton Hall,** p. 316, remains a sterling example.

Stately homes such as Howard and Houghton were increasingly prized during the 18th century, and much time and money were devoted to their grand design and furnishing. Naturally, the decorative arts soon achieved prominence, notably with the **Chippendale** family of cabinetmakers. Thomas Chippendale (1718-79) studied his trade in Yorkshire before opening a studio in London in the mid-1700s. He was never wealthy but always highly regarded, most celebrated for his designs of Rococo and Neoclassical furniture. His son continued to run the Chippendale firm successfully into the 19th century. Another wildly popular decorative arts firm was the **Wedgwood** ceramic manufactory, founded in 1759 by Josiah Wedgwood (1730-95). Josiah was an innovative ceramics artist who took 5000 experiments to perfect his recipe for Jasper, the familiar white porcelain that can be stained with deep color and built up with bas-relief ornament. Stately homes tended to have just as stately **gardens.** The most famous green thumb of the late 18th century was **Lancelot "Capability" Brown** (1716-1783), whose back-to-nature style revolutionized landscape design. His parks can be seen at over 200 English estates, including magnificent **Blenheim Palace,** redesigned by Brown in 1764 (p. 263).

THE NINETEENTH CENTURY: TRADITION AND MODERNITY

Landscape painting peaked in the 19th century, when **J.M.W. Turner** (1775-1851) and **John Constable** (1776-1837) glorified the English countryside with their romantic and luminous oil paintings. Reacting to the popularity of genre painter **David Wilkie**'s (1785-1841) darkly expressive, urban scenes, the three young artists **William Holman Hunt** (1827-1910), **Dante Gabriel Rossetti** (1828-82), and **Sir John Everett Millais** (1829-96) founded the Italian-inspired Pre-Raphaelite Brotherhood in 1848. They depicted subjects both lofty and literary in clear, vibrant colors by applying paint over a white preparatory ground. Perhaps most exciting, though slow to amass a following, was the invention of a method of **photography,** the calotype, by **William Henry Fox Talbot** (1800-1877). His first surviving paper negative dates from 1835, four years before Daguerre presented his own photographic discoveries in Paris. The soft-focus portraits and literary tableaus of **Julia Margaret Cameron** (1815-79), one of a group of photographers loosely known as the Aristocratic Amateurs, were linked thematically to the work of the Pre-Raphaelites. The field of illustration also flourished in this period, typified by the lampoons of Punch cartoonist **John Leech** (1817-64), the illuminated manuscripts of prophetic poet **William Blake** (1757-1827), the haunting, exaggerated imagery of **Aubrey Beardsley** (1872-98), and the satirical musings of **Sir John Tenniel** (1820-1914), who provided the whimsical plates for Lewis Carroll's *Alice's Adventures in Wonderland*.

Meanwhile, the architect developed as an independent professional during the 19th century. Though associated with a legacy of workhouses and factories, the **Industrial Revolution** provided the new materials and building methods for a machine age. Joseph Paxton's glass-and-iron **Crystal Palace**, erected in London for the Great Exhibition of 1851 (p. 70), was a startling masterpiece of early industrial design. Also characteristic of 19th-century architecture was a dizzying, almost schizophrenic eclecticism. Fine examples of the range of styles favored include the Gothic **Houses of Parliament** (p. 111), the Egyptian-flavored **Marshall's Woollen Mill** in Leeds, and the **British Museum,** a Greek revivalist's dream (p. 131). Toward the end of the century, **William Morris** (1834-96) rebelled against the machine craze and sought inspiration in England's more rural past, exploring methods of traditional design in the **Arts and Crafts** movement. Championing the architect and designer as artist and emphasizing the quality and character of materials, the movement achieved special prominence in landscape design. The classic cottage garden, with its geometric beds and patches of wildflowers, may be its most ubiquitous legacy (see Sissinghurst, p. 156).

THE TWENTIETH CENTURY AND BRITAIN TODAY

The photo-based canvases of **Walter Sickert** (1860-1942) greatly influenced British figurative painters of the 20th century. Sickert, among the last of the Victorians, was a harbinger of modernism in his awareness of international styles. **Wyndham Lewis** (1882-1957) was one of the first British artists to show an active interest in the Cubism and Expressionism of the Continent. By 1913 he was popularly thought of as the leader of the British avant-garde, and in the following year he published his Vorticist manifesto. Celebrating the dynamism of machines and the vitality of the time, **Vorticism** sought to dispel the lingering inertia of the Victorian age. Despite ties to literary figures Ezra Pound and T.S. Eliot, the movement lost its momentum during WWI, but many examples may be seen in the collection of the Tate Britain (p. 132). In opposition to the Vorticists' cosmopolitan consciousness, an art colony developed at **St. Ives** (p. 241) that tried to avoid the influences of industrialization by emphasizing Cornwall's distance from London. Artists such as the painter **Ben Nicholson** (1894-1982) and the sculptor **Barbara Hepworth** (1903-1975) married notions of the traditional and modern artist with abstract works shaped by their experiences of nature. The languorous nude sculptures of **Henry Moore** (1898-1986) furthered the cause of modernism in England, gaining the artist international recognition (see the Henry Moore Institute, p. 382).

After WWII England's art scene became increasingly experimental, involved in a livelier exchange with movements in Europe and America. The unsettling carnality of **Francis Bacon** (1909-1992) and the edgy realism of **Lucian Freud** (b. 1922), Sigmund's grandson, have transformed British portraiture, while Pop artist **David Hockney** (b. 1937) infused an American-born movement with British wit. More recently, the multimedia artist **Damien Hirst** (b.1965) has startled international audiences with such installations as a shark suspended in formaldehyde solution. Installation artist and sculptor **Rachel Whiteread** (b. 1963), known for her unusual use of materials like resin and cement, became the first woman to be honored with the prestigious Turner Prize. Hirst, Whiteread, and their precocious peers were dubbed the **Young British Artists,** or YBAs, in the 1990s. Much of their work, widely varied but characterized by a conceptualist humor and self-consciousness of craft, was brought together in the controversial *Sensation* exhibition of 1997. Debate has also raged over recent architectural developments in London. Richard Rodger's metallic **Lloyd's Building** (p. 121) echoes his Pompidou Center in Paris, while the recent docklands development of **Canary Wharf** is a tad modern for some tastes. The **Tate Modern** (p. 132), on the other hand, holds an enormous collection of 20th-century international art in the breathtakingly redesigned Bankside Power Station, a must-see in Southwark. Infinitely less popular is Greenwich's **Millennium Dome.** Supporters praise its monumental size and futuristic decor, but detractors insist it looks like a giant breast.

Inspired by the hip street energy of London in the 1960s along with movements like Op and Pop Art, England's **fashion designers** have achieved international fame. A revolution was sparked when **Mary Quant** (b. 1934) invented the miniskirt. **Vivienne Westwood** (b. 1941) is credited with originating punk fashion in the early 1970s, and her label is still known for its references to costume history. The most recent string of young British designers are taking the reigns at prestigious prewar fashion houses, creating sharply tailored, avant-garde clothes. **John Galliano** (b. 1960) designs for the House of Dior in Paris, as well as for his own line; **Alexander McQueen** (b. 1970), named British Designer of the Year in 2001, headed the House of Givenchy until last fall, also in Paris; **Stella McCartney** (b. 1972), daughter of Paul and Linda, designs to wild success for a third Parisian house, Chloe.

FILM

British film has endured an uneven history, marked by cycles of relative independence from Hollywood followed by increasing drains of talent to America. WWII inspired a more nationally orientated state of affairs, as the government commissioned a series of propaganda films, including stage impresario **Laurence Olivier**'s smashing *Henry V* (1944). Master of suspense **Alfred Hitchcock** snared audiences with films produced on both sides of the Atlantic, including *Dial M for Murder* (1954) and *Psycho* (1960). The 60s phenomenon of "swingin' London" created new momentum for the British film industry and jump-started international interest in British culture. American Richard Lester made pop stars into film stars in the **Beatles**' *A Hard Day's Night* (1963), and Scot **Sean Connery** downed the first of many martinis as **James Bond** in *Dr. No* (1962).

Elaborate costume drama and offbeat independent films have come to represent contemporary British film. The saga of **Hugh Hudson**'s *Chariots of Fire* (1981) and **Richard Attenborough**'s *Gandhi* (1982) swept the Oscars in successive years. Director-producer team **Merchant-Ivory** have led the way in adaptations of British novels like Forster's *A Room with a View* (1986). **Kenneth Branagh** has focused his talents on adapting Shakespeare for the screen, with glossy, acclaimed works such as *Hamlet* (1996). In the same year, indie flick *Trainspotting* sparked drug-fueled controversy and inspired a techno-fueled following. The dashing **Guy Ritchie,** Madonna's new husband, has tapped into earlier cinematic conventions with his dizzying *Lock, Stock and Two Smoking Barrels* (1998) and cleverly scripted *Snatch* (2000). **Mike Leigh**'s subtle, deeply affecting work, such as *Secrets and Lies* (1995), is internationally acclaimed. Of timely interest, gorgeous Alnwick Castle (p. 418) is the backdrop for the first Harry Potter movie.

ENGLAND

MUSIC

CLASSICAL

England was long called "a land without music," a tag not entirely deserved. Though the country may have failed to produce an original composer for centuries following the Renaissance, England always remained receptive to influences from abroad. In the middle ages, traveling **minstrels** improvised freelance performances in the courts of the rich, often incorporating **ballads,** short narrative folk songs from the country, into their entertainments. During the Renaissance, all published music, by royal decree, came from the printing presses of anthem writer **Thomas Tallis** (1550-1640), known as the "Father of English Cathedral Music" for his enormous, seminal output. Tallis's one-time student and partner **William Byrd** (1543-1623) gave the Italians a run for their money by composing motets and psalms in Latin and English. During the same creative period, **Thomas Morley** (1557-1602) developed the quintessential British madrigal, and the melodies for solo voice and lute in **John Dowland**'s (1563-1626) collection of airs are as light as, well, air. **Thomas Weelkes** (1575-1623) and **John Wilbye** (1574-1638) continued these motet and madrigal traditions into the 16th and 17th centuries, and later **Henry Purcell** (1659-1695) rang in the baroque with instrumental music for Shakespeare's plays as well as England's first great opera, *Dido and Aeneas*.

The 18th century, regarded as England's musical Dark Age, welcomed the visits of the foreign geniuses Mozart, Haydn, and the nationally-challenged **George Frideric Handel,** a German composer who wrote operas in the Italian style but spent most of his life in Britain. Thanks to Handel's influence, England experienced a wave of **operamania** in the early 1700s, but enthusiasm waned when listeners realized they couldn't understand what the performers were saying. **William Boyce** (1710-79) embraced the vernacular with his three-volume collection of early English cathedral music, but the real turning point occurred when **John Gay** satirized the operahouse in *The Beggar's Opera* (1727), a low-brow comedy in which Italianate arias were set to English folk-tunes.

In the 19th century, **Sir William Sterndale Bennett** (1816-75) wrote sprightly piano compositions bearing the influence of his friend Mendelssohn, but today's audiences are more familiar with the operettas of **W.S. Gilbert** (1836-1911) and **Arthur Sullivan** (1842-1900); the pair were rumored to hate each other, but they managed to produce gems filled with social satire and farce, such as *The Mikado* and *The Pirates of Penzance*. A second renaissance of more serious music began under **Edward Elgar** (1857-1934), whose pomp is outweighed by circumstances of eloquence in his *Enigma Variations*. **Gustav Holst** (1874-1934), in contrast to his suites for military band, adapted Neoclassical methods and folk materials to Romantic moods in *The Planets*.

Also borrowing elements from folk melodies, **Ralph Vaughan Williams** (1872-1958) and **John Ireland** (1879-1962) brought musical modernism to the island, while composer **William Walton**'s (1902-83) world conducting tours erased the "not for export" stamp so long attached to British music. The world wars provided adequate fodder for this continued musical resurgence, provoking **Benjamin Britten**'s (1913-76) heartbreaking *War Requiem* and **Michael Tippett**'s (1905-98) humanitarian oratorio, *A Child of Our Time*. Present stalwarts **Peter Maxwell Davies** (b. 1934), whose symphonies evoke Medieval and Renaissance themes, and **Harrison Birtwistle** (b. 1934), are also valued for sponsoring performances of contemporary compositions. **Richard Rodney Bennett** (b. 1936) has experimented with 12-tone methods of writing, while **Jonathan Harvey** (b. 1939) added electronics to the mix in his choral/instrumental works. On the British stage, **Oliver Knussen** (b. 1952) set Maurice Sendak's *Where the Wild Things Are* to music in his one-act opera, and **Andrew Lloyd Webber** (b. 1948) has transformed musical theater with his blend of opera, popular music, and falling chandeliers. **Brian Ferneyhough** (b. 1943), **Anthony Powers** (b. 1953), and

Philip Grange (b. 1956) stand at the fore of England's contemporary classical scene. On a more traditional note, the wildly popular **Proms** at Royal Albert Hall (p. 144) afford a rousing evening surrounded by Brits waving flags, blowing whistles, and singing along to their favorite national songs.

POPULAR

THE BRITISH ARE COMING. Despite its mediocre classical record, Britain has revolutionized the popular scene and continues to export the vanguard in musical innovation. Invaded by American blues and rock 'n' roll following WWII, Britain staged an offensive of its own as the **British Invasion** groups of the 60s returned rock to America with a more daring, controversial sound. From Liverpool (p. 332) and then London, the **Beatles** were the ultimate trendsetters, endlessly creative and still influential more than 30 years after their break-up. The edgier lyrics and grittier sound of the **Rolling Stones** shifted teens' thoughts from "I Wanna Hold Your Hand" to "Let's Spend the Night Together," while the **Kinks** spurned drugs and vulgarity with their hard-driving sound and lyrics to match. Urban "mods," who liked speed and androgyny, embraced the "rock operas" of **The Who,** which chronicled the rival factions of British youth culture, and the psychedelia-meets-Motown sounds of the **Yardbirds,** whose members included 70s guitar heroes Eric Clapton of **Cream** and Jimmy Page of **Led Zeppelin.**

ANARCHY IN THE UK. British rock schismed in the mid-70s, as the theatrical excesses of **glam rock** performers like **Queen, Elton John,** and **Gary Glitter** contrasted with the conceptual, album-oriented **art rock** emanating from **Pink Floyd,** Phil Collins's **Genesis,** and Brian Eno's **Roxy Music.** Despite (or perhaps because of) England's conservative national character, homosexuality became central to the flamboyant scene. **David Bowie** flitted through personae, the male lead of goth poseurs **The Damned** sang "He gives me head," and the fans who sent it up the charts were surprised to learn that the **Buzzcocks'** Pete Shelley wrote "Ever Fallen in Love?" about a man.

With civil unrest on the rise due to high unemployment and an energy crisis, dissonant **punk rock** emerged from Britain's industrial centers as a counter to self-indulgence. **Stiff Little Fingers** performed on benefit albums for striking miners; the **Clash** produced political punk with leftist leanings; and Paul Weller of the **Jam** chronicled the plight of the proletariat with resolutely British lyrics. Meanwhile, the **Sex Pistols,** though they became emblematic of the movement, sprang from the capitalist marketing it despised. After they were brought together by Malcolm McLaren to promote his King's Road boutique, "Sex," the Pistols' angry 1977 single "God Save the Queen" topped the charts despite being banned in the UK. Their fame peaked when lead **Johnny Rotten** cursed during a televised interview with the BBC, but plummeted when bassist **Sid Vicious** died of a heroin overdose in 1979. Sharing punk's anti-establishment impulses, the metal of **Ozzy Osbourne** and **Iron Maiden** was much less acclaimed but still attracted a cult following. Sheffield's **Def Leppard** carried the hardrock-big-hair ethic through the 80s.

PAINT IT BLACK. The punk movement evolved in numerous offshoots after the death of Vicious. Against the backdrop of Thatcher's conservatism, student bands such as **Wire** and the **Gang of Four,** who formed at Leeds University, continued punk's political legacy with articulate lyrics and dissonant guitar riffs inspired by Free Jazz. Gloom colored the poetic rock of Manchester's **Joy Division,** while the **Cure** shook teens everywhere. Taking darkness to its painted extreme, **goth** bands like **Siouxie and the Banshees** and Nick Cave and the Bad Seeds combined synthesizers with *Addams Family* attire in acknowledgment of punk's commercialization. Meanwhile, **Elvis Costello** and **Squeeze** found that punk had cleared the ground for smart pop, which stayed bitingly British even as it conquered world charts.

ENGLAND

I WANT MY MTV. Buoyed by a booming economy, British bands continued to achieve popular success on both sides of the Atlantic thanks to the 1980s advent of America's Music Television. **Dire Straits** introduced the first computer-animated music video, while **Duran Duran,** the **Eurythmics, Boy George, Tears for Fears,** the **Pet Shop Boys,** and the **Police** enjoyed many top-10 hits. When asked why rock stars marry supermodels, Duran Duran member Simon Le Bon captured the spirit of the age by replying, "Because they can." Prompted by the keyboard swagger of Germany's Kraftwerk, a swarm of bubbly **New Romantics** such as the **Human League** celebrated lipstick and synthesizers, while the producing machine of Stock, Aitken and Waterman churned out a string of embarrassingly catchy hits by **Rick Astley** and **Bananarama,** among others. **Wham!,** where George Michael got his start, managed to be equally embarrassing on their own-own.

RAVING MADCHESTER. Manchester was England's most influential center of musical innovation in the mid- to late-80s. The melancholy musings of **The Smiths** were matched by the bittersweet beats of **New Order** (formerly Joy Division), while another Mancunian, Mark E. Smith, founded influential indie band **The Fall.** At the end of the decade, a crop of guitar-noise bands from the city galvanized the early **rave** movement. Sweaty, mop-topped youths dropped Ecstasy and danced maniacally to the "Madchester" sounds of the **Stone Roses, The Happy Mondays,** and **The Charlatans.** As the scene exploded world-wide, DJs such as **Carl Cox** and **Paul Oakenfold** became stars in their own right, while a kaleidoscope of club sounds followed. Big-Beat practitioners the **Chemical Brothers** and **Fatboy Slim** drew dance music crowds; **Basement Jaxx** revolutionized the genre known as **house;** and **Roni Size and Reprazent** dominated the drum-and-bass scene. **Trip-hop,** which refers to the downtempo Bristol sound of **Massive Attack, Tricky,** and **Portishead,** provides a mellower alternative, while **Jamiroquai** blends dance music with ska, reggae, and funk.

COMMON PEOPLE. Home to the original boy band, England revived fresh-faced bubblegum pop with **Take That,** survived by the extremely successful Robbie Williams. On the female front, the **Spice Girls** swept the pre-teen crowd with their "Girl Power" rally and astonishingly clever lyrics ("What I really really really want is zig-a-zig-ah!"). Since the mid-90s, most other English bands have fallen under the Britpop label. Beatles-esque bands the **Verve** and **Oasis** cherish dreams of rock 'n' roll stardom, leaving trashed hotel rooms in their wake, while the campy **Pulp** and wry **Blur** embrace suburban boredom. The tremendous popularity of American **grunge rock** inspired a host of poseurs in the UK, beginning with **Bush** but reaching maturity with Oxford's **Radiohead.** Renowned as conceptual innovators, Radiohead continues the tradition of English creativity in the new millenium.

GET YER ROCKS OFF If you're looking for road tunes, you could do worse than to pick something from this selection of albums.

British Invasion: The Beatles, *Sergeant Pepper's Lonely Hearts Club Band;* The Rolling Stones, *Beggar's Banquet;* and *Something Else by the Kinks.*

Punk/post-punk: The Clash, *London Calling;* Joy Division, *Permanent;* and The Sex Pistols, *Never Mind the Bollocks, Here's the Sex Pistols.*

Synth-pop: Duran Duran, *Decade;* Pet Shop Boys, *Discography;* The Police, *Every Breath You Take: The Singles;* and *(The Best of) New Order.*

Indie: The Smiths, *The Queen is Dead;* Blur, *Parklife;* Oasis, *What's the Story (Morning Glory);* Pulp, *Different Class;* and Radiohead, *OK Computer.*

Dance: Fatboy Slim, *On the Floor at the Boutique;* Massive Attack, *Blue Lines;* Portishead, *Dummy;* and Roni Size and Reprazent, *New Forms.*

FLAKES AND FRUITS

FLAKES AND FRUITS British food has character (of one sort or another), and the traditional snack menu is a unique hodgepodge of sweets, crisps, and squashes. **Cadbury's chocolate** bars to die for include Flake, Crunchie (made out of honeycombed magic), and the classic Dairy Milk. **Sweets** come in many forms—the fizzy Refreshers, the chewy Wine Gums, or frosted Fruit Pastilles. Potato chips, or **crisps** as they are known in England, are not just salted, but take on a range of flavors, from Prawn Cocktail to Cheese 'n' Onion. All this sugar and salt washes down with a bottle of Ribena, a blackcurrant manna from heaven. This beverage belongs to a family of drinks known as **squash,** fruit-based syrups watered down to drink.

FOOD AND TEA

English cooking, like the English climate, is a training for life's unavoidable hardships.
    —R.P. Lister

British cuisine's deservedly modest reputation redeems itself in the few specialties without which the world's palate would be sadly incomplete. Even the dish names range from the redundantly bland to the curiously vivid: there are the basic rice, Yorkshire, and bread puddings, alongside the inestimable Hobnob, bubble and squeak, and spotted dick.

Britons like to start their day off heartily with the famous **English breakfast,** served in most B&Bs across the country. Meat is a mainstay of any traditional British meal, and this cholesterol-filled repast, with its fried eggs, fried ham, fried bacon, fried sausage, fried bread, marmalade, grilled tomatoes and mushrooms, and (in winter) porridge, is no exception. You will want a strong "cuppa" (tea) to wash it all down, for, unlike its French and Italian counterparts, British coffee is far from exceptional. The best native dishes for lunch or dinner are **roasts**—beef, lamb, and Wiltshire hams. **Bangers and mash** uses up left-over sausages and potatoes, while **bubble and squeak** does the same for cabbage and potatoes. Vegetables, often boiled into a flavorless, textureless mound, are often the weakest part of the meal. Beware the British salad—it often consists of a few limp lettuce leaves mixed with an abundance of sweetened mayonnaise called "salad cream."

The British like their **desserts** exceedingly sweet and gloopy. Fools, sponges, trifles, and puddings of endless variety will satiate even the severest of sweet teeth. **Fruit trifle** is a combination of all the best things in life: cake, custard, jam, whipped cream, fresh fruit, and sherry. **Treacle tart** and **spotted dick** (a spongy cake with raisins) are mini-feasts as well. For a lighter end to one's meal, **fools** (whipped cream blended with fruit) and airy cakes called **sponges** are delicious. Most desserts are served with large dollops of thick, yellow custard or whipped cream.

Pub grub is fast, filling, and a fine option for budget travelers. Hot meals vary from **Cornish pasties** (PAH-stee: meat and veggies wrapped in pastry) to the hearty **steak and kidney pie.** The inexpensive **ploughman's lunch,** a staple in country pubs, is simply cheese, bread, pickled gherkin, chutney, and pickled onion. More cheap culinary options abound at the perennial chippy—deep fried **fish and chips** are served in a cone of paper, dripping with grease, salt, and vinegar. In recent years, restaurant chains have sprung up in the larger cities. You can always find a reliable if slightly pricey meal in establishments such as All Bar One, Café Rouge, Pizza Express, or Dôme, while light snacks are available at Prêt-à-Manger. **Outdoor markets** and **supermarkets** (such as Marks & Spencer, Waitrose, and Tesco) provide another source of cheap food, especially for picnics—try Stilton cheese with digestive biscuits and find a suitably picturesque view.

ENGLAND

Britain's history of imperialism has resulted in an abundance of excellent ethnic food throughout the country. For a welcome alternative to traditional British food, try Chinese, Greek, and especially Indian cuisines—Britain offers some of the best **tandoori and curry** outside of India, particularly in London and the larger northern cities. Ethnic restaurants are widespread and tend to be open late—stopping for a quick *chicken tikka masala* on the way home from a night at the pub has become a common phenomenon, substituted occasionally by a nice *shish kebab*.

British "tea" refers both to a drink and a social ceremony. The ritual refreshment, accompanying almost every meal, is served strongly steeped and milky. The standard tea, colloquially known as a nice **cuppa,** is mass produced by PG Tips or Tetleys; more refined cups specify particular blends such as **Earl Grey, Darjeeling,** or **Lapsang Souchong.** The oft-stereotyped British ritual of afternoon **high tea,** served around 4pm, includes cooked meats, salad, sandwiches, and pastries. Fans of Victorianism will appreciate the dainty **cucumber sandwiches** served at classy tea joints like Fortnum and Mason's or the Savoy Hotel in London. **Cream tea,** a specialty of Cornwall and Devon, includes toast, shortbread, crumpets, scones, and jam, accompanied by clotted cream (a cross between whipped cream and butter). The summertime potion called **Pimms** is a punch of fruit juices and gin (the precise recipe is claimed to be a well-guarded secret), and often taken at teatime by the decadent set—think an edgier version of sangria. Many Britons take short tea breaks each day, including mornings ("elevenses"), but Sunday takes the cake for best tea day; the indulgent can while away a couple of hours over a pot of Earl Grey, a pile of buttered scones, and the Sunday newspaper supplements.

PUBS AND BEER

O Beer! O Hodgson, Guinness, Allsopp, Bass! Names that should be on every infant's tongue!
—S.C.L. Calverley

"As much of the history of England has been brought about in public houses as in the House of Commons," said Sir William Harcourt. You may not witness history in the making, but you will certainly absorb the spirit of the region if you pause within the four wood-panelled walls of a local tavern. The routine inspired by the pub is considerable; to stop in for a sharpener at lunchtime and then again after work is not uncommon. Thanks to this established pace, Brits rapidly develop affinities for neighborhood establishments, becoming loyal to their **locals.** Many pubs cater to a regular clientele—student discounts are common near university dorms, while village pubs maintain a sleepier atmosphere. Those seeking more variety head on a **pub crawl,** the British equivalent of bar hopping. The drinking age is 18, though it is skimpily enforced.

Bitter, named for its sharp, hoppy aftertaste, is the standard pub drink and should be hand-pumped or pulled from the tap at cellar temperature into government-stamped pint glasses (20oz.) or the more modest but socially scorned half-pints. Abbot's, Youngs, and Ruddles are dark and full-bodied southern examples, while worthy northern brews are Tetleys, John Smith, and Samuel Smith. **Real ale,** using top-fermenting yeast and drawn from a barrel, retains a die-hard cult of connoisseurs in the shadow of giant corporate breweries. Brown, pale, and India pale ales—less common varieties—all have a relatively heavy flavor with noticeable hop. **Stout,** the distinctive subspecies of ale, is rich, dark, and creamy; try the Irish Guinness (p. 671) with its silky foam head, rumored to be a recipe stolen from the older Beamish. Most draught ales and stouts are served at room temperature, so if you can't stand the heat, try a **lager,** the tasty European precursor of American beer. **Cider,** a fermented apple juice served sweet or dry, is one potent, cold, and tasty alternative to beer. Especially succulent brands include Strongbow, Blackthorn, Woodpecker, and the unrefined Scrumpy Jack. Variations on the standard pint include the **shandy,** a combination of beer and fizzy lemonade that no respectable drinker would go near; **black velvet,** a mating of stout and champagne; **black and tan,** layers of stout and ale; and **snakebite,** a murky mix of lager and cider with a dash of blackcurrant Ribena.

Visitors will learn to their dismay that government-imposed **closing times** force revelries to end early, especially in England. Drinking hours enforced during WWI to prevent munitions workers from arriving at the factory drunk are still in place; generally, drinks are served 11am-11pm Monday to Saturday, and from noon-3pm and 7-10:30pm on Sundays, though this varies from region to region. A bell 10 minutes or more before closing time signifies "last orders." T.S. Eliot knew the special agony of pub closings: many a drunkard has argued that the most painful words in all of *The Waste Land* come in its second part, with the publican-god's cry, "HURRY UP PLEASE IT'S TIME." Whether or not patrons consider the existential implications of the call, they know that just a handful of minutes remain to finish their beers before chairs go up and lights go down.

More recently, the government has been making noise about extending hours, or doing away with restrictions altogether, thus bringing the dream of the 24-hour pub a bit closer to reality. Many establishments, particularly in larger towns and cities, find ways around closing times anyway—serving food or having an entertainment license allows an establishment to serve alcohol later, so late-night wine bars are popular, and around pub-closing time people pack the clubs.

SPORT

Many evils may arise which God forbid.
  —King Edward II, banning football in London, 1314

FOOTBALL

The not-entirely-fair stereotype of English athletic performance is that the English are masters of inventing sports but only average players. **Football** (soccer), whose rules were formalized by the English Football Association (F.A.) in 1863, remains Britain's—and the world's—most popular sport. Tiny grounds dot the countryside, and grand, storied stadia attract thousands every weekend like the cathedrals they are. At the highest echelon of English football are the 20 clubs (teams) of the **Premier League,** which are populated with world-class players from Britain and abroad. Below the Premiership lie the three divisions of the Nationwide League. At the end of the season, the three clubs with the worst records in the Premiership face relegation to the First Division, whose top three clubs are promoted. The same process affects the teams of the Second Division, Third Division, lower divisions, and non-league clubs. The **F.A. Cup,** held every May on the hallowed turf of Wembley, is English football's premier knockout competition, and the ultimate achievement for an English football club is to "do the Double"—to win both the Premier League and the F.A. Cup in one season.

At present, the English Premier League is dominated by **Manchester United** (p. 342) and **Arsenal,** with Liverpool, Leeds, and Chelsea also leading the pack. Many English clubs are well known worldwide, and Manchester United ("Man U"), now owned by international news mogul Rupert Murdoch, is the red victory machine that every Brit loves to hate. Unfortunately, the four British international teams (England, Scotland, Wales, and Northern Ireland compete as separate countries) have not performed as well in World Cups and European Championships—England's 1966 World Cup victory being the glorious exception. The next World Cup tournament is slated for North and South Korea in 2003, so national team schedules will begin to fill with international qualifying matches and "friendlies."

Over half a million fans attend professional matches in Britain every weekend from mid-August to May, and they spend the few barren weeks of summer waiting for the publication of the coming season's **fixtures,** or match schedules. If you can get tickets, a match is well worth attending for a glimpse of British **football culture.** Fans with painted faces and dressed in team colors form a rowdy chorus of uncannily synchronized (and usually rude) songs and chants. Football passion achieves a level of religious fervor, and intracity club rivalries (Arsenal-Tottenham in London or Everton-Liverpool in Liverpool) have been known to divide families. Being a true football fan often involves a certain form of masochism, supporting a team across the country despite foul luck and foul weather. Excessive enthusiasm has, however, proved problematic. Violence and vandalism used to dog the game, causing tension between fans and the police who tried to control huge crowds in old stadia. **Hooligans** are usually on their worst behavior when the England national team plays abroad; things are a bit better at home, though far from perfect. The atmosphere in stadia has become safer now that clubs have been forced to convert to seating-only, rather than standing spaces in the once-infamous terraces. As a result, football has become more family-friendly, albeit pricier.

A LOAD OF BALLS

According to legend, **rugby** was born one glorious day in 1823 when William Webb Ellis, an inspired (or perhaps slightly confused) Rugby School student, picked up a soccer ball and ran it into the goal. Since then, rugby has evolved into a complex and subtle game. The first amateur **Rugby Union** was formed in 1871, and play, involving 15-man teams, started in 1895. **Rugby League,** a professional sport using modified rules and played by teams of 13, was soon formed. Although both variants now have professional and amateur teams, the rugby world remains separated into union and league; in Britain, the former is associated with Wales and the south of England, and the latter with northwest England. A *melée* of blood, mud, and drinking songs, rugby is exciting to watch, with no non-injury substitutions and little stoppage of play. An oval-shaped ball is carried or passed backward until the team is able to touch the ball down past the goal line (known as a "try" and worth five points) or kick it through the uprights (worth three points). The club season runs from September to May, while the culmination of international rugby union is the Rugby World Cup, last played in Cardiff, Wales in 1999.

While fanatically followed within the Commonwealth, **cricket** remains a confusing spectacle to the uninitiated. Though it might seem incomprehensible to those not raised on Marmite, its rules are actually quite simple. The game is played by two 11-player teams on a 22-yard green, marked by two **wickets** (three vertical stumps and two bails) at each end. In an innings, one team acts as **batsmen** and the other as **fielders.** The batting team sends up two batsmen, and a **bowler** from the fielding side throws the ball so that it bounces toward the wickets. The goal of the fielders is to try to get the batsmen out by **taking** the wickets (hitting the wickets so that the bails fall) or by catching the ball. The batsmen's goal is to make as many runs as they can while protecting their wickets, scoring every time they switch places. The teams switch positions once 10 batsmen are out; usually both sides bat twice. Matches last one to five days, with the biggest crowd-pullers being the one-day internationals of the Cricket World Cup, won by Australia in 1999. International games are known as Test matches; the **Ashes,** named for the remains of a cricket bail, are the prize in England's Test series with Australia. London's **Lords** cricket grounds is regarded as the spiritual home of the game.

When **tennis,** a sport with a long history, was becoming popular at the end of the 15th century, Henry VII played in black velvet. As the game developed, cooler white became the traditional color for players on the court. Today almost any high-tech garb goes. For two weeks in late June and early July, tennis buffs all over the world focus their attention on **Wimbledon,** home to the only Grand Slam event played on grass.

HORSES AND COURSES

Prized for their speed and grace, **horses** have pleased riders and observers alike in several arenas. Princess Anne competed in the 1976 Olympics in **equestrian,** which involves three days of competition in dressage, cross-country, and show-jumping. In late June, **polo** devotees flock to the **Royal Windsor Cup.** Horse-racing also pretends to noble status. An important society event, the **Royal Gold Cup Meeting** at **Ascot** has occurred in the second half of June for every summer since 1711, though some see it as an excuse for Brits of all strata to indulge in drinking and gambling while wearing over-the-top hats. Top hats also distinguish the famed **Derby** (DAR-bee), which has been run since 1780 on Epsom Racecourse, Surrey, on the first Saturday of June.

ENGLAND

Britain remains a force in rowing, and the annual **Henley Royal Regatta** is the most famous series of rowing races in the world. The five-day regatta ends on the first Sunday in July; Saturday is the most popular day, but some of the best races are the Sunday finals. The **Boat Race,** between eights from Oxford (p. 253) and Cambridge (p. 302), enacts the traditional rivalry between the schools. Britain is the center of Formula One racecar design, and the **British Grand Prix** is held every July. Meanwhile, the **T.T. races** bring hordes of screeching motorcycles to the Isle of Man in the first two weeks of June (p. 349).

THE MEDIA

PRINT

In a culture with a rich print-media history, the influence of newspapers remains enormous. The UK's plethora of national newspapers yields a range of political viewpoints. **The Times,** long a model of thoughtful discretion and mild infallibility, has turned Tory under the ownership of Rupert "Buy It" Murdoch. **The Daily Telegraph,** dubbed "Torygraph," is fairly conservative and old-fashioned. **The Guardian** leans left, while **The Independent** answers for its name. Of the infamous tabloids, **The Sun,** Murdoch-owned and better known for its page-three topless pin-up than for its reporting, is among the most influential. Among the others, **The Daily Mail, The Daily Express,** and **The London Evening Standard** (the only evening paper) make serious attempts at popular journalism, although the first two tend to position themselves as the conservative voice of Middle England. **The Daily Mirror, The News of the World,** and **The Star** are as shrill and lewd as *The Sun.* The best international news is in *The Times, The Guardian,* and *The Independent,* while **The Financial Times,** on pink paper, does more elegantly for the City what *The Wall Street Journal* does for Wall Street.

Although they share close association with their sister dailies, the **Sunday newspapers** are actually separate entities, with a subtly distinctive look and style. **The Sunday Times, The Sunday Telegraph, The Independent on Sunday,** and the highly polished **Observer,** the world's oldest paper and sister to *The Guardian,* publish multi-section papers with glossy magazines. Sunday editions offer detailed arts, sports, and news coverage, together with more "soft bits" than the dailies. If you're looking for events, *The Independent* publishes a supplement every Thursday, *The Guardian* on Saturday.

A quick glance around any High Street newsagent will prove Britain has no shortage of magazines. World affairs are covered with refreshing candor and wit by **The Economist. The New Statesman** on the left and **The Spectator** on the right cover politics and the arts with verve. The satirical **Private Eye** is subversive, hilarious, and overtly political. Some of the best music mags in the world are UK-based. **Melody Maker** and **New Musical Express** (NME) trace the latest trends; check them for concert news. **Q** covers a broader spectrum of rock music in excellent detail, while **Gramophone** focuses on classical music. Club kids should check out **Mixmag** and **Jockey Slut** for listings and dance music reviews, while **The Face** remains the UK's ultimate scene magazine. The indispensable London journal **Time Out** is the most comprehensive listings guide to the city and features fascinating pieces on British culture; its web site (www.timeout.co.uk) also keeps tabs on events in Dublin, Edinburgh, and Glasgow. Recent years have seen the explosion of "lad's magazines" such as **FHM** and **Loaded,** which feature scantily-clad women and articles on beer, "shagging," and "pulling" (see p. 751). Though meant for female readers, the British edition of **Vogue** features just as many scantily-clad women.

RADIO AND TELEVISION

The **BBC** (British Broadcasting Corporation, sometimes known as the Beeb) established its reputation for cleverly styled fairness with its radio services, and its World Service continues to provide citizens of countries around the world with a glimpse into British life. Within the UK, BBC **Radio 1** (98.8 FM) has ceded responsibilities of news coverage to its cousin **Radio 4** (93.5 FM) but continues to feature rock institution John Peel as well as current pop-rock with such radio personalities as Zoe Ball. Completing the BBC stable, **Radio 2** (89.1 FM) takes on easy listening and non-rock forms such as folk and jazz, **Radio 3** (91.3 FM) broadcasts classical music, and **Radio 5 Live** (693 MW/AM) carries mainly sports broadcasts. Each region also has a variety of local commercial broadcasting services.

British television has brought to the world such mighty comic wonders as *Monty Python's Flying Circus* and *Mr. Bean*, and continues to produce many programs of high quality. At the other end of things is Britain's current obsession with do-it-yourself (DIY) home-improvement shows, cooking programs, and voyeur TV—Britain has, after all, been struck by the *Survivor* craze along with the rest of us. A **licence fee** paid by all television owners in Britain ensures that BBC TV, which sent out the world's first broadcast in 1929, remains advertisement-free. National TV listings are slightly modified to fit different regions. A repository of wit and innovation, the BBC broadcasts on two national channels. **BBC1** carries news at 1pm, 6pm, and 9pm as well as various Britcoms. Telecast on **BBC2** are cultural programs and fledgling sitcoms (*Absolutely Fabulous* and the marvelous *Blackadder* both started here), along with the ubiquitous Teletubbies. **ITV,** Britain's first and most established commercial network, carries drama and comedy, along with its own news. **Channel 4** has the hilarious *Big Breakfast* morning show, highly respected arts programming, and imported American shows. **Channel 5,** the newest channel, features late-night sports shows and action movies at 9pm. In the world of satellite broadcasting, Rupert Murdoch's **Sky TV** shows football, futbol, soccer, and any other incarnations of the global game that it can find on its Sky Sports channel, while its Sky One channel features mostly American shows.

SOAPS AND SUDS Addiction to soaps broadcast over the airwaves is one typical marker of British identity. Britain pioneered the soap opera on radio with *The Archers*, the longest-running soap in the world. Set in the idyllic fictional village of Ambridge, *The Archers* chronicles the escapades of a farming family in its weekday broadcasts on Radio 4. It is television, however, that has become the preferred soaps purveyor. The most popular TV soaps, with almost 20 million viewers a week each, are *Eastenders* on BBC1 and *Coronation Street* on ITV, which chronicle the lives of rough-and-tumble working-class neighborhoods in London and Manchester, respectively. Public enthusiasm for these TV soaps has infected even the once-pastoral *Archers*, who now boast their own share of disasters and illicit love-affairs.

LONDON

 London's phone code is 020.

A man who is tired of London is tired of life; for there is in London all that life can afford.
   —Samuel Johnson

Ever an assault on the senses, London defies simple categorization. Those expecting tea-drinking, Royal-loving gardeners will quickly find London equally the province of black-clad slinky young things lounging in Soho bars, Indian takeaway owners in the East End, and pinstriped bankers in the City. While London abounds with remnants of Britain's long history, a trip to one of many futuristic boutiques will eclipse any impression—culled from bobbies, Beefeaters, and Big Ben—that London is chained to bygone days. Many pubs may close early, but London roars on, full throttle, around the clock, with 24hr. cafes and clubs pounding until the first light of the new day. One of the world's greatest centers for the arts, London dazzles with concert halls, theaters, museums, and bookshops. Trends bloom and die here—buy something in London and six months later you'll see it on the catwalks—and despite the stereotypes about British food, the city has steadily gained status as a culinary center. This is in no small measure due to London's large and diverse multinational population, ever-growing and ever renewing this city of the world with energy and optimism. For more detailed coverage of this great and good city, get thee to a bookstore for a copy of *Let's Go: London 2002*.

HIGHLIGHTS OF LONDON

ALL THE POSTCARD STUFF To catch the London unmissables, start at stately **Westminster Abbey** (p. 114), gaze upward at **St. Paul's Cathedral** (p. 112), watch your head at the imposing **Tower of London** (p. 113), do a spot of shopping and catch a bite in **Covent Garden** (p. 117), and follow up the sights with a night of **clubbing** (p. 146).

MUSEUMS Revel in the magnificent collections of London's museums, some of the finest in the world, including the **British Museum** (p. 131), the **National Gallery** (p. 131), and the quirky **Sir John Soane's Museum** (p. 134), idiosyncratic home of the architect of the Bank of England, replete with sarcophagi and green glass floors.

THEATER Forget the West End and turn your theatrical attention to **Shakespeare's Globe Theatre** (p. 122), where you can stand and jostle with the other "groundlings" or cram onto hard wooden benches while watching Shakespeare as it was meant to be.

INTERCITY TRANSPORTATION

FROM THE AIRPORTS

For information on international flights to London, see **By Plane**, p. 37.

HEATHROW

Ugly, sprawling, crowded, and chaotic, Heathrow (☎(0870) 000 0123) feels more like a shopping mall with a runway than the world's busiest international airport.

   Underground: ☎7222 1234. Heathrow's 2 Tube stations form a loop on the end of the **Piccadilly Line:** trains stop first at Terminal 4 and then at Terminals 1,2,3 before swinging back to central London. 40min.-1hr. from central London, every 4-5min. £3.50, under 16 £1.50.

Central London

● SIGHTS

Albert Memorial, 6	B4	
All Souls Langham Place, 16	C3	
Apsley House, 22	C4	
Bank of England, 95	F3	
Banqueting House, 40	D4	
The Barbican, 69	E3	
Bond St., 20	C4	
British Library, 66	D2	
British Museum, 64	D3	
Buckingham Palace, 24	C4	
Burlington House, 48	D4	
Cabinet War Rooms, 37	D4	
Chelsea Physic Garden, 28	C5	

Chinatown, 53	D3
Courtauld Institute Galleries, 58	D3
Design Museum, 90	F4
Fleet St., 80	E3
The Gilbert Collection, 57	D3
Gray's Inn, 68	E3
Green Park, 21	C4
Guildhall, 76	E3
Hayward Gallery, 43	D4
HMS Belfast, 91	F4
The Houses of Parliament, 33	D4
Hyde Park, 10	B4
ICA, 42	D4
Imperial War Museum, 89	E5

Jewel Tower, 31	D4
Kensington Gardens, 8	B4
Kensington Palace, 9	B4
Leicester Sq., 52	D3
Leighton House, 1	A4
Lincoln's Inn, 74	E3
London Eye, 38	D4
London Planetarium, 13	C3
London's Transport Museum, 61	D3
Madame Tussaud's, 14	C3
Marble Arch, 18	C3
Millennium Bridge, 85	E4
Monument, 94	F3
Museum of London, 72	E3

National Gallery, 46	D3
Natural History Museum	
National Portrait Gallery	
Old Bailey, 75	E3
Oxford St., 17	C3
Parliament Square, 35	
Piccadilly Circus, 54	D4
Queen's Gallery, 25	C4
Regent's Park, 11	C3
Regent St., 55	C3
Royal Academy, 49	D4
Royal Albert Hall, 5	B4
Royal Courts of Justice	
The Royal Hospital, 27	C5

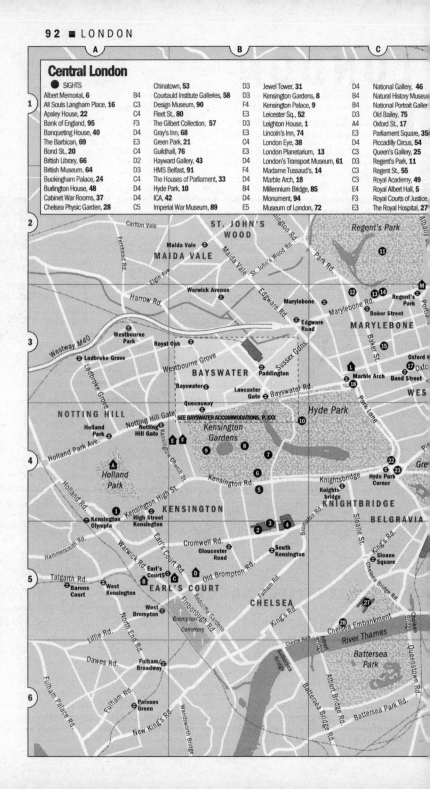

SEE BAYSWATER ACCOMMODATIONS, P. XXX

D   **E**   **F**

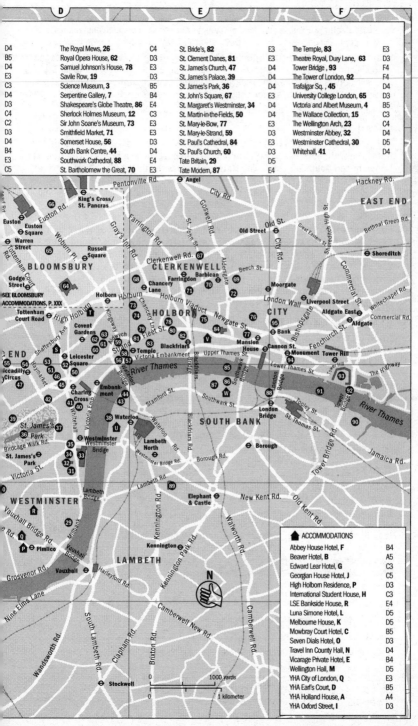

▲ ACCOMMODATIONS

Abbey House Hotel, **F**	B4
Beaver Hotel, **B**	A5
Edward Lear Hotel, **G**	C3
Georgian House Hotel, **J**	C5
High Holborn Residence, **P**	D3
International Student House, **H**	C3
LSE Bankside House, **R**	E4
Luna Simone Hotel, **L**	D5
Melbourne House, **K**	D5
Mowbray Court Hotel, **C**	B5
Seven Dials Hotel, **O**	D3
Travel Inn County Hall, **N**	D4
Vicarage Private Hotel, **E**	B4
Wellington Hall, **M**	D5
YHA City of London, **Q**	E3
YHA Earl's Court, **D**	B5
YHA Holland House, **A**	A4
YHA Oxford Street, **I**	D3

0   1000 yards
0   1 kilometer

Heathrow Express: ☎(0845) 600 1515. A speedy link to **Paddington station.** Buy tickets at Heathrow Express counters, on board, or at self-service machines; railpasses not accepted. 15min.; every 15min.; £12, return £22, £2 extra if bought on board.

Bus: The **Airbus A2** (☎(0870) 575 7777) crawls to **King's Cross,** stopping at various points on the way. 1¼-1½hr.; 2 per hr. 4am-8pm; £7, return £10. **National Express** (which operates Airbus) sends coaches to **Victoria Coach Station.** Contact and prices as above. 40min.-1hr., approx. 2 per hr.

Taxis: Licensed (black) cabs will cost at least £40 and take 50min.-1½hr.

GATWICK

Thirty miles south of London, Gatwick (☎(0870) 000 2468) may look distant, but three train services to London make transport there a breeze. The **train station** is in the **South Terminal.** The **Gatwick Express** (☎(0870) 000 2468) service to **Victoria station** would like you to think it's the only train to London (30-35min.; every 15min., every hr. midnight-5am; £10.50, return £20). In fact the cheaper **Connex** (☎(0870) 603 0405) commuter trains run the same route just as frequently and take only 7min. longer (37-42min.; £8.20, return £16.40). Additionally, **Thameslink** (☎(0845) 730 0400) commuter trains head regularly to **King's Cross,** stopping in **London Bridge** and **Blackfriars.** Beware that Thameslink stations typically have lots of stairs (50min.; every 15-30min.; £9.80, return £19.60). Gatwick's distance from London makes **road services** slow and unpredictable. The **Airbus A5** takes 1½hr. to travel to **Victoria Coach Station.** (For details, see bus transportation from Heathrow, above.) Taking a licensed **taxi** will take over an hour, and cost at least £90.

STANSTED AND LUTON

Charters and discount airlines often operate from London's secondary airports. **Stansted** (☎(0870) 000 0303) is halfway between London and Cambridge; the **Stansted Express** (☎(08457) 444422) offers frequent train service to **Liverpool St. station** (42min.; every 15-30min.; £13, return £20). The **Airbus A6/A7** runs 24hr. daily 2 per hr. to **Victoria station.** The A6 travels via the West End, the A7 via the City. (Contact and prices as for Heathrow. 1¼-1¾hr.) From **Luton Airport, Thameslink** commuter trains head to **King's Cross, Blackfriars,** and **London Bridge.** (Contact as for Gatwick; 30-50min.; every 15-30min.; £9.50, return £18.) **Green Line 757** (☎(0870) 608 7261) buses link Luton to the **West End** and **Victoria** (1-1¾hr.; 2 per hr. 8am-8pm, every hr. 8pm-midnight and 3am-8am; £8, return £13).

BY TRAIN

London's array of mainline stations dates from the Victorian era, when each railway company had its own London terminus; see the chart below for service information. All London termini are well served by bus and Tube. All major stations sell various **Railcards,** which offer regular discounts on train travel (see **By Train,** p. 37); they do *not* sell BritRail passes, which must be purchased abroad.

STATION	SERVES:
Charing Cross	Kent (Canterbury, Dover).
Euston	Northwest (Birmingham, Glasgow, Holyhead, Liverpool, Manchester).
King's Cross	Northeast (Cambridge, Edinburgh, Leeds, Newcastle, York).
Liverpool St.	East Anglia (Cambridge, Colchester, Ipswich, Norwich, Stansted).
Paddington	West (Oxford); southwest (Bristol, Cornwall); South Wales (Cardiff).
St. Pancras	The Midlands (Nottingham); northwest (Sheffield).
Victoria	South (Brighton, Canterbury, Dover, Hastings); Gatwick Airport.
Waterloo	South and southwest (Portsmouth, Salisbury); Paris and Brussels.

BY BUS

Most long-distance buses come into **Victoria Coach Station** (Tube: Victoria), Buckingham Palace Rd. **Green Line** coaches (☎(0870) 608 7261), which serve much of the area around London, leave from nearby **Eccleston Bridge** coach station behind Victoria train station.

▚ LOCAL TRANSPORTATION

Though locals are convinced of the opposite, London's transport system is one of the world's best: there's nary a spot not served by Tube, bus, or train. For 24hr. info and advice call 7222 1234 or click to www.transportforlondon.gov.uk.

ZONES. Public transport is divided into a series of concentric zones; ticket prices depend on the zones passed through during your journey. To confuse matters, there's a different zoning system depending on the type of transport. The Tube, rail, and DLR operate on a system of six zones, with Zone 1 being the most central. Buses reduce this to 4 zones, though Zones 1, 2, and 3 are the same as for the Tube. Almost everything of interest to visitors is found in Zones 1 and 2.

PASSES. You're almost bound to save money by investing in a travel pass. Passes work on the zone system (see above), and can be purchased at Tube, DLR, commuter rail stations, and at newsagents. Beware **ticket touts** hawking secondhand Travelcards and Bus Passes: you might save a few pounds, but there's no guarantee the ticket will work, and it's illegal—penalties are stiff. Note that all **passes expire** at 4:30am the morning after the printed expiry date. If you travel beyond the validity of your pass, you must purchase an **excess fare** at the start of your journey, which covers the fare from the last point included in your pass to your destination. Failure to do so counts as fare evasion. Passes include **One Day Travelcards**, valid for bus, Tube, DLR, and commuter rail services from 9:30am weekdays, all day weekends; **LT Cards**, which differ only in being valid before 9:30am; **Family Travelcards**, valid for one to two adults and one to four children traveling together; **Weekend** and **Weekly Travelcards**, valid two consecutive days on weekends and public holidays or seven consecutive days from date of purchase; and **Bus Passes**, valid only if you won't be using the Tube.

To qualify for child fares, teenagers **aged 14-15** must display a **child-rate Photocard** when purchasing tickets and traveling on public transportation. These can be obtained free of charge from any Tube station on presentation of proof of age and a passport-sized photo. Teenagers **aged 16-17** and full-time **students** at London colleges are eligible for 30% discounts on period Travelcard and Bus Passes: you'll need either a "16-17" Photocard (available at Tube stations) or a student Photocard, obtained through the qualifying educational establishment.

UNDERGROUND AND DOCKLANDS LIGHT RAILWAY

Universally known as **"the Tube,"** the Underground provides a fast and convenient way of getting around the capital. Within Zone 1, the Tube is best suited to longer journeys: adjacent stations are so close together that you might as well walk, and buses are cheaper and often get you closer to your destination. The **Docklands Light Railway** (DLR) is an overland version of the Tube running in East London, using driverless trains; the ticketing structure is the same. If you'll be using the Tube a lot, you'll save money with a **Travelcard** (see above). Regular ticket prices depend on two factors: how many zones traveled (see above), and whether you traveled through Zone 1. Tickets must be bought at the start of your journey and are valid only for the day of purchase (including return tickets). Keep your ticket for the entire journey; it will be checked on the way out and may be controlled at any time. A **carnet** is a pack of 10 tickets for travel in Zone 1, valid one year from the day of purchase (£11.50); otherwise a one-way trip in Zone 1 costs £1.50.

The Tube runs daily approximately 6am-midnight, giving clubbers that extra incentive to party till dawn. The exact time of the first and last train from each station is posted in the ticket hall: check if you plan on taking the Tube any time after 11:30pm. Trains run less frequently early mornings, late nights, and Sundays.

BUSES

Excellent signage makes the bus system easy to use even for those with no local knowledge; most stops display a map of local routes and nearby stops, together with a key to help you find the bus and stop you need faster than you can say "mind the gap." Officially bus stops come in two varieties, regular and request: supposedly buses must stop at regular stops (red logo on white background), but only pull up at request stops (white on red) if someone rings the bell, or someone at the bus stop indicates to the driver with an outstretched arm. In reality, it's safest to ring/indicate at all stops. On the older open-platform "Routemaster" buses, you're free to hop on and off whenever you like, but the risk is yours.

Buses run approximately 5:30am-midnight; a reduced network of **Night Buses** (see below) fills in the gap. Double-deckers generally run every 10-15min., while single-decker hoppers should come every 5-8min. These are averages, though—it's not uncommon to wait 30min. only for three buses to show up in a row.

On newer buses, show your pass or buy a ticket from the driver as you board: state your destination or just say the price. Older buses still use conductors, who make the rounds between stops to collect fares—they have android-like memories for remembering who's already paid. Despite the "exact change" warnings posted on buses, drivers and conductors give change, though a £5 note will elicit grumbles and anything larger risks refusal. Keep your ticket until you get off the bus, or you face a £5 **on-the-spot fine.** Trips including Zone 1 cost £1; journeys wholly outside Zone 1 cost 70p. Before 10pm, ages 5-15 pay 40p regardless of zones traveled; after 10pm they pay the adult fare. Fares for night buses are higher.

NIGHT BUSES. When honest folk are in bed, London's Night Buses comes out to ferry party-goers home. Night Bus route numbers are prefixed with an "N"; they typically operate more or less the same route as their daytime equivalents. Many routes start from Trafalgar Sq. (except on New Year's Eve, since that's where all the celebration happens). Most Night Buses operate 1-2 per hr. midnight-5:30am, when they miraculously revert to pumpkins. Night buses cost £1.50 for journeys including Zone 1 and £1 outside Zone 1.

SUBURBAN RAILWAYS

Almost nonexistent in the city center, in the suburbs London's commuter rail network is nearly as extensive as the Tube—and in much of South and East London it's the only option. Though trains run less frequently than the Tube—generally every 20-30min.—they can dramatically reduce journey times thanks to direct cross-town links, and service often continues later into the night. For journeys combining rail travel with Tube and DLR, you can buy a single ticket valid for the entire trip. Travelcards are also valid on most suburban rail services, though not on intercity lines that happen to make a few local stops.

TAXIS

Taxis in London come in two forms: classic licensed taxicabs, or **black cabs;** and **minicabs,** essentially private cars that offer pre-arranged pickups. As symbolic of London as gondolas are of Venice, "black cabs" are almost as expensive. That's because driving a London taxi is skilled work: your driver has studied for years to pass a rigorous exam called "The Knowledge" to prove he knows the name of every street in central London and how to get there by the shortest possible route. Cabs are specially designed for London's narrow streets and can turn on a sixpence—don't be afraid to hail one on the other side of the road. Available cabs are indicated by the blue "for hire" light by the driver and the orange "taxi" sign on the roof. **Pickups** attract a £1.20 supplement; dispatchers include Computer Cabs (☎ 7286 0286), Datacab (☎ 7727 7200), and Dial-a-Cab (☎ 7253 5000).

Anyone with a car and a driving license can set themselves up as a "minicab" company: while only licensed cabs can ply the streets for hire, there are no regulations concerning pre-arranged pickups. As a result, competition is fierce and prices are lower than licensed cabs—but unless you know a reliable company, ordering a minicab is something of a crapshoot, though there's rarely any danger involved (not counting the hair-raising driving skills of many drivers). Be especially careful with the dodgy drivers that turn up outside nightclubs at closing time—note down a number before you go out and call from the club, or arrange to be picked up in advance. Always agree on a price with the driver before getting in; some firms now have standardized price lists. One good firm is Teksi (☎8455 9999), offering 24hr. pickup anywhere in London.

▓ ORIENTATION

WEST END. Whether it's shopping, eating, theatergoing, or clubbing, the West End is London's popular heartland, with a wider variety of activities than anywhere else in the city. The well-heeled still live in **Mayfair** and socialize in neighboring **St. James**'s gentlemen's clubs. On the other side of Piccadilly Circus, **Soho** is London's nightlife nexus—and, around Old Compton St., its gay ground zero. **Oxford Street** has been London's premier shopping street for over 150 years. The more fashion conscious head to the boutiques of **Covent Garden,** southwest of Soho. South of Covent Garden, the **Strand** leads to majestic, pigeon-infested **Trafalgar Square.**

HOLBORN AND CLERKENWELL. London's second-oldest area, **Holborn** was the first part of the city settled by Saxons. Today Holborn is associated with two unholy professions: law and journalism. After seeing the sights, there's little to do here but sit in one of the many pubs once frequented by Samuel Johnson. North and east of Holborn, **Clerkenwell**'s heady combination of nightlife and restaurants, fuelled by a growing media presence, makes comparison with Soho hard to avoid.

CITY OF LONDON. The City is where London began, yet to most Londoners, Europe's most important financial center is now an outlying irrelevance. A quarter of a million people may work here during the day, but by night the City's population shrinks to a measly 8000, not even close to the number of tourists who daily storm St. Paul's Cathedral and the Tower of London.

SOUTH BANK. Close to the City, but long exempt from its party-pooping laws, this part of London was for centuries London's entertainment center, renowned for its theaters, cock-fighting, bull-baiting, and other less reputable diversions. The **"Millennium Mile"** stretches from the London Eye in the west to the swank restaurants of Butler's Wharf in the east, passing by the cultural powerhouses of the Festival Hall, Hayward Gallery, National Theatre, Tate Modern, and Shakespeare's Globe.

WESTMINSTER. Home to Parliament, the Prime Minister, and the Queen herself, Westminster exudes privilege. **Pimlico,** south of Victoria, is a quiet residential district with some of London's best B&Bs. Don't come here for food, shopping, or nightlife; but with some of London's top sights and trendier neighborhoods nearby, whatever you don't find in Westminster can't be far away.

CHELSEA. In the 1960s and 70s, Chelsea was the epitome of swinging London— the King's Road gave the world miniskirts and punk rock. A century earlier, Chelsea hummed to the discussions of Edgar Allen Poe, George Eliot, Dante Gabriel Rossetti, Oscar Wilde, J.M.W. Turner, John Singer Sargent, and James MacNeill Whistler. Stifled by a surfeit of wealth, today's Chelsea has little stomach for radicalism—these days, local luminaries include Hugh Grant, Liz Hurley, and a string of B-list celebrities, models, and trust-fund kids known as "Sloane Rangers."

KNIGHTSBRIDGE AND BELGRAVIA. Knightsbridge has been one of London's most desired addresses for centuries—Apsley House, the Duke of Wellington's former abode, revels in the address "No. 1, London." Like the locals, famed department stores Harrods and Harvey Nichols are secure in their sense of superiority. **Sloane Street**'s boutiques, meanwhile, have no need to envy their Bond St. cousins—if anything, they're glitzier and more exclusive. **Belgravia,** east of Sloane St., is a cultural desert of 19th-century mansions and apartments occupied by millionaires.

KENSINGTON AND EARL'S COURT. Until recently the stomping ground of Princess Diana, **Kensington** divides more or less equally between the label-obsessed consumer mecca of **Kensington High St.** in the west and the incredible array of museums and colleges of **South Kensington**'s "Albertopolis" in the east—no prizes for guessing which was Di's favorite. Both High St. and South Ken have a smattering of budget accommodations, but neither can compare with **Earl's Court**'s to the southwest, which combines cheap accommodations and food with good transport links to central London.

NOTTING HILL. For decades one of London's most vibrant, ethnically mixed neighborhoods, in the past few years (helped on by a certain movie) Notting Hill has become a victim of its own trendiness. Only at the edges can you catch glimpses of the old Notting Hill. Still, once a year, the whole neighborhood explodes with Caribbean color and sound during the Notting Hill Carnival, attended by over 2 million people.

BAYSWATER. Once London's most stylish neighborhood, Bayswater's downfall arrived with the Paddington canal and then the railway and the slums that grew up around them. Today, the area graciously accommodates thousands of travelers who bed down in the B&Bs that line the streets around **Queensway** and **Paddington.** Bayswater has also always been one of the most ethnically diverse London neighborhoods; it can rightly claim to be the original London home of those two English staples, curries and kebabs.

MARYLEBONE AND REGENT'S PARK. Marylebone is an elusive district; easy to find on a map, it lacks cohesion and a sense of identity. Largely residential and respectable, its best parts are the edges. Forming the northern border of Marylebone, **Regent's Park** is a giant and popular expanse of greenery surrounded by elegant Regency terraces. Nearby, **Marylebone Rd.** and **Baker St.** provide tourist thrills at the ever-popular Madame Tussaud's and the Sherlock Holmes Museum.

BLOOMSBURY. Home to dozens of universities, colleges, and specialist hospitals, not to mention both the British Museum and the British Library, Bloomsbury is London's undisputed intellectual powerhouse. In the early 20th century, the quiet squares and Georgian terraces resounded to the intellectual musings of the Bloomsbury Group, including T.S. Eliot, E.M. Forster, Virginia Woolf, Bertrand Russell, Vanessa Bell, and John Maynard Keynes; today, they house student halls and dozens of affordable accommodations, with lots of good restaurants nearby.

NORTH LONDON. Green and prosperous, North London's inner suburbs are some of London's older outlying communities: **Hampstead** and **Highgate** were pleasant country retreats for centuries before urban sprawl engulfed them, and they still retain their village feel. Closer to the center, **Camden Town** and **Islington** were for most of the 19th and 20th centuries grimy working-class areas, but in the 1980s their stock shot up and both are now solidly populated with wealthy liberals. In recent years, Islington's **Upper St.** has become one of London's top eating destinations, with over 100 restaurants within walking distance of Angel Tube. **Maida Vale** and **St. John's Wood** are wealthy extensions of Marylebone and Bayswater.

WEST LONDON. The garden of London, the area along the western riverbank stretches for miles before petering out in the hills and vales of the Thames valley. Historically, these reaches were fashionable spots for country retreats, and by the time you reach affluent **Richmond,** the river winds carelessly through the grounds of stately homes and former royal palaces on its way to **Hampton Court.**

SOUTH LONDON. Only developing since the 19th century, South London contains some of London's most dynamic neighborhoods in its Victorian railway muddle. **Brixton** is a vibrant melting pot where African, Caribbean, and English traditions collide and fuse—with London's highest concentration of under-40s, it's unsurprisingly home to thumping nightlife. Neighboring **Dulwich** couldn't be more different: the south's answer to Hampstead, this prosperous hilly village is where Margaret Thatcher chose to live out her days.

EAST LONDON. At Aldgate, the wealth of the city gives way to the historically impoverished **East End.** Older residents still remember when this was a predominantly Jewish neighborhood, but today it's solidly Bangladeshi. East of **Whitechapel,** the East End remains poor and working-class until you hit **Docklands.** Since the late 1980s, this vast manmade archipelago has become a city-within-a-city: the skyscrapers of **Canary Wharf** are establishing it as London's second financial center. Steeped in history, **Greenwich** is a beautiful district with a wealth of sights, though the **Millennium Dome**—while still visible—is closed to visitors.

🛈 PRACTICAL INFORMATION

TOURIST INFORMATION CENTRES

Britain Visitor Centre (www.visitbritain.com), 1 Regent St. Tube: Oxford Circus. Run by the British Tourist Association. Open M 9:30am-6:30pm, Tu-F 9am-6:30pm, Sa-Su 10am-4pm.

London Visitor Centres (www.londontouristboard.com). Run by the London Tourist Board. Books accommodations for £5; call 7932 2020 or email book@londontouristboard.co.uk. Tube station branches at: **Heathrow Terminals 1,2,3** (open Oct.-Aug. daily 8am-6pm; Sept. M-Sa 9am-7pm and Su 8am-6pm); **Liverpool St.** (open June-Sept. M-Sa 8am-7pm, Su 8am-6pm; Oct.-May daily 8am-6pm); **Victoria** (open Easter-Sept. M-Sa 8am-8pm, Su 8am-6pm; Oct.-Easter daily 8am-6pm); **Waterloo International** (open daily 8:30am-10:30pm).

EMERGENCY AND MEDICAL CARE

Emergency: Dial 999 from any phone. Always free.

Dental Care: Dental Emergency Care Service (☎7955 2186). Refers callers to the nearest open dental surgery. Open M-F 8:45am-3:30pm.

Samaritans: ☎(08457) 909090. 24hr. emotional support for depression and suicide.

Hospitals: For urgent care, go to the **Accident and Emergency** or **Casualty** ward of any of the following major hospitals; all are open 24hr., and treatment is free of charge. **Charing Cross,** Fulham Palace Rd., entrance on St. Dunstan's Rd. (☎8846 1234). Tube: Baron's Court or Hammersmith. **Royal London Hospital,** Whitechapel Rd. (☎7377 7000). Tube: Whitechapel. **Royal Free,** Pond St. (☎7794 0500). Tube: Belsize Park. **St. Thomas's,** Lambeth Palace Rd. (☎7928 9292). Tube: Waterloo. **University College Hospital,** Grafton Way (☎7387 9300). Tube: Warren St.

Pharmacies: Most chemists keep standard store hours (approx. M-Sa 9:30am-5:30pm); one "duty" chemist in each neighborhood will additionally open on Su, though hours may be limited. Late-night and 24hr. chemists are rare; one is **Zafash Pharmacy,** 233 Old Brompton Rd. (☎7373 2798). Tube: Earl's Court. Open 24hr.

Police: London is covered by 2 police forces: the **City of London Police** (☎7601 2222) for the City and the **Metropolitan Police** (☎7230 1212) for the rest.

COMMUNICATIONS

Internet Access: Most B&Bs and hostels now offer Internet access; however rates are lower at the scores of cyber cafes. **easyEverything** (☎7907 7800). Locations include 9-16 Tottenham Court Rd. (Tube: Tottenham Court Rd.); 7 Strand (Tube: Charing Cross); 358 Oxford St. (Tube: Bond St.); 9-13 Wilson Rd. (Tube: Victoria); 160-166 Kensington High St. (Tube: High St. Kensington). Prices vary with demand, from £1 per hr.; minimum charge £2. All open 24hr.

Post Office: Post offices are found on almost every major road. When sending mail to London, be sure to include the full post code, since London has 7 King's Roads, 8 Queen's Roads, and 2 Mandela Streets. The largest office is the **Trafalgar Square Post Office,** 24-28 William IV St., WC2N 4DL (☎7484 9304). Tube: Charing Cross. All mail sent Poste Restante or general delivery to unspecified post offices ends up here. Open M-Th and Sa 8am-8pm, F 8:30am-8pm.

⚑ ACCOMMODATIONS

Sorry folks, but this isn't going to be pretty. Just as real estate prices make Londoners clutch their heads and scream, hotels and hostels are incredibly expensive.

WEST END

▓ **High Holborn Residence,** 178 High Holborn, WC1V 7AA (☎ 7379 5589; fax 7379 5640; www.lse.ac.uk/vacations). Tube: Holborn or Tottenham Court Rd. Comfortable modern student residence near Covent Garden. "Flats" of 4-5 rooms, each with phone, sharing kitchen and bathroom. Laundry, bar, and TV and games room. Continental breakfast included. Open mid-June to late Sept. Singles £28-35; twins £47-57, with bath £57-67; triples with bath £67-77. Rates highest in July, lowest mid-Aug. to Sept. MC/V.

YHA Oxford Street, 14-18 Noel St. (☎ 7734 1618; fax 7734 1657; oxfordst@yha.org.uk). Tube: Oxford Circus. Small, sparse hostel with limited facilities but unbeatable location for Soho nightlife. Windowless TV lounge with Internet contrasts a light, well-equipped kitchen. Towels £3.50. Continental breakfast £3.30. Reserve at least 1 month ahead. 3- to 4-bed dorms £21.50, under 18 £17.50; twins £23.50.

Seven Dials Hotel, 7 Monmouth St., WC2H 9DA (☎ 7240 0823; fax 7681 0792). Tube: Covent Garden or Holborn. Fantastic location compensates for occasionally quirky accommodation. Rooms at front are brighter, with triple glazing to keep out the noise. All have TV, phone, kettle, and sink; most have ceiling fan. English breakfast included. Reserve well ahead. Singles £65, with shower £75, with bath £85; doubles £75/£85/£95; twin with bath £100; triple with bath £115. AmEx/MC/V.

CITY OF LONDON

YHA City of London, 36 Carter Ln., EC4V 5AB (☎ 7236 4965; fax 7236 7681). Tube: St. Paul's. In the frescoed former buildings of St. Paul's Choir School, within spitting distance of the cathedral. Single-sex dorms have interlocking bunks, sinks, and lockers. Secure luggage storage, currency exchange, laundry, and Internet access. English breakfast included. Reception 7am-11pm. Dorms: 3-4 beds £24.70, under 18 £21; 5-8 beds £23.50, £19.90; 10-15 beds £21.15, £18.90. Private room rates: singles £27.80, under 18 £23.70; doubles £51, £41 if includes 1 child under 16; triples £72, £61; quads £94, £82; quints £118, £102; sextuples £138, £123. MC/V.

SOUTH BANK

▓ **Travel Inn County Hall,** Belvedere Rd., SE1 7PB (☎ (0870) 238 3300; fax 7902 1619; www.travelinn.co.uk). Tube: Westminster or Waterloo. Don't expect any grand views—the river is hogged by a Marriott. Rooms clean and modern, with bathroom, kettle, and TV. Elevator, restaurant, and bar. Prices by the room, making it a great deal for families. Reserve at least 1 month ahead; cancel by 4pm on day of arrival. Continental breakfast £5, English £6, kids £3.50. Singles, doubles, and family rooms (2 adults and 2 kids) £75. AmEx/MC/V.

LSE Bankside House, 24 Sumner St., SE1 9JA (☎ 7633 9877; fax 7574 6730; www.lse.ac.uk/vacations). Tube: Southwark or London Bridge. Another of the London School of Economics' well-kept student halls, facing the back of the Tate Modern. Over 500 rooms, all with phone. Elevator, laundry, TV lounge, games room, and bar. Open July 6-Sept. 28, 2002. English breakfast included. Singles £28, with bath £41; twins with bath £55.50; triples with bath £81; quads with bath £93. MC/V.

WESTMINSTER

▓ **Luna Simone Hotel,** 47/49 Belgrave Rd. (☎ 7834 5897; fax 7828 2474; www.lunasimonehotel.com). Tube: Victoria or Pimlico. Victorian facade conceals ultra-modern rooms with TV, phone, kettle, and hair dryer. Some singles are cramped. English breakfast included. Reserve 2 weeks ahead; 48hr. cancellation policy. Singles £40, low season (Nov.-Easter) £35, with bath £35/45; doubles £80/60, with bath £65/50; triples with bath £100/80. 10% discount for stays over 7 nights in low season. MC/V.

Georgian House Hotel, 35 St. George's Drive, SW1V 4DG (☎7834 1438; fax 7976 6085; www.georgianhousehotel.co.uk). Tube: Victoria. Rooms are large and well equipped, with TV, phone, hair dryer, and kettle. Top-floor "student" rooms, available to all, are smaller with fewer fittings. Rooms in the annex, on Cambridge St., have bath but no phone. English breakfast included. Reserve 1 month ahead for Sa-Su and student rooms. Singles £36, student £26, with bath £49, annex £43; doubles £42, £48, £66, £56; triples £63, £69, £82, £72; quads with bath £90, student £70, annex £82; quints with bath £96. MC/V.

Melbourne House, 79 Belgrave Rd. (☎7828 3516; fax 7828 7120; www.melbourne-househotel.co.uk). Tube: Pimlico. Extraordinarily clean, well-kept establishment. Non-smoking rooms all have TV, phone, and kettle; their pride and joy is the superb basement double, with triangular bathtub large enough for two. Continental breakfast included. Reserve 2 weeks ahead. Singles £30, with bath £55; doubles with bath £75; triples with bath £95; quad with bath £110. MC/V (payment on arrival; cash preferred).

Wellington Hall, 71 Vincent Sq., SW1P 2PA (☎7834 4740, reservations 7928 3777; fax 7233 7709). Tube: Victoria. Edwardian building overlooking Westminster School's playing fields. Smallish rooms have sink; ask for one overlooking the square rather than the busy road at rear. What the bathrooms lack in privacy, the breakfast room makes up for in mock-Tudor magnificence. TV lounge, pool table, laundry, and bar. Open Easter and mid-June to mid-Sept. English breakfast included. Singles £27.50; twins £42.

KENSINGTON AND EARL'S COURT

YHA Earl's Court, 38 Bolton Gdns., SW5 0AQ (☎7373 7083; fax 7835 2034). Tube: Earl's Court. Rambling Victorian townhouse, more casual than most YHAs. Ongoing refurbishment is adding dozens more bathrooms. All dorms single sex. Garden, kitchen, laundry, 2 TV lounges, Internet access, and luggage storage. Reserve 1 month ahead. Continental breakfast £3.30. 3- to 16-bed dorms £18.50, under 18 £16.50; twins £51, including breakfast. AmEx/MC/V.

YHA Holland House, Holland Walk, W8 7QU (☎7937 0748; fax 7376 0667; hollandhouse@yha.org.uk). Tube: High St. Kensington or Holland Park. On the edge of Holland Park, accommodation is split between a 17th-century mansion and a less attractive 1970s unit; dorms in both are similar, with 12-20 interlocking bunks. Caters mostly to groups. Lockers, laundry, TV room, luggage storage, and kitchen. Breakfast included. Book 1 month ahead in summer. £20.50, under 18 £18.50. AmEx/MC/V.

▧ Vicarage Private Hotel, 10 Vicarage Gate, W8 4AG (☎7229 4030; fax 7792 5989; www.londonvicaragehotel.com). Tube: High St. Kensington. Beautifully kept Victorian house with ornate hallways, TV lounge, and superb rooms: cast-iron beds, solid wood furnishings, and luxuriant drapes, some with TV. English breakfast included. Reserve months ahead. Singles £45; doubles £74, with bath £98; triples £90; quads £98.

Abbey House Hotel, 11 Vicarage Gate, W8 4AG (☎7727 2594; fax 7727 1873; www.abbeyhousekensington.com). Tube: High St. Kensington. Spacious, pastel rooms with TV, desk, sink, and matching furniture. Very helpful staff. 5 bathrooms between 16 rooms. 24hr. free tea, coffee, and ice room. English breakfast included. Singles £45; doubles £74; triples £90; quads £100. Winter discounts available.

Beaver Hotel, 57-59 Philbeach Gdns. (☎7373 4553; fax 7373 4555). Tube: Earl's Court. From the talking elevator to separate smoking and nonsmoking TV lounges, the Beaver displays unusual attention to detail. Rooms range from basic basics with phone and washbasin to 2 new plush doubles with bath, matching curtains and bedspreads, TV, and hair dryer. English breakfast included. Singles £40, with bath £60; doubles with bath £85; triples with bath £99. Parking £8. AmEx/MC/V.

Mowbray Court Hotel, 28-32 Penywern Rd. (☎7373 8285 or 7370 3690; fax 7370 5693; www.m-c-hotel.mcmail.com). Tube: Earl's Court. Large B&B making a claim for hotel status with elevator and bar. Rooms vary from smallish to enormous; TV, trouser press, hair dryer, and phone. Continental breakfast included. Reserve well ahead for larger rooms. Singles £45, with bath £52; doubles £56/£67; triples £69/£80; quads £84/£95; quints £100/110; sextuples £115/£125. AmEx/MC/V.

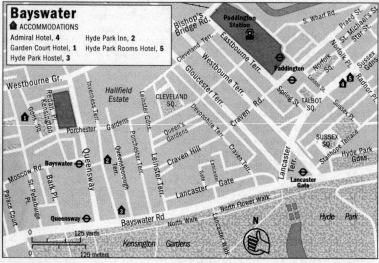

Bayswater

⌂ ACCOMMODATIONS

Admiral Hotel, **4**   Hyde Park Inn, **2**
Garden Court Hotel, **1**   Hyde Park Rooms Hotel, **5**
Hyde Park Hostel, **3**

BAYSWATER

Hyde Park Hostel, 2-6 Inverness Terr., W2 3HY (☎ 7229 5101; fax 7229 3170; www.astorhostels.com). Tube: Queensway or Bayswater. There's little room in these 12-bed women's and 18-bed mixed dorms, but smaller quarters are more spacious and bathrooms a cut above average. Internet access, hip late-bar with DJs and bands Th-Sa, cafeteria, kitchen, laundry, pool/TV lounge, secure luggage room. Continental breakfast and linen included. Ages 16-35 only. Reserve 2 weeks ahead for summer. 12-bed dorms £10-12; 10-beds £12.50-14; 8-beds £14-15.50; 6-beds £15-16.50; quads £16-17.50; twins £20-22.50 per person. MC/V.

Hyde Park Inn, 48-50 Inverness Terr., W2 3JA (☎ 7229 0000; fax 7229 8886; www.hydeparkinn.com). Very cheap and fairly cheerful. Smaller dorms are more spacious than the 10-bed room. Internet, laundry, kitchen, lockers (£1 per day), luggage storage (£1.50 per bag per day). Continental breakfast included. £10 deposit for linen and keys. 10-bed dorms £9-11; 8-beds £11-12; 6-beds £12-14; 4-beds £14.50-17; 3-beds £15.50-19; double and twins £18-21; singles £29-32. MC/V (2.5% surcharge).

Admiral Hotel, 143 Sussex Gdns., W2 2RY (☎ 7723 7309; fax 7723 8731; www.admiral143.demon.co.uk). Tube: Paddington. Beautifully kept B&B. 19 nonsmoking rooms with bathroom, TV, and kettle, decorated in summer colors. Haters of prefab cabins should request rooms with a "real" bathroom. Call 10-14 days ahead in summer. Singles £48, low season (Oct.-Mar.) £40; doubles £70, £55; triples £75-90; quads £88-100; quints £92-115. MC/V.

Hyde Park Rooms Hotel, 137 Sussex Gdns., W2 2RX (☎ 7723 0225; fax 7723 0965). Tube: Paddington. That rarest of species—a B&B run by a Londoner. White rooms with fluorescent-colored bedspreads all have sink and TV, and most benefit from solid wood furniture with tall wardrobes. The one quad is lit only by skylight, but makes it up in size. Timer-less electric-bar heating requires active temperature control. Reserve 2 weeks ahead in summer. Singles £30, with bath £40; doubles £40-45/£50-55; triples and quad £20 per person, with bath £24. AmEx/MC/V (5% surcharge).

Garden Court Hotel, 30-31 Kensington Gdns. Sq., W2 4BG (☎ 7229 2553; fax 7727 2749; www.gardencourthotel.co.uk). Tube: Bayswater or Queensway. The snazzy reception feels like a 3-star Tuscan resort; rooms are solidly English B&B, varying widely in size, but all decorated to a high standard and equipped with sink, TV, hair dryer, and phone. Guests have access to the patio garden. Reserve at least 1 week ahead in summer. English breakfast included. Singles £39, with bath £58; doubles £58/£88; triples £72/£99; family quad (2 double beds) £82/£120. MC/V.

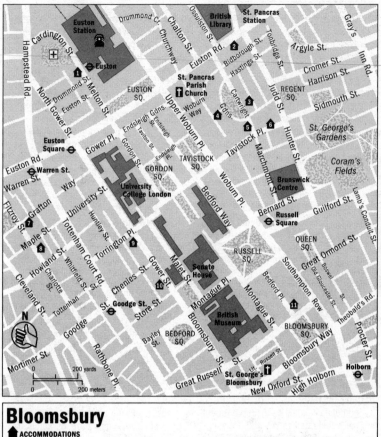

Bloomsbury

▲ **ACCOMMODATIONS**

Arosfa Hotel, **9**
Carr-Sanders Hall, **8**
Commonwealth Hall, **3**
Crescent Hotel, **4**

The Generator, **6**
George Hotel, **5**
Hotel Ibis Euston, **1**
Indian YMCA, **7**

The Langland Hotel, **10**
Pickwick Hall International
Backpackers, **11**

YHA St. Pancras
International, **2**

MARYLEBONE AND REGENT'S PARK

International Student House, 229 Great Portland St., W1B 1SH (☎ 7631 8300; fax 7631 8315; accom@ish.org.uk; www.ish.org.uk). Tube: Great Portland St. A thriving international metropolis near Regent's Park, minutes from Oxford Circus. Most rooms similar size—singles seem huge, bunk-bedded quads less so—with desk, sink, phone, and fridge. Spartan 8- to 10-bed dorms have sink and lockers. 3 bars, nightclub/venue, cafeteria, fitness center (£3 per day), cinema, Internet access, and laundry. Continental breakfast included except for dorms (£2); English breakfast £3. £10 key deposit. Reception M-F 7:45am-10:30pm, Sa-Su 8:30am-10:30pm. Reserve minimum 1 month ahead. Dorms £10; singles £31, with bath £33; twins £45/£51; triples £60; quads £70. Weekly rates (Sept.-May): singles £188; twins £280. MC/V.

Edward Lear Hotel, 28-30 Seymour St., W1H 5WD (☎ 7402 5401; fax 7706 3766; edwardlear@aol.com; www.edlear.com). Tube: Marble Arch. This was once the home of Ed Lear, though no owls nor pussies are here. The rooms may be basic, but you just have to face it: for the location it's really not dear. All rooms have phone, kettle, TV; in the lounge you can email free. Plus there's breakfast included, and so we concluded: this hotel gets three out of three. Singles £49, with shower £58; doubles £70, with shower £82, with bath and WC £93; triples £83, with shower £92, with bath and WC £105; family quad with bath £100, with bath and WC £110. MC/V.

BLOOMSBURY

■ **The Generator,** Compton Pl. (off 37 Tavistock Pl.), WC1H 9SD (☎7388 7666; fax 7388 7644; www.lhdr.demon.co.uk). Sleep in cell-like units with bare walls and metal bunks, relax in the "Turbine," complete with video games and pool tables, eat up at the "Fuel Stop," or interface with the 'net in the "Talking Head" quiet area. Late bar with free juke-box and big-screen TV. 8-bed basement dorms have lockers; upper floors have smaller rooms and slightly more privacy. Rules strictly enforced (e.g., no noise after 9pm), but with 800 beds, that's a necessity. Reserve for weekends. Dorms £15; Nov.-Feb. 7- to 8-bed rooms £19, Mar.-Oct. £21.50; 3- to 6-bed rooms £20, £22.50; twins (per person) £23, £26.50; singles £36.50, £41; prices 20% more over New Year. MC/V.

■ **Indian YMCA,** 41 Fitzroy Sq., W1T 6AQ (☎7387 0411; fax 7383 4735; www.indi-anymca.org). Tube: Warren St. or Great Portland St. Fantastic location by an attractive Georgian square. Standard student rooms, with desk, phone, and institutional shared bathrooms, but with prices including both continental breakfast and an Indian dinner, who needs charm? Deluxe rooms are larger, with TV, fridge, and kettle. £1 membership and 50p reservation fee payable on arrival. Reservations essential. Dorms £20; singles £33; doubles £46, with bath £52; deluxe doubles with bath £75. AmEx/MC/V.

YHA St. Pancras International, 79-81 Euston Rd., NW1 2QS (☎7388 9998; fax 7388 6766; stpancras@yha.org.uk). Tube: King's Cross/St. Pancras. Away from the seediest part of King's Cross, opposite the British Library. Triple glazing and comfortable wooden bunks provide a sound night's sleep. Most dorms have bathrooms and A/C. Kitchen, laundry, Internet access. English breakfast included. Dinner 6-9pm (£4.90). 10-day max. stay. Dorms £23.50, under 18 £19.90; twins £51; doubles and twins with bath £56; quads with bath £103. AmEx/MC/V.

Pickwick Hall International Backpackers, 7 Bedford Pl., WC1B 5JE (☎7323 4958). Tube: Tottenham Court Rd. or Russell Sq. Aside from the single 8-bedder, most accom-modation is in 2- to 3-bed single-sex "dorms," comparable to B&B rooms. No smoking, no food in the dorms, and no men on the top floor. TV lounge and kitchen open 7:30am-11:30pm. Laundry room. Continental breakfast included. Reception approx. 8-10am. Call 2-3 days ahead. Dorms £15 per person; singles £25; doubles £40; triples £54. £75 weekly dorm rates for stays over 1 month. AmEx/MC/V.

■ **Crescent Hotel,** 49-50 Cartwright Gdns. (☎7387 1515; fax 7383 2054; www.cresc-enthotelsoflondon.com). Tube: Russell Sq. A real family-run atmosphere, with artisti-cally decorated rooms and antiques in the hallways. All rooms have TV, kettle, and phone. Bathrobes lent out with £30 deposit; racquets and balls are available for use in the tennis courts in front of the hotel. Reserve 3 weeks ahead for weekends. Singles £43, with shower £48, with bath £70; doubles with bath £82; triples with bath £93; quads with bath £105. More for 1 night stays; discounts for over a week. MC/V.

■ **Arosfa Hotel,** 83 Gower St., WC1E 6HJ (☎/fax 7636 2115). Tube: Warren St. or Goodge St. The Iberian owners ensure that this small, nonsmoking B&B lives up to its Welsh name (meaning "place to rest"). Rooms of unusual shapes charm with framed mirrors and prints; all have TV and sinks. Garden in rear. English breakfast included. Reserve 1-2 months ahead with 1 night non-refundable deposit. Singles £37; doubles £50, with bath £66; triples £68/£79; quad with bath £92. MC/V (2% surcharge).

Carr-Saunders Hall, 18-24 Fitzroy St., W1T 4BN (☎7580 6338; fax 7580 4718; www.lse.ac.uk/vacations). Tube: Warren St. Large hall shows its age in places, but rooms are larger than in most student halls and have sink and phone. Breakfast on the panoramic roof terrace. TV lounge, games room, and elevator. English breakfast included. Reserve 6-8 weeks ahead for July-Aug. Open Easter and mid-June to mid-Sept. Singles summer £27, Easter £23.50; twins £45, £37, with bath £50, £42. MC/V.

Commonwealth Hall, 1-11 Cartwright Gardens, WC1H 9EB (☎7685 3500; deb-bie.hanks@commonwealthhall.lon.ac.uk). Tube: Russell Sq. Post-war block with 400 basic, slightly worn student singles, with phone but no sink; still, it's unbeatable value. Kitchen on each floor, elevators, bar, cafeteria, tennis and squash courts. Open Easter and mid-June to mid-Sept. Reserve 2 months ahead July-Aug.; no walk-ins. English breakfast included. Singles £22, half-board £26; students half-board £19. MC/V.

George Hotel, 58-60 Cartwright Gdns., WC1H 9EL (☎7387 8777; fax 7387 8666; ghotel@aol.com; www.georgehotel.com). Tube: Russell Sq. Meticulous rooms with satellite TV, kettle, phone, and sink. Forward-facing 1st-floor rooms are better than those in basement and rear. Delightful lounge (with Internet terminal) and dining room. Reserve 3 months ahead for summer. Singles £50, with shower £65, with shower and WC £75; doubles £69.50/£77/£90; triples £83/£91.50/£105; basic quads £95. 10% discount for stays over 7 days (Nov.-June only) and Internet bookings. MC/V.

Hotel Ibis Euston, 3 Cardington St., NW1 2LW (☎7304 7712, fax 7388 0001; H0921@accor-hotels.com; www.ibishotel.com). Tube: Euston. Predominantly French staff preside over the 350 spacious, modern rooms of this European hotel chain, with cable TV, A/C, phone, desk, and bathroom. 24hr. snack bar. Restaurant serves 2-course dinner (£8) 6-10:30pm. Breakfast £4.50. Doubles and twins £70. MC/V.

Langland Hotel, 29-31 Gower St., WC1E 6HG (☎7636 5801; fax 7580 2227; langlandhotel@lineone.net; www.langlandhotel.com). Tube: Goodge St. Family atmosphere, wood-framed beds, solid furniture, and plenty of spacious, sparkling bathrooms (cleaned twice daily) help this B&B stand out from its neighbors. All rooms have TV, kettle, and fan. Comfy satellite-TV lounge. Singles £40, with bath £55; doubles £50/£75; triples £70/£90; quads £90/£110; quint (no bath) £100. AmEx/MC/V.

NORTH, WEST, AND SOUTH LONDON

■**YHA Hampstead Heath,** 4 Wellgarth Rd., NW11 7HR (☎8458 9054; fax 8209 0546; hampstead@yha.org.uk). From Golders Green Tube (Zone 3), turn left into North End Rd.; Wellgarth Rd. is a 10min. walk up on the left. Out-of-the-way location is main disadvantage of this manorial hostel. Large garden, email, laundry, lockers, currency exchange, and self-service restaurant. Breakfast included. Reception 24hr. 4- to 6-bed dorms £19.90; doubles £46, family (at least one child under 18) £36; triples £67, £53; quads £82, £51; quints £101, £88; sextuples £121, £102. AmEx/MC/V.

■**Star Hotel,** 97-99 Shepherd's Bush Rd., W6 7LP (☎7603 2755; fax 7603 0948). Tube: Goldhawk Rd. or Hammersmith. Rooms relatively spacious and generally light; all have TV, kettle, and large bathroom while phones should be installed by 2002; refurbished rooms have solid wood furniture and granite bathroom floors. English breakfast included. Book 1 month ahead July-Aug. Singles £35-40; doubles £48-58; triples £66-75; quads £84-92; lower rates apply for longer stays. MC/V (3% surcharge).

◘ FOOD AND PUBS

Forget stale stereotypes: London's restaurants offer a gastronomic experience as diverse, stylish, and satisfying as you'll find anywhere on the planet—until you see the bill. Any restaurant charging under £10 for a main course is regarded as "cheap"; add drinks and service and you're nudging £15. That said, it *is* possible to eat cheaply—and eat well—in London. Lunchtime and early-evening **special offers** save cash, while **pub grub,** as elsewhere in Britain, offers a hearty lunch or dinner. Many of the best budget meals are found in the amazing variety of **ethnic restaurants.** For the best and cheapest ethnic food, head to the source: Whitechapel for Bengali baltis, Islington for Turkish *meze,* Marylebone for Lebanese *shwarma,* and Soho for Cantonese *dim sum.* The cheapest places to get the ingredients for your own meal in London are often the local **street markets;** there's generally at least one in each neighborhood. For night owls, the branches of **Hart's** supermarkets stay open 24hr. And if you're willing to splurge, the food halls of **Harrods, Harvey Nichols, Selfridges,** and **Fortnum and Mason**'s are attractions in their own right.

AFTERNOON TEA

A social ritual as much as a meal, this high point of English cuisine involves a long afternoon of sandwiches, scones, pastries, tinkling china, and restrained conversation. Perhaps the main attraction of afternoon tea today is the chance to lounge in sumptuous surroundings that at any other time would be beyond all but a Sultan's budget (though it's still not cheap).

Brown's, Albemarle St. (☎7493 6020). Tube: Green Park. Opened by Lord Byron's butler in 1837, Brown's was London's first luxury hotel and still oozes old-fashioned charm. Tea is taken in the cozy drawing room, with dark paneling and comfy settees. M-F sittings 3 and 4:45pm (book 1 week ahead for Th-F); Sa-Su tea served 3-4:45pm (no reservations). Set tea £23, with champagne £33. No jeans or trainers. AmEx/MC/V.

The Lanesborough, Hyde Park Corner (☎ 7259 5599). Tube: Hyde Park Corner. For sheer opulence, the Regency interior out-ritzes The Ritz. Afternoon tea is served in the oriental-fantasy Conservatory, with heavy silk furnishings, palm fronds, painted vases, and mannequin mandarins. No dress code. Set tea £22.50, champagne tea £26.50; scones with jam and clotted cream £6.50. Minimum charge £9.50 per person.

WEST END

🍴 **busaba eathai,** 106-110 Wardour St. (☎ 7255 8686). Wildly popular Thai eatery from the founder of Wagamama. *Busaba* is a Thai flower, while *eathai*...well, work it out. Get in line for great food (£5-8) at shared square tables in a cozy, wood-paneled room. Open M-Th noon-11pm, F-Sa noon-11:30pm, Su noon-10pm. AmEx/MC/V.

🍴 **Mô,** 23 Heddon St. (☎ 7434 4040). Tube: Piccadilly Circus or Oxford Circus. A "salad bar, tearoom, and bazaar," Mô transports you to Marrakesh. The interior is hung with traditional lanterns and festooned with Moroccan crafts, all for sale. Wash down 4 traditional salads, dips, and meats (£6) with sweet mint tea (£1.50). No reservations, but popular—arrive early or late. Open M-W 11am-11pm, Th-Sa noon-midnight.

🍴 **Mr. Kong,** 21 Lisle St. (☎ 7437 7341). Do people really eat "goose web with fish lips and sea cucumber," or is it just there to convince Westerners of this small restaurant's authenticity? In any case, you won't go wrong here. £7 minimum for dinner. Open daily noon-3am. AmEx/MC/V.

Bar Italia, 22 Frith St. (☎ 7437 4520). A fixture of the late-night Soho scene, immortalized by *Pulp,* and still *the* place for a post-club panini (£3.50-5). The large, loud TV is never turned off—appropriate, since John Logie Baird gave the first-ever demonstration of television upstairs in 1922. Open 24hr. except M 3-7am.

Lamb and Flag, 33 Rose St. (☎ 7497 9504). Once called the "Bucket of Blood" for the violence of the bare-knuckle fights held upstairs. The traditional dark-wood interior and no-music policy make it a great place for a quiet pint, though not after 6pm when the 2 floors (and courtyard) fill with local workers. Food daily noon-3pm. Live jazz upstairs Su from 7:30pm. Open M-Th 11am-11pm, F-Sa 11am-10:45pm, Su noon-10:30pm.

Old Compton Cafe, 34 Old Compton St. (☎ 7439 3309). Tube: Piccadilly Circus. *The* gay cafe, though you wouldn't know it from the tourist-filled outside tables (neither do the tourists). Salads and sandwiches £2-5. Open 24hr. Cash only.

Wong Kei, 41-43 Wardour St. (☎ 7437 3071). Tube: Piccadilly Circus or Leicester Sq. While renovations in 2001 have removed much of the kitsch charm of this Chinatown stalwart, little else has changed: the waiters remain as famously curt as ever, and prices absolutely rock-bottom. Be prepared to share a table. Won-ton noodle soup £2.50, roast duck and rice £3.50. Open daily noon-11:30pm. Cash only.

HOLBORN AND CLERKENWELL

🍴 **Bleeding Heart Tavern,** corner of Greville St. and Bleeding Heart Yard (☎ 7404 0333). This 2-level establishment is split between the laid-back upstairs pub with some brilliant beers (Adnams £2.40) and the cozy restaurant below, whose fresh roses and candles make a romantic backdrop to hearty and delicious Olde English fare (spit-roasted pork £8). Get 2 courses for £10 5-7:30pm. Tavern open M-F 11am-11pm. AmEx/MC/V.

🍴 **St. John,** 26 St. John St. (☎ 7251 0848). Tube: Farringdon. St. John has stormed the London restaurant scene, winning countless prizes for its eccentric English cuisine—they call it "nose to tail eating," and certainly few body parts are wasted. Prices in the posh restaurant are high (mains £14), but you can enjoy similar bounty (in smaller quantities) in the airy bar: lamb sandwich £5, roast bone-marrow salad £6, brawn (pig's feet and cow's head stew...yum) £5.50. Bar open M-F 11am-11pm, Sa 6-11pm. MC/V.

🍴 **Ye Olde Cheshire Cheese,** Wine Office Ct. by 145 Fleet St. (☎ 7353 6170). Tube: Blackfriars or St. Paul's. Dark labyrinth of oak-panelled rooms on 3 floors, dating from 1667 and one-time haunt of Johnson, Dickens, Mark Twain, and Theodore Roosevelt. Multiple bars and restaurants at every price range; sandwiches (£4-5) in the Cheshire bar at the back; meaty traditional dishes in the Chophouse (main courses £7-10); daily hot specials (£4.25) in the cellar bar; fancier cuisine in the Johnson Room (£7-12). Open M-F

11:30am-11pm, Sa 11:30am-3pm and 5:30-11pm, Su noon-3pm; food M-F noon-9:30pm, Sa noon-2:30pm and 6-9:30pm, Su noon-2:30pm. AmEx/MC/V.

Tinseltown 24-Hour Diner, 44-46 St. John St. (☎ 7689 2424) Tube: Farringdon. Cavernous underground haven for pre- and post-clubbers, Tinseltown's hours are more commendable than its burgers (£5.50) and shakes fare. Open 24hr.

CITY OF LONDON

The Place Below, St. Mary-le-Bow, Cheapside. (☎ 7329 0789) Tube: St. Paul's, Mansion House, or Bank. In the 11th-century crypt of St. Mary-le-Bow church, vegetarian dishes provide salvation for the weary traveler. Salads and hot dishes £6.50-7.50, sandwiches £5; takeaway £1-2 less. Open M-F 7:30am-4pm, with lunch 11:30am-2:30pm. MC/V.

Simpson's, Ball Court, off 38½ Cornhill (☎ 7626 9985). Tube: Bank. "Established 1757," this pub remains so traditional a man stands in the door to greet you. Different rooms divide the classes, from the basement wine bar (sandwiches £2-4) to the upstairs restaurants (traditional main dishes £6-7). Open M-F 11:30am-3pm.

SOUTH BANK

▩ **Cantina del Ponte,** 36c Shad Thames, Butler's Wharf (☎ 7403 5403). Tube: Tower Hill or London Bridge. Amazing riverside location by Tower Bridge. Given the quality of the Italian-style food (especially the desserts), the set menu is a bargain at £10 for 2 courses, £12 for 3 (available M-F noon-3pm and 6-7:30pm). Live Italian music Tu and Th nights. Open M-Sa noon-3pm and 6-10:45pm, Su noon-3pm and 6-9:45pm. MC/V.

▩ **Tas,** 72 Borough High St. (☎ 7403 7200; Tube: London Bridge) and 33 The Cut (☎ 7928 2111; Tube: Waterloo). Dynamic duo of stylish and affordable Turkish restaurants. Tasty stews and baked dishes—many vegetarian—outshine the respectable kebabs. Main courses £6-8; set menus include 2 courses for £7 and *mezes* (selection of starters) £7-10. Live music from 7:30pm. Fan-Tas-tic. Evening reservations essential. Open M-Sa 12:30-11:30pm, Su 12:30-10:30pm. AmEx/MC/V.

WESTMINSTER

▩ **Jenny Lo's Teahouse,** 14 Eccleston St. (☎ 7259 0399). Tube: Victoria. Long before noodle bars hit the big time, Jenny Lo was offering stripped-down Chinese fare at communal tables. Cha shao (pork noodle soup; £5) or sichuan aubergine (£5.75). Teas, blended in-house, are served in attractive hand-turned stoneware (from 85p). Open M-F 11:30am-3pm and 6-10pm; Sa noon-3pm and 6-10pm. £5 minimum. Cash only.

Red Lion, 48 Parliament St. (☎ 7930 5826). Tube: Westminster. *The* MPs' hangout, where the Chancellor's press secretary was infamously overheard leaking information in 1998. TVs carrying the Parliament cable channel allow MPs to listen to the debates, while a "division bell" alerts them to drink up when a vote is about to be taken. Despite the distinguished clientele, the food (sandwiches £3, hot dishes £6) is decidedly ordinary. Open M-Sa 11am-11pm, Su noon-7pm; food served daily noon-3pm. MC/V.

CHELSEA

▩ **New Culture Revolution,** 305 King's Rd. (☎ 7352 9281). See **North London,** p. 109.

Chelsea Bun Diner, 9a Limerston St. (☎ 7352 3635). Wannabe American diner with a West Coast twist. Pasta, chicken, burgers, and omelettes £6-8. Minimum £3.50 per person lunch, £5.50 dinner. Open M-Sa 7am-midnight, Su 9am-7pm. MC/V.

Stockpot, 273 King's Rd. (☎ 7486 9185). Another outpost of this unfeasibly cheap, reasonably tasty minichain. See below.

KNIGHTSBRIDGE AND BELGRAVIA

▩ **Stockpot,** 6 Basil St. (☎ 7589 8627). Tube: Knightsbridge. Many worse restaurants get away with charging twice the prices of this supercheap stalwart. No-frills pinewood interior is the setting for bargains like beef stroganoff (£3.65) and grilled lamb cutlets (£4.30). 2-course set menu £3.90. Open M-Sa 7:30am-11pm, Su noon-10:30pm.

Gloriette, 128 Brompton Rd. (☎ 7589 4750). Tube: Knightsbridge. Venerable *pâtisserie* that recently started serving hot meals. Leaf teas £2 per pot, delicious cakes and pastries £2.60-3.30, sandwiches £5-7. More substantial fare includes veal goulash (£7.50) and 2-course set meals (£8). Open M-F 7am-9pm, Sa 7am-8pm, Su 9am-6pm. MC/V.

KENSINGTON AND EARL'S COURT

■ **The Troubador,** 265 Old Brompton Rd. (☎ 7370 1434). Tube: Earl's Court. Cozy old-fashioned interior festooned with curios plus a shady rear garden. Sandwich platters with salad and crisps £4-5, pasta £5-7, hot specials £7-10. Also poetry and folk-music nights. Open daily 9am-midnight. MC/V.

The Orangery, Kensington Palace (☎ 7938 1406). Tube: High St. Kensington or Queensway. Built for Queen Anne's dinner parties, today this airy building is a popular setting for light lunches (£7-8) and afternoon teas (from £8). Open daily 10am-6pm. MC/V.

Raison d'Être, 18 Bute St. (☎ 7584 5008). Tube: South Kensington. Catering to the local French community, this stylish cafe offers a bewildering range of filled *baguettes* (£2.20-5) as well as a few *salades composées* (£3.50-4.70), all freshly made to order. Open M-F 8am-6pm, Sa 9:30am-4pm. Cash only.

NOTTING HILL

■ **George's Portobello Fish Bar,** 329 Portobello Rd. (☎ 8969 7895). Tube: Ladbroke Grove. George opened up here in 1961, and while the shop has gone through various incarnations (it's currently a 50s-style diner), the fish and chips (£4-5) is as good as ever. No inside seating. Open Su-F 11am-midnight, Sa 11am-9pm. Cash only.

Books for Cooks, 4 Blenheim Cres. (☎ 7221 1992). Tube: Ladbroke Grove. At lunchtime, chef-owner Eric and his crew of culinary pros "test" recipes from new titles, much to the enjoyment of customers (though the tables can make book-browsing a trifle tricky). There's no telling what will be on offer, but you can rely on the cakes (£2). Bookstore open M-Sa 10am-6pm; food available M-Sa 10am-2:30pm or so. Daily cookery workshops held in upstairs demo kitchen (£25; reservations essential). AmEx/MC/V.

BAYSWATER

■ **Royal China,** 13 Queensway (☎ 7221 2535) Tube: Bayswater or Queensway. The glitzy, swan-themed decor isn't mirrored in the prices. Renowned for London's best *dim sum* (£2-3 per dish; count on 3-4 dishes each). Set meals from £7-10. *Dim sum* served M-Sa noon-5pm, Su 11am-5pm; on weekends, arrive early or expect to wait 30-45min. Open M-Th noon-11pm, F-Sa noon-11:30pm, Su 11am-10pm. AmEx/MC/V.

■ **La Bottega del Gelato,** 127 Bayswater Rd. (☎ 7243 2443). Tube: Queensway. Now in his 70s, Quinto Barbieri still gets up at 4:30am every morning to make the best *gelati* this side of the Rubicon. Opposite Hyde Park, it's perfect for a post-prandial stroll. Scoops from £1.30. Open daily 10am-7pm, later in summer. Cash only.

Alounak Kebab, 44 Westbourne Grove (☎ 7229 0416). Tube: Bayswater or Royal Oak. With decor ranging from a golden rococo fountain to a silver pendulum clock, Alounak's decor is hard to define; the food, however, is thoroughly Persian. Slow-grilled kebabs (from £5.60) are served with mouthwateringly fluffy saffron rice or fresh flatbread, baked in the traditional clay oven by the door. Open daily noon-midnight. MC/V.

MARYLEBONE AND REGENT'S PARK

■ **Patogh,** 8 Crawford Pl. (☎ 7262 4015). Tube: Edgware Rd. *Patogh* is Persian for "meeting place," and this certainly is a focal point for London's Iranian community. The generous portions are out of proportion with the tiny space; order a *kebab-e-koobideh* (minced-lamb kebab) with bread to receive a delicious 12" flatbread strewn with grilled meat, herbs, and *torshi* (Iranian pickles). Open daily noon-midnight. Cash only.

■ **Giraffe,** 6-8 Blandford St. (☎ 7935 2333). Tube: Bond St. or Baker St. 2nd branch of the deservedly popular micro chain, with the same winning combination of delicious eats (mains around £8), modern decor, and great music. See **North London,** p. 109.

BLOOMSBURY

■ **Da Beppe,** 116 Tottenham Court Rd. (☎ 7387 6324). Tube: Warren St. Possibly the best Italian restaurant in London. Beppe himself keeps the patrons coming back for more with positively Texan-sized platters of authentic Italian delicacies. Choose from 34 pastas and risottos (£6.50-8.50), 20 pizzas (£5-8.50), and numerous specialty meats (£8.50-10). Open M-Sa noon-3pm and daily 6-11pm. AmEx/MC/V.

▓ **Diwana Bhel Poori House,** 121-123 Drummond St. (☎ 7387 5556). Tube: Warren St. or Euston. No frills or frippery here—just great, cheap south Indian vegetarian food. Why bother with the £5.10 lunch buffet (daily noon-2:30pm) when £4.85 will get you a *Paneer Dosa* (rice pancake filled with potato and cheese) that's more than enough? Open daily noon-11:30pm. AmEx/MC/V.

ECCo (Express Coffee Co.), 46 Goodge St. (☎ 7580 9250). 11" thin-crust pizzas, made to order, cost an incredible £3; sandwiches and baguettes, on in-store baked bread, cost from £1, and rolls from 50p. Buy any hot drink before noon and get a fresh-baked croissant for free. Pizzas available from noon on. Open daily 7am-11pm. Cash only.

The Lamb, 94 Lamb's Conduit St. (☎ 7405 0713). Tube: Russell Sq. Popular with doctors from the many nearby hospitals, regulars also include Peter O'Toole, and fading photos of past thespian tipplers line the walls. The "snob screens" around the bar originally provided privacy for "respectable" men meeting with ladies of ill-repute. Open M-Sa 11am-11pm, Su noon-10:30pm; food daily noon-2:30pm and M-Sa 6-9pm. MC/V.

NORTH LONDON

▓ **Le Crêperie de Hampstead,** 77 Hampstead High St. Tube: Hampstead. Watch as delicacies like Mushroom Garlic Cream (£3) or Banana Butterscotch Cream Dream (£2.40) are prepared before your eyes. 35p gets you gooey Belgian chocolate instead of sticky syrup. Open M-Th 11:45am-11pm, F-Su 11:45am-11:30pm. Cash only.

▓ **Tartuf,** 88 Upper St. (☎ 7288 0954). Tube: Angel. Have a fantastic cutlery-free experience with Alsatian *tartes flambées* (£5-6), a cross between a crepe and a pizza, only much tastier. Before 3pm get 1 savory and 1 sweet *tarte* for £4.90. Open M-F noon-3pm and 5-11:30pm, Sa-Su noon-11:30pm. MC/V.

▓ **Gallipoli,** 102 Upper St., and **Gallipoli Again,** 120 Upper St. (☎ 7359 0630). Tube: Angel. Hanging lamps and Anatolian pop complement such Turkish delights as "Iskender Kebab," grilled lamb served with yogurt and marinated pita bread (£7). Reserve F-Sa. Open M-Th 10am-11pm, F-Sa 10am-midnight, Su 10am-10:30pm. MC/V.

▓ **Giraffe,** 29-31 Essex Rd. (☎ 7359 5999; Tube: Angel) and 46 Rosslyn Hill (☎ 7435 0343; Tube: Hampstead). A giraffe theme, an eclectic international menu, and toe-tapping music make this a treat. Superb salads—try the sushi rice, avocado, and daikon (£4.30). "Giraffe Time" gives you 2 courses for £6.50 and 2-for-1 drinks M-F 5-7pm. Open M-F 8a-11:30pm, Sa 9am-11:30pm, Su 9am-11pm. AmEx/MC/V.

▓ **New Culture Revolution,** 43 Parkway (☎ 7267 2700). Tube: Camden Town. Prophetically named—when this small restaurant opened in 1994, serving simple bowls of noodles in a functional setting, East Asian food in London was still associated with greasy takeaways. Noodles, dumplings, and north-Chinese food all under £6. Open M-Th noon-3:30pm and 5:30-11pm, F noon-11pm, Sa-Su 1-11pm. AmEx/MC/V.

SOUTH LONDON

Cafe Bar and Juice Bar, 407 Coldharbour Ln. (☎ 7738 4141). Tube: Brixton. Huge portions of Caribbean food: "soul food special" (£5.50) is a feast of plantain, yams, and salad on 2 plates. Open Su-Th 10am-midnight, F-Sa 10am-1am. AmEx/MC/V.

Fujiyama, 7 Vining St. (☎ 7737 2369). Tube: Brixton. Warm wooden tables and red walls form the backdrop to all your favorite ramen, udon, and soba, plus curries and rice dishes (£5-7). Open Su-Th noon-11pm, F-Sa noon-midnight. AmEx/MC/V.

EAST LONDON

▓ **Grand Central,** 93 Great Eastern St. (☎ 7613 4228). Tube: Old St. You could spend all day here: start with waffles and maple syrup for breakfast (£3.40, served to noon), move on to an open-faced hot salt-beef sandwich (£5.25) for lunch, wild salmon hash (£6.50) for dinner, then relax with one of 26 different bourbons (£1.90-2.40) as the nighttime crowds pile in to hear DJs play the latest electronica, soul, hip-hop, house, and R&B. Open M-F 7:30am-midnight, Sa 10am-midnight, Su noon-10:30pm. MC/V.

LONDON

Aladin, 132 Brick Ln. (☎ 7247 8210). Tube: Aldgate East. One of Brick Lane's more popular balti joints—even the Prince of Wales has been here. The diner-style interior's pretty basic, but who cares when you can get a Camilla Parker Bowl of curry for £3-4. BYOB. Open daily 11:30am-11:30pm. Cash only.

Arkansas Cafe, Old Spitalfields Market (☎ 7377 6999). Tube: Liverpool St. or Aldgate East. Bubba spends his days lovingly tending his oak-fired pits at this indoor-outdoor BBQ shack. The beef is all hormone-free US meat, chickens free-range from France. Open M-F noon-2:30pm, Su noon-4pm. £5 minimum per head. MC/V.

◎ SIGHTS

ORGANIZED TOURS. The classic London tour is on an open-top double-decker—and in fine weather, it's undoubtedly the best way to get a good overview of the city. However, if booking in advance, you might prefer to insure against rain and choose a bus with a roof upstairs, since you'll see little from street level. **The Big Bus Company,** 48 Buckingham Palace Rd. (☎ 7233 9533; Tube: Victoria), runs hop-on/hop-off bus tours every 15min. including one-hour walking tours and a mini Thames cruise. (Tickets valid 24hr. from first use. £15, children £7.) **London Frog Tours,** County Hall (☎ 7928 3132; Tube: Waterloo or Westminster), operates a fleet of amphibious vehicles that follow an 80min. nonstop road tour with a splash into the Thames for a 30min. cruise. Tours depart County Hall, opposite the London Eye (£15, students and seniors £12, children £9). For a more in-depth account, **Original London Walks** (☎ 7624 9255) is the city's oldest and biggest walking-tour company, running 12-16 walks per day, from "Magical Mystery Tour" to nighttime "Jack the Ripper's Haunts" and guided visits to larger museums. Most walks last 2hr. (£5, students and seniors £4, children free.) Organized bicycle tours let you cover plenty of ground while still going to places double-decker buses can't. The **London Bicycle Tour Company** runs leisurely tours designed to keep contact with road traffic to a minimum; prices include bike hire, helmet, and comprehensive insurance. (Tours start from the LBTC store, Gabriel's Wharf. ☎ 7928 6838. Tube: Waterloo or Southwark. Royal West Sa 2pm; East Tour Su 2pm. Both 9 mi., 3½hr. Book in advance. £12.) **Catamaran Cruises** operates a nonstop sightseeing Thames cruise with recorded commentary, leaving year-round from Waterloo Pier and April to May from Embankment Pier. (☎ 7987 1185. July-Aug. £7, seniors £6.30, children £5; Sept.-June £6.70, £6, £4.70. 33% discount with Travelcard.)

MAJOR ATTRACTIONS

BUCKINGHAM PALACE

*At the end of the Mall, between **Westminster, Belgravia,** and **Mayfair.** ☎ 7839 1377. Tube: St. James's Park, Victoria, Green Park, or Hyde Park Corner.*

Originally built for the Dukes of Buckingham, Buckingham House was acquired by George III in 1762, and converted into full-scale palace by George IV. Even so, the palace was found to be too small for Victoria's growing brood; a solution was found by closing off the three-sided courtyard, concealing the best architecture with Edward Blore's uninspiring facade.

THE STATE ROOMS. The Palace opens to visitors for a two-month period every summer while the Royals are off sunning themselves; advance booking is recommended. Don't look for any insights into the Queen's personal life—the State Rooms are used only for formal occasions, such as entertaining visiting heads of state; as such, they are also the most sumptuous in the Palace, if not all of Britain. The **Galleries** display many of the finest pieces in the outstanding Royal Collection. New from 2001, Liz has also graciously allowed commoners into the **gardens**—keep off the grass! *(Enter on Buckingham Palace Rd. Tickets available from ☎ 7321 2233 or (from late July) the Ticket Office, Green Park. Open early Aug. to Sept. daily 9:30am-4:30pm. £11, seniors £9, children £5.50, under 5 free, families £27.50.)*

CHANGING OF THE GUARD. The Palace is protected by a detachment of Foot Guards in full dress uniform, (fake) bearskin hats and all. Accompanied by a band, the "New Guard" starts marching down Birdcage Walk from Wellington Barracks around 10:30am, while the "Old Guard" leaves St. James's Palace around 11:10am. When they meet at the central gates of the palace, the officers of the regiments then touch hands, symbolically exchanging keys, *et voilà*, the guard is officially changed. Show up well before 11:30am and stand directly in front of the palace; for a less-crowded close-up of the guards (but not the ceremony), watch along the routes of the troops between the Victoria Memorial and St. James's Palace or along Birdcage Walk. *(Apr.-Oct. daily; Nov.-Mar. every other day, provided the Queen is in residence, it's not raining too hard, and there are no pressing state functions. Free.)*

THE HOUSES OF PARLIAMENT

*Parliament Sq., in **Westminster**. Enter at St. Stephen's Gate, between Old and New Palace Yards. Tube: Westminster. Commons Info Office ☎ 7219 4272. Debates: open to all while Parliament is in session (Oct.-July); can be very busy. Advance tickets required for Prime Minister's Question Time (W 3-3:30pm). M-Th after 6pm and F are least busy. Lords usually sits M-W from 2:30pm, Th 3pm, occasionally F 11:30am; closing times vary. Commons sits M-W 2:30-10:30pm, Th 11:30am-7:30pm, F 9:30am-3pm. Tours for British residents held year-round M-W 9:30am-noon and F 2:30-5:30pm; contact your MP to book. Tours for non-residents are held Oct.-July F 3:30-5:30pm; apply in writing at least 4 weeks ahead to: Parliamentary Education Unit, Norman Shaw Building, SW1A 2TT (☎ 7219 4600; edunit@parliament.uk). Tours open to all Aug.-Sept. M-Sa 9:15am-4:30pm. Reserve through Ticketmaster (☎ 7344 9966) or in person from mid-July. £3.50.*

The Palace of Westminster, as the building in which Parliament sits is officially known, has been at the heart of English governance since the 11th century, when Edward the Confessor established his court here. William the Conqueror found the site to his liking, and under the Normans the palace was greatly extended. Westminster Hall aside, what little remained of the Norman palace was entirely destroyed in the massive conflagration of October 16, 1834; the rebuilding started in 1835 under the joint command of Charles Barry and Augustus Pugin. Access to the Palace has been restricted since a bomb killed an MP in 1979. If you're unable to gain a place on one of the rare tours don't despair: all are allowed in to see debates while the Houses are in session.

OUTSIDE THE HOUSES. Facing the statue of Cromwell, at about the midpoint of the complex, **Old Palace Yard** is the triangular area to the right. Once the site of executions, including those of Walter Raleigh and Guy Fawkes, today a statuesque Richard I lords it over parked cars. On the left, **New Palace Yard** is a good place to spy your favorite MPs as they enter the complex through the Members' entrance. Behind Cromwell squats **Westminster Hall,** the sole survivor of the 1834 fire. Unremarkable from the outside, the Hall's chief feature is a magnificent hammerbeam roof, constructed in 1394 and considered the finest timber roof ever made. During its centuries as a law court, famous defendants here included Thomas More and Charles I. These days, it sees use for public ceremonies and occasional exhibitions. The **Clock Tower** is universally mis-known as **Big Ben,** which name refers strictly to the bell within—it's named after the robustly proportioned Sir Benjamin Hall, who served as Commissioner of Works when the bell was cast in 1858.

DEBATING CHAMBERS. Visitors to the debating chambers must first pass through **St. Stephen's Hall,** which stands on the site of St. Stephen's Chapel. Formerly the king's private chapel, in 1550 St. Stephen's became the meeting place of the House of Commons. The Commons have since moved on, but four brass markers point out where the Speaker's Chair used to stand. At the end of the hall, the **Central Lobby** marks the separation of the two houses, with the Commons to the north and the Lords to the south. The ostentatious **House of Lords** is dominated by the sovereign's Throne of State under a gilt canopy. The Lord Chancellor presides over the Peers from the **Woolsack,** a red behemoth the size of a VW Beetle. Next to him rests the almost 6 ft. **Mace,** brought in to open the House each morning. In contrast is the restrained **House of Commons,** with simple green-backed benches under a plain wooden roof. This is not entirely due to the difference in class—the Commons was destroyed by bombs in 1941, and rebuilding took place during a time of post-war austerity. The Speaker sits at the center-rear of the chamber, with government MPs to his right and the opposition to his left. The front benches are reserved for government ministers and their opposition "shadows"; the Prime Minister and the Leader of the Opposition face off across their dispatch boxes. With room for only 437 out of 635 MPs, things can get hectic when all are present.

ST. PAUL'S CATHEDRAL

St. Paul's Churchyard, **City of London.** *Tube: St. Paul's, Mansion House, or Blackfriars.* ☎ *7246 8348. Audioguides £3.50, concessions £3. 1½hr. tours M-F 11, 11:30am, 1:30, 2pm; £2.50, students and seniors £2, children £1. Open M-Sa 8:30am-4pm; open for worship daily 7:15am-6pm. 45min. Evensong M-Sa 5pm (free); arrive at 4:50pm to be admitted to seats in the quire. Cathedral £5, students and seniors £4, children £2.50.*

Sir Christopher Wren's masterpiece is the fifth cathedral to occupy the site; the original was built in AD 604. Wren's succeeded "Old St. Paul's," begun in 1087 and with a steeple a third the height of the current 364 ft. dome. By 1666, when the Great Fire swept it away, Old St. Paul's was ripe for replacement, used as a marketplace and barracks during the Civil War. Even so, only in 1668 did the authorities invite Wren to design a new cathedral rather than restore the old one. When the bishops rejected his third design, Wren, with Charles II's support, just started building—sneakily, he had persuaded the king to let him make "necessary alterations" as work progressed, and the building that emerged from the scaffolding in 1708 bore little resemblance to the "Warrant Model" Charles had approved.

INTERIOR. The entrance leads to the north aisle of the **nave,** the largest space in the cathedral with seats for 2500 worshippers. Unlike at Westminster Abbey, no one is actually buried in the cathedral floor—the graves are all downstairs in the crypt. The second tallest freestanding **dome** in Europe (after St. Peter's in the Vatican) seems even larger from inside, exaggerated by the false perspective of the paintings on the inner surface. The stalls in the **quire** escaped a bomb, but the altar did not. It was replaced with the current marble **High Altar,** above which looms the mosaic of *Christ Seated in Majesty.* The north quire aisle holds Henry Moore's *Mother and Child.* One month after the sculpture's arrival, guides insisted a plaque be affixed because no one knew what it was. The statue of **John Donne** in the south quire aisle is one of the few monuments to survive from Old St. Paul's.

SCALING THE HEIGHTS. The dome is built in three parts: an inner brick dome, visible from the inside of the cathedral; an outer timber structure; and between the two a brick cone that carries the weight of the lantern on top. A network of stairs pierces the structure, carrying brave visitors up, up, and away. First stop is the narrow **Whispering Gallery,** reached by 259 shallow steps or (for those in need only) a small elevator—though it's not wheelchair accessible. Encircling the base of the inner dome, the gallery is a perfect resounding chamber: whisper into the wall, and your friend on the other side should be able to hear you. Well, they could if everyone else wasn't trying the same thing. From here, climb another 119 steps (this time steep and winding) to the **Stone Gallery,** outside the cathedral at the base of the outer dome. The heavy stone balustrade, not to mention taller modern buildings, results in an underwhelming view, so take a deep breath and persevere up the final 152 vertiginous steps to the **Golden Gallery** at the base of the lantern.

PLUMBING THE DEPTHS. In the other vertical direction, the crypt is saturated with tombs of great Britons. **Nelson** commands pride of place, with radiating galleries festooned with monuments to other military heroes, from Epstein's bust of **T.E. Lawrence** (of Arabia) and **Florence Nightingale.** The neighboring chamber contains **Wellington's** massive tomb. The rear of the crypt bears the graves of artists, including **William Blake, J.M.W. Turner,** and **Henry Moore,** crowded around the black slab concealing the body of **Christopher Wren.** Inscribed on the wall above is his famous epitaph: *Lector, si monumentum requiris circumspice* ("Reader, if you seek his monument, look around").

THE TOWER OF LONDON

Tower Hill, next to Tower Bridge, in the City of London. Tube: Tower Hill or DLR: Tower Gateway. ☎ 7709 0765. Audioguides £3. Free 1hr. tours meet near entrance 2 per hr. M-Sa 9:30am-3:30pm, Su 10am-3:30pm. Open Mar.-Oct. M-Sa 9am-5:30pm, Su 10am-5:30pm; Nov.-Feb. until 4:30pm. Last admission 30min. before close. £11.30, students and seniors £8.50, children £7.50, families £34. Tickets also sold at Tube stations; buy them in advance since queues at the door are horrendous.

The Tower of London, palace and prison of English monarchs for over 900 years, is steeped in blood and history. Conceived by William the Conqueror more to provide protection from than for his new subjects, his wooden palisade of 1067 was replaced in 1078 by a stone structure that grew into the White Tower. Yeomen Warders, or "Beefeaters"—a reference to their daily allowance of meat in former times—still guard the fortress, dressed in their blue everyday or red ceremonial uniforms. The fortress has been divided into seven self-contained areas, which can be visited in any order. A **Yeoman Warders' Tour** (see above) will fill you in on the Tower's history and legends.

WESTERN ENTRANCE AND WATERLANE. From **Middle Tower,** where today tickets are collected and bags searched, you pass over the moat (now a garden) and enter the **Outer Ward** though **Byward Tower.** Just beyond Byward Tower, the massive **Bell Tower** dates from 1190; the curfew bell has been rung here nightly for over 500 years. The stretch of the Outer Ward along the Thames is **Water Lane,** which until the 16th century was adjacent to the river. **Traitor's Gate** was built by Edward I for his personal use, but is now associated with the prisoner who passed through it.

MEDIEVAL PALACE. In this sequence of rooms, archaeologists have attempted to recreate the look and feel of the Tower during the reign of Edward I (1275-1279). The tour starts at **St. Thomas's Tower,** a half-timbered set of rooms above Traitor's Gate. In other rooms, costumed guides regale visitors. The tour also takes in **Wakefield Tower,** presented as a putative throne room. Tower lore claims that Henry VI was murdered while imprisoned here in 1471 by Edward IV, though recent evidence suggests he was kept in the adjacent **Lanthorn Tower.**

WALL WALK. The walk runs along the eastern wall constructed by Henry III in the mid-13th century. The wall is entered via **Salt Tower,** long used as a prison and said to be haunted—apparently dogs refuse to enter it. At the end of the walk is **Martin Tower,** home to a fascinating collection of retired crowns, *sans* gemstones along with paste models of some of the more famous jewels, including the Cullinan diamond, the largest ever found at 3106 carats. The stone was mailed third class from the Transvaal in an unmarked parcel, a scheme Scotland Yard believed was the safest way of getting it to London.

CROWN JEWELS. The queue at the Jewel House is a miracle of crowd management. After passing through room after room of video projections of the jewels in action, the crowd is finally ushered into the vault and onto moving walkways that whisk them past the crowns. Most of the items come from the Coronation regalia; while the eye is naturally drawn to the **Imperial State Crown,** home to the Stuart Sapphire along with 16 others, 2876 diamonds, 273 pearls, 11 emeralds, and a mere five rubies, don't miss the **Sceptre with the Cross,** topped with First Star of Africa, the largest quality cut diamond in the world. The **Queen Mother's Crown** is set with the Koh-I-Noor diamond, which legend claims will only bring luck to women.

WHITE TOWER. The Conqueror's original castle has served as royal residence, wardrobe, storehouse, records office, mint, armory, and prison. Visitors are given the option of long or short routes. The long version starts with the first-floor **Chapel of St. John the Evangelist.** The spacious hall next door was most likely the royal **bedchamber,** adjacent to the larger **Great Hall.** Today it houses a collection of armor and weapons: one look at Henry VIII's tournament suit will show why he never had any trouble remarrying. The visit then passes through more displays of weaponry before meeting up with the start of the short route. This trails through a set of historic misrepresentations, starting with the **Spanish Armory**—torture instruments displayed in the 17th century as being captured from the Spanish Armada (1588), but actually from the Tower's own armory.

TOWER GREEN. The grassy western side of the Inner Ward marks the site of the Tower's most famous executions, surrounded by residential buildings. The Tudor **Queen's House** (which will become the King's House when Charles ascends the throne) is occupied by the Governor of the Tower. Nearby, the **Beauchamp Tower** was usually reserved for high-class "guests," many of whom carved intricate inscriptions into the walls during their detention. On the north of Tower Green is the **Chapel Royal of St. Peter ad Vinculum.** Three Queens of England, Anne Boleyn, Catherine Howard, and Lady Jane Grey, are buried here, as well as Catholic martyrs Sir Thomas More and John Fisher. *(Open only by Yeoman tours or after 4:30pm.)* Across the green, **Bloody Tower** is named for the probability that here Richard III imprisoned and murdered his nephews, the rightful Edward V (aged 12) and his brother, before usurping the throne in 1483. In 1674, the bones of two children were unearthed nearby and subsequently reinterred in Westminster Abbey.

WESTMINSTER ABBEY

*Parliament Sq., **Westminster;** access Old Monastery, Cloister, and Garden from Dean's Yard, behind the Abbey. Tube: Westminster or St. James's Park. Abbey ☎ 7222 7110, Old Monastery 7222 5897. Audioguides £2. 1½hr. guided tours M-F 10, 11am, 2, 3pm; Sa 10, 11am; Apr.-Oct. also M-F 10:30am and 2:30pm. £3, including Old Monastery. Open: Abbey M-F 9am-4:45pm, Sa 9am-2:45pm; last admission 1hr. before close; Su for services only. Pyx Chamber and Museum daily 10:30am-4pm. Chapter House Apr.-Oct. daily 10am-5:30pm; Nov.-Mar. 10am-4pm. Cloisters daily 8am-6pm. Garden Apr.-Sept. Tu-Th 10am-6pm; Oct.-Mar. 10am-4pm. Abbey £6, students and seniors £3, under 11 free, families £12; entry to services is free. Old Monastery £2.50. Joint entry with abbey £1 extra on abbey prices. Cloisters and Garden free.*

On December 28, 1065, Edward the Confessor, last Saxon King of England, was buried in his still-unfinished abbey church of the West Monastery; almost exactly a year later, the abbey saw the coronation of William the Conqueror. Thus even before it was completed, the abbey's twin traditions as the figurative birthplace and literal resting place of royalty had been established. Later monarchs continued to add to the abbey, but the biggest change was constitutional rather than physical: in 1540 Henry VIII dissolved the monasteries, expelling the monks and stripping their wealth. Fortunately, Henry's respect for his royal forebears outweighed his vindictiveness against the Pope, and so uniquely among the great monastic centers of England, Westminster escaped destruction and desecration.

STONED On Christmas Day, 1950, daring Scottish patriot Ian Hamilton—posing as a visitor—hid himself in Westminster Abbey until it closed. He meant to steal the 200kg Stone of Scone and return it to Scotland, but as he approached the door near Poet's Corner to let in his three accomplices, he was detected by a watchman. Hamilton (now a prominent Scottish MP) talked fast enough to convince the watchman that he had been locked in involuntarily.

That same night the foursome forcibly entered the abbey and pulled the stone out of its wooden container, in the process inadvertently breaking the famed rock into two uneven pieces. Hamilton sent his girlfriend driving off to Scotland with the smaller piece, while he returned to deal with the larger piece. The remaining two accomplices had been instructed to drag the larger piece toward the cars, but when he returned Hamilton found only the stone. He lugged the piece to his car, and, while driving out of London, happened across his wayward accomplices. The stone was repaired in a Glasgow workyard, but the patriots were frustrated that they could not display it in a public place. On April 11, 1951, Hamilton and Company carried the stone to the altar at Arbroath Abbey where it was discovered and returned to England.

The final chapter of the story is that now-deceased Glasgow councilor Bertie Gray claimed, before he died, that the stone was copied and the one residing in the abbey was a fake. The real stone resides at Scone Palace, near Perth (see p. 558).

INSIDE THE ABBEY. Visitors enter through the **Great North Door** into **Statesman's Aisle,** littered with monuments to 18th- and 19th-century politicians. From here, the **ambulatory** leads past a string of side chapels to the left and the **Shrine of St. Edward** to the right. Around the Confessor's shrine, the **House of Kings** arrays the tombs of monarchs from Henry III (d. 1272) to Henry V (d. 1422). At the far end of the Shrine stands the **Coronation Chair,** built for Edward I; the shelf below the seat was made to house the Scottish Stone of Scone, which Edward brought south in 1296—the Stone was finally returned to Scotland 700 years later. Stairs lead from the chair to the **Lady Chapel,** now a Tudor mausoleum; the aisles on either side hold **Elizabeth I** in the north, and **Mary, Queen of Scots** in the south. Returning to the central part of the Lady Chapel, the nave is dominated by the carved wooden stalls of the **Order of the Bath;** at its end **Henry VII** lies within a wrought-iron screen. The south transept holds the abbey's most famous and popular attraction: **Poet's Corner.** Its founder member was buried here for reasons nothing to do with literary repute—**Chaucer** had a job in the abbey administration. Plaques at his feet commemorate both poets and prose writers, as does the stained-glass window above. At the very center of the abbey, a short flight of steps leads up to the **Sanctuary,** where coronations take place; the stall to the left of the altar is used by the Royal Family. Cordons prevent you from climbing up to admire the 13th-century Cosmati mosaic floor. After a detour through the cloisters, including optional visits to the Old Monastery and gardens (see below), visitors return to the **nave.** At the western end is the **Tomb of the Unknown Warrior,** bearing the remains of an unidentified WWI soldier, with an oration poured from molten bullets; just beyond is the simple grave of a well-known hero, **Winston Churchill.** Stretching eastward, the North Aisle starts with memorials to 20th-century Prime Ministers before transmuting into **"Scientist's Corner,"** even less of a corner than its poetic equivalent. Isaac Newton's massive monument, set into the left-hand quire screen, presides over a tide of physicists around his grave in the nave itself, while in the aisle biologists cluster around would-be pastor Charles Darwin.

OLD MONASTERY, CLOISTERS, AND GARDENS. Formerly a major monastery, the abbey complex stretches far beyond the church itself. Note that all the sights below are accessible through Dean's Yard without going through the abbey. The **Great Cloisters** hold yet more tombs and commemorative plaques; a passageway running off the southeastern corner leads to the idyllic **Little Cloister** and 900-year-old **College Gardens.** A door off the east cloister leads to the octagonal **Chapter House,** the original meeting place of the House of Commons, whose 13th-century tiled floor is the best-preserved in Europe. Dark and windowless, the **Pyx Chamber** is one of the few surviving parts of the original 11th-century monastic complex. Originally a chapel, it was converted into a treasury in the 13th century. Next door, the **Abbey Museum** is housed in the Norman undercroft. The self-proclaimed highlight of the collection is the array of **funeral effigies,** from the unhealthy-looking wooden models of the 14th century to fully-dressed 17th-century wax versions.

WEST END

OXFORD AND REGENT STREETS

Oscar Wilde famously quipped that London's famous shopping strip **Oxford Street** is "all street and no Oxford." **Regent Street** is more imposing, though none of Nash's original Regency arcades have survived. North of Regent St. near Oxford Circus, **Carnaby Street** was at the heart of Swinging London in the 1960s. After that psychedelic high followed 30 years as a lurid tourist trap; now Carnaby swings again for the naughty noughties with an influx of trendy boutiques. *(Tube: Oxford Circus.)*

ALL SOULS LANGHAM PLACE. Forced to make an ungainly kink in linking Regent St. to Portland Pl., Nash designed All Souls to soften the bend. Unlike any other church in London, the main building barely brushes against its circular entrance hall, whose central spire pierces a double wedding-cake tier of columns. A bust of Nash adorns the outside of the entrance hall. *(Tube: Oxford Circus.)*

MARBLE ARCH. Designed by Nash in 1828 as the front entrance to Buckingham Palace, extensions to the palace soon rendered Marble Arch useless, so it was moved to the present site as an entrance into Hyde Park. Then new roads cut the arch off, leaving it stranded forlornly on a traffic roundabout. Until 1783, this was the main execution site in London. *(Tube: Marble Arch.)*

MAYFAIR AND ST. JAMES'S

Long London's aristocratic quarter, many would-be sights, such as St. James's Palace and the gentlemen's clubs, are out-of-bounds to all but the most blue-blooded.

PICCADILLY CIRCUS, BOND ST., AND SAVILE ROW. Frilly ruffs were big business in the 16th century—one local tailor named his house after these "piccadills," and the name stuck. Clogged with traffic, Piccadilly is no longer the preferred address of gentlemen, as it was in the late 18th century, but it's still posh, with a capital P. *(Tube: Piccadilly Circus or Green Park. For details of Piccadilly Circus, see Soho, below.)* Running into Piccadilly, **Old Bond Street** is London's poshest shopping street; this end is dominated by art and jewelry dealers, while most of the designer boutiques are found on **New Bond Street,** nearer Oxford St. *(Tube: Bond St. or Green Park. Note that Bond St. Tube is not on Bond St.; exit right onto Oxford St., then take the 2nd right onto Bond St.)* **Savile Row,** running parallel to Bond St., is synonymous with elegant and expensive tailoring; less well known is that the **Beatles** performed their last ever live gig on the roof of no. 3 while filming of *Let It Be. (Tube: Piccadilly Circus.)*

BURLINGTON HOUSE. The only one of Piccadilly's aristocratic mansions to survive, Burlington House was built in 1665. Although the Earls of Burlington have since departed, it still has an aristocratic grandeur. Today, Burlington House is home to numerous regal societies, including the **Royal Academy** (see p. 136).

ST. JAMES'S CHURCH. William Blake was baptized in Wren church, whose exterior is now darkened by the soot of London's satanic mills. The current structure is largely a post-war reconstruction; the flowers, garlands, and cherubs by master carver Grinling Gibbons fortunately escaped the Blitz. *(Enter at 197 Piccadilly or on Jermyn St. ☎ 7734 4511. Church open daily 8am-7pm.)*

ST. JAMES'S PALACE. Built in 1536, St. James's is London's only remaining purpose-built palace (Buckingham Palace was a rough-and-ready conversion job). The massive gateway is one of the few original parts of the palace to survive. Unless your name starts with HRH, the only part of the palace you're likely to get into is the **Chapel Royal,** open for Sunday services from October to Easter at 8:30 and 11am. From Easter to September, services are held in the Inigo Jones-designed **Queen's Chapel,** across Marlborough Rd. from the palace.

SOHO

Soho has a history of welcoming all colors and creeds to its streets. Early settlers included French Huguenots fleeing religious persecution in the 17th century, but these days Soho is less gay Paris, more plain gay: a concentration of gay-owned restaurants and bars has turned **Old Compton Street** into the heart of gay London. A blue plaque at 28 Dean St. locates the two-room flat where **Karl Marx** lived with his wife, maid, and five children while writing *Das Kapital.*

PICCADILLY CIRCUS. Five of the West End's arteries merge and swirl around Piccadilly Circus, and the entire tourist population of London seems to bask under its lurid neon signs. The **statue of Eros** was dedicated to the Victorian philanthropist, Lord Shaftesbury: Eros originally pointed his arrow down Shaftesbury Ave., but recent restoration has put his aim significantly off. *(Tube: Piccadilly Circus.)*

LEICESTER SQUARE. Amusements at this entertainment nexus range from London's largest cinemas to the **Swiss Centre** glockenspiel, whose atonal renditions of Beethoven's *Moonlight Sonata* are enough to make even the tone-deaf weep. *(Rings M-F at noon, 6, 7, 8pm; Sa-Su noon, 2, 4, 5, 6, 7, 8pm.)* Be true to your inner tourist and get a henna tattoo or sit for a caricature. *(Tube: Leicester Sq. or Piccadilly Circus.)*

CHINATOWN. Pedestrianized, tourist-ridden **Gerrard Street,** with scroll-worked dragon gates and pagoda-capped phone booths, is the self-proclaimed heart of this tiny slice of Canton, but gritty **Lisle Street,** one block to the south, has a more authentic feel. Chinatown is most vibrant during the year's two major festivals: the Mid-Autumn Festival at the end of September, and the raucous Chinese New Year Festival in February. *(Between Leicester Sq., Shaftesbury Ave., and Charing Cross Rd.)*

COVENT GARDEN

On the very spot where, 350 years ago, Samuel Pepys saw the first Punch and Judy show in England, street performers entertain the thousands who flock here summer and winter, rain and shine, Londoner and tourist alike. *(Tube: Covent Garden.)*

ST. PAUL'S. Not to be confused with St. Paul's Cathedral, this simple Inigo Jones church is the sole remnant of the original square. Known as "the actor's church," the interior is festooned with plaques commemorating the achievements of thespians from Vivien Leigh to Tony Simpson ("inspired player of small parts"). The **churchyard's** leafy gardens belie its status as a plague burial ground—Margaret Ponteous, the first victim of the Great Plague, was buried here on April 12, 1665. *(On Covent Garden Piazza; enter via King St., Henrietta St., or Bedford St. ☎ 7836 5221. Open daily 8:30am-4:30pm.)*

THE ROYAL OPERA HOUSE. The Royal Opera House reopened in 2000 after a major expansion. During the day, the public is free to wander the ornate lobby of the original 1858 theater, as well as the enormous glass-roofed space of **Floral Hall.** From here, take the escalator to reach the **terrace** overlooking the Piazza, with great views of London. *(Enter on Bow St. or through "the Link" in the northeast of the Piazza. 1¼hr. backstage tours M-Sa 10:30am, 12:30, 2:30pm; reservations essential. Open daily 10am-3:30pm. £7, concessions £6. For performances, see p. 144.)*

THEATRE ROYAL, DRURY LANE. Founded in 1663, this is the oldest of London's surviving theaters. Charles II met Nell Gwynn here in 1655, while David Garrick ruled the roost in the 18th century. The theater even has a ghost—a corpse and dagger were found bricked up in the wall in the 19th century. This and other pieces of Drury Ln. lore are brought back to life in the actor-led backstage tours. *(Entrance on Catherine St. ☎ 7240 5357. Tours M-Tu, Th-F, Su 12:30, 2:15, 4:45pm; W and Sa 10:15am and noon. £7.50, children £5.50.)*

TRAFALGAR SQUARE AND THE STRAND

John Nash suggested laying out **Trafalgar Square** in 1820, but it took almost 50 years for London's largest traffic roundabout to take on its current appearance: Nelson arrived in 1843, and the bronze lions in 1867. The long-empty **fourth plinth** holds specially commissioned modern sculpture; the first half of 2002 will see Rachel Whiteread's inverted clear resin cast of the plinth itself. Every December the square hosts a giant **Christmas Tree,** donated by Norway as thanks for British assistance against the Nazis. *(Tube: Charing Cross or Leicester Sq.)*

ST. MARTIN-IN-THE-FIELDS. James Gibbs's 1720s creation is instantly recognizable as the model for countless Georgian churches in Britain and America. It's still the Queen's parish church; look for the royal box to the left of the altar. Handel and Mozart both performed here, and the church hosts frequent concerts. Downstairs the **crypt** has a life of its own, home to a cafe, bookshop, art gallery, and the ever-popular **London Brass Rubbing Centre.** *(St. Martin's Ln., in the northeast corner of Trafalgar Sq.; crypt entrance on Duncannon St. Tube: Leicester Sq. ☎ 7766 1100. Brass rubbing centre open M-Sa 10am-6pm, Su noon-6pm. Brass rubbing £5-8.)*

SOMERSET HOUSE. Completed in 1790, Somerset House was London's first purpose-built office block. Originally home to the Royal Academy, the Royal Society, and the Navy Board, the building now harbors the **Courtauld Institute Galleries** (see p. 133) and the **Gilbert Collection of Decorative Art** (see p. 134). Mid-December to mid-January, the central **Fountain Courtyard** is iced over to make an open-air rink. *(Strand, east of Waterloo Bridge. Tube: Charing Cross or Temple. ☎ 7845 4600, events 7845 4670. 45min. tours Tu, Th, Sa 11am and 3:15pm. £2.75. Courtyard open daily 7:30am-11pm.)*

ST. MARY-LE-STRAND. The slender steeple and elegant portico of this 1724 church rise above a sea of traffic. Designed by James Gibbs, the church overlooks the site of the original Maypole, claimed by Isaac Newton for a telescope stand. Inside, the Baroque decoration reflects not only the glory of God but also Gibbs's Roman architectural training. *(☎ 7836 3205. Open M-F 11am-4pm.)*

HOLBORN AND CLERKENWELL

Squeezed between the City and the West End, **Holborn**'s crush of streets hide many marvels, chiefly the four **Inns of Court,** venerable institutions providing apprentice-ships for law students and housing the chambers of practising barristers. Most were founded in the 13th century when a royal decree barred the clergy from the courts, giving rise to a class of professional advocates. Northeast of Holborn, **Clerkenwell** may be the new Soho, but in historical terms it's far older. From the 12th century until Henry VIII's break with Rome, Clerkenwell was dominated by the great monastic foundations of which traces can still be found.

INNS OF COURT

THE TEMPLE. South of Fleet St., this labyrinthine compound encompasses the inns of the Middle Temple, to the west, and the Inner Temple, neighboring it on the east—there was once also an Outer Temple, but it has long since gone. *(Between Fleet St., Essex St., Victoria Embankment, and Temple Ave./Bouvier St.; numerous passages lead from these streets into the Temple. Tube: Temple or Blackfriars.)* From 1185 until the order was dissolved in 1312, this land belonged to the crusading Knights Templar; sole survivor of this time is the **Temple Church,** built in the 12th century. Adjoining the round church is a Gothic nave, built in 1240, with an altar screen by Wren. *(☎ 7353 3470. Open W-Th 11am-4pm, Sa 9:30am-1:30pm, Su 12:45-4pm. Free.)* While the **Inner Temple** was leveled during the Blitz—with the exception of the Tudor **Inner Temple Gateway,** 16-17 Fleet St., all is reconstruction—the **Middle Temple** was hardly touched. **Middle Temple Hall,** closed to the public, still has its 1574 hammerbeam ceiling as well as dining table made from the hatch of Sir Francis Drake's *Golden Hinde.* According to Shakespeare's *Henry VI,* the red and white flowers that served as emblems throughout the Wars of the Roses were plucked in **Middle Temple Garden,** south of the hall. *(Middle Temple Garden open May-Sept. M-F noon-3pm. Free.)*

LINCOLN'S INN. Just east of **Lincoln's Inn Fields,** London's largest square, sprawl the grounds of Lincoln's Inn. John Donne, Thomas More, Walpole, Pitt, Glad-stone, and Disraeli are a few former Inn-mates. The main gates deposit you in **New Square,** appearing much as it did when built in the 1690s. Next to New Sq. are the **Old Buildings,** including the 15th-century **Old Hall** (closed to the public) where the Lord High Chancellor presided over the Court of Chancery from 1733 to 1873. The **Chapel,** whose foundation stone was laid in 1620 by John Donne, sits above an open undercroft—once a popular spot for abandoning babies, who would be brought up in the Inn under the surname Lincoln. *(Between Lincoln's Inn Fields and Chancery Lane. Tube: Chancery Lane or Holborn. Gardens open M-F noon-2:30pm. Free.)*

GRAY'S INN. The exterior of Gray's Inn does not inspire joy—Dickens dubbed it "that stronghold of melancholy." Entering through the 1688 **gatehouse** on High Holborn, you pass the 16th-century **hall** to your right; its screen was carved from the timbers of a Spanish galleon. Francis Bacon maintained chambers here and is the purported designer of the expansive **gardens.** *(Between Theobald's Rd., Jockey's Fields, High Holborn, and Gray's Inn Rd. Tube: Chancery Lane. Gardens open M-F noon-2:30pm.)*

FLEET STREET

Named for the river (now underground) that flows from Hampstead to the Thames, Fleet Street's association with publishing goes back to the days when Thomas Caxton's successor Wyken de Worde relocated from Westminster to the precincts of St. Bride's church (below). Times—or rather *The Times*—have changed: Rupert Murdoch's 1986 move to Docklands initiated a mass exodus. Though "Fleet Street" is still synonymous with the British press, the famous facades, such as the *Daily Telegraph's* Greek and Egyptian Revival building and the *Daily Express's* Art Deco manse, now house offices. *(Tube: Temple.)*

ST. BRIDE'S. The unusual spire of Wren's 1675 church is the world's most imitated piece of architecture; a local baker even modeled a wedding cake on the multi-tiered structure. Dubbed "the printers' cathedral" since 1531, when Wyken de Worde set up his press here, literary associations include Pepys, baptized here, and Milton, who lived in the churchyard. The crypt, closed in 1853 following a cholera epidemic, was reopened during the post-Blitz restoration 1952; displays include the baker's wife's wedding dress and the remains of a Roman pavement. *(St. Bride's Ave., off Fleet St. Open daily 8am-4:45pm. Free.)*

SAMUEL JOHNSON'S HOUSE. Samuel Johnson, a self-described "shrine to the English language," lived here from 1748 to 1759, completing his dictionary, the first definitive English lexicon, even though rumor falsely insists that he omitted "sausage." He compiled this amazing document by reading all the great books of the age and marking the words he wanted included in the dictionary with black pen. *(17 Gough Sq.; follow the signs down the alley opposite 54 Fleet St. ☎ 7353 3745. Expected to reopen by late 2001; call for hours and prices.)*

ROYAL COURTS OF JUSTICE. Straddling the official division between the City of Westminster and the City of London is this elaborate neo-Gothic structure, designed in 1874 by G.E. Street; the courtrooms are open to the public during cases. In the Great Hall, you stand on the largest mosaic floor in Europe. At the top of the stairs at the rear of the hall is a small exhibition dedicated to the history of legal costume, including the wigs. *(Where the Strand becomes Fleet St. Tube: Temple or Chancery Lane. ☎ 7936 6000. Open M-F 9am-6pm, last admission 4:30pm; cases start 10am, with a break for lunch 1-2pm. Free.)*

CLERKENWELL

ST. JOHN'S SQUARE. Bisected by the busy Clerkenwell Rd., St. John's Square occupies the sight of the 12th-century **Priory of St. John,** formerly the English seat of the crusading Knights Hospitallers. Arching grandly over the entrance to St. John's Sq. is 16th-century **St. John's Gate,** with an odd mixture of artifacts relating to the original priory and Knights Hospitallers and hi-tech displays detailing the exploits of the modern-day British Order of St. John. Join a tour to see the upstairs council chamber and the **priory church,** complete with 12th-century crypt and the 1480 Weston Triptych. *(St. John's Ln. ☎ 7253 6644. Tours Tu and F-Sa 11am and 2:30pm; £4, seniors £3. Gate open M-F 10am-5pm, Sa 10am-4pm; church open only for tours. Free.)*

ST. BARTHOLOMEW THE GREAT. Visitors must enter through a 13th-century arch, disguised as a Tudor house, to reach this Norman gem. Hogarth was baptized in the 15th-century font, and Benjamin Franklin worked at a printers' in the Lady's Chapel. The tomb near the altar belongs to **Rahere,** who in 1123 founded both the church and **St. Bartholomew's Hospital** across the street. *(Little Britain, off West Smithfield. Tube: Barbican or Farringdon. ☎ 7606 5171. Open Sept.-July M-F 8:30am-5pm, Sa 10:30am-1:30pm, Su 8am-1pm and 2-8pm; Aug. closed M. Free.)*

SMITHFIELD MARKET. On the site of medieval St. Bartholomew's Fair, Smithfield has been London's main meat market since the 19th century. The association with butchery predates the Victorians: Wat Tyler, leader of the Peasants' Revolt, and William "Braveheart" Wallace were among those executed here in the Middle Ages. *(Charterhouse St. Tube: Barbican or Farringdon. Open M-F 4-10am.)*

THE CITY OF LONDON

The **City of London Information Centre,** St. Paul's Churchyard (☎ 7332 1456; Tube: St. Paul's) sells tickets to sights and shows and gives info on municipal events. One of the largest is the **Lord Mayor's Show,** held each year on the second Saturday of November. Open Apr.-Sept. daily 9:30am-5pm; Oct.-Mar. M-F 9:30am-5pm, Sa 9:30am-12:30pm.

The City of London (or "the City") is the oldest part of London—for most of its 2000 years, this *was* London, the rest being outlying villages—but its appearance is much newer. Following the Great Fire of 1666 and the Blitz of 1940-43, the financial area underwent a cosmetic rearrangement that left little of its history behind.

LUDGATE HILL AND AROUND

Legend holds that London takes its name from the mythical King Lud, supposedly buried beneath Lud Gate, one of the original Roman entryways into the City. As the City's highest spot, Ludgate Hill was the obvious spot to build **St. Paul's Cathedral** (see **Major Attractions,** p. 112), which still towers above its surroundings.

OLD BAILEY. Technically the Central Criminal Courts, the Old Bailey crouches under a copper dome and a wide-eyed figure of Justice. The current building is the third courthouse on the site; the previous two were incorporated into notorious Newgate Prison, only demolished in 1902. William Penn, founder of Pennsylvania, was tried here for evangelizing in 1670. After declaring him "not guilty," the jury was imprisoned. This led to the establishment of the "rights of juries to give their verdict according to their convictions." *(Corner of Old Bailey and Newgate St.; public entry via Warwick Passage. Tube: St. Paul's.* ☎ *7248 3277. Open M-F 10:30am-1pm and 2-4:30pm. No cameras, drinks, food, electronics, or large bags; there are no cloakroom facilities.)*

ST. MARY-LE-BOW. Another Wren creation, St. Mary's is most famous for its Great Bell—true-blue cockneys are born within their range. The church had to be almost completely rebuilt after the Blitz, but the 11th-century crypt, whose "bows" (arches) gave the church its epithet, survived. Since the 12th century, it has hosted the Court of Arches, where the Archbishop of Canterbury swears in bishops. Today, **The Place Below** restaurant (see p. 107) shares space with the court. *(Cheapside, by Bow Ln. Tube: St. Paul's or Mansion House.* ☎ *7246 5139. Open M-F 6:30am-6pm. Free.)*

OTHER SIGHTS. Dwelling incongruously in the shadow of the Temple Court building are the remains of the 3rd-century Roman **Temple of Mithras,** discovered during construction work in 1954 and shifted up 18 ft. to current street level. *(Queen Victoria St. Tube: Mansion House or Bank.)* Built in 1450, **St. Sepulchre-without-Newgate** (i.e., outside) was gutted in the Great Fire; the interior dates from 1670. Captain John Smith, of *Pocahontas* fame, is buried inside. Also in the church is the bell of Newgate Prison, rung outside the cells of the condemned on the eve of their execution. *(Holborn Viaduct, opposite the Old Bailey.* ☎ *7248 3826. Open Tu and Th noon-2pm, W 11am-3pm, and for concerts. Free.)* Adjacent to the original Ludgate (demolished 1720), **St. Martin-within-Ludgate** claims to have been founded around AD 700 by a shadowy "King Cadwalla." Rebuilt by Wren in 1684, its most notable features are the narrow spire, intended as a foil to St. Paul's, and the Grinling Gibbons woodwork inside. *(Ludgate Hill.* ☎ *7248 6054. Open M-F 11am-3pm.)*

GUILDHALL AND LONDON WALL

GUILDHALL. This vast Gothic hall, dating from 1440, is where the representatives of the City's 102 guilds, from the Fletchers (arrow-makers) to the Information Technologists, meet at the **Court of Common Council,** presided over by the Lord Mayor bedecked in traditional robes and followed by a sword-wielding entourage; the Court is held in public every third Thursday of the month. *(Off Gresham St. Tube: St. Paul's, Moorgate, or Bank.* ☎ *7606 3030. Open May-Sept. M-F 10am-5pm, Sa-Su 10am-4pm; Oct.-Apr. closed Su; last admission 30min. before close. Free.)*

THE BARBICAN. In the aftermath of WWII, the Corporation of London decided to develop this bomb-flattened 35-acre plot as a textbook piece of reintegration. At the center of the resulting concrete labyrinth is the **Barbican Centre** cultural complex. Described at its 1982 opening as "the City's gift to the nation," it incorporates a concert hall, two theaters, a cinema, three art galleries, and cafeterias, bars, and restaurants—if you can find any of them. *(Main entrance on Silk St. From Tube: Moorgate or Barbican, follow the yellow painted lines. ☎ 7638 8891. For more on events, see Museums and Galleries, p. 131, and Entertainment, p. 141. Open M-Sa 9am-11pm, Su 10:30am-11pm.)*

BANK TO THE TOWER

"Bank" refers to *the* Bank—the **Bank of England** (see below). Around this convergence of six streets stand hallowed institutions: the **Stock Exchange,** on Throgmorton St.; the neoclassical **Royal Exchange,** between Cornhill and Threadneedle St., founded in 1566 as Britain's first mercantile exchange; and the 18th-century **Mansion House,** on Walbrook, the official residence of the Lord Mayor.

BANK OF ENGLAND. Government financial difficulties led to the founding of the "Old Lady of Threadneedle St." in 1694, as a way of raising money without raising taxes—the bank's creditors supplied £1.2 million, and the national debt was born. The windowless outer wall, 8 ft. thick, is the only remnant of Sir John Soane's 1788 building; above it rises the current 1925 edifice. Top-hatted guards in pink tailsuits direct those who wander into the main entrance to the **Bank of England Museum** (see p. 134) around the corner. *(Threadneedle St. Tube: Bank.)*

MONUMENT. The only non-ecclesiastical Wren building in the City, this Doric pillar topped with a gilded flaming urn is a lasting reminder of the Great Fire. Erected in 1677, the 202 ft. column stands exactly that distance from the bakery on Pudding Lane where fire first broke out. The column offers an expansive view of London; bring stern resolution to climb its 311 steps. *(Monument St. Tube: Monument. ☎ 7626 2717. Open daily 10am-6pm. £1.50, children 50p. Joint with Tower Bridge Experience (see below) £6.75, children £4.25.)*

TOWER BRIDGE. Perhaps the most iconic symbol of London—which helps explain why tourists often mistake it for its plainer upriver sibling, London Bridge. Folklore claims that when London Bridge was sold and moved brick-by-brick to Arizona to make way for a replacement, the Americans thought they were getting Tower Bridge. For a deeper understanding of the history and technology behind the bridge, the **Tower Bridge Experience** offers a cutesy introduction. Don't expect too much of the view—iron latticework gets in the way. *(Entrance to the Tower Bridge Experience is through the west side (upriver) of the North Tower. Tube: Tower Hill or London Bridge. ☎ 7378 1928, lifting schedule 7378 7700. Open Apr.-Oct. daily 10am-6:30pm; Nov.-Mar. 9:30am-6pm; last admission 1¼hr. before close. £6.25, concessions £4.25, families £18.25.)*

OTHER LOCAL SIGHTS. St. Stephen Walbrook (built 1672-9) is arguably Wren's finest church. The plain exterior gives no inkling of the wide dome that floats above Henry Moore's mysterious 1985 freeform altar. *(39 Walbrook. Tube: Bank or Cannon St. ☎ 7283 4444. Open M-Th 9am-4pm, F 9am-3pm. Free.)* The most famous modern structure in the City is **Lloyd's of London,** built by Richard Rogers in 1986. With metal ducts, lifts, and chutes on the outside, it wears its heart (or at least its internal organs) on its sleeve. *(Leadenhall. Tube: Bank.)* **All Hallows-by-the-Tower** bears its longevity with pride, incorporating a Saxon arch from AD 675 and a Roman pavement in the undercroft "museum." Samuel Pepys witnessed the Great Fire from its tower, while American associations include John Quincy Adams, who married here, and William Penn, baptized here in 1644. *(Byward St. Tube: Tower Hill. ☎ 7481 2928. Church open M-F 9am-5:45pm, Sa-Su 10am-5pm. Crypt M-Sa 11am-4pm, Su 1-4pm. Free.)*

LONDON

THE SOUTH BANK

LONDON EYE. Also known as the Millennium Wheel, at 443 ft. the London Eye is the biggest observational wheel in the world. The ellipsoid glass "pods" give uninterrupted views from the top of each 30min. revolution: on clear days you can see to Windsor in the west. *(Jubilee Gardens, between County Hall and the Festival Hall. Tube: Waterloo or Westminster. ☎ (0870) 500 0600. Open late May to early Sept. daily 9:30am-10pm; Apr. to late May and rest of Sept. 10:30am-8pm; Jan.-Mar. and Oct.-Dec. 10:30am-7pm; ticket office opens 30min. earlier. Ticket office in corner of County Hall; advance booking recommended. July-Sept. £9.50, seniors £7.50; Oct.-June £9, £7; children £5 year-round.)*

THE SOUTH BANK CENTRE. Sprawling on either side of Waterloo Bridge along the Thames, this symphony of concrete is Britain's premier cultural center. Its nucleus is the **Royal Festival Hall,** a classic piece of white 1950s architecture. Close by the Festival Hall, the **Purcell Room** and **Queen Elizabeth Hall** cater for smaller concerts, while just behind it the spiky ceiling of the **Hayward Gallery** shelters excellent shows of modern art. On the embankment beneath Waterloo Bridge, the **National Film Theatre** offers London's most varied cinematic fare, while past the bridge looms the **National Theatre.** To find out how one of the world's largest, most modern theaters operates, join an hour-long backstage tour. *(On the riverbank between Hungerford and Waterloo Bridges. Tube: Waterloo or Embankment. For Festival Hall, Purcell Room, Queen Elizabeth Hall, and National Film Theatre, see p. 142; for Hayward Gallery, see p. 136. National Theatre ☎ 7452 3400. Tours M-Sa 10:15am, 12:15 or 12:30, 5:15 or 5:30pm, depending on performances. £5, students and seniors £4.25.)*

TATE MODERN AND THE MILLENNIUM BRIDGE. Squarely opposite each other on Bankside are the biggest success and most abject failure of London's millennial celebrations. **Tate Modern** (see p. 132), created from the shell of the former Bankside power station, is visually arresting as its contents are thought-provoking. Built to link the Tate to the City, the **Millennium Bridge** was not only completed six months too late for the Y2K festivities, but following a literally shaky debut closed down within days. Engineers promised to fix it in weeks, but a year later no progress had been made; with luck, it will finally reopen sometime in 2002. *(Queen's Walk, Bankside. Tube: Southwark, Blackfriars, or (across the bridge) St. Paul's.)*

SHAKESPEARE'S GLOBE THEATRE. In the shadow of Tate Modern, the half-timbered Globe (opened 1997) rises just 650m from where the original burned down in 1613. Try to arrive in time for a tour of the theater itself, given mornings only during the performance season. *(Bankside. Tube: Southwark or London Bridge. ☎ 7902 1500. Open May-Sept. daily 9am-noon and 1-4pm (exhibition only); Oct.-Apr. 10am-5pm. £7.50, students £6, children £5, families £23; 50p less when no tour operates. See also p. 142.)* Nearby lie the ruins of the 1587 **Rose Theatre,** Bankside's first, where both Shakespeare and Marlowe performed. The site was rediscovered in 1989; not much is left, though the outline is clearly visible. *(56 Park St. ☎ 7593 0026. Open daily 11am-5pm. £4, students and seniors £3, children £2, families £10; £1 off with same-day Globe exhibition ticket.)*

SOUTHWARK CATHEDRAL. Though Christians have worshipped here since AD 606, the church of St. Saviour only made cathedral status in 1905. The new **Visitor Centre** houses a hi-tech historical exhibition on the area. The oldest complete part of the cathedral itself is the **retrochoir,** separated from the main choir by a 16th-century **altar screen.** The **north aisle** holds the richly painted tomb of John Gower (d. 1408), the "first English poet," while across the 19th-century nave, the **south aisle** bears a window and monument to William Shakespeare, whose brother Ed is buried here. *(Montague Close. Tube: London Bridge. ☎ 7367 6700. Open daily 8am-6pm; exhibition 10am-6pm. Cathedral free (£2.50 donation); exhibition £3, seniors and students £2.50, children £1.50, families £12. Camera permit £1.50, video £5.)*

HMS BELFAST. This enormous battleship led the bombardment of Normandy during D-Day and supported UN forces in Korea before graciously retiring in 1965. Kids will love clambering over the decks and aiming the anti-aircraft guns at dive-bombing seagulls. Dozens of narrow passages, steep staircases, and ladders make exploring the boat a physical challenge in itself. *(At the end of Morgans Ln. off Tooley St. Tube: London Bridge. ☎ 7940 6300. Open Mar.-Oct. daily 10am-6pm; Nov.-Feb. 10am-5pm; last admission 45min. before close. £5.40, students and seniors £4, children free.)*

OTHER SOUTH BANK SIGHTS. County Hall, almost opposite the Houses of Parliament, houses two of London's most advertised and least impressive sights, the **London Aquarium** and **Dalí Universe.** *(Westminster Bridge Rd. Tube: Westminster or Waterloo. Aquarium: ☎ 7967 8000. Open daily 10am-6pm, last admission 5pm. £8.50, students and seniors £6.50, children £5, families £24. Dalí: ☎ 7620 2720. Open daily 10am-5:30pm. £8.50, students and seniors £6, children £5, families £22.)* **Vinopolis** is a Dionysian Disneyland offering patrons an interactive (yes, that means samples) tour of the world's wine regions. *(1 Bank End. Tube: London Bridge. ☎ (0870) 444 4777. Open M 11am-8pm, Tu-F and Su 11am-6pm, Sa 11am-9pm. £11.50, seniors £10.50, children £5.)* The **Old Operating Theatre and Herb Garret** is bizarrely located in the loft of an 18th-century church. The oldest operating theater in the world is accompanied by a fearsome array of saws, knives, and primitive surgical instruments, such as a trepanning drill, used to relieve headaches by boring a hole in the skull. *(9a St. Thomas's St. Tube: London Bridge. ☎ 7955 4791. Open daily 10:30am-4:45pm. £3.50, concessions £2.50, children £1.75, families £8.)* For less authentic horrors, the **London Dungeon** is always mobbed with thousands of kids waiting to revel in tasteful displays about Jack the Ripper, the Fire of London, and anything else remotely connected to horror and Britain. *(28-34 Tooley St. Tube: London Bridge. ☎ (0870) 846 0666. Open mid-July to Sept. daily 10:30am-8pm (last admission); Apr. to mid-July and Sept.-Oct. 10:30am-5:30pm; Nov.-Mar. 10:30am-5pm. £11, students £9.50, seniors and children £7; advance tickets £1 extra.)*

WESTMINSTER

WHITEHALL

A long stretch of imposing facades housing government ministries, "Whitehall" is synonymous with the British civil service. From 1532 until a devastating fire in 1698, however, it was the home of the monarchy and one of the greatest palaces in Europe. Today all that remains are Henry VIII's wine cellars, hidden under the monolithic **Ministry of Defence** and viewable only on written application, and Inigo Jones's **Banqueting House** (see below). Opposite Banqueting House, the burnished hussars of the Household Cavalry stand guard at **Horseguards.** The guard is changed weekdays at 11am, Saturdays at 10am, with a dismount for inspection daily at 4pm. Where Whitehall becomes Parliament St., gates mark the entrance to **Downing Street;** no. 10 is the official residence of the Prime Minister, but Tony Blair's family is too big, so he's swapped with Chancellor Gordon Brown, at no 11. *(Between Trafalgar Sq. and Parliament Sq. Tube: Westminster, Embankment, or Charing Cross.)*

BANQUETING HOUSE. All that remains of the Palace of Whitehall, Banqueting House was built in 1622 by Inigo Jones for James I. Essentially a one-up, one-down affair—the vaulted undercroft below and the great hall above—Banqueting House is still used for state dinners. Charles I commissioned Rubens to paint the great ceiling panels with scenes extolling the monarchy; unfortunately for him, Parliament wasn't impressed, and on January 27, 1649, Charles stepped out of the window on the first-floor landing onto the scaffold where he was beheaded. *(Whitehall, opposite Horseguards. ☎ 7930 4179. Open M-Sa 10am-5pm, last admission 4:30pm. £3.90, students and seniors £3.10, children £2.30.)*

PARLIAMENT SQUARE

Laid out in 1750, Parliament Square rapidly became the focal point for opposition to the government. Today, demonstrators are dissuaded by a continuous stream of heavy traffic, with no pedestrian crossings. Standing opposite the **Houses of Parliament** (see p. 111), Winston Churchill was famously given a turf mohican during the May 2000 anti-capitalist demonstrations. South of the square rises **Westminster Abbey** (see p. 114) while to the west looms the great dome of **Methodist Central Hall,** where the United Nations first met in 1946. (Tube: Westminster.)

ST. MARGARET'S WESTMINSTER. Literally in Westminster Abbey's shadow, since 1614 St. Margaret's has been the official church of the House of Commons. The **Milton Window** (1888), to the right of the main entrance above the North Aisle, shows the poet (married here in 1608) dictating *Paradise Lost* to his daughters. The **East Window** above the altar celebrates the wedding of Henry VIII to Catherine of Aragon. Opposite, the **West Window** commemorates Sir Walter Raleigh, executed across the street in 1618 and now lying in the chancel. *(Tube: Westminster.* ☎ *7222 6382. Open M-F 9:30am-3:45pm, Sa 9:30am-1:45pm, Su 2-5pm. Free.)*

JEWEL TOWER. Cut off from the Houses of Parliament by Millbank, Jewel Tower is a lone survivor of the medieval Palace of Westminster. Built by Edward III in 1365-6, from 1621 to 1869 it was used to store the parliamentary archives (now in Victoria Tower, across the street). These days it houses the **Parliament Past and Present** exhibition, which explains the history and workings of Parliament. *(Tube: Westminster.* ☎ *7222 2219. Open Apr.-Sept. daily 10am-6pm; Oct. 10am-5pm; Nov.-Mar. 10am-4pm. £1.60, students and seniors £1.20, children 80p, under 5 free.)*

OTHER WESTMINSTER SIGHTS

WESTMINSTER CATHEDRAL. Following Henry VIII's break with Rome, London's Catholic community remained without a cathedral for over three centuries until 1887, when the Church purchased a derelict prison as the site from which the neo-Byzantine church was to rise. The architect's plan outran available funds; by 1903, when work stopped, the interior remained unfinished. The three blackened brick domes contrast dramatically with the swirling marble of the lower walls and the magnificence of the side chapels. A lift carries visitors up the striped 273 ft. **bell tower** for a view of Westminster, the river, and Kensington. *(Cathedral Piazza, off Victoria St. Tube: Victoria.* ☎ *7798 9055. Cathedral open daily 7am-7pm. Suggested donation £2. Bell Tower open Apr.-Nov. daily 9am-5pm; Dec.-Mar. Th-Su £2, concessions £1, families £5.)*

THE ROYAL MEWS. Doubling as a museum and a working carriage house, the Mews' main attraction is the Queen's collection of coaches, from the "glass coach" used to carry Diana to her wedding to the four-ton **Gold State Coach.** Kids will enjoy a chance to get up close to the carriage horses, each named personally by the Queen. As a working mews, horses and carriages are liable to be absent without notice, and opening hours are subject to change. *(Buckingham Palace Rd. Tube: St. James's Park or Victoria.* ☎ *7839 1377. Open M-Th noon-4pm, last admission 3:30pm. £4, seniors £3.60, under 17 £2.60, families £11.80.)*

ST. JAMES'S PARK AND GREEN PARK. The run-up to Buckingham Palace is flanked by two expanses of greenery. **St. James's Park,** acquired along with St. James's Palace by Henry VIII in 1531, owes its informal appearance to a re-landscaping by Nash in 1827. Across the Mall, **Green Park** is the creation of Charles II; "Constitution Hill" refers not to the king's interest in political theory, but to his daily exercises. *(The Mall. Open daily 5am-midnight.)*

CHELSEA

*The only **Tube** station in Chelsea is Sloane Sq.; from here **buses** #11, 19, 22, 211, and 319 run down the King's Rd.*

The stomping ground of the Sloane Ranger—well-bred, dim-witted aristocratic scions—Chelsea nevertheless retains a unique vibrancy. Henry VIII's right-hand man (and later victim) Sir Thomas More was the first big-name resident in the 16th century, but it was in the 19th century that the neighborhood became an artistic hothouse: **Cheyne Walk** was home to Turner, George Eliot, Dante Gabriel Rossetti, and more recently Mick Jagger (at no. 48); Oscar Wilde, Sargent, Whistler, and Bertrand Russell lived on **Tite Street;** while Brunel, Mark Twain, Henry James, T.S. Eliot, and William Morris were also Chelsea residents at one time.

THE ROYAL HOSPITAL. Charles II established the Hospital—designed by Christopher Wren—as a retirement community for army veterans ("hospital" meaning a place of shelter) in 1692. It remains a military institution, with the uniformed "Chelsea Pensioners" arranged in companies under the command of a retired officer. French canons from Waterloo guard its open south side of **Figure Court,** named for Grinling Gibbons's statue of Charles II, while the north is divided between the **chapel** and the **Great Hall.** The outhouses harbor a small **museum,** detailing the history and the hospital's everyday life, and a display of medals. *(Royal Hospital Rd. ☎ 7881 5204. Open M-Sa 10am-noon and 2-4pm; Apr.-Sept. also Su 2-4pm. Free.)*

CHELSEA PHYSIC GARDEN. Founded in 1673 to provide medicinal herbs, the Physic Garden was the staging post from which tea was introduced to India and cotton to America. Today it remains a living repository of all manner of plants, from opium poppies to carrots. *(66 Royal Hospital Rd.; entrance on Swan Walk. ☎ 7352 5646. Open early Apr. to late Oct. W noon-5pm, Su 2-6pm; M-F noon-5pm during Chelsea Flower Show (late May) and Chelsea Festival (mid-June). £4, students and children £2.)*

OTHER CHELSEA SIGHTS. With four sides at 90°, **Sloane Sq.** serves as the eastern end of the **King's Road,** until 1829 a private royal route from Hampton Court to Whitehall. The 60s were launched here in 1955 when Mary Quant dropped the miniskirt on an unsuspecting world; two decades later the Sex Pistols snarled their way out of Malcolm McLaren's boutique at the **World's End,** 430 King's Rd. In **Carlyle's House,** which remains much as it was during Thomas Carlyle's lifetime, the historian, writer, and "Sage of Chelsea" entertained Dickens, Tennyson, George Eliot, and Ruskin. *(24 Cheyne Row. ☎ 7352 7087. Open Apr.-Oct. W-Su 11am-5pm, last admission 4:30pm. £3.50, under 16 £1.75.)* Where Cheyne Walk spills onto Chelsea Embankment stands **Chelsea Old Church,** looking remarkably new following post-WWII restoration. Fortunately, the bombs spared the southern chapel, designed by Thomas More in the 16th century. Henry VIII is reported to have married Jane Seymour here before the official wedding took place. *(Old Church St. Open Tu-F 1:30-5:30pm and for services Su 8, 10, 11am, 12:15, 6pm.)*

KNIGHTSBRIDGE AND BELGRAVIA

Now home to London's most expensive stores, it's hard to imagine that in the 18th century **Knightsbridge** was a racy district known for its taverns and its highwaymen. Neighboring **Belgravia** was catapulted to respectability by the presence of royalty at nearby Buckingham Palace in the 1820s. **Belgrave Square,** the setting for *My Fair Lady,* is the most impressive of the set-pieces, now so expensive that the aristocracy has had to sell out to foreign governments—this is embassyland.

APSLEY HOUSE. "No. 1, London" was bought in 1817 by the Duke of Wellington, whose heirs still occupy the top floor. On display is Wellington's outstanding collection of art, much of it given in gratitude by the crowned heads of Europe following the battle of Waterloo. The majority of paintings hang in the **Waterloo Gallery,** where the Duke would hold his annual Waterloo banquet. In the basement an entire cabinet is filled with Wellington's medals, while another holds newspaper caricatures from Wellington's later political career—his nickname "the Iron Duke" comes not from his steadfastness in battle, but from the metal shutters put up to protect him from egg-throwing political opponents. *(Hyde Park Corner. Tube: Hyde Park Corner. ☎ 7499 5676 Open Tu-Su 11am-5pm. £4.50, students and seniors £3, children free.)*

THE WELLINGTON ARCH. At the center of London's most infamous intersection, the Wellington Arch was built in 1825 as the "Green Park Arch." In 1838 it was dedicated to the Duke of Wellington and eight years later encumbered by a gigantic statue of the Duke, much to the horror of its architect, Decimus Burton. Wellington's statue was finally replaced in 1910 by the *Quadriga of Peace,* designed by army vet Adrian Joens. Inside the arch, exhibitions on the building's history and the changing nature of war memorials play second fiddle to the viewing platforms. *(Hyde Park Corner. Tube: Hyde Park Corner. ☎ 7930 2726. Open Apr.-Sept. W-Su 10am-6pm; Oct. 10am-5pm; Nov.-Mar. 10am-4pm. £2.50, students and seniors £1.90, children £1.30.)*

KENSINGTON AND EARL'S COURT

Nobody took much notice of Kensington before 1689, when the newly crowned William III and Mary II moved into Kensington Palace and high society tagged along. The next significant date in Kensington's history was 1851, when the Great Exhibition brought in enough money to finance its museums and colleges. In Kensington's southwestern corner, Earl's Court is a grimier district that earned the nickname "Kangaroo Valley" in the 1960s and 1970s for its popularity with Australian expats.

KENSINGTON PALACE. In 1689, William and Mary commissioned Christopher Wren to remodel Nottingham House into a proper palace; parts are still in use as a royal residence—Princess Diana was the most famous recent inhabitant. Inside, the **Royal Ceremonial Dress Collection** displays the intricate costumes required of courtiers in the 19th and early 20th century, together with a number of the Queen's demure evening gowns and Diana's racier numbers. After the dresses, you enter the **State Apartments.** Hanoverian economy is evident in the *trompe l'oeil* decoration throughout, carried out by William Kent for George I. *(Eastern edge of Kensington Gardens; enter through the park. Tube: High St. Kensington or Queensway. ☎ 7937 9561. Open Mar.-Oct. daily 10am-5pm; Nov.-Feb. 10am-4pm; last admission 1hr. before close. £8.80, students and seniors £6.90, children £6.30, families £26.80.)*

HYDE PARK AND KENSINGTON GARDENS. Surrounded by London's wealthiest neighborhoods, giant Hyde Park has served as the model for city parks around the world, including Central Park in New York and Paris's Bois de Boulogne. **Kensington Gardens,** contiguous with Hyde Park and originally part of it, was created in the late 17th century when William and Mary set up in Kensington Palace. Officially known as the Long Water west of the Serpentine Bridge, the 41-acre **Serpentine** was created in 1730. From the number of people who pay to row and swim here, you'd think it was the fountain of youth. South of Long Water, some way from the lake itself, the **Serpentine Gallery** displays contemporary art (see p. 137). Running south of the Serpentine, the dirt track of **Rotten Row** stretches westward from Hyde Park Corner. Originally *Route du Roi* or "King's Road," it was the first English thoroughfare lit at night to deter crime. At the northeastern corner of the park, near Marble Arch, proselytizers, politicos, and flat-out crazies dispense their knowledge to bemused tourists at **Speaker's Corner** on Sundays. *(Framed by Kensington Rd., Knightsbridge, Park Ln., and Bayswater Rd. Tube: Queensway, Lancaster Gate, Marble Arch, Hyde Park Corner, or High St. Kensington. ☎ 7298 2100. Hyde Park open daily 5am-midnight. Kensington Gdns. open dawn-dusk. Both free.)*

"ALBERTOPOLIS". The Great Exhibition of 1851 was the brainchild of Prince Albert, Queen Victoria's husband; by the time the exhibition closed, a year later, six million people (as many as visited the Millennium Dome in 2000) had passed through, and the organizers were left with a $200,000 profit. Again at Albert's suggestion, the cash was used to buy 86 acres of land in South Kensington to be dedicated to institutions promoting British arts and sciences. Along with the trio of the **Victoria and Albert Museum** (p. 133), the **Science Museum** (p. 135), and the **Natural History Museum** (p. 135), most famous is the **Royal Albert Hall,** an all-purpose venue that has hosted a full-length marathon and the first public display of electric lighting, as well as the annual **Proms** music festival (see p. 144). The odd array of discs hanging from the ceiling is an attempt to solve the hall's booming echo. *(Kensington Gore. Tube: South Kensington or High St. Kensington. Box office ☎ 7589 8212.)* Opposite the hall, the prince is commemorated by Gilbert Scott's **Albert Memorial,** either nightmarish or fairy-tale, depending on your opinion of Victorian High Gothic. *(Kensington Gore. 45min. tours Su 2 and 3pm; £3.50, concessions £3. Reservations ☎ 7495 0916.)*

MARYLEBONE AND REGENT'S PARK

Marylebone's most famous resident (and address) never existed; **221b Baker Street** was the fictional lodging house of Sherlock Holmes. 221 Baker St. is actually the headquarters of the Abbey National bank (there was never a 221b). A little farther down the street, the **Sherlock Holmes Museum** (see p. 135) gives its address out as 221b, although some sleuthing will reveal that it in fact stands at no. 239.

MADAME TUSSAUD'S AND THE LONDON PLANETARIUM. Back in the 18th century, Mrs. T got her big break with a string of commissions for death masks of guillotined aristos, including a freshly beheaded **Marie Antoinette.** Despite its revolutionary beginnings, the display of waxworks positively fawns over royalty and other more and less worthy celebrities. Like a giant green silicon-filled breast, the Planetarium rises alluringly next to Madame Tussaud's masculine bulk. As cinematic spectacle, it's tough to beat, but entertainment values have completely swamped any educational ideals the Planetarium formerly aspired to. Unless you enjoy spending hours waiting outside, book ahead or get together with at least 9 others and save time and money by using the group entrance. *(Marylebone Rd. Tube: Baker St. ☎(0870) 400 3000. Open M-F 10am-5:30pm, Sa-Su 9:30am-5:30pm. Planetarium shows 2 per hr. Tickets sold at both Madame Tussaud's and Planetarium. Madame Tussaud's £11.50, seniors £9, children £8. Planetarium £6.50, £5.10, £4.35. Combined £14, £10.80, £9.50. Advance booking £1 extra; groups approx. £1 less per person.)*

REGENT'S PARK. Perhaps London's most attractive and most popular park, with a wide range of landscapes from soccer-scarred fields to Italian-style formal gardens. It's all very different from John Nash's vision of wealthy villas hidden among exclusive gardens; fortunately for us common folk, Parliament intervened in 1811 and guaranteed the space would remain open to all. *(Tube: Baker St., Regent's Park, Gt. Portland St., or Camden Town. ☎7486 7905. Open daily from 6am. Seasonal closings: Jan. 6pm; Feb. 7pm; Mar. 8pm (after clocks change); Apr. and Aug. 9pm; May-July 9:30pm; Sept. 8pm; Oct. 7pm (5:30pm after clocks change); Nov.-Dec. 4:30pm. Free.)*

BLOOMSBURY

ACADEMIA. The strip of land along **Gower St.** and immediately to its west is London's academic heartland. Established in 1828 to provide an education to those excluded from Oxford and Cambridge, **University College London** was the first in Britain to admit Catholics, Jews, and women. The embalmed body of founder **Jeremy Bentham** has occupied the South Cloister since 1850. *(Main entrance on Gower St. South Cloister entrance through the courtyard. Tube: Warren St. or Euston Sq.)* Now the administrative HQ of the University of London, **Senate House** was the model for the Ministry of Truth in *1984*—George Orwell worked there as part of the BBC propaganda unit in WWII. *(At the southern end of Malet St. Tube: Goodge St. or Russell Sq.)*

▨**BRITISH LIBRARY.** Castigated by traditionalists for being too modern and by modernists for being too traditional, since its 1998 opening the new British Library building has won plaudits from visitors and users alike for its stunning interior. The heart of the library is underground, with space for 12 million books on 200 mi. of shelving; the above-ground brick building is home to the reading rooms, an engrossing museum (see p. 135), and 65,000 volumes of George III's **King's Library,** displayed in a glass cube. *(96 Euston Rd. Tube: King's Cross. ☎7412 7332. Tours M, W, F 3pm; Sa 10:30am and 3pm; £5, concessions £3.50. Tours including reading rooms Tu 6:30pm and Su 11:30am and 3pm; £6, £4.50. Reservations recommended for all tours. Open M and W-F 9:30am-6pm, Tu 9:30am-8pm, Sa 9:30am-5pm, Su 11am-5pm. Free.)*

OTHER BLOOMSBURY SIGHTS. Next to the modern British Library are the soaring Gothic spires of **St. Pancras Station.** Formerly housing the Midland Grand Hotel, today Sir George Gilbert Scott's facade is but a hollow shell awaiting redevelopment as a Marriott. *(Euston Rd. Tube: King's Cross/St. Pancras.)* Started in 1816, **St. Pancras Parish Church** is a replica of the 2500-year-old Erectheon in Athens, with an octagonal tower based on the Acropolis's Tower of the Winds. *(On the corner of Euston Rd. and Upper Woburn Pl. Tube: Euston.)* The shrapnel-scarred Corinthian portico of Hawksmoor's 1730 **St. George's Bloomsbury** is in desperate need of repair, but the interior is in perfect condition. Anthony Trollope was baptized before the gilded mahogany altar, also the setting of Dickens's *Bloomsbury Christening. (Bloomsbury Way. Tube: Russell Square. Open M-Sa 9:30am-5:30pm.)*

NORTH LONDON

CAMDEN TOWN

An island of good, honest tawdriness in an increasingly affluent sea, Camden Town has effortlessly thrown off attempts at gentrification thanks to the ever-growing **Camden Market** (see p. 140). Now London's fourth most popular tourist attraction, on weekends the market presents a variety of life unmatched even by **London Zoo**, a serene jaunt up the **Regent's Canal** from the market's nerve center in Camden Lock.

HAMPSTEAD

Hampstead first caught the attention of well-heeled Londoners in the 17th century, when it became fashionable to take the waters at Hampstead Wells, on the site of **Well Walk** today. In the 1930s, Hampstead found itself at the forefront of a European avant-garde in flight from fascism. Residents such as Aldous Huxley, Piet Mondrian, Barbara Hepworth, and Sigmund Freud lent the area a cachet that grows to this day.

HAMPSTEAD HEATH. Hampstead Heath is one of the last remaining traditional commons in England, open to all since at least 1312. **Parliament Hill** is the highest open space in London, with excellent views across the city. Farther north, ◨**Kenwood** is a picture-perfect 18th-century country estate, designed by Robert Adams for the first Earl of Mansfield and home to the impressive **Iveagh Bequest** (see p. 135) of Old Masters. *(Tube: Hampstead or Rail: Hampstead Heath. Heath open 24hr. Kenwood open daily 8am-8pm; Oct.-Mar. closes 4pm.)*

KEATS HOUSE. While living here between 1818 and 1820, John Keats produced some of his finest work, including Ode to a Nightingale and fell in love with and married his neighbor, Fanny Brawne. Inside, poems lie scattered about the reconstructed rooms. *(Keats Grove. Tube: Hampstead or Rail: Hampstead Heath. ☎ 7435 2062. Tours Sa-Su 3pm. Open May-Oct. Tu-Su noon-5pm. £3, students and seniors £1.50, children free.)*

OTHER HAMPSTEAD SIGHTS. Looking like an unimposing 1950s-style miniblock, **Two Willow Road** was built in 1939 as the avant-garde home of architect Ernö Goldfinger. Ian Fleming hated it so much, he named a *James Bond* villain after him. From within, the house is a masterpiece of modernist living, designed by Goldfinger down to the last teaspoon. *(Off South End Green, near Rail: Hampstead Heath (Zone 3); 15min. walk from Hampstead Tube (Zone 2). ☎ 7435 6166. Open Apr.-Oct. Th-Sa noon-5pm; 1hr. guided tours every 45min. 12:15-4pm. £4.30, children £2.15.)*

WEST LONDON

ROYAL BOTANICAL GARDENS, KEW. Founded in 1759 by Princess Augusta as an addendum to Kew Palace, the Royal Botanical Gardens have since expanded to swallow the palace grounds entirely, now extending in a 300-acre swathe along the Thames. No ordinary park, Kew is a leading center for plant science, thanks in no small part to its living collection of thousands of flowers, fruits, trees, and vegetables from across the globe. The three great **conservatories** and their smaller offshoots, housing a staggering variety of plants ill-suited to the English climate, are the highlight of the gardens. Most famous is the steamy **Palm House**, home to "The Oldest Pot Plant In The World," which is not at all what it sounds like but interesting nonetheless. The **Temperate House** is the largest ornamental greenhouse in the world, although the **Princess of Wales Conservatory,** opened by Diana but named for Augusta, has a larger area, thanks to its innovative structure. The interior is divided into 10 different climate zones, including one entirely devoted to orchids. *(Main entrance and visitors center is at Victoria Gate. Tube: Kew Gardens (Zone 3). ☎8940 5622. "Explorer" hop-on/hop-off shuttle makes 35min. rounds of the gardens; first shuttle departs Victoria Gate 11am, last 3:35pm. £2.50, children £1.50. Open Apr.-Aug. M-F 9:30am-6:30pm, Sa-Su 9:30-7:30pm; Sept.-Oct. daily 9:30am-6pm; Nov.-Mar. 9:30am-4:15pm. Greenhouses close Apr.-Oct. 5:30pm; Nov.-Mar. 3:45pm; last admission 30min. before close. £6.50, "late entry" (45min. before close) £4.50; students and seniors £4.50; children free.)*

HAMPTON COURT PALACE. Although a monarch hasn't lived here for 250 years, Hampton Court exudes regal charm. Cardinal Wolsey built the first palace here in 1514, showing the young Henry VIII how to act the part of a splendid and powerful ruler—a lesson Henry learned all too well, confiscating it in 1528, and embarking on a massive building program. In 1689, William III and Mary II employed Christopher Wren to bring Hampton Court up to date, but less than 50 years later George II abandoned the palace for good. The **palace** is divided into six 45min.-1hr. routes, all starting at **Clock Court,** where you can pick up a program of the day's events and an audioguide. In **Henry VIII's State Apartments,** only the massive Great Hall and exquisite Chapel Royal hint at the magnificence of Henry's court. Below, the **Tudor Kitchens** offer insight into how Henry ate himself to a 54" waist. Predating Henry's additions, the 16th-century **Wolsey Rooms** are complemented by Renaissance masterpieces, including a boyish self-portrait by Raphael. Most impressive are Wren's **King's Apartments,** restored following a 1986 fire to their original appearance under William III. Mary II's death postponed the completion of the **Queen's Apartments** until 1734. Last and least, the **Georgian Rooms** were created by William Kent for George II's family. Scarcely less impressive are the **gardens.** Secreted away in the neighboring Lower Orangery is Mantegna's series **The Triumphs of Caesar** (1484-1505). One of the most important works of the Italian Renaissance, it's displayed in semi-darkness to protect the fragile colors. North of the palace, the **Wilderness,** a pseudo-natural area earmarked for picnickers, holds the ever-popular **maze,** planted in 1714. Its small size belies its devilish design; "solve" it by getting to the middle and back. *(Take the train from Waterloo (32min., 2 per hr., day return £4) or a boat from Westminster Pier (4hr.; 4 per day; £10, return £14); to leave time to see the palace, take the boat one way and return by train. ☎(020) 8781 9500. Open mid-Mar. to late Oct. M 10:15am-6pm, Tu-Su 9:30am-6pm; late Oct. to mid-Mar. until 4:30pm; last admission 45min. before close. Palace and gardens £10.80, students and seniors £8.30, children £7.20, families £32.20. Maze only £2.90, children £1.90. Gardens (excluding south gardens) free.)*

EAST LONDON

WHITECHAPEL AND THE EAST END

The boundary between the East End and City of London is as sharp today as it was when Aldgate and Bishopsgate were real gateways in the wall separating the rich and powerful City from the poorer quarters to the east. The best reason to visit are its vibrant **markets** (see p. 140), which draw shoppers from all over London.

CHRIST CHURCH. Now an island of Anglicanism amid a spectrum of other traditions, Christ Church is Nicholas Hawksmoor's largest church and considered by many to be his masterpiece. Alas, this 1714 building is in a sorry state; derelict since 1957, only now is it slowly being restored to its former glory. *(Commercial St., opposite Spitalfields market. Tube: Liverpool St. ☎7247 7202.)*

BRICK LANE. In Brick Lane, even the street signs are written in Bengali: this is the epicenter of Bangladeshi Britain. Most famous for its vibrant Sunday market and scores of curry houses, Brick Ln. has recently become the unlikely center of the East End's creative renaissance: the former **Truman Brewery,** at no. 91 and 150, is now occupied by design and media consultants, sleek stores, and a cafe-bar-club trio that together form one of London's hottest nightspots. *(Tube: Shoreditch (open only in rush hour), Aldgate East, or Liverpool St.)*

DOCKLANDS

Countering heritage-obsessed Greenwich across the Thames, brash young Docklands is the largest commercial development in Europe. From the 19th century to the 1960s, this man-made archipelago was the commercial heart of the British Empire, with cargoes from across the world being loaded and unloaded in a never-ending stream of activity. In 1981, the Conservative government founded the London Docklands Development Corporation (LDDC) to redevelop the area. The showpiece is **Canary Wharf,** with Britain's highest skyscraper, the 800 ft., pyramid-topped **One Canada Square.** Under the tower, the vast **Canada Place** and **Cabot Square** malls suck in shoppers from all over London, while the dockside plaza is lined with pricey corporate drinking and eating haunts. *(Tube/DLR: Canary Wharf.)*

GREENWICH

*All sights are closest to DLR: Cutty Sark. The **Greenwich Tourist Information Centre,** Pepys House, 2 Cutty Sark Gdns. (☎(0870) 608 2000) offers the usual services and a slick exhibition on local history. Walking tours leave the center daily at 12:15 and 2:15pm. (£4, students and seniors £3, children free.) Open daily 10am-5pm.*

Seat of the Royal Navy until 1998, Greenwich's position as the "home of time" is intimately connected to its maritime heritage—the Royal Observatory, site of the Prime Meridian, was originally founded to produce the accurate star-charts essential to navigation. If you're planning on spending a day or two sightseeing in Greenwich, consider buying the **Greenwich Passport Ticket,** giving entry to the National Maritime Museum, the Royal Observatory, and the Cutty Sark. *(Available at the Tourist Information Centre and participating sights. Ticket valid on any 2 days within 1 year of issue. £12, students and seniors £9.60.)*

RIVER TRIPS. Many people enhance their experience with a 1hr. **boat** trip from Westminster. Travelcard holders get 33% off riverboat fares. **City Cruises** operates from Westminster Pier to Greenwich via the Tower of London. *(☎7930 9033. Apr.-Oct. daily every 40min. 10am-5:40pm; last departure from Greenwich 5:35pm. £6, all-day "rover" ticket £7.50; children £3, £3.75; families £19.50.)* **Westminster Passenger Association** boats also head from Westminster Pier for Greenwich. Their "Sail&Rail" deal combines a one-way trip between Westminster and Greenwich with unlimited all-day travel on the DLR. *(☎7930 4097. Apr. to early Oct. daily every 3min. 10:30am-5pm, last departure from Greenwich 6pm, from Thames Barrier 3:30pm. To Greenwich £6, return £7.50, Sail&Rail £8.30; seniors £4.80, £6, £7; children £3, £3.75, £4.20; families £15.65, £19.50, £23.)*

ROYAL OBSERVATORY GREENWICH. Charles II founded the Royal Observatory in 1675 to find a way of calculating longitude at sea. Though the problem was eventually solved without reference to the sky, the connection lives on—the **Prime Meridian** (which marks 0° longitude) started out as the axis along which the astronomers' telescopes swung. Next to the meridian, Wren's **Flamstead House** retains its original interior in **Octagon Room,** with wraparound windows designed to accommodate long telescopes. Next to the Meridian Building's telescope display, climb the **Observatory Dome** to see the 28" telescope, constructed in 1893 and still the world's 7th largest refracting 'scope. It hasn't been used since 1954, but you can see the stars at the **Planetarium** in the South Building. *(At the top of Greenwich Park, a steep climb from the National Maritime Museum; for an easier walk, take The Avenue from the top of King William Walk. ☎8312 6565. Open daily 10am-5pm, last admission 4:30pm. £6, students £4.80, seniors and children free. With National Maritime Museum and Queen's House £10.50, £8.40, free. For Greenwich Passport ticket, see above. Planetarium £2 extra, concessions £1.50.)*

OTHER GREENWICH SIGHTS. Now part of the National Maritime Museum (see p. 136), Inigo Jones' **Queen's House** was commissioned in 1616 by Anne of Denmark, James I's queen, but only completed 22 years later for Charles I's wife Henrietta Maria. The house was built on the site of a gateway into the former Palace of Placentia, which explains the unusual design straddling a roadway. *(At the foot of Greenwich Park, on Trafalgar Rd.)* Last of the great tea clippers, even landlubbers will appreciate the **Cutty Sark**'s thoroughbred lines—she was the fastest ship of her time, making the round-trip from China in only 120 days. The deck and cabins have been restored to their 19th-century prime, while the hold houses an exhibition on the ship's history and a collection of figureheads. *(King William Walk, by Greenwich Pier. ☎8858 3445. Open daily 10am-5pm, last admission 4:30pm. £3.50, concessions £2.50, families £8.50.)* Close by the Cutty Sark, **Gypsy Moth** is a 54 ft. craft in which 64-year-old Francis Chichester sailed solo around the globe in 1966, covering nearly 30,000 mi.

ROYAL NAVAL COLLEGE. On the site of Henry VIII's Palace of Placentia, the Royal Naval College was founded by William III in 1694 as the Royal Hospital for Seamen, along the same lines as the army's Royal Hospital in Chelsea (see p. 125). In 1873 it was converted into the Royal Naval College, but in 1998 Greenwich's naval association ended when the University of Greenwich blew in. To Mary II's insistence that the new buildings not restrict the view from the Queen's House, Wren responded with two symmetrical wings separated by a colonnaded walkway. Buy a ticket to gain access to the **Painted Hall,** which took Sir James Thornhill 19 years to complete, and the simple **chapel,** with Benjamin West's painting of a shipwrecked St. Paul. *(King William Walk. ☎ 8269 4744. Open M-Sa noon-5pm, Su 12:30-5pm. £3, students and seniors £2, children free.)*

🏛 MUSEUMS AND GALLERIES

Centuries as the capital of an empire upon which the sun never set, together with a decidedly English penchant for collecting, have endowed London with a spectacular set of museums. Even better, after a decade which saw museum prices rise, the government plans to return all major collections to free admission by November 2001.

MAJOR COLLECTIONS
BRITISH MUSEUM

Great Russell St., Bloomsbury. Rear entrance on Montague St. Tube: Tottenham Court Rd., Russell Sq., or Holborn. ☎ 7323 8000. Audioguides £2.50. Free tours start at Great Court info desk. Highlights Tour (1½hr.): M-Sa 10:30am and 1pm; Su 11am, 12:30, 1:30, 2:30, 4pm. Advanced booking recommended. £7, concessions £4. Focus tour: (1hr.): M-W and Sa 3:15pm; Th-F 3:15, 5:30, 7pm; Su 4:30pm. £5, concessions £3. Open: Great Court M 9am-6pm, Tu-W and Su 9am-9pm, Th-Sa 9am-11pm. Galleries Sa-W 10am-5:30pm, Th-F 10am-8:30pm. Admission free; £2 suggested donation. Temporary exhibitions around £7, concessions £3.50.

The funny thing about the British Museum is that there's almost nothing British in it. Founded in 1753 as the personal collection of Sir Hans Sloane, in 1824 work started on the current Neoclassical building, which took another 30 years to construct. The opening of the **Great Court** in December 2000—the largest covered square in Europe—finally restored to the museum its focal point, the enormous rotunda of the **Reading Room,** whose desks have shouldered the weight of research by Marx, Lenin, and Trotsky, plus most major British writers and intellectuals.

The most famous items in the collection are found in the **Western Galleries;** here Room 4 harbors an unrivalled collection of Egyptian sculpture, including the **Rosetta Stone,** and Room 18 is entirely devoted to the **Elgin Marbles,** carved under the direction of Phidias, ancient Greece's greatest sculptor. Other highlights include giant **Assyrian** and **Babylonian** reliefs, the Roman **Portland Vase,** and bits and bobs from two Wonders of the Ancient World, the **Temple of Artemis** at Ephesus and the **Mausoleum of Halikarnassos.** Just when you thought you'd nailed antiquity, the **Northern Galleries** strike back with eight rooms of **mummies** and **sarcophagi** and nine of artifacts from the ancient Near East, including the **Oxus Treasure** from Iran. Also in the northern wing are the excellent **African** and **Islamic** galleries, the giant **Asian** collections, and the frankly pathetic **Americas** collection. The upper level of the **South** and **East Galleries** is dedicated to ancient and medieval **Europe,** some of which is actually British. The preserved body of **Lindow Man,** an Iron Age Celt, was sacrificed in a gruesome ritual (Room 50) and treasures excavated from the **Sutton Hoo Burial Ship** fill Room 41. Next door, Room 42 is home to the enigmatic **Lewis Chessmen,** an 800-year-old chess set mysteriously abandoned in Scotland (see p. 611).

NATIONAL GALLERY

Main entrance on north side of Trafalgar Sq. Tube: Charing Cross or Leicester Sq. ☎ 7747 2885. Audioguides free; £4 suggested donation. Tours start at Sainsbury Wing info desk. 1hr. gallery tours daily 11:30am and 2:30pm, W also 6:30pm; free. Open Th-Tu 10am-6pm, W 10am-9pm; Sainsbury Wing exhibitions until 10pm. Free; some temporary exhibitions £6-7, seniors £4-5, students and children £2-3.

The National Gallery was founded by an Act of Parliament in 1824, with 38 pictures displayed in a townhouse; it grew so rapidly in size and popularity that it was decided to construct a purpose-built gallery in 1838. The most recent extension is the massive **Sainsbury Wing,** which Prince Charles described as "a monstrous carbuncle on the face of a much-loved and elegant friend." Its climate-controlled rooms house the oldest, most fragile paintings, including the 14th-century English *Wilton Diptych*, Botticelli's *Venus and Mars*, and the *Leonardo Cartoon*, a detailed preparatory drawing by Leonardo da Vinci for a never-executed painting. With paintings from 1510 to 1600, the **West Wing** is dominated by the Italian **High Renaissance** and **early Flemish** art. In room 8, the artistic forces of Rome and Florence fight it out, with versions of the *Madonna and Child* by Raphael and Michelangelo. The **North Wing** spans the **17th century,** with an exceptional Flemish works spread over 10 rooms. Room 23 boasts 17 Rembrandts; the famous *Self Portrait at 63* gazes knowingly at his *Self Portrait at 34*. The **East Wing,** home to paintings from **1700-1900,** is the most popular in the gallery, thanks to the array of Impressionists including Van Gogh's *Sunflowers* in Room 45 and two of Monet's *Waterlilies* in Room 43. A reminder that there was art on this side of the Channel too, room 34 flies the flag with six luminescent Turners, from the stormy realism of *Dutch Boats in a Gale* to the blur of *Margate from the Sea*.

TATE BRITAIN

Millbank, near Vauxhall Bridge, in Westminster. Tube: Pimlico. ☎ 7887 8008. Audioguides £1. 1hr. tours free: highlights M-F 2:30 and 3:30pm, Sa 3pm; Turner M-F 11:30am. Open daily 10am-5pm. Free; special exhibitions £3-5.

The original Tate opened in 1897 as a showcase for "modern" British art—modern being extended back to 1790 to allow the inclusion of the Turner bequest of 282 oils and 19,000 watercolors. Before long, the remit had expanded to include contemporary art from all over the world, as well as British art from the Middle Ages on. Despite numerous expansions, it was clear that the dual role was too much for one building; the problem was resolved in 1999 with the relocation of almost all the contemporary art to the new Tate Modern at Bankside (see below). At the same time, the original Tate was rechristened Tate Britain, and rededicated to British art—a tag which also includes foreign artists working in Britain and Brits working abroad. The **Clore Gallery** continues to display the Turner Bequest; other painters to feature heavily are William Blake, John Constable, Joshua Reynolds, Dante Gabriel Rossetti, John Hodgkin, Lucien Freud, and David Hockney. Sculptors are less well represented, though Jacob Epstein's *Jacob and the Angel* (1940-41), in the Sackler Octagon, is a favorite with the crowds. Recent BritArt is mostly absent, having been transferred to the Tate Modern. However, the annual **Turner Prize** for contemporary art is still held here. The shortlisted works go on show from early November to mid-January every year.

TATE MODERN

Bankside, on the South Bank; main entrance on Holland St.; secondary entrance on Queen's Walk. Tube: Southwark or Blackfriar's. ☎ 7887 8888. Audioguides £1. Tours meet on the gallery concourses; free. History/Memory/Society 10:30am, level 3; Nude/Body/Action 11:30am, level 3; Landscape/Matter/Environment 2:30pm, level 5; Still Life/Object/Real Life 3:30pm, level 5. Open Su-Th 10am-6pm, F-Sa 10am-10pm. Free; special exhibitions £5-7, concessions £1 off.

Since opening in May 2000, Tate Modern has been credited with single-handedly reversing the long-term decline in museum-going numbers in Britain. The largest modern art museum in the world, its most striking aspect is the building, formerly Bankside power station. A conversion by Swiss firm Herzog and de Meuron has added a seventh floor with wraparound views of north and south London, and turned the old **Turbine Hall** into an immense atrium that often overpowers the installations commissioned for it. For all its popularity, the Tate has been criticized for its controversial curatorial method, which groups works according to themes rather than period or artist: the four overarching divisions are **Still Life/**

Object/Real Life and Landscape/Matter/Environment on level 3, and Nude/Action/Body and History/Memory/Society on level 5. Even skeptics admit that this arrangement throws up some interesting contrasts. The achievement of the thematic display is that it forces visitors into contact with an exceptionally wide range of art. It's now impossible to see the Tate's more famous pieces, which include Marcel Duchamp's *Large Glass* and Picasso's *Weeping Woman*, without also confronting challenging and invigorating works by little-known contemporary artists.

VICTORIA AND ALBERT

Main entrance on Cromwell Rd., in Kensington. Tube: South Kensington. ☎ 7942 2000. Free tours meet at rear of main entrance. Introductory tours daily 10:30, 11:30am, 1:30, 2:30pm; W also 4:30pm. Focus tours daily 12:30 and 1:30pm; subjects change every 6 weeks. Free 45min.-1hr. gallery talks daily 1pm. Talks, tours, and live music W from 6:30pm; last F of month also fashion shows, debates, and DJs. Open Th-Tu 10am-5:45pm, W and last F of month 10am-10pm. Free, except some special exhibitions.

Founded in 1852 to encourage excellence in art and design, the V&A is the largest museum of the decorative (and not so decorative) arts in the world—as befits an institution dedicated to displaying "the fine and applied arts of all countries, all styles, all periods." The subject of a £31 million refit, the vast **British Galleries** hold a series of recreated rooms from every period between 1500 and 1900, mirrored by the vast **Dress Collection**, a dazzling array of the finest *haute couture* through the ages.

The ground-floor **European** collections range from 4th-century Byzantine tapestry to Alfonse Mucha posters; if you only see one thing in the museum, make it the **Raphael Gallery**, hung with six massive paintings commissioned by Leo X in 1515. The **Sculpture Gallery**, home to Canova's *Three Graces* (1814-17), is not to be confused with the **Cast Courts**, a plaster-cast collection of the world's sculptural greatest hits, from Trajan's Column to Michelangelo's *David*. The V&A's **Asian** collections are particularly formidable—if the choice of objects occasionally seems to rely on national cliches (Indian temple carvings, Persian carpets, Chinese porcelain, Japanese ceramics), it says more about how the V&A has formed opinion than followed it.

In contrast to the geographically laid-out ground floor, the **upper levels** are mostly arranged by material; here you'll find specialist galleries devoted to everything from jewelry to musical instruments to stained glass. An exception to the materially themed arrangements is the large **20th-century** collections, featuring design classics from Salvador Dalí's 1936 "Mae West" sofa lips to a pair of 1990s rubber hotpants.

The 6-level **Henry Cole** wing is home to the V&A's collection of British paintings, including some 350 works by Constable and numerous Turners. Also here is a display of **Rodin** bronzes, donated by the artist in 1914, and the "world's greatest collection" of miniature portraits, including Holbein's **Anne of Cleves.** The Frank Lloyd Wright gallery contains a full-size recreation of the office commissioned by Edgar J. Kauffmann for his Pittsburgh department store in 1935.

OTHER PERMANENT COLLECTIONS

WEST END

■ **THE COURTAULD INSTITUTE GALLERIES.** The Courtauld's small but outstanding collection ranges from early 14th-century Italian works to 20th-century abstractions, focusing on Impressionism; masterpieces including Manet's *A Bar at the Follies Bergères*, van Gogh's *Self Portrait with Bandaged Ear*, and Cézanne's *The Card Players*. *(Somerset House, Strand. Tube: Charing Cross or Temple. ☎ 7848 2549. Open M-Sa 10am-6pm, Su noon-6pm. £4, UK seniors £3, under 18 free; free to all M 10am-2pm. Joint ticket with Gilbert Collection £7, seniors £5.)*

■ **LONDON'S TRANSPORT MUSEUM.** Informative *and* fun, kids and adults too will find themselves engrossed in the history of London's public transportation system. Clamber over dozens of buses before trying your hand at driving a Tube-train simulator. *(Southeast corner of Covent Garden Piazza. Tube: Covent Garden or Charing Cross. ☎ 7565 7299. Open Sa-Th 10am-6pm, F 11am-6pm; last admission 5:15pm. £6, students and seniors £4, children free with adult.)*

NATIONAL PORTRAIT GALLERY. This artistic *Who's Who* in Britain began in 1856 as "the fulfillment of a patriotic and moral ideal." To see the paintings in historical order, take the long escalator to the top-floor Tudor gallery and work your way around and down to the contemporary works on the ground floor. The size of the collection, however, makes a complete tour of the gallery a long and exhausting prospect, not helped by endless galleries of bewhiskered Victorians. Contemporary Britain is represented on the ground floor; whether Posh Spice and Fatboy Slim will still be on show in 50 years is debatable. *(St. Martin's Pl., at the start of Charing Cross Rd. Tube: Leicester Sq. or Charing Cross. ☎ 7312 2463. Audioguides free; £4 suggested donation. Open M-W and Sa-Su 10am-6pm, Th-F 10am-9pm. Free; exhibitions £0-5.)*

THE GILBERT COLLECTION. On the lower level of Somerset House, the Gilbert Collection of Decorative Arts opened in 2000 to widespread acclaim. Make sure to pick up a free audioguide and magnifying glass as you enter—the latter is invaluable for studying the displays of micromosaics and ornate "Gold Boxes," bejewelled 18th-century snuff-boxes. *(Enter from Somerset House, Strand, or from Victoria Embankment. Tube: Temple. ☎ 7420 9400. Open M-Sa 10am-6pm, Su noon-6pm. £4, students and seniors £3, under 18 free. Joint admission with Courtauld £7, seniors £3.)*

HOLBORN AND CLERKENWELL

SIR JOHN SOANE'S MUSEUM. Eccentric architect John Soane let his imagination run free when designing this intriguing museum for his own collection of art and antiquities. Idiosyncratic cupolas cast light on a bewildering panoply of ancient carvings; in the Picture Room, multiple Hogarths hang from fold-out panels. *(13 Lincoln's Inn Fields. Tours Sa 2:30pm, tickets sold from 2pm. £3. Open Tu-Sa 10am-5pm; first Tu of month also 6-9pm. Free; £1 donation requested.)*

CITY OF LONDON

■ **MUSEUM OF LONDON.** Perched in the corner of the Barbican complex (see p. 121), this engrossing collection traces the history of London from its foundations to the present day, with a particularly strong array of Roman objects. The largest item on show is the gold-plated **Lord Mayor's State Coach**, built in 1757. *(London Wall; enter through the Barbican or from Aldersgate. Tube: St. Paul's or Barbican. ☎ 7600 3699. 30min. gallery tours Tu 2:30pm. Free. Open M-Sa 10am-5:50pm, Su noon-5:50pm; last admission 5:30pm. £5, concessions £3, under 17 free; tickets valid 1 year from date of issue.)*

BANK OF ENGLAND MUSEUM. Housed within the bank itself (see p. 121), the museum traces its history from the events leading up to its foundation in 1694 to the present day. *(Bartholomew Ln. Tube: Bank. ☎ 7601 5545. Open M-F 10am-5pm. Free.)*

SOUTH BANK

DESIGN MUSEUM. Housed in a classic Art Deco riverfront building, this thoroughly contemporary museum explores the development of mass-market design with a constantly changing selection of objects; most fun are the dozens of funky chairs that patrons are encouraged to try out. *(28 Shad Thames, Butler's Wharf. Tube: Tower Hill or London Bridge. ☎ 7403 6933. Open daily 10am-6pm, last entry 5:15pm. £5.50, students £4.50, seniors and children £4, families £15.)*

WESTMINSTER

CABINET WAR ROOMS. For six tense years, Churchill, his cabinet and generals, and dozens of support staff lived and worked in these dank underground quarters; the day after the war ended in 1945 they were abandoned, shut up, and left undisturbed for decades until their reopening in 1981. Highlights include the small room containing the top-secret transatlantic hotline—the official line was that it was Churchill's personal loo. *(Clive Steps, King Charles St. Tube: Westminster. ☎ 7930 6961. Open Apr.-Sept. daily 9:30am-6pm; Oct.-Mar. 10am-6pm; last admission 5:15pm. £5.40, students and seniors £3.90, children free.)*

QUEEN'S GALLERY. The Queen's Gallery will open in spring 2002, displaying works from the richly endowed Royal Collection. Five rooms will also be dedicated to exhibitions of paintings, prints, furniture, decorative arts, and jewelry. *(Buckingham Palace Rd. Tube: St. James's Park. For hours and prices, call Buckingham Palace, ☎ 7839 1377.)*

KENSINGTON AND EARL'S COURT

◼ NATURAL HISTORY MUSEUM. Architecturally the most impressive of the South Kensington trio, this cathedral-like building is home to an outstanding array of animals and minerals, though few plants. Highlights include the remarkably realistic T-Rex (complete with bad breath) in the **Dinosaur** exhibit, the engrossing interactive **Human Biology** gallery, and the giant **Mammals** hall. *(Cromwell Rd. ☎ 7942 5000. Tube: South Kensington. Free 45min. highlights tours noon, 1, 2, 3pm; reserve places at the main info desk. Open M-Sa 10am-5:50pm, Su 11am-5:50pm; last admission 5:30pm. Free.)*

SCIENCE MUSEUM. An odd mix of state-of-the-art interactive displays, impressive historical artifacts, and some truly mind-numbing galleries (standard weights and measures?). Most impressive is the gigantic **Making of the Modern World** hall, a collection of pioneering contraptions from "Puffing Billy" (1815), the oldest surviving steam locomotive, to the Apollo 10 command module. The hi-tech exhibits of the blue-lit **Wellcome Wing** are literally overshadowed by the overhead curve of the vast **IMAX** cinema. *(Exhibition Rd. ☎ (0870) 870 4868, IMAX (0870) 870 4771. Tube: South Kensington. IMAX: shows every 1-1¼hr., M-F 10:45am-4:25pm, Sa-Su 11am-5:50pm. Call for prices and bookings. Open daily 10am-6pm. Free.)*

MARYLEBONE AND REGENT'S PARK

◼ THE WALLACE COLLECTION. Housed in palatial Hertford House, this is a stunning array of paintings, porcelain, and medieval armor. The **first floor** is home to a world-renowned collection of 18th-century French art as well as the **Great Gallery**, whose 17th-century works include Frans Hals's *Laughing Cavalier*, along with paintings by Rembrandt, van Dyck, and Rubens. *(Hertford House, Manchester Sq. Tube: Bond St. or Marble Arch. ☎ 7563 9500. Free 1hr. tours of the collection given W and Sa 11:30pm and Su 3pm. Free talks are held M-F 1pm. Open M-Sa 10am-5pm, Su noon-5pm.)*

SHERLOCK HOLMES MUSEUM. It takes a master sleuth to deduce that this meticulously recreated home-from-Holmes is entirely fictional. Or was he? The house fits Dr. Watson's descriptions so perfectly that the premise "once you have excluded the impossible, whatever remains, however unlikely, must be the truth," leads you to the conclusion that this truly was Holmes's home. *(Marked "221b Baker St."; actually at 239. Tube: Baker St. ☎ 7935 8866. Open daily 9:30am-6:30pm. £6, children £4.)*

BLOOMSBURY

◼ BRITISH LIBRARY GALLERIES. The British Library presents an appropriately stunning display of books and manuscripts, from the 2nd-century *Unknown Gospel* to the Beatles' hand-scrawled lyrics of *Paperback Writer*. Other highlights include a Gutenberg Bible, Joyce's handwritten draft of *Finnegan's Wake*, and pages from Leonardo da Vinci's notebooks. *(For practical information, see p. 127.)*

NORTH LONDON

◼ THE IVEAGH BEQUEST. A stout collection bequeathed to the nation by Edward Guinness, Earl of Iveagh, the Kenwood setting (see p. 128) and the magnificent pictures make it one of the finest small galleries in London. Highlights include works by Rembrandt, Vermeer, Turner, and Botticelli. *(Kenwood House, Highgate (Zone 3); for directions, see p. 128. Open Apr.-Sept. Sa-Tu and Th 10am-6pm; W and F 10:30am-6pm; Oct. until 5pm; Nov.-Mar. until 4pm. Free.)*

◼ ROYAL AIR FORCE MUSEUM. Exhibitions detail every aspect of life for those fighting in and against the RAF, but the real stars are the planes—scores of 'em, from wood-and-cloth biplanes of 1914 to 1980s Harriers. *(Grahame Park Way. From Tube: Colindale (Zone 4), turn left and walk about 10min. ☎ 8205 2266. Open daily 10am-6pm; last admission 5:30pm. £7.50, students £4.90, seniors and children free; half-price after 4:30pm.)*

SOUTH LONDON

■ **IMPERIAL WAR MUSEUM.** A pair of massive 15-inch naval guns guard the entrance to the Imperial War Museum; formerly the infamous lunatic asylum known as Bedlam, today it illustrates another type of human madness. The commendably un-jingoistic exhibits follow every aspect of war from 1914, covering conflicts both large and small. Most impressive is the **Holocaust Exhibition,** a two-floors exposition of Nazi atrocities against not only Jews, but also gays, gypsies, and the disabled. *(Lambeth Rd., Lambeth. Tube: Lambeth North or Elephant and Castle. ☎ 7416 5320. Open daily 10am-6pm. £6.50, students £5.50, seniors and children free; free for all after 4:30pm.)*

■ **DULWICH PICTURE GALLERY.** Designed by Sir John Soane, this marvelous array of Old Masters was England's first public art gallery. Rubens and van Dyck feature prominently, as does Rembrandt's *Portrait of a Young Man*, believed to be his son. *(Gallery Rd., Dulwich. Rail: North Dulwich or West Dulwich plus well-signed 10min. walk, or Tube: Brixton and bus P4 to the door. ☎ 8693 5254. Open Tu-F 10am-5pm, Sa-Su 11am-5pm. £4, seniors £3, students and children free; free for all F.)*

EAST LONDON

■ **NATIONAL MARITIME MUSEUM AND QUEEN'S HOUSE.** The NMM's exceptionally broad-ranging displays cover almost every aspect of seafaring history. Child-friendliness is achieved by designing the galleries to resemble a nautical theme park—once your kids get into the **All Hands** interactive gallery, you'll find it hard to get them out again. Pride of the naval displays is the **Nelson Room,** which tells the stirring tale of one 12-year-old midshipman's rise through the ranks. *(Trafalgar Rd., between the Royal Naval College and Greenwich Park. DLR: Cutty Sark. ☎ 8858 4422. Open June to early Sept. daily 10am-6pm; early Sept. to May 10am-5pm; last admission 30min. before close. £7.50, after 4:30pm £6; students £6, £4.80; seniors and children free. Combined ticket with Queen's House and Royal Observatory £10.50, students £8.40, seniors and children free. For Greenwich Passport ticket, see p. 130.)* The collection of the NMM is kept in the **Queen's House** (see also **Sights,** p. 130); the galleries of past admirals take second place to Inigo Jones's architecture. *(£1, seniors and under 16 free.)*

MAJOR EXHIBITION SPACES

▨ **Institute of Contemporary Arts (ICA),** Nash House, the Mall (☎ 7930 3647). Tube: Charing Cross or St. James's Park. A grand Neoclassical pediment in London's most conservative neighborhood is the last place you'd expect to find Britain's national center for the contemporary arts—at least it's conveniently located for attacking the establishment. Open M noon-11pm, Tu-Sa noon-1am, Su noon-10:30pm; galleries close 7:30pm. "Day membership," giving access to galleries and cafe-bar, M-F £1.50, Sa-Su £2.50. Cinema £6.50, before 5pm £4.50; concessions £5.50, £3.50.

▨ **Royal Academy,** Burlington House, Piccadilly (☎ 7300 8000). Tube: Piccadilly Circus or Green Park. Founded in 1768 as both an art school and meeting place for Britain's foremost artists, the Academy holds outstanding exhibitions on all manner of art. Anyone can submit a piece for inclusion in the **Summer Exhibition** (June-Aug.), held every year since 1769. Open Sa-Th 10am-6pm, F 10am-10pm. Around £7, concessions £1-4 less.

▨ **Saatchi Gallery,** 98a Boundary Rd. (☎ 7624 8299). From St. John's Wood Tube, head down Grove End Rd., turn right into Abbey Rd.; Boundary Rd. is about a 12min. walk up on the left. A changing array of works from Charles Saatchi's vast collection of contemporary British art. The only permanent piece on display is Richard Wilson's 1987 installation *20:50,* a whole room filled with 2.5 ft. of used oil. Open Sept.-July Th-Su noon-6pm. £5, concessions £3, under 12 free.

Hayward Gallery, South Bank Centre (☎ 7960 4242). Tube: Waterloo. Behind the Royal Festival Hall, this stark modernist block is the South Bank Centre's appropriately high-powered artistic wing. Contemporary art predominates. Open Th-M 10am-6pm, Tu-W 10am-8pm. £7, concessions £5, under 12 free.

Serpentine Gallery, off West Carriage Drive, Kensington Gdns. (☎ 7402 6075). Tube: South Kensington, Lancaster Gate, or High St. Kensington. The unlikely venue for top contemporary art shows. Open daily 10am-6pm. Free; £1 donation requested.

Whitechapel Art Gallery, Whitechapel High St. (☎ 7377 7888). Tube: Aldgate East. Long the sole artistic beacon in a culturally and materially impoverished area, now at the forefront of the East End's buzzing art scene. Excellent, often controversial shows of contemporary art on 2 floors. Open Tu and Th-Su 11am-5pm, W 11am-8pm. Free.

▣ SHOPPING

From its earliest days, London has been a trading city, and today even more so than at the Empire's height, London's economy is truly international. Thanks to the eclectic taste of Londoners, the range of goods is unmatched anywhere.

DEPARTMENT STORES AND MAJOR CHAINS

As in most prosperous cities, London retailing is dominated by giant department stores and own-label chains. Most chain stores have a flagship on or near **Oxford St.**, often with a second flagship in **Covent Garden.**

DEPARTMENT STORES

Liberty, 210-220 Regent St.; main entrance on Gt. Marlborough St. (☎ 7734 1234). Tube: Oxford Circus. Focus on top-quality design and handicrafts. Enormous hat department, a whole hall of scarves, and small but perfectly formed cosmetics department. Open M-W 10am-6:30pm, Th-Sa 10am-7pm, Su noon-6pm. AmEx/MC/V.

Fortnum and Mason, 181 Piccadilly (☎ 7734 8040). Tube: Green Park or Piccadilly Circus. Founded in 1707, Fortnum's is famed for its sumptuous food hall, with liveried clerks, chandeliers, and fountains. Few make it to the upper floors that complete London's smallest, snootiest department store. Open M-Sa 10am-6:30pm. AmEx/MC/V.

Hamley's, 188-189 Regent St. (☎ 7734 3161). Tube: Oxford Circus. 7 floors filled with every conceivable toy and game; dozens of strategically placed product demonstrations are guaranteed to turn mummy's darling into a snarling, toy-demanding menace. Open M-F 10am-8pm, Sa 9:30am-8pm, Su noon-6pm. AmEx/MC/V.

Harrods, 87-135 Old Brompton Rd. (☎ 7730 1234). Tube: Knightsbridge. Huge and bewildering, the only thing bigger than the store itself is the mark-up on the goods—it's no wonder only tourists and oil sheikhs actually shop here (even the bathrooms cost £1). Open M-Sa 10am-7pm. AmEx/MC/V/your soul.

Harvey Nichols, 109-125 Knightsbridge (☎ 7235 5000). Tube: Knightsbridge. Imagine Bond St., Rue-St-Honoré, and Fifth Avenue all rolled up and turned into 5 floors of fashion, from the biggest names to the hippest contemporary unknowns. Open M-Tu and Sa 10am-7pm, W-F 10am-8pm, Su noon-6pm. AmEx/MC/V.

Selfridges, 400 Oxford St. (☎ 7629 1234). Tube: Bond St. The total department store. Expensive fashion departments cover the gamut from traditional tweeds to space-age clubwear; the cosmetics department is especially vast. 14 eateries, a hair salon, a bureau de change, and even a hotel. Massive Jan. and July sales. Open M-W 10am-7pm, Th-F 10am-8pm, Sa 9:30am-7pm, Su noon-6pm. AmEx/MC/V.

CHAINS

Lush (☎ (01202) 668545). 5 locations, including Garden Piazza (Tube: Covent Garden) and 40 Carnaby St. (Tube: Oxford Circus) All-natural cosmetics that look good enough to eat; soap is hand-cut from blocks masquerading as cakes and cheeses (£3-5), facial masks scooped from guacamole-like tubs. Vegan cosmetics are marked by a green dot.

FCUK, flagship at 396 Oxford St. (☎ 7529 7766). Tube: Bond St. The shop formerly known as French Connection needs no introduction. Open M-W and F-Sa 10am-8pm, Th 10am-9pm, Su noon-6pm. AmEx/MC/V.

Jigsaw (☎ 8392 5678). 13 locations: flagship at 126 New Bond St. (Tube: Bond St.). The essence of Britishness, distilled into quality mid-priced womenswear. Bond St. store open M-W and F-Sa 10am-6:30pm, Th 10am-7:30pm, Su noon-6pm. AmEx/MC/V.

Muji, flagship at 41 Carnaby St. (☎ 7287 7323). Tube: Oxford Circus. Minimalist lifestyle stores, with a Zen take on everything from clothes to kitchenwear. Carnaby St. open M-W and Sa 10am-7pm, Th 10am-8:30pm, F 10am-8pm, Su noon-6pm. AmEx/MC/V.

Topshop/Top Man/Miss Selfridge, flagship at 214 Oxford St. (☎ 7927 0000). Tube: Oxford Circus. Cheap fashions for young people—over-25s will feel middle-aged. The flagship store brings them all under one roof; Topshop dominates with strappy shoes and skimpy clubwear over 3 floors. Miss Selfridge has an even younger, girlier feel; Top Man is all shiny Ts and cargo pants, with free foosball. 10% student discount. Oxford St. store open M-W and F-Sa 9am-8pm, Th 9am-9pm, Su noon-6pm. AmEx/MC/V.

WEST END

OXFORD AND REGENT STREETS

Aside from the department stores and mainstream chains of Oxford St. and Regent St., fashionable boutiques line pedestrian **South Molton Street,** stretching south into Mayfair from Bond St. Tube, and **Foubert's Place,** near youth-oriented Carnaby St.

Browns Labels for Less, 50 South Molton St. (☎ 7514 0052). Tube: Bond St. Small range of remainders from the Browns empire, but unbelievable reductions: D&G pants from £180 to £30. Open M-W and F-Sa 10am-6:30pm, Th 10am-7pm. AmEx/MC/V.

HMV, 150 Oxford St., W1 (☎ 7631 3423). Tube: Oxford Circus. 3 massive floors; exceptional range of dance music. Open M-Sa 9am-8pm, Su noon-6pm. AmEx/MC/V.

Proibito Sale Shop, 9 Gees Court, St. Christopher's Pl. (☎ 7409 2769) and 42 South Molton St. (☎ 7491 3244). Tube: Bond St. for both. Casualwear from top designer names for up to 70% off—get a pair of Valentino jeans for only £35. Open M-W 10am-6:30pm, Th 10am-7:30pm, F-Sa 10am-7pm, Su noon-6pm. AmEx/MC/V.

Virgin Megastore, 14-16 Oxford St., W1 (☎ 7631 1234). Tube: Tottenham Court Rd. Join the line for the free PS2 consoles or surf the Internet for £4 per hr., including soft drink. Oh, lots of music, too. Open M-Sa 9:30am-10pm, Su noon-6pm. AmEx/MC/V.

MAYFAIR

Mayfair's aristocratic pedigree is evident in the scores of high-priced boutiques, many bearing Royal Warrants to indicate their status as official palace suppliers. **Bond Street** is the location of choice for the biggest names. Less mainstream designers set up shop on **Conduit Street,** where Old Bond St. meets New Bond St.; here you'll find Vivienne Westwood, Alexander McQueen, and Yohji Yamamoto.

Paul Smith Sale Shop, 23 Avery Row. Tube: Bond St. Smallish range of last-season and clearance items from the acknowledged master of modern British menswear. Open M-W and F-Sa 10am-6pm, Th 10am-7pm. AmEx/MC/V.

Sotheran's of Sackville Street, 2-5 Sackville St. (☎ 7439 6151). Tube: Piccadilly Circus. Founded in 1761; while the hushed atmosphere and locked shelves give an impression of exclusivity, there are plenty of affordable books, and the staff is charming. Open M-F 9:30am-6pm, Sa 10am-4pm. AmEx/MC/V.

Waterstone's, 203-206 Piccadilly (☎ 7851 2400). Tube: Piccadilly Circus. Europe's largest bookshop, on 8 floors, with cafe, Internet station, and posh basement restaurant. Open M-Sa 10am-11pm, Su noon-6pm. AmEx/MC/V.

SOHO

Despite Soho's eternal trendiness, it's never been much of a shopping destination—between all the bars and cafes, there's precious little space left for boutiques. The main exception to this are the record stores of **D'Arblay Street** and **Berwick Street** and the musical instrument and equipment shops of **Denmark Street.**

Black Market, 25 D'Arblay St. (☎ 7437 0478). Tube: Oxford Circus. All-vinyl dance emporium; house and garage upstairs, phenomenal drum and bass section below. Open M-Sa 11am-7pm.

Daddy Kool, 12 Berwick St. (☎7437 3535). Tube: Oxford Circus or Piccadilly Circus. The basement has Soho's best reggae collection, with loads of obscure 7" and LPs. Open M-F 10:30am-7pm, Sa 10am-6pm. MC/V.

Sister Ray, 94 Berwick St. (☎7287 8385). Tube: Oxford Circus, Piccadilly Circus, or Tottenham Court Rd. Rare outlet for indie and alternative music on both vinyl and CD; lots of goth, metal, and punk. Open M-Sa 9:30am-8pm, Su 11am-5pm. MC/V.

Uptown Records, 3 D'Arblay St. (☎7434 3639). Tube: Oxford Circus. Ever wondered what DJs do in the daytime? You'll find lots of them working in this small all-vinyl store, advising shoppers on the latest house, garage, and hip-hop happenings. Open M-W and F-Sa 10:30am-7pm, Th 10:30am-8pm. AmEx/MC/V.

COVENT GARDEN

Covent Garden is increasingly mainstream, though there are still enough quirky shops left to make it worth a wander. North of the piazza, **Floral Street** is firmly established as the smartest street in the area, with top designer names next to up-and-coming brands. Ever popular, **Neal Street** is a top destination for funky footwear and mid-priced club clobber, though the fashion focus has shifted to nearby **Shorts Gardens, Earlham,** and **Monmouth Streets.**

Dr. Marten's Dept. Store, 1-4 King St. (☎7497 1460). Tourist-packed 5-tiered megastore, with baby docs, papa docs, and the classic yellow-stitched boots. Open M-W and F-Sa 10am-7pm, Th 10:30am-8pm, Su noon-6pm. AmEx/MC/V.

Miss Sixty, 39 Neal St. (☎7836 3789). The newest Italian clothing craze. Bright, patterned, and skin-hugging female fashions in a laid-back and sexy style. Open M-W and F-Sa 10am-6:30pm, Th 10am-7:30pm, Su noon-6pm. AmEx/MC/V.

Office, 57 Neal St. (☎7379 1896). The largest outlet of London's foremost fashion footwear retailer, stylish *and* wearable. The **sale shop** at 61 St. Martin's Ln. (☎7497 0390; Tube: Leicester Sq.) has a more conventional selection, though there are some good deals to be found. Neal St. store open M-W and F-Sa 10am-7pm, Th 10am-8pm, Su noon-6pm. Sale shop open M-Sa 10am-7pm, Su noon-6pm. MC/V.

CHELSEA, KNIGHTSBRIDGE, AND BELGRAVIA

No serious shopper can ignore Chelsea. If **Sloane Square** is well, too sloaney (the English equivalent of US preppy), the **King's Road,** with one-off boutiques at all price ranges, is all things to all shoppers. **Knightsbridge**'s main shopping arteries are the **Old Brompton Road,** with upmarket chains between **Harvey Nichols** and **Harrods** (see **Department Stores,** above), and **Sloane Street,** full of exclusive boutiques.

World's End, 430 King's Rd. (☎7352 6551). The fountain of cool, this boutique's past incarnations include SEX, the proto-punk store that gave birth to the Sex Pistols. Vivienne Westwood still runs the sloping-floored boutique, though the clothes are now as unaffordable as they are unwearable. Open M-Sa 10am-6pm. AmEx/MC/V.

NOTTING HILL

The best reason to visit Notting Hill is **Portobello Market,** which brings an influx of color and vivacity to an otherwise gentrified area. The "Market" is actually several distinct markets occupying different parts of the street and operating on different days; Saturdays, when all come together in a mile-long row, is the best day to visit.

The Markets: Antiques market, north along Portobello from Chepstow Villas to Elgin Crescent. Tube: Notting Hill Gate. Most of what's on display outside is cheapish bric-a-brac, little of it truly rare or very old. (Sa 7am-5pm.) **General market,** Elgin Cres. to Lancaster Rd. Tube: Westbourne Park or Ladbroke Grove. Food, flowers, and household essentials. (M-W 8am-6pm, Th 9am-1pm, F-Sa 7am-7pm.) **Clothes market,** north of Lancaster Rd. Tube: Ladbroke Grove. Wide selection of secondhand clothes, New Age bangles, and cheap clubwear. (F-Sa 8am-3pm.)

LONDON

The Travel Bookshop, 13-15 Blenheim Cres. (☎7229 5260). The specialist bookshop featured in *Notting Hill*, today besieged by Grantophiles in search of instant karma. Open M-Sa 10am-6pm, Su 11am-4pm. MC/V.

Dolly Diamond, 51 Pembridge Rd. (☎7792 2479). Tube: Notting Hill Gate. Jackie Onassis or Audrey Hepburn? Choose your look from the great selection of classic 50s-70s clothes and elegant 20s-40s evening gowns. Open M-F 10:30am-6:30pm, Sa 9:30am-6:30pm, Su 11am-5pm. "Cash preferred."

BLOOMSBURY

Besides intellectuals, Bloomsbury's main commodity is **books;** the streets around the British Museum in particular are crammed with specialist and cut-price bookshops. If you're after **electronics** equipment, head to **Tottenham Court Rd.**

▨ **Delta of Venus,** 151 Drummond St. (☎7387 3037). Tube: Warren St. or Euston. Small but unbeatable array of vintage clothes spanning the 1960s to the early 80s. Dresses £18-40, shirts £10-18, rummage box £3 per item. Open M-Sa 11am-7pm. MC/V.

Gay's the Word, 66 Marchmont St. (☎7278 7654). Tube: Russell Sq. One of only 2 specialist gay and lesbian bookshops in the UK. Also well endowed with erotic postcards, serious movies, and free mags. Open M-Sa 10am-6:30pm, Su 2-6pm. AmEx/MC/V.

Unsworths, 12 Bloomsbury St. (☎7436 9836). Tube: Tottenham Court Rd. Up to 90% off publishers' prices on a wide range of literature and academic books, many US-sourced, with an emphasis on the humanities. Used and antiquarian books downstairs. Open M-Sa 10am-8pm, Su noon-8pm. AmEx/MC/V.

NORTH LONDON

In **Camden Town,** you'll find hundreds of identical stores flogging the same chunky shoes and leather trousers they've been selling for years. Arrive early and have a game plan—amid the dross there are genuine bargains and incredible avant-garde finds, but you have to dig deep.

▨ **Cyberdog/Cybercity,** arch 14, Stables Market (☎7482 2842). Tube: Camden Town. Unbelievable club clothes for superior life forms. Alien gods and goddesses will want to try on the fluorescent body-armor or steel corsets with rubber breast hoses. Open M-F 11am-6pm, Sa-Su 10am-7pm. AmEx/MC/V.

Camden Markets, off Camden High St. and Chalk Farm Rd. Tube: Camden Town.

Stables Market, nearest Chalk Farm and the best of the bunch. Some of the most outrageous club- and fetish-wear ever made, plus a good selection of vintage clothes. Most shops open daily.

Camden Lock Market, from the railway bridge to the canal. Arranged around a food-filled courtyard on the Regent's Canal, mostly indoor shops sell pricier items such as carpets, and household goods. Most stalls operate F or Sa-Su only.

Camden Canal Market, down the tunnel opposite Camden Lock, starts out promisingly with jewelry and watches, then degenerates rapidly into sub-par club clothes and tourist trinkets. Open F-Su.

The Camden Markets, the nearest to Camden Tube, and correspondingly the most crowded and least innovative. Jeans, sweaters, and designer fakes at average prices. Open F-Su.

Camden Passage, Islington High St. Tube: Angel. Turn right from the tube; it's the alley-way that starts behind "The Mall" antiques gallery on Upper St. Not to be confused with Camden Market (see above). *The* place for antiques, especially old prints and drawings. Shops vastly outnumber stalls; both tend to open only W and Sa, 8:30am-6pm.

SOUTH LONDON

If you're looking for the fruits of West Indian cultures, **Brixton** is the place to be.

Brixton Market, along Electric Ave., Pope's Rd., and Brixton Station Rd., as well as indoors in Granville Arcade and Market Row. Tube: Brixton. Nowhere is Brixton's ethnic heritage more evident. Open M-Tu and Th-Sa 8:30am-5pm, W 8:30am-1pm.

Red Records, 500 Brixton Rd., SW2 (☎7274 4476). Tube: Brixton. Impressive collection of reggae, hip-hop, soul, garage, and jazz on new and used vinyl, CD, and tape. Open M-Sa 9:30am-8pm. AmEx/MC/V.

EAST LONDON

In East London, the **street-market** tradition is alive and well, helped along by large immigrant communities; the South Asian-dominated Brick Lane and Petticoat Lane are justly famous.

Brick Lane Market. Tube: Shoreditch or Aldgate East. Famous weekly market with a South Asian flair (food, rugs, spices, bolts of fabric, strains of sitar). Open Su 8am-2pm.

Petticoat Lane Market. Tube: Liverpool St., Aldgate, or Aldgate East. Block after block of cheap clothing, with lots of leather jackets around Aldgate East. The real action begins at about 9:30am. Open Su 9am-2pm; starts shutting down around noon.

Spitalfields Market. Tube: Shoreditch or Liverpool St. Formerly one of London's main wholesale vegetable markets, now a new-agey crafts market with a wide range of foods. Crafts market M-F 11am-3:30pm, Su 10am-5pm. Organic market F and Su 10am-5pm.

⟁ ENTERTAINMENT

On any given day or night in London, you can choose from the widest range of entertainment a city can offer. The West End is perhaps the world's theater capital, supplemented by an adventurous "fringe" and a justly famous National Theatre, while new bands spring eternal from the fountain of London's many music venues. Whatever you're planning to do, *Time Out* magazine's weekly listings will be indispensable (£2.20, every W).

THEATER

The stage for a national dramatic tradition over 500 years old, London theaters maintain unrivaled breadth of choice. At a **West End** theater (a term referring to all the major stages, whether or not they're actually in the West End), you can expect a professional, if mainstream production, top-quality performers, and (usually) comfortable seats. **Off-West End** theaters tend to present more challenging work, while remaining as professional as their West End brethren. The **Fringe** refers to the scores of smaller, less commercial theaters, often just a room in a pub basement with a few benches and a team of dedicated amateurs.

The **Leicester Square Half-Price Ticket Booth** is run by the theaters themselves and releases (genuine!) half-price tickets on the day of the show. The only catch is that you have to buy them in person, in cash, with no choice in seating (most expensive tickets sold first) and no way of knowing in advance what shows will have tickets available that day. Even so, it's phenomenally popular—come early and be prepared to wait, especially Saturday. (South side of Leicester Sq.—look for the long lines. Tube: Leicester Sq. £2 booking fee per ticket. Max. 4 tickets per person. Open M-Sa 10am-7pm, Su noon-2:30pm.)

OTHER WEST END AND REPERTORY COMPANIES

Barbican Theatre, Barbican; main entrance on Silk St. (general box office ☎ 7638 8891, cinema hotline 7382 7000). Tube: Barbican or Moorgate. A futuristic auditorium seating 1166 in steeply raked, forward-leaning balconies. From Oct. 2001 to May 2002, the **Royal Shakespeare Company** will be spending its last season in residence at the Barbican. Prices vary with seat, day, and production. £6-30, cheapest M-F evening and Sa matinee. Student and senior standbys from 9am day of performance. In the same complex, **The Pit** is primarily experimental. £10-15 depending on production.

National Theatre, just downriver of Waterloo bridge (info ☎ 7452 3400, box office 7452 3000). Tube: Waterloo, Embankment, or Temple. Since opening in 1963, the National has been at the forefront of British theater. The **Olivier** stage seats 1160, the **Lyttelton** 890, and the experimental **Cottesloe** 300. Box office open M-Sa 10am-8pm. Complex pricing scheme; basically £10-30, day seats (from 10am) £10-13, standby (2hr. before curtain) £15; concessions £8-15.

Open-Air Theatre, Inner Circle, Regents Park (☎ 7486 2431). Tube: Baker St. Bring blankets and waterproofs to this open-air stage. Program runs early June to early Sept. Performances M-Sa 8pm; 2:30pm matinees May-June and Sept. Th and Sa and Aug. daily. £8.50-23; families £12 per person for best available seat, minimum 4 people with at least 1 under 16; student and senior standby £8 from 1hr. before curtain.

Royal Court Theatre, Sloane Sq. (☎ 7565 5000). Called "the most important theater in Europe" by the *New York Times,* dedicated to new writing and innovative interpretations of classics. Main stage £5-25; concessions £9 in advance, £5 on the day; standing places 10p 1hr. before curtain. Upstairs £5-15, concessions £9. M all seats £5.

Sadler's Wells, Rosebery Ave. (☎ 7863 8000). Tube: Angel. London's premier dance space, with everything from classical ballet to contemporary tap, plus occasional operas. £8.50-40; student, senior, and under 16 standbys £8.50-15 1hr. before curtain (cash only). Box office open M-Sa 9am-8:30pm.

Shakespeare's Globe Theatre, 21 New Globe Walk (☎ 7401 9919). Tube: Southwark or London Bridge. A faithful reproduction of the original 16th-century playhouse where Shakespeare himself performed. Choose between backless wooden benches or stand through a performance as a "groundling." For tours, see **Sights,** p. 122. Performances mid-May to late Sept. Tu-Sa 7:30pm, Su 6:30pm; from June also Tu-Sa 2pm, Su 1pm. Box office open M-Sa 10am-6pm, 8pm on performance days. Seats £11-27, concessions £9-23; yard (i.e., standing) £5.

MAJOR FRINGE THEATERS

The Almeida, Almeida St. (☎ 7359 4404). Tube: Angel or Highbury and Islington. During renovations (until May 2002), productions are held in a disused coach depot at Omega Pl., off Caledonian Rd. Hollywood stars, including Kevin Spacey and Nicole Kidman, queue up to prove their acting cred here. Box office open 9:30am-curtain. M-Sa 7:30pm, with matinee Sa 3pm. £6-27.50; students and seniors £7-11.

Donmar Warehouse, 41 Earlham St. (☎ 7369 1732). Tube: Covent Garden. Serious contemporary theatre. £14-35; concessions standby £12 30min. before curtain.

Young Vic, 66 The Cut (☎ 7928 6363). Tube: Waterloo. The theater—with only 8 rows of seats surrounding the flat stage—can be unnervingly intimate. Box office open M-Sa 10am-8pm. £10-12, seniors £8-10, students and children £5-7.

CINEMA

London's film scene offers everything. The heart of the celluloid monster is **Leicester Square** (p. 116), where the latest releases premiere a day before hitting the city's chains, while the dominant mainstream cinema chain is **Odeon** (☎ (0870) 5050 007). Tickets to West End cinemas cost £8-10; weekday screenings before 5pm are usually cheaper. The following cinemas have less mainstream offerings:

Electric Cinema, 191 Portobello Rd. (info ☎ 7727 9958, tickets 7229 8688). Tube: Ladbroke Grove. London's oldest purpose-built cinema (1910) has been restored to its original baroque splendor. Independent and international films, with late-night blockbuster reruns Sa 11pm, and classics and double bills Su 2pm. Features M-F £6.50, Sa-Su £7.50, students and seniors M-F before 6pm and children all day £4; luxury seats M-F £7.50, Sa-Su £8.50; 2-seat sofa £16, £18. Double bills and late shows £5.50.

ICA Cinema, Nash House. See **Museums,** p. 136.

Lux Cinema, 2-4 Hoxton Sq. (☎ 7684 0200). Tube: Old St. The place to go for something obscure or peculiar. Shows usually W-Su evenings. £6, concessions £4.

National Film Theatre (NFT), on the south bank, right underneath Waterloo Bridge (☎ 7928 3232; www.bfi.org.uk). Tube: Waterloo, Embankment, or Temple. One of the world's leading cinemas, with a mind-boggling array of films. 6 different movies hit the 3 screens every evening, starting around 6pm. All films £6.85, concessions £5.25.

The Prince Charles, Leicester Pl. (☎ 7957 4009 or 7420 0000). Tube: Leicester Sq. *Sing-a-long-a-Sound-of-Music,* where Von Trappists dress as everything from nuns to "Ray, a drop of golden sun" (F 7:30pm, Su 2pm; £12.50, children £8), and the live-troupe accompanied *Rocky Horror Picture Show* (F 11:45pm; £6, students £3) are both London institutions. £3.50, M-F before 5pm £1.75, M evenings £2.

COMEDY

Capital of a nation famed for its sense of humor, London takes its comedy seriously. On any given night of the week, you'll find at least 10 comedy clubs in operation; check listings in *Time Out* or a newspaper to keep up to speed. Summertime comedy seekers should note that London empties of comedians in **August,** when most head to Edinburgh to take part in the annual festival.

Comedy Store, 1a Oxendon St., SW1 (TicketMaster ☎ 7344 0234). Tube: Piccadilly Circus. The UK's top comedy club sowed the seeds that gave rise to *Ab Fab, Whose Line is it Anyway,* and *Blackadder,* while Robin Williams did frequent impromptu acts in the 1980s. Tu *Cutting Edge* (contemporary satire), W and Su ◧ Comedy Store Players improvisation, Th-Sa standup. Bar at back sells food (burger £5.60). Shows Tu-Su 8pm plus midnight Sa. Book ahead. 18+. £12-15, students and seniors £8.

Comedy Cafe, 66 Rivington St. (☎ 7739 5706). Health warning: prolonged exposure may lead to uncontrollable laughter. Skip the food (burgers £7) and save up your cash for beers (£2.50-3). Reserve F-Sa. Doors 7pm, show 9pm, dancing to 2am. W free try-out night, Th £3, F £10, Sa £12.

MUSIC
ROCK AND POP

Birthplace of the Rolling Stones, the Sex Pistols, Madness, and the Chemical Brothers, home to Madonna and Paul McCartney, London is a town steeped in rock 'n' roll.

Brixton Academy, 211 Stockwell Rd. (Ticketweb ☎ 7771 2000). Tube: Brixton. 1929 ex-theater; sloping floor ensures everyone can see the band. Covers all the bases from the Pogues to Senegalese stars. 4300 capacity. Box office open only on performance evenings. £10-15, sometimes up to £30. Cash only at the door.

Dublin Castle, 94 Parkway (☎ 8806 2668). It's Madness in the back room every Tu, with a Blur of record execs and talent scouts on the lookout for the next big thing at *Club Fandango.* 3 bands nightly 8:45-11pm; doors 8:30pm. £5, students £4.

Forum, 9-11 Highgate Rd. (☎ 7284 1001, box office 7344 0044). Tube: Kentish Town. Turn right and cross the road. Lavish Art Deco theater with great sound and views. Van Morrison, Bjork, Oasis, Jamiroquai, and others have played this 2000-capacity space. When no gigs are on, a cheesy 60s-80s disco takes over Sa (10pm-2am; £8).

London Astoria (LA1), 157 Charing Cross Rd. (☎ 7344 0044). Tube: Tottenham Court Rd. Originally a pickle factory, the Astoria was a strip club and music hall before turning to full-time rock venue in the late 1980s. 2000 capacity. F-Sa hosts the popular G-A-Y clubnight (see p. 148). £10-20.

The Water Rats, 328 Grays Inn Rd. (☎ 7837 7269). Tube: King's Cross/St. Pancras. A pub-cafe by day, a stomping venue for top new talent by night. Oasis were signed here after performing their first London gig. Open for coffee M-F 8am-noon, surprisingly good lunches (£4-6) M-F noon-2pm, and music M-Sa 8pm-midnight (cover £5, students £4).

CLASSICAL

Home to four world-class orchestras, three major concert halls, two opera houses, two ballet companies, and more chamber ensembles than you could Simon Rattle your baton at, London is ground zero for serious music—and there's no need to break the bank. To hear some of the world's top choirs for free, head to Westminster Abbey (p. 114) or St. Paul's Cathedral (p. 112) for Evensong.

Barbican Hall, details as for Barbican Theatre (p. 141). Tube: Barbican or Moorgate. One of Europe's leading concert halls. The resident **London Symphony Orchestra** plays over 80 concerts a year. Tickets £6-35.

English National Opera, at the Coliseum, St. Martin's Lane (☎ 7632 8300). Tube: Charing Cross or Leicester Sq. All the classics, plus contemporary and avant-garde work. All works sung in English. £6-60; under 18 half-price with adult. Day seats for the dress-circle (£29) and balcony (£3) released M-F 10am (12:30pm by phone); max. 2 per person. Standbys from 3hr. before curtain; students £12.50, seniors £18, Sa also available to general public for £28. If all seats are sold, standing places are available for £3.

The Proms, at the Royal Albert Hall (see **Sights,** p. 126). This summer season of classical music has been held every year since 1895, with concerts every night from mid-July to mid-September. "Promenade" refers to the tradition of selling dirt-cheap standing tickets, but it's the presence of up to 1000 dedicated prommers that gives the concerts their unique atmosphere. Lines for standing places often start mid-afternoon. Tickets go on sale in mid-May (£5-30); standing places sold from 1½hr. before the concert (£3).

Royal Opera House, Bow St. (☎ 7304 4000). Tube: Covent Garden. Known as "Covent Garden" to aficionados, the Royal Opera House is also home to the **Royal Ballet.** Productions tend to be conservative but lavish. Box office open daily 10am-8pm. Best seats £100+, but standing room and restricted-view seating in the upper balconies can be under £5. Concessions standby 4hr. before curtain £12.50-15. 67 day seats £10-40 from 10am on day of performance.

South Bank Centre, on the south bank of the Thames between Hungerford and Waterloo bridges (☎ 7960 4242). Tube: Waterloo or Embankment. All manner of "serious" music is on the program here; the **London Philharmonic** is the orchestra-in-residence for the **Royal Festival Hall.** Tickets for all events can be purchased from the Royal Festival Hall box office (open daily 10am-9pm; phones M-Sa 9am-9pm, Su 9:30am-9pm); Queen Elizabeth Hall and Purcell Room box offices open 45min. before performance. Some discounts for concessions; standbys may also be released 2hr. before performance (check at 7921 0973).

Wigmore Hall, 36 Wigmore St. (☎ 7935 2141). Tube: Oxford Circus. London's premier chamber-music venue, in a beautiful setting with excellent acoustics; occasional jazz recitals. Box office open Nov. to mid-Mar. M-Sa 10am-8:30pm, Su 10:30am-5pm; mid-Mar. to Oct. 10:30am-8pm. Phone bookings close 1½-2hr. earlier; £1 supplement. Concerts most nights 7:30pm; £8-20, student and senior standby £8-10 1hr. before start (cash only). Daytime concerts Su 11:30am (£9) and M 1pm (£8, seniors £6).

JAZZ, FOLK, AND WORLD

When it comes to **jazz,** this ain't Chicago, but top clubs still pull in big-name performers. **Folk** (which in London usually means **Irish**) and **world** music keep an even lower profile, mostly restricted to pubs and community centers. International performers occasionally make appearances at major concert halls such as the **South Bank Centre,** the **Barbican,** and the **Wigmore Hall** (see **Classical Music,** above).

Jazz Cafe, 5 Parkway (☎ 7916 6060; tickets 7344 0044). Tube: Camden Town. With a crowded front bar and balcony restaurant, this would be a popular nightspot even without the top jazz, soul, funk, and Latin performers (tickets £10-16). Jazzy club nights follow the show F-Sa (£8-9) and every other Su (free). Bring your horn to the jam session Su noon-4pm (£1). Open M-Th 7pm-1am, F-Sa 7pm-2am, Su 7pm-midnight. MC/V.

Pizza Express Jazz Club, 10 Dean St. (☎ 7439 8722). Tube: Tottenham Court Rd. Underneath a branch of the popular chain, diners tuck into pizza while feasting their ears on music. Atmospheric lighting and a laid-back atmosphere make for a great date spot. Doors normally open 7:45pm, with music 9-11:30pm; some F-Sa have 2 shows, with doors opening at 6 and 10pm. Cover (£12-20) added to the bill. MC/V.

Ronnie Scott's, 47 Frith St. (☎ 7439 0747). Tube: Tottenham Court Rd. or Piccadilly Circus. London's oldest and most famous jazz club. 2 bands alternate 2 sets every night M-Sa, support starting at 9:30pm and the headline around 11pm; Su brings lesser-known bands from 8:30pm. Reservations often essential. Food £5-14, cocktails £7-8. Box office open M-Sa 11am-6pm. Club open M-Sa 8:30pm-3am, Su 7:30-11:30pm. £15 M-Th, £20 F-Sa, £8-12 Su; students M-W £9. AmEx/MC/V.

The Swan, 215 Clapham Rd. (☎ 7978 9778). Tube: Stockwell. Opposite the Tube. Large, dark pub with music every night; some F-Su a 2nd band plays upstairs. M traditional Irish; Tu "Celtic jazz;" W antipodean night; Th-Su Irish rock. Music starts 9:30pm. Open M-W 5-11:30pm, Th 5pm-2am, F 5pm-3am, Sa 7pm-3am, Su 7pm-2am. Free M-Th; F £5, £2.50 before 9pm; Sa £6, £3 before 9pm; Su £4, free before 10pm.

⚄ NIGHTLIFE

The West End, and in particular **Soho,** is the scene of most of London's after-dark action, with hundreds of bars and clubs, from the glitzy (and best avoided) Leicester Sq. tourist traps such as the Hippodrome and Equinox to semi-secret underground clubs. Soho is also the center of London's **gay** and **lesbian** scene—you'll find more gay bars in the few streets around Old Compton St. than in the rest of the city put together. The other major axis of London nightlife is **Shoreditch** and **Hoxton** (collectively known as Shoho) in East London; dead until a few years ago, this is now London's most cutting-edge, fashionable area, though parts are still pretty deprived. As such, style and attitude are essential; most bars and clubs here are for posing as much as for getting on down. Outside these two areas, **Notting Hill, Brixton** (in South London), and **Camden Town** and **Islington** (both in North London) have a sprinkling of decent nightspots.

BARS

In London these days, drinking is the new dancing, and bars are the new nightclubs. An explosion of club-bars has invaded the previously forgotten zone between pubs and clubs, offering seriously stylish surroundings and top-flight DJs together with plentiful lounging space. Usually, club-bars are open from noon or early evening, allowing you to skip the cover charge (if there is one) by arriving early and staying put as the scene shifts around you. On the other hand, they tend to close earlier than clubs, usually between midnight and 2am, so you'll need to move on to a "real" nightclub for serious action.

⚄ **Filthy MacNasty's Whisky Cafe,** 68 Amwell St. (☎ 7837 6067). Tube: Angel. This small, friendly Irish pub is frequented by a galaxy of stars—Shane MacGowan and U2 regularly stop by, while Johnny Depp, Kate Moss, and Ewan McGregor are known to drop in. Actually 2 bars with separate entrances, linked by the passage marked "toilets." Live rock 'n' roll Tu 8:30pm, Su 3 and 8:30pm; *Vox 'n' Roll*, Tu-W 8:30pm, is one of London's top literary events, with readings by well-known authors. Wide range of whiskies around £2. Open M-Sa 11am-11pm, Su noon-10:30pm.

⚄ **Freud,** 198 Shaftesbury Ave. (☎ 7240 9933). Invigorate your psyche in this offbeat underground hipster hangout. Sand-blasted walls occasionally echo to live music (including from the didgeridoo-playing waiters). Cheap cocktails (from £3.40). Light meals 11am-4:30pm (£3.50-6). Open M-Sa 11am-11pm, Su noon-10:30pm. MC/V.

⚄ **Grand Central,** 93 Great Eastern St. See **Food and Pubs,** p. 109.

⚄ **Soshomatch,** 2 Tabernacle St. (☎ 7920 0701). Tube: Moorgate or Old St. A 2-floor bar/restaurant that converts into a stylish club Th-Sa, Soshomatch is perfect for those seeking to combine a DJ-driven atmosphere with acres of comfy leather couches. Th *Love is...* swings from rare groove to jazz and disco to house (10pm-2am; free); F *Ripped* world-influenced cutting-edge house (10pm-2am; £5, free before 10pm); Sa *Mind Fluid* brain-melting nu-jazz to tribal voices to house (6pm-2am; £5, free before 9pm). Open M-W 11am-midnight, Th-Sa 11am-2pm. AmEx/MC/V.

AKA, 18 West Central St. (☎ 7419 9199), next to The End (see **Nightclubs,** below). Tube: Tottenham Ct. Rd. or Holborn. There's nowhere like the candlelit island lounge, high above the main action, for people watching. Cocktails £6-7. Free movies projected on the back wall M 7:30pm; it's "members only," but you can join at the door. Tu *Armaghetto* live jazz, funk, and soul (£4); W alternates between "hiphopfunkacidbreakselectrodubfunkyhouseplease" and tech-house; F rocks to 21st-century soul (£5). Dress nicely! Open Su-F 6pm-3am; food until 1am.

Dogstar, 389 Coldharbour Ln. (☎ 7733 7515). Tube: Brixton. One of the first nightspots to cash in on Brixton's new-found popularity as a bohemian hang-out. At 9pm, the tables are cleared from the dance-floor to make the metamorphosis from bar to club. M *Nubient* ambient chill-out session; Tu *Bullitt* hip-hop; W *Rude* deep 'n' dirty house; Th *DFX* drum 'n' bass; F -Sa varied house-oriented nights; Su *Negligée* ironically plays 60s-80s pop. Su-Th free; F £5, £4 10-11pm, free before 10pm; Sa £7, £5 10-11pm, free before 10pm. Open Su-Th noon-2am, F-Sa noon-4am.

Shoreditch Electricity Showrooms, 39a Hoxton Sq. (☎ 7739 6934). Tube: Old St. If you wanted to know where the super-cool go, this is the answer. Massive windows make it great for posing, while giant photomurals peer down from the walls and hanging (plastic) flowers cascade over the bar. DJs shake the downstairs floor with various musical eclectica F-Sa from 9pm (free). Bottled beer £2.70-3. Food served 1-3:45pm, e.g. crispy squid (£5) or merguez sausages (£7.25). Open Tu-W noon-11pm, Th noon-midnight, F-Sa noon-1am, Su noon-10:30pm. AmEx/MC/V.

The Social, 5 Little Portland St. (☎ 7636 4992). Tube: Oxford Circus. Tiny DJ-driven bar in the narrow space under the Little Portland St. pavement—glass tiles overhead let in the moonlight. A media-crowd favorite, with too many packed into the tiny "dance-floor" to do anything but yell at each other. Cocktails £4.80, shooters £3. DJs nightly from 7pm. No cover. Open M-Sa noon-midnight, Su 5-10:30pm.

NIGHTCLUBS

Every major DJ in the world either lives in London or makes frequent visits to the city. While the US may have introduced house music to the world, the UK has taken the lead in developing and experimenting with new types of dance music, and club culture in London is all-pervasive. Such is the variety and fast-changing nature of London nightlife that even weekly publications have trouble keeping up—*Time Out*, the Londoner's clubbing bible, only lists about half the club happenings in London on any given night.

DRESS. London clubs often fall into one of two categories: those for dancing, and those for posing. In the former, dress codes are generally relaxed; it's not uncommon to find clubbers dressed in nothing fancier than jeans, a stylish T-shirt, and trainers (sneakers), although women are usually expected to make more of an effort. At posers' clubs, however, dress is crucial, and what's expected depends very much on the scene. If you're not sure what to wear, call up the club beforehand (although answers like "New York super-funk glam" aren't always that helpful); otherwise, black and slinky is generally safe. The exception to the easy categorization are retro and theme nights, when you have to work a bit harder.

PLANNING. London clubbing revolves around promoters and the nights they organize rather than the bricks-and-mortar clubs themselves. This gives London clubbing both its incredible range and its infuriating ephemerality; top nights come, go, and move around unpredictably. To stay on top of things, comb through the listings in *Time Out* and the *Guide* supplement to the *Guardian* newspaper on Saturdays; *Time Out* also prints the weekly "TOP" club pass (look in the clubbing section), which gives you discounts on entry to many of the week's shenanigans. Working out how to get home afterwards is crucial; remember that the Tube and regular buses stop shortly after midnight, and after 1am black cabs are like gold dust. If there's no convenient Night Bus home, ask the club in advance if they can order a **minicab** (unlicensed taxicab) for you on the night; otherwise, order your own before you leave. Although it's technically illegal for minicabs to ply for hire, whispered calls of "taxi" or honking horns signal their presence—however, you've no guarantee that the driver is reputable or even insured. If you have no other option, agree on a price before you get in, and never ride alone.

■ **Bug Bar,** Crypt, St. Matthew's Church (☎ 7738 3184). Tube: Brixton. The antithesis of most self-labeled "cool" nightspots, the Bug's super laid-back, friendly crowd gives this whitewashed former church crypt a genuine vibe. W live acts, from poetry slams to breakbeats (7pm-1am; £3-4, free before 8pm); Th *Sessions* funk, jazz, and R&B (7pm-1am; free); F *Chew the Fat* rare beats and breaks (7pm-3am; £6, £4 9-11pm, free before 9pm); Sa various one-offs, from hip-hop to jazz (7pm-3am; £6, £4 9-11pm, free before 9pm); Su *Simply Boogie* garage, R&B, funk, hip-hop, and "boogie classics" (7pm-2am; free).

■ **Fabric,** 77a Charterhouse St. (☎ 7336 8898). Tube: Farringdon. Bigger than a B52 and 100 times as loud. When they power up the underfoot subwoofer, lights dim across London. 3 dance-floors, chill-out beds, multiple bars, and unisex toilets crammed with up to 2500 dance-crazed Londoners. Yow. Various monthlies F (9:30pm-5am; £10-15), Sa *Fabric Live* (9:30pm-7am; £12).

Notting Hill Arts Club, 21 Notting Hill Gate (☎7460 4459). Tube: Notting Hill Gate. No-frills basement that's consistently the coolest nightspot in the city. Tu *Bemsha!* live Latin beats and jazz improv (6pm-1am; £5, free before 8pm); W *Poptones presents...* live new signings with dance favorites; Th alternates *Soleal* afro-latin beats, hip-hop, and jazz with *Future World Funk* global beatfest (6pm-1am; £5, free before 8pm); F *Inspiration Information* black music from jazz to hip-hop (6pm-2am; £6, free before 8pm, £5 8-10pm); Sa daytime *Rough Trade Sessions* live music from new and established acts (4-8pm; free); Sa evenings a number of one-offs and monthly nights; Su acclaimed *Lazy Dog* journey from deep house to soul (4-11pm; £5, free before 6pm).

Scala, 275 Pentonville Rd. (☎7833 2022, tickets 7771 2000). Tube: Kings Cross. Huge main floor embraces its cinematic past: DJs spin from the projectionist's box, ramped balconies provide a multi-level dance experience, and a giant screen pulsates with mood-enhancing visuals as pyramids of speakers detonate the bass. F *Popstarz* gay/mixed eclectica (10pm-5am; £10); Sa were in flux at press time but tend to be house-dominated; every other Su *Latin 8* provides 6hr. of hip-swinging salsa with a free dance workshop 8:30-9:30pm (8pm-2am; £8). Dress up.

93 Feet East, 150 Brick Lane (☎7247 3293). Tube: Aldgate East or Liverpool St. One of the hottest new clubs in East London. Barn-like main dance-floor, sofa-strewn upstairs room, plus the hard-to-find chill-out space with curved wooden benches topped with bean-bag cushions. W *Rumbamumba* salsas to a live Latin band (7-11pm, £5, students £3); Th *Anokha* acclaimed world dance mixes (9pm-3am; £7); fortnightly F *Haywire* techno and Euro-house (9pm-3am; £8, £7 students and before 11pm) alternates with *Mr. Scruff's* "Keep it unreal" (10pm-3am; free); Sa's a grab-bag (9pm-2am; £5-10).

333, 333 Old St. (☎7739 5949). Tube: Old St. The definitive Shoho hangout; get out the thick-rimmed specs, dye your hair, and arrive early. F monthlies include *Menage à Trois,* with 3 promoters on 3 floors taking you from basement techno-trance to first-floor funkadelia (10pm-5am; £10, £5 before 11pm); Sa *Revolver* brings eclectic funky dance on the main floor, while in true Warhol fashion anyone can get 15min. of fame upstairs—BYO music (10pm-5am; £10, £5 before 11pm).

Cargo, Kingsland Viaduct, 83 Rivington St. (☎7739 3440). Tube: Old Street. Despite the superclub trimmings—2 enormous arched rooms, fab acoustics, movie projectors, and an intimate candle-lit lounge—Cargo is crippled by a 1am license. On the plus side, the place is kicking by 9:30pm. Strong Latin lineup includes Tu *Cubanito* and deep Latin house F at *Barrio,* both mixing DJs and live music. Onsite restaurant serves world food day and night (£2-5). Open M-F noon-1am, Sa 6pm-1am, Su noon-midnight; sets from 8pm M-Sa, 6pm Su. Normally £3-7.

The Fridge, Town Hall Parade, Brixton Hill, SW2 (☎7326 5100). Tube: Brixton. Turn left from the station and bear right at the fork onto Brixton Hill. The giant split-level dance-floor and the stepped wraparound balcony bar give it away as a former cinema. F *Escape from Samsara* total trance glo-stick madness (10pm-6am; £14, £9 before 11pm); Sa usually gay nights, including *Love Muscle* "hot and steamy fun" every other week (10am-6pm; £13). After parties Sa-Su mornings from 5:30am at the Fridge Bar.

The End, 16A West Central St. (☎7419 9199). Tube: Tottenham Court Rd. or Holborn. With speaker walls capable of some earth-shattering bass on 2 dance-floors, The End is best known as a house-and-garage hotspot. M *Trash* glam rock to cutting edge (10pm-3am; £4); Th *Atelier* gay-friendly festival of funky house (9pm-4am; £7, £5 before 11pm); Sa *As One* joins up with AKA to provide 3 floors and 4 bars of futuristic dance (10pm-6am; £15 in advance); Su *Riot* all-day celebration of hard house (2pm-midnight; £7, £5 before 5pm). F one-offs and mega monthlies.

Herbal, 12-14 Kingsland Rd. (☎7613 4462). Tube: Old Street. Herbal is one of the few East London clubs to retain a relaxed, friendly feel unfazed by the neighborhood's rapid climb/decline into the fashionable limelight. Wide range of varying one-offs and monthlies, never over £5. Fixtures include: W *turntable anarchy* (£2); Th *PM Scientists* deep house (£3) alternating with *Groove Armada* funkfest (£5); 2nd F of the month *Carpet* drum'n'bass (£3, free before 11pm); Sa monthlies include *Voodoo* hip-hop (1st and 3rd; £5, £3 before 10pm), interspersed with *Stumble* deep house (2nd; £5) and *Warm Leatherette* punk, disco, and electronica (4th; £5). All nights run 7:30pm-2am.

Ministry of Sound, 103 Gaunt St. (☎ 7378 6528). Tube: Elephant and Castle. Take the exit for South Bank University. The granddaddy of all serious clubbing—arrive early or queue all night. Emphasis on dancing rather than decor, with a massive main room, smaller 2nd dance-floor, and overhead balcony bar (often VIP only). Dress code generally casual, but famously unsmiling doorstaff make it sensible to err on the side of smartness (*no* sports shoes!). F *Smoove* garage and R&B (10:30pm-6am; £12); Sa *Rulin* US and vocal house (midnight-9am; £15).

Sound, 10 Wardour St. (☎ 7287 1010). Tube: Leicester Sq. or Piccadilly Circus. A cheesy Leicester Sq. location can't keep this swinger down. A real labyrinth of a club, with the large, loud main room and balcony bar on the 1st and 2nd floors, a ground floor bar, and a basement restaurant and semi-separate club with its own entrance on Leicester Sq. Th *Bliss* R&B, soul, and UK garage (10pm-3am; £8, £5 before 11pm); F *Funk* pure R&B (10pm-4am; £12, £10 before 11:30pm); Sa ▨ *Carwash* super-70s retro fest—funky dress a must (10pm-4:30am; £12, £5 after 2am).

Velvet Room, 143 Charing Cross Rd. (☎ 7734 4687). Tube: Tottenham Court Rd. Small, showing its age, and packed even midweek—if people don't come for the single dance-floor or dated decor, they must be here for the music. M *Off the Hook* brings R&B and hip-hop to a gay audience (10pm-3am; £5); Tu *Syndicate* garage (10:30pm-3am; £7); W ▨ *Swerve*, with Brazilian beats from fantastic Fabio (10pm-2:30am; £8, students £4.); Th *Ultimate Bass* funky techno (10pm-3am; £6, £4 before 11:30pm), F *House and Trance* (10pm-4:30am; £10, £7 before 11pm, £5 after 2:30am); Sa *Big and Clever* house (10pm-4am; £10, £8 before 11pm).

GAY AND LESBIAN

The Box, 32-34 Monmouth St. (☎ 7240 5828). Recently renovated, this spacious gay/ mixed bar-brasserie is popular with a stylish media/fashion crowd. Daily changing food specials (main courses around £9). They're very proud of their Ally McBeal-style unisex toilets. Also sells club tix. Open M-Sa 11am-11pm, Su 7-10:30pm. MC/V.

Candy Bar, 23-24 Bateman St., on the corner of Greek St. (☎ 7437 1977). Tube: Tottenham Ct. Rd. The UK's first full-time lesbian den, with a groovy bar and a basement dance-floor. DJs W-Su. Tu *Loose* striptease; W funk, soul, and disco; Th R&B and garage; F uplifting house; Sa house, funk, and soul; Su pop, retro, and indie. Open M-Tu 5pm-1am, W-F 5pm-3am, Sa 3pm-3am, Su 5-11pm. F-Sa £5 after 9pm.

Comptons of Soho, 53 Old Compton St. (☎ 7479 7461). Tube: Leicester Sq. or Piccadilly Circus. Soho's "official" gay pub is always busy with a no-nonsense male crowd of all ages. Horseshoe bar encourages the exchange of meaningful glances, while upstairs (opens 6pm) offers a mellower scene with pool table. Open M-Sa 11am-11pm, Su noon-10:30pm. MC/V.

First Out, 52 St. Giles High St. (☎ 7240 8042). Tube: Tottenham Court Rd. Skip the ground-floor cafe serving so-so veggie standards (lasagna £4.25) and head down to the funky-but-friendly basement bar. Predominantly lesbian, but plenty of gay men too except F, when the women-only *Girl Friday* takes over. Open M-Sa 10am-11pm, Su 11am-10:30pm. Cash only.

G-A-Y (☎ (0906) 100 0160). M and Th at the Mean Fiddler, 165 Charing Cross Rd., F-Sa at the Astoria (see p. 143). Tube: Tottenham Court Rd. London's biggest gay and lesbian night, 4 nights a week. Frequently besieged by teenage girls on weekend nights— bands to have played include the Spice Girls and Boyzone—but the majority-gay door policy keeps the atmosphere camp. M *Pink Pounder* 90s classics with 70s-80s faves in the bar (10:30pm-4am; £1 with flyer or ad, available at most gay bars, students free); Th *Music Factory* house, dance, and a little pop (11pm-4am; £1 with flyer or ad, students free); F *Camp Attack* attitude-free 70s and 80s cheese (11pm-4am; £3); Sa *G-A-Y* big night out, rocking the capacity crowd with commercial-dance DJs, and live pop performances (10:30pm-5am; £10).

Heaven, The Arches, Craven Terr. (☎7930 2020). Tube: Charing Cross or Embankment. Though running regular mixed nights, "the world's most famous gay disco" dispels any doubts about its orientation with ubiquitous racks of *boyz* magazines. Labyrinthine interior rewards explorers. M mixed *Popcorn* with chart-toppers, 70s-80s disco hits, commercial house, and £1.50 drinks (10:30pm-3am; £4); W gay *Fruit Machine* house, garage, soul, and swing (10:30pm-3am; £6, £4 before 11:30pm); F mixed *There* hard house and trance danceathon (10:30pm-6am; £10); Sa gay/lesbian *Heaven* dance, trance, house, and disco (10pm-5:30am; £12).

Ku Bar, 75 Charing Cross Rd. (☎7437 4303). Tube: Leicester Sq. Don't be fooled by the naked-lady mosaic; this fashionable hangout is definitely gay, attracting well-dressed, younger men and those that love them. Drinks deals include cocktail pitchers £7 before 9pm, Carlsberg £1 per bottle all day M-F. Get your tickets to *G-A-Y.* (see above) here and skip the queue. Pints from £2.70. Open M-Sa 12:30-11pm, Su 12:30-10:30pm.

Vespa Lounge, St. Giles Circus (☎7836 8956). Tube: Tottenham Court Rd. Above the Conservatory restaurant, at the foot of Centrepoint tower. Relaxed lesbian lounge bar with blue walls, comfy seats, pool table. Thai food supplied by downstairs restaurant. "Laughing Cows" comedy night first Su of month (£5-8), plus occasional theme nights. Gay men welcome as guests. Open M-Sa 6-11pm, Su 6-10:30pm.

LONDON

SOUTH ENGLAND

South England's sprawling pastures unfold with a history that asserts Britain's island heritage and expresses a continental link deeper than the Channel Tunnel. Early Britons settled the counties of Kent, Sussex, and Hampshire after crossing the English Channel the hard way. The later, modestly titled European tourist William the Conqueror left his mark in the form of intimidating castles and inspiring cathedrals, many built around settlements begun by Romans. More recently, German bombings during WWII uncovered long-buried evidence of Caesar's invasion. Victorian mansions balance atop seaside cliffs and the masts of restored ships spike the skyline, summoning a chorus of voices from England's naval and literary past. Geoffrey Chaucer's pilgrims colored the way to Canterbury with their bawdy tales. Jane Austen's acerbic pen scratched in an archipelago of houses near the southern downs and borders. Charles Dickens drew mammoth novels from his early experiences in Portsmouth, while E.M. Forster, Virginia Woolf, and other Bloomsburyites vacationed and lived near the South Downs.

HIGHLIGHTS OF SOUTH ENGLAND

CANTERBURY CATHEDRAL Wend your way to the cathedral that has inspired pilgrims since the 12th century (p. 154).

BRIGHTON Stroll through the beach's carnival madness and take a tour of Brighton's pan-Asian Royal Pavilion (p. 164).

DOVER CLIFFS Don't miss the famous chalk-white cliffs of Dover, one of the first glimpses of England for ferry travelers (p. 157).

SOUTH DOWNS WAY Hike the salty slopes and sleep among Bronze Age burial mounds (p. 164).

KENT

CANTERBURY ☎01227

And specially from every shires ende
Of engelond to caunterbury they wende.
     —Geoffrey Chaucer, *Prologue to The Canterbury Tales.*

Archbishop Thomas à Becket met his demise in Canterbury Cathedral in 1170 after an irate Henry II asked, "Will no one rid me of this troublesome priest?" Tom had dared to stand up for individual rights and freedoms, and a few of the king's henchmen took the hint. The site of one of Britain's most gruesome executions has since become the focus of countless pilgrimages dedicated to the "hooly blisful martir," masterfully captured by Geoffrey Chaucer in his ribald *Canterbury Tales*. Today, visitors come to admire the grand cathedral as well as to discover the city's earthly, living charms.

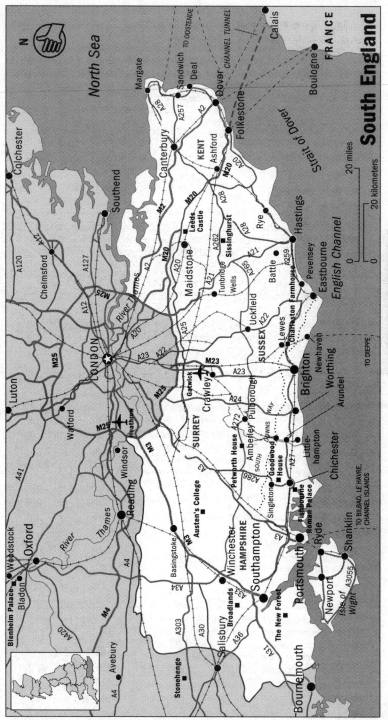

South England

SOUTH ENGLAND

⌷ THE SHIPMAN'S TALE

Trains: East Station, Station Rd. East, off Castle St., southwest of town. Open M-Sa 6:10am-8:20pm, Su 6:10am-9:20pm. **Connex South Trains** (☎(08457) 484950) from **London Victoria** (1½hr.; 2 per hr.; £15.70, day return £16.10). **West Station,** Station Rd. West, off St. Dunstan's St. Open M-F 6:15am-8pm, Sa 6:30am-8pm, Su 7:15am-9:30pm. Connex South Trains from **London Charing Cross** and **London Waterloo** to Canterbury West (1½hr.; every hr.; £15.70, day return £16.10). Ask everyone in your compartment to tell one story each way.

Buses: Bus Station, St. George's Ln. (☎472082). Open M-Sa 8:15am-5:15pm. **National Express** (☎(08705) 808080) **buses** from **London** (2hr., every hr., £6-8). Book tickets by 5pm. **Explorer** tickets allow one day's unlimited bus travel in Kent for the price of a single ticket (£6.50, seniors and children £4.50, families £13.60). Canterbury, on the rail and bus lines from Dover and Folkestone, is often a first stop for travelers from the Continent (see **Dover,** p. 157).

Taxis: Longport (☎458885). Open daily 7am-2am.

Bike Rental: Byways Bicycle Hire, 2 Admiralty Walk (☎277397). Owner delivers from home office; call at any reasonable hour. £10 per day, £50 per week. £50 deposit. **Downland Cycle Hire,** West Station (☎479543). Reserve in advance. £10 per adult per day, £7 per child. Bike trailers £6 per day. £25 deposit.

⚹⚹ ⁊ THE REEVE'S TALE

Canterbury center is roughly circular, as defined by the eroding city wall. An unbroken street crosses the city from northwest to southeast, changing names from **St. Peter's St.** to **High St.** to **The Parade** to **St. George's St.**

Tourist Information Centre: 34 St. Margaret's St. (☎766567; fax 459840; canterburyinformation@canterbury.gov.uk). Bursting with maps and guides. "Book a bed ahead" service £2.50 and 10% deposit (☎780063). Open M-Sa 9:30am-5:30pm, Su 10am-4pm.

Tours: 1½hr. guided tours of the city from the tourist information centre (TIC) Apr.-Oct. daily at 2pm; additional tours July-Aug. M-Sa at 11:30am. £3.50, students and seniors £3, under 14 free, families £8.50. The TIC has info on hot-air balloon tours.

Financial Services: Banks mingle near the big-name department stores. **Lloyds TSB,** 49 High St. (☎451681). Open M-Tu and Th 9am-5pm, W 9:30am-5pm, F 9am-6pm, Sa 9am-12:30pm. **Bureau de change** closes 30min. before bank. **Thomas Cook,** 14 Mercery Ln. (☎767656). Open Th-Tu 9am-5:30pm, W 10am-5:30pm.

Launderette: 36 St. Peter's St. (☎786911). Open M-Sa 8:30am-5:45pm.

Police: Old Dover Rd. (☎762055), outside the eastern city wall.

Hospital: Kent and Canterbury Hospital (☎766877), off Ethelbert Rd.

Internet Access: I2M Internet Cafe, corner of St. Dunstan's St. and Station Rd. West (☎478778). Cheap and fast at £3 per hr. Open M-Sa 10am-6pm, Su noon-5pm.

Post Office: 28 High St. (☎473811), across from Best Ln. Open M-Sa 8:30am-5:30pm. **Postal Code:** CT1 2BA.

⌷ THE INNKEEPER'S TALE

Canterbury is busy and singles are scarce; reserve ahead or arrive by mid-morning. B&Bs cluster around High St. and near West Station. The cheaper B&Bs (£18-20) on **New Dover Rd.,** ½ mi. from East Station, fill fast. Turn right as you leave the station and continue up the main artery, which becomes Upper Bridge St. At the second roundabout, turn right onto St. George's Pl., which becomes New Dover Rd.

The Tudor House, 6 Best Ln. (☎765650), off High St. Recline by a Tudor fireplace in this 16th-century home. Front rooms have stellar cathedral views. Bike and boat rental £3 per half-day, £5 per day. Singles £18; doubles £36, with bath £44; family rooms £50.

Hampton House, 40 New Dover Rd. (☎464912). Luxurious house with quiet rooms and heavenly mattresses. Tea and coffee room service and English breakfast. £20-25 per person in summer. Singles can be more expensive. Off-season prices vary.

Kipps, A Place to Sleep, 40 Nunnery Fields (☎786121; fax 766992; kipps@FSB-dial.co.uk), a 5-10min. walk from the city center. Comfortable place for a kip, with terrific self-catering kitchen. Towels £1. Washer (£2.80) and dryer (90p). Key deposit £10. Dorms £11-13; singles £15; doubles £28. Weekly rates and family discounts available.

Let's Stay, 26 New Dover Rd. (☎463628). Hostel-style lodgings in delightful Irish hostess's home. Vegetarian breakfast available; engaging conversation included. Ask about the origin of the name! Reception hours vary—call before arrival. Beds £11 per person.

YHA Canterbury, 54 New Dover Rd. (☎462911; fax 470752; canterbury@yha.org.uk), ¾ mi. from East Station and ½ mi. southeast of the bus station. 86 beds. Laundry facilities. Lockers £1 plus deposit. Kitchen; meals also available. Relaxing lounge with Internet access (50p per 6min.) and games. Bureau de change. Reception 7:30-10am and 1-11pm. Book at least two weeks in advance in summer. Dorms £11, under 18 £7.90.

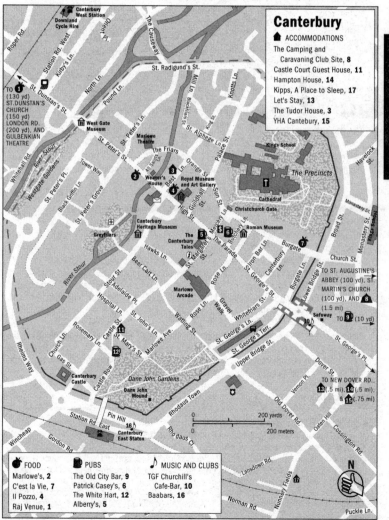

Canterbury

🏠 ACCOMMODATIONS

The Camping and
    Caravaning Club Site, **8**
Castle Court Guest House, **11**
Hampton House, **14**
Kipps, A Place to Sleep, **17**
Let's Stay, **13**
The Tudor House, **3**
YHA Cantebury, **15**

SOUTH ENGLAND

🍴 FOOD

Marlowe's, **2**
C'est la Vie, **7**
Il Pozzo, **4**
Raj Venue, **1**

🍺 PUBS

The Old City Bar, **9**
Patrick Casey's, **6**
The White Hart, **12**
Alberry's, **5**

🎵 MUSIC AND CLUBS

TGF Churchill's
    Cafe-Bar, **10**
Baabars, **16**

Castle Court Guest House, 8 Castle St. (☎/fax 463441), a few minutes from Eastgate in the old town. Cream-colored walls guard this quiet B&B; *Let's Go* users get 10% off. Vegetarian breakfast available. Singles £22; doubles and twins £36, with bath £42.

Camping: The Camping and Caravaning Club Site, Bekesbourne Ln. (☎463216), off the A257 (Sandwich Rd.), 1½ mi. east of the city center. Take Longport Rd. from the city wall. Good facilities. Open year-round. £4.75 pitch fee; £5.30 per person.

■ THE COOK'S TALE

The **Safeway** supermarket, St. George's Pl., is 4min. from the town center. (☎769335. Open M-Sa 8am-8pm, Su 10am-4pm.)

Marlowe's, 55 St. Peter's St. (☎462194). English food with Mexican improvisations. Choose from 8 toppings for 8 oz. burgers (£6.60) or select a veggie dish (£6.35-9). Try the Steak and Strawberry special for £6. Open daily 11:30am-10:30pm.

C'est la Vie, 17b Burgate (☎457525). Fresh, inventive sandwiches for takeaway (£1.90-2.20). 10% student discount before noon or after 2pm. Open daily 9am-6pm.

Il Pozzo, 15 Best Ln. (☎450154). Distinguishes itself from scads of Italian restaurants with richly sauced, aromatic food. Somewhat more expensive (main courses around £11) but superlative. Open M-Sa noon-2pm and 7-10pm. MC/V.

Raj Venue, 92 St. Dunstan's St. (☎462653). Fairly portioned Indian food (many dishes £4.50-7) will please the gourmet, and the 10% student discount will please the cash-strapped traveler. Open daily noon-2:30pm and 6-11:30pm.

■ PUBS AND CLUBS

The Old City Bar, Oaten Hill Pl. (☎766882). Students and twentysomethings pack both pub beer garden. BBQ and live music on weekends. Open daily noon-11pm; food served noon-2:30pm.

Patrick Casey's, Butchery Ln. (☎463252). With a vast menu of traditional Irish foods and amply flowing beverages, Casey's warms a traveler's stomach. Live folk music Th and F nights at 9pm, Su at 8:30pm. Open M-Sa 11am-11pm, Su noon-10:30pm.

The White Hart, Worthgate Pl. (☎765091), near East Station. Congenial pub with home-made lunch specials and sweets (£4.50-6), plus some of Canterbury's best bitters (£1.80). Enjoy both in the city's largest beer garden. Open daily 10am-11pm.

Alberry's, 38 St. Margaret's St. (☎452378). A stylish wine bar that pours late into the evening. Happy hour 5:30-7pm. Open M-W noon-11pm, Th noon-1am, F-Sa noon-2am.

TGF Churchill's Cafe-Bar, St. George's Pl. (☎761276). Mix a touch of the 1940s with Hollywood glam, add a dash of everything from classic rock to garage, and get one of the most refreshing clubs around. M student night, W live tribute band, Th party night. Dress smart casual, no jeans or trainers F-Sa. Free M and Th-Sa before 9pm, Tu-W before 8pm. Open M-W 7pm-1am, Th-Sa 7pm-2am.

Baabars, 15 Station Rd. East (☎761233). 3-way split personality on weekends: Baa-bars, the charty and party first floor; the Bizz, the all-dance 3rd floor; leaving the Works musically and architecturally in between. No jeans or trainers F-Su. Cover £3-6. Open M-Th 7pm-2am, F-Sa 7pm-3am (bar closes at 2am), Su 7pm-11:30pm.

◉ SIGHTS

■ CANTERBURY CATHEDRAL

☎762862. *Cathedral open Easter-Sept. M-Sa 9am-6:30pm, Su 12:30-2:30pm and 4:30-5:30pm; Oct.-Easter M-Sa 9am-5pm, Su 12:30-2:30pm and 4:30-5:30pm. Evensong M-F 5:30pm, Sa 3:15pm, Su 6:30pm. Precincts open daily 7am-9pm. £3.50, concessions £2.50. Visitors are charged at the gate; after hours you may wander the precincts for free, but not the building, unless you happen to be an Anglican bishop. 75min. tours 4 per day, fewer off season; £3, students and seniors £2, children £1.20; check the nave or welcome center for times. Self-guided tour booklet £1.25. 25min. audio tour £2.50. Photography permit £2.*

Money collected from pilgrims funded most of Canterbury Cathedral's wonders, including the early Gothic nave, constructed mostly between the 13th and 15th centuries on a site allegedly consecrated by St. Augustine 700 years earlier. Among the nave's entombed residents are Henry IV, his wife Joan of Navarre, and the Black Prince. A taste for the macabre has drawn the curious since 1170, when Archbishop Thomas à Becket was beheaded at the cathedral with a strike so forceful it broke the axe-blade. The murder site is closed off by a rail—a kind of permanent police line—around the Altar of the Sword's Point, while a 14min. audiovisual re-creation of the homicide plays just off the cloisters (shown continuously 10am-4pm; £1, students and seniors 70p, children 50p). In the adjacent **Trinity Chapel,** a solitary candle marks where Becket's body lay until 1538, when Henry VIII burned his remains and destroyed the shrine to show how he dealt with unruly bishops. Keep alert for an orange-striped cat known as Tom padding across a tomb or napping in a pew. The mysterious kitty comes and goes as he pleases, and is most famous for trailing the Archbishop during a televised high mass.

In a structure plagued by fire and rebuilt time and again, the **Norman crypt,** a huge 12th-century chapel, remains intact. The **Corona Tower,** 105 steps above the easternmost apse, recently reopened after renovations (60p, children 30p). Under the **Bell Harry Tower**—at the crossing of the nave and western transepts—perpendicular arches support intricate 15th-century fan vaulting.

OTHER SIGHTS

THE CANTERBURY TALES. Let the gap-toothed Wife of Bath and her waxen companions entertain you in an abbreviated version of the Tales, complete with smells of sweat, hay, and general grime. The museum reenacts the journey of Chaucer's pilgrims, only this time with headsets and in several languages. *(St. Margaret's St.* ☎ *479227. Open July-Aug. daily 9am-5.30pm; Mar.-June and Sept.-Oct. 9:30am-5:30pm; Nov.-Feb. Su-F 10am-4:30pm, Sa 9:30am-5:30pm. £5.90, concessions £4.90, families £18.50.)*

ST. AUGUSTINE'S ABBEY. Soaring arches and crumbling walls are all that remain of what was once among the greatest abbeys in Europe, built in AD 598. Don't miss St. Augustine's humble tomb under a pile of rocks. Exhibits and a free audio tour reveal the abbey's history as burial place, royal palace, pleasure garden, and World Heritage Site. *(Outside the city wall near the cathedral.* ☎ *767345. Open Apr.-Oct. daily 10am-6pm; Nov.-Mar. 10am-4pm. £2.60, students and seniors £2, children £1.30.)*

CHURCH OF ST. MARTIN. In this parish church, the oldest in Britain, Pagan King Æthelbert was married to the Christian French Princess Bertha in AD 562, paving the way for England's conversion to Christianity. Joseph Conrad is buried here, sleeping in darkness. *(North Holmes St.* ☎ *459482. Open M-Su 9am-5pm. Free.)*

CANTERBURY HERITAGE MUSEUM. Housed in the medieval Poor Priests' Hospital, the museum spans Canterbury's history, from St. Thomas to WWII bombings to beloved children's-book character Rupert Bear, the creation of local artist Mary Tourtel. *(Stour St.* ☎ *452747. Open June-Oct. M-Sa 10:30am-5pm, Su 1:30-5pm; Nov.-May M-Sa 10:30am-5pm. £1.90, concessions £1.20.)*

WEST GATE MUSEUM. The remainder of medieval Canterbury bunches near the West Gate, through which pilgrims traditionally entered the city and one of the few medieval fortifications to survive wartime blitz. Just within it, the museum, a former prison surrounded by well-tended gardens, keeps armor, old weapons, a faux prisoner, and commanding views of the city. *(☎ 452747. Open M-Sa 11am-12:30pm and 1:30-3:30pm. £1, students and seniors 65p, children 50p, families £2.30.)*

GREYFRIARS. England's first Franciscan friary, Greyfriars was built over the River Stour in 1267 by Franciscan monks who arrived in the country in 1224, two years before Francis of Assisi died. A small museum devoted to the local order and a chapel are found inside the simple building. For a quiet break, walk to Greyfriars's riverside gardens. *(Stour St. Open in summer M-F 2-4pm. Free.)*

BEST OF THE REST. Home of the Huguenots during the 15th century, the **Weaver's House,** 1 St. Peter's St., features an authentic witch-dunking stool swinging above the river. **Weaver's River Tours** runs 30min. cruises leaving from the house several times per day. (☎ 464660. £4, student and seniors £3.50, children £3.) The **Roman Museum,** Butchery Ln., houses hairpins, building fragments, and other artifacts from Roman Canterbury in a hands-on exhibit. (☎ 785575. Open June-Oct. M-Sa 10am-5pm, Su 1:30-5pm; Nov.-May M-Sa 10am-5pm. Last admission 4pm. £2.50, concessions £1.60.) The **Royal Museum and Art Gallery** showcases new local talents and recounts the history of the "Buffs," one of the oldest regiments of the British Army. (In the public library on 18 High St. ☎ 452747. Open M-Sa 10am-5pm. Free.)

Near the city walls to the southwest lie the **Dane John Mound and Gardens,** now a park, and the massive, solemn remnants of the Norman **Canterbury Castle,** built for William the Conqueror. Outside the city walls to the northwest, the vaults of **St. Dunstan's Church,** north of St. Dunstan's St., contain a relic said to be the head of *Utopia* author Sir Thomas More. Legend has it that his daughter bribed the executioner at the Tower of London to obtain the head for burial.

♫ ENTERTAINMENT

For up-to-date entertainment listings, pick up *What, Where, When,* free at the TIC, or call 767744 for the recorded "Leisure Line." Buskers, especially along St. Peter's St. and High St., play Vivaldi streetside while young bands of impromptu players ramble from corner to corner, acting out the most absurd of Chaucer's scenes.

The task of regaling pilgrims with stories today falls to the **Marlowe Theatre,** The Friars, which stages touring London productions. (☎ 787787. Box office open M-Sa 10am-9pm. Tickets £6.50-22. Concessions available.) The **Gulbenkian Theatre,** at the University of Kent, University Rd., west of town on St. Dunstan's St., stages a range of productions. (☎ 769075. Box office open M-F 10:30am-5:30pm. Tickets £5-21. Unsold tickets available from 7pm on performance evening for £5.)

For information on summer arts events and the October **Canterbury Festival**—two full weeks (Oct. 12-26 in 2002) of drama, opera, cabaret, chamber music, dance, and exhibitions inspired by French culture—contact Canterbury Festival, Christ Church Gate, The Precincts, Canterbury, Kent CT1 2EE (☎ 452853). The **Chaucer Festival Spring Pilgrimage** (☎ 470379) in April brings a medieval fair and period-costumed performers. The **Stour Music Festival,** a popular celebration of Renaissance and Baroque music, lasts for 10 days at the end of June in Ashford, 5 mi. southwest of Canterbury. The festival takes place in and around All Saint's Boughton Aluph Church, on the A28 and accessible by rail from West Station. Call the Canterbury bookings office a month in advance for tickets (☎ 455600; £5-14).

▨ DAYTRIPS FROM CANTERBURY

▨ SISSINGHURST CASTLE GARDEN

Catch a train from Canterbury West to Staplehurst station, where local buses #4 and 5 run to Sissinghurst Garden. ☎ (01580) 710700; info line 710701. Open Apr. to mid-Oct. Tu-F 1-6:30pm, Sa-Su 10am-6:30pm; last admission 1hr. before close. £6.50, children £3. A timed ticket system prevents overcrowding.

A masterpiece of floral design and execution by Vita Sackville-West and her husband, Harold Nicholson, both of Bloomsbury Group fame, Sissinghurst is Britain's most popular garden. The flowers that spill into narrow paths in an overwhelming mosaic of color may seem like the chaotic victory of Mother Nature, but the garden is organized according to the best-laid of human plans, profoundly influenced by Gertrude Jekyll's cottage-style landscape design and the Arts and Crafts movement of the early 20th century. After savoring the serenity of the White Garden of fiery Cottage Garden, stroll along the moat to forested, tranquil lakes.

LEEDS CASTLE

23 mi. southwest of Canterbury on the A20 London-Folkestone road near Maidstone. Trains run from Canterbury West Station to Bearsted and a shuttle runs between the station and the castle (return £3.20). ☎(01622) 765400 or (0870) 600 8880. Castle open Mar.-Oct. daily 11am-7:30pm; Nov.-Feb. 10:15am-5:30pm. Grounds open Mar.-Oct. daily 10am-7pm; Nov.-Feb. 10am-5pm. Last admission 2hr. before close. Castle and grounds £10, students and seniors £8.50, children £6.50, families £29. Grounds only £8.50, students and seniors £7, children £5.20, families £24. Reduced rates for disabled travelers.

Billed as "the Loveliest Castle in the World," Leeds was built immediately after the Norman Conquest and remained a favorite royal property until Edward VI sold it for a song. His father, Henry VIII, had made the castle a lavish dwelling whose 500 acres of woodlands and gardens still host unusual waterfowl, including black swans. The ground floor is the quintessential royal Tudor residence, in sharp contrast the more modern second floor. One wing displays an alarming collection of medieval dog collars. Outdoors, lose yourself in a **maze** of 2400 yew trees, though the sculpted grounds, gardens, and forests are practically a maze in themselves.

DOVER ☎01304

And thence to France shall we convey you safe,
And bring you back, charming the narrow seas.
—William Shakespeare, *Henry V*

From Celtic invaders to the Channel Tunnel, the white chalk cliffs of Dover have been—and will remain—the first impression made upon many a traveler to England. Though the city's tranquility has been disrupted by the puttering of ferries and the hum of hovercraft, the splendor of this transport hub survives in its magnificent castle and the unforgettable promontories it guards. To be sure, urban Dover has sacrificed whatever charm it once possessed to the business of getting travelers in and out fast, but a few minutes' walk along the beach will restore any visitor's childhood imaginings of stalwart lighthouses and Norman ruins.

▐ GETTING THERE AND CROSSING THE CHANNEL

Trains: Priory Station, Station Approach Rd. Ticket office open M-Sa 4:15am-11:20pm, Su 6:15am-11:20pm. Trains (☎(08457) 484950) from **London Victoria, Waterloo East, London Bridge,** and **Charing Cross** (2hr., 2 per hr., £21) and **Canterbury** (20min., 2 per hr., £4.90). Check schedules to see which trains branch off en route.

Buses: Pencester Rd., between York St. and Maison Dieu Rd. (☎(01304) 240024). Ticket office open M-Tu and Th-F 8:45am-5:15pm, W 8:45am-4pm, Sa 8:30am-noon. The tourist information centre (TIC) also sells tickets. **National Express** (☎(08705) 808080) from **London,** continuing to the Eastern Docks after stopping at Pencester Rd. (2¾hr., 23 per day, £10). **Stagecoach** (☎(01227) 472082) from **Canterbury** (45min., £4.40) and **Deal** (40min., £3). A bus from **Folkestone,** the termination point for Channel Tunnel trains, runs 2 per hr. (30min., £2.60).

Ferries: Major companies operate ships from the Eastern Docks to **Calais** and **Oostend, Belgium,** and the Dover TIC offers a ferry booking service. **P&O Stena** lines (☎(08706) 000600; www.posl.com) to Calais for £26 (departing 35 times per day); **SeaFrance** (☎(08705) 711711; www.seafrance.com) for £17 (departing 15 times daily). Special deals are common in summer. **Hovercrafts** leave from the Hoverport at the Prince of Wales Pier for Calais, foot passengers £27 one way. Free bus service leaves Priory Station for the docks 45min. to 1hr. before sailing time. (See **By Ferry,** p. 35, for complete ferry and hovercraft information.) The **Channel Tunnel** offers passenger service on Eurostar and car transport on Le Shuttle to and from the continent (see **By Train,** p. 37).

Taxis: Central Taxi Service (☎240 0441). 24hr.

🛈 PRACTICAL INFORMATION

Tourist Information Centre: Townwall St. (☎205108; fax 245409), a block from shore. Multilingual staff sells ferry and hovercraft tickets; after hours call for a list of accommodations. Open daily 9am-6pm.

Tours: Guide Friday (☎205108) operates 1hr. hop-on/hop-off tours with convenient stops at the train station, TIC, Market Sq., and Dover castle. Runs daily 10am-4pm. £6.50, students and seniors £5.50, children £2.50, families £15.50. **White Cliffs Boat Tour** (☎/fax 271388) sails every hr. from the Marina. £5, children £3, families £12.

Financial Services: Several **banks,** generally open M-F 9:30am-4:30pm, bump elbows in Market Sq. **Thomas Cook,** 3 Cannon St. (☎204215), has a **bureau de change.** Open M-Tu and Th-Sa 9am-5:30pm, W 10am-5:30pm.

Launderette: Cherry Tree Ave. (☎242822), off London Rd., beyond the hostel. Change machine and soap (30p). Open daily 8am-8pm, last wash 7:15pm.

Police: Ladywell St. (☎240055), off High St.

Hospital: (☎201624). Take bus #D9 or D5 from outside the post office to the Buckland Hospital on Coomb Valley Rd., northwest of town.

Internet Access: Library, Biggin St. (☎204241). Free, maximum 1hr.; call ahead to book. Open M-Tu and Th 9:30am-6pm, W 9:30am-1pm, F 9:30am-7pm, Sa 9:30am-5pm. **Cyber Communication International Ltd.** 10p per min., £6 per hr. Maybe the Internet is cheaper in France. Open M-W 10am-7pm, Th-Sa 9am-8pm, Su 10am-5pm. MC/V.

Post Office: 68 Pencester Rd. (☎241747), by the bus station, inside Alldays. Open M-F 8:30am-5:30pm, Sa 8:30am-noon. **Postal Code:** CT16 1PB.

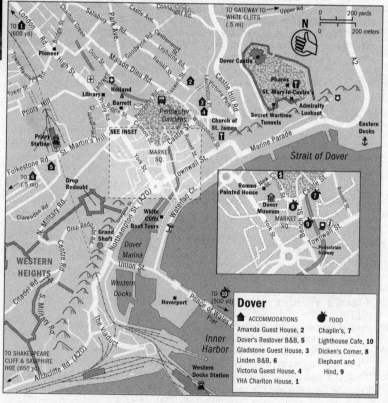

Dover

🏠 ACCOMMODATIONS
Amanda Guest House, 2
Dover's Restover B&B, 5
Gladstone Guest House, 3
Linden B&B, 6
Victoria Guest House, 4
YHA Charlton House, 1

🍴 FOOD
Chaplin's, 7
Lighthouse Cafe, 10
Dicken's Corner, 8
Elephant and Hind, 9

ACCOMMODATIONS

Rooms are difficult to find in high season, so plan ahead—the ferry terminal makes an ugly and unsafe campground. The cheaper B&Bs congregate on **Folkestone Rd.** past the train station, quite a walk from the center of town. Some of them stay open all night; if the lights are on, ring the bell. During the day, pricier B&Bs are near the center of town on **Castle St.** A "White Cliffs Association" plaque outside signals quality, moderately priced rooms. Most B&Bs ask for a deposit.

YHA Charlton House, 306 London Rd. (☎201314; fax 202236), with overflow at **14 Goodwyne Rd.** (closer to town center). ½ mi. from the train station; turn left onto Folkestone Rd., then left again at the roundabout onto High St., which becomes London Rd. 69 beds, 2-10 beds per room. Lounge and game room with pool table. Kitchen, forceful showers, and lockers. Overflow building has 60 beds, kitchen, and lounge area. You may have to wait a bit after ringing for staff. Same prices as main hostel, but bring exact change. Lockout 10am-1pm. Curfew 11pm. Dorms £11, under 18 £7.80.

Gladstone Guest House, 3 Laureston Pl. (☎208457; kud3gladstone@aol.com). Tasteful rooms with cherry finish hand-created by the owner, some with views of rolling hills and fish ponds. Singles £25-28; doubles £44-48. Under 10 free. Families £18 per person.

Dover's Restover Bed & Breakfast, 69 Folkestone Rd. (☎206031; fax 216052), across from the train station. Well-equipped rooms, pleasant service, and full English breakfast. £22-30 per person, off season £15-20.

Victoria Guest House, 1 Laureston Pl. (☎/fax 205140; WHam101496@aol.com). Well-traveled hosts extend a friendly welcome, but think twice about complaining of sore muscles; your neighbor might have just swum the Channel. Victorian rooms in an excellent location. No singles. Doubles £30-46; family room £50-56. Special 5-day rates.

Amanda Guest House, 4 Harold St. (☎201711; pageant@port-of-dover.com). Hall bathrooms are a small price to pay for elegant Victorian light fixtures and marble fireplaces in a house built by the former mayor. Twins £34-36; family room £50.

Linden Bed & Breakfast, 231 Folkestone Rd. (☎205449; fax 212499; lindenrog@aol.com). Plush B&B makes every effort to accommodate its guests—ask for courtesy pickup from the train station and docks. £24-28 per person, off season £22.

Camping: Harthorn Farm (☎852658), at Martin Mill Station off the A258 between Dover and Deal. Near the railway; follow the brown campground signs from the train station. 250 pitches. June to mid-Sept. £13 per 2 people with car and tent; mid-Sept. to Oct. and Mar.-May £3 per additional person. Without car £4 per person. Electricity £2.

FOOD

Despite (or perhaps because of) the proximity of the Continent, Dover's cuisine remains staunchly English. Grease fires rage in the fish-and-chip shops on London Rd. and Biggin St. Get groceries at **Pioneer,** on the corner of Bridge St. and High St. (Open M-F 8:30am-10pm, Sa 7:30am-10pm, Su 10am-4pm.) For health food, swing by **Holland & Barrett,** 35 Biggin St. (☎241426. Open M-Sa 9am-5:30pm. MC/V.)

Chaplin's, 2 Church St. (☎204870). Pictures of Charlie in a classic diner. Shoe leather is (sadly) not on the menu, but you won't miss it with specials like their English kidney pie (£5 with vegetables). Open daily 8:30am-9pm, off season until 8.30pm.

The Lighthouse Cafe and Tea Room (☎242028), at the end of Prince of Wales Pier. Basic fish-and-chips fare, but not a basic location: a view of Dover castle, beaches, and the White Cliffs as you sip tea from ½ mi. offshore. Worth the visit for the vista alone. Open in summer daily 10am-5:30pm; a sign at the pier's start tells you if they're open.

Dickens' Corner, 7 Market Sq. (☎206692). The ground floor bustles as channelers browse baguettes and sandwiches (£3-4) while the upstairs tearoom moves at a more refined pace. People-watch from the tables outside. Open M-Sa 9am-5:30pm.

SOUTH ENGLAND

Elephant and Hind, Market Sq. Toss back your favorite ale while shooting pool or chatting it up in this lively pub in the center of town. Impressive meal deals for a mere £1-3, served M-F noon-2:30pm. Open M-Sa 10am-11pm, Su noon-10pm.

👁 SIGHTS

DOVER CASTLE. The view from Castle Hill Rd., on the east side of town, reveals why Dover Castle is famed both for its magnificent setting and for its impregnability. Many have launched assaults on the castle by land, sea, and air. The French tried in 1216, as did the English themselves during the Civil Wars in the 17th century, and the Germans in WWI and II; all efforts failed. Boulogne, 22 mi. away across the Channel, can (barely) be seen on clear days from the castle's top; it was from that coast that the Germans launched rocket bombs in WWII. These "doodle-bug" missiles destroyed the **Church of St. James,** the ruins of which crumble at the base of Castle Hill. Beside **St. Mary-in-Castro's,** a tiled Saxon church, the **Pharos** towers as the tallest remaining Roman edifice in Britain, built in 43 BC, and the only Roman lighthouse in existence. Take a moment to climb to the platform of the **Admiralty Lookout** for unsurpassable views of the cliffs and harbor; 50p gets you a binocular look at France. The ☒**Secret Wartime Tunnels** constitute an impressive 3½ mi. labyrinth only recently declassified. Originally built in the late 18th century to defend Britain from attack by Napoleon, the vast network of burrows occupies five stories and served as the base for the evacuation of Allied troops from Dunkirk in WWII. The lowest level, not yet open to the public, was intended to house the government in 1962 should the Cuban Missile Crisis have triggered WWIII. Tours fill quickly, and there is usually a long wait, so check in before visiting the rest of the Castle. *(Buses from the town center run Apr.-Sept. daily every hr. (55p); otherwise, scale Castle Hill. There's a pedestrian ramp and stairs by the first Castle sign. Open daily Apr.-Sept. 10am-6pm; Oct. 10am-5pm; Nov.-Mar. 10am-4pm. £7, concessions £5.30, children £3.50, families £17.50. Prices include the tour of the (not-so) secret tunnels.)*

DOVER MUSEUM. An engaging museum that renders even the Bronze Age exciting. The first floor depicts Dover's Roman days as Dubras, an important colonial outpost, while the third floor's high-tech gallery (mind the polar bear) features the Dover Bronze Age Boat, the oldest seafaring vessel yet discovered. At 3600 years, it's older than Moses. *(Market Sq. ☎201066; fax 241186. Open Apr.-Oct. daily 10am-6pm; Nov.-Mar. 10am-5:30pm. £1.75, concessions 95p, families £4.50. 50% YHA discount.)*

THE WHITE CLIFFS. Covering most of the surrounding coastline, the white cliffs make a beautiful backdrop for a stroll along the pebbly beach. A few miles west of Dover, the whitest, steepest, and most famous of them all is known as **Shakespeare Cliff** because it is traditionally identified as the site of eyeless Gloucester's battle with the brink in *King Lear*. *(25min. by foot along Snargate St.)* To the east of Dover, past Dover Castle, the **Gateway to the White Cliffs** overlooks the Straits of Dover and serves as informative starting point for exploration. *(Buses and Guide Friday go to Langdon Cliff at least every hr. (55p). ☎202746. Open Mar.-Oct. 10am-5pm; Nov.-Feb. 11am-4pm.)*

THE GRAND SHAFT. This 140 ft. triple spiral staircase was shot through the rock in Napoleonic times to link the army on the Western Heights with the city center. The first stairwell was for "officers and their ladies," the second for "sergeants and their wives," the last for "soldiers and their women." *(Snargate St. ☎201200. Ascend July-Aug. W-Su 2-5pm; on bank holidays 10am-5pm. £1.50, seniors and children £1.)*

OTHER SIGHTS. Recent excavations have unearthed a remarkably well-preserved **Roman painted house** off Cannon St. near Market Sq. It's the oldest Roman house in Britain, complete with underground central heating and indoor plumbing. *(New St. ☎203279. Open Apr.-Sept. Tu-Su 10am-5pm. £2, concessions 80p.)* Dozens of **cliff walks** lie within a short distance of the town center; consult the TIC for trail info. For more startling views, take the A20 toward Folkestone to **Samphire Hoe,** a well-groomed park planted in the summer of 1997 from material dug from the Channel Tunnel.

PLAYING WITH YOUR FOOD The northernmost of the Cinque Ports, **Sandwich** first tasted fame when the 4th Earl of Sandwich popularized the culinary masterpiece of the same name. A hardcore gambler, the Earl was usually too busy playing cards to bother himself with such superfluity as knives or forks; instead, he'd often ask for meals between two slices of bread so he could eat from one hand and play rummy with the other. It's unlikely that the Earl was the first to slap together viands and carbs, but the tradition can't be traced father back. Since this gastronomical revolution 250 years ago, not much has happened to the tiny town. Don't bother visiting—that is, if you don't mind missing lunch.

◪ DAYTRIP FROM DOVER

DEAL

*Trains from Dover Priory arrive in Deal Station at least every hr. (15min., £3). The **tourist information centre,** Town Hall, High St., books beds for a 10% deposit and provides the free Deal Historic Town Trails, which details 10 walks in the area. (☎(01304) 369576. Open Oct.-May M-F 9am-12:30pm and 1:30-5pm; June-Sept. also Sa 10am-2pm.)*

Julius Caesar came ashore with an invasion force at Deal in 55 BC, and the area's 16th-century castles represent Henry VIII's attempt to prevent similar occurrences. Quiet and serene today, Deal makes a pleasant daytrip with its close proximity to castles and beaches *sans* ferry traffic. **Deal Castle,** south of town at the corner of Victoria Rd. and Deal Castle Rd., is the largest of Henry VIII's constructions for the Cinque Ports defensive system. Meant to serve as an imposing bulwark against the French, it holds a symmetrical maze of corridors and cells guaranteed to entangle potential visitors. Note the medieval subliminal advertising: the castle's six buttresses form the distinctive shape of the Tudor Rose, Henry's family symbol. (☎(01304) 372762. Free audio tour. Open Apr.-Sept. daily 10am-6pm; Oct.-Mar. W-Su 10am-4pm. £3.10, concessions £2.30, children £1.60.) **Walmer Castle,** ½ mi. south of Deal via the beachfront pedestrian path or the A258, is the best-preserved and most elegant of Henry VIII's citadels. Walmer has since been transformed into a country estate which, since the 1700s, has been the official residence of the Lords Warden of the Cinque Ports: notable Wardens past include the Duke of Wellington (whose famed boots are on display), William Pitt, and Winston Churchill. The post is currently filled by the Queen Mum, who usually moves into Walmer for part of July; the beautiful gardens are planted with her favorite flowers. (☎(01304) 364288. Worthwhile 30min. audio tour free. Open Apr.-Sept. daily 10am-6pm; Oct. 10am-dusk; Nov.-Mar. W-Su 10am-4pm; call ahead in July, when the castle is often closed. £5, students and seniors £4, children £2.75.) Perhaps the most famous restaurant in Kent, **Dunkerley's Bistro,** 19 Beach St., overlooks the sea. Residents from all over the region flood in to dine on local fish for around £12. (☎375016. Open Tu-Sa noon-2:30pm and 6-10pm, Su noon-9:30pm.)

SUSSEX

RYE ☎01797

Settled before the Roman invasion, Rye's status soared with its admission to the elite Membership of the Cinque Ports, a defensive organization initiated by Edward the Confessor and still in operation today. As though Rye were getting too big for its boots, nature interfered and choked the waterways with silt—according to local myth, Rye's name derives from the French *la rie*, the waste spot. Throughout the 18th century, the town was best known for its bands of smugglers, who darted past royal authorities to stash contraband in an elaborate network of secret cellars and passageways. Today's Rye (pop. 4350) maintains much of its former affluence, its cobblestone streets and half-timbered houses making the town one of the most beautiful in the kingdom.

 TRANSPORTATION. Trains (☎ (08457) 484950) puff into the station off Cinque Port St. from: **London Bridge** (1½hr., £17.60); **Brighton** (1¾hr., £12); **Eastbourne** (1hr., £6.90); **Dover** (1¾hr., £9.80). **National Express** (☎ (08705) 808080) runs from **London** (£12). **Buses** (☎ 223343) covering south England stop in the train station's car park.

 ORIENTATION AND PRACTICAL INFORMATION. Rye sits at the mouth of the River Rother. To get to the tourist information centre (TIC) from the station, steer yourself to Cinque Port St. proper, and turn right onto Wish St.; turn left onto the Strand Quay and the TIC is on the left. To reach the oldest part of town, hike 5min. up Market Rd. to High St., Lion St., and Mermaid St.

The **tourist information centre** (TIC), Rye Heritage Centre, Strand Quay, distributes the free *Rye: 1066 Country* guide, which lists sights and accommodations. (☎ 226696; fax 223460; www.rye.org.uk. Open mid-Mar. to Oct. daily 9am-5:30pm; Nov.-Feb. M-F 10am-3pm, Sa-Su 10am-4pm.) The TIC also shows a "laser and light film" (a movie, in normalspeak) about Rye's smuggling past and hands out self-guided audio tours. (£2, concessions £1.50.) Other services include: **banks** on High St.; a **launderette,** in Ropewalk Arcade (open daily 8:30am-6pm); the **police,** Cinque Port St. (☎ 222112); **Internet access** at the **library** (☎ 223355; £1.50 per 30min.; open M and W 9:30am-5:30pm, Th 9:30am-12:30pm, F 9:30am-6pm, Sa 9:30am-5pm); and the **post office,** 22-24 Cinque Port St. (☎ 222163; open M-Tu and Th-F 8:30am-5:30pm, W and Sa 9am-5:30pm). **Postal code:** TN31 7AA.

 ACCOMMODATIONS. The area's only **YHA Youth Hostel,** Rye Rd., is 7 mi. from Rye, 5 mi. from Hastings. From Rye, head down the A259 past Winchelsea and Icklesham (look for the sign on the right). Alternatively, take bus #711 from Rye to the White Hart in Guestling (M-Sa roughly 2 per hr., summer also Su every 2hr., last bus around 7:45pm; £1.85). From the White Hart, the hostel is downhill on the left on Rye Rd. You can also take the train to Three Oaks (£1.90), the third stop from Rye toward Hastings, and follow the signs 1½ mi. (☎ 812373; fax 814273. 51 beds with 4-12 per room. Open July-Aug. daily, Mar.-June and Sept.-Oct. 6 days per week—call ahead since the one day it's closed varies; Nov.-Dec. F-Sa. Dorms £9.50, under 18 £6.70.) The hostel also has **camping** (£4.75 per pitch).

Rye's many inexpensive **B&Bs** are often away from the center, either on the roads past the train station or on **Winchelsea Rd.,** across the river from the TIC (about a 10min. walk); call ahead and you may get a ride. To reach the B&B at beautiful **Glencoe Farms,** West Undercliff, exit right from the train station and turn right on Ferry Rd. across the tracks; after Ferry Rd. becomes Udimore Rd., West Undercliff comes up on the left; follow the signs to the farm (10-15min.). The farm has friendly owners, livestock to pet, and three airy rooms with bath—book well ahead. (☎ 224347. £18 per person.) The Beatles will always rock at Richard and Jane McGowan's **Amberley Bed and Breakfast,** 51 Winchelsea Rd., located conveniently near town. (☎ 225693. £20 per person.) **Vine Cottage Bed and Breakfast,** 25a Udimore Rd., offers privacy and comfort, and attends to guests in English, Spanish, or German. (☎ 222822. Singles £22; doubles £34; reduced rates for students.)

 FOOD. For groceries, visit **Budgens,** across from the train station. (Open M-Sa 8am-10pm, Su 10am-4pm.) At the bend of one of Rye's most charming streets, **Ye Olde Bell Inn,** 33 The Mint, serves toasted sandwiches (£2-2.50) and other dainties in an English cottage garden. (☎ 223323. Open M-Th 11am-11pm, F-Sa 11am-midnight, Su 11am-10:30pm.) In continued obedience to thy sweete toothe (and fake Old English), climb to **Ye Olde Tuck Shoppe,** 9 Market St., to sample their homemade fudge and heavenly cakes. (☎ 222230. Open M-Sa 9:30am-5:30pm, Su 10am-5:30pm.) **Jempson's Coffee House and Bakery,** 45 Cinque Port St., offers a mouthwatering assortment of pastries and lunch dishes. (☎ 223986. Open M-Sa 8am-6pm.)

SOUTH ENGLAND

◙🎵 SIGHTS AND ENTERTAINMENT. Well-preserved half-timbered homes jus-tify Rye's frequent role as picturesque backdrop in English cinema. At the top of the hill, for a further turn of the screw, Henry James wrote his later novels while living in **Lamb House,** at the corner of West St. and Mermaid St. (Open Apr.-Oct. W and Sa 2-6pm. £2.60, children £1.30.) Before descending the hill, check out **St. Mary's Church,** at the top of Lion St., a huge 12th-century parish church that houses one of the oldest functioning clocks in the country. A climb up the tower steps reveals a terrific view of the river valley, but avoid the ascent when the bell is about to ring—your ears may never forgive you. (☎222430. Open M-W and F 9am-6pm, Th 10:40am-6pm, Sa 9am-5:30pm, Su 11:40am-5:30pm. £2.50, students and seniors £1.50.) Around the corner from the church, **Ypres Tower** (EE-pres), built in 1350, was intended to fortify the town against invaders from the sea. Since then it has served as a jail and now contains the **Rye Museum.** (☎226728. Open Apr.-Oct. M and Th-F 10am-1pm and 2-5pm, Sa-Su 10:30am-1pm and 2-5pm; Nov.-Mar. Sa-Su 10:30am-3:30pm. Combined ticket to tower and museum £2.90, students and seniors £2, children £1.50, families £5.) A walk down Mermaid St. leads to the famed **Mermaid Inn,** where smugglers once cavorted until dawn before vanishing into the secret tunnels underneath the Inn. (☎223065. Open M-Sa 11am-11pm, Su noon-10:30pm.) You can watch potters mold the famous Rye pottery at the many shops sprinkled through the town. During its **festival** in the first two weeks of September, Rye celebrates art, theater, and music. (☎227338. Tickets £4-14.)

🎯 DAYTRIPS FROM RYE

HASTINGS

*Trains arrive from Rye daily (20min., every 45min., £3). The **tourist information centre** books accommodations at Queens Sq. and The Stade; follow the signs from the station. (☎(01424) 781111; fax 781186; www.hastings.gov.uk. Open Apr.-Oct. M-F 8:30am-6:15pm, Sa 9am-5pm, Su 10am-4:30pm; Nov.-Mar. M and F 8:30am-6:15pm, Tu-Th 8:30am-5pm, Sa 9am-5pm, Su 10am-4:30pm.)*

Having given up its name and identity to a decisive battle (see p. 67), Hastings still revels in its thousand-year-old claim to fame. Looming above town, the fragmentary remains of **Hastings Castle,** built by William the Conqueror, mark the spot where the French duke's troops camped before trouncing the Saxons. The castle met its demise in the 13th century, when part of the cliff collapsed and took half the fortifications with it; during WWII, Germans finished the job by dropping excess explosives on Hastings before returning home. Catch the **1066 Story,** an interactive display on the famous spat between William the Conqueror and Harold, and visit the castle's underground "dungeons." (Take the East or West Hill Cliff lifts to the top of the hill. Return 80p, concessions 40p. Castle ☎(01424) 781111. Open daily 10am-5pm. £3.20, students and seniors £2.60, children £2.10.) Before heading back to sea level, duck into St. Clements Caves for the **Smuggler's Adventure.** An historical-site-cum-theme-park, these miles of caves and tunnels were once the heart of the Sussex smuggling ring. A ghostly apparition of Hairy Jack is your guide through this spooky lair. (☎(01424) 422964. Open daily 10am-6pm, last admission 5:30pm. £5.35, students and seniors £4.25, children £3.50, families £14.75.) Hastings is also famous for its **Net Shops,** clusters of tall, slim black buildings used by fishermen for storage and found nowhere else in Britain. More information on the area's nautical past can be found in a variety of museums, most notably the **Shipwreck Heritage Centre.** (☎(01424) 437452. Open Apr.-Oct. daily 10am-5pm; Feb.-Mar. 10am-4pm. Free.)

BATTLE

*Bus #5 runs directly to the Battle Abbey from Hastings, near the bank buildings (20min.; M-Sa every hr., Su every 2hr.; £4.90). The **tourist information centre,** 88 High St., opposite Battle Abbey, books accommodations. (☎(01424) 773721; fax 773436; battletic@rother.gov.uk. Open Apr.-Sept. daily 10am-6pm; Oct.-Mar. M-Sa 10am-4pm.)*

Appropriately renamed after the little tiff between Normans and Anglo-Saxons that took place in 1066, the town of Battle makes a fine expedition from Rye. To commemorate his victory in the Battle of Hastings, William the Conqueror had **Battle Abbey** built in 1094, spitefully positioning its high altar upon the very spot where Harold was felled by an arrow in the eye (see p. 67). The town grew prosperous enough to survive Henry VIII's closing the abbey in 1538. Little remains apart from the gate and a handsome series of 13th-century common quarters. (☎ (01424) 773792. Open Apr.-Sept. daily 10am-6pm; Oct. 10am-5pm; Nov.-Mar. 10am-4pm. £5, students and seniors £3.50, children £2.50, families £11.50.) The battlefield where Harold's troops were taken by surprise is now a pasture trampled only by sheep. In summer, you can take a free audio tour of the abbey and walk the **battlefield trail,** a one-mile jaunt up and down the green hillside.

PEVENSEY

Trains run hourly from Rye and Hastings to Pevensey (£5.60). There is no tourist information centre (TIC)—for info on the town, call the TIC in nearby Boship (☎ (1323) 442667).

William the Conqueror's march to Battle began from **Pevensey Castle,** a Roman fortress once called Anderita already 800 years old when the Normans landed. Considered one of the best examples of Roman building in England, the original walls—12 ft. thick and 30 ft. high—are all that's left. (☎ (01323) 762604. Open Apr.-Sept. daily 10am-6pm; Oct. 10am-5pm; Nov.-Mar. W-Su 10am-4pm. £3, students and seniors £2.30, children £1.80.) The best part of Pevensey owes its origins to commerce rather than conquest. The **Mint House,** on High St., begun as a mint under the Normans, was transformed by Henry VIII's physician into a country retreat, and eventually became a smugglers' den, complete with sliding ceiling panels. It now teems with Victorian miscellany, stuffed birds, and other fascinating oddities worth the price of admission in themselves. (☎ (01323) 762337. Open M-F 9am-5pm, Sa 10:30am-4:30pm. £1.50, children 50p.)

SOUTH DOWNS WAY

Meandering through the rolling hills and livestock-laden greens that typify pastoral England, The South Downs Way, perhaps Britain's most famous hiking trail, stretches from Eastbourne west toward Portsmouth and Winchester, never far from coastal towns yet rarely crossing into civilization's domain. Robbed of some of its bucolic innocence during the air raids of WWII, the sparse soil and light vegetation of the Downs once provided land that prehistoric tribes could cultivate. Forts and settlements now dot the former paths of Bronze and Iron Age tribes, who were followed by Romans, Saxons, and Normans. Fertile ground for legend, the windswept slopes and salt-sprayed cliffs of the Downs have borne words as prodigiously as flowers, from *The Domesday Book* to A.A. Milne.

▐ TRANSPORTATION

Trains (☎ (08457) 484950) run to **Eastbourne** from **London Victoria** (1½hr., 2 per hr., £19.70) and to **Petersfield** from **London Waterloo** (1hr., 3 per hr., £19.70). From the west, take a train to **Amberly** (via **Horsham**), where the Way greets the River Arun. Eastbourne's helpful **Bus Stop Shop,** Arndale Centre, dispenses info on local buses that travel to the Way. From the train station, turn left onto Terminus Rd.; Arndale Centre is on the left. (☎ (01323) 416416. Open M-Sa 9am-5pm.)

Walking the entire path takes about 10 days, but public transportation makes it possible to traipse just a segment of the trail. **Trains** connect **Lewes** to **Southease** (3 per hr., £3), while **County Bus** #1232 heads from Lewes to **Kingston** (20min., 6 per day, £2.10) and **Rodmell** (15min., 1 per day, £1.70). Bus #126 runs 5 times per day from **Eastbourne** to **Alfriston** (40min., £2.80) and **Wilmington** (30min., £3.10). For bus schedules, call Eastbourne Buses (☎ (01323) 416416) or East Sussex County Busline (☎ (01273) 474747).

Cycling has long been a popular means of seeing the downlands: D.H. Lawrence cycled the Way in 1909, visiting his friend Rudyard Kipling. Except for a brief section of the Way stretching from Alfriston to Eastbourne, and the western section between Brighton and Winchester, cycling and **horse riding** are permitted. **Cuckmore Cycle Company** has four locations in the Way. (☎(01323) 870310. Bikes £3.50 per hr., £20 per day.) **Audiburn Riding Stables,** Ashcombe Ln., conducts guided one-hour horseback tours. (☎(01273) 474398. £15 per person.)

✴🛈 ORIENTATION AND PRACTICAL INFORMATION

Serious hikers will want to begin their exploration in **Eastbourne,** the official start of the Way, which offers accommodations and local services.

Tourist Information Centres:

Eastbourne: Cornfield Rd. (☎(01323) 411400). Provides vague maps (free) and detailed 1:50,000 Ordnance Survey Landranger maps (#185 and 197-99 are the most useful; around £5). Also sells a number of guides (see below). Open M-Sa 9am-6pm, Su 10am-1pm.

Lewes: 187 High St. (☎(01273) 483448). Books rooms and sells Ordnance Survey maps and guides (see below). Open M-F 9am-5pm, Sa 10am-5pm; summer also Su 10am-2pm.

Financial Services: All major banks are located in **Eastbourne** town center. Be sure to pick up your sterling before hitting the trail. **Thomas Cook,** 101 Terminus Rd. (☎(1323) 725431). Open M-Tu and Th-Sa 9am-5:30pm, W 10am-5:30pm.

Guidebooks and Outdoor Supplies: The **Eastbourne** and **Lewes** Tourist Information **Centres** sell *On Foot in East Sussex* (£3.20) and *Along the South Downs Way* (£5), useful for trekkers; *Exploring East Sussex* (£2) lists various guided walks and cycle rides; *The South Downs Way* photocopied edition (£2) has info on accommodations. **Millets Leisure,** 146 Terminus Rd., Eastbourne (☎(1323) 723840), stocks camping supplies and Ordnance Survey Maps. Open M-Sa 9am-5:30pm, Su 10:30am-4pm. Near the middle of the Way, outdoors shops abound in **Brighton.**

🏠 ACCOMMODATIONS

There are few towns along the Way, and B&Bs fill quickly. Consider making daytrips along parts of the Way; Brighton makes a good base. For **B&Bs** in nearby towns, try Brighton (p. 164), Lewes (see p. 173), Arundel (see p. 174), or Southcliff Ave. in Eastbourne. **Camping** on the Way is permitted with the landowner's permission. Fortunately, the following four **YHA youth hostels** lie along or near the Way, each within a day's walk of the next. Be sure to call at least 2-3 weeks ahead; the hostels are often full at the same time. Unless noted, all the hostels listed here have a 10am-5pm lockout and an 11pm curfew. For other hostels near the Way, check the **Accommodations** sections in Brighton (p. 167) or Arundel (p. 174).

YHA Eastbourne: East Dean Rd., Eastbourne, East Sussex (☎/fax 721081). Converted golf clubhouse on the A259 between South Downs Way and the Seven Sisters, about 3 mi. from Beachy Head. From Eastbourne Station, turn right and follow the A259 (marked Seaford/Brighton) for 1½ mi.; even pro cyclists gasp at the steep hill leading to the hostel. Buses #711-712 depart from Shelter H on Terminus Rd., left of the station (95p). Spare, clean rooms with bunks. Breakfast £3.75. Open July-Sept. daily; Apr.-June Th-M; closed Oct.-Mar. Dorms £11, under 18 £7.40.

YHA Alfriston: Frog Firle, Alfriston, Polegate, East Sussex (☎870423; fax 870615; alfriston@yha.org.uk). 1½ mi. from the Way and from Alfriston, 8 mi. from Eastbourne. At the market cross, turn left at the sign marking "South Downs Way" and pass the village green toward the White Bridge. Follow the overgrown riverside path to Litlington footbridge and turn right along the path; the hostel is at the end of the path in a stone house with bovine neighbors. Authentic Tudor wood. Open July-Aug. daily; Feb.-June and Sept.-Oct. M-Sa; Nov.-Dec. F-Sa. Dorms £11, under 18 £7.40.

YHA Telescombe: Bank Cottages, Telescombe, Lewes, East Sussex (☎/fax (01273) 301357). 1 mi. from Rodmell, 2 mi. from Way, 12 mi. from Alfriston. From Rodmell (see below), follow signs directly to hostel. 18th-century house and cheery staff. Open July-Aug. daily; Easter-June W-M; closed Sept.-Easter. Dorms £10.80, under 18 £7.

YHA Truleigh Hill: Tottington Barn, Truleigh Hill, Shoreham-by-Sea, West Sussex (☎(01903) 813419; fax 812016). At the center of the Way, 10 mi. from Brighton. Modern building with sharp, clean rooms on 4½ acres. Open June-Sept. daily; Apr.-May and Sept.-Oct. Tu-Sa. Dorms £11, under 18 £8.

🏃 HIKING THE SOUTH DOWNS WAY

EASTBOURNE TO ALFRISTON

The best place to begin walking the Way is the Victorian seaside city of **Eastbourne,** which lives in the shelter of **Beachy Head,** the path's official starting point. (No beach here: *beau chef* means "fine headland.") The open-topped bus #3, from Terminus Rd. in Eastbourne, brings you to the top of Beachy Head (Su-F 9 per day, £2), though you can save money and gain scenic vistas by asking to be let off at the bottom and climbing it yourself. Make the strenuous ascent and follow the fields ever upward past some inquisitively bent trees to reach the cliffs. Mountaineers claim that Beachy Head, 543 ft. above the sea, has the same vertiginous effects as Alpine ridges. Whatever breath you have left after the climb will certainly be taken away by the view of the **Seven Sisters,** a series of chalk ridges carved by centuries of receding waters and surpassing the Head in majesty. The queenly sisters hold court about 4½ mi. away, over a windswept series of hills. From Beachy Head, the path winds past a number of *tumuli*—the burial mounds of Bronze Age peoples constructed around 1500 BC—but the overgrown bush makes them impossible to distinguish. To reach **Alfriston,** follow the Way 4 mi. over a path reputedly used by smugglers who docked among the cliffs. You can also take bus #711 or 712 from Terminus Rd. in Eastbourne (35min., M-Sa 6 per day, £1.10).

Another option is the shorter **bridleway path** to Alfriston (8 mi., as opposed to the 11 mi. coastal jaunt). The bridleway can be joined from a path just below the **YHA Alfriston** hostel (see p. 165) and passes through the village of **Wilmington** and by its famous **Long Man,** a 260 ft. earth sculpture of mysterious origins. Varyingly attributed to prehistoric peoples, Romans, 14th-century monks, and aliens, the Long Man is best viewed from a distance and is almost invisible when you first come over his hillside on the Way. It is rumored that Victorian prudes robbed the fellow of male attributes that might have elucidated his name. Proceeding back through the Long Man's gate and onto the South Downs Way path over Windover Hill will lead you to **Alfriston,** a sleepy one-road village called "the last of the old towns."

ALFRISTON TO FORTY ACRE LANE

From Alfriston town center, join the Way behind the Star Inn, on High St. (the *only* street), and continue 7 mi. to **Southease** among hills so green and vast, one might fear Julie Andrews lurks tunefully over the next ridge. The Way directly crosses **Firle Beacon,** with a mound at the top said to contain a giant's silver coffin. Reaching Southease, proceed north ¾ mi. to **Rodmell.** A Merchant-Ivory set of a town, Rodmell's single street contains **Monk's House,** home of Leonard and Virginia Woolf from 1919 until their deaths. The house retains its intimacy and most of the original furnishings; the tiled fireplace in Virginia's bedroom was painted by Vanessa Bell. The faithful can retrace the writer's last steps to the River Ouse (1 mi.), where she committed "the one experience I shall never describe"; her ashes nourish a fig tree in the garden. (Open Apr.-Oct. W and Sa 2-5:30pm. £3, children £1.50, families £16.) For information, call the regional **National Trust** office (☎(01892) 890651). The **YHA Telescombe** hostel (see p. 166) is 1 mi. south of Rodmell.

The closest that the Way actually comes to **Lewes** (LEW-is) is at the village of **Kingston** to the southwest—here is where hikers from **Brighton** should pick up the trail. A stone at the parish boundary, called **Nan Kemp's Corner,** feeds one of the more macabre Downs legends: townspeople whisper that a woman named Nan Kemp, jealous of her husband's affection for their newborn, roasted it for him to eat, then killed herself at the site of the present stone. Look for the signs to **YHA Truleigh Hill** (see p. 166) if you're in need of a warm bed. From Kingston, continue on an eight-mile stretch of the Way to **Pyecombe,** which brings you to **Ditchling Beacon,** the highest point in East Sussex's Downs. The hill was one in a series that relayed the message of the defeat of the Spanish Armada to Elizabeth I. Another eight-mile amble from Pyecombe to **Upper Beeding** takes you to **Devil's Dyke,** a dramatic chalk cliff that looks like a hillside cross section. Local legend says that the Dyke was built by Lucifer himself to let the sea into the Weald and float away all Christian churches. The Prince of Darkness was interrupted by the light of an old woman's candle, which, in a moment of diabolic weakness, he thought was the sun; frightened, he fled before he could finish the job. On the path from Upper Beeding to **Washington** lies the grove of **Chanctonbury Ring**—trees planted in the 18th century around a 3rd-century Roman template, built on a previous Celtic one.

Completing the 6½ mi. trek from Washington to **Amberly** brings you to a path leading to **Burpham,** from which the **YHA Warningcamp** (see p. 174) is accessible by a three-mile walk. The 19 mi. of orchids and spiked rampion fields from Amberly to **Buriton,** passing through **Cocking,** complete the Way to the northwest. Southward, across the River Arun to **Littleton Down,** are views of the Weald and the North Downs. The spire of Chichester Cathedral (p. 176) marks the beginning of **Forty Acre Lane,** the Way's final arm, which touches the West Sussex-Hampshire border.

BRIGHTON ☎ 01273

In Lydia's imagination, a visit to Brighton comprised every possibility of earthly happiness.
　　—Jane Austen, *Pride and Prejudice*

The undisputed home of the dirty weekend, Brighton (pop. 180,000) relishes its reputation for the risqué. According to legend, the future King George IV sidled into Brighton around 1784 for some hanky-panky. Having staged a fake wedding with a certain "Mrs. Jones" (Maria Fitzherbert), he headed off to the farmhouse known today as the Royal Pavilion, and the royal rumpus began. Since then, Brighton has turned a blind eye to some of the more scandalous activities that occur along its shores, as holiday-goers and locals alike peel it off—all off—at England's first bathing beach. Kemp Town (jokingly called Camp Town), among other areas of Brighton, has a thriving gay and lesbian population, while the immense student crowd, augmented by flocks of foreign youth purportedly learning English, feeds Brighton's notorious clubbing scene. Lovingly known as "London-by-the-Sea," Brighton's open demeanor and youthful spirit ensure a memorable sojourn.

▛ TRANSPORTATION

Trains: Brighton Station, uphill at the northern end of Queen's Rd. Ticket office open 24hr. Travel center open M-Sa 8:15am-6pm. **Trains** (☎(08457) 484950) from: **London** (1¼hr., 6 per hr., £10.50); **Arundel** (50min.; 3 per hr.; £6.10, day return £6.20); **Portsmouth** (1½hr., every hr., £11.70); **Rye** (1½hr., every hr., £11.30).

Buses: Stop at Pool Valley, at the southern angle of Old Steine. Tickets and info at **One Stop Travel,** 16 Old Steine (☎700406). Open M-F 8:30am-5:45pm, Sa 9am-5pm; June-Sept. also Su 11am-4:30pm. AmEx/MC/V. **National Express** (☎(08705) 808080) buses come from **London** (2hr., 15 per day, £8 return).

SOUTH ENGLAND

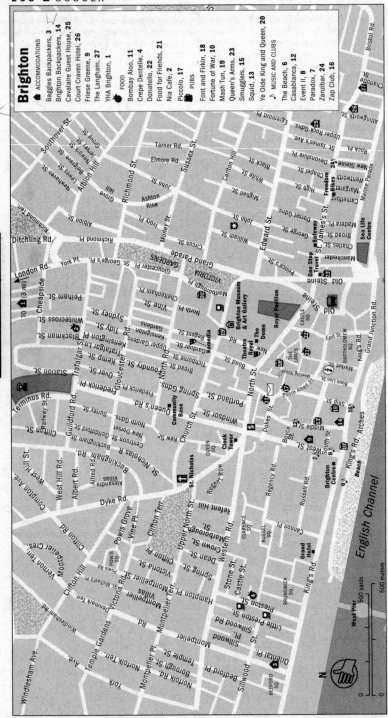

Brighton

♣ ACCOMMODATIONS
Baggies Backpackers, 3
Brighton Backpackers, 14
Cavalaire Guest House, 25
Court Craven Hotel, 26
Friese Greene, 9
The Langham, 27
YHA Brighton, 1

● FOOD
Bombay Aloo, 11
Crepe Dentelle, 4
Donatello, 22
Food for Friends, 21
Nia Cafe, 2
Piccolo, 17

■ PUBS
Font and Firkin, 18
Fortune of War, 10
Mash Tun, 19
Queen's Arms, 23
Smugglers, 15
Squid, 13
Ye Olde King and Queen, 20

♪ MUSIC AND CLUBS
The Beach, 6
Casablanca, 12
Event II, 8
Paradox, 7
Zanzibar, 24
Zap Club, 16

English Channel

West Pier

500 yards
500 metres

N

Public Transportation: Local buses operated by **Brighton and Hove** (☎886200) congregate around Old Steine. The tourist information centre (TIC) can give route and price information for most buses, though all carriers charge £1 in the central area.

Taxis: Brighton Taxis (☎202020). 24hr.

Bike Rental: Freedom Bikes, 108 St. James's St. (☎681698). £10 per day for a snazzy mountain bike, £50 per week. £50 deposit. Open Oct.-May M-Sa 9:30am-5:30pm. Vendors on the **waterfront** also rent small watercraft, bikes, and in-line skates, but the prices are higher and the quality somewhat lower.

▚▞ ORIENTATION AND PRACTICAL INFORMATION

Queen's Rd. connects the train station to the English Channel, becoming **West St.** at the intersection with **Western St.** halfway down the slope. Funky stores and alternative restaurants cluster around **Trafalgar St.** The narrow streets of **the Lanes,** a pedestrian shopping area, provide an anarchic setting for Brighton's nighttime carousing; turn left off **Prince Albert St.** before the TIC. **Old Steine,** a road and a square, runs in front of the **Royal Pavilion,** while **King's Rd.** parallels the waterfront.

TOURIST, FINANCIAL, AND LOCAL SERVICES

Tourist Information Centre: 10 Bartholomew Sq. (☎(0906) 711 2255; fax 292594; www.visitbrighton.com). Enthusiastic staff vends materials on practically any subject, books National Express tickets, and reserves rooms at B&Bs for £1 plus 10% deposit. Open M-Tu and Th-F 9am-5pm, W and Sa 10am-5pm; Mar.-Oct. also Su 10am-4pm.

Tours: Walking tours leave from the TIC June-Aug. £3. **Guide Friday** (☎746205) gives 1hr. bus tours departing Palace Pier, the train station, and a few other sites 2 per hr. £7, students and seniors £5.50, children £3, families £16.50.

Financial Services: Banks line North St., near Old Steine. **Thomas Cook,** 58 North St. (☎325711). Open M-Tu and Th-Sa 9am-5:30pm, W 10am-5:30pm. **American Express,** 82 North St. (☎321242). Open M-Tu and Th-Sa 9am-5pm, W 9:30am-5pm.

Disabled Information: Snowdon House, 3 Rutland Gdns., Hove (☎203016). Open M-F 10am-4pm. The **TIC,** above, has a phenomenal printout detailing local services.

Launderette: 5 Palace Rd. (☎327972). Open daily 8am-8pm.

EMERGENCY AND COMMUNICATIONS

Police: John St. (☎606744).

Community Centre: Community Base, 173 Queen's Rd. (☎234002). Enthusiastic reception has contact information for support centers and hotlines.

Hospital: Royal Sussex County, Eastern Rd. (☎696955), parallel to Marine Parade.

Internet Access: Foobar, 37 Preston St. Full-fledged cafe with cozy couches. £2.70 per hr. 10am-6pm, £2 per hr. 6-11pm. Open M-Sa 10am-11pm, Su 11am-11pm. Down the street, **Pursuit Internet** (☎823282) has lower prices for students. 4p per min. before noon and 5-10pm, 5p noon-5pm; students 3p, 4p. Open daily 10am-10pm. Also, the **Library,** Church St. (☎296971), across from the Brighton Museum. £1.50 per 30min. Open M and Th-F 9:30am-5pm, Tu 9:30am-7pm, Sa 9:30am-4pm.

Post Office: 51 Ship St. (☎573209), off Prince Albert St. **Bureau de change;** £1 commission with student ID. Open M-Sa 9am-5:30pm. **Postal Code:** BN1 1BA.

▛ ACCOMMODATIONS

Brighton's best budget beds are in its four hostels. B&Bs and cheaper hotels begin at £18-20. Many mid-range B&Bs line **Madeira Pl.,** and the shabbier B&Bs and hotels collect west of **West Pier** and east of **Palace Pier.** There is a huge number of B&Bs in **Kemp Town,** the neighborhood east of Palace Pier that runs perpendicular to the sea. Frequent conventions make rooms scarce—book early or consult the TIC upon arrival. The TIC also keeps a list of guest houses owned and operated by gays or lesbians. Rooms may be cheaper in the **Hove** area, just west of Brighton.

SOUTH ENGLAND

▨ **Baggies Backpackers,** 33 Oriental Pl. (☎733740; guest phone ☎203611). From the town center, go past West Pier along King's Rd.; Oriental Pl. will be on your right. Live blues and jazz, spontaneous parties and pot lucks, and exquisite murals set the tone for this mellow hostel. Talking, singing, and drinking in the candlelit lounge often beats a seedy club-hop. Vast video collection. 50 beds in spacious coed and single-sex dorms, some doubles. Kitchen and laundry. Key deposit £5. Dorms £11; doubles £27.

▨ **Brighton Backpackers Hostel,** 75-76 Middle St. (☎777717; fax 887778; stay@bright-onbackpackers.com). Lively independent hostel with international flavor and great location. Gregarious owner Miles plays guitar as resident parakeets chirp along. Pool table, Internet access (£1.50 per 30min.), and TV lounge for Sunday-night *Simpsons* rituals. The quieter annex faces the ocean. 4- to 8-bed coed and single-sex dorms. Inexpensive meals. Kitchen and laundry. No reservations. Dorms £11, weekly £60; doubles £25.

The Langham, 16-17 Charlotte St. (☎682123; fax 682843; www.langhambrighton.co.uk), off Marine Parade. 20 rooms connected by ultra-pink halls steps from the Channel. Luxurious hotel quality for B&B prices. Dorms Apr.-Oct. M-Th £20 per person, F-Su £30; Nov.-Mar. M-Th £15 per person, F-Su £25.

Friese Greene, 20 Middle St. (☎747551). Bohemian, family-run hostel in the heart of Brighton's nightlife attracts serious partiers and seasoned travelers. £5 deposit for key and linen. Laundry, kitchen, pool, and TV. Dorms £11. Weekly £55.

YHA Brighton, Patcham Pl. (☎556196). 4 mi. north on the main London Rd; take Patcham bus #5 or 5A from Old Steine (stop E) to the Black Lion Hotel (£1.40). Georgian country house filled with friendly staff. Good jumping-off point for the South Downs Way (see p. 164), but not the place if you want to party late. Laundry. Lockout 10am-5pm. Curfew 11pm. Often full; call ahead July-Aug. Closed Jan. Dorms £11, under 18 £7.

Cavalaire Guest House, 34 Upper Rock Gdns. (☎696899; fax 600504). Comfortable rooms ideal for a lazy weekend in town. Wonderful breakfast choices, from tropical to vegetarian. All rooms with TV. Internet £5 per hr. Singles £25; doubles £42-55.

Court Craven Hotel, 2 Atlingworth St. (☎607710), off Marine Parade. A well-decorated guest house in Kemp Town for gay and lesbian travelers. Clean and elegant, with a bar and deluxe kitchen. Singles £20-22; doubles £40-45, though prices vary.

◧ FOOD

Except for the picks below, the Lanes area is full of suspiciously trendy places waiting to gobble tourists' cash. The fish-and-chip shops along the beach or north of the Lanes offer better value. Get groceries at **Safeway,** 6 St. James's St. (☎570363. Open M-Sa 8am-9pm, Su 11am-5pm.) For sugar cravings, Brighton Rock Candy is available at any of the multitude of shops claiming to have invented it.

Donatello, 1-3 Brighton Pl. (☎775477). A hot people-watching spot on fringe of the Lanes. Gain a few pounds sampling the 3-course special (£8.25). Delicious (and big!) pizza £4-6. Reservations advised. Open daily 11:30am-11:30pm. AmEx/MC/V.

Nia Cafe, 87 Trafalgar St. (☎671371). Generous helpings (£4-6) are the norm in this hip cafe near the Laine, the Lanes' cooler counterpart. Open daily 10am-8pm. MC/V.

Crepe Dentelle, 65 Preston St. (☎323224). Sweet and savory crepes (£3-5) and galettes (£4-7). Takeaway 20% off. Open M-F 10am-3pm and 6-10pm, Sa-Su noon-10pm.

Food for Friends, 17a-18 Prince Albert St. (☎202310). Well-seasoned vegetarian food includes heavenly salad specials (£2.25-3.55) and the "Taster" (£5.20), a bit of every main course. 20% student discount. Open M-Sa 8am-10pm, Su 9:15am-10pm.

Piccolo, 56 Ship St. (☎380380). Benvenuto a Piccolo, home of great pizza toppings and even better dough (£3.30). Open daily noon-midnight. MC/V.

Bombay Aloo, 39 Ship St. (☎776038). Pure buffet and purely vegetarian in this inventive Indian restaurant. £5 all-you-can-eat from 18 steaming vats (£3.50 between 3:15-5:15pm). Open daily noon-midnight.

◉ ◢ SIGHTS AND BEACHES

In 1750, Dr. Richard Russell wrote a treatise on the merits of drinking seawater and bathing in brine to treat glandular disease; before then, sea-swimming was thought nearly suicidal. Thus began the transformation of the sleepy village of Brighthelmstone into a fashionable town with a decidedly hedonistic bent. Although an early-90s recession hit Brighton hard, the town has nearly completed a revitalization of its waterfront, and tourism is bouncing back brighter than ever.

ROYAL PAVILION. Perhaps it's wrong to reduce an entire city to one of its parts, but the proudly extravagant Royal Pavilion may be credited with much of Brighton's present gaudiness. George IV, then Prince of Wales, enlisted architect John Nash to turn an ordinary farm villa into the Oriental/Indian/Gothic/Georgian palace visible today. Rumor has it that George wept tears of joy upon entering it, proving that wealth does not give one taste. After living there for a month, Queen Victoria decided to have it demolished—proving that wealth does not deny one taste—until the town offered to buy the royal playground. Note the life-size portrait of George IV just after the King's Apartments: what looks like a brilliant oil painting is actually an exact replica, in mosaic, of a portrait the Protestant George IV once sent to the Pope. The Pope was not amused, and the mosaic was his response. Enjoy the pavilion from the surrounding parks by renting a deck chair (£1), or take in the view and a sandwich at **Queen Adelaide's Tea Room** inside. (☎ 290900. Open June-Sept. daily 10am-6pm; Oct.-May 10am-5pm. Guided tours 11:30am and 2:30pm, £1.25. Audio tour £1. Admission £5.20, students and seniors £3.75, children £3.20.)

SUN OF A BEACH. Brighton's main attraction is, of course, the beach, but those who associate the word "beach" with sand and sun may be sorely disappointed. The weather can be quite nippy even in June and July, and the closest thing to sand here are fist-sized brown rocks. Even in 70°F (21°C) weather with overcast skies, beach-goers gamely strip to bikinis and lifeguards don sunglasses, fighting for their patch of rock during high season. To visit **Telescombe Beach,** 4½ mi. east of Palace Pier, follow the sign for "Telescombe Cliffs" before the Telescombe Tavern.

PIER AND OTHER PIERS. The Pavilion's gaudiness permeates to the beachfront, where the relatively new Palace Pier, the fourth largest tourist attraction in England, has slot machines, video games, and condom dispensers galore, with a roller coaster thrown in for good measure. **Volk's Railway,** Britain's first 3 ft. gauge electric train, shuttles along the waterfront. (☎ 681061. Open Apr.-Sept. daily 11am-6pm. Rides £1.50, children £1.) The **Grand Hotel,** King's Rd., home to many political conventions, has been rebuilt since a 1984 IRA bombing that killed five but left then-Prime Minister Margaret Thatcher unscathed. Farther along, the once lavish, now decrepit **West Pier** lies abandoned out in the sea. Full-scale renovation was set to begin in the spring of 1999, but the abrupt collapse of part of the pier put a wrinkle in the plans. (☎ 207610. West Pier tour M-F 1:30pm; Sa-Su noon, 1:30, 3pm. £10, concessions £7.50.) A short walk along the coast past West Pier leads to **Hove.**

BRIGHTON MUSEUM AND ART GALLERY. More edifying than most of the town's attractions, this gallery, expected to reopen in 2002 after renovations, features paintings, English pottery, and Art Deco and Art Nouveau collections. In the fine **Willett Collection of Pottery,** post-modern porcelains and neolithic relics simultaneously reflect the varied faces of this seaside escape. (Church St., around the corner from the Pavilion. ☎ 290900. Open M-Tu and Th-Sa 10am-5pm, Su 2-5pm. Free.)

THE LANES. Small fishermen's cottages once thrived in the Lanes, a jumble of 17th-century streets—some no wider than 3 ft.—south of North St. in the heart of Old Brighton. Now filled with overpriced antique jewelry shops, the Lanes have lost some of their charm. Those looking for fresher shopping opportunities should head toward **North Laines,** off Trafalgar St., where alternative merchandise and colorful cafes still dominate. On Saturdays, the area is closed to traffic and cafe tables and street performances take over.

SEA LIFE CENTRE. Although England's largest aquarium has freed its dolphins, Missie and Silver, many other sea creatures remain trapped in large glass tanks for your viewing pleasure. *(Marine Parade, near Palace Pier. ☎ 604234. Open daily 9am-5pm, last admission 4pm. £6.50, seniors £4.45, children £4.25.)*

OTHER SIGHTS. To escape Brighton's frivolity, head to **St. Nicholas's Church,** on Dyke Rd., which dates from 1370. Its 12th-century baptismal font is thought to be the most beautiful Norman carving in Sussex. **St. Bartholomew's Church,** on Ann St., was originally called "The Barn" or "Noah's Ark"—one look at it and you'll see why. This little-known hiccup of Victorian genius rises higher than Westminster Abbey, to 135 ft. To get there, take bus #5, 5A, or 5B from Old Steine.

■ PUBS

J.B. Priestley once wisely noted that Brighton was "a fine place either to restore your health, or . . . to ruin it again"; the city's sea of alcohol presents ample opportunity to demonstrate Priestley's latter point. Brighton is a student town, and where there are students there are cheap drinks. Many pubs offer fantastic drink specials during the week—some budget-minded travelers find no reason to go out on weekends, when places get crowded and expensive. Revelers taking on the Lanes congregate in front of pubs on the beach between West Pier and Palace Pier.

Font and Firkin, Union St., the Lanes (☎ 747727). The altar in this former parish house now honors the gods of rock. Worshipers libate many a pint of ale and are rewarded for their devotion by a monthly Elvis appearance. Live entertainment W and F-Sa. Food served until 8:30pm. Open M-Sa noon-11pm, Su noon-10:30pm. MC/V.

Ye Olde King and Queen, Marlborough Pl. (☎ 607207). TV football, groovy dance-floor, beautiful beer garden, and multiple bars. Open M-Sa 11am-11pm, Su noon-10:30pm.

Smugglers, 10 Ship St. A pirate's den with a techno beat. Bedsteads, 2 dance-floors, velvet couches, and vodka-bottle chandeliers make this pub a raucous place to drink. Pints £1.60. Happy hour M-F noon-8pm. Open M-Sa noon-11pm, Su 7:30-10:30pm.

Fortune of War, 157 King's Road Arches (☎ 205065), beneath King's Rd. by the beach. Grab a Guinness and relax on the sand—the spot to be at sunset. Open M-Sa 10:30am-11pm, Su 11am-10:30pm.

Mash Tun, 1 Church St. (☎ 684951). Alternative pub attracts an eclectic student crowd with "friendly food, tasty bar staff; real music, groovy ales." Sample their hot chocolate and dark rum concoction (£2.90). Open M-Sa noon-11pm, Su noon-10:30pm. MC/V.

Squid, 78 Middle St. (☎ 727114). Next door to Backpackers hostel and linked to Zap Club. Packed with pre-clubbers. Open M-F 5-11pm, Sa 3-11pm, Su 3-10:30pm.

Queen's Arms, 8 George St. (☎ 696873). Draws an enthusiastic gay and lesbian crowd with its Sa night cabaret. Fairly inexpensive pints (£2.30). Entertainment nightly; check the board outside. Open M-Sa 1-11pm, Su 2-10:30pm.

■ ♫ NIGHTLIFE AND ENTERTAINMENT

For info on hot-and-happening scenes, *The Punter*, a monthly found at pubs, newsagents, and record stores, details evening events, as does *What's On*, a poster-sized flysheet found at record stores and pubs. Gay and lesbian venues can be found in the latest issues of *Gay Times* (£2.75) or *Capital Gay* (free), available at newsstands; *What's On* also highlights gay-friendly events.

Although the Lanes are the most vibrant part of town at night, with outdoor concerts, jugglers, and mimes, they are not necessarily the safest. The City Council spent £5 million installing surveillance equipment along the seafront and major streets to ensure safety during late-night partying, but still try to avoid walking alone late at night through Brighton's spaghetti-style streets. **Night buses** #N97-99 run infrequently but reliably in the early morning, picking up passengers at Old Steine and in front of many clubs, usually hitting each spot twice between 1 and 2:30am (£2.50). 24hr. cab companies are always a more expensive option.

CLUBS

Brighton is the hometown of Norman Cook, better known as Fatboy Slim, and major dance record label Skint Records, so these Brightonians know a thing or two about dance music. Most clubs are open M-Sa 9pm-2am; after 2am the party moves to the waterfront. Like pubs, many clubs have student discounts on weeknights and then raise prices on weekends. Covers usually run $4-10.

The Beach, 171-181 King's Rd. Arches (☎ 722272). Adds monstrous big beat to the music on the shore. Fatboy Slim still mixes here on some F nights, when the club is known as The Boutique and queues begin at 8-9pm.

Casablanca, Middle St. (☎ 321817). Plays live jazz and less electronically-oriented tunes to a mix of students and late-twentysomethings. Get ready to sweat it again, Sam.

Zap Club, King's Rd. Arches (☎ 202407). This cavernous space under the arches of World War II tunnels is the place to be for hard-core grinding to rave and house music.

Paradox, West St. (☎ 321628). Perhaps the paradox is that despite its commercialism, Paradox remains one of Brighton's mainstays. The exception is the monthly "Wild Fruit" gay night—popular among people of all persuasions.

Event II, West St. (☎ 732627). Among the most technically armed and massively populated, Event II spent over £1 million adding all electric trimmings to its already immense dance-floor. Crammed with the down-from-London crowd looking for wild thrills; experienced Brighton clubbers tend to head for less conventional venues.

Zanzibar, 129 St. James's St. (☎ 622100). Gay clubbers flock to this zany club for fun nightly entertainment and a constant flow of brew. Check the billing outside for the week's special events.

MUSIC, THEATER, AND FESTIVALS

Brighton Centre, King's Rd. (☎ 290131), and **The Dome,** 29 New Rd. (☎ 709709), host Brighton's biggest events, from Chippendales shows to music concerts. (Both offices open M-Sa 10am-5:30pm.) The TIC also sells tickets. Local plays and touring London productions take the stage at the **Theatre Royal** on New Rd., a Victorian beauty with a plush interior. (☎ 328488; fax 765507. Tickets $6-20. Open M-Sa 10am-8pm.) **Komedia,** on Gardner St., houses a cafe, bar, theater, comedy club, and cabaret. (☎ 647100. Tickets $5-8; discounts available. Standby tickets 15min. before curtain. Box office open M-Sa 11am and Su 10am to start of last show.)

The **Brighton Festival** (☎ 292950, box office 709709), held each May, is one of the largest festivals in England, celebrating music, film, and other art forms. Gays and lesbians celebrate the concurrent **Brighton Pride Festival** (☎ 730562). For more info or a program of events, contact the TIC.

◪ DAYTRIPS FROM BRIGHTON

LEWES

Trains leave for Lewes from Brighton's Queen's Rd. Station (10min., return £3).

The historic town of Lewes, second home to Thomas Paine, author of *Rights of Man*, has an appealing location in the Sussex chalklands and makes a perfect jumping-off point for South Downs Way hiking trails (see p. 164). The views from the flower-strewn ruins of the Norman **Lewes Castle,** High St., 5min. northwest of the train station, merit as much of a visit as do the remains. (☎ (01273) 486290. Open M-Sa 10am-5:30pm or dusk, Su 11am-5:30pm or dusk.) The 15th-century **Anne of Cleves House Museum,** Southover High St., 15min. from the castle, celebrates the clever woman who got the house in her divorce from Henry VIII without losing her head. (☎ (01273) 474610. Open Feb.-Oct. M-Sa 10am-5pm, Su noon-5pm; Nov.-Feb. Tu, Th, Sa 10am-5pm.) A combination ticket buys entrance into both the Castle and Museum for $5.50, students and seniors $4.80, children $2.70, families $13.50.

THE CHARLESTON FARMHOUSE

South of Lewes, off the A27. Bus #125 leaves the Lewes bus station for Charleston 6 times per day; get a timetable from the Lewes TIC. Farmhouse ☎(01323) 811265. Open July-Aug. W-Sa 11:30am-6pm, Su 2-6pm; Apr.-June and Sept.-Oct. W-Su 2-6pm. Last admission 5pm. £5.50, concessions £4; Connoisseur Fridays £6.50, no concessions. Garden only £2, children £1.

The Charleston Farmhouse was the country retreat of the Bloomsbury Group. Originally lacking amenities such as electricity and a telephone, Charleston soon became a center for literary, artistic, and intellectual life in Britain. Frequent guests included art theorist Clive Bell, novelist Virginia Woolf, and economist John Maynard Keynes, who terrorized the help with his "time experiments," setting all the clocks off an hour. Today the beautiful farmhouse and gardens highlight the domestic decorative art of Vanessa Bell and Duncan Grant. On Fridays, visitors may take a peak at Bell's studio and take longer guided tours.

ARUNDEL ☎01903

Arundel (pop. 3200) sits in the shadow of towers and spires, but the town refuses to let those landmarks dim its character. The romantic castle does draw most visitors (with good reason), and wearisome antique shops do clutter the streets. However, observers will find that the town's storybook beauty stems less from souvenir shops than from the rippling River Arun and the town's idyllic hillside location, a perfect place from which to explore the surrounding countryside.

TRANSPORTATION AND PRACTICAL INFORMATION

Trains (☎(08457) 484950) arrive from: **London Victoria** (1½hr.; 2 per hr.; £12, day return £16.10); **Chichester** (20min.; 2 per hr.; £3.40, day return £3.90); **Portsmouth** (50min.; every hr.; £7.40, day return £7.80); **Brighton** (1hr.; 3 per hr.; £6.10, day return £6.20). Many routes require connections at **Littlehampton** to the south or **Barnham** to the west. **Buses** stop across from the Norfolk Arms on High St., and come from **Littlehampton** (#702; M-Sa 2 per hr., Su every hr.). Arundel doesn't have any local **bike stores,** but two-wheelers can be hired for £12.50 per day at **Wests,** in nearby Angmering (☎(01903) 770649). Call **Castle Cars** for a **taxi.** (☎884444. 24hr.)

The friendly **tourist information centre** (TIC), 61 High St., dispenses the free *Town Guide.* (☎882268. Open Oct.-Easter daily 10am-3pm; Easter-Oct. M 9:30am-5pm, Tu-Su 9am-5pm.) Other services include: **Lloyds TSB,** 14 High St. (☎717221; open M-F 9:30am-4:30pm); the **police,** on the Causeway; and the **post office,** 2-4 High St. (☎882113; open M-F 9am-5:30pm, Sa 9am-12:30pm). **Postal code:** BN18 9AA.

ACCOMMODATIONS AND CAMPING

B&Bs are consistent with Arundel's elegance, and are priced accordingly (singles £25-30). During summer, reserve ahead to avoid anxiety and a severe gouging of the wallet. The TIC maintains an up-to-date list of vacancies outside its entrance.

Arundel House, 11 High St. (☎882136; arundelhouse@btinternet.com). Moderately priced with immoderate luxuries, including 400-year-old architecture and an incredible location. Singles, doubles, and twins all have bathrooms and TVs. £20 per person.

Arden House, 4 Queens Ln. (☎882544). 8 rooms of rosy hue, some with wood-beamed ceilings, in a convenient location. Help yourself to a pot of tea. TV in all rooms. Singles £25-30, depending on season and availability; doubles £40, with bath £44.

YHA Warningcamp (☎882204; fax 870615), ½ mi. out of town. Turn left from the train station and right at the "Public Footpath" sign, making another right onto the path. Follow the trail and the River Arun until you cross the railroad tracks, then go through the gate, and make a left to the hostel. A Georgian house with aqua-green interior. Single-sex and coed showers with private changing booths. Huge kitchen and laundry facilities. Lockout 10am-5pm. Curfew 11pm. Open July-Aug. daily; Sept.-Oct. Tu-Sa; Nov.-Dec. F-Sa; Apr.-June M-Sa. Dorms £9.50, under 18 £6.50, camping £4.

Camping: Ship and Anchor Site (☎(01243) 551262), 2 mi. from Arundel on Ford Rd. along the River Arun. Inglorious field with pub and shops nearby. Open Apr.-Sept. £3.50 per person, children £1.75. £1.50 per vehicle. Showers free.

♺ FOOD

Arundel's pubs and tea shops are generally a bit expensive, and generally unremarkable. A few fruit and bread peddlers line High St. and Tarrant St. The supermarket **Alldays,** 17 Queen St., honors its name, selling food practically all day. (Open M-Sa 6:30am-11pm, Su 7:30am-11pm.)

Belinda's, 13 Tarrant St. (☎882977). Locals frequent this 16th-century tearoom for its large selection of traditional English fare. Linger over cream teas (£2) and Belinda's famous homemade jam. Open Tu-Sa 9am-5pm, Su 11am-5:30pm.

White Hart, 12 Queen St. (☎882374). Serves pub grub and local ales (£2.20 per pint). Main courses, though slightly pricey (£7-8), are good; seek out homemade specials and vegetarian selections. Open M-F 11am-3pm and 5:30-11pm, Sa-Su 11am-11pm.

Castle Tandoori, 3 Mill Ln. (☎884224). Dishes out an all-you-can-eat buffet of spicy Indian cuisine for £10 (Th-Su 6-11pm). Open daily noon-2:30pm and 6pm-midnight.

Country Life Cafe, Tarrant Sq. (☎883456). Quality vegetarian, vegan, and other options for around £4. Open M-W and F-Sa 10:30am-5pm, Su 11am-5pm.

👁 SIGHTS AND FESTIVALS

Poised above town like the backdrop of a fairy tale, ▨**Arundel Castle** is lord of the skyline. The castle, seat of the Duke of Norfolk, was built in the 11th century but heavily damaged during the Civil Wars because the Duke was, like his successors, the highest-ranking Catholic in the aristocracy. The castle was restored piecemeal by the dukes who called it home in the 18th and 19th centuries and may be the best-preserved castle in the land. Winding passages and 131 steps lead to the keep, with breathtaking vistas of the town below and the emerald countryside beyond. Portraits by Van Dyck, Overbech, and others stare from the **Barons' Hall** while the many photographs of the current Duke and his family lend the place an air of home-sweet-castle. The 122 ft. library, meticulously carved in the late 18th century, along with the family chapel, will make you want to marry nobility. Don't overlook the graphically termed death warrant served against one of the Duke's ancestors by agreeable Elizabeth I. (☎882173. Open Apr.-Oct. Su-F noon-5pm, last entry 4pm. £7.50, seniors £6.50, children £5, families £21. Grounds only £3.)

Along the river across from the castle, a placard recounts the troubled past of the monks of **Blackfriars,** the Dominican priory whose remains are nearby. Atop the same hill as Arundel Castle, the **Cathedral of Our Lady and St. Philip Howard,** a Catholic cathedral, was designed by Joseph Hansom, inventor of the hansom cab. The French Gothic building is more impressive from the outside than from within. Though executed for cheering on the Spanish Armada in 1588, St. Philip occupies an honored place in the north transept. During **Corpus Christi** (May 31, 2002), thousands of flowers are laid in a pattern stretching 93 ft. down the center aisle in a tradition dating to 1873. (☎882297. Open summer daily 9am-6pm; winter 9am-dusk. Free.) Concealed observation enclosures at the **Wildfowl and Wetlands Trust Centre,** less than 1 mi. past the castle on Mill Rd., permit visitors to "come nose to beak with nature"—just make sure nature doesn't nip back. Over 12,000 birds roost on 60 acres. (☎883355. Open summer daily 9:30am-5pm; winter 9:30am-4:30pm. Last entry 1hr. before close. £4.75, students and seniors £3.75, children £2.75.)

In late August, Arundel castle is the centerpiece of the **Arundel Festival,** 10 days of musical, Shakespearean, and artistic shows. The **Festival Fringe** simultaneously offers free or inexpensive events. Tickets for both go on sale six to eight weeks before the festivals begin. (☎883690; box office 883474. Tickets up to £20.)

TREADING THE LINE Many can define the word "schism"—a division within a church—but few can describe what one looks like. Those few must have visited Arundel's **Parish Church of St. Nicholas** (☎882262; open dawn-dusk), across from the Cathedral of Our Lady and St. Philip Howard. The church, built in 1380, straddles a property line such that when the Anglican Church broke from the Roman Catholic Church, the western portion of the parish fell under the Church of England's control, while the eastern portion remained property of the Catholic Duke of Norfolk. Hence, though the western portion still operates as an Anglican place of worship, the eastern portion, called the Fitzalan Chapel (access from castle grounds), remains a Catholic burial chamber. Today, a glass wall separates the two spiritually diverse arenas, making the building the only example in England of two faiths operating under one roof.

🔼 DAYTRIP FROM ARUNDEL: PETWORTH HOUSE

Take the train to Pulborough (10min.) and walk the remaining 2 mi. to the house or catch bus #1. Ask for directions at the TIC. House ☎(01798) 342207. Open Apr.-Oct. M-W and Sa-Su 1-5:30pm, last admission 4:30pm; extra rooms shown M-W. Grounds open daily 8am-dusk. House and grounds £6, children £3. Grounds only £1.50, children free.

Situated among acres of sculpted gardens and lawns designed by Capability Brown, Petworth House has one of the greatest art collections in the UK. J.M.W. Turner often painted the house and landscape, and many of his iridescent works hang alongside canvases by Van Dyck, Bosch, Dahl, Jones, Blake, and Reynolds. The House is also famous for the Petworth Chaucer, an early 15th-century manuscript of Chaucer's *Canterbury Tales*. Grinling Gibbons's intricate carvings fill the legendary **Carving Room,** as does a multitude of scaffolding and tarp since woodworm was discovered in its precious motifs.

CHICHESTER ☎01243

Confined for centuries within eroding Roman walls, the citizens of well-preserved Chichester (pop. 30,000) take pride in their town's position as a center of English culture. The settlement still thrives on its markets (cattle, corn, and others), and all roads still lead to the ornate Market Cross, a gift from Bishop Storey in 1501, but Chichester's chief attractions include one of the country's best theaters, an arts festival, a host of gallery exhibits, and a nearby summer motor-racing spectacular. The quirky cathedral provides more permanent delight, while the nearby Fishbourne Roman Palace is one of the better ancient attractions in the region.

◧ TRANSPORTATION

Chichester is 45 mi. southwest of London and 15 mi. east of Portsmouth. **Trains** (☎(08457) 484950) service Southgate station from: **London Victoria** (1½hr.; 3 per hr.; £16.90, day return £17.20); **Portsmouth** (40min.; 2-3 per hr.; £4.80, day return £4.90); **Brighton** (50min.; 2-3 per hr.; £7.80, day return £8.10). The **bus station** (☎(01903) 237661) also lies on Southgate. **National Express** (☎(08705) 808080) buses come from **London** (1 per day, return £9). **Stagecoach Coastline** buses connect Chichester with **Portsmouth** (#700-701, 1hr., 2 per hr., £4) and **Brighton** (#702, 3hr., 2 per hr., £4.60). An **Explorer** ticket grants a day's unlimited travel on buses servicing southern England from Kent to Salisbury. (£5.25, seniors £3.85, children £2.60, families £10.50). For **taxis**, call **Central Cars of Chichester,** 30 South St. (☎(0800) 789432).

✴🔢 ORIENTATION AND PRACTICAL INFORMATION

Four Roman streets named for their compass directions divide Chichester into quadrants that converge at **Market Cross.** To reach the **tourist information centre** (TIC), 29a South St., from the train station, turn left as you exit onto South-

SOUTH ENGLAND

Got ISIC?

SIC is your passport to the world.

Accepted at over 17,000 locations worldwide.

Great benefits at home and abroad!

apply for your International Student, Teacher or Youth Identity Card

CALL 1-800-2COUNCIL
CLICK www.counciltravel.com
VISIT your local Council Travel office

ring this ad into your local Council Travel office and receive
a free Council Travel/ISIC t-shirt! *(while supplies last)*

gate, which turns into South St. Check the computer terminal (available 24hr.) in the front window for accommodations or use the booking service inside. (☎775888; fax 539449; www.chichesterweb.co.uk. Open July-Aug. M-Sa 9:15am-5:15pm, Su 10am-4pm; Sept.-June M-Sa 9:15am-5:15pm.) **Guided tours** of the city depart from the TIC. (May-Sept. Tu 11am, Sa 2:30pm. £2.) Other services include: **banks** on East St.; **Thomas Cook,** 40 East St. (☎536733; 2% commission; open M and W-Sa 9am-5:30pm, Tu 10am-5:30pm); a **launderette,** 11 Eastgate (open daily 8am-8pm, last wash 7pm); the **police,** Kingsham Rd. (☎(0845) 607 0999); **Internet access** at **Junction Club,** 2 Southgate (☎776644; £1.50 per 30min.; open M-F 10am-10pm, Sa 10am-8pm, Su 11am-4pm); and the **post office,** 10 West St., with a **bureau de change** (☎771736; open M 8:45am-5:30pm, Tu-Sa 9am-5:30pm). **Postal code:** PO19 1AB.

🏠🍴 ACCOMMODATIONS AND FOOD

B&Bs are abundant, but cheap rooms are rare, especially on big racecourse weekends; plan on paying around £20, and expect a 15min. walk to the town center. **Hedgehogs,** 45 Whyke Ln., close to the town center, has cozy rooms, a cheerful black labrador, and happy hedgehog paraphernalia. (☎780022. No smoking. Singles £23-24; doubles £36-38.) **Bayleaf,** 16 Whyke Rd., welcomes guests with colorful geraniums, freshly squeezed orange juice, and sugared grapefruits. (☎774330. No smoking. £23 per person.) Pitch your tent at **Southern Leisure Centre,** Vinnetrow Rd., a 15min. walk southeast of town. (☎787715. Clean facilities with showers and laundry. Open Apr.-Oct. £3 per person; pitch fee £8-10.)

A **market** convenes in the parking lot off Market Ave. every Wednesday and Saturday. **Bakeries** line North St., while groceries await at **Iceland,** 55 South St. (Open M-Th and Sa 8:30am-7pm, F 8:30am-8pm, Su 10am-4pm.) The town's best eateries congregate around the cathedral and tend to gouge the pocket. Patrons gulp ales and delectable pub chow beneath soaring ceilings and stained glass at the **Slurping Toad,** West St., set in the parish church across from the cathedral. (☎539637. Drinks £1.50 Tu-F 5:30-8:30pm. Open M-Sa 11am-11pm.) Twentysomethings mingle with the pre-theater crowd at **Woodies Wine Bar and Brasserie,** 10 St. Pancras, the oldest wine bar in Sussex. A sandwich and glass of wine (or pint of ale) cost £4.50, main courses £7-10. (☎779895. Open M-Sa noon-2:30pm and 6-11pm, Su 6-11pm.) The **Pasta Factory,** 6 South St. (☎785764), rolls out fresh pasta daily; its cannelloni inspire pleasant dreams for weeks (£8). **Maison Blanc Boulangerie and Patisserie,** 56 South St., fills pastries from eclairs to passionata (chocolate croissant £1) and builds sandwiches on organic bread for £4. (☎539292. Open M-F 8:45am-5:30pm, Sa 8:45am-6pm; June-Sept. also Su 9am-5pm.)

👁 SIGHTS

Begun in 1091, **Chichester Cathedral,** west of the 15th-century market cross, is an architectural grab-bag spanning over 1000 years. Norman arches frame Reformation stained glass, a floor cutaway reveals a Roman mosaic, and Queen Elizabeth II and Prince Philip peer from the newly renovated West Front. A stained-glass depiction by Marc Chagall of Psalm 150 celebrates music and the arts in vibrant colors. Less sanguine, one of Cromwell's soldiers plucks out the eye of Edward IV in the South Transept. Also in the cathedral is an incredibly rare depiction of medieval hand-holding in the 14th-century effigy of Earl Richard Fitzalan, which inspired Larkin's poem "An Arundel Tomb," now displayed on a nearby pillar. The statue of St. Richard, former bishop of Chichester, guards the entrance in a "No pictures, please" pose. (☎782595. Open summer daily 7:30am-7pm; winter 7:30am-5pm. Tours from the West Door Apr.-Oct. M-Sa 11am and 2:15pm. Evensong M-Sa 5:30pm, Su 3:30pm. Free lunchtime concerts Tu. £2 donation encouraged.)

Chichester's other attractions include the **Pallants,** a quiet area with elegant 18th- and 19th-century houses in the quadrant between South St. and East St. **The Pallant House,** 9 North Pallant, is an impeccably restored Queen Anne building attributed to Sir Christopher Wren that draws visitors for its collection of 20th-century art. Native painters such as Ben Nicholson and Lucien Freud are well represented, though a few foreign faces like Picasso and Cézanne make an appearance. A vigorous schedule of temporary exhibitions, concerts, and gallery talks ensures daily events of interest. (Open Tu-Sa 10am-5pm, last admission 4pm. Free guided tours Sa 3pm. £4, students £2.50, seniors £3, children free.)

♫ ENTERTAINMENT AND FESTIVALS

Unexpectedly located in a residential neighborhood north of town, the **Chichester Festival Theatre,** Oaklands Park (☎781312), is the cultural center of Chichester. Founded by Sir Laurence Olivier, the internationally renowned venue has attracted such artists as Maggie Smith, Peter Ustinov, Kathleen Turner, and Julie Christie. The newer **Minerva Studio Theatre** is a smaller space for more intimate productions, including theater in the round. The **Theatre Restaurant and Cafe** caters to patrons from 12:30pm on matinee days, 5:30pm for evening shows. (Box office open M-Sa 9am-8pm, or until 6pm non-performance days. Tickets £15-20, 60 seats available at box office at 10am on day of show £6-8, max. 2 tickets per person.)

During the first two weeks in July, artists and musicians collaborate to produce one of the finest spells of concentrated creativity in England: the **Chichester Festivities.** A full program is published in April. (☎780192. Tickets from £2. Box office, 23 South St., open mid-May until the festival's end M-Sa 10am-5:30pm.)

🏃 DAYTRIPS FROM CHICHESTER

FISHBOURNE ROMAN PALACE. Built around AD 80, possibly as the home of a local king, the palace is the largest domestic Roman building found in Britain; archaeologists believe the original residents possessed wealth of Pompeian proportions. The remains include the country's oldest mosaic floors and a formal garden replanted according to the original excavated plans. *(2 mi. from Ave. de Chartres roundabout in Chichester; walk west along Westgate, which becomes Fishbourne Rd. (the A259) for 1½ mi., or take bus #11, 56, or 700 from Chichester center. Buses stop at Salthill Rd., 5min. from the palace. Fishbourne train station is also 5min. from the palace. ☎(01243) 785859. Open Aug. daily 10am-6pm; Mar.-July and Sept.-Oct. 10am-5pm; Feb. and Nov.-Dec. 10am-4pm; Jan. Su 10am-4pm. £4.50, students and seniors £3.90, children £2.40, families £11.70.)*

GOODWOOD. Three mi. northeast of Chichester, splendid Canalettos, Reynoldses, and Stubbses vie for attention in the 18th-century home of the Duke of Richmond. The sculpture collection is world-famous. *(Take bus #268 from Chichester, and follow the signs 1 mi. ☎(01243) 755040. Open Aug. Su-Th 1-5pm; Apr.-July and Sept. Su-M 1-5pm. £6.50, seniors £6, children 12-18 £3, under 12 free.)* The rich and famous prefer **Racing at Goodwood,** an equestrian tradition celebrating its 200-year anniversary in 2002. Festivities begin July 31. *(☎755055.)* Motorcars rumble in the younger **Festival of Speed** in July and the **Motorcar Revival Race** in September. *(☎755022.)*

WEALD AND DOWNLAND OPEN AIR MUSEUM. For a leisurely stroll through a village unlike any other in England, head to this 50-acre museum in Singleton. Over the past 25 years, 40 buildings representing different eras in British history have been removed from their original sites and reconstructed here. Visitors can time travel from a medieval farmstead to a Tudor market hall to a Victorian rural school. *(7 mi. north of Chichester off the A286. ☎(01243) 811348. Open Mar.-Oct. daily 10:30am-6pm, last admission 5pm; Nov.-Feb. W and Sa-Su 10:30am-4pm. Special combined bus and admission ticket available from bus driver. £7, children £4.)*

HAMPSHIRE

PORTSMOUTH   ☎ 023

Don't talk to me about the naval tradition. It's nothing but rum, sodomy, and the
lash.
   —Winston Churchill

Set Victorian seaside holidays against prostitutes, drunkards, and a bloody lot of
cursing sailors, and the 900-year history of Portsmouth (pop. 190,500) will emerge.
Henry VIII's *Mary Rose*, which sank in 1545 and was raised 437 years later, epitomizes an incomparable naval heritage in a city that will appeal most to those fasci-
nated by the storied saga of the Royal Navy. On the seafront, older visitors relive
D-Day while fresh faces learn of the days when Britannia truly ruled the waves.

▐ TRANSPORTATION

Trains: Portsmouth and Southsea Station, Commercial Rd., in the city center. Travel
center open M-F 8:40am-6pm, Sa 8:40am-4:30pm. Office open M-Sa 5:40am-8:30pm,
Su 6:40am-8:40pm. **Portsmouth Harbour Station,** The Hard, ¾ mi. away at the end of
the line. Ferries to the Isle of Wight. Office open M-F 5:50am-7:30pm, Sa 6am-7:30pm,
Su 6:40am-8:10pm. **Trains** (☎(08457) 484950) go to both stations from **London
Waterloo** (1½hr.; 3 per hr.; £20, day return £21) and **Chichester** (40min.; 2 per hr.;
£4, day return £4.90).

Buses: The Hard Interchange, The Hard, next to the Harbour train station. **National
Express** (☎(08705) 808080) rumbles from **London** (2½hr., every hr., £10.50) and
Salisbury (2hr., every hr., £8.25). Office open M-F 7:45am-5pm, Sa 7:45am-4pm.

Ferries: Wight Link (☎(0870) 582 7744) chugs to the Isle of Wight from the harbor
(15min.; 1-2 per hr.; return £11.70, children £5.60). **Hovertravel** (☎9281 1000)
departs from Clarence Esplanade for Ryde, Isle of Wight (9min.; 2 per hr.; return
£10.90, children £5.60). For services to the **Continent,** consult **By Ferry,** p. 35.

Public Transportation: A reliable and comprehensive bus system connects the city.
Local bus companies **First Provincial** (☎9286 2412) and **Stagecoach** (☎(01903)
237661) run throughout. Daily pass £2, weekly pass £10.

Taxis: Aqua Cars (☎9281 8123). **Streamline Taxis** (☎9281 1111).

✳ ▐ ORIENTATION AND PRACTICAL INFORMATION

Portsmouth sprawls along the coast for miles—Portsmouth, Old Portsmouth, and
the resort community of Southsea can seem like altogether different cities. Major
sights in Portsmouth cluster at **The Hard, Old Portsmouth** (near the Portsmouth and
Southsea train station and Commercial Rd.), and **Southsea Esplanade.**

Tourist Information Centre: The Hard (☎9282 6722; fax 92822693; www.visitports-
mouth.co.uk), by the historic ships. Bursting with brochures; the library map is worth the
20p. Free accommodations booking. **Seasonal offices** (☎832464) near the Sea Life
Centre and Clarence Esplanade. Open Apr.-Sept. daily 9:30am-5:45pm.

Tours: Guide Friday buses stop 2 per hr. at major points of interest. A ticket entitles you
to get on and off as you please, 10am-6pm. £7, students and seniors £5.50, children
£3. **Waterbus** (☎9282 2584) offers 1hr. guided rides in Portsmouth Harbour from The
Hard. Tours 9:30am-4:30pm. £3.50, seniors and students £3, children £2.

Financial Services: Banks clump around the Commercial Rd. shopping precinct, north of
Portsmouth and Southsea Station, including **Lloyds TSB.** Open M-Tu and Th-F 9am-
5pm, W 9:30am-5pm, Sa 9:30am-12:30pm. **American Express,** 110 Commercial Rd.
(☎9286 5865). Open M-Tu and Th-F 9am-5:30pm, W 9:30am-7:30pm, Sa 9am-5pm.

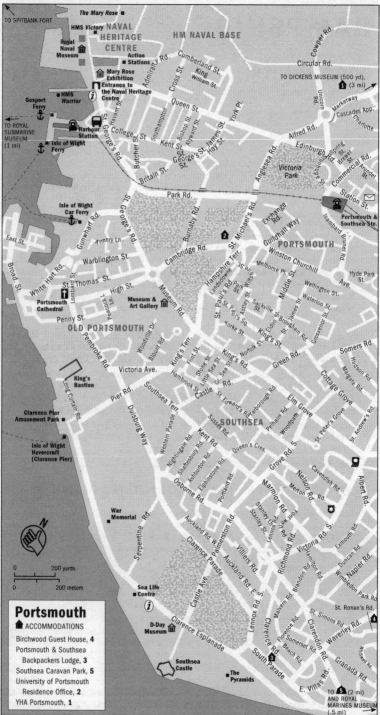

The Mary Rose ■

HMS *Victory* ■ **NAVAL**
HERITAGE
Royal   **CENTRE**
Naval
Museum

HM NAVAL BASE

TO SPITBANK FORT

Action
Stations ■

Mary Rose
Exhibition
Entrance to
the Naval Heritage
Centre

Admiral Rd.
Cumberland St.
King
William St.
Cross St.
Queen St.
York Pl.

TO DICKENS MUSEUM (500 yd),
(3 mi)

Gosport
Ferry

■ HMS
Warrior

Harbour
Station

TO ROYAL
SUBMARINE
MUSEUM
(1 mi)

■ Isle of Wight
Ferry

St. George's Rd.

St. Paul's Rd.

Southampton Rd.

Butcher St.

Kent St.
George's
St.
St. James's St.
Hay St.
Britain St.

Alward St.
Buxton Rd.

Alfred Rd.

Edinburgh Rd.

Anglesea Rd.

Spring
Brewer

Commercial Rd.

Arundel Rd.

Charlotte

Cascades App.

Marketway

Unicorn Rd.

Victoria
Park

Park Rd.

Isle of Wight
Car Ferry

Gunwharf Rd.

Armory Ln.

Warblington St.

White Hart Rd.

Broad St.

East St.

St. George's Rd.

Burnaby Rd.

Cambridge Rd.

2 ■

St. Michael's Rd.

Exchange
Rd.

Guildhall Way

Station
Rd.

Portsmouth &
Southsea Stn.

Isambard Brunel Rd.

PORTSMOUTH

Winston Churchill

Hampshire Terr.

Landsdowne

St. Paul's Rd.

Melbone Pl.

Wellington St.

Waterloo St.

Hyde Park
St.

Lombard St.
Pembroke Rd.
Penny St.
High St.
St. Thomas' St.

Portsmouth
Cathedral

Peacock

Museum Rd.

Museum &
Art Gallery ■

OLD PORTSMOUTH

Woodville Dr.

Blount Rd.

King's Terr.

Flint St.

Stone St.

Hambrook St.

Little Sea Rd.

Yorke St.

St. Paul's Sq.

Sackville St.

St. Paul's Rd.
Kidden St.
Astley St.

St. Edward's Rd.

Norfolk St.

King's Rd.

King's Rd.

Middle St.

Brougham Rd.

James St.

Goodwood

Green Rd.

Somers Rd.

Hudson Rd.

Margate Rd.

Cottage Grove

King's
Bastion

Victoria Ave.

Pier Rd.

Southsea Terr.

Duisburg Way

Long Curtain Rd.

Castle

Gr. Sea Rd.

Sussex Rd.

SOUTHSEA

Elm Grove

Peham Rd.

Woodpath

St. Peter's Grove

St. Andrew's Rd.

Clarence Pier
Amusement Park ■

Isle of Wight
Hovercraft
(Clarence Pier)

Western Parade

Nightingale Rd.

Shaftesbury Rd.

Ashburton Rd.

Elphinstone Rd.

Kent Rd.

Queen's Cres.

Portland Rd.

Grove Rd.

Nelson Rd.

Merton Rd.

Cavendish Rd.

Albert Rd.

War
Memorial ■

Osborne Rd.

Marmion Rd.

Stanley Rd.

Stanley St.

Victoria Rd. S.

Exmouth Rd.

Duncan Rd.

Napier Rd.

Serpentine Rd.

Auckland Rd. W.
Palmerston Rd.

Villiers Rd.

Richmond Rd.

Clarendon Rd.

Wimbledon Park Rd.

Sea Life
Centre ■

Clarence Parade

Castle Ave.

Auckland Rd. E.

Lennox Rd. S.

Malvern Rd.

Brandon Rd.

Florence Rd.

Somerset Rd.

Beach Rd.

St. Simons Rd.

St. Ronan's Rd.

4

D-Day
Museum ■

Clarence Esplanade

South Parade

3

Waverley Rd.

Granada Rd.

Southsea
Castle

■ The
Pyramids

E. Villas Rd.

TO 5 (2 mi)
AND ROYAL
MARINES MUSEUM
(.5 mi)

0 —— 200 yards
0 —— 200 meters

SOUTH ENGLAND

Launderette: Laundrycare, 121 Elm Grove. Open M-Su 8am-6pm, last wash 4:45pm.

Police: Winston Churchill Ave. (☎9283 9333).

Hospital: QA Hospital (☎9228 6000) handles emergencies. Also **St. Mary's Hospital,** Milton Rd. (☎9282 2331).

Internet Access: The Cyber Cafe (☎9266 4158), corner of Victoria Rd. South and Albert Rd. Members 2p per min., nonmembers 4p. Membership free. Open M-Tu and Th-Sa 11am-9pm, W 1:30-9pm, Su noon-6pm. **The Online Cafe** has 2 locations in Southsea, 163 Elm Grove (☎9283 2206) and 23 Highland Rd. (☎9286 1221). £3 per hr. Open daily 10am-9pm.

Post Office: Slindon St. (☎9283 5201), near the train station. Open M and Th 8:45am-5:30pm, Tu-W and F-Sa 9am-5:30pm. **Postal Code:** PO1 1AA.

ACCOMMODATIONS

Moderately priced B&Bs (around £20) clutter **Southsea,** Portsmouth's contiguous resort town, 1½ mi. east of The Hard along the coast. Many are located along Waverly Rd., Clarendon Rd., and South Parade. If you're arriving via the Portsmouth and Southsea Station, catch one of the frequent buses on Commercial Rd. (#16 and #5 are good choices). If your ferry or train arrives at Portsmouth Harbor, hop aboard one of the several buses that makes the pilgrimage from The Hard to South Parade (such as #5). Cheaper lodgings lie two or three blocks inland—Whitwell Rd., Granada Rd., St. Roman's Rd., and Malvern Rd. all have a fair sprinkling.

Portsmouth and Southsea Backpackers Lodge, 4 Florence Rd. (☎/fax 9283 2495). Take any Southsea bus and get off at The Strand. Immaculate rooms in a 4-story home. Pan-European crowd and energetic owners; backpackers have been known to come for 2 days and stay for 2 months. Comfy lounge, wooden bunks, satellite TV, and Internet access (£1 per 15min.) make for a social environment. Deluxe kitchen and well-stocked grocery counter. Laundry facilities (£2). Dorms £10; doubles £22, with bath £25.

Birchwood Guest House, 44 Waverly Rd. (☎9281 1337). A touch of quiet elegance in a city of carnivals and sailors. Bright, spacious rooms recently refurbished with aboriginal art. Incredibly personable hosts invite guests to unwind with a drink in the lounge. Ample breakfast included. Singles and quads £18-20 per person; doubles, triples, and quads with bath £20-30 per person.

YHA Portsmouth, Wymering Manor, Old Wymering Ln., Medina Rd., Cosham (☎9237 5661). From Cosham train station, make a right and walk up High St.; turn left on Wayte St. and cross the roundabout to Medina Rd. After 6 blocks, Old Wymering Ln. is on your right; the hostel is across from the church. From Portsmouth, take any bus (#1, 3, 40, and others) to Cosham station and follow the signs. Though far from town, this former home of Catherine Parr, sixth wife of Henry VIII, features exquisitely detailed woodwork and architecture. Sleep in a Tudor drawing room. 58 beds. Lockout 10am-5pm. Curfew 11pm. Open Feb.-Aug. daily; Sept.-Nov. F-Sa. Dorms £9.50, under 18 £6.50.

University of Portsmouth Halls of Residence, Nuffield Centre, St. Michael's Rd. (☎9284 3178), overlooking Southsea Common. 15min. from The Hard. Small, modern rooms in **Burrel House, Rees Hall,** or **Harry Law Hall,** all reasonably convenient. Booking ahead is highly recommended, but last-minute arrivals should head over to Rees Hall directly (take bus #5). Singles and twins available mid-July to Sept. Rooms £22.25 per person with full English breakfast (cheaper with self-catering).

Camping: Southsea Caravan Park, Melville Rd., Southsea (☎9273 5070). At the eastern end of seafront, 5-6 mi. from The Hard. Pretty site with toilets, showers, laundry facilities, shop, restaurant-bar, and pool. No reservations, but call ahead for availability. 2-person tent £8-9 per night; after Sept. from £7.

🔼🔽 FOOD AND PUBS

Good restaurants reside along the waterfront, Palmerston Rd., Clarendon Rd., and **between** the shopping districts in Southsea and on Commercial Rd. There is no **drought** of pubs in Portsmouth to provide the weary sailor with galley fare and a bottle of gin, especially near The Hard or along Palmerston. Ethnic foods add spice to the scene on Albert Rd. The **Tesco** supermarket awaits on Craswell St., just off the town center, and has a habit of cutting prices to ridiculous levels just before closing. (☎ 839222. Open 24hr. between M 7am and Sa 10pm, Su 10am-4pm.)

Country Kitchen, 59a Marmion Rd. (☎ 9232 1148). Savory vegetarian and vegan dishes (around £4.50) and un-decadent desserts please the taste buds and the wallet. Genial service. Open daily 9:30am-5pm.

Brown's, 9 Clarendon Rd. (☎ 9282 2617). The coffee will keep you wide-eyed for days at this local favorite, which serves fresh English food in relaxed surroundings. Omelettes £3-4, all-day brunch £4. Open M-Sa 9:30am-5pm, Su 11am-3pm.

One Eyed Dog (☎ 9282 7188), corner of Elm Grove and Victoria Rd. South. This bright blue cross between a pub and a trendy bar draws a steady flow of twentysomethings afternoon and night. The place to sate your thirst but not your hunger pains (bar snacks only). Open M-F 3:30-11pm, Sa noon-11pm, Su noon-10:30pm.

The Outback Bar, Ashley Pl. (☎ 9282 3497), off Clarendon Rd. in Southsea. Jumping with Aussie energy, The Outback will satisfy any hankering for kangaroo steak. Happy "hour" all day Tu for women and Su for everyone. Open daily noon-11pm.

The Elms, 128 Elm Grove (☎ 9281 8123). The proud, rainbow-bedecked center of the Portsmouth gay and lesbian community—and one of the busiest spots in town to boot. DJ or live music F-Sa. 18+. Open M-Sa 11am-11pm, Su noon-10:30pm.

👁 🎵 SIGHTS AND ENTERTAINMENT

Portsmouth overflows with magnificent ships and seafaring relics. The bulk of sights worth seeing anchor near The Hard, delighting war buffs, intriguing historians, and looking like some pretty big boats to the rest of the world. In summer, the colorful boardwalk attracts the attention of landlubbers.

◼ NAVAL HERITAGE CENTRE

*In the Naval Yard. Entrance next to the TIC on The Hard; follow the signs to Portsmouth Historic Ships. ☎ 9286 1512 or 9286 1533. Ships open Mar.-Oct. daily 10am-5:30pm; Nov.-Feb. 10am-5pm. Last entry to many sights 4:45pm. Each sight £6-6.50, seniors £5.30-5.80, children £4.50-4.80. If you plan to see more than 2 sights, the **Passport ticket** gives one-time entrance to every site and is valid for a year. £17.50, seniors £15.50, children £12.50.*

Admirals and historians will want to plunge head first into the unparalleled Naval Heritage Centre, which brings together a virtual armada of Britain's most storied ships and nautical artifacts. Resurrect the past with these floating monuments to Britain's former majesty of the seas—even the staunchest army man can't help but be awed by the history within these hulls. The five galleries of the **Royal Naval Museum** fill in the historical gaps between the three ships.

MARY ROSE. The center includes one of England's earliest warships, Henry VIII's *Mary Rose.* Henry was particularly fond of her, but like many other of Henry's women, the *Mary Rose* died before her time—she sank after setting sail from Portsmouth in July 1545. Not until 1982 was Henry's flagship raised from her watery grave. The eerie, skeletal hulk is now continuously sprayed with a waxy preservative mixture designed slowly to dry the timber over a total of 20 years (five to go!). Thousands of artifacts discovered with the ship are on display in the **Mary Rose Exhibition** gallery by the Centre's entrance.

HMS VICTORY. Napoleon must be rolling in his tiny grave to know that the HMS Victory is still afloat. Cinching Britain's reputation as queen of the waves with its defeat of Napoleon's forces at Trafalgar in 1805, the *Victory* embodies the order and invincible regimentation of Admiral Nelson's Navy. It vividly portrays the dismal, cramped conditions for press-ganged recruits, and the spot where Nelson expired has become a veritable shrine for the Royal Navy. *Victory* is only on view via a guided tour—be sure to check your admission ticket for your time slot.

HMS WARRIOR. Eclipsed by its neighbor, the HMS Warrior provides an intriguing companion to the *Victory*. The pride of Queen Victoria's navy and the first iron-clad battleship in the world, *Warrior* never saw battle. Nonetheless, a respectful Napoleon III called it "The Black Snake among the Rabbits in the Channel."

ACTION STATIONS. Scale walls, navigate enemy seas, pilot a helicopter, and experience other simulated trials of naval fire in this high-tech new addition to the dockyards. The 24min. Omni film *Command Approved* reveals a "typical" day aboard a Type 23 frigate: missiles and bravado fly as the ship engages in an all-out war with evil modern-day island pirates.

OTHER NAVAL SIGHTS

Not surprisingly, Portsmouth's collection of museums rarely deals with more than the sea and its inhabitants. **Spitbank Fort** has protected Portsmouth through two World Wars and remains relatively unscathed. Boats depart from the Historic Dockyard. *(25min. crossing. Runs Easter-Oct. W and Sa 1:30pm, Su 2pm. Trips £6.50, concessions £5.)* The **Royal Navy Submarine Museum** surfaces in Britain's only walk-on submarine, the **HMS Alliance,** and provides tours of this underwater habitat. The Gosport ferry continuously crosses from the Harbour train station (£1.80); then follow the signs or take bus #9 to Haslar Hospital. *(☎9252 9217. £3.75, concessions £2.50, families £10.)* The **Royal Marines Museum** chronicles the 400 years in which the British Empire was established—and then lost. It includes a prodigious display of medals, a jungle tour (look out for scorpions), and an animated marine in drag. *(☎9281 9385. Open Nov.-Mar. daily 10am-4:30pm; Apr.-Oct. 10am-5pm. £4, children £2.25.)*

THE BEST OF THE REST

SOUTHSEA. The ■**D-Day Museum,** on Clarence Esplanade, is a creative museum that leads visitors through life-size dioramas of the 1944 invasion. It also houses the Overlord Embroidery, a latter-day Bayeux Tapestry (but 41 ft. longer) commissioned in 1968 to recount the Allied victory. *(☎9282 7261. Open Apr.-Sept. daily 10am-5:30pm; Oct.-Mar. 10am-5pm. £5, seniors £3.75, students £3, families £13. Admission and special events during the anniversary week of D-Day (June 6) £2.50. Audioguide to embroidery 50p.)* **Southsea Castle,** built by Henry VIII at the point of Clarence Esplanade, was an active fortress into the 20th century. Don't miss the secret underground tunnels. *(Open Apr.-Sept. daily 10am-5:30pm. £2.50, senior £1.80, students and children £1.50, families £2.50.)* Aquariums are declining in popularity, but the **Sea Life Centre** has retained a healthy squad of squid and such. *(☎9287 5222. Open in summer daily 10am-7pm; winter 10am-5pm. £6, seniors £5.50, students £5, children £4.50.)*

CHARLES DICKENS BIRTHPLACE MUSEUM. Charles Dickens was born in Portsmouth, returning later to derive inspiration for *Nicholas Nickleby*. His birthplace is today an uninspired museum. The only authentic Dickens artifacts in the Regency-style house are the couch on which he died (transplanted from Kent) and a lock of his precious hair. *(393 Old Commercial Rd., ¾ mi. north of Portsmouth and Southsea station. ☎9282 7261. Open Apr.-Oct. daily 10am-5:30pm; Nov.-Dec. and Feb. 7, Dickens's Birthday, 10am-5pm. £2.50, seniors £1.80, students and children £1.50, families £6.50.)*

FESTIVALS. Several annual festivals heat up Portsmouth during the summer. Don't miss the **Tall Ships Race** in 2002. This international flotilla is due to cross the finish line at Portsmouth August 15-18. In early June, the circus comes to town. Late August brings both the **Southsea Show** (☎9283 4158) and the **Kite Festival** (☎9283 4158). In the absence of a lively event, the Southsea shoreline, dotted with parks, flower beds, and war memorials, makes for a wonderfully peaceful stroll.

ISLE OF WIGHT   ☎ 01983

> She thinks of nothing but the Isle of Wight and she calls it the Island, as if there
> were no other island in the world.
> —Jane Austen, *Mansfield Park*

Far more tranquil and sun-splashed than its mother island to the north, the Isle of
Wight offers travelers stunning scenery, bright sandy beaches, and peaceful family
breaks. The life of the Isle has softened the hardest of hearts through the centuries, from Queen Victoria, who reportedly found much amusement here (and little
elsewhere), to Karl Marx, who exclaimed the island "a little paradise!" Best known
for its shores of stone and sand, the Isle of Wight also shelters much inland beauty.

▐ TRANSPORTATION

Ferries: Wight Link (☎(0870) 582 7744) ferry services include: **Lymington** to
Yarmouth (return £9, children £4.80); **Portsmouth Harbour** to **Fishbourne** (return £9,
children £4.80); **Portsmouth Harbour** to **Ryde** (15min.; return £11.70, children
£5.60). **Red Funnel** ferries (☎(023) 8033 4010) steam from **Southampton** to **East
Cowes** (every hr.; return £8.20, children £4.30). **Hovertravel** (☎(023) 9281 1000)
sails from **Southsea** to **Ryde** (9min.; 34 per day; return £10.90, children £5.60).

Public Transportation: Trains and buses run throughout the island. The **Island Line** train
service (☎562492) is limited to the eastern end of the island, including Ryde, Brading,
Sandown, Shanklin, and a few points in between. **Southern Vectis** buses (☎827005)
cover the entire island; **tourist information centres** (TICs) and **Travel Centres**
(☎827005) in Cowes, Shanklin, Ryde, and Newport sell the complete service timetable
(50p). Buy tickets on board. The **Island Rover** ticket gives you unlimited bus travel (1-
day £6.70, children £3.35; 2-day £10.90, children £5.45).

Car Rental: South Wight Rentals, 10 Osborne Rd. (☎864263), in Shanklin, offers free
pickup and drop-off. Rentals from £25 per day. Open daily 8:30am-5:30pm. **Solent
Self Drive,** Marghams Garage, Crocker St., Newport (☎282050 or (0800) 724734).
Also at Red Funnel Terminal, West Cowes. Rates from £29 per day, £51 per weekend,
£175 per week.

Bike Rental: Solent Self Drive (see above). £9 per day, £40 deposit. **Island Cycle Hire,**
17 Beachfield Rd. (☎363134), in Sandown. £8-12 per day, £30-40 per week; ID plus
£25 deposit. Open Apr.-Sept. daily 9am-5pm; Oct.-Mar. 5-6 days a week 9am-5pm.

✦ ☑ ORIENTATION AND PRACTICAL INFORMATION

The Isle of Wight is 23 mi. by 13 mi. and shaped like a diamond, with towns clustered along the coasts. **Ryde** and **Cowes** are to the north, **Sandown, Shanklin,** and
Ventnor lie along the east coast heading south, and **Yarmouth** is on the west coast.
The capital, **Newport,** sits in the center, at the origin of the River Medina. These are
the best places to find TICs, accommodations, and bus service.

Tourist Information Centres: Each supplies an individual town map as well as the free
Isle of Wight Official Pocket Guide. A **general inquiry service** (☎813818; fax 863047;
www.islandbreaks.co.uk) directs questions to one of the seven regional offices listed
below—call this number first. TICs tend to close earlier than their posted hours in the
slower winter months. For accommodations, call the central booking line (☎813813).

Cowes: Fountain Quay (☎291914), in the alleyway next to the ferry terminal for RedJet (to
Southampton). Open Tu-Sa 9am-5:30pm, extended hours July-Aug.; Cowes week (1st week in
Aug.) daily 8am-8pm.

Newport: The Guildhall, High St. (☎525450), follow signs from the bus station. Open M-Sa 9am-
5:30pm, Su 10am-4pm.

Ryde: Western Esplanade (☎562905), at the corner with Union St., opposite Ryde Pier and the bus
station. Open M-Sa 9am-5:30pm, Su 9am-5pm.

SOUTH ENGLAND

Sandown: 8 High St. (☎403886), across from Boots Pharmacy. Open Apr.-Oct. M-Sa 9am-5:30pm, Su 9am-5pm; Nov.-Mar. daily 9am-5pm.

Shanklin: 67 High St. (☎862942). Open Apr.-Oct. M-Sa 9am-5:30pm, Su 9am-5pm; Nov.-Mar. daily 9am-5pm.

Ventnor: 34 High St. (☎853625). Open Apr.-Oct. M-Tu and Th-Sa 10am-3pm. Call the central line for winter hours.

Yarmouth: The Quay (☎813818), follow the signs from the ferry stop. Open M-Sa 9am-5:30pm, Su 9am-5pm.

Financial Services: Banks can be found in all major town centers. Make sure you stock up on cash, as cash machines are rare in the smaller towns.

Police: ☎528000.

Medical Assistance: St. Mary's Hospital (☎524081), in Newport. Disabled travelers can seek assistance from **Dial Office** (☎522823).

Internet Access: The idea of peddling Internet access is beginning to catch on at the Isle of Wight; ask the local TIC for the nearest location. Sandown has its own **Internet Cafe,** 16-18 Melville St. (☎408294), off High St. by the pier, and is your best bet for fast service. £1.75 per 30min. Open Tu-Sa 11am-6pm. **Lord Louis Library** (☎823800) in Newport and the **Ryde Library** (☎562170) in Ryde also have connections. Both offer access for £3 per 30min. or £5 per hr.; book in advance.

Post Office: Post offices are found in every town center.

▌ ACCOMMODATIONS AND CAMPING

Accommodations on the Isle of Wight tend to require a two-night minimum stay. Prices range from decent to absurd, often depending on proximity to the shore. Budget travelers should try one of the YHA Youth Hostels at either end of the island, look into less-visited areas, or try their luck with the Isle's **Accommodation Booking Service** (☎813813).

YHA Sandown, The Firs, Fitzroy St., Sandown (☎402651; fax 403565). Follow the signs from town center or, from the train station, take Station Ave. until Fitzroy St. on the right. Ultra-clean new dorm, kitchen and lounge facilities by one of the more popular Wight beaches: a pleasant respite from a hard day's sunbathing. Luggage storage and wet-weather shelter available during lockout hours (10am-5pm). Open mid-Apr. to Sept. daily; mid-Feb. to mid-Apr. and Sept. W-Su. Dorms £11, under 18 £7.90.

YHA Totland Bay, Hurst Hill, Totland Bay (☎752165; fax 756443), on the west end of the island. Take Southern Vectis buses #7 or 7A to Totland War Memorial; turn left up Weston Rd., and take the 2nd left onto Hurst Hill. Hostel is on the left. Comfortable lodgings in a fantastic location. Cliffs, walking trails, and Alum Bay are all close by. Open Mar.-June M-Sa; July-Aug. daily; Sept.-Oct. F-Sa. Dorms £11, under 18 £7.90.

Seaward Guest House, 14 George St., Ryde (☎563168; seaward@FSBDial.co.uk). Friendly proprietor and dog provide airy, pastel rooms and a hearty breakfast, near the hovercraft, bus, and train stations. Singles £18-£20; doubles £30-36, with bath £36-44.

Camping: Check the free Isle of Wight *Camping and Touring Guide*, available from all TICs; sites are plentiful. **Beaper Farm Camping Site** (☎615210), between Ryde and Sandown, accessible by bus #7. Sheltered by a grove of trees, with 150 pitches, electricity hookups, showers, and laundry facilities. 2-person tent £7.

▐ FOOD

Hungry travelers throughout the Isle of Wight can begin their hunt for food on the local High St. or Esplanade; these commonly named roads often feature uncommonly excellent restaurants. Locally caught fish is a specialty. *The Official Guide to Eating Out*, free and distributed by TICs, offers additional dining options. Supermarkets are in most large cities, and thirsty vacationers need not look far for a pub, since the island harbors nearly one public house for every square mile. When using **Ryde** as a center for island exploration, feast on exquisite gourmet baguettes and pastries (£1.30-£3.30) from the **Baguette Factory,** 24 Cross St. (☎611115. Open M-Sa 8:30am-4pm.) **S. Fowler & Co.,** 41-43 Union St., buzzes with tourists and locals alike, and no wonder, with plenty of meals under £5, including several vegetarian options. (☎613937. Open daily 10am-8pm. AmEx/MC/V.)

⊙ SIGHTS

Wight's natural treasures are especially prominent in the west, with rolling hill-sides, multicolored beaches, and the famous Needles (below); bus #7, 7a, or 7b to Alum Bay catches breathtaking views while it whisks along cliff roads. Zoos specialize in everything from butterflies to dinosaurs to tigers, and there is a museum dedicated to the art of smuggling. All these sights are listed in the *Official Pocket Guide* and are bound to delight, but don't miss the following must-see sights.

OSBORNE HOUSE. The image of Queen Victoria as a stern monarch in perpetual mourning is shattered by the spacious splendor of Osborne House, the backdrop for the 1997 film *Mrs. Brown.* Completed in 1846, the house was meant to serve as a "modest" country home providing refuge from affairs of state. Victoria used it as a long-term retreat after Albert's death in 1861 and died here herself in 1901. Mementos and family pictures give the home an unusual personal touch; meanwhile, the India Exhibit in the resplendent white **Durbar Room** speaks to the Queen's public persona. A free **horse-and-carriage ride** through the manicured grounds and gardens passes the children's Swiss Cottage. *(Take Southern Vectis bus #4 or 5 from Ryde or Newport. ☎200022. Open Apr.-Sept. daily 10am-6pm; Oct. 10am-5pm; Feb.-Mar. and Nov. to mid-Dec. booked tours only. House and grounds £7.20, students and seniors £5.40, under 16 £3.60. Grounds £3.80, £2.90, £1.90.)*

CARISBROOKE CASTLE. If whoever controls the castle controls the island, then the six Carisbrooke donkeys are the rightful rulers of Wight. The Norman castle's most famous resident, however, was here not as a ruler but as a prisoner. Suffering numerous defeats in the Civil War, Charles I fled to Carisbrooke in 1647, where he was captured and imprisoned until his execution. Charles did not accept his fate lying down; visitors climbing through the ruins can still see the window in which the deposed king got stuck while trying to escape. A museum details the structure's history, including the **Tennyson Room,** containing the poet's hat, desk, cloak, and, more morbidly, funeral pall. *(From Newport, with the bus station on your left follow Upper St. James St. until turning right onto Trafalgar St. Bear left onto Castle Rd., which becomes Castle Hill. ☎522107. Open Apr.-Sept. daily 10am-6pm; Oct. 10am-5pm; Nov.-Mar. 10am-4pm. £4.50, students and seniors £3.40, children £2.30, families £11.30. Tour £1, children 50p.)*

ALUM BAY AND THE NEEDLES. Some of the Isle of Wight's most charmed sights predate both Victorians and Normans. On the western tip of the island, the white chalk **Needles** jut into a dark sea. The third rock supports a lighthouse manned until 1997. Local cruises in **Alum Bay** afford a good view of the Needles. The pleasure park may distract you from the natural beauty of the bay, but a **chairlift** runs down to the base of the cliffs to the famous colored beaches (used by Victorians in paint pigments) and back (return £3, children £2).

WALKING AND CYCLING. Walkers and cyclists enjoy the coastal path stretching from **Totland,** past lighthouses both modern and medieval at **St. Catherine's Point,** to **St. Lawrence** at the southern end of the island. Explore the island's 500 mi. of well-maintained footpaths during the annual **Walking Festival** (mid-May) and **Cycling Festival** (mid-June), when participants pace along scenic routes or race over strenuous courses. Visit the TICs for more details. Racing ships speed past the coastline in the regatta that takes place during **Cowes Week** in early August.

WINCHESTER ☎ 01962

Best known for its dramatic cathedral, Winchester (pop. 32,800) traces its origins to Roman times, when it was the walled city of Venta Belgarum. Both Alfred the Great and William the Conqueror deemed the town the center of their kingdoms, and monks painstakingly prepared the *Domesday Book* for William here (see **Christians, Vikings, and Normans, O My!**, p. 67). During the Great Plague of 1665, Charles II moved his court to Winchester, from where he frequently checked on the well-being of his London properties and less often on that of his dying subjects. In the more recent past, Jane Austen and John Keats both lived and wrote in town, and Winchester inspired Keats's much-adored "To Autumn." While its grandest days have passed, Winchester has managed to polish some luster into its old walls. Locals amble through quiet gardens along the River Itchen, and the pedestrian area bustles with students and shoppers.

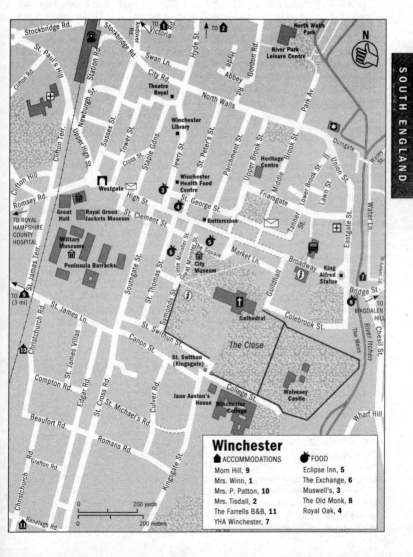

SOUTH ENGLAND

Winchester

🏠 ACCOMMODATIONS

Morn Hill, **9**
Mrs. Winn, **1**
Mrs. P. Patton, **10**
Mrs. Tisdall, **2**
The Farrells B&B, **11**
YHA Winchester, **7**

🍎 FOOD

Eclipse Inn, **5**
The Exchange, **6**
Muswell's, **3**
The Old Monk, **8**
Royal Oak, **4**

0   200 yards
0   200 meters

⊟ TRANSPORTATION

Just north of Southampton, Winchester makes an excellent daytrip from **Salisbury,** 25 mi. away, or **Portsmouth,** 27 mi. away. However, beautiful river walks and Winchester's own daytrips might tempt you to stay the night.

Trains: Winchester Station, Station Hill, northwest of the city center. Tourist center open M-F 9am-6pm, Sa 9am-5pm, Su 9am-4:30pm. Ticket counter open M-F 6am-8:30pm, Sa 6am-7:30pm, Su 7am-8:30pm. Trains (☎(0457) 484950) from: **London Waterloo** (1hr., 2 per hr., £16.60); **Portsmouth** (1hr., every hr., £7); **Brighton** (1½hr., every hr., £16.10). Be prepared to change trains at Basingstoke or Fareham.

Buses: Buses stop either inside the **bus station** or outside on Broadway, the end of High St. near Alfred's statue. (Open M 7:30am-5:30pm, Tu-F 8:30am-5:30pm, Sa 8:30am-12:30pm.) **National Express** (☎(08705) 808080) runs buses from **London** via **Heathrow** (1½hr., 7 per day, £12) and **Oxford** (2½hr., 2 per day, £6.75). **Hampshire Stagecoach** (☎(01256) 464501) heads to: **Southampton** (#47, 50min., 2 per hr., return £2.90); **Salisbury** (#68, 45min., 7 per day, return £4.45); **Portsmouth** (#69, 1½hr., 12 per day, return £4.45). **Explorer** tickets are available for bus travel in Hampshire and Wiltshire for £5.25, seniors £3.85, children £2.60, families £10.50.

Local Transportation: Local buses (☎(01256) 464501) stop by the bus and train stations. Ask for a timetable of all Winchester buses at the tourist information centre (TIC).

Taxis: Francis Taxis (☎884343) collect by the market.

✦🛈 ORIENTATION AND PRACTICAL INFORMATION

Winchester's major (and commercial) axis, **High St.,** stretches from the statue of Alfred the Great at one end to the arch of **West Gate** at the other. The city's bigger roads stem off High St., which transforms into **Broadway** as you approach Alfred.

Tourist Information Centre: The Guildhall, Broadway (☎840500; fax 850348; www.winchester.gov.uk), across from the bus station. Stocks free maps, seasonal *What's On* guides, and city guides (£1). **Walking tours** £3, children free. Helpful multilingual staff book accommodations for £3 plus a 10% deposit. Open June-Sept. M-Sa 10am-6pm, Su 11am-2pm; Oct.-May M-Sa 10am-5pm.

Financial Services: Major banks, including **Barclays** and **Lloyds TSB,** cluster around the junction of Jewry St. and High St. **Thomas Cook,** 30 High St. (☎841661 for travel information). Open M-Tu and Th-Sa 9am-5:30pm, W 10am-5:30pm.

Launderette: 27 Garbett Rd., Winnall (☎840658). Climb Magdalen Hill, and continue straight as it changes to Alresford Rd. Turn left on Winnall Manor Rd., and follow until Garbett Rd. on your left. 25p for soap, £2 per load. Open M-F 8am-8pm, Sa 8am-6pm, Su 10am-4pm. Last wash 1hr. before close.

Police: North Walls (☎868100), near the intersection with Middle Brook St.

Hospital: St. Paul's Hospital, St. Paul's Hill. **Royal Hampshire County,** Romsey Rd. (☎863535), at St. James Ln.

Internet Access: Mailboxes Etc., 80 High St. (☎622133). £3 per 30min. Reservations suggested. Open M-F 8:30am-6pm, Sa 10am-3pm. The **Winchester Library,** Jewry St. (☎853909), also has a terminal, starting at £1 per 15min. Open M-Tu and F 9:30am-7pm, W-Th 9:30am-5pm, Sa 9:30am-4pm.

Post Office: Middle Brook St. (☎854004). Turn off High St. at Marks and Spencer. **Bureau de change.** Open M-Sa 9am-5:30pm. **Postal Code:** SO23 8WA.

⌂ ACCOMMODATIONS AND CAMPING

Winchester's B&Bs cluster half a mile southwest of the TIC, near Ranelagh Rd., on the corner of Christchurch Rd. and St. Cross Rd. Buses #29 and 47 make the journey from the town center to Ranelagh Rd. twice every hour; bus #69 runs the same route once per hour. Many pubs also offer accommodations, but try to book early, especially in the summer. A steady stream of Londoners drives up prices all over town, making Winchester's youth hostel particularly attractive.

YHA Winchester, 1 Water Ln. (☎853723). Located in an 18th-century watermill perched atop the rush of the River Itchen. A "simple" hostel, which means creative bed arrangements between the mill's roofbeams. Kitchen available. Lockout 10am-5pm. Stringent 11pm curfew. Open July-Aug. daily; mid-Feb. to June and Sept.-Oct. M-Sa. Dorms £9.25, students £8.25, under 18 £7.

Mrs. P. Patton, 12 Christchurch Rd. (☎854272), between St. James Ln. and Beaufort Rd., 5min. from the cathedral on a silent street of stately houses. Graceful double rooms, recently repainted and refurbished. Look for the partridge-in-a-pear-tree curtains in the bedroom on the right. Shared bathrooms. Singles £25-28; doubles £33-40.

The Farrells B&B, 5 Ranelagh Rd. (☎/fax 869555), 10min. walk from town off Christchurch Rd. Furniture a mother would rave over in a well-kept home. Feels instantly welcoming, with decades of family photos on the wall. 3 doubles are let out as singles in the off season (or after 6pm). £20 per person, with bath £22.

Mrs. Winn, 2 North Hill Close (☎864926). Comfortable, cheap rooms just up the road from the train station. The price of proximity is the dull rumble of coaches. Still, it's tended by 2 warm hosts with an affection for backpackers and other budget travelers. Mind the teddy bears as you climb the stairs. £16 per person.

Mrs. Tisdall, 32 Hyde St. (☎851621), a 5min. walk from town on Jewry St., which becomes Hyde St. Conveniently located between the train station and the town center. Large, airy rooms in an 18th-century townhouse. Singles £26; doubles £34-36. 10% discount for *Let's Go* users.

Camping: Morn Hill Caravan Club Site, Morn Hill (☎869877), 3 mi. east of Winchester off A31, toward New Forest. Mainly for caravans, so extra facilities are limited. Open Apr.-Oct. Campers £6.20-13.80 per night, tents at warden's discretion. Call ahead.

🍴🍺 FOOD AND PUBS

High St. and St. George's St. are home to several food markets, fast-food venues, and tea houses. Jewry St. serves up more substantial restaurants, as well as the **Winchester Health Food Centre,** 41 Jewry St. (☎851113. Open M-F 9:15am-5:45pm, Sa 9am-5:30pm.) **Sainsbury's,** at Middle Brook St. off High St., hawks groceries. (☎861792. Open M-Th 8am-6:30pm, F 8am-9pm, Sa 7:30am-6pm.) If you're looking for a **market,** vendors sell fruits and vegetables on Middle Brook St., behind Marks and Spencer and across from the town library. (Open W-Sa 8am-6pm.)

Muswell's, 8-9 Jewry St. (☎842414). Zany bartenders, toe-tapping dance tunes, deals on meals, and rotating student nights draw a youthful pub crowd. Snag an open-air table to people-watch by day or take a drink at night. Su all-day happy hour. Open M-Sa 11am-11pm, Su noon-10:30pm.

The Eclipse Inn, The Square (☎865676). Winchester's smallest pub, in a 16th-century rectory that the claustrophobic should avoid. Pub grub (from £4) attracts many regulars and, supposedly, a ghost or two. Open M-Sa 11am-11pm, Su 10:30am-noon; food served M-Sa noon-2:30pm and 6-9pm, Su 12:30-3pm.

The Old Monk, 1 High St. (☎855111), next to the River Itchen. Enjoy a meal or a drink on the riverside patio or lounge inside on plush leather chairs. Hundreds of students flock here after class and stay into the night. 2 courses for £6.49. Open M-Sa 11am-midnight, Su noon-10:30pm.

Royal Oak, Royal Oak Passage (☎842701), next to the Godbegot House off High St. Despite its refurbished gleam, this is yet another pub that claims to be the kingdom's oldest. Descend into the 900-year-old subterranean foundations and enjoy the locally brewed hogshead cask ale (£1.75) and English cuisine (£3-6). Open daily 11am-11pm; food served noon-5pm. AmEx/MC/V.

SOUTH ENGLAND

The Exchange, 9 Southgate St. (☎854718). A wild menu, with crocodile, vegan nut, and (for the truly adventurous) beef burgers. Discounts for students and seniors. Open M-Sa 10am-11pm, Su noon-11pm; last call for food orders 2pm.

🔆 SIGHTS

WINCHESTER CATHEDRAL. Duck through the archway (note the stones from William the Conqueror's palace), pass through the square, and behold the 900-year-old cathedral. At a length of 556 ft., it's the longest medieval building in Europe. Magnificent tiles, roped off for preservation, cover much of the floor near the chancel. Jane Austen's tomb rests in the northern aisle of the nave; while gazing at her memorial plaque, don't walk past (or over) Jane herself, buried in the floor. Near the front of the cathedral is a glimmering icon screen, complete with a "How to Pray to Icons" guide. The stained glass window in the rear seems oddly cubist—Cromwell's soldiers smashed the original window in the 17th century, and though the glass pieces have been reinserted, the pattern got lost in the shuffle. *(5 The Close. ☎857225 or 857208. Open daily 7:15am-5:30pm; visiting encouraged after 8:30am. East End closes at 5pm. Free 50min. tours depart from the west end of nave daily 10am-3pm. 75min. tower tours also available. Suggested donation £3.50, students and seniors £2.30, children 50p, families £7. Photography permit £2.)*

The **Norman crypt,** supposedly the oldest, and definitely one of the finest in England, can only be viewed in the summer by guided tour. The crypt contains the statues of two of Winchester's most famous figures: Bishop William of Wykeham, founder of Winchester College, England's first public school, and St. Swithun, patron saint of weather. St. Swithun was interred at the cathedral against his will; in retaliation, the saint brought torrents down on the culprits for 40 days. Supposedly, if it rains on July 15 (St. Swithun's Day), it will rain for the next 40 days. Considering this is England, it might anyway. The **Triforium Gallery** at the south transept contains several relics. The 12th-century *Winchester Bible* resides in the **Library**. Outside to the south of the cathedral is tiny **St. Swithun's Chapel,** rebuilt in the 16th century, nestled above **King's Gate.** *(Free 20min. crypt tours depart from crypt door. Gallery and Library open M-Sa 11am-4:30pm. £1, students 50p, families £2.)*

GREAT HALL. Henry III built his castle on the remains of an earlier fortress of William the Conqueror, and it became a favorite haunt for early royals. What remains is the Great Hall, a gloriously intact medieval structure (unlike its counterpart down the road at Wolvesey), which contains a Round Table modeled after King Arthur's and dated six centuries after his legendary reign. Henry VIII tried to pass the table off as authentic to Holy Roman Emperor Charles V, but the repainted "Arthur," resembling Henry himself, fooled no one. *(At the end of High St. atop Castle Hill. Open Mar.-Oct. daily 10am-5pm; Nov.-Feb. M-F 10am-5pm, Sa-Su 10am-4pm. Free.)*

MILITARY MUSEUMS. Just through **Queen Eleanor's Garden,** in the Peninsula Barracks, five military museums detail the story of the city and the country's military power. The **Royal Greenjackets Museum** is the must-see of the bunch. Explore 400 years of British imperial history while taking on a French guillotine, testing your marksmanship (10p), and ducking German artillery fire. The heart of the museum is the 276 sq. ft. diorama of the Battle of Waterloo containing 21,500 tiny soldiers and their 9600 steeds. *(☎828549. Open M-Sa 10am-1pm and 2-5pm, Su noon-4pm. £2, seniors and children £1, families £6. Hours for the other 4 museums vary.)*

WOLVESEY CASTLE. Though some may find the walk along the river to **Wolvesey Castle** more enjoyable than the site itself, its ruins provide a glimpse into the historic relationship of church and state. The Norman bishop used to live here, exerting influence over the surrounding area. The current bishop still lives in the newer mansion next door, but exerts considerably less secular power. *(☎252000. Open Apr.-Oct. daily 10am-6pm. £1.90, students and seniors £1.40, children £1.)*

CITY MUSEUM. Pristine, interactive galleries explore Winchester's past, from its days as the Roman Venta Belgarum through the Anglo-Saxon invasion and Middle Ages to the present. The Roman gallery is the most impressive, crammed with dazzling artifacts including a rare complete floor mosaic from the local ruins of a Roman villa. (☎848269. Open Apr.-Oct. M-Sa 10am-5pm, Su noon-5pm; Nov.-Mar. Tu-Sa 10am-4pm, Su noon-4pm. Free.)

WALKS. The **Buttercross,** 12 High St., is a good starting point for a walking tour of the town. The statue of St. John, William of Wykeham, and King Alfred derives its name from the shadow it cast over the 15th-century market to keep butter cool. Another ideal walk is along the **River Itchen,** the same taken by poet John Keats; directions and his poem "To Autumn" are available at the TIC for 50p. For a lovely view of the city, including the ruins of Wolvesey Castle, climb to **St. Giles's Hill Viewpoint** at sunset. Pass the Mill and take Bridge St. to the gate marked Magdalen Hill; follow the paths up from there.

♫ ENTERTAINMENT AND FESTIVALS

Weekend nights attract hordes of revelers to bars along **Broadway** and **High St.** For a different type of fun, and since the weather won't let you stay dry anyway, go aquatic at **River Park Leisure Centre.** The park contains a huge pool, as well as Twister the Water Slide, included in the price of a swim. (☎848700. Open daily 6:30am-11pm. £2, concessions £1.)

In all its Edwardian glory, **Theatre Royal,** Jewry St., hosts regional dramatic companies and concerts. Late May features the **Homelands Music Festival,** and though smaller than Glastonbury's summer music orgy, bands still play to sell-out crowds. Acquire tickets from the TIC. In early July, the **Hat Fair** (☎849841), the longest running street festival in Britain, fills a weekend with free theater, street performances, and peculiar headgear.

⮊ DAYTRIPS FROM WINCHESTER

AUSTEN'S COTTAGE. Jane Austen lived in the meek village of **Chawton,** 15 mi. northeast of Winchester, from 1809 to 1817. Visitors have come in droves since the release of several film versions of her novels. It was here that she penned *Pride and Prejudice, Emma, Northanger Abbey,* and *Persuasion,* and some manuscripts, as well as other personal belongings, are on display. A creak was deliberately left in the door to warn Austen so she could hide her writing amid her needlework. (Take Hampshire bus #X64 (M-Sa 11 per day, return £4.50), or London and Country bus #65 on Su, from the bus station. Ask to be let off at Chawton roundabout and follow the brown signs. ☎/fax (01420) 83262. Open Mar.-Dec. daily 11am-4:30pm; Jan.-Feb. Sa-Su 11am-4:30pm. £3.50, concessions £3, under 18 £1.)

THE NEW FOREST. The New Forest, 20 mi. southwest of Winchester in **Lyndhurst,** was William the Conqueror's 145 sq. mi. personal hunting ground and remains, 1000 years later, an idyllic example of rural England. The **Rufus Stone** (near Brook and Cadnam) marks the spot where William's son was accidentally slain. Today, wild ponies, donkeys, and deer wander freely, and safely, alongside winding country roads. The **Museum and Visitor Centre** has a list of campsites. (Take bus #66 to Romsey (every hr.) and transfer to a Lyndhurst bus; Su use bus #X66 (mid-May to mid-Sept., 3 per day, return £4.10). Or take a train to Southampton and then a bus to Lyndhurst. Visitor Centre ☎(023) 8028 2269. Open daily 10am-6pm. £2.50, seniors £2, children £1.50, families £6.50.)

SOUTHWEST ENGLAND

Chiefly agricultural, the southwest's rolling hills and salty sea air provide a refreshing change from city rhythms. In England's West Country, mists of legend shroud the counties of Dorset, Devon, and Cornwall almost as densely as the fog drifting in from the Atlantic. King Arthur was allegedly born at Tintagel on Cornwall's northern coast and is said to have battled Mordred on Bodmin Moor. One hamlet purports to be the site of Camelot, another claims to be the resting place of the Holy Grail, and no fewer than three small lakes are identified as the grave of Arthur's sword, Excalibur. In a more modern myth, the ghost of Sherlock Holmes still pursues the Hound of the Baskervilles across Dartmoor.

Legends aside, the southwest has been a place of refuge for several distinct peoples, all of whom left their mark on land and culture. Cornwall was the last holdout of the Celts in England, while stone circles and the excavated remnants of even older Neolithic communities leave volumes to the imagination. Farther northeast, Somerset, Avon, and Wiltshire are defined by other eras, from Salisbury's medieval cathedral to Bath's Roman baths to enigmatic Stonehenge.

HIGHLIGHTS OF SOUTHWEST ENGLAND

STONEHENGE Puzzle over one of the most astounding engineering feats of the 2nd millennium BC and one of the world's great mysteries (p. 198).

BATH Dally in the world of 18th-century pleasure-seekers who repaved this Roman spa town with their elegant buildings and improper behavior (p. 200).

TINTAGEL Tackle the steep, slippery cliffs leading to Merlin's Cave in the reputed birthplace of King Arthur (p. 234).

ST. IVES Ride the surf or contemplate modernist sculpture in Cornwall's sophisticated coastal beacon (p. 241).

▐ TRANSPORTATION IN SOUTHWEST ENGLAND

It's usually easier to get to Somerset, Avon, and Wiltshire than to regions farther southwest. **Trains** (☎ (08457) 484950) offer fast and frequent service from London and the North. The region's primary east-west line from **London Paddington** passes through **Taunton, Exeter,** and **Plymouth,** ending at **Penzance.** Frequent trains connect London to Bath, Bristol, and Salisbury. Trains from the north pass through **Bristol,** although it may be more convenient to travel through London. Branch lines connect **St. Ives, Newquay, Falmouth,** and **Barnstaple** to the network. As elsewhere in Britain, day return fares are often only slightly more expensive than single fares.

A variety of **Rail Rover passes** (☎ (08457) 484950) can be used in the region: the **Freedom of the Southwest Rover** covers the area from Bristol Parkway through Salisbury and down to Weymouth, covering all of Cornwall, Devon, Somerset, and parts of Avon and Dorset (8 days in 15 £71.50). The **Devon Rail Rover** is bounded by and includes travel on the Taunton-Exmouth line on the east and the Gunnislake-Plymouth line in the west (3 days in 7 £30, 8 in 15 £46.50). The **Cornish Rail Rover** is bounded by the Gunnislake-Plymouth line (3 days in 7 £25.50, 8 in 15 £40).

Buses can be few and far between; plan carefully. **National Express** (☎ (08705) 808080) runs to major points along the north coast via **Bristol** and to points along the south coast (including **Penzance**) via **Exeter** and **Plymouth.** For journeys within the region, local bus services are usually less expensive and more extensive than

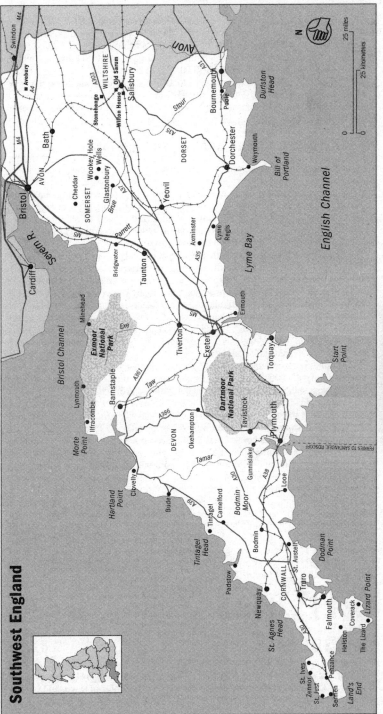

Southwest England

trains. All the large regional bus companies—**Western National** (☎ (01209) 719988) in Cornwall and south Devon, **Southern National** in Somerset and West Dorset, **Devon General** and **Badgerline** (☎ (0117) 955 3231) in Somerset and Avon—sell **Explorer** or **Day Rambler** tickets, which allow a full day's travel on any bus within their region for £4-6 (3-day Explorer £16.50, 7-day £29.50).

When making travel plans, phone ahead in the off season: branch-line **train** service shuts down on winter Sundays, and many lines don't run between September and March. As train or bus passes don't always cover all of the southwest's worthwhile spots, you may find yourself renting a bike or walking to a point of interest.

■ HIKING AND BIKING AROUND THE REGION

Distances between towns in southwestern England are so short that you can travel through the region on your own steam. The narrow roads and hilly landscape can make biking difficult, but hardy cyclists will find the quiet lanes and countryside rewarding terrain. If you're walking or cycling, on- or off-road, bring along a large-scale **Ordnance Survey** map and an impregnable windbreaker to shield you from foul weather. When hiking through countryside, respect the property of local residents, whose livelihood depends on the land you're crossing.

The **South-West Peninsula Coast Path,** the longest coastal path in England, originates in Dorset and passes through South Devon, Cornwall, and North Devon, ending in Somerset. Winding past cliffs, caves, beaches, and resort colonies, it takes several months to walk in its entirety. However, journeys of any length are possible, as buses serve most points along the route, and hostels and B&Bs are spaced at intervals of 5-25 mi. Many rivers intersect the path, so you'll have to take a ferry or wade through the crossings; check times carefully to avoid being stranded. Some sections of the trail are difficult enough to dissuade all but the most ambitious, so before you set out consult tourist officials to make sure that the area you want to visit is well marked. Most tourist information centres sell guides and Ordnance Survey maps covering appropriate sections of the path, which is generally smooth enough to cover by bike. Rental shops can often suggest three- to seven-day cycling routes along the coast.

The path is divided into four parts. The **Dorset Coast Path,** stretching from Lyme Regis to Poole Harbor, can be negotiated in a few days; the *Purbeck Outdoor Leisure Map* or Ordnance Survey Landranger series maps #193-195 (1:50,000) will help planning. The **South Devon Coast Path** picks up near Paignton and continues through Plymouth, tracing spectacular cliffs, wide estuaries, and remote bays set off by lush vegetation and wildflowers. The **Cornwall Coast Path,** with some of the most rugged stretches, starts in Plymouth (a ferry takes you on to Cremyll), rounds the southwestern tip of Britain, and continues up the northern Atlantic coast to Bude. The magnificent Cornish cliffs here harbor a vast range of birds and marine life. The final section, the **Somerset and North Devon Coastal Path,** extends from Bude through Exmoor National Park to Minehead. The least arduous of the four, it features the highest seaside cliffs in southwestern England. On the way, the path passes Culbone and England's smallest church, the 100 ft. dunes of Saunton Sands, and the steep cobbled streets of Clovelly Village on Hartland Point, with pubs dating back to the 1500s.

WILTSHIRE

SALISBURY   ☎ 01722

That all roads in Salisbury (pop. 37,000) seem to lead to its cathedral gates is no accident. Salisbury's small grid of streets was carefully charted by Bishop Poore in the early 13th century. The cathedral is the geographic center of town, and the Salisbury Stake the highest spire in England. If one architectural wonder is not enough for you, nearby Stonehenge has intrigued visitors for thousands of years.

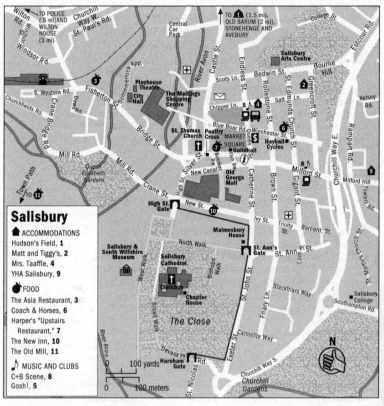

Salisbury

🏠 ACCOMMODATIONS
Hudson's Field, **1**
Matt and Tiggy's, **2**
Mrs. Taaffle, **4**
YHA Salisbury, **9**

🍎 FOOD
The Asia Restaurant, **3**
Coach & Horses, **6**
Harper's "Upstairs
    Restaurant," **7**
The New Inn, **10**
The Old Mill, **11**

🎵 MUSIC AND CLUBS
C+B Scene, **8**
Gosh!, **5**

TRANSPORTATION

Trains: South Western Rd. (☎(02380) 213600), west of town across the River Avon. Ticket office open M-Sa 5:30am-8pm, Su 7:30am-8:45pm. Trains (☎(08457) 484950) from most major towns, including: **London Waterloo** (1½hr., every hr., £22-30); **Southampton** (40min., 2 per hr., £8); **Winchester** (1½hr., every hr., £11.50); **Portsmouth and Southsea** (1½hr., every hr., £11-13).

Buses: Bus Station, 8 Endless St. (☎336855). Open M-F 8:15am-5:30pm, Sa 8:15am-5:15pm. **National Express** (☎(08705) 808080) runs from **London** (2¾hr.; 4 per day; £12.20, return £13.10). Buy tickets at the TIC. **Wilts and Dorset** (☎336855) from **Bath** (#X4, 2hr., 6 per day, £3.20). An **Explorer** ticket is good for a day's worth of travel on **Wilts and Dorset** buses and some **Hampshire, Provincial,** and **Solent Blue** buses (£5.25, seniors £3.85, children £2.60, families £10.50).

Taxis: Taxis cruise by the train station and New Canal. **A and B Taxis** (☎744744) provides wheelchair-friendly service. **505050 Value Cars** (☎505050) runs 24hr.

Bike Rental: Hayball Cycles, 26-30 Winchester St. (☎411378). £9 per day, £2.50 overnight, £55 per week. Cash deposit £25. Open M-Sa 9am-5:30pm. For routes and services call the **Walking and Cycling Hotline** (☎623255).

PRACTICAL INFORMATION

Tourist Information Centre: Fish Row (☎334956; fax 422059; www.visitsalisbury.com), in the Guildhall in Market Sq. Extremely helpful staff. National Express ticket service. Books rooms for a 10% deposit. Open June-Sept. M-Sa 9:30am-6pm, Su 10:30am-

4:30pm; Oct.-Apr. M-Sa 9:30am-5pm; May M-Sa 9:30am-5pm, Su 10:30am-4:30pm. 1½hr. **city tours** leave Apr.-Oct. 11am and 8pm; £2.50, children £1.

Financial Services: Banks are easily found. **Thomas Cook,** 18-19 Queen St. (☎313500). Open M-Tu and Th-Sa 9am-5:30pm, W 10am-5:30pm.

Launderette: Washing Well, 28 Chipper Ln. (☎421874). Open daily 8am-9pm.

Police: Wilton Rd. (☎411444).

Internet Access: Starlight Internet Cafe, 1 Endless St. (☎349359) at Market Sq. £1 per 15min. Open Mar.-Aug. daily 9:30am-10pm; Sept.-Feb. 9:30am-7pm. **ICafe,** 30 Milford St. (☎320050). Funky music and fishtank. £2 per 30min. minimum fee; 20% student discount. Open M-Sa 9am-11pm, Su 10am-11pm. **YHA Salisbury** (see below).

Post Office: 24 Castle St. (☎413051), at Chipper Ln. **Bureau de change.** Open M-Sa 9am-5:30pm. **Postal Code:** SP1 1AB.

ACCOMMODATIONS AND CAMPING

Salisbury's proximity to much-frequented Stonehenge breeds B&Bs, most of them comfortable and reasonably priced, though they fill quickly in summer.

YHA Salisbury, Milford Hill House, Milford Hill (☎327572; fax 330446). 74 beds. Tucked into a cedar grove with 4 kitchenettes, TV lounge, Internet access (£2.50 per 30min.), and cafeteria (breakfast £3.30, dinner under £4). Lockout 10am-1pm. Curfew 11:30pm. The first place to fill in summer; make a reservation. Dorms £11, under 18 £7.60; annex £10, under 18 £6.90. **Camping** £7 per person.

Matt and Tiggy's, 51 Salt Ln. (☎327443), just up from the bus station. A welcoming 450-year-old home with warped floors and ceiling beams and an overflow house nearby; both are remarkably convenient. Mellow, hostel-style, 2-, 3-, and 4-person rooms; no bunk beds. Breakfast £2.50. Sheets £1. Dorms £11-12.

Mrs. Taaffe, 34 Salt Ln. (☎326141), also near the bus station. Convenient to city center. Cozy rooms with TV. Shared bathroom. Singles £16; doubles £32.

Camping: Hudson's Field, Castle Rd. (☎320713). Between Salisbury and Stonehenge. Modern, clean, and well located. Vehicle curfew 11pm. Pitches £5 per night, higher July-Aug. £5 per person; May-June £4; Mar.-Apr. and Sept. £3.50.

FOOD AND PUBS

The most jaded pub dweller can find a pleasing venue among Salisbury's 60-odd watering holes. Most serve cheap food (£4-6) and live music (free). **Market Sq.** in the town center fills on Tuesdays and Saturdays, with vendors hawking everything from peaches to posters. (Open 7am-4pm.) A **Sainsbury's** supermarket is at The Maltings. (☎332282. Open M-Th 8am-8pm, F 8am-9pm, Sa 7:30am-7pm, Su 10am-4pm.) **Salisbury Health Foods,** Queen St., is near the TIC. (Open M-Sa 9am-5:30pm.)

■ **Harper's "Upstairs Restaurant,"** 6-7 Ox Rd., Market Sq. (☎333118). Their slogan is "real food is our speciality," but their true speciality is really *good* food. Inventive English and international dishes (£6-10) make a hearty meal, as does the "8B48" (2 generous courses for £8 before 8pm, £6.50 for seniors 50+). Open M-F noon-2pm and 6-9:30pm, Sa noon-2pm and 6-10pm, Su 6-9pm. AmEx/MC/V.

The Old Mill, Town Path (☎327517), atop the River Nadder at the end of a scenic 10min. stroll along Town Path through the Harnem Water Meadows. The ideal setting for an outdoor drink, with real ales from Salisbury's Hopback Brewery on tap. Open M-Sa 11am-11pm, Su noon-10:30pm.

Coach & Horses, Winchester St. (☎336254). Meals and drinks flow nonstop, drawing families during the day and a louder crowd at night to what may be Salisbury's oldest pub, open since 1382. Open M-Sa 11am-11pm.

The Asia Restaurant, 90 Fisherton St. (☎327628). Indian food so generously spiced it can be smelled from across the street. Open daily noon-3pm and 5:30pm-midnight.

The New Inn, 41-47 New St. (☎327679), forged the way for nonsmoking pubs in Britain. Enjoy your brew or vegetarian meal with a cathedral view. Open M-Sa 11am-3pm and 6-11pm; Su noon-3pm and 7-11pm; last food orders at 2pm and 10pm. MC/V.

🔆 SIGHTS

🖼 SALISBURY CATHEDRAL

33 The Close. ☎555120. Open June-Aug. M-Sa 7:15am-8:15pm, Su 7:15am-6:15pm; Sept.-May daily 7:15am-6:15pm. Suggested donation £3.50, students and seniors £2.50, children £2, families £8. Evensong M-Sa 5:30pm, Su 3pm. Free tours May-Oct. M-Sa 9:30am-4:45pm, Su 4-6:15pm; Nov.-Feb. M-Sa 10am-4pm; more often in summer. 1½hr. roof and tower tours May-Sept. M-Sa 11am, 2, 3pm, Su 4:30pm; June-Aug. M-Sa also 6:30pm; winter hours vary. £3, concessions £2. Call ahead.

Salisbury Cathedral rises from its grassy close to a neck-breaking height of 404 ft. In 1320, architects imagined that the higher a building climbed, the closer it came to God. Built in just 38 years, rather than the usual centuries taken to construct cathedrals, Salisbury Cathedral has a singular and weighty design. The bases of the marble pillars bend inward under the strain of 6400 tons of limestone—if a pillar rings when you knock on it, you should probably move away. Nearly 700 years have left the cathedral in need of structural and surface repair, and scaffolding shrouds parts of the outer walls where the stone is disintegrating (note the avalanche warning signs). Once inside, head to the wooden tomb of William Longespee, Earl of Salisbury (d. 1226), rare in a universe of stone sarcophagi. The chapel houses the oldest functioning mechanical clock, a strange collection of wheels and ropes that has ticked 500 million times over the last 600 years. A tiny stone figure rests in the nave. Legend has it either that a boy bishop is entombed on the spot or that it covers the heart of Richard Poore, founder of the cathedral. The incongruously abstract window at the eastern end, gleaming in rich jewel-like tones, is dedicated to prisoners of conscience, for whom a prayer is said each day.

Much to King John's chagrin, the best-preserved of the four surviving copies of the *Magna Carta* rests in the **Chapter House** and is still legible (that is, if you can read medieval Latin). Named for the practice of reading a Bible chapter at meetings there, the House is surrounded by detailed friezes. In one standout, Noah fills his ark and releases the dove while Cain bludgeons his fair brother's head with what looks like a pickaxe. Ask a guide for a complete list of the relief figures. *(Open June-Aug. M-Sa 9:30am-7:45pm, Su 9:30am-5:30pm; Sept.-May daily 9:30am-5:30pm. Free.)*

OTHER SIGHTS

SALISBURY AND SOUTH WILTSHIRE MUSEUM. The museum houses a mixture of artwork, including Turner's fine watercolors of the cathedral, and random oddities, such as period fashion and doll houses. The worthwhile Stonehenge exhibit shares an extensive amount of history—not bad, seeing as the structure's still a complete mystery. *(65 The Close, along the West Walk. ☎332151. Open July-Aug. M-Sa 10am-5pm, Su 2-5pm; Sept.-June M-Sa 10am-5pm. £3.50, under 16 £1, family £7.90.)*

MALMESBURY HOUSE. Handel once lived in this well-preserved house, but not even the composer of *The Messiah* shall reign eternally—the house is currently a private residence. Tours are by appointment only, but pause by on your way to the cathedral to admire Handel's recital room above the gate and the Julian Calendar (11 days too short) on the outer wall. *(St. Ann's Gate on St. John's St. ☎327027.)*

🎵 🎭 ENTERTAINMENT, NIGHTLIFE, AND FESTIVALS

Salisbury's repertory theater company puts on shows at the **Playhouse,** Malthouse Ln., over the bridge off Fisherton St. (☎320333. Box office open daily 10am-6pm. $8.50-14, concessions $2 less. Half-price tickets available same day.) The **Salisbury Arts Centre,** Bedwin St., offers music, theater, and exhibitions throughout the year. (☎321744. Box office open Tu-Sa 10am-4pm. From $5.) In the summer there are free Sunday **concerts** in various parks; call the TIC for info.

SOUTHWEST ENGLAND

For a little nightlife, head to **Gosh!**, 6 Endless St., a funky restaurant and club with Tuesday foam parties (kids' party 7-10pm, £2; adults 10:30pm-2am, £1). Other entertainments vary. (☎505905. Open M-Sa 11am-2am, Su noon-12:30am. Cover £0-5.) **C+B Scene,** 29 Millford St., is a favorite bar among the young and trendy. Innovative fare is served to a pulsing beat. (☎502397. Open W-Sa 6pm-midnight.)

The **Salisbury Festival** features dance exhibitions, music, and wine-tasting for two weeks in late May and early June. Contact the Festival Box Office at the Playhouse. (☎320333; www.salisburyfestival.co.uk. From £2.50.)

◪ DAYTRIPS FROM SALISBURY

OLD SARUM. At Old Sarum, the prehistoric precursor to Salisbury, an Iron Age fort evolved into a Saxon town, then a Norman fortress. In the 13th century, church officials moved the settlement into the neighboring valley, where they built Salisbury Cathedral. Old Sarum was the most notorious of the "rotten boroughs" eliminated by the Reform Act of 1832. Now a windswept mound strewn with stone ruins, it is still an atmospheric spot with perfect country views. Look for the annual apparition of the crop circle, a detailed wheatfield imprint supposedly left by celestial visitors. *(Off the A345, 2 mi. north of town. Buses #3 and 6-9 run every 15min. from Salisbury. ☎335398. Open July-Aug. M-Sa 10am-5pm, Su 2-5pm; Apr.-June and Sept.-Oct. M-Sa 10am-5pm; Nov.-Mar. M-Sa 10am-4pm. £2, students and seniors £1.50, children £1.)*

WILTON HOUSE. Declared by James I to be "the finest house in the land," the home of the Earl of Pembroke showcases paintings by Van Dyck, Rembrandt, and Rubens. Rembrandt's portrait of his mother has returned to the Great Ante Room after she was stolen and MIA for eight years, then discovered in the trunk of a London car. The house's impressive—nay, outrageous—interior was designed in part by Inigo Jones. The Tudor kitchen and Victorian laundry shed new light on the domestic arts (complete with automated rat). Before touring the house, watch the introductory film narrated by a dead nun. *(3 mi. west of Salisbury on the A30. Take bus #60 or 61 outside Salisbury's Marks and Spencer M-Sa every 10min., Su every hr. ☎746720. Open Easter-Oct. daily 10:30am-5:30pm; last admission 4:30pm. House and grounds £7.25, students and seniors £6.25, children £4.50, families £20. Grounds only £3.75, children £2.75.)*

NEAR SALISBURY

STONEHENGE
You may put a hundred questions to these rough-hewn giants as they bend in grim contemplation of their fellow companions; but your curiosity falls dead in the vast sunny stillness that shrouds them and the strange monument, with all its unspoken memories, becomes simply a heart-stirring picture in a land of pictures.
　　—Henry James

Surely the gentle giants on Salisbury's even plain will fascinate us for millennia to come. A ring of submerged colossi amid swaying grass and indifferent sheep, Stonehenge stands unperturbed by whipping winds. The present stones—22 ft. high—comprise the fifth temple constructed on the site. The first probably consisted of an arch and circular earthwork furrowed in 3050 BC, and was in use for about 500 years. Its relics are the **Aubrey Holes** (white patches in the earth) and the **Heel Stone** (the rough block standing outside the circle). The next monument consisted of about 60 stones imported up the River Avon from Wales around 2100 BC and used to mark astronomical directions. This was likely composed of two concentric circles and two horseshoes of megaliths, both enclosed by earthworks. The present shape, once a complete circle, dates from about 1500 BC. Stonehenge must have seemed old even to the Celts and Romans.

The monument is still more impressive considering that its stones, some of which weigh 45 tons, are thought to have been erected by an infinitely tedious process of rope-and-log leverage. The most famous Stonehenge legend holds that the circle was built of Irish stones magically transported by Merlin. Other tales alternately attribute the monument to giants, Phoenicians, Mycenaean Greeks, Druids, Romans, Danes, and aliens. Whether the rocks traveled by land, water, or flying saucer, Bronze Age builders possessed more technology than we can explain.

Many peoples have worshipped at the Stonehenge site, from late Neolithic and early Bronze Age chieftains to contemporary mystics. In 300 BC, Druids arrived from the Continent and claimed Stonehenge as their shrine. Today, Druids are permitted to enter Stonehenge on the Summer Solstice to perform their ceremonial exercises. In the last few years, however, new-age mystics have beaten them to the spot; in 1999 this led to conflicts with the police and eventual arrests, but the past two celebrations have proved considerably more peaceful.

☐ TRANSPORTATION. Getting to Stonehenge, 8 mi. northwest of Salisbury, doesn't require much effort—as long as you don't have a 45-ton rock in tow. **Wilts and Dorset** (☎336855) runs several **buses,** including daily service from the Salisbury train station (#3, 40min., return £5.25). The first bus leaves Salisbury at 8:45am (Su 10:35am), and the last leaves Stonehenge at 6:30pm (Su 5:45pm). For the same price as a Salisbury-Stonehenge return, get an **Explorer** ticket that allows you to travel all day on any bus, including those stopping by **Avebury,** Stonehenge's less-crowded cousin (see below), and Old Sarum (see p. 198). **Guide Friday,** with Wilts and Dorset, runs a **tour bus** from Salisbury (3 per day, £6-12.50).

The most scenic walking or cycling route from Salisbury is the **Woodford Valley Route** through Woodford and Wilsford. Go north on Castle Rd., bear left just before Victoria Park onto Stratford Rd., and follow the road over the bridge through Lower, Middle, and Upper Woodford. After about 9 mi., turn left onto the A303 for the last mile. If Stonehenge isn't enough rock for you, keep your eyes peeled to your right in Wilsford for the Jacobean mansion that belongs to singer Sting.

◐ ON THE ROCKS? NEAT! Admission to Stonehenge includes a 40min. audio tour that uses handsets resembling cellular telephones. The effect may be more haunting than Stonehenge itself—a bizarre march of tourists who seem engaged in business calls. Nonetheless, the tour is helpful, and includes arguments between a shepherd and his mother about the stones' origins. English Heritage also offers free guided tours (30min.) throughout the day. You can admire the rocks free of charge from the roadside or from Amesbury Hill, 1½ mi. up the A303; it's worth the walk to view the coterie of giants looming in the distance. *(☎(01980) 624715. Open June-Aug. daily 9am-7pm; mid-Mar. to May and Sept. to mid-Oct. 9:30am-6pm; mid-Oct. to mid-Mar. 9:30am-4pm. £4.20, students and seniors £3.20, children £2.50, families £10.60.)*

AVEBURY

The small village that has sprouted within the **stone circle** at Avebury gives a more intimate feel to this sight than is found at Stonehenge, 18½ mi. south. Visitors can weave among the megaliths and even picnic in their midst. With stones that date from 2500 BC, Avebury's sprawling titans are 500 years older than their favored (and smaller) cousins at Stonehenge. Taking perhaps centuries to build, the circle has remained true to its original form and a mystery to the archaeologists, mathematicians, and astronomers who have studied it so stubbornly. Just outside the circle, curious **Silbury Hill** rises from the ground. Europe's largest manmade mound has baffled researchers, and its date, 2660 BC, was only determined by the serendipitous excavation of a flying ant. The **Alexander Keillor Museum** details the history of the stone circle and its environs. *(Buses #5 and 6 run from Salisbury, 6 per day, £3.90. ☎(01672) 539250. Open Apr.-Oct. daily 10am-6pm; Nov.-Mar. 10am-4pm. £2.50.)* Locate the Avebury **tourist information centre** through the car park by following the signs. *(☎(01672) 539425. Open W-Sa 10am-5pm, Su 10am-4pm.)*

SOMERSET AND AVON

BATH ☎ 01225

A visit to the spa city of Bath (pop. 83,000) remains *de rigeur*, even if it is now more of a museum—or a museum's gift shop—than a resort. But expensive trinkets can't conceal Bath's sophistication. Early in their occupation of Britain, the Romans built an elaborate complex of baths to house the curative waters at the town they called Aquae Sulis. In 1701, Queen Anne's trip to the hot springs reestablished the city as a prominent meeting place for artists, politicians, and intellectuals. More than lofty talk was exchanged, though, as Bath became a social capital second only to London, its scandalous scene immortalized by authors as diverse as Fielding, Austen, and Dickens. Bath's Georgian architecture, heavily bombed in WWII, has been painstakingly restored so that today every thoroughfare remains utterly elegant, even if more hair salons than literary salons grace its fair streets.

▚ TRANSPORTATION

Trains: Railway Pl., at the south end of Manvers St. Booking office open M-F 5:30am-8:30pm, Sa 6am-8:30pm, Su 7:45am-8:30pm. Travel center open M-F 8am-7pm, Sa 9am-6pm, Su 9:30am-6pm. Trains (☎(08457) 484950) from: **London Paddington** (1½hr., 2 per hr., £34); **London Waterloo** (2¼hr., 4 per day, £21); **Bristol** (15min., 3 per hr., £4.60); **Exeter** (1¼hr., every hr., £21.50).

Buses: Station at Manvers St. (☎464446). Ticket office open M-F 8:30am-5:30pm, Sa 8:30am-4:30pm; Information Centre M-Sa 9am-5:30pm; National Express office M-Sa 8:30am-5pm. **Luggage storage** during ticket office hours (£2 per 2 days). **National Express** (☎(08705) 808080) from: **London** (3hr., 9 per day, £11.50) and **Oxford** (2hr., 6 per day, £12). **Badgerline** buses sell a **Day Rambler** ticket for unlimited bus travel in the region (£5.30, seniors and children £3.75).

Taxis: Abbey Radio (☎444446) or **Orange Grove Taxis** (☎447777).

Bike Rental: Avon Valley Bike Hire (☎461880), behind the train station. £9 per half-day, £14 per day. Steep £350 credit card deposit. Open Apr.-Oct. daily 9am-5:30pm; Nov.-Mar. M-Sa 9am-5:30pm, Su 10am-5pm.

Boat Rental: Bath Boating Station (☎466407), at the end of Forester Rd., about ½ mi. north of town. Punts and canoes £5 per person per hr., £1.50 each additional hr. Open in summer daily 9am-9pm; winter 9am-5:30pm.

✳ 🛈 ORIENTATION AND PRACTICAL INFORMATION

The beautiful **Pulteney Bridge** and **North Parade Bridge** span the River Avon, which bends around the city. The **Roman Baths,** the **Pump Room,** and **Bath Abbey** cluster in the city center, while the **Royal Crescent** and **The Circus** lie to the northwest.

Tourist Information Centre: Abbey Chambers (☎477101; fax 477787; tourism@bathnes.co.uk). Books accommodations for £2.50 plus 10% deposit. Town map and mini-guide 50p. Pick up *This Month in Bath* (free) for event listings. Open May-Sept. M-Sa 9:30am-6pm, Su 10am-4pm; Oct.-Apr. M-Sa 9:30am-5pm, Su 10am-4pm.

Tours: The Mayor's Honorary Guides lead free **walking tours** from the Abbey Churchyard daily at 10:30am and 2pm. The **Bizarre Bath Walking Tour** (☎335124) begins at the Huntsman Inn at North Parade Passage nightly at 8pm (1¼hr.). Tours vary from mildly amusing to hysterically funny and include absolutely no historical content; £4.50, students £4. **Guide Friday** (☎444102) runs narrated 1hr. hop-on/hop-off bus tours, departing from the bus station every 12min. 9:15am-5:30pm; £9, students and seniors £6.90, children £3.70. **Mad Max Tours** (☎465674) sends young people on daytrips to Wiltshire, including Stonehenge and the Cotswolds. Departs 8:45am from the statue on Cheap St., stops at the YHA hostel at 8:50am. Book ahead. Tours £14.

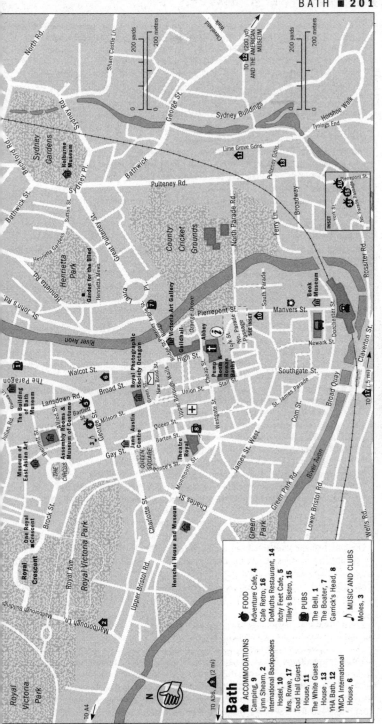

SOUTHWEST ENGLAND

Bath

ACCOMMODATIONS
Camping, 9
Lynn Shearn, 2
International Backpackers
Hostel, 10
Mrs. Rowe, 17
Toad Hall Guest
House, 11
The White Guest
House, 13
YHA Bath, 12
YMCA International
House, 6

FOOD
Adventure Cafe, 4
Cafe Retro, 16
DeMuths Restaurant, 14
Itchy Feet Cafe, 5
Tilley's Bistro, 15

PUBS
The Bell, 1
The Boater, 7
Garrick's Head, 8

MUSIC AND CLUBS
Moles, 3

Financial Services: Banks are ubiquitous; try **Lloyds TSB,** 47 Milsom St. (☎310256). Open M-Tu and Th-F 9am-5pm, W 9:30am-5pm, Sa 9:30am-12:30pm. **Thomas Cook,** 20 New Bond St. (☎492000). Open M-Tu and Th-Sa 9am-5:30pm, W 10am-5:30pm. **American Express,** 5 Bridge St. (☎444757), just before Pulteney Bridge. Open M-Sa 9am-5:30pm. **Branch** (☎424416) in the tourist information centre (TIC).

Launderette: Spruce Goose, Margaret's Buildings, off Brock St. Small load £2, large load £3, soap 60p. Open daily 8am-9pm, last wash 8pm.

Police: Manvers St. (☎444343), near the train and bus stations.

Hospital: Royal United Hospital, Coombe Park, in Weston (☎428331). Take bus #14, 16, or 17 from the train or bus station.

Internet Access: Click Internet Cafe, 19 Broad St. (☎337711). £2.50 per 30min. Open daily 10am-10pm. Also at the **International Backpackers Hostel** (☎446787). 50p per 15min. Open daily 8am-midnight; see below.

Post Office: 21-25 New Bond St. (☎445358), across from the Podium Shopping Centre. **Bureau de change.** Open M-Sa 9am-5:30pm. **Postal Code:** BA1 1A5.

▐ ACCOMMODATIONS AND CAMPING

Bath's well-to-do visitors drive up prices. B&Bs cluster on **Pulteney Rd.** and **Pulteney Gdns.** From the stations, walk up Manvers St., which becomes Pierrepont St., right onto North Parade Rd., and past the cricket ground to Pulteney Rd. For a more relaxed setting, continue past Pulteney Gdns. (or take the footpath from behind the train station) to **Widcombe Hill;** the steep climb has prices to match. A walk west toward Royal Victoria Park on **Crescent Gdns.** reveals another front of B&Bs.

🐌 **Lynn Shearn,** Prior House, 3 Marlborough Ln. (☎313587; fax 443543; keith@shearns.freeserve.co.uk). Take bus #14 from the train station to Hinton Garage (6 per hr.) or make the 12min. walk; look for 2 black signs. Friendly proprietors and inviting rooms, complete with boardgames and hairdryers. Familial breakfast ensues around a large dining table. No smoking. Doubles/twins from £40, with bath £45.

YHA Bath, Bathwick Hill (☎465674; fax 482947; bath@yha.org.uk). From North Parade Rd., turn left onto Pulteney Rd., then right onto Bathwick Hill. A footpath takes the hardy up a never-ending hill to the hostel (a steep 20min. walk). Save your energy for the city: Badgerline "University" bus #18 (6 per hr. until midnight; return £1) runs to the hostel from the bus station or the Orange Grove roundabout. Secluded Italianate mansion overlooking the city. 124 beds. TV, Internet access (£2.50 per 30min.), laundry, lockers. In summer reserve a week in advance. Dorms £11, under 18 £7.75.

International Backpackers Hostel, 13 Pierrepont St. (☎446787; fax 446305; info@backpackers-uk.demon.co.uk). Extremely convenient location, up the street from the stations and 3 blocks from the baths. A self-proclaimed "totally fun-packed mad place to stay." Each room and bed is identified by a music genre and artist ("I'm sleeping in Rap"). A pool table, game room, and bar fill the even more manic basement. Internet access in attached cafe (see above). Breakfast £1. Laundry £3. Dorms £12.

Toad Hall Guest House, 6 Lime Grove (☎/fax 423254). A florid, friendly B&B with 3 comfortable doubles (1 can be let as a single) and hearty breakfasts. Single £20-25; doubles £38-42; discount for stay of 2 nights or more.

Mrs. Rowe, 7 Widcombe Cres. (☎422726), off Widcombe Hill. In the southeast, uphill from the stations and 10min. from city center. The height of elegance with a view to match. Singles £26; twins £44; doubles with bath £46.

The White Guest House, 23 Pulteney Gdns. (☎426075). A homey B&B with flower-filled patio. All rooms have TV and bath. £2 off if you tell the owners *Let's Go* sent you, 10% off if you stay 3 or more nights. Singles £25-30; doubles £45-50. Prices lower Nov.-Apr.

YMCA International House, Broad Street Pl. (☎325900). Men and women accepted. Central location (3min. from TIC). 210 beds. Continental breakfast included. Sheet rental £1.50 in dorms; sheets included in private rooms. Heavily booked in summer. Dorms £11; singles £16 for 1 night, £14 per night for 2 nights or more; doubles £28 for 1 night, £26 per night for 2 nights or more; triples £39.

SOUTHWEST ENGLAND

Camping: Newton Mill Camping, Newton Rd. (☎333909; fax 461556), 2½ mi. west of city center off the A36. Take bus #5 from the bus station (5 per hr., return £1.60) to Twerton and ask to be let off at the campsite. 105 car and caravan sites in an idyllic stream-side setting. Shop, laundry, restaurant, and free showers. No reservation necessary for individual campers; drivers should book a week ahead. July-Aug. £4.75 per person; Sept.-June £4.25. Tent, car, and 2 people £12 July-Aug.; £10 Sept.-June.

▶ FOOD

Although most restaurants in Bath are expensive and elegant, decently priced cafes and restaurants dot the city. For fruits and vegetables, visit the **Guildhall Market,** between High St. and Grand Parade. (Open M-Sa 8am-5:30pm.) Find picnic fare at **Waitrose Supermarket's** excellent salad bar in the Podium on High St. across from the post office. (Open M-F 8:30am-8pm, Sa 8:30am-7pm, Su 11am-5pm.)

■Tilleys Bistro, 3 North Parade Passage (☎484200). Savor Tilleys's impressive French creations and large selection of English and vegetarian fare. Mushroom crepes under £5. Open M-Sa noon-2:30pm and 6:30-11pm, Su 6:30-10:30pm.

Demuths Restaurant, 2 North Parade Passage (☎446059), off Abbey Green. Creative vegetarian and vegan dishes even the most devoted carnivore would enjoy. Lemon yellow walls may inspire you to try the luscious lemon sponge (£2.50). Main courses around £8. Open daily 10am-10pm.

Adventure Cafe, 5 Princes Buildings, George St. (☎462038). Brave the elements at a spindly outdoor table or take a window seat for ample views of passersby. Brightly lit cafe with salads and sandwiches (from £2.50). Casual, satisfying fare takes the worry out of any lunching adventure. Open M-F 9am-5pm, Sa 8am-5pm, Su 11am-4pm.

Cafe Retro, 18 York St. (☎339347). Not that retro, but compensates with delicious dishes and lunch specials. Swing by for one of their towering club sandwiches (£5); after 6pm, prices rise as steeply as Bathwick Hill. Open daily 10am-11pm.

The Pump Room, Abbey Churchyard (☎444477). Exercises its monopoly over Bath Spa drinking water (50p per glass) in a palatial Victorian ballroom. Cream tea (£6.75) is served from 2:30pm until closing; weekend reservations are essential. Open Apr.-Sept. daily 9am-6pm; Oct.-Mar. 9:30am-5pm.

The Walrus and the Carpenter, 28 Barton St. (☎314864). Lewis Carroll's characters watch over this trendy poster-plastered bistro. No talking oysters here, but the steak kebabs and ample salad options are popular lunch choices. Main courses £5-12. Open M-Sa noon-2:30pm and 6-11pm, Su noon-11pm.

Itchy Feet Cafe, 4 Bartlett St. (☎337987). This cyber cafe and adventure travel shop purveys sandwiches and smoothies to an exuberant clientele. Stacked sandwiches for slim prices (salad and sandwich £3). Open M-Sa 10am-6pm, Su 11am-5pm.

◉ SIGHTS

THE ROMAN BATHS. In 1880, sewer diggers inadvertently uncovered the first glimpse of what excavation has shown to be a splendid model of advanced Roman engineering. Most of the outside complex, however, is not Roman, but a Georgian dream of what Romans might have built. Penny-pinching travelers can view one of the baths in the complex for free by entering through the **Pump Room** (see above).

Underneath the baths, the ■**museum** makes up for the entrance price with its display on Roman building design, including central heating and internal plumbing. Bath flourished for nearly 400 years as a Roman spa city, and walkways wind visitors through the remains of their sprawling bath complex. Attentive eyes will connect the strands of recovered artifacts and structural remnants to imagine the society that spun them. Read the various recovered curses that Romans cast into Minerva's spring. Tradition promised that if the curse floated on the water, it would be visited back upon the curser. The Romans neatly avoided this by writing their ill wishes on lead. *(Stall St. ☎477759. Open Apr.-July and Sept. daily 9am-6pm; Aug. 9am-6pm and 8-10pm; Oct.-Mar. 9:30am-5pm. Last admission 30min. before close. Hourly guided tours and audio tours included. £7.50, seniors and students £6.50, children £4.20, families £18.50. Joint ticket to the Baths and the Museum of Costume £9.50, seniors and students £8.50, children £5.50, families £25.)*

BATH ABBEY. On a site that once contained a Saxon cathedral three times as large, the 15th-century abbey still towers over its neighbors. An anomaly among the city's Roman and Georgian sights, the abbey saw the crowning of King Edgar, "first king of all England," in AD 973. The whimsical west facade sports angels climbing ladders up to heaven and two angels climbing down. Tombstones cover every possible surface save sanctuary and ceiling. Peruse the protruding markers—they reveal the eerie and mysterious ways various Brits and Yanks met their ends—and play "Trivial Pursuit: New Testament Edition" with the 56 stained-glass scenes of Jesus's life at the church's east end. *(Next to the Baths. ☎477752. Open M-Sa 9am-4:30pm, Su 1-2:30pm and 4:30-5:30pm. Requested donation £1.50.)* Below the abbey, the **Heritage Vaults** detail the abbey's history and importance. Among the exhibits are statues from the original facade and a nifty disappearing diorama. *(☎422462. Open M-Sa 10am-4pm, last admission 3:30pm. £2, students and seniors £1, children free.)*

THE MUSEUM OF COSTUME AND ASSEMBLY ROOMS. This museum hosts a dazzling, albeit motionless, parade of 400 years of catwalk fashions, with everything from silver tissue garments to Queen Victoria's "generously cut" wedding gown. The wardrobe is so vast that only a tenth of the phenomenal archive can be displayed at any one time. *(Bennett St. ☎477752. Open daily 10am-5pm. £4.20, seniors £3.75, children £3. For info on joint ticket with the Roman Baths, see above.)* The museum is in the basement of the **Assembly Rooms,** which staged fashionable events in the 18th century. Although WWII ravaged the rooms, renovations duplicate the originals in fine detail. *(☎477789. Open daily 10am-5pm. Free.)*

JANE AUSTEN CENTRE. Austen lived in Bath from 1801 to 1806 (at 13 Queen Sq.) and thought it a "dismal sight," although she still managed to write *Northanger Abbey* and *Persuasion* here. The center organizes Austen's references to Bath, and invites dilettantes and devotees alike to visit the city as it was in 1806. *(40 Gay St. ☎443000. Open Apr.-Sept. M-Sa 10am-5:30pm, Su 10:30am-5:30pm; Oct.-Mar. M-Sa 10am-5pm, Su 10:30am-5pm. £4, seniors and students £3, children £2, families £10.)* **Tours** of the sights in her novels run three days per week from the center, according to demand. *(£3.50, seniors and students £2.50, children £2, families £8.)*

HISTORIC BUILDINGS. In the city's residential northwest corner, Beau Nash's contemporaries John Wood, father and son, made the Georgian rowhouse a design with which to be reckoned. Walk up Gay St. to **The Circus,** which has attracted illustrious residents for two centuries. Blue plaques mark the houses of Thomas Gainsborough, William Pitt the Elder (who was MP for Bath), and Dr. Livingstone. Proceed from there up Brock St. to Royal Crescent, a half-moon of Georgian townhouses, stopping at the oasis of book, art, and antique stores at **Margaret's Building** on the way. The interior of **One Royal Crescent** has been painstakingly restored to a near-perfect replica of a 1770 townhouse, authentic to the last teacup and butter knife. *(1 Royal Cres. ☎428126. Open mid-Feb. to Oct. Tu-Su 10:30am-5pm; Nov. Tu-Su 10:30am-4pm. £4, concessions £3.50, families £10.)* Climb the 156 steps of **Beckford's Tower** for stupendous views. *(Lansdowne Rd. ☎338727. £2, concessions £1.)*

THE AMERICAN MUSEUM. Homesick Yankees and vicarious visitors to the States will enjoy this museum dedicated to the history of American domestic life. A series of furnished rooms are transplanted from historically significant homes, including a cozy Revolutionary War-era kitchen with a working beehive oven. *(Claverton Manor. Climb Bathwick Hill, or let bus #18 (£1.20) save you the steep 2 mi. trudge. ☎460503. Museum open late Mar. to Oct. Tu-Su 2-5pm. Gardens open late Mar. to Oct. Tu-F 1-6pm, Sa-Su noon-6pm; also M in Aug. House, grounds, and galleries £5.50, students and seniors £5, children £3. Grounds, Folk Art, and New Galleries only £3, children £2.)*

OTHER MUSEUMS AND GALLERIES. The **Victoria Art Gallery** holds a diverse collection of works including Old Masters and British art, such as Thomas Barker's "The Bride of Death"—Victorian melodrama at its sappiest. The "Cabinets of Curiosities" feature unusual and amusing artifacts. *(Bridge St., next to the Pulteney Bridge. ☎477772. Open Tu-F 10am-5:30pm, Sa 10am-5pm, Su 2-5pm. Free.)* Away from the tourist-trafficked abbey and baths, the **Royal Photographic Society Octagon Galleries** hosts well-executed contemporary exhibits and traces the history of photography from daguerreotypes to holograms. *(Milsom St. ☎462841. Open daily 9:30am-5:30pm, last admission 4:45pm. £4, concessions £2, families £8.)* **The Museum of East Asian Art** displays objects from 5000 BC onward and has an amazing collection of jade and rhino-horn carvings. *(12 Bennett St. ☎464640. Open Tu-Sa 10am-5pm, Su noon-5pm; last admission 4:30pm. £3.50, students £2.50, seniors £3, children £1, under 6 free, families £8.)* The **Building of Bath Museum,** on the Paragon, recounts in precise, scale-model detail how the city's masterful Georgian architecture progressed from the drawing board to the drawing room. *(☎333895. Open mid-Feb. to Nov. Tu-Su 10:30am-5pm. £3.50, students and seniors £2.50, children £1.50.)*

GARDENS AND PARKS. Consult a map or the TIC's *Borders, Beds, and Shrubberies* brochure to locate the many stretches of cultivated green scattered throughout the city. Next to Royal Crescent, **Royal Victoria Park** contains one of the finest collections of trees in the country, and its botanical gardens nurture 5000 species of plants from all over the globe. For bird aficionados, there's also an aviary. *(Open M-Sa 9am-dusk, Su 10am-dusk. Free.)* **Henrietta Park,** laid in 1897 to celebrate Queen Victoria's Diamond Jubilee, was later redesigned as a garden for the blind—only the most fragrant flowers and shrubs were chosen for its tranquil grounds. Walk a few blocks beyond the Pulteney Bridge to Henrietta Rd. *(Free.)*

🝮🝮 PUBS AND CLUBS

Luring the backpacker contingent, the **Pig and Fiddle,** on the corner of Saracen St. and Broad St., brings in a young crowd for pints around its generous patio, while **The Garrick's Head,** St. John's Pl. (☎448819), is a scoping ground for the stage door of the Theatre Royal. **The Boater,** 9 Argyle St. (☎464211), overlooks the river with a view of the lit Pulteney Bridge. Its basement has become a shrine to the vodka-Red Bull combination. (All pubs open M-Sa 11am-11pm, Su noon-10:30pm.) Bath nights wake up at **The Bell,** 103 Walcot St., an artsy pub that challenges its clientele to talk over the live jazz, blues, funk, and reggae. (☎460426. Open daily 11am-11pm.)

Bath clubbing peaks at **Babylon,** Kingston Rd., an unpretentious techno and electronica venue with an energetic crowd. (☎400404. Cover £3-5. Open Tu 8pm-1am, Th varies, F-Sa 9:30pm-3am.) At 14 George St., underground **Moles** pounds out a mix of soul, funk, and house. (☎404445. Cover £5. Open M-Sa 9pm-2am.)

🎵 ENTERTAINMENT AND FESTIVALS

In summer, buskers (street musicians) perform in the Abbey Churchyard, and a brass band often graces the Parade Gardens. The magnificent **Theatre Royal,** Sawclose, Beau Nash's old haunt at the south end of Barton St., showcases opera and theater. (☎448844. Box office open M-Sa 10am-8pm, Su noon-8pm. Tickets £8-22; standby tickets £5; discounts for seniors and students M-Th.)

The renowned **Bath International Festival of the Arts** (☎463362) induces city-wide merriment during two weeks of concerts and exhibits in May and June; book well in advance for the simultaneous **Bath International Music Festival,** with world-class symphony orchestras, choruses, and jazz. (Box office ☎463362. Open M-Sa 9:30am-5:30pm.) The **Contemporary Art Fair** opens the festival by bringing together the work of over 700 British artists. For a brochure or reservations, write to the Bath Festivals Office, 2 Church St., Abbey Green, Bath BA1 1NL. The concurrent **Fringe Festival** (☎480097) celebrates music, dance, and liberal politics. The **Literature Festival** in late February, the **Balloon Fiesta** in mid-May, and the **Film Festival** in October are all popular events. Stay abreast of current entertainment news by picking up *Venue* or *The Bath Chronicle*, available at the TIC and around town.

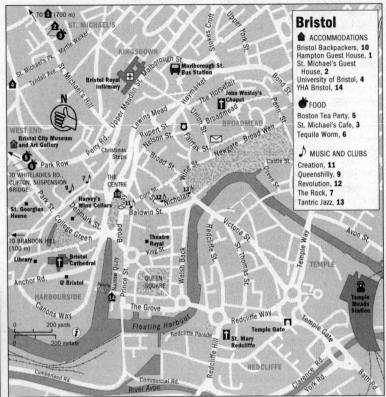

Bristol

🏠 ACCOMMODATIONS

Bristol Backpackers, **10**
Hampton Guest House, **1**
St. Michael's Guest
  House, **2**
University of Bristol, **4**
YHA Bristol, **14**

🍎 FOOD

Boston Tea Party, **5**
St. Michael's Cafe, **3**
Tequila Worm, **6**

♪ MUSIC AND CLUBS

Creation, **11**
Queenshilly, **9**
Revolution, **12**
The Rock, **7**
Tantric Jazz, **13**

BRISTOL

☎ 0117

Bristol's wealth and one-time status as a second city to London grew from its lucrative slave and sugar-cane trades with the West Indies and the Americas. Still the southwest's largest city, Bristol (pop. 401,000) hums as a working business center by day and springs to life by night. Pubs, clubs (dance music pioneers Massive Attack and Portishead grew up here), and late-night eateries cluster near the educational and commercial districts. Though much of Bristol's architectural might was felled by the bombs of WWII, some impressive sites remain, while others, like the high-tech @Bristol, have been added. Despite a rebuilt city center and lavish quay front, Bristol remains largely undiscovered by tourists, making its lack of pretension and hopping nightlife one of Britain's best-kept secrets.

▐ TRANSPORTATION

Trains: Bristol Temple Meads Station (☎929 4255). Ticket office open M-Sa 5:30am-9:30pm, Su 6:45am-9:30pm. **Luggage storage** £2 per item. Open M-Sa 8:30am-9:30pm, Su 9:30am-9:30pm. Trains (☎(08457) 484950) from: **London Paddington** (1½hr., 2 per hr., £36); **Bath** (15min., 3 per hr., £4.60); **Cardiff** (50min., 2 per hr., £8.90); **Manchester** (3½hr., every hr., £41). Another station, **Bristol Parkway,** is far, far away; make sure to get off at Temple Meads.

Buses: Marlborough St. Bus Station (☎955 3231). Information shop open M-F 7:30am-6pm and Sa 10am-5:30pm. Travel center open M-F 8:30am-6pm, Sa 8:30am-5pm. **National Express** (☎(08705) 808080) from: **London** (2½hr., 21 per day, £10); **Cardiff** (1¼hr., 11 per day, £4.50); **Birmingham** (2hr., every 2hr., £14); **Manchester** (5hr. via Birmingham, 8 per day, £22).

Public Transportation: Badgerline (☎955 3231) buses run in the city. A **Rambler** ticket buys unlimited travel for a day (£5.30, seniors and children £3.75, families £10.60).

Taxis: Yellow Cab Company (☎963 1414).

✦🛈 ORIENTATION AND PRACTICAL INFORMATION

Bristol is a sprawling mass of neighborhoods. The shopping and commerce center is the **Broadmead** district, while **Corn St., Baldwin St., Quay St., St. Augustine's Parade,** and **Broad St.** run through the oldest part of the city. To get to **Cotham,** take St. Michael's Hill. **Park St.** (which becomes **Queens Rd.**) offers nighttime entertainment and takes you into the tiny **Clifton** neighborhood. Wander northwest of Broadmead in the direction of the **St. Pauls** neighborhood to find more nightlife options.

Tourist Information Centre: The Annex, Wildscreen Walk, Harbourside (☎926 0767; fax 929 7703; www.visitbristol.co.uk), next to Explore@Bristol. Books accommodations for £3 and a 10% deposit and sells tickets for local attractions (booking hotline ☎946 2222). Guided walking **tours** (1hr.) Apr.-Oct.; £3, children £2. Open July-Aug. M-W and Sa-Su 10am-6pm, Th-F 10am-8pm; Sept.-July daily 10am-6pm.

Financial Services: Banks include **HSBC,** 11a Broadmead. Open M and W-F 9am-5pm, Th 9am-7pm, Sa 9:30am-3:30pm. **American Express,** 31 Union St. (☎927 7788). Open M-Sa 9am-5pm. Also at 74 Queens Rd. (☎975 1751). Open M-Sa 9am-5pm.

Police: Nelson St. (☎927 7777).

Hospital: Bristol Royal Infirmary, Upper Maudlin St. (☎923 0000).

Internet Access: Internet Exchange, 23-25 Queens Rd. (☎929 8026). 12p per min. for nonmembers; 7p with free membership. Open M-F 8:30am-10pm, Sa 9am-7pm, Su 11am-6pm. Access is free at the **library,** St. George's Rd., next to Bristol Cathedral. Open M-Tu and Th 9:30am-7:30pm, W and F-Sa 9:30am-5pm, Su 1-4pm.

Post Office: The Galleries, Wine St. (☎925 2322), inside the shopping center. Open M-Sa 9am-5:30pm. **Postal Code:** BS1 3XX.

🏠 ACCOMMODATIONS

Budget B&Bs are nearly impossible to find; nearby Bath may have cheaper accommodations. Upscale lodgings can be found in **Clifton** and nearby **Cliftonwode,** as well as **Cotham.** There are a few B&Bs in the **St. Paul's** neighborhood, but travelers should note that the area is difficult to navigate and potentially unsafe.

■ **Bristol Backpackers,** 17 St. Stephen's St. (☎925 7900; www.bristolbackpackers.co.uk). Hot off the presses, this backpacker's dream occupies an old newspaper building. Every comfort, with sociable dorms in an equally sociable part of town: let the sounds of nearby clubs be your techno-lullaby. 2 lounges, one with medieval city walls and basement bar. Internet access 15p per 5min. Dorms £12.50 per person.

YHA Bristol, Hayman House, 14 Narrow Quay (☎922 1659; fax 927 3789; bristol@yha.org.uk). This 88-bed hostel inhabits a beautifully renovated warehouse on the waterfront. Excellent city-center location, bureau de change, free luggage storage (bring a padlock), laundry facilities, and games. Arrange late-night entry beforehand for post-midnight returns. Book ahead, especially in summer. Dorms £12.15, under 18 £8.35.

Hampton Guest House, 124 Hampton Rd. (☎973 6392), 1½ mi. from the city center. Walk northeast on St. Michael's Hill until reaching Hampton Rd. Large, clean rooms in a plush B&B. Singles £21; doubles £34.

St. Michael's Guest House, 145 St. Michael's Hill (☎907 7820), above St. Michael's Cafe. A 10min. walk from the city center, though cable TV and fairly spacious rooms are your reward. Book in advance. Singles £25; doubles £35; triples £45.

University of Bristol (☎926 5698). Dorm-style accommodations close to the action of the city center, only during summer months and Easter. Around £21 per person.

🗋 FOOD

Boston Tea Party, 75 Park St. (☎929 8601). Contrary to historical precedent, the exquisite coffees and lattes stay *inside* the cups. Lunch options include a bevy of sandwiches (try the Thai chicken sandwich for £3.25), though dinner prices may inspire tea-themed protests in the nearby harbor (£13 for 2 courses, £15 for 3). Open M 7am-6pm, Tu-Sa 7am-10pm, Su 9am-7pm.

Tequila Worm, 64 Park St. (☎921 0373). Mexican food at its searing best, with great enchiladas (£8-11). The upstairs bar has a salsa DJ. 2 meals for the price of 1 M-F 5-7pm. Restaurant open M-Sa 5pm-midnight, Su 5-11:30pm; bar open Th-Sa until 2am.

St. Michael's Cafe, 145 St. Michael's Hill (☎907 7804). Murals of Elvis swagger over huge breakfasts (£3.50-5), veggie meals (under £4), and milkshakes in this American-style diner. Open M-F 7:30am-7:30pm, Sa 8am-4pm, Su 9am-3pm.

Pizza on the Hill, 122 St. Michael's Hill (☎929 3675). Gourmet pizzas in a laid-back environment provide tasty fuel for a night of pubbing or clubbing. Toppings range from chicken to duck to a harvest of veggies (from £6). Happy hour 6-7:30pm.

Three Sugar Loaves, 2 Christmas Steps (☎929 2431). Samuel Pepys did his drinking in this friendly pub, among low ceilings and dislocated wooden beams. Main courses £2-4.50. Pub open M-Sa 11am-11pm; food served M-F noon-2:30pm.

👁 SIGHTS

CLIFTON SUSPENSION BRIDGE. Isambard Kingdom Brunel had a prodigious career as engineer-architect, designing London's Paddington Station. His famous bridge, an architectural masterpiece spanning the Avon Gorge, can be reached via a pleasant walk through the Clifton neighborhood. Brunel's genius becomes clearer to the architecturally clueless upon perusing the Bridge House Visitor's Centre, nearby on Sion Pl., which documents the bridge's history and explains the finer points of bridge engineering. (☎974 4664. Open Apr.-Sept. daily 10am-5pm; Oct.-Mar. M-F 11am-4pm, Sa-Su 11am-5pm. £1.50, seniors £1.30, under 16 £1, families £3.80.)

@BRISTOL. The three related complexes of Bristol's newest attraction have been widening visitors' eyes since July of 2000. **Explore** educates with interactive biology exhibits such as the virtual journey of an egg-bound sperm. **Wildscreen** traces the history of evolution with live critters and multimedia presentations. The **IMAX theater** screens films on everything from dinosaurs to *The Simpsons*. (Explore Ln., Harbourside. ☎915 5000. Explore open daily 10am-6pm; Wildscreen 10am-6pm; IMAX 10am-9pm. Single sight £6.50, children £4.50; 2 sights £11, £8; all 3 sights £15.50, £11.)

CHURCHES. John Wesley's Chapel, the world's oldest Methodist building, sits incongruously opposite The Galleries, Bristol's shopping shrine. Note the chair fashioned from an inverted elm trunk. (☎926 4740. Open M-Sa 10am-4pm.) **Bristol Cathedral,** on the College Green, was begun in 1298 and in 1542 was named the Cathedral Church of the Holy and Undivided Trinity. The surrounding College Green receives swarms of students, skateboarders, and suntanners. (☎926 4879. Open daily 8am-6pm. Evensong 5:15pm. Suggested donation £2.) Elizabeth I termed the medieval church of **St. Mary Redcliffe,** 10 Redcliffe Parade West, the "fairest, goodliest, and most famous Parish Church in England." Supported by buttresses, it sits above the "floating harbour" and is the burial site of Admiral William Penn (father of the founder of Pennsylvania). Samuel Johnson once got stuck in one of the spiral staircases. (☎929 1487. Open summer M-Sa 8am-8pm, Su 7:30am-8pm; winter M-Sa 8am-5:30pm, Su 7:30am-8pm. Donations requested.)

CITY MUSEUM AND ART GALLERY. Covering all the bases from minerals to mummies, the City Museum, though less electrifying than @Bristol, impresses. The art gallery also exceeds expectations, sampling many styles and periods, including local modern art. (Queens Rd. ☎922 3571. Open daily 10am-5pm. Free.)

BRANDON HILL. A left turn off Park St. onto Great George St. leads to Brandon Hill, one of the most peaceful, secluded sights in Bristol. Snaking pathways climb through flower beds up to **Cabot Tower,** a monument commemorating the 400th anniversary of explorer John Cabot's arrival in North America. The tower offers a bird's-eye view of local sights to anyone willing to ascend the steep stairs; bronze etchings also point toward not-so-local sights, such as Helsinki, only 1250 mi. away. (☎922 3719. Open daily until dusk. Free.)

🎵 ENTERTAINMENT AND FESTIVALS

Britain's oldest theater, the **Theatre Royal,** King St. (☎987 7877), was rebuked for encouraging wickedness until King George III finally approved of the actors' antics. The Old Vic, the famous London repertory company, takes the stage regularly. Backstage tours are available. The **Hippodrome,** St. Augustine's Parade, presents the latest plays and concerts. (☎(0870) 607 7500. Box office open M-F 8:30am-10pm, Sa 8:30am-9:30pm, Su 10am-8pm.) In July, the amazingly popular **Bristol Community Festival** explodes with a wide range of musical performances. (Free, but £2 charitable donation encouraged.) Contact the TIC for details.

🌙 NIGHTLIFE

With state-of-the-art sound systems and a reputation for inventive electronica, Bristol's fluorescent venues pump the finest techno through the city's heart. Thousands of university students maintain the energetic vibe.

The Rock, Frogmore St. (☎927 9227). This seductive, factory-style space lures big-name DJs like Seb Fontaine and Paul Oakenfold. Open F-Sa 10pm-4am, cover £5-10; Su 4pm-midnight, no cover; M-W 10pm-2am, cover £2-4; Th 10pm-3am, cover £4-5.

Creation, 13-21 Baldwin St. (☎922 7177). The silver-tube entrance draws trendier club-goers, college students, and sometimes Fatboy Slim. Weekend queues are long, so come early. Cover £5-10. Open F-Sa 10pm-4am.

Revolution, The Old Fish Market, St. Nicholas St. (☎930 4335). Any dissent in this Red-tinted club drowns in the liquid goodness of exotically flavored vodkas. Live DJs nightly. No cover. Open daily until 2am.

Tantric Jazz, 39-41 St. Nicholas St. (☎940 2304). Chilled live jazz in a maroon lounge draws a diverse, mellow crowd. Live performances nightly.

Queenshilly, 9 Frogmore St. (☎926 4342). Save your shillings for the numerous cocktail options at one of Bristol's more popular gay-friendly clubs. Commercial dance and techno induce widespread glee. Cover £2-3. Open Tu-Sa until 2am.

WELLS ☎01749

Named for the natural springs at its center, Wells (pop. 10,000) is humbled by its magnificent cathedral. The town, lined with petite Tudor buildings and golden sandstone shops, is a charming, if self-consciously classy, stopover in Somerset.

▣ TRANSPORTATION

Trains leave Wells enough alone, but **buses** stop at the **Princes Rd. Depot.** (☎673084. Office open M-Tu and Th-F 9am-5pm, W and Sa 9:30am-1pm.) **Badgerline** (Bath ☎(01225) 464446, Bristol (0117) 955 3231) runs from **Bath** (#173; 1¼hr.; M-Sa every hr., Su every 3hr.; £3) and **Bristol** (#376 and 676; 1hr.; M-Sa every hr., Su every 3hr.; £3). If you'll be skipping around in the area, buy a **Day Rambler** (£5.30, seniors and children £3.75). **Bakers Dolphin** (☎679000) runs fast buses from **London** (2hr., 1 per day, £17). **Wookey Taxis** (☎678039) and **A Taxis** (☎670200) scurry through Wells's cramped streets. Rent bicycles at **Bike City,** 31 Broad St. (☎671711. £7 per half-day, £9 per day, £40 per week. Deposit £50. Open M-Sa 9am-5:30pm.)

🛈 PRACTICAL INFORMATION

The **tourist information centre** (TIC), in the Town Hall on Market Pl., books rooms for a 10% deposit and has free bus timetables. From the bus station, turn left onto Priory Rd., which becomes Broad St. and eventually merges with High St. Market Pl. is the top of High St. (☎672552; fax 670869. Open Apr.-Oct. daily 9:30am-5:30pm; Nov.-Mar. 10am-4pm.) Other services include: **banks** on High St. and Market Pl., including **HSBC**, 1 Market Pl. (☎316700; open M-F 9:15am-4:45pm); **Thomas Cook**, 8 High St., near the cathedral (☎313000; open M-Sa 9am-5:30pm); **Wells Launderette**, 39 St. Cuthbert St. (☎(01458) 835804; open daily 7am-8pm, last wash 7pm); the **police**, Glastonbury Rd. (☎(01934) 635252); **Wells and District Cottage Hospital**, St. Thomas St. (☎673154); **Internet access** at **d'e.c@fe**, South St., in the YMCA building (☎679757; £2 per 30min., students £1.50; open M and W-Th 10am-3pm, Tu and F 10am-5pm); and the **post office**, Market Pl. (☎677825; open M and W-F 9am-5:30pm, Tu 9:30am-5:30pm, Sa 9am-12:30pm). **Postal code:** BA5 2RA.

⌂ ACCOMMODATIONS

B&Bs in Wells are lovely but expensive; most offer only doubles and prefer longer stays, so you may have to daytrip from Bath. The closest **YHA Youth Hostels** and **campgrounds** are 10 mi. away in Wookey Hole and Cheddar (see **Near Wells**, p. 211).

▧ Richmond House, 2 Chamberlain St. (☎676438). Brass mirrors and an antique fireplace—and that's just the bathroom. Vegetarian breakfast available, including bubble and squeak. Flexible proprietors help travelers organize area treks. £22 per person.

Number Nine, 9 Chamberlain St. (☎672270; number9@ukf.net). Rose-ringed Georgian house has enormous rooms with TVs and baths. Ask Mrs. Elliott to show you her artwork. Singles £22, sometimes less in off season; doubles £38.

The Old Poor House, 7a St. Andrew St. (☎675052, mobile (0831) 811070). Please sir, can I have a B&B? Miss Helen Bowley keeps tidy rooms up the street from the cathedral. From £20 per person.

Bay Tree House, 85 Portway (☎677933). Homey atmosphere and pleasant conversation on the outskirts of town. Singles £25; doubles £36, £10 extra for 3rd person.

🍴 FOOD

Assemble a picnic at the **market** behind the bus stops (open W and Sa 8:30am-4pm), or purchase tasty breads, cheeses, and other provisions at **Laurelbank Dairy Co.**, 14 Queens St. (☎679803; open M-Sa 9am-5:30pm). A **Tesco** supermarket is at Princes Rd. (Open M-W 8:30am-8pm, Th-F 8:30am-9pm, Sa 8am-8pm, Su 10am-4pm.) **Boxer's Restaurant** and **The Fountain**, 1 St. Thomas St., behind the cathedral, are a restaurant-pub dynamic duo. The Fountain has a good selection of brews; at the renowned Boxer's Restaurant upstairs, some dishes approach stratospheric prices (£11), but their warm chicken salad is delicious at £6.75. (☎672317. Open M-Sa 6-10pm, Su 7-9:30pm.) Find great home-cooked pizzas (£1.85 per slice) and quiches (£1.70) at **The Good Earth**, 4 Priory Rd. The adjoining takeaway sells soups for £1-1.65, and salads for £1.55-2.75. (☎678600. Open M-Sa 9:30am-5:30pm.)

👁 SIGHTS

CATHEDRAL CHURCH OF ST. ANDREW. The 13th-century church in the center of town anchors a fantastically preserved cathedral complex, with a bishop's palace, vicar's close, and chapter house. Atop the 14th-century astronomical clock in the north transept, a pair of jousting, mechanical knights duke it out every 15min.—the same unfortunate rider is unseated each time. Walter Raleigh, Dean of Wells and nephew to the Sir, was murdered in the deanery where he had been imprisoned for his Royalist bent. The **Wells Cathedral School Choir**—one of the best in the country—sings services from September to April; visiting choirs assume the honor through summer break. Pick up the leaflet *Music in Wells Cathedral* at the cathedral or TIC for concert details and ticket information; many lunchtime performances are free. *(☎674483. Open in summer daily 7:15am-8:30pm if there's no concert; winter until 6pm. Free guided tours 10:15, 11:15am, 12:15, 2:15, 3:15pm. Evensong M-Sa 5:15pm, Su 3pm. Suggested donation £4, students and seniors £2.50, children £1.)*

BISHOP'S PALACE. A humble parish priest's abode, the palace was built in the 13th century. Ralph of Shrewsbury (1329-63) was alarmed by village riots a little later and built the moat and walls to protect himself. The mute swans in the moat are trained to pull a bell-rope when they want to be fed; visitors are encouraged to feed them brown and wholemeal bread (but not white—they get sick). The palace **gardens** surround the springs that give the city its name—an ideal setting for a champagne picnic. *(Near the cathedral. ☎678691. Open Aug. daily 10:30am-6pm; Easter-July and Sept.-Oct. Tu-F 10am-6pm, Su 2-6pm. Palace and gardens £3, students £1.50, seniors £2, children free.)* **Vicar's Close,** behind the cathedral, is reputedly the oldest street of houses in Europe; the houses date from 1363, their chimneys from 1470. **St. Andrew's Well,** bubbling up in the palace grounds, produces 40 gallons of spring water per second. Bishop Beckynton controlled the flow in the 15th century, harnessing the water and power for use, though today the liquid glides unfettered.

WELLS MUSEUM. North of the cathedral green and left of the cathedral's entrance, the refurbished museum contains remnants of the cathedral's decor, including its statuary. The statues look ill-proportioned but are designed to appear normal when viewed from below. Also on display are an alabaster "crystal ball" and the bones of an elderly woman, found in nearby Wookey Hole Caves, supposedly those of the legendary "Witch of Wookey Hole." *(8 Cathedral Green. ☎673477. Open July-Aug. daily 10am-8pm; Easter-Oct. 10am-5:30pm; Nov.-Easter W-Su 11am-4pm. £2.50, students and seniors £2, children and disabled £1, families £6.)*

NEAR WELLS: WOOKEY HOLE AND CHEDDAR

A short journey from Wells brings you to a vale of cheese, in every sense of the word. Admission to the **Wookey Hole Caves and Papermill,** 2 mi. northwest of Wells, combines a guided visit to the subterranean labyrinth, its walls adorned with prehistoric sketches, and a tour of the working paper mill, including its practicing craftsmen and collection of wooden carousel animals. *(☎672243. Open daily 10am-5pm. £7.30, children £4.30.)* **Camp** beside a brook at nearby **Homestead Park.** *(☎(01749) 673022. £9 per tent, car, and 2 people; £3 per additional person.)*

The **Cheddar Gorge,** formed by the River Yeo (YO!) in the hills northeast of the town of **Cheddar,** may be worth a daytrip, depending on your sensibilities and tolerance for overcrowded, touristy tea shops. Take bus #126 from Wells (20min., M-Sa every hr., £1.60) and follow the signs to **Jacob's Ladder,** a 322-step lookout. A view of the hills to the north and the broad plain to the south rewards the intrepid climber. (£2.50, children £2.) At the foot of the cliffs huddle the **Cheddar Showcaves,** England's finest. Feast your eyes on stalactites, stalagmites, and Cheddar Man, a 9000-year-old skeleton typical of the Stone Agers who settled in the Gorge. *(☎(01934) 742343. Caves open May to mid-Sept. daily 10am-5pm; mid-Sept. to Apr. 10:30am-4:30pm. Caves, Jacob's Ladder, and open-top bus ride around the Gorge £7.90, children £5, families £21.50; discount tickets available from Wells TIC.)*

If you plan to see both Wookey Hole and Cheddar, buy a **Day Rambler** in Wells (see p. 209). Cheddar's **tourist information centre** is at the base of Cheddar Gorge. *(☎(01934) 744071. Open Feb.-Nov. daily 10am-5pm; Dec.-Jan. Su 10am-5pm.)* The town's **YHA Youth Hostel,** Hillfield, is in a Victorian stone house off the Hayes, three blocks from the bus stop up Tweentown Rd. and ½ mi. from Cheddar Gorge. *(☎(01934) 742494. No lockout if staying more than one night. Curfew 11pm. Open July-Aug. daily; May-June and Sept.-Oct. M-Sa; Feb.-Mar. and Nov.-Dec. Sa-Su. Dorms £9.80, under 18 £6.75.)* The hostel is served by frequent buses from Wells (#126 and 826; M-Sa every hr. until 5:40pm; £1.20). Camp at **Bucklegrove Caravan and Camping Park,** in Rodney Stoke, near Cheddar. *(☎(01934) 870261. Open Mar.-Oct. daily. From £5 for tent and 2 people.)*

SOUTHWEST ENGLAND

ABBEY ROAD Glastonbury has been the backdrop to almost 2000 years of Christian history and legend. Joseph of Arimathea is said to have built the original wattle-and-daub church on this site in AD 63; larger churches were successively raised (and razed), until the current abbey was erected in 1184. Its sixth and final abbot, Richard Whiting, refused to obey Henry VIII's order that all Catholic churches be dissolved. In a characteristic display of religious tolerance, Henry had Whiting hanged, drawn, and quartered on Glastonbury Tor. The abbey has claimed two national patron saints as its own, St. Patrick of Ireland and St. George of England—St. Patrick is said to be buried here and St. George to have slain his dragon just around the corner. St. Dunstan hails from Glastonbury, where he served the diocese. In 1191, the remains of King Arthur and Queen Guinevere were "discovered" just in time for an abbey rebuilding campaign; their bones were reinterred in the church in 1276.

In 1170, Henry II declared Cheddar cheese the best in England. Today, cheese enthusiasts nibble at **Chewton Cheese Dairy,** north of Wells on the A39. Take bus #126 toward Bristol and get off at Cheddar Rd., just outside Wells. (☎(01761) 241666. Open Apr.-Sept. daily 9am-5pm; Oct.-Mar. daily 9am-4pm. Best time to view cheese-making 11:30am-2pm. No cheese-making Th and Su. Free.)

GLASTONBURY ☎01458

The reputed birthplace of Christianity in England and a seat of Arthurian myth, Glastonbury (pop. 6900) is an idiosyncratic intersection of mysticism and religion. According to legend, Jesus, Joseph of Arimathea, and Saints Augustine and Patrick all came here, and people pilgrimage to the stark **Glastonbury Tor,** where some believe the Messiah is slated to return. Other myths hold that the area is the resting place of the Holy Grail, that the Tor is the Isle of Avalon, where King Arthur sleeps, and that the Tor contains a passage to the underworld. Glastonbury's streets bustle in the morning with old women buying curative herbs and Osiris candles, not milk and vegetables. Grow your hair, suspend your disbelief, and join hands with Glastonbury's subculture of hippies and spiritualists.

▐ TRANSPORTATION. Glastonbury has no train station; most **buses** stop in front of the town hall. **Baker's Dolphin** (☎(01934) 616000) buses arrive from **London** (3¼hr., 1 per day, £5). **Badgerline** bus #376 runs from **Bristol** (1½hr.; every hr., Su every 3hr.; £4.50), and #163, 167, 168, 378, and 379 come from **Wells** (£2.70). From **Bath,** change at Wells (£4). For information on other Badgerline services, call their Bristol (☎(0117) 955 3231), Bath (☎(01225) 464446), or Wells (☎(01749) 673084) offices. **Explorer Passes** let you travel a full day on Badgerline buses (£5.30, seniors and children £3.75). **Southern National** (☎(01823) 272033) buses take travelers to points south, such as **Lyme Regis** and **Weymouth.**

▐ ORIENTATION AND PRACTICAL INFORMATION. Glastonbury is 6 mi. southwest of Wells on the A39 and 22 mi. northeast of Taunton on the A361. The compact town is bounded by **High St.** in the north, **Bere Ln.** in the south, **Magdalene St.** in the west, and **Wells Rd.** in the east. To get to the **tourist information centre** (TIC), The Tribunal, 9 High St., from the bus stop, turn right onto High St.; the TIC is on the left through the alleyway. They'll book rooms for a 10% deposit; after hours find the B&B list behind the building in St. John's car park. (☎832954; fax 832949. Open Apr.-Sept. Su-Th 10am-5pm, F-Sa 10am-5:30pm; Oct.-Mar. Su-Th 10am-4pm, F-Sa 10am-4:30pm.) Other services include: **banks** on High St., including **Barclays,** 21-23 High St. (☎582200; open M-F 9:30am-4:30pm); the **police** in the nearby town of Street at 1 West End (☎(01823) 337911); **Internet access** at **Glastonbury Backpackers** and **Cafe Galatea** (see below); and the **post office,** 35-37 High St. (☎831536; open M-F 9:30am-5pm, Sa 9am-1pm). **Postal code:** BA6 9HG.

◙ ACCOMMODATIONS. Single rooms are rare in Glastonbury. The nearest youth hostel is the **YHA Street,** The Chalet, Ivythorn Hill St., off the B3151 in the town of Street. Take Badgerline bus #376 to Loythorn Rd. and walk 1 mi. The hostel is a Swiss-style chalet with views of Glastonbury Tor, Sedgemoor, and the Mendip Hills. (☎442961. Lockout 10am-5pm. Curfew 11pm. Open July-Aug. daily; Apr.-June and Sept. W-Su. Dorms £9.25, under 18 £6.50.) The rooms at ◙**Glastonbury Backpackers,** in the Crown Hotel, Market Pl., are color-themed; the attached restaurant and bar (sushi, anyone?) and friendly staff complement a great location. Lucky "Bridal Suite" guests get jungle-print sheets and ceiling mirror. (☎833353. Internet access £3 per 30min., £5 per hr., £1 minimum charge. Dorms £10; doubles £26-30.) For private bathrooms, lovely gardens, and lovelier proprietors, call upon Mr. and Mrs. Hankins at **Blake House,** 3 Bove Town. Chat about your travels and immortalize your visit with a pin on their world map. (☎831680. Substantial continental breakfast included. From £19 per person.) Clean, bright rooms with TVs await at **The Bolt Hole,** 32 Chilkwell St., opposite the Chalice Well, a 15min. walk from the town center. (☎832800. £18 per person.) **Tamarac,** 8 Wells Rd., Mrs. Talbot's modern house on a central residential street, has biscuits in every room and plenty of novels to peruse. (☎834327. Singles £25; doubles £38; triples £57.)

◖ FOOD. Find food for a picnic at the **Truckle of Cheese** deli, 33 High St. (☎832116; open M-Sa 9am-5:30pm) and **Heritage Fine Foods,** 34 High St. (open M-Sa 7am-9pm, Su 8am-9pm). ◙**Rainbow's End,** 17a High St., serves vegetarian and wholefood specials. The menu changes depending on the chef's creative whims; try her £2 broccoli and cheddar quiche. (☎833896. Open daily 9am-4pm.) The age of Aquarius meets the age of technology at **Cafe Galatea,** 8 High St., a wholefood vegetarian-vegan cafe and cyberspace station. (☎834284. Internet access £1 per 10min., £5 per hr. Open M 11am-6pm, W-Th 11am-9pm, F 11am-10pm, Sa 10:30am-10pm, Su 10:30am-9pm.) **Burns the Bread,** 14 High St., does the opposite, whipping up the best chocolate muffins for miles. (☎831532. Open daily 7am-5pm.)

◙ SIGHTS. The ruins of **Glastonbury Abbey** behind the archway on Magdalene St. seem to have been carelessly discarded by a giant. The oldest Christian foundation and once the most important abbey in England, it was constructed "so as to entice even the dullest minds to prayer." A model of the abbey in 1539 recreates its pre-Henry VIII appearance. New-age religion finds an outlet in the open-air masses periodically held among the ruins. (☎832267. Open June-Aug. daily 9am-6pm; Sept.-May 9:30am-6pm. £3, students and seniors £2.50, children £1, families £6.50.)

Present-day pagan pilgrimage site **Glastonbury Tor** towers over Somerset's flatlands. Visible miles away, the Tor was known in its earlier incarnation as St. Michael's Chapel and is supposedly the site of the mystical Isle of Avalon, where King Arthur sleeps but will reappear when his country needs him most. Once surrounded by water, the Tor at times resumes its island appearance, rising supernaturally from the morning fog. From the top of the hill you can survey the Wiltshire Downs and the Mendips. To reach the Tor, turn right at the top of High St. and continue up to Chilkwell St., turning left onto Wellhouse Ln.; take the first right up the hill. In summer, the **Glastonbury Tor Bus** takes weary pilgrims around for 50p.

On the way down from the Tor, the **Chalice Well** on the corner of Wellhouse Ln. is the supposed resting place of the Holy Grail. Legend once held that the well ran with Christ's blood; in these post-Nietzsche days, rust deposits at the source turn the water red. Ancient mystics saw the iron-red water mingling with white water from a nearby well as a form of sexual imagery. The spring now tumbles through a tiered garden of hollyhocks, climbing vines, and dark yew trees. (Open Easter-Oct. daily 10am-6pm; Nov.-Feb. 1-4pm. £1.50, children and seniors 75p.)

Head down Bere Ln. to Hill Head to reach **Wearyall Hill,** where legend has it that the staff of St. Joseph of Arimathea bloomed and became the **Glastonbury Thorn.** The Thorn has grown on Wearyall Hill since Saxon times, blooming each year at Christmas and Easter—and, it's alleged, in the presence of royalty. Consequently, horticulturists here and abroad (where offshoots of the Thorn are planted) spend considerable time making sure that trees flower during visits by the Queen. Five miles east, Worthy Farm is the site of the annual **Glastonbury Festival** (www.glaston-buryfestivals.co.uk), Britain's largest summer music festival.

THE DORSET COAST

BOURNEMOUTH   ☎01202

At only 190 years old, Bournemouth (pop. 150,000) is an infant among English cities. In summer months, the seaside resort, made popular by its healing pine scents and curative sea-baths, is invaded by daytrippers and active retirees for its expansive beach and coastal ravines. Come nightfall, clubs and boardwalk entertainment attract families and students.

▐ **TRANSPORTATION.** Bournemouth is 104 mi. southwest of London; the Isle of Wight, 15 mi. to the west, helps shelter the city from the usual dismal English weather. The **train station** lies on Holdenhurst Rd. (Travel center open M-F 8am-5pm, Sa 9am-6pm, Su 9am-5:30pm.) Trains (☎ (08457) 484950) bring vacationers from: **London Waterloo** (1¾hr., 3 per hr., £27.20); **Dorchester** (40min., every hr., £7); **Bristol** (2½hr., every hr., £20.60). **Buses** pull up near The Square from: **London** (2½hr., every hr., £12); **Dorchester** (1¼hr., 3 per day, £4.50); **Bristol** (3¼hr., 1 per day, £11.75). Purchase **National Express** (☎(08705) 808080) tickets at the tourist information centre (TIC). **Central Taxis** (☎394455) run 24hr.

▐ **PRACTICAL INFORMATION.** The **tourist information centre,** Westover Rd., books rooms for a 10% deposit and leads free guided **walks.** (☎ (0906) 802 0234, premium rate; fax (01273) 696933. 1½hr. walks May-Sept. M-F 10:30am, Su 2:30pm. Open July-Aug. M-Sa 9:30am-7pm, Su 10:30am-4pm; Sept.-June M-Sa 9:30am-5:30pm.) Other services include: **banks** in The Square; **Thomas Cook,** on Richmond Hill (open M-Sa 9am-5:30pm); **American Express,** in the Christchurch Rd. pedestrian area (open M-F 9:30am-5:30pm, Sa 9am-5pm); a **launderette,** 172 Commercial Rd. (wash £2.40 per load; open daily 8am-9pm); the **police,** Madeira Rd. (☎552099); **Bournemouth Hospital** (☎303626), Castle Land East, Littledown; **Internet access** at **Click 'n' Link,** 248 Old Christchurch Rd. (☎780444; £2 per hr.); and the **post office,** Post Office Rd., off Richmond Hill (open M-Sa 9am-5:30pm). **Postal Code:** BH1 2BU.

▐▐ **ACCOMMODATIONS AND FOOD.** In true seaside-resort fashion, most quality Bournemouth **B&Bs** range from mildly pricey to ludicrously expensive. In the **Boscombe** neighborhood, a string of family villas have been converted into affordable B&Bs; follow the road signs from the train station (20min.). **Bournemouth Backpackers,** 3 Frances Rd., a small and friendly independent hostel, has the most reasonable rates. The informative proprietor helps guests obtain cheap bus passes to surrounding sights. (☎299491. Kitchen. £8-15 per person.) **Campers** enjoy the facilities at **Merley Court Park,** Merley, Wimborne, 8 mi. north of town on the A341. (☎881488; fax 881484. £12 per couple.)

Bournemouth has a smorgasbord of restaurants; **Christchurch Rd.** is particularly diverse. The cacti may be fake at **Coriander,** 22 Richmond Hill, but the Mexican cuisine is as authentic as it comes. Spice up your meal with sizzling fajitas (£5-8) or green coriander soup. (☎552202. Open daily noon-10:30pm.) At **CH2,** 37 Exeter Rd., modern decor, inexpensive lunch specials, and fusion cuisine are a reactive combination. (Open daily noon-2:30pm and 6-10:30pm.) The best in creamy goodness, **Shake Away,** 7 Post Office Rd., serves over 100 flavors of milkshakes (£1.95), from marshmallow to pecan popcorn. (☎310105. Open daily 9am-5:30pm.)

◉◪ **SIGHTS AND BEACHES.** The **Russell-Cotes Art Gallery and Museum,** East Cliff, houses a remarkable collection of Victorian art and sculpture. The building itself is a fine example of Victorian architecture, influenced by the Japanese exhibit inside. (☎451800. Open Tu-Su 10am-5pm. Free.) The **Shelley Rooms,** Beechwood Avenue, Boscombe, contain a small collection of Percy Bysshe Shelley memorabilia that only the poet's die-hard fans will appreciate. (☎451500. Open Tu-Su 2-5pm. Free.) For more of the Shelley clan, the remains of Mary Shelley, author of *Frankenstein,* rest in **St. Peter's** parish church, on the corner of Hilton Rd.

Bournemouth's main draw is the 7 mi. of clean, sandy shoreline known as **Bournemouth Beach.** Though the area surrounding **Bournemouth Pier** (☎451781) has been spoiled by cheap amusements, a short walk takes sunbathers to relatively uncrowded spots where they can rent bungalows and deck chairs for the afternoon. Less marine-minded, the internationally themed gardens of **Compton Acres,** Canford Cliffs Rd., Poole, are worth the money for the horticulturally inclined. (Open Mar.-Oct. daily 10am-5pm. £4.95, seniors £3.95, children £2.45.)

▣ **ENTERTAINMENT AND FESTIVALS.** Swarms of foreign-language students and young vacationers have revitalized Bournemouth's nightlife. Many bars and clubs line **Christchurch Rd.** The clientele may not be as savage as the names imply, but a good-sized crowd parties to mainstream club beats at **The Zoo** and **The Cage,** under the same roof on Firvale Rd., off Christchurch Rd. (☎311178. Open M, W, F-Sa 9pm-1am.) A little remodeling has transformed a theater into **The Opera House,** 57 Christchurch Rd., which attracts a stylish crowd. (Cover £4-10. Open Th-Su 9pm-1am, sometimes later.) Every summer Wednesday since 1896, 15,000 candles have lit up the Lower Gardens during the **Flowers by Candlelight Festival.** Bournemouth's **music festival** (☎451702) is in late June.

DORCHESTER   ☎01305

Every city has its favorite children, but in Dorchester, Thomas Hardy is an only son, and the locals indulge his spirit to the point of spoiling it. Pub regulars will share time-worn stories about the author whose sober statue overlooks the town's main street, and most businesses, from inns to shoe stores, manage to incorporate "Hardy" into their names. Those travelers not Hardy-hooked will hardly be hooked by Dorchester. The sleepy city that inspired Hardy's fictional "Casterbridge" has seen more prosperous times, though Dorchester *is* far from the madding crowd.

◪ **TRANSPORTATION**

The county seat of Dorset, Dorchester is 120 mi. southwest of London. Most **trains** (☎(08457) 484950) come into **Dorchester South,** off Weymouth Ave., which runs southwest from the bottom of South St. (Ticket office open M-F 6:05am-8pm, Sa 6:40am-8pm, Su 8:40am-7pm.) Trains run from **London Waterloo** (2½hr., 14 per day, £32.40). Some trains arrive at the unstaffed **Dorchester West,** also off Weymouth Ave., including those from **Weymouth** (15min., 20 per day, £2.50). Dorchester is easily accessible by **bus,** although it lacks a bus station. **National Express** (☎(08705) 808080) travels from **London** (3¾hr., 1 per day, £13) and **Exeter** (2hr., 1 per day, £10.50); tickets are sold at the tourist information centre (TIC). **Southern National** (☎(01392) 382800) #X53 is a better bargain from **Exeter** (M-Sa 4 per day, return £3.20). The **Wilts & Dorset bus** (☎673555) comes from **Salisbury** via **Blandsford** (4 per day, £4.50). **Dorchester Coachways** (☎262992), Grove Trading Estate, provides local service and makes daily trips to **London** (return £17.50). **Dorchester Cycles,** 31a Great Western Rd., rents **bikes.** (☎268787. £5 per half-day, £10 per day, £50 per week. Credit card deposit. Open M-Sa 9am-5:30pm.)

SOUTHWEST ENGLAND

✦❷ ORIENTATION AND PRACTICAL INFORMATION

The intersection of **High West** with **South St.** (which eventually becomes **Cornhill St.**) serves as the unofficial center of town. The main **shopping district** extends southward along South St. The **tourist information centre,** 11 Antelope Walk, sells helpful maps and walking tour pamphlets (10p-£5), as well as tickets for local and regional buses. From South Station, follow the brown signs; from West Station, turn right onto Great Western Rd. and left onto South St. (☎267992. Open Apr.-Oct. M-Sa 9am-5pm, Su 10am-3pm; Nov.-Mar. M-Sa 9am-4pm.) **Walking tours** leave from the TIC. (Mid-June to mid-Sept. M, W, Su 2pm; Th 6:30pm. £3, students and seniors £2.75, children free.) The **Thomas Hardy Experience,** booked through the TIC, guides visitors over every inch of town remotely connected to the author. (Tours M and W 10:30am, Tu 2:30pm. £10.) Other services include: **Barclays bank,** 10 South St. (☎326700; open M-Tu and Th-F 9am-5pm, W 10am-5pm); a **launderette,** 16c High East St. (wash £2.60-3; open daily 8am-7pm); the **police,** Weymouth Ave. (☎251212); **West Dorset Hospital,** Dames Rd. (☎251150); free **Internet access** at the **library,** Colliton Park, off The Grove (☎224448; open M 10am-7pm, Tu-W and F 9:30am-7pm, Th 9:30am-5pm, Sa 9am-4pm); and the **post office,** 43 South St., with a **bureau de change** (☎251093; open M-Sa 9am-5:30pm). **Postal code:** DT1 1DH.

▐ ACCOMMODATIONS AND CAMPING

The nearest **YHA Youth Hostel** is several miles away at **Litton Cheney.** (☎(01308) 482340. Open Jan.-Sept. Tu-Su. Dorms £10, under 18 £6.90.) Lodging in Dorchester is pricey (£15-18), and no B&Bs are especially plush. Most have only two rooms to let; call ahead to secure one of the scarce singles.

Maumbury Cottage, 9 Maumbury Rd. (☎266726). Close to both train stations, kind Mrs. Wade lets 1 single, 1 double, and 1 twin. Lucky guests will hear Hardy stories and get a free tour of town. Jolly good English breakfast included. Rooms £17 per person.

The White House, 9 Queens Ave. (☎266714), off Maumbury Rd. Quite possibly the largest guest rooms in southern England; unfortunately, there are only 2 of them, with bath and TV. £18 per person.

Barbara Broadway, 11 Sydenham Way (☎260248). The Broadways open their tiny home with big enthusiasm. Singles £18; double and twin £26.

Camping: Giant's Head Caravan and Camping Park, Old Sherborne Rd. (☎(01300) 341242), Cerne Abbas, 8 mi. north of Dorchester. Head out of town on The Grove and bear right onto Old Sherborne Rd. Showers, laundry, and electric points. Open Apr.-Oct. 2 people and tent £5-7.

◨▥ FOOD AND PUBS

The eateries along **High West St.** and **High East St.** provide a range of options, and an inordinately large number of **bakeries** lurk in the alleys off **South St.** Find groceries at the **market,** in the parking lot near South Station (open W 8am-3pm), or **Waitrose,** in the Tudor Arcade off South St. (open M-W and Sa 8:30am-6pm, Th-F 8:30am-8pm; in summer also Su 10am-4pm). **Mount Stevens,** 8 Cornwall St., bakes shelves of pastries and Belgian buns for under £1. (Open M-Sa 8am-5pm.) The **Potter Inn,** 19 Durngate St., puts whole orchards into their apple cake (£1.20) and serves towering sandwiches and homemade ice cream on a sunny, secluded patio. (☎260312. Open M-Sa 9:30am-5pm; July-Aug. also Su 11am-4pm.)

Dorchester barely dabbles in nightlife, but decent pubs include **The Sun Inn,** at the junction of Old Sherbourne Rd. and Lower Burton, which has terrific grub. (☎250445. Open M-Sa 11am-3pm and 5:30-11pm; food served M-Sa noon-2pm and 6:30-10pm, Su noon-2pm and 6:30-10:30pm.) Heed the warning to "duck or grouse" when entering the **King's Arms,** 30 High East St., then have a pint in this historic inn, featured in Hardy's *Mayor of Casterbridge.* (☎265353. Open M-F 11am-3pm and 5:30-11pm, Sa 11am-11pm, Su 11am-3pm and 7-10:30pm.)

👁 SIGHTS

Dorchester's half-dozen Hardy attractions can't quite compete with the compelling sights in the hills just outside of town, where two vastly different periods—Roman Britain and Hardy's Wessex—collide. The restless traveler, preferably in possession of a bike, can negotiate both in a day. In town, at the **Dorset County Museum,** 66 High West St., a replica of Hardy's study joins the relics of Dorchester's other keepers—the Druids, Romans, and Saxons. (☎262735. Open M-Sa 10am-5pm; May-Oct. also Su 10am-5pm. £3.30, students and seniors £2.20, children £1.60, families £8.20.) Hardy designed the home **Max Gate,** at Arlington Ave. and Syward Rd., and wrote *Tess of the D'Urbervilles* and *Jude the Obscure* there. (☎262538. Drawing room and garden open Apr.-Sept. Su-M and W 2-5pm. £2, children £1.)

The next stop for a Hardy adventurer is ever-so-small **Stinsford Church,** northeast of town in Stinsford Village. Follow the London Rd., which becomes Stinsford Hill. At the roundabout, proceed onto the continuation of Stinsford Hill and take the first right on Church Ln. The churchyard is just over the hill. Hardy was christened in the church, and his family plot can be found in the yard. Hardy's heart alone is buried here, for his ashes lie in Westminster Abbey (see p. 114). Nearby rests the classicist Cecil Day Lewis (Daniel's dad), who asked to be buried near the author.

Scattered ruins outside of town recall Dorchester's status as a former Roman stronghold. Just past the entrance to South Station sprawl the **Maumbury Rings,** a Bronze Age monument with a grassy, gaping maw used as an amphitheater by the Romans. The complete foundation and mosaic floor of a **Roman Town House** are at the back of the County Hall complex, near the Top o' Town roundabout. (Enter the parking lot and walk all the way back; the gate, marked by black signs, is unlocked during daylight hours.) The only remaining fragment of the **Roman Wall** is on Albert Rd., a short walk to the south. Look carefully, or you'll pass right by. The most significant of Dorchester's ancient ruins is **Maiden Castle,** a fortification dating from 3000 BC that was seized by the Romans in AD 44. The "castle" is really a fortified hilltop patrolled by sheep. There is no bus transport, but the local shuttle to Vespasian Way goes halfway (every 15min. from Trinity St.). Alternatively, take a scenic hike (2 mi.) from the center of town down Maiden Castle Rd.

Neither Roman nor Hardy-related, the **Keep Military Museum of Devon and Dorset,** Bridport Rd., collects uniforms and memorabilia from the Devon and Dorset regiments. See the desk swiped from Hitler's study. (☎264066. Open M-Sa 9:30am-5pm; July-Aug. also Su 10am-4pm. £2.50, concessions £1.50, families £7.50.)

LYME REGIS   ☎01297

Known as the "Pearl of Dorset," Lyme Regis (pop. 3500) perches precariously on the face of a coastal hillside. Steep climbs, startling views, and natural beauty entice budget travelers and would-be beach bums to this quiet hamlet, where you can hear the sigh of waves from the main road. The stark coast and curving Cobb have inspired many: it was here that Jane Austen worked and vacationed and that Whistler painted *The Master Smith* and *The Little Rose.* More recently, native John Fowles set his neo-Victorian novel *The French Lieutenant's Woman* in Lyme Regis, and part of the movie was filmed on location.

🚍🚊 TRANSPORTATION AND PRACTICAL INFORMATION. Lyme Regis makes a fine daytrip from Exeter. To reach Lyme by **train** (☎(08457) 484950), stop at **Axminster** (5 mi. north of Lyme on the A35) and transfer to **Southern National** (☎(01305) 783645) bus #31 or X31 (every hr., £1.50). Southern National bus #X53 goes directly to Lyme from **Exeter** (£4.40).

The **tourist information centre** (TIC) sits on Church St. at Guildhall St. and helps locate lodgings. Walk downhill from the bus stop, turn left onto Bridge St., and walk straight ahead. (☎442138. Open M-F 10am-6pm; in summer also Sa-Su 10am-5pm.) Other services include: **banks** on Broad St., including **Lloyds TSB,** 54 Broad St. (open M-Tu and Th-F 9am-4:30pm, W 9:30am-4:30pm); **Internet access** at **LymeNet,**

Church St. (☎444570; M-F £3 per 30min., Sa free; open M-Th 9am-8pm, F 9am-4pm, Sa 10am-1pm); a **launderette,** Lyme Close (☎443461; wash £2, soap 20p; open daily 8am-9pm); the **police,** Hill Rd. (☎442603); **Axminster Hospital,** Chard Rd. (☎32071), Axminster; and the **post office,** 37 Broad St. (☎442836; open M-F 8:30am-5:30pm, Sa 8:30am-6pm). **Postal code:** DT7 3QF.

▐▝▐ ACCOMMODATIONS AND FOOD. The **Newhaven Hotel,** at the start of Pound St., has ocean glimpses, a cheerful hostess, and impressive breakfasts, including omelettes and smoked mackerel fillet. (☎442499. In summer £19.50 per person; winter £17.) **Camp** at **Hook Farm,** a 25min. walk along the River Exe footpath. (☎442801. £2 per person, additional £1 each for tent and car.)

Coffee shops and greengrocers line **Broad St.,** the town's main strip, and fish and chips sizzle where the **Cobb** meets **Marine Parade.** Pubs along Broad St. offer generous portions of food amid dark-wooded decor; try **The Volunteer Inn,** 31 Broad St. (☎442214), or the **Royal Lion,** 60 Broad St. (☎445622). For excellent seafood (fresh crab £6.50) and a view, stroll down to the **Cobb Arms** pub on Marine Parade. (☎443242. Open daily 7am-11pm; food served until 9pm.)

◙▐ SIGHTS AND ENTERTAINMENT. Lyme's stone **Cobb,** a large rock seawall, curves out from the land to cradle the small harbor. In Jane Austen's *Persuasion,* Louisa Musgrove suffered an unfortunate fall here, brightening Anne Elliot's prospects. A few years ago, a man who fell off the Cobb evoked national scandal by suing the government for £96,000, presumably charging that the rocks were negligent for getting wet. Footpaths wind along the coast toward Seaton and over clifftops to Charmouth. The **Marine Aquarium** on the Cobb features luminescent and frighteningly magnified models of plankton. (☎443678. Open May-Oct. daily 10am-5pm; later in July-Aug. £1.50, students and seniors £1, children £1, under 5 free.) History buff Richard J. Fox, former world-champion town crier, conducts **tours** dressed in 17th-century military regalia on Tuesdays in July and August at 3pm. Inquire at Country Stocks, 53 Broad St., or meet at the Guildhall. (☎443568. 1½hr. tours £1.50, children £1.20.) The **Philpot Museum,** Bridge St., refurbished under Sir David Attenborough's auspices, houses local fossils and chronicles Lyme Regis's geological and cultural histories. (☎443370. Open Apr.-Oct. M-Sa 10am-5pm, Su 10am-noon and 2:30-5pm. £1.20, students and seniors £1, children 50p.)

Langmoor Gardens, accessible from Pound St., overlook the ocean, their lonely palm trees standing like exiles from across the sea. Follow the signs and turn left off Coombe St. to reach the **Riverside Walk,** a short path with lovely garden views flanked on both sides by the Lym. A small stone memorial marks where the Lepers' Hospital once stood. In summer, several **festivals** visit Lyme Regis, popular among them a **Jazz Festival** (early July) and a **Regatta Carnival** (early Aug.).

DEVON

EXETER ☎01392

In 1068, the inhabitants of Exeter earned the respect of William the Conqueror, holding their own against his forces for 18 days. When the wells within the city ran dry, the Exonians used wine for cooking, bathing, and (of course) drinking, which might explain why the city finally fell. As years went by, Exeter's cathedral (built in 1133) made it the religious center of the southwest and eventually the county seat of Devon, only to be flattened in a few days of Nazi bombing in 1942. Frantic rebuilding has made Exeter (pop. 110,000) an odd mixture of the venerable and the banal: Roman and Norman ruins poke from parking lots, and the cash registers of a bustling department store stand atop a medieval catacomb.

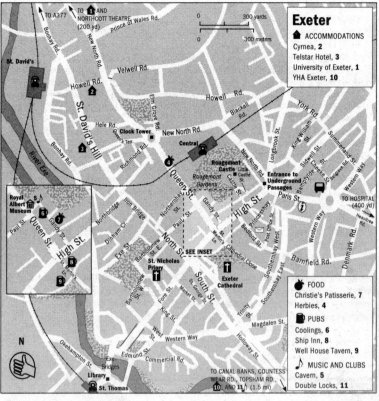

Exeter

🏠 ACCOMMODATIONS
Cyrnea, **2**
Telstar Hotel, **3**
University of Exeter, **1**
YHA Exeter, **10**

🍎 FOOD
Christie's Patisserie, **7**
Herbies, **4**

🍺 PUBS
Coolings, **6**
Ship Inn, **8**
Well House Tavern, **9**

♪ MUSIC AND CLUBS
Cavern, **5**
Double Locks, **11**

SOUTHWEST ENGLAND

▭ TRANSPORTATION

Trains and buses travel to Exeter from London and Bristol and transfer here for trips to the rest of Devon and Cornwall.

Trains: Exeter St. David's Station, St. David's Hill. Ticket office open M-F 5:45am-8:40pm, Sa 6:15am-8pm, Su 8am-8:40pm. Trains (☎(08457) 484950) from **London Paddington** (2½hr., 2 per hr., £39) and **Bristol** (1½hr., every hr., £13.60). **Exeter Central Station,** Queen St., next to Northernhay Gardens. Office open daily 8am-6pm. From **London Waterloo** (3hr., 6 per day, £38.30).

Buses: Bus station, Paris St. (☎256231), off High St. Office open M-Sa 8:30am-6pm, Su 9am-5pm. 24hr. **lockers** (50p-£2). **National Express** (☎(08705) 808080) from: **London** (4hr., every 1½hr., return £16); **Bristol** (2¾hr., 7 per day, £10.50); **Bath** (2¾hr., 3 per day, £13).

Public Transportation: Minibuses shuttle between city areas. An **Exeter Freedom Ticket** allows unlimited travel (£2.50 per day, £8.25 per week; weekly passes require 2 passport-sized photos).

Taxis: Capital (☎433453) and **City Central** (☎434343).

🛈 PRACTICAL INFORMATION

Tourist Information Centre: At the Civic Centre in the City Council Building, Paris St. (☎265700), behind the bus station. Books accommodations for a 10% deposit. Open M-Sa 9am-5pm; summer also Su 10am-4pm.

Tours: An institution for over a decade, the Exeter City Council's 1½hr. themed **walking tours** (☎265203) are frequented as often by locals as tourists and are the best way to explore this idiosyncratic city. Most walks leave from the front of the Royal Clarence Hotel on High St.; the "Port of Exeter" tour departs from the Quay House Visitor Centre on the Quay. Apr.-Oct. 4-5 per day; Nov.-Mar. 11am and 2pm. Free.

Financial Services: Banks are easy to find, including **Barclays,** 20 High St. (☎602200). Open M-W and F 9am-5pm, Th 10am-5pm, Sa 9:30am-noon. **Thomas Cook,** 9 Princesshay (☎601300). Open M-W and F 9am-5:30pm, Th 10am-5:30pm. **American Express,** 21-23 Princesshay (☎493222). Open M-W and F 9am-5:30pm, Th 9:30am-5:30pm, Sa 9am-5pm.

Launderette: St. David's Launderette, 24 St. David's Hill (☎274459), between the town center and train station. Bring soap and 20p coins. Open daily 8am-9pm, last wash 8pm.

Police: Heavitree Rd. (☎(0990) 777444), 3 blocks past the junction of Heavitree Rd., Western Way, and Paris St.

Internet Access: Hyperactive, Castle St. (☎201544), off High St., in Central Station. £2.50 per 30min., students £2.25. Open M-F 10:30am-7:30pm, Sa 10am-6pm, Su noon-6pm. The **library** books free 20min. slots on the computer.

Post Office: Bedford St. (☎423401). Open M-Sa 9am-5:30pm. **Postal Code:** EX1 1AA.

■ ACCOMMODATIONS AND CAMPING

Exeter's less expensive B&Bs flourish on **St. David's Hill,** between the train station and the center of town, as well as on **Howell Rd.,** closer to Central Station. There are also limited accommodations at the **University of Exeter** (☎211500).

YHA Exeter, 47 Countess Wear Rd. (☎873329; fax 876939), 2 mi. southeast of the city center off Topsham Rd. Take minibus K or T from High St. to the Countess Wear Post Office (97p). Follow Exe Vale Rd. to the end and turn left. Spacious, cheery hostel. Reception 8-10am and 5-10pm. No curfew, but ask for the door code. Dorms £11, under 18 £7.75. About 10 **campsites** at half the price of dorm beds.

Telstar Hotel, 77 St. David's Hill (☎272466; reception@telstar-hotel.co.uk). Eager-to-please owners (and their amiable black dog) usher you into large, comfortable rooms. Full breakfast includes a fresh fruit salad. Book a week ahead in summer. Singles £20, less in off season; doubles from £36.

Cyrnea, 73 Howell Rd. (☎/fax 438386). Friendly, open atmosphere. If Mr. Budge is home when you call, he may pick you up from the station. £15-17 per person.

■ FOOD AND PUBS

St. George's Market, 91 High St., sells fresh produce and meats (open M-Tu and Th-Sa 8am-5pm, W 8am-3pm), while **Sainsbury's** is in the Guildhall Shopping Centre off High St. (☎217129. Open M-W and F 8am-6:30pm, Th 8am-7pm, Sa 7:30am-6pm, Su 10:30am-4:30pm.) Exeter suffers from a dearth of cheap restaurants, though there are a few near Central Station along **Queen St.** At **Herbies,** 15 North St., you'll find leafy delights for £3-4. (☎258473. Open M 11am-2:30pm, Tu-F 11am-2:30pm and 6-9:30pm, Sa 10:30am-4pm and 6-9:30pm.) **Christie's Patisserie,** 29 Gandy St., serves hefty, made-to-order sandwiches (£1.35-1.60) and savories (most under £1) with a vegetarian spin. (☎423003. Open M-F 8am-5pm, Sa 8am-5:30pm.)

A skeleton guards the medieval well in the basement of the **Well House Tavern,** on Cathedral Close (an annex of the ancient and blue-blood-haunted Royal Clarence Hotel), while hearty ale flows upstairs. (☎319953. Open M-Sa 11am-11pm, Su noon-10:30pm; food served noon-2pm.) When Sir Francis Drake wasn't aboard his own ship, he preferred no place to the **Ship Inn,** 1-3 St. Martin's Ln., off High St. Burgers cost less in the pub and snack bar downstairs; upstairs is more expensive. Look for their many promotions. (☎272040. Open M-Sa 11am-11pm, Su noon-10:30pm.) Duck into **Coolings,** 11 Gandy St., for a relaxed atmosphere and young local crowd. (☎434184. Open daily 9:30am-11pm; food served until 5:30pm.)

👁 SIGHTS

EXETER CATHEDRAL. The west front holds hundreds of stone figures in various states of mutilation, crowned by a statue of St. Peter as a virile, naked fisherman. Inside, effigy tombs, including cadavers, line the walls, and shattered flagstones mark the chapel in which a German bomb landed in 1942. When the intricate 15th-century clock strikes one, look for the tiny hole in the wooden door beneath, where the bishop's cat once ran in after mice (hence the rhyme "Hickory Dickory Dock"). The building has been extensively (and expensively) restored, thanks to a staunch campaign by locals and the patronage of Prince Charles. The 60 ft. **Bishop's Throne,** made without nails, was disassembled in 1640 and again during WWII to save it from destruction. A collection of manuscripts, donated to the cathedral in the 11th century by the munificent Bishop Leofric and known to modern scholars as the **Exeter Book,** is the richest treasury of early Anglo-Saxon poetry in the world. The book is on display in the cathedral library. Ask at the information desk about the shortcut. *(☎ 255573. Cathedral open daily 7am-6:30pm. Library open M-F 2-5pm. Evensong services M-F 5:30pm, Sa-Su 3pm. Free guided tours Apr.-Oct. M-F 11:30am and 2:30pm, Sa 11am. Requested donation £2.50, seniors £1, families £5.)*

ST. NICHOLAS PRIORY. The 900-year-old building used to enclose much of today's High St. It has a medieval guest hall and kitchen, along with a timeworn toilet seat young Arthur himself couldn't lift. *(Take the alleyway next to The Mint at 154 Fore St. ☎ 665870. Open Easter-Oct. M, W, Sa 2:30-4:30pm. 50p.)*

THE ROYAL ALBERT MUSEUM. To learn what reduced St. Nicholas Abbey to its remaining priory, explore the museum's thorough reconstruction of Exeter and Devon's past. The museum also has a stuffed elephant from Kenya and an impressive collection of exotic butterflies. *(Queen St. ☎ 265858. Open M-Sa 10am-5pm. Free.)*

THE UNDERGROUND PASSAGES. Six hundred years ago, the church built underground passages to deliver clean water to the church community. Not to be outdone, wealthy merchants built their own subterranean piping network. Although the pipes are long since pilfered, visitors can now explore the passages, which are two by six feet and contain doors built by Cavaliers from 1642 to 1646 to keep out besieging Roundheads—this site is not for the claustrophobic. *(Accessible from Romangate Passage next to Boots on High St. ☎ 265887. Open July-Sept. M-Sa 10am-5:30pm; Oct.-June Tu-F 2-5pm, Sa 10am-5pm. 2 tours per hr.; last tour 4:30pm. Book tickets in person by noon during July and Aug. Tours £3.75, concessions £2.75, families £11.)*

OTHER SIGHTS. Upon penetrating the city, William the Conqueror built **Rougemont Castle** on Castle St. to keep the locals in check. The ruins between High St. and Central Station include a gatehouse dating from 1070. The immaculate flower-beds of Regency-era **Rougemont Gardens** surround the remaining castle walls. Due to security at the adjacent court building, tourists can only view the ruins from a non-photogenic angle below; there are no good views unless you're on trial. *(Free. Crime does not pay.)* The expansive 17th-century **Northernhay Gardens** unfold just beyond the castle and the preserved **Roman city walls.**

🎵 ENTERTAINMENT AND FESTIVALS

The Cavern, 83-84 Queen St., in a brick cellar decorated with comic-book camp, hosts up-and-coming bands nightly; check the kiosks plastered in fluorescent paper on High St. for details. *(☎ 495370. Cover £0-8. Open Su-Th 8:30pm-1am, F-Sa 8:30pm-2am; cafe open M-Sa 11am-2:30pm.)* Exeter's students hang out at **Double Locks,** on Canal Banks toward Topsham from the Exe Bridges. An hourly daytime boat leaves from the Quay. *(☎ 256947. Open M-Sa 11am-11pm, Su noon-10:30pm.)* The professional **Northcott Theatre** company, based on Stocker Rd. at the University of Exeter, performs throughout the year. *(☎ 493493. Tickets £7-15, student standbys £6.)* The **Arts Booking and Information Centre** *(☎ 211080)*, opposite Boots just off High St., supplies monthly listings of cultural events in the city. The **Exeter Festival** features concerts, opera, lectures, and an explosion of theater for three weeks in July (call the Arts Centre for details). Pick up your spirits at the three-day **Blues Festival** during the second May bank holiday; contact the TIC for details.

EXMOOR NATIONAL PARK

Once a royal hunting preserve, Exmoor is among the smallest of Britain's national parks, covering 265 sq. mi. on the north coast of England's southwestern peninsula. Dramatic sea-swept cliffs fringe moors cloaked in purple heather where sheep and cattle graze. Wild ponies still roam, and England's last herds of red deer graze in woodlands between the river valleys. Although over 80% of Exmoor is privately owned (as in most British national parks), the territory is accommodating to respectful hikers and bikers.

▐ GETTING THERE

You'll get to Exmoor with fewer gray hairs if you grab a copy of the *Exmoor and West Somerset Public Transportation Guide,* free from tourist information centres (TICs). The guide provides bus timetables as well as vague but well-meaning walking maps. Exmoor's western gateway, **Barnstaple,** is a good hiking base. **Trains** (☎(08457) 484950) arrive in town from **Exeter St. David's** (1hr., every hr., £10.10). **National Express** (☎(08705) 808080) **buses** come from **London** (5hr., 3 per day, £27) and **Bristol** (2½hr., 2 per day, £18.60). Catch **Western National** (☎(01208) 79898) bus #86 to Barnstaple from **Plymouth** (2½hr., 2 per day, £4.10). **Stagecoach** bus #315 rolls from **Exeter** to **Ilfracombe** (2¼hr., M-Sa 2 per day, £6). For more information, call the bus station in Plymouth (☎(01752) 222666) or Exeter (☎(01392) 256231).

You can reach **Minehead,** Exmoor's eastern gateway, by **Southern National** (☎(01935) 476233) **bus** #600 from **Porlock** (7 per day, £1.45) and #928 from **Taunton** (1¼hr.; M-Sa every hr., Su 4 per day; £3.20). To get to Taunton, take the train from **Exeter** (25min., £7). **West Somerset Railway** (☎(01643) 704996), a private line, runs to **Minehead** from **Bishops Lydeard,** 4 mi. from Taunton (1¼hr.; July-Aug. 4-7 per day, May-June and Sept.-Oct. 4 per day; £5.40). Buses shuttle to Bishops Lydeard from the Taunton train station.

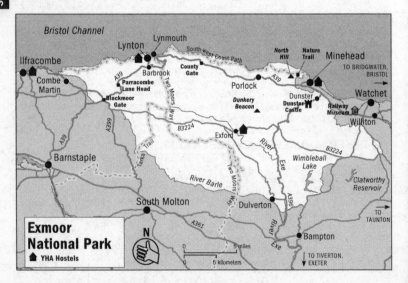

▣ LOCAL TRANSPORTATION

Although getting to the outskirts of Exmoor by public transportation is relatively easy, bus service within the park is erratic. Again, the *Exmoor and West Somerset Public Transportation Guide*, found at all TICs near Exmoor, is invaluable. Buses from **Minehead** run to: **Ilfracombe** (Devon Bus #300; 2hr., M-F 2 per day, £4.70); **Williton** (Bryants Coaches #305-7; 30min., M-Sa every hr., £1.10); **Dunster** (Southern National #34; M-Sa every hr., 65p). **North Devon Bus** (☎(01271) 45444) runs from **Barnstaple** to **Ilfracombe** (M-Sa 2 per hr., £1.60) and from **Ilfracombe** to **Combe Martin** (1 per day, 80p). *Accessible Exmoor*, free from National Park Information Centres, provides a thorough guide to the park for disabled visitors.

Relatively flat, Exmoor is best toured on **foot** or by **bike**; large parts of the park are reserved for cyclists. Two long-distance paths are the **Somerset and North Devon Coast Path** for hikers and the **coastal path,** which follows the ghost of the Barnstaple railroad, for bikers. Both routes pass through or near the towns of (west to east) Ilfracombe, Combe Martin, Lynton, Porlock, Minehead, and Williton. The **Tarka Trail** traces a 180 mi. figure-eight (starting in Barnstaple), 31 mi. of which are bicycle-friendly.

▣ PRACTICAL INFORMATION

The National Park Information Centres listed below supply detailed large-scale Ordnance Survey maps of the region (£5.25), bus timetables, and the invaluable *Exmoor Visitor*. The centers offer themed guided walks of 1½-10 mi. Always be prepared for a sudden rainstorm. Sea winds create volatile weather, and thunderstorms burst without warning. Be sure to stock up on food and equipment in the larger towns, as stores in coastal villages have smaller selections.

NATIONAL PARK INFORMATION CENTRES

Combe Martin: Seacot, Cross St. (☎/fax (01271) 883319), 3 mi. east of Ilfracombe. Open Easter-Sept. daily 10am-5pm; until 7pm in peak season.

County Gate: A39, Countisbury (☎(01598) 741321), 7 mi. east of Lynton. Open Apr.-Sept. daily 10am-5pm; Oct. 10am-4pm.

Dulverton: Dulverton Heritage Centre, The Guildhall, Fore St. (☎(01398) 323841). Open Apr.-Oct. daily 10am-5pm; limited winter hours.

Dunster: Dunster Steep Car Park (☎(01643) 821835), 2 mi. east of Minehead. Open Apr.-Oct. daily 10am-5pm; limited winter hours.

Lynmouth: The Esplanade (☎(01598) 752509). Open Apr.-July and Sept.-Oct. daily 10am-5pm; Aug. 10am-6pm; limited winter hours.

TOURIST INFORMATION CENTRES

Barnstaple: 36 Boutport St. (☎(01271) 375000). Open Apr.-Oct. M-Sa 9:30am-5pm.

Ilfracombe: The Landmark Seafront, in the Landmark Theatre (☎(01271) 863001). Open Easter-Sept. M 9:30am-showtime, Tu-F 10am-showtime, Sa 11am-7pm, Su 10am-8:15pm; Nov.-Easter M-F 10am-5pm.

Lynton and Hunmouth: Town Hall (☎(01598) 752225), Lynton. Also has info on Lynmouth. Open Easter-Oct. daily 9:30am-6pm; Nov.-Mar. M-Sa 9:30am-1:30pm.

Minehead: 17 Friday St. (☎(01643) 702624). Open July-Aug. M-Sa 9:30am-5:30pm; Apr.-June and Sept.-Oct. 9:30am-5pm; Nov.-Mar. M-Sa 10am-4pm.

▣ ACCOMMODATIONS

Rain or shine, hostels and B&Bs (£14-16) fill up quickly; check listings and the *Exmoor Visitor* at the TIC. At busy times, **camping** may be the easiest way to see the park. The *Exmoor Visitor* lists several caravan parks that accept tents, but campsites that don't advertise are easy to find, especially near coastal towns. Most

SOUTHWEST ENGLAND

land is private; before pitching a tent, ask the owner's permission. The quality of Exmoor's **YHA Youth Hostels** varies widely according to proprietor and location. In general, you can expect small accommodations with a kitchen, day lockout (usually 10am-5pm), curfew (around 11pm-midnight), and no laundry facilities.

YHA Crowcombe: (☎/fax (01984) 667249), Crowcombe Heathfield. A large house in the woods on the Taunton-Minehead Rd., 2 mi. from Crowcombe Heathfield below Quantock Hills. Turn onto the road marked "Crowcombe Station & Lydeard St. Lawrence." The hostel is 1 mi. down the road, on the left. Open mid-Apr. to early May and July-Aug. daily; early May to June F-W. Dorms £9.25, under 18 £6.50.

YHA Elmscott: (☎(01237) 441367; fax 441910), 4 mi. southwest of Hartland village by footpath. Extremely difficult to find—get a map before you go. On weekends bus #199 goes to Hartland. Call for off-season times. Dorms £10, under 18 £6.90.

YHA Exford: Withypoole Rd. (☎(01643) 831288; fax 831650), Exe Mead, Exford. This superior hostel is next to the River Exe bridge, the first road on the left, in the center of the moorland. Laundry facilities. Open July-Aug. daily; mid-Feb. to June and Sept.-Oct. M-Sa. Dorms £11, under 18 £7.75.

YHA Ilfracombe: 1 Hillsborough Terr. (☎(01271) 865337; fax 862652), Ilfracombe. Take Red bus #3, 30, or 123 from Barnstaple, just off the main road. Georgian house with a view of the Welsh coast. Family rooms available. Open Mar.-Oct. daily. Dorms £10, under 18 £6.90.

YHA Lynton: (☎(01598) 753237; fax 753305), Lynbridge, Lynton. Take Red bus #309 or 310 from Barnstaple to Castle Hill Car Park. A former Lyn West valley hotel. Open July-Aug. daily; Sept.-Oct. Th-M; mid-Feb. to June W-M. Dorms £10, under 18 £6.90.

YHA Minehead: (☎(01643) 702595; fax 703016), Alcombe Combe, Minehead, 2 mi. from the town center. Follow Friday St. as it becomes Alcombe Rd., turn right on Brook St. and follow to Manor Rd. (30min.). From Taunton, take the Minehead bus to Alcombe; the bus stops 1 mi. from the hostel. Spacious grounds. Open July-Aug. daily; mid-Apr. to June M-Sa. Dorms £10, under 18 £6.90.

YHA Quantock Hills: (☎/fax (01278) 741224), Sevenacres, Holford, Bridgwater, 1½ mi. past the Alfoxton Park Hotel in Holford—keep right after passing through the gate by the hotel stables. From Kilze, take Pardlestone Ln. by the post office for 1 mi., then follow signs. Country house overlooking Bridgwater Bay. Open mid-July to Aug. daily. Dorms £9.25, under 18 £6.50.

BARNSTAPLE ☎01271

Although Barnstaple, just outside the park, isn't the only suitable hiking base, it is the largest town in the region, a transport center, and the best place to get gear. The town holds a **tourist information centre** (TIC; see above). There are daily markets at the **Pannier Market,** while **Giovanni's,** 35 Boutport St. (☎321274), next to the TIC, serves up Italian fare (from £6). **Tarka Trail,** conveniently located at the head of the coastal bike path, **rents bikes.** From the center of town, cross the bridge and take the second left after the bridge at the roundabout; Tarka is by the train station. (☎324202. £6.50-8.50 per day. Open daily 9:30am-5pm.) The coastal path provides level cycling for 15 mi. where the old Barnstaple rail tracks used to run.

Two good places to begin traipsing into the forest close to Barnstaple are **Blackmoor Gate,** 9 mi. northwest of Barnstaple, and **Parracombe,** 2 mi. farther northwest along the road. Both are on Filer's Barnstaple-Lynton bus line.

MINEHEAD AND DUNSTER ☎01643

Only a mile from the park's eastern boundary, **Minehead** boasts an informative **nature trail** with labeled vegetation. Other well-marked paths weave through North Hill, an easy walk from the town center. The **South-West Peninsula Coast Path,** Britain's longest National Trail, ends in Minehead.

The village of **Dunster** lies 3 mi. east of Minehead, and buses from Minehead stop at its base every hr. in summer. **Dunster Castle** (☎821314) towers over the former 17th-century yarn market. Home to the Luttrell family for six centuries, the elaborate interior includes a not-to-be-missed 16th-century portrait of Sir John Luttrell wading buck-naked through the surf. (☎821314. Open Apr.-Sept. Sa-W 11am-5pm; Oct. 11am-4pm. Subtropical gardens open Apr.-Sept. daily 10am-5pm; Oct.-Mar. 11am-4pm. £6, children £3. Grounds only £3, children £1.50, families £7.50.)

DARTMOOR NATIONAL PARK

Dartmoor National Park, south of Exmoor and 10 mi. west of Exeter, is strewn with remnants of the past, from oddly balanced granite tors to Neolithic rock formations. Ramblers through the 367 sq. mi. of green hills and gray skies may also find the skeleton of a once-flourishing tin-mining industry and the heavily guarded Princetown prison. Its rough terrain and harsh climate have allowed the park to remain largely untouched for centuries, except by sheep and native wild ponies. Many spirits linger in Dartmoor's mystical bleakness, the most famous being the canine immortalized in Sir Arthur Conan Doyle's *Hound of the Baskervilles*.

▐ TRANSPORTATION

Buses are infrequent and often erratic: plan well ahead, using the schedules available at every tourist information centre (TIC). The best day to travel is Sunday, when frequencies increase and the **Sunday Rover** allows unlimited bus travel (£5, seniors and

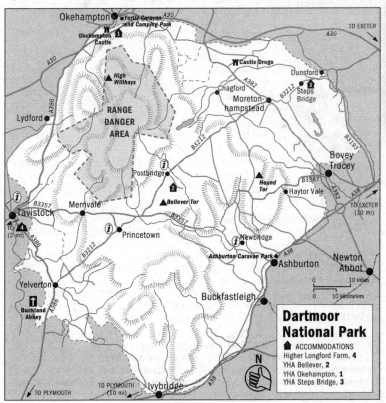

Dartmoor National Park

▲ ACCOMMODATIONS
Higher Longford Farm, **4**
YHA Bellever, **2**
YHA Okehampton, **1**
YHA Steps Bridge, **3**

SOUTHWEST ENGLAND

students £4.50, children £3). The **Transmoor Link,** a.k.a. **Stagecoach Devon** (☎(01392) 427711) bus #82 (late May to Sept.; M-Sa 3 per day, Su 5 per day; £5) cuts through the middle of the park on its southwest-northeast route between **Plymouth** and **Exeter,** passing through **Yelverton** at the southwest corner of the park, and **Princetown, Postbridge, Moretonhampstead,** and **Steps Bridge** at the northeast. Stagecoach Devon bus #X38 also binds **Exeter** and **Plymouth,** stopping in **Buckfastleigh** and **Ashburton** along the park's southern edge (M-Sa 8 per day, Su 6 per day; £4.85). Sit on the right-hand side for the views. **Plymouth Buses** (☎(01752) 222221) #X80 and **Western National** #88 and X88 run from **Ivybridge** (30min.; 3 per hr.). Plymouth Buses also run from **Tavistock,** north of Yelverton on the park's western edge (#83, 84, 86; 1hr.; 4 per hr.), and **Okehampton,** on the northern edge (#86; M-F 9 per day, Su 2 per day).

For more information, contact the **Exeter bus station** (☎(01392) 256231), the **Devon County Council's Public Transportation Helpline** (☎(01392) 382800 or (01271) 382800; open M-F 8:30am-5pm), or any National Park Information Centre (see below). The invaluable *Dartmoor Public Transportation Guide,* in bus stations or TICs, contains relevant bus routes and useful phone numbers and suggests walking routes. Once you've reached the park's perimeter, make your way on bike or foot, as buses require careful planning. A 30 mi. drive across the park takes 3hr.; the bus stops every time a sheep crosses its path. In winter, snow often renders the park and its tortuous roads impassable. **Hitchhikers** report that rides are frequent, but *Let's Go* does not recommend hitchhiking as a safe mode of transport.

🔢 PRACTICAL INFORMATION

The National Park Authority conducts walks (2-6hr., £2-4) from many locations. Check the *Dartmoor Visitor,* found at the **National Park Information Centres** below:

Haytor: (☎(01364) 661520), near Leonard's Bridge. In the bottom end of a car park just off the B3387. Open in summer daily 10am-5pm.

Ivybridge: (☎(01752) 897035). Books accommodations within 10 mi. for a 10% deposit, beyond 10 mi. for an additional £3 fee. Open July-Aug. M-F 9am-5pm, Sa 10am-4pm, Su 10am-2pm; Sept.-June M-Sa 9am-5pm.

Okehampton: 3 West St. (☎(01837) 53020), in the courtyard adjacent to the White Hart Hotel. Books beds in person only for a £3 fee. Open June-Aug. daily 10am-5pm; Apr. and Sept.-Oct. M-Sa 10am-5pm.

Newbridge: (☎(01364) 631303), in the Riverside car park. Books accommodations for a £2 deposit. Open Easter-Oct. daily 10am-5pm.

Postbridge: (☎(01822) 880272), in a car park off the B3212 Moretonhampstead-Yelverton Rd. Open roughly Apr.-Oct. daily 10am-5pm; Nov.-Mar. Sa-Su 10am-4pm.

Princetown (High Moorland Visitor Centre): (☎(01822) 890414), in the former Duchy Hotel. Open in summer daily 10am-5pm; winter 10am-4pm.

Tavistock: Town Hall, Bedford Sq. (☎(01822) 612938). Books accommodations for a £3-3.50 fee. Open Easter-Oct. M-Sa 10am-5pm; Nov.-Easter M-Tu and F-Sa 10am-4pm.

🏠 ACCOMMODATIONS AND CAMPING

B&BS AND HOSTELS

B&B signs often appear on pubs and farmhouses along the roads. All the National Park Information Centres provide free accommodations lists, and the Tavistock, Ivybridge, and Okehampton centers book rooms. The YHA hostels in the park are:

YHA Bellever: (☎(01822) 880227; fax 880302), a mile southeast of Postbridge village on bus #82 from Plymouth or Exeter to Postbridge. Ask to be let off as close to the hostel as possible, then go west from Postbridge on the B3212 and make a left on Bellever. Walk 20-25min. to the hostel. First Western #98 from Tavistock also stops right outside the hostel. In the heart of the park and very popular. Open July-Aug. daily; Sept.-Oct. Tu-Sa; Apr.-June M-Sa. Dorms £10, under 18 £6.90.

YHA Okehampton: Klondyke Rd. (☎(01837) 53916; fax 53965; okehampton@yha.org.uk). From the TIC, turn onto George St., right onto Station Rd., and continue under the bridge. Offers occasional rock-climbing trips. Open Feb.-Nov. Dorms £11, under 18 £7.50; doubles £24.50.

YHA Steps Bridge: (☎(01647) 252435; fax 252948), a mile southwest of Dunsford on the B3212, near the eastern edge of the park. Take bus #359 from Exeter, get off at Steps Bridge, and hike up the steep drive. The warden cooks vegetarian delights in this cabin in the woods. Open mid-Apr. to Aug. Dorms £8.50, under 18 £5.75.

CAMPING

Although official campsites exist, many travelers camp on the open moor. Dartmoor land is privately owned, so ask permission before crossing or camping on land. Backpack camping is permitted on non-enclosed moor land more than 100 yd. away from the road or out of sight of inhabited areas and farmhouses. Pitching is prohibited in common areas used for recreation. Campers may only stay for one night in a single spot. Don't build fires in the moors or climb fences or walls unless posted signs say you may do so. If using the official campsites below, call ahead for reservations, especially in summer.

Ashburton Caravan Park (☎(01364) 652552), Waterleat, Ashburton. 1½ mi. from town; head north on North St. and follow the signs. July-Aug. £10 per 2-person tent, £6 per single; Easter-June and Sept.-Oct. £4 per single, £7.50 per 2-person tent.

Higher Longford Farm (☎(01822) 613360), Moorshop, Tavistock. 2 mi. from Tavistock toward Princetown on the B3357. Office open daily 10am-5pm. £7.50 for first adult, £2 per additional adult.

River Dart Country Park (☎(01364) 652511), Holne Park, Ashburton. Lush surroundings and heated swimming pool. Open Apr.-Sept. £6.50 per adult, £5.15 per child.

Yertiz Caravan and Camping Park, Exeter Rd. (☎(01837) 52281), Okehampton. ¾ mi. east of Okehampton, off the A30, on the brow of a hill near the Esso garage. July-Aug. £2.75 per person; Sept.-June £2.25; 50p per additional camper.

◪ HIKING AND OTHER ACTIVITIES

Visitors should not underestimate Dartmoor's moody weather and treacherous terrain. Ordnance Survey Outdoor Leisure Map #28 (1:25,000; £6.50), a compass, and waterproof garb are essential; mists descend without warning, and there is no shelter away from the roads. Stick to the marked paths. The *Dartmoor Visitor*, free at Park Centres, is almost as indispensable as a bus schedule, providing maps and information on accommodations and food. Centres also offer detailed walking guides, some with map supplements (50p to £9). The official **Dartmoor Rescue Group** is on call at ☎999. See **Wilderness Safety,** p. 54, for more information.

Dartmoor's roads are hilly but good for cycling. Fishing, canoeing, and climbing are also popular. For **canoeing** arrangements, contact Mr. Chamberlain, **Mountain Stream Activities,** Hexworthy (☎(01364) 646000). For **horse riding,** contact **Sherberton Stables,** Hexworthy (☎(01364) 631276; £7.50 per hr.), or **Moorland Riding Stables,** Will Farm, Peter Tavy, Tavistock (☎(01822) 810293; £6 per hr., £18 per day).

> **WARNING.** The Ministry of Defense uses much of the northern moor for target practice; consult the *Dartmoor Visitor* or an Ordnance Survey map for the boundaries of the danger area and check the weekly firing timetable, available in National Park Information Centres and tourist information centres, hostels and campsites, police stations, pubs, and the Friday papers. Danger areas, marked by red-and-white posts, change yearly, so be sure your information is up-to-date.

◉ SIGHTS

Postbridge and **Princetown** hover at the southern edge of the park's north-central plateau. Dartmoor's forbidding maximum-security **prison** looms over Princetown, the larger of the two towns. Frenchmen from the Napoleonic Wars and Americans who fought to annex Canada in 1812 once languished within its walls. Princetown and its prison stand isolated by miles of bleak moorland, the setting for one of the most famous of the Sherlock Holmes tales, *Hound of the Baskervilles*, which emerged from an ancient Dartmoor legend of a gigantic, glowing pooch. Several peaks crown the northern moor, the highest of which is **High Willhays** at 2038 ft. **Merrivale** lies 4 mi. outside Princetown, with knee-high Neolithic stone circles; to get there, take bus #172 (M-Sa 2 per day, Su 3 per day; return £1.25).

The rugged eastern part of the park gathers around **Haytor Vale.** Two miles north lie Dartmoor's celebrated medieval ruins at **Hound Tor,** where excavations unearthed the remains of 13th-century huts and longhouses. Check the *Dartmoor Visitor* for guided walks and bus routes. Sir Francis Drake was born west of Hay Tor at **Tavistock.** South of Hay Tor, 2¾ mi. outside **Yelverton,** is **Buckland Abbey,** off Milton Combe Rd. Cistercian monks built the abbey in 1273; Drake later bought it for his private palace. The exterior and grounds, including the huge **Tithe Barn,** make for an interesting wander, but you may not want to bother with the lusterless interior. (☎ (01822) 853607. Open Apr.-Oct. M-W and F-Su 10:30am-5:30pm; Nov.-Mar. Sa-Su 2-5pm. £4.40, students and seniors £2.30. Grounds only £2.10, students and seniors £1.10.) The last castle built in England isn't Norman or Tudor. It's **Castle Drogo,** built between 1910 and 1930 by tea baron Julius Drewe. Convinced that he was a direct descendant of a Norman baron who had arrived in the 11th century with William the Conqueror, Drewe constructed this granite fortress in the style of his supposed ancestor. (☎ (01647) 433306. Open Apr.-Oct. Sa-Th 11am-5:30pm. Grounds open daily 10:30am-5:30pm. £5.40. Grounds only £2.60.)

TORQUAY   ☎ 01803

The largest city in the Torbay resort region—the self-proclaimed "English Riviera"—Torquay isn't quite as glamorous as the French original, but does have friendly beaches, abundant palm trees, and stimulating nightlife. Resident supersleuth Agatha Christie schemed here, and it was in Torquay that the fictional Basil Fawlty ran his madcap hotel. Semitropical when it doesn't rain, Torquay serves as a base for exploring the sunnier parts of the southwestern English coast.

◪ **TRANSPORTATION AND PRACTICAL INFORMATION.** Torquay's **train station** is off Rathmore Rd., near the Torre Abbey gardens. Trains (☎ (08457) 484950) arrive from: **London Paddington** (3½hr., 3 per day, £52.50); **London Waterloo** (4hr., 5 per day, £52.50); **Exeter** (45min., 2 per hr., £6.60); **Plymouth** (1hr., 2 per day, £7.30); **Bristol** (2hr., 4 per day, £21). **Buses** depart from the Pavilion; the nearby resort towns of **Paignton** and **Brixham** are accessible by the #12 bus. Call 213213 24hr. for a **taxi.** The **tourist information centre** (TIC), Vaughan Parade, arranges theater bookings, discounted tickets for nearby attractions, and accommodations for a 10% deposit. (☎ (0906) 680 1268; fax 214885; torquay.tic@torbay.gov.uk. Open summer M-Sa 9:30am-6pm, Su 10am-6pm; winter M-Sa 9:30am-5pm.) Other services include: **banks** on Fleet St., including **Barclays** (open M-Sa 9am-4:30pm); **Thomas Cook,** Union St. (☎ 352140; open M-Sa 9am-5:30pm); a **launderette,** 63 Princes Rd., off Market St. (£2 per load, soap 40p; open M-F 9am-7pm, Sa 9am-6pm, Su 9am-3pm); the **police,** South St. (☎ (0990) 777444); **Torbay Hospital,** Newton Rd. (☎ 614567); **Internet access** at **Cyberpoint,** 240 Union St. (☎ 297675; £2.50 per 30min.; open M and W 9:15am-5:30pm, Tu and Th 9:15am-7pm, F 9:15am-6:30pm, Sa 10am-6:30pm); and the **post office** (open M-Sa 9am-5:30pm). **Postal Code:** TQ2 5JG.

ACCOMMODATIONS AND FOOD. Though the hotel in *Fawlty Towers* was in Torquay, most accommodations today promise budget-busting prices rather than side-splitting humor. Since Torquay is a resort town, book well in advance for July and August. A number of **B&Bs** line Abbey Rd. and Morgan Ave., such as the amiable **Rosemont Guest House,** 5 Morgan Ave. (☎295475. Singles £15.) At **Torquay Backpackers,** 119 Abbey Rd., ever-accommodating Jane fosters a cozy environment. (☎299924. Dorms £7-10; doubles £18-20. Weekly rates available.)

Buy groceries at **Somerfield,** Union Square. (Open M-Sa 8:30am-8pm, Su 10am-4pm.) ✉**Number Seven,** Beacon Terr., is the place to splurge for dinner. This fish-obsessed bistro serves superb seafood in a simple setting. (☎295055. Open W-Sa 12:45-1:45pm and 6-10pm.) Many pubs, including **Hole in the Wall,** near Park Lane, serve surprisingly good meals in a youthful atmosphere. The waterfront is lined with cheap cafes and restaurants perfect for the beach-goer. **Breezes,** Torbay Rd., by the Princess Theatre, has wonderful sandwiches. (Open daily from noon.)

SIGHTS. To get out of the sun, head for **Torre Abbey,** Kings Dr. Founded in 1196 as a monastery and converted into a private mansion in the 16th century, the building now serves as a museum. Check out the recreation of Agatha Christie's study. (☎293593. Open Easter-Oct. daily 9:30am-6pm, last admission 5pm. £3, students and seniors £2.50, children £1.50, families £7.25.) For more on Agatha and Torquay's history, visit the **Torquay Museum,** Museum Rd. (☎293975. Open M-F 10am-4:45pm; Easter-Oct. also Sa 10am-4:45pm and Su 1:30-4:45pm. £2.) Residential and public **gardens** throughout Torquay are filled with palm trees and other subtropical plants not normally associated with (or found in) the British Isles.

BEACHES AND ENTERTAINMENT. There are clear distinctions between the English Riviera and its more established French cousin—the weather, for one. Yet spotty skies lend Torquay beaches a beauty of their own, and the slightest hint of sun thrills waiting crowds. **Torre Abbey Sands** draws the hordes, but better beaches lie north, where **Oddicombe, Maidencombe,** and **Watcombe** are peaceful and sandy. When the sun dips and beaches empty, nightlife options wake. **The Piazza,** Braddons Hill, has a lively atmosphere and livelier bands that keep locals loyal. (☎295212. Open M-Sa 11am-11pm, Su 11am-10:30pm.) Among nightclubs, **Claires,** Torwood St., stands out with popular house music (cover £3-5; open Th-Sa), while the **Monastery,** Torwood Gardens Rd. (☎298020), is an impiously late-night club that offers a few extra hours of hardcore dancing.

PLYMOUTH ☎01752

Immortalized by those hasty to leave it behind—the English fleet that defeated the Spanish Armada in 1588, explorers Sir Francis Drake, Captain Cook, the Pilgrims, and millions of emigrants to the United States and New Zealand—Plymouth (pop. 250,000) is no longer a point of immediate departure. Massive air raids during WWII left the city only the cracked shell of a naval capital, but among its rectilinear rows of buildings and awkward modern thoroughfares, patches of Plymouth's rich history still merit the day's exploration.

GETTING THERE AND SAILING AWAY

Plymouth lies on the southern coast between Dartmoor National Park and the Cornwall peninsula, on the London-Penzance train line.

Trains: Plymouth Station, North Rd. Ticket office open M-F 5:30am-8:30pm, Sa 5:30am-7pm, Su 9:30am-8:30pm. Western National buses #14, 16B, 72, 83, and 84 connect to the city center. (It's a long walk—take a bus.) Trains (☎(08457) 484950) arrive from: **London Paddington** (4hr., 17 per day, £60); **Penzance** (2hr., 21 per day, £10.30); **Bristol** (3hr., 18 per day, £44).

SOUTHWEST ENGLAND

Buses: Bretonside Station, Western National Office (☎222666). **Lockers** 50p-£2. Information office open M-Sa 7am-7pm, Su 9am-5pm. **National Express** (☎(08705) 808080) from **London** (4½hr., £20) and **Bristol** (2½hr., £18.50). **Stagecoach Devon** bus #X38 from **Exeter** via **Dartmoor** (1¼hr.; M-Sa 8 per day, Su 6 per day; £4.85).

Ferries: Millbay Docks. City buses #33 and 34 go to the docks (west of the city center at the mouth of the River Tamar). Follow signs to the ferry stand, a 15min. walk from the bus stop. Taxi to the terminal £3. Buy tickets at least 24hr. in advance, though foot passengers may need to come only 2hr. ahead. Check in 1hr. before departure, 2hr. for disabled travelers. **Brittany Ferries** (☎(0990) 360360) to **Roscoff, France** (6hr., 12 per week, £20-58) and **Santander, Spain** (24hr., 1-2 per week, return £80-145).

Public Transportation: Hoppa and **Citybus** buses from Royal Parade (70p-£1.80).

Taxis: Plymouth Taxis (☎606060).

Bike Rental: Caramba! 8-9 Quay Rd., The Barbican (☎201544). £10 per day, £60 per week. Credit card deposit £150—ay Caramba! Open M-Sa 10am-5pm, Su 10am-4pm.

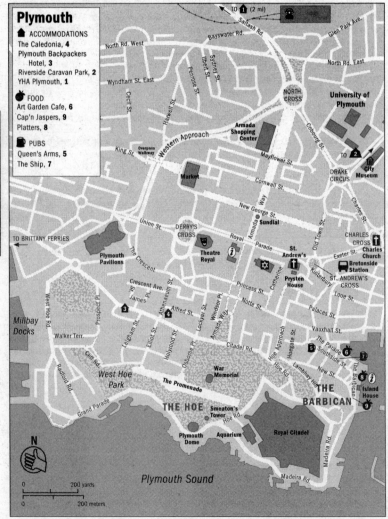

Plymouth

🏠 ACCOMMODATIONS
The Caledonia, **4**
Plymouth Backpackers
  Hotel, **3**
Riverside Caravan Park, **2**
YHA Plymouth, **1**

🍴 FOOD
Art Garden Cafe, **6**
Cap'n Jaspers, **9**
Platters, **8**

🍺 PUBS
Queen's Arms, **5**
The Ship, **7**

SOUTHWEST ENGLAND

✱🔢 ORIENTATION AND PRACTICAL INFORMATION

Plymouth's center, wedged between the River Tamar and Plymouth Sound, combines lush grass and bleak buildings. Almost all the attractions and shops are scattered in a rough semicircle around the city's crown jewel, the **Hoe** (or "High Place"), the area along the coastal road overlooking the harbor. The city center and cobbled streets of the **Barbican** quake with tourists and shoppers.

Tourist Information Centre: Island House, 9 The Barbican (☎304849; fax 257955), Sutton Harbour. In a building said to have housed the Pilgrims just before their departure on the *Mayflower* (look for a list of those on the boat). Books accommodations. Free map. Open M-Sa 9am-5pm, Su 10am-4pm.

Tours: Guide Friday bus tours (☎222221) leave every 20min. from stations near the Barbican and the Hoe. £5.50, students and seniors £4.50, children £1.50, families £9. **Boat cruises** around the harbor depart sporadically from spots near the *Mayflower* shrine on the Barbican; check boards there for times and prices.

Financial Services: Banks are plentiful along Royal Parade and Armada Way. **Thomas Cook,** 9 Old Town St. (☎667245), opposite the post office. Open M-Sa 9am-5:30pm. **American Express,** 139 Armada Way (☎228708), in the plaza formed by New George St. and Armada Way. Open M-Sa 9am-5pm.

Launderette: Hoegate Laundromat, 55 Notte St. (☎223031). Small loads £2; soap 70p. Open M-Th 8am-8pm, F-Su 8am-7pm; last wash 1hr. before close.

Police: Charles St. (☎(0990) 777444), near Charles Cross bus station.

Hospital: Derriford Hospital, Derriford (☎777111). About 5 mi. north of the city center. Take bus #10, 11, or 15 from Royal Parade in front of Dingles.

Internet Access: Cyber Cafe, 15-17 PTCI House, Union St. (☎201830). Make reservations. £2.50 per 30min.; 20% student discount. Open M-Th 9am-8pm, F-Sa 9am-4pm.

Post Office: 5 St. Andrew's Cross. Open M-Sa 9am-5:30pm. **Postal Code:** PL1 1AB.

▟ ACCOMMODATIONS AND CAMPING

Inexpensive B&Bs grace **Citadel Rd.** and **Athenaeum St.** between the west end of Royal Parade and the Hoe. Rooms tend to be small but cheap (£12-15 per person).

YHA Plymouth, Belmont House, Belmont Pl., Stoke (☎562189; fax 605360; plymouth@yha.org.uk), 2 mi. from the city center. Take bus #15 or 81 from the train station or Royal Parade to Stoke; it's on your left. Space and elegance in a mansion with beautiful grounds. Lockout 10am-5pm. Curfew 11pm, but a door code allows later access. Book in advance. Dorms £11, under 18 £7.75.

Plymouth Backpackers Hotel, 172 Citadel Rd. (☎225158; fax 207847), 2 blocks from the west end of the Hoe. Basic dorms and laid-back atmosphere in a hostel that attracts a mix of travelers from backpackers to their grandparents. Free showers; baths £1.50. Laundry service. Smoking allowed downstairs. Dorms £8.50, 3 days £22, weekly £50; singles £10; triples £27.

The Caledonia, 27 Athenaeum St. (☎229052). Elegantly furnished, well-kept bedrooms in a central location. Ample breakfast included. Singles £17; twins from £30.

Camping: Riverside Caravan Park, Longbridge Rd., Marsh Mills (☎344122). Take bus #21 or 51 from the city center toward Exeter. July-Aug. £3 per person, £4 per pitch; Sept.-June £3 per person, £3.50 per pitch, £7 per car.

🍴🍷 FOOD AND PUBS

The largest supermarket in town is **Sainsbury's,** in the Armada Shopping Centre, at the top of Armada Way. (☎674767. Open M-Sa 8am-8pm, Su 10am-4pm.) Pick up picnic fixings at **Plymouth Market,** an indoor bazaar at the west end of New George St. (☎264904. Open M-Tu and Th-Sa 8am-5:30pm, W 8am-4:30pm.)

Platters, 12 The Barbican (☎227262). You didn't think we'd neglect to include a chippy in a port town, did you? Grab great fish and chips for £3. Open daily 11:30am-11pm.

Art Garden Cafe, Parade Quay Rd. Standing out among the seaside cafes, this colorful restaurant offers filling sandwiches and baps (£1.90-2.25). Take a seat on the patio or enjoy the artwork inside. Open M-F 9am-5pm, Sa 9am-6pm, Su 9:30am-6pm.

Cap'n Jaspers, a stand by the Barbican side of the Harbour. Sells local catch to schools of sea dogs and tourists. Gobble sandwiches at picnic tables guarded by seagulls. Burgers from £1.10, half-yard hot dog £3, famous crab-rolls £1.85. Good for breakfast too. Open M-Sa 6:30am-11:45pm, Su 10am-11:45pm.

Crawl through pubs on Southside St. on the way to the Barbican. **The Ship,** almost at the end of Southside St., serves seaside spirits with some fishing nets hanging about. (☎667604. Open M-Sa 11am-11pm, Su 11am-10:40pm.) A thirtysomething crowd frequents the **Queen's Arms** on Southside St. at Friar's Ln., while the younger set sips at **The Bank** near the cinema.

◉ SIGHTS

THE HOE. The Hoe has provided tremendous views long before it oversaw the battle with the Spanish Armada. Climb the spiral steps and leaning ladders to the balcony of **Smeaton's Tower** for ferocious blasts of wind from the Channel and a magnificent impression of Plymouth and the Royal Citadel. Originally a lighthouse 14 mi. offshore, the 72 ft. tower was moved to its present site in 1882. Legend has it that Sir Francis Drake was playing bowls on the Hoe in 1588 when he heard that the Armada had entered the Channel. English through and through, Drake finished his game before hoisting sail. *(Tower open Easter-Sept. 10:30am-6pm, last admission 5pm. 75p, seniors 55p, children 40p, free with admission ticket to the Plymouth Dome.)*

MAYFLOWER STEPS. A plaque and American flag mark the spot on the Barbican where the **Pilgrims** set off in 1620 for their historic voyage to the New World. Subsequent departures have been marked as well, including Sir Humphrey Gilbert's voyage to Newfoundland, Sir Walter Raleigh's attempt to colonize North Carolina, and Captain Cook's voyage to Australia and New Zealand.

PRYSTEN HOUSE. Standing behind bombed-out **St. Andrews Church,** this 15th-century house contains an 11th-century tapestry alongside the **New World Tapestry,** which narrates the story of North American settlement and which, when finished, will be the longest in the world. Add your own stitch for £1. *(Open Apr.-Oct. M-Sa 10am-3:30pm. 50p, seniors and children 25p.)*

CHARLES CHURCH. The blackened shell of Charles Church, destroyed by a bomb in 1941, stands in the middle of the Charles Cross traffic circle half a block east of the bus station. The roofless walls are Plymouth's memorial to her citizens killed in the Blitz; grass grows where the altar used to stand. Keys to the ruin are available from the chief inspector's office at the Bretonside Bus Station.

OTHER SIGHTS. The **National Marine Aquarium,** The Barbican, takes care to provide a unique marine experience with high-tech gadgetry and an immense recreation of a coral reef. (☎220084. Open Apr.-Oct. 10am-6pm; Nov.-Mar. 10am-4pm. £6.75, students and seniors £5.20, children £4, families £19.) **Plymouth Gin,** Southside St., is England's oldest active gin brewery, at it since 1793. 40min. tours scour the still-active distillery and give historical tidbits. (☎665292. Open Easter-Dec. M-Sa 10:30am-4pm. £2.75, concessions £2.25, families £7; 50p discounts off bottles of gin with ticket.) In 1762, the local Jewish community built a **synagogue** (☎301955) on Catherine St. behind St. Andrew's Church. Still active, it is the oldest Ashkenazi synagogue in the English-speaking world. The building isn't clearly labeled; from the church, turn right into the alley behind the Eyeland Express store.

🎵 ENTERTAINMENT AND FESTIVALS

The **Theatre Royal,** on Royal Parade, has one of the West Country's best stages, featuring ballet, opera, and West End touring companies, including the Royal National Theatre. Limited discount tickets are available, usually for midweek performances. (☎267222. From £12, student standby 30min. before curtain from £10.) Plymouth's festivals revolve around its harbor, from the **August Navy Days,** a celebration of Plymouth's great ships, to the myriad boat rallies and regattas in summer. The **British National Fireworks Championship** explodes in early August.

CORNWALL

Cornwall's ethereal landscape doesn't feel quite like England. Indeed, the southwest corner's isolation made it a favored place for Celtic migration in the face of Saxon conquest, and, though the Cornish language is no longer spoken, the area remains fiercely protective of its distinctive past. Westward movement continues today, albeit in different forms: now, tourists jockey for rays on the beaches of Penzance, St. Ives, and Newquay, some of the sandiest and surfiest in northern Europe. Cornwall is also home to a rich collection of Stone Age and Iron Age monuments, along with the pasty (PAH-stee), the region's ubiquitous stuffed turnover.

📳 TRANSPORTATION

Penzance is the southwestern terminus of Britain's **trains** (☎(08457) 484950) and the best base for the region. The main rail line from **Plymouth** to **Penzance** bypasses coastal towns, but connecting rail service reaches **Newquay, Falmouth,** and **St. Ives.** Trains are frequent and distances short enough that you can make even Newquay a daytrip. **Rail Rover** tickets make it easier still (3 days in 7 £25.50, 8 in 15 £40).

The **Western National bus** network is similarly thorough, although the interior is not served as well as the coast. Buses run frequently from **Penzance** to **Land's End** and **St. Ives** and from **St. Ives** to **Newquay,** stopping in the smaller towns along these routes. Pick up a set of timetables at any Cornwall bus station (20p). Many buses don't run on Sundays, and many run only May-Sept.; call Western National (☎(01209) 719988) to check. **Explorer tickets** are an excellent value for those making long-distance trips or hopping from town to town (£6 per day, seniors £4); they are also available in three- and seven-day forms (£16.50 and £29.50 respectively). Cyclists may not relish the narrow roads, but the cliff paths, with their evenly spaced hostels, make for easy hiking. For serious hikers, the famous **Land's End-John O' Groats** cross-Britain walking route begins here.

BODMIN MOOR

Like Dartmoor and Exmoor to the east, Bodmin Moor is high country, containing Cornwall's loftiest points—Rough Tor (1311 ft.) and Brown Willy (1377 ft.). The region is rich with ancient remains, such as the stone hut circles that litter the base of Rough Tor. Some maintain that Camelford, at the moor's northern edge, is the site of King Arthur's Camelot, and that Arthur and his illegitimate son Mordred fought each other at Slaughter Bridge, a mile north of town. If you keep to designated paths in this romantic land, we guarantee the sheep won't prosecute.

📳 TRANSPORTATION

Bodmin Moor spreads north of **Bodmin** town toward coastal **Tintagel** and **Camelford** and **Launceston,** both inland. Bodmin is the area's point of entry, accessible from all directions, though it is not a good place to start hiking. **Trains** (☎(08457) 484950) stop at **Bodmin Parkway** from **London Paddington** (4hr., every hr., £61.50) and **Ply-**

mouth (35min., 2 per hr., £7). **National Express** (☎(08705) 808080) **buses** arrive from **Plymouth** (1½hr., 3 per day, £3.75). The town is served directly by buses from **Padstow** on the north coast (M-Sa 10 per day) and **St. Austell** to the south (M-Sa 12 per day). **Western National** (☎(01208) 79898) #X4 service arrives at the Mt. Folly bus stop by the Bodmin post office from **Tintagel** via **Camelford** (1hr., every hr., £2.70).

Since Bodmin is not a national park, it lacks National Park Visitor Centres dedicated to the area; visit local tourist information centres (TICs) instead. **Hiking** is convenient, especially from Camelford, and is the only way to reach the tors, which give grand views of the boulder-strewn expanse. **Bikes** can be hired in surrounding towns. **Hitchhiking** is dangerous, especially on the narrow A roads, which leave drivers with only six inches of road shoulder space—hardly enough to stand.

▐ ACCOMMODATIONS

B&Bs may be booked through the Bodmin TIC (☎(01208) 76616). **Colliford Tavern,** Colliford Lake, St. Neot, Liskeard, in the middle of the moorland, offers **B&B.** (☎(01208) 821335. Open Easter-Dec. From £37.50 per person; room only from £31.50 per person.) The nearest youth **hostels** are on the beautiful northern coast of Cornwall, a few miles northwest of the moor; both have a 10am-5pm lockout and 11pm curfew. **YHA Boscastle Harbour,** Palace Stables, Boscastle Harbour, is set among steep green hills and flowery riverbanks. Take bus #X9 from Exeter, #125 from Bodmin or Wadebridge, or #X4 from Bude. (☎(01840) 250287; fax 250615. Self-catering. Open June-Aug. daily; Sept.-Oct. and mid-Apr. to May W-Su. Dorms £10, under 18 £6.90.) For directions to **YHA Tintagel,** see p. 235.

BODMIN ☎01208

The unremarkable town of Bodmin (pop. 14,500) is the last supply stop before venturing out to Arthurian stomping grounds. Hidden in surrounding forests, the stately mansion **Lanhydrock,** built in the 1600s and gutted by fire in 1881, is surrounded by elaborate formal gardens. Inside, magnificent plasterwork ceilings portraying scenes from the Old Testament overhang plush Victorian furnishings. From Bodmin, take Western National bus #55 (£2) or walk 2½ mi. southeast on the A38. (☎73320. Open Apr.-Oct. Tu-Su 11am-5:30pm. £6.40, children £3.20, families £16. Grounds only £3.20, children £1.60.)

To reach town from the **Bodmin Parkway Station,** 5 mi. away on the A38, take Western National bus #55 (£1.20) or call **ABTaxis** (☎75000; £4.50 between station and town). The **tourist information centre** (TIC), at the Mount Folly Car Park, sells Ordnance Survey maps of the area for £5. (☎76616. Open M-Sa 10am-5pm.) Other services include: **banks** on Fore St.; the **police** (☎(0990) 777444), up Priory Rd., past the ATS car parks; and the **post office,** St. Nicholas St., beyond the TIC up Crinnicks Hill (☎72638; open M-F 9am-5:30pm, Sa 9am-12:30pm). **Postal code:** PL3 1AA.

A mile north of town, camp at the **Camping and Caravanning Club,** Old Callywith Rd., with laundry, showers, and a shop. (☎73834. Open Mar.-Oct. £2.75-4.05 per person, nonmembers £4.30 per pitch. Electricity £1.60.)

CAMELFORD ☎01840

Warning: those who imagined Camelot as a sweeping Utopia will be disappointed by miniscule Camelford, 13 mi. north of Bodmin. Tiny **Slaughter Bridge,** inlaid with hunks of petrified wood a mile north of town, marks the site where Arthur supposedly fell. Folks at the Camelford **tourist information centre,** in the North Cornwall Museum, can tell you how to find the inscribed stone marking his alleged grave. (☎212954. Open Apr.-Sept. M-Sa 10am-5pm.) From the center of town, **Rough Tor** is a 1¼hr. walk amid mist and nervous sheep; take Rough Tor Rd. to the end. The climb is not arduous until the 300 ft. ascent at the top, where stacked granite boulders form steps and passageways, offering a wind-ravaged lookout over the moor. To get to Camelford from **Bodmin,** take **Western National** bus #X4 (1hr.; M, W, F 2 per day; £2.70) or #55 to Wadebridge bus station (40min., 7-8 per day, £1.70) and transfer to #22 to Camelford (1hr., 7-8 per day, £2).

TINTAGEL
☎ 01840

More enjoyable than Camelford, Tintagel, 6 mi. northwest, is both the name of a village and of the ■fortress of Arthurian legend. Roman and medieval ruins cling to a headland besieged by the Atlantic; some have already collapsed into the sea. Below, Merlin's cave is worth the climb, but check for low-tide times and be careful on the steep cliffs. Even if you don't buy into the legends, the views are haunting. (Castle open July-Aug. daily 10am-7pm; Apr.-June and Sept. 10am-6pm; Oct. 10am-5pm; Nov.-Mar. 10am-4pm. £3, students and seniors £2.20, children £1.50.)

Inland, the one-road village is lined with gift shops. In **King Arthur's Great Hall of Chivalry,** Fore St., an antechamber tells Arthur's story with spotlights and a "mist of time" laid down by a humidifier. The great hall houses not one, not two, but *three* Round Tables. (☎770526. Open in summer daily 10am-5pm; winter 10am-dusk. £2.75, children £2.) The **Tintagel Visitor Centre,** Bossiney Rd., affords glimpses of the village's geological and mythical roots. (☎779084. Open M-Sa 9am-5pm, Su 10am-4pm. Free.) Escape gaudy homages to Arthur by taking a pleasant 1½ mi. walk through ■**St. Nectan's Glen** to its cascading 60 ft. waterfall. Pass the Visitor Centre out of town as you head toward Bossiney. About ¾ mi. later, take the footpath on your right across from the Ocean Cove caravan park and follow signs through the woods. (Open daily 10am-6:30pm.)

Tintagel has no tourist information centre. To get from town to **YHA Tintagel,** at Dunderhole Point, walk ¼ mi. past the 900-year-old St. Materiana's Church, then bear left through the cemetery and keep close to the shore. After 250 yd., look for the hostel's chimney, located in a hollow by the sea. You'll find a kitchen, spectacular sea views, and one happy owner. (☎770334; fax 770733. Open June-Aug. daily; Apr.-May and Sept. Th-Tu. Dorms £9.80, under 18 £6.75.)

FALMOUTH
☎ 01326

Seven rivers flow into the port of Falmouth (pop. 18,300), guarded by two spectacular castles. In the 16th and 17th centuries, Falmouth's ruthless Killigrews built a name on piracy and murder. The Killigrews were loyal to none but themselves; a particularly faithless clansman sold Pendennis Castle to the Spanish. Though only souvenir shops now skirmish in Falmouth, the 450-year-old fortresses of Pendennis and St. Mawes still eye each other across the narrow harbor, like two retired soldiers in seafront chairs straddling one of the world's deepest natural harbors.

■ TRANSPORTATION

Falmouth is about 60 mi. west of Plymouth along England's southern coast.

Trains: 3 small **stations,** all stops on the Truro-Falmouth line. **Penmere Halt** is a 10min. walk northwest from town, though it's the closest stop to the tourist information centre (TIC); **Dell-Falmouth Town** is east of the center and close to budget B&B-land; **Falmouth Docks** is nearest the hostel and Pendennis Castle. None of the stations sells tickets; instead, head for **Newell's Travel Agency,** 26 Killigrew St., on The Moor, a large traffic island on Killigrew St. (☎315066. Open M-F 9am-5:30pm, Sa 9am-4pm.) Trains (☎(08457) 484950) from: **London Paddington** (5½hr., every hr., £64); **Truro** (22min., every hr., £2.60); **Plymouth** (2hr.; M-Sa 17 per day, in summer Su 9 per day; £9.70); **Exeter** (3½hr., 6 per day, £24).

Buses: Out-of-town and local **Hoppa buses** stop opposite the TIC at **The Moor,** the Killigrew St. traffic island, perpendicular to the harbor. **National Express** (☎(08705) 808080) from **London** (6½hr., 2 per day, £34.50) and **Plymouth** (2¼hr., 2 per day, £5.25). **Western National** (☎(01209) 719 9880) from **Truro** (#88A, 89, X89, and X90; M-Sa 2 per hr., Su every hr.; £2.20) and **Helston** (#2 and 2A; 7 per day, £3.50). National Express schedules and tickets at Newell's Travel Agency (see above).

Ferries: Check signs on Prince of Wales Pier and Custom House Quay for boats and ferries; several make runs around the bay, most charging £4.30.

Taxis: Falmouth & Penryn Radio Taxi (☎315194).

Hitchhiking: Hitchhikers report good conditions 1½ mi. out of town at Dracaena Ave., where the streets are wider. *Let's Go* does not recommend hitchhiking.

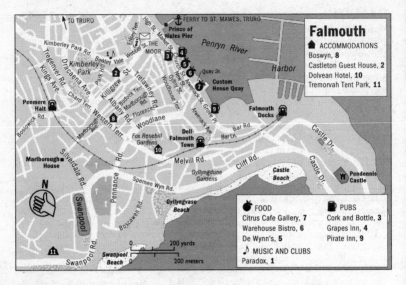

⚡ 🛈 ORIENTATION AND PRACTICAL INFORMATION

The exceptional **tourist information centre**, 28 Killigrew St., The Moor, books beds for a 10% deposit and has information on the Lizard Peninsula. From inland, follow signs to Killigrew Rd. or Kimberley Park Rd., then go downhill toward the river. (☎(08700) 110018; fax (08700) 110019. Open Apr.-Sept. M-Sa 9:30am-5:30pm; July-Aug. also Su 10am-2pm; Oct.-Mar. M-F 9am-5:30pm.) Other services include: **banks** on Killigrew St., including **Lloyds TSB**, 11-12 Killigrew St. (☎212600; open M-Tu and Th-F 9am-5pm, W 9:30am-5pm); the nearest **police station** (☎213432), in Penryn; **Falmouth Hospital** (☎434700), on Trescobeas Rd.; **Internet access** at the **Seaview Inn**, Woodhouse Terr. (£2 per 30min; open M-F 11:30am-3pm and 6-11pm, Sa 11am-11pm, Su noon-10:30pm), and the **library**, on The Moor (☎314901; £2 per hr.; open M-Tu and Th-F 9:30am-6pm, Sa 9:30am-12:30pm); and the **post office**, on The Moor (☎312525; open M-F 9am-5:30pm, Sa 9am-12:30pm). **Postal code:** TR11 3RB.

🏠 ACCOMMODATIONS AND CAMPING

The **B&Bs** on Cliff Rd. and Castle Dr. have great views of the cliffs; reserve ahead and expect to pay for the thrill (from £25). B&Bs closer to town are cheaper, but lack beach access and views. At the **Dolvean Hotel,** 50 Melvill Rd., Paul pampers guests with luxurious views of the beach and a short walk to the shore, as well as biscuits and chocolates by your bedside in the morning. (☎313658; fax 313995; reservation@dolvean.freeserve.co.uk. All rooms with bath. £25 per person. AmEx/MC/V.) Find comfortable accommodations with TVs in 200-year-old **Castleton Guest House**, 68 Killigrew St. Vegetarians may request alternatives to the English breakfast; everyone may request umbrellas for the English weather. (☎311072. From £18 per person.) **Boswyn**, Western Terr., is a plush set-up fanned by sea breezes only a block from the beach. Comfortable rooms, all with bath, and a gregarious owner welcome you. (☎314667. £18.50 per person.) If you're camping, try **Tremorvah Tent Park**, Swanpool Rd., just past Swanpool Beach and reachable by Hoppa bus #6 (2 per hr.), a lovely hillside spot with laundry and showers. (☎318311. £3 per night, 50p per car. Weekly: £18, July-Aug. £20.)

THE PASTY'S PAST You've watched them being baked. You've read the recipes. Maybe you've even tried them for lunch. But what exactly *are* they? Besides being a concoction of savories and sweets stuffed into a pastry turnover pocket, pasties are a rich part of Cornwall's history, once a source of crucial sustenance in Cornwall's mining towns. Originally baked so rock-hard that they wouldn't break if dropped down a mine shaft, pasties provided a complete and balanced meal for miners. Their ridged crusts made a perfect grip for dirty fingers, allowing workers to eat the soot-free filling and toss the crust later. Pasties also played a part in keeping Cornwall safe: according to legend, the devil refused to cross into Cornwall for fear of being diced and baked into pasties by the local housewives. Talk about paranoid!

FOOD

You won't escape Falmouth without picking up a classic Cornish pasty at any bakery, coffeehouse, or waterfront barbershop. ("Welcome to the bank. Pasty?") The local **W.C. Rowe** and **Pengenna** bakeries vie for the title of best pasty-makers in the city. Look on the blackboard menus of the various bistros and small restaurants that line Church St. for deals. A **Tesco** supermarket is on The Moor. (Open M-Tu and Sa 8:30am-5:30pm, W-F 8am-8pm, Su 10am-4pm.) The **Citrus Cafe Gallery,** 6 Arwenack St., serves refreshing milkshakes (90p), homemade doughnuts, and filling lunches (£3) with flair. (☎318585. Open M-W 10am-6pm, Th-Sa 10am-10pm, Su noon-4pm.) The **Warehouse Bistro** is slightly pricier, with three-course "value meals" from £9.45. (Open daily 6-10pm.) **De Wynn's 19th-Century Coffee House,** 55 Church St., delivers exotic teas and exquisite cakes (£2) in a painfully dainty setting. (☎319259. Open M-Sa 10am-5pm, Su 11am-4pm.)

SIGHTS AND BEACHES

Pendennis Castle, built by Henry VIII to keep French frigates out of Falmouth, now features a walk-through diorama that assaults the senses with waxen gunners bellowing incoherently through artificial fog. Better views and ventilation are to be found on the battlements. (☎316594. Open July-Aug. daily 9am-6pm; Apr.-June and Sept. 10am-6pm; Oct. 10am-5pm; Nov.-Mar. 10am-4pm. £3.80, students and seniors £2.90, children £1.90.) An occasionally wet 20min. ferry ride across the channel ends among the thatched roofs and aspiring tropical gardens of **St. Mawes** village. (☎313201. Ferries depart from Town Pier and the Quay in summer 2 per hr., less often in winter. Return £3.50.) On St. Mawes, the well-preserved **St. Mawes Castle** was built by Henry VIII to blow holes through any Frenchman spared by Pendennis's gunners. Henry's stone minion is now a six-story playset popular with schoolchildren, and though the tower is worth climbing, Pendennis wins the battle for superior views. (Open Apr.-Sept. daily 10am-6pm; Oct. 10am-5pm; Nov.-Mar. F-Tu 10am-1pm and 2-4pm. 1hr. audio tour included. £2.50, students and seniors £1.90, children £1.30.)

To taste the surf, head to one of Falmouth's three beaches; if morning skies are gray, be vigilant until noon, and the Cornish weather might surprise you. **Castle Beach,** on Pendennis Head, is too pebbly for swimming or sunbathing, but low tide reveals a labyrinth of seaweed and tidepools. **Gyllyngvase Beach** is the sandiest and has the best facilities, making it popular with families and windsurfers.

PUBS AND ENTERTAINMENT

For a fairly small town, Falmouth has a surprisingly vibrant social scene. Swill your rum at the **Pirate Inn** on Grove Pl., opposite the Killigrew Monument and the Quay, where local bands perform live every night. (Open M-Th 7pm-midnight, F-Sa 7pm-1am, Su 7-10:30pm.) Falmouth's hottest club, **Paradox,** on The Moor, is best on weekends when good-sized crowds groove to rock and chart music. (☎314453.

Cover £3. Open daily 9pm-1am.) On Friday and Saturday nights, the Bacchanalian crowd at **The Cork and Bottle,** 67 Church St. (☎316909), vies to match that of **The Grapes Inn** (☎314704), across the road at 64 Church St. (Both open M-Sa 11am-11pm, Su noon-10:30pm.) The **Falmouth Arts Centre,** Church St., hosts exhibitions, concerts, theater, and films. (☎212300. Theater tickets around £5.) The first two weeks of August are livened by **Carnival** and **Regatta Weeks.**

NEAR FALMOUTH: THE LIZARD PENINSULA

Once a leper colony, the Lizard Peninsula between Falmouth and Penzance enjoys relative isolation, untrampled by tourists. Although the peninsula's name isn't helping the tourist information centre corner the herpetophobic market, visitors will probably not encounter reptilia. "Lizard" is a corruption of Old Cornish "Lys ardh," meaning "the high place." A scaly line of cliffs and caves striped with serpentine paths leads to **Lizard Point** (see below), the southernmost prong of England, where the Atlantic becomes the English Channel. Inland, the heath of **Goonhilly Downs** is riven by slices of purple rock: the Lizard's rare minerals produce soil that yields exotic flora. Pay a visit to **Earth Station Goonhilly,** the world's largest satellite station, which offers exhibits, films, a shuttle tour through the satellites' perimeters, and a free "Internet Zone." (☎(0800) 679593. Open daily 10am-6pm. £4, seniors £3, children £2.50.) A mile and a half from Mullion, a village on Lizard's west coast, waves swirl around rocky **Mullion Cove,** lined with steep but climbable cliffs. Hundreds of seabirds nest on **Mullion Island,** 250 yd. off the cove.

Access to the peninsula is tedious; take **Western National bus** #2 or 2A from **Falmouth** or **Penzance** to **Helston** (1hr., 2 per hr., £3), then one of the **Truronian** (☎(01872) 273453) lines down to Mullion and the Lizard (1hr., 6 per day, £2.25 and £2.45 respectively). **Bus tours** (£5.70, children £3.80) of the peninsula leave **Penzance** (Tu 11am) and **St. Ives** (Tu 11:30am). For information on bus service into the peninsula, call Camborne (☎(01209) 719988). **Driving** access is via the A30383 from the A394. The tiny town of **The Lizard** has capitalized handily on its unique claim to fame, enjoying a roaring (or at least hissing) trade in "serpentine sales and gifts." Snaking out of the town is the path to ▧**Lizard Point,** where perilous cliffside paths slither past wildflowers. A small information booth near the car park vends walking maps for a small fee.

Contact the **Helston tourist information centre,** in front of the Coinagehall bus stop, if you'd like to stay the night, and pick up the free *Guide to the Lizard Peninsula.* (☎565431. Open M-F 10am-1pm and 2-5pm, Sa 10am-1pm and 2-4:45pm.) Stock up on cash in Helston—elsewhere, **banks** and **cash machines** are rare. **YHA Coverack,** to the southeast, is the Lizard's only hostel; take Truronian bus #T3 from Helston to Coverack Village. (☎280687; fax 280119. Open July-Aug. daily; Apr.-June F-W. £10, under 18 £6.90.) At **Henry's Campsite,** Shetland ponies jostle campers. (☎290596. £3 per 1-person tent, £5 per 2-person, each additional person 50p.)

PENZANCE   ☎01736

Penzance is the very model of an ancient English pirate town: water-logged and unabashed. The city's armada of souvenir shops wages countless raids on tourist doubloons and sometimes makes Penzance feel as authentic as the wooden pirates on a Disney ride. But with glorious sunsets and mildly bawdy pubs, it's difficult not to enjoy this irreverent, swashbuckling town.

▛ TRANSPORTATION

Trains: Wharf Rd., at the head of Albert Pier. Ticket office open M-Sa 6:15am-6pm, Su 8:15am-6pm. Trains (☎(08457) 484950) from: **London** (5½hr., every hr., £54); **Plymouth** (2hr., every hr., £10); **Exeter** (3hr., every hr., £19); and on another line from **Newquay** (2hr., 6 per day via Par, £11.40) and **St. Ives** (25min., 3-4 per day, £4.30). Other St. Ives trains change at **St. Erth** (25min., every hr., £4.30).

Buses: Wharf Rd. (☎(01209) 719988), at the head of Albert Pier. Information and ticket office open M-F 8:30am-4:45pm, Sa 8:15am-3pm, Su 9:30am-12:30pm. **National Express** (☎(08705) 808080) from: **London** via **Heathrow** (8hr., 8 per day, £27) and **Plymouth** via **Truro** (3hr., 2 per hr., £6).

⚡🛈 ORIENTATION AND PRACTICAL INFORMATION

Penzance's train station, bus station, and tourist information centre (TIC) stand conveniently together on **Wharf Rd.**, adjacent to the harbor and town. **Market Jew St.** is laden with well-stocked bakeries and ill-stacked bookstores (the street's name is a corruption of the Cornish "Marghas Yow," meaning "Market Thursday"). It mutates into **Alverton St.**, then **Alverton Rd.**, then changes face again to become the A30, the road to Land's End. **Chapel St.**, a cobblestone row of antique shops and pubs, descends from the town center into a welter of alleys near the docks.

Tourist Information Centre: Station Rd. (☎362207), between the train and bus stations. Books beds for a 10% deposit. Free map of Penzance. Open in summer M-F 9am-5pm, Sa 9am-4pm, Su 10am-1pm; in winter M-F 9am-5pm, Sa 10am-1pm.

Tours: The TIC arranges minibus tours of attractions in west Cornwall, led by the mirthful **Harry Safari** (see p. 241). **National Express, Western National,** and **Cornwall** buses offer guided tours of the area. **Western National** (☎(01209) 719988) tours include weekly trips from Penzance to King Arthur's Country (Boscastle and Tintagel; Th 9:30am; £7.20, children £4.80), fishing villages (W 9:30am; £6, children £4), and the Lizard Peninsula (M 11am; £6, children £4).

Financial Services: Barclays, 8-9 Market Jew St. (☎362271). Open M-Tu and Th-F 9am-5pm, W 10am-5pm, Sa 9:30am-noon.

Launderette: Polyclean, on the corner of Leskinnick St. and Market Jew St. Soap available. Open daily 8am-8pm.

Police: Penalverne Dr. (☎(0990) 777444), off Alverton St.

Hospital: West Cornwall Hospital, St. Clare St. (☎874000). Take bus #10, 10A, 11, 11A, or 11D.

Internet Access: Penzance Public Library, Morrab Rd. Email 50p per 15min., net surfing £2.50 per 30min.

Post Office: 113 Market Jew St. (☎363284). Open M-F 9am-5:30pm, Sa 9am-12:30pm. **Postal Code:** TR18 2LB.

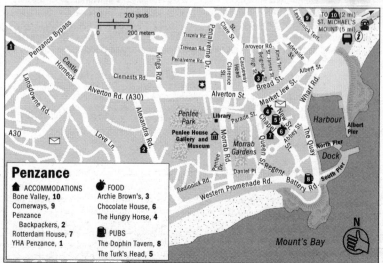

Penzance

🔺 ACCOMMODATIONS
Bone Valley, **10**
Cornerways, **9**
Penzance
  Backpackers, **2**
Rotterdam House, **7**
YHA Penzance, **1**

🍴 FOOD
Archie Brown's, **3**
Chocolate House, **6**
The Hungry Horse, **4**

🍺 PUBS
The Dophin Tavern, **8**
The Turk's Head, **5**

Mount's Bay

ACCOMMODATIONS AND CAMPING

Penzance's fleet of B&Bs (£14-20) occupies the hills above the Esplanade and beach, primarily **Morrab Rd.** between Alverton St. and Western Promenade Rd. Also check out the side streets off **Chapel St.** and, farther out, **Alexandra Rd.** Camping areas blanket the west Cornwall peninsula.

Penzance Backpackers, Blue Dolphin, Alexandra Rd. (☎363836; fax 363844; pzbackpack@ndirect.co.uk). Relaxed and eclectic with 29 beds. Internet access (8p per min.) and ample lounge. Laundry and kitchen facilities. Dorms £8-9; doubles £18-22.

YHA Penzance, Castle Horneck (☎362666; fax 362663; penzance@yha.org.uk). A 30min. walk, or take Hoppa bus #B and hop off at Pirate Inn, or Albert's Taxi from the train or bus stations (£2.30). A restored 18th-century mansion. Effusive staff, classy lounge, kitchen, and laundry. Reception 3-11pm. Lockout 10am-1pm. Dorms £11, under 18 £7.75. **Campsites** in the backyard for £5, including use of hostel facilities.

Cornerways, 5 Leskinnick St. (☎364645), a block from the train station. You're in luck—you'll get a warm B&B welcome from the entire royal family, past and present, on porcelain. Friendly proprietress offers vegetarian breakfast. All rooms with bath. Book weeks ahead. Singles £23; twins £40; triples £54.

Rotterdam House, 27 Chapel St. (☎/fax 332362). Comfortable rooms and congenial owners—what else do you need? How about smoked haddock for breakfast and a house built by Grandpa Brontë? Book well ahead, especially in summer. £15 per person.

Camping: Bone Valley, Heamoor, Penzance (☎360313). Family-run site 2 mi. from the city center. July-Aug. £5 per person; Sept.-June £4.50 per person. £1 per car.

FOOD AND PUBS

Expect to pay at least £7 for Penzance's excellent seafood dinners along **The Quay. Market Jew St.** fare is unexciting and expensive. The best buys are in coffee shops and local eateries on smaller streets and alleys, far from the hustle of town.

☒ The Turk's Head, 49 Chapel St. (☎363093). A 13th-century pub (Penzance's oldest), sacked by Spanish pirates in 1595. A smuggler's tunnel allegedly wound here from the harbor in the 17th century. Locals drift in to sample great meats (main courses around £6). Food served M-Sa 11am-2:30pm and 6-10pm, Su noon-2:30pm and 6-10pm.

☒ Archie Brown's, Bread St. (☎362828), above Richard's Health Food Store. Heralded by a colorful banner, this innovative vegetarian cafe makes creative meals at pleasing prices. Favorites include falafel wrap with salad (£4.50), the daily vegan soup, and homity pie. Open M-Sa 9:30am-5pm, also F for more expensive dinners (£15).

The Hungry Horse, Old Bakehouse Ln. (☎363446), in an alley off Chapel St. Pizzas from £4, chargrilled specialties like swordfish steak or herb-roasted chicken from £8.50. It's worth the splurge. Open M-Sa 7-10pm.

Chocolate House, 44 Chapel St. (☎368243). An Eden for chocoholics: try to forget your dentist. A box of their Cornish chocs is £2-14. Reasonably priced soups and sandwiches are also served in the classy cafe. Open M-Sa 10am-5pm.

The Dolphin Tavern, The Quay (☎364106). Supposedly haunted by a sea captain's ghost, this pub was the first place tobacco was smoked in Britain. Down a pint with quality grub (£4-8) next to the harbor. Open M-Sa 11am-11pm, Su 11am-10:30pm.

SIGHTS

Penzance's attractions are enjoyable but few. Most museums reside on or near Chapel St. Follow in the swashbuckling steps of the pirates of Penzance and use the city as a port for sailing out to Cornwall's more scenic landscapes.

THE MARITIME MUSEUM. A life-like stone sailor greets visitors to this museum, which bears a resemblance to a 17th-century galleon, complete with low ceilings and plastic cannons. The museum holds shelves of corroded coins, plates, spoons, a reconstructed man-o'-war, and other wreckage recovered in the 1960s from the *Association* and the *Colossus*, ships that sank off the Isles of Scilly in the 18th century. *(19 Chapel St. Open M-Tu and Th-F 11am-4pm, W 11am-2pm. £2, seniors £1.50, children £1, families £5.)*

ST. MICHAEL'S MOUNT. In AD 495, the archangel St. Michael supposedly appeared to some fishermen on Marazion, a small island across the bay from Penzance. A Benedictine monastery was built on the spot, and today St. Michael's Mount sits offshore, with a church and castle at its peak and a village at its base. The Mount is essentially a smaller and squatter version of the more celebrated Mont St. Michel, across the English Channel in Normandy. The castle's interior is unspectacular (see if you can spot Oliver Cromwell's bib); however, the grounds are lovely, and the 30-story views captivating. Joachim von Ribbentrop, Hitler's foreign minister, had it picked out as his personal residence after the conquest of England. *(Take bus #2 or 2A to Marazion and turn right at the post office, toward the harbor (M-Sa 3 per hr., return 80p). Access to the mount is by the painfully uneven, seaweed-strewn causeway or by ferry (return £1, children 50p, goats and sheep 50p) during high tide. ☎ 710507. Open Apr.-Oct. M-F 10:30am-5:30pm, in summer also most weekends; Nov.-Mar. in good weather. Last admission 4:45pm. £4.40, children £2.20, families £12.)*

OTHER SIGHTS. The **Penlee House Gallery and Museum,** on Morrab Rd., rotates new exhibits through elegantly sparse galleries every few months. Look for the 18th-century Scold's Bridle, a menacing discouragement of loose lips. *(☎363625. Open M-Sa 10:30am-4:30pm. £2, students and seniors £1, children free.)* The bizarre and gaudily painted facade of the **Egyptian House,** near the top of Chapel St., pokes fun at itself and at the 1830s craze for Egyptian ornamentation.

🎵 ENTERTAINMENT AND FESTIVALS

It's almost compulsory for people with an interest in 1) Cornish history, 2) touring with a folk band, or 3) riotous jokes about Neolithic man to take a tour with ▨**Harry Safari.** It's a corny trip through the Cornish wilds, stone circles, and Neolithic community, and far superior to soporific bus rides on the A30. *(☎711427. Tours 4hr., Su-F 1 per day. £12.50, £10 for YHA hostelers.)*

For seven weeks during the summer, natives and tourists flock to the open-air ▨**Minack Theatre,** 9 mi. from Penzance, which puts on performances from Shakespeare to the inevitable *Pirates of Penzance*. Hacked into a cliffside at Porthcurno, the theater reportedly appeared in a dream of Rowena Cade, a Victorian who enlisted the help of sympathetic souls and constructed the surreal amphitheater "with her own hands." A bus runs from the TIC on Wednesdays (£9.50, children £6, including show tickets). For other buses, call Western National (☎(01209) 719988), Mount's Bay Coaches (☎363320), or Oates Travel (☎795343). Access by car is via the B3283. (Visitor center ☎381081. Ticket office open M-F 9:30am-8pm, Sa-Su 9:30am-5:30pm; closed noon-4:30pm during matinees. Performances £5-6, children £2.50-3; matinees £2, seniors £1.50, youths £1, children free.) Bacchus visits the city in June during the pagan **Golowan Festival,** featuring bonfires, fireworks, and the election of the mock Mayor of the Quay.

ST. IVES   ☎01736

> As I was going to St. Ives, I met a man with seven wives.
> Each wife had seven sacks, each sack had seven cats,
> Each cat had seven kits. Kittens, cats, sacks, and wives,
> How many were going to St. Ives?

Only one, of course. But medieval St. Ives (pop. 11,100), perched 10 mi. north of Penzance on a spit of land edged by pastel beaches and azure waters, has attracted plenty of visitors for centuries. The town's cobbled alleyways, colored by overflowing flowerpots, drew a colony of painters and sculptors in the 1920s; today, their legacy fills the windows of countless local art galleries, including a branch of the Tate. Virginia Woolf too was bewitched by the energy of the Atlantic at St. Ives: her masterpiece *To the Lighthouse* is thought to refer to the Godrevy Lighthouse in the distance, disappearing and reappearing in the morning fog.

■ TRANSPORTATION AND PRACTICAL INFORMATION. Trains (☎ (08457) 484950) on the Plymouth-Penzance line run from **St. Erth** (10min., 2 per hr., £3), where they connect to **Penzance** and **Truro.** Intermittent trains come directly from **Penzance** (M-F 6 per day, Sa-Su 3-4 per day). **National Express** (☎ (08705) 808080) **buses** stop in St. Ives on their way between **Plymouth** and **Penzance** (6 per day). **Western National** (☎ (01208) 798798) arrives from **Penzance** (#16; 3 per hr., off season M-Sa only; £2.50) and **Newquay** (#57 or X2). **Store luggage** at the **St. Ives Travel Agency** (£1.50; open M-F 9am-5:30pm, Sa 9am-5pm) or at the **Western National Office,** at the Malakoff (£1-2; open M-Sa 9am-5pm, Su 9am-2pm).

The **tourist information centre** (TIC) is in the Guildhall on Street-an-Pol. From the bus or train station, walk to the foot of Tregenna Hill and turn right on Street-an-Pol. The staff books beds for a 10% deposit and sells 10p maps of St. Ives's medieval maze—trust us, you'll need one. (☎ 796297. Open M-Sa 9:30am-6pm, Su 10am-1pm; closed Sa-Su in winter.) Wednesday evenings at 6pm (July-Aug. only), weave up one alley and down another on a **walking tour** that departs from the bus station. (☎ 796389. 1½hr. £3.) **Windansea Surf Shop,** 25 Fore St., rents and repairs bikes and surfboards. (☎ 794830. Surfboards and wetsuits £5 per day, £25 per week. £5 deposit. Open daily 9:30am-9:30pm.) Other services include: **Barclays bank,** High St., across from the post office (☎ 362261; open M-Tu and Th-F 9:30am-4:30pm, W 10am-4:30pm); **Internet access** at **TEK,** 3-4 Tregenna Hill (☎ 799416; £1 per 10min., £5 per hr.; open in summer daily 9am-9pm; winter 10am-7pm) and at **St. Ives International Backpackers** (10p per min., £5 per hr.; see below); and the **post office,** 1 Tregenna Pl. (☎ 795004; open M-F 9am-5:30pm, Sa 9am-1pm). **Postal code:** TR26 1AA.

▐ ACCOMMODATIONS. B&Bs await on **Park Ave.** and **Tregenna Terr.;** for fine sea views, try **Clodgy View** and **West Pl.** Prices usually dip for rooms farther from the water and higher up the gusty hillside. **St. Ives International Backpackers,** The Stenmack, funkifies a 19th-century Methodist church. There's a free shuttle service for those staying at its sister hostel in Newquay. (☎/fax 799444. Dorms £12 high season, £8 off season. Weekly: £40-45.) **Harbour Lights,** Court Cocking, Fore St., occupies a 536-year-old building 30 ft. from the sea on one of the oldest streets in St. Ives and features canopied beds and TVs. (☎ 795525. Rooms £18 per person; 10% student discount.) Somewhat more tranquil, **Downlong Cottage,** 95 Backroad East., is also 3min. from the beach. (☎ 798107. Rooms £15-18 per person.) If you can't find a room, seek one of the £15 B&Bs in **Carbis Bay** (20min. by coastal walk or 3min. by train on the St. Ives-Penzance line; return £1). Places to **camp** abound in nearby **Hayle;** try **Trevalgan Camping Park** (☎ 796433), with laundry and cooking facilities and access to the coastal path, or **Ayr Holiday Park** (☎ 795855), at the top of Bullans Ln. (Sites £4.50-7.)

■ FOOD AND PUBS. Stock up on groceries at **Spar,** Tregenna Pl. (Open daily 7am-10pm.) **Fore St.** is packed with small bakeries, each hawking its own interpretation of the pasty. Many eateries also sell Cornish cream teas; try one for £2.60 at **Bumble's Tea Room,** Digey Sq., near the Tate. (☎ 797977. Open M-Sa 10am-5pm; summer also Su 11am-4pm.) Miniscule **Ferrell's Bakery,** 64 Fore St., bakes a delicious pasty as well as a saffron bun (40p) rumored to be Cornwall's best. (☎ 797703. Open daily 9am-5:30pm.) Earning the scorn of pasty purists, the chocolate and banana pasty (£1.40) at **Granny's Pasties,** 9 Fore St., does for pasties what color did for TV. (☎ 793470. Open daily 9am-5:30pm; summer 9am-9pm.) For the pastyweary, **The Cafe,** Island Sq., changes a consonant with vegetarian meals such as spinach and feta pasta for around £7. (☎ 793621. Open daily 11am-3pm and 7-10pm.) Beer has flowed at **The Sloop,** on the corner of Fish St. and The Wharf, since 1312. (☎ 796584. Open daily 11am-11pm; food served noon-3pm and 6-8:45pm.)

■ SIGHTS AND BEACHES. The modernist fruits of this art colony by the sea are on display at the **Tate Gallery,** on Porthmeor Beach. Like its sister, the Tate Modern in London (see p. 132), the gallery focuses on abstract art (mainly local, in constantly shifting displays); its seafront location successfully integrates art and the environment that inspired it. (☎ 796226. Open Tu-Su 10:30am-5:30pm; July-Aug. also M 10:30am-that inspired it. (☎796226. Open Tu-Su 10:30am-5:30pm; July-Aug. also M 10:30am-5:30pm. Free tours M-F 2:30pm. £4, students and seniors £2.50, children free.) Under the protective wing of the Tate, the nearby **Barbara Hepworth Museum and Sculpture Garden** shows Hepworth's landmark 20th-century abstractions in her former studio and lush garden. (Same hours as Tate. £3.50, students and seniors £1.80, children free. Same-day admission to both museums £6, students and seniors £3.30.) For information on the town's innumerable other galleries, check the TIC's *Arts Guide* (£1).

The sun-god accepts burnt offerings of British skin at a number of beaches. Follow the hill down from the train station to **Porthmaster Beach,** a white, sandy expanse with tamer waves perfect for the families that crowd it on warm days. Some people enjoy tanning around the harbor, but the tourists wandering Wharf Rd. make it less intimate than **Porthguidden Beach,** hugged by the jutting arms of the island. **Porthmeor Beach,** below the Tate, attracts surfers but has less appealing sands. Find a perch onshore to admire the bewitching Godrevy Lighthouse; **boats** occasionally head to the lighthouse from The Wharf. Check with the TIC or look at the blackboards that pepper the pier (£6, children £4).

FROM ST. IVES TO LAND'S END

The Penwith Peninsula scrolls into the Celtic Sea at **Land's End,** Britain's southernmost point. Unfortunately, protective efforts could not prevent the area's transformation into a zone of outlandish commercial booty. Land's End is now a tourist park of rides and plastic phenomena, but a look out to the dramatic granite cliffs and sea will remind you why you came. **Western National** (☎(01208) 798798) **buses** run to Land's End from **Penzance** (1hr., every hr., £3) and **St. Ives** (35min., 3 per day, £2). For those unafraid of hills and hell-bent drivers, **biking** is the best way to tour the region, affording glimpses of sparkling coastlines.

ST. JUST. North of Land's End on Cape Cornwall, the craggy coast of St. Just (pop. 2700) remains fairly untouched by tourism. Derelict copper and tin mines define this former mining center, while the ever-present Neolithic stone circles poke unobtrusively out of the landscape. Two- to four-mile hikes are outlined in leaflets in most tourist information centres (TICs), but the dramatic cliff path wrapping the entire coast unveils the best of Cornwall. The **YHA Land's End,** at Letcha Vean, occupies three pristine acres with many sea views. From the bus station's rear exit, turn left and follow the lane to its end, past the chapel and farm. (☎(01736) 788437; fax 787337. Daytime lockout. Open Mar.-Oct. daily. Dorms £10, under 18 £6.90.) **Buses** #10, 10A, 10B, or 11 run from the **Penzance** bus station.

SENNEN. Just 1½ mi. from Land's End, or 9 mi. from Penzance on the A30, in the tiny hamlet of Sennen, **Land's End Backpackers and Guest House,** White Sands Lodge, dazzles with its Crayola-bright walls and communal spirit. Their adjoining **restaurant** whips up an array of meals that brings in a drive-by trade of young and old diners tired of pub grub. (☎/fax (01736) 871776. Restaurant open 8am-10pm. English or vegetarian breakfast £4. Dorms £10; private guest house singles £14.50; doubles with bath £35. Camping £6.) Give 'em a ring and they may pick you up from the Penzance bus or train station, or take Western National #1 or 1A from **Penzance** or **Land's End** (1hr., 12 per day) or #15 from **Land's End** (5min., 1 per day).

ZENNOR. Legend has it that at the tiny village of Zennor (accessible by bus from St. Ives), a mermaid, drawn by the singing of a young man, returned to the sea with him in tow. On misty evenings, locals claim to see and hear the happy pair; a mermaid is carved on one of the benches of the local church. **The Old Chapel Backpackers Hostel,** a beautiful and immaculate independent hostel, is close to hiking and 4 mi. from the beaches at St. Ives's. (☎(01736) 798307. Dorms £10.)

ANCIENT MONUMENTS. Inland on the Penwith Peninsula, some of the least-tarnished Stone and Iron Age monuments in England lie along the Land's End-St. Ives bus route. Once covered by mounds of earth, the quoits (also called cromlechs or dolmens) are thought to be burial chambers from 2500 BC. The **Zennor Quoit** is named for the village. The **Lanyon Quoit,** off the Morvah-Penzance road about 3 mi. from each town, is one of the area's most impressive megaliths.

The famous stone near Morvah (on the Land's End-St. Ives bus route) with a hole through the middle has the Cornish name **Mên-an-Tol,** or "stone with a hole through the middle." The doughnut is allegedly endowed with curative powers: climbing through the aperture supposedly remedies backaches, assures easy childbirth, or induces any alteration in physiology your heart desires. The best-preserved Iron Age village in Britain is at **Chysauster,** about 4 mi. from both Penzance and Zennor. Take Western National bus #16 (4 per day, £1.60) or the 2½ mi. footpath off the B3311 near Gulval. (☎(0831) 757934. Open Apr.-Oct. daily 10am-6pm. £1.60, students and seniors £1.20, children 80p.)

NEWQUAY   ☎01637

At Newquay (NEW-key; pop. 30,000) station, a range of hairstyles disembark: bald, bleached-blond, blue. Sheathed surfboards strapped to their backs, athletes head straight for the beach. Others, imposter surfers in Airwalks, race to the pubs. Partiers here, families there, tackiness everywhere, Newquay swells to 100,000 in summer with holidaymakers. The surf *is* great—among Europe's best—and the parties *do* throb late into the night. Just watch your step around Newquay's treacherous tourist traps.

▐⌐ TRANSPORTATION

Trains: Cliff Rd. **Luggage storage** £1 per item. Open daily 8:30am-3pm. Buy train tickets at the station from **LSA Travel** (☎877180). Open M-F 9am-5pm, Sa 9am-4pm. Getting to Newquay from the main London-Penzance line requires a quick stopover in **Par.** Trains (☎(08457) 484950) arrive from: Par (50min., every hr., £4.30); **Plymouth** (2hr., every hr., £8.10); **Penzance** (2hr., every hr., £10.30).

Buses: 1 East St. Western National ticket office open M-F 9am-8pm, Sa 8:30am-5:30pm, Su 9am-1pm and 2-8pm. **National Express** (☎(08705) 808080) from **London** (5¾hr., 3 per day, £26.50). **Western National** (☎(01208) 798798) from **St. Austell** (45min.; 2 per hr., off season M-Sa only; £3); **Bodmin** (2hr., 3 per day, £3.50); **St. Ives** (2hr., June-Sept. 1 per day, £5). Call Jody at **Roadland Trip Overland Tours** (☎(0800) 056 0505) for whimsical, £25 trips to London.

Bike Rental: Newquay International Backpackers, 69-73 Tower Rd. (☎879366). £2.50 per hr., £10 per day, £50 per week.

▐ PRACTICAL INFORMATION

The **tourist information centre** (TIC) is on Marcus Hill; facing the street from the train station, turn left and go four blocks. It sells street maps for 50p and *What's On in Newquay* for £1. (☎854022; fax 854030; info@newquay.co.uk. Open M-Sa 9am-6pm, Su 9am-4pm; closed earlier in winter.) Get a board at **Fistral Surf,** 1 Beacon Rd., which rents all the surf paraphernalia one needs to bust the rippingest British tubes, mate. (☎850520. Board £5 per day, £25 per week; wetsuit £5 per day, £20 per week. Open daily 9am-6pm; until 10pm in summer.) **Surf condition updates** (☎(0891) 360360) cost 50p per min. Other services include: **Newquay Hospital,** St. Thomas Rd. (☎893600); **Internet access** at **Newquay International Backpackers** (10p per min.) and **Emoceanl Surf,** 2 Grover Ln. (☎851121; £1.50 per 15min.; open daily 9am-6pm); and the **post office,** 31-33 East St. (☎873364; open M-F 9am-5:30pm, Sa 9am-12:30pm). **Postal code:** TR7 1BU.

ACCOMMODATIONS AND CAMPING

The local YHA Youth Hostel closed a few years ago, partly because its curfew was incompatible with the town's nocturnal habits, but Newquay's surfer subculture has spurred loads of **independent hostels.** Be wary of choosing a place to stay based solely on proximity to the beach: while some hostels are well kept and offer initiation into the ways of the wetsuited, others are dark, dirty, and unwelcoming. Many advertise £5 beds to seduce surfers into staying, but that often translates into a 6-by-1 ft. rectangle of mattress-less, grimy floor space. Hordes of **B&Bs** (around £14 per night) gather near Fistral Beach and closer to town in the avenues near the bus station, bounded by East St. and Mount Wise.

Newquay International Backpackers, 69-73 Tower Rd. (☎879366; backpacker@dial.pipex.com). Welcomes surf bunnies and hydrophobes alike. International crowd parties late into the night. Guests get clean dorms, discounts on area pubs, clubs, and restaurants, and free shuttle service to and from the sister hostel in St. Ives. Internet access 10p per min. Dorms £10, less in winter.

Seagull Cottage, 98 Fore St. (☎875648). Rooms close to Fistral Beach, a scone's throw from town. Breakfast with a jungle of parrots. £16 per person, off season £10.

Quebec Hotel, 34 Grosvenor Ave. (☎874430). A good night's rest awaits in this B&B's comfy beds. Singles £15, with bath £25; doubles £30-60.

Camping: Trevelgue Caravan and Camping Park (☎851851), in Porth. Sites £4.80-5.50 per person. Or try **Hendra Tourist Park** (☎875778), 2 mi. east of town on the A392 beyond the Lane Theatre. From Trenance Gdns., go under the viaduct and past the boating lake, then turn left. Bus #58 runs directly from the town center 2 per hr. Families and couples only. Sites £3-5 per person. Electricity £2.75.

FOOD AND PUBS

Restaurants in Newquay tend to be quick, bland, and costly. For a cheap alternative, head for pubs with dinner specials between 5-7pm or craft a meal at **Somerfield** supermarket, off Fore St. (☎876006. Open M-Sa 8am-11pm, Su 11am-5pm.)

Ye Olde Dolphin, 39-47 Fore St. (☎874262). Newquay's abysmal restaurants count at least one jewel. Meals can get a bit dear here, but take advantage of their 6-8pm specials, including a 3-course meal for £9. Open daily 6-11pm.

Food for Thought, 33b Beachfield Ave. (☎871717), at the corner of Bank St. and Beachfield Ave. A late-night stop for clubbers and surf bums. Grills burgers, stuffs sandwiches, and cultivates salads for £2-3. Open daily 8:30am-1:30am.

Boston's, 28-30 East St. (☎852626). Tasty pizzas from £3, though nothing Beantown about them. Open Su-Th 8:30am-11:30pm, F-Sa 8:30am-1:30am.

The Red Lion, North Quay Hill (☎872195). Transcendent pub grub, with most homemade specials under £6. Food served daily noon-9pm.

BEACHES

After a 3000 mi. trip across the Atlantic, winds descend on **Fistral Beach** with a vengeance, creating what most consider the best surfing conditions in Europe. The shores are less cluttered than the sea, where throngs of wetsuited surfers pile in between the troughs and crests all year. Ominous skies often forecast the liveliest surf, which can tumble from heights of 12 ft. on the best of days. Just in case the waters get too fierce, lifeguards roam the white sands May through September 10am-6pm. On the bay side, **Towan Beach** and **Great Western Beach** are thronged with families, lured by tamer waters. Nearby, enticing **Lusty Glaze Beach** attracts beach-goers of all ages.

🎵 NIGHTLIFE AND ENTERTAINMENT

The party beast stirs at 9pm and reigns uncontested through the wee hours of the morning. The pilgrimage trail of surfer bars begins on North Quay Hill at the corner of Tower Rd. and Fore St. All spots listed below exceed critical density at the end of July and the beginning of August.

The Red Lion, North Quay Hill (☎872195), at Tower Rd. and Fore St. Surfers and a young international crowd jam at this traditional first stop on the clubbing tour.

Sailors, 111-117 Fore St. (☎872838), next to the Red Lion. Sets the pace with 2 levels, 4 bars, 24 video screens, a disco night on Th, and no dearth of tanned flesh. Dress is smarter, but still casual, like everything in Newquay. Cover £4-6 before 11pm, up to £10 on busy nights.

Bertie's, East St. (☎872255). Shake what your momma gave you at this old standby. Commercial tunes and cool crowd. Open M-Sa 9:30pm-2am, Su 7-10pm.

San Francisco Rock Cafe, Grover Ln. (☎878800). Dance what's left of your legs to American classics. Cover around £2. Open M-W 11am-12:30am, Th-Su 11am-1:30am, Su noon-10:30pm.

If surfing and clubbing wear you out, **The Lane Theatre** presents a midsummer night's drama. (☎876945. Book tickets M-W 9:30am-2:30pm. £5-6.) Comedians and musicians also often entertain by the beach.

Mooooore Room.

Real American Airlines deals for students and faculty, online at StudentUniverse. Earn AAdvantage miles and enjoy *more room throughout Coach only on American**.

StudentUniverse.com

featuring
American Airlines

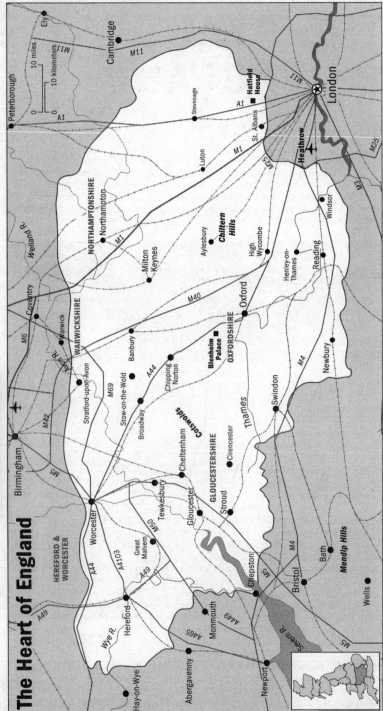

HEART OF ENGLAND

The Heart of England

THE HEART OF ENGLAND

The patchwork pastures and half-timbered houses that characterize the countryside west of London are the stuff that stereotypes are made of. So many of England's heaviest hitters are here: elegant, medieval Oxford, Britain's oldest university town; sweet and tourist-swamped Stratford-upon-Avon, Shakespeare's famous home; and the impossibly picturesque villages of the Cotswolds, scattered among river-riven hills. It takes a wily traveler to avoid the touring hordes in this too-perfect landscape, but whether you're pestered by schoolchildren in a classic cottage garden or inundated by oohs and aahs in front of a charming Tudor facade, you will always know just where you are. England. At the heart of it.

HIGHLIGHTS OF THE HEART OF ENGLAND

OXFORD Bask in eight centuries of brilliance at a university rich in architectural flights-of-fancy and bizarre traditions (p. 253).

WINDSOR Let your jaw drop as you explore one of the world's most divine royal residences (p. 251).

STRATFORD-UPON-AVON Shuffle off to Shakespeare's hometown, where tourist trails honor the Bard's footsteps and the world-renowned Royal Shakespeare Company venerates his every syllable (p. 264).

THAMES VALLEY

ST. ALBANS ☎ 01727

From the Catuvellauni tribe to Julius Caesar, William the Conqueror to the royal houses of York and Lancaster, everyone who was anyone has wanted to set St. Albans on fire or make it their magnificent capital—usually a little of both. The first English Christian martyr, the Roman soldier Alban, was beheaded here for sheltering a priest; his consolation prize was eternal salvation and, better still, having Britain's second most significant Roman town named for him.

◪ TRANSPORTATION. St. Albans has two **train stations;** City Station, the main one, is not to be confused with Abbey Station, which runs a single-schedule local service. **Trains** (☎ (08457) 484950) enter City Station from **London King's Cross** (20min., 4 per hr., £6.90). To get from City Station to the town center turn right out of the station and then right onto Victoria Rd., or avoid the long uphill hike by hopping any "Into Town" bus (60p). **National Express** (☎ (08705) 808080), which arrives from **London** several times per hr. (30-45min., £5.40) and local **Sovereign** (☎ 854732) **buses** usually stop at both City Station and along St. Peter's St.

◪◪ ORIENTATION AND PRACTICAL INFORMATION. Leaving City Station, **Hatfield Rd.** to the left and **Victoria St.** to the right both head uphill to the town center; they are intersected perpendicularly by the main drag, which morphs from **St. Peter's St.** to **Checquer St.** to **Holywell Hill** to **St. Stephen's Hill** as it descends the slope. The columned **tourist information centre** (TIC), Market

Place, St. Peter's St., has a free map and a sights-filled miniguide (25p); they also book accommodations for £1.50 and 10% deposit. (☎864511; fax 863533; www.stalbans.gov.uk. Open Apr.-Oct. M-Sa 9:30am-5:30pm; July-Sept. also Su 10:30am-4pm; Nov.-Mar. M-Sa 10am-4pm.) Other services include: all major **banks** along St. Peter's St.; the **police station,** Victoria St. (☎796000); free **Internet access** at the **library,** The Maltings, near the TIC (☎860000; open M-Sa 9am-5:30pm; call ahead to reserve a slot); and the **post office,** 2 Beaconsfield Rd. (☎860110). **Postal Code:** AL1 3RA.

⚑🏠 ACCOMMODATIONS AND FOOD. Reasonable lodgings, mainly **B&Bs** (around £25), are scattered and often unmarked. The saints at the TIC offer the exhausted traveler a free accommodations guide. By City Station, **Mrs. Murphy,** 478 Hatfield Rd., keeps rooms graced by small touches of luxury. (☎842216. Singles £25; doubles and twins £40-50; family rooms £40-60.) **Mrs. Nicol,** 178 London Rd., the next road over from Victoria St., opens her beautiful, old home to guests, with cable TV to boot. (☎846726. Singles £25; doubles and twins £45.)

Pick from mountains of fresh fruit and veggies at the famous **market** (W and Sa by the TIC); otherwise journey to **Iceland,** Victoria St., for daily staples. (Open M-W 9am-7pm, Th-F 9am-8pm, Sa 8:30am-6pm, Su 10am-4pm.) For lunch, a pint, or pure curiosity's sake, visit **Ye Olde Fighting Cocks,** Abbey Mill Ln., through the double arch by the cathedral. This bizarre octagonal building, with 7th-century foundations, is the oldest pub in England, and among the liveliest. Underground tunnels, used by the monks to flee Henry VIII's thugs at the time of the Dissolution, run from cathedral to pub. (☎865830. Open M-Sa noon-11pm, Su noon-10:30pm.) Flowers tumble into the lazy River Ver and assertive ducks waddle at the **Waffle House,** Kingsbury Watermill, St. Michael's St., toward the Roman quarter. Choose from a host of creative meat-lover, vegetarian, or sweet-tooth toppings for £3.50-5.50. (☎853502. Open summer M-Sa 10am-6pm, Su 11am-6pm; winter M-Sa 10am-5pm, Su 11am-5pm.) St. Albans is home to the **Campaign for Real Ale** (to pay homage, go to Hatfield Rd.), meaning pubs are plentiful and good ale even more so.

◎ SIGHTS. The Saxon-Norman-Gothic-Victorian **⛫Cathedral of St. Alban** is one-of-a-kind. Built on the foundations of a Saxon parish, the 1077 Norman design still dominates. At 300 ft. the medieval nave is the longest in Britain, and the splendid wooden roof one of the largest. The tower ceiling features the white and red roses of the houses of York and Lancaster, allegedly the first time both were depicted together: the ceiling was painted while the outcome of the battle between the two was uncertain, so the abbot, not a betting man, opted for both. Rare Norman murals and other original wall colorings have survived. In defiance of Henry VIII and Cromwell stands the shrine of St. Alban, its fragments at long last reassembled. (☎860780. Open M-Sa 10:30am-5pm, Su 1-5pm. Suggested donation £2.50.)

From the cathedral, follow Fishpool St. over the river and uphill as it becomes St. Michael's St. to visit the **⛫Verulamium Museum.** Homes of the rich and poor of Roman Britain have been painstakingly recreated around mosaics and painted wall plasters discovered in the area. (☎751810. Open M-Sa 10am-5:30pm, Su 2-5:30pm; last admission 5pm. £3.20, concessions £1.85, families £8.05.) Nearby, the remains of one of five **Roman theaters** built in England is unique for its stage. The lucky will catch archaeologists working on further excavations. (☎835035. Open daily 10am-5pm. £1.50, students and seniors £1, children 50p.)

With over 30,000 roses, the **Gardens of the Rose** is the "flagship garden" of the Royal National Rose Society. Roses conquer sweeps of field and scale tall buildings in a single bound. (☎850461. Open June-Sept. M-Sa 9am-5pm, Su 10am-6pm. £4, seniors £3.50, children £1.50, families £10.)

◪ DAYTRIP FROM ST. ALBANS

HATFIELD HOUSE

Bus #S06 connects St. Albans and Hatfield House (20min., 1-3 per hr., return £1.90). Hatfield train station, directly across from the main gate, makes the house easily accessible from destinations other than St. Albans, but not from St. Albans itself. ☎(01707) 262823. House open late Mar. to late Sept. Tu-F 10am-4pm, Sa-Su 1-4:30pm. Grounds open late Mar. to late Sept. Tu-Su 11am-6pm. Excellent free guided tours Tu-F. £6.60, children £3.30. Grounds only £4, children £3. Prices rise for "Connoisseurs Friday," when tours are longer and more gardens are open: £10, grounds only £6.

Built for the Bishop of Ely in 1497, Hatfield was acquired by Henry VIII as a residence for the royal children. Of all the Tudor offspring, however, the house is most associated with Queen Elizabeth I. It was here that the future queen spent much of her turbulent childhood; here that she was placed under house arrest for suspected treason by order of her sister, Queen Mary; here that, while reading in the garden, she received word of Mary's death and thus of her own ascension to the throne; and here that the young queen held her first Council of State. Hatfield still boasts two famous portraits of Elizabeth I, and, though the silk stockings attributed to Elizabeth are fakes, the gloves are real. Keep an eye out for the queen's 22 ft. long family tree, tracing her lineage to Adam and Eve via Noah, Julius Caesar, King Arthur, and King Lear. All that remains of Elizabeth's palace is the Great Hall; the rest was razed to make way for the magnificent mansion that dominates the estate today, which, in a final homage to Elizabeth, was designed in the shape of an 'E' by chief minister to James I and first Earl of Salisbury Sir Robert Cecil.

WINDSOR ☎01753

The town of Windsor and the attached village of Eton are entirely overshadowed by their two bastions of the British class system, Windsor Castle and Eton College. Residential Windsor spread out from the castle in the Middle Ages and is now thick with specialty shops, tea houses, and pubs, all of which wear a certain charm. However, time is far better spent at the stupendous sights nearby.

▤ TRANSPORTATION

Windsor is best seen as a daytrip from London. Two train stations lie near Windsor Castle, and signs point the way into town. **Trains** (☎(08457) 484950) pull into **Windsor and Eton Central** from **London Victoria** and **Paddington** via **Slough** (50min., 2 per hr., day return £6.90). Trains arrive at **Windsor and Eton Riverside** from **London Waterloo** (50min., 2 per hr., day return £6.90). **Green Line** (☎8668 7261) **buses** #700 and 702 arrive at **Central** from London's Eccleston Bridge (1-1½hr., day return £5.50-6.70).

✴◪ ORIENTATION AND PRACTICAL INFORMATION

Windsor village slopes in a crescent from the foot of its castle. **High St.** spans the hilltop, then becomes **Thames St.** at the statue of Queen Victoria and moves downhill to the river; the main shopping area, **Peascod St.**, meets High St. at the statue.

Tourist Information Centre: 24 High St. (☎743900; fax 743904; www.windsor.gov.uk), near Queen Victoria. Sells useful local maps and guides (50p-£1.50) and has a wall of free brochures. Also sells tickets to Legoland (prices below). Books rooms (☎743907; windsor.accomodation@rbwm.gov.uk) for a £3 fee and 10% deposit. Open May-June daily 10am-5pm; July-Aug. M-F 9:30am-6pm, Sa 10am-5:30pm, Su 10am-5pm; Sept. M-Sa 10am-5pm, Su 10am-4pm; Oct.-Apr. Su-F 10am-4pm, Sa 10am-5pm.

Police: Alma Rd. (☎831990). Heading down Peascod St., turn right onto St. Marks Rd.

Internet Access: Central Station (open M-Sa 9:30am-5:30pm); **Tower Records,** on Peascod St. (open M-Sa 10am-5:30pm); and **YHA Windsor** all have slot-machine Internet access stations (£2.50 per 30min., minimum deposit 50p).

🏠🏠 ACCOMMODATIONS AND FOOD

If you intend to spend the night, the cheapest place in town is the **YHA Windsor,** Edgeworth House, Mill Ln., a well-marked 20min. walk from the castle along the Thames. Ringed by lush trees, the YHA has a kitchen, TV lounge, and Internet access. (☎861710; fax 832100. Dorms £11, under 18 £7.50.) The tourist information centre (TIC) locates more expensive **B&B** accommodations for a £3 fee.

Curiously, fast-food joints dominate the downhill end of historic High St. **The Waterman's Arms,** Brocas St., is just over the bridge into Eton, next to the boat house. Founded in 1542, it's still a local favorite. Cod and chips are £4.50, while sandwiches run £2-3. (☎861001. Open M-Sa noon-2:30pm and 6-11pm, Su noon-3pm and 7-10pm.) The tiny **Crooked Tea House** lists decidedly to its right at 52 High St. Splurge on high tea (£7), sample a tea fruit infusion (£1.70), or snack on cakes and sandwiches for under £5. (☎857534. Open M-Sa 10am-5:30pm. MC/V.)

👁 SIGHTS

WINDSOR CASTLE

24hr. info ☎831118. Audio tours (£3.50) and multilingual guidebooks (£4.50) available. Open Apr.-Oct. daily 10am-5:30pm, last entry 4pm; Nov.-Mar. 10am-4pm, last entry 3pm. Allow roughly 2hr. £11, over 60 £9, under 17 £5.50, families £27.50.

The largest and oldest continuously inhabited castle in the world, Windsor features some of the most sumptuous rooms in Europe and some of the rarest artwork in the Western tradition. Built high above the Thames by William the Conqueror in the 1070s and 1080s as a fortress rather than as a residence, 40 reigning monarchs have since left their mark, and the castle has expanded over the course of nine centuries. Windsor is a working castle, and members of the Royal Family often stay here for weekends and special ceremonies. The Queen is officially in residence for the month of April and a week in June; when she visits, the Royal Standard flies over the tower instead of the Union Jack. As a practical consequence of the Royals' residence, large areas of the castle will be unavailable to visitors, usually without warning. The steep admission prices are lowered on these occasions, but it is wise to call before visiting in any case. Visitors can watch the **Changing of the Guard** in front of the Guard Room at 11am (summer M-Sa; winter alternate days M-Sa). The Guards can also be seen at 10:50am and 11:30am as they march to and from the ceremony through the streets of Windsor.

UPPER WARD. The upper ward is reached through the Norman tower and gate (built by Edward III from 1359-60). Stand in the left line to enter the ward (it's worth the wait) to detour past **Queen Mary's Doll House,** an exact replica of a grand home on a 1:12 scale, with tiny classics in its library handwritten by their original authors, as well as fully functioning plumbing and electrical systems. Continue on to the opulent **state apartments,** used for ceremonial events and official entertainment. The rooms are decorated with art from the dense Royal Collection, including works by Holbein, Rubens, Rembrandt, van Dyck, and Queen Victoria herself. The **Queen's Drawing Room** features famous portraits of Henry VIII, Elizabeth I, and Bloody Mary, but don't miss smaller details like the silver dragon doorknobs. A fire on the Queen's anniversary in 1992 destroyed the **Lantern Room,** the **Grand Reception Room,** and the stunning **St. George's Hall,** all fully restored for her 1997 anniversary.

MIDDLE AND LOWER WARD. The middle ward is dominated by the **Round Tower** and its moat-cum-rose-garden. A stroll to the lower ward brings you to **St. George's Chapel,** a 15th-century structure with delicate vaulting and an exquisite wall of stained glass dedicated to the Order of the Garter. Used for the marriage of Sophie and Prince Edward, the chapel is the repository of the bones of Edward's ancestors. Ten sovereigns lie here, including George V, Queen Mary, Edward IV, Charles I, and Henry VI. Henry VIII rests below a remarkably humble stone.

OTHER SIGHTS

ETON COLLEGE. Eton College, founded by Henry VI in 1440 as a college for paupers, is England's preeminent public—which is to say, private—school. The Queen is the sole (honorary) female Old Etonian. Eton boys still wear tailcoats to class and solemnly raise one finger in greeting to any teacher they pass. Despite its position at the apex of the British class system, Eton has shaped some notable dissidents and revolutionaries, including Aldous Huxley, George Orwell, and former Liberal Party leader Jeremy Thorpe. Wander the schoolyard, a central quad where Etonians have gambolled for centuries under the gaze of a statuesque Henry VI. The quad is circled by 25 houses for approximately 1250 students. King's Scholars, students selected for full scholarship based on exam scores, live in the house known as "College," in the courtyard of College Chapel. *(Down Thames St., across Windsor Bridge, and along Eton High St. ☎671177. Tours daily 2:15 and 3:15pm; £4, under 16 £3.10. Open July-Aug. and late Mar. to mid-Apr. daily 10:30am-4:30pm; other months 2-4:30pm; schedule depends on academic calendar. £3, under 16 £2.25.)*

LEGOLAND WINDSOR. A whimsical and expensive addition to the town, this imaginatively landscaped amusement park will wow the 11-and-under set with its rides, playgrounds, and circuses. Adults are wowed in turn by Miniland, which took 100 workers three years and 25 million blocks to craft. The replica of the City of London includes a 6 ft. St. Paul's, as well as every other major city landmark. The Lego buses that motor along the reduced streets without hitting a car or building are a marvel. *(☎(08705) 040404. Open Mar. to mid-July and Sept. to early Nov. daily 10am-5pm or 6pm; mid-July to Aug. 10am-7pm; consult schedule beforehand. £18.50, children £15.50, seniors £12.50. Shuttle from the castle £2.50, children 5-15 £1.25, under 5 free.)*

OXFORD   ☎01865

Oxford has been home to a near-millennium of scholarship—22 British prime ministers and numerous other world leaders have been educated here. A scholarly community formed in the 11th century, but it was in 1167 that Henry II founded the actual university, Britain's first. After a tiff with Thomas à Becket, Henry ordered the return of English students from Paris so that "there may never be wanting a succession of persons duly qualified for the service of God in church and state." Today trucks barrel, bus brakes screech, and bicycles scrape past the pedestrians stuffing the streets. Despite the touring crowds, Oxford has an irrepressible grandeur, and there are pockets of sweet quiet to lift the spirits: the basement room of Blackwell's Bookshop, the impeccable galleries of the Ashmolean, and the perfectly maintained quadrangles of Oxford's 39 colleges.

⌐ TRANSPORTATION

Trains: Botley Rd. (☎794422), down Park End. Ticket office open M-F 6am-8pm, Sa 6:45am-8pm, Su 7:45am-8pm. Trains (☎(08457) 484950) from **London Paddington** (1hr., 2-4 per hr., day return £14.80).

Buses: Bus Station, Gloucester Green. **Stagecoach Express** (☎(01604) 620077) from **Cambridge** (2¾hr.; every hr.; day return £8.75, concessions £6.50). **Stagecoach Oxford** (☎772250) operates the **Oxford Tube** to **London** (1½hr.; 1-6 per hr.; next-day return £7.50, concessions £6.50; return £9.50). **Oxford CityLink** (☎785400) from: **London** (1¾hr.; 1-4 per hr.; next-day return £7.50, concessions £6.50); **Gatwick** (2hr.; every hr. daytime, every 2hr. at night; next-day return £19, children £9.50); **Heathrow** (2 per hr.; day return £12, children £6). **National Express** (☎(08705) 808080) from **London** (1¾hr., 2 per hr., £7) and **Cambridge** (3¼hr., every hr., £8).

Public Transportation: Most local services board around Carfax. The **Oxford Bus Company** (☎785400) and **Stagecoach Oxford** (☎772250) have swift and frequent service. The Oxford Bus Company operates **Park & Ride** and **Cityline.** Cityline buses #4, 4A, 4B, and 4C go down Iffley Rd.; 13A, 13B, and 13C up Marston Rd.; 2A, 2B, 2C, 2D up Banbury Rd.; 16 and 35 down Abingdon Rd.; 5, 5A, and 5F down Cowley Rd. Fares are low (most 70p). Day and week passes available from bus drivers or at the bus station.

Taxis: Radio Taxi (☎242424). **ABC** (☎770681).

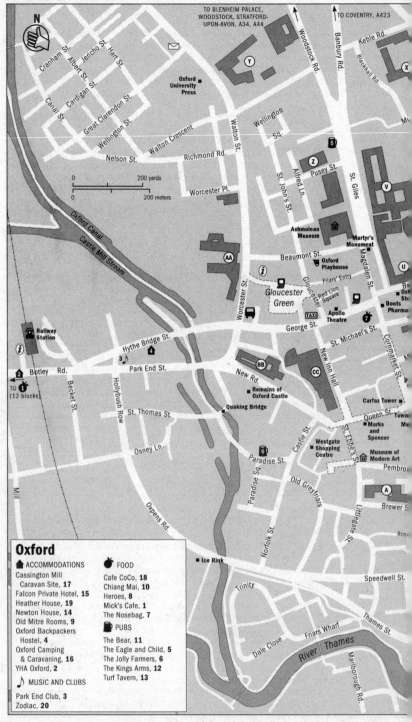

N

TO BLENHEIM PALACE, WOODSTOCK, STRATFORD-UPON-AVON, A34, A44

TO COVENTRY, A423

Keble Rd.

Blackhall Rd.

Woodstock Rd.

Banbury Rd.

Cranham St.

Jericho St.

Hart St.

Albert St.

Cardigan St.

Canal St.

Great Clarendon St.

Wellington St.

Canal St.

Oxford University Press

Walton St.

Wellington Sq.

Walton Crescent

Nelson St.

Walton Crescent

Richmond Rd.

Pusey St.

Alfred Ln.

St. John's St.

St. Giles

Worcester Pl.

Ashmolean Museum

Martyr's Monument

Magdalen St.

Beaumont St.

Oxford Playhouse

Worcester St.

Friars' Entry

Gloucester Green

Red Lion Square

Boots Pharma

George St.

Apollo Theatre

TAXI

St. Michael's St.

Railway Station

Hythe Bridge St.

Park End St.

New Inn Hall

Cornmarket St.

Botley Rd.

Becket St.

New Rd.

Remains of Oxford Castle

Carfax Tower

TO (12 blocks)

Hollybush Row

St. Thomas St.

Quaking Bridge

Castle St.

Queen St.

Marks and Spencer

Town

Osney Ln.

St. Ebbe's St.

Westgate Shopping Centre

Museum of Modern Art

Paradise St.

Paradise Sq.

Old Greyfriars

Pembro

Oxens Rd.

Norfolk St.

Littlegate St.

Brewer S

Mill

Ice Rink

Trinity

River Thames

Thames St.

Speedwell St.

Dale Close

Friars Wharf

Marlborough Rd.

0 200 yards
0 200 meters

Oxford

ACCOMMODATIONS

Cassington Mill
  Caravan Site, **17**
Falcon Private Hotel, **15**
Heather House, **19**
Newton House, **14**
Old Mitre Rooms, **9**
Oxford Backpackers
  Hostel, **4**
Oxford Camping
  & Caravaning, **16**
YHA Oxford, **2**

♪ **MUSIC AND CLUBS**

Park End Club, **3**
Zodiac, **20**

FOOD

Cafe CoCo, **18**
Chiang Mai, **10**
Heroes, **8**
Mick's Cafe, **1**
The Nosebag, **7**

PUBS

The Bear, **11**
The Eagle and Child, **5**
The Jolly Farmers, **6**
The Kings Arms, **12**
Turf Tavern, **13**

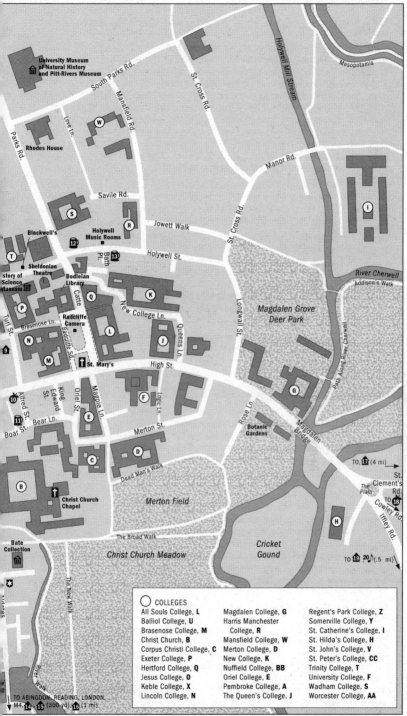

University Museum of Natural History and Pitt-Rivers Museum

South Parks Rd.

Mansfield Rd.

St. Cross Rd.

Love Ln.

Parks Rd.

Rhodes House

Mesopotamia

Holywell Mill Stream

Manor Rd.

Savile Rd.

W

Jowett Walk

St. Cross Rd.

I

S

Holywell Music Rooms

R

Blackwell's

12

13

Holywell St.

Bath Pl.

River Cherwell

Addison's Walk

story of Science Museum

Sheldonian Theatre

Bodleian Library

T

Catte

New College Ln.

K

Q

Magdalen Grove Deer Park

Longwall St.

Path Along River Cherwell

Radcliffe Camera

P

Brasenose Ln.

Turl St.

N

L

M

Radcliffe Sq.

St. Mary's

Queens Ln.

J

High St.

9

Alfred St.

King Edward St.

10

Oriel St.

Magpie Ln.

F

G

11

Bear Ln.

Boar St.

E

Logic Ln.

Merton St.

Rose Ln.

Botanic Gardens

Magdalen Bridge

C

D

Dead Man's Walk

TO **17** (4 mi)

St. Clement's Rd.

B

Christ Church Chapel

Merton Field

The Plain

TO **18**

Cowley Rd.

Iffley Rd.

Bate Collection

The Broad Walk

Christ Church Meadow

Cricket Gound

H

The New Walk

TO **20** (.5 mi)

River

TO ABINGDON, READING, LONDON, M4, **(300 yd)** **(1 mi)**

○ COLLEGES

All Souls College, **L**
Balliol College, **U**
Brasenose College, **M**
Christ Church, **B**
Corpus Christi College, **C**
Exeter College, **P**
Hertford College, **Q**
Jesus College, **O**
Keble College, **X**
Lincoln College, **N**

Magdalen College, **G**
Harris Manchester College, **R**
Mansfield College, **W**
Merton College, **D**
New College, **K**
Nuffield College, **BB**
Oriel College, **E**
Pembroke College, **A**
The Queen's College, **J**

Regent's Park College, **Z**
Somerville College, **Y**
St. Catherine's College, **I**
St. Hilda's College, **H**
St. John's College, **V**
St. Peter's College, **CC**
Trinity College, **T**
University College, **F**
Wadham College, **S**
Worcester College, **AA**

◼◼ ⓘ ORIENTATION AND PRACTICAL INFORMATION

Queen St., High St., St. Aldates, and **Cornmarket St.** meet at right angles at **Carfax,** the town center. Oxford extends some 3 mi. around colossal Carfax Tower, but the colleges are all within a mile of each other, mainly east of Carfax along High St. and Broad St. The bus and train stations and tourist information centre (TIC) are to the northwest. Past the east end of High St. over Magdalen Bridge, East Oxford runs along Cowley Rd. and Iffley Rd. Abingdon Rd. leads to South Oxford, while upscale residences surround Woodstock Rd. and Banbury Rd. to the north.

When on foot, especially near Carfax, enjoy the pedestrian zone; beware, however, that from 6pm to 10am bikes are allowed to intrude. College parks and quads remain sacrosanct. For cyclists, the *Cycle into Oxford* pamphlet, with excellent maps of the city and its hinterland, is free at the TIC.

Tourist Information Centre: The Old School, Gloucester Green (☎726871; fax 240261), beside the bus station. A pamphleteer's paradise. The busy staff books rooms for £2.50 and a refundable 10% deposit. Accommodations list 60p. Valuable street map and guide £1. Open M-Sa 9:30am-5pm; Easter-Oct. also Su 10am-3:30pm.

Tours: A 2hr. **walking tour** on the history of Oxford University leaves daily from the TIC, providing access to some colleges that are otherwise closed to visitors. 2-5 per day, 10:30am-2pm. £5, children £3. **Guide Friday** (☎790522) runs bus tours from the train station. Tours every 15min. 9:30am-6pm. £8.50, students and seniors £7, children £2.50. **The Oxford Classic Tour** (☎(01235) 819393), another bus service, charges less and will hand you earphones in the language of your choice. £7, students and seniors £5, children £2. Both bus tours allow hop-on/hop-off access all day.

Budget Travel: STA Travel, 36 George St. (☎792800). Open M-W and F 9am-5:30pm, Th 10am-5:30pm, Sa 11am-5pm. **UC Campus,** 105 St. Aldates (☎242067). Open M-Tu and Th-F 9am-5:30pm, W 10am-5:30pm, Sa 10am-5pm.

Financial Services: Many banks line Carfax. **Barclays** is on 54 Cornmarket St. Open M-Tu and Th-F 9am-5pm, W 9:30am-5pm, Sa 9:30am-noon. The **Marks and Spencer** offers a **bureau de change** in their upstairs customer service area, no commission. **American Express,** 4 Queen St. (☎207101). Open M-Tu and Th-F 9am-5:30pm, W 9:30am-5:30pm, Sa 9am-5pm, call for Su hours. **Bureau de change** open July-Aug.

Luggage Storage: Pensioners' Club in Gloucester Green (☎242237), by the bus station. Luggage can be left from several hours to several weeks. £1-2 donation requested. Open M-Sa 9am-4:45pm.

Launderette: Clean-o-Fine, North Parade (☎553631). Open daily 7:30am-10pm, last wash 9:30pm. Washer load £2.20-3, soap 20p-£1.

Police: St. Aldates and Speedwell St. (☎266000).

Hospital: John Radcliffe Hospital, Headley Way (☎741166). Bus #13B or 14A.

Internet Access: Internet Exchange, 8-12 George St. (☎241601). Located west of the bus station on George St. 8am-noon 8p per min., noon-7pm 7p per min., 7pm-close 5p per min. Open M-Sa 8am-8pm, Su 10am-7pm. **Pickwick Papers,** 90 Gloucester Green (☎793149). Adjacent to the bus station. £1 per 15min. Open daily 4:30pm-6:30pm.

Post Office: 102-104 St. Aldates (☎202863). Open M-F 9am-5:30pm, Sa 9am-6pm. **Bureau de change. Postal Code:** OX1.

⌂ ACCOMMODATIONS AND CAMPING

Book at least a week ahead from June to September, especially for singles, and be prepared to mail in a deposit or give a credit card number. B&Bs line the main roads out of town and are reachable by Cityline buses (or a 15-45min. walk for the energetic). The 300s on Banbury Rd. stand north of town and are reachable by buses #2A, 2C, and 2D. Cheaper B&Bs lie in the 200s and 300s on Iffley Rd. (bus #4), between 250 and 350 Cowley Rd. (buses #51 or 52), and on Abingdon Rd. in South Oxford (bus #16). Wherever you go, expect to pay £20-25 per person, with singles hitting the £30 mark. If it's late and you're homeless, call the Oxford Association of Hotels and Guest Houses at one of the following numbers: 721561 (East Oxford), 862138 (West Oxford), 554374 (North Oxford), or 244268 (South Oxford).

Oxford Backpackers Hostel, 9a Hythe Bridge St. (☎ 721761). Right between the bus and train stations, this lively independent hostel nurtures the best qualities of backpacker social-life with inexpensive bar, pool table, constant music, and colorful murals. Many of the staff are backpackers themselves and offer advice on mastering the Oxford scene. Linens provided, but no towels. Kitchen, laundry facilities (£2.50), and Internet access (£1.50 per 15min.). Guests must show passport. Dorms £11-12 per night.

YHA Youth Hostel, 2a Botley Rd. (☎ 762997; fax 769402). An immediate right from the train station onto Botley Rd. Superb location and bright surroundings. Generous rooms and facilities include kitchen, laundry, supplies store, and lockers. Most rooms have 4-6 bunks. Breakfast included. Dorms £18, under 18 £13.50, £1 off for students.

Heather House, 192 Iffley Rd. (☎/fax 249757). Walk 20min. or take the bus marked "Rose Hill" from the bus or train stations or Carfax Tower (70p). Vivian, the vibrant proprietress, keeps modern rooms sparkling, and her matchless repository of advice and information will remind you why you love to travel. Singles £30 for 1 night, 2nd night £27; doubles with bath £58 for 1 night, 2nd night £54. Cheaper for longer stays.

Sportsview Guest House, 106-110 Abingdon Rd. (☎244268; stay@sportsview-guest-house.freeserve.co.uk). Mr. and Mrs. Saini have fostered a relaxed environment for 55 years. Across from the Queens College sportsgrounds, the house provides a cheerful, green view. Singles £28-37; doubles £42-62; triples £72-81; family rooms £95.

Falcon Private Hotel, 88-90 Abingdon Rd (☎511122; reservations@thefalconhotel.freeserve.co.uk; www.oxfordcity.co.uk/hotels/falcon). Falcon Hotel is a great place to nest while exploring Oxford. Recently refurbished with an impressive slew of facilities: TV, phone, alarm clock, shower, tea/coffee. Singles £36; twins £56; doubles £58-68.

Old Mitre Rooms, 4b Turl St. (☎279821; fax 279963). Lincoln College dorms with shaggy green carpet. Some Lincoln Quad views. Open July to early Sept. Singles with bath £32; twins £48.50, with bath £53; triples/family rooms with bath £63.50.

Newton House, 82-84 Abingdon Rd. (☎240561), ½mi. from town. Take any Abingdon bus across Folly Bridge. Affable proprietor and dark wardrobes await Narnia fans. All rooms with TV. Singles £48; doubles £54-64, with bath £58; varies with season.

Camping: Oxford Camping and Caravaning, 426 Abingdon Rd. (☎244088, call 8am-8pm), behind the Touchwoods camping store. 84 sites. Toilet and laundry facilities. £4.90-£6.25 per tent. Showers free. 2-night max. stay for nonmembers. **Cassington Mill Caravan Site,** Eynsham Rd., Cassington (☎881081), about 4mi. northwest on the A40. 87 pitches and hot showers. £8 for large tents, £6.50 for small tents.

◖ FOOD

The proprietors of Oxford's swank, bulging eateries know they have a captive market: students fed up with fetid college food are easily seduced by a bevy of budget options. If you're cooking for yourself, the **Covered Market** between Market St. and Carfax has fresh produce, deli goods, breads, and even shoe leather. (Open M-Sa 8am-5:30pm.) Keep an eye out for after-hours **kebab vans** (hummus and chips £1.50), usually at Broad St., High St., Queen St., and St. Aldates.

Across Magdalen Bridge, there are cheap restaurants along the first four blocks of Cowley Rd., from the funky **Hi-Lo Jamaican Eating House,** 70 Cowley Rd. (☎725984), to the Bangladeshi cuisine of **Dhaka,** 186 Cowley Rd. (☎202011), and the authentic Thai savories of **The Pak Fook,** 100 Cowley Rd. (☎247958). Near Somerville College, seek out **Jamal's Tandoori Restaurant,** 108 Walton St. (☎310102).

Cafe CoCo, 23 Cowley Rd. (☎200232). Lively atmosphere and great Mediterranean menu. Try the Merguez (spicy lamb-and-beef sausages with veggies, salad, and tzatziki) for £7.50. Main courses £6-8.50. Open daily 10am-11pm.

The Nosebag, 6-8 St. Michael's St. (☎721033). A different gourmet-grade menu each night, served cafeteria-style in this 15th-century stone building. Good vegetarian selection. Lunch under £6.50, dinner under £8. Open M 9:30am-5:30pm, Tu-Th 9:30am-10pm, F-Sa 9:30am-10:30pm, Su 9:30am-9pm. **The Saddlebag Cafe** downstairs sells sandwiches, salads, and cakes during the day (£3-5.50). Open M-Su 9:30am-5:30pm, sandwiches served until 5pm.

Chiang Mai, 130a High St. (☎202233), tucked down an alley. Broad menu of Thai food in half-timbered surroundings. Adventurous? Try the jungle curry with wild rabbit (£7). Open M-Sa noon-2:30pm and 6-11pm, Su noon-3pm and 6-10pm.

Mick's Cafe, Cripley Rd. (☎728693), off Botley Rd next to the train station. This little diner serves up big breakfasts of bigger value. Various combination platters (choice of eggs, sausage, bacon, beans, toast, and more for £1.60+) and a distinct ambiance (entertaining murals of the owners and employees) make Mick's popular with locals and students. Open M-F 6am-2pm, Sa 7am-1pm, Su 8am-1pm.

Harvey's of Oxford, 58 High St. (☎723152), near Magdalen College. One of Oxford's better takeaways. Cherry-apple flapjacks 85p, mighty sandwiches £1.60-3, and a great variety of coffees. Open M-F 8am-7pm, Sa 8am-6pm, Su 8:30am-6pm.

Heroes, 8 Ship St. (☎723459). Where students dine on sandwiches, freshly baked breads, and a plethora of meat-and-cheese fillings (£1.90-3.65). Best for takeaway, but there's a small eat-in area. Open M-F 8am-9pm, Sa 8:30am-5pm, Su 10am-6pm.

▼ PUBS

Pubs far outnumber colleges in Oxford—some even consider them the city's prime attraction. Most open by noon, begin to fill around 5pm, and close at 11pm (10:30pm on Sundays). Food is sometimes served only during lunch and dinner hours (roughly noon-2pm and 6-8pm). Be ready to pub crawl. Many pubs are so small that a single band of merry students will squeeze out other patrons, while just around the corner, others have several spacious rooms.

▨ Turf Tavern, 4 Bath Pl. (☎243235), off Holywell St. Arguably the most popular student bar in Oxford (they call it "the Turf"), this 13th-century pub is tucked against ruins of the city wall. A maze of rooms and 2 terraces are intimate until the student crowd arrives. Open M-Sa 11am-11pm, Su noon-10:30pm; hot food served in back room noon-8pm.

Duke of Cambridge, 5-6 Little Clarendon St. (☎558173). Oxford's choice cocktail lounge, where patrons pay homage to the rival Dukedom. Sophisticated decor gets lost in the buzz of happy hour bliss. Half off all cocktails daily 5-8:30pm. Open M-F noon-11pm, Sa 10am-11pm, Su 10am-10:30pm.

The Eagle and Child, 49 St. Giles (☎310154). One of Oxford's most historic pubs, this archipelago of paneled alcoves welcomed C.S. Lewis and J.R.R. Tolkien. *The Chronicles of Narnia* and *The Hobbit* were first read aloud here. Settle into a dim niche of your own to observe distinguished dons and students alike. The front has more flavor than the newer back conservatory. Open M-Sa 11am-11pm, Su 11am-10:30pm; food served noon-2:30pm and 5-7:30pm.

The Kings Arms, Holywell St. (☎242369). Oxford's unofficial student union. The coffee room at the front lets quieter folk avoid the merry masses at the back. Open M-Sa 10:30am-11pm, Su 10:30am-10:30pm; coffee bar closes 5:30pm.

The Bear, Alfred St. (☎721783). Over 5000 neckties from famous patrons and Oxford students cover nearly every flat surface of this tiny pub, established in 1242. During the day, the clients are older than the neckwear, and the young sit out back. Open M-Sa noon-11pm, Su noon-10:30pm.

The Jolly Farmers, 20 Paradise St. (☎793759). Take Queen St. from Carfax, turn left on Castle St., then right on Paradise St. One of Oxfordshire's first gay and lesbian pubs, featuring occasional comedy, female impersonators, and male strippers. Crowded with students and twentysomethings, especially on weekends; significantly more sedate in the student-free summer. Open M-Sa noon-11pm, Su 12:30-10:30pm.

OXFORD MADE EASY Oxford undergraduates study for three years, each year consisting of three eight-week terms; more time is spent on holiday than at school. The university itself has no official, central campus. Though central facilities—libraries, laboratories, and faculties—are established and maintained by the university, Oxford's independent colleges, where students live and learn simultaneously (at least in theory), are scattered throughout the city. Students must dress in formal wear called **sub fusc** for all official university events, including exams; carnations are obligatory. At the end of their last academic year, students from all the colleges assemble for degree examinations, a gruelling three-week ordeal that takes place in the Examination Schools on High Street in late June and early July. Each year university authorities do their best to quell the vigorous post-examination celebrations in the street. Each year they fail. The authorities, that is.

SIGHTS

Oxford first earned its name as a place where oxen could ford the Thames, and two of **Oxford University**'s famous sons, Lewis Carroll and C.S. Lewis, later sat near the stone-bridged waters of the Isis (as the Thames is known here) dreaming of crossings through mirrors and wardrobes. The university has also been a breeding ground for England's leaders. Christ Church College alone has produced 13 prime ministers, while St. John's College was home to collegiate rocker Tony Blair.

In summer, hordes of international students arrive for university programs, and the chatter is a thousand-tongued Babel of anything but British English. The TIC sells a map (£1) and the *Welcome to Oxford* guide (£1) that list the colleges' public visiting hours, but even these can be rescinded without explanation or notice. Some colleges also charge admission. Don't bother trying to sneak into Christ Church outside opening hours, even after cleverly hiding your backpack and copy of *Let's Go*: bouncers sporting bowler hats and stationed 50 ft. apart will squint their eyes and kick you out. Other colleges have been known to be less vigilant near the back gates. Coddle the porters or you will get nowhere.

CHRIST CHURCH COLLEGE
Just down St. Aldates St. from Carfax. ☎276492. Open M-Sa 9:30am-5:30pm, Su 11:30am-5:30pm; closed Christmas. Services Su 8, 10, 11:15am, and 6pm; weekdays 7:30am and 6pm. £2.50, concessions £1.50, families £6.

An intimidating pile of stone, "The House" has Oxford's grandest quad and its most socially distinguished students. In June, hush while navigating the narrow strip open to tourists, lest you be rebuked by irritable undergrads prepping for exams. Charles I made Christ Church his capital for three and a half years during the Civil Wars, escaping dressed as a servant when the city was besieged.

CHRIST CHURCH CHAPEL. Also the city's cathedral, it's the smallest in England. In AD 730, Oxford's patron saint, St. Frideswide, built a nunnery on this site in honor of two miracles: the blinding of a troublesome suitor and his subsequent recovery. A stained-glass window (c. 1320) depicts Thomas à Becket kneeling in supplication moments before being gorily dispatched in Canterbury Cathedral. A rather incongruous toilet floats in the background of an 1870 window showing St. Frideswide's death. The Reverend Charles Dodgson (a.k.a. Lewis Carroll) was friendly with Dean Liddell of Christ Church—as well as his daughter, Alice—and visited the family in the gardens of the Dean's house. From the largest tree in the garden (which is private but visible from the cathedral), the Cheshire Cat first grinned; the White Rabbit can be spotted fretting in the stained glass of the hall.

TOM QUAD. The site of undergraduate lily-pond dunking, Tom Quad adjoins the chapel grounds. The quad takes its name from Great Tom, the seven-ton bell in Tom Tower, which has faithfully rung 101 strokes (the original number of students) at 9:05pm (the original undergraduate curfew) every evening since 1682. Sixty coats of arms preside over the ceiling beneath the tower. Nearby, the fanvaulted college hall holds portraits of some of Christ Church's most famous alums—Sir Philip Sidney, William Penn, John Ruskin, John Locke, and a bored-looking W.H. Auden in a corner by the kitchen.

OTHER SIGHTS. Through an archway (to your left as you face the cathedral) lie **Peckwater Quad** and the most elegant Palladian building in Oxford. Look here for faded rowing standings chalked on the walls and for Christ Church's library, closed to visitors. Spreading east and south from the main entrance, **Christ Church Meadow** compensates for Oxford's lack of "backs" (the riverside gardens in Cambridge). A fenced portion of the meadow contains a herd of American longhorn cattle, given by Bill Clinton on a visit to the city.

Housed in the Canterbury Quad, the **Christ Church Picture Gallery** is a swell collection of Italian, Dutch, and Flemish paintings, starring Tintoretto and Vermeer. *(Enter on Oriel Sq. and at Canterbury Gate; visitors to the gallery only should enter through Canterbury Gate off Oriel St. ☎202429. Open Apr.-Sept. M-Sa 10:30am-1pm and 2-5:30pm, Su 2-5:30pm; Oct.-Mar. closes at 4:30pm. £1, students and seniors 50p.)*

OTHER COLLEGES

MERTON COLLEGE. Merton has a fine garden and a library with the first printed Welsh Bible. J.R.R. Tolkien lectured here, inventing the language of Elvish in his spare time. The college's **Mob Quad** is Oxford's oldest and least impressive, dating from the 14th century, but nearby **St. Alban's Quad** has some of the university's best gargoyles. Residents of Crown Prince Narahito's native Japan visit daily to identify the rooms he inhabited in his Merton days. *(Merton St. ☎276310. Open M-F 2-4pm, Sa-Su 10am-4pm. Closed around Easter and Christmas and on some Saturdays. Free.)*

UNIVERSITY COLLEGE. This 1249 soot-blackened college vies with Merton for the title of oldest, claiming Alfred the Great as its founder. Percy Bysshe Shelley was expelled for writing the pamphlet *The Necessity of Atheism* but has since been immortalized in a prominent monument, to the right as you enter. Bill Clinton spent his Rhodes days here; his rooms at 46 Leckford Rd. are a tour guide's endless source of smoked-but-didn't-inhale jokes. *(High St. ☎276619.)*

ORIEL AND CORPUS CHRISTI COLLEGES. Oriel College (a.k.a. "The House of the Blessed Mary the Virgin in Oxford") is wedged between High St. and Merton St. and was once the turf of Sir Walter Raleigh. *(☎276555. Open daily 2-5pm. Free.)* South of Oriel, **Corpus Christi College** surrounds a sundialed quad. The garden wall reveals a gate built for visits between Charles I and his queen, residents at adjacent Christ Church and Merton during the Civil Wars. *(☎276700. Open daily 1:30-4:30pm. Free.)*

ALL SOULS COLLEGE. A graduate college with a prodigious endowment, All Souls is reputed to have the most heavenly wine cellar in Oxford. Candidates who survive the difficult admission exams get invited to dinner, where it is ensured that they are "well-born, well-bred, and only moderately learned." **The Great Quad,** with its fastidious lawn and two spare spires, may be Oxford's most serene. *(Corner of High St. and Catte St. ☎279379. Open M-F 2-4:30pm; closed Aug. Free.)*

QUEEN'S COLLEGE. Around since 1341, Queen's was rebuilt by Wren and Hawksmoor in the 17th and 18th centuries in the distinctive Queen Anne style. A trumpet call summons students to dinner, where a boar's head graces the table at Christmas. The latter tradition supposedly commemorates an early student of the college who, attacked by a boar on the outskirts of Oxford, choked his assailant to death with a volume of Aristotle. Alumni include starry-eyed Edmund Halley and the more earthly Jeremy Bentham. *(High St. ☎279121. Closed to the public, except for those on authorized tours from the TIC.)*

MAGDALEN COLLEGE. With extensive grounds and flower-laced quads, Magdalen (MAUD-lin) is considered Oxford's handsomest college. The college boasts a deer park flanked by the River Cherwell and Addison's Walk, a circular path that touches the river's opposite bank. The college's decadent spiritual patron is alumnus Oscar Wilde. Marking, on the other hand, a personal decline, Edward Gibbon declared the 14 months he spent here "the most idle and unprofitable of my whole career." *(On High St. near the River Cherwell.* ☎ *276000. Open July-Sept. M-F noon-6pm, Sa-Su 2-6pm; Oct.-June 2-5pm. Apr.-Sept. £2, concessions £1; Oct.-Mar. free.)*

TRINITY COLLEGE. Founded in 1555, Trinity has a splendid Baroque chapel with a limewood altarpiece, cedar lattices, and cherubim-spotted pediments. The college's series of eccentric presidents includes Ralph Kettell, who would come to dinner with a pair of scissors and chop anyone's hair that he deemed too long. *(Broad St.* ☎ *279900. Open daily 10:30am-noon and 2-4pm. £2, concessions £1.)*

BALLIOL COLLEGE. Students at Balliol preserve the semblance of tradition by hurling abuse over the wall at their conservative Trinity College rivals. Matthew Arnold, Gerard Manley Hopkins, Aldous Huxley, and Adam Smith were all sons of Balliol's mismatched spires. The interior gates of the college bear scorch marks from the immolations of 16th-century Protestant martyrs (the pyres were built a few yards from the college, where a small cross set into Broad St. rattles cyclists today), and a mulberry tree planted by Elizabeth I still shades slumbering students. *(Broad St.* ☎ *277777. Open daily 2-5pm term only. £1, students and children free.)*

NEW COLLEGE. Founded by William of Wykeham as "late" as 1379, this is one of Oxford's most prestigious colleges. A croquet garden is ringed by part of the old city wall, and every three years the City of Oxford's mayor visits for a ceremonial inspection to ascertain the wall's state of repair. The bell tower has gargoyles of the Seven Deadly Sins on one side, the Seven Virtues on the other, all equally grotesque. A former warden, Rev. William Spooner, is now remembered as the unintentional inventor of "spoonerisms"; he rebuked a student who had "hissed all the mystery lectures" and "tasted the whole worm." *(New College Ln. From Carfax, head down High St. and turn onto Catte St.; New College Ln. is to the right.* ☎ *279555. Open daily Easter-Oct. 11am-5pm; Nov.-Easter 2-4pm, use the Holywell St. Gate. £1.50 in the summer.)*

SOMERVILLE COLLEGE. Somerville is Oxford's most famous once-women's college, with alumnae including Indira Gandhi and Margaret Thatcher, though women were not granted degrees at all until 1920—Cambridge held out until 1948. Today, all of Oxford's colleges are coed except St. Hilda's, which remains women-only. *(Woodstock Rd. From Carfax, head down Cornmarket St. which becomes Magdalen St., St. Giles, and finally Woodstock Rd.* ☎ *270600. Open daily 2-5:30pm. Free.)*

KEBLE COLLEGE. Designed by architect William Butterfield, the college's intricately patterned red brick, known as "The Fair Isle Sweater," was deemed "actively ugly" by architecture guru Sir Nikolaus Pevsner. Through a passageway to the left, the **Hayward** and **deBreyne Buildings** squat on the tarmac like black plexiglass spaceships. *(Corner of Keble and Park St.* ☎ *272727. Open M-Sa 2-5pm. Free.)*

OTHER SIGHTS

▨**ASHMOLEAN MUSEUM.** The grand Ashmolean, the finest classical collection outside London, was Britain's first public museum when it opened in 1683. Familiar favorites include da Vinci, Monet, Manet, van Gogh, Michelangelo, Rodin, and Matisse. Renovated ground-floor galleries also house a previously homeless collection of ancient Islamic, Greek, and Far Eastern artwork. *(Beaumont St. From Carfax, head up Cornmarket St., which becomes Magdalen St.; Beaumont St. is on the left.* ☎ *278000. Open Tu-Sa 10am-5pm, Su 2-5pm. Extended summer hours; call for details. Free.)*

BODLEIAN LIBRARY. Oxford's principal reading and research library has over five million books and 50,000 manuscripts. Sir Thomas Bodley endowed the library's first wing in 1602 on a site that had housed university libraries since 1488. The institution has since grown to fill the immense **Old Library** complex, the round **Radcliffe Camera** next door, and two newer buildings on Broad St. The Bodleian receives a copy of every book printed in Great Britain. Admission to the reading rooms is by ticket only. If you can prove you're a scholar (a student ID may be sufficient, but a letter of introduction from your college is encouraged), present two passport photos, and promise not to light any fires, the Admissions Office will issue a two-day pass for £3. No one has ever been permitted to take out a book, not even Cromwell. Well, especially not Cromwell. *(Catte St. Take High St. and turn left on Catte. ☎ 277224. Library open M-F 9am-6pm, Sa 9am-1pm. Tours leave from the Divinity School, across the street; in summer M-F 4 per day, Sa-Su 2 per day; in winter 2 per day. Tours £3.50.)*

SHELDONIAN THEATRE. This Roman-style auditorium was designed by Christopher Wren while a teenager. Graduation ceremonies, conducted in Latin, take place in the Sheldonian and can be witnessed with permission from one of the "bulldogs" (bowler-hatted university officers). The cupola gives an inspiring view of Oxford's scattered quads. The ivy-crowned stone heads on the fence behind the Sheldonian do not represent emperors: they are a 20th-century study of beards. *(Broad St. ☎ 277299. Open roughly M-Sa 10am-12:30pm and 2-4:30pm. £1.50, children £1.)*

BLACKWELL'S BOOKSTORE. Guinness lists it as the largest four-walled space devoted to bookselling anywhere in the world. The basement room swallows the building and underpins the foundations of Trinity College next door. *(48-50 Broad St. ☎ 792792. Open M and W-Sa 9am-6pm, Tu 9:30am-6pm, Su 11am-5pm.)*

CARFAX TOWER. A hike up this tower's 99 spiral stairs affords a fantastic city vista from the only present-day reminder of medieval St. Martin's Church. *(Corner of Queen St. and Cornmarket St. ☎ 792653. Open Apr.-Oct. daily 10am-5:30pm; Nov.-Mar. 10am-3:30pm. £1.20, under 16 60p.)*

THE BOTANIC GARDEN. Plants have flourished here for three centuries. The path connecting the Botanic Garden to Christ Church Meadow provides a view of the Thames and cricket grounds on the opposite bank. *(From Carfax, head down High St.; the Garden is on the right. Open Apr.-Sept. daily 9am-5pm; Oct.-Mar. 9am-4:30pm. Glasshouses open daily 2-4pm. Late June to early Sept. £2, children free; free the rest of the year.)*

THE MUSEUM OF OXFORD. From hands-on exhibits to the skeleton of a murderer dissected at Christ Church, the museum provides an in-depth, if self-congratulatory, look at Oxford's birth and growth. *(St. Aldates. ☎ 815559. Open Tu-F 10am-4pm, Sa 10am-5pm. £2, students and seniors £1.50, children 50p, families £5; audio tour £1.)*

THE OXFORD STORY. The Oxford Story hauls visitors in medievalized seats through dioramas that recreate Oxford's past. Share the pleasures of a 13th-century student making merry with a wench. It's a bit excessive when you can stay outside and see real stone-ringed quads instead of fiberglass imitations. *(6 Broad St. ☎ 790055. Open July-Aug. daily 9am-6pm; Apr.-June and Sept.-Oct. 9:30am-5pm; Nov.-Mar. M-F 10am-4:30pm, Sa-Su 10am-5pm. Closed Christmas. £5.70, concessions £4.70.)*

BEST OF THE REST. Although the **Museum of Modern Art** has no permanent collection, it hosts solid international traveling shows. *(30 Pembroke St. ☎ 722733. Open Tu-W and F-Su 11am-6pm, Th 11am-9pm. £2.50, students and seniors £1.50, children free. Free for all on W 11am-1pm and Th 6-9pm.)* The **Bate Collection of Historical Instruments** rests in the Faculty of Music. *(St. Aldates St., before Folly Bridge. ☎ 276139. Open M-F 2-5pm. Free.)* The **Museum of the History of Science** holds a radiant collection of sundials and countless clocks. *(Broad St. ☎ 277280. Call for hours. Free.)* Across from Keble College stands the cast-iron-and-glass **University Museum of Natural History.** *(Parks Rd. ☎ 272950. Open daily noon-5pm. Free.)* At the attached **Pitt-Rivers Museum,** behold an eclectic ethnography and natural history collection that includes shrunken heads and rare butterflies. *(☎ 270949. Open M-Sa 1-4:30pm, Su 2-4:30pm. Free.)*

🎵🎭 ENTERTAINMENT AND NIGHTLIFE

Like pubs, public transit in Oxford shuts down sometime after 11pm, but nightlife can last until 3am. Check *This Month in Oxford* (free at the TIC) for upcoming events. *Daily Information*, posted in the TIC, most colleges, and some hostels, provides pointers, and pubs often have their own brochures.

Music: Centuries of tradition give Oxford a quality music scene. Attend a concert or an Evensong service at a college—**New College Choir** is one of the best boy choirs around—or a performance at the **Holywell Music Rooms** (on Holywell St.), the oldest in the country. The **City of Oxford Orchestra** (☎744457), the professional symphony orchestra, plays a subscription series at the Sheldonian and in college chapels during summer. Concerts once a month; tickets £10-15, 25% student discount. The **Apollo Theatre**, George St. (☎(08706) 063500), presents a wide range of performances, from lounge-lizard jazz to the Welsh National Opera, which visits in late Mar., late June, and Oct. Open M-Sa 10am-6pm on non-performance days, until 8pm on show days. Tickets from £10; discounts for students and seniors.

Theaters: The **Oxford Playhouse,** 11-12 Beaumont St. (☎798600), hosts bands, dance troupes, and the Oxford Stage Company. Tickets from £6; standby tickets for seniors (matinees only) and students (any show time) on day of show with cash. The **Oxford Union**, St. Michael's St. (☎778119), puts up solid theater productions. Tickets £8, concessions £5. The university itself offers marvelous entertainment; college theatre groups often stage productions in gardens or cloisters.

Clubs and Cafe-bars: Head up **Walton St.** or down **Cowley Rd.**, the most self-indulgent of Oxford's neighborhoods—both areas provide late-night clubs and a jumble of ethnic restaurants, exotic shops, and used bookstores. The **Zodiac,** 193 Cowley Rd. (☎726336), has crazy themes nightly and the best live gigs around for a cover of £5 and up. Headliners have included Rage Against the Machine and Dido. **Freud's,** 119 Walton St. (☎311171), in the former St. Paul's Parish Church (stained-glass windows included), is a cafe by day and club by night. Open M-Tu until 11pm, W-Th 1am, F-Sa 2am, Su 10:30pm. The bartenders at **Thirst,** Park End St. (☎242044), dazzle their parched patrons with enough cocktail magic to put Tom Cruise to shame. Open M-Sa 5pm-1am. Across from Thirst, **Park End** is a flashy favorite of students and locals that cranks out commercial techno and house. Smart clubwear, please. Cover £2-5.

Punting and Cruises: A traditional pastime in Oxford is **punting** on the River Thames (known in Oxford as the Isis) or on the River Cherwell (CHAR-wul). Before venturing out, punters receive a tall pole, a small oar, and an advisory against falling into the river. Our own set of advisories: avoid creating an obstacle course for irate rowers; don't jump into one of the canals, as you could wind up with a tetanus shot and stitches; and don't be surprised if you come upon **Parson's Pleasure,** a small riverside area where men sometimes sunbathe nude. **Magdalen Bridge Boat Co.,** Magdalen Bridge (☎202643), east of Carfax along High St., rents M-F £9 per hr., Sa-Su £10 per hr. Deposit £20 plus ID. Open Mar.-Nov. daily 10am-9pm.

Festivals: The university celebrates **Eights Week** at the end of May, when all the colleges enter crews in bumping races and beautiful people sip champagne on the banks. In early September, **St. Giles Fair** invades one of Oxford's main streets with an old-fashioned carnival, complete with Victorian roundabout and whirligigs. Daybreak on **May Day** (May 1) cues one of Oxford's sweetest moments: the Magdalen College Choir sings madrigals from the top of the tower, and the town indulges in morris dancing, beating the bounds, and other age-old rituals of merrymaking—pubs open at 7am.

🏛 DAYTRIP FROM OXFORD: BLENHEIM PALACE

In the town of Woodstock, 8 mi. north of Oxford on the A44. Stagecoach Express (☎(01865) 772250) runs to Blenheim Palace from Gloucester Green bus station (20min., return £3.50). ☎(01993) 811091. House open mid-Mar. to Oct. daily 10:30am-5:30pm. Grounds open year-round 9am-9pm. Last admission 4:45pm. £9, students and seniors £7, children £4.50.

The largest private home in England (and one of the loveliest), Blenheim Palace (BLEN-em) was built in honor of the Duke of Marlborough's victory over Louis XIV at the Battle of Blenheim in 1704 and as a token of Queen Anne's friendship with the Duke's wife, Sarah. The 11th Duke of Marlborough now calls the palace home. His rent is a single French franc, payable each year to the Crown—not a bad deal for 187 furnished rooms. High archways and marble floors accentuate the pleasing artwork inside, including wall-size tapestries of 17th- and 18th-century battle scenes. **Winston Churchill,** a member of the Marlborough family, spent his early years here before being packed off to boarding school, and his baby curls are still on view. 2100 glorious acres circumscribe fantastic gardens, roaming goats, and a lake, all designed by landscaper **"Capability" Brown** (well, except the goats—he wasn't *that* capable). Blenheim is on display in Kenneth Branagh's 4hr. film of *Hamlet* (1996); less recently, Geoffrey Chaucer lived in neighboring Woodstock, and Winston Churchill rests in the nearby village churchyard of **Bladon.**

THE WESTERN HEART

STRATFORD-UPON-AVON ☎01789

> The remarkable thing about Shakespeare is that he is really very good—in spite of all the people who say he is very good.
> —Robert Graves, British poet and novelist

Shakespeare lived here. This fluke of fate has made Stratford-upon-Avon a town more visited than most. Knickknack huts hawk "Will Power" T-shirts, and proprietors tout the dozen-odd properties linked, however tenuously, to the Bard and his extended family. Though all the perfumes of Arabia may not sweeten the exhaust from tour buses, behind their sound and fury there still survives Stratford-besides-Shakespeare, worthwhile in its own right for the grace of the weeping Avon and for the pin-drop of silence before a soliloquy in the Royal Shakespeare Theatre.

■ JOURNEY'S END

Trains: Station Rd., off Alcester Rd. Ticket office open M-Sa 6am-10:55pm, Su 9:45am-6:30pm. **Thames Trains** (☎(08457) 484950) from: **London Paddington** (2¼hr., 7-10 per day, return £22.50); **Warwick** (25min., £2.60); **Birmingham** (1hr., £3.60).

Buses: Riverside Car Park, off Bridgeway Rd. near the Leisure Centre, receives **National Express** (☎(08705) 808080) buses from **London** (3hr., 3-4 per day, £11). Buy National Express tickets at the tourist information centre (TIC). **Stagecoach** runs buses into Gloucester Green Station from **Oxford** (day return £5.25).

Public Transportation: Local **Stratford Blue** bus services stop on Wood St.

Taxis: Main Taxis (☎415111) or **Taxiline** (☎266100). Both 24hr.

Bike Rental: Clarke's Cycle Rental (☎205057), the corner of Guild St. and Union St. £10 per day, £40 per week. Deposit £75 or credit card. Open M-Sa 9am-5pm.

Boat Rental: Stratford Marina, Clopton Bridge (☎269669). Rowboats £5 per hr.; 6-seater motorboats £7 per 30min. **Behind the RST.** Rowboats £6 per hr.

☎ HERE CEASE MORE QUESTIONS

Tourist Information Centre: Bridgefoot (☎293127, bed booking hotline 415061). Maps, guidebooks, tickets, and accommodations list. Books rooms for £3 and 10% deposit. Open Apr.-Oct. M-Sa 9am-6pm, Su 11am-5pm; Nov.-Mar. M-Sa 9am-5pm.

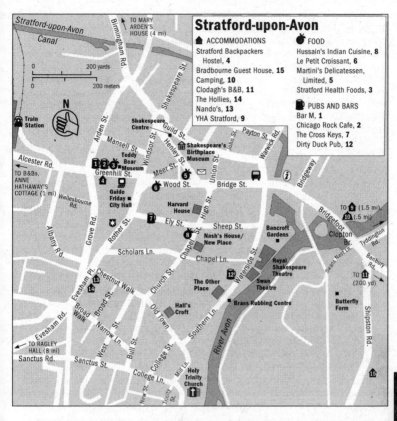

Stratford-upon-Avon

🏠 ACCOMMODATIONS
Stratford Backpackers
 Hostel, **4**
Bradbourne Guest House, **15**
Camping, **10**
Clodagh's B&B, **11**
The Hollies, **14**
Nando's, **13**
YHA Stratford, **9**

🍴 FOOD
Hussain's Indian Cuisine, **8**
Le Petit Croissant, **6**
Martini's Delicatessen,
 Limited, **5**
Stratford Health Foods, **3**

🍺 PUBS AND BARS
Bar M, **1**
Chicago Rock Cafe, **2**
The Cross Keys, **7**
Dirty Duck Pub, **12**

Tours: Guide Friday, Civic Hall, 14 Rother St. (☎294466). Transport to all Shakespeare-related houses. 4-5 tours per hr. depart daily from shrines around town. £9, students and seniors £7, children £5. They also go to the **Cotswolds** (£17.50, students and seniors £15, children £8) and **Warwick Castle** (£17.50, £15, £8; castle admission included). Office open daily 9am-5:30pm.

American Express: (☎415856; fax 262411), in the TIC. Open same hours.

Launderette: Sparklean (☎269075), the corner of Bull St. and College Ln. Near B&Bs. Bring change. Wash £2.50, dry 20p per 4min. Open daily 8am-9pm, last wash 8pm.

Police: Rother St. (☎414111).

Hospital: Stratford-upon-Avon Hospital, Arden St. (☎205831), off Alcester Rd.

Internet Access: Java Cafe, 28 Greenhill St. (☎263400). £3 per 30min., £5 per hr.; students and seniors £2.50 and £4. Also cheap international phone calls. Open M and W 10am-5:30pm, Tu 11am-5:30pm, Th 10am-6pm, F 10am-7pm, Sa 11am-6pm.

Post Office: 2-3 Henley St. (☎414939). **Bureau de change.** Open M-F 8:30am-5:30pm, Sa 8:30am-6pm; June-Aug. also Su 10am-3pm. **Postal Code:** CV37 6PU.

🔪 TO SLEEP, PERCHANCE TO DREAM

To B&B or not to B&B? This hamlet has tons of them, but singles are hard to find. B&Bs in the £15-26 range line **Grove Rd., Evesham Pl.,** and **Evesham Rd.** Or try **Shipston Rd.** and **Banbury Rd.** across the river, a 15-20min. walk from the station.

OFF YER ROCKER 1999 marked the passing of David Sutch, founder of one of Britain's more dynamic political parties, the **Official Monster Raving Loony Party (OMRLP).** Screaming Lord Sutch, as David Sutch was known, began his political career as the National Teenage Party's candidate for Stratford-upon-Avon. After brief membership in both the Young Ideas Party and the Go to Blazes Party, Sutch founded the OMRLP in 1980. Although initially dismissed as a "Shakespearean antic for the TV age," the OMRLP enjoyed surprising success in the 1990 by-election, beating the Social Democrats in one constituency.

The Loonies will fight on, despite the death of their leader—Alan "Howling Lord" Hope fought for a seat in parliament in a 1999 by-election, while Baron von Thunderclap, previously the party's spokesman for transport/saving the dodo/decimal time, has assumed temporary leadership. Meanwhile, 13-year-old Oliver Hewitt has been asked to become the junior party chairman after chaining himself to the railings of Downing St., protesting that children should not be made to study algebra. Hewitt is being groomed to take over party leadership in 2010.

Stratford Backpackers Hostel, 33 Greenhill St. (☎/fax 263838). 3-story hostel for sociable Shakespearean pilgrims, near restaurants, pubs, and the Bard's birthplace. Lounge, pool table, TV room, kitchen, and storage. Photo ID required. Dorms £12 first night, additional nights £11; £1 off if you come from the Oxford Backpackers Hotel.

YHA Stratford, Hemmingford House, Wellesbourne Rd., Alveston (☎297093; stratford@yha.org.uk), 2 mi. from Stratford. Follow the B4086 35min. from the town center, or take bus #X18 from the Bridge St. stop (every hr., £1.70). Large, attractive grounds and a 200-year-old building with RSC photos. Friendly staff offers Shakespearean wisdom and full English breakfasts. With return bus fare, this may cost as much as some B&Bs. 130 beds. Kitchen and Internet access (£2.50 per 30min.). Reception 24hr., but midnight lockout. B&B style £15.50, under 18 £11.50; dinner £5 extra.

Clodagh's B&B, 34 Banbury Rd. (☎269714; clodagh@lycosmail.com). Amazing value. Once Clodagh takes you into her home, you'll be tempted to stay longer than planned. Superb showers and Internet access. Singles £16.50; doubles £33.

Bradbourne Guest House, 44 Shipston Rd. (☎204178), 8min. walk from the center. Recently redecorated Tudor-style home with a pleasant conservatory. Breakfast includes veggie dishes. Cable TV in every room. Singles £30; doubles £50. Rates lower Oct.-Apr.

The Hollies, 16 Evesham Pl. (☎266857). From mint walls to creeping ivy, green prevails. Hosted by a warm and attentive proprietor for whom the guest house is a labor of love. Spacious and well decorated. Doubles £35, with bath £45.

Nando's, 18 Evesham Pl. (☎/fax 204907). Friendly owners. Comfortable rooms all have TVs; most have private bathrooms. Singles £22; doubles £48. Rates lower in winter.

Camping: Riverside Caravan Park, Tiddington Rd. (☎292312), 30min. from town center, 1 mi. east of Stratford on the B4086. Sunset views on the Avon, but often crowded. Village pub is a 3-4min. walk. Showers. Open Easter-Oct. Tent and 2 people £7, each additional person £1.

◖ FOOD OF LOVE

Baguette stores and bakeries are scattered like itinerant minstrels, while a **Safeway** supermarket beckons on Alcester Rd., just across the bridge past the train station. (Open M-Th and Sa 8am-9pm, F 8am-10pm, Su 10am-4pm.) A **market** convenes at the intersection of Rother St. and Wood St. (Open F 8:30am-4:30pm.)

De:alto, 13 Waterside (☎298326). A trendy anachronism in this historical town, De:alto's decor will make the chic New Yorker in you feel at home. Pizza £5.60-6, salad £5.60-7, calzones £6.15. Open M-Th noon-10pm, F-Sa noon-11pm, Su 2-9:30pm.

Hussain's Indian Cuisine, 6a Chapel St. (☎267506). Stratford's best Indian cuisine, with a slew of tandoori prepared as you like it. A favorite of Ben Kingsley. The chicken tikka masala is fabulous. 3-course lunch £6. Main courses £6.50 and up. 15% discount for takeaway. Open Th-Su 12:30-2:30pm and daily 5pm-midnight.

Martini's Delicatessen Limited, 3A The Minories (☎414474). In a corner of the Minories shopping center, Martini's whips up gourmet pizza slices (£1.60), salads, pastas, and sandwiches (from £2.20). Takeaway with limited seating outdoors.

Le Petit Croissant, 17 Wood St. (☎292333). A great place for breakfast or lunch, with delicious baked treats such as tarts, baguettes, and quiches (from 80p). Sandwiches are sold in back (from £3). Open M-Sa 8am-6pm.

Stratford Health Foods, 10 Greenhill St. (☎292353). The "Whole Food Takeaway" includes sausage rolls (45p), veggie samosas (57p), and "healthy" desserts like freshly baked chocolate brownies (50p). Open M and W-Sa 9am-5:30pm, Tu 9:30am-5:30pm.

▨ DRINK DEEP ERE YOU DEPART

▨ **Dirty Duck Pub,** Waterside (☎297312). Originally called "The Black Swan," the pub was rechristened by alliterative Americans during WWII. River view outside, huge bust of Shakespeare within. Theater crowds abound, and the actors themselves make frequent entrances. Pub lunch £3-9; dinner £6-20. Open M-Sa 11am-11pm, Su noon-10:30pm.

Bar M, 1 Arden St. (☎297641). A pub by day; the silvered staircase leads to a clubby dance area at night. Various promotions, such as £1 drinks with £5 cover on weekends. Open M and Th noon-1am, Tu-W noon-midnight, F-Sa noon-2am, Su noon-10:30pm.

The Cross Keys, Ely St. (☎293909). Always lively. The patio has a giant sports-tuned TV. Open M-Sa 11am-11pm, Su 11am-10:30pm; food served noon-3pm and 5-8pm.

Chicago Rock Cafe, 8 Greenhill St. (☎293344). A modern bar popular with locals. Specials most nights: M 2-for-1 drinks, Tu karaoke, W live bands, Th half-price cocktails, F-Sa party. Open M-Th 11:30am-11:30pm, F-Sa 11:30am-12:30am, Su noon-10:30pm.

◉ THE GILDED MONUMENTS

TO BE
Stratford's Will-centered sights are best seen before 11am, when the daytrippers arrive, or after 4pm, when the hurly-burly's done. Bardolatry peaks at 2pm. The five official **Shakespeare properties** are Shakespeare's Birthplace, Hall's Croft, Nash's House and New Place, Anne Hathaway's Cottage, and Mary Arden's House. Diehard fans should buy the **combination ticket.** (☎204016. £12, students and seniors £11, children £6.) If you don't want to visit every shrine (dark-timbered roof beams start to look the same no matter who lived under them), buy a **Shakespeare's Town Heritage Trail** ticket, which covers the Birthplace, Hall's Croft, and Nash's House and New Place (£8.50, students and seniors £7.50, children £4.20).

SHAKESPEARE'S BIRTHPLACE. The only sight in town directly associated with the Bard includes an exhibit on the glove-making career of Will's father, aside from the requisite period re-creation and life-and-works celebration. Join such distinguished pilgrims as Charles Dickens by signing the guestbook. *(Henley St. ☎204016. Open Mar. 20-Oct. 19 M-Sa 9am-5pm, Su 9:30am-5pm; Oct. 20-Mar. 19 M-Sa 9:30am-4pm, Su 10am-4pm. £6, students and seniors £5.50, children £2.50, families £15.)*

HALL'S CROFT. Dr. John Hall married Shakespeare's oldest daughter Susanna. He also garnered fame in his own right as one of the first doctors to keep detailed records of his patients. The Croft features an exhibit on Hall and medicine in Shakespeare's time—frogs were a frequent prescription. *(Old Town. Open Mar. 20-Oct. 19 M-Sa 9:30am-5pm, Su 10am-5pm; Oct. 20-Mar. 19 M-Sa 10am-4pm, Su 10:30am-4pm. £3.50, students and seniors £3, children £1.70, families £8.50.)*

NASH'S HOUSE AND NEW PLACE. Tenuous Shakespeare Connection Alert: Thomas Nash was the first husband of Shakespeare's granddaughter Elizabeth, the last of the playwright's descendants. Nash's House holds a local history collection. The adjacent **New Place** was Stratford's hippest home when Shakespeare bought it in 1597 after writing some hits in London. Only the foundations remain after a disgruntled 19th-century owner razed the building when excessive tourism drove him over the edge. Admission to Nash's House allows you to view the plot and remains of New Place. *(Chapel St. Open Mar. 20-Oct. 19 M-Sa 9:30am-5pm, Su 10am-5pm; Oct. 20-Mar. 19 M-Sa 10am-4pm, Su 10:30am-4pm. £3.50, students and seniors £3, children £1.70, families £8.50.)* Down Chapel St. from Nash's House, the sculpted bushes, manicured lawn, and abundant flowers of the **Great Garden of New Place** offer a peaceful retreat from Stratford's mobbed streets. *(Open M-Sa 9am-dusk, Su 10am-dusk. Free.)*

SHAKESPEARE'S GRAVE. The least crowded way to pay homage to the institution himself is to visit his little, little grave in **Holy Trinity Church,** though groups still pack the arched door at peak hours. Beware the epitaph's curse: a 17th-century tradition holds that Shakespeare wrote it himself. The church also harbors the graves of his wife and his daughter Susanna. *(Trinity St. £1, students and children 50p.)*

AROUND THE ROYAL SHAKESPEARE THEATRE. In the free **Royal Shakespeare Theatre Gardens,** south of the theater, the **RST Summer House** runs a **brass-rubbing studio,** an alternative to plastic Shakespeare memorabilia. Watching the serene rowers between the RST and Clopton Bridge, you'd never guess that about six million buses rumble behind you. *(☎ 297671. Open Apr.-Sept. daily 10am-6pm; Oct.-Mar. 11am-4pm. Prices of rubbing plates 95p-£4 and higher; materials included.)*

ANNE HATHAWAY'S COTTAGE. The birthplace of Shakespeare's wife lies about 1 mi. from Stratford in **Shottery;** take the ill-marked footpaths north. This is probably the fairy-tale, thatched-roof cottage you saw on the travel agent's poster. Entrance entitles you to sit on a bench Will may or may not have also sat on. View from outside if you've seen the birthplace. *(☎ 292100. Open Mar.-Oct. daily 9am-5pm; Nov.-Feb. 9:30am-4:30pm. £4.50, students and seniors £4, children £2.)*

MARY ARDEN'S HOUSE. This farmhouse, restored in the style a 19th-century entrepreneur determined to be that of Shakespeare's mother, is 4 mi. from Stratford in Wilmcote. A brief history recounts how Mary Arden abandoned a sheepshearing fortune to marry Shakespeare's dad. *(Connected by footpath to Anne Hathaway's Cottage. ☎ 293455. Open Mar.-Oct. M-Sa 9:30am-5pm, Su 10am-5pm; Nov.-Feb. M-Sa 10am-4pm, Su 10:30am-4pm. £5.50, students and seniors £5, children £2.50, families £13.50.)*

NOT TO BE

If you're bored of the Bard, fear not—non-Shakespearean sights *are* available (if not particularly exciting) in Stratford.

TEDDY BEAR MUSEUM. The museum boasts thousands of stuffed, ceramic, and painted bears. Though most went to children in Yugoslavia, 12 of the "Diana bears" (left in front of Kensington Palace), rest near the original Fozzie Bear, who was given by Jim Henson and now waves goodbye. *(Exit, pursued by a bear. 19 Greenhill St. ☎ 293160. Open daily 9:30am-6pm. £2.25, students and seniors £1.75, children £1.)*

HARVARD HOUSE. Period pieces and pewter punctuate this authentic Tudor building, vaguely connected with the man who lends his name to the American college that owns it (his mother lived here). The "Harvard-only" guestbook contains the names of such notables as Morgan Rodman. *(High St. ☎ 204507. Open May-Sept. M-Sa 10am-4:30pm, Su 10:30am-4:30pm. Free.)*

STRATFORD-UPON-AVON BUTTERFLY FARM. Swarms of butterflies (and some less appealing insects and arachnids) flutter through tropicalized surroundings, while swarms of schoolchildren colonize the museum shop next door. *(Off Swan's Nest Ln. at Tramway Walk, across the river from the TIC. ☎ 299288. Open in summer daily 10am-6pm; winter 10am-dusk. £3.75, students and seniors £3.25, children £2.75.)*

RAGLEY HALL. Eight miles from Stratford on Evesham Rd. (the A435), Ragley Hall houses the Earl and Countess of Yarmouth. Set in a stunning 400-acre park, the estate holds a collection of paintings and a captivating maze. *(Take a bus to Alcester (M-Sa 5 per day), walk 1 mi. to the gates, then ½ mi. up the drive. ☎ 762090. Open July-Aug. daily 11am-5pm; Apr.-Oct. Th-Su 11am-5pm. £5, students and seniors £4.50, children £3.50.)*

🎵 THE PLAY'S THE THING

THE ROYAL SHAKESPEARE COMPANY
The box office in the foyer of the Royal Shakespeare Theatre handles ticketing for all three theaters. ☎ 403403, 24hr. recording ☎ 403404; www.rsc.org.uk. Open M-Sa 9am-8pm. Tickets for RST £5-40; Swan £5-36; Other Place £10-20. RST and Swan have £5 standing room tickets; under 25 get half-price same-day tickets; and £8-12 student and senior same-day standbys exist in principle—be ready to pounce.

One of the world's most acclaimed repertories, the Royal Shakespeare Company sells well over one million tickets each year, and claims Kenneth Branagh and Ralph Fiennes as recent sons. In Stratford, it performs in three theaters: the Royal Shakespeare, the Swan, and The Other Place. A group gathers outside about 20min. before opening for same-day sales (matinee tickets are easier to secure). A happy few get customer returns and standing-room tickets for evening shows; queue 1-2hr. before curtain. **Disabled travelers** should call in advance to advise the box office of their needs; some performances feature sign language interpretation or audio description. The RSC conducts **backstage tours** that cram groups into the wooden "O"s of the RST and the Swan. *(☎ 412602. Tours daily 1:30 and 5:30pm, and after performances. £4, students and seniors £3.)*

Royal Shakespeare Theatre, Waterside, across from Chapel Ln. He was born on Henley St., died at New Place, and lives on at the RST, which towers over slanting willows on Waterside. The boards of the RST are graced only by the great man's plays: lesser playwrights are relegated to the other stages.

The Swan Theatre, Waterside, across from Chapel Ln. The RSC took the shell of burnt-out Memorial Theatre and renovated it as Shakespeare's Globe for productions of Renaissance and Restoration plays. Smaller and more intimate than the RST.

The Other Place, on Southern Ln. The RSC's newest branch produces avant-garde premieres, and modern, rarely performed plays in an experimental black-box theater.

FESTIVALS
Astonishingly, for two weeks in July the **Stratford Festival** celebrates artistic achievement other than Shakespeare's, from music to poetry. Tickets (when required) can be purchased from the Festival box office on Rother St. (☎ 414513). The modern, well-respected **Shakespeare Centre,** Henley St., hosts an annual **Poetry Festival** every Sunday evening in July and August. Over the past few years, Seamus Heaney, Ted Hughes, and Derek Walcott have put in appearances. (☎ 204016. Open M-F 9am-5pm. Tickets £7.) The center also has a library and a bookshop.

WORCESTER ☎ 01905

Worcester (WOO-ster) sits over the Severn between Cheltenham and Birmingham, but lacks the former's gentility and the latter's pace. The city's name (pop. 95,000) has been made famous by Worcestershire sauce and Worcester porcelain, and the city itself was the site of the Civil Wars' final battle and birthplace of the composer Elgar. But, beyond the beautiful cathedral, Worcester's sights are lackluster.

🚋 TRANSPORTATION

The city's main **train station** sits at the edge of the town center on Foregate St. (Ticket window open M-Sa 6am-11:20pm, Su 6:30am-11:05pm. Travel center open M-Sa 9am-4pm.) Trains also pull into the **Shrub Hill Station** (mainly serving the

HEART OF ENGLAND

southwest) just outside town. To get to town from Shrub Hill (a 15min. walk), turn right onto Shrub Hill Rd., then left onto Tolladine Rd., which becomes Lowesmoor; follow Lowesmoor to St. Nicholas St., which intersects The Foregate, the town's main drag. (Ticket window open M-Sa 5:30am-7pm, Su 7am-7pm. Travel center open M-Sa 9am-4pm.) **Trains** (☎(08457) 484950) travel to Worcester from: **London** (2½hr.; every hr.; £22.80, return £38.90); **Birmingham** (2 per hr. 9am-6pm, day return £5.40); **Cheltenham** (30min., every 2hr., £5.50).

The **bus station** is at Angel Pl. near the Crowngate Shopping Centre. **National Express** (☎(08705) 808080) **buses** run from: **London Paddington** (4hr., 1 per day, £14.50); **Birmingham** (1hr.; every hr.; £3, return £3.50); **Bristol** (1½hr.; 2 per day; £8.10, return £10). **Midland Red West** (☎763888) is the regional bus company; their **Day Rover** allows unlimited one-day travel within Worcestershire (£4.60, seniors £3.60, children £3.10, families £9.20). **Associated Radio Taxis** is at ☎763939. **Peddlers,** 46-48 Barbourne Rd., rents **bikes.** (☎24238. £8 per day, £30 per week; mountain bikes £15, £60. Deposit £50. Open M-Sa 9:30am-5:45pm, Su 9:30am-4:30pm.)

■ ↗ ORIENTATION AND PRACTICAL INFORMATION

The city center is bounded by the train station to the north and the cathedral to the south. A fickle street runs between the two, switching names along the way from **Barbourne Rd.** to **The Tything** to **Foregate St.** to **The Foregate** to **The Cross** to **High St.** To reach the tourist information centre (TIC) from the train station, turn left onto **Foregate St.** From the bus station, turn left onto **Broad St.** and right onto **The Cross.**

The helpful **tourist information centre,** The Guildhall, High St., sells the *Worcester Visitor* guide for 75p and books beds for a 10% deposit. (☎726311; fax 722481. Open M-Sa 10am-5:30pm.) 1½hr. **tours** leave from the TIC. (May-Sept. W 11am and 2:30pm. £3, children £1.50.) Other services include: **Barclays,** 54 High St. (☎684828; open M-Tu and Th-F 9am-5pm, W 9:30am-5pm, Sa 9:30am-12:30pm); **Severn Laun-Dri,** 22 Barbourne Rd. (wash £2-3, dry from £1; open daily 9am-8pm, last wash 7pm); the **police,** Deansway (☎(08457) 444888), behind the Guildhall, across from St. Andrew's Park; **Ronkswood Hospital,** Newtown Rd. (☎763333; take bus #29D and #31A); and the **post office,** 8-10 Foregate St., next to the train station, with a **bureau de change** (☎(08457) 223344; open M-Sa 9am-5:30pm). **Postal code:** WR1.

♠ ACCOMMODATIONS AND CAMPING

B&B prices in Worcester are high, as proprietors cater to businessmen or to Londoners looking for a weekend in the country. Try your luck on **Barbourne Rd.,** the fifth manifestation of High St., about a 15-20min. walk from the city center. The nearest **YHA Youth Hostel** is 7 mi. away in the town of Malvern, 12min. by train (see p. 271). **Osbourne House,** 17 Chestnut Walk, has TVs and electronic, touch-operated showers in every bedroom, three types of cookies on your nightstand, and brilliant marmalade. (☎/fax 22296. Doubles £40, with bath £45; available to singles for £24.) Monty Python fans will appreciate the name of the **Shrubbery Guest House,** 38 Barbourne Rd. Everyone else will appreciate the expert way Mrs. Law makes guests feel at home. (☎24871; fax 23620. TVs. Singles £20; doubles £40, with bath £45.) Riverside **Ketch Caravan Park,** Bath Rd., has a restaurant, phones, toilets, and showers. Take the A38 2 mi. south of Worcester or local bus #32, every 10min. (☎820430. Open Easter-Oct. £6-8 per tent, £8 per caravan. Electricity £1.75.)

◑ ▤ FOOD AND PUBS

A **Sainsbury's** is tucked into the Lynchgate Shopping Centre off High St. (☎21731. Open M-Th 8am-6pm, F 8am-7pm, Sa 8am-6pm.) **Mealcheapen St.** offers food deals, plus bonus fun with street-name puns. Good Indian restaurants fills **The Tything.** At **Clockwatchers,** 20 Mealcheapen St., farm-fresh sandwiches start at £1.60 takeaway (eat-in £2.50-3), and bagels are only 75p. (☎611662. Open M-Sa 8:30am-5pm). **Natu-ral Break,** off Foregate St. at The Hopmarket, provides organic respite in the form of sandwiches and quiches from £2.75. (☎26654. Open M-Sa 9am-5pm.) **The Cardinal's Hat,** 31 Friar St., is Worcester's oldest pub, dating from 1482. Sit in front of open fires sipping ales (£1.60-2) brewed onsite. (☎22423. Open daily 11am-11pm.) For pint-sized entertainment, the pub scene on **Friar St.** is popular.

🔆 SIGHTS

Worcester Cathedral, founded in AD 680, towers majestically by the River Severn at the southern end of High St. Over the years, the buttresses supporting the central nave have deteriorated and the central tower is in danger of collapsing. Renovation attempts are underway, but even steel rods set into the tower's base do not detract from the awe-inspiring Norman detail of the nave and quire. To the delight of schoolchildren and *Let's Go* researchers, Bishop Freake (1516-91) has his tomb in the south wall. The quire contains intricate 14th-century misericords and the tomb of King John; copies of the *Magna Carta* wait outside. **Wulston's Crypt** is an entire underground level with its own chapel. Be sure to take the free tour for an enriching visit. (☎28854. Cathedral open daily 7:30am-6:30pm; choral Evensong M-F 5:30pm, Su 4pm. Free tours May-Sept.; tower tours Sa, late July also M-Th. Suggested donation £2, tower tours £2.)

Retrace the 1651 Battle of Worcester at the **Commandery,** Sidbury Rd., Sit in on the trial of Charles I and choose whether to sign the king's death warrant. Your vote counts. (☎36182. Open M-Sa 10am-5pm, Su 1:30-5pm. £3.70, seniors and children £2.60, families £9.90.) The **Royal Worcester Porcelain Company,** southeast of the cathedral on Severn St., manufacturer of the famous blue-red-and-gold-patterned bone china, has serviced the royal family since George III visited in 1788. Porcelain junkies can visit the adjacent **Worcester Museum of Porcelain,** which has the largest collection in England. (☎23221. Open M-Sa 9am-5:30pm. Tours M-F at regular intervals; £5, no children under 11. Museum £3, students £2.25, under 5 free. Museum and tour £8, seniors and students £6.75.) The **Worcester City Museum and Art Gallery,** Foregate St., near the post office, has a military exhibit; Hitler's clock, found in his office when it was captured by the Worcester Regiment in 1945 and frozen at 5:51, is the highlight. (☎25371. Open M-W and F 9:30am-5:30pm, Sa 9:30am-5pm. Free.) Behind the Guildhall, all that remains of St. Andrew's Church is a 245 ft. spire, known locally as the **Glover's Needle** because of the area's ties with glove-making. Among the half-timbered buildings on **Friar Street** stands the **Museum of Local Life,** showcasing past centuries of Worcester life. (☎722349. Open M-W and F-Sa 10:30am-5pm. £1.50, concessions 75p, families £3.25.)

Three miles south of town, **Elgar's Birthplace Museum** is filled with manuscripts and memorabilia of the composer. Midland Red West bus #419/420 makes the journey (10min., return £1.80). From the Crown East Church bus stop walk 15min. to the museum. Otherwise, cycle 6 mi. along the Elgar trail. (☎333224. Open May-Sept. Th-Tu 10:30am-6pm; Oct. to mid-Jan. and mid-Feb. to Apr. Th-Tu 1:30-4:30pm. £3.50, students £1.75, seniors £2.60, children 1.50p.)

NEAR WORCESTER: MALVERN ☎01684

The name Malvern refers collectively to the contiguous towns of Great Malvern, West Malvern, Malvern Link, Malvern Wells, and Little Malvern, all of which hug the base and the eastern side of the Malvern Hills. The tops of the Malvern Hills peek over the A4108 southwest of Worcester and offer 8 mi. of accessible trails and quasi-divine visions of greenery. **Great Malvern,** a Victorian spa town, was built around the 11th-century **church** on Abbey Rd. Benedictine monks rebuilt the structure in the 15th century, adding stained-glass windows. (Suggested donation £1.) On the steep hillside above town, **St. Ann's Well** supplies the famous restorative "Malvern waters" that fueled Great Malvern's halcyon days. The beautifully redone **Malvern Theatres** on Grange Rd. host plays, including top-quality London theatre by the Almeida Company in August. (☎892277. Box office open M-Sa 9:30am-8pm. Tickets £10-20, student discounts £1-9 off.)

HEART OF ENGLAND

The **Worcestershire Way** slips through the Malverns for 36 mi. to Kingsford County Park in the north. The **Countryside Service** (☎(01905) 766493), in the County Hall in Worcester, will tell you about hiking in the area. **Trains** (25min., 10 per day) and **Midland Red West** (M-Sa 2 per hr., hourly on Su) come from **Worcester**. The **tourist information centre**, 21 Church St., by the post office, ably assists in hill navigation. (☎892289; fax 892872. Short-distance walk pamphlets 30p. Open daily 10am-5pm.) The **YHA Hatherly Youth Hostel**, 18 Peachfield Rd., in Malvern Wells, holds 59 beds and a TV lounge. Take Citibus #42 from Great Malvern or walk 20min. from the train station. (☎569131; fax 565205. Lockout 10am-5pm. Curfew 11pm. Open mid-Feb. to Oct. daily; Nov.-Dec. F-Sa. £10, under 18 £6.90.)

CHELTENHAM   ☎01242

A spa town second only to Bath, Cheltenham (pop. 107,000) wears a carefree sophistication. Manicured gardens of bursting red line walkways, while well-dressed yuppies tread the crowded Promenade. Cheltenham's Laura Ashley-esque quality is a break from the touristed centers of Bath and Stratford and the industrial megaliths of the Midlands. A useful launching pad into the Cotswolds, this city also has a student population that brings the pubs and clubs to life at night.

▛ TRANSPORTATION

Cheltenham lies 43 mi. south of Birmingham, and makes an excellent stopover for cyclists and walkers traveling the Cotswolds. The tourist information center (TIC) stocks a free *Getting There* pamphlet with detailed information on area travel.

Trains: Cheltenham Spa Station, on Queen's Rd. at Gloucester Rd. Ticket office open M-F 5:45am-8:15pm, Sa 5:45am-7:15pm, Su 8:15am-8:15pm. Trains (☎(08457) 484950) from: **London** (2½hr., every hr., £31.50); **Birmingham** (30min., 2 per hr., £12.60); **Bath** (1½hr., every hr., £11.10); **Exeter** (2hr., every 2hr., £28.50).

Buses: Royal Well, Royal Well Rd. National Express office open M-Sa 9am-5:30pm. **Luggage lockers** £1-2. **National Express** (☎(08705) 808080) from: **London** (3hr., every hr., £10.50); **Bristol** (1¼hr., every 2hr., £6.50); **Exeter** (3½hr., every 2hr., £18). **Swanbrook Coaches** (☎(01452) 712386) from **Oxford** (1½hr., return £8).

Taxis: Central Taxi (☎228877). **Associated Taxis** (☎(01452) 311700). Taxis wait outside the bus station all day; there's a free phone in the train station.

✴ ▛ ORIENTATION AND PRACTICAL INFORMATION

Most attractions in Cheltenham are within walking distance of the town's center. The TIC is on **The Promenade,** a pedestrian-only walkway one block east of the bus station. From the train station, walk down Queen's Rd. and bear left onto Lansdown Rd. Head left again at the Rotunda onto Montpellier Walk, which leads to The Promenade. Save yourself the 15min. walk and hop a frequent F or G bus (8 per hr., 75p). A free city-center bus service is available from the Royal Well station.

Tourist Information Centre: Municipal Offices, 77 The Promenade (☎522878; accommodations booking 517110; fax 515535; www.visitcheltenham.gov.uk). Well-organized staff sells National Express tickets and books accommodations for a 10% deposit. B&B vacancies posted outside after hours. Open M-Sa 9:30am-5:15pm. **Tours** leave from the office late June to mid-Sept. 1¼hr., M-F 11am, £2.50.

Financial Services: Banks are everywhere; try **Lloyds TSB,** 130 High St. (☎518169). Open M-Tu and Th-F 9am-5pm, W 9:30am-5pm, Sa 9am-12:30pm.

Launderette: Soap-n-Suds, 312 High St. (☎512107). Open daily 7:30am-8pm, last wash 7pm.

Police: Holland House, 840 Lansdown Rd. (☎521321).

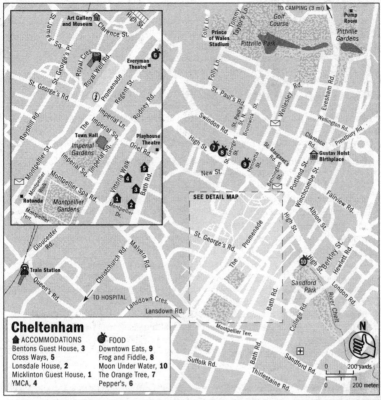

Cheltenham

ACCOMMODATIONS	FOOD
Bentons Guest House, 3	Downtown Eats, 9
Cross Ways, 5	Frog and Fiddle, 8
Lonsdale House, 2	Moon Under Water, 10
Micklinton Guest House, 1	The Orange Tree, 7
YMCA, 4	Pepper's, 6

Hospital: Cheltenham General, Sandford Rd. (☎222222). Follow the Bath Rd. south-west from town and turn left onto Sandford Rd. Emergency entrance on College Rd.

Internet Access: Rendezvous Cyber Cafe, 16 Portland St. (☎577893). £1 per 15min. Open M-Sa 9am-5:30pm, Tu and Th also 6-9pm.

Post Office: 225-227 High St. (☎526056). Open M-Sa 9am-5:30pm. **Bureau de change. Postal Code:** GL50.

ACCOMMODATIONS

Standards in Cheltenham's B&Bs tend to be high, but so do the prices. A handful of B&Bs can be found in the **Montpellier** area and along **Bath Rd.,** a five-minute walk from the town center. The TIC publishes a thick accommodations booklet.

Cross Ways, 57 Bath Rd. (☎527683; fax 577226; crossways@btinternet.com). A warm and inviting proprietress. Admire the floral decorations—she made the bedding and curtains herself. Rooms with TVs, cookies, and tea. Tasty breakfast. £22-25 per person.

YMCA, Vittoria Walk (☎524024; fax 232365). At the town hall, turn left onto the Promenade and walk 3 blocks; Vittoria Walk is on the right. Men and women accepted. A backpackers paradise, the well-kept singles are complete with full kitchen. Convenient location and free breakfast. Book ahead. Office open 24hr., but if you want B&B, arrive before 9:30pm. Porter admits guests after 11pm. Singles £15, £13.80 after first night.

Bentons Guest House, 71 Bath Rd. (☎517417; fax 577744). Floral patterns everywhere, from the exuberant gardens to the spotless rooms with TVs. Platter-sized plates can barely hold the breakfast. £25-35 per person, depending on season and facilities.

Lonsdale House, 16 Montpellier Dr. (☎232379; lonsdale-house@hotmail.com). Large home with a bounty of singles. Comfortable, spacious rooms stocked with TVs and English literary classics. Singles £21; doubles with bath £49.

Micklinton Guest House, 12 Montpellier Dr. (☎520000; fax 704056; dobeid@cableinet.co). Less frilly than the average B&B, but still cozy. They even have menus at breakfast. All rooms with TV. Singles £20-24, doubles £40-44.

☕🍴 FOOD AND PUBS

Fruit stands, butchers, and bakeries dot **High St.,** while down the road, **Tesco** has it all under one roof. (☎847400. Open M-Tu and Sa 7:30am-7pm, W-F 7:30am-8pm, Su 11am-5pm.) A **market** takes place on Henrietta St. on Thursday mornings.

Pepper's Cafe-Bar, Regent St. (☎573488). A local hangout that combines English pub and trendy Californian cafe. Salsa dancing F nights until 1am. Creative sandwiches start at £4, and salads are around £5. Open M-Sa 8am-11pm, Su 9am-10:30pm.

Choirs Restaurant, 5-6 Well Walk (☎235578). The French owner serves lunch (under £7) in a setting as dainty as the delicious food; prices rise after 7pm.

The Orange Tree, 317 High St. (☎234232). Proudly health-conscious. Follow a hummus sandwich with organic beer. Main courses £8. Weekend reservations recommended. Open M 9:30am-4pm, Tu-Th 9:30am-9pm, F-Sa 9:30am-10pm, Su 11am-3pm.

Moon Under Water, 16-28 Bath Rd. (☎583945). The romantic name and running waterfall whisper of romance, though the indelicate menu deflects some of cupid's arrows. Delicious nachos, chips, and juicy burgers. Dine on their outdoor patio, which overlooks Sandford Park. Open daily 11am-11pm; food served until 10pm.

Downtown Eats, 293 High St. (☎516388). Simple takeaway sandwiches (90p-£1.80) perfect for a picnic in the Montpellier or Imperial Gardens. Open M-Sa 8am-3:30pm.

Frog and Fiddle, 315 High St. (☎701156; fax 701157). Chill on the big blue couches or examine the art in the upstairs gallery. Students fill the pub's cavernous back rooms. Often pre-club promotions M-W and Su. Open M-Sa 11am-11pm, Su noon-10:30pm.

👁 SIGHTS

Cheltenham proudly possesses the only naturally **alkaline water** in Britain. Crazy George III took the waters in 1788; in the 19th century the Duke of Wellington claimed that the spring cured his "disordered liver." You don't need an illness to enjoy the diuretic and laxative effects of the waters at the **town hall.** (Open M-F 9:30am-5:30pm. Water tasting free.) Two blocks from the bus station on Clarence St., the **Cheltenham Art Gallery and Museum** specializes in the Arts and Crafts movement. In addition to its extensive pottery collection, it features an interesting exhibit on England's urban prosperity over the past 1000 years. (☎237431. Open M-Sa 10am-5:20pm. Free.) The **Gustav Holst Birthplace Museum,** 4 Clarence Rd. (*not* Clarence St.), portrays the composer's early life in his largely unchanged home. See the piano at which he composed *The Planets* (and hear them, too). Follow the signs to the bus station, then walk one block to Clarence Rd. (☎524846. Open Tu-Sa 10am-4:20pm. £2.50, concessions £1.25.) A walk down Clarence St. and a left at St. James Sq. will bring you to the house in which **Tennyson** wrote *In Memoriam.* No museum here—the house is in disrepair, with windows thickly crusted, one and all. Downtowners and dogs sunbathe among the exquisite blooms of the **Imperial Gardens,** just past the Promenade away from the center of town.

🎵 FESTIVALS

The indispensable *What's On* poster, displayed on kiosks and at the TIC, lists many concerts, plays, tours, sporting events, and evening hot-spots. The **Cheltenham International Festival of Music** in July celebrates modern classical works, as well as opera. The Fringe branch of the Festival features jazz, rock, and world premieres; many performances are free. Full details are available in March from the box office, Town Hall, Imperial Sq., Cheltenham GL50 1QA. (☎227979. Tickets £2-19.) The **Cheltenham Cricket Festival,** the oldest in the country, commences in early July. Purchase tickets at the gate and inquire about game times at the TIC, or call 514420. October heralds the fortnight-long **Cheltenham Festival of Literature.** Recent guests have included Seamus Heaney, P.D. James, and Stephen Spender. For a full program of events, write to the Town Hall or call the 24hr. Festival Box Office. (☎237979. Advance tickets £1.50-4.) The **National Hunt,** a horseracing event, starts in the winter and culminates in March, when the population of Cheltenham nearly doubles—you can find over 50,000 people per day at the race course.

🔁 DAYTRIP FROM CHELTENHAM: TEWKESBURY

Ten miles northwest of Cheltenham, at the confluence of the Rivers Avon and Severn, Tewkesbury merits an excursion for its stately **abbey.** Consecrated in 1121, the well-proportioned building, illuminated by 14th-century stained glass, captures the beautiful power of Norman (or "English Romanesque") architecture. During the Battle of Tewkesbury, some Lancastrians tried to seek refuge in the abbey. The monks attempted to protect them, but the Yorks killed the monks as well, and the abbey had to be reconsecrated. The abbey stands today only because townsfolk raised £453 to save it from the dissolution planned by Henry VIII. (☎(01684) 850959. Open in summer M-Sa 7:30am-6:30pm, Su 7:30am-7pm; in winter daily 7:30am-5:30pm. Services Su at 8, 9:15, 11am, and 6pm. Requested donation £2.) Small museums dot the village, including the **Tewkesbury Town Museum,** 64 Barton St., charmingly petite with an exhibit on the 1471 Battle of Tewkesbury. (☎(01684) 295027. Open daily 10am-4pm. £1, seniors 50p, children 75p.) The **Little Museum,** Church St., is a merchant's cottage built in 1450 and restored five centuries later. (☎(01684) 297174. Open Apr.-Oct. Tu-Sa 10am-5pm. Free.) Once an Iron Age fort, the **Country Park,** Crickley Hill, offers ethereal views and archaeological finds.

Tewkesbury makes a leisurely day trip from Cheltenham and can be adequately visited in a few hours. **Cheltenham District** (☎(01242) 522021) bus #41 departs from Cheltenham (M-F every hr. until 7pm, Sa 2 per hr.; return £2.15). The town's **tourist information centre** is in the Town Museum. It sells a 10p town map and a 20p pamphlet outlining walks through Tewkesbury's alley-like streets. (☎(01684) 295027. Open daily 9am-5pm, Su 10am-4pm.) The **post office** is at 99-100 High St. (☎(01684) 293232. Open M-F 9am-5:30pm, Sa 9am-4pm.) **Postal code:** GL20. To stay the night, **Hanbury Guest House,** Barton Rd., 5min. from the town center on the left, has comfortable rooms whose quilts and curtains contribute to a homemade ambience. (☎(01684) 299911. Doubles £36, with bath £40.)

THE COTSWOLDS

The Cotswolds have deviated little from their etymological roots—"Cotswolds" means "sheep enclosure in rolling hillsides." These vivid, verdant hills enfold tiny towns with names longer than their main streets and barely touched by modern life, save for periodic strings of antique shops and summer tourists. Saxon villages and Roman settlements, hewn straight from the famed Cotswold Stone, link a series of trails accessible to walkers and cyclists. The Cotswolds are not just for outdoors enthusiasts, however; anyone with an interest in rural England will find something here. The towns seem like scenes preserved from a rustic past, and brilliant greens, golds, and purples lend their color to the area.

▟ TRANSPORTATION

If you like to travel spontaneously, a bike or car is a must in the Cotswolds, since there's a paucity of public transport. Decide beforehand which villages you aim to hit, as those in the so-called "Northern" Cotswolds (Stow-on-the-Wold, Bourton-on-the-Water, Moreton-in-Marsh) are more easily reached via Cheltenham, while the "Southern" Cotswolds (notably Slimbridge and Painswick) are served more

HEART OF ENGLAND

frequently by Gloucester. The Gloucester tourist information centre (TIC) has transport information, and the Cheltenham TIC provides the invaluable *Getting There from Cheltenham* pamphlet.

Trains frequent the area's major gateways (Cheltenham, Bath, and Gloucester), but Moreton-in-Marsh and Charlbury are the only villages with train stations. **Trains** (☎ (08457) 484950) depart from **Oxford** for **Moreton-in-Marsh** (30min., every hr., £7.50) and **Charlbury** (20min., every hr., £3.80). Several **bus** companies operating under the auspices of the county government cover the Gloucestershire Cotswolds, which includes most of the range, though many buses run only one or two days per week. Two regular services are **Pulham's Coaches** (☎ (01451) 820369) from **Cheltenham** to **Moreton-in-Marsh** (1hr., M-Sa 7 per day, £1.50) via **Bourton-on-the-Water** and **Stow-on-the-Wold**, and **Castleway's Coaches** (☎ (01242) 602949) from **Cheltenham** to **Broadway** (50min., M-Sa 4 per day, £1.80) via **Winchcombe**. The indispensable *Connection* timetable is free at bus stations and TICs. Various **coach tours** run to the Cotswolds from Cheltenham, Cirencester, Gloucester, and Tewkesbury.

If you want your own wheels, **Country Lanes Cycle Centre** rents bikes at the Moreton-in-Marsh train station. Phone ahead—bikes are popular in these rolling hills. (☎ (01608) 650065. £14 per day, plus two pieces of ID and refundable deposit. Gear and maps included. Open daily 9:30am-5:30pm.) **Stow Cycle Hire** delivers bikes for no additional charge. (☎ (01451) 832291. £8.50 per half-day, £12.50 per day.)

✴ 🛈 ORIENTATION AND PRACTICAL INFORMATION

The Cotswolds lie mostly in Gloucestershire, bounded by **Banbury** in the northeast, **Bradford-on-Avon** in the southwest, **Cheltenham** in the north, and **Malmesbury** in the south. The range hardly towers; a few areas in the north and west rise above 1000 ft., but the average Cotswold hill reaches only 600 ft. A 52 mi. unbroken ridge, **The Edge,** dominates the western reaches of the Cotswolds. The best bases from which to explore the region are **Cheltenham, Cirencester,** and **Moreton-in-Marsh.**

Tourist Information Centres: There are many in the area, all of which provide maps and pamphlets and book accommodations, usually for a 10% deposit.

Bath: Abbey Chambers (☎ (01225) 477101). Open June-Sept. M-Tu and F-Sa 9:30am-6pm, W-Th 9:45am-6pm, Su 10am-4pm; Oct.-May M-Sa 9am-5pm, Su 10am-4pm.

Bourton-on-the-Water: 5 Station Rd. (☎ (01451) 810597). Open M-Sa 10am-1pm and 2-5:30pm.

Broadway: 1 Cotswold Court (☎ (01386) 852937). Open Mar.-Oct. M-Sa 10am-1pm and 2-5pm.

Cheltenham: 77 The Promenade (☎ (01242) 522878; accommodations booking (01242) 517110; www.visitcheltenham.gov.uk). Open M-Sa 9:30am-5:15pm.

Chipping Campden: Rosary Court, High St. (☎ (01386) 841206). Open daily 10am-5:30pm.

Cirencester: Corn Hall, Market Pl. (☎ (01285) 654180; fax 641182). Open Apr.-Oct. M 9:45am-5:30pm, Tu-Sa 9:30am-5:30pm; Nov.-Mar. daily 9:30am-5pm.

Gloucester: 28 Southgate St. (☎ (01452) 421188). Open M-Sa 10am-5pm.

Stow-on-the-Wold: Hollis House, The Square (☎ (01451) 831082). Open Easter-Oct. M-Sa 9:30am-5:30pm, Su 10:30am-4pm; Nov.-Easter M-Sa 9:30am-4:30pm.

Winchcombe: Town Hall (☎ (01242) 602925). Open Apr.-Oct. M-Sa 10am-1pm and 2-5pm, Su 10am-1:30pm and 2-4pm.

🏠 🍴 ACCOMMODATIONS AND FOOD

The *Cotswold Way Handbook and Accommodation List* (£2) details many **B&Bs.** They are usually spaced in villages 3 mi. apart and offer friendly lodgings to trekkers. If you're not hiking, pick up the cheaper *Cotswolds Accommodation Guide* (50p). Savvy backpackers stay outside the larger towns to enjoy the silence and the prices. **Campsites** congregate close to Cheltenham; Bourton-on-the-Water, Stow-on-the-Wold, and Moreton-in-Marsh also provide convenient places to rough it. When in doubt, consult the *Gloucestershire Caravan and Camping Guide* (free at local TICs). The **YHA** has two **youth hostels** in the area, both of which serve meals and have a 10am-5pm lockout:

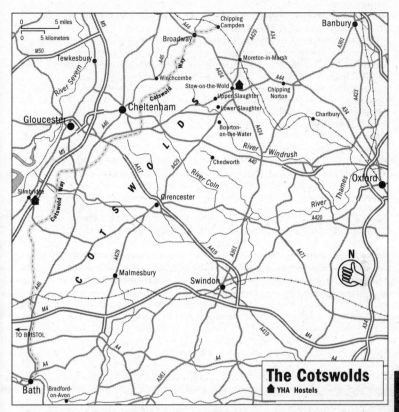

The Cotswolds
⌂ YHA Hostels

Slimbridge: Shepherd's Patch (☎(01453) 890275; fax 890625), across from the Tudor Arms Pub. Off the A38 and the M5, 4 mi. from the Cotswold Way and ½ mi. from the Wild Fowl Trust Reserve and Wetlands Centre. The nearest train station (Cam and Dursley) is 3½ mi. away; it's easier to take a bus from Gloucester. Comes complete with its own ponds and wildfowl. 56 beds, small store. Open Feb.-Oct. F-Sa, but call to verify, as the hostel is sometimes open during the week. Dorms £10.10, under 18 £6.95.

Stow-on-the-Wold: The Square (☎(01451) 830497). In the center of Stow, between the White Hart Hotel and the Old Stocks. On the A424 highway; Pulham's bus stops every hour from Cheltenham (17 mi.), Moreton-in-Marsh (4 mi.), and Bourton-on-the-Water. 49 beds in bright rooms with wooden bunks, most with attached bathrooms. Helpful warden. Kitchen. Open Apr.-Oct. daily; Nov. and Feb. F-Sa; Mar. M-Sa. Dorms £10.85, students £9.85, under 18 £7.40.

Supermarkets, takeaways, and full-fledged restaurants call larger towns like Cirencester home, while smaller towns have "if-we-don't-have-it-you-don't-need-it" general stores, as well as numerous tea shops that cater to tourists. Country pubs crop up in villages along the way.

🔲 HIKING THROUGH COTSWOLD VILLAGES

Experience the Cotswolds as the English have for centuries—by treading well-worn footpaths from village to village. Speed-walking will enable you to see several settlements in a day, which proves especially convenient for daytrippers. TIC shelves strain under the weight of various walking guides. Bear in mind that the Northern Cotswolds have a decidedly different feel from the Southern; many think the former are more picturesque, while the latter are less congested. Look for spring festivities such as cheese rolling or woolsack races. TICs sell the *Cotswold Map and Guidebook in One* (£5) and give out *Guided Walks and Events in the Cotswolds*. Ordnance Survey Outdoor Leisure Map #45 covers the Cotswolds (1:25,000; £6.50). The Cotswolds Voluntary Warden Service conducts **guided walks** through the Cotswolds, some with an historical bent. (1½-7½hr. Free.)

Those in search of long-distance hiking routes can choose from a handful of carefully marked trails. B&Bs and pubs rest conveniently within reach of the **Cotswold Way** and the **Oxfordshire Way.** The more extensive Cotswold Way spans just over 100 mi. from Bath to Chipping Campden. The entire walk can be done in a week at a pace of about 15 mi. per day. Pockmarks and gravel make certain sections of the path unsuitable for biking or horseback riding, and many sections cross pasture land; try not to disturb the sheep and cattle. Consult the **Cotswold Voluntary Warden Service** (☎ (01452) 425674) for details. The Oxfordshire Way (65 mi.) runs between the popular hyphen-havens of Bourton-on-the-Water and Henley-on-Thames, site of the famed annual regatta (p. 89). A comprehensive *Walker's Guide* can be found in TICs. Mince over cowpats while wending from Bourton-on-the-Water to Lower and Upper Slaughter along the **Warden's Way** (a half-day). Adventurous souls can continue on to Winchcombe for a total of about 14 mi.

Local roads are perfect for biking, and the rolling hills welcome casual and hardy cyclers alike; the closely spaced, tiny villages make ideal watering holes. TICs sell trail guides specially designed for the cyclist. Parts of the footpaths of the Oxfordshire Way are hospitable to cyclists, too, if slightly rut-ridden.

CHIPPING CAMPDEN. Years ago, quiet Chipping Campden was the capital of the Cotswold wool trade: the village became a one-time market center ("chipping" means "market"). Currently the town is famous for its **Cotswold Olympic Games** at **Dovers Hill,** featuring the obscure "sport" of shin-kicking. This sadistic activity was prohibited from 1852 to 1952 but has since been enthusiastically revived in late May and early June (buy tickets on game day). The **Church of St. James,** a signposted stroll from High St. (5min.), provides some architectural diversity.

BROADWAY. Only 3 mi. west of Chipping Campden, restored Tudor, Jacobean, and Georgian buildings with thatch or Cotswold-tile roofs give Broadway a museum-like air, while numerous antique shops and boutiques provide surprising shopping options. **Broadway Tower** enchanted the likes of decorator-designer-poet William Morris and his pre-Raphaelite comrade Dante Gabriel Rossetti. Built in the late 1700s in a superfluous attempt to intensify the beauty of the landscape, the tower affords a view of 12 counties. (☎ (01386) 852390. Open early Apr. to late Oct. daily 10:30am-5pm. £4, students and seniors £3, children £2.30, families £11.50.)

STOW-ON-THE-WOLD. Stow-on-the-Wold hides languidly in the hills. Despite a reluctant concession to progress—a Tesco supermarket has opened to the tune of ardent local objection—its fine views of the surrounding countryside mean it will never be mistaken for anything but the sweet Cotswold village it is. Bind your feet in the village's authentic stocks and snap a photo (or watch every other tourist do it while remaining cool and aloof yourself). Near the stocks stands a **YHA Youth Hostel** (see p. 276). If the hostel's full, head to the B&B of **Rosemary Quinn,** 22 Glebe Close, to find a warm welcome and beds laden with cushy quilts and pillows. (☎ (01451) 830042; ro@quinn.freeserve.co.uk. £18.50 per person.) Rugged simplicity defines **Pear Tree Cottage,** on High St., in an old stone house with comfortable rooms. (☎ (01451) 831210. Doubles £30-40.) Replenish glucose at **The Organic Shop** across from the hostel, or down a pint at **The King's Arms** across the way.

THE SLAUGHTERS. Like the proverbial lamb, you can travel a few miles southwest to the Slaughters (Upper and Lower), a pair of peaceful villages connected by footpaths. Fortunately, your visit will be heralded by a host of lively sheep, not an unhinged butcher. The **Old Mill** at Lower Slaughter scoops water from the river that flows placidly past.

BOURTON-ON-THE-WATER. Rather inexplicably touted as the "Venice of the Cotswolds" (no gondolas, just a picturesque stream and a series of footbridges), Bourton hosts its share of affluent tourists. Many of the larger trails, including the Cotswold and Oxfordshire Ways, converge here. Follow signs to the scale model of Bourton, an incredibly accurate, if miniature, labor of love and patience. Between the olfactory heaven and hell of rose-laden gates and dung-strewn fields, **The Cotswold Perfumery,** on Victoria St., houses a theater equipped with "Smelly Vision," a system that releases actual scents as they're mentioned on screen. (☎ (01451) 820698. Open M-Sa 9:30am-5:30pm, Su 10:30am-5:30pm; sometimes later in summer. £1.75, concessions £1.50, families £6.50.)

CIRENCESTER. One of the larger villages, and sometimes regarded as the capital of the region, Cirencester (SI-ruhn-ses-ter) is the site of Corinium, a once important Roman town founded in AD 49. Cirencester today caters to its older population; younger travelers should stay elsewhere and make it a daytrip. Although only scraps of the amphitheater still exist, the **Corinium Museum,** on Park St., has culled a formidable collection of Roman paraphernalia, including a hare mosaic. (☎ (01285) 655611. Open Apr.-Oct. M-Sa 10am-5pm, Su 2-5pm; Nov.-Mar. Tu-Sa 10am-5pm, Su 2-5pm. £2.50, students £1, seniors £2, children 80p, families £5.) The second longest yew hedge in England bounds Lord Bathwist's mansion in the center of town; the garden is scattered with Roman ruins.

The **Cirencester Parish Church** is Gloucestershire's largest. A "wool church," the money to build it came from wealthy wool merchants in the region. (Open daily 10am-5pm. Morning Prayer before opening, Evening Prayer around 4:45pm. Donation requested.) On Fridays, the entire town turns into a frenetic antique market; a smaller crafts fair appears on Saturdays inside Corn Hall, near the **tourist information centre** at Market Pl. Pricey **B&Bs** cluster a few minutes from town along Victoria Rd. Stop by the **Golden Cross** on Black Jack St. or the **Crown** at West Market Pl. near the abbey for a pint.

CHEDWORTH. Tucked away in the Chedworth hills southwest of Cheltenham, Chedworth contains the well-preserved **Chedworth Roman Villa,** equidistant from Cirencester and Northleach off the A429. The famed Roman mosaics in the villa were discovered in 1864 when a gamekeeper noticed fragments of tile revealed by clever rabbits. The site now displays a water shrine and two bathhouses just above the River Coln. (☎ (01242) 890256; recorded info (01684) 855371. Open Mar.-Nov. Tu-Su and bank holidays 10am-5pm. £3.40, children £1.70, families £8.50.)

SLIMBRIDGE. Slimbridge, 12½ mi. southwest of Gloucester off the A38, is the site of the largest of seven **Wildfowl Trust** centers in Britain. Sir Peter Scott has developed the world's biggest collection of wildfowl here, with over 180 different species. All six varieties of flamingos nest here, and white-fronted geese visit from Siberia. In the tropical house, hummingbirds skim through jungle foliage. The visitor center has exhibits and food. (☎ (01453) 890333. Open in summer daily 9:30am-5pm; winter 9:30am-4pm. £5.75, students and seniors, £4.75, children £3.50, families £15.) **YHA Slimbridge** (p. 277) benefits from Sir Peter's ornithological efforts as well, hosting flocks of its own.

Just south of Slimbridge on the A38 rises the massive **Berkeley Castle** (BARK-lay), ancestral home of the Berkeley family, founders of the university in California. This stone fortress has impressive towers, a dungeon, and a timber-vaulted Great Hall, where barons of the West Country met before forcing King John to sign the *Magna Carta*. (☎ (01453) 810332. Open July-Aug. M-Sa 11am-5pm, Su 1-5pm; June and Sept. Tu-Sa 11am-5pm, Su 2-5pm; Apr.-May Tu-Su 1-5pm; Oct. Su 1-4:30pm. £5.40, students and seniors £4.40, children £2.90, families £14.50.)

SUDELEY CASTLE. West of Stow-on-the-Wold and 6 mi. north of Cheltenham on the A46 lies **Sudeley Castle,** neighboring the town of Winchcombe. Once the manor estate of King Ethelred the Unready, the castle was a prized possession in the Middle Ages, with lush woodland, a royal deer park, and later Charles I's gloriously

> **LIKE A ROLLING STONE** According to legend, the curious grouping that comprises the Rollright Stones near Chipping Norton were created when an evil witch told an ambitious king, "Seven long strides shalt thou take / If Long Compton thou canst see, then King of England thou shalt be. / If Long Compton thou cannot see, then King of England thou shalt not be." The king bounded up the hill but found a large stone blocking his view. To ensure the accuracy of her prophecy, the witch turned all the king's party, including the poor king himself, into stone. Today the king stone, an 8 ft. loner, is still surrounded by his circle of men, 77 stones 100 ft. in diameter. The group of stones ¼ mi. west, known as the Whispering Knights, are said to have been a group of knights who were plotting treason. Too bad the beleaguered king couldn't just climb the Broadway Tower.

carved four-poster bed. The Queen's Garden is streamlined by a pair of yew-hedge corridors leading to rose and herb beds, while the newly planted Knot Garden was inspired by a pattern on a gown worn by Queen Elizabeth. **St. Mary's Chapel** contains the tomb of Henry VIII's Queen Katherine Parr. Present occupants Lord and Lady Ashcombe welcome you and your admission fee to their home. (☎ (01242) 602308. Open Mar.-Oct. daily 10:30am-5:30pm. ₤6.20, seniors ₤5.20, children ₤3.20. Grounds only ₤4.70, seniors ₤3.70, children ₤2.50, families ₤17.)

PREHISTORIC REMAINS. Archaeologists have unearthed some 70 ancient habitation sites in the Cotswolds. **Belas Knap**, a 4000-year-old burial mound, stands 1½ mi. southwest of Sudeley Castle, accessible from the Cotswold Way. The **Rollright Stones**, off the A34 between Chipping Norton and Long Compton (a 4½ mi. walk from Chipping Norton), are a 100 ft. wide ring of 11 stones (see **Like a Rolling Stone,** below). Consult Ordnance Survey Tourist Map #8 (₤4.50) for other sites.

HEREFORD   ☎01432

A square of activity in the bucolic patchwork of the Wye River region, Hereford (HAIR-uh-fuhd; pop. 60,000) was for centuries an important market town. The town still sells its rural wares in its busy center, from cider pressed in its orchards to the white-faced Hereford cattle and sheep that gather in the livestock market every Wednesday. A pedestrian center and narrow streets make Hereford a town best seen on foot, while excellent bus and rail connections make it a springboard westward into the Wye Valley on the Welsh-English border (see p. 435).

▐ TRANSPORTATION. The **train** and **bus stations** are both located on Commercial Rd. Trains (☎ (08457) 484950) arrive from: **London Paddington** (2¾hr., every hr., ₤33); **Abergavenny** (25min., 2 per hr., ₤5.60); **Shrewsbury** (1hr., every hr., ₤11.20); **Cardiff** (1hr., every hr., ₤11.70); **Chepstow** via **Newport** (1½hr., every 2hr., ₤13.20). **National Express** (☎ (08705) 808080) runs buses from **London** (4hr., 3 per day, ₤13.50) and **Birmingham** (2hr., 1 per day, ₤6.25). A few steps past the tourist information centre (TIC) along Broad St. is the **bus stop** for local services. **Stagecoach Red and White** (☎ (01633) 838856) bus #20 connects Hereford from **Newport** and the **Wye Valley** (M-Sa 4 per day). Bus #39 comes in from **Brecon** via **Hay-on-Wye** (1¾hr., M-Sa 5 per day, ₤5). On Sundays, **Yeoman's** bus #40 takes over (2 per day). For bus info, pick up the free *Herefordshire Public Transport Map and Guide* at the TIC.

▐ PRACTICAL INFORMATION. The **tourist information centre**, 1 King St., in front of the cathedral, books beds for ₤1 and a 10% deposit on the first night's stay. (☎ 268430; fax 342662. Open M-Sa 9am-5pm; May-Sept. also Su 10am-4pm.) **Walking tours** leave from the TIC. (1½hr. Mid-May to mid-Sept. M-Sa 11am, Su 2:30pm. ₤2, seniors and children ₤1, under 12 free.) **Cathedral Cruises** runs 40min. **river tours.** (☎ 358957. Mar.-Oct. Subject to weather.) Other services include: **Barclays bank,** Broad St. (open M-W and F 9am-5pm, Th 10am-5pm, Sa 9:30am-noon); **Thomas**

Cook, St. Peter's St., near the Old House (☎422500; open M-Tu and Th-Sa 9am-5:30pm, W 10am-5:30pm); the **Coin-op Launder Centre,** 136 Eign St. (☎269610; open daily 6am-7pm); the **County Hospital** (☎ 355444); **Internet access** at the **Pi Shop,** 17 King St. (☎377444; nonmembers £2 per 30min., members £1 per 30min.; open M and W-Sa 9am-9pm, Tu 9am-10pm, Su 10am-5pm); and the **post office,** 20 Broad St., next to the bus stop (☎273611; open M-Th 9am-5:30pm, F 9:30am-5:30pm, Sa 9am-12:30pm). **Postal code:** HR4 9HQ.

▚▐ ACCOMMODATIONS AND FOOD. Cheap lodgings in Hereford are scarce and mediocre; your best bet is to walk to the **B&Bs** (from £20) at the T-junction at the end of Bodenham Rd. **Bourvrie House,** 26 Victoria St., will supply you with a clean and simple room a mere 5min. from downtown. (☎266265. TVs. Singles £20; doubles £18.50 per person; family room £23 per person.) A bit farther away, at the **Holly Tree,** 19-21 Barton Rd., TVs also await in every room. (☎357845. Singles £22; doubles £44. No smoking.) For local flavor eat at the **Black Lion Inn,** 31 Bridge St., a friendly pub with a generous menu. The award-winning (we're serious) plough-man's lunches start at £5.50. (☎354016. Open M-Sa 11am-11pm, Su noon-10:30pm. Food served M-Sa noon-8pm, Su noon-3pm.) The **Cafe@All Saints,** in the All Saints' Church on High St., puts local ingredients to work. Lunch on a quiche and salad for £5 or a cider tart for £2. (☎370415. Open M-Sa 8:30am-5:30pm.)

◪ SIGHTS. Rising above surrounding greens, the heavy rose walls of the 11th-century **Hereford Cathedral** enclose a light and airy sanctuary and museum. Most visitors flock to see the **Mappa Mundi,** a map of the world drawn on animal skin around 1290 and now enclosed in a secure display chamber. Sodom and Gomorrah lie drowned in the Dead Sea, a tipsy polar bear staggers about Norway, and the Bonnacon, a mythical bull-horse, discharges flaming dung, literally laying waste to large parts of Syria. In the **Chained Library,** 1500 rare and extremely old books are linked to their shelves by slender chains. (☎374209. Cathedral open daily until Evensong. Mappa Mundi and Chained Library open May-Sept. M-Sa 10am-4:15pm, Su 11am-3:15pm; Oct.-Apr. M-Sa 11am-3:15pm. Cathedral admission free; Mappa Mundi and library £4, concessions £3.50, families £10.)

The steeples of St. Peter's Church and All Saints' Church act as bookends to the pedestrian **High Town,** an old market place turned modern shopping plaza. Half-tim-bered Tudor buildings once lined High Town, but only the 17th-century **Old House** remains fully intact. A former butcher's shop, the Old House has creaky wooden floors that now support loads of antique furniture. (☎260694. Open Apr.-Sept. Tu-Sa 10am-5pm, Su 10am-4pm; Oct.-Mar. Tu-Sa 10am-5pm. Free.) "Cheers!", written in several languages, greets visitors to the **Cider Museum** on Pomona Pl., where you can learn about traditional cider-making. (☎354207. Open Apr.-Oct. M-Sa 10am-5:30pm; Nov.-Dec. M-Sa 11am-3pm; Jan.-Mar. Tu-Sa 11am-3pm. £2.50.)

▚ NIGHTLIFE. Those looking for a night out on the town will find that Hereford offers decent if unspectacular options. **Booth Hall** on East St., where St. Peter's St. meets High Town, is a pub that cranks up the music in the evenings and brings in a DJ on Sunday nights—but only Sunday nights. (☎344487. Open M-Sa 11am-11:30pm, Su 7-10:30pm.) **Eros,** 100 Commercial Rd., has a Wednesday student night and 80s rock Thursday; the crowd tends toward youngish. (☎353868. Open W-Th 9pm-1am, F-Sa 9pm-2am.)

HEART OF ENGLAND

THE MIDLANDS

Mention "the Midlands," and you'll invariably evoke images grim, urban, and decidedly sunless. But *go* to the Midlands and you may be surprised by the unique industrial heritage and quiet grandeur of this smokestacked pocket. Warwick's storybook castle and Lincoln's breathtaking cathedral are two of Britain's stand-out attractions, while the entire towns of Tudor Shrewsbury and Georgian Stamford are considered architectural wonders. Even Birmingham, the region's much-maligned center, has its saving graces, among them lively nightlife and the seat of the Cadbury chocolate empire. But perhaps Ironbridge and its chain of museums best personify the Midlands: deep in the Severn Valley, this World Heritage Site commemorates the region's innovative role in 18th-century iron production, a history rich with soot but fascinatingly gray.

HIGHLIGHTS OF THE MIDLANDS

IRONBRIDGE Admire the world's first cast-iron bridge and explore other living museums at this monument to Britain's Industrial Revolution (p. 287).

LINCOLN Climb your way to Lincoln's cathedral, once Europe's tallest building and now the stunning centerpiece of this city-on-a-hill (p. 295).

STAMFORD Stroll through the streets of this impeccable stone town on your way to Burghley House, one of Britain's most lavish stately homes (p. 299).

WEST MIDLANDS

WARWICK   ☎ 01926

Most tourists who reach Warwick (WAR-rick) come only to visit the famous castle, a rewarding daytrip from Birmingham or Stratford. Those with more time, however, may be compelled to stay the night by the town's unique architectural heritage, with buildings that pre- and post-date the Great Fire of 1694.

THE MIDLANDS

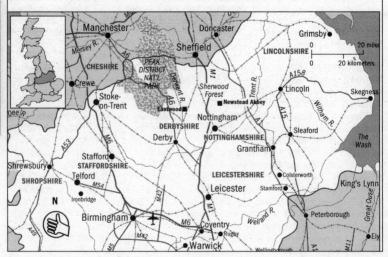

⚏⚐ TRANSPORTATION AND PRACTICAL INFORMATION. The Warwick **train station** sits on Coventry Rd. (Ticket office open M-Sa 6am-10:30pm, Su 8:30am-10pm.) Several **trains** (☎(08457) 484950) run daily from: **London Marylebone** (2½hr.; 2 per hr.; £24.50, day return £19.50); **Stratford** (20min., every hr., £2.50); **Birmingham** (40min., every hr., £3.50). **National Express** (☎(08705) 808080) **buses** stop in Old Square from **London** (3hr., 3 per day, £11); buy tickets at **Coop Travel,** Market St. (☎410709). **Stagecoach Midland Red** (☎(01788) 535555) buses stop at Market Place from **Stratford** (#X16, 30min., every hr.) and **Coventry** (#X18, 1hr., every hr.). **Warwickshire Traveline** (☎562036) has local bus info. For cabs, try **Tudor Taxi** (☎495000).

The **tourist information centre** (TIC), Court House, Jury St., books rooms for £2.50 plus a 10% deposit, and stocks a 30p guided map and a free town map. (☎492212; fax 494837; www.warwick-uk.co.uk. Open daily 9:30am-4:30pm.) **Tours** leave from the TIC on Sunday at 10:45am and some Mondays at 2:30pm. Other services include: **Barclays,** 5 High St. (☎303000; open M-F 9am-5pm); **Warwick Hospital,** Lakin Rd. (☎495321); the **police station,** Priory Rd. (☎410111); and the **post office,** Westgate House, 45 Brook St. (☎491061). **Postal code:** CV34 4BL.

⚐⚊ ACCOMMODATIONS AND FOOD. A stay near the castle can be pricey, but **Emscote Rd.** has cheaper options. From the train station, turn right onto Coventry Rd. and left at the Crown's Hotel onto Cotton End, which becomes Emscote Rd. (10min. walk). The humorous, young proprietor of **Westham Guest House,** 76 Emscote Rd., maintains a laid-back atmosphere. (☎491756; westhamhouse@aol.com. Singles £18; doubles £32, with bath £36-40.) At **Park House Guest House,** 17 Emscote Rd., all rooms have attached baths. (☎494359. Singles £20-25; doubles £36-40.) **Avon Guest House,** 7 Emscote Rd., has standard rooms across from the beautiful green of St. Nicholas Park. (☎491367. Singles £20; doubles £22, some with bath.) **Ashburton Guest House,** 74 Emscote Rd., is bright and modern, with a polished dining room. (☎401082. Singles £20; doubles with bath £40.)

For a sit-down meal, the **Crown Hotel Pub,** 4-6 Coventry Rd., down St. Nicholas St. from the castle, has sandwich-and-chips lunch specials (from £2) and dinners (burger £4.50) in a traditional pub. (☎492087. Open M-Sa 11am-11pm, Su noon-10:30pm.) Ten minutes from the city center, **The Roebuck,** Smith St. (☎494900), readies cheap "quick serve dishes" (£3.75-4.75) and desserts, in addition to a traditional menu. For **medieval banquets** call Warwick Castle (☎495421).

◙ SIGHTS. Many medievalists, architects, and fire-breathing dragons regard **❊Warwick Castle** as England's finest. Climb 530 steps to the top of its towers and see the countryside unfold like a fairytale kingdom of hobbits and elves. The dungeons are manned by life-size wax soldiers preparing for battle, while "knights" and "craftsmen" discuss their trades. (☎495421, 24hr. recording 406600. Open Apr.-Oct. daily 10am-6pm; Nov.-Mar. 10am-5pm. Lockers £1. Mid-May to early Sept. £11.50, students £8.60, seniors £8.20, children £6.75, families £30; Mar. to early May and early Sept. to mid-Feb. around £1 cheaper.)

Warwick's other sights are not as impressive as the castle, but not as expensive either. **St. Mary's Church,** Church St., keeps the grave of Fulke Greville, who's said to haunt the castle's Watergate Tower. In 1571, Lord Leycester acquired the buildings of the **Lord Leycester Hospital,** 60 High St., to house 12 old soldiers who had fought with him in the Netherlands; today, seven retired veterans still live inside. (☎491422. Open Easter-Oct. Tu-Su 10am-5pm; Oct.-Easter 10am-4pm. £2.75, students and seniors £2, children £1.50.) The **Warwickshire Museum,** in the Shirehall, is of good quality for a free museum, with displays on archaeology and natural history. (☎410410. Open M-Sa 10am-5:30pm. Free.) **St. John's Museum,** on St. John's St., houses Victorian costumes and musical instruments. (☎410410. Open Tu-Sa 10am-12:30pm and 1:30-5:30pm; May-Sept. also Su 2:30-5pm. Free.)

THE MIDLANDS

NEAR WARWICK: COVENTRY   ☎ 024

Twelve miles northeast of Warwick swells Coventry. Bombed during WWII, it has rebuilt itself, unprettily but effectively, into a modern city and transportation hub. The phrase "sent to Coventry" means to receive the silent treatment, an expression that arose from Royalist/Puritan antagonism during the Civil Wars. Now Coventry is united around its two **cathedrals**—the destroyed and the resurrected. Shards of the old cathedral are visible through the glass "west wall" (actually the south wall) of the new, which was dedicated in 1962 to the strains of Benjamin Britten's *War Requiem*. (☎7622 7597. Open daily 9:30am-4:30pm. Requested donation £3. Visitor center open M-Sa 10am-4pm. £2, concessions £1, families £5.) The **Museum of British Road Transport,** Hales St., displays the largest collection of British cars in the world. (☎7683 2422. Open daily 10am-4:30pm. Free.)

Coventry has a pedestrian-only downtown that resembles a shopping mall, littered with fast-food shops. Those staying in Coventry can visit the **Coventry Tourism Centre,** Bayley Ln., which books accommodations for an 8% deposit. (☎7622 7264; fax 7622 7255. Open Easter-Oct. M-F 9:30am-5pm, Sa-Su 10am-4:30pm; Nov.-Easter M-F 9:30am-4:30pm, Sa-Su 10am-4:30pm.) Once home to **Lady Godiva,** the city honors her memory with a week-long June festival featuring a (fully clothed) parade.

BIRMINGHAM   ☎ 0121

Castle-scouring, monument-seeking history buffs, move on—no great battles were fought in Birmingham, and no medieval landmarks are situated here. Birmingham, industrial heart of the Midlands, is resolutely modern in style, packing its city center with convention-goers and three-piece suits. Britain's second most populous city proper is a transport hub surrounded by ugly ring roads, but efforts at civic renovation have improved things somewhat. Witness the elegant fountain of Victoria Sq. or the chi-chi cafes along redeveloped canal banks. Cadbury World offers some daytime diversion, but it isn't until night that the city, fueled by world-class entertainers and a young university crowd, comes alive.

▐ TRANSPORTATION

Birmingham snares a clutch of train and bus lines between London, central Wales, southwest England, and points north.

Flights: Birmingham International Airport (☎767 5511). Free transfer to the nearby Birmingham International train station for connections to New St. Station and London.

Trains: New St. Station, Britain's busiest. Trains (☎(08457) 484950) from: **London Euston** (2hr., 2 per hr., £22.50); **Nottingham** (1¼hr., 2-4 per hr., £8.20); **Oxford** (1¼hr., 1-2 per hr., £14.20); **Liverpool Lime St.** (1½hr., 1-2 per hr., £18.50); **Manchester Piccadilly** (2½hr., every hr., £14.20). Others pull into **Moor St.** and **Snow Hill** stations. A red path guides travelers between New St. and Moor St. (10min. walk).

Buses: Digbeth Station, Digbeth. Open 24hr. **Luggage storage** £1-3. National Express office open M-Sa 7:15am-7pm, Su 8:15am-7pm. **National Express** (☎(08705) 808080) from: **London** (3¼hr., every hr., return £15); **Cardiff** (2¼hr., 4 per day, return £18.75); **Liverpool** (2½hr., 15 per day, return £11); **Manchester** (2½hr., every 2hr., return £12.50). Buses also stop at Colmore Row and Bull Ring.

Public Transportation: Information at **Centro** (☎200 2700), in New St. Station. Stocks local transit map and bus schedules. Bus and train day pass £5; bus only £2.50, children £1.70. Open daily 7:30am-10:30pm.

❈▐ ORIENTATION AND PRACTICAL INFORMATION

Streets beyond the central district can be dangerous. As always, take care at night.

Tourist Information Centre: 2 City Arcade (☎643 2514; fax 616 1038). Books rooms for 10% deposit for English tourist board accommodations, £2 fee for other listings. Sells theater and National Express tickets. Open M-Sa 9:30am-5:30pm. **Branch,** Victoria Sq. (☎693 6300; fax 693 9600). Open M-Sa 9:30am-6pm, Su 10am-4pm.

Birmingham

🏠 ACCOMMODATIONS

Cook House, **8**
Woodville House, **7**

🍎 FOOD

Ipanema, **5**
Warehouse Cafe, **2**
Wine Republic, **1**

♪ MUSIC AND CLUBS

Bakers, **6**
Nightingale, **9**
Rat and Parrot,**4**
Stoodibakers, **3**

Tours: Guide Friday (☎ 693 6300) runs 1½hr. hop-on/hop-off bus tours, departing from Waterloo St. daily every hr. 10am-4pm. £7.50, students and seniors £6.50, children £2.50, under 5 free.

Financial Services: Barclays, 56 New St. (☎ 480 2351). Open M-Tu and Th-F 9:30am-4:30pm, W 10am-4:30pm. **American Express,** Bank House, 8 Cherry St. (☎ 644 5533). Open M-F 8:30am-5:30pm, Sa 9am-5pm.

Police: Lloyd House, Colmore Circus, Queensway (☎ 626 5000).

Internet Access: NetAdventure Cyber Cafe, 68-70 Dalton St. (☎ 693 6655), off Newton St. £3 per hr., £1 minimum. **Input Output Centres,** Central Library, Chamberlain Sq. (☎ 233 2230), near Colmore Row. £1 per 15min. Open M-F 9am-8pm, Sa 10am-5pm.

Post Office: 1 Pinfold St., Victoria Sq. (☎ 643 5542). **Bureau de change.** Open M-F 8:30am-5:30pm, Sa 8:30am-6pm. **Postal Code:** B2 4AA.

🏠 ACCOMMODATIONS

Despite its size, Birmingham has no hostels; the tourist information centre (TIC) has good B&B listings. B&Bs line **Hagley Rd.,** reachable by bus #9, 109, or 139. Hagley Rd. is a major thoroughfare, so you'll drift off to the sounds of passing traffic. Call to reserve a place at the YMCAs or YWCAs, as they're often booked solid.

Grasmere Guest House, 37 Serpentine Rd., Harborne (☎/fax 427 4546). Take bus #22, 23, or 103 from Colmore Row to the Duke of York pub. Turn right off Harborne Rd. onto Serpentine Rd. A bit far out, but the chatty proprietor offers tidy rooms and a lovely back garden. Board games in lounge and tea and biscuits every night at 9:30pm. No smoking. £15 per person, with bath additional £10 per room.

Cook House, 425 Hagley Rd. (☎429 1916). Take bus #9 or 139 from Colmore Row and tell the driver to stop before the Quantum Pub. Walk back 1-2min. Informative proprietor welcomes travelers into his large Victorian home. Rooms with TVs, tea/coffee, and sinks. £20 per person; doubles available.

Woodville House, 39 Portland Rd., Edgbaston (☎454 0274). Take bus #128 or 129 from Colmore Row in the city center (10min.). Comfortable and well located. Must ring bell for late-night entry. All rooms with TV. Singles £18; doubles £30, with bath £35.

YMCA: 200 Bunburg Rd. (☎475 6218); bus #61, 62 or 63 to Church Rd., Northfield; and 300 Reservoir Rd. (☎373 1937); bus #104 to Six Ways in Erdington. Basic rooms in decent areas. Both men and women accepted, must be over 18 and a member (£1). Breakfast included; dinner £3.50. Singles £15.50; weekly with dinner £117.

YWCA: Alexandra Residential Centre, 27 Norfolk Rd. (☎454 8134). Take bus #9, 126, 140, or 258 from Broad St. or Corporation St. and get off outside Liberty's nightclub; Norfolk Rd. is on your left. Singles £10; weekly small room £52.55, large room £57. Also at 5 Stone Rd. (☎440 5345). Take bus #61, 62, or 63 to Bristol Rd. Ask the bus driver to announce the stop if possible; it's not clearly marked. Be wary in the neighborhood, especially after dark. Women and men accepted. Week-long stays only £56.15.

◖ FOOD

Birmingham is most proud of **balti**, a Kashmiri-Pakistani cuisine invented here by immigrants from the subcontinent and cooked in a special pan. Brochures at the TIC map out the city's numerous balti restaurants. Most of the best are southeast of the city center in Birmingham's "Balti Triangle."

Warehouse Cafe, 54 Allison St. (☎633 0261), off Digbeth above the Friends of the Earth office. Chill atmosphere and lunchtime veggie burgers (£2) keep locals loyal. Bowl of soup and (organic) roll £2. Vegan items. Open M-F 11am-3pm, Sa 11am-4pm.

Al Frash, 186 Ladypool Rd. (☎753 3120). One of Brum's Balti Triangle restaurants. Tasty, generous portions of balti chicken for £3.90. Open daily 5pm-1am.

Wine Republic, Centenary Square (☎644 6464), next to Symphony Hall and the Repertory Theatre. Get free tapas in outdoor dining area 5:30-9:30pm. Panini £4.50, pasta £6.50; over 40 wines available. Open M-Sa 11am-11pm, also Su when there's a show.

Ipanema, 60 Broad St. (☎643 5577). Daytime diners swing to samba and salsa and spy on busy Broad St. as they munch authentic Latin American cuisine. A club by night.

◓ SIGHTS

Twelve minutes south of town by rail lies ▉**Cadbury World**, a cavity-prompting celebration of the chocolate firm and its enlightened treatment of workers. Sniff your way through the story of chocolate's roots in the Mayan rainforests, but be prepared to fend off hordes of schoolchildren; then indulge in a 400g chocolate bar (£2). Take a train from New St. to Bournville or bus #83, 84, or 85 from the center. (☎451 4180. Open daily 10am-3pm; closed certain days Nov.-Feb. £8, students and seniors £6.50, children £6, families £24. Usually includes 3 free chocolate bars.)

The **City Museum and Art Gallery,** Chamberlain Sq. off Colmore Row, supports **Big Brum,** northern cousin to London's Big Ben, and houses costumes, pre-Raphaelite paintings, and William Blake's illustrations of Dante's *Inferno*. The interactive *Light on Science* makes science palatable for kids and adults alike; check out the skeleton riding a bike. (☎303 2834. Open M-Th and Sa 10am-5pm, F 10:30am-5pm, Su 12:30-5pm. Free.) The **Barber Institute of Fine Arts,** in the University of Birmingham on Edgbaston Park Rd., displays works by artists as diverse as Rubens, Renoir, and Magritte. Take bus #61, 62, or 63 from the city center. (☎414 7333. Open M-Sa 10am-5pm, Su 2-5pm. Free.)

THE MIDLANDS

The more than 100 jewelry shops that line the **Jewellery Quarter** hammer out almost all of Britain's jewelry. The **Museum of the Jewellery Quarter,** 77-79 Vyse St., Hockley (signposted from the city center), lets visitors tour an old factory and watch skilled jewelers. (☎554 3598. Open M-F 10am-4pm, Sa 11am-5pm. £2.50, concessions £2.) The **National Sea Life Centre,** The Waters Edge, Brindleyplace, overlooks the canal network and has the world's first fully transparent 360° underwater tunnel. (☎633 4700. Open daily from 10am. £8, seniors and children 5.50.)

ENTERTAINMENT AND FESTIVALS

BARS AND CLUBS
Broad St. is lined with trendy cafe-bars and clubs. A thriving gay-friendly scene has arisen in the area around **Essex St.** Pick up the bimonthly *What's On* or the monthly *Leap* to discover the latest hotspots. Clubbers on a budget should grab a guide to public transport's Night Network from the Centro office in New St. Station—**night buses** generally run hourly until 3:30am on Friday and Saturday nights.

Stoodibakers, 192 Broad St. (☎643 5100). Alluringly dark decor prompts much drinking, posturing, and occasional dancing. Dress is trendy. Cover £4 F-Sa after 9:30pm.

Bakers, 162 Broad St. (☎633 3839). Savor the deep beats of Brum's favorite late-night house venue, complete with black lighting. "Horny" on F (unless otherwise noted) with female DJs (£4-5), "Republica" on Sa (£5-7). Open F 10pm-2:30am, Sa 10pm-4am.

Rat and Parrot, 200 Broad St. (☎643 7130). Angels herald the resurgence of Brum's hip-hop and R&B scene. The fashionable sip, step, and survey. No trainers/sneakers, jeans, or sportswear. Usually free. Club atmosphere Th-Sa 9pm-1am.

Nightingale, Essex House, Kent St. (☎622 1718). 2 frenzied dance-floors, jazz lounge, and billiard room attract a predominantly gay crowd from all over the UK. Weekend cover £5, weekdays £1. Open Tu-W 10pm-2am, F-Sa 9pm-4am, Su 9pm-1am.

MUSIC AND THEATER

City of Birmingham Symphony Orchestra (☎780 3333) plays in superb Symphony Hall at the Convention Centre on Broad St. Box office open M-F 10am-8pm, Sa 10am-10pm; Su hours dependent on show times. Tickets £5-32; some concessions and group discounts; student standbys £7.50 after 1pm on concert days.

Hippodrome Theatre, Hurst St. (☎622 7486). Originally a music hall featuring big-name vaudeville artists, the theater now stages West End musicals and quality opera. Call for hours and ticket prices.

Birmingham Repertory Theatre, Centenary Sq. (☎236 4455), on Broad St. A less grandiose, but still celebrated, theater. Open M-Sa 9:30am-8pm, Su 4-8pm on performance days. Tickets £7-20, half-price standby tickets for students and UB40 cardholders.

The **Birmingham Jazz Festival** (☎454 7020) brings over 200 jazz bands, singers, and instrumentalists to town during the first two weeks of July; book through the TIC.

IRONBRIDGE ☎01952

While mucking about in his furnace workshop in 1709, a Coalbrookdale man discovered a way to smelt iron ore using coke (coal residue) instead of expensive charcoal. Abraham Darby's discovery made possible the mass production of iron: soon these wooded hills became a smoke-belching inferno, and the Industrial Revolution was born. From this Shropshire valley came the world's first iron rails and, in 1799, the first cast-iron bridge. No industry remains, but the mines and ironworks are now museums collectively designated a World Heritage Site.

⬛ TRANSPORTATION. The nearest **train** station is at **Telford,** 20min. from Shrewsbury on the Birmingham-Shrewsbury-Chester line (M-Sa 1-4 per hr., Su every hr.). The best (well, only) way to reach Ironbridge directly is by **bus.** Timetables are notoriously temperamental; even the *Rural Bus Network,* a free booklet available at tourist information centres (TICs), is not always up-to-date. For bus information, call the TIC or the Telford Travelink (☎200005). **Midlands North** (☎(08457) 056005) bus #96 stops at Ironbridge from **Telford** (15min., M-Sa 6 per day, £2.20) and **Shrewsbury** (40min.; M-Sa 6 per day, Su 5 per day; £1.80). The Sunday bus from Shrewsbury also stops at **Coalbrookdale, Blists Hill,** and **Coalport. Arriva** (☎(08456) 015395) bus #99 runs on the Wellington-Bridgnorth route, stopping at **Ironbridge** and **Coalbrookdale** from **Telford** (25min., M-Sa 16 per day, £2.20). Arriva #76 (20min., M-Sa 5 per day) and 77 (20min., M-Sa 4 per day) provide crucial, albeit spotty, service between Coalbrookdale and Coalport, both home to YHA hostels, stopping at the Ironbridge Museum of the Gorge en route. Note that not all buses begin or terminate in Coalport; get a timetable at the Ironbridge TIC.

⬛ ORIENTATION AND PRACTICAL INFORMATION. Ironbridge is the name of both the river gorge around which several villages cluster and the village at the center. The nine **Ironbridge Gorge Museums** huddle on the banks of the Severn valley in an area covering 6 sq. mi.; some are difficult to reach without a car, since buses stop only at selected points and bike rental stores are conspicuously absent. The museums group in three main areas. Central **Ironbridge** is home to the TIC and the Iron Bridge and Tollhouse; the Museum of the Gorge is ½ mi. to the west. Some 2 mi. northwest of the bridge is **Coalbrookdale,** where you'll find the Coalbrookdale Museum of Iron and the Darby Houses. Two miles east of the bridge, past the Jackfield Tile Museum, the village of **Coalport** is home to the Coalport China Museum and the Tar Tunnel. A mile north of Coalport is **Blists Hill Victorian Town.**

The friendly staff at the **tourist information centre,** the Wharfage, in Ironbridge, provides the free 66-page tome *Ironbridge Gorge Visitor Guide,* books accommodations for a 10% deposit, and commiserates with you over bus schedules. (☎432166 or toll-free (0800) 590258; fax 432204; www.ironbridge.org.uk. Open M-F 9am-5pm, Sa-Su 10am-5pm.) There are **no banks** or **cash machines** anywhere in Ironbridge. The **post office** is on The Square in Ironbridge. (Open M-Tu and Th-F 9am-1pm and 2-5:30pm, W 9am-1pm, Sa 9am-12:30pm.) **Postal code:** TF8 7AQ.

⬛ ACCOMMODATIONS AND FOOD. The two buildings of the **YHA Ironbridge Gorge** grace the valley's opposite ends, 3 mi. apart. The hostel in **Coalbrookdale** inhabits a remodeled schoolhouse built by the Darby family and is near the Ironbridge TIC. Walk past the Museum of the Gorge and turn right toward Coalbrookdale; the YHA will be on your right. The hostel in **Coalport,** next to the Coalport China Museum, is a renovated china factory equipped with laundry facilities, Internet access, and a restaurant. Both buildings are reached by Arriva bus #76, and Coalbrookdale is also a stop on #77; see **Transportation,** above. (Both ☎588755; fax 588722; ironbridge@yha.org.uk. Dorms £11.25, children £8.)

Besides the hostels, budget accommodations are practically non-existent. The few B&Bs in the Ironbridge area charge upwards of £22 per person, and solo travelers can expect to pay at least £30 for a single room. With a prime location in Ironbridge village, **Eley's of Ironbridge,** 13 Tontine Hill, has rooms that include bath, color TV, and great views of the bridge. (☎432541. Singles £35-40; doubles £45-55.) One of the cheaper B&Bs is **Coalbrookdale Villa,** Paradise St., an elegant Gothic house about 10min. from Ironbridge. The kind proprietress strives to supply every cereal you could desire. (☎/fax 433450. Singles £45; doubles £52-56.) The nearest campsite is the **Severn Gorge Caravan Park,** 3 mi. from Ironbridge and 1 mi. north of the Blists Hill Victorian Town on Bridgnorth Rd. in Tweedale. (☎684789. 1-person tent £7.35, 2-person tent £10.50. Electricity £2.30-2.60. Showers free.)

Oliver's Vegetarian Bistro, 33 High St., offers a varied menu (main courses £4-7) in a cozy setting. (☎433086. Open Tu-F 7-11pm, Sa 11am-3pm and 7-11pm, Su 11am-5pm.) The steak-and-kidney pie at the **Horse and Jockey** pub, 15 Jockey Bank, is said to be the best in Britain (£5.25). Walk 5min. from Ironbridge toward Madeley. (☎433798. Open daily noon-2:30pm and 7-11pm; food served until 9:30pm.)

▥ **MUSEUMS.** There's not much more to Ironbridge than the **Ironbridge Gorge Museums,** but you'd be hard-pressed to find a better portrayal of Britain's unique industrial heritage. Count on spending at least two days to cover the lot. If visiting all nine museums, buy an **Ironbridge Passport** from any of them, which admits you once to each of the museums on any dates you choose (£10, seniors £9, students and children £6, families £30; YHA members 10% discount). The major museums are open year-round daily 10am-5pm, while smaller museums such as the Darby Houses, the Iron Bridge Tollhouse, and the Broseley Pipeworks are open only limited hours November through March; call the TIC for more information.

The **Iron Bridge,** built in 1779 by Abraham Darby III to world-wide attention, crosses a deep gorge of the River Severn. At its southern end, a small exhibit in the **Tollhouse** describes the bridge's history and how even royals had to pay the toll. (☎884391. Free.) A 10min. walk from Ironbridge village, the **Museum of the Gorge** provides a brief introduction to the area's history and is a good place to begin the day's exploring. (☎432405. £2, students and children £1, seniors £1.50.) In Coalbrookdale to the northwest, the **Coalbrookdale Museum of Iron,** once a great warehouse, recreates the furnace of Abraham Darby I where the whole brouhaha began, traces the history of iron use through millennia, and exhibits iron products beyond your wildest imagination. (☎433418. £4.60, seniors £3.90, students and children £2.90.) Nearby, the **Darby Houses** model the pleasant quarters of a 19th-century ironmaster. (☎432551. £2.65, seniors £2, students and children £1.50.) In Coalport to the west, the **Coalport China Museum** and **Jackfield Tile Museum** show the products of the porcelain and tile industries that moved in when iron production tailed off; both offer demonstrations and workshops. (China ☎580650; Tile 882030. Both £3.90, students and children £2.25, seniors £3.60.) Don a hard-hat at the eerie **Tar Tunnel,** constructed to connect the Blists Hill mines to the Severn, where workers were surprised to discover that smudgy natural bitumen dripped from the walls. (☎580827. £1, students and children 50p, seniors 80p.) After eyeing a lot of iron, which, quite frankly, tends not to hold up its end of the conversation, make haste to the open-air **Blists Hill Victorian Town,** where you can chat with real actors going about their make-believe business, as well as exchange your silly 20th-century money for serious Victorian shillings and brass farthings with which to buy ale. (☎582050. £7.50, students and children £5, seniors £7.)

SHREWSBURY ☎01743

A town "islanded in Severn stream," in the words of poet A.E. Housman, Shrewsbury (SHROWS-bree; pop. 59,000) has been occupied by many peoples. The semi-circular patch of land was first settled by pugnacious Saxons, who decided to call it Scrobbesbyrig, and then by Roger de Montgomery, second-in-command to William the Conqueror, who sashayed up from Hastings in the 11th century. By the 16th century, wool-rich Shrewsburyites had redecorated, raising distinctive timber houses later made accessible by the railways that grew like weeds over Victorian England. Taking a bit of a breather today, Shrewsbury continues to attract architectural buffs and travelers in transit with its stereotypically English streetscapes.

▐ TRANSPORTATION

The **train station,** a splendid neo-Gothic building, is at the end of Castle St. (Ticket office open M-Sa 5:30am-10pm, Su 7:30am-8:30pm.) **Trains** (☎(08457) 484950) run from: **London** (3hr., 1-2 per hr., £31.30); **Wolverhampton** (30-50min., 1-3 per hr., £5.40); **Aberystwyth,** on the Cambrian Coaster (2hr.; M-Sa 8 per day, Su 5 per day;

£11.40); **Swansea,** on the Heart of Wales Line (3½hr.; M-Sa 3 per day, Su 1 per day; £15.20); most of North Wales via **Wrexham General** and **Chester** (1hr.; M-Sa 14 per day, Su 6 per day; £6). The **bus station** is at Raven Meadows, parallel to Pride Hill. (☎244496. Office open M-F 8:30am-5:30pm, Sa 8:30am-4pm.) **National Express** (☎(08705) 808080) **buses** arrive from: **London** (4½hr., 2 per day, £13.50); **Llangollen** (1hr., 1 per day, £3); **Birmingham** (1½hr., 2 per day, £4). The *Shrewsbury Public Transport Guide* is free at the bus station and the tourist information centre (TIC). **Taxis** queue in front of the train station, or call **Access Taxis** at 360606.

◆✦🔃 ORIENTATION AND PRACTICAL INFORMATION

The **River Severn** encircles Shrewsbury's town center in a horseshoe shape, with the curve pointing south. The town's central axis runs from the train station in the northeast to Quarry Park in the southwest: starting as **Castle Gates,** the road becomes **Castle St.** near the station, then the pedestrian-only **Pride Hill,** then **Shoplatch,** and finally **St. John's Hill.** Signposts help travelers navigate.

Tourist Information Centre: Music Hall, The Square (☎281200; fax 281213; www.shrewsburytourism.co.uk), across from the Market Bldg. Get free town maps, buy National Express tickets, and book accommodations for £1.50 and a 10% deposit. Oversized town trail leaflets (95p), the new *Shrewsbury Guide* (£2.50), and piles of brochures. Open May-Sept. M-Sa 10am-6pm, Su 10am-4pm; Oct.-Apr. M-Sa 10am-5pm.

Tours: Historic 30min. walking tours from the TIC pass through Shrewsbury's "shuts" (lanes that could be shut) and uncover the etymology of Grope Lane. May-Sept. M-Sa 11am and 2:40pm; Oct. M-Sa 2:30pm; Nov.-Apr. Sa only. £2.50, children £1.

Financial Services: Barclays, corner of Castle St. and St. Mary's St. Open M-Tu and Th-F 9am-5pm, W 10am-5pm, Sa 9:30am-1pm. **Thomas Cook** (☎842000), corner of Pride Hill and Butcher Row. Open M-Tu and Th-Sa 9am-5:30pm, W 10am-5:30pm.

Launderette: Stidgers Wishy Washy, Monkmoor Rd. (☎355151), off Abbey Foregate. No soap, and proud of it. M-F service wash only, Sa-Su self-service permitted. Wash £3, dry 20p per 3min.; service £7 per load. Open M-F 7:30am-5pm, Sa 10am-4pm, Su 10am-2pm; last wishy washy 1hr. before close.

Police: Raven Meadows. Open M-Sa 9am-5pm. Also Clive Rd. (☎232888), Monkmoor.

Hospital: Shrewsbury Hospital, Mytton Oak Rd. (☎261138).

Internet Access: PC+, 11 Abbey Foregate (☎242135), over the English Bridge. £2 per 30min. Open M-Sa 9am-5pm. **Shrewsbury Library,** Castle Gates (☎255300). £1 per 15min. (ID required). Open M and W 9:30am-5pm, Tu and F 9:30am-7:30pm, Th 9:30am-1pm, Sa 9:30am-4pm.

Post Office: St. Mary's St. (☎362925), just off Pride Hill. **Bureau de change.** Open M-Sa 9am-5:30pm. **Postal Code:** SY1 1DE.

♠♣ ACCOMMODATIONS AND FOOD

The **YHA Shrewsbury,** The Woodlands, Abbey Foregate, is 1½ mi. from the city center. Cross the English Bridge, pass the abbey, and head down Abbey Foregate. Alternatively, catch bus #8 or 26 from the center and get off at Shirehall before the Lord Hill's Column roundabout. This Victorian house has laundry facilities and a pool table. (☎360179; fax 357423; shrewsbury@yha.org.uk. Lockout 10am-5pm. Curfew 11pm. Open Feb.-Oct. M-Sa. Dorms £9.25, under 18 £6.50.) Several **B&Bs** (£18-22) lie between Abbey Foregate and Monkmoor Rd. Comely **Glyndene,** Park Terr., has an elaborate bell-pull and tasteful rooms with TVs. From the bridge, follow the road left of the abbey. (☎352488; www.glyndene.co.uk. £18-20 per person.) Two doors down, **Allandale** hangs its walls with prints of wide-eyed babies and cityscapes. (☎240173. £20 per person.) **Abbey Lodge,** 68 Abbey Foregate, has standard rooms with TVs. (☎/fax 235832. Singles £18; doubles with bath £42.50.)

Lunch crowds queue at **Subs,** Wyle Cop, which prepares excellent hot panini (£3) and a wide range of pasta dishes in the £2-3 range. (☎241620. Open Tu-Sa 9am-4pm.) **The Good Life Wholefood Restaurant,** Barracks Passage, off Wyle Cop, serves vegetarian dishes in a 14th-century building near the Lion Hotel. (☎350455. Open M-Sa 9:30am-4:30pm.) At the **King's Head** pub, Mardol St., admire a medieval wall painting of the Last Supper and the £3.45 full roast dinner. (☎362843. Open M-Sa 10:30am-11pm, Su noon-11pm; food served M-Sa 11am-7pm, Su noon-7pm.)

🄖 SIGHTS

Shrewsbury's biggest attraction is undoubtedly its architecture. Tudoresque houses dot the central shopping district and rally in full force at the **Bear Steps,** which start in the alley on High St. across from the Square. At the end of Castle St., the riverside acres of **Quarry Park** explode with bright flowers. According to local law, sheep can graze anywhere; a number infiltrate the churchyard at **St. Mary's.** Shrewsbury also makes a habit of honoring its native sons, and memorials pepper the city. Check out **Darwin's statue** opposite the castle, the colossal **Lord Hill Column** at the end of Abbey Foregate, and the **Clive of India** outside Market Sq.

The original earth-and-timber version of **Shrewsbury Castle,** near the train station, was constructed in 1083 by William the Conqueror's buddy Roger de Montgomery, who demolished 50 Saxon houses to make way for it. It has since been replaced by the Great Hall, a more durable stone building now home to the **Shropshire Regimental Museum.** Climb **Laura's Tower** for a grand view of town. (☎358516. Museum and tower open Easter-Sept. Tu-Sa 10am-5pm, Su 10am-4pm; Oct.-Easter Tu-Sa only. Grounds open Easter-Sept. daily 9am-5pm; Oct.-Easter M-Sa only. £2, seniors £1, students and children free. Grounds free.) The **Shrewsbury Museum and Art Gallery,** Barker St., off Shoplatch, displays Iron Age log boats, a silver mirror from AD 130, and a recreation of King Arthur's sword, Excalibur. (☎361196. Open Easter-Sept. Tu-Sa 10am-5pm, Su 10am-4pm; Oct.-Easter Tu-Sa 10am-4pm. Free.)

Beyond the English Bridge, the 919-year-old **Shrewsbury Abbey** holds the remains of a shrine to St. Winefride, a 7th-century princess who was beheaded, then miraculously re-capitated to become an abbess and patroness of North Wales and Shrewsbury. A memorial to local boy and WWI poet Wilfred Owen lies in the garden. (☎232723. Open Easter-Oct. daily 9:30am-5:30pm; Nov.-Easter 10:30am-3pm.)

EAST MIDLANDS

NOTTINGHAM   ☎0115

Nottingham (pop. 261,500) maintains its age-old tradition, created by the mythical Robin Hood and his band of merry men, of taking from the rich. The modern city uses Robin Hood as an economic tool, luring tourists with little substance but plenty of thrill. Don't be fooled: Nottinghamshire has produced more famed residents than its socially conscious outlaws, including Lord Byron, D.H. Lawrence, and Jesse Boot, whose name appears on pharmacies England-wide. Navigating Nottingham today you'll more likely see savvy urban youths than either merry men or club-footed poets, as the city is also home to 20,000 university students.

▟ TRANSPORTATION

Trains: Nottingham Station, Carrington St., south of the city, across the canal. Trains (☎(08457) 484950) arrive from: **London St. Pancras** (2hr., every hr., £37); **Sheffield** (50min., every hr., £8.20); **Lincoln** (1hr.; M-Sa 32 per day, Su 7 per day; £7).

Buses: Broad Marsh Bus Station (☎950 3665), between Collin St. and Canal St. Ticket and info booth open M-F 9am-5:30pm. **Victoria Bus Station,** at the corner of York St. and Cairn St. **National Express** (☎(08705) 808080) speeds to Broad Marsh from **London** (3hr., 7 per day, £15) and **Sheffield** (1¼hr., every hr., £9). **Nottinghamshire County Council Buses** link points throughout the county.

Public Transportation: For short urban journeys, hop on a **Nottingham City Transport** bus (40, 70, or 90p tickets). All-day local bus passes £2.50. For public transit info call **Nottinghamshire Buses Hotline** (☎924 0000). Open daily 7am-8pm.

ORIENTATION AND PRACTICAL INFORMATION

Nottingham is a busy city and its streets are confusing. Its hub is **Old Market Sq.**, a plaza near the Council House (beware of the pigeons). The train and bus stations lie to the extreme south. The trendy neighborhood of **Hockley** is east of the center.

Tourist Information Centre: 1-4 Smithy Row (☎915 5330), off Old Market Sq. Many reference guides, tour listings, a free city map, and the free *What's On* entertainment guide. Books rooms before 4:30pm for a £3 fee and 10% deposit. Open M-F 9am-5:30pm, Sa 9am-5pm; Aug.-Sept. also Su 10am-3pm.

Tours: The **Nottingham Experience** (☎(0410) 293348) leads 30min. tours, leaving from the castle gatehouse. Tours Easter-Oct. daily 10am-4pm; £3, concessions £2.50.

Financial Services: Barclays, 2 High St. Open M-Tu and Th-F 9am-5pm, W 10am-5:30pm, Sa 9:30am-3:30pm. **Thomas Cook,** 4 Long Row (☎909 3000). Offers budget travel services. Open M-Tu and Th-Sa 9am-5pm, W 9:30am-5:30pm. **American Express,** 2 Victoria St. (☎(08706) 001060). Open M-Tu and Th-F 9am-5:30pm, W 9:30am-5:30pm, Sa 9am-5pm.

Launderette: Brights, 150 Mansfield Rd. (☎948 3670), near the Igloo hostel. Open M-F 8:30am-7pm, Sa 8:30am-6pm, Su 9:30am-5pm. Last wash 1hr. before close.

Police: North Church St. (☎948 2999).

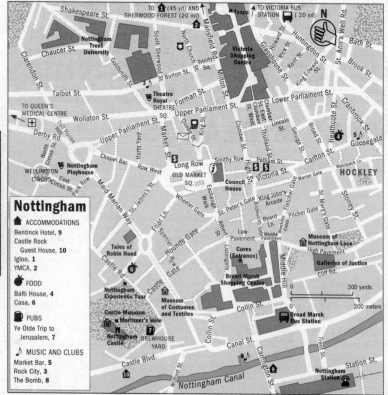

THE MIDLANDS

Nottingham

ACCOMMODATIONS
Bentinck Hotel, 9
Castle Rock
  Guest House, 10
Igloo, 1
YMCA, 2

FOOD
Balti House, 4
Casa, 6

PUBS
Ye Olde Trip to
  Jerusalem, 7

MUSIC AND CLUBS
Market Bar, 5
Rock City, 3
The Bomb, 8

Hospital: Queen's Medical Center, Derby Rd. (☎924 9924).

Internet Access: Alphacafe, 4 Queen St. (☎956 6988). 16+ terminals, stylish setting. £2 per hr. before noon, £4 per hr. after. Open M-F 9:30am-8:30pm, Sa 10am-7pm.

Post Office: Queen St. (☎947 4311). Open M-Sa 9am-5:30pm. **Bureau de change.** **Postal Code:** NG1 2BN.

ACCOMMODATIONS

A number of guest houses cluster along **Goldsmith St.** (near Nottingham Trent University) and charge ₤18-22 per person.

Igloo, 110 Mansfield Rd. (☎947 5250; reception@igloohostel.co.uk), on the north side of town. From the train station, take bus #90 to Mansfield Rd. From the TIC, walk right to Clumber St., then take a left and walk straight for 10min. Homey hostel operated by an experienced backpacker. Dorm-style with lively orange and green walls. TV lounge, kitchen, and 2 black cats. Sleepsacks available. Curfew 3am. £12 per person.

YMCA, 4 Shakespeare St. (☎956 7600; admin@nottingham.ymca.org.uk). Large building with bland decor on a busy street, but the youthful atmosphere is inviting. Breakfast included. Key deposit £5. Dorms £11; singles £16.

Castle Rock Guest House, 79 Castle Blvd. (☎948 2116). 5min. walk from the train station, without having to negotiate those nasty hills. Clean double and family rooms with TVs. Attentive hostess. £17-25 per person.

Bentinck Hotel, Station St. (☎958 0285), directly across from the train station. Great location makes up for worn carpets. Clean rooms with TVs. Singles £18; doubles £32.

FOOD

Quick, inexpensive bites are easily found on **Milton St.** and **Mansfield Rd.** Gaggles of sandwich shops, trendy cafes, and ethnic eateries line **Goosegate.** There is a **Tesco** supermarket in the Victoria Shopping Centre off Mansfield Rd. (Open M-Tu and Th-Sa 8am-7pm, W 8am-8pm, Su 11am-5pm.)

Ye Olde Trip to Jerusalem, 1 Brewhouse Yard (☎947 3171). Yet another pub claiming the title "Oldest Inn in England," this one pulled its first drink in 1189. Soldiers stopped here en route to the Crusades. Locally known as "The Trip," the pub is carved into Nottingham Castle's sandstone base: watch your head on the 6 ft. ceiling. Open M-Sa 11am-11pm, Su noon-10:30pm; food served M-F 9am-5pm, Sa-Su noon-6pm.

Casa, 12-18 Friar Ln. Fine service in expansive surroundings. Scan stylish patrons and passersby as you munch fresh sandwiches (£4-6). Open daily noon-10:30pm.

Balti House, 35 Heathcote St. (☎947 2871). This tandoori treasure trove sizzles above and beyond the throngs of Indian dives around town. Open daily 6-10pm.

SIGHTS

▨THE GALLERIES OF JUSTICE. An innovative museum experience at its interactive best. The Crime and Punishment Galleries drag unsuspecting visitors before a merciless court, throw them behind bars, and let them see the English prison system through the eyes of the convicted. Tourists are regularly sentenced to Australia; Australians may not use this as a free return ticket. You can then switch sides and help solve criminal investigations in the Police Galleries. *(High Pavement. ☎952 0558. Open Tu-Su 10am-5pm. About 2hr. long; last admission to Crime and Punishment 3pm, Police Galleries 4pm. £6.95, students and seniors £5.95, children £5.25, families £19.95.)*

NOTTINGHAM CASTLE. Originally constructed in 1068 by William the Conqueror, the remains of the castle top a sandstone rise south of the city center. In 1642, Charles I raised his standard against Parliament here, kicking off the Civil Wars. For his troubles, the king was beheaded and the castle destroyed. What's left now houses the ▨**Castle Museum and Art Gallery,** a refreshing collection of historical exhibits, Victorian art, silver, and the regimental memorabilia of the Sherwood Foresters. (☎915 3700. *Open Mar.-Oct. daily 10am-5pm; Nov.-Feb. Sa-Th 10am-5pm. Admission M-Th free; Sa-Su £2, concessions £1, families £5, free for disabled visitors.*) While you're there, check out **Mortimer's Hole,** the 100m underground passageway that leads from the base of the cliff to the castle. After Mortimer and Queen Isabella murdered Edward II, they retreated to Nottingham Castle. Edward III created the passageway to sneak up on the castle and capture his father's assassin. (☎915 3700. *50min. tours daily 2 and 3pm from the Castle Museum entrance. £2, concessions £1.*)

THE UNDERGROUND SCENE. Beneath Nottingham lie hundreds of ancient caves. As early as the 10th century, Nottingham dwellers dug homes out of the soft and porous "Sherwood sandstones" on which the city rests. Even in medieval times, the caves were often preferred to more conventional housing—they required no building materials and incurred lower taxes. While cave residency dwindled during the Industrial Revolution, Nottingham citizens (and pub owners) continued to use some for storage, and during WWII many caves were converted to air-raid shelters. Visitors can tour one cave complex, surreally situated beneath the Broad Marsh Shopping Centre. The 40min. audio tour of the "Tigguo Cobauc," or "City of Caves," includes a trip through Britain's only underground medieval tannery—authentic smells included. (☎924 1424. *Open M-Sa 10am-5pm, Su 11am-5pm. £3.75, concessions £2.75, families £11.50.*)

TALES OF ROBIN HOOD. Well, there had to be something in Nottingham commemorating the man. Cable cars will carry you and your five-year-old through Robin's amusement-park version of Sherwood Forest. (*30-38 Maid Marion Way.* ☎948 3284. *Open daily 10am-6pm, last admission 4:30pm. £5.95, students and seniors £4.95, children £3.95, families £17.75.*)

THE LACE INDUSTRY. A local myth holds that there are five women for every Nottingham man. This unlikely ratio springs from Nottingham's lace industry, which employed thousands of young women during the mid-19th century. The **Museum of Nottingham Lace,** 3-5 High Pavement, uses a working 1850s spinning machine to show how the material was woven into the social fabric of the city. Demonstrations take place daily from 11am to 1pm and 1:30 to 3:30pm. (☎989 7365. *Open daily 10am-5pm. £2.95, students and seniors £2.50, children £1.95. 50min. audio tour requires £1.95 deposit.*)

♫ ENTERTAINMENT

Thirty-plus clubs, and even more pubs, blanket the city. Nights, covers, and crowds vary, but students can be found everywhere. Sunday salsa parties fill the **Market Bar,** 16-22 Goosegate, Hockley (☎924 1780), when most other clubs are closed. **Rock City,** 8 Talbot St., entertains with local bands and mainstream rock. "Damaging" Thursday nights offer metal appreciation, and Saturdays are alternative. (☎950 0102. Cover £3-4. Open M-Sa 8:30pm-2am.) **The Bomb,** 45 Bridlesmith Gate, plays house, garage, and hip-hop and has a "trainers ok, but no check shirt casualties please" dress code. (☎950 6667. Cover £1-3. Open M-Sa 10:30pm-2am.) The **Theatre Royal** (☎989 5555), at Theatre Sq., and **Nottingham Playhouse** (☎941 9419), at Wellington Circus, offer musicals and dramas (tickets from £6).

▨ DAYTRIPS FROM NOTTINGHAM

▨ NEWSTEAD ABBEY

Bus #757 travels from Nottingham's Victoria Bus Station to the abbey gates (35min., 2 per hr., return £3.25). House and gardens lie 1 mi. from gates. ☎(01623) 793557. *House open Apr.-Sept. daily noon-5pm. Grounds open year-round 9am-dusk. House and grounds £4, students and seniors £2, under 16 £1.50. Grounds only £2, concessions £1.*

North of Nottingham in the village of **Linby** stands **Newstead Abbey,** ancestral estate of Romantic poet Lord Byron. Byron took residence as a 10-year-old and remained here until forced to sell. Many of his personal effects stayed behind, including a replica of "Byron's skullcap," an ancient human cranium unearthed at Newstead in 1806, which Byron had coated in silver, inscribed with verse, and filled with wine before its mysterious reinterment in 1863. Lively peacocks hold court in the gracious gardens, and the staff stands ready to enlighten those who step indoors.

SHERWOOD FOREST

Buses #33 and 36 leave Victoria Bus Station in Nottingham for the Sherwood Forest Visitors Centre (1hr., every 2hr., £4.50). ☎(01623) 823202. Centre open Apr.-Oct. daily 10:30am-5pm; Nov.-Mar. 10:30am-4:30pm. Forest open year-round dawn-dusk. Free.

To the north spreads famed Sherwood Forest, considerably thinned since the 13th century. The **Sherwood Forest Visitor Centre** has a small museum, but beware the multitude of children circling with mini-archery sets. To escape the crowds, take the 3½ mi. walk from the Centre. The medieval-style **Robin Hood Festival,** run by the Visitors Centre, stages a jousting tournament each August.

EASTWOOD

6 mi. west of Nottingham. Rainbow bus #1 leaves from Victoria Bus Station for Eastwood (40min.; every 10min. 7am-6pm, 2 per hr. 6-11:30pm; £3.50).

D.H. Lawrence was an Eastwood native and schoolteacher who went on to write controversial poetry and prose. Once he was banned from the bookshelves, now he's buried in Westminster Abbey. The **D.H. Lawrence Birthplace Museum** fills his childhood home at 8A Victoria St., near Mansfield Rd. (☎(01773) 717353. Open Apr.-Oct. daily 10am-5pm; Nov.-Mar. 10am-4pm. £2, concessions £1.20.) The **Sons and Lovers Cottage,** 28 Garden Rd. (☎(0151) 653 8710), where young Lawrence lived from 1887 to 1891, is free and open by appointment to die-hard fans.

LINCOLN   ☎01522

Medieval streets climb their cobbled way past half-timbered homes to Lincoln's dominating 12th-century cathedral, itself a relative newcomer in a town built for retired Roman legionnaires. Lincoln (pop. 90,000), often thought of as a cold industrial town, does not draw tourists, but those who do make the trip, and the steep uphill climb to the city's peak, will consider it worthwhile.

▐ TRANSPORTATION

Trains: Central Station, St. Mary's St. Ticket office open M-Sa 5:45am-7:30pm, Su 10:30am-9:20pm. Travel center open M-Sa 9am-5pm. Trains (☎(08457) 484950) on the Doncaster-London line from: **London King's Cross** (2½hr.; M-Sa every hr., Su every 2hr.; return £40.50); **Nottingham** (1hr.; M-Sa 2 per hr., Su 7 per day; return £5.85); **Leeds** (2hr.; every 2½hr., return £17.70).

Buses: City Bus Station, Melville St. off St. Mary's St., opposite the train station. Open M-F 8:30am-5pm, Sa 9am-1:45pm. **National Express** (☎(08705) 808080) from: **London** (5hr., 2 per day, £18) and **Nottingham** (1¼hr.; 1-2 per hr.; £13). For information on rural Lincolnshire bus services, contact the Lincolnshire Roadcar station on St. Mark St. (☎522255). Open M-F 8:30am-5pm, Sa 8:30am-4:30pm.

Travel Hotline: ☎553135. Open M-Th 8am-5:15pm, F 8am-4:45pm.

▌▌ ORIENTATION AND PRACTICAL INFORMATION

Roman and Norman military engineers were attracted to the summit of **Castle Hill;** later railway engineers preferred its base. Thus, Lincoln has an affluent acropolis to the north and a cottage-filled lower town near the tracks. The tourist information centre (TIC) and major sights lie at the junction of Steep Hill and Castle Hill.

Tourist Information Centre: 9 Castle Hill (☎529828; fax 579055; www.lincoln-info.org.uk). Books rooms for 10% deposit. Pick up a free map and glossy city miniguide (25p). Open M-Th 9:30am-5:30pm, F 9:30am-5pm, Sa-Su 10am-5pm. Another **branch** (☎579056) is on the corner of Cornhill and High St. Same hours on M-Sa, closed Su.

Tours: 1hr. tours depart from the TIC July-Aug. daily 11am and 2pm; Sept.-Oct. and Apr.-June only Sa-Su. £2.50, children £1.50. **Guide Friday** (☎522255) runs bus tours all around the city, at least 1 per hr. during summer. Hop on at any of the many stops. Tours 50min. £6, students and seniors £4.50, children £2.50.

Financial Services: Barclays, 316 High St. (☎343555), and other banks line High St. Open M-Tu and Th-F 9am-5pm, W 10am-5pm, Sa 9:30am-12:30pm. **Thomas Cook,** 4 Cornhill Pavement (☎346400). Open M-Tu and Th-Sa 9am-5:30pm, W 10am-5:30pm.

Launderette: Burton Laundries, 8 Burton Rd. (☎543498), at Westgate near the cathedral. Dry cleaning. Open daily from 8:30am; M-F last wash 7pm, Sa-Su last wash 4pm.

Police: West Parade (☎882222), near the town hall.

Hospital: Lincoln County Hospital, Greenwell Rd. (☎512512).

Internet Access: Central Library, Free School Ln. (☎510800), between Saltergate and Silver St. Of the 3 terminals, 1 must be reserved ahead (£3 per hr.), while the others are for drop-in use (£1 per 15min.). Open M-F 9:30am-7pm, Sa 9:30am-4pm. **Sun Cafe,** 7a St. Mary (☎579067), across from the train station. 3 computers in a self-appointed center for the arts. £4 per hr. Open M-Sa 9am-6pm, Su noon-5pm.

Post Office: Cornhill (☎532288), just off High St. **Bureau de change,** no commission. Open M-F 9am-5:30pm, Sa 9am-5pm. **Postal Code:** LN5 7XX.

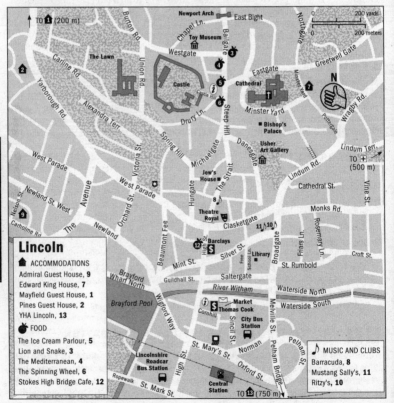

Lincoln

🏠 ACCOMMODATIONS
Admiral Guest House, **9**
Edward King House, **7**
Mayfield Guest House, **1**
Pines Guest House, **2**
YHA Lincoln, **13**

🍴 FOOD
The Ice Cream Parlour, **5**
Lion and Snake, **3**
The Mediterranean, **4**
The Spinning Wheel, **6**
Stokes High Bridge Cafe, **12**

🎵 MUSIC AND CLUBS
Barracuda, **8**
Mustang Sally's, **11**
Ritzy's, **10**

ACCOMMODATIONS

B&Bs line **Carline** and **Yarborough Rd.,** west of the castle, most for £17-20 per person. Consult the accommodations list in the window of the branch TIC.

YHA Lincoln, 77 South Park Ave. (☎522076; fax 567424), opposite South Common at the end of Canwick Rd. Veer right from the station, turn right onto Pelham Bridge (which becomes Canwick Rd.), and again after the traffic lights at South Park Ave. 47-bed Victorian villa with a solarium and view of meandering ponies. Lockout 10am-5pm. Curfew 11pm. Open Feb.-Oct. Dorms £11, under 18 £7.40.

Mayfield Guest House, 213 Yarborough Rd. (☎/fax 533732). Entrance behind house on Mill Rd., a 20min. walk from train station and near the Ellis Mill, a working windmill. If you have a backpack, spare yourself and take bus #7 or 8 (60p). A bright Victorian mansion with large rooms and fluffy quilts. Panoramic breakfast-room view of countryside. No smoking. Singles £19-25; doubles £38-40.

Admiral Guest House, 18 Nelson St. (☎/fax 544467), in the lower part of town. From the railway station, take Wigford Way across the canal, then take the immediate steps down to the canal and walk along Brayford Wharf North; turn left onto Carholme Rd. and right onto Nelson St. Mrs. Robertson's decor is so nautical, you'll think you're at sea. A must for Lord Nelson devotees. Cable TV. Singles £18; doubles £35.

Edward King House, Minster Yard (☎528778), next to the Bishop's Palace. The diocese runs this place, so bibles replace TVs in the rooms. The views are divine, the breakfast room and building immaculate, and the city center location miraculous. Continental breakfast included, English breakfast £3. £20 per person.

Pines Guest House, 104 Yarborough Rd. (☎/fax 532985). Take bus #7 or 8 to Yarborough Rd. or walk 15min. from the train station. Turn left, then veer right onto Wigford Way, which becomes Newland; take a right onto The Avenue and a left onto Yarborough Rd. Large, thickly carpeted B&B. All rooms have TV, but you'll probably spend your time hanging out in the game room at the pool table and full bar. Singles from £16; twins and doubles £32, with bath £36.

FOOD

The **market,** at Sincil St. near the TIC branch office, sells local fruits, veggies, and oddities. (Open M-F 9am-4pm, Sa 9am-4:30pm.) A variety of restaurants, tearooms, and takeaways grace **High St.,** tempting those trekking up the hill to take a break. Or hold out for the pubs that abound on **Bailgate St.,** on the other side of the hill.

The Ice Cream Parlour, at the base of Bailgate. This tiny, traditional shop scoops out first-rate homemade ice cream and sorbets. A cone of coconut costs a modest 90p. Open M-Th 10:30am-6pm, F-Su 9:30am-sunset.

The Spinning Wheel, 39 Steep Hill (☎522463), a block south of the TIC in a leaning, half-timbered building. Tea (80-90p) and vegetarian dishes (£4-5) are nicely priced; others are a bit steeper, but filling (from £6). Open daily 11:30am-10pm.

The Mediterranean, 14 Bailgate St. (☎546464). Snappy decor, candy-colored wrought-iron tables, and fresh flowers accompany inventive dishes from around the world. Starters and lunch run £3-5 with dinner from £4. Open M-F noon-2:30pm and 6-10:30pm, Sa noon-3pm and 6-10:30pm, Su noon-4pm and 6-10:30pm.

Stokes High Bridge Cafe, 207 High St. (☎513825). Busy tearoom in a Tudor-style house-cum-bridge, displayed on many a postcard. Sit by a window, watch swans float by on the green canal, and munch steak pie (£4.50). 2-course lunch (£5.40) served 11:30am-2pm; tea served 9:30am-5pm. Coffee shop downstairs, open daily 9am-5pm.

Lion and Snake, 79 Bailgate St. (☎523770), by the cathedral. Alluring pub with picnic tables for a restorative pint and 2-course meal (£3.95). Famed daily roast £4.25. Open M-Sa 11am-11pm, Su noon-10:30pm; food served M-F noon-6pm, Sa-Su noon-3pm.

🔍 SIGHTS

LINCOLN CATHEDRAL. While the rest of Lincoln endured a millennium of rumblings and crumblings in which Roman barricades, bishops' palaces, and conquerors' castles were erected and destroyed, the undefeated king of the hill is magnificent Lincoln Cathedral. Although construction began in 1072, the cathedral wasn't completed until three centuries later, when it towered over Europe as the continent's tallest building. The cathedral's many enduring, and endearing, features include the imp in the Angel Choir, who turned to stone while attempting to chat with the angels. A treasury room displays ancient sacred silver and a shrine to child martyr Sir Hugh, mentioned in Chaucer's *Prioress's Tale* and Marlowe's *The Jew of Malta*. Other rotating exhibits reside in a library designed by Christopher Wren. (☎544544. *Open June-Aug. M-Sa 7:15am-8pm; Su 7:15am-6pm; Sept.-May M-Sa 7:15am-6pm, Su 7:15am-5pm. Free tours depart May-Aug. daily 11am, 1, 3pm; Sept.-Apr. Sa only, same times. Cathedral £3.50, concessions £3. Library M-F free; Sa-Su £1, children free.*)

LINCOLN CASTLE. Home to one of four surviving copies of the *Magna Carta*, the grandiloquent ancestor of all modern constitutions, this 1068 castle was also the house of pain for inmates of Victorian Castle Prison. A cheerful tour guide leads the "Prison Experience," among other walks. (☎511068. *Open Apr.-Oct. M-Sa 9:30am-5:30pm; Su 11am-5:30pm; Nov.-Mar. M-Sa 9:30am-4pm, Su 11am-4pm. Tours Apr.-Oct. 11am-2pm. £2.50, seniors and students £1.50, children £1, families £6.50.*)

BISHOP'S PALACE. Rather than destroy the traces of Lincoln's ancient imperial settlers, pragmatic Lincolnites of the Middle Ages put them to good use. The medieval Bishop's Palace was originally wedged between the walls of the upper and lower Roman Cities. Thanks to 12th-century cleric Bishop Chesney, a passageway through the upper city wall links the palace remains to Lincoln Cathedral at the top of the hill. The palace itself, in Chesney's time the seat of England's largest diocese, is now an English Heritage sight with peaceful ruins, vineyards, and long views over greater Lincoln. (☎527468. *Open Apr.-Oct. daily 10am-6pm; Nov.-Mar. Sa-Su 10am-4pm. £2.50, concessions £1.90, children £1.30.*)

THE INCREDIBLY FANTASTIC OLD TOY SHOW. This humble museum is the perfect setting for a child's fantasy or a horror movie, with a collection of antique toys and modern market marvels. (*26 Westgate.* ☎520534. *Open Apr.-Sept. Tu-Sa 11am-5pm; Oct.-Dec. Sa 11am-5pm, Su noon-4pm. £2.20, students and seniors £1.80, children £1.20.*)

🎵 ENTERTAINMENT

Lincoln's nightlife is respectable. Clubs usually open from 9pm to 2am, charge a £1-3 cover, and play a mix of chart, house, and garage, with the occasional touch of underground. Head for **High St.,** and watch for **The Barracuda Club,** 780-781 High St. (☎525828). On the corner of Silver St. and Flaxengate, **Mustang Sally's** has a range of theme nights. Next door, **Ritzy** (☎522314) is popular, meaning more techno and dance and longer lines at the door.

For less strenuous entertainment, pick up the monthly *What's On in Lincoln* at the TIC, or ask at the cathedral about choral and organ performances. The **Theatre Royal,** Clasketgate at the corner of High St., stages all manner of drama and musical year-round. (☎525555. *Box office open M-Sa 10am-6pm. Tickets £7-16.50, some student discounts.*) **The Lawn,** on Union Rd. by the castle, hosts regular outdoor music and dance events. (☎560306. *Open Apr.-Sept. M-F 9am-5pm, Sa-Su 10am-5pm; Oct.-Mar. M-F 9am-4:30pm, Sa-Su 10am-4pm. Free.*) Late July brings **Medieval Weekend** and August supports the relatively new **Lincoln Early Music Festival.**

⚡ DAYTRIPS FROM LINCOLN

COLSTERWORTH. At Colsterworth stands **Woolsthorpe Manor,** birthplace of Sir Isaac Newton. Young Newton would scribble his early intellectual musings on the wall, a habit Mama Newton must have found adorable, since visitors can still peep at Isaac's graffiti. It was here, under an apple tree, that the scientist conceptualized gravity and dreamt up calculus, the bane of students everywhere. The barn holds a new **Sir Isaac Newton Science Discovery Centre,** a fantastic hands-on exhibit. *(7 mi. south of Grantham. Trains reach Colsterworth from Grantham (15min., every hr., day return £3.20). Lincolnshire Roadcar also runs from Grantham (20min., every 2-3hr., day return £2.50). ☎(01476) 860338. Open Apr.-Oct. W-Su 1-5pm. Manor £3.30, children £1.60, families £8.20. Discovery Centre £2, children £1, families £5.)*

GRANTHAM. It was in Grantham that Sir Isaac Newton attended the **King's School,** on Brook St., and left a carving of his schoolboy signature in a windowsill. *(☎(01476) 563180. Open by appointment only. Free, but donations accepted.)* The **Grantham Museum,** on St. Peter's Hill by the TIC, has exhibits on Newton's life and work and a video exhibit on another Grantham progeny, Margaret Thatcher. *(25 mi. south of Lincoln. Trains reach Grantham from Lincoln (45min., every hr., day return £2.50). Lincolnshire Roadcar (☎522255) buses run from Lincoln's St. Mark St. bus station (#601; 1¼hr.; M-Sa every hr., Su less frequent; day return £4). ☎(01476) 568783. Open M-Sa 10am-5pm. Free.)*

STAMFORD   ☎01780

The finest scene between London and Edinburgh.
　　—Sir Walter Scott

William the Conqueror built a castle at Stamford, since destroyed during a string of nasty sieges and now the site of the bus station. Renegade scholars abandoned Oxford in 1333 and came to Stamford to found a new school; the school floundered, and two years later the scholars sulkily returned home. Despite such pitfalls, sweetly tiny Stamford lures travelers today with its architecture. Norman arches frame crooked alleys between striking Georgian facades, earning Stamford its reputation as the most splendid stone town in England.

🚉 TRANSPORTATION AND PRACTICAL INFORMATION. Stamford teeters on the edge of Lincolnshire, with Cambridgeshire ready to break its fall. **Trains** (☎(08457) 484950) stop at **Stamford Station,** at the southern end of town, calling from **London King's Cross** (2hr., 1-2 per hr., £36.50); **Cambridge** (1hr., 1-2 per hr., £12.40); **Lincoln** (1½hr., every hr., £16.70). **Buses** gather at Sheepmarket, off All Saints' St. (☎554571. Office open M-Sa 9am-5:30pm.) **National Express** (☎(0990) 808080) makes the trip from **London** (2½hr., 1 per day, £12).

To reach the **tourist information centre** (TIC), in the Stamford Arts Centre on St. Mary's St., follow Garrett Rd. from the train station over the River Welland and continue uphill to a right at Castle St.; Castle St. becomes St. Mary's St. The TIC has a town map (£2) and trail guide (75p) and books beds for free. After hours, check the list in the front window. (☎755611. Open M-Sa 9:30am-5pm; Apr.-Oct. also Su 11am-4pm.) Other services include: **banks** along High St.; the **police,** North St. (☎752222); the **hospital,** Ryhall Rd. (☎764151); **Internet access** at **Rush** (see below); and the **post office,** 9 All Saints' Pl. (☎763294). **Postal code:** PE9 2EY.

🏠 ACCOMMODATIONS AND FOOD. Beauty is priceless, at least in Stamford; consider basing yourself in Cambridge or Lincoln to avoid high **B&B** prices. Budget B&Bs stay on the outskirts; call ahead, and you may be offered a ride. Try **Birch House,** 4 Lonsdale Rd., where each room has been individually decorated

with artful zest. (☎754876. ₤20 per person.) Gracious rooms wait at the home of **Jo and Peter Unsworth,** 10 Waterside, north of Stamford. (☎764459. ₤20 per person.)

For groceries hit **Tesco,** 46-51 High St. (☎683000. Open M-W and Sa 7:30am-5:30pm, Th-F 7:30am-6:30pm, Su 10am-4pm.) Check email between rounds of giant outdoor chess at **Rush,** St. Mary's St., or munch creative sandwiches (under ₤3) while surfing the web. (☎767874. Internet ₤3 per hr. Open M-Th 9am-6pm, F-Sa 9am-8pm, Su 10am-6pm.) Savor a pot of tea (95p) or an afternoon specialty (₤3-5.25) with your favorite bear at **Paddington's,** Ironmonger St. (☎751110. Open M-Sa 9am-5:30pm.) Once the Midlands's most famous coaching inn (look for the waiting rooms for London and York as you enter), **The George** commands High St. St. Martin's. (☎750700. Food served at the bar daily noon-2:30pm.)

▣ ☐ SIGHTS AND ENTERTAINMENT. Stamford's overriding point of interest is ▨**Burghley House,** England's largest Elizabethan mansion, a 1 mi. walk from Stamford along Burghley Park; blue signs mark the path from High St. St. Martin's. Thickly wooded forests give way to the white palace, poised on rolling lawns and ringed with gardens (of Capability Brown's design, of course). The house was the prized creation of William Cecil, Lord High Treasurer of England and advisor to Queen Elizabeth I, who designed and built much of it himself. Eighteen state rooms display a splendid collection of art and furnishings, as well as costumes from the recent Merchant-Ivory movie, Henry James's *The Golden Bowl.* The famous **Heaven Room** and infamous **Hell Staircase** are both masterworks of Antonio Verrio: giant murals of spectacularly spirited ancient gods ascend the walls of the former, while sinners of every shape and hue descend the latter—Dante would be proud. Don't miss Burghley's newest addition, the 12-acre **Sculpture Garden,** which showcases rare flowers and contemporary sculpture. (☎752451. House open Apr.-Oct. daily 11am-4:30pm; shown by tour M-F. Sculpture Garden open daily 11am-4pm. Park open daily dawn-dusk. ₤6.80, seniors ₤6.30, children free.)

The quirky **Stamford Museum,** Broad St., charts the town's history from Saxon days through the Georgian high period, during which most of the existing buildings were constructed. One exhibit, of dubious taste and complete with wax figures, concerns Daniel Lambert, England's fattest man, who died in Stamford and was buried in the graveyard of St. Martin's. Vaudeville novelty Tom Thumb came to Stamford to perform while standing in the armhole of Lambert's waistcoat. (☎766317. Open M-Sa 10am-5pm; Apr.-Sept. also Su 2-5pm. Free.) On the way to Burghley House, pay a visit to the Cecil family, who slumber in their Romanesque tombs beneath twinkling stained glass at **St. Martin's Church,** High St. St. Martin's. (☎751233. Open daily 9am-4pm. Free.)

The **Stamford Arts Centre,** St. Mary's St., hosts local productions and national touring companies. (☎763203. Box office open M-Sa 10am-5pm.) The famous **Stamford Shakespeare Festival** is based at Elizabethan **Tolethorpe Hall** from June to August. (☎756133. Box office open M-Sa 9:30am-8pm; tickets also available from the Stamford Arts Centre. M-Th ₤10, concessions ₤9; F-Sa ₤13, no concessions.)

EAST ANGLIA

The plush farmland and watery flats of East Anglia stretch northeast from London, cloaking the counties of Cambridgeshire, Norfolk, and Suffolk, as well as parts of Essex. Literally England's newest landscape, the vast plains of the Fens were drained as late as the 1820s. From Norwich east to the English Channel, the water that once drenched enormous medieval peat bogs was channeled into the maze of waterways known as the Norfolk Broads, now a National Park. Continental-style windmills helped maintain the drained Fens, and some survivors still mark the marshes. Farther inland and 800 years earlier, Norman invaders had made their way to the elevated mound at Ely, building a stunning cathedral from stone transported by boat across then-flooded fenland. In the 15th century, in a village to the south, renegade scholars from Oxford set up shop along the River Cam. Eventually granted a royal imprimatur, they built a university. Farther northeast, the imposing houses and magnificent "wool churches" of small towns in Norfolk and Suffolk stand as testament to their past as thriving wool centers. But despite the obvious impact humans have made on this region, much of the rustic beauty that inspired the landscape paintings of natives Constable and Gainsborough remains.

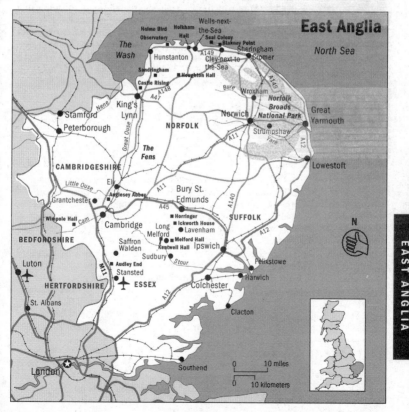

HIGHLIGHTS OF EAST ANGLIA

CAMBRIDGE Stroll among the colleges (but keep off the grass!) in this picturesque university town, one of the world's best-known reserves of learning (p. 302).

ELY CATHEDRAL Gaze skyward at this medieval masterwork, still breathtaking as it towers over former fenland (p. 313).

NORWICH Mind your map in this twisting, wool-trading town, once the largest in Anglo-Saxon England, where markets and festivals have endured for centuries (p. 323).

▐ TRANSPORTATION IN EAST ANGLIA

A **combined Anglia Plus Pass** (about £60, discount with Railcard), available only at stations within East Anglia, entitles you to a week's unlimited travel on all **train** routes in the region. A **regular Anglia Plus Pass** allows a week of unlimited travel within either Norfolk or Suffolk (£29). Both zones are covered by their own one- and three-day passes (£9 and £20). All Anglia Plus passes also grant free travel on various lines of the Norwich, Ipswich, and Great Yarmouth local **bus** services. The **Out 'n' About** ticket allows unlimited day travel on the Stagecoach Cambuses (£5, students £3.60, children £3). However, you may end up paying with your time; buses run infrequently.

East Anglia's flat terrain and relatively low annual rainfall please cyclists and hikers, though rental bikes can be difficult to procure outside of Cambridge and Norwich. The area's two longest and most popular walking trails, together covering 200 mi., are the **Peddar's Way,** which runs from Knettishall Heath to Holme and includes the Norfolk coast path, and the **Weaver's Way,** an extended trail that traverses the north coast from Cromer to Great Yarmouth. Both cross a town with a train or bus station about every 10 mi. Tourist information centres (TICs) in Norwich, Bury St. Edmunds, and several Suffolk villages issue guides for the Weaver's Way. For the Peddar's Way, pick up *Peddar's Way and Norfolk Coast Path.*

CAMBRIDGESHIRE

CAMBRIDGE ☎ 01223

Cambridge (pop. 105,000) has weathered many winds of change. Once inhabited by Romans, this trading town endured a series of nasty Viking raids before the Normans arrived in the 11th century. The 13th century brought Oxford's refugees, an influx that would alter the city more than any military conquest. In contrast to museum-oriented, metropolitan Oxford, Cambridge is determined to retain its pastoral academic robes. As the tourist information centre will tell you, the city manages, rather than encourages, visitors. In recent decades, the University of Cambridge has ceased to be an exclusive preserve of upper-class sons, bringing the student ratios for state school pupils and women to more just levels. Some old upper-crust traditions are slipping, too: students now only bedeck themselves in gown and cravat for meal times once a week. At exams' end, Cambridge explodes with Pimms-soaked glee, and May Week (in mid-June, naturally) launches a swirl of cocktail parties and balls in celebration of pending graduation ceremonies.

▐ TRANSPORTATION

Trains: Station Rd. Purchase tickets daily 5am-11pm. **Trains** (☎ (08457) 484950) run from **London King's Cross** (45min., 2 per hr., £14.90) and **London Liverpool St.** (1¼hr., 2 per hr., £14.90).

Buses: Drummer St. Station—more a street than a station. Ticket booth open daily 8:45am-5:30pm; tickets also often available on board. **National Express** (☎(08705) 808080) arrives from **London** (2hr., 17 per day, from £8). **Jetlink** coach service runs hourly shuttles to Drummer St. from: **Heathrow Airport** (2hr., £21); **Gatwick Airport** (3hr., £20); **Stansted Airport** (45min., £9). **Stagecoach Express** (☎(01604) 620077) runs from **Oxford** (2¾hr., 10-12 per day, from £7).

Public Transportation: Cambus (☎423554) zooms from the train station to the city center (85p) and around town (85p-£1.60). **Whippet Coaches** (☎(01480) 463792) runs daytrips from town.

Taxis: Cabco (☎312444). **Camtax** (☎313131). Both 24hr.

Bike Rental: Mike's Bikes, 28 Mill Rd. (☎312591). £8 per day, £10 per week, £50 deposit; reduced prices for extended rentals. Lock, light, and basket included. Open M-Sa 9am-6pm, Su 10am-4pm. The tourist information centre has a full list of bike shops.

⚡️🛈 ORIENTATION AND PRACTICAL INFORMATION

About 60 mi. north of London, Cambridge has two main avenues, both suffering from multiple personality disorder. The main shopping street starts at **Magdalene Bridge** and becomes **Bridge St., Sidney St., St. Andrew's St., Regent St.,** and **Hills Rd.** The other—alternately **St. John's St., Trinity St., King's Parade,** and **Trumpington St.**— is the academic thoroughfare. The two streets cross at **St. John's College.** From the bus station at **Drummer St.,** a stroll down **Emmanuel St.** will land you in the shopping district near the tourist information centre (TIC). To get to the heart of things from the train station on **Station Rd.,** turn right onto Hills Rd. and continue straight.

The primary mode of transport in Cambridge is the **bicycle.** This city claims to have more bikes per person than any other place in Britain. A series of one-way streets and an armada of foreign teenagers used to riding on the wrong side of the road complicate summer transport. If riding, use hand signals and heed road signs; if walking, look both ways—and behind, above, and under—twice before crossing.

Tourist Information Centre: Wheeler St. (☎322640; fax 457588; www.tourismcambridge.com), a block south of Market Sq. Mini-guide 40p, maps 20p. *Cambridge: The Official Guide* gives a clear map of the town center as well as suggested walks and commercial listings (£3.95). Maps of area cycling tours £4. Books rooms for £3 and a 10% deposit. Advance booking hotline (at least 5 days in advance; ☎457581; M-F 9:30am-4pm). Open Apr.-Oct. M-F 10am-5:30pm, Sa 10am-5pm, Su 11am-4pm; Nov.-Mar. M-F 10am-5:30pm, Sa 10am-5pm.

Tours: Informative 2hr. walking tours of the city and some colleges leave from the TIC. Call for times. Tours are well narrated but often enter only 1 college—usually King's. £7, children £4. Special **Drama Tour** in July and Aug. led by guides in period dress (Tu 6:30pm; £4.50). **Guide Friday** (☎362444) runs its 1hr. hop-on/hop-off **bus tours** every 15-30min. Apr.-Oct. £8.50, students and seniors £7, children £2.50, families £19.50.

Budget Travel: STA Travel, 38 Sidney St. (☎366966). Open M-W and F 9am-5:30pm, Th 10am-5:30pm, Sa 11am-5pm.

Financial Services: Banks line Market Sq. and St. Andrew's St. **Lloyds TSB,** 3 Sidney St. Open M-Tu and Th-F 9am-5pm, W 9:30am-5pm, Sa 10am-1pm. **Thomas Cook,** 8 St. Andrew's St. (☎366141). Open M-Tu and Th-Sa 9am-5:30pm, W 10am-5:30pm. **American Express,** 25 Sidney St. (☎(08706) 001060). Open M-Tu and Th-F 9am-5:30pm, W 9:30am-5:30pm, Sa 9am-5pm.

Launderette: Clean Machine, 22 Burleigh St. (☎578009). Open daily 8am-8pm.

Police: Parkside (☎358966).

Hospital: Addenbrookes, Hills Rd. (☎245151). Catch Cambus #4, 5, or 5a from Emmanuel St. (£1) and get off where Hills Rd. intersects Long Rd.

Internet Access: International Telecom Centre, 2 Wheeler St. (☎357358). £1 for first 33min., then 3p per min. 9am-noon or 4p noon-10pm. £1 minimum. Open daily 9am-10pm. **CB1,** 32 Mill Rd. (☎576306), near the hostel. 5p per min. Open daily 10am-8pm.

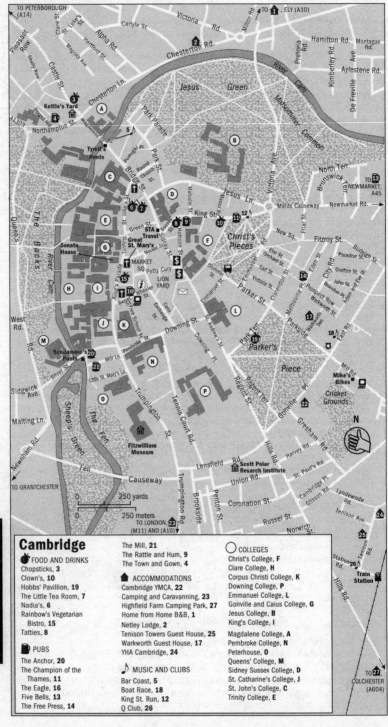

Cambridge

🍴 **FOOD AND DRINKS**
Chopsticks, **3**
Clown's, **10**
Hobbs' Pavillion, **19**
The Little Tea Room, **7**
Nadia's, **6**
Rainbow's Vegetarian
Bistro, **15**
Tatties, **8**

🍺 **PUBS**
The Anchor, **20**
The Champion of the
Thames, **11**
The Eagle, **16**
Five Bells, **13**
The Free Press, **14**

The Mill, **21**
The Rattle and Hum, **9**
The Town and Gown, **4**

🏠 **ACCOMMODATIONS**
Cambridge YMCA, **22**
Camping and Caravanning, **23**
Highfield Farm Camping Park, **27**
Home from Home B&B, **1**
Netley Lodge, **2**
Tenison Towers Guest House, **25**
Warkworth Guest House, **17**
YHA Cambridge, **24**

🎵 **MUSIC AND CLUBS**
Bar Coast, **5**
Boat Race, **18**
King St. Run, **12**
Q Club, **26**

⭕ **COLLEGES**
Christ's College, **F**
Clare College, **H**
Corpus Christi College, **K**
Downing College, **P**
Emmanuel College, **L**
Gonville and Caius College, **G**
Jesus College, **B**
King's College, **I**

Magdalene College, **A**
Pembroke College, **N**
Peterhouse, **O**
Queens' College, **M**
Sidney Sussex College, **D**
St. Catharine's College, **J**
St. John's College, **C**
Trinity College, **E**

Post Office: 9-11 St. Andrew's St. (☎323325). Open M-Sa 9am-5:30pm. **Postal Code:** CB2 3AA.

ACCOMMODATIONS AND CAMPING

Rooms are scarce, which makes prices high and quality low. Most B&Bs aren't in the town center; many around **Portugal St.** and **Tenison Rd.** house students during the academic year and are open to visitors in July and August. If one is full, ask about others nearby, as they're often unmarked. Pick up a guide from the TIC (50p) or check the list in the window after it closes. Cheaper accommodations in **Ely** (see **p. 313**) make it a good base for exploring Cambridge.

YHA Cambridge, 97 Tenison Rd. (☎354601; fax 312780; cambridge@yha.org.uk). A relaxed, welcoming atmosphere, although more showers wouldn't hurt. 100 beds, mostly 3-4 per room; a few doubles. Rock music filters through a well-equipped kitchen. Laundry facilities. TV lounge. **Bureau de change.** Breakfast £3.50, packed lunch £2.80-3.65. Call well ahead. Dorms £15.10, under 18 £11.40.

Cambridge YMCA, Gonville Pl. (☎356998; fax 312749; admin@camymca.org.uk). Men and women welcome. Well-located, large, clean rooms, if slightly industrial. Breakfast included. Singles £23; shared room (usually doubles) £18.50.

Tenison Towers Guest House, 148 Tenison Rd. (☎566511). Blue is the word at Tenison Towers, where fresh flowers grace airy rooms 2 blocks from the train station. Mrs. Chance keeps an impeccable house. Singles and doubles £20-25 per person.

Home from Home B&B, 39 Milton Rd. (☎323555). A 20min. walk from the center. Spotless rooms, TVs, showers. English breakfast with fruit, cereal, and croissants. Yum. Biscuits and hot chocolate in every room. Yum. Call ahead with a credit card for reservations. Yum. Singles from £35; doubles from £48; discounts for longer stays.

Netley Lodge, 112 Chesterton Rd. (☎363845). Plush red carpets and a conservatory lush with greenery welcome you. Roses inside and out—hostess Mrs. Mikolajczyk is a study in elegance. Singles £22-24; doubles £40.

Warkworth Guest House, Warkworth Terr. (☎363682). Sunny rooms near the bus station; the spot for those seeking more privacy than the nearby hostels, but it'll cost you. Packed lunch on request. Singles £30, with bath £35; twins £55/£60.

Highfield Farm Camping Park, Long Rd., Comberton (☎262308). Head west on the A603 3 mi., then turn right on the B1046 to Comberton for 1 mi., or take Cambus #118 (every 45min.) from the Drummer St. bus station and ask to be let off at Highfield Farm. Cozy field with flush toilets, showers, and laundry. Open Apr.-Oct. £7 per tent, with car £8.75; off season £6.25, £7.25.

Camping and Caravanning Club Site, 19 Cabbage Moor, Great Shelford (☎841185). Head 3 mi. south on the M11, then left onto the A1301 for ¾ mi., or take Cambus #102 or 103 to Westfield Rd. Excellent site with facilities for the disabled. Open Mar.-Oct. Call ahead. £5.70 per member, children £2; nonmember pitch fee £4.50.

FOOD

Market Square has bright pyramids of fruit and vegetables, cheaper than those in supermarkets. (Market open M-Sa usually 9:30am-4:30pm.) Students get beer and cornflakes at **Sainsbury's,** 44 Sidney St. (☎366891. Open M-F 8am-9pm, Sa 7:30am-9pm, Su 11am-5pm.) Cheap Indian and Greek fare sates hearty appetites (make sure you don't meet the Christ's College football club out for its ritual curry night). South of town, Hills Rd. and Mill Rd. brim with good, budget restaurants.

Nadia's, 11 St. John's St. (☎460961). An uncommonly good bakery with reasonable prices and a divine smell. Wonderful flapjacks and quiches (80p-£1.25). Sandwiches (£1.75) and muffins (75p) are a brunch unto themselves. Takeaway only. Open daily 8:30am-5pm. Also at 16 Silver St. and 20 King's Parade.

Hobbs' Pavillion, Parker's Piece (☎367480), off Park Terr. Renowned for imaginative, rectangular pancakes. Hobbs' feels like a stylish living room, with a view across Parker's Piece, jaunty jazz music, and a Mars Bar and ice cream pancake for £4—you won't need to eat again for weeks. Open Tu-Sa noon-2:15pm and 6-9:45pm. No credit cards.

Rainbow's Vegetarian Bistro, 9a King's Parade (☎321551). Duck under the rainbow sign on King's Parade. A tiny, creative burrow featuring delicious international vegan and vegetarian fare, all for £6.25. Open M-Sa 11am-11pm, last order 10:30pm.

Clown's, 54 King St. (☎355711). Cheerful staff adds the final dash of color to this humming spot—children's renderings of clowns plaster the walls, as do adoring odes by local regulars. Cakes, toasties, even lasagna £1-6. Open daily 7:30am-midnight.

The Little Tea Room, 1 All Saints' Passage (☎366033), off Trinity St. Hopelessly pretentious, yet the place to go for afternoon tea. Heroic waitstaff navigate 2 tightly packed rooms to serve tip-top teas. Open M-Sa 10am-5:30pm, Su 1-5:30pm.

Tatties, 11 Sussex St. (☎323399). Dedicated to one of England's most popular dishes—the terrific jacket potatoes make up for the fast-food ambiance. Fillings from butter (£2) to Philly cheese and smoked salmon (£5.75). Open M-Sa 8:30am-7pm, Su 10am-5pm.

Chopsticks, 5 Castle St. (☎356150). A dim exterior makes way for tasty Chinese dishes within. 2-course lunch with tea at an unbeatable £6. Open M 5:30-11pm, Tu-Su noon-2:30pm and 5:30-11pm.

📰 PUBS

King St. has a diverse collection of pubs and used to host the King St. Run, for which contestants ran the length of the street stopping at each of the 13 pubs to down a pint. The winner was the first to cross the finish line on his own two feet. Most pubs stay open from 11am to 11pm, Sundays noon to 10:30pm. The local brewery, Greene King, supplies many of them with the popular bitters IPA (India Pale Ale) and Abbott.

The Eagle, Benet St. (☎505020). Have a pint in Cambridge's oldest pub. This was where Watson and Crick first rushed in breathless to announce their discovery of the DNA double helix. The barmaid insisted they settle their 4-shilling tab before she'd serve them a toast. During WWII, British and American pilots stood on each other's shoulders to burn their initials into the ceiling of the RAF room with Zippos.

The Mill, Mill Ln. (☎357026), off Silver St. Bridge. Claims the riverside park as its own on spring nights for punt- and people-watching. In summer, it fills with the odd remaining student and hordes of international youth.

The Anchor, Silver St. (☎353554). Another undergraduate watering hole crowded day and night, the Anchor allows you to savor a pint while watching amateur punters collide under Silver St. Bridge. Open M-Sa 11am-11pm, Su 1-10:30pm.

The Rattle and Hum, 4 King St. (☎505015). A prerequisite for hitting the clubs, with a DJ spinning dance tunes 7 nights a week. Th karaoke night.

The Champion of the Thames, 68 King St. (☎352043). The size of a broom closet and filled with regulars; the bartender tells the customer personally when a phone call comes in. Bring your own food.

The Free Press, Prospect Row (☎368337), behind the police station. Named after an abolitionist newspaper, it now sponsors a local boat club in the Amateur Rowing Association. Mostly a local haunt. No smoking!

The Town and Gown, Poundhill (☎353791), just off Northampton St. Gay men gather in this classically English pub. Strong community feel and a warm welcome. Open M-F 11am-3pm and 7-11pm, Sa 11am-11pm, Su noon-10:30pm.

Five Bells, 126-128 Newmarket Rd. (☎314019). Primarily gay clientele fills the beer garden for buzzing afternoons and lively nights. Open M-F 11am-3pm and 7-11pm, Sa 11am-11pm, Su noon-10:30pm.

M.A.? B.S.! Cambridge graduates are eligible for the world's easiest master's degrees: after spending three and one-third years out in the Real World, a graduate sends £15 to the university. Provided that said graduate is not in the custody of one of Her Majesty's Prisons, the grad receives an M.A. without further ado, making Cambridge the world's simplest correspondence school.

⑥ COLLEGES AND OTHER SIGHTS

Cambridge is an architect's fantasia, packing some of England's most breathtaking monuments into less than 1 sq. mi. The soaring **King's College Chapel** and the post-card-familiar St. John's **Bridge of Sighs** are sightseeing staples, while more obscure college courts veil undiscovered treats. Most historic buildings are on the east bank of the Cam between Magdalene Bridge and Silver St. The gardens, meadows, and cows of the **Backs** lend a pastoral air to the west bank.

The **University of Cambridge** has three eight-week terms: Michaelmas (Oct.-Dec.), Lent (Jan.-Mar.), and Easter (Apr.-June). Visitors can gain access to most of the college grounds daily from 9am to 5:30pm, though many close to sightseers during the Easter term, and virtually all are closed during exam period (mid-May to mid-June); your best bet is to call ahead (☎331100) for hours. If you have time for only a few colleges, **King's, Trinity, Queens', Christ's, St. John's,** and **Jesus** should top your list, though the Britain-in-a-week traveler could see 12 or 14 colleges in a few hours—most cluster around the center of town. Porters (plump bowler-bedecked ex-servicemen) maintain security. Those who appear like Cambridge undergrads (i.e. no traveler's backpack, no camera, and definitely no Cambridge sweatshirt) can often wander freely through most college grounds after hours. For maximum camouflage carry a plastic bag from Sainsbury's and wear your rucksack over one shoulder. The fastest way to mark yourself as a target for the security guards is to trample the sacred grass of the college courtyards, a privilege granted only to senior members. In summer, a few undergrads stay to work or study, but most skip town, leaving it to 5000 PhD students and mobs of foreign teenagers.

KING'S COLLEGE

King's Parade. ☎331100. Chapel and grounds open M-Sa 9:30am-4:30pm, Su 9:30am-2:30pm. Listing of services and musical events available at porter's lodge, £1. Evensong 5:30pm most nights. Contact TIC for tours. £3.50, concessions £2.50, under 12 free.

King's College was founded by Henry VI in 1441 as partner to a school he had established near Windsor, and it wasn't until 1861 that students from schools other than Eton were allowed to compete for scholarships. But King's is now the most socially liberal of the Cambridge colleges, drawing more of its students from state schools than any other; the college was also the site of the student riots of 1968. As a result, Cambridge's best-known college is its least traditional—there are no formal dinners or white-tie balls, and interior corridors are coated with lurid graffiti.

Little of this is noticeable to visitors, who descend in droves on the Gothic spectacular that is **King's College Chapel.** One of England's more pious monarchs, Henry VI cleared the center of medieval Cambridge for the foundation of the college, and he intended this chapel to be England's finest. If you stand at the southwest corner of the courtyard, you can see where Henry's master mason left off and work under the Tudors began—the earlier stone is off-white. The elaborate wall that separates the college grounds from King's Parade was not part of the original plans, but a 19th-century addition; originally the chapel and grounds were hidden behind a row of shops and houses. The chapel's interior is a single chamber cleft by a carved choir screen whose design was destroyed by its Italian creators, fearful of replication. Heralding angels hover against the world's largest fan-vaulted ceiling, described by Wordsworth as a "branching roof self-poised, and scooped into ten thousand cells where light and shade repose." The chapel also houses a few works of sacrilege—look for the 15th-century graffiti on the wall to the right of the altar and the devilish portrait of a craftsman's estranged wife on the choir screen.

Behind the altar hangs Rubens's *Adoration of the Magi* (1639), the most expensive painting ever auctioned at the time of its purchase and subsequently given as a gift to the college. The canvas has been protected by an electronic alarm since an attack by a crazed chisel-wielder several years ago. Free musical recitals often play at the chapel, and schedules are kept at the entrance. The classic view of the chapel and the adjacent **Gibbs Building** is had from the riverbank. As you picnic by the water, think of those who have gone before you: John Maynard Keynes kept watch over the college finances, Alan Turing invented the digital computer, and E.M. Forster used his undergraduate experiences as fuel for *The Longest Journey* and *Maurice*; Salman Rushdie also felt the college's grounds beneath his feet. In early June the university posts the names and final grades of every student in the Georgian **Senate House** opposite the King's College chapel, designed by Gibbs and built in the 1720s; about a week later, degree ceremonies are held there.

TRINITY COLLEGE

Trinity St. ☎ 338400. Chapel and courtyard open daily 10am-5pm. Wren Library open M-F noon-2pm, Sa 10:30am-12:30pm. Easter-Oct. £1.75, otherwise free.

Henry VIII, not to be outdone by Henry VI, intended the College of the Holy and Undivided Trinity to be the largest and richest of all the Cambridge colleges. Founded in 1546 shortly before Henry VIII's death, the college has amply fulfilled his wish, being today Britain's third largest landowner (after the Queen and the Church of England); legend holds that it is possible to walk from Cambridge to Oxford without stepping off Trinity land.

The alma mater of Sir Isaac Newton, who lived in E staircase for 30 years, the college boasts an illustrious list of alumni: literati include John Dryden, Lord Byron, Lord Alfred Tennyson, A.E. Housman, and Vladimir Nabokov; while James Clerk Maxwell, who discovered the laws of electromagnetism, atom-splitter Ernest Rutherford, philosopher Ludwig Wittgenstein, and Indian statesman Jawaharlal Nehru also studied here.

The heart of the college is the aptly named **Great Court,** the world's largest enclosed courtyard. Great Court is reached from Trinity St. through **Great Gate,** a castle-like gateway fronted by a statue of Henry VIII grasping a wooden chair leg—the original scepter was stolen years ago as a student prank and never recovered. If you want to be taken as a student (and skip the entrance fee), enter confidently through the smaller door on the right—only tourists use the main gate. On the west side of the court stands the door **chapel,** whose interior is lined with plaques naming famous alums, and the **King's Gate** tower. The tower is home to what William Wordsworth called the "loquacious clock that speaks with male and female voice"; try to run around the court during the 24 strikes of midday—Great Court is the site of the original race against the clock made famous in the movie *Chariots of Fire.* The **fountain** (1602) in the center of the court is the only one in Cambridge, and Lord Byron used to bathe nude in it. The eccentric poet kept a bear as a pet (college rules only forbade cats and dogs) and claimed it would take his fellowship exams for him. The south side of the court is home to the palatial **Master's Lodge** and the cathedral-like **Great Hall** (another original name), where students and dons dine under the gaze of Henry VIII and hundreds of grotesque carved faces.

On the other side of the Hall is the exquisite Renaissance facade of **Nevile's Court.** Newton measured the speed of sound by timing the echo in the cloisters that lead to Sir Christopher's **Wren Library** (1695). While the college's collection has long outgrown the building, it is still used to house old books and precious manuscripts; those on view include alumnus **A.A. Milne**'s original handwritten copies of *Winnie the Pooh* and Newton's own copy of his *Principia.* The library is dominated by a large stained-glass window of who else but Newton being presented to George III. Adjacent to Nevile's Court, pass through the drab, neo-Gothic **New Court** (Prince Charles lived in E staircase) to get to the Backs where you can rent **punts** or simply enjoy the view of the Wren Library and St. John's college from **Trinity Bridge.**

DUCKING AND DINING While you're wondering at the height of the ceiling in Trinity's Great Hall, take time to search for a fake duck hanging from the rafters. While no one is sure how the tradition started, it has become a challenge for undergraduates to try to scale the ceiling and move the duck around. Success is rewarded with membership in the ultra-secretive Mallard Society; failure (if you're discovered mid-mallard moving), with immediate expulsion from the college. While the College disapproves of this risky pastime, student lore claims that the president of the society is none other than the Dean—the very man who expels those caught in the act.

OTHER COLLEGES

ST. JOHN'S COLLEGE. Established in 1511 by Lady Margaret Beaufort, mother of Henry VIII, St. John's is one of seven Cambridge colleges founded by women. The striking brick-and-stone gatehouse bears Lady Margaret's heraldic emblem. St. John's centers around a paved plaza rather than a grassy courtyard, and the **Bridge of Sighs** (nothing like the one in Venice) connects the older part of the college to the towering neo-Gothic extravagance of **New Court,** which is likened by some to a wedding cake in silhouette. The **School of Pythagoras,** a 12th-century pile of wood and stone thought the oldest complete building in Cambridge, hides in St. John's Gardens. *(St. John's St. ☎ 338600. Chapel and grounds open daily 10am-4:45pm. Evensong 6:30pm most nights. £2, students and seniors £1.20, families £4.)*

QUEENS' COLLEGE. Founded not once, but twice—by Queen Margaret of Anjou in 1448 and Elizabeth Woodville in 1465—Queens' College has the only unaltered Tudor courtyard in Cambridge. According to myth, the **Mathematical Bridge,** just past Cloister Court, was built in 1749 without a single bolt or nail, relying on mathematical principle. A meddling Victorian is said to have taken the bridge apart to see how it worked, and the inevitable occurred—he had to put it back together using steel rivets every two inches. Cambridge students may be good, but not that good: the bridge was made with bolts from the beginning. *(Silver St. ☎ 335511. College open Mar.-Oct. daily 10am-4:30pm. Closed during exams. £1.)*

CLARE COLLEGE. Clare's coat-of-arms, golden teardrops ringing a black border, recalls the college's founding in 1326 by thrice-widowed, 29-year-old Lady Elizabeth de Clare. Misery has not shrouded the college indefinitely, however, for Clare has some of the most cheerful gardens in Cambridge. The gardens lie across elegant Clare Bridge. Walk through the **Old Court,** designed by Wren, for a view of the University Library, where 82 mi. of shelves hold books arranged according to size rather than subject. *(Trinity Ln. ☎ 333200. College open daily 10am-5pm. Old Court open during exams after 4:45pm to groups of 3 or fewer. £2, under 10 free.)*

CHRIST'S COLLEGE. Founded as "God's-house" in 1448 and renamed in 1505, Christ's has since won fame for its association with John Milton and for its gardens. Charles Darwin studied at Christ's before dealing a blow to its religious origins—his rooms (unmarked and closed to visitors) were on G staircase in First Court. **New Court,** on King St., is one of Cambridge's most modern structures; its symmetrical concrete walls and dark windows make it look like the amalgam of a pyramid, Polaroid camera, and typewriter. Bowing to pressure from aesthetically offended Cantabrigians, a wall was built to block the view of the building from all sides except the inner courtyard of the college. *(St. Andrews St. ☎ 334900. Gardens open in summer M-F 9:30am-noon; term-time M-F 9am-4:30pm. Free.)*

JESUS COLLEGE. Spacious Jesus has preserved an enormous amount of medieval work from as far back as 1496. Beyond the high-walled walk called the "Chimny" lies a three-sided court fringed with colorful gardens. Through the arch on the right sit the remains of a gloomy medieval nunnery. Pre-Raphaelite stained glass by Edward Burne-Jones and ceilings by William Morris decorate the chapel. *(Jesus Ln. ☎ 339339. Courtyard open 9am-6pm; closed during exams to groups of 3 or more.)*

MAGDALENE COLLEGE. Inhabiting a 15th-century Benedictine hostel, Magdalene (MAUD-lin), sometime home of Christian allegorist C.S. Lewis when he wasn't at Oxford, has retained its religious emphasis. Take a peek at **Pepys Library,** in the second court; the library displays the noted statesman and prolific diarist's collections. *(Magdalene St. ☎332100. Library open Easter-Aug. 11:30am-12:30pm and 2:30-3:30pm; Sept.-Easter M-Sa 11:30am-12:30pm. Courtyards closed during exams. Free.)*

SMALLER COLLEGES. Thomas Gray wrote his *Elegy in a Country Churchyard* while staying in **Peterhouse,** Trumpington St., the oldest and smallest college, founded in 1294. *(☎338200. Call for opening hours.)* In contrast, **Robinson College,** across the river on Grange Rd., is the newest. Founded in 1977, this modern-medieval brick pastiche sits just behind the university library. Bronze plants writhe about the door of the college chapel. *(☎339100. Call for opening hours.)* **Corpus Christi College,** Trumpington St., founded in 1352 by the common people, contains the dreariest and oldest courtyard in Cambridge, forthrightly called Old Court and unaltered since its enclosure. The library, on the other hand, maintains the snazziest collection of Anglo-Saxon manuscripts in England, among them the Parker Manuscript of the *Anglo-Saxon Chronicle.* Alums include Sir Francis Drake and Christopher Marlowe. *(☎338000. Courtyard open until 6pm; closed during exams.)*

The 1347 **Pembroke College,** next to Corpus Christi, harbors the earliest architectural effort of Sir Christopher Wren and counts Edmund Spenser, Ted Hughes, and Eric Idle among its grads. *(☎338100. Courtyard open until 6pm; closed during exams.)* **Downing College,** Regent St., was founded in 1807, and is pleasantly isolated. *(☎334800. Courtyard open until 6pm.)* A chapel designed by Sir Christopher Wren dominates the front court of 1584 **Emmanuel College,** St. Andrews St., known to its residents as "Emma." John Harvard, benefactor of the New England university, attended Emmanuel. Among alumni with more tangible accomplishments is John Cleese. *(☎334200. Courtyard open until 6pm.)*

MUSEUMS AND CHURCHES

■**FITZWILLIAM MUSEUM.** A welcome break from the academia of the colleges, the Fitzwilliam Museum fills an immense Neoclassical building, built in 1875 to house Viscount Fitzwilliam's collection. The mosaic floors could be a display of their own. A goulash of Egyptian, Chinese, Japanese, and Greek antiquities bides its time downstairs, joined by a muster of 16th-century German armor. The **Founder's Library** is a must-see, housing an intimate collection of French Impressionists. The drawing room shows William Blake's books and woodcuts. Call to inquire about lunchtime and evening concerts. *(Trumpington St. ☎332900. Open Tu-Sa 10am-5pm, Su 2:15-5pm. Guided tours Sa 2:30pm. Suggested donation £3. Tours £3.)*

OTHER MUSEUMS. ▨**Kettle's Yard,** at the corner of Castle St. and Northampton St., keeps early 20th-century art. The gallery rotates its shows, but the house, created in 1956 by Tate curator Jim Ede as "a refuge of peace and order," is a quiet constant. *(☎352124. House open Apr.-Sept. Tu-Sa 1:30-4:30pm, Su 2-4:30pm; Oct.-Mar. Tu-Su 2-4pm. Gallery open year-round Tu-Su 11:30am-5pm. Free.)* The **Scott Polar Research Institute,** Lensfield Rd., commemorates icy expeditions with photographic and artistic accounts and memorabilia. *(☎336540. Open M-Sa 2:30-4pm. Free.)*

CHURCHES. The **Round Church (Holy Sepulchre),** where Bridge St. meets St. John's St., is one of five surviving circular churches in England, built in 1130 (and later rebuilt) on the pattern of the Church of the Holy Sepulchre in Jerusalem. *(☎311602. Free.)* It merits comparison with **St. Benet's,** a rough Saxon church on Benet St., built in 1050 and the oldest structure in Cambridge. It once had a spire, but spire-building was a technology the Normans lacked, so they spitefully knocked it down. *(☎353903. Free.)* The tower of **Great St. Mary's Church,** off King's Parade, asserts the best view of the broad greens and the colleges. Pray that the 12 bells don't ring while you're ascending the 123 tightly packed spiral steps. *(Tower open M-Sa 9:30am-5pm, Su 12:30-5pm. £1.85, children 60p, families £4.20.)*

ENTERTAINMENT AND FESTIVALS

PUNTING. Punts (flat-bottomed boats propelled by a pole) are a favored form of hands-on entertainment in Cambridge. Punters take two routes—one from Magdalene Bridge to Silver St., the other from Silver St. to Grantchester. On the first route, the shorter, busier, and more interesting of the two, you'll pass the colleges and the Backs. Beware that punt-bombing—jumping from bridges into the river alongside a punt, thereby tipping its occupants—is an art form. **Tyrell's,** Magdalene Bridge (☎(01480) 413517), has punts and rowboats for £8 per hr. plus a £40 deposit. At **Scudamore's,** Silver St. Bridge (☎359750), punts are £10 per hr. plus a £50 deposit. Student-punted **tours** (about £20) are another option. Inquire at the TIC for a complete list of companies.

THEATER. The Arts Box Office (☎503333) handles ticket sales for the **Arts Theatre,** around the corner from the TIC, which stages traveling productions, and the **ADC Theatre** (Amateur Dramatic Club; ☎359547), Park St., which offers lively performances of student-produced plays as well as term-time movies and the Folk Festival. The **Cambridge Shakespeare Festival,** in association with the festival at that other university, features plays in open-air repertory throughout July and August. Tickets are available from the Arts Box Office or at the Corn Exchange (£10, concessions £7). You can get an earful at the **Corn Exchange,** at the corner of Wheeler St. and Corn Exchange St. across from the TIC, a venue for band, jazz, and classical concerts. The box office also has info about other local events. (☎357851. Open M-Sa 10am-6pm, till 9pm on performance evenings; Su 6-9pm on performance days only. £7.50-24, some student standbys 50% off on day of show.)

NIGHTLIFE. At dusk, **Evensong** begins at King's College Chapel, a breathtaking treat for day-worn spirits—not to mention a good way to sneak into the college grounds free of charge. (M-Sa 5:30pm, Su 3:30pm. Don't forget Evensong at other colleges, notably St. John's, Caius, and Clare.) **Pubs** constitute the core of Cambridge nightlife. The **Boat Race,** 170 East Rd., a packed and popular joint near the police station, features a variety of live music every evening. (☎508533. Opens 8pm. Usually free, but call ahead.) **Bar Coast,** Quayside, offers free, frequent dance nights, from disco to "uplifting house and garage." (☎556961. Opens 8-9pm.) **Q Club,** 1-3 Station Rd., is home to gifted DJs and host to live bands. (☎315466. Opens 8-9pm. Cover varies.) The quintessential college pub, but with club hours, **King St. Run,** King St., packs in the student crowd amid university kitsch. (☎328900. Open M-Sa 11am-1am, Su noon-10:30pm.) Students, bartenders, and the latest issue of the term-time *Varsity* (20p) will be your best sources of information. The TIC also stocks useful brochures.

MAY WEEK. During the first two weeks of June, students celebrate the end of the term with May Week (a May of the mind), crammed with concerts, plays, and elaborate balls followed by recuperative riverside breakfasts. The college boat clubs compete in an eyebrow-raising series of races known as the **bumps.** Crews line up along the river (rather than across it) and attempt to ram the boat in front before being bumped from behind. May Week's artistic height is the famous **Footlights Revue,** a collection of comedy skits; performers have included future Monty Python members John Cleese, Eric Idle, and Graham Chapman.

FESTIVALS. Midsummer Fair, dating from the 16th century, appropriates the Midsummer Common for five days in the third week of June. The free **Strawberry Fair** (☎560160), on the first Saturday in June, attracts a crowd with food, music, and body piercing. Address inquiries to the TIC. During the rest of the summer, Cambridge caters more to tourists than students. **Summer in the City** and **Camfest** brighten the last two weeks of July with a series of concerts and special exhibits culminating in a huge weekend celebration, the **Cambridge Folk Festival** (☎357851). Book tickets well in advance (about £38); camping on the grounds is £5-18 extra.

▶ DAYTRIPS FROM CAMBRIDGE

GRANTCHESTER

To reach Grantchester Meadows from Cambridge, take the path that follows the River Cam. Grantchester lies a mile from the meadows; ask the way at a neighborhood shop or follow the blue bike-path signs (45min. by foot). If you have the energy to pole or paddle your way, rent a punt or canoe from Scudamore's Boatyards (see p. 311). Or hop on Stagecoach Cambus #118 and hop off at the town's bus stand (9-11 per day from Drummer St., return £1.20).

In 1912, Rupert Brooke wrote "Grantchester! Ah Grantchester! There's peace and holy quiet there." His words from "The Old Vicarage" hold true today, as Grantchester is a mecca for Cambridge literary types. The gentle Cam and swaying seas of grass rejuvenate after bustling Cambridge. Brooke's home at the **Old Vicarage** is now owned by novelist and erstwhile London-mayor-wannabe Jeffrey Archer and closed to the public. The weathered 14th-century **Parish Church of St. Andrew and St. Mary,** on Millway, is beautifully intimate and not to be missed. The main village pub, the **Rupert Brooke,** 2 Broadway, will reward the famished for their efforts. (☎840295. Open M-F 11am-3pm, Sa 11am-11pm, Su noon-10:30pm.) Or wend your way to the idyllic **Orchard Tea Gardens** on Mill Way, once the leisurely Sunday haunt of the "neo-Pagans," a Grantchester offshoot of the famous Bloomsbury Group, including Brooke, Wittgenstein, and Keynes. Outdoor plays are occasionally performed on summer evenings; ask at the Cambridge TIC. (☎845788. Open daily 10am-7pm; year-round indoor and outdoor seating.)

ANGLESEY ABBEY

6 mi. north of Cambridge on the B1102 (signposted from the A14). Buses #111 and 122 run from Drummer St. (25min., every hr.); ask to be let off at Lode Crossroads. ☎/fax 811200. House open Easter to mid-Oct. W-Su and bank holidays 1-5pm. Gardens open Easter to mid-Oct. W-Su and bank holidays 10:30am-5:30pm. Last admission 4:30pm. W-F £6.10, children £3.05; Sa-Su £7.10, children £3.55.

Northeast of Cambridge, 12th-century Anglesey Abbey has been remodeled to house the priceless exotica of the first Lord Fairhaven. One of the niftiest clocks in the universe sits inconspicuously on the bookcase beyond the library's fireplace, but don't worry if you miss it—there are 55 other clocks to enjoy along with a multitude of bizarre tokens and trifles not seen in the typical stately home. In the 100-acre gardens, trees punctuate lines of clipped hedges and manicured lawns.

OTHER DAYTRIPS

WIMPOLE HALL. Cambridgeshire's most elegant mansion lies 10 mi. southwest of Cambridge. The hall holds works by Gibbs, Flitcroft, and Joane, and outside an intricate Chinese bridge crosses the lake set in 60 acres of **gardens** designed by Capability Brown. *(Whippet Bus #175 from Drummer St. (35min., £2). ☎207257. Open Apr.-Nov. T-Th and Sa-Su 1-5pm. £5.90, children £2.70. Gardens £2.50.)* **Wimpole's Home Farm** brims with Longhorn and Gloucester cattle, Soay sheep, and Tamworth pigs. *(☎208987. Open Apr.-Nov. Tu-Th and Sa-Su 10:30am-5pm. Farm £4.70, children £2.70. Estate ticket for hall and farm £8.50, children £4.20, families £21.)*

AUDLEY END. The house "too big for a king" proves that even the monarchy has its limits. The magnificent Jacobean hall is but a quarter of the house's former size—it once extended down to the river, where part of the Cam was redirected by Capability Brown. The grand halls display case after case of stuffed animals, including some extinct species. *(Trains leave Cambridge every hr. for Audley End Station. ☎(01799) 522842. House open Apr.-Sept. W-Su and bank holidays noon-5pm; Oct. W-Su 11am-4pm. Grounds open Apr.-Sept. 11am-6pm; Oct. 11am-4pm. Last admission 1hr. before close. £6.75, concessions £5.10, children £3.40, families £16.90. Grounds only £4, concessions £3, children £2, families £10. Free 15min. introductory talk in the Great Hall.)*

SAFFRON WALDEN. Dating from the Saxon invasions and possibly the Neolithic and Bronze Ages, the market town of Saffron Walden (pop. 15,000) lies 15 mi. south of Cambridge in Essex (take Cambus #102) and 1 mi. west of Audley End House (signs mark the way). It was named for the saffron that was sold here and the Anglo-Saxon word for "wooded valley." The town is best known for the "pargetting" (plaster molding) of its Tudor buildings and its two mazes, a Victorian hedge maze and ancient earthen maze. The **tourist information centre**, 1 Market Pl., Market Sq., stocks a free map marking all points of interest. (☎ (01799) 510444. Open Apr.-Oct. M-Sa 9:30am-5:30pm; Nov.-Mar. M-Sa 10am-5pm.) The **YHA Youth Hostel,** 1 Myddylton Pl., in the north part of town, occupies one of the town's oldest buildings. (☎ (01799) 523117. Lockout 10am-5pm. Curfew 11pm. Open July-Aug. daily; Apr.-June and mid-Sept. to Oct. Tu-Sa; Mar. F-Sa. £9, under 18 £6.20.)

ELY   ☎ 01353

The prosperous town of Ely (EEL-ee) was an island until its fens, now rich flatlands, were drained in the 17th century. Legend has it that the city got its name when St. Dunstan transformed local monks into eels for their lack of piety. The more likely story claims that "Elig" (eel island) was named for the eels that once darted through its surrounding waters. Here, brave Hereward the Wake stood against Norman invaders, earning the title "last of all the English." Worth a visit for its spectacular cathedral alone, Ely also makes a quiet base for visiting Cambridge.

 TRANSPORTATION. Ely is the junction for **trains** (☎ (08457) 484950) between London and various points in East Anglia, including **Cambridge** (20min., every hr., day return £3.40) and **Norwich** (1½hr., every hr., £10.80). **Cambus** (☎ (01223) 423554) #X9 arrives at Market St. from **Cambridge** (30min., every hr., £3.40).

 ORIENTATION AND PRACTICAL INFORMATION. Ely's two major streets run parallel to the cathedral; the town's sights and businesses line **High St.** and **Market St.,** with Cromwell's House and some shops trailing behind on **St. Mary's St.** To reach the cathedral and **tourist information centre** (TIC) from the train station, walk up Station Rd. and continue up Back Hill. The TIC shares and operates the Cromwell House, 29 St. Mary's St. Its staff books rooms for a 10% deposit and £1 fee; call at least two days in advance. (☎ 662062. Open Apr.-Sept. daily 10am-5:30pm; Oct.-Mar. M-Sa 10am-5pm.) They also sell a combination admission ticket, the **Passport to Ely,** that lets you into Ely Cathedral, Cromwell House, Ely Museum, and the Stained Glass Museum (£9, students and children £7). Other services include: the **police,** Nutholt Ln. (☎ (01223) 358966); **Internet access** at **Ely Computer Supplies,** 17 Broad St. (☎ 668863; £2.50 per 30min.), and the **library,** 6 The Cloisters, just off Market Pl. (☎ 662350; free, but often a long wait); and the **post office,** in Lloyd's Chemist on 19 High St. (☎ 669946). **Postal code:** CB7 4HF.

 ACCOMMODATIONS AND FOOD. Cheaper accommodations make Ely a good base for exploring Cambridge. **B&B** options include **The Post House,** 12a Egremont St., which has elegant rooms and a sinfully strong shower. (☎ 667184. TVs. No smoking. From £19.) **Jane's B&B,** 82 Broad St. (☎ 667609), flaunts a homey flat complete with kitchen for only £18-20 per person. Close to the train station and river, **Mr. and Mrs. Friend-Smith's,** 31 Egremont St., lets rooms with garden views. (☎ 663118. From £23.) Camp among spuds and sugar beet with a view of the cathedral at **Braham Farm,** Cambridge Rd., off the A10, 1 mi. from the city center. (☎ 662386. Toilets and cold water. £3 per tent. Electricity hook-up £1.50 per night.)

Most shops close down on Tuesday afternoons in winter. On Thursdays and Saturdays 8am-4pm, stock up on provisions at the **market** in Market Pl. **Waitrose Supermarket,** Brays Ln., hides behind a Georgian facade. (☎ 668800. Open M-Tu and Sa 8:30am-6pm, W-Th 8:30am-8pm, F 8:30am-9pm, Su 10am-4pm.) The **Minster Tavern,** Minster Pl., opposite the cathedral, is popular for lunches. (☎ 652901. £3-7. Open M-Sa 11am-11pm, noon-10:30pm.) **The Steeplegate,** 16-18 High St., serves tea and snacks in two rooms built over a medieval undercroft. (☎664731. Open M-Sa 10am-4:30pm. No smoking.) **The Almonry,** just off the corner of High St. and Brays Ln., serves well-heeled basics for £6-7; eat outside for a stunning garden and cathedral vista. (☎666360. Open M-Sa 10am-5pm, Su 11am-5pm.)

▣ **SIGHTS.** The towers of massive ▣**Ely Cathedral** are impossible to miss for miles around. The cathedral was founded in 1081, on the spot where St. Ethelreda had formed a religious community four centuries before, and was redecorated in the 19th century, when the elaborate ceiling above the nave and many of the stained-glass windows were completed. Upon entering, don't overlook the tiled floor maze; the correct path is 260 ft. long. In 1322, the original Norman tower collapsed, later replaced by the present Octagon Altar, topped by the lantern tower. The eight-sided cupola appears to burst into mid-air but is in fact held up by eight stone pillars (total weight 400 tons). Headless figures in the Lady Chapel and empty grottoes recall destructive visits by Reformation iconoclasts. In the south transept lies the tomb of Dean of Ely, Humphrey Tyndall, an eternal PR boost for the monarchy: heir to the throne of Bohemia, Humphrey refused the kingdom, saying he'd "rather be Queen Elizabeth's subject than a foreign prince." Keep an eye out, too, for the tomb of one of Ely's former bishops, who strikes a pose more becoming of a Playgirl model than a servant of God. Incongruous but beautifully rendered stained-glass windows depict pilots and planes from both World Wars. (☎667735. Open Easter-Sept. daily 7am-7pm; Oct.-Easter M-F 7:30am-6:30pm, Su 7:30am-5pm. Evensong M-Sa 5:30pm, Su 3:45pm. Tours of the Octagon May-Sept. 3 per day, £2.50. Free tours of the West Tower July-Aug. 4 per day. Free ground tours also 4 per day. £4, concessions £2.50.)

The brilliant **Stained Glass Museum** overlooks the nave of the cathedral and details the history of the art form while displaying over a hundred of its finest examples. (☎660347. Open Easter-Oct. M-F 10:30am-5pm, Sa 10:30am-5:30pm, Su noon-6pm; Nov.-Easter M-F 10:30am-4:30pm, Sa 10:30am-5pm, Su noon-4:30pm. £3.50, concessions £2.50, families £7.) The brass-rubbing center is free, but you pay for the materials. (Open July-Aug. daily 10:30am-4pm, Su noon-3pm. Materials £1.70-8.70.) Monastic buildings around the cathedral are still in use: the **infirmary** houses one of the resident canons, and the **bishop's palace** is a home for children with disabilities. The remaining buildings are used by the **King's School,** one of the older public (read: private) schools in England.

For an architectural tour of Ely, follow the path outlined by the TIC's free *Town Trail* pamphlet. **Ely Museum,** at the Old Gaol on the corner of Market St. and Lynn Rd., tells the story of the fenland city and its people, highlighting the saga of the swamp-draining project that created the present landscape. (☎666655. Open in summer 10:30am-5:30pm; winter 10:30am-4:30pm. £2, concessions £1.25.) **Oliver Cromwell's House,** 29 St. Mary's St., has been immortalized with wax figures, 17th-century decor, and a "haunted" bedroom, replete with fake ghost—it's more entertainment than hard-hitting history. (☎662062. Open Apr.-Sept. daily 10am-5:30pm; Oct.-Mar. M-Sa 10am-5pm, Su 11am-3pm. £3.50, concessions £2.75, families £7.)

NORFOLK

KING'S LYNN ☎01553

King's Lynn (pop. 35,500) was one of England's foremost 16th-century ports. Four hundred years later, the once mighty current of the Great Ouse (OOze, as in slime) river has slowed to a leisurely flow, and the town has slowed its pace to match. This dockside city borrows its Germanic look from trading partners such as Hamburg and Bremen; the earth tones of the flat East Anglian countryside meet with a somber red-brick facade. The town slumbers early and heavily, and the sights can be dry, but King's Lynn makes a perfect stopover for hikers exploring the region and anyone in search of rest and relaxation.

🖳🔃 TRANSPORTATION AND PRACTICAL INFORMATION

Trains (☎ (08457) 484950) steam into the **station** on Blackfriars Rd. from: **London King's Cross** (1½hr., 19 per day, day return £23.70); **Cambridge** (1hr., 20 per day, return £8.10); **Peterborough** (1hr., 6 per day, return £9). **Buses** arrive at the **Vancouver Centre** (☎772343; office open M-F 8:30am-5pm, Sa 8:30am-noon and 1-5pm). **First Eastern Counties** (☎ (01603) 660553) buses travel from: **Norwich** (#X94, 1½hr., 8 per day, £4.70) and **Peterborough** (1¼hr., 11 per day, £5). **National Express** (☎ (08705) 808080) runs once daily from **London** (£11).

The **tourist information centre** (TIC), in the Custom House, on the corner of King St. and Purfleet beneath the gigantic "i" flag, books rooms for a 10% deposit and provides bus and train info. From the train station, walk down Waterloo St. until reaching the bus station, then veer left onto New Conduit St., which turns into Purfleet. (☎763044. Open M-Sa 9:15am-5pm, Su 10:15am-5pm.) Buy National Express tickets from **West Norfolk Travel**, 2 King St. (☎772910. Open M-Sa 9am-5pm. MC/V.) Other services include: the **police** (☎691211), at the corner of St. James and London Rd.; the **hospital** (☎613613), located on Gayton Rd.; and the **post office**, at Baxter's Plain on the corner of Broad St. and New Conduit St. **Postal code:** PE30 1YB.

🏠🍴 ACCOMMODATIONS AND FOOD

The quayside **YHA King's Lynn** (☎772461; fax 764312), a short walk from the train and bus stations, occupies part of 16th-century Thoresby College, on College Ln., opposite the Old Gaol House. Its location, river view, and friendly staff make the hostel your best bet. It often fills, so call ahead, and keep your eyes peeled: it's easy to miss. (No smoking. Lockout 10am-5pm. Curfew 11pm. Open May-Aug. daily; Apr. and Sept.-Oct. W-Su. £9.25, under 18 £6.40.) **B&Bs** are a hike from the city center; the less expensive ones span **Gaywood Rd.** and **Tennyson Ave.** Seven gracious rooms fill Victorian **Fairlight Lodge,** 79 Goodwins Rd. (☎762234. £17-24 per person.) Lodgings at **Maranatha-Havana Guest House,** 115 Gaywood Rd., are plush, and ground floor rooms are with bath. (☎774596. £16-22 per person.)

King's Lynn restaurants operate on their own sweet time, and many close on Sunday. A **Sainsbury's** supermarket is at St. Dominic's Sq., Vancouver Centre. (☎772104. Open M-W 8am-8pm, Th-F 8am-9pm, Sa 7:30am-8pm, Su 10am-4pm.) For fresh fruit, visit the **markets** (Tu and Sa 8:30am-4pm) held at larger Tuesday Market Pl., on the north end of High St., or at Saturday Market Pl. Inexpensive Italian meals await at **Antonio's** on Baxter's Plain, off Tower St. (Open Tu-Sa noon-3pm and 6:30-11pm.) Quiet **Archers,** a few steps up Purfleet from the TIC, serves tasty lunches and teas. (☎764411. Open M-Sa 9am-5pm.) The **Seven Sisters** pub presides at the top of Extons Rd. and feels nicely out of the way after a stroll from the town center through The Walks. (Open M-Sa 11am-11pm, Su noon-10:30pm.)

🎥🎵 SIGHTS AND ENTERTAINMENT

The sights of King's Lynn pale in comparison to neighboring Norwich, but a walking tour (guide 30p from the TIC) is rewarding on a fine day. The 15th-century **Guildhall of St. George,** 27-29 King St., near the Tuesday Market, is said to be the last surviving building where Shakespeare appeared in his own play; it now hosts the **King's Lynn Arts Centre.** There are no tours or plaques, so just wander around yourself. (☎774725, Arts Centre 764864. Open M-F 10am-2pm. Free.)

At the **Tales of the Old Gaol House,** Saturday Market Pl., an audioguide tells of Lynn's murderers, robbers, and witches; look for the mugs of Mussolini and Hitler in the book of wanted "local" criminals. The Regalia Room displays the 14th-century "King John Cup" and other treasures from King's Lynn's past. (☎774297. Open Apr.-Oct. daily 10am-5pm; Nov.-Mar. F-Tu 10am-5pm. £2.40, concessions £1.70.) **St. Margaret's Church,** across from the Gaol House on Saturday Market Pl., was built in 1101. Peaceful **Tower Gardens** ensconce Greyfriars Tower on one side of St. James' St., while **The Walks,** on the other side, stretch away from the town center.

The **Corn Exchange** at Tuesday Market Pl. sells tickets for music, dance, and theater events. (☎764864. Open M-Sa 10am-6pm and at evening showtimes, Su 1hr. prior to show. Shows usually 8pm.) During the last half of July, the Guildhall hosts the **King's Lynn Festival,** an orgy of classical and jazz music, along with ballet, puppet shows, and films. Get schedules at the Festival Office, 5 Thoresby College, Queen St. PE30 1HX. (Info ☎767557, tickets 764864. Box office open M-F 10am-5pm, Sa 10am-1pm and 2-4pm. Tickets £3-10.)

◪ DAYTRIPS FROM KING'S LYNN

The stomping grounds of the wealthy give way to wilder country as the road leading north from King's Lynn bends east to flank the Norfolk coast.

SANDRINGHAM. Sandringham has been a royal home since 1862. The Edwardian interior includes halls lined with weaponry, ornate ceilings, and detailed Spanish tapestries; the grounds boast flowing lawns, neat gardens, and a lovely lake; and the museum touts the big-game trophies of George V and royal cars owned by Edward VII in 1900 and Prince Charles in 1990. George once described the place as "dear old Sandringham, the place I love better than anywhere else in the world." Its 600 acres are open to the public when not in use by the royals. It's usually closed in June; ask at the King's Lynn TIC. The best time to visit, though, is during the **flower show** in the last week of July. *(10 mi. north of King's Lynn. First Eastern Counties buses #411 and 414 arrive from King's Lynn (25 min.; M-Sa 8 per day, last return 6pm; Su 5 per day, last return 8:30pm; return £3.35). ☎(01553) 772675. Open Apr.-Sept. 11am-4:45pm. Admission to house, grounds, and museum £6, seniors and students £4.50, children £3.50, families £15.50. Museum and grounds only £5, seniors and students £4, children £3, families £13.)*

CASTLE RISING. Closer to King's Lynn, this solid keep set atop massive earthworks was home to Queen Isabella, "She-Wolf of France," after she plotted the murder of her husband, Edward II. The beautiful view, navigable ruins, and informative tour make the easy trip worthwhile. *(First Eastern Counties buses run from King's Lynn (#410 and 411; 15min.; M-Sa 16 per day, last return 8:45pm; #415, Su 11 per day, return £2). ☎(01553) 631330. Open Apr.-Oct. daily 10am-6pm; Nov.-Mar. W-Su 10am-4pm. Admission and audio tour £3.25, students and seniors £2.50, children £1.60, families £9.)*

HOUGHTON HALL. Built in the mid-18th century for Sir Robert Walpole, the first prime minister of England, Houghton Hall is a magnificent example of Palladian architecture, a style all the rage in Georgian England. Its rooms, designed and decorated by James Gibbs and William Kent, were intended to reflect the grandeur of the prime minister's office, and still include original tapestries, paintings, a famous model soldier collection, and "the most sublime bed ever designed." *(14 mi. northeast of King's Lynn. Take First Eastern Counties bus #411 (45min., M-Sa 2 per day, return £3.75). ☎(01485) 528569. Open Easter to late Sept. Th, Su, and bank holidays 2-5:30pm; gate closes 5pm. Admission to house and grounds £6, children £2.)*

NEAR KING'S LYNN: THE NORTHERN NORFOLK COAST

The northern Norfolk Coast is a blissfully tranquil expanse of British seashore. The occasional windmill or mansion dots untamed beaches, sand dunes, and salt marshes, while sailboats slumber and wading birds balance in boggy harbors. Those with eight to 12 days can traverse the 93 mi. **Norfolk Coast Path.** The National Trail begins 16 mi. north of King's Lynn at **Hunstanton,** spans east to **Wells-next-the-Sea** and then **Sheringham** and the **Norfolk Broads** (see p. 322), finishing near **Cromer.** The trail and its villages are also fine daytrips. The **Norfolk Coast Hopper,** Norfolk Green Coach #36, makes daily stops between Hunstanton and Sheringham. (☎(0845) 300 6116. 1½hr.; every hr. in summer, fewer in winter; all-day ticket £4.)

The highlight of the coast is the boisterous ◪**Blakeney Point Seal Colony.** Though accessible by a four-mile footpath from **Cley-next-the-Sea,** the seals would much rather their admirers visit by boat. **Temple's Ferry Service** runs trips from Morston Harbour, bookable from nearby towns. (☎(01263) 740791. 1-1½hr. trips £5, children £3.50.) Nearer to Hunstanton, the **Scolt Head Island Reserve** and the **Holme Bird Observatory** are also superb. Holme is 3 mi. east; buses run from Hunstanton to Holme's Crossing in summer only (12min.). To visit Scolt Head Island go via Brancaster Staithe (an Anglo-Saxon word meaning "pier"), 10 mi. east along the A149.

For a taste of luxury, **Holkham Hall**, 2 mi. west of Wells-next-the-Sea, is the Palladian home of the Earl of Leicester. Marvel at the massive marble hall before getting lost in the amusing **Bygones Museum**, which assembles over 4000 knickknacks from the family's past. The labyrinthine grounds attract all sorts of wildlife, from heron to deer. (☎ (01328) 710227. Open Apr.-Sept. Su-Th 1-5pm. Combined hall and museum £8, children £4. Hall or museum each £5, children £2.50.)

The Norfolk Coast makes an easy daytrip from **King's Lynn**, though **Hunstanton,** at the beginning of the coast, is a more intimate touring base. Buses #410 and 411 run from Vancouver Centre in King's Lynn to Hunstanton (2hr.; M-Sa 2 per hr., Su every 2hr.; £2.80, return £3.70). For details on the Northern Norfolk Coast, maps, and bus schedules, consult the Hunstanton **tourist information centre** (TIC), Town Hall, The Green. (24hr. ☎ (01485) 532610. Open Apr.-Sept. daily 9:30am-5pm; Oct.-Mar. 10:30am-4pm.) The **National Trail Office,** 6 Station Road, Wells-next-the-Sea, has expert advice on hiking the Norfolk Coast Path. (☎ (01328) 711533. Open daily 9am-5pm.) Budget accommodations along the coast are rather scarce, but the kind folks at the King's Lynn or Hunstanton TICs can help you find something suitable for a 10% deposit. On the coast, your best bet is the **YHA Youth Hostel,** 15 Avenue Rd., well signposted from the center of Hunstanton. (☎ (01485) 532061. Open July-Aug. daily; Easter-June M-Sa; Sept.-Oct. Tu-Sa. Dorms £10, under 18 £6.85.)

NORWICH ☎01603

In the mood to lose your way? Try navigating the dizzying medieval streets of Norwich (NOR-rich) as they wind outwards from the Norman castle, past the cathedral, and to the scattered fragments of the 14th-century city wall. Even though Norwich retains the hallmarks of an ancient city, a university and active art community ensure that it is also thoroughly modern. One sign of the times: Norwich once had a church for every Sunday and a pub for every day of the year, but now only 36 churches coexist with 380 pubs. Clearly, the hum of "England's city in the country" has not yet abated, with a daily market almost a millennium old still thriving alongside busy art galleries and nightlife.

▐ TRANSPORTATION

Easily accessible by bus, coach, or train, Norwich makes a decent base for touring both urban and rural East Anglia, particularly the Norfolk Broads.

Trains: Corner of Riverside and Thorpe Rd., 15min. from the city center, which is connected by bus (40p). Ticket window open M-Sa 4:45am-8:45pm, Su 6:45am-8:45pm. Information open M-Sa 9am-7pm, Su 10:15am-5:30pm. **Anglia Railways** (☎ (08457) 484950) from: **London Liverpool St.** (2hr., M-Sa 30 per day, £31); **Great Yarmouth** (30min.; M-Sa 12 per day, Su 6 per day; return £4-5.30); **Peterborough** (1½hr.; M-Sa 15 per day, Su 8 per day; return £11.60-15.10); **Cambridge** (1½hr., 12 per day, £10.90-11.40). Under 16 ride at half-price.

Buses: Station (☎660553), on Surrey St. off St. Stephen St., southwest of the castle. **Luggage storage** in the cafeteria £1-3. Information center and ticket desk open M-F 8am-5:30pm, Sa 9am-5:15pm. **National Express** (☎ (08705) 808080) from **London** (3hr., 7 per day, £14.20) and **Cambridge** (2hr., 1 per day, day return £10). **Cambridge Coach Services** (☎ (01223) 423900) from **Cambridge** (#74; 2hr.; 4 per day; £9.10, students and seniors £7, children £4.65). **First Eastern Counties** (☎ (08456) 020121) travels to King's Lynn, Peterborough, and other Norfolk towns; **Ranger tickets** give 1 day of unlimited travel (£6, seniors £4.70, children £4, families £11.50).

Norfolk Bus Information Centre (NORBIC): Castle Meadow, across from the stretch of bus stops. (☎ (0845) 3006116). Open M-Sa 8:30am-5pm.

Taxis: Express Taxis (☎767626). 24hr. 1 wheelchair taxi, limited hr. (☎300300). **Canary Taxis** (☎414243) has a 24hr. wheelchair taxi.

✦ ᷟ ORIENTATION AND PRACTICAL INFORMATION

Want to find your way around Norwich? Get a map, and pray. The city's planner must have had a wobbly hand, for although sights are fairly close together and walking is an efficient way to get around, the twisty streets are guaranteed to confuse. Take care in the center of town after dark.

Tourist Information Centre: The Forum, Millennium Plain, Bethel St. (☎666071; fax 765389; www.norwich.gov.uk). Stocks brochures about the region and a 30p city guide map. Books rooms for £3 and a 10% deposit. Luggage storage £2.50 plus £3 key deposit. Open June-Sept. M-Sa 9:30am-5pm; Oct.-May M-F 9:30am-4:30pm, Sa 9:30am-1pm and 1:30-4:30pm. **Walking tours** (1½hr.) Apr.-Oct.; £2.50, children £1.

Financial Services: Banks line **London St.** and **Bank Plain,** including **Barclays,** 36 Bank Plain (☎244500). Open M-Tu and Th-F 9am-4:30pm, W 10am-4:30pm. **Thomas Cook,** 15 St. Stephen's St. (☎241200). Open M-Tu and Th-F 9am-5:30pm, W 10am-5:30pm, Sa 10am-4pm.

Launderette: Laundromat, 179a Dereham Rd. (☎626685). Change and soap (20p) available. Open M-Sa 8am-8pm, Su 10am-7pm; last wash 1½hr. before closing.

Police: Bethel St. (☎768769).

Hospital: Norfolk and Norwich Hospital (☎286286), corner of Brunswick Rd. and St. Stephen's Rd.

Internet Access: Cyber cafes in Norwich are quick to kick the cyberbucket; ask the TIC for an up-to-date list of access sites. **Cybercand,** 14 Bank St. (☎619091), has fast terminals. Open M-F 10am-8pm, Sa 1-6pm. Members £2 per hr., nonmembers £4; get the £5 membership if planning to use Internet for more than 2hr. More high-speed connections await at **Cafe Connect,** Queens Rd. (☎611699), by the bus station. £4 per hr. Open daily 8:30am-6pm. The one spot that isn't going anywhere is the **Lending Library,** Ber St. (☎215215). Sign up for a temporary membership and surf for free. Open M-F 10am-8pm, Sa 9am-5pm; reserve ahead.

Post Office: Castle Mall, 84-85 Castle Meadow Walk (☎761635). **Bureau de change.** Open M-F 9am-5:30pm, Sa 9am-6pm. **Branches** at Queen St. (☎220278) and 13-17 Bank Plain (☎220228). Open M-F 9am-5:30pm, Sa 9am-12:30pm. **Postal Code:** NR1 3DD.

ᷟ ACCOMMODATIONS AND CAMPING

Cheap ($17-20) and convenient lodgings are located on **Stracey Rd.,** a five-minute walk from the train station. Instead of taking a left onto Prince of Wales Rd., turn left onto Thorpe Rd., walk two blocks up (away from the bridge), and go right onto Stracey Rd. Many pleasant B&Bs in the $18-24 range line **Earlham Rd.** and **Unthank Rd.,** but they're at least a 20min. hike westward from downtown and even farther from the train station. Most guest houses on both streets appear when house numbers reach the 100s. B&Bs may also be found along **Dereham Rd.:** follow St. Benedict's St., which eventually becomes Dereham Rd.

Beaufort Lodge, 62 Earlham Rd. (☎/fax 627928). This new B&B promises plushly-carpeted, wide-windowed rooms at gently indulgent prices. The lovely hosts feed you tea, coffee, and cookies after fetching you from the station. Color TV. No smoking. Singles £35; doubles from £50.

YHA Norwich, 112 Turner Rd. (☎627647). From the train station, cross the river and wait at the shelter in front of the Furniture Store for bus #19 or 20 (ask for the Earl of Leicester stop; 80p), or walk 1½ mi. from the city center. Drag your bones along Prince of Wales Rd. until Bank Plain, then turn right and continue as the road becomes Dereham Rd. Upon reaching the Earl of Leicester Pub, turn right onto Turner Rd.; the hostel

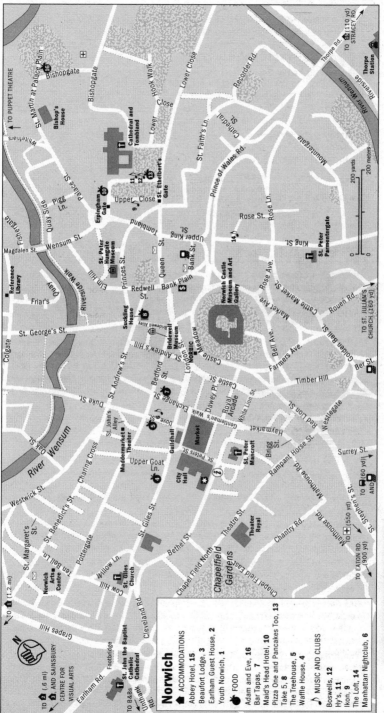

TO ★ (110 yd)
STRACEY RD.

Thorpe Rd.

Thorpe
Station

Riverside

River Wensum

St. Martin at Palace Plain

Bishopgate

TO PUPPET THEATRE

Bishop's
House

Whitefriars

Cathedral and
Tombland

Lower Hook Walk

Lower Close

Close

Recorder Rd.

St. Faith's Ln.

Cathedral St.

Mountergate

Palace St.

St. Ethelbert's
Gate

Upper Close

Prince of Wales Rd.

Pigg Ln.

Quay Side

Erpingham
Gate

Rose St.

Rose St.

Rose Ln.

Fishergate

Magdalen St.

Wensum St.

Tombland

Upper King St.

King St.

St. Peter
Parmentergate

Reference
Library

Elm Hill

St. Peter
Hungate Museum

Princes St.

Queen St.

Bank St.

Norwich Castle
Museum and Art
Gallery

Rose Ave.

Friar's

Redwell
St.

Bank Plain

Market Ave.

Rose Ave.

Rouen Rd.

Colgate

St. George's St.

Suckling
House

Bridewell Alley

Bridewell
Museum

St. Andrew's Hill

London St.

Castle
Meadow

Cattle Market St.

Bell Ave.

Farmers Ave.

TO ST. JULIAN'S
CHURCH (160 yd)

Golden Ball St.

NORWICH

St. Andrew's St.

Bedford
St.

Castle St.

Timber Hill

Ber St.

River Wensum

Duke St.

Charing Cross

St. John's
Alley

Dove St.

Exchange St.

Davey Pl.

Royal
Arcade

White Lion St.

Westlegate

Red Lion St.

Westwick St.

Maddermarket
Theater

Upper Goat
Ln.

Guildhall

Gentleman's Walk

Market

St. Peter
Mancroft

Haymarket

Surrey St.

Rampant Horse St.

Brigg St.

St. Benedict's St.

Charing Cross

St. Giles St.

City
Hall

St. Peters St.

Matthouse Rd.

TO ★ (160 yd)
AND ★

TO ★ (550 yd)
St. Stephen's St.

St. Margaret's
St.

Ten Bell Ln.

Pottergate

Willow Ln.

St. Giles
Church

Theatre St.

Bethel St.

Chapel Field North

Chapel Field
Gardens

Chapel Field East

Theater
Royal

Chantry Rd.

Westwick St.

Cow Hill

Norwich Arts
Centre

St. Giles
Catholic
Church

TO EATON RD.
(900 yd)

Cleveland Rd.

TO ① (1.2 mi)

Grapes Hill

N

St. John the Baptist
Catholic Cathedral

Footbridge

Earlham Rd.

Unthank Rd.

TO ② (.6 mi)
② AND SAINSBURY
CENTRE FOR
VISUAL ARTS

TO B&Bs

200 yards

200 meters

Norwich

⌂ ACCOMMODATIONS
Abbey Hotel, **15**
Beaufort Lodge, **3**
Earlham Guest House, **2**
Youth Norwich, **1**

♦ FOOD
Adam and Eve, **16**
Bar Tapas, **7**
Maid's Head Hotel, **10**
Pizza One and Pancakes Too, **13**
Take 5, **8**
The Treehouse, **5**
Waffle House, **4**

♪ MUSIC AND CLUBS
Boswells, **12**
Hy's, **11**
Ikon, **9**
The Loft, **14**
Manhattan Nightclub, **6**

is the last building on your right. Clean rooms of varying sizes (2-8 bunks per room). Internet access £2.50 per 30min. Luggage storage. Lockout 10am-5pm. Curfew 11pm, but guests can arrange to stay out late. Often full July-Aug.; call ahead. Open Jan. to mid-Dec. daily. Dorms £10, under 18 £6.90.

Earlham Guest House, 147 Earlham Rd. (☎459469). Take bus #26 or 27 from the city center and ask to get off at The Mitre pub. The guest house of friendly hosts Mr. and Mrs. Wright stands out from surrounding B&B's for its cozy lounge and refreshing garden. The tasteful blue-and-pastel rooms each have TV, tea and coffee maker, and wash basin. No smoking. Singles £21; doubles and twins £21-24 per person.

The Abbey Hotel, 16 Stracey Rd. (☎/fax 612915), 5min. from the train station up Thorpe Rd. A TV and wash basin await in every quiet room of this clean, yellow building. Singles £20-29; doubles £40-54; ask about reduced rates.

Camping: Closest is the **Lakenham** campsite, Martineau Ln. (☎620060; no calls after 8pm), 1mi. south of the city center. First Eastern Counties buses #9, 29, and 32 stop nearby. Cars can't enter after 11pm. Toilets and showers; facilities for disabled travelers. July-Aug. £4 per adult, £2 per child; Easter-June £3.80, £1.80; Sept.-Easter £3, children free. Pitch fee £3.50. Family deals available.

🍴🍺 FOOD AND PUBS

In the heart of the city and just a stone's throw from the castle spreads one of England's largest and oldest **open-air markets.** (Open M-Sa roughly 8:30am-4:30pm.) Feast your gut on everything from fresh fruits and cheeses to ice cream (jewelry and knickknacks are harder to digest). **Tesco Metro** is alongside the market square on St. Giles St. (Open M-Sa 7:30am-8pm, Su 11am-5pm.)

⊠ The Treehouse, 14 Dove St. (☎763258). Eat fresh vegetarian cuisine on earthenware plates while stuffed parrots eye you hungrily from their perches. Daily menu with creative specials £4.80-6.25; bowl of assorted salads and wholebread £3.70. The store downstairs sells healthy victuals. Open M-W 11:30am-5pm, Th-Sa 11:30am-9pm.

Pizza One and Pancakes Too, 24 Tombland (☎621583), by the cathedral. Creative pizza and crepe dishes. Have a 4-cheese "charity pizza" (£5) and 50p goes to the charity-of-the-month; order the banana-dog (£2) and ask questions later. Ingest any meal and get free admission to neighboring clubs Boswell's and Hy's (see p. 321). Students get 20% off entrees. Open M-W noon-10pm, Th noon-10:30pm, F-Sa noon-11pm, Su noon-9pm.

The Waffle House, 39 St. Giles St. (☎612790). A family restaurant with wicker galore. Astounding Belgian waffles (wholemeal or white) made with organic ingredients and fillings from ham, cheese, and mushrooms to tuna and bean sprouts (£2.15-5.75). Fruity milkshakes go well with a sweet waffle for dessert. 20% student discount. Open M-Th 10am-10pm, F-Sa 10am-11pm, Su 11am-9pm.

Bar Tapas, 16-20 Exchange St. (☎764077). Experience the rhythm of South America and the spirit of Spain in this flag-adorned eatery. Try the authentic *Tortilla Española to Brochetta da Gambas* (£3-5). Open M-W 10:30am-6pm, Th-Sa 10:30am-11pm.

The Adam and Eve, Bishopgate (☎667423), behind the cathedral at the Palace St. end of Riverside Walk. Norwich's first pub (est. 1249) is older than sin and still one of its most pleasing watering holes. Half-pint of cider £1.10. Cheese-drenched jacket potatoes and other treats served noon to 7pm. Open M-Sa 11am-11pm, Su noon-10:30pm.

Take 5, St. Andrews Hill (☎763099), off St. Andrews St. in the old Suckling House. One of the best spots for an evening drink in town isn't even a pub—it's a cafe, restaurant, and exhibition center in a fantastic 14th-century building with a hidden cobblestone courtyard. Open M-Sa 10:30am-11pm. Bar only Su 6-10:30pm.

The Maid's Head Hotel (☎209955), Tombland. One of the poshest hotels in Norwich serves an amazing lunch deal. The "Best of British Menu" (affectionately called BOB), a luxurious two-course meal served in a luminated atrium, costs only £9.95. Open for lunch daily noon-2pm; dinner M-Th 6-11pm, F-Sa 5-11pm, Su 6:30-10:30pm.

👁 SIGHTS

NORWICH CASTLE MUSEUM AND ART GALLERY. The original Norwich Castle was built in 1089 by a Norman monarchy intent on subduing the Saxon city. Its current exterior dates from an 1830s restoration, though last year's £12 million refurbishment is the largest in the castle's history. It was here that English nobles forced King John to sign the *Magna Carta* in 1215, curbing the power of the monarchy. Now, the Castle Museum in the castle keep has a hands-on exhibit that brings new life to Norman rule, while the archaeology gallery displays relics of Queen Boudicca, a first-century feminist who rebelled against the Romans. The art gallery contains a collection of oil paintings and watercolors by the Norwich school. (☎493636. Open July-Aug. 10am-7pm, Su noon-5pm; Sept.-June 10am-5pm, Su 2-5pm. Museum and gallery £4.70, students and seniors £4.10, children £3.50, families £13.90.)

NORWICH CATHEDRAL AND TOMBLAND. The castle and the Norman Norwich Cathedral dominate the skyline. The cathedral, built by an 11th-century bishop as penance for having bought his episcopacy, features unusual two-story cloisters (the only ones of their kind in England) and flying buttresses that help support the second tallest spire in the country (315ft.; the Salisbury Stake is the tallest). Use the mirror in the nave to examine the overhead bosses carved with biblical scenes. In summer, the cathedral frequently hosts orchestral concerts and art exhibitions. (☎764385. Open mid-May to mid-Sept. daily 7:30am-7pm; mid-Sept. to mid-May 7:30am-6pm. Evensong M-F 5:15pm. Free tours May-Oct. 2-3 per day, Sa-Su 3:30pm. £3 suggested donation.) Though it sounds like a macabre amusement park, **Tombland,** which runs in front of the Cathedral Park, is the burial site of thousands of victims of the Great Plague and now a nightclub hotspot. Connection? You decide.

BRIDEWELL MUSEUM. This museum displays the history of local industry, turning back time by recreating an early 19th-century pharmacy, public bar, and tap room, among other common locales of the past. The enchanting medieval building has its own storied history, serving at various times as a merchant's house, mayor's mansion, factory, warehouse, and prison: still visible are dates and initials carved in the courtyard. (Bridewell Alley, off St. Andrew's St. ☎667228. Open Apr.-Sept. M-Sa 10am-5pm, Su 2-5pm. £2.50, students and seniors £2, children £1.50, families £6.50.)

ST. JULIAN'S CHURCH. Long before Aphra Behn held a pen, a 14th-century nun named Juliana of Norwich took up a cell of her own here and became the first known woman to write a book in English. Her 20-year work, *Revelations of Divine Love*, is based on her mystic experiences as an anchoress at this church, where you can visit her lonely cell and shrine. (Between King St. and Rouen Rd. ☎767380. Open May-Sept. daily 8am-5:30pm; Oct.-Apr. 8am-4pm. Free.)

SAINSBURY CENTRE FOR VISUAL ARTS. Standing at the University of East Anglia, 3 mi. west of town on Earlham Rd., this center was destroyed during the English Reformation and restored after WWII. Sir Sainsbury (of the supermarket chain) donated his superb collection of art, including works by Picasso, Bacon, and other modern artists, to the university in 1973. The award-winning building was designed by Sir Norman Foster. (Take any university-bound bus, such as #26, and ask for the Constable Terr. stop. ☎456060. Open Tu-Su 11am-5pm. £2, concessions £1.)

🎵 ENTERTAINMENT

Norwich offers a rich array of cultural activities, especially in summer. The TIC, as well as many cafes and B&Bs, has information on all things vaguely entertaining. Next to the Assembly House on Theatre St., the Art Deco **Theatre Royal** houses touring opera and ballet companies, as well as London-based theater troupes such as the Royal Shakespeare Company and Royal National Theatre. (☎630000. Box office open M-Sa 9:30am-8pm, until 6pm on non-performance days. Tickets £3-17, some concessions.) The home of the Norwich Players, **Maddermarket Theatre** stages high-quality amateur drama in an Elizabethan-style theater. Adhering to a bizarre tradition, all actors remain anonymous, adding new meaning to "Who's Who in the Cast." (☎620917. 1 St. John's Alley. Box office open M-Sa 10am-9pm; on non-performance days M-F 10am-5pm, Sa 10am-1pm. Tickets £7, under 25 and seniors £5.) The **Norwich Arts Centre**, between Reeves Yard St. and Benedicts St., is the city's most versatile venue, hosting folk and world music, ballet, and comedy. (☎660352. Box office open M-Sa 9am-10pm. Tickets £4-12, concessions available.) The **Norwich Puppet Theatre**, St. James, Whitefriars, comes in handy with shows for all ages. (☎629921. Box office open M-F 9:30am-5pm, Sa 1hr. prior to show. Tickets £5-6, children £4.) Ask the TIC for a free guide to the City Council's free summer presentations of **Theatre in the Parks** (☎212137).

The **Norfolk and Norwich Festival**—an extravaganza of theater, dance, music, and visual arts—explodes in mid-October. **Picture This,** in mid-June, offers two weeks of open artists' studios around the county. Pick up leaflets at the TIC or call 764764 for information and tickets. July welcomes the **LEAP Dance Festival** (mostly contemporary dance). Norwich's outdoor parks also host a stream of other **festivals** and **folk fairs** in summer.

▣ NIGHTLIFE

Many pubs and clubs offer live music, while some, like the "cafe-music bar" **Boswells**, 24 Tombland, near the cathedral, hyphenate the two. Live bands entertain Monday through Saturday 9pm-midnight, when a disco takes over until 2am. (☎626099. 18+. Cover Tu-Sa £1-3 after 9pm. Open M-Sa noon-2am, Su noon-6pm.) Slide (electrically) to **Hy's,** next door, where theme nights bring anything from salsa rhythms to disco beats. Tuesday is student night. (☎621155. Tu and Th-Sa 18+; W 7-11pm 14-17. Cover £1-4. Open Tu-Sa 9pm-2am.) Nearby **Ikon**, on Tombland across from the Maid's Head Hotel, goes retro Wednesday, party Friday, and explodes with dance on Saturday. (☎621541. 18+. Cover £1-4. Open W 10pm-2am, F-Sa 9:30pm-2am.) **Manhattan Nightclub** on Dove St., with its Sunday night "Exclusive Chilled-out Zone," is another hotspot. (☎629060. 18+. Open F-Su 9pm-4am, Su 9pm-2am.) **The Loft,** on Rose St., is a relaxed, gay-friendly club with live music downstairs and soul and funk wafting from the loft. (☎623559. 18+, occasional 16+ nights. Open Th-F 10:30pm-2am, Sa 10pm-3am, Su 8:30pm-midnight.) On **Prince of Wales Rd.,** near the city center, five more clubs within two blocks jockey for social position. The **City Rail Link**, a service of First Eastern Counties (☎(08456) 020121), whisks tired partiers between the university and the train station, stopping close to all of the above venues (1-2 per hr.; runs all night Tu-Sa, last bus Su-M 2:30am).

▣ DAYTRIPS FROM NORWICH

NORFOLK BROADS NATIONAL PARK

To reach the Broads, take a train from Norwich, Lowestoft, or Great Yarmouth to the smaller towns of Beccles, Cantley, Lingwood, Oulton Broad, Salhouse, or Wroxham. From Norwich, First Eastern Counties buses leave from the corner of St. Stephen's St. and Surrey St. to: **Wroxham** *(#54; 40 min.; M-Sa every hr., Su every 1½hr.; return £2.70);* **Horning** *(#723 or 726, 45min., 4 per day, £3.20);* **Potter Heigham** *(#723-726, 1hr., 4 per day, return £3.30);* **Strumpshaw** *(#30-33, 30min., M-Sa 8 per day, return £2.20);* **other Broads towns** *(#705, M-F 1 per day in the evening).*

Though London and other southern towns have pirated away much of northern East Anglia's marine commerce, folk around here still seek out seafaring adventures. Birds and beasts flock to the national parkland of the **Norfolk Broads,** a watery maze of navigable marshlands, where traffic in narrow waterways hidden by hedgerows conjures a surreal image of sailboats floating through fields. The broads didn't occur naturally, but were formed in medieval times when peat was dug out to use for fuel. Over the centuries, water levels rose and the shallow lakes or "broads" were born. With their unique ecology and birdlife, the marshes and the hills nearby beckon nature enthusiasts traveling by foot, cycle, or boat. Exercise care when walking about the Broads, a designated environmentally sensitive area; continual abuse by humans has damaged the marshlands tremendously.

Among the many **nature trails** that pass through the Broads, **Cockshoot Broad** lets you birdwatch, a circular walk around **Ranworth** points out the Broads' various flora, and **Upton Fen** is popular for its bugs. Hikers can challenge themselves with the 56 mi. long **Weaver's Way** between Cromer and Great Yarmouth. By collecting stamps along the trek, the hardy receive an exclusive woven patch upon completion. Girl scouts eat your heart out. The small village of **Strumpshaw,** with its bird reserve, is especially popular among birdwatchers. (☎(01603) 715191. Open daily 9am-9pm or dusk. £3.25.)

Numerous companies offer **cruises** around the Broads. **Broads Tours** of Wroxham, on the right-hand side before the town bridge, runs an excellent 1-2hr. trip. (☎(01603) 782207. Office open daily 9am-5:30pm. Tours July-Aug. 7 per day, Sept.-June 11:30am and 2pm. £4.60-6.25, children £3.40-5.) **Southern River Steamers,** 65 Trafford Rd., gives cruises from Norwich to Surlingham Broad, leaving from quays near the cathedral and train station. (☎(01603) 624051. 30min. to 3¼hr. excursions leaving periodically May-Sept. 11am-5:30pm. £1.60-6.70, children 80p-£4.30.) Certain areas of the Broads are accessible only by car or bike; the pamphlet *Broads Bike Hire,* available at the Wroxham TIC, lists rental shops. The most convenient place to rent a cycle is **Camelot Craft** in Wroxham, though it's best to call ahead; follow Station Rd. to the river and take a left onto The Rhond. (☎(01603) 783096. £5 per half-day, £8 per day. Open daily 9am-5pm.)

Wroxham, 10min. from Norwich by train, is the best base for information-gathering and preliminary exploration of some of the area's most pristine wetlands. To reach the **Wroxham and Hoveton Broads Information Centre** from the train station and town bus stop, take a right down Station Rd. and walk about 90 yd. Knowledgeable Broads rangers answer questions and supply travelers with maps, guides, and contact information. Pick up free copies of *The Broadcaster,* which outlines local happenings; *The Broad Sheet,* for more recent Broads news; and *The Broad Miniguide,* which recommends certain sights and includes a map. The office also has lists of boat rentals and campsites scattered throughout the area, and books guest houses and hotels around the park. (☎/fax (01603) 782281. Open Easter-Oct. M-Sa 9am-1pm and 2-5pm.)

SUFFOLK AND ESSEX

BURY ST. EDMUNDS   ☎01284

In AD 869, Viking invaders tied the Saxon monarch King Edmund to a tree, used him for target practice, and then beheaded him. Approximately 350 years later, 25 barons met in the Abbey of St. Edmund to sow the seeds of democracy, swearing to force King John to sign the *Magna Carta.* From these two defining moments in English history, Bury St. Edmunds came to be known as "shrine of a king, cradle of the law," and is now a charmingly intimate small English town.

▣ TRANSPORTATION. Bury makes a good daytrip from either Norwich or Cambridge, especially if you include a jaunt to Lavenham, Sudbury, Long Melford, or any of the other historic villages in Western Suffolk. **Trains** (☎(08457) 484950) arrive from: **London Liverpool St.** (2hr., every 1-2 hr., return £29.40); **Colchester** (1hr., every 1½hr., return £12.75); **Felixstowe** (1¼hr., 2 per hr., return £11). **National Express** (☎(08705) 808080) **buses** come from **London** (2hr., 2 per day, £11). **R.W. Chenery** (☎(01379) 741221) runs an express bus from **London Victoria** once per day (£13). **Cambus** (☎(01223) 423554) #X11 runs from Drummer St. in **Cambridge** (55min.; M-Sa every 2hr., Su every 4hr.; return £4.50). The area around Bury is explorable by bike, but rentals are difficult to come by. Try **Barton's Bicycles,** 5 Marrio's Walk, Stowmarket; call a few days in advance. (☎(01449) 677195. Bikes £8 per day, £35 per week. Open M-Sa 9am-5:30pm.)

■ ⓘ ORIENTATION AND PRACTICAL INFORMATION. Laid out according to the original 12th-century plan, Bury's streets are easier to untangle than those of neighboring towns. The folks at the **tourist information centre** (TIC), 6 Angel Hill, will happily supply you with maps, an accommodations list, and a copy of *What's On.* (☎ 764667; fax 757084. Open Easter-Oct. M-Sa 9:30am-5:30pm, Su 10am-3pm; Nov.-Easter M-F 10am-4pm, Sa 10am-1pm.) To reach the TIC from the train station, follow Northgate St. through the roundabout; turn right onto Mustow St. and walk up to Angel Hill. From the bus station, follow St. Andrew's St. to Brentgovel St., turn right at Lower Baxtel St. and then left onto Abbeygate St. The TIC runs 1½hr. guided **walking tours** of the city (June-Sept. Su-F 2:30pm; £2.50). Banks in town include **Lloyds,** on Buttermarket St., half a block from the marketplace. (☎ (0845) 303 0105. Open M-Tu and Th-F 9am-5pm, W 9:30am-5pm, Sa 9:30am-12:30pm.) **Thomas Cook** is at 43b Cornhill St. (☎ 752184. Open M and W-Sa 9am-5:30pm, Tu 10am-5:30pm.) The **post office** is at 17-18 Cornhill St. (☎ 701095. Open M-F 9am-5:30pm, Sa 9am-12:30pm.) **Postal code:** IP33 1AA.

ⓝ ⓒ ACCOMMODATIONS AND FOOD. The TIC books B&Bs in town or on a nearby farm (£18-25). Sling that heavy pack over your shoulder with a smile: the charming home of **Mrs. Montanari,** 6 Orchard St., is a mere 2min. from the bus station. (☎ 750191. Singles £20; doubles £36.) **Mrs. Norton,** 16 Cannon St., provides a warm welcome on a quiet, centrally located street. (☎ 761776. Singles £18, additional nights £17; twins £32, £31.)

For groceries, head down Cornhill St. from the post office to the **Iceland** supermarket. (Open M-W and Sa 8:30am-6pm, Th-F 8:30am-7pm.) Quiet Bury bustles on **market** days (W and Sa 9am-4pm). Pints go for £1.80 at the pint-sized **Nutshell,** Abbeygate at the Traverse (☎ 764867), the world's smallest pub. The hostess speaks with reverence about her entry in the pages of the *Guinness Book of World Records,* created when the 15-by-17 ft. pub squeezed 102 people and one dog between its tiny walls. A crowd of locals lead the budget eater into **The Baker's Oven,** 11 Abbeygate St. (☎ 754001), where you can munch on scrumptious toasties filled with tomatoes, ham, and eggs, and a side salad for under £3.

ⓖ ⓙ SIGHTS AND ENTERTAINMENT. A few hours of whimsical wandering reveal Bury's prized charms. Along Crown St., across from the TIC on the soggy banks of the River Lark, lie the beautiful and extensive ruins of the **▨Abbey of St. Edmund,** 11th-century home to cadres of foraging ducks. The weathered, massive pillars look like stone refugees from Easter Island. It was here that the 25 *Magna Carta* barons met in 1214 to discuss their letter to the king. The formal gardens next to the remains won the 1999 Britain in Bloom and Nations in Bloom competitions and are at their best in late June. Be sure to see the aviary and the Olde English Rose Garden of Frances Hodgson Burnett's dreams. (Ruins and garden open M-Sa 7am-sunset, Su 9am-sunset. Free.) At the TIC, pick up an audio tour of the ruins to hear a 12th-century monk named Jocelin tell stories of executions with slightly too much glee. (45min. tour £1.50, concessions £1.)

Next door, the interior of the delightful 16th-century **St. Edmundsbury Cathedral** is bathed in magnificent color; take care to look heavenward and admire the wooden ceiling designed in East Anglian style. The cherub overhanging the entrance, allegedly pilfered years before, was "rediscovered" by a Bury businessman in a Belgian antique shop. (☎ 754933. Open June-Aug. daily 8:30am-8pm; Sept.-May 8:30am-6pm. Evensong W-Sa 5:30pm, Su 3:30pm. Suggested donation £2.)

The **Manor House Museum** borders the abbey gardens to the south. This elegant Georgian house, a must-see if you're cuckoo for clocks, contains dozens of synchronized timepieces, including a replica of the first rolling-ball clock. The museum also houses an impressive collection of Victorian and 1920s costumes. (☎ 757076. Open Su-W noon-5pm. £2.50, concessions £1.50.) The **Moyses' Hall Museum,** Corn Hill in the marketplace, is hopelessly devoted to its collection of historical junk, including a mummified cat and a violin made out of a horse's skull.

Superstitious highlights include artifacts from the 1828 murder of local Maria Marten, such as a book covered with the murderer's skin. Afraid that an evil criminal might slip unnoticed into heaven, the people of the time were convinced that skinning the murderer would expose his soul so that no one would mistake him. (☎757488. Open M-Sa 10am-5pm, Su 2-5pm. £2, concessions £1.50, families £6, free after 4pm.) To spark up your stay, visit in mid-May, when the town's annual **festival** brings three weeks of music, street entertainment, and a firework finale.

▶ DAYTRIPS FROM BURY ST. EDMUNDS

Three miles southwest of Bury in the village of Horringer, **Ickworth House,** the capacious home of the Marquis of Bristol, is a Neoclassical oddity. Dominated by a 106 ft. rotunda, the opulent state rooms are filled with 18th-century French furniture and more portraits than you could possibly absorb, including some by Titian, Velasquez, and Gainsborough. The classical Italian garden is splendid, and the manor's sheep quite cordial. **First Eastern Counties** (☎ (01284) 766171) **buses** #141-144 leave St. Andrew's Station in Bury for Horringer and Ickworth nine times per day Monday through Saturday; a return ticket costs £3.10. (☎ (01284) 735270. House open late Mar. to Oct. Tu-W, F-Su, and bank holidays 1-5pm. Gardens open late Mar. to Oct. daily 10am-5pm; Nov.-Mar. M-F 10am-4pm. Park open year-round daily 7am-7pm. £5.70, children £2.50. Park and gardens only £2.50, children 80p.)

Turrets and moats await those who visit **Long Melford,** a mile-long Suffolk village graced by two Tudor mansions. The more impressive of the two, **Melford Hall** has retained much of its original Elizabethan exterior and panelled banquet hall. Peek at the Victorian bedrooms before exploring the well-manicured lawns and colorful gardens. (☎ (01787) 880286. Open May-Sept. W-Th and Sa-Su 2-5:30pm; Apr. and Oct. Sa-Su 2-5:30pm. £4.40.) More amusing than stately, **Kentwell Hall** is filled with authentically costumed guides; visitors too are sometimes asked to come in Tudor costume. (☎ (01787) 310207. Open Mar.-May and Sept.-Oct. Su noon-5pm; July-Aug. daily noon-5pm. £5.50, students £3.40, seniors £4.70.) While in the area, stop by the **Long Melford Church,** between the two mansions, erected in 1484 by funding from opulent wool merchants. Long Melford is accessible from Bury by **H.C. Chambers bus** #753 (☎ (01787) 227233; catch the bus near the train station).

HARWICH AND FELIXSTOWE

Continent-bound travelers head south to **Harwich** (HAR-idge), a ferry depot for trips to Holland, Germany, and Scandinavia, and to **Felixstowe,** where boats sail to Belgium (see **By Ferry,** p. 35). Both are easily accessible by train and bus. Call the **Harwich tourist information centre,** Iconfield Park, Parkeston for details about ferries. (☎ (01255) 506139. Open Apr.-Sept. daily 9am-7pm; Oct.-Mar. M-Sa 9am-4pm.) The **Felixstowe tourist information centre** is on the seafront. (☎ (01394) 276770. Open M-F 9am-5:30pm, Sa-Su 9:30am-5:30pm.)

COLCHESTER   ☎01206

England's oldest recorded town, Colchester (pop. 89,000) has been so thoroughly beaten on so many occasions it's a wonder everyone hasn't packed up and left. The Trinovantes tribe, the town's first inhabitants, were conquered by the Romans, who were slaughtered by the Iceni (led by Queen Boudicca), who were pillaged by the Saxons, who were finally flogged by the Normans. However, the most recent invader to rush down from the hills has been the modern consumer. A pedestrian-only shopping center now sits on what was once a Roman market, a Norman stronghold, and a medieval weaving center. Colchester's historical sites pale somewhat in comparison to those of other towns, but this oldest of settlements entices with England's largest castle keep and musketball-ridden pubs.

☎☏ TRANSPORTATION AND PRACTICAL INFORMATION. Colchester is best visited as a daytrip from London or nearby East Anglian towns. **Trains** (☎ (08457) 484950) pull into **North Station** from **London Liverpool St.** (45min., every 15min., £23.30) and **Cambridge** (2hr., 2 per hr., £28.20). North Station lies a good 2 mi. from town (as opposed to Town Station, which services regional trains); **local buses** frequently make the uphill trip (#1 is a good choice, 80p). **Buses** from **London** (2¼hr., 4 per day, £9) and **Cambridge** (2hr., 1 per day, £7) pull into the **Bus Authority**, Queen St. (☎ 282645), around the corner from the tourist information centre (TIC).

Said **TIC,** 1 Queen St., across the street from the castle, books rooms two days in advance for a 10% deposit and leads two-hour **tours** of the city. (June-Sept. 11am. £2.50, students and seniors £2, children £1.25.) Pick up a free map and copies of local magazines *The Sticks* and *The Grapevine,* which list music in pubs. (☎ 282920. Open Easter-Nov. M-Tu and Th-Sa 9:30am-6pm, W 10am-6pm, Su 10am-5pm; Dec.-Easter M-Sa 10am-5pm.) Other services include: **banks** on High St.; the **police,** 10 Southway (☎ 762212); **Internet access** at **Webs Netcafe,** with speedy connections two blocks from the TIC (☎ 560400; £2 per hr.); and the **post office,** 68-70 North Hill (☎ 549807). **Postal code:** CO1 1AA.

☏☐ ACCOMMODATIONS AND FOOD. Since the YHA Youth Hostel packed up and left town six years ago, Colchester has had no substitute for the penny-pinching traveler. The cheapest place to stay in town is the **Scheregate Hotel,** 36 Osborne St., whose large and spotless rooms are equipped with TVs. (☎ 573034. Shared bathroom. Singles £20-25, breakfast included.)

The **Sainsbury's** supermarket is on Priory Walk, off Queen St. (Open M-W 8am-6:30pm, Th-F 8am-7pm, Sa 7:30am-6:30pm.) Surprisingly elegant, **The Thai Dragon,** 35 East Hill, has a full lunch for only £5.50. Dinner is pricier (main courses £4-8), but the traditional dishes are quite tasty. (☎ 863414. Open M-Sa noon-2:30pm and 6-11pm, Su noon-2:30pm and 6-10:30pm.) **Jackpots,** along Red Lion Walk off High St., dishes out jacket potatoes (£3-5.50) and a £4 "classic dish" of lasagna, vegetarian chili, or macaroni and cheese with a side potato. (☎ 549990. Open M-Sa 8am-5pm.)

☑ SIGHTS. A Norman fortress built by William the Conqueror upon the ruins of a Roman Temple, **Colchester Castle** now houses the dynamic ▧**Castle Museum,** where interactive displays help you see, touch, and hear history. Act out a short scene behind Roman theater masks, try on Roman battle gear, and experience a chilling witch confession in the dungeon. A tour takes you to the depths of the Roman foundations and the heights of the Norman towers. (☎ 282939. Castle open M-Sa 10am-5pm; Mar.-Nov. also Su 11am-5pm. Last admission 4:30pm. 5 tours per day £1.20, children 60p. Castle £3.90, concessions £2.60, families £10.50.)

The castle is flanked by two lesser museums. In a Georgian townhouse built in 1718, the freshly renovated **Hollytrees Museum** displays a cache of 18th-century knickknacks from toys and games to musical instruments and scientific equipment. (☎ 282939. Open M-Sa 10am-5pm, Su 11am-5pm. Free.) Marveling at a fine collection of 18th-century grandfather clocks in **Tymperleys Clock Museum,** off Trinity St., is a decent way to pass the time. Tick. That is, unless constant ticking drives you mad. Tock. (Open M-Sa 10am-5pm, Su 11am-5pm. Free.)

NORTHWEST ENGLAND

The 19th century swept Northwest England in an industrial coal cloud, revolutionizing quiet village life. By the end of the 1800s, the "dark satanic mills" that horrified William Blake had overrun the region's cities, and, as D.H. Lawrence put it, mines were "like black studs on the countryside, linked by a loop of fine chain, the railway." Prosperity followed where smokestacks led, and the cities of the northwest became the world's wool and linen workshops. The later decline of heavy industry affected Merseyside, Lancashire, and Manchester as it did urban areas elsewhere in Britain, if not more so. But urban life and a strong youth culture inspired creativity, and today the region possesses an innovative music and arts scene: Liverpool and Manchester alone produced four of Q magazine's top-ten biggest rock stars of the century. Add to that a large student population and through-the-roof nightlife, and you'll begin to understand the reinvigorated northwest. If you need a break from frenetic activity, the Peak District to the east provides respite, as does Cumbria to the north, where the Lake District possesses the stunning crags and waters that sent the Romantic poets into pensive meditation.

HIGHLIGHTS OF NORTHWEST ENGLAND

LIVERPOOL Don't miss Liverpool, **Beatles** fans: virtually every pub, restaurant, and corner claims some connection to the Fab Four (p. 332).

MANCHESTER Revel in the wealth of Manchester nightlife, where trendy cafe-bars morph into late-night venues for dancing and drinking (p. 343).

LAKE DISTRICT Explore the dramatic peaks and sparkling lakes of this National Park, one of the country's most beautiful regions and inspiration for the poetry of Wordsworth, Coleridge, and Romantics everywhere (p. 361).

NORTHWEST CITIES

CHESTER ☎ 01244

With fashionable chain stores behind mock-medieval facades, tour guides in Roman armor, a town crier in full uniform, and a Barclays bank in a wing of the cathedral, Chester resembles an American theme-park pastiche of Ye Olde English Towne. Built by Romans, Chester was later a base for Plantagenet campaigns against the Welsh—old town law states that Welshmen wandering the streets after 9pm can be beheaded—and developed trading connections throughout continental Europe. Silt blocked the River Dee in the 17th century, and Chester, crowded but lovely, commercial but lively, was left to turn its archaism into a selling point.

▐ TRANSPORTATION

Chester serves as a rail gateway to Wales through the North Wales train line. The train and bus stations both lie 15min. to the north, outside the walls.

Trains: City Rd. Office open M-Sa 5:30am-12:30am, Su 8am-midnight. Trains (☎(08457) 484950) from: **London Euston** (2½hr.; M-F 2 per hr., Sa-Su every hr.; £48.40); **Manchester Piccadilly** (1hr.; M-F 2 per hr., Sa-Su every hr.; £8.80); **Holyhead** in Wales (1½hr.; M-F every hr., Sa-Su 9 per day; £16.70); **Birmingham** (1¾hr.; M-F 2 per hr., Sa-Su every hr.; £10.70). Frequent **Merseyrail** service makes Chester an easy daytrip from **Liverpool** (1½hr.; M-F 2 per hr., Sa-Su every hr.; £3.20).

Buses: Delamere St. (☎381515), north of the city wall off Northgate St. Office open M-Sa 8:30am-5pm. **National Express** (☎(08705) 808080) from: **London** (5½hr., 5-6 per day, £16.50); **Manchester** (1¼hr., 3 per day, £4.50); **Birmingham** (2hr., 5 per day, £8.50); **Blackpool** (3½hr., 4 per day, £7.50-8.70). **Huxley Coaches** (☎(01948) 770661) #C56 to Foregate St. from **Wrexham** (M-Sa, £2.35).

Public Transportation: Call 602666 for local bus info, daily 8am-8pm. Routes are detailed in 12 *Bus Times* booklets, available free at the tourist information centre (TIC).

Taxis: Radio Taxis (☎372372).

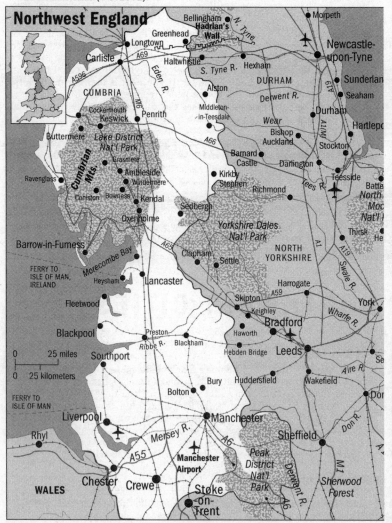

ORIENTATION AND PRACTICAL INFORMATION

Chester's center is bound by a medieval **city wall** and breached by seven gates. **St. Peter's Cross** is formed by **Eastgate St., Northgate St., Watergate St.,** and **Bridge St.,** which crosses the Dee. **The Groves,** a left before the bridge, hugs the river for a mile. From the train station, take the Citylink minibus, free with a rail ticket, to **Foregate St.** (every 6min.). Enter the walls at **Eastgate St.** and turn right onto **Northgate St.** From the bus station, turn left onto **Upper Northgate St.** and enter **Northgate.**

Tourist Information Centre: Town Hall, Northgate St. (☎402111; www.chestertourism.com). **Chester Visitor Centre,** Vicars Ln. (☎402111; fax 403188), opposite the Roman amphitheater. Both open May-Oct. M-Sa 9am-5pm, Su 10am-4pm; Nov.-Apr. M-Sa 10am-5pm, Su 10am-4pm. Both book accommodations for a £3 fee and sell city maps for £1. Pick up *What's on in Chester* for information on upcoming events.

Tours: Chester has more tours than intact Roman columns. A legionnaire in full armor leads the **Roman Tour.** (June-Aug. Th-Sa 1:45pm from the Visitor Centre, 2pm from the TIC. £2.50, concessions £2, families £7.) The open-top **Guide Friday** (☎347457) buses do their usual schtick with hop-on/hop-off service. (4 per hr. £7, students and seniors £6.50, children £2.50, families £16.50.) Beings ghoulish and ghastly lurk on the **Ghost Hunter Trail.** (June-Oct. Th-Sa 7:30pm from the TIC; after 5:30pm, buy tickets at the Coach and Horse pub on Northgate St. £3.50, concessions £2, families £9.) For a run-down of Chester's history, try the **Pastfinder Tour,** also from the TIC. (May-Oct. daily 10:45am and 2:30pm; Nov.-Apr. Sa-Su 2:30pm. £3, concessions £2.50.)

Financial Services: Barclays, 35 Eastgate St. Open M-F 9am-5pm, Sa 9:30am-3:30pm. **Thomas Cook** (☎593500) has 2 branches on Bridge St., 1 with a **bureau de change.** Open M-Tu and Th-Sa 9am-5:30pm, W 10am-5:30pm, Su 11am-4pm.

Launderette: 56 Garden Ln. (☎371406). Turn left off Northgate St., then right off Canal St. Open daily 9am-6pm, last wash 4:30pm.

Police: Grosvenor Rd. (☎350222).

Hospital: Countess of Chester (West Chester) Hospital, Liverpool Rd. (☎365000). Take bus #40A from the station or #3 from the Bus Exchange.

Internet Access: Public Library, beside the Town Hall (☎329798). First hr. free, then £1 per hr. Open M and Th 9:30am-7pm, Tu-W and F 9:30am-5pm, Sa 9:30am-1pm. **i-station,** Rufus Court (☎401680). £2 per 30min., though rates vary. Open 8am-10pm.

Post Office: 2 St. John St. (☎348315), off Foregate St. **Bureau de change** and photo booth. Open M-Sa 9am-5:30pm. **Postal Code:** CH1 1AA.

ACCOMMODATIONS

B&Bs (£20 and up) concentrate on **Hoole Rd.,** a five-minute walk from the train station (turn right from the exit, climb the steps to Hoole Rd., and turn right over the train tracks), and **Brook St.** (right from the train station exit, then the first left). Bus #53 (6 per hr.) runs to the area from the city center.

YHA Chester, Hough Green House, 40 Hough Green (☎680056; fax 681204; chester@yha.org.uk), 1½ mi. from the city center. Cross the river on Grosvenor Rd. and turn right at the roundabout (40min.) or take bus #7 or 16 from the Bus Exchange and ask for the hostel. Renovated Victorian house with laundry and Internet access. Thunderous showers restore lost youth. Breakfast included. Reception 7am-10:30pm. Open mid-Jan. to mid-Dec. Dorms £14.50, under 18 £11.25. Twins and family rooms available.

Laburnum Guest House, 2 St. Anne St. (☎/fax 380313), across from the bus station. 4 sparkling rooms, all stocked with TV and bath, rest as close to the town center as you can get without braving legions of shoppers. £21 per person.

Lloyds Guest House, 108 Brook St. (☎325838; fax 317491), near the train station. 21 rooms, all with TV. Singles £20; doubles with bath £35.

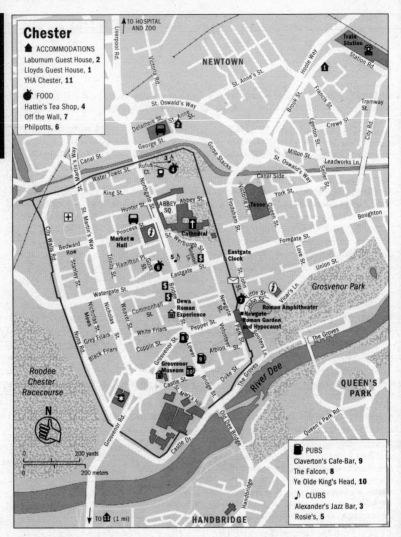

Chester

▲ ACCOMMODATIONS
Laburnum Guest House, **2**
Lloyds Guest House, **1**
YHA Chester, **11**

🍎 FOOD
Hattie's Tea Shop, **4**
Off the Wall, **7**
Philpotts, **6**

🍴 PUBS
Claverton's Cafe-Bar, **9**
The Falcon, **8**
Ye Olde King's Head, **10**

♪ CLUBS
Alexander's Jazz Bar, **3**
Rosie's, **5**

🍴 FOOD

Tesco supermarket hides at the end of an alley off Frodsham St. (Open M-Sa 7am-9pm, Su 11am-5pm.) The town's **market,** beside the Bus Exchange on Princess St., numbers fruit and vegetables among its bargains. (☎402340. Open M-Sa 8am-5pm.) Picnic in the shade of lovely **Grosvenor Park**—its sloping, flowered acres contain neither Roman artifacts nor tourists. From Bridge St., turn left onto Pepper St., cross under Newgate, pass the amphitheater, and enter on your right.

Philpotts, 2 Goss St. (☎345123), off Watergate St. Stuffs tuna, sweet corn, and Somerset brie into baguettes (£1.60-2.30). Pastas also available. Open M-Sa 8am-2:30pm.

Off the Wall, 12 St. John's St. (☎348964). Typical pub exterior, atypical menu. Crispy barbecue chicken with cheese (£3.75). Food served Su-Th noon-4pm, F-Sa noon-5pm.

Hattie's Tea Shop, 5 Rufus Court (☎345173), off Northgate St. Scrumptious home-made cakes and a £4.55 "giant topless" ham salad sandwich. Open July-Aug. M-Sa 9:30am-5pm, Su 11am-4pm; Sept.-June M-Sa 9:30am-5pm, Su 10:30am-4pm.

👁 SIGHTS

ARCHITECTURE. Chester's faux-medieval architecture is its main attraction, although the wannabe Tudor buildings fail to hide that the city center is really a vast outdoor shopping mall. While a few structures are of Tudor age, the black-and-white paint is a strictly Victorian phenomenon. On summer Saturdays a bizarre variety of street musicians, from cowpoke trios to accordion-wielding matrons, sets up shop. Climb the town's famous **city walls** or the **rows** of Bridge St., Watergate St., and Eastgate St., where walkways provide access to another tier of storefronts above street-level. Some historians theorize that Edward I imported the tiered design from Constantinople, which he visited while crusading. **Northgate,** with a fine view of the Welsh hills, was rebuilt in 1808 to house the city's jail 30 ft. underground. The bridge outside the gate is dubbed the Bridge of Sighs; it carried doomed convicts from jail to chapel for their last mass, although a good number jumped into the canal and swam for it before railings were installed.

CHESTER CATHEDRAL. In 1092, Hugh Lupus, newly named Earl of Chester, founded a Benedictine abbey here on the site of a church dedicated in AD 907 to St. Werburgh, a Mercian princess who passed up royal comfort for a nunnery and who resurrected geese as a hobby. A Gothic facelift in 1250 set off a flurry of makeovers, transforming the Romanesque cathedral into a stunning architectural hodgepodge. Intersecting stone arches, "The Crown of Stone," support the tower, and stained-glass windows blaze throughout. The quire showcases some of the finest 14th-century woodwork in Britain and an enormous pipe organ. Find peace in the grassy cloister, a monastic courtyard with a lovely fountain. *(Just off Northgate St. ☎324756. Free guided tours May-Oct. daily. Open 8am-6pm. Suggested donation £3.)*

ROMAN SIGHTS. By AD 43, most of Britannia had been conquered by the Romans, and Deva (modern-day Chester) was a strategic outpost of considerable importance. At the **Grosvenor Museum,** watch the animated video to see what life in Deva was like. *(27 Grosvenor St. ☎402008. Open M-Sa 10:30am-5pm, Su 2-5pm. Free.)* Outside Newgate, find the unimpressive base of the largest **Roman amphitheater** in Britain. Excavated in 1960, it once accommodated the legion at Deva for gladiatorial bouts, but now looks like an oversized tiger trap. *(Always open. Free.)* Next door, the **Roman Garden and Hypocaust** offers picnic space on shaded grass lined with stunted Roman columns. The final stop on a Roman tour is the half-hearted **Dewa Roman Experience.** Learn how Romans pronounced the letter "v" and examine exposed archaeological digs. *(Pierpoint Ln. ☎343407. Open daily 9am-5pm. £4, seniors and students £3.50, children £2.25, families £11.)*

OTHER SIGHTS. Chester Zoo, one of Europe's largest, goes to great lengths to justify its captive inmates. Over half the zoo's species are endangered, and its many enclosures are decorated with self-congratulatory plaques. *(Take Crosville bus #8 or 8X from the Bus Exchange behind the town hall (return £2). ☎380280. Open high season 10am-7pm, last entry 5pm. Open until 5:30pm in off season, last entry 3:30pm. £10, seniors and children £8, families £36, YHA members £9.)*

🍺🍸 PUBS AND NIGHTLIFE

Chester has some 30 pubs; many parrot Ye Olde English decor, and almost all are open Monday through Saturday from noon to 11pm and Sunday from noon to 10:30pm. Watering holes group on Lower Bridge and Watergate St. Traditionalists head to **Ye Olde King's Head,** 48-50 Lower Bridge St. (☎324855), where an assortment of steins hangs from beams in a restored 17th-century house. For a cheap pint, try upstairs at **The Falcon,** 6 Lower Bridge St. (☎314555), whose black-and-white timber tilts a little too precariously. **Claverton's Cafe-Bar,** on Lower Bridge St., has cozy couches that attract a chic, female-strong crowd on weekends. (☎319760. Sometimes closes early on weekdays. Pints £1.90.)

Join the twentysomethings that crowd **Rosie's,** a three-floor club at Northgate Row. The ground-level pub is littered with Route 66 signs, commercial dance music inundates the floor above, while funk and soul fill the upper echelon. Arrive between 8 and 10pm on weekends and down four drinks for £5. (☎327141. M student night, Tu-W first floor only, Th-F second and third floors, Sa all three floors open. Cover £4-6; Tu-W free. F-Sa 20+. Pub open Tu-Sa 8pm-1am; club open Th-Sa 9:30pm-2am.) **Alexander's Jazz Bar,** Rufus Court, off Northgate St., hosts jazz and blues bands, in summer often nightly. Saturday is comedy night. (☎340005. Cover £5-6. Open M-Th 11am-midnight, F-Sa 11am-12:30am, Su 11am-10:30pm.)

🎵 ENTERTAINMENT AND FESTIVALS

On sporadic spring and summer weekends, England's oldest horse races are held on the **Roodee,** formerly the Roman harbor. Lodgings fill quickly on these weekends; call or email the TIC for schedules and advance booking. (☎304600. Entrance from £4.) During the last week in June and the first week of July, Chester hosts a **Sports Festival** (☎348365). Celebrations center on a river carnival and raft race down the winding Dee. The **Chester Summer Music Festival** draws classical musicians to the cathedral in late July. (Box office ☎320700. Ticket prices vary.) Check the TIC's free monthly *What's On in Chester* for other events.

LIVERPOOL   ☎ 0151

On the banks of the Mersey, Liverpool (pop. 520,000) opened England's first commercial docks in 1715. Much of the its early wealth was amassed through the slave trade, but it was the Lancashire cotton industry that bolstered the city's growth. Unfortunately, Liverpool's shipping dominance drew attention in WWII as it became Britain's second most heavily bombed city, and the decline of the Empire and the advent of cheap air travel dealt further blows. In the 1980s, high unemployment and government scandals inhibited the revival of prosperity and enthusiasm. Yet despite the poverty of some of the city's outlying suburbs, central Liverpool is increasingly vibrant. A transformed Albert Dock studded with restaurants and museums, two enormous cathedrals, and mad nightlife make Liverpool a great destination for travelers. Scousers—as Liverpudlians are colloquially known—are usually happy to introduce you to their dialect and humor and to discuss the relative merits of Liverpool's two football teams. Oh, yeah—and the Beatles.

🎫 TICKET TO RIDE

Trains: Lime St. Station. Ticket office open M-Sa 5:15am-12:30am, Su 7:15am-12:30pm. Trains (☎(08457) 484950) from: **London Euston** (3hr.; M-Sa every hr., Su 10 per day; £48.40); **Chester** (45min., 2 per hr., £3.20); **Manchester Piccadilly** (1½hr., 2 per hr., £7.20); **Birmingham** (1¾hr.; M-F 5 per day, Sa 2 per day, Su 3 per day; £18.50). The smaller **Moorfields, James St.,** and **Central** train stations serve mainly as transfer points to local **Merseyrail** trains (including service to Chester).

Buses: Norton St. Station receives **National Express** (☎(08705) 808080) from: **London** (4½hr., 5 per day, £16.50); **Manchester** (1hr., 1-2 per hr., £4.50); **Birmingham** (2½hr., 5 per day, £7.50). Other buses stop at **Queen Sq.** and **Paradise St.** stations.

Ferries: Liverpool Sea Terminal, Pier Head, north of Albert Dock. Open daily 9am-5pm. The **Isle of Man Steam Packet Company** (☎(08705) 523523) runs ferries from Princess Dock to the Isle of Man and Dublin (see **Isle of Man: Getting There,** p. 347).

Local Transportation: Private buses blanket the city and the Merseyside area. Consult the transport mavens at **Mersey Travel** (☎236 7676) in the tourist information centre (TIC). Open M and W-Sa 9am-5:30pm, Tu 10am-5:30pm, Su 10:30am-4:30pm.

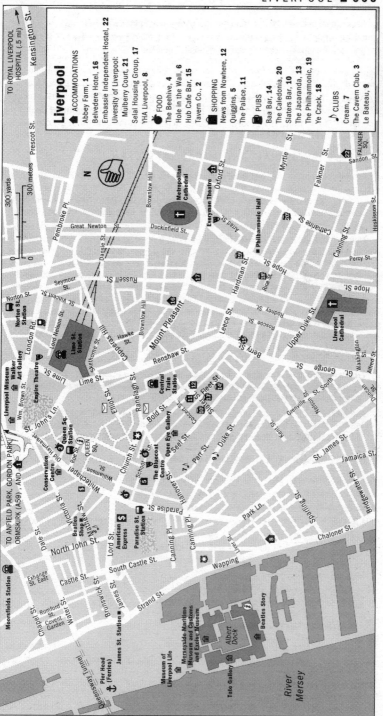

Liverpool

♠ ACCOMMODATIONS
Abbey Farm, **1**
Belvedere Hotel, **16**
Embassie Independent Hostel, **22**
University of Liverpool:
   Mulberry Court, **21**
   Selal Housing Group, **17**
YHA Liverpool, **8**

♦ FOOD
The Beehive, **4**
Hole in the Wall, **6**
Hub Cafe Bar, **15**
Tavern Co., **2**

■ SHOPPING
News from Nowhere, **12**
Quiggins, **5**
The Palace, **11**

▮ PUBS
Baa Bar, **14**
The Caledonia, **20**
Slaters Bar, **10**
The Jacaranda, **13**
The Philharmonic, **19**
Ye Crack, **18**

♪ CLUBS
Cream, **7**
The Cavern Club, **3**
Le Bateau, **9**

Taxis: Local taxis are cheap and efficient. Try **Mersey Cabs** (☎207 2222).

Bike Rental: The **Hub Cafe-Bar** (p. 335) has an attached cycle store (☎708 8819). £8 per day. Passport or driver's license deposit. Open M-Sa 10am-6pm.

✴ ❷ HELP!

Liverpool's central district is surprisingly pedestrian-friendly. There are two clusters of museums: on **William Brown St.**, near Lime St. Station, and at **Albert Dock**, on the river. These flank the central shopping district, whose central axis comprises **Bold St., Church St.**, and **Lord St.**

TOURIST, FINANCIAL, AND LOCAL SERVICES

Tourist Information Centre: Queen Square Centre (☎(0906) 680 6886, premium rate call; fax 707 0986; www.visitliverpool.com), in Queen Sq. Sells the handy *Visitor Guide to Liverpool and Merseyside* (£1.50). Books beds for a 10% deposit. Open M and W-Sa 9am-5:30pm, Tu 10am-5:30pm, Su 10:30am-4:30pm. **Branch, Atlantic Dock Centre,** Atlantic Pavilion, Albert Dock (☎(0906) 680 6886). Open daily 10am-5:30pm.

Tours: Expert guide **Phil Hughes** (☎236 9091, mobile (07961) 511223) runs personalized Beatles tours for the lucky 8 that fit in his van. (3-4hr.; 1-2 per day; £11.50, private tours £65.) The yellow-and-blue **Magical Mystery Tour** (☎709 3285) bus takes 40 fans to Fab-Four sights, leaving from the Queens Sq. TIC and picking up outside the Beatles Story Museum 15min. later. (2hr.; mid-July to Aug. 2 per day, Sept. to mid-July 1 per day; £11, £15 Beatles Combo Ticket includes admission to the Beatles Story Museum. Book ahead.) For those interested in non-Beatles sights (if such people exist), **Liverpool Duck Tours** (☎708 7799) runs rings around the city's center in amphibious WWI-era vehicles. (Mid-Feb. to Oct. 8 per day, Nov.-Dec. call for details; £9, students and seniors £7, children £6, families £25.) Numerous other bus tours (from £4) and walking tours (£3, concessions £2) run in summer; the TIC has the leaflets to prove it.

Financial Services: Barclays, 9-11 Whitechapel (☎(08457) 555 555). Open M-Tu and Th-Sa 9:30am-5pm, W 10am-5pm. **American Express,** 54 Lord St. (☎702 4505), has a **bureau de change.** Open M-F 9am-5:30pm, Sa 9am-5pm.

Launderette: There are no launderettes downtown, though the **YHA**, next to Albert Dock, often allows non-residents to use its facilities. Alternatively, head to the **Caledonia Laundromatic Super Pub** and do your wash in style (see **Come Together,** below).

EMERGENCY AND COMMUNICATIONS

Police: Canning Pl. (☎709 6010). **Cop Shop** (outpost) on Church St. (☎777 4045).

Crisis Lines: The Samaritans (☎(0845) 790 9090). 24hr.

Hospital: Royal Liverpool Hospital, Prescot St. (☎706 2000).

Internet Access: Central Library, William Brown St. (☎233 5835). Free. Open M-Sa 9am-5pm, Su noon-5pm. **Planet Electra,** 36 London Rd. (☎708 0303). £2.50 per 30min.; 20% student discount. Open M-W and Sa 10am-5:30pm, Th 10am-7:30pm, F 10am-6pm. And **Caledonia Laundromatic Super Pub** (see **Come Together,** below).

Post Office: 42-44 Houghton Way (☎709 6971), in St. John's Shopping Centre (below the Radio City Tower). **Branch** in the splendid Lyceum building on Bold St. Both open M-Sa 9am-5:30pm. **Postal Code:** L1 1AA.

▗ A HARD DAY'S NIGHT

Your best bet for cheap accommodations lies east of the city center. **Lord Nelson St.**, adjacent to the train station, is lined with modest hotels, and similar establishments are found along **Mount Pleasant**, one block from Brownlow Hill and the bus stop. Liverpool's hostels are full of young music-loving travelers, but stay only at places approved by the TIC. Demand for rooms is highest in early April for the Grand National Race and during the Beatles Convention at the end of August.

Embassie Independent Hostel, 1 Falkner Sq. (☎ 707 1089). 15-20min. walk or £3 taxi from the bus and train stations. Feels like a laid-back student's flat, with laundry, satellite TV, pool table, and kitchen, plus all the toast and jam you can eat. Ask the energetic staff—many of whom came for a night years ago—for pub-crawling tips, or talk them into coming with you. Dorms £13.50 first night, £12.50 each additional night.

YHA Liverpool, 25 Tabley St., off The Wapping (☎ 709 8888; fax 709 0417; liverpool@yha.org.uk). Upscale digs on 3 Beatles-themed floors, next to Albert Dock. Rooms with double beds a good choice for families. Laundry, kitchen, Internet access, currency exchange, and restaurant. Breakfast included. Dorms £18, under 18 £13.50.

Selal Housing Group, 1 Rodney St. (☎ 709 7791), off Mt. Pleasant. This former YWCA accepts both men and women. Mostly single rooms, spacious but somewhat sterile. A few doubles are available. Kitchen and laundry facilities. £12 per person.

Belvedere Hotel, 83 Mt. Pleasant (☎ 709 2356). This family-run guest house in the city center has small, comfortable rooms with TVs. Breakfast included. £20 per person.

University of Liverpool: Mulberry Court, Oxford St. (☎ 794 3298). Clean but spartan self-catering accommodations with bath for £16 per person. The university-wide conference office (☎ 794 6440) has information on other halls open to travelers (£15 including continental breakfast). All university accommodations open July-Sept.

Camping: Abbey Farm, Dark Ln., Ormskirk (☎(01695) 572686), on the northern rail line from Lime St. Station. A £2.50 taxi from Ormskirk Station. £5 per 1-person tent, £6.50 per 2-person tent. Electricity £1.50. Showers free.

🍫 SAVOY TRUFFLE

Trendy cafes and well-priced Indian restaurants line **Bold St.** and **Hardman St.,** while takeaways crowd **Hardnon St.** and **Berry St.** Many eateries are open until 3am. Try **St. John's Market,** at the top of the shopping mall, for produce and local color.

Tavern Co., Queen Sq. (☎ 709 1070), near the TIC. Hearty burritos and creative taco salads £5-7 in a wine-bar atmosphere. Open M-Sa noon-11pm, Su noon-10:30pm; food served M-Th and Su until 10pm, F-Sa until 11pm.

The Beehive, 7 Paradise St. (☎ 709 5875). The book-lined walls of this city-center pub offer an escape from the shopping masses and a tasty 2-meals-for-£5 deal. Open M-Sa 11am-11pm, Su noon-10:30pm; food served M-Sa 11am-11pm, Su noon-3pm.

Hub Cafe Bar, Berry St. (☎ 709 7495). Full of character: furniture made from bicycle parts and a homemade "Big Wac" veggie burger (£4.20). Live music Th-Sa 9-11pm. Open M-W 10am-7pm, Th-Sa 10am-11pm; kitchen closes at 6pm.

Hole in the Wall, School Ln. (☎ 709 7733). This self-described "coffee lounge" serves lip-smacking sandwiches and sweets (£3-4.50) on 2 floors. Open daily noon-6pm.

🎡 MAGICAL MYSTERY TOUR

With first-rate museums, unusual cathedrals, and the twin religions of football and the Beatles, Liverpool wills the tourist to fall in love with the North. **Hope St.,** southeast of the city center, connects Liverpool's two 20th-century cathedrals. Most other sights are located on **Albert Dock,** an open rectangle of Victorian warehouses now stocked with offices, restaurants, and museums. Those visiting only the attractions on the dock can purchase a **Waterfront Pass** from the Atlantic Pavilion branch TIC (£10, concessions £6). It includes admission to the Beatles Story, the Merseyside Maritime Museum, the Museum of Liverpool Life, and a Mersey Ferries cruise, and gets a £1 discount on Liverpool Duck Tours (see **Help!,** above).

THE BEATLES STORY. Walk-through recreations of Hamburg, the Cavern Club (complete with "basement smells"), and a shiny Yellow Submarine trace the rise and—sigh—fall of the band. Audiovisuals will leave you nostalgic and primed for the gift shop. (*Albert Dock.* ☎709 1963. *Open Apr.-Oct. daily 10am-6pm; Nov.-Mar. 10am-5pm; last admission 1hr. before close. £8, concessions £5.45, families £19.*) For other Beatles-themed locales, get the **Beatles Map** (£2.50) at the TIC: it takes you to Strawberry Fields and Penny Lane. Souvenir hunters can raid the **Beatles Shop**, stuffed with memorabilia on Beatles-packed Mathew St. below a small shrine to the boys. *(31 Mathew St. ☎ 236 8066. Open M-Sa 9:30am-5:30pm, Su 11am-4pm.)*

MERSEYSIDE MARITIME MUSEUM. Liverpool's heyday as a major port has passed, but the six impressive floors of this museum allow you to explore the cramped hull of a slave trader's ship or a dimly lit dockside street. Fans of a certain movie starring Leonardo DiCaprio can see items recovered from the "unsinkable" ship. Attached to the Maritime Museum is the **H.M. Customs and Excise Museum**, with an intriguing array of confiscated goods from would-be smugglers, including a fountain pen that shoots chili powder and a teddy bear full of cocaine. *(Albert Dock. ☎ 478 4499. Open daily 10am-5pm. Free.)*

TATE GALLERY. The intimate Liverpool branch of the now-national institution contains a select range of 20th-century artwork. Works by British artists that have included Lucian Freud, Damien Hirst, and Francis Bacon dominate the ground floor, while the floor above shows a rotating collection from the gallery's archives. By prior arrangement, the staff will fit the visually impaired with special gloves and allow them to touch some of the art. *(Albert Dock. ☎ 702 7400. Open Tu-Su 10am-6pm. Free. Some special exhibits charge admission, usually £3, concessions £2.)*

METROPOLITAN CATHEDRAL OF CHRIST THE KING. Dubbed "Paddy's Wigwam" by locals, the city's Roman Catholic cathedral looks more like an upside-down funnel than a house of worship. A quick step inside proves you can't judge a cathedral by its resemblance to a kitchen utensil. Neon-blue stained glass casts a glow over the circular interior, and modern sculptures fill niches and chapels. The cathedral sticks to most traditions—the organists weren't allowed to play pop music until a 1981 memorial service for John Lennon. *(Mt. Pleasant. ☎ 709 9222. Open in summer M-F 8am-6pm, Sa-Su 8:30am-6pm; winter M-F 8am-6pm, Sa 8:30am-6pm, Su 8:30am-5pm. Free.)*

LIVERPOOL CATHEDRAL. Begun in 1904, completed in 1978, this Anglican cathedral is *vast*, featuring the highest Gothic arches ever built (107 ft.), the largest vault and organ (9704 pipes), and the highest and heaviest bells in the world. Take two lifts and climb the final 108 stairs to the top of the tower for a view stretching to Wales. *(Upper Duke St. ☎ 709 6271. Cathedral open daily 9am-6pm; tower open 11am-4pm, weather permitting. Suggested Cathedral donation £2.50. Tower admission £2, children £1.)*

THE MUSEUM OF LIVERPOOL LIFE. This museum tells of Liverpool's history of stormy labor struggles and race relations, as well as the city's sporting and soap-opera heritage. A TV runs footage from legendary football matches between Liverpool and Everton, while a plaque commemorates Grand National-winning horses. *(Albert Dock. ☎ 478 4080. Open daily 10am-5pm. Free.)*

WALKER ART GALLERY. This stately gallery reopens in February 2002, after more than a year's renovation. The huge collection includes medieval works and a variety of impressive post-Impressionist and pre-Raphaelite paintings. Temporary exhibits for 2002 include George Romney (Feb.-Apr.), while Paul McCartney's work will be on display starting in May. *(William Brown St. ☎ 478 4199. Open M-Sa 10am-5pm, Su noon-4pm. Free.)*

CONSERVATION CENTRE. A small interactive museum below the conservation studios and labs for the National Museum and Galleries of Merseyside, the Centre provides insight into the processes of art conservation, restoration, and preservation. Hands-on exhibits are particularly engaging for children. *(Whitechapel. ☎ 478 4999. Open M-Sa 10am-5pm, Su noon-5pm. Free. Tours W and Sa 2 and 3pm cost extra.)*

LIVERPOOL AND EVERTON FOOTBALL CLUBS. If not for the Beatles, you're probably here for the football. The rivalry between the city's two main clubs is deep and passionate. **Liverpool** and **Everton** both offer tours of their grounds (Anfield and Goodison Park, respectively) and match tickets when available. Book in advance. *(Both stadia can be reached by bus #26 from the city center. Liverpool ☎ 260 6677. Everton ☎ 330 2277. Liverpool tour, including entrance to their museum, £8.50, concessions £5.50, families £23. Everton tour £5.50, concessions £3.50. Match tickets from £14.)*

🗷 COME TOGETHER

Two of the Liverpool's most notable products—football fans and rock musicians—were born of pub culture. The city has continued to incorporate these traditions into its present pub renaissance. **Slater St.** in particular brims with £1 pints.

The Philharmonic, 36 Hope St. (☎707 2837). John Lennon once said the worst thing about being famous was "not being able to get a quiet pint at the Phil." The non-celebrities among us can still get that silent beer. Worth a walk-through just to see some of Britain's most ornate bathrooms. Open M-Sa noon-11pm, Su noon-10:30pm.

The Jacaranda, 21-23 Slater St. (☎707 8281). The site of the first paid Beatles gig, the Jac's basement was painted by original Beatle Stuart Sutcliffe. Live bands still play, and a small dance-floor lets you kick loose. Open M-Sa noon-2am, Su noon-10:30pm.

The Caledonia Laundromatic Super Pub (☎709 9567), corner of Catherine St. and Caledonia St. Half-launderette, half-pub, this funky multi-tasker *hasn't* been visited by the Beatles—boy did they miss out. 2 computers with free Internet access squat atop clothes driers-turned-fishbowls. £3 buys a wash, dry, and free coffee. Food (under £3) and pints (under £2) are cheap. DJs nightly. Open M-Sa noon-11pm, Su noon-10:30pm; food served noon-8pm.

Slaters Bar, 26 Slater St. (☎708 6990). Cheap drinks (pints start at £1.10) and a young crowd by the jukebox. Open M-Sa 11am-2am, Su noon-10:30pm.

Baa Bar, 43-45 Fleet St. (☎707 0610), off Bold St. This gay-friendly establishment is popular for its cappuccino by day (£1.20) and cheap beer by night (bottles £1). Open M-Sa 10am-2am.

Ye Crack, 13 Rice St. (☎709 4171). Where John Lennon used to finish off lathery pints; ask about how he later got banned. Ethnic food theme nights M-Th and fabulous beer garden out back. Open M-Sa 11:30am-11pm, Su noon-7pm.

🎵 PLEASE PLEASE ME

Consult the *Liverpool Echo*, an evening paper sold by street vendors, for up-to-date information on events, especially in the *What's On* section of Friday editions (32p). The emporia of **Quiggins,** 12-16 School Ln. (☎709 2462), and the **Palace,** 6-10 Slater St., both sell hipster paraphernalia and have tons of flyers detailing the club scene. For alternative events, check the bulletin board in the **Everyman Bistro,** 9-11 Hope St., where bohemian happenings often occur in the attached **Third Room.** (☎708 9545. Open M-Th noon-midnight, F-Sa noon-2am.) Read and inquire about events at gay and lesbian clubs in **News From Nowhere,** 96 Bold St., a feminist bookshop run by a women's cooperative. (☎708 7270. Open M-Sa 10am-5:45pm.)

On weekend nights, the downtown area, especially Mathew St., Church St., and Bold St., overflows with pubbers and clubbers. Window-shop venues to find what you like, and dress smartly to avoid provoking the army of bouncers. Also try to avoid wandering into dark alleys, as high concentrations of drunken revelers are prime targets for street theft.

CLUBS

🗷 **Cream** (☎709 1693), in Wolstonholme Sq., off Parr St. In a word, *brilliant*. The queue goes on forever because people travel from all over Britain (and the world) to come to this renowned superclub. Steep prices, but it's an amazing party. Cover £11. Open Sa, plus last F of the month 10pm-4am.

The Cavern Club, 10 Mathew St. (☎236 9091). The Fab Four made these narrow, brick-lined premises famous. A larger, more conventional space still hosts live bands (Th-F 8pm-2am, Sa 2-11pm). No cover until 10pm, £2 10-11pm, £4 11pm-2am. Club open Th-F 6pm-2am, Sa 6pm-3am; pub open M-Sa from noon.

Le Bateau, 62 Duke St. (☎709 6508), swings with 60s music upstairs at **Uptight,** and loosens up with a mellow club downstairs. Cover £5. Open roughly F-Sa 9pm-3am.

MUSIC, THEATER, AND FESTIVALS

⬛ Bluecoat Centre (information line ☎ 709 5297, box office 707 9393), off School Ln. Begun in 1717 as a charity school and now Liverpool's performing arts center. An art-school atmosphere permeates the exhibition spaces. Offers workshops in art, dance, and music; linger in the cafe and used bookstore. Open M-Sa 9am-5:30pm; box office open M-F 11am-4pm; gallery open Tu-Sa 10:30am-5pm.

Philharmonic Hall, Hope St. (☎ 709 3789). The **Royal Liverpool Philharmonic,** one of England's better orchestras, performs here along with an array of others, including jazz and funk bands. Box office open M-Sa 10am-5:30pm, Su noon-5pm. Tickets from £13-25, though student prices are as low as £5. Concessions half-price on day of show.

Liverpool Empire Theatre, Lime St. (☎ (0870) 606 3536), hosts a variety of dramatic performances, welcoming such famous troupes as the Royal Shakespeare Company. Box office open M-Sa 10am-8pm on performance days, otherwise M-Sa 10am-6pm; also Su 1hr. before show. Tickets normally £5-35, concessions available.

Everyman Theatre (☎ 709 4776), at the corner of Hope St. and Oxford St., provides space for adventurous contemporary productions. Box office open M-F 10am-6pm, Sa noon-6pm. Tickets from £7, some concessions.

Festivals: Liverpool hosts many conventions and festivals throughout the year, ranging from the **Mersey River Festival** (mid-June) to the **International Street Theatre Festival** (early Aug.). At the end of August, a week-long **Beatles Convention** draws pop fans and bewildered entomologists from around the world.

MANCHESTER
☎ 0161

The Industrial Revolution transformed the unremarkable village of Manchester into a northern hub, now Britain's second-largest urban area. A center of manufacturing and production in the 19th century, the city became a hotbed of liberal politics, its deplorable working-class conditions arousing the indignation of everyone from Frederic Engels (who called it "Hell on Earth") to John Ruskin (who called it a "devil's darkness"). Now a hotbed of electronic beats and post-industrial glitz, Manchester has risen phoenix-like from factory soot to savor its reputation as one of the hippest spots in England. Though dodgy in parts, the city is undergoing a gradual gentrification and is accessible to the street smart. With few comely corners, Manchester proves that it's not just the pretty who are popular, attracting thousands to its vibrant arts and nightlife scenes.

▐ TRANSPORTATION

Flights: Manchester International Airport (☎ 489 3000; international arrivals (0839) 888747, domestic arrivals (0839) 888757, both 50p per min.). Trains (25min.; 4 per hr., all day; £2.50) and buses #44 and 105 head to Piccadilly.

Trains: Manchester Piccadilly, London Rd., serves mostly trains from the south, east, and Scotland. Travel center open M-Sa 8am-8:30pm, Su 11am-7pm. Trains (☎ (08457) 484950) from: **London Euston** (2½hr., at least every hr., £84.50); **York** (40min., 2 per hr., £15.80); **Chester** (1hr., every hr., £8.50); **Birmingham** (1¾hr., 2 per hr., £14.20); **Edinburgh** (4hr.; 12 per day; £41.60 via Carlisle, £51.50 via York). **Manchester Victoria,** Victoria St., serves mostly trains from the west and north. Travel center open M-Sa 8:30am-6pm. From **Liverpool** (50min., 2 per hr., £6.95). Both stations open 24hr. and connected by Metrolink.

Buses: Chorlton St. Coach Station, Chorlton St. Office open M-F 7:15am-7pm, Sa-Su 7:15am-6:15pm. Luggage storage £2; open daily 9am-6pm. **National Express** (☎ (08705) 808080) from: **London** (4-5hr., 7 per day, £15); **Liverpool** (50min., every hr., £4); **Leeds** (1hr., every hr., £5.50); **Sheffield** (1½hr., 6 per day, £5.75).

Public Transportation: Piccadilly Gardens is home to about 50 bus stops. Pick up a free route map from the TIC. **Buses** generally run until 11:30pm, weekends until 2:30am. Office open M-Sa 7am-6pm, Su 10am-6pm. All-day ticket £3. **Metrolink** trams

(☎205 2000) link 8 stops in the city center with Altrincham in the southwest, Bury in the northeast, and Eccles in the west (every 5-15min., £1-5). Combined bus and tram ticket £5. **GMPTE information line:** ☎228 7811; www.gmpte.gov.uk. Open 8am-8pm.

Taxis: Mantax (☎236 5133).

✦ ℹ ORIENTATION AND PRACTICAL INFORMATION

The city center is an odd polygon formed by **Victoria Station** to the north, **Piccadilly Station** to the east, **G-Mex** and the canals to the south, and the **River Irwell** to the west. The area is fairly compact, but the many by-ways require a good map. Most streets bear illuminated, poster-sized maps, and Mancunians are generally helpful.

Tourist Information Centre: Manchester Visitor Centre, Town Hall Extension, Lloyd St. (☎234 3157, 24hr. info (0891) 715533). Helpful staff books accommodations (£2.50 plus 10% deposit). Free literature includes a city map, the *Manchester Pocket Guide*, the *Greater Manchester Network Map*, and *What's On*, which lists local events. City **tour** information also available. Open M-Sa 10am-5:30pm, Su 11am-4pm.

Financial Services: Banks include **Barclays,** 51 Mosley St. (☎228 3322). Open M-Tu and Th-F 9:30am-4:30pm, W 10am-4:30pm. **Thomas Cook,** 2 Oxford St. (☎236 8575) and 23 Market St. Open M-W and F-Sa 9am-5:30pm, Th 10am-5:30pm. **American Express,** 10-12 St. Mary's Gate (☎833 0121). Open M-F 9am-5:30pm, Sa 9am-4pm.

Launderette: Mr. Bubbles, 246 Wilmslow Rd. (☎257 2640). Change and soap available. Open daily 8am-8pm, last wash 7pm.

Police: Chester House, Bootle St. (☎872 5050 or 273 2081).

Crisis Lines: Samaritans, 72-74 Oxford St. (☎236 8000).

Hospital: Manchester Royal Infirmary, Oxford Rd. (☎276 1234).

Internet Access: interc@fe, Piccadilly Sq. (☎832 8666), on the first floor of Debenhams department store. £1.50 per 30min., first 30min. free with food or drink purchase. Open M, W, F 9:30am-5:30pm; Tu 10am-5:30pm; Th 9:30am-7:30pm; Sa 9am-5:30pm; Su 11am-4:30pm. Also **YHA Manchester** (see below).

Post Office: 26 Spring Gdns. (☎839 0687). Open M-Tu and Th-F 8:30am-6pm, W 9am-6pm, Sa 8:30am-7pm. Poste Restante (☎834 8605) has a separate entrance. Open M-F 6am-5:30pm, Sa 6am-12:30pm. **Postal Code:** M2 2AA.

⌂ ACCOMMODATIONS

Cheap stays in the city center are hard to find, though summer offers the possibility of **student housing,** a decently priced option. The highest concentration of budget lodgings is found 2-3 mi. south in the suburbs of **Fallowfield, Withington,** and **Didsbury;** take bus #40, 42, or 157. For a £2.50 fee and 10% deposit, the staff at the tourist information centre (TIC) can scour the town for rooms within your price range, sometimes getting better rates and special prices. Browse the free booklet *Where to Stay,* available at the TIC, for listings.

YHA Manchester, Potato Wharf, Castlefield (☎839 9960; fax 835 2054; manchester@yha.org.uk). Take bus #33 from Piccadilly Gardens toward Wigan. Raising hosteling to swanky heights. Good security. Members' kitchen and restaurant. Lockers £1-2. Laundry £1.50 per load. Internet access £2.50 per 30min. Currency exchange. Reception open 7am-11:30pm. Dorms £18, under 18 £13.10; £1 student discount.

Woodies Backpackers Hostel, 19 Blossom St., Ancoats (☎/fax 228 3456; backpackers@woodiesuk.freeserve.co.uk). The hostel is just beyond the Duke of Edinburgh pub on Blossom St. in a ghost-like part of town. Comfortable dorm accommodations with TV lounge, kitchen, laundry, free luggage storage, and friendly, well-traveled staff. Good security, but stay within the area. Singles £17; dorms £12 per night, £60 per week.

Manchester Conference Centre and Hotel, Sackville St. (☎/fax 955 8000). B&B-style lodgings attached to a pricier hotel. Open mid-June to Sept. Singles £40 with breakfast; book through the TIC and pay £20 for room only, booking fee included.

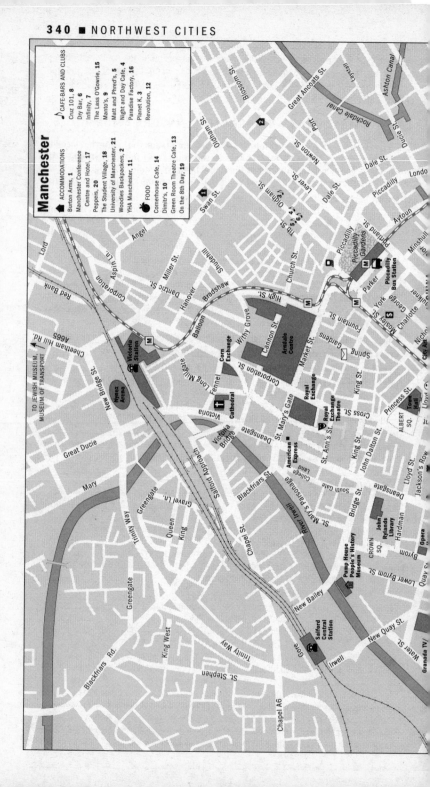

Manchester

♪ CAFE-BARS AND CLUBS
Cruz 101, 8
Dry Bar, 6
Infinity, 7
The Lass O'Gowrie, 15
Manto's, 9
Matt and Phed's, 5
Night and Day Cafe, 4
Paradise Factory, 16
Planet K, 3
Revolution, 12

♠ ACCOMMODATIONS
Burton Arms, 1
Manchester Conference Centre and Hotel, 17
Peppers, 20
The Student Village, 18
University of Manchester, 21
Woodies Backpackers, 2
YHA Manchester, 11

● FOOD
Cornerhouse Cafe, 14
Dimitri's, 10
Green Room Theatre Cafe, 13
On the 8th Day, 19

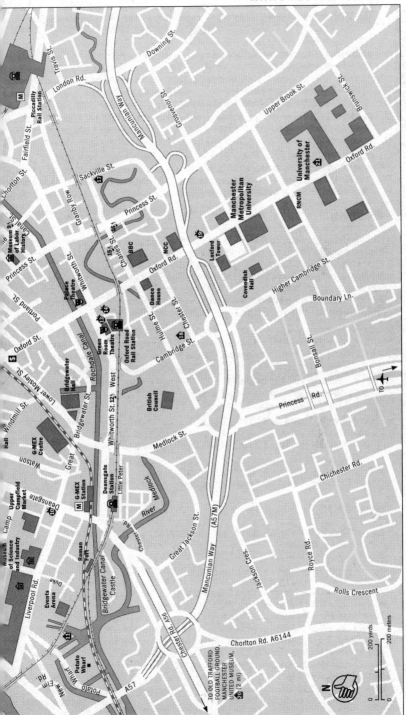

The Student Village, Lower Chatham St. (☎236 1776; www.thestudentvillage.com). A 10min. walk from St. Peter's Sq. Nothing outstanding about these 1039 summer rooms but the price. Singles £17, £15 for students.

University of Manchester: St. Gabriels Hall, 1-3 Oxford Pl., Victoria Park (☎224 7061). Self-catering dorms during school vacations. Reserve a week or more in advance with deposit. 3-day minimum stay. Singles £8.25, students £7; twins £16.45, students £14. If full, try **Woolton Hall,** Whitsorth Ln., Fallowfield (☎224 7244). For more info contact the **University Accommodation Office** (☎275 2888). Open M-F 9:30am-5pm.

Peppers, 17 Great Stone Rd., Stretford (☎/fax 848 9770). Take the Metrolink to Old Trafford (12min.), walk past the cricket ground and turn left, then take the first right onto Great Stone Rd. Simple hostel accommodations a bit out of the way. Internet access. £3 key deposit. Dorms £8; twins £10 per person.

Burton Arms, 31 Swan St. (☎/fax 834 3455). Basic rooms above a pub on a busy street. A 15min. walk from both train stations and St. Peter's Sq. Full English breakfast included. £19.50 per person, with bath £25.

🍴 FOOD

Outwit the pricey Chinatown restaurants by eating the multi-course "Business-man's Lunch" offered by most (M-F noon-2pm; £4-8, with or without briefcase and masculine gender). Better yet, visit **Curry Mile,** a stretch of Asian restaurants on Wilmslow Rd., for cheap, quality eats. Come evening, hip youths and yuppies wine and dine in the cafe-bars (see p. 343). For nocturnal appetites, kebab/burger/fish-and-chips joints on **Whitworth St. West** are open until 4am. A **Tesco** supermarket waits on Market St. (☎835 3339. Open M-Sa 8am-8pm, Su 11am-5pm.)

Cornerhouse Cafe, 70 Oxford St. (☎228 7621). Part of the Cornerhouse Arts Centre, it features a bar, 3 galleries, 3 arthouse cinemas, and trendy crowds. Main courses from £3.50, desserts from 70p. Open daily 11am-8:30pm; hot meals served noon-2:30pm and 5-7pm; bar open M-Sa noon-11pm, Su noon-10:30pm.

On the 8th Day, 107-111 Oxford Rd. (☎273 1850). An eclectic menu of vegetarian and vegan fare popular with students. Most meals under £4. Student discounts sweeten the pot. Open M-F 9am-7pm, Sa 10am-4:30pm.

Green Room Theatre Cafe, 54-56 Whitworth St. West (☎950 5777). Hip, minimalist decor. Menu includes "leafy herby salad" and no red meat. Snacks £1.50-4.25. Delectable main courses from £5. Food served M-Sa noon-3pm and 6-7:45pm.

Dimitri's, Campfield Arcade, Tonman St. (☎839 3319). Greek delicacies for plebeians and soap-opera divas alike (there's a TV studio next door). 2 appetizers make a meal (£3.65-5.45). 20% off drinks during happy hour (5-7pm). Open daily 11am-midnight.

👁 SIGHTS

Few of Manchester's buildings are notable—postcards mostly portray the front of trams—but an exception is the neo-Gothic **Manchester Town Hall,** at St. Peter's Sq. Behind the Town Hall Extension, the **Central Library** is the city's crown jewel. One of the largest municipal libraries in Europe, the domed building has a music and theater library, a language and literature library, and the UK's second-largest Judaica collection. The **Library Theatre Company** puts on several shows a year. (Library ☎234 1900; theater 236 7110. Open M-Th 10am-8pm, F-Sa 10am-5pm.) The **John Rylands Library,** 150 Deansgate, keeps rare books; its most famous holding is the St. John Fragment, a piece of New Testament writing from the 2nd century AD. (☎834 5343. Open M-F 10am-5:30pm, Sa 10am-1pm. Free. Tours W at noon £1.)

The **City Art Galleries** (☎236 5244) are closed for renovations for the foreseeable future. In the **Museum of Science and Industry,** Liverpool Rd. in Castlefield, working steam engines and looms provide a dramatic vision of the power, danger, and noise of Britain's industrialization. (☎832 1830. Open daily 10am-5pm. £6.50, concessions £3.50.) The Spanish and Portuguese synagogue-turned-**Jewish Museum,**

190 Cheetham Hill Rd., traces the history of the city's sizeable Jewish community and offers city tours. (☎834 9879. Open M-Th 10:30am-4pm, Su 10:30am-5pm. £3.25, concessions £2.50, families £8.) Loved and reviled, Manchester United is England's reigning football team. The **Manchester United Museum and Tour Centre,** Sir Matt Busby Way, at the Old Trafford football stadium (follow signs up Warwick Rd. from the Old Trafford Metrolink stop), displays memorabilia from the club's inception in 1878 to its recent trophy-hogging success. The museum's religious fervor may just convert you. (☎868 8631. Open daily 9am-5pm. Tours every 10min., 9:40am-4:30pm. Museum £5.50, seniors and children £3.75. With tour £8.50, £5.75.)

🎵 MUSIC, THEATER, AND FESTIVALS

Besides those listed below, Manchester's other major concert venue is the **Nynex Arena** (☎950 8000), behind Victoria Station.

Royal Exchange Theatre (☎833 9833) has returned to St. Ann's Sq., a few years after an IRA bomb destroyed the original building. The theater stages Shakespeare and world premieres of original works. Box office open M-Sa 9:30am-7:30pm. M-Th and Sa tickets £7-23, concessions £5 when booked 3 days in advance; separate concession rates apply to W and Sa matinees.

G-Mex, Lower Mosley St. (☎832 9000). The Greater Manchester Exhibition and Event Centre hosts pop, jazz, and classical concerts in a renovated train station; the front side closely resembles the head of space villain Darth Vader.

Bridgewater Hall (☎907 9000), across from the G-Mex. The new glass-and-metal home for the superb Hallé Orchestra, directed by Kent Nagano.

Palace Theatre, Oxford St. (☎242 2503). Caters to more classical tastes in theater, opera, and ballet. Box office open M-Sa 10am-6pm, until 8pm on performance days; Su 2hr. before performance. Some student discounts.

The **Boddington Manchester Festival of the Arts and Television** takes place in September and October. **The Manchester Festival** (www.the-manchester-festival.org.uk) runs all summer long, with dramatic, musical, and multimedia events. Call the Central Library (☎234 1944) for information on both events. The Gay Village also hosts a number of festivals, most notably **Mardi Gras** (☎237 3237), in late August, which raises money for AIDS relief. The **Independence Festival** (☎234 3160) convenes millions of disabled people for a giant celebration in early September.

🎭 NIGHTLIFE

CAFE-BARS

Many of Manchester's excellent lunchtime spots morph into pre-club drinking venues, or even become clubs themselves. Classifications are murky: in the **Clubs** section, Generation X has a good cafe-bar; in the **Food** section, the Cornerhouse and Green Room Cafes both offer stylish locales for the chic to drink. Below are our picks for the hippest spots.

The Lass O'Gowrie, 36 Charles St. (☎273 6932). Traditional pubs aren't passé when the evening crowd is this lively. BBC personalities trickle in from the neighboring studio. Good food at amazing prices (£1-3). Open M-Sa 11am-11pm, Su 11:30am-10:30pm; food served 9am-7pm.

Night and Day Cafe, Oldham St. (☎236 4597). A lounge, live music venue, and club, this retro haven provides an alternative to the gum-chewing, processed-pop crowd found elsewhere in the city. Club Carnaby, the 2nd F of each month, is a psychedelic 60s throwback. Cover £3 after 8:30pm. Open M-Sa 11am-2am.

Dry Bar, 28-30 Oldham St. (☎236 9840). Founded by Factory Records and the band New Order, this sleek super-long bar draws beautiful people after dark. Too cool for a sign; look for big wooden doors. Older R&B, hip-hop, and non-mainstream tunes. Happy hour M-F 4-9pm, Su all day. Open M-Th noon-1am, F-Sa noon-2am, Su noon-10:30pm.

CLUBS

Manchester's clubbing and live music scene remains a national trendsetter. Centered around **Oldham St.**, the **Northern Quarter** is the city's youthful outlet for live music, its alternative vibe and underground clothing shops drawing a hip crowd. Moody, candlelit **Matt and Phreds,** 85 Oldham St. (☎661 7494), is one of the city's few all-jazz venues. Don't forget to collect flyers—they often get you a discount. **Afflecks Palace,** 52 Church St., supplies paraphernalia from punk to funk; the walls of the stairway are postered with event notices. (☎834 2039. Open M-F 10am-5:30pm, Sa 10am-6pm.) Just up Oldham St., **Fat City** sells drum 'n' bass and hip-hop records and various tickets and passes. (☎237 1181. Open M-Sa 10am-5:30pm.)

At night, streets in the Northern Quarter are dimly lit. If you're crossing from Piccadilly to Swan St. or Great Ancoats St., use Oldham St., where the bright late-night clubs (and their bouncers) provide reassurance. There's also no shame in short taxi trips at night in this town.

■ **Infinity,** Peter St. (☎839 1112). Circular lights form an electric halo over a decadent dance-floor. Garage, house, and trance complete the £3 million refurbishment. Dress supersmart. Open M-W 9am-2pm (cover £2-4), Th-Sa 9pm-3am (£4 on Th, £6-8 F-Sa).

Generation X, 11-13 New Wakefield St. (☎236 4899). If you're "mad for it," house and breakbeat play on the roof terrace; the cafe-bar below features more conventional music. W "Hey Gringo" has salsa, funk, and fusion (£3). Mellow out at **Regeneration,** its *après*-clubbing Su chill-down. Cover £6-8. Open F-Sa until 2am, Su noon-10:30pm.

Revolution, Deansgate Locks (☎839 7569). Revolution leads an army of upstart bars and clubs on Deansgate with its Red decor (look for the bust of Lenin). Unrivaled vodka selection. DJs nightly. No cover unless special promotion. Open daily 11am-2am.

Planet K, 46-50 Oldham St. (☎839 9941). The principal club of the Northern Quarter, and a space for big-name DJs. A too-cool-for-you underground crowd fills the industrial dance-floor. Open W 10pm-2am (cover £2 after 11pm), Th-Sa 10pm-3am (£3-8).

THE GAY VILLAGE

Gay and lesbian clubbers will want to check out The Gay Village, northeast of Princess St. Evening crowds fill the bars lining **Canal St.,** in the heart of the area, which is also lovely and lively during the day. When weather cooperates, the bars are busy but empty, with patrons flooding the sidewalk tables.

■ **Cruz 101,** 101 Princess St. (☎237 1554). Fun and sexy cruisers teach a lesson in attitude at the Village's current champion of nightlife. Commercial dance gets bodies moving. Smart casual. Cover £2 M, Tu-Th free, F £3, Sa £5. Open M-Sa 10:30pm-2:30am.

Manto's, 46 Canal St. (☎236 2667), fills its classy purple interior with all ages, genders, and orientations. DJs F-Su. Extreme late-night fun during Sa night/Su morning "Breakfast Club" 2:30-6am. Cover £5-6.

Paradise Factory, 114-116 Princess St. (☎228 2966). The site for 2 of the biggest nights in Manchester's gay scene—"DirtyCityDiscos" (F) and "Creme Brulée" (Sa)—plays a mix of house, commercial dance, and more. Look for the shiny purple tiles around the entrance. Tu student night. Cover varies £4-8.

BLACKPOOL   ☎01253

Once a resort for the well-to-do, Blackpool has embraced its modern fame as King of Tack. The present gaudy era began with the railways built in the 1840s, along with the introduction of open-air dancing (1870) and electric street lighting (1879). By the end of the 19th century, droves of working-class Brits from Lancashire and Yorkshire arrived for a raucous holiday. Today, the town's amusements are numbingly numerous—7 mi. of hyperactive promenade with dinosaurs, roller coasters, palm-readers, fruit machines, donkey rides, fun palaces, 24hr. cabarets, and the occasional beach. With the possible exception of Las Vegas, Blackpool, for all its unabashed tackiness (or, more likely, because of it), is unrivaled worldwide as a tasteless dispenser of uninhibited fun of the piss-drunk, lounge-act variety.

▢ TRANSPORTATION

Trains: Blackpool North Station (☎620385), 4 blocks down Talbot Rd. from North Pier. Travel center open daily 8am-8pm. **Trains** (☎(08457) 484950) arrive from: **London Euston** (change at Preston; 4hr.; every hr.; £43, return £44); **Manchester** (1¼hr., 2 per hr., £9.50); **Liverpool** (1½hr., every hr., £10.65).

Buses: Talbot Rd. station dispenses National Express information. Open M-Sa 8:15am-midnight, Su 10am-6pm. **National Express** (☎(08705) 808080) **buses** from: **London** (6½hr., 6 per day, £18.75); **Liverpool** (1½hr., 4 per day, £5.50); **Manchester** (2hr., 5 per day, £6); **Chester** (4hr., 3 per day, £8).

Public Transportation: Local trains utilize Blackpool South and Pleasure Beach stations. **Local bus** info is available at Talbot Rd. station. Single from the Tower to Pleasure Beach 90p. Bus #1 covers the Promenade every 8min. A 1-day **Travelcard** buys unlimited travel on local buses and **vintage trams.** £4.25, seniors and children £3.75.

▨ PRACTICAL INFORMATION

Tourist Information Centre: 1 Clifton St. (☎478222; fax 478210). Books beds for £2 plus 10% deposit. Smoking dragon sculpture and free street maps. Open May-Nov. M-Sa 9am-5pm, Su 10am-4pm; Nov.-Apr. M-Sa 8:45am-4:45pm. **Branches** on the Promenade, near the Tower (☎478222), and 87a Coronation St. (☎403223), across from Pleasure Beach, open May-Nov. M-Sa 9:15am-5pm, Su 10:15am-3:30pm.

Financial Services: Banks are easy to find, especially along **Corporation St.**

Launderette: Corner of Albert Rd. and Regent Rd. Open M-F 9am-4pm, Sa 10am-2pm.

Internet Access: Blackpool Public Library (☎478111), on the corner of Queen St. and Abingdon St. £1 per 30min. Open M, W, F-Sa 10am-5pm; Tu and Th 10am-7pm. **CafeNet,** 16 Deansgate (☎625003), off Abingdon St. 75p per 15min. Open Su-W 10am-5pm, Th-Sa 10am-7pm.

Post Office: 26-30 Abingdon St. (☎622888). Accepts Poste Restante for letters only. Open M-Sa 9am-5:30pm. **Postal code:** FY1 1AA.

▮▢ ACCOMMODATIONS AND FOOD

With over 3500 guest houses and 120,000 beds, you won't have trouble finding a room, except on weekends during the Illuminations (see p. 346). Budget-friendly B&Bs dominate the blocks behind the Promenade between the North and Central Piers (£10-14). Pick up the free Bible-sized *Blackpool Have the Time of Your Life* at the tourist information centre (TIC) for an impressive list.

▨ **Manor Grove Hotel,** 24 Leopold Grove (☎625577; www.manorgrovehotel.com). From the bus or train station, head to the sea on Talbot Rd., turn left on Topping St., and right on Church St.; Leopold Grove is 1 block on the left (10min.). Familial atmosphere, professional service. Spacious rooms are modem accessible, with TV, phone, and bath. Hearty English breakfast. July-Dec. £19 per person; Jan.-June £18. AmEx/MC/V.

Clarron House, 22 Leopold Grove (☎623748). Next door to the Manor Grove Hotel. Your chip-heavy, dance-weary body will thank you for the comfy beds. All rooms with TV. Apr.-June £14 per person; July-Aug. £15; Sept.-Nov. £16-18; Jan.-Mar. £13.

Silver Birch Hotel, 39 Hull Rd. (☎622125). From the bus and train stations, head down Talbot Rd. to the ocean, take a left on Market St., pass the Tower, and turn left. You can also enter from Albert Rd. The maternal proprietress has spoiled guests with warm hospitality for 23 years. TV in every room. Breakfast £3. £10 per person, with bath £13.

York House, 30 South King St. (☎624200). Follow the Manor Grove directions, but turn left on Church St.; South King St. is 1 block down on the right. Bay windows, tall ceilings, and aristocratic red decor. Rooms with TV and bath £16.50 per person.

You know you're in Blackpool when McDonald's starts looking like class. The **Iceland** supermarket, 1 Dickson Rd., is across from the bus station. (☎293051. Open M-F 8:30am-8pm, Sa 8:30am-5:30pm, Su 10am-4pm.) Loaves from **Sayers the Baker,** 1 Birley St., make for lovely picnics in the 256 acres of **Stanley Park,** a mile east of the Tower. (☎624913. Open M-Sa 8:30am-5pm.) Blackpool's branch of **Harry Ramsden's,** on the corner of the Promenade and Church St., is a step up from most fast-food fare: the fish and chips aren't floating in grease. (☎294386. Open M-Th and Su 11:30am-7:30pm, F-Sa 11:30am-9pm.)

◉ ♫ SIGHTS AND ENTERTAINMENT

No fewer than 36 nightclubs, 38,000 theater seats, several circuses, and still more roller coasters squat along the **Promenade,** served by Britain's first electric tram line. Even the three 19th-century piers are stacked with ferris wheels and chip shops. The only thing the hedonistic hordes don't come for is the ocean.

PLEASURE BEACH. Around 7.1 million people visit the sprawling 40-acre amusement park annually, second in Europe only to EuroDisney. Pleasure Beach is known for its historic wooden roller coasters—the twin-track **Grand National** (c. 1935) is something of a mecca for coaster enthusiasts, and the **Big Dipper** was invented here. Thousands of thrill-seekers line up for the aptly named **Big One,** and aren't disappointed. Their screams vie with the seagulls' cries, as the 235 ft. steel behemoth, tall enough to merit aircraft warning lights, sends them down a heart-stopping 65° slope at 87 mph—the highest, steepest, and fastest in the world. Although admission to the themeless park is free, the rides themselves aren't— kiddy rides go for £1, most coasters cost £2.10, and the Big One is a whopping £4.20. The pay-as-you-ride system does mean queues are shorter than at other amusement parks, and discount ticket books are available. By night, Pleasure Beach has illusion shows and family-geared acts in a "Las Vegas-style theatre." *(Across from South Pier.* ☎*(0870) 444 5566. A book of £20 Ride Tickets buys £25 of rides. Opens daily at 10-11am; closing time varies. Call ahead or check posted times at the entrance.)*

BLACKPOOL TOWER. When a London businessman visited the 1890 Paris World Exposition, he returned determined to erect Eiffel Tower imitations throughout Britain. Only Blackpool embraced his enthusiasm, and in 1894 the 560 ft. Tower graced the city's skyline. Unfortunately, it looks more like a sooty junkheap find than France's sleek symbol of modernism. **Towerworld** at its base is a bizarre microcosm of Blackpool's eclectic tackiness, with a motley crew of attractions: a black-lit aquarium, motorized dinosaur ride, insanely large jungle gym, daily circus show (Easter-Oct. only), arcade games, and casino. Couples (mostly senior citizens) dance sedately and somewhat surreally in the ornate Victorian ballroom, complete with Wurlitzer organ. *(☎622242. Open June-Oct. daily 10am-11pm; Nov.-May 10am-6pm. Easter-Oct. £10, seniors and children £5; Nov.-Easter £5, children £3. Tower only Easter to mid-July £6.50, children £4; mid-July to Nov. £7.50, £6.)*

THE ILLUMINATIONS. Blackpool, the first electric town in Britain, consummates its crazed love affair with bright lights in the orgiastic **Illuminations.** The display takes place over 5 mi. of the Promenade from September to early November. In a colossal waste of electricity, 72 mi. of cables light up the tower, promenade, star-encased faces of Hollywood actors, corporate emblems, and garish placards.

NIGHTLIFE. Between North and Central Piers, Blackpool's famous **Golden Mile** shines with more neon than gold, hosting scores of sultry theaters, cabaret bars, and bingo halls. Crisscrossed by laser beams, the dance-floors of the UK's largest nightclub, **The Palace,** Central Promenade, pack in up to 3000 revelers for 70s night on Thursday. (☎626281. Cover £1-9. Open Th-Sa 9pm-2am.) The more upscale **Main Entrance,** directly below the Palace, only holds 1000. (☎292335. Cover £2-12. Open M-Tu and Th-Sa 9pm-2am, second Su of the month 9pm-midnight.)

ISLE OF MAN
☎ 01624

Isle of Man

[Map of the Isle of Man showing: Point of Ayre, The Ayres, Bride, Ramsey Bay, Andreas, Jurby, Ramsey, Maughold, Sulby, TT Circuit, Ballaugh, Kirk Michael, Snaefell, Laxey, Lonan, Laxey Bay, St. Patrick's Isle, Peel, Tynwald Hill, Greeba, Onchan, Contrary Head, St. John's, Crosby, Douglas, Douglas Bay, Foxdale, Braaid, Douglas Head, Port Soderick, Ballasalla, Bradda Head, Colby, Ronaldsway Airport, Port Erin, Castletown, Derbyhaven, Cregneash, Port St. Mary, Scarlett Point, Castletown Bay, Dreswick Point, Spanish Head, Calf Sound, Calf of Man; with roads A1, A2, A3, A5, B10, TT Circuit; ferry routes TO BELFAST (SEACAT), TO HEYSHAM, TO LIVERPOOL, TO DUBLIN; scale 5 miles / 5 kilometers; N compass]

The Isle of Man is a droplet of land (33 by 13 mi.) in the middle of the Irish Sea. While the 75,000 Manx swear allegiance to Queen Elizabeth, they are not a part of the UK and have their own parliament, flag, currency, and language. Vikings landed on Man in the 9th century and established the Isle's parliament, **Tynwald Court.** After the last Viking king died in 1266, Scottish and English lords fought for power, and in 1405 home rule ended when the English "Lords of Man" took control. Smugglers contributed to an economic boom until England's Isle of Man Purchase Act (1765) sent the island spinning into poverty. Man's rejuvenation began in 1828, when self-government was restored, and today independent Man controls its own internal affairs and finances while remaining a crown protectorate.

Ringed by cliffs and sliced by valleys, Man can be explored in a few days. The island caters more to families than backpackers, but draws all types when motorcyclists descend for the famous **T.T. races.** Much of the fauna is unique, including multi-horned **Manx Loghtan sheep** and tailless **Manx cats.** Man's most famous (and odorous) delicacy is the **kipper,** herring smoked over oak chips. The **Manx language,** a cousin of Irish and Scots Gaelic, is heard when Manx laws are proclaimed each year on July 5, and the **three-legs-of-Man** emblem appears on every available surface, asserting the proud and singular identity of this tiny island nation.

✕ GETTING THERE

Flights: Ronaldsway Airport (☎821600), 10 mi. southwest of Douglas on the coast road. Buses #1, 1C, and 2 connect to Douglas (25min., 1-3 per hr.), while several others stop at points around the island. **Manx Airlines** (☎824313, UK (08457) 256256, Ireland (01) 260 1588; www.manx-airlines.com) flies from London, Dublin, Glasgow, Manchester, and other airports in Britain and Ireland. **British European** (UK ☎(08705) 676676; Ireland (1890) 925532) also serves the isle.

Ferries: Douglas Sea Terminal. Travel Shop open M-Sa 9am-5pm, and at times of sailing. The **Isle of Man Steam Packet Company** (☎646645 or (08705) 523523) runs the only ferries to the isle, sailing from: **Belfast** (2¾hr.; Apr.-Sept. 2 per week, usually W and Su); **Liverpool** (2½hr.; Apr.-Oct. 1-3 per day, Nov.-Mar. 3 per week); **Dublin** (2¾hr.; Apr.-Dec. 3 per week, usually Tu, Th, Sa); **Heysham,** Lancashire (2½-3½hr., 2 per day). Fares are higher in summer and on weekends (£25-51, students and seniors £19-51, children £12-25). Book in advance for discounts. Combination tickets can save money on round-trips; purchase **Sail & Rail** tickets from train stations or the Isle of Man Steam Packet and **Sail & Coach** tickets from National Express bus stations.

▐ LOCAL TRANSPORTATION

The Isle of Man may have more cars per person than anywhere else in the world except Los Angeles, but it also has an extensive system of public transportation run by **Isle of Man Transport** (☎663366), in Douglas. Their **Travel Shop,** on Lord St. next to the bus station, has details on all government-run transportation, including free maps and schedules and discount tickets. (☎662525. Open M and W 10am-5:45pm, Tu and Th 8am-3:45pm, Sa 8am-3:30pm.) The Travel Shop and the Douglas tourist information centre (TIC) sell **Island Explorer tickets,** which provide unlimited travel on most of the Isle of Man Transport bus and train services, as well as horse trams (1-day £8, 3-day £18, 5-day £26, 7-day £32; children half-price).

The island's size makes it easy to get around by **bike.** The southern three-quarters of the island are covered in challenging hills—manageable, but worthy of Man's status as professional terrain. TICs provide a free map of six one-day cycle trails. Locals claim that the Isle of Man is one of the safer places for **hitchhiking,** though *Let's Go* does not recommend it.

Trains: Isle of Man Railways (☎663366) runs along the east coast from Port Erin to Ramsey (Easter-Oct., limited service in winter). The 1874 **Steam Railway** runs from Douglas to Port Erin via Castletown. The 1899 **Electric Railway** runs from Douglas to Ramsey. The **Mountain Railway** runs to **Snaefell,** the island's highest peak (2036 ft.); trains #1 and 2 are the oldest in the world.

Buses: Frequent buses connect every island hamlet. Douglas is the center of the island's bus empire. Pick up a free copy of the *Isle of Man Transport Timetables* at the TIC for all bus and train info. An Island Explorer ticket may save you money (see above).

Tours: Isle of Man Bus Tour Company, Central Promenade (☎674301), in Douglas, provides several tours, including the popular "Round the Island" departing from Douglas W and F 10:15am and returning at 5pm (£12, children £6). Office open 45min. before tour departures.

▐ PRACTICAL INFORMATION

Manx **currency** is equivalent in value to British currency but not accepted outside the Isle; notes and coins from England, Scotland, and Northern Ireland can be used in Man. Manx coins are reissued each year with different and often bizarre designs—we're talking dirtbikes and cell phones, here. When preparing to leave the island, you can ask for your change in UK tender and usually get it. **Manx stamps** are also unusual (the eagle-eyed will notice that the Queen's head bears no crown). BT phonecards don't work on Man; post offices and newsagents sell Manx Telecom **phonecards** instead. The Isle shares Britain's **international dialing code,** 44.

▐ HIKING AND WALKING ON THE ISLE OF MAN

The government maintains three long-distance trails, marked by the three-legs-of-Man symbol. **Raad ny Foillan** ("Road of the Gull") is a 90 mi. path around the island marked with seagull signs. The ◪**Port Erin to Castletown route** is a spectacular hike (12 mi.) offering the very best of the island's south: sandy beaches, cliffs, and splashing surf. **Bayr ny Skeddan** ("The Herring Road"), once used by Manx fishermen, covers the less spectacular 14 mi. between Peel in the west and Castletown in the east. It overlaps the **Millennium Way,** which goes from Castletown to Ramsey along the course of the 14th-century Royal Highway for 28 mi., ending a mile from Ramsey's Parliament Sq. For a shorter walk, follow signs in **Port Erin** to the nature trail that leads to a coastal peak; this easy climb offers a terrific view of the island and of the **Calf of Man,** the small land mass and bird sanctuary off the isle's southern tip. The Douglas TIC has maps and free leaflets detailing island walks.

■ EVENTS

The island's economy relies heavily on tourism, so there are always festivals celebrating everything from jazz to angling. The TIC stocks a calendar of events; ask for the biannual *What's on the Isle of Man*. Each year, the first two weeks of June turn Man into a merry motorcycling beast for the **T.T. (Tourist Trophy) Races.** The population doubles, the Steam Packet Co. schedules extra ferries, and Manx Radio is replaced by its evil twin, "Radio T.T." The races originated in 1904 when the tourist-hungry government passed the **Road Closure Act,** under which roads could be closed and speed-limits lifted for a motor race. Today there are 600 racers and 40,000 fans. The circuit consists of 38 mi. of hairpin turns and mountain climbs, and the winner gets his name (no "her" yet) and make of motorcycle engraved on the same silver "tourist trophy" that has been used since 1907. The T.T. season is a nonstop two-week party, embraced by locals as part of their national identity.

The **Isle of Man International Cycling Week** usually occurs around the T.T. Race weeks and uses the same tracks. Established in 1936, it is now the most respected bicycle race in the British Isles. **Southern "100" Motorcycle Races** (☎822546) take place over three days in mid-July: more bikers, more fun, this time based in Castletown, the self-proclaimed "Road Racing Capital of the World." The Isle also celebrates at **Tynwald Fair,** which sees the pronouncement of new laws on July 5, Manx National Day. Representatives don British wigs and robes to read the laws, but they do so in the Manx tongue upon a remote hill of ancient significance. The holiday takes place as part of the week-long **Manx Heritage Festival.**

DOUGLAS   ☎01624

Recent capital of an ancient island, Douglas (pop. 22,000) has leveled the natural Manx landscape under a square mile of concrete promenades and narrow Victorian townhouses. In the last century, Douglas bloomed as a seaside resort, but today it profits most from the savvy businessmen who hurry down the promenade from nine to five. It remains a solid spot from which to explore the island.

⨂ TRANSPORTATION. Ferries arrive at the **Sea Terminal,** at the southern end of town near the bus station. **Isle of Man Transport,** Banks Circus (☎663366), runs local trains and buses (see **Local Transportation,** p. 348). Slow but inexpensive horse-drawn **trams** run down The Promenade between the bus and Electric Railway station in summer. Stops are posted every 200 yd. or so. (☎675522. Continuous service June-Aug. daily 9:10am-8:50pm; Sept.-May 9:10am-6:30pm.) Motorized **buses** also run along The Promenade, connecting the bus and Steam Railway stations with the Electric Railway (65p). For taxis, call **A-1 Taxis** (☎663344) or **Telecabs** (☎621111), both open 24hr. There are several car rental companies in Douglas; the TIC has fliers. **Eurocycles,** 8a Victoria Rd., off Broadway, rents **bikes.** (☎624909. Call ahead in summer. Open M-Sa 9am-6pm.)

◪ ORIENTATION AND PRACTICAL INFORMATION. Douglas stretches for 2 mi. along the seafront, from **Douglas Head** in the south to the **Electric Railway** terminal in the north. Douglas Head is separated from the rest of town by the River Douglas, which flows into the harbor. The ferry and bus terminals lie just north of the river. **The Promenade** bends from ferry terminal to Electric Railway terminal along the crescent of beach. **Nobles Park** is the site of recreation facilities and the start of the T.T. course. The shopping district spreads out around pedestrianized **Strand St.**

The **tourist information centre** (TIC), in the Sea Terminal Bldg., books accommodations for free on a walk-in basis. (☎686766; www.gov.im/tourism. Open Easter-Sept. daily 9:15am-7pm; Oct.-Easter M-Th 9am-5:30pm, F 9am-5pm.) Other services include: **Lloyds TSB** bank, 78 Strand St. (☎(08456) 035013; open M-F 9:30am-4:30pm, Sa 9:30am-12:30pm); **Thomas Cook,** 7/8A Strand St. (☎626288; open M-W and F-Sa 9am-5:30pm, Th 10am-5:30pm); the **police,** Glencrutchery Rd. (☎631212);

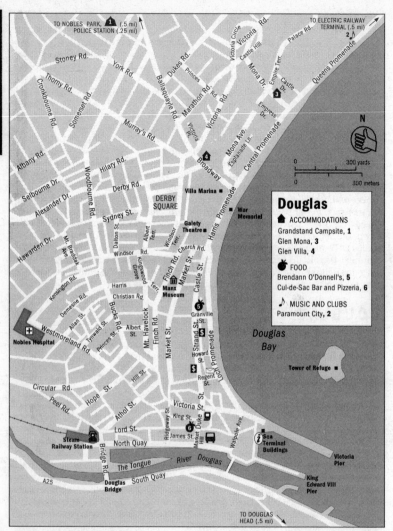

Douglas

🏠 **ACCOMMODATIONS**
Grandstand Campsite, **1**
Glen Mona, **3**
Glen Villa, **4**

🍎 **FOOD**
Brendann O'Donnell's, **5**
Cul-de-Sac Bar and Pizzeria, **6**

🎵 **MUSIC AND CLUBS**
Paramount City, **2**

Nobles Isle of Man Hospital, Westmoreland Rd. (☎642642); **Internet access at Fee-gan's Lounge,** 22 Duke St., off Lord St. near the bus station (☎679280; £1 per 15min.; open M-F 9am-7pm, Sa 9am-5pm); and the **post office,** Regent St. (☎686141; open M and W-F 9am-5:30pm, Tu 9:30am-5:30pm, Sa 9am-12:30pm). **Postal Code:** IM1 2EA.

🏠🍴 ACCOMMODATIONS AND FOOD. Douglas is overrun with B&Bs and hotels. During T.T. race weeks, they raise their rates and fill a year in advance. **Glen Villa,** 5 Broadway, near the grassy lawns of the Villa Marina Gardens, has comfortable rooms with TVs and halls lined with racing photos. From the sea terminal, head down The Promenade past the War Memorial and turn onto Broadway. (☎673394. £20 per person.) The **Glen Mona,** 6 Mona Drive, is a family-run hotel up The Promenade with 17 pleasant rooms. (☎676755. £17 per person; singles £20.) **Grandstand Campsite** is behind the T.T. races' start and finish line. (☎621132. Office open M-F 9am-5pm. Site open mid-June to mid-Aug. and Sept. £6 per pitch. Laundry £2. Showers £1.) It's closed during the T.T. races and Grand Prix week, but other campsites around the island open then—ask the TIC for a list.

Cheap grill and chip shops proliferate along The Promenade, Duke St., Strand St., and Castle St. For groceries, try the **Safeway,** Chester St. (☎673039. Open M-W 8:30am-8pm, Th-F 8:30am-9pm, Sa 8am-8pm, Su 9am-6pm.) The **Cul-de-Sac Bar and Pizzeria,** 3 Market Hill, by North Quay, has lots o' pizza (Hawaiian pizza £7.50), more than 125 flavors of vodka (toffee vodka £1.85), the largest selection of beer on the island, and free live music on weekends. Enough said. (☎623737. Live music Th-Sa 9pm-2am. Open Su-Th 11am-2pm and 5pm-midnight, F-Sa 11am-2pm and 5pm-2am.) At **Brendann O'Donnell's,** 16-18 Strand St., Guinness posters and traditional music quickly remind you of the owner's loyalty and the Isle's proximity to Ireland. (☎621566. Open Su-Th noon-11pm, F-Sa noon-midnight.)

◨◪ SIGHTS AND ENTERTAINMENT. From the shopping district, signs point mysteriously to the Chester St. parking garage, where an elevator ride to the roof leads you across a footbridge to the entrance of the **Manx Museum.** This fascinating gallery chronicles the history of the island since the Ice Age, with geological and taxidermic displays and a pair of arguing rocks. (☎648000. Open M-Sa 10am-5pm. Free.) Past the Villa Marina Gardens on Harris Promenade sits the **Gaiety Theatre.** Designed in 1900 and recently restored, the theater shone during Douglas's seaside resort days. To see the nifty antique machinery you'll have to take a guided **tour.** (☎625001. 1½hr. tours Sa 10:15am; July-Aug. also Tu and Th 1:45pm. £3, children £1; advance booking recommended. Performances Mar.-Dec. Box office open M-Sa 10am-4:30pm and 1hr. before performances. Tickets £13-15; discounts for seniors and children.) The distant sandcastle-like structure sitting in Douglas Bay is the **Tower of Refuge,** closed to the public.

Most of the late-night **clubs** in Douglas are 21+ and free until 10 or 11pm, with a £2-5 cover thereafter. Paramount City, Queens Promenade (☎622447), houses two nightclubs: the upstairs **Director's Bar** plays favorites from the 50s to the 90s, while the downstairs **Dark Room** plays chart and dance music. (No jeans, t-shirts, or sportswear. Cover £3-4. Open F-Sa 8pm-2:15am.)

PEEL ☎01624

Considered the "cradle of Manx heritage" and headquarters of the Manx kipper industry, Peel is a beautiful fishing town on the west coast of Man. Twisting streets and salt-soaked stone buildings remain practically unchanged since the days fishermen sailed from here to the Hebrides. Romantic **◨Peel Castle,** situated atop the gentle height of **St. Patrick's Isle,** is easily reached from the mainland by pedestrian causeway. Not as grand as its British counterparts, the castle has served the Lords of Man quite nicely for centuries. The damp, eerie **Bishop's Dungeon** was used to punish sinners for such offenses as missing church. Footpaths ring the ruins before dipping to a stretch of beach and skimming the rocks of **Peel Hill.** (Open Easter-Oct. daily 10am-5pm; winter hours vary. £3, children £1.50, families £7.50; includes audioguide.) Across the narrow harbor is the impressive **House of Manannan,** a link in the island-wide Story of Man museum series, emphasizing the role of the sea in Manx history with engaging reconstructions and informative video footage. (☎648000. Open daily 10am-5pm, last admission 3:30pm. £5, children £2.50, families £12.50.) **Moore's Traditional Curers,** on Mill Rd. off East Quay, is one of Peel's two **kipper factories.** The largest of its kind in Europe, the 1880 structure once produced 250,000 kippers a day. Alas, the kipper industry isn't what it used to be. (☎843622. Tours run Apr.-Oct. daily 2 and 3:30pm. £2, children £1.)

Buses (☎662525) come to the station on Atholl St. from **Douglas** (#4, 5A, 6, 6A, 7; 35min.; M-Sa 1-2 per hr., Su 11 per day; return £3) and **Port Erin** (#8; 55min.; M-Sa 3 per day, Su 2 per day; return £3.10). Some buses leave from around the corner outside the town hall on Derby Rd., and all buses do so on Sundays and after 6pm on weekdays. The **tourist information centre** is in the Town Hall, Derby Rd. (☎842341. Open M-Th 8:45am-5pm, F 8:45am-4:30pm.)

Seabourne House, Mt. Morrison, offers nine rooms with TVs and stupendous views of the Irish sea. (☎842571. May-Sept. £14.50 per person; Oct.-Apr. £15.) **Peel Camping Park,** Derby Rd., has laundry facilities. (☎842341; fax 844010. Open May-Sept. £3.75 per person.) The town's two **Shoprite** grocery stores are on Derby Rd.

Peak District National Park   ♠ YHA Hostels

Axe Edge Moor, **26**	Haddon Hall, **30**	Peak Cavern, **22**
Birchinlee Pasture, **12**	Hartington Upper Quarter, **23**	Raven's Low, **25**
Black Ashop Moor, **13**	Hobson Moss, **10**	Saddleworth, **3**
Blue John Cavern, **19**	Hope Woodlands, **11**	Shining Clough Mass, **7**
Broomhead Moor, **9**	Jacob's Ladder, **18**	Shining Tor (elevation 1854), **23**
Chatsworth House, **29**	Kinder Low (elevation 2077), **16**	Thor's Cave, **27**
Derwent Moors, **14**	Longsett Moors, **6**	Thurlstone Moor, **5**
Dick Hill, **4**	Mam Tor, **21**	Treak Cliff Cavern, **20**
Edale Head, **17**	Margery Hill (elevation 1793), **8**	Wessenden Head Moor, **2**
Edale Moor, **15**	Middle Hills, **27**	Wessenden Moor, **1**

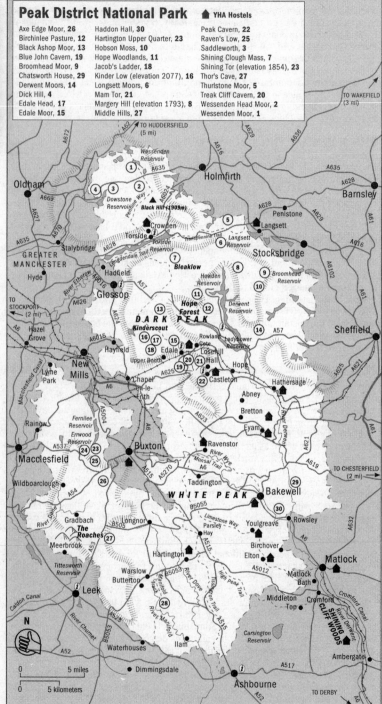

(open M-Th 8:30am-6:30pm, F 8:30am-8pm, Sa 8am-6pm) and in the center of town on Michael St. (open M-F 8:30am-8pm, Sa 8am-7pm, Su 10am-5pm). The **Harbour Lights Cafe and Tearoom,** Shore Rd., provides the chance to try a Peel kipper. (☎897216. Main courses £6-8. Open Tu-Su 10am-5pm.) A visit to the beach would not be complete without a stop at **Davidson's Ice Cream Parlour,** 1 Castle Court. Two enormous scoops of tasty Manx ice cream cost an unheard-of £1. (☎844761. Open Apr.-Sept. daily 10am-9pm; Oct.-Mar. 10am-7:30pm.)

PEAK DISTRICT NATIONAL PARK

Named in 1951 as Britain's first national park, Peak boasts 555 sq. mi. of ambitious hills; devoid of mountains, the area derives its name from the Old English *peac,* meaning "hill." In the **Dark Peak** area to the north, deep groughs (gullies) gouge the hard peat moorland below gloomy cliffs, while friendlier footpaths wicker the rocky hillsides and village clusters of the **Northern Peak** area. The rolls of the southern **White Peak** cradle abandoned millstones and stately country homes. A green cushion between the hard industrial giants of Manchester, Sheffield, and Nottingham, the park serves as playground to its millions of urban neighbors. Trampled trails attest to the park's popularity, as it attracts 20 million annual visitors. The park's southern regions accommodate hikers with gentler terrain and better transport links, but travelers seeking solitude should point their compasses toward the bleaker northern moors, beyond the reaches of commuter rail lines.

■ TRANSPORTATION

Trains (☎(08457) 484950) seem intimidated by the rustic splendor of the park; only three lines enter its boundaries, and only one dares to cross. One line goes from **Derby** to **Matlock,** on the park's southeastern edge (M-Sa 13-14 per day, Su 6 per day). From the west, a train runs from **Manchester** to **Buxton** (1hr., every hr., £5.30). The **Hope Valley line** (1½hr.; M-F 15 per day, Sa 17 per day, Su 9 per day) runs from Manchester across the park via **Edale** (£6.30), **Hope** (near Castleton), and **Hathersage,** terminating in **Sheffield** (£10.40). Both lines from Manchester enter the park at **New Mills**—the Buxton line at Newtown Station and the Hope Valley line at Central Station. A 20min. signposted walk separates the stations.

A sturdy pair of legs is more than sufficient for inter-village journeys, but if you must depend upon the rare train or the infrequent bus, Derbyshire County Council's *Peak District Timetable* (60p) is invaluable. The timetable includes all bus and train routes as well as a large map and information on various day-long bus tickets, cycle hire, youth hostels, tourist information centres (TICs), and hospitals. **Buses** make a noble effort to connect the scattered towns of the Peak District. The public transportation information line, **Traveline** (☎(0870) 6082608), offers solutions and sympathy. Coverage of many routes actually improves on Sundays, especially in summer. **Trent** (☎(01773) 7122765) bus TP, the "Transpeak," winds for 3hr. between **Manchester** and **Nottingham,** stopping at **Buxton, Bakewell, Matlock, Derby,** and other towns in between. **First PMT** (☎(01782) 207999) #X18 runs from **Sheffield** to **Bakewell** (45min., M-Sa 5 per day) and **Buxton** (1¼hr., M-Sa 5 per day) en route to **Keele** (3¼hr.; M-Sa 5 per day, Su 4 per day). **First Mainline** (☎(01709) 515151) #272 and **Stagecoach East Midland** (☎(01246) 211007) #273 and 274 both reach **Castleton** from **Sheffield** (40-55min.; 15 per day, Su 17 per day; £2.30). Stagecoach East Midland also runs between **Sheffield** and **Buxton** via **Eyam** (#65; 1¼hr.; M-Sa 5 per day, Su 3 per day; £2.90) and from **Bakewell** to **Castleton** (#173; 45min.; M-Sa 4-5 per day, Su 3 per day; £2.10).

If you're going to use public transport, pick one of the half-dozen bargain day tickets available; they're clearly explained in the *Timetables* booklet, and several have their own brochures at the TIC. The best deal is the **Derbyshire Wayfarer** (£7.25, seniors and children £3.65, families £12), which allows one day of train and bus travel through the Peak District north to Sheffield and south to Derby. The plain **Wayfarer** (£7, seniors and children £3.50, families £12), gives one unlimited day's travel within Greater Manchester and the Peak District as far east as Matlock (including Buxton, Bakewell, Castleton, Edale, and Eyam). Both passes are sold at Manchester train stations and National Park Information Centres.

🔋 PRACTICAL INFORMATION

Daytime facilities in the Peak District generally stay open through the winter due to the proximity of large cities. Some B&Bs and youth hostels welcome travelers until December. Most TICs book accommodations for a 10% deposit.

NATIONAL PARK INFORMATION CENTRES
All carry detailed walking guides and fun facts on the park.

Bakewell: Old Market Hall (☎(01629) 813227; fax 814782), at Bridge St. From the bus stop, put the Rutland Arms hotel behind you and the Bath Gardens on your left and walk a block down Bridge St. Doubles as the TIC. Good selection of maps and books accommodations. Open Mar.-Oct. daily 9:30am-5:30pm; Nov.-Feb. 10am-5pm.

Castleton: (☎/fax (01433) 620679), Castle St., near the church. From the bus stop, follow the road past the post office into town and turn left at the youth hostel sign. Open Apr.-Oct. daily 10am-1pm and 2-5:30pm; Nov.-Mar. Sa-Su 10am-5pm.

Edale: (☎(01433) 670207; fax 670216), Fieldhead, between the rail station and village. Open Apr.-Oct. daily 9am-1pm and 2:30-5:30pm; Nov.-Mar. closes at 5pm.

Fairholmes: (☎(01433) 650953), Upper Derwent Valley, near Derwent Dam. Open Apr.-Oct. daily 9:30am-5pm; Nov.-Mar. Sa-Su 10am-4:30pm.

TOURIST INFORMATION CENTRES

Ashbourne: 13 The Market Pl. (☎(01335) 343666; fax 300638). Open Mar.-Oct. daily 9:30am-5:30pm; Nov.-Feb. M-Sa 10am-4pm.

Buxton: The Crescent (☎(01298) 25106). Open Mar.-Oct. daily 9:30am-5pm; Nov.-Feb. 10am-4pm.

Matlock: Crown Square (☎(01629) 583388). Open Mar.-Oct. daily 9:30am-5pm; Nov.-Feb. 10am-4pm.

Matlock Bath: The Pavilion (☎(01629) 55082), along the main road. Open Mar.-Oct. daily 9:30am-5pm; Nov.-Feb. Sa-Su 10am-4pm, though hours vary.

🏠 ACCOMMODATIONS

National Park Information Centres and TICs distribute free park-wide and regional accommodations guides; a camping guide costs 30p. **B&Bs** are plentiful and cheap (from £14), as are **youth hostels** (around £8). Most hostels are not open every day of the week. **Buxton, Bakewell,** and **Matlock Bath** are particularly well stocked with inexpensive B&Bs. Many farmers allow **camping** on their land, sometimes for a small fee; remember to ask first and leave the site as you found it.

YHA YOUTH HOSTELS
The Peak District has almost 20 hostels, many of which are listed below, but don't let numbers fool you—most fill quickly with enthusiastic school groups, so call ahead to reserve a space. Hostels lie within a day's hike of one another and sell maps detailing routes to neighboring hostels. Alternatively, the *Peak District Timetables* (60p at TICs) lists both YHAs and the bus services to them. Unless noted, the hostels serve meals and have a 10am-5pm lockout and 11pm curfew. Most offer a £1 **student discount.** Three of the smaller ones (Bretton, Langsett, and Shining Cliff) book through the central **YHA Diary** office (☎(01629) 592707); only call the hostels directly for general information or for lodging within the following week.

Bakewell: Fly Hill (☎/fax (01629) 812313). A 5min. walk from the town center. Surrounded by bountiful pots of flowers, this 28-bed hostel delivers huge meals. Open Mar.-Oct. M-Sa; Nov.-Feb. daily. Dorms £10, under 18 £6.90.

Bretton: (☎(01433) 631856). Self-catering hostel 2 mi. from Eyam atop Eyam Edge (1250 ft.). A heck of a view. Take bus #65, 66, or 67 to Foolow. Face the pub and follow the sign to Bretton up the hill on the left. Open mid-July to Aug. daily; Sept.-Oct. and Easter to mid-July F-Sa. Dorms £8.50, under 18 £5.75.

Buxton: Sherbrook Lodge, Harpur Hill Rd. (☎/fax (01298) 22287). From the train station, follow Terrace Rd. as it becomes London Rd.; turn right at the YHA sign (25min.). If your pack's too heavy, take bus #185 or 186 from the train station toward Harpur Hill and ask for the hostel (5min., 2 per hr.). Open Apr.-Oct. M-Sa; Nov.-Dec. M and Th-Su; Feb.-Mar. F-Sa. Dorms £8.50, under 18 £5.75.

Castleton: Castleton Hall (☎(01433) 620235). Pretty country house and attached vicarage in the heart of town. The vicarage has nicer rooms with baths and no curfew. Internet access. Book way in advance. Open Feb. to late Dec. daily. Beds £11.25, under 18 £8; vicarage dorms £13.75, under 18 £10.25.

Crowden-in-Longdendale: (☎/fax (01457) 852135), Crowden, Hadfield, Hyde. Take National Express #350, which runs from Liverpool to Nottingham, and get off at Crowden (3 per day); the hostel is a clear 200 yd. away. Open Apr.-Sept. Th-Tu; Oct. F-M; Nov. F-Sa. Dorms £8.20, under 18 £5.65.

Edale: (☎(01433) 670302; fax 670243), Rowland Cote, Nether Booth, Edale, 2 mi. from Edale village. From the train station, turn right and then left onto the main road; follow to Nether Booth, where a sign points the way. Includes a climbing tower. Travelers arriving at the train station between 4-8pm can arrange to be picked up. No lockout. Dorms £11, under 18 £7.75.

Elton: Elton Old Hall, Main St. (☎/fax (01629) 650394). Catch bus #172, which runs from Matlock to Bakewell, to the Elton stop (M-Sa 7-9 per day). Self-catering. Open Easter-Oct. Tu-Sa. Dorms £8.50, under 18 £5.75.

Eyam: (☎(01433) 630335, fax 639202), Hawkhill Rd. Walk down the main road from the square, pass the church, and look for the sign on your right. With turret and oaken door, this is more castle than hostel. Internet access. Open mid-July to mid-Sept. daily; mid-Sept. to Oct. and mid-Feb. to June M-Sa; Nov. F-Sa. Dorms £11, under 18 £7.75.

Hartington Hall: Hall Bank (☎(01298) 84223; fax 84415), Hartington. 122 beds in a 17th-century manor house with oak paneling. Bonnie Prince Charlie once slept here, *sans* YHA membership. Internet, laundry, restaurant, TV lounge, and playground. Dorms £13.75, under 18 £9.75.

Hathersage: Castleton Rd. (☎(01433) 650493). Stone building with white-framed windows and creeping ivy. Open Apr.-Oct. M-Sa. Dorms £10, under 18 £6.90.

Langsett: (☎(01226) 761548). 5 mi. from Penistone. Be grateful for Yorkshire Traction buses #23 and 24, which stop outside the hostel on their circular routes to and from Barnsley (M-Sa every hr., Su 15 per day). Self-catering. Open mid-July to Aug. daily; Sept. to mid-July F-Sa. Dorms £8.50, under 18 £5.75.

Matlock: 40 Bank Rd. (☎(01629) 582983; fax 583484). Matlock is a regional train and bus depot. Conveniently located hostel with rooms named after popular Peak District sights. Internet and laundry facilities. No lockout. Open Nov.-Jan. Tu-Sa; Feb.-Oct. daily. Dorms £11, under 18 £7.75.

Ravenstor: (☎(01298) 871826; fax 871275), ½ mi. from Millers Dale. Bus #65 (Buxton-Sheffield) and #66 (Buxton-Chesterfield) will stop at the YHA (both M-Sa 10 per day, Su 7 per day). The National Trust-owned house includes Internet access, bar, TV, and games room. Open mid-July to Aug. daily; Feb.-July and Sept.-Nov. F-Sa and school holidays. Dorms £11.25, under 18 £8.

Shining Cliff: (☎/fax (01629) 760827), Shining Cliff Woods, 2 mi. from Ambergate. A mile from the road in a pristine forest; call for directions or visit www.yha.org.uk. Trains and buses reach Ambergate. Self-catering. Bring food and a flashlight. Open mid-July to Aug., Easter holiday, and bank holidays only. Dorms £8.50, under 18 £5.75.

Youlgreave: Fountain Sq. (☎/fax (01629) 636518). Open Apr.-Oct. M-Sa; Nov. to mid-Dec. and Feb.-Mar. F-Sa. Dorms £11, under 18 £7.75.

CAMPING BARNS

The 13 YHA-operated **camping barns** are simple night shelters, providing a sleeping platform, water tap, and toilet (£3.60 per person). Bring a sleeping bag and the usual camping equipment. You must book and pay ahead with the **Camping Barns Reservation Office,** 6 King St., Clitheroe, Lancashire BB7 2EP (☎(01200) 420102; fax 420103; campbarnsyha@enterprise.net). You may pay over the phone with a credit card, or they'll hold your reservation for five days while you mail in a booking form; such forms are available in camping barn booklets, distributed free at National Park Information Centres. Camping barns can be found in: **Abney,** between Eyam and Castleton; **Alstonefield,** between Dovedale and Manifold Valley; **Birchover,** near Matlock off the B5056; **Butterton,** near the southern end of the park, along the Manifold track; **Edale; Losehill,** near Castleton; **Middleton-By-Youlgreave; Nab End,** in Hollinsclough; **One Ash Grange,** in Monyash; **Taddington,** on Main Rd.; **Underbank,** in Wildboarclough; and **Upper Booth,** near Eyam.

⬛ HIKING AND BIKING

The central park is marvelous territory for rambling. Settlement is sparser and buses fewer north of Edale in the land of the Kinder Scout plateau, the great Derwent reservoirs, and the gritty cliffs and peat moorlands. From Edale, the **Pennine Way** (see p. 373) runs north to Kirk Yetholm, across the Scottish border. Be advised that warm clothing and the customary supplies and precautions should be taken (see **Wilderness Safety,** p. 35). Also, the land is privately owned, so be respectful and stay on designated paths. Ramblers' guidebooks and the park's invaluable free newspaper, the *Peakland Post,* are available at National Park Information Centres. Contact the **Peak District National Park Office,** Aldern House, Barlow Rd., Bakewell, Derbyshire DE45 1AE (☎(01629) 816200; www.peakdistrictnpa.gov.uk), for information and a list of publications.

The park authority operates six **Cycle Hire Centres.** A free brochure, *Peak Cycle Hire,* available free at National Park Information Centres, includes phone numbers, opening hours, and locations. They can be found in **Ashbourne** (☎(01335) 343156), on Mapleton Ln.; **Derwent** (☎(01433) 651261), near the Fairholmes Information Centre; **Hayfield** (☎(01663) 746222), on Station Rd. in the Sett Valley; **Middleton Top** (☎(01629) 823204), at the visitor center; **Parsley Hay** (☎(01298) 84493), in Buxton; and **Waterhouses** (☎(01538) 308609), in the Old Station Car Park between Ashbourne and Leek on the A523, near the southern end of the Manifold Truck. (Most open Apr.-Sept. daily 9:30am-6pm; Oct.-Mar. call for hours. £7 per 3hr., £10 per day. Helmet included. £20 deposit; £100 deposit for tandem bike. 10% discount for YHA members, seniors, and Wayfarer ticket holders.)

NOT FROM NOTTINGHAM Robin Hood fans may have
thought that Kevin Costner's portrayal of the Prince of Thieves as some sort of American prospector was a unique travesty, but Kevin isn't the only one confused about the origin of Robin and his merry men. The bandits didn't come from Nottingham, as is often supposed, but from the Peak District, the more plebeian base from which they made sporadic and fruitful strikes on nearby Nottingham. "Little John" (the study of his remains has proved him a physical giant) is buried in Hathersage, where a corner pub is now emblazoned with his name. It was also in tiny Hathersage that Charlotte Brontë saw another formidable band of men: the twelve apostles eerily painted on a cupboard at the home of one of her acquaintances, Thomas Eyre. Charlotte's mind bore both cupboard and surname back to Haworth where she recreated them in *Jane Eyre.*

CASTLETON
☎01433

For such a small town, Castleton (pop. 705) lays claim to an unnatural amount of natural beauty—and, naturally, to the unnatural number of tourists that follow. The town's main attraction are caverns carved by Ice Age rivers once mined for lead and later for Blue John, a semi-precious mineral found only in these hills. Buses don't service the caverns on weekdays, but on weekends #260 makes a loop between Edale and Castleton, stopping at Blue John, Speedwell, and Treak Cliff Caverns (Sa-Su 8-9 per day). The cavern entrances are all within walking distance of one another. As you leave town on Cross St. (which becomes Buxton Rd.), formerly the A625, you'll pass a large sign on the left for Peak Cavern. Ten minutes later, road signs appear for the others.

Although it's not the first cavern on the road out of Castleton, ◙**Treak Cliff Cavern** is the one most worth visiting, with Blue John seams coursing through its ceilings and fantastical chambers of stalagmites and stalagtites. The mandatory tour is excellent. (☎620571. Tours 40min., every 15-30min. £5.50, seniors £5, students and YHA members £4.50, children £3.) Just outside Castleton, in the gorge beneath the castle ruins, **Peak Cavern** features the largest aperture in Britain. Decorously known in the 18th century as the "Devil's Arse," the cavern now features tours by guides pale and wry-humored from long days in Old Harry's Sphincter. (☎620285. Open Easter-Oct. daily 10am-5pm; Nov.-Easter Sa-Su 10am-5pm; last tour 4pm. 1hr. tours £5, students and seniors £4, children £3, families £14.) Be advised that all caverns are the temperature of an average refrigerator. Speedwell and Blue John, less interesting caves with inferior tours, involve very steep stair-climbs.

William Peveril, son of William the Conqueror, chose a visually arresting and defensively ideal setting in which to build **Peveril Castle.** Not much of the 11th- and 12th-century castle remains, but the ruins, including a hollowed keep, crown a dramatic peak overlooking the town. (☎620613. Open Apr.-Oct. daily 10am-6pm; Nov.-Mar. W-Su 10am-4pm. Last admission 30min. before close. £2.30, students and seniors £1.70, children £1.20.)

Castleton lies 2 mi. west of the **Hope** train station (don't ask for Castleton train station, or you'll end up in a suburb of Manchester), and **buses** arrive from Sheffield, Buxton, and Bakewell (see p. 353). Hikers looking for a challenge can set off southward from Castleton on the 26 mi. **Limestone Way Trail** to Matlock. Castleton's **National Park Information Centre** (see p. 354) stocks maps and brochures on local walks (most under £1). The nearest **bank** and **cash machine** lie 6 mi. east in **Hathersage.** Ramblers preparing to assault the moorlands should visit the **Peveril Outdoor Shop,** off the market place by the hostel. (☎620320. Open M-F 9:30am-5pm, Sa-Su 9:30am-6pm.) The **post office,** How Ln., near the bus stop, is in a convenience store. (☎620241. Open M-Tu and Th-F 7am-1pm and 2-5:30pm, W 7am-12:30pm, Sa 7:30am-12:30pm.) **Postal code:** S33 8WJ.

The super **YHA Castleton** and its torrential showers wait by the castle entrance (see p. 354). Those seeking B&B privacy can try ivy-walled **Cryer House,** Castle St., where Mr. and Mrs. Skelton keep two lovely rooms with TVs and a tea shop. (☎/ fax 620244; FleeSkel@aol.com. Doubles with bath £44.)

EDALE AND THE NORTHERN DARK PEAK AREA
☎01433

The deep dale of the River Noe cradles a collection of hamlets known as **Edale.** The area offers little in the way of civilization besides a church, rail stop, cafe, pub, school, and nearby youth hostel. Its environs, however, are among the most spectacular in northern England. The northern Dark Peak area is wild hill country, with vast moors like **Kinder Scout** and **Bleaklow** left undisturbed by motor traffic. In these mazes of black peat hags and groughs, paths are scarce and weather-worn. The rare town huddles in the crook of a valley, with provisions and shelter for weary hikers. Less experienced hikers should stick to Edale and southern paths.

On summer weekends Edale brims with hikers and campers preparing to tackle the **Pennine Way** (which passes out of the Peak District and into the Yorkshire Dales after a 3- to 4-day hike; see p. 373), or to trek one of the shorter (1½-8½ mi.) trails detailed in the National Park Authority's *8 Walks Around Edale* (£1.20). The relatively undemanding 3½ mi. path to **Castleton** begins 70 yd. down the road from the TIC toward the town and affords a breathtaking view of the Edale Valley (Dark Peak) and the Hope Valley (White Peak). A flagstone detour with still more spectacular views runs along the ridge between these valleys to **Mam Tor**, a decaying Iron Age hillside fort that receives over 250,000 annual visitors. The hill is known locally as the "shivering mountain" for its shale sides; one such shiver left the road below permanently blocked. Cliffs on three sides beckon fearless hanggliders from near and far.

Edale lies on the Hope Valley rail line between Manchester and Sheffield and is served by **trains** every one or two hours (from Manchester 45min.; Sheffield 35min.). Stop at the huge **National Park Information Centre** (see p. 354), near the train station, for weather forecasts and training with a map and compass. Unless you reserve centuries ahead, your tent could be your best friend in this town, as popular 139-bed **YHA Edale** is the only place to stay (see p. 354). Take a right 70 yd. up the road from the National Park Information Centre toward the town and follow the path to the hostel. Campers can try **Fieldhead**, behind the TIC. (☎670386. £3.40 per person, children £2.40, cars £1.20. Showers 50p.)

BAKEWELL   ☎01629

Fifteen miles southwest of Sheffield and 30 mi. southeast of Manchester, Bakewell makes the best spot from which to explore the region and to transfer along more elaborate bus routes. Located near several scenic walks through the White Peaks, the town itself is best known as the birthplace of Bakewell pudding. The pudding was created in the 1860s when a flustered cook at the Rutland Arms Hotel tried, in spite of his town's name, to make a tart by pouring an egg mixture over strawberry jam instead of mixing it into the dough. Some have suggested that Jane Austen stayed in the Rutland Arms and based the town in *Pride and Prejudice* on Bakewell. Bakewell's stone buildings are huddled around a handful of narrow streets and a central square bursting with flowers, wrapped by a lazy bend in the River Wye. Ducks scuttle beneath the five graceful arches of the **medieval bridge** (c. 1300). On the hill above town, **All Saints Church** lies in a crowded park of gravestones and carved cross fragments. In the south transept, three very curious human gargoyles guard the remains of Anglo-Saxon and Norman headstones. Nearby, a 16th-century timber-frame house encased in stone shelters the **Old House Museum**, which displays a modest collection of 19th-century toys, blacksmith equipment, and early 20th-century cameras. (☎813165. Open July-Aug. daily 11am-4pm; Apr.-June and Sept.-Oct. 1:30-4pm. £2.50, children £1, under 5 free.)

Buses arrive in Rutland Sq. from: **Sheffield** (#X18 and 240; 1hr.; M-Sa 13-14 per day, Su 10-12 per day); **Manchester** via **Buxton** (#TP; 1½hr., 6 per day, £2.90); **Matlock**, site of the nearest train station (#172, R61, TP; 40-50min., 1-3 per hr.). Bakewell has a **National Park Information Centre** that doubles as a **tourist information centre** (TIC), at the intersection of Bridge St. and Market St. (see p. 354). Other services include: an **HSBC bank**, Rutland Sq. (open M-F 9:30am-5pm); **camping supplies** at **Yeoman's**, 1 Royal Oak Pl., off Matlock St. (☎815371; open M-Sa 9am-5:30pm, Su 10am-5pm); **Bakewell Launderama**, Water St., off Rutland Sq. (open daily 7:30am-7pm, last wash 6pm); the **police**, Granby Rd. (☎812504); **Internet access** at **Bakewell Public Library**, Orme Court, above the swimming pool (☎812267; £1.50 per 30min.; open M-Tu 10am-5pm, W and F 10am-7pm, Th 10am-1pm, Sa 9:30am-4pm); and the **post office**, Unit 1 Granby Croft, in the **Spar** supermarket on Granby Rd. (☎815112; open M-F 8:30am-6pm, Sa 8:30am-3pm). **Postal code:** DE45 1ES.

The comfy **YHA Bakewell**, on Fly Hill, is a short walk from the TIC (see p. 354). **B&Bs** are plentiful considering the village's size, but expect to pay about £20 per person; *The Derbyshire Dales Accommodation Guide*, free at the TIC, lists

B&Bs in the area. Entire villages pour into Bakewell's **market,** held since 1330 off Bridge St. (Open M 9am-4pm; follow the doomed mooing of 3000 cows.) Cafes aim to cash in on Bakewell's confectionery reputation. **The Old Original Bakewell Pudding Shop,** Rutland Sq., sells sinful desserts under a vaulted ceiling. Skip lunch and order the £5 full afternoon tea, which includes sandwiches, two fruit scones with jam and cream, a Bakewell pudding, and tea. (☎812193. Open July-Aug. daily 8:30am-9pm; Sept.-June M-Th 9am-6pm, F-Sa 8:30am-9pm.) The **Extra Foodstore** is on the corner of Granby Rd. and Market St. (Open M-Sa 8am-10pm, Su 10am-4pm.) **The Australian,** Granby Rd., off Matlock St., draws a lively, grizzled crowd and serves Outback Bruce Burgers (£4.50), Billy Can Soup (£2.25), and other Aussie-themed meals. (☎814909. Open daily 11am-11pm.)

🔀 DAYTRIPS FROM BAKEWELL

🏛 CHATSWORTH HOUSE

Take bus #179 directly to the house (2 per day) or ask the TIC about other buses that stop close by. ☎(01246) 565300. 1½hr. audio tour £2.50. Open Apr.-Dec. daily 11am-5:30pm, last admission 4:30pm. £7, students and seniors £5.75, children £3, families £17.25. Gardens only £4, students and seniors £3, children £1.75, families £9.50.

Near Bakewell unfold the 100 breathtaking acres of Chatsworth House, home of the Duke and Duchess of Devonshire. The rolling grounds beg for a walk, with their cascade fountain—each step designed to make a different sound—hedge maze, and lagoon. The house's 26 ornate rooms are decorated with works of art; in one, late 17th-century paintings by Laguerre detail the life of Julius Caesar. Between 1570 and 1581, Mary stayed in the **Queen of Scots Rooms** during while under the custody of 6th Earl of Shrewsbury; they cost an extra £1.

HADDON HALL

From Bakewell, walk down Matlock St. as it becomes Haddon Rd. and then the A6 or take one of the buses that stops outside the gate (among them #171, 172, 179, and TP; ask the TIC for details). ☎812855. Open Apr.-Sept. daily 10:30am-5pm; Oct. M-Th 10:30am-5pm. £5.90, seniors £5, children £3, families £15.

Two miles southwest of Bakewell, the Duke of Rutland's Haddon Hall may be recognizable to visitors as the setting of several movies, including Franco Zefferelli's 1996 *Jane Eyre* and *The Princess Bride.* The house lends itself to cinematic romance because it has been so little altered since the reign of Henry VIII, preserving the wood-lined Long Gallery and frescoed chapel. Think about springing £2.50 for a guidebook, as the infrequent wall text tends to be unsatisfying.

EYAM

Take bus #175 from Bakewell, stand D (20min., 3-4 per day, £1.45) or #65/66 from Buxton (40min., M-Sa 11 per day, £2.15).

Just 5 mi. north of Bakewell, the hamlet of Eyam (Ee-yum) underwent a self-imposed quarantine when the plague spread here from London in 1665, during which a supposed 259 of its 350 residents died a bubonic death. Plaques on old houses tally the numbers that died in each, and makeshift graves lie in strangely vibrant gardens (victims were buried quickly to prevent the disease's spread). The first three victims perished in the flower-ringed **Plague Cottages,** Edgeview Rd. The tiny **Eyam Museum,** on Hawkhill Rd., commemorates all the grisly details, including touching final letters and heroic stories. (☎(01433) 631371. Open Apr.-Oct. Tu-Su 10am-4:30pm. £1.50, seniors and children £1, families £4.25.) **Eyam Hall,** on Edgeview Rd., 100 yd. west of the church, traces the owner's family history in a 17th-century manor house. The hall boasts a wall-to-wall tapestry room, an eight-line love stanza carved into the library window, and a 1675 pop-up human anatomy textbook. (☎(01433) 631976. Open June-Aug. Tu-Th and Su 11am-4pm. £4.25, students and seniors £3.75, children £3.25, families £13.50.) Eyam's **YHA Youth Hostel** plants its flag 800m above the town on Hawkhill Rd. (see p. 354).

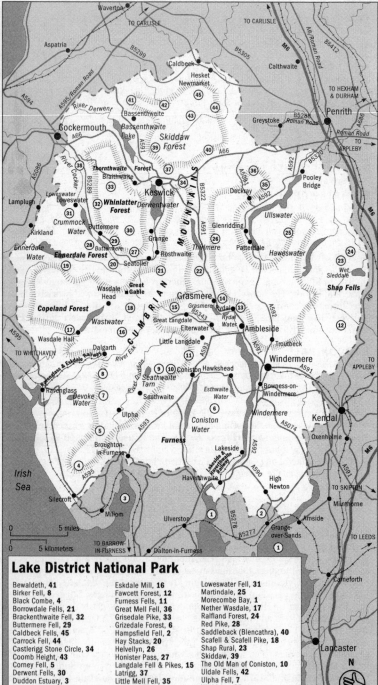

Lake District National Park

Bewaldeth, **41**
Birker Fell, **8**
Black Combe, **4**
Borrowdale Fells, **21**
Brackenthwaite Fell, **32**
Buttermere Fell, **29**
Caldbeck Fells, **45**
Carrock Fell, **44**
Castlerigg Stone Circle, **34**
Coomb Height, **43**
Corney Fell, **5**
Derwent Fells, **30**
Duddon Estuary, **3**
Ennerdale Fell, **19**

Eskdale Mill, **16**
Fawcett Forest, **12**
Furness Fells, **11**
Great Mell Fell, **36**
Grisedale Pike, **33**
Grizedale Forest, **6**
Hampsfield Fell, **2**
Hay Stacks, **20**
Helvellyn, **26**
Honister Pass, **27**
Langdale Fell & Pikes, **15**
Latrigg, **37**
Little Mell Fell, **35**
Lorton Vale, **38**

Loweswater Fell, **31**
Martindale, **25**
Morecombe Bay, **1**
Nether Wasdale, **17**
Ralfland Forest, **24**
Red Pike, **28**
Saddleback (Blencathra), **40**
Scafell & Scafell Pike, **18**
Shap Rural, **23**
Skiddaw, **39**
The Old Man of Coniston, **10**
Uldale Fells, **42**
Ulpha Fell, **7**
Wythburn, **22**

N

CUMBRIA

LAKE DISTRICT NATIONAL PARK

Quite possibly the most beautiful place in England, the Lake District was gouged by glaciers during the last ice age. Jagged peaks and windswept fells stand in desolate splendor, and water wends its way in every direction, from hillside torrents to gurgling peat-filled rivers. The shores are busy, but less packed than one would expect for a region where tourism employs 85% of the local population—and has since 1951, when the Lake District became England's largest National Park. Little development blights the landscape: on only one lake, Windermere, can visitors zoom around in noisy motorboats. Though in summer, hikers, bikers, and boaters almost equal sheep in number (and with four million sheep, that's quite a feat), there is always in this northwestern corner of the realm some lonely upland fell or quiet cove where your footprints seem the first for generations.

✈ GETTING THERE

Trains: The **Preston-Lancaster-Carlisle** line (connecting with **Leeds** at Lancaster) runs south to north along the eastern edge of the park, while the **Barrow-Carlisle** line serves the western coast. Hikes from stations along the Barrow-Carlisle line access the remote western or southern area. On the Preston-Carlisle line, **Oxenholme,** south of the Lake District, and **Penrith,** just west, are hubs served by most major bus routes. Trains (☎(08457) 484950) to **Oxenholme** from: **London Euston** (4-5hr.; M-Sa 16 per day, Su 11 per day; £59.60); **Manchester Piccadilly** (2hr.; M-F 6 per day, Sa 5 per day, Su 7 per day; £12.70); **Edinburgh** (2½-3hr., 6 per day, £30.80); **Birmingham** (2½hr., 1-2 per hr., £37.30). A short branch line covers the 10 mi. to **Windermere** from Oxenholme (20min., every hr., £3.50). There is also direct service to Windermere from **Manchester Piccadilly** (2½hr.; 3-4 per day; £12.50, return £12.60).

Buses: National Express (☎(08705) 808080) arrives in **Windermere** from **London** (7½hr.; 1 per day; £26, return £32) and **Birmingham** (4½hr.; 1 per day; £24.50, return £30). The buses continue north through **Ambleside** and **Grasmere** to **Keswick.** Call the Windermere tourist information centre (TIC) at (015394) 46499 for more info.

⌨ LOCAL TRANSPORTATION

Buses: Stagecoach Cumberland (☎(01946) 63222) serves over 25 towns and villages. The essential *Lakeland Explorer* magazine, free from TICs, presents up-to-date timetables, clear maps, and walking routes. **"Lakeslink"** bus #555 travels from **Kendal** to **Keswick,** stopping at **Windermere, Ambleside,** and **Grasmere** (M-Sa 11 per day, Su 5 per day; £2-4), and the open-top **"Lakeland Experience"** bus #599 passes between **Bowness** and **Grasmere** (30min.; M-Sa 11 per day, Su 5 per day; £3.25). Also consult *Getting Around Cumbria and the Lake District* (free from TICs). An **Explorer** ticket offers unlimited travel on all area Stagecoach buses. The 4-day pass usually saves travelers money over 2- or 3-day stays. 1-day £6.50, seniors and children £4.50, families £13; 4-day £15, seniors and children £11.

YHA Minibus: The YHA hostel at **Ambleside** provides a minibus service (☎(015394) 32304) between hostels in **Windermere, Ambleside, Hawkshead, Coniston Holly How, Elterwater, Langdale,** and **Grasmere** (2 per day, £2.50; schedules available at hostels). You can send your pack with the bus and enjoy the inter-hostel walk. Trips from the Windermere train station to Windermere and Ambleside hostels are free.

Tours: For those who wish to explore the park with minimal effort, **Mountain Goat** (☎(015394) 45161), downhill from the TIC in Windermere, does the climbing for you in a series of off-the-beaten-track, themed bus tours (£9-26). **Lakes Supertours,** 1 High

St. (☎(015394) 42751), across the road from Mountain Goat in the Lakes Hotel, runs similar half- and full-day tours, with witty local drivers (£15-16.50 per half-day; £24 per day). Free pickup in the Bowness-Ambleside area. Call daily 8am-9pm. The **Lakeside and Haverthwaite Railway** (☎(015395) 31594) runs a sightseeing trip by steam train.

✦ℹ️ ORIENTATION AND PRACTICAL INFORMATION

The major lakes diverge like spokes of a wheel from Wordsworth's village of Grasmere, south of Keswick and north of Ambleside on the A591. Derwentwater is one of the most beautiful lakes, Wastwater the most bewitchingly wild, and Windermere the largest, though bludgeoned by condos and marinas. The towns of Windermere, Ambleside, Grasmere, and Keswick make good touring bases, but the farther west you go from the A591, the more countryside you'll have to yourself.

The following **National Park Information Centres** dispense free information and town maps on the camping-barn network, secure fishing licenses, book accommodations (10% deposit for local bookings; non-local bookings an additional £3 fee), and often exchange currency. *Lake District Holidays 2002* lists accommodations, sights, and entertainment (free).

National Park Visitor Centre: (☎(015394) 46601). In Brockhole, halfway between Windermere and Ambleside. Most buses stop at the site. An introduction to the Lake District with exhibits, talks, films, and special events in this recently renovated house. Open Easter-Oct. daily 10am-5pm, plus most weekends in winter.

Ambleside Waterhead: (☎(015394) 32729; fax 31728). Walk south on Lake Rd. or Borrans Rd. from town to the pier. Open Easter-Oct. daily 9:30am-5:30pm.

Bowness Bay: Glebe Rd. (☎(015394) 42895). Bureau de change. Open July-Aug. daily 9:30am-6pm; Apr.-June and Sept.-Oct. 9am-5:30pm; Nov.-Mar. F-Su 10am-4pm.

Coniston: Ruskin Ave. (☎(015394) 41533; fax 41802), behind the Tilberthwaite Ave. bus stop. Bureau de change. Open Easter-Oct. daily 9:30am-5:30pm; Nov.-Easter Sa-Su 10am-3:30pm.

Grasmere: Redbank Rd. (☎(015394) 35245; fax 35057). Bureau de change. Open Easter-Oct. daily 9:30am-5:30pm; Nov.-Easter Sa-Su 10am-4pm.

Hawkshead: Main Car Park (☎(015394) 36525; fax 36349). Bureau de change. Open July-Aug. daily 9:30am-6pm; Easter-June and Sept.-Oct. 9:30am-5:30pm; Nov.-Easter Sa-Su 10am-3:30pm.

Keswick: Moot Hall, Market Sq. (☎(017687) 72645). Bureau de change. Open Aug. daily 9:30am-6pm; Sept.-July 9:30am-5:30pm.

Pooley Bridge: The Square (☎(017684) 86530). Bureau de change. Open Easter-Oct. daily 10am-1pm and 1:30-5pm.

Seatoller Barn: Borrowdale (☎(017687) 77294), at the foot of Honister Pass. Open Easter-Oct. daily 10am-5pm.

Ullswater: Main Car Park, Glenridding, Penrith (☎(017684) 82414), on the main road through town. Open Apr.-Oct. daily 9am-6pm; Nov.-Mar. Sa-Su 9:30am-4pm.

🏠 ACCOMMODATIONS

Though **B&Bs** line every street in every town (£17-25) and the Lakes have the highest concentration of hostels in the world, lodgings in the Lake District fill in July and August; reserve well in advance for weekend stays. TICs and National Park Centres book rooms for a 10% deposit. **Campers** should pick up the YHA's *Camping Barns in England* (free) and call or write ahead to reserve space at the Lake District's 12 **camping barns.** (Lakeland Barns Booking Office, Moot Hall, Market Sq., Keswick CA12 4JR. ☎(017687) 72645; fax 75043. Prices start at £3.50.) Twenty-six **YHA Youth Hostels** provide accommodations in the park, but many differ radically in facilities and style. Reception is usually closed 10am-5pm, though public areas and restrooms are accessible throughout the day. The YHA **minibus** travels between the bigger hostels (see **Local Transportation,** p. 361). The Ambleside hostel provides a free Lake District-wide booking service. (☎(015394) 31117. Open daily 9am-6pm; credit card required to reserve a bed.) The following is a selection of park hostels; see the YHA handbook for others.

▨ Ambleside: Waterhead, Ambleside (☎(015394) 32304; fax 34408; ambleside@yha.org.uk), 1 mi. south of Ambleside on Windermere Rd. (the A591), 3 mi. north of Windermere on the Lake's northern shores. Bus #555 stops in front of this mother of all hostels. 245 beds in a superbly refurbished old hotel. Distinctive country-club feel—you can even swim off the pier. Books tours, rents mountain bikes, exchanges currency, and operates the YHA shuttle. Internet access £2.50 per 30min. Mar.-Oct. no curfew; Nov.-Feb. midnight. Dorms £13.50, under 18 £9.50.

Black Sail: Black Sail Hut, Ennerdale, Cleator (☎(0411) 108450). Splendidly set in the hills. Take CMS bus #79 from Keswick to Seatoller and walk 3½ mi. from there. Alternatively, walk up the forest track in the Ennerdake valley or take the mountain walk over Black Sail Pass from Wastwater. 18 beds. Chilly outdoor showers. No heat or electricity in the bedrooms. Open July-Aug. daily; Apr.-June and Sept.-Oct. Tu-Sa. Dorms £9.25, under 18 £6.50.

Buttermere: King George VI Memorial Hostel, Buttermere (☎(017687) 70245; fax 70231), ¼ mi. south of the village on the B5289. A tranquil setting with lounges, dining room, and kitchen. 70 beds. Lockout 10am-1pm. Open Apr.-Aug. daily; Sept.-Dec. Tu-Sa; Jan.-Feb. F-Sa; Feb.-Mar. Tu-Sa. Dorms £11, under 18 £7.75.

Cockermouth: Double Mills, Cockermouth (☎/fax (01900) 822561), in the town center off Fern Bank at Parkside Ave. Converted 17th-century water mill. 28 beds. Open Apr.-Oct. daily. Dorms £8.50, under 18 £5.75.

Coniston (Holly How): Far End (☎(015394) 41323; fax 41803; conistonhh@yha.org.uk), just north of Coniston village at the junction of Hawkshead Rd. and Ambleside Rd. Modernized country house a good base for walking and watersports. 60 beds. Curfew 11pm. Open Apr. and July-Sept. daily; May-June and Oct.-Nov. and mid-Jan. to Mar. F-Su. Dorms £10, under 18 £6.90.

Coniston Coppermines: Coppermines House (☎/fax (015394) 41261), northwest along the Churchbeck River, 1¼ mi. from Coniston. No need to venture into the hills; the rugged journey to the hostel is itself a scenic challenge. Basic 28-bed hostel in the mine manager's house, overlooking the water. Open June-Aug. daily; Apr.-May and Sept.-Oct. Tu-Sa. Dorms £9.25, under 18 £6.50.

▨ Derwentwater: Barrow House, Borrowdale (☎(017687) 77246; fax 77396), 2 mi. south of Keswick on the B5289. Take bus #79 to Seatoller, or take the Keswick-bound ferry. It's worth the inconvenience to stay in this 90-bed, 200-year-old house with its own waterfall. Open Jan. to early Dec. daily. Dorms £11, under 18 £7.75.

Eskdale: (☎(019467) 23219; fax 23163). In a quiet valley 1½ mi. east of Boot on the Ravenglass-Eskdale railway, adjacent to Hardknot Pass. 50 beds. Laundry, kitchen, showers. Open Mar.-Oct. daily. Dorms £10, under 18 £6.90.

Grasmere: (☎(015394) 35316; fax 35798; grasmerebh@yha.org.uk). 2 buildings. **Butterlip How,** Easedale Rd. Follow road to Easedale 150 yd. and turn right down sign-posted drive. 80-bed Victorian house north of Grasmere village. Open Apr.-Oct. daily; Nov.-Jan. F-Sa; Feb.-Mar Tu-Sa. Dorms £12.50, under 18 £8.50. **Thorney How.** Follow Easedale Rd. ½ mi. and turn right at the fork; hostel is ¼ mi. down on the left. 48-bed farmhouse with a kindly staff. No lockout. Open Apr.-Sept. daily; mid-Feb. to Mar. and Oct.-Dec. Th-M. Dorms £10, under 18 £6.90.

Hawkshead: Esthwaite Lodge (☎(015394) 36293; fax 36720; hawkshead@yha.org.uk), 1 mi. south of Hawkshead village. Bus #505 from Ambleside stops at the village center. Follow Newby Bridge Road to this Regency mansion overlooking Esthwaite Water. Caters to families. 115 beds. Lockout 10am-noon. Open Apr.-Oct. daily; Nov. to mid-Dec. F-Sa; mid-Feb. to Mar. Tu-Sa. Dorms £11, under 18 £7.75.

Honister Hause: (☎/fax (017687) 77267), near Seatoller. A gray building at the summit of imposing **Honister Pass,** 9 mi. south of Keswick. May-Oct. bus #77 takes you there from Keswick; #79 stops within 1½ mi. Continue along Honister Pass and follow the signs. 26 beds. Open Apr.-Aug. daily. Dorms £9.25, under 18 £6.50.

Keswick: Station Rd. (☎(017687) 72484; fax 74129; keswick@yha.org.uk). From the TIC, bear left down Station Rd.; look for the YHA sign on the left. 91 beds in a former hotel with balconies over a river, clean rooms, and a decent kitchen. 6 showers, laundry facilities, TV, and game room. Lockout 10am-1pm. Curfew 11pm. Open daily year-round. Dorms £11, under 18 £7.75.

Wastwater: Wasdale Hall, Wasdale (☎(019467) 26222; fax 26056), ½ mi. east of Nether Wasdale. A 50-bed half-timbered house on the water. Climber's paradise. Bus #6 from Whitehaven to Seascale stops 5 mi. away in the Viking village of Gosforth; follow the signs for Nether Wasdale and then Wastwater YHA. Alternatively, take the postbus from Seascale to Wasdale Head, which passes the hostel. Open Apr.-Oct. daily; Nov.-Dec. F-Sa; Jan.-Mar. Th-M. Dorms £10, under 18 £6.90.

Windermere: High Cross, Bridge Ln., Troutbeck (☎(015394) 43543; fax 47165; windermere@yha.org.uk), 1 mi. north of Windermere off the A591. Ambleside bus stops in Troutbeck Bridge; walk ¾ mi. uphill to the hostel, or catch the YHA shuttle from the train station. Spacious, 73-bed house with panoramic views. Mountain bikes for rent. Internet access £6 per hr. Open mid-Feb. to Oct. daily. Dorms £11, under 18 £7.75.

⚡ HIKING, BIKING, AND CLIMBING

Outdoor enthusiasts outnumber water molecules in the Lake District. Park information centres have guidebooks for all occasions—mountain-bike trails, pleasant family walks, tough climbs, and hikes ending at pubs. Among the many available pamphlets is *Countryside Access for People with Limited Mobility* (75p). Hostels are also an excellent source of information, with large maps and posters on the walls and free advice from experienced staff.

If you plan to go on a long or difficult outing, check first with the Park Service, call **weather information** (24hr. ☎(017687) 75757; YHAs also post daily forecasts), and leave a route plan with your B&B proprietor or hostel warden before setting out. Steep slopes and reliably unreliable weather can quickly reduce visibility to 5 ft. A good map, compass, and the ability to use them are necessities. The 1:25,000 Ordnance Survey Outdoor Leisure Maps #4-7 detail the four quadrants of the Lake District (£6.50), while the 1:50,000 Ordnance Survey Landranger Maps #89-91 and 96-98 chart every hillock and bend in the road (£5.25). A public right-of-way does not always mean a path, and vice versa.

Any **cyclist** planning an extensive stay in the Lake District should consider investing in the *Ordnance Survey Cycle Tours* (£10), which provides detailed maps of on- and off-trail routes. The circular **Cumbria Cycle Way** tours some of Cumbria's less-traveled areas via a 259 mi. route from Carlisle in the north and around the park's outskirts. Pick up *The Cumbria Cycle Way* (£6) from a TIC for details.

WINDERMERE AND BOWNESS ☎015394

Windermere and its sidekick, Bowness-on-Windermere (combined pop. 10,000), fill to the gills with vacationers in July and August when sailboats and water-skiers swarm the lake. Both towns are popular with families, as much for their year-round celebration of Peter Rabbit as for their gang of belligerent swans.

📱 TRANSPORTATION AND PRACTICAL INFORMATION. Flanking the lake, Bowness is an easy 1½ mi. walk south of Windermere, which is by the train station. From the station, turn left onto High St., then right on Main St.; walk through downtown to New Rd., which becomes Lake Rd., leading pierward. Windermere's **train station** is also the town's primary **bus depot. Lakeland Experience** bus #599 runs to Bowness (3 per hr., £1). For information on getting to Windermere, see **Getting There,** p. 361. Call **Windermere Taxis** (☎42355) for a cab, and rent new bikes from **Country Lanes Cycle Hire,** at the train station. (☎(015394) 44544. £9 per half-day, £14 per day; £2 discount with train ticket. Open Easter-Oct. daily 9am-5:30pm.)

The Windermere **tourist information centre** (TIC), next to the train station, stocks guides to lake walks (30p), books **National Express** tickets, sells **Stageland Explorer** passes, books accommodations (10% deposit for local lodgings, £3 fee for beds outside Cumbria), and exchanges currency for a £2.50 commission. (☎46499. Open July-Aug. daily 9am-7:30pm; Easter-June and Sept.-Oct. 9am-6pm; Nov.-Easter 9am-5pm.) The **Bowness Bay National Park Information Centre** provides similar services and has a display on the Lake District's topology (see p. 362). Other services include: **banks** in both towns—stock up before heading out; **NatWest,** across from the TIC in Windermere (open M-Tu and Th-F 9am-4:30pm, W 9:30am-4:30pm); **luggage storage** at **Darryl's Cafe,** 14 Church St. (☎42894; £1 per bag; open W-M 8am-7pm); a **launderette** on Main Rd. (wash £2, dry 20p per 4min.; open M-F 9am-6pm, Sa 9am-5pm); the **police,** Lake Rd. (☎(01539) 722611); **Internet access** at **Triarom,** Birch St., near the post office (☎44639; £1 per 10min., £5 per hr.; open M-Sa 9:30am-5:30pm); and the **post office,** 21 Crescent Rd. (☎43245; open M-F 9am-5:30pm, Sa 9am-12:30pm). **Postal code:** LA23 1AA.

▐▐ ACCOMMODATIONS AND FOOD. Windermere and Bowness have more **B&Bs** than the hills have sheep. Nevertheless, those who neglect to book ahead risk sleeping in cold, lonely fields amid cowpats and wool tufts. Windermere's YHA Youth Hostel is 1 mi. north of town; see p. 364. To reach the social **Lake District Backpackers Hostel,** on High St., exit the train station and turn left on High St.; look for the sign on the right as you descend the hill. The friendly hostel has a great common room and lively atmosphere. (☎46374. Reception 9am-1pm and 5-9pm. Dorms £11-13.) **Brendan Chase,** 1-3 College Rd., has beautifully furnished rooms in two Edwardian townhouses. (☎45638. £12.50-25 per person.) Other fine B&Bs include the elegant **Village House,** 5 Victoria St. (☎46041; £12-19 per person); the centrally-located **Haven,** 10 Birch St. (☎44017; £19-21 per person); and the homey, family-run **Greenriggs,** 8 Upper Oak St. (☎42265; singles £14-25; doubles £36-50). The nearest campground, **Limefitt Park,** 4½ mi. north of Bowness on the A592 just below the Kirkstone path, has most amenities, except for public transport. Only couples may stay at the campground, with or without children, though exceptions are sometimes made. (☎32300. 2-person tent and car £12.)

All groceries great and small pepper the area. **Booths Supermarket** is housed in Windermere's Old Station at the end of Cross St. (☎46114. Open M-F 8:30am-8pm, Sa 8:30am-7pm, Su 10am-4pm.) The selection at **Booker's,** on Lake Rd. in Bowness is fit for a Bacchanalian revel—bountiful fresh fruit and loads of liquor. (☎88798. Open daily 8am-10pm.) In Windermere, vegetarians are catered to in the bright blue and yellow **Wild Oats** cafe on Main Rd. Sandwiches with salad are £2, main courses such as chicken curry only £4.50, and breakfast is served all day. (☎43583. Open daily 10am-9pm.)

◙ SIGHTS. A number of boating companies are located at Bowness Pier. **Windermere Lake Cruises** runs its own **Lake Information Centre** (☎43360; fax 43468) at the north end of the pier that vends maps and accommodation guides and rents rowboats or motorboats. The center also books passage on popular lake cruises. From Easter to October, boats sail north to Waterhead Pier in Ambleside (30min.; about 2 per hr. 9am-6pm; return £6, children £3) and south to Lakeside (40min., every hr. 9am-5pm; return £6.20, children £3.60). "Freedom of the Lake" all-day passes are also available (£10.50, children £5.25, families £26.80). In town, **The World of Beatrix Potter,** in the Old Laundry Theatre complex, Crag Bow, induces nausea with overly cute displays. Unless you're five, feel as if you're five, or are inextricably bound to a five-year-old, explore other sights. (☎88444. Open Easter-Sept. daily 10am-5:30pm; Oct.-Easter 10am-4:30pm. £3.50, children £2.) If bunnies aren't your thing, spend a couple of hours trekking to **Orrest Head,** a popular walk. Two and a half miles long, the ramble affords one of the best views in the Lake District; it begins opposite the TIC on the other side of the A591 (follow the signs). A guide to the walk is available at the TIC (30p).

BEFORE THERE WERE POWERBARS About the only thing more common in Lakeland than lakes is the hiking essential locals call mint cake. The marbly white snack assumes myriad forms, but the original recipe dates back to 1913 when James Wilson of Kendal boiled sugar, peppermint oil, and a touch of salt in an open copper pan to create the most saccharine of power foods. Since then, Kendal Mint Cakes have accompanied English expeditioners to the top of Mount Everest and deep into the Sahara Desert. At 95 grams of sugar per serving, you'd better save room for a toothbrush.

AMBLESIDE
☎ 015394

Just under a mile north of the tip of Windermere lake, Ambleside (pop. 9000) has adapted to the tourist influx without selling its soul to the industry. Oft-times dubbed "anorak capital of England" for its numerous outdoors stores (14 at last count), Ambleside focuses on enjoying the Lake District rather than on milking tourists' last pound for a rustic hat.

🖪🛂 TRANSPORTATION AND PRACTICAL INFORMATION. For information on getting to Ambleside, see **Local Transportation**, p. 361. **Buses** stop on Kelsick Rd. (☎32231. Open M-W and F-Sa 10am-6pm.) **Lakeslink** bus #555 runs from **Grasmere, Windermere,** and **Keswick** (every hr., £2-6.50). Buses #505 and 506 join the town to **Hawkshead** and **Coniston** (M-Sa 10 per day, Su 3 per day; £2.55). Rent bikes from **Ghyllside Cycles,** The Slack. (☎(015394) 33592. £12.50 per day, £50 per week. ID deposit. Discounts for rentals longer than 3 days. Open Apr.-Oct. daily 9am-5:30pm; Nov.-Apr. closed Tu.)

The **tourist information centre** (TIC) is in the Central Building on Market Cross. It offers identical services to the TIC in Windermere (see p. 364), including a **bureau de change**. Book accommodations online at www.amblesideonline.co.uk. (☎31576. Open daily 9am-5:30pm.) The **National Park Information Centre** at Waterhead also exchanges currency. (£3 per transaction. Open Easter-Oct. daily 9:30am-5:30pm.) Other services include: **Barclays bank,** on Market Pl. (open M-W and F 9:30am-4:30pm, Th 10am-4:30pm); the **launderette,** across from the bus station on Kelsick Rd. (open M-F 10am-7pm, Sa 10am-6pm); and the **post office,** Market Pl. (☎32267; open M-F 9am-5:30pm, Sa 9am-12:30pm). **Postal code:** LA22 9BU.

🖪🔾 ACCOMMODATIONS AND FOOD. There are almost as many **B&Bs** and guest houses here as private residences. Most B&Bs cost £18-20 and fill up quickly in summer. Some cluster on Church St. and Compston Rd.; others line the busier Lake Rd. leading in from Windermere. Ambleside's ◼**YHA Youth Hostel** resides near the steamer pier at Waterhead, a pleasant one-mile walk from the town center (see p. 362). **Shirland, Linda's B&B,** on Compston Rd., has four rooms with TV, cramped attic space for three, and a private, hostel-style bunkhouse. (☎32999. No singles. £14-15 per person, without breakfast £10.) Hospitable Mr. and Mrs. Richardson run **3 Cambridge Villas,** on Church St. next to the TIC, and are famous for their vegetarian breakfasts. (☎32307. £16 per person, with bath £20.) Across the street, the Irelands have hotel-style lodgings at **Melrose Hotel,** Church St. (☎32500. £15-25 per person.) **Camp** at **Hawkshead Hall Farm,** 5 mi. south of Ambleside off the B5286. (☎36221. Open Mar.-Nov. £1 per person, £1 per tent, £1 per car.)

Ambleside specializes in trail food, from the omnipresent **mint cakes** (see **Before There Were Powerbars,** p. 366) to gourmet sandwiches. Assemble your own picnic at the Wednesday **market** on King St. or at the **Co-op Village Store,** Compston Rd. (☎33124. Open M-Sa 8:30am-6pm, Su 10am-4pm.) The **Golden Rule** (☎32257), on Smithy Brow, taps good local beer; try the Coniston Brew (£2).

🖪🔾 SIGHTS AND HIKING. Ambleside's only noteworthy sight is the tiny **House on the Bridge,** off Rydal Rd.; actually, house and bridge are one and the same. About four paces long and one pace wide, it was once inhabited by a basket weaver, his wife, and six children. It now houses one lone representative of the National Trust, and even he looks cramped. (☎32617. Open Apr.-Oct. daily 10am-5pm. Free.) If you're feeling homesick for the city, head for the **Homes of Football Photographic Gallery,** 100 Lake Rd., where a great many panoramic photos of urban soccer shrines grace the walls. (☎34440. Open daily 10am-6pm. Free.) You can view the surrounding landscape most vividly from the middle of the lake; rent a rowboat at the Waterhead pier, and float by the splendor of **Horseshoe Falls.** (Boat rental £3 per hr., each additional person £1.50.)

Great **hikes** extend in all directions from Ambleside. Hidden trail markings, steep slopes, and weather-sensitive visibility all make a good map and compass necessary. The mountain rescue service averages two to three crises a day in this area; don't let yourself be one. For an introduction to the area, try one of the excellent warden-guided **walks** which leave from Ambleside and Grasmere's National Park Information Centres and TICs. Bring a sweater, rain gear, sturdy walking shoes or boots, lunch, and water to fuel you for the four- to six-hour rambles of varying degrees of difficulty. From the oft-trodden top of **Loughrigg,** there are views of higher surrounding fells—it's only a 2½ mi. hike from Ambleside, with a 3½ mi. circuit descent (trail map at TIC 30p). For gentler, shorter hikes, *Ambleside Walks in the Countryside* (30p) lists three easy walks from the town center.

CONISTON   ☎015394

Less touristed than its nearby counterparts, Coniston retains the rustic feel of the region's past; its fells to the north and lake to the south make it popular with hikers and cyclists. On rainy days, the town is known for the former residency of writer-artist-philosopher-critic-social-reformer John Ruskin. At the **John Ruskin Museum,** on Yewdale Rd., admire the sketches, photographs, and geological hammers of said writer-etc.-etc. (☎41164. Open Easter-Nov. daily 10am-5:30pm. £3, children £1.75, families £8.50.) Ruskin's **gravestone** is in St. Andrew's Churchyard. **Brantwood,** Ruskin's manor from 1872, looks across the lake at Coniston and the Old Man; it holds Ruskin's art, as well as prose works by Tolstoy, Proust, and Gandhi. (☎41396. Open mid-Mar. to mid-Nov. daily 11am-5:30pm; mid-Nov. to mid-Mar. W-Su 11am-4pm. £4, students £2.10, under 18 £1. Gardens only £2.) The easiest way to reach Brantwood is by water: the **Coniston Launch** travels to and from Brantwood. (☎36216. Apr.-Oct. 6-8 per day. Return £3.60. Combined £6.90 ticket for ferry and admission, students £5.70, children £2.70, families £18.50.) In the hamlet of Hawkshead, 4 mi. east of Coniston, imagine pulling Wordsworth's hair and passing him notes at the **Hawkshead Grammar School,** on Main St., where the poet studied from 1779 to 1787. (Open Easter-Oct. M-Sa 10am-12:30pm and 1:30-5pm, Su 1-5pm. £2, children 50p.)

Around the turn of the century, a thriving copper mining industry sprang up in the hills surrounding Coniston. The mines have since been abandoned, but hikers of moderate skill level still explore the **Coppermines** area in search of the "American's stope"—an old copper mine shaft named in honor of an American who leapt over it twice successfully and survived a 160 ft. fall the third time (*Let's Go* does not recommend 160 ft. falls). More ambitious hikers tackle the steep **Old Man** (5 mi. round-trip), or the less lofty but equally vertical **Yewdale Fells.** Both trails terminate at the top of nearby bluffs and offer incredible views of the surrounding lakes and countryside. Cyclists roll down the 40 mi. of forest tracks criss-crossing through **Grizedale Forest,** an ecosystem-cum-art-gallery dotted with hundreds of sculptures by local artists. For serious mountaineering, **Dow Crag** is a vaulting rock formation begging to be tamed. Be sure to gather the proper equipment and inform the TIC of your plans.

> # A LITTLE LAKE DISTRICT... If you stay in the Lake District
> for a few days, you're bound to hear this trivia question from locals: How many lakes
> are there in the Lake District? (Hint: there's a map on p. 360)

> **...HUMOR** Answer: Only one, Bassenthwaite Lake. The rest are known only by name, or are followed by "Water." No one ever said the locals were funny.

Coniston is accessible by **bus** #505 or 506 (the "Coniston Rambler"), which begins in Kendal and turns, twists, stops, and starts between Windermere, Bowness Pier, Ambleside, and sometimes Hawkshead on its way to Coniston and the lake (from Ambleside 45min.; M-Sa 10 per day, Su 3-6 per day; £2-6.50). Buses stop at the corner of Tilberthwaite and Ruskin Ave. Coniston's **tourist information centre,** on Ruskin Ave., poses as a **National Park Information Centre.** (☎41533. Open Easter-Oct. daily 9:30am-5:30pm; Nov.-Easter Sa-Su 10am-3:30pm.) Other services include: bike rental from **Summitreks,** 14 Yewdale Rd. (☎41212. £9 per half-day, £13 per day); a **Barclays bank** bereft of cash machines, Bridge End (☎41249; open M-F 9:30am-3:30pm); and the **post office,** Yewdale Rd. (☎41259; open M-F 9am-12:30pm and 1:30-5:30pm, W closes at 5pm, Sa 9am-noon). **Postal code:** LA21 8DU.

Accommodations are available at **YHA Holly How** (see p. 363) or the rugged **YHA Coppermines** (see p. 363). Hikers and climbers will find their ideal hosts in the ice-, rock-, and mineshaft-climbing proprietors of **Holmthwaite,** on Tilberthwaite Ave. Large rooms and lots of advice make for excellent resting and hiking. (☎41231. £19 per person; discounts for stays over 3 nights.) For **groceries,** head to the **Coop** on Yewdale St. (☎41247. Open M-Sa 9am-9pm, Su 10am-8pm.)

GRASMERE ☎015394

With a lake and a poet all to itself, the attractive village of Grasmere has its share of camera-clicking tourists. The sightseers crowd in at midday to visit the Wordsworth home, grave, and museum, but in the quiet mornings and evenings the peace that the poet so enjoyed graciously returns. The early 17th-century ▧**Dove Cottage,** where Wordsworth lived with his wife and his sister Dorothy from 1799 to 1808, is almost exactly as Wordsworth left it. A multitude of guides provide 20min. tours. Next door, the outstanding **Wordsworth Museum** includes pages of his handwritten poetry and info on his Romantic contemporaries. The cottage is 10min. from the center of Grasmere. Bus #555 stops here hourly en route to Ambleside or Keswick, and open-top bus #599 (£2.50-6.50) stops every 20min. (☎35544. Open mid-Feb. to mid-Jan. daily 9:30am-5pm. Cottage and museum £5, students and YHA members £4.20, seniors £4.70, children £2.50. Museum alone £2.50, children £1.25.) A 40min. hike, starting at Dove Cottage, up the **Old Coffin Trail** toward Ambleside (or one bus stop nearer to Ambleside on bus #555) leads to ▧**Rydal Mount,** the poet's home from 1813 until his death in 1850. The small hut in which the poet frequently composed verses lies across the garden terrace, designed by Wordsworth himself. (☎33002. Open Mar.-Oct. daily 9:30am-5pm; Nov.-Feb. W-M 10am-4pm. £3.75, students and seniors £3.25, children £1.75.) Down Grasmere's Redbank Rd., hydrophiles can hire rowboats for the deep green lake. (Open summer daily 10am-5pm. £2-4 per person depending on size of group; £10 deposit.) Hydrophiles of a different sort can purchase a pot of tea (80p) at the same port and direct a Romantic gaze across the water at the fells.

As Wordsworth well knew, Grasmere is a good base for walkers. A steep two-hour scramble (up Easedale Rd. until it ends, then follow the signs) leads to the top of **Helm Cragg,** dubbed by locals "the lion and the lamb." Can you find that magic angle? Hint: the lion is lying beside the lamb. Walk to the other side and it's supposed to look like a woman playing an organ. The six-mile **Wordsworth Walk** circumnavigates the two lakes of the Rothay River, passing the poet's grave, Dove Cottage, and Rydal Mount. Star-seeking fell-climbers tackle the path from Rydal to Legburthwaite (near Keswick) in an athletic day, passing the towering Great Rigg and Helvellyn on the way. Bus #555 returns ramblers to Ambleside (£2).

The combined **tourist information centre** and **National Park Information Centre** is in town on Redbank Rd. The staff of experienced hikers frequently hosts free guided walks on summer Sundays; details are in the *Events 2002* magazine. It also **exchanges currency** for £3 per transaction. (☎35245; fax 35057. Open Easter-Oct. daily 9:30am-5:30pm; Nov.-Easter Sa-Su 12:30-5:30pm.)

There are two **Grasmere YHA Youth Hostel** buildings within an eight-minute walk: **Butterlip How** and **Thorney How** (see p. 363). All B&Bs in town cost at least £17 and fill up quickly, so hope that the **Glenthorne Quaker Guest House**, ¼ mi. up Easedale Rd. and past the Butterlip How hostel, has a place for thee. Most rooms are clean, spacious singles. (☎35389. Optional 15min. Quaker meeting each morning. B&B £21, full board £39.50.) **Newby's Deli**, Red Lion Sq., packs superb sandwiches from £1.25. (☎35248. Open M-Sa 9am-5:30pm.) Sarah Nelson's famous Grasmere Gingerbread, a staple since 1854, is a bargain at 22p in **Church Cottage**, outside St. Oswald's Church. (☎35428. Open Easter-Nov. M-Sa 9:15am-5:30pm, Su 12:30-5:30pm; Nov.-Easter M-Sa 9:15am-5pm, Su 12:30-5:30pm.)

KESWICK
☎017687

Sandwiched between towering Skiddaw peak and the northern edge of Derwentwater, Keswick (KEZ-ick) rivals Windermere as the Lake District's tourist capital. However, with a ban on motorboating on its beautiful lake, Keswick surpasses its competitors in tranquil charm.

▼ PRACTICAL INFORMATION. For information on how to get to Keswick, see **Local Transportation**, p. 361. The **National Park Information Centre**, Moot Hall, behind the clock tower in Market Sq., sells a lodgings booklet (£1), hands out free town maps, and books B&Bs for a 10% deposit. They also **exchange currency** for £3. (☎72645. Open Aug. daily 9:30am-6pm; Sept.-July 9:30am-5:30pm.) A variety of **guided walks** leave from the park information centre, including the popular "Keswick Ramble" that leaves daily at 10:15am and lasts about seven hr. (Bring lunch and rain gear. £5, children £2.) Serious climbers should inquire about taking special trips. Book a tour of the area at the **Mountain Goat Office**, in the car park. (☎73962. Open Apr.-Oct. M-F 9am-5pm, Sa-Su 9am-4:30pm; Nov.-Mar. M-F 9am-4:30pm). **Keswick Mountain Bikes**, just out of town in Southey Hill Industrial Estate, rents cycles. (☎(017687) 75202. £10 per half-day, £13 per day. Open daily 9am-5:30pm.) Other services include: **Barclays bank**, Market Sq. (☎864221; open M-Tu and Th-F 9:30am-4:30pm, W 10am-4:30pm); the **launderette**, Main St., west of the mini-roundabout (open daily from 7:30am, last wash 7pm); the **police** (☎(01900) 602422), Bank St.; and the multitasking **post office**, 48 Main St., at the corner of Bank St. and Market Pl., where you can reserve **National Express** tickets or get **Internet access** (☎72269; £2.50 per 30min.; open May-Oct. M-Sa 8:30am-8pm, Su 10:30am-4pm; Nov.-Apr. M-Sa 8:30am-5:30pm). **Postal code:** CA12 5JJ.

▼⏢ ACCOMMODATIONS AND FOOD. The **Keswick** and **Derwentwater YHA Youth Hostels** grace this small town (see p. 363). Vast quantities of **B&Bs** nestle between Station St., St. John St.-Ambleside Rd., and Penrith Rd. No-frills **Elmtree Lodge**, 16 Leonard St., at Church St., promises quiet slumber. (☎74710. £18 per person, £15 without breakfast.) **Century House**, 17 Church St., has bright peaches-and-cream bedrooms in a Victorian-style house. (☎72843. £20 per person.) Lacy curtains and floral prints decorate the **Dorchester Guest House**, 17 Southey St. (☎73256. £18 per person, with bath £25.) **Campers** can pitch a tent at **Castlerigg Hall**, 1 mi. southeast of Keswick on the Windermere bus route, equipped with phones, toilets, and showers. (☎72437. Open Apr.-Nov. £3.70 per person, £2 per child, £1.50 per car.)

Sundance Wholefoods, 33 Main St., sells nature-friendly groceries at Market Pl. (☎74712. Open summer daily 9am-6pm; winter roughly 9am-5pm.) For meatless treats, grab excellent sandwiches for £3 at **Lakeland Pedlar**, in an alley off Main St. (☎74492. Open July-Sept. daily 9am-8pm; Oct.-Apr. daily 10am-4pm; May-June M-F 10am-4pm, Sa-Su 9am-4:30pm.) Those in the know frequent the lively **Dog & Gun**, just past Moot Hall on Market Pl., for its vegetarian fare. (☎73463. Open M-Sa 11am-11pm, Su noon-10:30pm; food served noon-9pm.) **Ye Olde Queen's Head**, behind the Queen's Hotel on Main St., is perfect for unwinding over a pint. (☎73333. Open M-Sa 11am-11pm, Su 11am-10:30pm; happy hour 6-7pm.)

NORTHWEST ENGLAND

⚑ HIKES. An excellent two- to three-hour amble for average hikers begins and ends in the town center. From Keswick, leave Market Place by Borrowdale Rd. and turn right onto Lake Rd., passing the boathouses by the lakeshore. A footpath continues to **Friar's Crag,** a rocky promontory with views of Derwentwater (praised by literary giants Ruskin, Wordsworth, and *Let's Go*), and then to the **Jaws of Borrowdale,** where the valley narrows between steep, tooth-like hills. After conquering the fells, retrace the path back to the boat landings, and take the trail on the right into **Cockshott Wood,** following it to the top of **Castle Head** for rewarding views. To return to Keswick, trudge onwards until Springs Rd.; at the end of the road, turn left onto Ambleside Rd. to arrive at Market Place. Another standout dayhike visits the **Castlerigg Stone Circle,** a neolithic henge dating back nearly 5000 years. Archaeologists believe it may have been used as a place of worship, astronomical observatory, or trading center. Leave Keswick Market Place on Ambleside Rd., and turn right onto Springs Rd. (approximately 800 yd.). The two-mile footpath starts at Springs Farm, and terminates at the main highway into town.

WESTERN LAKE DISTRICT

With comparatively few visitors and spectacular, windswept scenery, the Western Lake District is delightful. Getting there is not, unless you have a car or like to climb steep hills while carrying a heavy pack. Approach the remote southern villages of **Eskdale** and **Wasdale** from Ravenglass (or less easily from Coniston). The Ravenglass-Eskdale railway (☎ (01229) 717171) stops in Boot, 1½ mi. from **YHA Eskdale** (see p. 363). There are a few B&Bs at Wasdale Head. Facing the famous and forbidding Wastwater Screes is the fetching but oh-so-remote **YHA Wastwater** (see p. 364). Climb the nearby **Whin Rigg** or venture over to the many waterfalls of **Greendale Valley.**

While the mountain blockade across the Western Lake District can be breached from the south, the best approach is from the north. From Keswick, take bus #79 (30min.; M-Sa 18 per day, Su 10 per day; £2.45) 8 mi. to Seatoller, hike 1¼ mi. south to **Seathwaite,** and pick your mountain. To climb craggy **Great Gable** (2949 ft.) and its sidekick **Green Gable** (2628 ft.; no pigtailed redheads in sight) follow the trail on your left, which climbs steeply along the side of a waterfall (2¼ mi. up from Seathwaite to the summit). Bus #79 also goes 1½ mi. beyond Seatoller to the harrowing **Honister Pass,** which holds **YHA Honister Hause** on its summit (see p. 363).

Set in a splendid valley between two mountain lakes on the other side of Honister Pass, **Buttermere** is a remote town that doubles as a fishing hole. It's reachable by bus #77 from Keswick (30min., 4 per day, £2.45). Nearby, **Sour Milk Gill Falls** curdles from the slopes of Red Pike. The hike up **Hay Stacks** is tough, but the summit delivers bone-chilling views of surrounding mountains. **Red Pike** (2479 ft.), **High Stile** (2644 ft.), and **High Cragg** are the three main challenges for ambitious hikers in the area. Those more sensible might take a constitutional up **Ranndale Knotts.** The **YHA Buttermere** grants a hiker's reprieve (see p. 363). **Sike Farm** in the village offers B&B and camping. (☎ (017687) 70222. £18 per person, discount for longer stays. Camping £4.50 per person. Showers 20p.) **Crag Foot Cottage** is a wonderfully friendly B&B. (☎ (017687) 70220. £18 per person, discount for longer stays.) South of Buttermere, **Ennerdale Forest** shades a mountain valley and, at its southeastern edge, 1½ mi. from Great Gable, the remote **YHA Black Sail** (see p. 363).

CARLISLE   ☎ 01228

Nicknamed "The Key of England" for its strategic position in the Borderlands between England and Scotland, Carlisle (pop. 72,000) has been bloodied by over 2000 years of conquests and battles. The likes of Emperor Hadrian, Mary, Queen of Scots, Robert the Bruce, and Bonnie Prince Charlie have all lorded over Cumbria's principal city. Today, Carlisle remains an ideal stopover for more peaceful border crossings, as well as a good base for examining Hadrian's Wall (see p. 415).

LIAR, LIAR, PINT'S ON FIRE Every third Thursday in November at Santon Bridge, near Eskdale in the Western Lake District, noses grow a little when the local pub hosts the "Biggest Liar in the World" competition. The contest was started in the 1920s by one William Rishden, proprietor of the Wasdale Head Inn a few miles from Santon Bridge and the self-styled greatest liar in the world. Many a weary traveler would come to Rishden's inn, spend a comfortable night, and then get hopelessly lost the next day due to Rishden's entirely fictional directions and hiking suggestions. One year, after taking part in the contest for over a decade, Rishden refused to enter. Curious, his competitors asked him why. "I cannot tell a lie," said Rishden. He was promptly awarded first prize.

TRANSPORTATION. Carlisle's **train station** lies on Botchergate, diagonally across from the citadel. (Ticket office open M-Sa 5am-11:30pm, Su 9:30am-11:30pm.) **Trains** (☎(08457) 484950) arrive from: **London Euston** (4hr., every hr., £67.40); **Newcastle** (1½hr.; M-Sa every hr., Su 9 per day; £10.10); **Edinburgh** (2hr., every hr., £30.20); **Glasgow** (2½hr., every hr., £20.70); **Leeds** (2¾hr., 5-6 per day, £21.10). The **bus station,** on the corner of Lowther St. and Lonsdale St., books National Express or local tickets. (Open M-Sa 8:30am-6:30pm, Su 9:45am-5:30pm.) **National Express** (☎(08705) 808080) **buses** arrive from **London** (9½hr., 1 per day, £25). **Stagecoach Cumberland** (☎(01946) 63222) bus #555 drives in from **Keswick** in the Lake District (1¼hr.; M-Sa 3 per day, Su 2 per day; £4.85); the company also offers **bus excursions** to the **Lake District, Northumberland,** and **Scotland.** The 150 mi. **Cumbria Cycle Way** runs along the outskirts of the Lake District through Carlisle (see p. 364). **Bike rental** is available at **Scotby Cycles,** 30 Bridge St. (☎(0800) 783 2312. £12 per day. £20 deposit. Open M-Sa 9am-5:30pm.)

ORIENTATION AND PRACTICAL INFORMATION. Carlisle's city center is a pedestrian zone formed by **English St., Scotch St.,** and **Bank St.** The **tourist information centre** (TIC) lies in the middle of this triangle at Old Town Hall, Green Market. To get there from the train station, turn left and walk about three blocks (Botchergate becomes English St.), then cross the Old Town Square. To get to the TIC from the bus station, cross Lowther St., walk through the shopping center, and go right. The TIC **exchanges currency** and has day-long **luggage storage** for 75p per bag. Booking a room there, for a 10% deposit (plus £3 fee for booking outside Cumbria), gets you a free coupon book for discounts at restaurants and entertainment venues. (☎625600; fax 625604. Open July-Aug. M-Sa 9:30am-6pm, Su 10:30am-4pm; May-June and Sept. M-Sa 9:30am-5pm, Su 10:30am-4pm; Mar.-Apr. and Oct. M-Sa 9:30am-5pm; Nov.-Feb. M-Sa 10am-4pm.) Other services include: **Barclays bank,** 33 English St. (☎604400; open M-Tu and Th-F 9:30am-5pm, W 10am-5pm, Sa 9:30am-noon); **Internet access** at Carlisle Library, 11 Globe Ln., off Scotch St. (☎607310; £1 per 30min.; open M-F 9:30am-7pm, Sa 9:30am-4pm); and the **post office,** 20-34 Warwick Rd., which also has a **bureau de change** (☎512410; open M-Sa 9am-5:30pm). **Postal code:** CA1 1AB.

ACCOMMODATIONS AND FOOD. Warwick Rd., running east out of the city, has many B&Bs. **Cornerways Guest House,** 107 Warwick Rd., sports a sky-lit staircase and three floors of big rooms with patterned carpets and high ceilings. (☎521733. £15-16 per person, with bath £18.) At the nearby **Calreena Guest House,** 123 Warwick Rd., parade downstairs on crimson carpets to an excellent breakfast. (☎525020. Singles £16; doubles £30.) The **Howard House,** 27 Howard Pl., off Warwick Rd., delivers the royal treatment with curtained, four-post beds. (☎/fax 529159. £17 per person, with bath £21.) **Chatsworth Guest House,** 22 Chatsworth Sq., left off Chiswick St. from the bus station, has large rooms in an antique house. (☎524023. Singles £25; doubles and families £38.)

The fairground interior of the **Market Hall,** off Scotch St., holds fresh fruit, vegetables, and baked goods. (Open M-Sa 8am-5pm.) **Zorba Greek Restaurant,** 68 Warwick Rd., tosses a mean Greek salad for only £2.50. (☎592227. Open daily 5:30-10:30pm, also Tu-Sa noon-2pm.) The **Crown & Mitre Hotel,** English St. (☎525491), sells a healthy portion of their dish of the day for only £3.50 during lunch hours (noon-2pm). In the evening, students, regulars and tourists mix in the plush blue-and-maroon interior of **The Boardroom,** Paternoster Row, near the cathedral. Nonstop jukebox tunes and the occasional live music make for an upbeat atmosphere. (☎527695. Open M-Sa 11am-11pm, Su noon-10:30pm; food served 11am-8pm.)

◨ **SIGHTS.** The **Tullie House** museum and art gallery on Castle St. houses acclaimed exhibits on Hadrian's Wall and other areas of local history, plus a large enough collection of old shoes to make Imelda Marcos jealous. (☎534781. Open M-Sa 10am-5pm, Su noon-5pm; Nov.-Mar. M-Sa 10am-4pm, Su noon-4pm. £3.75, seniors and children £2.75, students £2.25.) Built in 1092 by William II with stones from Hadrian's Wall, **Carlisle Castle** looms in the northwest corner of the city. Mary, Queen of Scots was imprisoned here until Elizabeth I wanted her a wee bit farther from the border. Hundreds incarcerated in the dungeons of the castle after the 1745 Jacobite rebellion stayed alive by slurping water that collected in the trenches of the dark stone walls. Observe these "licking stones" as you learn about forms of torture employed against the Scots. (☎591922. Open Apr.-Sept. daily 9:30am-6pm; Oct. 10am-6pm; Nov.-Mar. 10am-4pm. Guided tours June and Sept. Su 12:30 and 2pm; July also Su 11am. £1.40, children 70p. £3.10, students and seniors £2.30, children £1.60.)

Carlisle's **cathedral,** founded in 1122, contains some fine 14th-century stained glass and the Brougham Triptych, a beautifully carved Flemish altarpiece. Sir Walter Scott married his French sweetheart on Christmas Eve, 1797, in what is now called the Border Regiment Chapel. (☎548151. Open M-Sa 7:30am-6:15pm, Su 7:30am-5pm. Evensong during school year M-F 5:30pm. Suggested donation £2.)

NORTHEAST ENGLAND

With Scotland to the north and the North Sea to the east, this corner of England has always been border country. Hadrian's Wall marks skirmishes with fierce northern tribes, and the area's three national parks, some of the most removed countryside in England, retain their frontier ruggedness. No trail tests hikers like the Pennine Way, Britain's first and longest official long-distance path. An extensive network of shorter paths accommodates ramblers of all levels, crisscrossing the heather-flecked moors of the Brontës' imagination to the rolling dales beloved by James Herriot. The isolation of the northeast testifies to its agricultural bent, where even the growth of textile manufacturing sprang from the extensive presence of sheep. But while the principal urban areas of Yorkshire and Tyne and Wear (including Leeds, York, and Newcastle) may have grown out of the wool and coal industries, and bear the 19th-century scars to prove it, today their refurbished city centers accommodate visitors with great energy.

HIGHLIGHTS OF NORTHEAST ENGLAND

YORK MINSTER Don't miss the splendid Minster, Britain's largest Gothic cathedral, which contains half of England's medieval stained glass and the largest medieval glass window in the world (p. 388).

NATIONAL PARKS Wander the emerald valleys and stone walls of the **Yorkshire Dales** (p. 382) or brave the winds and haunting desolation of the **North York Moors** (p. 394).

NEWCASTLE Sample the pubs and clubs of this gritty city, home of the famed brown ale, where crowded dance-floors and lively locals make the nightlife legendary (p. 407).

HADRIAN'S WALL Admire the remains of Hadrian's massive construction, which once delineated the northernmost border of the Roman Empire (p. 415).

PENNINE WAY

Like England's spine, the Pennine Peaks arch up the center of Britain from the Peak District National Park to the Scottish border. Britain's first long-distance trail, the 268 mi. Pennine Way begins at Edale, traverses the boggy plateau of **Kinder Scout,** then passes into the **Yorkshire Dales** at Malham to reemerge at the 2273 ft. Pen-y-Ghent peak. The northern section crosses the **High Pennines,** a 20 mi. stretch from below Barnard Castle to Hadrian's Wall, terminating at Kirk Yetholm across the Scottish border. The moorland of this often desolate landscape has fostered a rebellious population. They erected chapels in defiance of Canterbury, embraced socialism in the face of textile barons, and broke the will of private-property absolutists by winning public right-of-way access for these very trails.

🥾 HIKING

Hikers have completed the way in as few as 10 days, but most spend three weeks on the trail. The less ambitious can make brief but rewarding forays on well-traveled walkways from major towns. The unusual limestone formations in the Yorkshire Dales and the lonely moor of Kinder Scout are highlights.

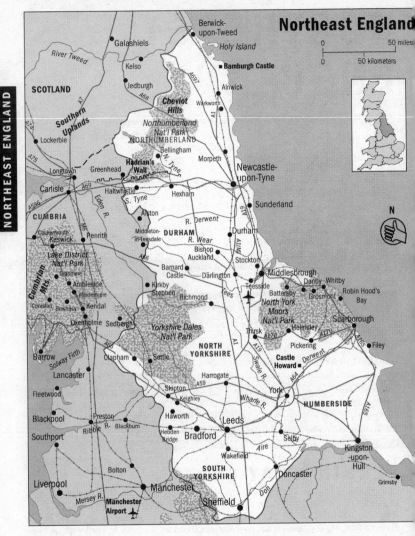

Northeast England

Wainwright's *Pennine Way Companion* (£10), a pocket-sized volume available from bookstores, is a worthwhile supplement to Ordnance Survey maps (£6-8), available from National Park Information Centres and tourist information centres (TICs). Sudden storms can reduce visibility to under 20 ft., leave low-level paths swampy, and sink you knee-deep in peat. Those in the know recommend staying away from the Pennines in the winter unless you're a hardcore Hiker. Bring a map and compass and know how to use them. Rain gear, warm clothing, and extra food are also essential. Consult **Wilderness Safety**, p. 54, for more advice.

■ ACCOMMODATIONS AND CAMPING

YHA Youth Hostels are spaced within a day's hike (7-29 mi.) of one another. The handy YHA **Pennine Way Package** allows you to book a route of 18 or more hostels along the walk (booking 50p per stamped hostel) and provides useful advice on paths and equipment. Send a self-addressed envelope to YHA Northern Region, P.O. Box 11, Matlock, Derbyshire DE4 2XA (☎(01629) 825850). Any National Park Information Centre or TIC can supply details on trails and alternate accommodations. The *Pennine Way Accommodations Guide* (90p) is invaluable.

YHA YOUTH HOSTELS

The following hostels are arranged alphabetically by town, with the distance from the nearest southerly hostel listed. Lockout for all is 10am-5pm, curfew is 11pm, and breakfast and evening meals are served, unless otherwise noted.

Alston: The Firs, Alston (☎/fax (01434) 381509), 22 mi. from Dufton. Open Apr.-Aug. daily; Sept.-Oct. Tu-Sa. Dorms £9.25, under 18 £6.50.

Baldersdale: Blackton, Baldersdale (☎/fax (01833) 650629), 15 mi. from Keld in a converted stone farmhouse overlooking Blackton Reservoir. Open Apr.-Aug. daily; Sept.-Oct. F-Tu. Dorms £8.15, under 18 £5.65.

Bellingham: 14 mi. from Once Brewed in Northumberland. See p. 414.

Byrness: 15 mi. from Bellingham, Northumberland. See p. 414.

Crowden-in-Longdendale: 15 mi. from Edale in the Peak District. See p. 357.

Dufton: Redstones, Dufton, Appleby (☎(017683) 51236; fax 53798), 12 mi. from Langdon Beck. Shop in hostel. Open July-Aug. daily; May-June Th-M; Apr. and Sept.-Oct. F-Tu. Dorms £9.25, under 18 £6.50.

Earby: 9-13 Birch Hall Ln. (☎/fax (01282) 842349), 15 mi. from Haworth. Open July-Aug. daily; Apr.-June and Sept.-Oct. M-W and F-Su. Dorms £9.25, under 18 £6.50.

Edale: (☎(01433) 670302), in the Peak District. See p. 357.

Greenhead: 17 mi. from Alston. See p. 416.

Hawes: 19 mi. from Stainforth in the Yorkshire Dales. See p. 385.

Haworth: 1 mi. from town. See p. 380.

Keld: 9 mi. from Hawes in the Yorkshire Dales. See p. 385.

Kirk Yetholm (SYHA): (☎(01573) 420631), 27 mi. from Byrness. See p. 525.

Langdon Beck: Forest-in-Teesdale (☎(01833) 622228; fax 622372), 15 mi. from Baldersdale. Shop in hostel. Open mid-July to Aug. daily; Apr. to mid-July M-Sa; mid-Feb. to Mar. and Sept.-Oct. Tu-Sa; Nov. F-Sa. Dorms £9.80, under 18 £6.75.

Malham: 15 mi. from Earby in the Yorkshire Dales. See p. 385.

Mankinholes: Todmorden (☎/fax (01706) 812340), 24 mi. from Crowden. Shop in hostel. Open mid-Mar. to Aug. M-Sa; Sept.-Oct. Tu-Sa; Feb. to mid-Mar. and Nov. F-Sa. Dorms £8.15, under 18 £5.65.

Once Brewed: 7 mi. east of Greenhead. See p. 416.

Stainforth: 8 mi. from Malham in the Yorkshire Dales. See p. 385.

CAMPING BARNS

In the High Pennines, the YHA operates three **camping barns,** hollow stone buildings on private farms with wooden sleeping platforms, (very) cold water, and a toilet. The telephone numbers below are for confirming arrival times *only;* book with YHA Camping Barns, 16 Shawbridge St., Clitheroe, BB7 1LZ (☎(01200) 420102).

Holwick Barn: Mr. and Mrs. Scott, Low Way Farm, Holwick (☎(01833) 640506), 3 mi. north of Middleton-in-Teesdale. Sleeps 20. £5 per person.

Wearhead Barn: Mr. Walton, Blackcleugh Farm, Wearhead (☎(01388) 537395), 1 mi. from Cowshill. No electric lights. Sleeps 12. £3.55 per person.

Witton Barn: Witton Estate, Witton-le-Wear (☎(01388) 488322), just off the Weardale Way. Sleeps 15. £3.50 per person.

NORTHEAST ENGLAND

YORKSHIRE

SHEFFIELD ☎ **0114**

Sheffield (pop. 530,000) rose to fame in a flurry of chopping, scooping, carving, and spreading. While Manchester was clothing the world, Sheffield was setting its table, first with hand-crafted flatware, then with mass-produced cutlery, and eventually with stainless steel, invented here. As 20th-century industry moved elsewhere, economic depression, made familiar by *The Full Monty*, set in. Though a dearth of city-center accommodations foils any overnight aspirations of the budget traveler, Sheffield, with its three new town squares and numerous art galleries, represents the last bastion of urbanity and nightlife before the Peak District.

▐▌ ▐▌ TRANSPORTATION AND PRACTICAL INFORMATION

Sheffield lies on the M1 motorway, about 30 mi. east of Manchester and 25 mi. south of Leeds. **Midland Station** is on Sheaf St., near Sheaf Sq. Luggage storage lockers are £1-3. **Trains** (☎(08457) 484950) arrive from: **London St. Pancras** (2-3hr., 1-2 per hr., £46); **Manchester** (1hr., every hr., £10.75); **York** (1¼hr., every hr., £12.10); **Birmingham** (1½hr., 1-2 per hr., £18.50); **Liverpool** via **Stockpool** (1¾hr., every hr., £13.90). The major **bus station** in town is the **Interchange**, between Pond St. and Sheaf St. (☎275 4905. Open M-F 8am-5:30pm. Lockers £1-2.) **National Express** (☎(08705) 808080) travels from: **London** (3½hr., 8 per day, £12); **Nottingham** (1¼hr., every hr., £9); **Birmingham** (2½hr., 6 per day, £13). The **Supertram**, Sheffield's modern transport system, covers the town. (☎272 8282. 1-day £1.90, 7-day £6.30.)

Sheffield's **tourist information centre** (TIC), 1 Tudor Sq., off Surrey St., books rooms for a 10% deposit. Ask for a free copy of *It's Happening In Sheffield*. (☎221 1900, bookings 201 1011; fax 201 1020; www.sheffieldcity.co.uk. Open M-Th 9:30am-5:15pm, F 10:30am-5:15pm, Sa 9:30am-4:15pm.) Other services include: **banks** along Pinstone St. and Church St.; **American Express**, 20 Charles St. (☎275 1144; open M and W-F 9am-5:30pm, Tu 9:30am-5:30pm, Sa 9am-5pm); the **police**, West Bar (☎220 2020); **Northern General Hospital**, Herries Rd. (☎243 4343); **Internet access** at **Havana Bistro** (see below); and the **post office**, Fitzalan Sq. (☎733525; open M 9am-5:30pm, Tu-Sa 8:30am-5:30pm). **Postal code:** S1 1AB.

▐▌ ▐▌ ACCOMMODATIONS AND FOOD

Sheffield doesn't exactly roll out the red carpet, nor even a worn welcome mat, for the budget traveler. If you don't mind the 30min. commute by train, try the **youth hostel** in **Hathersage** (see p. 355). The booklet *It's Happening in Sheffield*, free at the TIC, has thorough accommodations listings. Unless you opt to nest above a pub, expect a hilly westward hike from the city, where B&Bs cost at least £18.

The **YMCA**, 20 Victoria Rd., between Broomhall Rd. and Victoria Rd., has clean rooms on a quiet street a few blocks from the university. Men and women are accepted. Take bus #60 to Hallamshire Hospital, bear left on Clarkehouse Rd. to Park Ln., turn left again and then right onto the unmarked Victoria Rd. (☎268 4807. Continental breakfast. 18+. Singles £17. Weekly £74.) **Rutland Arms**, 86 Brown St., near the train and bus stations, offers clean rooms above a friendly pub, all with bath. (☎272 9003; fax 273 1425. Breakfast included. Singles £23.50; doubles £37; family room £47.) Feel at home at the **House of Elliott**, 465 Manchester Rd., with plush carpets and free rides on the rocking horse—you'll forget you're in industria. Take bus #51 from the City Hall or Leopold St. to Crosspool. (☎268 1677. Continental breakfast. £20 for first night, £18 for subsequent nights.)

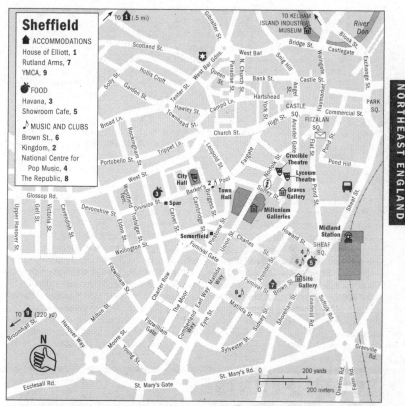

Sheffield

🏠 ACCOMMODATIONS
House of Elliott, **1**
Rutland Arms, **7**
YMCA, **9**

🍴 FOOD
Havana, **3**
Showroom Cafe, **5**

♪ MUSIC AND CLUBS
Brown St., **6**
Kingdom, **2**
National Centre for
Pop Music, **4**
The Republic, **8**

Cheap nourishment in the city center is hard to come by; head for the student haunts on **Ecclesall Rd.** or the ubiquitous cafe-bars on **Division St.** and **Devonshire St.,** where clubbers prepare for the night ahead. The **Spar** supermarket, at the intersection of Holly St. and Division St., is open 24hr. **Havana Bistro,** 32-34 Division St., concocts out-of-the-ordinary cyber fare, such as chicken goujons and melted brie for $3.50. (☎249 5452. Internet $1 per 15min., $3 per hr. Open M-Th 10am-10pm, F-Sa 10am-7pm, Su 11am-6pm.) **The Showroom Cafe-Bar,** 7 Paternoster Row, draws sophists to its minimalist interior. Lounge on the couch over the large and tasty chicken dishes, burgers, and stir-fry ($6.25-7.50) before watching one of the art-house films next door. (☎275 3588. Open M-Sa 11am-11pm, Su noon-10:30pm.)

🔍 SIGHTS

Sheffield's cultural reputation has energized with the opening of the ◪**Millennium Galleries,** Arundel Gate. Two of the galleries host national and international exhibitions, including for 2002 "Movies on the Move" (Feb.-May), "The Power of the Poster" (June-Sept.), and the "National Exhibition of Theatre Design" (Oct.-Dec.). In 1875, Victorian critic John Ruskin established a museum to show the working class that "life without industry is guilt, and industry without art is brutality." That museum, now the Millennium Galleries' excellent **Ruskin Gallery,** merges nature, architecture, and industry to challenge our perceptions. The final permanent gallery celebrates **Metalwork.** Before groaning with boredom, take a closer look; this isn't your typical shop class. (☎278 2600. Open M-Sa 10am-5pm, Su 11am-5pm; extended hours for special exhibits. General admission free. Special exhibits usually $4, students and seniors $3, children $2, families $9.)

The **Kelham Island Industrial Museum,** Alma St., studies the strong hand and dirty glove of Sheffield's industrial movement. Take bus #53 from the Interchange to Nursery St.; turn left on Corporation St., right on Alma St., and wind 200 yd. through an industrial park to the museum on the right. (☎272 2106. Open M-Th 10am-4pm, last admission 3pm; Su 11am-4:45pm, last admission 3:45pm. £3.50, students and seniors £2.50, children £2, families £8, disabled free.)

The ⬛**Graves Gallery,** on Surrey St. above the public library, dedicates a room to post-war British art, another to romantic and Impressionist works, and leaves its remaining six open to traveling exhibitions. "Leonardo da Vinci: A Jubilee Celebration" is scheduled for July 12-Sept. 21, 2002. (☎278 2600. Open M-Sa 10am-5pm; off season closed M. Free.) The **Site Gallery,** 1 Brown St., is dedicated to contemporary art, showcasing terrific shows of media art and photography. (☎281 2077. Open Tu-F 11am-6pm, Sa 11am-5:30pm, Su 1-5pm. Free.)

🎵 ENTERTAINMENT

At night, the **Crucible** and **Lyceum Theatres,** both in Tudor Sq. and sharing a box office on Norfolk St., stage musicals, plays, and dance shows, many of which are West End transfers. (☎249 6000. 20% concessions discount; same-day tickets £5.)

Most **clubs** are in the southeastern section of the city, around Matilda St.; *It's Happening in Sheffield* has current nightclub listings. Once a museum, the garish **National Centre for Popular Music,** Paternoster Row, intermittently serves as a nightclub. The party spills out into the courtyard and across to buzzing **Brown St.,** 60 Brown St. (☎279 6959. Cover £2-7. Cafe open M-F noon-4pm. Club open Th-F 9pm-3am, Sa 9pm-4am.) **The Republic,** 112 Arundel St., hosts Sheffield's largest party with its Saturday bash, "Gatecrasher." (☎276 6777. Cover M and Th £2-3, F £3-5, Sa £10-15 after 10:30pm. Open M and Th-F 10pm-2am, Sa 10pm-6am.) **Kingdom,** Barker's Pool across from City Hall, was voted the UK's best discotheque by the National Association of Discotheques—no joke. (☎278 8811. Cover £3-6. Open W 9pm-2am, Th-F 9pm-3am, Sa 9pm-6am.)

SOUTH PENNINES

Prepared by their dog-eared copies of *Wuthering Heights* for bleak and isolated vistas, visitors to the South Pennines may be surprised by the domesticated feel of this landscape. The villages of Haworth and Hebden Bridge have elbowed into the gorse-strewn moorlands, and the deserted, heathery slopes unfolding quietly between the towns are patterned into well-cultivated fields.

▐ TRANSPORTATION

The proximity of the South Pennines to Leeds and Bradford makes transport fairly easy. Two train lines (☎(08457) 484950) frequent the region. The Claverdale Line reaches Hebden Bridge and Mytholmroyd between Leeds and Manchester or Blackpool. Transpennine Express reaches Hebden Bridge from Newcastle-upon-Tyne, Manchester, and Liverpool (every hr. 7am-9pm, fewer on Su). The Airedale Line, from Leeds, stops at Keighley (KEETH-lee), 5 mi. north of Haworth, en route to Carlisle or Morecambe. The private steam-hauled trains of the Keighley and Worth Valley Railway (☎(01535) 645214) run a special route from Keighley to Oxenhope, passing through Haworth.

Local **bus** questions are answered by the **Metro Travel Centre.** (☎(0113) 245 7676. Open M-Sa 8am-7pm, Su 9am-5:30pm.) **West Yorkshire Buses** #663, 664, and 665 go to **Haworth** from **Keighley** and **Bradford. Keighley and District Travel** (☎(01535) 603284) bus #500 travels from **Hebden Bridge** to **Haworth** (30min., 4-5 per day).

Tourist information centres (TICs) hold a wide selection of trail guides. The **Worth Way** traces a 5½ mi. route from Keighley to Oxenhope; ride the steam train back to your starting point. From Haworth to Hebden Bridge, choose a trail from the TIC's *Two Walks Linking Haworth and Hebden Bridge* (30p), which guides visitors on the dark and verdant paths that inspired the Brontë sisters.

HEBDEN BRIDGE ☎01422

An historic gritstone village on a hillside, Hebden Bridge lies close to the Pennine Way and the circular 50 mi. Calderdale Way. Originally a three-farm cluster, the medieval hamlet stitched its way to modest expansion in the booming textile years of the 18th and 19th centuries, and many of the trademark "double-decker" houses of this period are still standing. Today, Hebden Bridge has few sights; most visitors use it as a starting point for day (or longer) hikes.

Calder Valley Cruising gives horse-drawn boat trips along the recently restored Rochdale Canal. (☎845557. Office open M-F 10am-noon; Easter-Oct. also Sa-Su 11am-5pm. 2-3 trips per day in summer; call in advance. £6, students and seniors £5, children £3, families £14.) From Hebden Bridge, you can make day hikes to the villages of **Blackshaw Head, Cragg Vale,** or **Hepstonstall.** Hepstonstall holds the remains of Sylvia Plath (after her death, husband Ted Hughes moved to nearby Mytholmroyd), and the ruins of a 13th-century church and a 1764 chapel, the oldest Methodist house of worship in the world. Trails also wind to the National Trust's **Harcastle Crags** (☎844518), a ravine-crossed wooded valley known locally as Little Switzerland, 1½ mi. northwest along the A6033. Pick up *Walks Around Hebden Bridge* (40p) from the TIC for scenic half-day hikes.

Hebden Bridge lies about halfway along the Manchester-Leeds line, with hourly **train** service in both directions. **Buses** stop at the train station and on New Rd. The **tourist information centre,** 1 Bridge Gate, distributes 40p walking guides. (☎843831; www.hebdenbridge.co.uk/tourist-info. Open Easter-Sept. M-Sa 10am-5pm, Su 11am-5pm; Oct.-Easter daily 10am-4pm.) **Internet access** is available at **Java Cafe,** New Rd. (£1 per 20min.) The **post office** is on Holme St. (☎842366. Open M-F 9am-5:30pm, Sa 9am-12:30pm.) **Postal code:** HX7 8AA.

At the **B&B** of photographer **Claire McNamee,** 1 Primrose Terr., and her painter husband, the simply furnished rooms are hung with the owners' works of art. (☎844747. £14 per person.) Lace doilies enhance the meals (around £4) at **Watergate Tea Shop,** 9 Bridge Gate. (☎842978. Open Su-F 10:30am-5pm, Sa 7am-9:30pm.) Purchase groceries at **Spar,** Crown St. (Open M-Sa 8am-11pm, Su 8am-10:30pm.)

HAWORTH ☎01535

> I can hardly tell you how the time gets on at Haworth. There is no event whatever to mark its progress. One day resembles another . . .
> —Charlotte Brontë

Haworth's (HAH-wuth) *raison d'être* stands at the top of its hill—the parsonage that overlooks Brontë-land. A cobbled main street milks all association with the Brontës: tearooms and souvenir shops fall over themselves to solicit the crowds in their ascent to the wuthering heights of the Brontë home. The village today wants for wandering heroines, but a moving echo of the wind-swept moors remains.

☐☑ TRANSPORTATION AND PRACTICAL INFORMATION. The **train station** (☎(01535) 645214) only runs the private steam-hauled trains of the Keighley and Worth Valley Railway. **Trains** come from **Keighley** (20min.; daily mid-June to Aug., call for other times; return £6). **West Yorkshire buses** (☎(0113) 245 7676) #663-665 stop at the base of Main St. from **Keighley** and **Bradford. Keighley and District Travel** (☎(01535) 603284) bus #500 comes from **Hebden Bridge** (30min., 4-5 per day).

The **tourist information centre** (TIC), 2-4 West Ln., at Main St.'s breathless summit, provides the useful *Three Walks from the Centre of Haworth* (30p), the town's mini-guide (35p), and books beds for a 10% deposit. (☎642329; fax 647721. Open Easter-Oct. daily 9:30am-5:30pm; Nov.-Easter 9:30am-5pm.) The **post office,** 98 Main St., is the only place to **exchange currency.** (☎644589. Open M and W-F 9am-1pm and 2-5:30pm, Tu 9am-1pm, Sa 9am-12:30pm.) **Postal code:** BD22 8DP.

🏠🍴 ACCOMMODATIONS AND FOOD. The elegant **YHA Haworth**, Longlands Dr., Lees Ln., is 1 mi. from the TIC in a Victorian mansion. (☎642234; fax 643023. Meals £3-5. Open mid-Feb. to Nov. daily; early Nov. to mid-Dec. M-Sa. Dorms £10, under 18 £6.90.) **B&Bs** (£15-17) await on Main St., downhill from the TIC. **Ashmount**, Mytholmes Ln., built by the doctor who attended Charlotte Brontë's death, has sweeping views. (☎645726. Singles £25; doubles £39; triples £50.) The **Ebor House**, Lees Ln., was built in 1850 for a nearby mill-owner. Walk from the train station down Mill Hey, which becomes Lees Ln. (☎645869. Singles £16; doubles £30.)

When combined, **Snowden's**, 98 Main St. (☎643214), and **Southams**, 123 Main St. (☎643196), form an adequate grocery. **The Black Bull**, a pub once frequented by the errant Branwell Brontë, is a stone's throw from the TIC. For reasonably priced restaurants, skip Main St. and head to **Mill Hey**, near the steam-railway station.

🔎 SIGHTS. Down a tiny land behind the village church, the tasteful **Brontë Parsonage** details the lives of Charlotte, Emily, Anne, and Branwell. Quiet rooms, including the dining room where the sisters penned their classics *Wuthering Heights* and *Jane Eyre*, contain original furnishings and mementos like Charlotte's minuscule boots and mittens. An exhibition traces the Brontës' humble origins in Ireland—their real name, either Brunty or Prunty, was changed out of veneration for Lord Nelson, the Duke of Brontë. (☎642323. Open Apr.-Sept. daily 10am-5:30pm; Oct.-Mar. 11am-5pm; call for hours Jan.-Feb. £4.50, students and seniors £3.30, children £1.40, families £10.) A footpath behind the church leads uphill toward the pleasant (if untempestuous) **Brontë Falls**, a 2½ mi. hike.

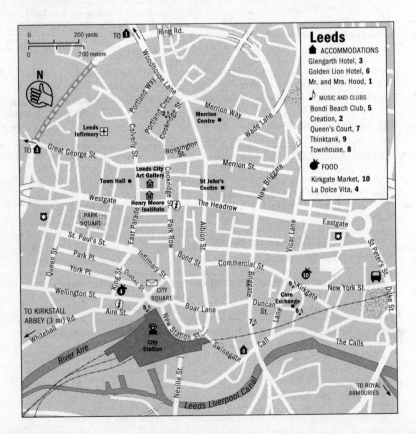

Leeds

🏠 **ACCOMMODATIONS**
Glengarth Hotel, **3**
Golden Lion Hotel, **6**
Mr. and Mrs. Hood, **1**

♪ MUSIC AND CLUBS
Bondi Beach Club, **5**
Creation, **2**
Queen's Court, **7**
Thinktank, **9**
Townhouse, **8**

🍴 **FOOD**
Kirkgate Market, **10**
La Dolce Vita, **4**

LEEDS

☎0113

Leeds (pop. 700,000) bloomed with textile-based prosperity in the ornate Victorian period, and today its building facades feature a curious cast of stone lions, griffins, and cherubs. Although most textile jobs have moved overseas, Britain's fourth-largest city has experienced a glamorous economic revival. The birthplace of Marks & Spencer now sports blocks of shops (including the north's sole branch of Harvey Nichols), a dynamic arts scene, and extravagant new nightlife venues, making this hip college hub worth a few days' exploration.

🔁 TRANSPORTATION AND PRACTICAL INFORMATION

Trains: City Station, City Sq. Ticket office open M-Sa 8am-8pm, Su 9am-6pm. Luggage storage. Trains (☎(08457) 484950) from: **London King's Cross** (2½hr., every hr., £56); **Bradford** (20min., 4 per hr., £2.15); **Manchester** (1½hr., 2 per hr., £10); **York** (2hr., 2 per hr., £6.50).

Buses: York St., behind Kirkgate Market. Office open M-F 8:30am-5:30pm, Sa 8:30am-4:30pm. Luggage storage. **National Express** (☎(08705) 808080) serves Leeds from most major cities. For local bus info, call **Metroline** at 245 7676.

Tourist Information Centre: Gateway Yorkshire, at the train station (☎242 5242; fax 246 8246). Books beds for £1.25 and a 10% deposit. Open M-Sa 9:30am-6pm, Su 10am-4pm. **Branch,** at the bus station. Open M-F 9:45am-5:30pm, Sa 9am-4:30pm.

Financial Services: Every conceivable **bank** lies on Park Row.

Police: Millgarth (☎(0845) 606 0606).

Internet Access: Leeds Central Library, the Headrow (☎247 8274). Free. Open M and W 9am-8pm, Tu and F 9am-5:30pm, Th 9:30am-5:30pm, Sa 10am-5pm.

Post Office: City Sq. (☎372853). Open M-Sa 9am-5:30pm. **Postal code:** LS1 2UH.

🏠 ACCOMMODATIONS

There are no hostels in Leeds, and finding a budget B&B often requires a hefty bus ride into suburbs like **Headingly** or **Halton.** Many well-located hotels offer discounts to clubbers and weekend visitors; the TIC lists such hotels and their specials.

Mr. and Mrs. Hood, 17 Cottage Rd., Headingly (☎275 5575). Take bus #93 or 96 from Infirmary St. The Hoods will charm you with conversation over coffee. Cooked breakfast includes homemade bread and marmalade. Singles £18; doubles £36.

Holme Leigh Guest House, 19 Pinfold Ln., Halton (☎260 7889). Take bus #40 from Boar Ln., across from the train station, to Temple Walk and continue up Pinfold Ln. (5min.). A Victorian home on a quiet street. Singles from £23; doubles from £35.

Golden Lion Hotel, 2 Lower Briggate (☎243 6454; info@goldenlion-hotel-leeds.com). This attractive, newly restored hotel pampers guests with room service, satellite TV, and convenient location. £32 per night, minimum 2-night stay.

Glengarth Hotel, 162 Woodsley Rd. (☎245 7940). A 15min. walk from the city center, or £4 cab ride. Adequate sleeping quarters and a traditional English breakfast. All rooms with TV and bath. Singles £30; doubles £36-50; family rooms £50-70.

🍴 FOOD

Kirkgate Market, at the south end of town. Sample the wares of butchers and bakers at Europe's largest indoor market. Open M-Sa 9am-5:30pm, W 9am-1pm.

La Dolce Vita, 130-134 Vicar Ln. (☎242 0565). Traditional Italian ambience complete with checkered tablecloths and a certain *amore.* 3-course lunches £5.55. Open M-Th noon-2:30pm and 5:30-11pm, F-Sa noon-2:30pm and 5:30-11:30pm, Su 6-11pm.

The Cornish Pasty Bakery, 54 Boar Ln. (☎420121). Caters to college students and business types on the go. Hot pastry pockets with assorted fillings 70p-£1.69.

👁 ▢ SIGHTS AND SHOPPING

One of the most touristed sights in Leeds, the ▨**Royal Armouries,** on Armouries Dr. by the waterfront, stakes its place among the world's best collections of arms and armor. The museum edifies through life-size recreations of battle scenes, battle simulations that put visitors in command, and demonstrations by staff in period dress. (☎220 1999. Open Apr.-Oct. daily 10:30am-5:30pm; Nov.-Mar. M-F 10:30am-4:30pm, Sa-Su 10:30am-5:30pm. £4.90, students and seniors £3.90.)

Leeds's massive library and two art museums, clustered across from the Victorian **Town Hall,** form the city's artistic center. The **Leeds City Art Gallery,** on the corner of the Headrow and East Parade, features one of the best permanent collections of 20th-century British art outside London. (☎247 8248. Open M-Tu and Th-Sa 10am-5pm, W 10am-8pm, Su 1-5pm. Free.) The adjacent **Henry Moore Institute,** 74 Headrow, holds excellent traveling sculpture exhibitions in its solemn building. (☎234 3158. Open M-Tu and Th-Sa 10am-5:30pm, W 10am-9pm, Su 1-5pm. Free.) The well-maintained ruins of 12th-century **Kirkstall Abbey,** Kirkstall Rd., along the River Aire, 3 mi. west of the city center, inspired J.M.W. Turner. Buses #732-736 reach the abbey. (☎275 5821. Open daily dawn-dusk. Free.)

Leeds is widely known for its shopping, and some of the malls and stores are sights in their own right. The colosseum-esque **Cornmarket Exchange,** at the corner of Duncan St. and Call Ln., houses three balconied floors of shops with the latest in hip, alterna-, and clubwear. The only British branch of **Harvey Nichols** (Harvey Nicks, dahling!) outside of London awaits in the posh Arcade Shopping Centre.

🔊 NIGHTLIFE

Leeds's nose for the trendy is exemplified by its nightlife. Come evening, moody cafe-bars morph into nightclubs that lure the city's swank (and wannabe-swank) into a neon heaven of commercial dance, house, indie-rock, and hip-hop music. Find up-to-date club listings in the monthly *Absolute Leeds,* available at the TIC.

Creation, 55 Cockridge St. (☎242 7272). A stylish newcomer, Creation's light show makes for superb eye candy, while house, retro, and commercial dance music fill the 3 floors. Outdoor balcony. Smart casual dress. No cover before 10pm, £3-8 after.

Townhouse, Assembly St. (☎219 4000). 3 stories struggle to contain the crazed collegiate crowd. A DJ spins dance on the 3rd floor. No cover. Club atmosphere picks up around 10pm and ends at 2am. Food served until 2pm.

Thinktank, Call Ln. (☎234 0980). Punk and indie rock venue for those who prefer bands like Vomit—and those who'd rather vomit than listen to the chirping techno beats that dominate the rest of Leeds's nightlife. Casual dress. Cover £3-6. Open 10pm-2am.

Queen's Court, 167-168 Lower Briggate (☎245 9449). Squeeze into your tightest outfit and show off that gym-toned bod. . .or suck it in. Prowling eyes rove Leeds's premier, ever-so-chic gay venue. M £2 cover upstairs; Tu-Th no cover; F £5 cover upstairs; Sa £6 cover upstairs. Open M and F-Sa 10pm-4am, Tu-Th 10pm-2am.

Bondi Beach Club, Queens Bldg. at City Sq. (☎243 4733). Wishful thinking made reality, the Bondi nurtures—or invents?—Leeds's latent beach culture. Find surfboards, bikini-clad girls, and, most importantly, a revolving dance-floor.

YORKSHIRE DALES NATIONAL PARK

A swath of emerald hills and valleys, the Yorkshire Dales National Park is liberally laced with sparkling rivers, subterranean caverns, and innumerable stone walls. The beauty of the dales, valleys formed by swift rivers and lazy glacial flows, is enhanced by traces of earlier residents: abandoned castles, stone farm houses, and tiny villages are scattered throughout. Bronze and Iron Age tribes blazed winding "green lanes," footpaths that remain upon the moorland tops; Romans

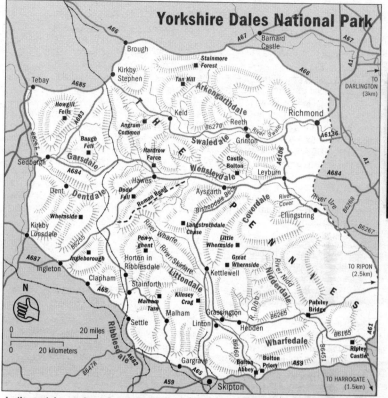

Yorkshire Dales National Park

built straight roads and stout hill-forts; and 18th-century workers pieced together the countless stone walls. While the Yorkshire Dales are a National Park, visitors should be aware that the land is not purely recreational—99% is privately owned and used for farming or other purposes. However, most property owners are willing to share the wealth of some of England's most marvelous countryside.

⌂ TRANSPORTATION

The most convenient way to enter the park is through Skipton, from where buses venture into smaller villages. **Trains** (☎ (08457) 484950) run to **Skipton** from: **Bradford** (40min., 2 per hr., £3.40); **Leeds** (40min., 2 per hr., £4.80); **Carlisle** (2hr., every 2hr., £11.20); **Morecambe** (2hr., 6-10 per day, £10.20). The **Settle-Carlisle Railway** (☎ (01729) 822007), one of England's most scenic train routes, slices through **Skipton, Garsdale,** and **Kirkby Stephen** (Settle to Carlisle 1¾hr., £16.20). **National Express** (☎ (08705) 808080) **buses** run to **Skipton** from **London** (1 per day, £12.40). **First Leeds** (☎ (0113) 242 0922) #84 travels from **Leeds** (1¼hr., every hr., £2).

For those without a car and not keen on hiking long distances, good luck. Those relying on public transport to get around the Dales should procure the *Dales Connection* timetable published by the North Yorkshire County Council (public transportation hotline ☎ (0870) 608 2608), free at any tourist information centre or National Park Information Centre. Get this in advance and plan your journey accordingly, since many **inter-village buses** run only a few times per week and tend to hibernate in winter. **Pride of the Dales** (☎ (01756) 753123) bus #72 connects **Skipton** to **Grassington,** sometimes continuing to **Kettlewell** (M-Sa every hr., Su 3 per day;

return £4.50). **Pennine Bus** (☎(01756) 749215) connects **Skipton** to **Settle** (#580; M-F every hr., Sa every 2hr.; return £6.90) and **Malham** (#210; M-Sa 4 per day, in summer also Su; return £6). Other villages are served less regularly, but **postbuses** run once per day to scheduled towns. If you miss your bus, you may have to walk. **Hitchhikers** complain that pickups are infrequent; *Let's Go* does not recommend hitching.

✦🛈 ORIENTATION AND PRACTICAL INFORMATION

Sampling the Dales requires several days, a pair of sturdy feet, and careful planning. In the south of the park, **Skipton** serves as a transport hub and provides goods and services not available in the smaller villages. **Grassington** and **Linton**, just north, are scenic bases for exploring southern Wharfedale. **Malham** is a sensible starting point for forays into western Wharfedale and Eastern Ribblesdale. To explore Wensleydale and Swaledale in the north, move out from **Hawes** or **Leyburn.**

The following **National Park Information Centres** are staffed by Dales devotees. Pick up the invaluable annual park guide, *The Visitor 2002*, and *The Yorkshire Dales Official Guide* (both free), along with numerous maps and walking guides. *The Visitor* highlights various guided walks and events sponsored by the National Park. In addition, most towns have tourist information centres (TICs).

Aysgarth Falls: (☎(01969) 663424; aysgarth@ytbtic.co.uk), in Wensleydale, a mile east of the village. Open Apr.-Oct. daily 9:30am-5:15pm; Nov.-Mar. Sa-Su 10am-5pm.

Clapham: (☎(015242) 51419; clapham@ytbtic.co.uk), in the village center. Open Apr.-Oct. daily 10am-5pm.

Grassington: Hebden Rd., Wharfedale (☎(01756) 752774; grassington@ytbtic.co.uk). 24hr. computer info. Open Apr.-Oct. daily 9:30am-5:15pm; off-season hours vary.

Hawes: Station Yard, Wensleydale (☎(01969) 667450; hawes@ytbic.co.uk). 24hr. computer information point. Open Apr.-Oct. daily 10am-5pm; some off-season weekends.

Malham: Malhamdale (☎(01729) 830363; malham@ytbtic.co.uk), at the southern end of the village. Open Apr.-Oct. daily 9:30am-5:15pm; Nov.-Mar. Sa-Su 10am-4pm.

Reeth: (☎(01748) 850252; reeth@ytbtic.co.uk), in the Green. Open Apr.-Oct. daily 10am-5pm; also off-season weekends with reduced hours.

Sedbergh: 72 Main St. (☎(01539) 620125; sedbergh@yorkshiredales.org.uk). Open Apr.-Oct. daily 9:30am-5:15pm; Nov.-Mar F-Sa 10am-4pm.

⌂ ACCOMMODATIONS AND CAMPING

Hostels, converted barns, tents, and B&Bs are all good options in the Dales. The free *Yorkshire Dales Accommodation Guide* is available at National Park Information Centres and TICs. Ask TICs about area caravan and camping sites.

The Yorkshire Dales area hosts 12 **YHA Youth Hostels.** Hawes, Keld, and Malham lie on the Pennine Way (see p. 373). Ingleton, on the western edge of the park, is a good jumping-off point to the Lake District. Linton, Stainforth, Kettlewell, Dentdale, Aysgarth Falls, and Grinton Lodge sit a few miles off the Pennine Way. Ellingstring, near Ripon, and Kirkby Stephen, north of Hawes, are both served by rail, but are set a little farther from the hiking trail. Hostel employees will often call other YHA hostels to help you find a bed for the next night.

Aysgarth Falls: (☎(01969) 663260; fax 663110), ½ mi. east of Aysgarth on the A684 to Leyburn. Lockout 10am-1pm. Reception from 5pm. Open Apr.-Oct. daily; Nov.-Mar. Sa-Su. Dorms £9.25, under 18 £6.50.

Dentdale: (☎(015396) 25251; fax 25068), Cowgill, on Dentdale Rd. 6 mi. east of Dent, 2 mi. from the Hawes-Ingleton Rd. On the River Dee. Open July-Aug. daily; Sept.-Oct. and Mar. F-Tu; Nov.-Feb. Sa-Su; Apr.-June F-W. Dorms £9.25, under 18 £6.50.

Ellingstring: Lilac Cottage (☎(01677) 460216), in the village. 18 beds. No smoking. Self-catering. Lockout 10am-5pm. Open July-Aug. daily; Apr.-June and Sept.-Oct. M-Th, groups only F-Su. Dorms £6.75, under 18 £4.75.

Grinton: Grinton Lodge (☎(01748) 884206; fax 884876), on the "Herriot Way," ¾ mi. south of Grinton on the Reeth-Leyburn Rd. Lockout 10am-1pm. Reception from 5pm. Open Apr.-Sept. daily; Oct. M-Sa; Nov.-Mar. F-Sa. Dorms £10, under 18 £6.90.

Hawes: Lancaster Terr. (☎(01969) 667368; fax 667723), west of Hawes on Ingleton Rd., uphill from town. 54 beds, enthusiastic staff. Meals £3-4. Open July-Aug. daily; Apr.-June and Sept.-Oct. Tu-Sa; Mar. and Nov.-Dec. F-Sa. Dorms £10, under 18 £6.90.

Ingleton: Greta Tower (☎(015242) 41444; fax 41854), downhill from Market Sq. Reception closed noon-5pm. 58 beds. Open Apr.-Aug. daily; Sept.-Oct. M-Sa; Nov.-Mar. F-Su. Dorms £11, under 18 £7.90.

Keld: Keld Lodge (☎(01748) 886259; fax 886013), Upper Swaledale, Richmond, west of Keld village. 40 beds. Open Apr.-Aug. daily; Sept.-Oct. W-Su; Jan.-Mar. and Nov. F-M. Dorms £9.25, under 18 £6.40.

Kettlewell: Whernside House (☎(01756) 760232; fax 760402), in the village center. 54 beds. Open Apr.-Sept. daily; Oct.-Mar. F-Su. Dorms £10, under 18 £6.90.

Kirkby Stephen: Fletcher Hill, Market St. (☎(017683) 71793; fax 72236). In a former chapel. 44 beds. Kitchen. Laundry. Open July-Aug. daily; Apr.-June and Sept.-Oct. Th-M. Dorms £9.25, under 18 £6.40.

Linton: The Old Rectory (☎/fax (01756) 752400), Linton-in-Craven, next to the village green. Skipton-Grassington buses #71 and 72 pass near the hostel, a 17th-century stone rectory. Friendly staff. Lockout 10am-5pm. Open June-Aug. daily; Apr.-May and Sept.-Oct. M-Sa; Jan.-Feb. and Nov. to mid-Dec. M-Th. Dorms £10, under 18 £6.90.

Malham: John Dower Memorial Hostel (☎(01729) 830321; fax 830551), at Malham Tarn. 2 lounges and storage lockers. 82 beds. Dorms £11, under 18 £7.60.

Stainforth: "Taitlands" (☎(01729) 823577; fax 825404), 2 mi. north of Settle, ¼ mi. south of Stainforth. Georgian house with walled garden. 50 beds. Open Apr.-Oct. daily; Feb.-Mar. and Nov. F-Sa. Dorms £11, under 18 £7.60.

Numerous **Dales Barns,** converted barns split up hostel-style into smaller bunk rooms, cost £5-7 per night. Most have showers, kitchens, and drying rooms. For lists of barns, ask at a TIC. Book weeks in advance with individual barns and get specific directions and locations along the trails when you call to book. **Airton Quaker Hostel** (☎(01729) 830263; £6, under 16 £3.50), **Barden Bunk Barn** (☎(01756) 720330; £6), and **Grange Farm Barn** (☎(01756) 760259; £6.50, under 18 £5.50) are all a few miles from Skipton. **Dub Cote** (☎(01729) 860238; £7) is in Horton Village, near Settle; **Hill Top Farm** (☎(01729) 830320; £7) in Malham; and **Skirfare Bridge** (☎(01756) 752465; £7) in Northcote Farm, Kilnsey, north of Grassington on the B6265. **Craken House Farm** (☎(01969) 622204; £6) stands ½ mi. south of Leyburn.

Campgrounds are hard to reach on foot, but farmers may let you use their stretch of dale. In **Skipton,** try Howarth Farm Camping and Caravan Site. (☎(01756) 720226. £6 per tent.) In **Grassington,** try Wood Nook. (☎(01756) 752412. 2-person tent £8.) In **Hawes,** try Bainbridge Ings, ½ mi. out of town on the Old Gale back road. (☎(01969) 667354. Open Apr.-Oct. 2-person tent and car £6.50, additional person 50p. Showers 20p.) In **Richmond,** try Brompton-on-Swale Caravan Park. (☎(01748) 824629. Open Apr.-Oct. 2-person tent £6, with car £7.75.) In **Aysgarth,** try Street Head Caravan Park. (☎(01969) 663472. 2-person tent and car £8.)

⛰ HIKING

Since buses are infrequent, and the scenery breathtaking, hiking remains the best way to see the Dales. The park's seven National Park Information Centres can help you prepare for a trek along one of three long-distance footpaths; make sure to procure decent maps before setting out. The challenging 270 mi. **Pennine Way** (see p. 373) curls from Gargrave in the south to Tan Hill in the north, passing Malham, Pen-y-ghent, Hawes, Keld, and most of the major attractions of the Dales. The more manageable 84 mi. **Dales Way** runs from Bradford and Leeds past Ilkley, through Wharfedale via Grassington and Whernside, and by Sedbergh on its way to the Lake District; it crosses the Pennine Way near Dodd Fell. The 190 mi. **Coast-to-Coast Walk** stretches from Richmond to Kirkby Stephen.

> **▼ SHAKE YER BOOTY.** Be aware that all the Dales are filled with **shake holes,** small depressions similar to grassy potholes—often unmarked—that indicate underground caverns. They can give way and may kill you if the cavern is large. Ordnance Survey maps and a compass are essential, especially on smaller, unmarked trails. See **Wilderness Safety,** p. 54, for other important tips.

The National Park Information Centres also detail walks only a few miles long. The park authority encourages visitors to keep to designated walks and to avoid falling into hidden mineshafts. Definitely take a **map** and **trail guide**; stone walls and hills all look similar after a while, and you'll need some way of retracing your steps. Don't forget to leave gates as you find them, lest you unleash hoards of grazing sheep and cows. The centers sell leaflets (₤1) covering over 30 short routes, beginning at Ingleton, Longstone Common, Malham, Aysgarth Falls, Grassington's Centre, Clapham's Centre, and other points. The YHA produces a series of leaflets on day-long walks between hostels (available from hostels for 30p). Many hostel employees are also avid walkers, so ask for suggestions. For those wishing to cycle, National Park Information Centres list rental stores and sell route cards plotting the **Yorkshire Dales Cycleway,** a series of six 20 mi. routes connecting the dales (₤2.50); bicycles are forbidden on public footpaths. **Ordnance Survey** maps are available for most smaller paths and can be purchased at any center or hiking supply store (₤4.50-8). If you're worried your pack may hold you back, the **Pennine Way/Dales Way Baggage Courier** will lighten your load as you trek through the Dales. (☎(01729) 830463, mobile (0411) 835322. ₤5-10 per bag.)

SKIPTON ☎01756

Skipton (pop. 13,000) is a transfer or sleeping point; once you've gathered your gear, skip town and head for the Dales. Empty **Skipton Castle** is the main sight, and one of the most complete medieval castles in England, much to the chagrin of the parliamentarians, whose three-year civil-war siege—the longest in British history—failed. (☎792442. Open Mar.-Sept. M-Sa 10am-6pm, Su noon-6pm; Oct.-Feb. closes 4pm. ₤4.20, students and seniors ₤3.60, children ₤2.10.)

Skipton's **train station** is ¼ mi. west of the city center on Broughton Rd. **Buses** stop on Keighley St. between Hirds Yard and Waller Hill, behind Sunwin House. Rent and repair mountain bikes at **Dave Ferguson Cycles,** 1 Brook St., off Gargrave Rd. (☎795367. ₤8 per half-day, ₤14 per day. ₤40 deposit. Open daily 9am-5:30pm.) The **tourist information centre,** 35 Coach St., books accommodations for a 10% deposit and sells National Express tickets and maps. (☎792809; fax 700709. Open M-F 10am-5pm, Sa 9am-5pm, Su 11am-3:30pm.) Get camping supplies at **George Fisher's,** by the TIC on Coach St. (☎794305. Open M and W-Sa 9am-5:30pm, Tu 10am-5:30pm, Su 10am-4pm.) Other services include: **HSBC bank,** 61 High St. (open M-F 9:30am-4:30pm) and the **post office** in a **supermarket** at Sunwin House, 8 Swadford St. (☎792724. Open M-F 9am-5:30pm, Sa 9am-4pm). **Postal Code:** B23 1JH.

B&Bs are moderately priced and easy to find—just look along Keighley Rd. The affable Hardings will be moving from **Cravendale House,** 57 Keighley Rd. (☎795129), across the way to **Carlton House,** 46 Keighley Rd., where blue vases and canopy beds reign supreme. (☎700921. Singles ₤25; doubles ₤40; ₤18 per person off season.) **Alton House,** 5 Salisbury St., features books, beds, benevolent proprietors, and TVs. (☎794780. Singles ₤17.50-20; doubles ₤35-40; discounts on longer stays.) Load up on fresh gooseberries and cheese at the **market,** which floods High St. (Open M, W, F-Sa.) The renowned **Bizzie Lizzies,** 36 Swadford St., serves exceptional fish and chips. (☎793189. Open summer M-F 11:30am-10pm, Su noon-10pm; winter M-F 11:30am-8pm, Su noon-8pm.) **Healthy Life,** 10 High St., near the church, peddles revitalizing snacks, including vegetarian haggis; the cafe upstairs, **Herbs,** serves sandwiches for ₤2. (☎790619. Store open M and W-Sa 8:30am-5:30pm, Tu 10am-5pm; cafe open M and W-Sa 9:30am-4:45pm.)

WHARFEDALE AND GRASSINGTON ☎01756

Wharfedale, created by the river Wharfe, is best explored using lovely Grassington as a base. Spectacular **Kilnsey Crag** lies 3½ mi. from Grassington toward Kettlewell; *Wharfedale Walk #8*, from the park centre, guides you there through a deep gorge and Bronze Age burial mounds. The **Stump Cross Caverns**, adorned with stalagmites and glistening rock curtains, are 5 mi. east of Grassington toward Pateley Bridge. Dress warmly, as it gets chilly down under. (☎752780. Open Mar.-Oct. daily 10am-4pm; Nov.-Feb. Sa-Su 10am-4pm. ₤4.40, children ₤2.50.) The second half of June brings the art and music of the annual **Grassington Festival** (☎753068).

Pride of the Dales **bus** service arrives from Skipton (#72; M-Sa every hr., Su 4 per day; day return ₤4.50). The **National Park Information Centre**, Hebden Rd., stocks the useful *Grassington Footpath Map* (₤1.30), the standard park trail guides (₤1), and gives occasional guided walks. (☎752774. Open Apr.-Oct. daily 9:30am-5:15pm; call for winter hours. Walks Mar.-Oct. ₤2-3, children ₤1-1.50.) **The Mountaineer**, Pletts Barn Centre, at the top of Main St., sells outdoor gear. (☎752266. Open daily 10am-5pm.) **Barclays bank** is at the corner of Main St. and Hebden Rd. (Open M-Tu and Th-F 9:30am-3:30pm, W 10am-3:30pm.) The **post office** is at 15 Main St. (☎752226. Open M-F 9am-5:30pm, Sa 9am-12:30pm.) **Postal Code:** BD23 5AD.

Florrie Whitehead, 16 Wood Ln., supplies excellent B&B and legendary hospitality. (☎752841. ₤16 per person.) **Burtree,** a few steps from the information centre on the corner of Hebden Rd. and Sedber Ln., is a cottage with a glorious garden. (☎752442. ₤17 per person.) Pubs and tea shops pack Main St., including **Picnic's Cafe,** 10 Main St., which serves traditional hot meals for ₤1.25-4.45; takeaway is available. (☎753342. Open in summer daily 10am-5:30pm; winter 10am-3:30pm.)

MALHAMDALE ☎01729

Limestone cliffs and gorges slice the pastoral valley of Malhamdale, creating spectacular natural sights within easy walking distance of one another. A four-hour hike from the information centre will take you past the stunning pavement of **Malham Cove,** a massive limestone cliff, to **Malham Tarn,** Yorkshire's second-largest natural lake. Two miles from Malham is the equally impressive **Gordale Scar,** cut in the last Ice Age by a rampaging glacier. Catch all of these beauties in *A Walk in Malhamdale* (leaflet #1), available from Malham's **National Park Information Centre** (☎830363; open Apr.-Oct. daily 9:30am-5:15pm; Nov.-Mar. Sa-Su 10am-4pm) or the superior-grade **YHA Youth Hostel,** thronged by Pennine Way followers (see p. 385). **Townhead Farm,** the last farm before Malham Cove, provides tent sites with showers (50p) and toilets. (☎830287. ₤3 per person, ₤1.50 per tent, ₤1.50 per car.)

INGLETON ☎015242

North of Malham, the high peaks and cliffs of **Ingleborough, Pen-y-ghent,** and **Whernside** form the Alpes Penninae. The 24 mi. **Three Peaks Walk** connecting the Alpes begins and ends in **Horton in Ribblesdale** at the clock of the **Pen-y-ghent Cafe,** a hiker's haunt with mammoth mugs of tea. The best place to break your journey is **Ingleton** (pop. 2000), near the middle of the trek, where the local **tourist information centre,** in the community center car park, books rooms. (☎41049. Open Apr.-Oct. daily 10am-4:30pm.) The 4½ mi. walk through the Ingleton Waterfalls is one of the park's most popular routes. Pick up the walk leaflet from the TIC or check out the Ingleton town trail sign in the center. Ingleton has a **YHA Youth Hostel** (see p. 385). Several small **B&Bs** on Main St. charge around ₤15, or a mile walk brings you to **Stacksteads Farm,** Butterthorne Rd., which offers B&B and a bunk barn with 22 beds. (☎41386. Self-catering. Rooms ₤17; barn ₤9.)

WENSLEYDALE AND HAWES ☎01969

The northerly Wensleydale landscape of potholes, caves, clints, and grikes melts into a broad sash of fertile dairyland. Base your ventures in **Hawes,** which has a **National Park Information Centre** (☎667450; see p. 384). Spit out 40p at the Green Dragon Pub to gain access to the trail to the **Hardrow Force** waterfall (1 mi. north along the Pennine Way). If you're tired of natural landscapes, the **Dales Countryside Museum,** in the same building as the National Park Information Centre, chronicles the history of "real Dalespeople." (☎667494. Open Apr.-Oct. daily 10am-5pm; winter 10am-4pm. £2, concessions £1.) ▧**Cumbria Classic Coaches** (☎(01539) 623254) runs various trips around the Dales in a vintage 1934 bus. The solid form of **Castle Bolton** graces Wensleydale—explore it from dungeon to 100 ft. battlements. It's a nice day's walk from YHA Aysgarth. (☎623981. Open Mar.-Nov. daily 10am-5pm. £4.50, concessions £3.50.) Pubs, takeaways, and a **Barclays bank** (open M, W, F 9:30am-3:30pm; Tu 9:30am-4:30pm; Th 10am-4:30pm) are along Main St. A **YHA Youth Hostel** (see p. 385) is in town, and **B&Bs** (£17-21) line Main St., too; check the list outside town hall each afternoon.

Farther north, Swaledale is known for picture-perfect barns and meadows. Also worthwhile are Aysgarth Falls to the east—rolling in tiers down the Yoredale Rocks—and the natural terrace of the Shawl of Leyburn. A **National Park Information Centre** idles in the car park above Aysgarth Falls (☎663424; see p. 384), and **Leyburn** has a **tourist information centre.** (☎623069. Open Easter-Sept. daily 9:30am-5:30pm; Oct.-Easter M-Sa 9:30am-noon and 1-4pm.) Both Aysgarth and Leyburn are serviced by United **buses** #156-157 from Hawes to Richmond (30-40min., every hr., return £3.90). The **YHA Youth Hostel** is ½ mi. east of the village (see p. 384).

YORK   ☎01904

The history of York is the history of England.
—King George VI, then Duke of York

With a pace suitable for ambling and its tallest building a cathedral, York is as different from nearby Leeds as it is from its new American namesake. Although its well-preserved city walls have foiled many, York fails to impede its present-day hordes of visitors. In AD 71, the Romans founded Eboracum as a military and administrative base for Northern England; the town remained important as Anglo-Saxon "Eoforwic" and Viking "Jorvik." William the Conqueror permitted York's Archbishop to officiate at his consecration. In 1069, York thanked him by joining with the Danes to massacre 3000 men in the Conqueror's garrison, producing just some of the ghosts in the self-proclaimed "most haunted city in the world." Current marauders, brandishing zoom cameras, are after York's compact collection of rich historical sights, including Britain's largest Gothic cathedral. The city manages to roll out the red carpet without sacrificing the authenticity of its heritage.

▛ TRANSPORTATION

Trains: York Station, Station Rd. Travel center and information office open M-Sa 8am-7:45pm, Su 9am-7:45pm. Ticket office open M-Sa 5:45am-10:15pm, Su 7:30am-10:10pm. **Luggage storage** £2-4; open M-Sa 8:30am-8:30pm, Su 9:10am-8:30pm. Trains (☎(08457) 484950) from: **London King's Cross** (2hr., 2 per hr., £61); **Scarborough** (50min., 2 per hr., £9.30); **Newcastle** (1hr., 2 per hr., £14.60); **Manchester Piccadilly** (1½hr., 2 per hr., £16.10); **Edinburgh** (2-3hr., 2 per hr., £49).

Buses: (☎551400). Stations at Rougier St., Exhibition Sq., the train station, and on Piccadilly. **National Express** (☎(08705) 808080) from: **London** (4½hr., 6 per day, £17); **Manchester** (3hr., 6 per day, £8); **Edinburgh** (5hr., 2 per day, £22).

Local Transportation: Call **First York** (☎622992, bus times 551400) for info. Ticket office open M-Sa 8:30am-4:30pm. **Yorkshire Coastliner** (☎(0113) 244 8976 or (01653) 692556) runs buses from the train station to Castle Howard (see p. 394).

Boats: Several companies along the River Ouse near Lendal, Ouse, and Skeldergate Bridges offer 1hr. cruises, including **YorkBoat,** Lendal Bridge (☎628324). Easter-Oct. trips depart 2 per hr.; Feb.-Mar. and Nov. at least 2 trips per day at 11am and 12:30pm, call ahead. £5, seniors £4.50, children £2.50. Office opens 10:30am.

Taxis: Station Taxis (☎ 623332 or 628197). 24hr.

Bike Rental: Bob Trotter, 13 Lord Mayor's Walk (☎ 622868). From £8 per day plus £50 deposit. Open M-Sa 9am-5:30pm, Su 10am-4pm.

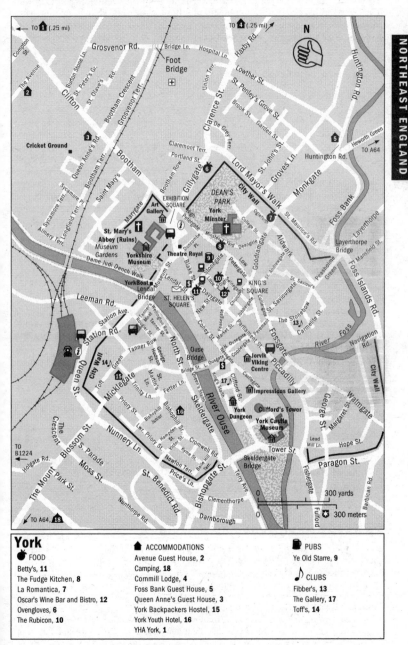

York

🍎 FOOD

Betty's, **11**
The Fudge Kitchen, **8**
La Romantica, **7**
Oscar's Wine Bar and Bistro, **12**
Ovengloves, **6**
The Rubicon, **10**

🛏 ACCOMMODATIONS

Avenue Guest House, **2**
Camping, **18**
Cornmill Lodge, **4**
Foss Bank Guest House, **5**
Queen Anne's Guest House, **3**
York Backpackers Hostel, **15**
York Youth Hotel, **16**
YHA York, **1**

🍺 PUBS

Ye Old Starre, **9**

🎵 CLUBS

Fibber's, **13**
The Gallery, **17**
Toff's, **14**

✦ 🔋 ORIENTATION AND PRACTICAL INFORMATION

York's streets now present a greater obstacle than the ancient walls ever did. They're winding, short, rarely labeled, and the longer ones change names every block or so. Fortunately, most attractions lie within the city walls, so you can't get too lost, and the **Minster,** visible from seemingly every point, provides an easy marker. The River Ouse (OOze) cuts through the city, curving west to south. The city center lies between the Ouse and the Minster; **Coney St., Parliament St.,** and **Stonegate** are the main thoroughfares.

Tourist Information Centre: De Grey Rooms, Exhibition Sq. (☎621756; www.york-tourism.co.uk). Books rooms for £3 plus a 10% deposit. The *York Visitor Guide* (50p) includes "Where to Stay" and "What to See" sections, and a detailed map. *Snickelways of York* (£5) is an offbeat self-tour guide. Open June-Oct. daily 9am-6pm; Nov.-May 9am-5pm. **Branch,** in the train station, has a **bureau de change.** Open June-Oct. M-Sa 9am-8pm, Su 9am-5pm; Nov.-May daily 9am-5pm. **York Visitor and Conference Bureau,** 20 George Hudson St., offers similar services. Room booking £4 plus a 10% deposit. Open M-Sa 9am-5:30pm; in summer also Su 10am-4pm.

Tours: A free 2hr. **walking tour,** offered daily by the Association of Voluntary Guides (☎630284). Meet in front of the York City Art Gallery, across from the TIC; tour times posted outside the TIC. A bewildering array of **ghost tours** all offer similar experiences. Brave the 1hr. **Ghost Hunt of York** (☎608700), which meets on Shambles daily 7:30pm. £3, children £2. **York Pullman** (☎622992) runs a variety of regional half- and full-day tours of the Yorkshire Dales and Moors (£7-20). **Guide Friday** (☎640896) leads its familiar open-roof bus tours; hop on at places throughout town. £7, students and seniors £6, children £2.50, families £16. **CitySightseeing** (☎692505) cruises the town in a similar hop-on/hop-off fashion. £5, concessions £3.50, families £10.

Financial Services: Banks fill Coney St. **Thomas Cook,** 4 Nessgate (☎653626). Open M and W-Sa 9am-5:30pm, Tu 10am-5:30pm. **American Express,** 6 Stonegate (☎670030). Open M-F 9am-5:30pm, Sa 9am-5pm; in summer **bureau de change** also open Su 10:30am-4:30pm.

Launderette: Haxby Road Washeteria, 124 Haxby Rd. (☎623379). Open M-F 8am-6pm, Sa 8am-5:30pm, Su 8am-4:30pm. Last wash 2hr. before close.

Police: Fulford Rd. (☎631321).

Hospital: York District Hospital (☎631313), off Wigginton Rd. Take bus #1, 2, 3, or 18 from Exhibition Sq. and ask for the hospital stop.

Internet Access: Cafe of the Evil Eye, 42 Stonegate (☎640002), is shockingly cheap at £1 per hr. **Gateway Internet Cafe,** 26 Swinegate (☎646446). 50p quick check, £1.50 per 15min., £4 per hr. 20% student discount. Open M-Sa 10am-8pm, Su noon-4pm. **Internet Exchange,** 13 Stonegate (☎638808). £1.50 per 15min., £5 per hr.

Post Office: 22 Lendal (☎617285). **Bureau de change.** Open M-Tu 8:30am-5:30pm, W-Sa 9am-5:30pm. **Postal Code:** YO1 2DA.

🏠 ACCOMMODATIONS AND CAMPING

Competition for inexpensive B&Bs (from £18) is fierce during summer. The TICs and the York Visitor and Conference Bureau may help. B&Bs are concentrated on the side streets along **Bootham** and **Clifton,** in the **Mount** area down Blossom St., and on **Bishopsthorpe Rd.,** due south of town. Book weeks ahead in summer.

🏠 **Avenue Guest House,** 6 The Avenue (☎620575; allen@avenuegh.fsnet.co.uk), off Clifton on a quiet, residential side street. Enthusiastic hosts provide immaculate rooms surrounding an impressive spiral staircase. Soft beds and plush towels make it a step up without being pricey. Some family rooms with baths. All rooms with TV. Singles £15-17; doubles £28-32, with bath £30-40; cheaper in off season.

York Backpackers Hostel, 88-90 Micklegate (☎/fax 627720; yorkbackpackers@cwcom.net). Fun atmosphere in a stately, 18th-century mansion. Kitchen and laundry facilities. Internet access £2.50 per 30min. TV lounge. "Dungeon Bar" open 3 nights per week, long after the pubs close. Dorms £9-12; doubles £30.

YHA York (☎653147), Water End, Clifton, 1 mi. from town center. From Exhibition Sq., walk ¾ mi. on Bootham and take a left at Water End; from the train station follow the river footpath "Dame Judi Dench," which connects to Water End; or take a bus to Clifton Green and walk ¼ mi. down Water End. Excellent facilities, but pricey. 156 beds. Reception 7am-10:30pm. Bedroom lockout 10am-1pm. Open mid-Jan. to mid-Dec. Dorms £16, under 18 £12; singles £18.50; twins £37; family rooms £52 or £78.

York Youth Hotel, 11-15 Bishophill Senior (☎625904). A well-located hostel, but picky travelers beware: the open shower takes you back to your gym class days. Much of the building is often booked by youth groups. Sleeps 120. Continental breakfast £2, English breakfast £3. Sheets £1. Laundry facilities. Key deposit £5. Bar open 9pm-1am. Reception 24hr. Dorms £9-11; singles £13-14; twins £24-33.

Foss Bank Guest House, 16 Huntington Rd. (☎635548). Walk or take bus #B5 or B6 from the train station. Comfortable beds and wooden desks in clean rooms by the River Foss. Doubles are particularly luxurious. All rooms have showers and sinks. Some with bathtub, some with TV. No smoking. Singles £17-19; doubles £37-44.

Queen Anne's Guest House, 24 Queen Anne's Rd. (☎629389), a short walk out Bootham from Exhibition Sq. Spotless single and double rooms with TVs; some doubles with bath. Large breakfasts fit for a queen. Singles from £16; doubles £32.

Cornmill Lodge, 120 Haxby Rd. (☎620566; cornmill_lodge@hotmail.com). From Exhibition Sq. go up Gillygate to Clarence St. and then Haxby Rd., or take bus #A1 from the station. Purify body and soul in this quiet, vegetarian B&B. Clean, convivial rooms with TV. Singles from £20; doubles from £40.

Camping: Riverside Caravan and Camping Park (☎705812), York Marine Services, Ferry Ln., Bishopthorpe, 2 mi. south of York off the A64. Take bus #23 from the bus station and ask the driver to let you off at the campsite (2 per hr., return £1.30). Pleasant riverside site. July-Aug. £8 per 2-person tent; Sept.-June £7.

FOOD AND PUBS

Greengrocers peddle at **Newgate market** between Parliament St. and Shambles. (Open M-Sa 9am-5pm; Apr.-Dec. also Su 9am-4:30pm.) There are more **pubs** in the center of York than gargoyles on the Minster's east wall. Most are packed on weekend nights, and all serve bar meals during the day.

The Fudge Kitchen, High Petergate (☎652643). Over 20 scrumptious flavors of homemade fudge, from Vintage Vanilla to Banoffee. Nibble a free sample while they make the fudge before your very eyes. Sold by the slice (£2.50-3). Open M-Sa 10am-5:30pm.

Oscar's Wine Bar and Bistro, 8 Little Stonegate (☎652002), off Stonegate. Hearty pub grub in massive portions (£6-8) will keep you going for a week. This popular pub has a swank courtyard, varied menu, and lively mood. Live jazz and blues M nights. Happy hour Su-M 4pm-close, Tu-F 5-7pm. Open daily 11am-11pm.

Ovengloves, 74 Gillygate (☎625184). Get a sandwich on the go for an itsy-bitsy price at this excellent takeaway bakery and delicatessen. Pies and pasties 65p, filled rolls made to order £1-1.20. Open M-Sa 8am-5:30pm.

La Romantica, 14 Goodramgate (☎626236). Candles dripping over wine bottles and Italian music in the background create a sensuous setting, but the friendly staff at La Romantica realize the quickest way to a traveler's heart is through his or her stomach. Generous servings of pasta and pizza (£5) or a large portion of both together (£7) will reinvigorate. Open M-Sa noon-2:30pm and 5:30-11pm, Su 5:30-10:30pm.

The Rubicon, 5 Little Stonegate (☎676076), off Stonegate. Upscale vegetarian restaurant has creative lunches (£3.50-5), such as butterbean and hazelnut pâté, and sandwiches (£3.50). Vegan and gluten-free options. Open daily 11am-10pm.

Ye Old Starre, 40 Stonegate (☎ 623063). The city's oldest pub, with a license that dates back to 1644. The best pub meals (£4-5), with sumptuous *chili con carne,* bursting Guinness pie, and giant Yorkshire puddings for lunch, plus a pleasant inner courtyard. Open M-Sa 11am-11pm, Su noon-3pm and 7-10:30pm.

Betty's, 6-8 St. Helens Sq. Traditional cream tea (pot of tea and 2 scones £5) is served in a terrifically refined atmosphere. Also serves lunch and dinner (£3-8). Live piano music daily 6-9pm. Open daily 9am-9pm.

☉ SIGHTS

The best introduction to York is a 2½ mi. walk along its **medieval walls,** especially the northeast section. Beware the tourist stampede, which weakens only in the early morning and just before the walls and gates close at dusk.

■ YORK MINSTER

Due north—you can't miss it. ☎ 639347. Open in summer daily 7am-8:30pm; winter 7am-6pm. Evensong M-F 5pm, Sa-Su 4pm. Tours 9:30am-3:30pm. Requested donation £3.

Everyone and everything in York converges at York Minster, the largest Gothic cathedral in Britain. The present structure, erected between 1220 and 1470, was preceded by the Roman fortress where Constantine the Great was hailed emperor in 306 and the Saxon church where King Edwin converted to Christianity in 627. Within this Minster, Miles Coverdale translated and published the first complete printed English Bible in 1535. An estimated half of all the medieval stained glass in England glitters as it holds the walls together. The **Great East Window,** constructed from 1405 to 1408 and depicting both the beginning and the end of the world in over a hundred small scenes, is the largest single medieval glass window in the world—it's as big as a tennis court. Also world-famous, although nobody seems to know why, is the **Monkey's Funeral,** the fifth window to the left upon entering the cathedral (look in the bottom right corner).

CENTRAL TOWER. It's a mere 275 steps up to the top of the tower, but ascents are only allowed during a five-minute period every 30min., as the stairs can't let two people pass. *(Open June-Sept. daily 9:30am-6:30pm; Mar. and Nov. 10am-4:30pm; Apr. and Oct. 10am-5:30pm; May 10am-6pm. £3, children £1.)*

THE FOUNDATIONS, CRYPT, AND TREASURY. Displays narrate how the central tower began to crack apart in 1967. You can tour the huge concrete and steel foundations inserted by engineers, remnants of the previous buildings they unearthed, and treasured items of the cathedral. Plunge to the **Roman level** to explore the remains of the Roman headquarters and town, including the spot where Constantine the Great was proclaimed Emperor. Along the way, duck into the crypt, which isn't a crypt at all but rather the altar of the Saxon-Norman church, with the shrine of **St. William** and the 12th-century **Doomstone** upon which the cathedral was built. *(Open June-Sept. daily 9:30am-6:30pm; Mar. and Nov. 10am-4:30pm; Apr. and Oct. 10am-5:30pm; May 10am-6pm. £3, students and seniors £2.60, children £1, families £6.50.)*

CHAPTER HOUSE AND LIBRARY. If you like grotesque medieval carvings, the Chapter House is the place to be. Every minute figure is unique, from mischievous demons to a three-faced woman; keep an eye out for the tiny Virgin Mary, so small it went unnoticed by Cromwell's idol-smashing thugs. Pick up the safari guide (20p) on your way in to help your hunt. The Minster Library, designed by Christopher Wren, guards manuscripts at the far corner of the grounds. *(Chapter House open June-Sept. daily 9:30am-6:30pm; Mar. and Nov. 10am-4:30pm; Apr. and Oct. 10am-5:30pm; May 10am-6pm. £1, concessions 80p. Library open M-Th 10am-4pm, F 10am-noon. Free.)*

OTHER SIGHTS

▧ YORK CASTLE MUSEUM. Housed in a former debtor's prison, the huge York Castle Museum lives up to its billing as Britain's premier museum dedicated to everyday life. The brainchild of eccentric collector Dr. John Kirk, who began collecting items during his housecalls from the 1890s to the 1920s, the museum now puts objects from the past into context. It contains **Kirkgate,** an intricately reconstructed Victorian shopping street complete with carriage, and **Half Moon Court,** its Edwardian counterpart. *(The Eye of York.* ☎ *653611. Open Apr.-Oct. daily 9:30am-5pm; Nov.-Mar. 9:30am-4:30pm. £5.75, concessions £3.50, families £16.)*

CLIFFORD'S TOWER. This tower is one of the last remaining pieces of York Castle, and a chilling reminder of the worst outbreak of anti-Semitic violence in English history. In 1190, Christian merchants tried to erase their debts to Jewish bankers by destroying York's Jewish community. On the last Sabbath before Passover, 150 Jews took refuge in a tower that previously stood on this site and, faced with the prospect of starvation or butchery, committed suicide. Visitors can read informative billboards along a wall walk with panoramic views. *(Tower St.* ☎ *601901. Open July-Aug. daily 9:30am-7pm; Apr.-June and Sept. 10am-6pm; Oct. 10am-5pm; Nov.-Mar. 10am-4pm. £2, students and seniors £1.50, children £1, families £5.)*

JORVIK VIKING CENTRE. The Viking Centre is one of the busiest places in York; visit early or late to avoid lines, or book at least 24hr. in advance. Visitors ride through the York of AD 948, past artifacts and painfully accurate smells. *(Coppergate.* ☎ *643211; for advance booking, call 543403 M-F 9am-5pm. Open Apr.-Oct. daily 9am-5:30pm; Nov.-Dec. 10am-4:30pm; Jan.-Mar. Su-F 9am-3:30pm, Sa 9am-4:30pm. Last admission 1hr. before close. £7, concessions £6, children £5, families £21.50.)*

YORKSHIRE MUSEUM. Hidden in 10 gorgeous acres of **gardens,** the Yorkshire Museum presents Roman, Anglo-Saxon, and Viking artifacts, as well as the $2.5 million **Middleham Jewel** (c. 1450), a gold amulet engraved with the Trinity and the nativity and set with an enormous sapphire. In the gardens, children chase pigeons into reclining lovers among the haunting ruins of **St. Mary's Abbey,** once the most influential Benedictine monastery in northern England. Visit the basement to get the lowdown on abbey life. *(Enter from Museum St. or Marygate.* ☎ *551800. Open daily 10am-5pm. £4, concessions £3, families £11.50. Gardens, pigeons, and abbey ruins free.)*

BEST OF THE REST. The **York City Art Gallery,** on Exhibition Sq. across from the TIC, has an uneven collection of Continental work, a better selection of English painters (including William Etty, York native and pioneer of the English painted nude), and a sprinkling of pottery. *(☎ 551861. Open daily 10am-5pm, last admission 4:30pm. £2, concessions £1.50.)* The morbidly inclined should try **York Dungeon,** 12 Clifford St. Learn the story of Guy Fawkes and Dick Turpin, stare at sore-ridden bodies in the Plague exhibit and mangled wax figures in the Torture exhibit—who's ready for lunch? *(☎ 632599. Open Apr.-Sept. daily 10am-5:30pm; Oct.-Mar. 10am-4:30pm. £6, students and seniors £4.50, children £4.)*

🎜 ENTERTAINMENT AND FESTIVALS

The monthly *What's On* and *Artscene* guides, available at the TIC, have listings of live music, theater, cinema, and exhibitions. A **Ghost Tour of York** makes a lively start to the evening (see p. 390). In **King's Square** and on **Stonegate,** barbershop quartets share the pavement with jugglers, magicians, and soapboxers. Next to the TIC on St. Leonards Pl., the **Theatre Royal** stages productions. *(☎ 623568; 24hr. info 610041. Box office open M-Sa 10am-8pm. $6-30, student standbys day of show $4.)*

York's dressy new club, **The Gallery,** 12 Clifford St., has two dance-floors and six bars. (☎647947. Cover varies. Open F-W 9:30pm-2am, Th 10pm-2am.) The excellent **Toff's,** 3-5 Toft Green, plays mainly dance and house music. (☎620203. No trainers. Cover £3.50, free F before 10:30pm. Open M-Sa 9pm-2am.) **Fibber's,** Stonebow House, the Stonebow, doesn't lie about the quality of live music playing nightly at 8pm. (☎466148. *What's On* lists guest bands and events.)

The Minster and local churches host a series of **summer concerts.** Celebrate Purcell and friends in July at the **York Early Music Festival** (☎658338). York recently revived a tradition of many centuries past, performing the **York Mystery Plays** in the nave of the minster during June and July every fourth year. The next performances will be in 2004. (☎635444 for more information.)

DAYTRIP FROM YORK

CASTLE HOWARD
15 mi. northeast of York. Yorkshire Coastliner bus #842 runs half-day excursions to the castle (5 per day, return £4.50); a bus ticket gets reduced admission. ☎(01653) 648333. Open mid-Mar. to Nov. daily 11am-4:30pm; gardens mid-Mar. to Nov. daily 10am-6:30pm. Chapel services Sa-Su 5:15pm, 10min. £7.50, students and seniors £6.75, children £4.50. Gardens only £4.50, children £2.50.

Castle Howard, still inhabited by the Howard family, made its TV debut as the home of the Marchmains in the BBC adaptation of Evelyn Waugh's *Brideshead Revisited.* Grand halls (including a spectacular entrance with marble floors) and stairways are festooned with portraits of the Howard ancestors in full regalia and cluttered with Roman busts. The **long gallery** provides a dwarfing promenade between enormous windows and shelves stuffed with books. Head to the chapel for the kaleidoscopic stained glass. More stunning than the castle itself are its 999 acres of glorious grounds, including luxurious rose gardens, fountains, and lakes, all roamed by raucous peacocks. Be sure to see the domed **Temple of the Four Winds,** whose hilltop perch offers views of rolling hills, still waters, and lazy cows.

NORTH YORK MOORS NATIONAL PARK

Imagining Heathcliff and Dracula upon Yorkshire's windy moors requires no suspension of disbelief: these heathered expanses and cliff-lined coasts have changed little since inspiring the Brontë sisters (see p. 75) and Bram Stoker. Unlike the lush valleys of the Yorkshire Dales, the vistas of the Moors provide a beauty more passionate than pastoral. Wayfarers pace the flagstone "trods," once used by journeying monks, or guide themselves by stone crosses, erected to protect early pilgrims.

The kidney-shaped park, 30 mi. north of York, encompasses the Vale of Pickering in the south, the Vales of York and Mowbray in the west, the flat Cleveland and Teeside Plains in the north, and the rugged North Sea coastline in the east. Though no town serves as an obvious base, each has unique advantages. On the seaside, Whitby and Scarborough, flooded with vacationers, are sizeable towns with coastal dayhikes for walkers of all levels. Farther inland, from Pickering, visitors can ride the popular North York Moors Railway and see the park without breaking a sweat. Quiet Helmsley retains more of the spirit of the moors, being closer to the park and well-served by the park-wide Moorsbus. Danby feels like it's in the middle of nowhere, but as home to a National Park Information Centre and numerous trailheads it provides the most rugged base for penetrating the park's interior.

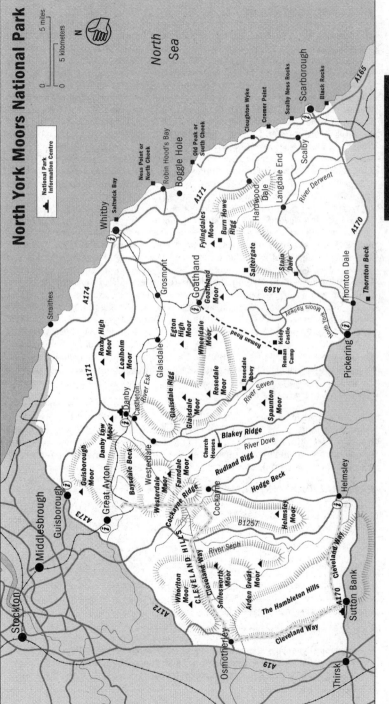

North York Moors National Park

▲ National Park
Information Centre

N

0 5 miles
0 5 kilometers

North Sea

Scarborough
Black Rocks
Scalby Ness Rocks
Cromer Point
Cloughton Wyke
Scalby
Langdale End
River Derwent
A165
A170

Old Peak or South Cheek
Boggle Hole
Robin Hood's Bay
Ness Point or North Cheek
Saltwick Bay
Whitby

Hardwood Dale
Langdale End
A171
Fylingdales Moor
Burn Howe Rigg
Saltergate
Stain Dale
Thornton Dale
Thornton Beck
A169

Straithes
A174

Grosmont
Goathland
Goathland Moor
Roman Road
North York Moors Railway
Kelde Castle
Roman Camp
Pickering

Roxby High Moor
Lealholm Moor
Egton High Moor
Wheeldale Moor
Glaisdale
Glaisdale Rigg
River Esk
Castleton
Danby
Danby Low Moor
Rosedale Moor
Rosedale Abbey
Glaisdale Moor
River Seven
Spaunton Moor

Guisborough Moor
Great Ayton
Baysdale Beck
Westerdale
Westerdale Moor
Farndale Moor
Blakey Ridge
Church Houses
River Dove
Rudland Rigg
Hodge Beck
Cockayne
Cockayne Ridge
A173
A171
A172

Middlesbrough
Guisborough
Stockton

Helmsley
Helmsley Moor
B1257
Cleveland Way
River Seph
Whorlton Moor
CLEVELAND HILLS
Snilesworth Moor
Arden Great Moor
The Hambleton Hills
Cleveland Way
Sutton Bank
A170
A19
Osmotherley
Thirsk

▐ TRANSPORTATION

The *Moors Connections* pamphlet, free at tourist information centres (TICs) and National Park Information Centres covers bus and rail service in glorious detail—service varies by season and is minimal in winter. The North York Moors public transport infoline also provides timetables (☎ (0870) 608 2608; 3-8p per min.).

Train (☎ (08457) 484950) service is limited but efficient; two lines enter the park. The **Northern Spirit** cuts through the park from the north, running from **Newcastle** to **Whitby**, via **Castleton, Danby,** and **Grosmont** (3hr., 4 per day, £9). The **Transpennine Express** provides southerly access, connecting **York** and **Scarborough** (45min., 2 per hr., £10). More tourist attraction than budget transportation, the steam-hauled **North York Moors Railway** (☎ (01751) 472508) links the north and south, chugging from **Pickering** to **Grosmont** via **Levisham** and **Goathland** (1hr., 5 per day, all-day pass £10). **Goathland Station** is famous for its appearances in the YTV series *Heartbeat*.

Buses cover more turf and run more frequently than trains. **Yorkshire Coastliner** (☎ (0113) 244 8976) serves many useful routes: pick up the free *Yorkshire Coastliner Timetable* at information centers or bus stations. Bus #840 travels between **Leeds, York,** and **Whitby**, with many stops at villages along the way (3hr., 5 per day), while bus #843 runs between **Leeds, York,** and **Scarborough** (3hr., every hr.). **Arriva** bus #93 journeys between **Middlesborough, Whitby,** and **Scarborough** (2hr., 2 per hr.). The Scarborough and District bus #128 covers **Scarborough, Pickering,** and **Helmsley** (1½hr., every hr.). On Sundays and Bank Mondays from April to September, additional **Moorsbus** services scour the Moors, connecting Scarborough, Pickering, Helmsley, and Danby to everything in between (all-day pass £2.50).

The Moors are steep, and **cycling** around them a challenge, but the paths on the plateaus are pleasant. TICs and National Park Information Centres offer several guides to cycling in the Moors (£1.80-7). The **Whitby to Scarborough Coastal Railtrail** (guidebook 30p), with sea views, refreshment stops, and sections for all skill levels, is especially popular. As biking on footpaths is destructive and dangerous, cycles should be used on roads and bridleways only.

▐ PRACTICAL INFORMATION

Along with the free *Moors Connections*, the *North York Moors Visitor Guide* (50p) is as crucial as sturdy shoes for exploring the park. Available at all TICs and National Park Information Centres, it contains useful advice and lists attractions, events, and accommodations throughout the Moors. In general, TICs in the area are outstandingly helpful, and they've got the awards to prove it.

NATIONAL PARK INFORMATION CENTRES

Danby: The Moors Centre (☎ (01287) 660654). From the train station, turn right as you leave the platform, left after you pass the gate, and right at the crossroads before the Duke of Wellington Pub; the Centre is a ½ mi. ahead on the right (20min.). Northern Spirit Middlesbrough-Whitby connection also stops at Danby. The largest National Park Information Centre in the Moors. Open Apr.-July and Sept.-Oct. daily 10am-5pm; Aug. 10am-5:30pm; Nov.-Dec. and Mar. 11am-4pm; Jan.-Feb. Sa-Su 11am-4pm.

Sutton Bank: (☎ (01845) 597426), 6 mi. east of Thirsk on the A170. Take the M3 or 128 bus from Helmsley. Open Apr.-Oct. daily 10am-5pm; Mar. and Nov.-Dec. 11am-4pm; Jan.-Feb. Sa-Su 11am-4pm.

TOURIST INFORMATION CENTRES

Goathland: The Village Store and Outdoor Centre (☎ (01947) 896207). Open Easter-Oct. daily 10am-5pm; Nov.-Easter M-W and F-Su 10am-4pm.

Great Ayton: High Green Car Park (☎ (01642) 722835). Open Apr.-Oct. M-Sa 10am-4pm, Su 1-4pm.

Guisborough: Priory Grounds, Church St. (☎(01287) 633801). Open Apr.-Sept. Tu-Su 9am-5pm; Oct.-Mar. W-Su 9am-5pm. Closed daily noon-12:30pm (F noon-1pm).

Helmsley: Town Hall, Market Pl. (☎(01439) 770173), in the town center. Open Mar.-Sept. daily 9:30am-6pm; Oct. 9:30am-5:30pm; Nov.-Feb. F-Su 10am-4pm.

Pickering: The Ropery (☎(01751) 473791), beside the library. Open Mar.-Oct. M-Sa 9:30am-6pm, Su 9:30am-5:30pm; Nov.-Feb. M-Sa 10am-4:30pm.

Scarborough: Unit 3, Pavilion House, Valley Bridge Rd. (☎(01723) 373333), across from the train station. Open May-Sept. daily 9:30am-6pm; Oct.-Apr. 10am-4:30pm.

Whitby: Station Sq., Langborne Rd. (☎(01947) 602674), across from the train station. Open May-Sept. daily 9:30am-6pm; Oct.-Apr. 10am-12:30pm and 1-4:30pm.

ACCOMMODATIONS AND CAMPING

Local TICs book beds for a small fee and 10% deposit. **B&Bs** in the National Park are listed under the appropriate towns. The following **YHA Youth Hostels** provide lodging in the Moors; reservations are strongly recommended, especially in summer. Most offer meals at fixed prices (breakfast £2.85, packed lunch £3, evening meal £4.25) and require a hostel card, which can be purchased for £3. Clearly named bus stops are rare; tell drivers where you're headed when you board.

Boggle Hole: (☎(01947) 880352; fax 880987), Mill Beck, Fylingthorpe. Easy access to Cleveland Way and Coast-to-Coast trails. 19th-century mill in a ravine on Robin Hood's Bay. Curfew 11pm. Open daily Feb. to mid-Nov. Dorms £10, under 18 £6.80.

Helmsley: (☎/fax (01439) 770433). From Market Pl. walk along Bondgate Rd., turn left onto Carlton Rd., and left again at Carlton Ln.; hostel is on the left. Lockout 10am-5pm. Curfew 11pm. Open Apr.-Aug. daily; Sept.-Oct. M-Sa. Dorms £9.50, under 18 £6.15.

Lockton: The Old School (☎(01751) 460376), off the Pickering-Whitby Rd. Take Coastliner bus #840 from Whitby. New, self-catering hostel. Open July-Aug. daily; June and Sept. M-Sa. Dorms £7, under 18 £4.80.

Osmotherley: (☎(01609) 883575; fax 883715), Cote Ghyll, Northallerton. Between Stockton and Thirsk, just northeast of Osmotherley. Dorms £10, under 18 £6.80.

Scarborough: The White House, Burniston Rd. (☎(01723) 361176; fax 500054), 2 mi. from Scarborough. Take bus #3 from the train station. By foot, follow the signs on Royal Albert Drive ½ mi. past the Promenade. In a former mill on a river, 10min. from the sea. Open Mar.-Aug. daily; Sept.-Oct. M-Sa. Dorms £8.15, under 18 £5.90.

Whitby: (☎(01947) 602878; fax 825146). 12th-century stone building next to the abbey, atop 199 mossy steps. Moor-bound school groups often fill the place until mid-July, so call ahead. Family rooms available. Lockout 10am-5pm. Curfew 11pm. Open Apr.-Oct. daily; Feb.-Mar. and Nov. to mid-Dec. F-Sa. Dorms £9.50, under 18 £6.15.

The YHA operates four **camping barns** in the Moors, in **Farndale,** Oakhouse farmyard (☎(01751) 433053); **Kildale,** on the Cleveland Way (☎(016427) 22135); **Sinnington,** on the edge of the park between Pickering and Helmsley (☎(01751) 473792); and **Westerdale,** in Broadgate Farm (☎(01287) 660259). These "stone tents" provide a roof, water, and toilets. A good sleeping bag, flashlight, and cooking equipment are essential. For listings, pick up the free *Stay in a Camping Barn* leaflet from information centers or contact the **YHA Northern Region,** P.O. Box 11, Matlock, Derbyshire DE4 2XA (☎(01629) 825850). Reservations must be made in advance. The barns all cost £3.25-4.75 per person. Barns sleep 12, are open for arrival at 4pm, and must be vacated by 10am.

HIKING AND BIKING

Hiking is the best way to travel these vast tracts of moor. Wrapping fully around the national park, the 93 mi. **Cleveland Way** is the yellow brick road of the North York Moors. A particularly well-marked and breathtaking portion of the Way is the 20 mi. trail between Whitby and Scarborough, the perfect day hike: wavering hills on one side, tranquil sea on the other, and miles of shoreline cliffs stretching ahead and falling behind. Ambitious hikers might consider tackling the 79 mi. **Wolds Way,** a stunning coastal hike that extends from Scarborough southward to the sandstone cliffs of Filey, or the shorter and unofficial 37 mi. **White Rose.** The **Crosses Walks,** an annual group hike, beginning in Danby, crosses the largest and most impressive moors before terminating in Castleton (contact the National Park Information Centre in Danby for dates). From Helmsley to Filey, the 35 mi. **Esk Valley Trail** hugs the lowlands near the railway track, its flat terrain ideal for inexperienced hikers. Since trails are not always marked or even visible, all hikers should carry a detailed map and compass (see **Wilderness Safety,** p. 54).

The amount of tourist literature on the North York Moors is astounding. The *Waymark* guides (30-40p), produced by the National Park authority, detail short (up to half-day) walks starting from villages or points of interest. The Ordnance Survey Tourist Map #2 (£4.25) covers the whole park, but may be too general for hikers; the 1:25,000 Outdoor Leisure sheets 26 and 27 (£6) are more precise. Before hitting the trails, consult more expensive books (£3-6) and get good advice (£0) from tourist officials. **Disabled travelers** should call the Disablement Action Group (☎ (01947) 821001) for guidance.

Cyclists roll gleefully through the **North Riding Forest Park,** located in the middle of the Moors between Pickering, Scarborough, and Sleights. The park holds mountain-bike paths for riders of all skill levels and short walking trails; the beginning of some of these are accessible by train. For details, inquire at the **Forest District Office,** Crossgates Ln., Pickering. (☎ (01751) 472295. Open July-Aug. M-F 10am-5:30pm; Easter-June and Sept.-Oct. 10am-4:30pm.) Pick up a list of cycle hire stores from a TIC, or check *The Moors Visitor.*

The Moors can be horribly hot or bitterly cold in the summer. Call the Danby National Park Information Centre (☎ (02187) 660654) for the **weather forecast** before setting out, but be aware that it reports on all of northeast England. The weather can vary dramatically even within the park. Bring raingear.

WHITBY ☎ 01947

Straddling a harbor between two desolate headlands, the seaside resort town of Whitby (pop. 14,000) has been the muse for many a struggling oddball. Here Caedmon sang the first English hymns, Bram Stoker conjured evil, and Lewis Carroll wrote *The Walrus and the Carpenter* while eating oysters. One of two English ports where the midsummer sun can be seen both rising and setting over the sea, this former whaling outpost inspired Captain Cook to set sail for Australia in the 18th century. The strip of slot-machines, gift shops, and fish-and-chips huts now lends a circus-like atmosphere to Whitby, giving the town an inexplicable charm.

■■ **ORIENTATION AND PRACTICAL INFORMATION. Trains** and **buses** stop at **Station Sq.** on **Endeavour Wharf,** on the west side of the River Esk; you can also flag Scarborough and County buses along Longhorne Rd. (Station Sq. office ☎ 602146. Luggage storage £1. Open daily 9am-5pm.) Whitby's **tourist information centre** (TIC) is at Station Sq. across Longhorne Rd. (see p. 397). Other services include: **National Westminster Bank,** 79 Baxtergate (☎ (0845) 609 0001; open M-F 9am-4:30pm); the **police** (☎ 603443), Spring Hill; **Internet access** at **New Tech Computer Systems,** off Flowergate through the archway beside the Lloyds TSB bank (☎ 602825; £1 per 10min.; open daily 10am-5:30pm) and at **Java,** Flowergate (£3 per 30min., £5 per hr.; open daily 7:30am-10pm); and the **post office** at the back of the **Whitby North Eastern Superstore** on Endeavour Wharf (post office ☎ 602327; open M-Sa 8:30am-5:30pm; store ☎ 600710; open M-Sa 8am-8pm, Su 10am-4pm). **Postal code:** YO21 1DN.

■■ **ACCOMMODATIONS AND FOOD.** The hilltop **YHA Whitby** (☎ 602878) has incredible views (see p. 397). Another hostel, **Harbour Grange,** off Spital Bridge about 7min. from Station Sq., has a riverside patio, kitchen, and homey decor for a great price. Walk south on Church St. and look right just after Green Ln. (☎600817. No smoking. Curfew 11:30pm. Dorms £8, with sheets £9.) **B&Bs** mass on the western cliff, along **Bellevue Terr.** and adjacent roads. At the **Jaydee Guest House**, 15 John St., the friendly Nicholsons offer pleasant conversation, great views of the city center, and a nautically inclined dining room. (☎605422. £17-20 per person.) Camp at the **Northcliffe Caravan Park**, 3 mi. south of town in High Hawkser. Take bus 93A from the bus station (£1), or head down the A171 and turn onto the B1447. (☎880477. Laundry facilities. July-Aug. £10.50 for tent and car; Apr.-June and Sept. £7; Oct.-Mar. £6. Electricity £2. Showers free.)

On the east side of the river, turn left at either Sandgate or Church St. to find the **market** (Tu and Sa 9am-4pm). █**Shepherd's Purse,** 95 Church St., serves a wealth of tasty vegetarian morsels in the funky cafe and tea garden in back. (☎820228. Open daily 10am-5pm and 6:30-10:30pm.) For superb food in a relaxed atmosphere, **The Vintner** awaits at 42a Flowergate. Specials go for £8-9; try the leek and roquefort canneloni. (☎601166. Open M-Tu 5:30-9:30pm, W-Sa noon-2:30pm and 5:30-9:30pm, Su noon-8:30pm. Reduced hours Nov.-Mar.) **Abbey Steps Tea Room,** 117 Church Street, serves traditional English teas (£1 per pot) and homemade scones (£1-2) beneath its collection of Staffordshire porcelain. (Open daily 10am-5pm.)

▣♫ SIGHTS AND ENTERTAINMENT. With marvelous views of the bay below, **Whitby Abbey** and **St. Mary's Churchyard** balance atop a hill buffeted by shrieking winds. Bram Stoker was a frequent visitor to Whitby, and the abbey and graveyard are believed to have inspired *Dracula.* The abbey's nonfictional history begins in AD 675 when St. Hilda founded a monastery here, only to be burned by Vikings in 867. The present structure dates to 1078. (☎603568. Open Apr.-Sept. daily 10am-6pm; Oct.-Mar. 10am-4pm. £3, students and seniors £2, children £1.) Next to the abbey, the peculiar box pews of **St. Mary's Church** merit a visit. (☎603421. Open July-Aug. daily 10am-5pm; in winter closes at 2pm. Suggested donation £1.)

Westward from Station Sq. on Bagdale, **Pannett Art Gallery and Whitby Museum,** in Pannett Park, has an impressive collection of model ships and "domestic bygones," but the fossils—including a 20 ft. *Ichthyosaurus Crassimanus*—put this place on the map. (Open May-Sept. M-Sa 9:30am-5:30pm, Su 2-5pm; Oct.-Apr. Tu 10am-1pm, W-Sa 10am-4pm, Su 2-4pm. Museum £2, children £1, families £5. Gallery free.) At East Terr., a bronze statue of **Captain Cook** overlooks the harbor. Charts in his left hand, sextant in his right, he squints toward Australia, the continent he charted. His memorial **museum,** on Grape Ln. across the river, contains original letters, drawings, and other navigational instruments. (☎601900. Open Apr.-Oct. daily 9:45am-5pm. £3, seniors £2.50, children £2, families £8.) Nearby, the self-explanatory **Whalebone Arch** pays tribute to the 17th-century whaling industry.

The western cliffs cradle the **Whitby Pavilion Theatre,** which stages family-oriented entertainment and amateur productions in summer. (☎604855. Box office open M-Sa 10am-4:30pm. Tickets £3-7.) Whitby takes pride in its annual August **Folk Festival** (☎708424), which offers 200 hours of dance, concerts, and workshops. The *What's On* brochure at the TIC lists other events around town.

NEAR WHITBY: DANBY AND CASTLETON

To the west of Whitby, villages like Grosmont, Danby, Castleton, and Kildale are easily accessible by the Northern Spirit Middlesbrough-Whitby connection. At **Danby,** visit the Moors Centre, the mother of all National Park Information Centres (see p. 396). You can also ascend the 1400 ft. **Danby Rigg** to the top of **Danby High Moor,** or make the easy hour-long walk to **Danby Castle,** a jumble of roofless 14th-century stones attached to a working farm. (Free, information pamphlet £1.) Other hikes in the area include the **Castleton** and **Glaisdale Riggs,** which are also accessible from the train stations at Castleton, Glaisdale, and Lealholme. Farther afield, walk from the Little Ayton train station (on the Esk Valley line) or from Newton-under-Roseberry to the summit of **Roseberry Topping** (not a dessert, but deserted).

SCARBOROUGH ☎ 01723

It all started in 1626 when Mrs. Tanyzin Farrer stumbled upon natural springs under a cliff near town. The bitter tasting stuff seemed to cure minor ailments, and soon "taking the water" became a medically accepted prescription—and popular pastime. Nearly four centuries later, English families still flock to Scarborough, one of England's first seaside resorts. During the summer months, when it feels as if the entire country has fled to the coast, lively pubs entertain hikers after a day in the Moors and the colorful boardwalk offers plenty of amusement. Beyond these diversions, Scarborough's wind-whipped beach scene is a little over-familiar.

⁊ PRACTICAL INFORMATION. The **tourist information centre** (TIC) is on Valley Bridge Rd., across from the train station. (☎373333. Open May-Sept. daily 9:30am-6pm; Oct.-Apr. 10am-4:30pm.) Other services include: **banks,** which crowd St. Nicholas St.; the **police** (☎500300), at the corner of Northway and Victoria Rd.; **Internet access** at **Complete Computing,** 14 Northway (☎500501; £3 per 30min., £5 per hr.; open M-F 9am-5:30pm, Sa 9am-5pm); and the **post office,** 11-15 Aberdeen Walk (☎381311; open M-F 9am-5:30pm, Sa 9am-12:30pm). **Postal code:** YO11 1AB.

⌂❑ ACCOMMODATIONS AND FOOD. YHA Scarborough is 2 mi. from town (see p. 397). Reasonable **B&Bs** (£17-20) can be found along Blenheim Terr., Rutland Terr., and the northern end of Castle Rd. The **Avenwood Hotel,** 129 Castle Rd., ideally located between North and South Bays near the castle, provides those sought-after sea views. (☎374640. July-Aug. £20 per person; Sept.-June £19.) The **Dene Lea Hotel,** 7 Rutland Terr., satisfies the senses with rustic quarters and a well-stocked bar. (☎361495. July-Aug. £20 per person; Sept.-June £19.) Centrally located two blocks from the train station, the **Terrace Hotel,** 69 Westborough, has spotless rooms and a friendly staff. Guests congregate in the happening bar and lounge. (☎374937. £20 per person for one night, £19 per night for multiple nights.)

For cheap meals, visit the **Public Market Hall,** an indoor market between Friargate and Cross St. (Open roughly 9am-5pm.) Locals swear by **Mother Hubbards,** 43 Westborough, the place to go for fish and chips. Fresh haddock served with bread and butter, and tea or coffee, costs only $4.25, $3.25 after 3pm. (☎376109. Open M-Sa 11am-6:45pm.) Wrought-iron garden chairs face the sea at the bright **Gala Coffee Bar,** 5 Museum Terr., where homebaked goodies like a banana toastie or fruit scone with cream cost £1.25. (Open daily 10am-5:30pm.)

◙♫ SIGHTS AND ENTERTAINMENT. A glimpse at the cliffs separating North and South Bay makes clear why Scarborough was long a strategic stronghold. **▧Scarborough Castle** was built by Henry II around 1160 on a site once home to a Roman signal station and Viking fort. The castle's fascinating history of stubborn sieges and defiant defenses is more than matched by tremendous views over town and sea. (☎372451. Open Apr.-Sept. daily 10am-6pm; Oct. 10am-5pm; Nov.-Mar. W-Su 10am-4pm. £2.30, students and seniors £1.70, children £1.20; includes 40min. audio tour.) Just down the hill, the cemetery of 12th-century **St. Mary's Parish Church,** across Church Ln., holds the grave of Anne Brontë, who passed away in Scarborough in 1849. (☎500541. Open May-Sept. M-F 10am-4pm, Su 1-4pm.)

The **Stephen Joseph Theatre** (☎370541), on the corner of Westborough and Northway, premiered much of Alan Ayckbourn's work, including *How the Other Half Loves*. As an actor in the theater, Ayckbourn often complained about his parts. When the director told him to write a better play, Ayckbourn usually did.

PICKERING ☎ 01751

Compared to Helmsley or Scarborough, heavily sedated Pickering (pop. 8000) offers little in the way of sights or entertainment, but the town is a more convenient base for exploring the national park and the **Dalby Forest,** a wildlife habitat outside of town. Pickering's main draw is the touristy **North York Moors Railway.** Nicknamed the "Heartbeat" Railway, the steam-hauled train journeys to the center of the Moors with scenic walks waiting at every stop; pick up *Walks from the Train* (80p) at the TIC. (☎472508. All-day pass £10.) Originally built in fear of Northern invasions, **Pickering Castle** soon became a favorite royal hunting spot. A short exhibition explains harsh measures such as the Forest Law: "Whosoever should slay hart or hind should be blinded. . . ." Remnants of the Norman castle still command an inspiring view. (☎474989. Open Apr.-Sept. daily 10am-1pm and 2-6pm; Oct.-Mar. W-Su 10am-1pm and 2-4pm. £2.30, students and seniors £1.70, children £1.20, under 5 free.) The **Parish Church of St. Peter and St. Paul** is a squat Norman building with a 15th-century gothic spire. Its medieval frescoes are in surprisingly good condition. (Open dawn-dusk. Suggested donation £1.)

Pickering's **tourist information centre** (TIC) is at The Ropery (see p. 397). Other services include: **Barclays bank,** 41 Market Pl. (☎(0345) 550088; open M-W and F 9:30am-4:30pm, Th 10am-4:30pm); **Internet access** at the **library,** next to the TIC (open M-T and Th 9:30am-5pm, F 9:30am-7:30pm, Sa 9:30am-12:30pm); and the **post office,** 7 Market Pl., inside Morland's Newsagents, with a **bureau de change** (☎(0345) 223344; open M-F 9am-5:30pm, Sa 9am-12:30pm). **Postal code:** YO18 7AA.

The TIC stocks a free list of accommodations, including farmhouses. For the Yorkshire experience, stay with the attentive Lovedays in **Clent House,** a restored 18th-century guest house on a picturesque street near the castle. (☎477928. Singles £20; doubles £32.) **Wayside Caravan Park,** Wrelton, 2½ mi. down the Pickering-Helmsley Rd., is a well-maintained site with beautiful park views. (☎472608. £7 per person. Extra person £1.25.) For gourmet food in a smart-casual setting, try **White Swan,** 7 Burgate. (Main meals £7-10; dinner served daily 7-9pm.)

HELMSLEY   ☎01439

Helmsley is a market town that's maintained the look and feel of its medieval past, despite its crafts shops and outdoor galleries. The main attraction is **Helmsley Castle,** built around 1120 in case the Scots ever got restless. They did, but the castle only saw military action during the Civil War, when the Parliamentarians blew the place in half—explaining its present-day appearance. (☎770442. Open daily 10am-1pm and 2-4pm; Apr.-Sept. until 6pm. £2.30, students and seniors £1.70, children £1.20.) The **Walled Garden** behind the castle contains over a hundred varieties of clematis, which, statistically, is England's favorite flower. (☎771427. Open Apr.-Oct. daily 10:30am-5pm; Nov.-Mar. F-Su noon-4pm. £2, students and seniors £1, children free.) **Duncombe Park,** ¾ mi. south on Buckingham Sq., is home to the lavish 18th-century villa of Lord and Lady Feversham. Informative guides point out family portraits, but you may spot the noble twosome themselves—they still live here. (☎770213. Open Apr.-Oct. M-Th and Su 10:30am-6pm; May-Sept. also F 10:30am-6pm. £6. Gardens only £4, children £2.)

A 3½ mi. walk out of town, or a quick ride on the Moorsbus to the Cleveland Way stop, leads to the stunning 12th-century **Rievaulx Abbey** (REE-vo). Established by monks from Burgundy, the abbey was an aesthetic masterpiece until Thomas Mannus, first Earl of Rutland, initiated a swift decay, stripping it of valuables, including the roof. It is now one of the most spectacular ruins in the country. Pick up Weymark Walk #20 guide (40p) at the TIC for more info. (☎798228. Open July-Aug. daily 9:30am-7pm; Apr.-June and Sept. 10am-6pm; Oct. 10am-5pm; Nov.-Mar. 10am-4pm. £3.60, students and seniors £2.70, children £1.80.) In late July and early August, music, drama, and literary talks color the **Reydale Festival** (☎771518).

The town centers around Market Pl., where buses stop and you'll find the **tourist information centre** (see p. 397). Other services include: **Barclays bank,** at the corner of Bandgate and Bridge St. (open M-W and F 9:30am-3:30pm, Th 10am-3:30pm); the **police** (☎(01439) 692424), at the corner of Ashdale Rd. and The Crescent; and the **post office,** Bridge St., across from Borgate (open M-Tu and Th-F 9am-12:30pm, 1:30-5:30pm; W and Sa 9am-12:30pm). **Postal code:** YO6 5BG

Helmsley is graced by a **YHA Youth Hostel** (☎/fax 770433; see p. 397) and **B&Bs. Mrs. Swift's,** Stillworth House, 1 Church St., lets large rooms in a Georgian townhouse near the main square. (☎(01439) 771072. Singles £20; doubles £30.) Those exploring the fern-lined **Newtondale Gorge** and the lush **Newtondale Forest** in the National Park (via the scenic North York Moors Railway from the Newtondale or Levisham stations) can lodge at **YHA Lockton** (☎(01751) 460376; see p. 397). Take York City District (☎(01904) 624161) bus #840 or 842 from Pickering or Whitby. An English teacher's nightmare, **Nice Things,** 10 Market Pl., does its name justice with a homemade quiche, jacket potato, and side salad for the kind price of £4. (☎771997. Open M-F 9:15am-5:30pm, Sa-Su 9:15am-6:30pm.)

COUNTY DURHAM

DURHAM   ☎0191

The commanding presence of England's greatest Norman cathedral lends grandeur to small-town Durham (pop. 90,000). For 800 years, the Bishops of Durham ruled the county from this town, with their own currency, army, and courts. In the 1830s, new rulers, otherwise known as students of Durham University, took over the hilltop city. Durham slows during summer recess, but the town is by no means a sleepy haven—tourists and festival-goers maintain the lively atmosphere, flowing steadily into the narrow streets that spiral up toward the cathedral.

▉ TRANSPORTATION

Durham lies 20 mi. south of Newcastle on the A167 and an equal distance north of Darlington. The **train station** is on a steep hill west of town. (☎232 6262. Ticket office open M-F 6am-9pm, Sa 6am-8pm, Su 7:30am-9pm. Advance ticket sales M-Sa 8:30am-5:45pm, Su 10am-5:45pm.) **Trains** (☎(08457) 484950) arrive from: **London King's Cross** (3hr., every hr., £75); **Newcastle** (20min.; 2 per hr.; £5, day return £9.50); **York** (1hr.; 2 per hr.; £20, return £28). The **bus station** is on North Rd., across Framwellgate Bridge from the city center. (☎384 3323. Office open M-F 9am-5pm, Sa 9am-4pm.) **National Express** (☎(08705) 808080) runs from: **London** (5½hr., 5-6 per day, £20.50); **Leeds** (2½hr., 3 per day, £17); **Edinburgh** (4½hr., 1 per day, £19.50). **Go Northern** and **United** run a joint bus service #722-723 from the Eldon Sq. station in **Newcastle** (1hr., every 10min., £3.50). **Arriva** buses serve most local routes (£1-1.50). Rent bicycles at the bright yellow **Cycle Force,** 29 Claypath. (☎384 0319. £12 per day. £35 deposit. Open M-W and F 9am-5:30pm, Th 9am-7pm, Sa 9am-5pm.)

▉ ORIENTATION AND PRACTICAL INFORMATION

The **River Wear** coils around Durham, creating a partial moat crossed by a handful of footbridges. With its cobblestone medieval streets, Durham is pedestrian-friendly, though hills may create difficulties for those carrying heavy packs.

To reach the **tourist information centre** (TIC), Market Pl., from the train station, descend the hill on Station Approach and take the steps on the left down to the Millburngate Bridge roundabout; cross the bridge and turn right at the first intersection into Market Pl. (☎384 3720; fax 386 3015. Open July-Aug. M-Sa 10am-5:30pm, Su 11am-4pm; June and Sept. M-Sa 10am-5:30pm; Oct.-May M-Sa 10am-5pm.) Other services include: **banks** in Market Pl.; the **police,** New Elvet (☎386 4222); **Internet access** at Reality-X Durham, 1 Framwellgate Bridge (☎384 5700; £3 per 30min.; open daily 10am-8pm) and at **Saints,** Back Silver St., behind the TIC (☎386 7700; £2.50 for 30min.; open daily 10am-6pm); and the **post office,** 33 Silver St., with a **bureau de change** (open M-Sa 9am-5:30pm). **Postal code:** DH1 3RE.

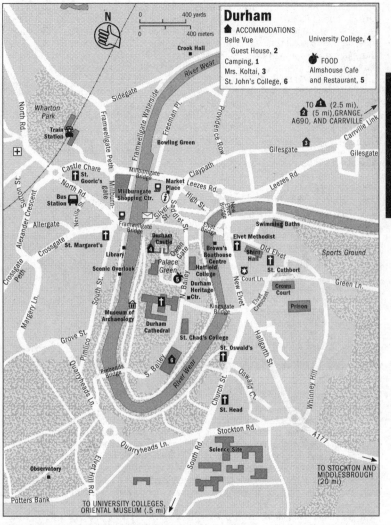

Durham

ACCOMMODATIONS
Belle Vue
   Guest House, **2**
Camping, **1**
Mrs. Koltai, **3**
St. John's College, **6**
University College, **4**

FOOD
Almshouse Cafe
and Restaurant, **5**

TO ▲ (2.5 mi),
② (5 mi), GRANGE,
A690, AND CARRVILLE

ACCOMMODATIONS AND FOOD

Durham is without hostels, but the large supply of inexpensive and often beautiful **dormitory rooms** is a boon for summer travelers. Others merely tour it, but you can pretend to be lord or lady of the ⬛**University College** dorms in Durham Castle as you eat breakfast in the enormous dining hall. (☎374 3863; fax 374 7470. Singles from $20.50 per person; doubles from $41.) On a cobbled street behind Durham Cathedral, **St. John's College**, 3 South Bailey, offers B&B in single and twin dorm rooms—vie for a room in the spacious theology students' section or in riverside Cruddas House. (☎374 3566; fax 374 3573. Singles £19.25; doubles £38.50.) Contact the **Durham University Conference and Tourism Office** for further availability information. (☎374 3454. Rooms open July-Sept. and around Easter and Christmas; breakfast included.) Bilingual **Mrs. Koltai,** 10 Gilesgate, explains breakfast options in English and Spanish at her cozy B&B, a steep uphill walk from the TIC. (☎/fax 386 2026.

Singles £20; doubles £36.) **Belle Vue Guest House,** 4 Belle Vue Terr., 5min. from the city on bus #59-59A to Dragonville Industrial Estate, has comfortable rooms. (☎386 4800. Singles £17.50; doubles £34.) **Camp** at the **Grange,** Meadow Ln., Carrville, on the A690 off the A1, 2½ mi. away. Take bus #220 to Rumpsite Hotel; follow the signs to the campground. (☎384 4778; fax 383 9161. Office open daily 8:30am-8pm. £4.20 per person, £1.25 per child. Laundry facilities. Showers free.)

At the **Indoor Market** off Market Pl., find the butcher, baker, and candlestick maker. (Open M-Sa 9am-5pm.) Students congregate over sandwiches or pastas for £2.50-4 in the 16th-century courtyard of **Vennel's,** next to Waterstone's in Saddler's Yd. (Open daily 9:30am-5pm.) The crowded **Almshouse Cafe and Restaurant,** 10 Palace Green, near the cathedral, serves delicious specials for £4-6. (☎361 1054. Open daily in summer 9am-8pm; winter 9am-5:30pm; meals served noon-2:30pm and 5:30-8pm.) Dine on Thai cuisine (£7-10) with unrivaled cathedral and river views at **Numjai,** 19 Millburngate. (☎386 2020. Open daily noon-2:30pm and 5:30-8pm.)

⊙ SIGHTS

▨ DURHAM CATHEDRAL

Crowning the hill in the middle of the city. ☎386 4266. Open June-Sept. M-Sa 9:30am-8pm, Su 12:30-8pm; Oct.-May M-Sa 9:30am-6pm, Su 12:30-5pm. Tours daily 10:30am and 2:30pm; Aug. also 11:30am. Suggested donation £3.

Built in 1093, the extraordinary Durham Cathedral stands, in the words of Sir Walter Scott, as "half church of God, half castle 'gainst the Scot." It is considered the finest Norman cathedral in the world, and the pamphlet on its layout, history, and architecture (60p) is invaluable. Behind the choir is the Tomb of Saint Cuthbert, who died in AD 687 and was buried on Holy Island; Danish raiders in the 9th century sent the island's monks packing, and they carried the saint's body with them as they fled. After wandering for 120 years, a vision in 995 led the monks to Durham, where the cathedral was built to shelter the saint's shrine. The central tower of the resulting structure reaches 218 ft. and is supported by 22 ft. intricately carved stone pillars. Next to the choir, the Bishop's Throne has been the subject of intense criticism since it stands nearly three inches higher than the Pope's throne at the Vatican. Opposite the choir lies the tomb of the Venerable Bede, author of the 8th-century *Ecclesiastical History of the English People,* the first history of England. During the church's time as a monastery, women had to stay behind the strip of black marble that separates Bede's tomb from the main part of the church. The marble itself contains hundreds of white blemishes which are actually fossilized plants and animals. The spectacular view from the top of the **Tower** is well worth the 325-step climb it takes to get there. *(Open mid-Apr. to Sept. 9:30am-4pm; Oct. to mid-Apr. M-Sa 10am-3pm weather permitting. £2, under 16 £1, families £5.)* The **Monks' Dormitory** off the cloister houses pre-Conquest stones and casts of crosses under an enormous 600-year-old timber roof that took over 21 oaks to build. *(Open Apr.-Sept. M-Sa 10am-3:30pm, Su 12:30-3:30pm. 80p, children 20p, families £1.50.)* The **Treasures of St. Cuthbert** holds the relics of St. Cuthbert, holy manuscripts dating back 1300 years, and the rings and seals of the all-powerful Bishops. *(Open year-round M-Sa 10am-4:30pm, Su 2-4:30pm. £2, students and seniors £1.50, children 50p, families £5.)*

OTHER SIGHTS

DURHAM CASTLE. For centuries a key fortress of the county's Prince Bishops, the castle is today a splendid residence for students at the university or summer sojourners; see **Accommodations,** p. 356. *(Next to the cathedral. ☎374 3800. Admission by tour only; call ahead for specific times, or visit the info booth outside the gates. Tours Mar.-Sept. daily 10am-12:30pm and 2-4pm; Oct.-Feb. M, W, Sa-Su 2-4pm. £3, children £2, families £6.50.)*

BEST OF THE REST. On the river bank between the Framwellgate Bridge and Prebends Bridge, the **Museum of Archaeology** showcases an impressive collection of Roman stone altars alongside finds from the prehistoric period to the present. *(☎374 3623. Open Apr.-Oct. daily 11am-4pm; Nov.-Mar. M and Th-F 12:30-3pm, Sa-Su*

11:30am-3:30pm. £1, concessions 50p, families £2.50.) Across the river and off South Rd. on Elvet Hill lies the interesting **Oriental Museum,** the only museum in Britain dedicated to Oriental art. *(☎374 7911. Open M-F 10am-5pm, Sa-Su noon-5pm. £1.50, seniors and children 75p, students free.)* A stroll along Framwellgate Waterside reaches **Crook Hall,** Frankland Ln. Built in the 13th century, this humble medieval manor occupies an enchanting position on the banks of the Wear. *(☎384 8023. Open May-Sept. Su 1-5pm; late July to early Sept. Su-F 1-5pm. £3.75, concessions £2.75, families £9.75.)*

🎵 ENTERTAINMENT AND FESTIVALS

Brown's Boathouse Centres, Elvet Bridge, rents rowboats in which you can trace the horseshoe curve of the River Wear. *(☎386 3779 or 386 9525. £2.50 per hr., children £1.25. Deposit £5.)* For a less arduous journey, the center runs a 1hr. cruise on the **Prince Bishop River Cruiser.** (Easter-Sept. daily; times depend on weather and university boating events. £3.50, children £1.50.)

After-hours entertainment in Durham is closely tied to university life; when students depart for the holidays, most nightlife follows suit. The intersection of **Crossgate** and **North Rd.,** across Framwellgate Bridge, is a good place to be at 10pm. A young crowd fills the popular **Hogshead** pub, 58 Saddler St., which has a fine selection of wines and a wall filled with the theatrical history of Durham. *(☎386 9550. Open M-Sa 11am-11pm, Su noon-10:30pm.)* The sporty riverside **Coach and Eight,** Bridge House, Framwellgate Bridge, is enormous and has a giant-screen TV to match. *(☎386 3284. Disco W and F-Su. Open M-Sa noon-11pm, Su noon-10:30pm.)* **Traveller's Rest,** 72 Claypath, offers a quiet sanctuary with an attractive selection of ales. *(☎386 5370. Open daily noon-3pm and 6-11pm.)* **Colpitts,** Colpitts Terr., is perfectly suited to live music. Mondays are Irish, Thursdays folk, and local acts and an open mic fill weekends. *(☎386 991. Open M-Sa noon-11pm, Su noon-10:30pm.)*

The TIC stocks the free pamphlet *What's On,* a great source of information on festivals and local events. Durham holds a **folk festival** in August with singing and clog dancing. Many events are free; others cost £2-7. **Camping** is free along the river during festival weekends (F-Su). Other major events include the **Durham Regatta** in the middle of June, held since 1834, and a sodden **beer festival** (the second largest in the country) in early September. Call the TIC for details on all festivals.

HIGH PENNINES

The area known as the High Pennines stretches north to south about 20 mi. west of Durham City, from below Barnard Castle to Hadrian's Wall. This vast landscape straddles the counties of Cumbria, Durham, and Northumbria and gives rise to the great northern rivers: the Tees, Tyne, Derwent, and Wear, whose sources perch high in the moorlands. Unlike the neighboring Yorkshire Dales, access to this region is limited, and it remains largely untouched by the frenetic tourist trade. Open moorland, tree-lined slopes, quiet stone villages, and waterfalls greet visitors to Derwent Valley and the region's other dales. The Pennine Way walking path crosses each dale as it winds up to Hadrian's Wall and the Scottish border.

🚌 TRANSPORTATION

Given the livestock-laden pastures and relatively level roads that greet the explorer here, the area is best suited to **hiking** and **biking.** Cars can successfully navigate the roads, but buses tackle the region with distressing hesitancy. Four motorways bound the region: the A66 along Darlington's latitude in the south; the A6 or M6 from Penrith to Carlisle in the west; the A69 from Carlisle to Newcastle to the north; and in the east the A167 from Newcastle through Durham and Darlington. The B6277 cuts a diagonal through the area, running northwest from Barnard Castle through Middleton-in-Teesdale to Alston. **Arriva** (☎(0345) 124125) buses #75 and 76 run from **Darlington** to **Barnard Castle** (45min., 2 per hr., £2.45);

Primrose bus #352 connects **Durham** and **Barnard Castle** via **Bishop Auckland** (40min.-1hr., 1 per day, £2.55). **Arriva** bus #5 runs directly from **Durham** to **Bishop Auckland** (40min., every hr., £2.50), and changes to **Go Northern** bus #8, connecting **Bishop Auckland** and **Barnard Castle** (50min., 10 per day, £2.55). The **Explorer North East** pass, available on any bus service, gives unlimited rides for one day from Berwick-upon-Tweed and Newcastle down to Whitby, and from Barnard Castle across to Sunderland (£5.25, seniors and children £4.25, families £10.50).

BARNARD CASTLE   ☎01833

Twenty miles southwest of Durham along the River Tees, Barnard Castle, the name of both the peaceful market town and its English Heritage ruins, is the best base for exploring the castles of Teesdale and the peaks of the North Pennine Hills. Along the river, the remains of the 12th-century Norman **castle** occupy six acres. (☎638212. Open Apr.-Sept. daily 10am-1pm and 2-6pm; Oct. 10am-1pm and 2-5pm; Nov.-Mar. M-Sa 10am-1pm and 2-4pm. Audio tour included. £2.30, students £1.70, children £1.20.) Past Newgate, the remarkable ◪**Bowes Museum** was built in the 19th century by John and Josephine Bowes to bring continental culture to England. The gallery now houses the couple's extensive and often curious private collection, including the largest gathering of Spanish paintings in Britain—El Greco's magnificent *Tears of St. Peter* among them—and a life-size mechanized silver swan (activated every day at 2 and 4pm), mentioned in Mark Twain's *Innocents Abroad*. (☎690606. Open daily 11am-5pm. Tours May-Aug. Tu-Sa 2 per day, Sept.-Oct. Sa-Su 1 per day. £4, concessions £3, families £12.) Dickens fans can follow the author's footsteps by car on **Dickens Drive,** a 25 mi. route that traces the path the author took in 1838 while researching *Nicholas Nickleby.* Pick up the free *In the Footsteps of Charles Dickens* from the tourist information centre. Northeast of Barnard Castle on the A688, **Raby Castle** (RAY-bee) is an imposing 14th-century fortress with a deer park. Take bus #75-76 (20min., 2 per hr., £1.50) toward Darlington. (☎660202. Open July-Sept. M-F and Su 1-5pm; May-June W and Su 1-5pm; park and gardens open same days 11am-5:30pm. £4, seniors £3, children £1.50, families £10. Park and gardens only £1.50, seniors and children £1.)

Five gracious and witty women manage the well-stocked **tourist information centre** (TIC), Woodleigh, Flatts Rd. (☎630262; fax 690909. Open Apr.-Oct. daily 10am-6pm; Nov.-Mar. 11am-4pm.) **Guided walks** of town leave from here. (1½hr.; late July to early Sept. Th 2:30pm. £1.50, seniors and children 75p.) **Banks** line Market Pl. The **post office,** 2 Galgate, has a **bureau de change.** (☎638247. Open M-F 9am-5:30pm, Sa 9am-12:30pm.) **Postal code:** DL12 8BE.

Barnard Castle has no youth hostel, but is blessed with superb **B&Bs,** many of which line Galgate. **Mrs. Kilgarrif,** 98 Galgate, offers satellite TV, an exercise room and sauna, and impressive knickknack collection. (☎637493. £21 per person, with bath £25.) **Mrs. Williamson,** 85 Galgate, rents comfortable rooms with TVs. (☎638757. Singles £25, with bath £32; doubles with bath £49.) The **Hayloft,** 27 Horsemarket, is an eclectic indoor market, with fruit and vegetables and a couple of cafes. **Stables Restaurant,** in the Hayloft, satisfies with sandwiches and salads (£3), along with other meals for under £4. (☎690670. Open daily 8:30am-5:30pm.)

▶ DAYTRIP FROM BARNARD CASTLE

BISHOP AUCKLAND. The town of Bishop Auckland is a major connection point for buses between Durham and Barnard Castle, and a brief stop en route shows a surprising amount beyond the bus station. Stroll down to **Auckland Castle,** presently the home of the county's Prince Bishops and of Europe's largest private chapel. The **Long Dining Room** holds an astounding collection of Francisco de Zubaran's paintings of Jacob and his 12 sons. (☎(01388) 609323. Open May-July 16 and Sept. F-Sa 2-5pm. Open July 17-Aug. 31 daily. Adults £3.50, concessions £2.50, under 12 free.) The **tourist information centre** stands in the town hall on Market Pl. (☎604922; fax 604960. Open M-F 10am-5pm, Sa 9am-4pm; May-Oct. also Su 1-4pm.)

THE GEORDIES What exactly is a Geordie (JOR-die)? Anyone born in the counties of Northumberland, Durham, or Tyne and Wear can claim Geordie status. But possessive as these sturdy Northerners are of their nickname, its origins are debatable. Try one of these:

1. During the Jacobite Rebellion of 1745, Newcastle's denizens supported George I, the reigning king, and were deemed "for George" by the Jacobites.

2. In 1815, George Stephenson invented the miner's lamp, which quickly gained favor among Northumberland miners. The lamp, and eventually the miners, became known as Geordies.

3. In 1826, Stephenson spoke before the Parliamentary Commission of Railways, and his dialect amused the snooty southerners, who began to call all keelmen carrying coal to the Thames "Geordies."

TYNE AND WEAR

NEWCASTLE-UPON-TYNE ☎ 0191

Unequivocally urban Newcastle (pop. 278,000) bills itself as a city of firsts. Beyond such contributions as the hydraulic crane and the steam locomotive, this gritty, industrial capital also brought us the world's first beauty contest and dog show, not to mention Sting (the first person to invoke Nabokov in a pop song). You won't find dreamy spires or evening hush here: what looks worn by day becomes full of energy by night, as locals, students, and tourists throng to Newcastle's (in)famous pubs and clubs. The most distinctive aspect of the city may be its citizens. Newcastle Geordies (see below) are proud of their accent, very proud of their football club, very, very proud of their brown ale, and usually happy to show you around.

▐ TRANSPORTATION

Newcastle is the last English stronghold before the Scottish border. The city lies 1½hr. north of York on the A19 and 1½hr. east of Carlisle on the A69. Edinburgh is straight up the coast along the A1, or through pastures and mountains via the A68.

Trains: Central Station, Neville St. (☎ (0345) 225225). Travel center sells same-day tickets daily 5:40am-9:15pm and advance tickets M-F 7am-7:50pm, Sa 7am-6:50pm, Su 8:40am-7:50pm. **Luggage storage** £2-4. Open daily 8am-6pm. Trains (☎ (08457) 484950) from: **London King's Cross** (3hr., every hr., £75); **Edinburgh** (1½hr.; M-Sa 23 per day, Su 16 per day; £33); **Carlisle** (1½hr.; M-Sa 15 per day, Su 9 per day; £10).

Buses: Gallowgate Coach Station (☎ 232 7021), off Percy St. Ticket office open M-Sa 8am-6pm. **National Express** (☎ (08705) 808080) from **London** (6hr., 6 per day, return £32) and **Edinburgh** (3hr., 3 per day, return £21). **Haymarket,** by the Metro stop, for local and regional service. Ticket office open M-F 8:30am-5:30pm, Sa 9am-4pm. **Northumbria** (☎ 212 3000) buses #505, 515, and 525 from **Berwick-upon-Tweed** (2½hr.; M-Sa every 2hr., Su 5 per day; £6.50).

Ferries: International Ferry Terminal, Royal Quays. DFDS Seaways (☎ (08705) 333 000) ferries daily to **Amsterdam, Gothenburg** and **Kristiansand** (see p. 35). Bus #327 serves all departures, leaving Central Station 2½hr. and 1¼hr. before each sailing. Take the Metro to Percy Main (£1.30) and walk 20min. to the quay, or take a taxi (£12).

Public Transportation: The **Metro** subway system (☎ 232 5325) runs from the city center to the coast and the airport. There are only a few stops in the city center. Tickets are purchased beforehand and checked on board. The **Day Saver** allows unlimited travel for one day (£3.75). First train around 6am; last train around 11:30pm.

Travel Information: Nexus Travel Line (☎232 5325) will keep you updated on local bus, train, and Metro information. Open M-Sa 8am-8pm, Su 9am-5pm.

Bike Rental: Newcastle Cycle Centre, 11 Westmorland Rd. (☎230 3022). £10 per day, £35 per week. £50 deposit. Open M-Sa 9am-5:30pm.

✳❷ ORIENTATION AND PRACTICAL INFORMATION

The free, full-color map of Newcastle available at the tourist information centre (TIC) is essential—streets shift direction and name without batting an eye. When in doubt, remember that the waterfront is at the bottom of every hill. The center of town is **Grey's Monument,** an 80 ft. stone pillar in **Monument Mall,** directly opposite **Eldon Sq.** The monument is dedicated to Charles, Earl of Grey, who nudged the steep 1832 Reform Bill through Parliament and mixed bergamot into Britain's tea.

Tourist Information Centre: Newcastle Information Centre, Central Exchange Bldgs., 132 Grainger St. (☎277 8000; fax 277 8010), facing Grey's Monument. Open M-W and F-Sa 9:30am-5:30pm, Th 9:30am-7:30pm; June-Sept. also Su 10am-4pm. **Branch** at Central Station. Open June-Sept. M-F 10am-8pm, Sa 9am-5pm; Oct.-May M-F 10am-5pm, Sa 9am-5pm.

Tours: Various themed city tours leave from the TIC generally W 6:45pm and Su 2:30pm, though times vary; check to be sure. £2, students and children £1.

Financial Services: Barclays, 7 Market St. (☎200 2000). Open M-Tu and Th-F 9am-5:30pm, W 10am-5:30pm, Sa 9:30am-12:30pm. **Thomas Cook,** 6 Northumberland St. (☎219 8000). Open M-Tu and F-Sa 9am-5:30pm, W 10am-5:30pm, Th 9am-8pm.

Launderette: Clayton Rd. Launderette, 4 Clayton Rd., Jesmond (☎281 5055), near the YHA Youth Hostel. Open M-Sa 8am-6pm, Su 8am-1pm.

Police: (☎214 6555), on the corner of Market St. and Pilgrim St.

Hospital: Royal Victoria Infirmary, Queen Victoria Rd. (☎232 5131).

Internet Access: McNulty's Internet Cafe, 26-30 Market St. (☎232 0922). £1.50 per 15min., Tu-W and F 9-11:30am free. Open M-Th 9am-7:30pm, F-Sa 9am-6pm.

Post Office: 24-26 Sidgate (☎(0345) 223344), in the Eldon Sq. Shopping Centre. Either enter by the monument and walk to the other end or enter at Blackett St. and take a right. **Bureau de change.** Open M-Sa 9am-5:30pm. **Postal Code:** NE1 7AB.

▐ ACCOMMODATIONS

The B&B scene is gasping for breath in Newcastle, which has plenty of dorm-style accommodations but few guest houses. Costlier lodgings neighbor the YHA Youth Hostel and YWCA in residential **Jesmond,** northeast of town via a three-minute Metro ride (80p). Slightly less expensive alternatives are scattered a few blocks to the north of Jesmond on **Osborne Rd.**

YHA Newcastle, 107 Jesmond Rd. (☎281 2570; fax 281 8779). Metro: Jesmond. Turn left onto Jesmond Rd. and walk past the traffic lights—it's on the left. The funky townhouse and lively atmosphere make this a good sightseeing base. Overrun by ferry traffic; call several days in advance. Lockout 10am-5pm. Curfew 11pm, but there's a late-entry code. Open Feb.-Dec. Dorms £11, students £10, under 18 £7.15.

University of Northumbria, Coach Ln. (☎227 4024; fax 227 3197). From the city center, go up Northumberland St. and take a right onto St. Mary's Pl., which leads into the University Library. The accommodations office is in Student Services in the library. Standard bed-basin-desk combos typical of college dormitories, but proximity to the city center a definite plus. No TVs; shared bathrooms. Breakfast included. Open late Mar. to mid-Apr. and June to mid-Sept. Singles £18.75; doubles £35.

Portland Guest House, 134 Sandyford Rd. (☎232 7868). From Jesmond Metro stop, turn left onto Jesmond Rd., then right onto Portland Terr.; the guest house is at the end. Modern townhouse in the heart of Jesmond with brightly colored rooms. Continental breakfast included. Singles from £18; doubles £37.

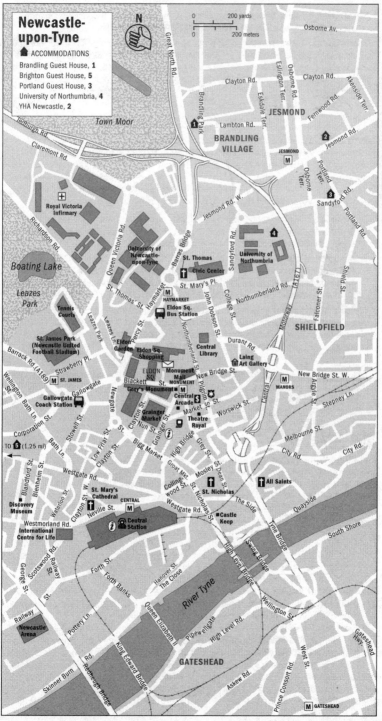

Newcastle-upon-Tyne

🏠 ACCOMMODATIONS
Brandling Guest House, **1**
Brighton Guest House, **5**
Portland Guest House, **3**
University of Northumbria, **4**
YHA Newcastle, **2**

Osborne Av.

Clayton Rd.   Clayton Rd.

Great North Rd.

0   200 yards
0   200 meters

Town Moor

Brandling Park

Lambton Rd.

JESMOND

Eslington Terr.
Eskdale Terr.
Osborne Rd.
Fernwood Rd.
Akenside Terr.
Jesmond Rd.

BRANDLING VILLAGE

JESMOND
Ⓜ

Jedburgh Rd.
Claremont Rd.

Richardson Rd.

Royal Victoria Infirmary ✚

Queen Victoria Rd.

Jesmond Rd. W.

Sandyford Rd.

Osborne Terr.

Portland Terr.

Sandyford

Portland Rd.

University of Newcastle-upon-Tyne

Barras Bridge
St. Thomas

University of Northumbria

Motorway (A167)

Shield St.

Boating Lake

St. Thomas' St.

Civic Center

Falconer St.

Leazes Park

St. Mary's Pl.

Northumberland Rd.

SHIELDFIELD

Haymarket

HAYMARKET
Ⓜ
Eldon Sq. Bus Station

John Dobson St.

College St.

Tennis Courts

Leazes Park

Percy St.

Northumberland St.

Durant Rd.

Central Library

New Bridge St. W.

St. James Park (Newcastle United Football Stadium)

Eldon Garden
Eldon Sq. Shopping

Central Library
Laing Art Gallery

Ⓜ MANORS

Barrack Rd. (A189)

Strawberry Pl.

ELDON SQ.
MONUMENT
Monument Mall

New Bridge St.

Ⓜ ST. JAMES

Blackett St.
Grey's Monument
Monument Ⓜ

St. Pilgrim St.

New Argyle St.

Stepney Ln.

Gallowgate Coach Station

Gallowgate
Newgate

Clayton St.
Grainger St.

Central Arcade

Market St.

Worswick St.

Melbourne St.

Wellington
Bath Ln.

Corporation St.

Stowell St.

Low Frias St.

Nun St.

Grainger Market

Theatre Royal

Grey St.

City Rd.   City Rd.

TO ⑤ (1.25 mi)

Bigg Market

High Bridge

Bath Ln.

Westgate Rd.

Groat Mkt.

Mosley St.

Dean St.

Blandford St.
Blenheim St.
Waterloo St.

Collingwood St.

St. Nicholas St.

All Saints

Clayton St.

St. Mary's Cathedral

CENTRAL

St. Nicholas

The Side

Quayside

Discovery Museum

Neville St.

Ⓜ

St. Nicholas St.

Castle Keep

South Shore

Westmorland Rd.
International Centre for Life

ℹ Central Station

Forth St.

Hanover St.

High Level Bridge

George St.

Railway St.

Forth Banks
The Close

Queen Elizabeth II

Swing Bridge

Tyne Bridge

Wellington St.

Gateshead Hwy.

Newcastle Arena

Pottery Ln.

River Tyne

Pipewellgate

High Level Rd.

Skinner Burn

King Edward Bridge Rd.
Redheugh Bridge

GATESHEAD

West St.

Askew Rd.

Prince Consort Rd.

Ⓜ GATESHEAD

The Brandling Guest House, 4 Brandling Park (☎281 3175). 9 spacious rooms on a quiet block of Jesmond, all with TV and sink. Singles and doubles £23-37.

The Brighton Guest House, 47-51 Brighton Grove, Fernham (☎273 3600; fax 226 0563), near the General Hospital. Either take a cheap taxi, a frequent bus (#10, 34-36, or 38) from the train station, or make the grueling 1½ mi. walk on Westgate Rd. and then left on Brighton Grove. The cheapest, largest rooms in town but well off the beaten track. All rooms with TV and sink. Singles from £16; doubles from £32.

⬛ FOOD

Every other restaurant in Newcastle has inexpensive pizza and pasta, and those in between serve everything from tandoori chicken to veggie burgers. Chinese eateries form a small Chinatown along **Stowell St.** near Gallowgate; all-you-can-eat specials for £4 to £6 are common. Many of the restaurants that line **Dean St.** serve cheap lunch specials. The **Grainger Indoor Market** is between Grainger St. and Grey St. near the monument. (Open M and W 7am-5pm, Tu and Th-Su 7am-5:30pm.)

Don Vito's, 82 Pilgrim St. (☎232 8923). Stands out among Italian eateries with generous pizzas and pastas for £4.75, replete with great toppings and inventive sauces. Try the *gnocchi*. Open M-F 11:45am-2pm and 5-10pm, Sa 11:45am-10:30pm.

Valley Junction 397, Archbold Terr. (☎281 6397), in the old station near the Jesmond Metro terminal. Sample Bengali-influenced cuisine while dining in an antique railway car. The Indian lager Kingfisher (£3.25) blends well with spinach-based paneers (£6-7). Vegan fare available. Open Tu-Sa noon-2pm and 6-11:30pm, Su 6-11:30pm.

Marco's Supernatural Vegetarian Restaurant, 2 Princess Sq. (☎261 2730). Facing the Central Library main entrance, take a left and go up the ramp; it's on your left. Expect more cheap delicious food and university types than paranormal activity. Main courses are £2.30-3.75. The quiche and two side salads are a bargain at £2.80. Vegan fare available. 10% student discount. Open daily 10:30am-10:30pm.

Fox Talbot, 46 Dean St. (☎230 2229). The earth tones and sheet-metal art may look too chi-chi for your budget, but this upscale eatery has terrific lunch deals: 2 courses and a glass of wine for under £5. Roast kangaroo, sweet potato chips, and red onion marmalade await the adventurous (£12). Open M-Sa 11am-11pm.

◔ SIGHTS

A combination of hoary old and resilient new, Newcastle's monuments blend in and out of the urban jungle. Between Central Station and the architectural masterpiece that is **Tyne Bridge** lingers the decrepit **Castle Keep.** The keep, at the foot of Dean St., is all that is left of the New Castle, erected in the 12th century on the site of a castle built in 1080 by Robert Curthose, bastard son of William the Conqueror. Oddly enough, the "New Castle" from which the city derives its name is in fact the older Curthose structure, not the 12th-century one. (☎232 7938. Open Apr.-Sept. Tu-Su 9:30am-5:30pm; Oct.-Mar. daily 9:30am-4:30pm. £1.50, concessions 50p.) Uphill on Mosley St., the **Cathedral Church of St. Nicholas** is topped with an elegant set of small towers around a double arch called "The Lantern," meant to resemble Jesus' crown of thorns. (Open M-F 7am-6pm, Sa 8am-4pm, Su 7am-noon and 4-7pm. Free.) The ⬛**Laing Art Gallery,** on New Bridge St., showcases an excellent collection of local art and a selection of fresh temporary exhibitions in a cutting-edge setting. (☎232 7734. Open M-Sa 10am-5pm, Su 2-5pm. Free.)

Newcastle has spearheaded its recent urban renewal with major projects showcasing science, technology, and the arts. Opened with fanfare in 2000, the extensively interactive **International Centre for Life** sprawls along Scotswood Rd. by the train station in Newcastle's own Times Square. Record your image at a photo caption station and watch yourself (d)evolve into a monkey or a jawed fish, among other prehistoric creatures. (☎243 8223, booking hotline 243 8201. Open daily 10am-6pm. £6.95, seniors and students £5.50, children £4.50, families £19.95.)

Gateshead Quay, opened in 2001, has rejuvenated the south bank. Snagging another first, the **Gateshead Millennium Bridge** is the only rotating bridge in the world, slowly opening like a giant eyelid to allow ships to pass. Nearby, the **Baltic Centre for Contemporary Art,** housed in a mid-century grain warehouse, is the largest center for contemporary visual art outside London, with 3 sq. km. of exhibition space. The unmissably metallic **Music Centre Gateshead** contains world-class music facilities and a permanent home for Northern Sinfonia, the Northumberland regional orchestra, and Folkworks, an agency dedicated to promoting traditional music (concert tickets £12). Daytrips from Newcastle include the castles at **Alnwick** and **Warkworth,** 20 mi. north by bus #518 (see p. 418), and **Hadrian's Wall** (see p. 415).

NIGHTLIFE AND ENTERTAINMENT

Home of the nectar known as brown ale, Newcastle's pub and club scene is legendary throughout England and, increasingly, the world at large. Nightlife is divided into two distinct areas: **Bigg Market,** a rowdy Geordie haven with the highest concentration of bars in all of England, and **Quayside** (KEY-side), which is slightly more relaxed and attracts local students. Be cautious at Bigg Market—this is where stocky footballer Paul "Gazza" Gascoigne got beaten up *twice* for deserting Newcastle, and underdressed student-types are frowned upon. The gay and lesbian scene centers around the corner of Waterloo St. and Sunderland St. in the city's southwest. *The Crack*, an offbeat magazine free at the TIC, has a calendar of live music and club events. The *Itchy Newcastle Insider's Guide* (£2.50) has more comprehensive information on shopping and clubbing. No matter what your plans, finish the night Newcastle-style with a kebab with extra chili sauce.

PUBS

Pubs are generally open M-Sa 11am-11pm and Su noon-6pm. Most pubs offer happy hours 4-8pm (Su 7-8pm).

Chase, 10-15 Sandhill (☎245 0055). Neon lighting and a fluorescent bar give this hopping pub its trendy rep. Designer drinks in a designer location under the Tyne Bridge.

Offshore 44, 40 Sandhill, Quayside (☎261 0921). Bearing an uncanny resemblance to a pirate's lair, this riverside pub blasts rock classics amid a decor of pirate chests, candles, and palm trees. Popular with the student crowd, yar.

Head of Steam, 2 Neville St. (☎232 4379). This split-level venue features the best in live soul, funk, and jazz reggae, as well as local DJs. Look for special mixing contests.

Fitzgeralds, 58-60 Grey Street (☎230 1350). An old-fashioned pub with a wood interior near the entertainment district, perfect for an afternoon cocktail or a pre-theater tipple.

CLUBS

Opening hours and special events vary with the season. Check the TIC or any of the numerous club gazettes doled out free at street-corners.

Tuxedo Princess, Hillgate Quay, Gateshead (☎477 8899). The hottest dance club in Newcastle is located on a decommissioned cruise ship under the Tyne Bridge. As if dancing on a boat weren't disorienting enough, one of this huge club's 2 dance-floors actually rotates. Open M and W-Sa 7:30pm-2am.

The Foundation, 57 Melbourne St. (☎261 8985). A flashy crowd fills this gutted factory warehouse with posh neon lighting and suspended balcony. Open M-Sa 7:30pm-2am.

The Baja Beach Club, Pipewellgate, Gateshead (☎477 6205). With a sandy beachfront on the River Tyne, Baja may be Newcastle's most crowded club. Along with the students, cheap drinks and chart-based music abound. Open M-Sa 8pm-2am.

Diva, New Bridge St. (☎261 2526). Home to the local punk scene, this small, rambunctious club spins James, the Charlatans, and the Roses. Very loud. 21+ on Sa. Open M-Sa 7:30pm-2am.

GAY AND LESBIAN

Rockshots 2, Waterloo St. (☎232 9648). Nationally renowned and the most exciting club in town. Ultra-modern decor and theme nights attract a varied clientele. W all you can drink for £7; Sa features the best DJs in house and garage. Open M-Sa 7pm-2am.

The Powerhouse, Waterloo St. (☎261 8874). The only exclusively gay club in all of Northeast England. Theme nights range from Cheap Booze Night to Classic Rock Night. Open M and Th 10pm-2am, Tu-W 11pm-1am, F-Sa 10am-3am.

The Village, Sunderland St. (☎261 8874), next to The Powerhouse. Described by locals as the "Champion Gay Bar," this pre-Powerhouse hangout has a seven-hour "happy hour" starting at noon. Open M-Sa noon-11pm and Su noon-6pm.

THEATER AND FESTIVALS

For seated entertainment, treat yourself to an evening at the lush gilt-and-velvet **Theatre Royal,** 100 Grey St. **The Royal Shakespeare Company** makes a month-long stop here, beginning the last week in September. (☎232 2061. Box office open M-Sa 10am-8pm. Tickets from £5-33; occasional discounts. Buy tickets for four or more plays and receive upper circle seats for only £7.) In the last full week of June, New-castle hosts **The Hoppings,** the largest seasonal fair in the world, with 28-30 acres of traveling showmen and general craziness. Call the TIC for more information.

NORTHUMBERLAND

NORTHUMBERLAND NATIONAL PARK

Northumberland is somewhat like Northumberland Avenue on the London version of Monopoly—tucked in the corner, not particularly sought after, and occasionally stacked with tiny houses. Perched at the edge of the Scottish frontier, these deso-late hills were once the site of skirmishes involving first territorial Romans, then Anglo-Saxons. Today, the 400 sq. mi. Northumberland National Park stretches south from the grassy Cheviot Hills near the border to the dolomitic crags of Whin Sill, where it includes part of Hadrian's Wall. Visitors are guaranteed a struggle with its poor public transport network, but this least populated and roughest-edged of all England's National Parks is blissfully free from tourist legions.

▐▌ TRANSPORTATION

As buses run more frequently up the coast than between the towns on the park's inland borders, Newcastle, Alnwick, and Berwick-upon-Tweed the best bases for exploration. On the park's border, Rothbury (southwest of Alnwick) and Wooler (northwest of Alnwick) enjoy the most frequent connections, halfway between "slightly accessible" and "left for dead" on the Access Meter. Postbuses creep like snails on somewhat erratic schedules; contact a post office for timetables.

Trains (☎(08457) 484950) run to **Berwick** from: **Newcastle** (1hr., 13 per day, £10.80); **York** (2hr.; M-F and Su 13 per day, Sa 16 per day; £29.80); **Edinburgh** (45min.; M-Sa 25 per day, Su 18 per day; £11.90). **Buses** are cheaper, if less comfort-able. Buses #505 and 515 go from **Newcastle** to **Berwick** via **Alnwick** (2hr., every 2hr., £11.25). From Alnwick, #501 leaves for **Craster,** going up the coast to Dunstan-burgh Castle, Seahouses, and Bamburgh Castle (2hr., every 2hr., £2.20-7). Bus #464 connects **Wooler** and **Berwick** (30min., 3-4 per day, £2.55); #469, 470, and 473 con-nect **Alnwick** and **Wooler** (45min., every hr., £3.75). Bus #416 runs from **Newcastle** to

Morpeth and **Rothbury** (M-Sa 8 per day, Su 2 per day; £2.40). Smart ramblers will invest in a **Northeast Explorer** ticket (£5.25, seniors and under 14 £4.25, families £10.50), good for unlimited one-day use on most local buses.

The major obstacle to area transport is the large military training area smack in the middle of the park, forcing all traffic to endure a significant detour. Hikers and bikers should be aware of this zone and steer clear—signs advise the avoidance of small, metallic objects as "they might explode and kill you." If you don't have a car or bicycle, staying overnight in Berwick, with its train and bus service, is your best bet. From there buses depart to most coastal hotspots. If you plan to village-hop, obtain the essential 256-page tome *Northumberland Public Transport Guide* (£1), available at any tourist information centre (TIC) or bus station, or by sending £1.75 to the Public Transport Office, County Hall, Morpeth, Northumberland NE61 2EF. (☎(0191) 212 3000. Open M-F 8am-5:15pm, Sa 8:30am-3pm.)

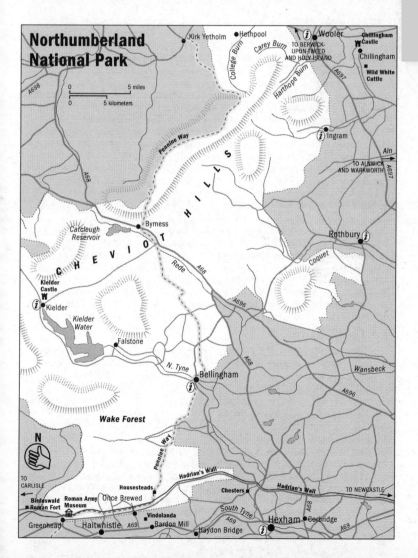

◪ THE PARK

THE SOUTH PARK

The south park embraces Hadrian's Wall (p. 415), Wark Forest, and strings of low hills. The main **National Park Information Centre** is in **Hexham.** (☎ (01434) 605225; see p. 417). The Pennine Way penetrates the park at **Greenhead,** a meek village on Hadrian's Wall 25 mi. east of Carlisle and 40 mi. west of Newcastle, which possesses a **YHA Youth Hostel** (☎ (016977) 47401; see p. 416). The path winds 7 mi. east to **Once Brewed,** home of the **YHA Once Brewed** (☎ (01434) 344360; see p. 416).

From Once Brewed, the path continues 14 mi. northeast to Bellingham (BELL-ing-um), due west of Morpeth. In town, the **YHA Bellingham,** Woodburn Rd., overlooks the village and countryside. (☎/fax (01434) 220313. Open July-Aug. daily; June and Sept.-Oct. M-Sa. Dorms £5.75, under 18 £3.60.) The Bellingham **tourist information centre,** Fountain Cottage, on Main St., details nearby walks, including a two-mile stroll through a ravine to the **Hareshaw Linn Waterfall.** (☎ (01434) 220616. Open June-Sept. M-Sa 10am-1pm and 2-6pm, Su 1-5pm; off-season hours reduced.)

Just outside the west boundary of the park lies **Kielder Water,** the largest man-made lake in Europe. From Bellingham, bus #814 (30min.; M-F 3-5 per day, Sa 2 per day; £2) and postbus #815 (45min.; M-F 2 per day, Sa 1 per day; 70p) run west to **Kielder,** on the northern tip of Kielder Water. **Water Cruises** run from docks on the lake. (☎ (01434) 240436. Tours July-Aug. 4 per day, 10am-6pm; off-season hours reduced. £4.50, children £3.30, families £17.) Built in 1775 by the Earl Percy, Duke of Northumberland, **Kielder Castle** now houses the **Kielder Castle Visitor Centre,** which holds exhibits on the park's flora and fauna and a small art gallery. (Open June-Aug. daily 9:30am-6pm; Mar.-May 10am-5pm; Sept.-Oct. 9:30am-5pm; Nov. to mid-Mar. Sa-Su 10am-3pm.) The **tourist information centre** at Tower Knowe, ¾ mi. from the village of **Falstone** on the southeastern shore, hosts a fishing tackle shop and restaurant. (☎ (01434) 240398; fax 250130. Open June-Aug. daily 9:30am-6pm; Mar.-May 10am-5pm; Sept.-Oct. 9:30am-5pm; Nov. to mid-Mar. Sa-Su 10am-3pm.)

High hills to the east and dense forests to the west accompany the 15 mi. Pennine stretch from Bellingham northwest to **Byrness,** home to a **YHA Youth Hostel,** 7 Otterburn Green, with a god-given drying room, cafe, and shop nearby. (☎ (01830) 520425. Open July-Aug. daily; Apr.-June and Sept. W.-M. Dorms £5.75, under 18 £3.60.) Bus #915 runs from **Bellingham** (45min., M-F 2 per day, £4). From Byrness, the Pennine Way finishes with a boggy 27 mi. stretch through the Cheviots. Since this area of the park is bereft of hostels until the trail's end in **Kirk Yetholm,** Scotland (☎ (01573) 420631; see p. 525), be sure to bring proper camping equipment.

THE NORTH PARK

At the northern boundary of the park, miles from the Pennine Way and semi-decent bus service, Wooler provides access to less strenuous daytrips into the **Cheviots**—a picturesque range of long dormant volcanos along the English-Scottish border—especially around the Glendale and Kyloe areas. Barring possession of a cycle or car, serious hikers can speed by taxi to trailheads at **Duns-dale, Mounthooly,** and **Hethpool,** each over 8 mi. away. Inquire at the TIC about taxis, or call **Glendale Taxis** (☎ (01668) 282292). The revamped **YHA Wooler,** 30 Cheviot St., has comfortable dorms 300 yd. uphill from the bus station and arranges group expeditions. (☎ (01668) 281365; fax 282368. Open Apr.-Aug. daily; Sept.-Oct. M-Sa; Mar. F.-Sa. Dorms £8.35, under 18 £5.65.) **Camp** at **High-burn House,** on Burnhouse St. near Wooler's High St. (☎ (01668) 281344. £4 per adult, 50p per child. Laundry facilities. Electricity £1.50. Showers 20p.) The **tourist information centre,** 11 Market Pl., suggests climbs in the Cheviots and gentler walks through the Happy and College Valleys. (☎ (01668) 282123. Open Apr.-Oct. M-Sa 10am-1pm and 2-5pm, Su 10am-2pm.)

Roughly 5 mi. southeast of Wooler, the quirky town of **Chillingham** struts its strange stuff. King Edward I stayed in **Chillingham Castle** while charting his campaign against William Wallace's rebellion. Among its present occupants is a collection of 15 ft. wide antlers from the now-extinct Irish elk. (☎ (01668) 215359. Open July-Aug. daily noon-5pm; May-June and Sept. W-M noon-5pm. Oct.-Apr. groups only by appointment. $4.30, seniors $3.80.) Next door to the castle graze the 60-odd **Wild White Cattle,** the total world endowment of entirely purebred cattle. Originally enclosed in 1235, the cattle have been inbred for over seven centuries, not a single heifer introduced from the outside. Sleek and broad-shouldered, they resemble other cows, but cannot be herded, will attack humans, and may even kill one of their own if he or she is touched by human hands. (☎ (01668) 215250. Warden-led tours 1-1½hr. Open Apr.-Oct. M and W-Sa 10am-noon and 2-5pm, Su 2-5pm. $3, students and seniors $2.50, children $1.) To get to Chillingham take a cab ($6.50) or bus #470, 473, or 871 from Wooler or Alnwick (20min., 3 per day, $1.10).

The nearest **National Park Visitor Centre** is 7 mi. south in **Ingram.** (☎/fax (01665) 578248. Open July-Aug. daily 10am-6pm; Mar.-June and Sept. 10am-5pm.) A **Gold Leaf Travel bus** runs between Wooler and Ingram every 1½hr. Twenty-five miles farther south of Wooler off the A697 on the B6341, the village of **Rothbury** sits in a densely wooded valley carved by the River Coquet, and has another **National Park Visitor Centre** networked with a **tourist information centre,** Church St. (☎/fax (01669) 620887. Open July-Aug. daily 10am-6pm; Apr.-June and Sept.-Oct. 10am-5pm.)

♫ FESTIVALS

In July, the **common ridings** are week-long festivals occurring in each Northumberland town at different times throughout the month. Locals dressed in their finest clothes parade on horseback through town and country accompanied by traditional marching bands and the Burgh Flag, a symbol of community spirit. The celebration commemorates the tradition of riding through a town's land holdings to establish and preserve boundaries and burgh rights.

HADRIAN'S WALL

When Roman Emperor Hadrian ordered that a wall be built in AD 122, official word went out that he wanted to mark his boundaries, but everyone knew he was just scared of the barbarians to the north (see **An Island to Call Their Own,** p. 67). Hadrian's unease created a permanent monument on the Roman frontier—first a V-shaped ditch 27 ft. wide, then a stone barrier 15 ft. high and 8-9 ft. across. Eight years, 17 milecastles (forts), 5500 cavalrymen, and 13,000 infantrymen later, Hadrian's Wall stretched unbroken for 73 mi. from modern-day Carlisle to Newcastle. The years have not been kind to Hadrian's project. Most of the wall's stones have been carted off and recycled into the surrounding structures, and the portions that remain stand at only half their original height. The highest concentration of remains scatters along the western part of the original wall, at the southern edge of Northumberland National Park (see p. 412).

▐ TRANSPORTATION. The wall is best accessed by car; failing that, **buses** are available. Between May and September, **Stagecoach Cumberland** (☎ (01946) 63222) sends the **Hadrian's Wall Bus,** a.k.a. #682, from English St. in **Carlisle** to **Hexham,** stopping at all the wall's major sights (2hr., 4 per day, $1.40-4.40). From **Newcastle,** bus #685 runs to **Carlisle** via **Hexham, Haltwhistle, Greenhead,** and other wall-related towns (2hr., 12 per day, $3.60-8.) A **Hadrian's Wall Bus Whole Day Rover ticket,** available from tourist information centres (TICs) or bus drivers, is a good idea for those planning to make numerous journeys within one day ($5.50, children $3, families $11). Another option is the **Hadrian's Wall Rover,** a 2-out-of-3-day ticket valid between Sunderland and Carlisle on the Tyne Valley train line, on the Hadrian's Wall Bus, and on the Tyne & Wear Metro ($13, children $6.50).

NORTHEAST ENGLAND

MAN-SIZED ROCKS Visitors to Hadrian's Wall often notice that all the blocks used in its construction are the same, user-friendly size. Historians know little about how the wall was built, but one theory suggests the following: although famous for their streamlined highways, the Romans had to construct winding roads to accommodate Britannia's hilly terrain and swamp-filled countryside. Since bends in the roads became perfect hiding places for brigands, Roman soldiers were under constant pressure to defend themselves while working for foreman Hadrian. Large stones that required two men to carry them were hazardous, as a sudden attack could cause one soldier to drop the stone, breaking the toes of the other (steel-toed sandals hadn't been invented yet). The stones we see today were probably cut to be just large enough for one person to carry, but small enough to be tossed away in the event of an ambush.

Trains (☎ (08457) 484950) run frequently between **Carlisle** and **Newcastle,** but stations all lie 1½-4 mi. from the wall; be prepared to hike to the nearest stones. Trains depart from **Carlisle** to: **Brampton,** 2 mi. from Lanercost and 5 mi. from Birdoswald (20min.; M-Sa 7 per day, Su 5 per day; £3.90, return £5.60); **Haltwhistle,** 2 mi. from Cawfields (35min.; M-Sa 12 per day, Su 7 per day; £4.85, return £6.60); **Bardon Mill,** 2 mi. from Vindolanda and 4½ mi. from Housesteads (40min.; M-Sa 7 per day, Su 5 per day; £5.40, return £9); **Hexham** (50min.; M-Sa 2 per hr., Su 9 per day; £7.10, return £12.10). Call **Northumberland Transport Enquiries** (☎ (01670) 533128) or **Cumbria Journey Planner** (☎ (01228) 606000) for more information.

■🛈 **ORIENTATION AND PRACTICAL INFORMATION.** Hadrian's Wall stands between the urban centers of Carlisle to the west and Newcastle to the east. The towns of **Greenhead, Haltwhistle, Once Brewed, Bardon Mill, Haydon Bridge, Hexham** (the hub of Hadrian's Wall transportation), and **Corbridge** lie somewhat parallel to the wall from west to east. The **Hexham tourist information centre** (TIC), at the bottom of the hill across from the abbey on Hallgate Road, offers accommodations booking as well as the useful pamphlets *The Essential Guide to Hadrian's Wall* (30p) and the free *Hadrian's Wall: Where to Stay for Walkers.* The **Northumberland National Park Information Centre** in **Once Brewed,** on Military Rd., is also helpful. (☎ (01434) 344396 or 344777. Open Mar.-Oct. daily 9:30am-5:30pm.)

🛏 **ACCOMMODATIONS.** Both **Carlisle** and **Hexham** have abundant B&Bs and make good bases for day journeys to the wall. Two youth hostels lie on the route of the Hadrian's Wall Bus. The **YHA Greenhead Youth Hostel,** 16 mi. east of Carlisle, is a converted chapel with modern facilities steps away from the wall. (☎/fax (016977) 47401. Lockout 10am-5pm. Open July-Aug. daily; Apr. to June M-Sa; Sept.-Oct. F-Tu. Dorms £8.10, under 18 £5.80.) The **YHA Once Brewed Youth Hostel,** Military Rd., Bardon Mill, has a central location 2½ mi. northwest of the Bardon Mill train station, 3 mi. from Housesteads Fort, 1 mi. from Vindolanda, and ½ mi. from the wall itself. (☎ (01434) 344360; fax 344045. Laundry and Internet. Binocular rental after 1pm. Lockout 10am-1pm. Open Apr.-Aug. daily; Sept.-Oct. M-Sa; Mar. F-Sa. Dorms £11, under 18 £7.50.) An independent hostel, the isolated **Hadrian Lodge** makes a good base for serious walkers; take a train to Haydon Bridge, then follow the main road uphill for 2½ mi. (☎ (01434) 688688. Breakfast £1.50-3.50. Kitchen and laundry facilities. Dorms £10; singles £23-28; doubles £42-45.)

◪ **SIGHTS.** Pick up the free *Visitors' Guide to Hadrian's Wall* from a TIC; **Supersaver tickets** are good for admission to both Vindolanda and the Roman Army Museum. (£5.85, students and seniors £4.80, children £4.20, families £18.) All sights listed below are accessible by the Hadrian's Wall Bus. If you have limited money or time, be sure to visit **Housesteads,** the most complete Roman fort in Britain, 5 mi. northeast of Bardon Mill on the B6318. The well-preserved ruins are freckled with informative billboards, and the site itself guards a good length of unbroken wall stretching far from the crowds. Sheep ignore the "Please keep off the walls" signs, but you shouldn't: walking on the wall is as dangerous for you as it is damaging to the wall. (☎(01434) 344363. Open Apr.-Sept. daily 10am-6pm; Oct. 10am-5pm; Nov.-Mar. 10am-4pm. £2.90, students and seniors £2.20, children £1.50.)

Constructed of stones permanently "borrowed" from the wall, the **Roman Army Museum** at Carvoran, ¾ mi. northeast of Greenhead, presents impressive stockpiles of artifacts, interactive stations, and a faux Roman Army recruiting video. (☎(016977) 47485. Open Apr.-Sept. daily 10am-6pm; Mar. and Oct. 10am-5pm; Nov.-Feb. 10am-4pm. £3.10, students and seniors £2.70, children £2.10.) Several well-preserved milecastles and bridges lie between Greenhead and **Birdoswald Roman Fort.** The fort itself, 15 mi. east of Carlisle, is the site of recent excavations, with views of wall, turret, and milecastle. An interactive visitor center introduces Hadrian's Wall and follows Birdoswald's 2000-year history. (☎(016977) 47602. Open Mar.-Nov. daily 10am-5:30pm; reduced hours in Nov. Museum and wall £2.50, students and seniors £2, children £1.50, families £6.50. Wall only £1, children 50p.) **Vindolanda,** 1½ mi. north of Bardon Mill and 1 mi. southeast of Once Brewed, is a fort and civilian settlement that predates the wall. Extensive excavations have revealed hundreds of inscribed wooden tablets that illuminate details of Roman life. (☎(01434) 344277. Open same hours as the Roman Army Museum. £3.90, students and seniors £3.30, children £2.80.) Dramatically situated on the cliffs of Maryport next to the Roman fort, the **Senhouse** museum houses Britain's oldest antiquarian collection, with revealing exhibits on Roman religion and warfare. (☎(01900) 816168. Open July-Oct. daily 10am-5pm; Nov.-Mar. F-Su 10.30am-4pm; Apr.-June Tu and Th-Su 10am-5pm. Adult £2, child 75p.) From Chollerford, 3 mi. north of Hexham, the best-preserved cavalry fort in Britain, **Chesters,** can be reached by a footpath leading ¼ mi. west. The extensive remains of a Roman bath house sidle the fort's riverside setting; a museum houses altars and sculptures from the wall. (☎(01434) 681379. Open Apr.-Sept. daily 9:30am-4pm; Oct. 10am-5pm; Nov.-Mar. 10am-4pm. £2.90, students and seniors £2.20, children £1.50.)

HEXHAM   ☎01434

West of Newcastle on the A69, well-heeled Hexham makes a fine base for exploring Hadrian's Wall, but also charms with its own sights. The cobbled town center coils around its impressively kept abbey, the **Priory Church of St. Andrew.** Built by Augustinian canons, the Abbey, as it's familiarly known, houses the 7th-century bishop's throne of St. Wilfrid. (☎602031. Open May-Sept. daily 9am-7pm; Oct.-Apr. daily 9am-5pm. Suggested donation £2.) Facing the abbey, the substantial 14th-century **Gatehouse Tower** recalls Hexham's turbulent past. For more corporeal evidence, sample the punishments of the **Border History Museum,** behind Market Pl. in the Old Gaol House. Built by decree in 1332, this early prison includes a dungeon and interactive stocks and pillory. (☎652349. Open Apr.-Oct. daily 10am-4:30pm; Feb.-Mar. and Nov. M-Tu and Sa 10am-4:30pm. Free.)

The **train station** is on Station Rd., 5min. from Market Pl. **Trains** (☎(08457) 484950) stop (M-Sa 15 per day, Su 9 per day) on their way between **Carlisle** (50min.; £7.10) and **Newcastle** (40min.; £4.50). The **bus station** is on Priestpopple Rd., south of Market Pl. From May to September, **Stagecoach Cumberland** (☎(01946) 63222) bus #682, a.k.a. the **Hadrian's Wall Bus,** runs from English St. in **Carlisle** along the wall's major sights, ending in Hexham (2hr., 4 per day, £1.40-4.40). Bus #685 runs from **Newcastle** (2hr., 12 per day, £3.60-8). See **Transportation,** p. 415.

Pass through the liberal arch of the Gatehouse Tower to reach the combined **tourist information centre** (TIC) and **Northumberland National Park Information Centre** in the Old Gaol House on Hallgate. It provides up-to-date information on visits to the wall, books accommodations for the Hexham area, and runs free guided walking tours from June to mid-September. (☎605225; fax 600325. Open mid-May to Sept. M-Sa 9am-6pm, Su 10am-5pm; Oct. to mid-May M-Sa 9am-5pm.) Other services include: **banks** along Battle Hill and Priestpopple Rd.; **Thomas Cook,** 12 Battle Hill (☎605233; open M and W-Sa 9am-5:30pm, Tu 10am-5:30pm); the **police,** Shaftoe Leages (☎604111); the **General Hospital,** Corbridge Rd. (☎655655); **Internet access** at **NBS The Computer Shop,** 10b Hencotes (☎600022; £1 per 10min.; open M-F 9:30am-5:30pm, Sa 9:30am-4:30pm); and the **post office,** Priestpopple Rd., hidden within Robbs of Hexham department store (☎602001; open M-Tu, Th, and Sa 8:30am-5:30pm, W 9am-5:30pm, F 8:30am-6pm). **Postal code:** NE46 1NA.

For a delightful stay, make your way up the flower-filled path to the antique-stuffed interior of Mrs. Boaden's **Number 18 B&B,** 18 Hexham Terr. (☎602265. Singles £17; doubles £34.) **Bunters Cafe,** 10 Hallgate, across from the TIC, serves a traditional English menu during the day (£2-5), plus a handful of Greek dishes (£3-4.50); by night, the cafe becomes **Athena's Mediterranean Restaurant,** with fewer of the English standards and slightly higher prices. (Cafe open M-Sa 10am-4:30pm, Su 10:45am-4:30pm; restaurant open Tu-Sa 6:30-9:30pm.) For fruits and vegetables, try **Stafford's Fruiterer and Florist,** at the top of Fore St. (☎602632. Open M-Sa 8am-5pm, Su 10am-4pm.) Across Market Pl., take in a quiet pint at the **Heart of All England** pub, Market St. (Open M-Sa 11am-11pm, Su 11am-10pm.)

ALNWICK AND WARKWORTH ☎01665

About 31 mi. north of Newcastle off the A1, the tiny town of **Alnwick** (AHN-ick; pop. 7400) settles quietly beside the magnificently preserved ⬛**Alnwick Castle,** a former Percy family stronghold and now home to the Duke and Duchess of Northumberland. This rugged Norman-fortification-turned-stately-home, featured in the films *Elizabeth* and *Harry Potter,* gives way to an ornate Italian Renaissance interior, circled by three small museums. (☎510777. Open Easter-Sept. daily 11am-5pm, last admission 4:15pm. £6.25, students and seniors £5.25, children £3.50, families £15.) Alnwick's well-supplied **tourist information centre** is at 2 The Shambles, Market Pl. (☎510665; fax 510477. Open July-Aug. M-Sa 9am-6:30pm, Su 9am-5pm; off season reduced.) **Barter Books,** one of Britain's largest secondhand bookshops, also provides **Internet access** under the circling tracks of a model train. (☎604888. £1.50 per 15min. Open July-Aug. daily 9am-7pm; Sept.-June M-W and F-Su 9am-5pm, Th 9am-7pm.) By the **bus station,** 10 Clayport St. (☎602182; open M-Sa 9am-5pm), is a **launderette,** 5 Clayport St. (☎604398; open M-F 8am-7pm, Sa-Su 9am-5pm). The **post office** is at 19 Market St. **Postal code:** NE66 155.

Stay with Mrs. Givens and her affectionate mutt at **The Tea Pot,** 8 Bondgate Without, and yes, that's a street name. (☎604473. £17-18 per person; £1 off if you mention *Let's Go.*) ⬛**The Town House** vegetarian restaurant, 15 Narrowgate, serves baguettes (£2.15) and other creative meals (£5-8) in a warm atmosphere decorated with wine-bottle candlesticks. (☎606336. Open M-F 10:30am-3pm, Sa 10am-4pm, Su from noon; F-Sa also from 6:30pm.) Get groceries at **Safeway,** beside the bus station. (☎510126. Open M-Th 8:30am-10pm, F 8am-10pm, Sa 8am-9pm, Su 9am-5pm.)

Seven mi. southeast of Alnwick, the evocative ruins of 12th-century **Warkworth Castle** guard the mouth of the River Coquet. The extraordinary 15th-century keep, foundation rubble, and largely intact curtain wall come to life in an excellent audio tour. (☎711423. Open Apr.-Sept. daily 10am-6pm; Oct. 10am-5pm; Nov.-Mar. 10am-1pm and 2-4pm. Adults £2.50, students and seniors £1.90, children £1.30. 40min. audio tour included.) Shakespeare set much of *Henry IV Part I* in Warkworth; the 14th-century **hermitage** carved from the Coquet cliffs is the reputed site of Harry Hotspur's baptism. The staff at the castle will row you there. (Open Apr.-Sept. W and Su 11am-5pm. £1.70, students and seniors £1.30, children 90p.)

BERWICK-UPON-TWEED ☎01289

Just south of the Scottish border, Berwick-upon-Tweed (BARE-ick) has changed hands more often than any town in Britain—14 times between 1100 and 1500 alone. The battle blood in town flows so hot that a popular local legend claims Berwick was at war with Russia for over 50 years. Supposedly Queen Victoria used her full title in the 1854 declaration of war, "Queen of Great Britain, Ireland, Berwick-upon-Tweed, and the British dominions beyond the sea," but neglected to include Berwick in the peace treaty. Most of the town's **castle** is buried beneath the train station, although the 13th-century **Breakneck Stairs,** opposite the terminal, can still be ascended for ocean views. (Open M-Sa 6:30am-7:50pm, Su 10:15am-7:30pm. Free.) For a sense of Berwick and its turbulent history, traverse the 16th-century **Elizabethan Walls,** built to encircle the Old Town. The town's most substantial sight is the tongue-twisting **Berwick Barracks** on the corner of Parade and Ravensdowne. The early 18th-century structures now contain a museum on military life, a crowded exhibit on Berwick's history, and a terrific contemporary art gallery, the **Berwick Gymnasium.** (☎304493. Open Apr.-Sept. daily 10am-6pm; Oct. 10am-4pm; Nov.-Mar. W-Su 10am-4pm. £2.70, students and seniors £2, children £1.40.) Berwick also makes a good base for exploring the fine houses and abbeys of the Scottish Borders, only a short bus ride away, and is the end of **St. Cuthbert's Way,** a hike that begins in Melrose (see p. 525).

The **Bus Information Shop,** at the uphill end of Marygate, sells National Express tickets. (☎307283. Open M-F 9am-5pm.) Buses stop at the **train station,** Golden Sq., Chapel St., or opposite the bus shop. The **tourist information centre,** 106 Marygate, books rooms for a 10% deposit. (☎330733; fax 330448. Open M-Sa 10am-6pm, Su 11am-4pm.) The **post office** (☎307596) is down the street. **Postal code:** TD15 1BH.

In need of scenic views of the River Tweed, luxurious baths, and antique-riddled rooms, all in an 18th-century former pub? Stay at the **White Swan,** 57 Castlegate. (☎305046. £16.50 per person.) Stock up on foodstuffs at the **North Eastern Co-Op,** 15 Marygate. (☎302596. Open M-Sa 9am-5:30pm.)

◪ DAYTRIPS FROM BERWICK-UPON-TWEED

HOLY ISLAND AND BAMBURGH CASTLE

Ten miles from Berwick-upon-Tweed, wind-swept ◪**Holy Island,** connected to the mainland at low tide by a causeway, rises just off the coast, an ideal daytrip for the romantically inclined. Seven years after Northumberland's King Edwin converted to Christianity in AD 627, the missionary Aidan arrived from the Scottish island of Iona to found England's first monastery, **Lindisfarne Priory,** the ruins of which still stand. (☎(01289) 389200. Open Apr.-Oct. daily 10am-6pm; Nov.-Mar. 10am-4pm. £2.90, students and seniors £2.20, children £1.50.) To save your shillings, the hill beyond the priory provides a good view of the remains. Also on the island, **Lindisfarne Castle** is a 16th-century fort later converted into a private residence. The castle's hilltop perch is spectacular from the outside, though its interior contains only a plain display of 19th-century furnishings. (☎(01289) 389244. Open Apr.-Oct. M-Th and Sa-Su noon-3pm, possibly 1½hr. earlier or later depending on tides. £4.20, families £10.50.) The island's most serene spot is also completely free: tiny **Saint Cuthbert's Island,** marked by a wooden cross 220 yd. off the coast of the priory, is where the famed saint took his hermitage when even the monastery proved too distracting. **Lindisfarne Mead,** a local concoction dating back to the Middle Ages that blends fermented honey with white wine, is still made by the island's monks.

Check tide tables at a TIC before you go, and bring a jacket; the wind can be so strong that birds fly as if intoxicated. You can cross the four-mile causeway only at low tide. Don't try swimming, as tidal currents are strong. Bus #477 (☎(0191) 212 3000) runs from Berwick to Holy Island (Feb.-Aug. 2-3 times per week, £1.90); schedules vary with the tides. Jim of **Jim's Taxis** (☎(01289) 302814, mobile (0977) 143530) can drive you over the causeway before the tide sweeps in.

◪**Bamburgh Castle,** a stunning Northumbrian landmark, straddles a rocky outcropping 25 mi. from Berwick. The castle's renovation began in the 1890s when it was acquired by the first Baron Armstrong. Today, the sumptuous interior contains one of the largest armories outside London. The public tour includes a glimpse of the ornate, vaulted ceilings of **King's Hall** and the eerie **catacombs** and **dungeon.** Reach the surrounding village by bus #515 from Berwick (25min., 8 per day, £2.75). Holy Island and Bamburgh Castle can be seen in a single day, though the tides make scheduling tight.

WALES (CYMRU)

> This nation, O King, may now as in former times, be harassed, and in a great
> measure weakened and destroyed by your and other Powers...but it can never be
> totally subdued through the wrath of man, unless the wrath of God shall concur.
> —an Old Man of Pencader to Henry II, quoted by Giraldus Cambrensis

Wales borders England, but if many of the 2.9 million Welsh people had their dru-
thers, they would be floating miles away. Since England solidified its control over
the country in 1282 with the murder of Prince Llywelyn ap Gruffydd (also known
as Llywelyn the Last), relations between the two have been marked by a powerful
unease—do not refer to the Welsh as "English." Until late in the 19th century,
schoolchildren were forbidden to speak Welsh in the classroom. Those who did
were made to wear a "Welsh Knot" around their necks, which was passed around
to the next child who dared speak Welsh; whoever was wearing the knot at the end
of the day would earn some form of punishment. Despite such dominance, Wales
clings steadfastly to its Celtic heritage, continuing a centuries-old struggle for
independence. The mellifluous Welsh language endures in conversation, commerce, and literature, both oral and written. As churning coal, steel, and slate
mines fell victim to Britain's faltering economy, Wales turned its economic eye
from heavy industry to tourism. Travelers come for the miles of sandy beaches,
grassy cliffs, and dramatic mountains that typify the rich landscape of this corner
of Britain, or to scan the numerous castles that dot the towns, remnants of long
battle with England. Against this striking backdrop, Welsh nationalists express
their dissatisfaction peacefully in the voting booths and in a celebration of their
distinctive culture and language at events like the Royal National Eisteddfod.

TRANSPORTATION

TRAINS

Britrail passes are accepted on all trains through Wales except narrow-gauge railways. Those traveling solely within Wales can purchase region-specific passes,
such as the **Freedom of Wales Flexipass** (8 days in 15 June-Sept. £92, Oct.-May £75; 4
days in 8 June-Sept. £55, Oct.-May £45), good on the entire Welsh network plus
Chester to Abergavenny via Crewe, and also valid on all buses (see below). The
Cambrian Coast Day Ranger (£6.60; £3.70 after 4:30pm) earns a day's rail travel from
Aberystwyth north to Pwllheli on the Llŷn Peninsula. The **Freedom of South Wales 7-
Day Flexi Rover** and **North and Mid Wales 7-Day Flexi Rover** cover both train and bus
travel; see **Buses,** below. Call **National Rail Enquiries** (☎ (08457) 484950) for train
information. **Narrow-gauge railways** tend to be attractions in themselves, rather than
actual means of transport. Trainspotters can purchase a **Great Little Trains of Wales
Wanderer** ticket, which gives unlimited travel on the Ffestiniog, Welsh Highland,
Bala Lake, Brecon Mountain, Talyllyn, Llanberis Lake, Welshpool and Llanfair, and
Vale of Rheidol lines. (4 days in 8 £35, 8 days in 15 £45, children half-price.)

BUSES

Pronouncing your destination properly will probably be the least of your problems
as you navigate the overlapping routes of Wales's 65 bus operators. Most of these
are local services; almost every region is dominated by one or two companies.
Life-saving regional public transport guides, available free in tourist information
centres (TICs), exist for many areas, but for others you'll have to consult an array
of small brochures. The free and very useful *Wales Bus, Rail, and Tourist Map
and Guide* provides information on bus routes, but not on timetables. Take all
bus schedules with a grain of salt, as buses can run late. Many local buses don't
run on Sunday, while some special tourist buses run *only* on summer Sundays.

Wales

TO DUN LAOGHAIRE, DUBLIN

Irish Sea

Amlwch

Liverpool

Birkenhead
Hoylake

R. Mersey

Holyhead

ANGLESEY

Conwy Bay Llandudno

Conwy

Dee Estuary

M53

M56

Holy Island

Penmon

Beaumaris

Llanfair P.G.

Bangor

Conwy

A55

Chester

A55

Trefriw

Llanwrstt *Brenig Reservoir*

A5

Caernarfon

Capel Curig

Menai Strait

Llanberis

Snowdon

Betws-y-Coed

Caernarfon Bay

Wrexham

LLŶN PENINSULA

Porthmadog

Blaenau Ffestiniog

Corwen

Llangollen

Chirk

Portmeirion

Dee

Cerniog

Pwllheli

Criccieth

Lake Bala

A5

Snowdonia National Park

Lake Vyrnwy

Tanat

Severn

Aberdaron

Abersoch

Harlech

A470

Cardigan Bay

Barmouth

Dolgellau

Dovey

Cader Idris

Shrewsbury

Aberdyfi

Machynlleth

Borth

Newtown

A470

A49

Severn

Aberystwyth

Wye

Ludlow

Knighton

CAMBRIAN MOUNTAINS

Rhayader

A470

Aberaeron

Llandrindod Wells

TO ROSSLARE HARBOR

Lampeter

Llanwrtyd Wells

Builth Wells

Cardigan

Teifi

A483

Clyro

Hereford

Hay-on-Wye

River Wye

A49

Fishguard

St. David's

Mynydd Preseli

Llandovery

Brecon

Black Mountains

PEMBROKESHIRE COAST NATIONAL PARK

St. Bride's Bay

Haverfordwest

Carmarthen

Llandeilo

A40

A40

Black Mountain

Brecon Beacons National Park

Abergavenny

Monmouth

A40

Amroth

Merthyr Tydfil

Tintern Wye Valley

A449

Pembroke

Tenby

Aberdare

Pontypool

Chepstow

Manorbier

Llanelli

Tawe

Cwmbran

Swansea

Port Talbot

Newport

Carmarthen Bay

GOWER PENINSULA

Mumbles

M4

Cardiff

R. Severn

Swansea Bay

Mouth of the Severn

TO CORK

Bristol

Barry

0   30 miles

0   30 kilometers

N

Bristol Channel

/////// **Narrow gauge rail**

TrawsCambria (☎(08706) 082608) bus #701 is the main north-south bus line. On it, you can travel from Cardiff or Swansea north to Machynlleth, Bangor, and Holyhead. BritRail and Freedom of Wales rail passes are valid on the bus. Within South Wales, **Cardiff Bus** (timetables ☎(08706) 082608, other enquiries (029) 2066 6444) blankets the area around Cardiff, while **Stagecoach Red and White** (☎(01633) 266336) buses serve the routes from Gloucester and Hereford in England west through the Wye Valley, past Abergavenny and Brecon. **First Cymru** (☎(08706) 082608) covers the Gower Peninsula and the rest of southwest Wales, including the Pembrokeshire Coast National Park.

Passes simplify bus fares. Cardiff Bus offers the **City Rider** day pass (£2.85, children £1.90, families £5.70; available from drivers) and one-week **Multiride** passes (£10.25, children £5.15; available at their office near the bus station). From Hereford south to Swansea and as far west as Carmarthen, one-day **Roverbus** tickets cover all bus travel on Stagecoach Red and White, First Cymru, Rhondda, and Silverline buses and can be purchased from bus drivers (£5, children £4). Long-distance and shuttle services such as TrawsCambria, National Express, and First Cymru Shuttles do not honor any rover tickets. The **Freedom of South Wales 7-Day Flexi Rover** offers bus and train travel throughout South Wales (7 days bus and any 3 days train, June-Sept. £35, Oct.-May £30).

In north Wales, **Arriva Cymru** (☎(08706) 082608) provides excellent service throughout most of the region. Buy the **One-Day Explorer** (£5, under 16 £3.50), valid north of Aberystwyth and as far east as Chester. If your travel is confined to the county of Gwynedd, extending from Machynlleth north to Holyhead and Llandudno, the Gwynedd **Red Rover** is a cheaper deal (£4.80, children £2.40). The **North and Mid Wales 7-Day Flexi Rover** offers bus and train travel throughout most of Wales above the imaginary Aberystwyth-Shrewsbury line, including free travel on the Ffestiniog Railway (3 days in 7 £28).

HIKING, BIKING, AND HITCHHIKING

Wales has hundreds of well-marked footpaths. *Walking in Wales*, at TICs, highlights interesting walks with sights and accommodations along the way. Long-distance **hikers** should buy 1:25,000 Ordnance Survey maps and bring proper equipment (see **Wilderness Safety**, p. 54). The **Offa's Dyke Path** (see p. 436) and the **Pembrokeshire Coast Path** (see p. 453) are popular long-distance walks. For more information, write to the **Countryside Council Wales**, 43 The Parade, Roth, Cardiff DF2 3UH, or visit their web site at www.ccw.gov.uk. **Bikers** in north Wales should obtain a copy of *Cyclists' Guide to North Wales* at TICs. *Let's Go* does not recommend **hitchhiking**, but many people choose this form of transport, especially in the summer. Cars stop most readily for hitchhikers who stand in lay-by (pull-off) areas along narrow roads.

LIFE AND TIMES

CELTS, ROMANS, AND NORMANS

As the western terminus of many waves of emigration, Wales has been influenced by a wide array of peoples since prehistoric times. Inhabitants from the Stone, Bronze, and Iron Ages left their mark on the Welsh landscape in the form of stone villages, forts covered in earth, *cromlechs* (standing stones also known as menhirs and dolmens), and partially subterranean burial chambers. It is the early **Celts** about whom we know the most, however, and who make Wales most distinct from her neighbors today. In the 4th and 3rd centuries BC, modern-day Wales witnessed two waves of Celtic immigration, the first from northern Europe and the second from the Iberian peninsula. By the time the **Romans** arrived in AD 50, the Celts had consolidated into four main tribes, with links to each other and to Celts in Ireland and Brittany. By AD 59, the Romans had invaded and established a fortress at Segontium (present-day Caernarfon), across the Menai Straits from Ynys Môn (Anglesey), the center of druidic, bardic, and warrior life in northern modern-day Wales.

Crossing the water, the Romans were faced with the bedlam of a Celtic attack, but having conquered Celts in France, Italy, and Spain, they weren't too impressed and proceeded to kill or capture all the residents. Though the Romans symbolically conquered the Celts, their domination was never fully consolidated, and Celtic resistance compelled the Romans to station two of their four legions in Britain along the modern-day Welsh border.

When the Romans finally departed Britannia in the early 5th century AD, they left not only towns, amphitheaters, roads, and mines, but also the Latin language and the first seeds of Christianity, both of which heavily influenced further development of Welsh scholarship and society. For the next 700 years, the Celts ruled themselves, doing their best to hold at bay invading Saxons, Irish, and Vikings, their efforts perhaps spearheaded by the legendary **King Arthur,** whose exploits were detailed by Geoffrey of Monmouth. Yet they were not, in the end, successful, for in the 8th century, King Offa of Mercia and his troops pushed what Celts remained in England into various western corners of Britain, such as Cornwall, Scotland, and Wales. To make sure the Celts stayed put, Offa built **Offa's Dyke,** a 150 mi. earthwork that still roughly marks the border between England and Wales. (The Welsh say it's there to keep the English out.) The newly contained Wales consisted of many Celtic kingdoms united by a single language, a uniform system of customary law, a shared social system based on kinship ties, and a ruling aristocracy linked by common ancestry and marriage, but the kingdoms did not achieve political unity until the time of Llywelyn ap Gruffydd in the 11th century.

THE ENGLISH CONQUEST

Within 50 years of William the Conqueror's invasion of England, one quarter of Wales had been subjugated by the Normans. The newcomers built a series of castles and market towns, introduced the feudal social system, and brought with them a variety of Continental monastic orders. Though the Welsh greeted the rule of the Christian Norman barons with less resistance than they had directed toward previous heathen invaders, conflict never subsided, and the Normans were unable to enter the heart of north Wales.

The English **Plantagenet** Kings invaded Wales throughout the 12th century, but it was not until 1282, when a soldier of **Edward I** (the Longshanks, of *Braveheart* fame) killed Prince **Llywelyn ap Gruffydd,** that independence symbolically ended. Llywelyn's head was taken to London, paraded through the streets wearing a crown of ivy, and displayed at the Tower of London, lest anyone dare imagine the Welsh still had a leader. Edward then appointed his son Prince of Wales, and in 1284 dubbed the Welsh **English subjects.** He would go on to use Welsh expertise with the longbow in his campaigns in Scotland and France. To keep the perennially unruly Welsh in check, Edward constructed a series of massive castles at strategic spots throughout Wales. The magnificent surviving fortresses at Conwy, Caernarfon, Harlech, and Beaumaris stand testament to his efforts.

In the early 15th century, the bold insurgent warfare of **Owain Glyndŵr** (Owen Glendower) temporarily freed Wales from English rule. Reigniting Welsh nationalism and rousing his compatriots to arms, Glyndŵr and his followers captured the castles at Conwy and Harlech, threatened the stronghold of Caenarfon, and convened a national parliament in Wales. While poverty, the Black Plague, and warfare ravaged the country, Glyndŵr created the ideal of a "unified" Wales that has captured the country's collective imagination ever since. But despite support from Ireland, Scotland, and France, by 1409 the rebellion had been reduced to a series of guerrilla raids. By 1417 Glyndŵr had disappeared into the mountains a fugitive, leaving only legend to guide his people. Though Wales had placed her hope in the Welsh-born **Henry VII** of the House of Tudor, who ascended the English throne in 1485, alliance with the Tudors did not bring independence.

Full integration with England came during Henry VIII's reign with the **Act of Union** of 1536, which granted the Welsh the same rights as English citizens and returned the administration of Wales to the local gentry. However, the price of power was assimilation. The act banished the distinctive Welsh legal and administrative system, officially "united and annexed" Wales, and sought to "extirpate all and singular the sinister usages and customs differing." Thus began the rise of the English language in Wales, which quickly became the language of the courts and government as well as the language of the gentry.

METHODISM AND THE INDUSTRIAL REVOLUTION

In the 18th and 19th centuries, religious shifts in Wales changed the nature of society. As the church in Wales became more anglicized and tithes grew more burdensome, the Welsh were ripe for the appeal of new Protestant sects. Nonconformists, Baptists, and Quakers all gained a foothold in Wales as early as the 17th century, but it was the 18th-century **Methodist revolution,** with its fiery preachers and austere lifestyle, that was most influential (by 1851, 80% of the populace was Methodist). Life in Wales centered on the chapel, not the church, where people created tight local communities through shared religion, heritage, and language. Chapel life remains one of the most distinctive features of Welsh society; the Sabbath closure of stores in parts of Wales (particularly in the north) is but one of the lasting effects.

The 19th century brought the **Industrial Revolution** to Wales, as industrialists from within and without sought to exploit coal veins in the south and iron and slate deposits in the north. New roads, canals, and—most importantly—steam railways were built throughout Wales to transport these raw materials, and the Welsh population grew from 450,000 to 1.16 million between 1750 and 1851. Especially in the south, pastoral landscapes were transformed into grim mining wastelands, and the workers who braved these dangerous workplaces faced lives of taxing work, poverty, and despair. Early attempts at unionism failed, and workers turned to violence to improve conditions. Welsh discontent was channeled into the **Chartist Movement,** which asked for political representation for all male members of society; its highest point was an uprising in Newport in 1839. Welsh society became characterized by two forces: a strongly leftist political consciousness—aided by the rise of organized labor—and large-scale emigration. Welsh miners and religious outgroups emigrated to America (founding particularly vibrant settlements in Pennsylvania), and in 1865 a group of Welsh men and women founded **Y Wladfa** (The Colony) in the Patagonia region of Argentina. Rural society was hardly more idyllic, and tenant farmers led the **Rebecca Riots** between 1839 and 1843.

The strength of the Liberal Party in Wales bolstered the career of **David Lloyd George,** who rose from being a rabble-rousing Welshman to Britain's Prime Minister (1916-22). Of the many Welshmen sent to fight the Great War on the Continent, over 35,000 never returned. This loss of a generation, combined with Prime Minister Winston Churchill's violent quelling of a Welsh **coal-miners' strike** and the economic depression of the 1930s (which spurred further emigration, and from which Welsh industry has never truly recovered), led to growing dissatisfaction.

MODERN POLITICS

Politics in Wales in the late 20th century have been especially characterized by nationalism and a vigorous campaign to retain one of Europe's oldest living modern languages. The establishment of Welsh language classes, publications, radio stations, and even a Welsh television channel (known as Sianel Pedwar Cymru, "Channel 4 Wales," or S4C for short), clearly indicates the energy invested in the Welsh language, the binding feature of the Welsh people today. In 1967, the **Welsh Language Act** established the right to use Welsh in the courts, while the 1988 **Education Reform Act** ensured that all children aged five to 16 in Wales would be introduced to the Welsh language in school.

Welsh nationalism has typically found its expression in the political realm: **Plaid Cymru,** the Welsh Nationalist Party, was founded in 1925 and has performed increasingly well since its founding, consistently garnering seats in Parliament. In the 1950s, a **Minister for Welsh Affairs** was made part of the national Cabinet, but Tory rule in the 1980s brought the legitimacy of rule from London into question, despite the fact that most of the Welsh seats were held by Labour and Plaid Cymru. On September 18, 1997, the Welsh voted in favor of devolution, but unlike their Scottish counterparts support for the idea was tepid, with only 50.3% voting 'yes' despite major governmental backing. Still, this was enough to lead to elections for the 60-seat Welsh Assembly (held in May 1999), which now has control over Wales's budget. A meager 46% voter turnout saw Labour take home a 28-seat plurality, and Plaid Cymru doing unexpectedly well with 17 seats.

LLITERATURE

The Welsh prefer philosophy to philology; music and poetry to both.
　　—T. Charles Williams

In Wales, as in other Celtic countries, much of the national literature stems from a vibrant bardic tradition. The earliest extant poetry in Welsh comes from 6th-century northern England, where the **cynfeirdd** (early poets), including the influential poet **Taliesin**, orally composed verse of praise for their patron lords. The *Gododdin*, a series of heroic lays totalling over 1000 lines and attributed to the poet **Aneirin**, is the most noted celebration of valor and heroism from this period. The 9th through 11th centuries brought emotional and often melancholy poetic sagas focusing on pseudo-historical figures such as the poet **Llywarch Hen, King Arthur,** and **Myrddin** (Merlin). Ushering in the most prolific period in Welsh literature, 12th-century monastic scribes compiled manuscripts in the Middle Welsh language. Most notable from this period is the collection of prose tales known as the **Mabinogion** (after a later translation by Lady Charlotte Guest). Under this title are the *Four Branches of the Mabinogi*, four loosely connected and highly dramatic tales of legendary Welsh figures, and seven other tales, including one of the earliest Arthurian stories in European literature, *Culwch ac Olwen*.

In the 14th century, Wales saw the development of the flexible poetic form *Cywydd* by **Dafydd ap Gwilym**. Often called the greatest Welsh poet, he combined playfulness, irony, and emotional depth in his verse, and continued to influence the works of later poets such as **Dafydd Nanmor** and **Iolo Goch** well through the 17th century. Yet a growing anglicizing of the Welsh gentry in the 18th century led to a decline in the tradition of courtly bards. Active composers of verse found their venue mainly at *eisteddfodau*, local poetry competitions, and the Royal National Eisteddfod (see **Ffestivals,** p. 427).

Modern Welsh literature has been influenced heavily in its use of language by Bishop William Morgan's 1588 **Welsh translation** of the Bible, which helped standardize Welsh and provided the foundation for literacy throughout Wales. A circle of Welsh romantic poets, **Y Beridd Newydd** (the New Poets), developed in the 19th century, including T. Gwynn Jones and W.J. Gruffydd. The horrors of WWI touched Wales as much as England and produced an anti-romantic poetic voice typified in the work of **Hedd Wyn,** who won the chief prize at the 1917 National Eisteddfod but was killed on the fields of France before accepting the honor.

The work of 20th-century Welsh writers (in both Welsh and English) features a compelling self-consciousness in addressing problematic questions of identity and national ideals. The incisive poetry of **R.S. Thomas** treads a fine line between a fierce defense of his proud heritage and a bitter rant against its claustrophobic provincialism. **Kate Roberts**'s short stories and novels, such as *Feet in Chains*, dramatize Welsh fortitude in the face of dire poverty. The best-known Welsh writer is, of course, Swansea's **Dylan Thomas,** who has become something of a national industry. His emotionally powerful poetry, as well as popular works like *A Child's Christmas in Wales* and the radio play *Under Milk Wood* (a microcosm of Wales told through a day in the life of a seaside town), describe his homeland with nostalgia, humor, and a tinge of bitterness. Wales's literary heritage is preserved in the **National Library of Wales** in Aberystwyth (p. 463), which receives (by law) a copy of every book published in Welsh in the UK.

MUSIC

Music in "the land of song" has always occupied an important place in cultural life. Not much is known about early Welsh music, but the fact that the Welsh word **canu** means both "to sing" and "to recite poetry" suggests an intimate historical connection between the spoken and the sung word. There is little extant Welsh music dating prior to the 17th century; nonetheless, historians know of three traditional instruments in medieval Wales: the harp, the pipe (hornpipe or bagpipe), and the **crwth,** a six-stringed oblong instrument played with a bow. Wales began to lose its indigenous music tradition when Welsh harpists were incorporated into England's 16th-century Tudor court; traditional playing died out by the 17th century. In the 18th century, the rise of chapels led to an energetic singing culture, as Welsh folk tunes were adapted to sacred songs of praise to God, and hymn-writers such as **Ann Griffiths** made their mark. Their works, sung in unison in the 18th century, became the basis for the harmony **choral singing** of the 19th and 20th centuries that is now Wales's best-known musical tradition. While many associate the all-male choir with Wales, both single-sex and mixed choirs are an integral part of social life, and singing festivals like the **cymanfa ganu** are found throughout Wales.

Today Welsh musical life includes much more than the chorus. Cardiff's **St. David's Hall** (opened in 1983 and regarded as one of the finest venues in Britain) regularly hosts both Welsh and international orchestras, and the **Welsh National Opera** has established a worldwide reputation, with the internationally renowned tenor **Bryn Terfel** as its star performer. Modern Welsh composers of orchestral and vocal works such as **Alun Hoddinott** and **William Mathias** have won respect in the classical genre; Mathias composed an anthem for the wedding of Prince Charles and the late Lady Diana.

Rock music (in both English and Welsh), as elsewhere, has been the voice of youth, although the two most famous Welsh pop music exports are the no longer youthful **Tom** "What's New Pussycat" **Jones** and **Shirley Bassey.** The 1990s have seen the rise of bands from Wales which combine Brit-pop sounds with a sometimes fierce nationalism, led by the **Manic Street Preachers.** Other bands with their share of hits include **Catatonia** (led by the dynamic Cerys Mathews), **Stereophonics,** and the **Super Furry Animals.** Good examples of the Welsh rock sound include the Manics' *Everything Must Go* and Catatonia's *International Velvet.*

FFOOD

Traditional Welsh cooking relies heavily on leeks (the national symbol), potatoes, onions, dairy products, lamb (considered the best in the world), pork, fish, and seaweed. Soups and stews are ubiquitous and often good. **Cawl** is a complex broth, generally accompanied by bread; most soups brim with leeks and generous helpings of lamb or beef. **Welsh rarebit** (also called "Welsh rabbit") is buttered toast topped with a thick, cheesy mustard-beer sauce. It's the baked goods that tempt most. Wales abounds with unique, tasty **breads. Crempogen** (griddle cakes), resembling miniature pancakes, are made with sour cream, studded with currants, and topped with butter. The adventurous should sample **laverbread,** not really bread at all but a cake-like slab made of seaweed. Those with a sweet tooth will love **bara brith,** a fruit and nut bread served with butter, or **teisennau hufen** (cream cakes), fluffy doughnut-like cakes filled with freshly whipped cream. **Cwrw** (beer) is another Welsh staple; **Brains S.A.** (p. 433) is the major brewer.

LLANGUAGE

The word "Welsh" comes from the Old English *wealh,* or "foreigner," and the language does seem alien to most English speakers. Though modern Welsh borrows significantly from English for vocabulary, as a member of the Celtic family of languages, *Cymraeg* is based on a grammatical system more closely related to Cornish and Breton. Out of a total population of three million, more than 500,000 people in Wales speak Welsh, and just over half are native speakers. Increasingly, Welsh is becoming the language of everyday life, especially north of Aberystwyth, but almost all Welsh speakers are bilingual.

Though English suffices nearly everywhere in Wales, it's a good idea to familiarize yourself with the language. Mastering Welsh pronunciation takes time. Welsh shares with German the deep, guttural **ch** heard in "Bach" or "loch." **Ll**—the oddest Welsh consonant—is produced by placing your tongue against the top of your mouth, as if you were going to say "l," and blowing. If this technique proves baffling, try saying "hl" (Hlan-GO-hlen for "Llangollen"). **Dd** is said either like the "th" in "there" or the "th" in "think" (hence the county of Gwynedd is pronounced the same way as Gwyneth Paltrow's first name). C and g are always hard. W is generally used as a vowel and sounds either like the "oo" in "drool" or "good." U is pronounced like the "e" in "he." Y trickily changes its sound with its placement in the word, sounding either like the "u" in "ugly" or the "i" in "ignoramus." F is spoken as a "v," as in "vertigo," and ff sounds exactly like the English "f." Emphasis nearly always falls on the penultimate syllable, and there are (happily) no silent letters.

Most Welsh place names are derived from prominent features of the landscape. *Afon* means river, *bedd* grave, *betws* or *llan* church or enclosure, *bryn* hill, *caer* fort, *ffordd* road, *glyn* glen or valley, *llyn* lake, *môr* sea, *mynydd* mountain, *pen* top or end, *pont* bridge, *tref* or *tre* town, and *ynys* island. *Mawr* is big, *bach* is little. The Welsh call their land *Cymru* (KUM-ree) and themselves *Cymry* ("compatriots"). Because of the Welsh system of letter mutation, many of these words will appear in usage with different initial consonants. **Welsh Words and Phrases,** p. 753, provides more information to aid you in your travels.

FFESTIVALS

The most significant of Welsh festivals is the **eisteddfod** (ice-TETH-vod), which literally means a sitting together or session. In practice, an eisteddfod is a competition of Welsh literature (chiefly poetry), music, and arts and crafts. Hundreds of local *eisteddfodau* (the plural) are held in Wales each year, generally lasting one to three days. The most important of these is the *Eisteddfod Genedlaethol Frenhinol Cymru*, or the **Royal National Eisteddfod** (held in St. David's from Aug. 3-10 in 2002; see below). Every July (July 8-14 in 2002), Wales turns its attention to the **International Musical Eisteddfod,** held in the small town of Llangollen (p. 492) in north Wales. This draws folk dancers, singers, and choirs from around the world for performance and competition. Though not focused on all things Welsh as is the Royal National Eisteddfod, the festival still epitomizes both Welsh hospitality and the Welsh love of music.

THE ROYAL NATIONAL EISTEDDFOD The Royal National Eisteddfod of Wales was established in 1568 by Elizabeth I to address her concern over the "intolerable multitude of vagrant and idle persons calling themselves minstrels, rhymers, and bards." Today the National Eisteddfod is a grand festival held the first week of August, alternating each year between a different location in North and South Wales. Its present incarnation owes much to the fancy of Iolo Morgannwg, poet and writer, who "invented" a tradition reaching back into the Druidic past of Wales. He created the *Gorsedd Beirdd*—an honorary group of great poets—who parade in white, green, and blue robes at two ceremonies, officiated by the "Archdruid," at which the winners of the crown and the chair (the two main poetry prizes) are introduced to the crowd amid much pomp. In recent years Eisteddfod events, which are conducted in Welsh, have made headsets available with translations for non-Welsh speakers. For information, write to the Eisteddfod Office, 40 Parc Ty Glas, Llanisien, Cardiff CF4 5WU or call (01222) 763777.

WALES

SOUTH WALES

South Wales is a master craftsman of natural landscapes. Its rivers carve lush valleys, its pastures quilt patches of gold and green, its peaks paint silhouettes, and its coastline welds rocky water to sandy beach. Ease of access to England has diluted the Celtic history of this region, but Welsh nationalism is gaining ground, and the native language is slipping back into the mainstream. Although Wales has suffered from the passing of the mining industry over the past thirty years, recent tourism has begun to revitalize the clustered market towns and gritty harbors. Ancient legends, towering castles, cliff-hanging chapels, and spectacular walking trails link the cities, towns, and treasures of South Wales. Along with sheep. Lots of sheep.

HIGHLIGHTS OF SOUTH WALES

CARDIFF Plunge into the vibrant cultural scene of one of Europe's youngest capitals, then scale majestic castle battlements north of the city (p. 428).

VALES AND HILLS Hike the Wye Valley for a fine view of **Tintern Abbey** (p. 437) and proceed north to the land of wild ponies in **Brecon Beacons National Park** (p. 442).

HAY-ON-WYE Browse bookshelves in a literary wonderland that boasts the largest secondhand bookstore in the world (p. 440).

ST. DAVID'S Savor the soft light in Britain's holiest city, at the tip of an ancient peninsula in cliff-mad **Pembrokeshire Coast National Park** (p. 457).

CARDIFF (CAERDYDD)   ☎029

Formerly a sleepy provincial town, Cardiff (pop. 321,000) emerged in the late 19th century as the main shipping port for Welsh coal. Its seaport became the world's busiest, sending coal from 300 mines to the rest of the world. An influx of sailors and merchants lent the Tiger Bay area a cosmopolitan diversity, though original settlers had arrived from abroad far earlier—stones from a 2000-year-old Roman town remain part of the walls of Cardiff Castle. Today, Cardiff is again the capital of a Welsh nation on the rise. Its center brims with theaters and clubs, while its rejuvenated bay is newly home to restaurants, a museum, and the Welsh National Assembly. Deeming itself "Europe's youngest capital," the city is growing to meet the needs of its proud populace and to secure a place on the international stage.

◧ TRANSPORTATION

Trains: Central Station, Central Sq., south of the city center, behind the bus station. Ticket office open M-Sa 5:45am-9:30pm, Su 6:45am-9:30pm. Trains (☎(08457) 484950) from: **Bristol** (45min., 3 per hr., £7); **Swansea** (1hr., 2 per hr., £8); **Bath** (1-1½hr., 3 per hr., £11.90); **London Paddington** (2hr., every hr., £37); **Birmingham** (2¼hr., 4 per hr., £26.50); **Edinburgh** (7hr., 7 per day, £100.80).

Buses: Central Station, on Wood St. National Express booking office and travel center. Show up at least 15min. before closing to book a ticket. Open M-Sa 7am-5:45pm, Su 9am-5:45pm. **National Express** (☎(0990) 808080) from: **Birmingham** (2½hr., 8 per day, £15.25); **Heathrow Airport** (3½hr., 17 per day, £29.50); **London** (3½hr., 7 per day, £14); **Gatwick Airport** (4¾hr., 17 per day, £32); **Manchester** (6hr., 5 per day, £27). Pick up a timetable from the bus station, or check the *Wales Bus, Rail and Tourist Map and Guide* (available at tourist information centres, or TICs) for further information. Competing regional bus lines sell an array of day and week passes.

Local Transportation: Cardiff Bus (Bws Caerdydd; bus times ☎(0870) 608 2608, other inquiries 2066 6444), in St. David's House, Wood St., runs a 4-zone network of orange buses in Cardiff and the surrounding area. Show up 5min. early at the bus stop; sched-

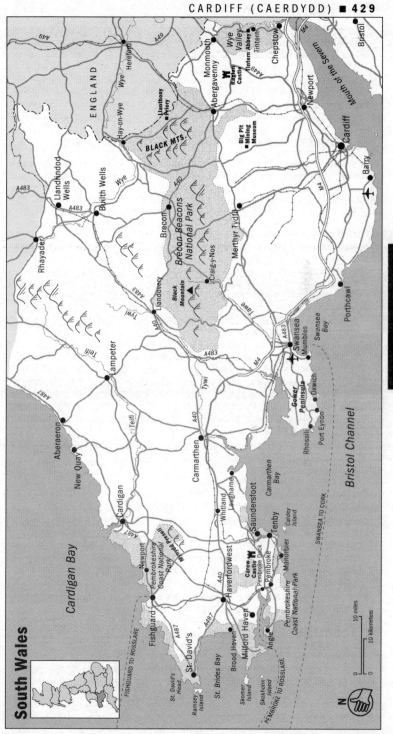

SOUTH WALES

ules can be unreliable. Service ends M-Sa 11:20pm, Su 11pm. Fares 55p-£1.35; reduced fares for seniors and children; fares 5-25p cheaper M-F 9:15am-3:45pm. Week-long **Multiride Passes** available (£10.25, children £5.15). **City Rider** tickets, which allow 1-day unlimited travel in the greater Cardiff area, can be purchased from drivers (£2.85, children £1.90, families £5.70). Pick up *A Guide to Bus Fares in Cardiff* from the bus office (open M and F 8am-5:30pm, Tu-Th and Sa 8:30am-5:30pm) or TIC.

Taxis: Premier (☎2077 7777), and **Dragon** (☎2033 3333). Taxi stands in front of the train and bus stations. Taxis often line up in front of major clubs late at night.

✳🛈 ORIENTATION AND PRACTICAL INFORMATION

Cardiff Castle stands in the city center, with **Bute Park** stretching behind it along the River Taff. Eastward along Park Pl. are the Civic Centre, university buildings, and National Museum. Shops, pedestrian walks, and indoor arcades cluster between **St. Mary St.** and **Queen St.**, southeast of the castle. The bus and train stations lie south of the center, by the River Taff. The redeveloping **Cardiff Bay** is farther south.

TOURIST, FINANCIAL, AND LOCAL SERVICES

Tourist Information Centre: 16 Wood St. (☎2022 7281; www.cardiffmarketing.co.uk), opposite the bus station. Home to a knowledgeable staff armed with brochures, maps, and oodles of information. Free accommodations list and map. Books rooms for a £1 fee. Ask for information about **walking tours.** Open July-Aug. M-Sa 9am-6pm, Su 10am-4pm; Sept.-June M-Sa 9am-5pm, Su 10am-4pm.

Tours: Leisurelink (☎2038 4291). 1hr. hop-on/hop-off bus tour departs every 20-30min. from the main gate of Cardiff Castle. Tours 10am-4pm and later. Ticket holders get discounts at some Cardiff sites. Purchase from driver or National Express window at bus station. £7, students and seniors £5.50, children £2.50, families £16.50, under 5 free. **Cardiff Cats** (☎2071 2693) water buses tour Cardiff Bay, the River Taff, and the River Ely year-round. Call for schedules.

Financial Services: Numerous banks line Queen St. and St. Mary St., including **Nationwide,** 26-27 St. Mary St. (☎2042 0200). Open M-F 9am-5pm, Sa 9am-noon. **Thomas Cook,** 16 Queen St. (☎2042 2500). Open M-Th and Sa 9am-5:30pm, F 10am-5:30pm. **American Express,** 3 Queen St. (☎(0870) 6001 0601). £2 commission for currency exchange. Open M-F 9am-5:30pm, Sa 9am-5pm.

Launderette: The TIC supplies a list of local launderettes including **Launderama,** 60 Lower Cathedral Rd. (☎2022 8326). Open Th-Tu 9:30am-5:30pm.

EMERGENCY AND COMMUNICATIONS

Police: King Edward VIII Ave. (☎2022 2111).

Hospital: University Hospital of Wales, Heath Park, North Cardiff (☎2074 7747).

Internet Access: Internet Exchange, 8 Church St. (☎2023 6048), by St. John's Church. £2 per hr., 1hr. minimum. Open M-Sa 9am-9pm, Su 10am-7pm. **Cardiff Internet Cafe,** 15-17 Wyndham Arcade (☎2023 2313), off St. Mary St. £1 for first 15min.; rate drops thereafter. Su £10. Open M-Sa 9:30am-9pm, Su 10am-7pm. **Cardiff Central Library,** St. David's Link (☎2038 2116), offers 30min. shifts of free access, 1 shift per person per day. Reserve in advance. Open M-W and F 9am-6pm, Th 9am-7pm, Sa 9am-5:30pm.

Post Office: 2-4 Hill's St. (☎2022 7305), off The Hayes. Open M-Sa 9am-5:30pm. **Bureau de change.** Money Gram wiring service. **Postal Code:** CF10.

📷 ACCOMMODATIONS AND CAMPING

Few budget accommodations lie in Cardiff's center, but the TIC lists reasonable B&Bs (£16-18) on the outskirts and books rooms for £1 and a 10% deposit. Many of the B&Bs that line lovely **Cathedral Rd.,** a short ride on bus #32 or a 15min. walk from the castle, are expensive (£25 and up); better bargains await on the side streets. Between June and September, **Cardiff University Student Housing** (☎2087 4864) lets out dorm rooms (from £6.50) to ID-bearing students, but call in advance.

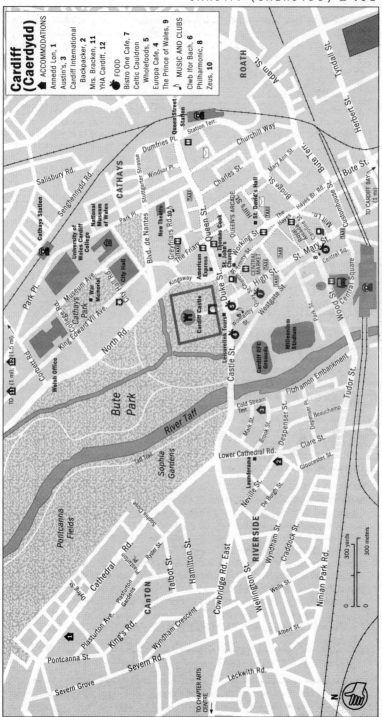

Cardiff (Caerdydd)

🏠 ACCOMMODATIONS
Annedd Lon, **1**
Austin's, **3**
Cardiff International Backpacker, **2**
Mrs. Bracken, **11**
YHA Cardiff, **12**

🍴 FOOD
Bistro One Cafe, **7**
Celtic Cauldron Wholefoods, **5**
Europa Cafe, **4**
The Prince of Wales, **9**

♪ MUSIC AND CLUBS
Clwb Ifor Bach, **6**
Philharmonic, **8**
Zeus, **10**

SOUTH WALES

▨ **Cardiff International Backpacker,** 98 Neville St. (☎2034 5577; fax 2023 0404). From Central Station, go down Wood St., cross the river, and turn right onto Fitzhamon Embankment. Turn left at the end of the road onto Despenser St. Everything a backpacker could want—kitchen, cable TV, pool table, bar staffed by locals, laundry facilities, Internet access (£1 for 15 minutes), bike rental (£7.50 per day; £5 deposit for helmet and lock), convenience store, and the occasional barbecue on the roof garden. Toast and tea included (7:30-10am). Locker deposit £5. Curfew Su-Th 2:30am, F-Sa open 24hr. 4- to 8-bed single-sex dorms £14, 3 nights £36; doubles £36; triples £42.

YHA Cardiff, 2 Wedal Rd., Roath Park (☎2046 2303), 20min. from the center on bus #80, 80B, or 82 from Central Station stand D3 (85p). Get off at the big roundabout, before the bridge, and head to the brick mansion on the left. British breakfast, lounge, kitchen, and Internet access (£2.50 for 30min.). Reception 7am-11pm. Check-out 10am. £13.50, under 18 £10.20, nonmembers £2 extra, students £1 off.

Annedd Lon, 157-159 Cathedral Rd. (☎2022 3349; fax 2064 0885). Proprietress Maria Tucker expanded these conjoined Victorian houses (built in 1894) to cater to budget travelers. Rooms in 157, the upscale half (£20 per person), have bath and British breakfast (don't you dare call it "English"); rooms in 159 (£18 per person) come with continental breakfast. All rooms have color TVs and sinks. No smoking.

Austin's, 11 Coldstream Terr. (☎2037 7148; fax 2037 7158; austins@hotel-cardiff.com). Off Castle St., 5min. from the castle, with views of the stadium and River Taff. All rooms have color TV, tea service, and sinks. Singles £20-25; doubles £30-39.

Mrs. Bracken, 302 Whitchurch Rd. (☎2062 1557). Take bus #35 from Wood St. opposite the bus station and ask to be let off at McJohn's (an auto shop), a 15min. ride (85p). A toilet-turned-flowerpot guards the door. Generous Irish proprietress welcomes with comfortable rooms and big breakfasts. TVs in all rooms. From £17 per person.

Camping: Acorn Camping and Caravanning, Rosedew Farm, Ham Ln. South, Llantwit Major (☎(01446) 794024). 1hr. by bus #X91 from Central Station, 15min. by foot from the Ham Ln. stop. May-Sept. £6 per night; Oct.-Apr. £7 per night. Electricity £2.

◨ ▨ FOOD AND PUBS

Budget travelers gleefully explore the stocked stalls of Victorian-style **Central Market,** in an arcade between St. Mary St. and Trinity St., where merchants sell everything from wigs to vegetables to Bibles. (Normally open M-Sa 8am-5pm.) For late-night fish and chips and kebabs, head to **Dorothy's,** or a host of similar food shops on **Caroline St.** (most open M-W until 3am and Th-Sa until 4am).

▨ **The Prince of Wales,** (☎2064 4449), at St. Mary St. and Wood St. A sweeping spiral staircase and balcony recall the building's previous life as an elegant theater, but the recently renovated Prince of Wales has all the pub amenities. Sip a pint at the bar (from £1.30) and sample the mixed grill (large platter of steaks and meats £5). Discounts on many beers 2-8pm. Rugby fans liven the evening scene. Open M-Sa 11am-11pm, Su noon-10:30pm; food served until 1hr. before close.

▨ **Celtic Cauldron Wholefoods,** 47-49 Castle Arcade (☎2038 7185), across from the castle. Try Welsh specialty laverbread, a seaweed concoction spread on toast (£2-4.60), or test your hunger with the Mighty Vegetarian For Two (£9.50). Open June-Aug. M-Sa 8:30am-9pm, Su 10am-4pm; Sept.-May M-Sa 8:30am-6pm, Su 11am-4pm.

Europa Cafe, 25 Castle St. (☎2066 7776), across from the castle, toward the river. Europa offers a coffeehouse brand of intellectualism, complete with poetry nights (most Sa), writers' group meetings (Tu 8:30pm), and mellow live music. Try the chocolate mocha (£2.20), choose a comfy sofa, and chat the evening away. Open Tu-Sa 11am-11pm, M 11am-6pm, Su noon-6pm. £2 cover on poetry nights.

Crumbs, 33 David Morgan Arcade (☎2039 5007). Tucked between St. Mary St. and The Hayes, this vegetarian restaurant serves salads (£2-3), delicious curry and brown rice (£4), and plenty of potatoes. Open M-F 10am-3pm, Sa 10am-4pm.

Bistro One Cafe, 4 Quay St. (☎2038 2914). Simple lunch options in a home-kitchen atmosphere. Jacket potatoes range from economical plain (£1.05) to top-of-the-line chicken curry (£2.55). Full menu available for takeaway. Open M-Sa 7:30am-5:30pm.

🍃 SIGHTS

CARDIFF CASTLE. The interior of Cardiff Castle is no less flamboyant than the strutting peacocks within its gates. The third Marquess of Bute employed William Burges, the most lavish of Victorian architect-designers, to restore the castle in mock-medieval style, each room brandishing a different theme. The castle also contains museums of the **1st Queen's Dragon Guards** and the **Welsh Regiment.** The climbable remnants of the Norman keep offer a sweeping view. (Castle St. ☎2087 8100. Open Mar.-Oct. daily 9:30am-6pm; Nov.-Feb. 9:30am-4:30pm. Last entry 1hr. before closing. Tours Mar.-Oct. every 20min., last tour 5pm; Nov.-Feb. 5 tours daily, last tour 3:15pm. £5.25, students £4.20, seniors and children £3.15, families £14.75 including tour.)

NATIONAL MUSEUM AND GALLERY OF WALES. Begin in the dazzling audiovisual exhibit on the evolution of Wales, which speeds you through millennia of geological transformation, before exploring the fine collection of European art and variety of ancient Welsh artifacts. (☎2039 7951. Open Tu-Su 10am-5pm. Free.)

CARDIFF BAY. Once the world's busiest seaport, Cardiff Bay lay derelict for decades before development replaced coal docks with shopping areas, restaurants, and the National Assembly. The **Visitor Centre,** known as "The Tube" for its unusual shape, gives free advice and a fine bay view. (Take bus #8 from Central Station stand W3 to the National Assembly building. ☎2046 3833. Open May-Sept. M-F 9:30am-5pm, Sa 10:30am-6pm; Oct.-Apr. M-F 9:30am-5pm, Sa 10:30am-5pm. Free.) The nearby timber edifice of the **Norwegian Church Arts Centre,** built by Norwegian sailors in the 19th century, now hosts concerts and exhibitions. (☎2045 4899. Open daily 10am-4pm and for evening events. Free.) Visit the **Pierhead Building,** built in 1887, to browse displays on the Welsh Assembly. (☎2089 8200. Open M-Th 9:30am-4:30pm, F 10am-4:30 pm, last entrance 30min. before closing. Free.) The temporary location of the **National Assembly of Wales,** next to the construction site for its permanent home, is open for tours. Assembly is in session on Tuesday and Wednesday and can be observed. (☎2089 8688 for tours, 2089 8200 for general information. Book tours in advance, or drop in weekdays 9am-4:30pm except Tu morning and W afternoon. Free.) Rambunctious children crowd **Techniquest,** an enormous hands-on science discovery museum. (☎2047 5475. Open M-F 9:30am-4:30pm, Sa-Su 10:30am-5pm. £5.50, concessions £3.80, families £15.75.)

CIVIC CENTRE. The stately Cardiff Civic Centre is set against the lawns of **Cathays Park.** Find the Functions Office, upstairs in **City Hall,** to pick up a brochure or inquire about tours. In the Hall of Welsh Heroes, St. David, patron saint of Wales, is flanked by Owain Glyndŵr, the Welsh rebel leader who razed Cardiff in 1404. (Across North Rd. from the castle. ☎2087 1727. Open M-F 8:30am-5pm. Free.)

BRAINS BREWERY. Cardiff's signature Thursday odor originates here. Its specialty is Brains S.A. (Special Ale), known to locals as "Brains Skull Attack," and served proudly by many a pub in the city. Call and ask for the marketing department to inquire about tours. (On Crawshay St. by the railway station. ☎2039 9022.)

🎵📷 ENTERTAINMENT AND NIGHTLIFE

CLUBS
Cardiff's club scene centers around the compact downtown area, so there's never much of a walk between clubs. Check out *Buzz!*, the free South Wales entertainment guide, for music listings, or find **St. Mary St.** and follow the crowd. **Thomson House,** near the TIC, publishes a useful *City Nights* guide (free) that lists restaurants, pubs, and clubs. Keep in mind that clubs don't start jumping until after 11pm. After dark, consider hailing a cab if you're leaving the city center.

Clwb Ifor Bach (a.k.a. the **Welsh Club**), 11 Womanby St. (☎2023 2199). This manic 3-tiered club offers everything from Motown tunes to video games. Bands such as Catatonia got their start performing here. Theme nights include "rock inferno" Tu, student night W, and hip-hop F. Cover £2-8. Open M-Th until 2am, F-Sa until 3am.

Philharmonic, 76-77 St. Mary St. (☎2023 0678). The "Philly" has a pub packed with dancers upstairs, a club downstairs; both play commercial dance and pop. Th is popular with students, F-Sa bring a slightly older crowd. No cover. Open M-Sa 11pm-3am.

Zeus, Greyfriars Rd. (☎2037 7014). A cavernous club whose 3rd floor pulses to 70s and 80s music on Th and commerical pop on Sa, when a dress code is enforced. Cover £2.50-5, free before 10:30pm with flier. Open Tu-Th 9pm-2:30am, F-Sa 9pm-3:30am.

Exit Club, 48 Charles St. (☎2064 0101). Where Cardiff's gay crowd dances the night away to chart favorites. Free before 9:30pm, £1.50 cover after. Open M-Su 6pm-2am.

ARTS

The elegant **Chapter Arts Centre,** Market Rd. in Canton, features an eclectic program of dance, drama, gallery shows, and film. Take bus #17, 18, or 19 from Castle St. up Cowbridge Rd. and get off opposite the Canton police station. (☎2030 4400. Box office open M-F 11am-8:30pm, Sa 1-8:30pm, Su 2-8:30pm. Cinema prices £4.20, students and seniors £2.90; discounts on early evening shows and W-Th matinees.) All types of dance and music, including the **BBC National Orchestra of Wales,** are found at modern **St. David's Hall,** The Hayes (☎2087 8444), considered one of Britain's finest concert venues. The **Sherman Theatre** (☎2064 6900), on Senghennydd Rd., stages contemporary plays and dance and serves as the home for a high-quality young people's theater group. (Box office open M-Sa 10am-6pm, Sa 10am-8pm on show nights. Comedy or opera show tickets £11, concessions £8, other shows £8, concessions £6.50.) **The New Theatre,** Park Pl. (☎2087 8889), off Queen St., is home to the **Welsh National Opera,** but also features musicals, plays, dance, and children's theater on its turn-of-the-century stage. (Box office open M-Sa 10am-8pm. Tickets from £7, some shows offer student standby.)

SPORTS

The gew-gaws that grace the **John Bachelor Statue,** at the corner of Hill's St. and The Hayes, is a gauge of Cardiff's festive atmosphere. Scarves, hats, and a clumsily grasped can of Brains S.A. signify sport-induced bacchanalia. **Rugby** matches are played at **Millennium Stadium,** Cardiff Arms Park; the 73,000-seater with retractable roof hosted the Rugby World Cup final in November 1999. (☎2082 2228 for tour info.) If you're lucky enough to catch the city in the fervor of a local match (fall is rugby season), call the Welsh Rugby Union (☎2039 0111) for ticket info.

◢ DAYTRIPS FROM CARDIFF

Cardiff Bus whisks travelers to nearby **Barry Island** to visit the fairgrounds and bask on sandy beaches (bus #354, 30min. boat to the island, every hr., £2 return). For those seeking pastoral diversion, the 55 mi. **Taff Trail** winds from Cardiff Bay through the Taff Valley to the heart of Brecon Beacons National Park (see p. 440). The Cardiff TIC has a free pamphlet on the route.

■ **CAERPHILLY CASTLE.** Eight miles north of Cardiff, this largest of Welsh castles floats above a mossy grove. Begun in 1268 by Norman warlord Gilbert de Clare, its water systems, concentric stone walls, catapults, and pivoting drawbridges made it the most technologically advanced fortification of its time. Today its main tower leans a precarious 10°, and ducks and kingfishers besiege the grounds. *(Take the train (20min., M-Sa 2 per hr., £2.50), or hourly bus #26, 71, or 72 from Central Station stand B3, and step off in the shadow of a massive curtain wall across the moat. ☎2088 3143. Open June-Sept. daily 9:30am-6pm; Apr.-May and Oct. 9:30am-5pm; Nov.-Mar. M-Sa 9:30am-4pm, Su 11am-4pm. Last admission 30min. before closing. £2.50, concessions £2, families £7.)*

MUSEUM OF WELSH LIFE. Four miles west of Cardiff in **St. Fagan's Park,** the open-air museum (called Amgueddfa Werin Cymru in Welsh) is home to more than 40 authentic buildings brought from all corners of Wales, some nearly 500 years old. They rest reassembled throughout the 100 acres of park as an interactive history lesson, staffed by traditionally garbed craftspeople. A guidebook ($1.95) is useful for those intent on seeing everything; others can simply take a day to wander the grounds. Stop by **St. Fagan's Castle,** and listen for Sarah, the Welsh-singing ghost that was once said to wander the place. *(Bus #32 runs to the museum hourly from Central Station stand B4 (20min., £1.10). ☎ 2057 3500. Open daily 10am-5pm. Free.)*

LLANDAFF CATHEDRAL. Two miles northwest of the city center, near the River Taff, the cathedral stands unassumingly amid stone paths and wildflowers. Built by Normans, used by Cromwell as an alehouse, restored by Victorians, and gutted by a German bomb, it is now an architectural mince pie—a stern and solid Norman arch behind the altar is overshadowed by an intrusive concrete arch from 1957. Take a walk around the cathedral's exterior to view the bomb's crater on the north side and the cemetery on the south side. Nearby lie the compact, ivy-covered ruins of the **Castle of the Bishops of Llandaff.** *(Take bus #63, 15min. from Central Station to the Black Lion Pub stop and walk up High St. or, walk down Cathedral Rd. and through Llandaff Fields, turn left onto Western Ave., right onto Cardiff Rd., and right onto Llandaff High St. Call 2056 4554 10am-3pm for tours or questions. Evensong daily 6pm. Open M-Su 7:30am-7pm. Free.)*

CASTELL COCH. Like its cousin in Cardiff, this 13th-century castle bears the ornate signature of Lord Bute and his renovator Burges, with butterflies on one ceiling, lascivious monkeys another, scenes from *Aesop's Fables* a third. Unlike the other Cardiff castles, Castell Coch occupies a secluded forest hillside, and connections to the Taff Trail offer hiking opportunities. *(Take bus #26 (25min., every hr.) from Central Station to Tongwynlais; a 15min. walk up Mill St. brings you to the castle. ☎ 2081 0101. Open Mar.-May daily 9am-5pm; May-Sept. 9:30am-6pm; Oct. 9:30am-5pm; Nov.-Mar. M-Sa 9:30am-4pm, Su 11am-4pm. £2.50, concessions £2, families £7; audio tour 50p extra.)*

WYE VALLEY

Crossing and recrossing the Welsh-English border, the Wye River (Afon Gwy) cuts through a tranquil valley, and legend-rich castles, abbeys, and trails trace the path from its spring in central Wales to its confluence with the Severn south of Chepstow. Cistercian monks found seclusion in these mountains, and Wordsworth escaped the "fever of the world" in these "steep cliffs" and "orchard tufts." Today visitors hike, pedal, paddle, and motor over fertile fields yet unsullied by tourism.

▟ TRANSPORTATION

The valley is best entered from the south at Chepstow. **Trains** (☎ (08457) 484950) chug to Chepstow from **Cardiff** and **Newport** (40min.; M-Sa 8 per day, Su 7 per day; £5.20). **National Express** (☎ (08705) 808080) **buses** ride to Chepstow from: **Newport** (30min., 6 per day, £2.25); **Cardiff** (50min., 5 per day, £3.25); **London** (2¼hr., 10 per day, £16.50). **Stagecoach Red and White** bus #69 loops between **Chepstow, Tintern,** and **Monmouth** (Chepstow-Monmouth M-Sa 7 per day; Monmouth-Chepstow M-F 10 per day, Sa 9 per day). **Phil Anslow Travel** (☎ (01495) 767999) bus #83 careens from **Monmouth** to **Abergavenny** (6 per day, 40min.). One-day **Network Rider** passes (£4.50, children and seniors £2.50, families £9), available on Stagecoach buses, might save you money. There is little Sunday bus service in the valley. Consult the indispensable *Wales Bus, Rail and Tourist Map and Guide,* or the even more indispensable *Discover the Wye Valley on Foot and by Bus* (30p), in area tourist information centres (TICs) for schedules. **Hitchhiking** is said to be possible on the A466 in the summer; some stand near the entrance to Tintern Abbey or by the Wye Bridge in Monmouth. *Let's Go* does not recommend hitchhiking.

LET THEM EAT CHEESE Don't be alarmed if you wake from an afternoon nap at St. Briavel's youth hostel to a rhythmic chant. The villagers gathered across the street leaping at flying chunks of cheese aren't preparing to storm the castle, but rather engaging in a mysterious ceremony unique to this tiny village.

In the 17th century, the English Earl of Hereford withdrew the local villagers' right to gather wood, but when his compassionate wife protested, the Earl backed down. As a gesture of thanks, his wife suggested that each villager contribute a penny to feed the poor. The ritual has since evolved from its charitable roots, and now residents from all social strata feast on the hurled cheese. Every Whitsunday, bread and cheese are distributed outside the Roman church to this chant: "St. Briavel's water and Whyrl's wheat are the best bread and water King John ever eat."

■ HIKING IN THE WYE VALLEY

The region rewards those who follow the Wye's example and wander the woods, gaining stunning vistas of the valley. Two main trails follow the river on either side, the Wye Valley Walk and Offa's Dyke Path. TICs disperse pamphlets, and those on long-distance hikes should carry Ordnance Survey maps (1:25,000; £6.75).

WYE VALLEY WALK. West of the river, the walk treks north from Chepstow via Hay-on-Wye to Prestatyn along wooded cliffs and farmland, eventually ending after 77 mi. in Rhayader. At **Symond's Yat**, 15½ mi. north of Chepstow, the hills drop away to a panorama of the Wye's horseshoe bends, seven counties, and a cliff where peregrine falcons make their eyrie every spring. *(Bus #W73 from Coleford Square DIY Shop, 6 per day.)* From **Eagle's Nest Lookout**, 3 mi. north of Chepstow, 365 steps descend steeply to the bank.

OFFA'S DYKE PATH. East of the river, the path starts in Sedbury's Cliffs and winds 177 mi. along the length of the Welsh-English border before finishing in Prestatyn; it is said to have been a trench originally dug to keep the English out. Trail maps (available at TICs) should be consulted before setting out, as some paths change grade suddenly and without warning. For info on the path, consult the **Offa's Dyke Association,** based halfway up the trail in Knighton (☎(01547) 528753; www.offasdyke.demon.co.uk).

ROYAL FOREST OF DEAN. This 20,000-acre forest, once the hunting grounds of Edward the Confessor and Williams I and II, lies east across the English border and is striped with hikes. Contact **Forest Enterprise** on Bank St. in Coleford, England, across the river from Monmouth (☎(01594) 833057; open M-Th 8:30am-5pm, F 8:30am-4pm) or the **Coleford tourist information centre,** High St. (☎(01594) 812388; open M-Sa 10am-5pm).

CHEPSTOW (CAS-GWENT)   ☎01291

Chepstow's strategic position at the mouth of the River Wye and the base of the Welsh-English border made it an important fortification in Norman times and a frontier town during the English Civil Wars. **Chepstow Castle,** Britain's oldest stone castle, was built by Earl William, a Norman companion of William the Conqueror. Its craggy face rises seamlessly from a cliff and casts a stern eye across the Wye to England. The **town wall** is in some places as thick as 7 ft. and as high as 15 ft. (☎624065. Open Apr.-May daily 9:30am-5pm; June-Sept. 9:30am-6pm; Oct.-Mar. M-Sa 9:30am-4pm, Su 11am-4pm. £3, concessions £2, families £8.) The second highest rising tide in the world (40-60 ft. per day) strands boats in mud under the **Wye Bridge** at the end of Bridge St. It was from these banks, at the **Wye Knot,** that Welsh emigrants and criminals set sail for Australia and America. The **Chepstow Festival,** held every other year, will take place for two weeks in July 2002, its open-air Shakespeare and musical events punctuated by armored battles and a spectacular sound-and-light show. Smaller exhibitions make up the odd years.

Chepstow's **train station** is on Station Rd., and **buses** stop above the town gate in front of the Somerfield supermarket. Both stations are unstaffed. Train and bus tickets are purchased onboard, except those for bus travel to major cities, which must be bought at **The Travel House,** 9 Moor St. (☎623031, M-Sa 9am-5:30 pm). The **tourist information centre** faces the castle from Bridge St. Ask about hikes, book accommodations, or pick up a "What's on Chepstow" flier. (☎623772; www.chepstow.co.uk. Open Apr.-Sept. daily 10am-5:30pm; Oct.-Mar. 10am-4:30pm.) Other services include: **Barclays bank,** Beaufort Sq. (☎(016) 3320 5000; open M-Tu and Th-F 9am-4:30pm, W 10am-4:30pm); **Chepstow Laundry Services,** 36 Moor St., near the bus station (☎626372; £2.80 per load, dryers 20p, soap £1.10; open M-F 8:30am-7pm, Sa 9:15am-5:30pm, Su 10am-4pm); the **police,** Moor St. (☎623993), across from the post office; the **Community Hospital** (24hr. ☎638800), west of town on Mounton Rd.; **Internet access** at the **Chepstow Library** on Manor Way in the town center (☎635730; £1.25 per 30min., £2 per hr.; open M and F 9:30am-5:30pm, Tu 10am-5:30pm, W-Th and Sa 9:30am-4pm); and the **post office,** Albion Sq. (☎622607; open M-F 9am-5:30pm, Sa 9am-12:30pm). **Postal code:** NP16.

The nearest **YHA Youth Hostel** is at **St. Briavel's Castle,** in England (see p. 437). In Chepstow, charismatic Eileen Grassby runs 🖪**Lower Hardwick House,** 300 yd. up Mt. Pleasant from the bus station. Her lemon-yellow Georgian mansion boasts arboreal gardens, and every wide window overlooks the river. (☎622162. Singles £18; doubles £30-36. Campers may pitch in the gardens for £5 per tent, with continental breakfast £7.50.) Or visit **Langcroft,** 71 St. Kingsmark Ave., where you can relax in the conservatory or before your own TV. (☎/fax 625569. £17 per person.)

TINTERN   ☎01291

Five miles north of Chepstow on the A466, the village of Tintern stretches out along a ½ mi. of road above the curving Wye. At one end, the haunting arches of 🖪**Tintern Abbey** "connect the landscape with the quiet of the sky," as Wordsworth famously wrote. Built by Cistercian monks in the 12th and 13th centuries as a center for religious austerity, the abbey became the richest in Wales until Henry VIII dissolved it and it fell into romantic ruin. Their stained glass long since vanished, the windows now provide an intimate connection to the nearby hills and dense trees. Arrive in the morning to avoid tourists and Wordsworth devotees. (☎689251. Open June-Sept. daily 9:30am-6pm; Apr.-May and Oct. 9:30am-5pm; Nov.-Mar. M-Sa 9:30am-4pm, Su 11am-4pm. £2.50, concessions £2, families £7. 45min. audio tours £1 plus £5 deposit.) If crowds overwhelm, get a copy of *Popular Walks Around Tintern* (£3) from the gift shop and head for the hills, or ask the gift shop employees for directions to the **Monk's Path** (2¼hr.) that winds around Tintern and the surrounding hills. A 1½hr. hike will get you to **Devil's Pulpit,** a huge stone from which Satan is said to have tempted the monks as they worked in the fields.

A mile north of the abbey on the A466 lies Tintern's **Old Station.** Once a stop on the Wye Valley Line, the out-of-service train station now holds a series of train carriages, one of which houses the **tourist information centre,** which can book accommodations for a £1 fee. (☎/fax 689566. Open Apr.-Oct. daily 10:30am-5:30pm.) The nearest **YHA Youth Hostel** is **St. Briavel's Castle,** 4 mi. northeast of Tintern across the English border. Once King John's hunting lodge, later a fortress against the marauding Welsh, the 12th-century castle maintains its medieval character. 15th-century graffiti marks one dorm's walls. From the A466 (bus #69 from Chepstow) or Offa's Dyke, follow signs for 2 mi. from Bigsweir Bridge to St. Briavel's. (☎(01594) 530272; fax 530849. Breakfast £3.20, pack lunch £2.80, dinner £4.80. Lockout 10am-5pm. Curfew 11:30pm. Dorms £10.85, under 18 £7.40.) The Wye courses just beyond the front hedge of the 400-year-old **Wye Barn Bed and Breakfast,** 200 yd. north of the abbey along a dirt road. (☎689456. Singles £22.50; doubles £40.) There are a number of B&Bs along the A466 throughout the village, many with river views. **Campers** can use the field next to the train station. (Toilets and water but no shower. £1.50 per person. Parking 50p per 3hr.)

SOUTH WALES

HAY-ON-WYE (Y GELLI)   ☎01497

Left to its own devices, Hay-on-Wye might have stayed a pretty freckle on the toes of the Black Mountains. The ambitious Richard Booth, however, had a vision. After establishing a secondhand bookstore in 1961, Booth vowed to transform Hay into a world-renowned Town of Books. From Hay Castle he now reigns over 40 antiquarian bookshops and countless bustling alleyways spilling over with second-hand volumes. This smallest of towns holds the largest of literary festivals every June, when book fever threatens to ignite the outlying grassy farmlands.

█▼ TRANSPORTATION AND PRACTICAL INFORMATION. The closest **train station** is in Hereford, England (see p. 280). **Stagecoach Red and White** (☎(01633) 838856) **bus** #39 stops at Hay as it travels between **Hereford** and **Brecon** (1hr. from Hereford to Hay, 40min. from Brecon; M-Sa 5 per day; £2.80-4.10). On Sundays, **Yeoman's** (☎(01432) 356202) bus #40 runs the same route twice (£4-5). The **tourist information centre** (TIC), on Oxford Rd. next to the bus stop, books beds for £2. Buy a copy of *Hay Bookworm* (£2) or take the *Secondhand & Antiquarian Booksellers & Printsellers* map and brochure (free) for help in the search for your dream book. (☎820144; www.hay-on-wye.co.uk. Open Apr.-Oct. daily 10am-1pm and 2-5pm; Nov.-Mar. 11am-1pm and 2-4pm.) Other services include: **Barclays bank**, Broad St. (open M-F 10am-4pm); a **launderette** (☎820360), just down from the bus stop on Bell Bank; **Internet Access** at **Hay Design & Print**, The Courtyard, 4 High Town (☎821058; £3 per hr.; open M and W-F 10am-1pm and 2-8pm, Tu 4-8pm, Sa-Su noon-8pm); and the **post office**, 3 High Town (open M and W-F 9am-1pm and 2-5:30pm, Tu 9am-1pm, Sa 9am-12:30pm). **Postal code:** HR3 5AE.

█▐ ACCOMMODATIONS AND FOOD. The **YHA Youth Hostel** nearest to Hay-on-Wye lies 8 mi. out of town at Capel-y-Ffin (see p. 444). Originally a 16th-century coaching inn, **The Bear**, Bear St., couples inglenook fireplaces with lovely rooms. Gracious hosts Sue Newall and Jon Field serve breakfast; order *crempog las* (vegetarian Welsh pancakes) the night before. (☎821302; fax 820506; www.thebear-hay-on-wye.co.uk. Rooms from £24.) Under the solid beams of 16th-century **Brookfield**, Brook St., each room gets its own Welsh name. (☎820518. Singles £25; doubles £36.) It's easy to **camp** near Hay along the **Wye Valley Walk** or **Offa's Dyke** (see p. 436). **Radnor's End Campsite,** on a tiny valley plateau, is the closest to town; cross Bridge St. and go 500 yd. to the right toward Clyro. (☎820780. £3 per person.)

At **The Granary,** Broad St., enjoy generous portions and a fine vegetarian selection. (☎820790. Main courses from £7.50. Open mid-July to Aug. daily 10am-9pm; Sept. to mid-July 9am-6pm.) **Oscars**, High Town, specializes in scones (£1-1.30), but also serves tasty meals. (☎821193. Open M-Su 10:30am-5:30pm.) Shoot pool as you wait to eat at the **Wheatsheaf Inn**, Lion St., the place to be on Friday nights. Happy hour gets you 30% off drinks. (☎820186. Happy hour M-F 4-6pm. M-Sa 11am-11pm, Su noon-10:30pm.; food served daily noon-2:30pm, M-F also 6-8:30pm.)

◪ SIGHTS. After weathering eight centuries of wars, fires, and neglect, Hay's **Norman castle** has been conquered by mobs of unruly first editions, courtesy of the castle branch of Richard Booth's bookshop. (Open summer daily 9:30am-6pm; winter 9am-5:30pm.) The town's myriad other shelves are a browser's paradise. Some specialize, like the **Poetry Bookshop**, Brook St. (☎821812), while others *specialize*, notably B&K Books, dedicated to beekeeping. Most vend a hodgepodge of used volumes, selling century-old editions for under £10. The townspeople throw a 10-day **literary festival** each year (May 31-June 9 in 2002), during which members of the literati such as Harold Pinter, Toni Morrison, and even Paul McCartney give readings. Literary buffs, be forewarned: festival crowds strain accommodations, and many readings charge hefty admission (£4-10). For less cerebral pursuits, **Celtic Canoes**, Newport St., rents and gives canoe instruction. (☎847422; mobile (0966) 505286. £13 per half-day, £20 per day.)

HAY'S DAY Hay-on-Wye straddles the England-Wales border. This indeterminate status, and the compelling logic that the independent city-states of Ancient Greece and Renaissance Italy were the world's greatest civilizations ever, led to Oxford-educated Richard Booth's grand April Fool's joke: a declaration of Hay's independence on April 1, 1977. Booth, owner of the largest secondhand bookstore in the world (Booth's Books acquires more books than all of Wales's universities and public libraries combined), made his proclamation as an attack on bureaucracy and big government, drawing national notice. Now Booth and his wife preside as King and Queen of Hay Castle. Turn up in Hay around April 1 to join the Independence Day celebrations.

ABERGAVENNY (Y FENNI)   ☎ 01873

The market town of Abergavenny (pop. 10,000) styles itself as the traditional gateway to Wales. Savvy visitors take this literally and travel straight through town on their way to the hills: the Black Mountains in the eastern third of Brecon Beacons National Park and the Seven Hills of Abergavenny.

▐ TRANSPORTATION. Trains (☎ (08457) 484950) run from: **London** (2½hr.; every hr.; Su-Th £33, F-Sa £43.50); **Newport** (20min., 2 per hr., £4.80); **Hereford** (25min., 2 per hr., £5.60); **Cardiff** (40min., every hr., £7.60); **Chepstow** (1hr., every 2hr., £8.30); **Bristol** (1¼hr., every 2hr., £7.60). To get to town from the train station, turn right at the end of Station Rd. and walk 15min. along Monmouth Rd. The bus station sits on Monmouth Rd., by the tourist information centre (TIC). **Stagecoach Red and White** (☎ (01633) 838856) **buses** roll in from: **Hereford** (#X4; 1hr., every 2hr., £4); **Newport** via **Cwmbran** (#X23 and X30; 45min., 2 per hr., £3.50); **Brecon** (#21; 1hr., 5 per day, £3); **Cardiff** (#X30; 1½hr., every hr., £4).

▐ PRACTICAL INFORMATION. The well-stocked **tourist information centre** (☎ 857588; fax 850217; www.abergavenny.co.uk; open Apr.-Oct. daily 10am-5:30pm; Nov.-Mar. 10am-4:30pm) shares space with the **National Park Information Centre** on Lower Cross St., by the bus station (☎ 853254; open Apr.-Oct. daily 9:30am-5:30pm). Purchase camping supplies at **Crickhowell Adventure Gear,** 14 High St. (☎ 856581. Open M-Sa 9am-1:30pm and 2:30-5:30pm, Su 10am-1:30pm and 2:30-4pm.) Other services include: **Barclays bank,** 57 Frogmore St. (open M-Tu and Th-F 9am-4:30pm, W 10am-4:30pm); the **police,** Tudor St. (☎ 852273); the **hospital,** Nevill Hall on Brecon Rd. (☎ 732732); **Internet access** at the **Public Library,** Library Square, Baker St. (☎ 735980; £1.25 per 30min., £2 per hr.; free 5min. for email) and **Celtic Computer Systems,** 20 Monk St. (☎ 858111; £5 per hr.; open M-Sa 9:30am-5pm); and the **post office,** with a **bureau de change,** St. John's Sq., where Tudor St. abuts Castle St. (☎ 223344; open M-F 9am-5:30pm, Sa 9am-12:30pm). **Postal code:** NP7 5EB.

▐▐ ACCOMMODATIONS AND FOOD. Black Sheep Backpackers, a stellar hostel in a former Great Western Hotel, caters to the weary backpacker's every need, with a kitchen, pool table, backyard barbecue, and Internet access (£1 per 15min). The friendly staff rents bikes (£8 per half-day, £14 per day) and organizes hikes. (☎ 859125. £10 per person; doubles £12.50 per person.) Expensive **B&Bs** (£18-20) wait on **Monmouth Rd.;** you're better off trying **Hereford Rd.,** 15min. from town. From the TIC, turn right at the Great George pub, continue on Monk St., and keep walking. The **Ivy Villa Guest House,** 43 Hereford Rd., provides TVs and British breakfast. (☎ 852473. Singles £16; doubles £30.) **Mrs. Bradley,** 10 Merthyr Rd., where Frogmore St. becomes Brecon Rd., keeps standard rooms with TVs. (☎ 852206. £12 per person with continental breakfast, £14 with cooked breakfast.)

On Tuesday, Friday, and Saturday mornings, the bustling **market** in Market Hall on Cross St. (☎ 735845) offers the best in fruit and vegetables, baked goods, and livestock trading; Wednesday brings a flea market. **Harry's Carvery** on St. John's St. loads crusty baguettes with fillings like honey-baked gammon and Stilton cheese for £1.50 and up. (☎852766. Open M-Sa 8:30am-4pm.) For a traditional pub with surprisingly good grub, head for **The Greyhound Vaults.** (☎858549. Food served W-M noon-2pm and 7-9pm, Su noon-2pm.)

◙⚠ SIGHTS AND OUTDOORS. Abergavenny's **castle** is a ruin, with views of the valley and mountains looming in the gaps between its walls. A 19th-century hunting lodge on the grounds houses the **Abergavenny Museum,** complete with a Victorian farmhouse kitchen. (☎854282. Museum open Mar.-Oct. M-Sa 11am-1pm and 2-5pm, Su 2-5pm; Nov.-Feb. M-Sa 11am-1pm and 2-4pm. £1, seniors and students 75p, children free. Grounds open daily 8am-dusk. Free.)

Abergavenny's real attractions lie in the hills that ring it; the excellent *Walks from Abergavenny* pamphlet (£2) details mountain climbs. **Blorenge** (1833 ft.), 2½ mi. southwest of town and the only thing that rhymes with orange, is the most massive by far. A path begins off the B4246, traversing valley woodlands to the upland area; it climbs the remaining 1500 ft. in 4½ mi. The trailhead to the top of **Sugar Loaf** (1955 ft.), 2½ mi. northwest, starts a mile west of town on the A40. Many report that it's easy to hitch a ride to the car park and start hikes from there. (*Let's Go* does not recommend hitchhiking.) The path to **Skirrid Fawr** (the Holy Mountain; 1595 ft.) lies northeast of town and starts 2 mi. down the B4521. The TIC has details on **pony trekking** in its comprehensive *Activity Wales* guide. Reputable local establishments include **Grange Trekking Centre** (☎890215; £16 per half-day, including instruction; £24 per day), **Wern Riding Center** (☎810899), and **Llanthony Riding and Trekking** (☎890359; £14 per half-day, £22 per day).

▨ DAYTRIPS FROM ABERGAVENNY

If traveling to the sights near Abergavenny by bus, a **network rider pass** (£4.50 per day for travel on all Stagecoach Red and White, Phil Anslow, and Cardiff buses) is usually cheaper than return tickets.

▨BIG PIT NATIONAL MINING MUSEUM FOR WALES. The silent hillsides of Blaenavon, 9 mi. southwest of Abergavenny, overlook a green valley scarred by fields of black. Descend a 300 ft. shaft to the subterranean workshops of a 19th-century coal mine operative until 1980, where ex-miners guide you with stories as grim as the surroundings. Dress warmly and wear sensible shoes. *(Take bus #X4 (13 per day) to Bryn Mawr, then #30 to Blaenavon (every 2hr.). ☎(01495) 790311. Open Mar.-Nov. daily 9:30am-5pm. Underground tours 10am-3:30pm. Free. Under 5 not admitted underground.)*

LLANTHONY PRIORY. All the megaliths in the Black Mountains are said to point toward ruined 12th-century Llanthony Priory, once helping errant friars find their way home. Founder William de Lacy doffed hunting gear and aristocratic title, taking to a contemplative life amid humbling natural beauty. The **YHA Capel-y-Ffin** (see p. 444) is another 4 mi. *(Take Stagecoach Red and White bus #X4 (M-Sa 6 per day) or follow the A465 to Llanfihangel Crucorney, where the B4423 begins. Most walk and some hitch the last 6 mi. to the priory, though Let's Go does not recommend hitchhiking. Always open. Free.)*

RAGLAN CASTLE. Between Abergavenny and Monmouth on the A40, Raglan is a baby among Welsh castles at only 565 years old. It was designed as a residence rather than a fortress, as the absence of arrow slits suggests. *(Take Stage Coach Red and White #83 from Abergavenny or Monmouth (20min.; M-Sa 6 per day, Su 4 per day), or #60 from Monmouth or Newport (40min. from Newport, 4 per day, £3-4.20). ☎(01291) 690228. Open June-Sept. daily 9:30am-6pm; Apr.-May and Oct. 9:30am-5pm; Nov.-Mar. M-Sa 9:30am-4pm, Su 11am-4pm; last admission 30min. before close. £2.50, concessions £2, families £7.)*

BRECON (ABERHONDDU)   ☎01874

Just north of the mountains, Brecon (pop. 8000) is the best base for hiking the Brecon Beacons. This quiet market town wears a temporary vibrancy during its exceptional **Jazz Festival** on the second weekend in August, attracting such luminaries as Branford Marsalis, Keb' Mo', and Van Morrison.

⌨ TRANSPORTATION. Brecon has no bus or train station, but **buses** arrive regularly at **The Bulwark** in the central square. Ask for bus schedules at the tourist information centre (TIC). **National Express** (☎(08705) 808080) **bus** #509 runs once a day from **London** (5hr., £17.50) via **Cardiff** (1¼hr., £2.75). **Stagecoach Red and White** (☎(01633) 838856) **buses** arrive from: **Swansea** (#63; 1½hr.; M-Sa 3 per day, Su 4 per day; £3.70); **Merthyr Tydfil** (#43; 40min.; M-Sa 6 per day, Su 2 per day; £2.40); **Abergavenny** and **Newport** (#21; M-Sa 6 per day, £2-4). To reach Brecon from **Cardiff**, take the #X4 or X40 to Merthyr Tydfil and transfer to #43 (2 per hr., £3.40). Bus #39 comes in from **Hereford** via **Hay-on-Wye** (M-Sa 5 per day, £2.80-4.10); on Sundays, **Yeomans** (☎(01432) 356202) follows the same route (#40, 2 per day, £4-5). Along the A40 from Abergavenny or the A470 from Merthyr Tydfil, **hitchhikers** stand near intersections; of course, *Let's Go* does not recommend hitchhiking.

🛈 PRACTICAL INFORMATION. The **tourist information centre** is located in the Cattle Market Car Park, across from Safeway; walk through Bethel Sq. off Lion St. to the car park. (☎622485; fax 625256. Open Easter-Oct. daily 10am-6pm; Nov.-Easter M-Sa 9:30am-5:30pm, Su 10am-4pm.) The TIC stocks an abundance of pamphlets, as does the **Brecon Beacons National Park Information Centre** in the same building. Skim a free copy of *Beacons Bannau*, the park's newspaper, for the latest news and events. (☎/fax 623156. Open Apr.-Sept. daily 9:30am-5:30pm.) **Brecon Cycle Centre,** 4 Ship St., rents mountain bikes and gives good advice for free. (☎622651. £15 per day, £25 per weekend.) **Bikes and Hikes** (see **Accommodations,** below) also rents equipment and organizes climbing, caving, and other gorge-oriented expeditions. (☎610071. £10 per half-day, £15 per day.) Other services include: **Barclays bank,** at the corner of St. Mary's St. and High St. (☎(01633) 20500; open M-Tu and Th-F 9am-4:30pm, W 10am-4:30pm); the **police,** Lion St. (☎622331); **Internet access** at **Brecon Branch Library,** Ship St. (☎623346; free, 1hr. maximum; call ahead to reserve), and **123 Computers,** 11 Watergate, though expected to move mid-2002 (☎611929; 99p per 30min.); and the **post office,** 6 Church Ln., off St. Mary St. (☎611113; open M-F 8:30am-5:30pm, Sa 8:30am-7:30pm). **Postal code:** LD3 7AS.

⌂ ACCOMMODATIONS. If you plan to visit during mid-August, book far in advance—the Jazz Festival claims every pillow in town. Only 2min. from the TIC and once an 18th-century sheriff's home, **⬛Bikes and Hikes,** the Struet, lives up to its name: the fabulous owners are outdoors enthusiasts, renting equipment and leading trips. (☎610071. Pool table, lounge, kitchen. £12.50 per person.) The nearest YHA hostel is **Ty'n-y-Caeau** (tin-uh-KAY-uh), 3 mi. from Brecon. From the town center, walk down The Watton and continue until the A40-A470 roundabout. Follow the branch leading to Abergavenny on the A40. Just after the roundabout, take the footpath to the left of the hamlet of **Groesffordd** (grohs-FORTH); then turn left onto the main road. Continue for 10-15min., bearing left at the fork; the hostel is on the right. A bus runs several times daily from Brecon to Groesffordd; alternatively, take the Brecon-Abergavenny bus and ask the driver to drop you at the footpath leading to Groesffordd. This Victorian mansion has gardens, a TV room, and Internet access. Lunch and dinner are offered to save guests a trip to town. (☎665270. Open July-Sept. daily; Oct.-June M-Sa. Dorms £10, under 18 £6.90.) **Mrs. J. Thomas's** signless B&B, 13 Alexandra Rd., rests behind the TIC. The warm proprietress has traveled to 27 countries, lived in 18, and collected exotic memorabilia from each. (☎624551. TVs. Open Feb.-Nov. From £17 per person.) Mrs. Parkin keeps original rooms at **Mulberry House,** 3 Priory Hill, across from the Cathedral. (☎624461. £17 per person.) For **camping** try **Brynich Caravan Park,** 1½ mi. east of town on the A40, signposted from the A40-A470 roundabout. (☎623325. Open Mar.-Oct. £4 per person, £7.50 with car.) During the Jazz Festival, additional campsites open on farms.

🏠 **FOOD. Cooperative Pioneer,** Lion St., has everything your pack could need. (☎625257. Open M-Sa 8am-9pm, Su 10am-4pm.) **St. Mary's Bakery,** 4 St. Mary St., sells yummy filled rolls and meat pasties for 75p-£1. (☎624311. Open M-F 7am-5pm, Sa 7am-2pm.) When the sun sets over the Beacons, try **The Camden Arms,** 21 The Watton, for drinks and grub. Be it a chip butty bap (£2) or a 10 oz. rumpsteak (£9.25), the food here deserves a hearty bottoms-up. (☎625845. Open daily noon-3pm and 6-11pm; food served noon-3pm and 6-9pm.)

🎭 **SIGHTS AND ENTERTAINMENT.** Wearing its 900 years of architectural fashion gracefully, **Brecon Cathedral** occupies a grove above the River Honddu. A nearby 16th-century tithe barn houses the **Heritage Centre,** which tells the cathedral's history. (Cathedral ☎623857, Heritage Centre 625222. Cathedral open daily 10am-Evensong, around 5:30pm. Heritage Centre open Mar.-Dec. daily 10:30am-4:30pm.) **The Royal Regiment of Wales Museum Brecon,** The Barracks, bursts with military paraphernalia, as countless weapons and medals adorn the walls. (☎613310. Open Apr.-Sept. daily 9am-5pm; Oct.-Mar. M-F 9am-5pm, last admission 4:15pm. £3, students and children free.) **Brecknock Museum and Art Gallery,** Captain's Walk, in the 1842 Assize Courthouse, has a full-size diorama of the Victorian Assize Court, among other exhibits. (☎624121. Open M-Sa M-F 10am-5pm, Sa 10am-1pm and 2-5pm; Apr.-Sept. also Su noon-5pm; Nov.-Feb. closes 4pm. £1, concessions 50p.) The **Brecon Jazz Gallery,** The Watton, is headquarters of the annual Jazz Festival and home to a small but engaging exhibit on the history of jazz. (☎625557; www.breconjazz.co.uk. Open M-F 10am-4pm. Free.) Set for August 9-11 in 2002, the **Brecon Jazz Festival** dubs itself "the only festival in Britain bigger than the town itself." Other festivals include **antique fairs** (last Sa of the month Feb.-Nov.) and **crafts fairs** in Market Hall on High St. (third Sa of the month Mar.-Dec.).

BRECON BEACONS NATIONAL PARK

Brecon Beacons National Park (Parc Cenedlaethol Bannau Brycheiniog) encompasses 519 sq. mi. of shorn peaks, well-watered forests, and windswept moorlands. The park divides into four regions: barren **Brecon Beacon,** where King Arthur's mountain fortress is thought to have stood; **Fforest Fawr,** with the spectacular waterfalls of Ystradfellte; the **Black Mountains** to the east; and the remote western **Black Mountain** (singular). The market towns on the fringe of the park, particularly Brecon and Abergavenny, make pleasant touring bases, but hostels allow easier access to the park's inner regions. Since crowds in the Brecon Beacons are less dense than in other Welsh parks, public transport is all the scarcer.

> The mountains are unprotected and in places difficult to scale. Cloud banks breed storms within minutes. In violent weather, do not shelter in caves or under isolated trees, which tend to draw lightning. A compass is essential: much of the park is trackless, and landmarks get lost in sudden mists. Never hike alone. If you're in trouble and can reach a telephone, dial 999. Otherwise, the standard six blasts on your whistle should summon help (three are the reply); a constant long blast will also indicate distress. See Wilderness Safety, p. 54.

🚆 TRANSPORTATION

The **train** line (☎(08457) 484950) from **London Paddington** to South Wales runs via Cardiff to **Abergavenny** at the park's southeastern corner and to **Merthyr Tydfil** on the southern edge. The **Heart of Wales** rail line passes through the towns of **Llandeilo** and **Llandovery** in the more remote Black Mountain region.

National Express (☎(08705) 808080) **bus** #509 runs once a day to Brecon, on the northern side of the park, from London and Cardiff (£18.50 from London). **Stagecoach Red and White** (☎(01685) 388216) **buses** cross the park en route to **Brecon**

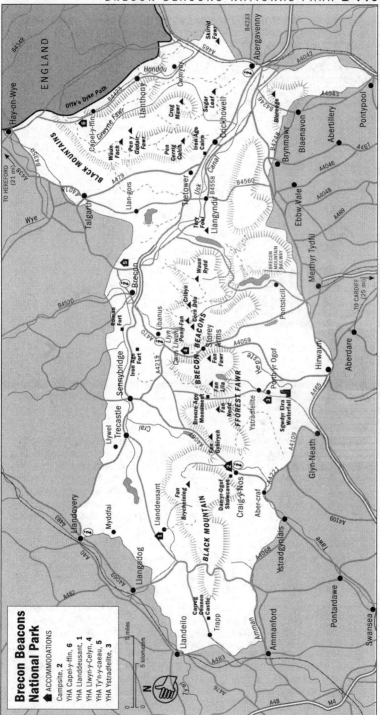

Brecon Beacons National Park

▲ ACCOMMODATIONS

Campsite, **2**
YHA Capel-y-ffin, **6**
YHA Llanddeusant, **1**
YHA Llwyn-y-Celyn, **4**
YHA Ty'n-y-caeau, **5**
YHA Ystradfellte, **3**

SOUTH WALES

from: **Cardiff** via **Merthyr Tydfil** (#X4 or X40, changing to #43; 1½hr.; #X4 and X40 2 per hr., #43 M-Sa 6 per day; £5-7); **Swansea** (#63; 1½hr.; M-F 2 per day, Sa 3 per day, Su 4 per day operated by Sixty Sixty Coaches; £4); **Abergavenny** (#21; 1hr., M-Sa 5 per day, £3-4.10); **Hay-on-Wye** (#39; 45min., M-Sa 6 per day, £2.80-4.10). **Yeomans** (☎ (01432) 356202) #40 runs from Hay-on-Wye on Sundays (2 per day, £4-5). **Brecon Bus Service** #760 runs twice on summer Sundays. The free, useful *Brecon Beacons: A Visitor's Guide* details bus coverage and describes walks accessible by public transport. **Brecon Cycle Centre,** Ship St., among others (see p. 440), rents mountain bikes. (☎(01874) 622651. £15 per day, £25 per weekend.) **Hitchhikers** say the going is tougher on the A470 than on minor roads, where drivers often stop to enjoy the view; *Let's Go* does not recommend hitchhiking.

🛈 PRACTICAL INFORMATION

Stop at a **National Park Information Centre** before venturing forth. While tourist information centres (TICs) are helpful in planning a route by car or bus, the park centres provide advice on hiking and biking. Free maps are available, but Ordnance Survey Outdoor Leisure Maps #12 and 13 (£6.50; 1:25,000) are indispensable for serious exploring and for reaching safety in bad weather. Consider registering with the police before setting out. The National Park staff usually conducts guided walks of varying difficulties between April and November; read through the free park newspaper for details. Centers also stock leaflets on everything from lovespoon carving (see **Gag Me with a Spoon,** p. 466) to sheepdog demonstrations.

NATIONAL PARK INFORMATION CENTRES

Libanus National Mountain Park Visitor Centre (Mountain Centre): Brecon Beacons (☎(01874) 623366; fax 624515). Catch Stagecoach Red and White Brecon-Merthyr bus #43 to Libanus, 5 mi. southwest of Brecon (8min., M-Sa 6 per day), and walk 1½ mi. uphill; on Su in July-Aug., take a shuttle to the front door (15min., June to mid-Sept. Su 6 per day) or Beacons Bus Service #7 (15min., July to mid-Sept. Su 2 per day), both from Brecon. Open July-Aug. M-F 9:30am-5pm, Sa-Su 9:30am-6pm; Apr.-June and Sept. daily 9:30am-5:30pm; Mar. and Oct. 9:30am-5pm; Nov.-Feb. 9:30am-4:30pm.

Abergavenny: see p. 439.

Brecon: see p. 441.

Craig-y-nos: At the Country Park, Pen-y-cae (☎/fax (01639) 730395). Take Silverline Bus #63, the Swansea-Brecon route, and ask to be dropped at Craig-y-nos (1½hr., M-Sa 3 per day). Open May-Aug. M-Th 10am-6pm, F-Su 10am-7pm; Mar.-Apr. and Sept.-Oct. M-F 10am-5pm, Sa-Su 10am-6pm; Nov.-Feb. M-F 10am-4pm, Sa-Su 10am-4:30pm.

Llandovery: Kings Rd. (☎(01550) 720693). Near the Black Mountain; take Heart of Wales train or bus #279 from Carmarthen. Open Easter-Sept. M-Sa 10am-1pm and 1:45-5:30pm, Su 2-5:30pm; Oct.-Easter M-Sa 10am-1pm and 1:45-4pm, Su 2-4pm.

🏠 ACCOMMODATIONS

B&Bs are sparse; the Brecon TIC's free *Where to Stay in Brecknockshire and Brecon Beacons National Park* lists a few. Scattered about the park are five **YHA Youth Hostels,** including **Ty'n-y-Caeau,** near Brecon (see p. 441). The other four are:

Capel-y-ffin (kap-EL-uh-fin; ☎(01873) 890650), near the River Honddu at the eastern edge of the Black Mountains along Offa's Dyke Path, 8 mi. from Hay-on-Wye. Take Stagecoach Red and White #39 (M-Sa 5 per day, £2.80-4.10) or Yeomans #40 (Su 2 per day, £4-5) from Hereford to Brecon, stop before Hay, and walk uphill; or take a taxi from Hay (Border Taxis ☎(01497) 821266; £12). Ideal for hikers and bikers, the road to the hostel climbs up Gospel Pass. Horseback riding trips leave from here in conjunction with Black Mountain Holidays. Lockout 10am-5pm, but daytime access to toilets and shelter from bad weather. Open July-Sept. daily; Oct. F-Tu; Nov. and Mar.-June F-Sa. Dorms £8.50, students £7.50, under 18 £5.75. **Camping** on grounds £5 per tent.

Llanddeusant (HLAN-thew-sont; ☎(01550) 740218). At the foot of isolated Black Mountain near Llangadog village; take the Trecastle-Llangadog road for 9 mi. off the A40. Lockout 10am-5pm. Curfew 11pm. Open mid-Apr. to Aug. daily. Dorms £8.50, students £7.50, under 18 £5.75.

Llwyn-y-Celyn (HLEWN-uh-kel-in; ☎(01874) 624261; fax 625916), 7 mi. south of Brecon, 2 mi. south of Libanus, and 2 mi. north of the Storey Arms car park on the A470. Take Stagecoach Red and White #43 from Brecon or Merthyr Tydfil (M-Sa every 2hr., Su 4 per day). Close to Pen-y-Fan and the Beacons range. Farmhouse near a nature trail. Lockout 10am-5pm, but access to lounges and toilets. Curfew 11pm. Open Easter-Aug. daily; Nov.-Easter F-Su. Dorms £9.25, students £8.25, under 18 £6.50.

Ystradfellte (uh-strahd-FELTH-tuh; ☎(01639) 720301), south of the woods and water-fall district, 3 mi. from the A4059 on a paved road; 4 mi. from the village of Penderyn; a 5min. walk from the Porth-yr-Ogof cave. Hard to reach by public transport except on Su in summer. Small 17th-century cottages. Kitchen. Open mid-July to Aug. daily; Apr. to mid-July and Sept.-Oct. F-Tu. Dorms £8.50, students £7.50, under 18 £5.75.

Commercial **campsites** are plentiful, but often difficult to reach without a car. *Where to Stay in Brecknockshire and Brecon Beacons National Park* lists 14 sites. Many offer laundry and grocery facilities, and all have parking and showers (£3-6 per tent). Farmers may let you camp on their land if you ask first and leave the site as you found it; be prepared to make a donation toward feeding the sheep. *Bunkhouse Accommodations In and Around the Brecon Beacons* (free at park information centres) provides info on more than 15 **bunkhouses.**

⬛ REGIONS OF THE NATIONAL PARK

THE BRECON BEACONS

At the center of the park, the Brecon Beacons lure hikers to pastoral slopes and stark peaks. A splendid view of the range complements an exhibit on its history at the **Mountain Centre** outside Libanus (see **National Park Information Centres,** p. 444). A pamphlet on walks around the center costs 50p; one stroll among daredevil sheep leads to the scant remains of an **Iron Age fort.** The most convenient route to the top of **Pen-y-Fan** (pen-uh-VAN), the highest mountain in southern Wales (2907 ft.), begins at **Storey Arms,** a car park and bus stop 5 mi. south of Libanus on the A470. Paths have eroded over time, and scree (loose rocks) shakes underfoot. A pleasanter hike starts in **Llanfaes,** a western suburb of Brecon. Walk the first 3 mi. from Llanfaes down Ffrwdgrech Rd. to the car park (take the middle fork after the first bridge). From the car park a trail to the peak passes **Llyn Cwm Llwch** (HLIN-koom-hlooch), a 2000 ft. glacial pool in the shadow of **Corn Ddu** (CORN-thee) peak. An arduous ridge path leads from Pen-y-Fan to other peaks in the Beacons.

The touristy **Brecon Mountain Railway,** Pant Station, Merthyr Tydfil, allows a glimpse of the south side of the Beacons as the narrow-gauge train runs north to Pontsticill. (☎(01685) 722988. Runs June to mid-Sept. daily 11am-4pm; Apr.-May and mid-Sept. to Oct. Tu-Th and Sa-Su. £6.80, seniors £6.20, children £3.40.)

THE WATERFALL DISTRICT (FFOREST FAWR)

Rivers tumble through rapids, gorges, and spectacular falls near **Ystradfellte,** about 7 mi. southwest of the Beacons. At **Porth-yr-Ogof** ("mouth of the cave"), less than 1 mi. from the YHA Ystradfellte (see p. 445), the River Mellte ducks into a cave at the base of the cliff and emerges as an icy pool. Swimming is decidedly *not* recommended: the stones are slippery, the pool deepens alarmingly, and dipping here has proved fatal in the past. Porth-yr-Ogof provides no solitude, and rubbish crowds the banks. Remote but worth the sweat is the **Sgwdyr Eira** waterfall (on the River Hepste ½ mi. from its confluence with the Mellte); you can stand behind thundering water in a cliff-face hollow, remaining dry as a bone. Follow the marked paths to the falls from Gwann Hepste. Hikers reach the waterfall district from the Beacons by crossing the A470 near the Llwyn-y-Celyn hostel, climbing

Craig Cerrig-gleisaid cliff and Fan Frynych peak, and descending along a rocky Roman road. The route crosses a nature reserve and some of the park's trackless heath. North of the falls, the pub in the village of Ystradfellte will renew your vigor.

Near **Abercrave,** between Swansea and Brecon off the A4067, the **Dan-yr-Ogof Showcaves** (☎(01639) 730284, 24hr. info 730801) reveal gargantuan stalagmites. From YHA Ystradfellte, 10 mi. of trails pass Fforest Fawr (headlands of the waterfall district) on their way to the caves. (Tours every 20min. Open Apr.-Oct. daily 10:30am-5pm, last admission 3pm. Tours £7.50, children £4.50, under 3 free.) A **campsite** nearby has full facilities (camping £4 per night; caravans £9 per night; electricity £1). Relax at the **Craig-y-nos Country Park,** ½ mi. away. (☎(01639) 730395. Open May-Sept. M-F 10am-6pm, Sa-Su 10am-7pm; Oct.-Apr. 10am-4pm. Free. Car park £2.) **Stagecoach Red and White** #63 (1½hr.; M-F 2per day, Sa 3 per day) stops at the hostel, caves, and campsite en route from Brecon to Swansea.

THE BLACK MOUNTAINS

Located in the easternmost section of the park, the Black Mountains are a group of long, lofty ridges offering 80 sq. mi. of solitude. Summits like **Waun Fach,** the highest point (2660 ft.), may seem dull and boggy, but the ridge-walks are unsurpassed. The 1:25,000 Ordnance Survey Outdoor Leisure Map #13 (£6.50) is essential.

Crickhowell, on the A40 and Stagecoach Red and White route #21 between Brecon and Abergavenny (M-Sa every 2-3hr.), is the best starting point for forays into the area. You can also explore by bus: Stagecoach Red and White bus #39 linking Brecon and Hay-on-Wye (see **Transportation,** p. 441) descends the north side of the Black Mountains. **Gospel Pass,** the park's highest mountain pass, often sees sun above the cloud cover. Nearby, **Offa's Dyke Path** (see **Hiking,** p. 436) sprints down the park's eastern boundary. The ridge valleys are dotted with churches, castles, and other ruins. There is almost no public transportation along valley routes.

SWANSEA (ABERTAWE)   ☎01792

Like most good paradoxes, native son Dylan Thomas's assessment of Wales's second city as "this ugly lovely town" is both logically impossible and very true. Endless rows of box houses creep uphill, offering travelers a worn hello. Yet, with its pedestrian-friendly streets and wide, sandy beach, Swansea (pop. 230,000) redeems itself of poor first impressions. Thomas aficionados need look no farther for satisfying sights, and, a haven for consumers and night-owls, Swansea serves as a transport hub for voyagers to the Gower and Ireland.

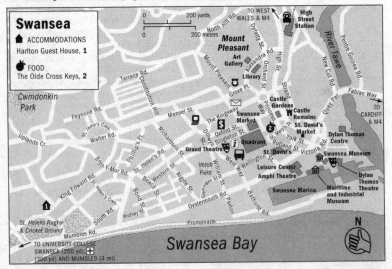

☐ GETTING THERE AND SAILING TO IRELAND. Swansea has direct connections to most major cities in Britain. At the **train station,** 35 High St., trains (☎(08457) 484950) arrive from: **Cardiff** (1hr., 1-2 per hr., £7.80); **London** (3hr., 1-2 per hr., £54); **Birmingham** (4hr., every hr., £31.40). The **Quadrant Bus Station** (☎475511) is near the Quadrant Shopping Centre and the tourist information centre (TIC). **National Express** (☎(08705) 808080) buses from: **London** (4¼hr., 5 per day., £17); **Cardiff** (1¼hr., 16 per day, £5); **Birmingham** (4hr., 4-5 per day, £22). **First Cymru** (☎(08706) 082608) buses cover the Gower Peninsula and the rest of southwest Wales; Monday to Friday a shuttle runs every hour to **Cardiff** (1hr., £6.50). A First Cymru **Day Saver** ticket (£4.50, children and seniors £3.50, families £9) allows unlimited travel for a day in the area; various **City Rider** tickets offer discounts on week-long travel in the Peninsula. **Stagecoach Buses** arrive from smaller towns around Wales, including **Brecon** (1½hr., 3 per day, £4.50). **Taxis** zip around town and down the bay to Mumbles courtesy of **Data Cabs** (☎474747) and **Glamtax** (☎652244). **Cork-Swansea ferries** (☎456116) leave for **Cork, Ireland,** from King's Dock (see **By Ferry,** p. 35). **Cruises** (☎(01446) 720656) leave from Swansea to **Ilfracombe** (£17.95) and other spots on the Bristol Channel from July to September.

◪ PRACTICAL INFORMATION. On the north side of the bus station, the **tourist information centre** (TIC) books rooms for £1 plus a 10% deposit and stocks free entertainment booklets, events calendars, and an excellent city map. (☎468321; fax 464602. Open M-Sa 9:30am-5:30pm, and sometimes Su in summer.) Other services include: **Barclays bank** on the Kingsway (☎(0800) 400100; open M-F 9am-5pm, Sa 9:30am-noon); **American Express,** 28 The Kingsway (☎455188; open M-F 9am-5pm, Sa 9am-4pm); **Lendart Launderette,** 91 Bryn-y-Mor Rd. (☎644682; wash £2.20, dry £1; open M-F 8am-8pm, Sa-Su 8am-6pm); the **police** (☎456999), at the bottom of Mt. Pleasant Hill; **Singleton Hospital** (☎205666), on Sketty Park Ln., which refers major ailments to more distant **Morriston Hospital** (☎702222); **Internet access** at the YMCA's **Cyber-Cafe,** 1 The Kingsway (☎652032; £1.50 per 30min.; open M-F 11am-3pm), or at the **Swansea Public Library,** Alexandra Rd., for the same rate (☎516753; book in advance; open M-W and F 9am-7pm, Th and Sa 9am-5pm); and the **post office,** 35 The Kingsway (open M-Sa 9am-5:30pm). **Postal code:** SA1 5LF.

☐☐ ACCOMMODATIONS AND FOOD. Inexpensive **B&Bs** and guest houses line **Oystermouth Rd.,** along the bay, but win no prizes for charm. **Harlton Guest House,** 89 King Edward's Rd., a mile out of town, is somewhat nicer. Bus #37 runs hourly from the bus station, or walk a mile from the city center. (☎466938. TVs. £10 per person, £12 with breakfast.) The closest hostel is the popular **YHA Port Eynon,** an hour out of town by bus (see **Accommodations,** p. 449). In high season, many travelers **camp** at sites along the Gower Peninsula.

Indian and Chinese takeaways line **St. Helen's Rd.,** and cafes dominate the **Oxford St.** pedestrian zone and **Wind St.**'s busy sidewalks. The city convenes to peruse everything from bread to CDs at the massive **Swansea Market,** on the other side of the Quadrant Shopping Centre from the bus station. (Open M-Th 8:30am-5:30pm, F-Sa 8am-5:30pm.) Those under 18 will find the doors of many traditional pubs closed, but **The Olde Cross Keys,** 12 St. Mary's St., lets kids—er, young adults—into their nonsmoking room for meals. (☎630921. Open M-Sa 11am-11pm, Su noon-10:30pm; food served M-Th 11am-8pm, F-Sa 8am-5:30pm, Su noon-6pm.)

◪ SIGHTS. The **castle,** reduced to humble ruins by Welsh rebel Owain Glyndŵr, lies between Wind St. and The Strand; it overlooks the **city square,** a motley extravaganza of street entertainers and people-watchers. As in Cardiff (Swansea's rival city), recent rebuilding has transformed the **maritime quarter** from a decaying dockland to an array of upscale apartment blocks and outdoor cafes. In the **Maritime and Industrial Museum,** vintage cars and grainy photos of tugboats share space with an exhibit on the world's first passenger railway, which chugged from Swansea to Oystermouth in 1807. Climb aboard the lightship **Helwick** docked outside and

WILD CHILD Son of Swansea's Cwmdonkin Dr., Dylan Thomas learned early that he could play with words. Walking to Aplans School with his mates, Dylan passed Mr. Brown's Butcher Shop, Mr. Green's Market, and Mrs. White's Bakery, convincing others that to own a shop on this street, your name had to be a color. The rhyme scheme of "Prologue" in *Collected Poems 1934-1952* divides the 102-line poem into two mirror-image verses: line one rhymes with line 102, line two rhymes with line 101, and so on. In *Under Milk Wood*, though, Dylan took his trickery too far for the refined tastes of the BBC. Originally written for radio presentation, the script was set in a fictitious Welsh town that Dylan intended to be "strangely simple and simply strange." The name he gave his town, Llareggub, certainly *looked* Welsh. However, when the work was first published in 1954, the spelling was changed to Llaryggub to disguise the fact that, when read backwards, Dylan's famous town says Buggerall.

admire the plush, pint-sized bunks. (☎650351. Museum open Tu-Su 10am-5pm. Boat open June-Aug. Th-Su 10am-5pm. Both free.) A pensive and bulbous-nosed **Dylan Thomas** sits at the end of the marina, and a full page of the *Swansea Bay* guide is devoted to shepherding iambic junkies along the **Dylan Thomas Uplands Trail** and **Dylan Thomas City Centre Trail** past the poet's favorite haunts. More detailed guidebooks to the trails (£1.50) are available at the **Dylan Thomas Centre,** Somerset Pl., which has a permanent exhibition on anything and everything Thomas. Scribble a few lines in the life-sized replica of Thomas's writing shed or examine the poet's only known painting, the surreal "Petition to the Government." In a video, Thomas claims he wasn't the world-class drinker and ladies' man he seemed. The Centre also presents dramatic, cinematic, and literary performances. (☎463980; box office 463932. Open Tu-Su 10:30am-4:30pm. Free.) **Swansea Museum,** Victoria Rd., is the oldest in Wales. Thomas described it as "a museum that should be in a museum." (☎653763. Open Tu-Su 10am-5pm, last admission 4pm. Free.)

🎭🎵 **ENTERTAINMENT AND NIGHTLIFE.** Evenings in Swansea are lively affairs, the downtown pedestrian area packed with theater-goers and clubbers. The bimonthly *What's On,* free at the TIC, lists events around town. The **Dylan Thomas Theatre,** along the marina, stages dramas and musicals. (☎473238. Tickets £5-7.) The **Grand Theatre,** on Singleton St., puts on operas, ballets, and concerts. (☎475715. Box office open 9:30am-8pm. Tickets £6-40, student discounts sometimes available on day of show.) The **Taliesin Arts Centre,** University College, hosts films, art shows, and dance. (☎296883. Box Office open Sept.-July M-F 10am-6pm, Sa noon-6pm, performance nights 6-8:15pm.) In mid-August, the village of Pontardawe, 8 mi. north of Swansea (take bus #120 or 125), floods with international folk and rock musicians for the **Pontardawe International Music Festival** (☎830200). During October, the **Swansea Festival** (☎205318, bookings 475715) presents a variety of classical concerts. No calendar would be complete without the annual **Dylan Thomas Celebration** (Oct. 27-Nov. 9 in 2002), with readings, shows, and lectures.

Nightlife in Swansea centers around the Kingsway, where swarms of students club-hop on weekend nights—just follow their lead. The enormous **Icon** and **Ritzy's** clubs, 72 The Kingsway, occupy the former Odeon Cinema, both popular on Monday student nights and "commercial dance night" Saturdays. (☎653142. Cover M and Th-F £1-3, Sa £5-6. Open M and Th 8pm-2:30am, F-Sa 8pm-4am.) About 5 mi. away, pubs on Mumbles Rd. are a beer-buyer's magnet (see **Entertainment,** p. 450).

THE GOWER PENINSULA ☎01792

Surrounded by sparkling waters, the limestone cliffs and white beaches of the 18 mi. Gower Peninsula are rife with unexpected finds. Crumbling castles and burial sites constellate the Cefn Bryn hills, while Mumbles, at its east end, is a major destination for pub crawlers. Best of all, the peninsula's proximity to Swansea (5 mi. from Mumbles) means you'll be spared a leg-breaking hike to get there.

☰ TRANSPORTATION. Buses overrun the peninsula from Swansea's **Quadrant Station. First Cymru** (☎(08706) 082608) buses #2 and 2A leave **Swansea** for Oystermouth Sq. in **Mumbles** (20min., 20 per hr., £1.55) and continue to lovely **Langland Bay** and then **Caswell Bay**. Buses #18 and 18d run to **Oxwich** (40min., every 2hr., return £3), while #18A lurches through the hills to **Rhossili** via **Port Eynon** (1hr., every 2hr., return £2.30). Bus #14 shuttles to **Pennard** (35min., every hr., 14 per day); bus #16 covers **North Gower**. On Sundays bus travel is difficult: only #18D crosses the peninsula, joined by #48 June through August. The First Cymru **Day Saver** is valid through the Gower and beyond (£4.80, concessions £3.50, families £9); the **Gower & City Rider** allows unlimited travel around the Peninsula for a week (£12, children £8.20). **Network Rider** passes are also accepted (see **Buses**, p. 420). **Hitchhiking** is said to be quicker than public transport and allows coastal views, while most buses follow inland routes. (*Let's Go* does not recommend hitchhiking.) The pleasant **Swansea Bikepath and Promenade** traces the coast from Swansea Bay to Mumbles pier. **Waterfront Bike Hire**, at the Boat Park on the Promenade in Mumbles, **rents bikes.** (☎495670. £3.50 per hr., £10 per day; helmets 50p. Discounts for families and children. Credit card deposit and 2 forms of ID required.)

◪ PRACTICAL INFORMATION. Most useful services on the Gower can be found in **Mumbles**. The **tourist information centre** (TIC) stands in a portacabin in the car park near the bus station. (☎361302; fax 363392. Open Easter-Oct. M-Sa 9:30am-5:30pm; July-Aug. also some Su.) Other services include: **Barclays bank**, Newton Rd. (☎492600; open M-Tu and Th-F 9am-4:30pm, W 10am-4:30pm); **A.A. Taxis** (☎360600); the **police**, Newton Rd. (☎456999), near Castle St.; **Internet access** at **Oystermouth Library**, Dunns Ln., up the street from the Mumbles TIC (☎368380; £1.50 per 30min.; open M-F 9:30am-1pm and 2-5:30pm, Sa 9:30am-1pm and 2-5pm); and the **post office**, 522 Mumbles Rd. (☎366821; open M-F 9am-12:30pm and 1:30-5:30pm, Sa 9am-12:30pm). **Postal code:** SA3 4HH.

⌂⌂ ACCOMMODATIONS AND FOOD. The farther west you go on the Gower, the more likely you are to find tourist-free campsites. **B&Bs** in Mumbles charge upwards of £18 and cluster on Mumbles Rd. and in the South End area (10min. from the TIC); singles are hard to find. With a prime quayside location, the gabled **Coast House**, 708 Mumbles Rd., has sunny rooms and sea views. (☎368702. Most rooms with TV and bath. Singles £20-23; doubles £38-44.) Behind it, **Rock Villa**, 1 George Bank, is comfortable, with a prized bay vista. (☎366794. Doubles £42-44.) Accommodations in nearby **Bishopston** are reachable by bus #14. To camp at **Three Cliffs Bay Caravan Park**, North Hills Farm, Penmaen, take bus #18 from Swansea. (☎371218. £4.50 per person. Families £10.50.) Port Eynon, west of Mumbles, hosts the no-frills **YHA Port Eynon**, a former lifeboat house on the beach; take bus #18A from Swansea. (☎/fax 390706. Reception from 5pm. Bedroom lockout 10am-5pm. Security-code entry after 11pm. Open July-Aug. daily; Apr.-June M-Sa; Sept.-Oct. Tu-Sa. £9.25, under 18 £6.50.) Beachside **camping** is possible at sites in Port Eynon.

In Mumbles, the **Somerfield** supermarket is at 512 Mumbles Rd. (Open daily 8am-10pm.) Head to busy **Verdi's**, Knab Rock, at the south end of Mumbles Rd., to savor homemade ice cream (from £2.60) in a people-watching paradise; the pricier restaurant serves pastas from £6.50. (☎369135. Open July-Aug. daily 10am-10pm; mid-Mar. to June 10am-9pm; Nov. to mid-Mar. M-W 10am-6pm, Th-Su 10am-9pm.) For a view of the Welsh cliffs, walk 2 mi. along the Bay Footpath to **Rother's Tor Cafe and Restaurant**, where you'll be rewarded with sandwiches (£3) on beachside tables. (Open July-Aug. daily 10am-9pm; Sept.-June 10am-5pm.) The Indian food at **Megna Restaurant**, 728 Mumbles Rd., tastes especially good on Sundays, when the buffet costs only £7. (☎361991. Open M-Sa 5:30pm-midnight, Su noon-10pm. Buffet Su noon-10pm.) **Hightide Cafe**, 61 Newton Rd., serves snacks all day and meals, like the Homemade Hoomoos (£4) and Spicy Vegetable Enchiladas (£5.80), from noon-3pm and in summer 6-9pm. (☎363462. Open July-Sept. M 9am-5pm, Tu-F 9am-9pm, Sa 10am-9pm, Su 11am-2pm and 6-8pm; Oct.-June M-Sa 9am-5pm, Su 11am-2pm.)

SOUTH WALES

◎ **SIGHTS.** Perched high above Mumbles, the battlements of 13th-century **Oystermouth Castle**, on Castle Ave. off Newton Rd., are overrun with birds and flowers. (☎368732. Open Apr. to mid-Sept. daily 11am-5pm, with occasional reenactments. £1, concessions 80p.) Picnickers should attempt the challenging ascent to the 56-acre **Mumbles Hill Nature Reserve,** an oasis of scrub, wildflowers, and rock overlooking Mumbles and the sea. The endless staircase begins by the George Hotel, a 10min. walk from the bus station on Mumbles Rd. Staff at the **Lovespoon Gallery,** 492 Mumbles Rd., tell you what to do if a wild-eyed Welshman lurches after you with a wooden spoon—they'll even sell you a spoon of your own (see **Gag Me with a Spoon,** p. 466). Lovespoons cost £2.20-170. (☎360132. Open M-Sa 10am-5:30pm.)

On the Gower Peninsula gorgeous **beaches** are a dime a dozen. From Southgate and Pennard, a half-hour walk along the Coast Path brings you to **Three Cliffs,** a secluded, cave-ridden beauty almost completely submerged at high tide. **Langland Bay, Caswell Bay, Oxwich Bay,** and **Port Eynon Bay** are all popular. To reach Langland, walk 45min. along the Bays Footpath that begins around the point of Mumbles Head. Caswell is another 45min., and Oxwich and Port Eynon are several miles beyond; buses #18 and 18A from Swansea sometimes make a stop. On the peninsula's western tip, green cliffs clutch the sexy curve of ◧**Rhossili Beach,** whose dramatic expanse makes overcrowding unlikely; take bus #18A from Swansea. At low tide, a causeway of tortured rock gives access to **Worm's Head,** a series of crags that looks like Nessie's Welsh cousin lumbering out to sea. **Llangennith Beach,** north of Rhossili, draws surfers from all over Wales.

🎭 **ENTERTAINMENT AND FESTIVALS.** A quiet fishing village by day, **Mumbles** is famous for its raucous pubs. The short stretch of **Mumbles Rd.** at Mumbles Head is lined with watering holes, some of them former haunts of the area's most famous dipsomaniac, Dylan Thomas. In University of Swansea parlance, to hang out on Mumbles Rd. is to "go mumbling"; to start at one end and have a pint at each pub is to "do the Mumbles Mile." Flower's, Usher's, Buckley's, and Felin Foel are the local real ales. The **Gower Festival** fills the peninsula's churches with the sounds of string quartets and Bach chorales during the last two weeks of July. The *What's On* guide, free at the Mumbles TIC, has details (☎468321; box office 475715).

TENBY (DINBYCH-Y-PYSGOD)   ☎01834

"Fair and fashionable" and nicknamed the Welsh Riviera, Tenby lives up to the good and bad implicit in its reputation. The soft-sanded beaches can be crowded—Tenby is largely a summer resort town, after all. But slip away to the shady sidewalk by the town wall or cross to an offshore island, and youthful, ancient Tenby will reward with history, ghost stories, and a perfect patch of sand.

◘ **TRANSPORTATION**

The five booklets of the *Public Transport Timetables for South Pembrokeshire,* available free at tourist information centres (TICs), list buses, trains, and ferries for the area, including Tenby, Pembroke, Saundersfoot, and Manorbier.

Trains: At the bottom of Warren St. Unstaffed. **Tenby Travel** (☎843214), in the Tenby Indoor Market between High St. and Upper Frog St., books tickets. Open M-Tu and Th-F 9am-5pm, W and Sa 9am-4pm. Trains (☎(08457) 484950), all M-F 8 per day, Sa 10 per day, Su 5 per day, from: **Pembroke** (30min., £3); **Carmarthen** (45min., £5.20); **Swansea** (1½hr., £8.10); **Cardiff** (2½hr., £13.90).

Buses: Buses leave from the multi-story car park on Upper Park Rd., next to Somerfield supermarket. **First Cymru** (☎(01792) 580580) arrives from **Haverfordwest** via **Pembroke** (#349, every hr. M-Sa until 5:30pm, £4). Or go from **Swansea** to **Carmarthen** (#X11 or X30, M-Sa every hr., £3.60) and transfer to **Silcox Coaches** bus #333 (2½hr., M-Sa 4 per day). A Silcox Coaches (☎842189) office is in the arcade between South Parade and Upper Frog St., across from the market hall. A First Cymru **Day Saver** (£4.80) or a **Cleddau Rider** (£11.90) buys unlimited daily or weekly travel west of Carmarthen. **National Express** (☎(08705) 808080) also runs from **Swansea** (#508).

Taxis: Local Taxis (☎ 844603). Taxis also congregate by the bus station.

✴🛈 ORIENTATION AND PRACTICAL INFORMATION

The old town is in the shape of a triangle pointing into the bay, with **North Beach** along the top edge, **Castle Beach** and **South Beach** along the bottom, and the train station on the back edge. From the station, **Warren St.** approaches town, becoming **White Lion** and continuing to North Beach. Like tines of a fork off White Lion, **South Parade**, **Upper Frog St.**, **Crackwell St.**, and **High St.** all lead toward South Beach. **The Croft** runs along North Beach, and the **Old Wall** runs along South Parade.

Tourist Information Centre: The Croft (☎ 842404; fax 845439), overlooking North Beach. Free accommodations list. Town maps 15p. Open June to mid-July daily 10am-5:30pm; mid-July to Aug. 10am-9pm; Sept.-May M-Sa 10am-4pm.

Financial Services: Barclays, 18 High St. (☎ (01437) 822400). Open M-W and F 9am-5pm, Th 10am-5pm.

Launderette: Fecci's, Lower Frog St. (☎ 842484). Change machine. Wash £1.60-2.60, dry 20p per 5min., soap 20p. Open daily 8:30am-9pm; last wash 8:30pm.

Police: Warren St. (☎ 842303), near the church off White Lion St.

Hospital: Tenby Cottage Hospital, Trafalgar Rd. (☎ 842040).

Internet Access: Tenby County Library, Greenhill Ave. (☎ 843934), is free. Best to book ahead. Open M and W-F 9:30am-1pm and 2-5pm, Tu 9:30am-1pm and 2-6pm, Sa 9:30am-12:30pm. **Webb-Computers,** Upper Park Rd. (☎ 844101), in front of Somerfield, costs £1 per 15min. Open M-Tu and Th-Sa 9:30am-5:30pm, W 9:30am-9pm; July-Aug. also Su 10am-5pm.

Post Office: Warren St. (☎ 843213), at South Parade. Open M-F 8:30am-5:30pm, Sa 8:30am-12:30pm. **Postal Code:** SA70 7JR.

🛏 ACCOMMODATIONS AND CAMPING

Warren St., outside the town wall near the train station, has loads of B&Bs for £18-22; the side streets of **Greenhill Ave.** and those off the Esplanade and Trafalgar Rd., are almost as well endowed. Or take a bus ride to **Saundersfoot** (#352, every hr.).

Hazlemere, 13 Warren St. (☎ 844691). Bright rooms and reams of tourist brochures. June-Aug. £16-18 per person; Sept.-May £15 per person. £4 extra for singles.

Lyndale, Warren St. (☎ 842836). The comfortable rooms may have you spending more time in bed than on the beach. £20-25 per person in summer; £18 in winter.

Langdon Guest House, Warren St. (☎ 843923). The family energy will recharge your battery as you enjoy the color TV. Easter-Aug. £18 per person; Sept.-Easter prices lower.

Camping: Meadow Farm (☎ 844829), at the top of The Croft, overlooking the town and North Beach. Open Easter-Oct. £4, accompanied children £1.50. Showers free.

🍴 FOOD

Tenby has plenty of restaurants, but many are so expensive you'll be tempted to drink the ketchup just to get your money's worth. Lunch specials can soften the blow, and there's always the banana split at any of the innumerable ice-cream parlors. Buy picnic goods at **Tenby Market Hall** between High St. and Upper Frog St. (open daily 8am-5pm; Oct.-June closed W afternoons and Su) or **Somerfield** supermarket, next to the bus station on Upper Park Rd. (☎ 843771; open M-Th and Sa 8am-8pm, F 8am-9pm; mid-July to Aug. until 10pm.)

▨ The Plantagenet, Quay Hill (☎ 842350). Hidden in an alley connecting Bridge St. and St. Julian's St.—a jungle of flowers betrays it in warmer months. Excellent Welsh and Continental cuisine. Sit under the 800-year-old, 40 ft. stone chimney. Lunchtime is preferable (£5-6.25), as dinner can be pricey (£12-17). Kids eat free before 7pm. Open Easter-Oct. daily 9:30am-12:30am; Nov.-Easter F-Su 9:30am-12:30am.

Candy, Crackwell St. (☎842052), on the corner of High St., leans like a captain's cabin over the sea. Go for salads (£4.90-5.40) and omelettes (£4.70-5.20) or try one of the "popular meals" (£3.50-5.50). Open Apr.-Oct. daily 9am-8:30pm.

Pam Pam, 2 Tudor Sq. (☎842946), satiates with hearty plates and brunch (£3.45-7) until 5:30pm. Dinner runs £6-13, vegetarian dishes £6-7. Open Easter-Oct. daily 10am-10:30pm; Nov.-Easter 10:30am-9pm.

The Sherma Balti (☎845045), below the Hilton pub just beyond the B&Bs on Warren St. Great Indian food (£4-10, takeaway 10% discount) with adventurous menu options. Open Su-Th 5pm-12:30am, F-Sa noon-1:30pm and 5pm-1am.

◖◉ BEACHES AND SIGHTS

Promenades and clifftop benches afford marvelous views, but most visitors zip straight to the sand. On a sunny day, **North Beach,** by the Croft, and **South Beach,** beyond the Esplanade, swarm with pensioners and naked toddlers. At the eastern tip of Tenby, **Castle Beach** reaches into caves that taunt the curious explorer, but only by evading the crowds and heading for rockier, less groomed sand will you find the treasure troves of Tenby sea shells. **DragonSports,** Castle Slipway on Castle Beach, provides equipment for sailing, waterskiing, and scuba diving. (☎843553. Open Easter to late Sept. daily 9am-late.) A variety of excursions leave from the harbor; check the kiosks at Castle Beach. **Coastal and Island Cruises** runs boat trips. (☎843545. Open Apr.-Oct. Trips £6, students and seniors £5, children £3.)

The three floors of the ▧**Tudor Merchant's House,** on Quay Hill off Bridge St., take historical display to the highest level, detailing the superstitions of a 16th-century Welsh household. Ever want to know how cutlery-care attracted murderers or why lefties were forbidden to stir the stew? (☎842279. Open Apr.-Sept. M-Tu and Th-Sa 10am-5pm, Su 1-5pm; Oct. M-Tu and Th-F 10am-3pm, Su noon-3pm. £1.80, children 90p.) The ruins of Tenby's **castle** rest at the summit of Castle Hill, almost fully surrounded by ocean. Views reach across Carmarthen Bay to Worm's Head on the Gower Peninsula, and sometimes all the way to Devon. At night, Tenby's spooks and ghouls share the streets with resort revelers; the 1½hr. **Ghost Walk of Tenby** departs from the Lifeboat Tavern in Tudor Sq. at 8pm. Buy tickets at Dales Music Shop, High St. (☎845841, last-minute booking (07970) 420734. Runs June-Sept. daily, advance booking suggested; Oct.-May M-Sa, advance booking required. £3.25, seniors and students £3, children £2.25, families £10.)

▶ DAYTRIPS FROM TENBY

CALDEY ISLAND. Three perfumed miles south of Tenby lies this saffron-sanded island. Site of an active monastery founded in the 6th century, the current building is the dogged third coming, as Vikings and Henry VIII sacked the first two. The land hosts a community of seabirds, seals, and 20 enterprising Cistercian monks, who produce perfume (£3.50-14.95) and chocolate (90p) for the island's several stores. The island's post office dispenses information and fake souvenir stamps. If the commercialism overwhelms you, take one of the several footpaths to the other side of the island. (*Caldey Boats sail from Tenby harbor.* ☎842296. *Runs June-Aug. M-F 9:45am-5:30pm. Cruises 20min.; 4 per hr.; return £7, seniors £6, children £3.*)

CAREW CASTLE. Strange, handsome Carew Castle, 5 mi. northwest of Tenby, is an odd mixture of Norman fortress and Elizabethan manor, where ruins of mighty stone mingle with windows of pretty glass. Nearby, one of Britain's three **tidal mills,** dating to 1558, turns by a medieval bridge and an 11th-century cross. Check *Coast to Coast,* free at most TICs, for events at the castle. (*Take Silcox bus #361 from Tenby to the castle (45min., M-Sa 5 per day). Castle* ☎(01646) 651782. *Open Apr. to early Nov. daily 10am-5pm. Tours usually 11am, noon, 2, 3pm. Mill and castle £2.80, seniors and children £1.90, families £7.50. Castle or mill only £1.90, seniors and children £1.40.*)

MANORBIER CASTLE. Between Tenby and Pembroke stands superbly preserved Manorbier Castle, a 13th-century Norman baron's palace where mood music drifts from the ceilings and wax figures fill the halls. A garden in the keep and a beach below the ramparts are equally inviting. (*Trains from Tenby and Pembroke run 10 per day. First Cymru bus #349 shuttles between Tenby, Manorbier, Pembroke, and Haverfordwest (M-Sa every hr., in summer also Su 4 per day). Castle ☎(01646) 621500. Open Easter-Sept. daily 10:30am-5:30pm. £2, seniors £1.50, children £1.*) Manorbier also has a **YHA Youth Hostel** (☎871803; see p. 454). The National Park authorities organize guided walks in the area, outlined in their free seasonal publication *Coast to Coast*.

DYLAN THOMAS BOAT HOUSE. Dylan Thomas spent his last four years in the boat house in **Laugharne** (LARN) at the mouth of the River Taff, about 15 mi. northeast of Tenby. The boat house, now fairly commercialized, displays Thomas's photographs, art, and books, and the shed where he wrote is just as he left it. (*Take First Cymru bus #351 to Laugharne (45min., every 2hr.). House ☎(01994) 427420. Open May-Oct. daily 10am-5pm; Nov.-Apr. 10:30am-3pm. £2.75, children £1, seniors £1.75, under 7 free.*)

PEMBROKESHIRE COAST NATIONAL PARK

The 225 sq. mi. of Pembrokeshire Coast National Park (Parc Cenedlaethol Arfordir Penfro), stretched along the water and scattered in inland pockets, are best known for dramatic coastal scenery. The park also features the wooded Gwaun Valley and prehistoric Celtic remnants deep in the Preseli Hills. But the coast remains the supreme draw: hikers from near and far follow 186 mi. of coastal path past secluded inlets, towering rocks overrun by birds, tiny chapels, squat cathedrals, and sheer cliffs that rise from the Atlantic surf.

⌁ TRANSPORTATION

The best place to enter the region is **Haverfordwest.** Buses offer more frequent and wide-ranging service than trains. The Dale Peninsula, southwest of Haverfordwest, is not served by public transport at all. While *Let's Go* does not recommend hitchhiking, hitchers rave about the area. Mountain bikes are an excellent means of transport on the one-lane roads. Do not, however, ride on the coastal path itself; it is illegal and extraordinarily dangerous, in that you might plummet over a cliff.

Trains: (☎(08457) 484950). To **Haverfordwest** from **London Paddington** (4¾hr.; M-F 7 per day, Sa 5 per day, Su varies; M-Th £44, F £61, Sa-Su varies) and **Cardiff** (2½hr., 7 per day, £13.90). Trains also run to **Fishguard** on the north coast and **Tenby** and **Pembroke Dock,** both on the south coast (change at Whitland).

Buses: There are many local bus providers; consult the 5 unnamed but useful bus-and-train transport booklets, available free at local TICs. **Richards Brothers** (☎(01239) 613756) runs from **Haverfordwest** to **St. David's** (#411; 45min., 13 per day., £2) and **Fishguard** (1½hr., 5 per day, £4). **First Cymru** (☎(01792) 580580) runs from **Haverfordwest** to **Milford Haven** (#302; 20min.; M-Sa 1-2 per hr., Su 8 per day; £1.90) and, in conjunction with **Silcox Coaches** (☎(01646) 683143), from **Haverfordwest** to **Broad Haven** (#311, 15min., M-Sa 5 per day, £1.45). A **West Wales Rover Ticket** (£4.60 per day, children £3.40, accompanied children £2.30) gets you virtually unlimited travel in **Pembrokeshire** and neighboring **Carmarthenshire** and **Ceredigion.**

Bike Rental: Voyages of Discovery, Cross Sq. (☎(01437) 721911), in St. David's, will rent you a bike for a half-day (£8) or day (£10). Open daily 8:30am-5pm.

Boat Rental: A number of **outdoor activity centers** rent canoes, kayaks, ponies, bikes, and other archaic means of transport (£10-20 per day); check the *Coast to Coast* newspaper, available at Park Information Centres, for locations. Among the most popular is **TYF Adventure,** which has stores in Tenby and St. David's.

PRACTICAL INFORMATION

The **National Park Information Centres** listed below sell 10 annotated maps covering the coastal path (from 45p each). National Park officers will aid your planning for free; ask about the guided walks offered by the park. Write for brochures to National Park Information Services, Pembrokeshire Coast National Park Head Office, Winch Ln., Haverfordwest, Pembrokeshire, Wales SA61 1PY (☎(01437) 764636; www.pembrokeshirecoast.org). For **weather info,** call any park office; in an emergency, contact **rescue rangers** by dialing 999 or 112.

NATIONAL PARK INFORMATION CENTRES

Haverfordwest: 40 High St. (☎(01437) 760136, 24hr. info 771455; fax 775140). Open Easter-Sept. M-Sa 10am-1pm and 1:45-5:30pm.

Newport, Pembrokeshire: Bank Cottages, Long St. (☎/fax (01239) 820912). Open Easter-Oct. M-Sa 10am-5:30pm.

St. David's: The Grove (☎(01437) 720392; fax 720099). Doubles as the town TIC. Open Easter-Oct. daily 9:30am-5:30pm; Nov.-Easter M-Sa 10am-4pm. Closed for 2 weeks in Jan.

TOURIST INFORMATION CENTRES

Fishguard: Town Hall, The Square (☎(01348) 873484; fax 875246). Open Easter-Oct. M-Sa 10am-5:30pm; Nov.-Easter M-Sa 10am-4pm.

Haverfordwest: 19 Old Bridge (☎(01437) 763110; fax 767738). Open Apr.-Aug. M-Sa 10am-5:30pm; Sept. 10am-5pm; Oct.-Mar. 10am-4pm.

Milford Haven: 94 Charles St. (☎(01646) 690866; fax 690655). Open Easter-Oct. M-Sa 10am-5pm.

Saundersfoot: The Barbecue, Harbour Car Park (☎(01834) 813672; fax 813673). Open Easter-Oct. daily 10am-5pm.

Tenby: The Croft (☎(01834) 842404; fax 845439). Open June to mid-July daily 10am-5:30pm; mid-July to Aug. 10am-9pm; Sept.-May M-Sa 10am-4pm.

ACCOMMODATIONS AND CAMPING

Spaced along the coastal path, the park's **YHA Youth Hostels** are all within a reasonable day's walk of one another. If you plan well ahead, you can book at all of the hostels at least 14 days beforehand for a £2.50 fee through the **West Wales Booking Bureau,** Anna Davis, YHA St. David's, Pembrokeshire SA62 6PR (☎(01629) 51061). Roads between Tenby, Pembroke, and St. David's teem with **B&Bs** (£14.50-30), but they are hard to secure in summer. The coast is lined with **campsites,** as many farmers convert fallow fields into summer sites (about £4 per tent); inquire before pitching. The Manorbier, Poppit Sands, and Pwll Deri hostels also allow camping.

YHA Broad Haven: (☎(01437) 781688; fax 781100), on St. Bride's Bay off the B4341. Take bus #311 from Haverfordwest and get off in Broad Haven (20min., 4-5 per day). 75 beds and some of the best facilities on the Walk. Washing machine (£1). Lockout 10am-1pm. Curfew 11pm. Open mid-Feb. to Oct. daily. Dorms £11.25, under 18 £8.

YHA Manorbier: Skrinkle Haven (☎(01834) 871803; fax 871101), near Manorbier Castle. From the train station, walk past the A4139 to the castle, make a left onto the B4585, a right up to the army camp, and follow the signs. Vigorous showers and laundry facilities. Lockout 10am-5pm. Curfew 11pm. Open mid-Feb. to Oct. daily. Dorms £10.85, under 18 £7.40. Camping £5.40.

YHA Marloes Sands: (☎/fax (01646) 636667), near the Dale Peninsula. A cluster of farm buildings on National Trust Property. Hiking's your best bet. Lockout 10am-5pm. Curfew 11pm. Open Apr.-Oct. daily. Dorms £7.35, under 18 £5.15.

YHA Pwll Deri: (☎(01348) 891385), on breathtaking cliffs around Strumble Head near Fishguard. Lockout 10am-5pm. Curfew 5pm. Open July-Aug. daily; Apr.-June and Sept.-Oct. W-Su. Dorms £8.10, under 18 £5.65. Camping £4.

YHA St. David's: (☎(01437) 720345; fax 721831), near St. David's Head. Take the 2 mi. path past the bishop's palace and look for the red-painted doors. Men stay in the cowshed, women in the stables, with extra rooms in the granary. Lockout 10am-5pm, but daytime access to dining hall. Curfew 11pm. Open mid-July to Aug. daily; Apr. to mid-July and Sept.-Oct. W-Su. Dorms £8.10, under 18 £5.65.

YHA Trevine: (☎(01348) 831414), between St. David's and Fishguard. Bus #411 stops at the hostel upon request. Lockout 10am-5pm. Curfew 11pm. Open July-Aug. daily; Apr.-June and Sept.-Oct. Tu-Sa. Dorms £8.10, under 18 £5.65.

🥾 HIKING

For short hikes, stick to the more accessible **St. David's Peninsula** in the northwest. Otherwise, set out on the 186 mi. **Coastal Path,** marked with acorn symbols along manageable terrain. It begins in the southeast at Amroth and continues west through Tenby to St. Govan's Head, where worn steps lead to █**St. Govan's Chapel** on its patch of cliff over crashing ocean. One myth has it that Arthurian knight Sir Gawain retreated here after the fall of Camelot. The waters of its well are said to heal ills and grant wishes, and no mortal can count its steps.

From here to the impressive **Elegug Stacks,** pinnacles of rock a bit offshore, the path passes natural sea arches, mile-wide lily pools at Bosherston, and limestone stacks. Unfortunately, the stretch from St. Govan's Head to the Stacks (6 mi.) can be closed to hikers for use as an artillery range. Call the **Castemartin Range Office** (☎(01646) 662367) or the **Pembroke National Visitor Centre** (☎(01646) 622388) for openings or check postings at the TIC in Tenby. For 10 mi. west of the Stacks the coast is permanently off-limits, and the path veers inland until **Freshwater West.**

From Freshwater West to **Angle Bay,** the coastline walk covers mild and pretty terrain. It breaks slightly at Milford Haven, where it's crossed by a channel running over 25 mi. inland. Geologists call it a "ria," or drowned river valley. From the Dale Peninsula, the path passes by the long, clean beaches of St. Bride's Bay, turns up to Newgale, and arrives at ancient **St. David's Head,** the site of pre-Cambrian formations and the oldest named feature on the coast of Wales. The ocean has carved away caves and secluded inlets, and the jagged terrain is awe-inspiring.

🏝 ISLANDS OFF THE PEMBROKESHIRE COAST

GRASSHOLM. On Grassholm, farthest from the shore, 35,000 pairs of gannets raise their young. **Dale Sailing Company** runs guided trips around, but not to, the island from Martin's Haven on the Dale Peninsula, often encountering Manx shearwaters and storm petrels along the way. (☎(01646) 601636. Times vary; call for information. £20. Reservations required.) The company also sails to the island of **Skomer,** a marine reserve and breeding ground for auks, seals, and puffins. (Apr.-Oct. Tu-Su. £6 boat fee, £6 landing fee; children £5 boat fee, no landing fee.)

RAMSEY ISLAND. Seals and rare seabirds live on Ramsey Island, off St. David's farther up the coast. On the east side of the island lurk the **Bitches,** a chain of offshore rocks where countless sailors have come to grief. **Thousand Islands Expeditions,** Cross Sq. (☎(01437) 721686 or (0800) 163621), in St. David's, sail from Whitesands Bay or St. Justinians around Ramsey Island. (1½hr.; Easter-Nov. daily, weather permitting; £12, children £6.) They also offer landing trips from St. Justinians (Easter-Oct. W-M 2 per day; £10, children £5.) The adventurous can brave the passages between the Bitches on a white-water jetboat trip (1hr.; £25, adults only) or a journey through the island's sea-caves, the longest in Wales (2hr.; £22.50, children £10). **Voyages of Discovery and Ramsey Island Cruises,** Cross Sq., St. David's, also runs tours around the island. (☎(01437) 721423. Tours in normal boats £8, seniors £6, children £4; in super-speedy inflatable boats £10, seniors £6, children £5.)

PEMBROKE (PENFRO) AND PEMBROKE DOCK ☎01646

Bounded by a towering Norman castle and 14th-century walls, Pembroke is not the military stronghold it once was. This former bastion of anti-Cromwell resistance now invites visitors for a peaceful stroll down Main St. Nearby Pembroke Dock, about 1½ mi. away, lacks the ancestry of its neighbor—the ferry to Rosslare, Ireland, is its greatest attraction today. Both towns are stepping stones to the Pembrokeshire Coast National Park, but Pembroke is the more popular place to stay.

▐ TRANSPORTATION. Pembroke's unstaffed **train station** rests on Lower Lamphey Rd. **Trains** (☎(08457) 484950) run to Pembroke and Pembroke Dock from **Tenby**, **Swansea**, and points farther east (2hr.; M-F 5 per day, Sa 7 per day, Su varies). In Pembroke, **buses** going east stop outside the Somerfield supermarket; those going north stop at the castle. **National Express** (☎(08705) 808080) arrives from **London** (#508, 6hr., 2 per day, £19.50) and **Cardiff** via **Swansea** (3½hr., 2 per day, £10.75). In Pembroke Dock, buses stop at the **Silcox Garage** (☎683143; open M-F 8:30am-5:30pm). Be sure to signal your stop clearly to the bus driver. **First Cymru** (☎(0870) 608 2608) stops in Pembroke and Pembroke Dock between **Tenby** and **Haverfordwest** (#349; 35-40 min.; M-Sa 21 per day, Su 2 per day; £1.80-2.25). **Irish Ferries** (☎(08705) 171717) and **Stena Sealink** (☎(08705) 707070) send ferries from Pembroke Dock to **Rosslare, Ireland** (return £9-22; see **By Ferry**, p. 35).

▰▯ ORIENTATION AND PRACTICAL INFORMATION. **Pembroke Castle** lies up the hill on the western end of **Main St.**; the street's other end fans into five roads from a roundabout. The **tourist information centre** (TIC) occupies a former slaughterhouse on Commons Rd. below the elevated heights of the town center and has displays on town history. They book accommodations for £1 and a 10% deposit, ferries for free, and sell town maps for 10p. (☎622388; fax 621396. Open Easter-June daily 10am-5pm; July-Oct. 10am-5:30pm.) Other services, divided between Pembroke and Pembroke Dock, include: a **Barclays bank** on 35 Main St. in Pembroke (☎(01437) 822400; open M and W-F 9am-5pm, Tu 10am-5pm); the Pembroke Dock **police**, Water St. (☎682121); the Pembroke Dock **hospital** (☎682114); **Internet access** at the Pembroke Dock **library** (☎686356); and the Pembroke **post office**, 49 Main St. (☎682737; open M-F 9am-5:30pm, Sa 9am-1pm). **Postal code:** SA71 4JT.

▐▐ ACCOMMODATIONS AND FOOD. The nearest **YHA Youth Hostel** is in Manorbier on the bus line between Tenby and Pembroke (see p. 454). The few B&Bs in Pembroke are scattered and singles are scarce; try to book ahead. Try the flower-covered **Beach House**, 78 Main St., for genuine hospitality and a comfortable TV lounge. (☎683740. £15 per person, children £5.) Originally a Victorian merchant's house, **Merton Place House**, 3 East Back, off Main St., has a large library and a medieval-style garden. (☎684796. Singles £20; doubles £35. Cheaper in winter.)

Gather a bargain feast at **Somerfield** on Main St. (Open M-Sa 8am-8pm, Su 10am-4pm.) Across the Northgate St. Bridge on your right is the **Watermans Arms**, 2 The Green, where you can sit by Mill Pond with a view of swans and the occasional carousing otter. (☎682718. Open Easter-Oct. daily noon-3pm and 6-11pm; food served noon-1:45pm and 7-9pm. Winter hours vary.) **Haven Coffee Shop**, 1 Westgate Hill, sells cheap sandwiches (baguettes £2.50), lunches, and coffees, with garden seating. (☎685784. Open M-F 10am-4pm.)

◲ SIGHTS. ▮**Pembroke Castle**, at the head of Main St., is a mighty fortress, authentically restored and a feast for the imagination. Imagine racing down snail shell staircases and high guard walks in the heat of battle; imagine hearing the first cries of baby Henry VII and the Tudor dynasty in one of the seven massive towers; imagine camera crews hauling across the immaculate inner courtyard while filming C.S. Lewis's *Chronicles of Narnia;* imagine a five-story stone-cold latrine tower. Climbing the 100 steps of Britain's most imposing Norman keep gives a fine view of rolling hills and a not-so-fine view of Pembroke Dock's smokestacks. The gatehouse runs a thorough exhibit on the castle's history. (☎684585. Castle open Apr.-Sept. daily 9:30am-6pm; Mar. and Oct. 10am-5pm; Nov.-Feb. 10am-4pm. Gatehouse open summer daily 9:30am-5pm; winter 10am-4pm. £3, seniors and children £2, families £8. Tours May-Aug. 4 per day; 50p, children free.)

ST. DAVID'S (TYDDEWI)   ☎01437

St. David's (pop. 1700) was once the largest and richest diocese in medieval Wales; it now stands proudly as Britain's smallest city. While you'll need to plan ahead to avoid being stranded, it's well worth the effort. There is a magical serenity about St. David's. In the Middle Ages, it was considered so holy that two pilgrimages here equaled one to Rome, and three equaled one to Jerusalem. Today's pilgrims come for the quiet coves and fiery sunsets over the Atlantic.

🖅🛂 TRANSPORTATION AND PRACTICAL INFORMATION. Pick up *1: Haverfordwest & St. David's Area*, which lists bus services, free at any Pembrokeshire County tourist information centre (TIC). The **Richards Bros.** (☎(01239) 613756) **Haverfordwest-Fishguard bus** hugs the coast, stopping at St. David's from both towns (#411; 50min.; M-Sa 5 per day, Su 2 per day). Several other buses also terminate at St. David's during the week. A **Day Explorer Pass** may be the cheapest return fare (£3.30, children £2.20). **Tony's Taxis** (☎720931) come when you call, and **Frank's Cabs** (☎721731) has minivans. The **National Park Information Centre,** The Grove, also doubles as the local TIC; the helpful staff will give you a local map or book you a bed for £1 plus a 10% deposit. (☎720392; fax 720099; www.stdavids.co.uk. Open Easter-Oct. daily 9:30am-5:30pm; Nov.-Easter M-Sa 10am-4pm.) Other services include: **Barclays,** corner of High St. and New St. (☎822400; open M-F 9:30am-4pm); the **police,** High St. (☎720233), or the **Haverfordwest police** (☎763355); the nearest **hospital,** in Haverfordwest (☎764545); and the **post office,** 13 New St. (☎720283; open M-F 9am-5:30pm, Sa 9am-1pm). **Postal code:** SA62 6SW.

🛏🍴 ACCOMMODATIONS AND FOOD. Rooms in St. David's are already filling, as the city will host the National Eisteddfod in 2002 (see p. 427). Book as early as possible. The **YHA Youth Hostel** lies 2 mi. northwest of town at the foot of a rocky outcrop near St. David's Head (see p. 455). **Pen Albro Bed and Breakfast,** 18 Goat St., has TVs and stereos in all rooms; doubles have Art Deco fireplaces and weddingcake canopied beds. (☎721865. £14.50 per person.) **The Coach House,** 15 High St., at the center of town, ranges from singles to bunk-bed rooms, all with TVs. A small cafe downstairs makes lunch easy. (☎720632. £15-20 per person; July-Aug. £20-25.)

Quick, affordable meals are had at **Prices,** Nun St. Choose among delicious takeaway sandwiches, breads, and pasties. The double burger is an unbeatable £2.50 once the clock hits 5pm and hot meals are served. (☎720219. Open in summer daily 7am-11pm; winter hours vary.) For excellent Welsh food, head for the elegant **Cartref,** in Cross Sq. Dinner starts at £8, but at lunch a toasted sandwich will only set you back £3.25. (☎720422. Open Mar.-May daily 11am-2:30pm and 6:30-8:30pm; June-Aug. 11am-3pm and 6-9pm.)

🗺 SIGHTS AND FESTIVALS. ◨St. David's Cathedral, perhaps the finest in Wales, stands in a hollow below the village. A few remnants of the 6th-century church linger in the 12th-century structure, and, like lakes on a lucid day, the tiled floors mirror the painted ceiling, whose wooden timbers release a live smell into the airy chambers. The reliquary holds the bones of St. David, the patron saint of Wales, and his comrade St. Justinian, who was killed on nearby Ramsey Island but managed to carry his own head back to the mainland for burial. In the St. Thomas à Becket chapel, the stained-glass window portrays three surly knights jabbing their swords at poor prostrate Becket. (Open 6am to around 5:30pm, and for evening services. Suggested donation £2, children £1.)

SOUTH WALES

The **Bishop's Palace,** across a bridged brook, was built from 1328 to 1347 by Bishop Henry Gower, a former chancellor of Oxford University, back when it was acceptable for a bishop to have the largest palace in Wales. The exhibition details why archaeologists love medieval cesspits. (☎720517. Open June-Sept. 9:30am-6pm; Oct. and Apr.-May 9:30am-5pm; Nov.-Mar. M-Sa 9:30am-4pm, Su noon-2pm. £2, concessions £1.50, families £5.50.) A half mile south of town, the walls of **St. Non's Chapel** mark the site of St. David's birth around AD 500. At the moment of his birth, the saint split a rock poised to fall on his mother. Water from the nearby well supposedly cures all ills; take Goat St. downhill and follow the signs to health and happiness. Tours run to **Ramsey Island,** off the coast (see p. 456).

The week of August 3-10, 2002, St. David's will host the **Royal National Eisteddfod,** which rotates among the towns of Wales each year. It is a rousing celebration of Welsh culture and language, and not a single bed will be available for miles.

FISHGUARD
☎01348

Victim of pirate attacks, star of the film *Moby Dick*, and harbor of the late *Lusitania*, modest Fishguard hasn't let its moments of celebrity go to its head. Its roots lie in Lower Town's herring trade, where merchants and smugglers made the money that moved the town up the cliff to Upper Fishguard. Now a ferry port, rumored passageways from Upper Town basements to smugglers' caves, cannon balls wedged in walls, and local pride keep Fishguard's 2000 residents lively.

⌐ TRANSPORTATION. Trains (☎(08457) 484950) pull into **Fishguard Harbour,** Goodwick, from **London** via **Bristol, Newport, Cardiff, Swansea,** and **Whitland** (4½hr., 1 per day). **Buses** stop at **Fishguard Sq.,** the town center. Ask at the tourist information centre (TIC) for *2: Fishguard and Cardigan Area,* a free bus and train timetable. From the north, take **Richards Bros.** (☎(01239) 613756) buses from **Aberystwyth** to **Cardigan** (#550 or 551, 2hr., M-Sa 10 per day) and then from **Cardigan** to **Fishguard** (#412, 45min., M-Sa 13 per day, £4.60). Take **First Cymru** (☎(01792) 580580) buses from **Tenby** or **Pembroke** to **Haverfordwest** (#349; 1hr.; M-Sa every hr., Su 2 per day; £2-4) and from **Haverfordwest** to **Fishguard** (#412, 45min., 1-2 per hr., £2). Two **ferries** (☎(08705) 707070 or (08705) 421107) run daily from **Rosslare, Ireland: Stena Sealink** (1¾hr.; 4 per day; £16-20, children £8-10) and **Superferry** (2 per day; £9-12, children £5-6). Call for reservations (see **By Ferry,** p. 45). **Town bus #410** shuttles the mile between Fishguard Harbour and Fishguard Sq. twice per hr. (5min., 41p), and **Merv's Taxis** (☎875129) are on call 24hr.

⓴ PRACTICAL INFORMATION. The **tourist information centre** (TIC), Town Hall, Main St., sells National Express tickets, ferry tickets, and books rooms for £1 and a 10% deposit. (☎873484; fax 875246. Open Easter-Oct. daily 10am-5:30pm.; Nov.-Easter M-Sa 10am-4pm.) Other services include: **Barclays,** across from the TIC (☎822400; fax 402999; open M-Tu and Th-F 9am-4:30pm, W 10am-4:30pm); the **police,** Brodog Terr. (☎872835); the nearest **hospital,** in Haverfordwest (☎(01437) 764545); **Dyfed Cleaning,** Brodog Terr. (☎872140; wash £2-3, dry 85p; open M-Sa 8:30am-5:30pm); **Internet access** at **Cyber Cafe,** The Parrog, in the Ocean Lab building (☎874737; £2 per 30min.; open 10am-6pm); and the **post office,** 57 West St. (☎873863; open M-F 9am-5:30pm, Sa 9am-12:30pm). **Postal Code:** SA65 9NG.

⌐⌐ ACCOMMODATIONS AND FOOD. B&Bs (£16-20) run up **High St.** and **Vergam Terr.** in Upper Fishguard. ◪**Harlton Guest House and Backpackers Lodge,** 21-23 Hamilton St., is intensely comfortable, with a book-lined TV lounge, toast-and-tea breakfasts, and Steve, the well-traveled host. (☎874797; www.fishguard-backpackers.com. Laundry, kitchen, and Internet access. Dorms £11; singles and doubles £13 per person; group discounts.) At peaceful **Avon House,** 76 High St., the rooms are large and fresh, as are the breakfasts. (☎874476. From £17.50 per person.)

If you come to Fishguard with dreams of fish and chips, rest easy: **Bursco's** (☎872008), Market Sq., fulfills that fantasy for £2.65. **Y Pantri**, 31 West St., rolls sandwiches, filled baguettes (£1.30), and corned beef pasties (85p) for uncommonly low prices. (☎872637. Open M-Sa 9am-5:30pm.) **Taj Mahal**, 22 High St., serves a celebrated cardamom-rich curry. Main dishes range from £3.50 to £7.50. (☎874593. Open M-Su 6-11:30pm, takeaway until midnight.) Not your average pub and converted barn, **The Old Coach House**, High St., has a mammoth menu of British and Italian fare for £3 to £10. (☎875429. Open M-Sa 11am-11pm, Su noon-10:30pm; food served noon-2pm and 6-9pm.)

◪ ◫ SIGHTS AND ENTERTAINMENT. The **Marine Walk**, a paved path undulating along the ocean cliffs, has exquisite overlooks of town and sea, as well as plaques on the town's rich history. Peer down, as Richard Burton and Gregory Peck did, on Lower Town, where both *Under Milk Wood* and *Moby Dick* were filmed. Ramblers can see Goodwick Harbour, where the flagship *Lusitania* began its monthly sails to America, and where the first flight from Britain to Ireland took off. Near the shores that saw the last invasion of Britain, the Bayeux-style **Last Invasion Tapestry** recounts the story. Stitched in 1997 by local women, the 100 ft. canvas depicts the unsuccessful French invasion of 1797, colored by the local legends that have evolved since. (Inquire at TIC for information on location and hours.)

In a glassy beachside building, **Ocean Lab**, The Parrog, features a 15min. show by the Henson Creature Shop, famous for their muppeteering. The simulation of a submarine trip to view prehistoric sea creatures is particularly suited to young children. Make use of the cyber cafe while you wait for your submarine show. (☎874737. Open Easter-Oct. daily 10am-6pm. Call for winter times. Submarine show every 45min.) During the day, picnickers and sun gluttons pebble protected **Goodwick Beach**. Inquire at the TIC about day-walks and tours into the **Preseli Hills**, ancient grounds that still support stone circles and a mysterious **standing stone**.

Fishguard nightlife can be a bit quiet early in the week, but weekends erupt into a pub scene of festival proportions. The **Old Coach House** (above) is the place to be, but all pubs along **High St.** see action—until 11pm, that is, at which time, by law, they must close. Some pubs allow patrons to remain beyond the hour of doom, but shut their doors to any potential newcomers. On Saturday nights, students stumble onto the buses that leave from the square at 11pm for the disco at the Brynawelon Country Hotel in nearby Letterston (☎840307).

FRENCH MISS In 1797, the last invasion of Britain took place, when two frigates and several smaller boats landed on the shores just outside Fishguard. Led by the Irish-American General Tate, this band of 1500 Frenchmen (800 of whom were convicts) gallantly aimed to spread a bit of the revolution that had seized their own country a few years earlier. But when the warriors landed, they set up headquarters in a farmhouse that was stocked for a wedding; the party favors more than quenched the soldiers' thirst. Tate's force, suddenly a drunken mob, couldn't hold out long enough to recover from the hangover. When the loftily intentioned heroes emerged from the farmhouse onto the fields of battle, they were met by hundreds of red-cloaked women who had assembled in the surrounding hills to witness the spectacle. Thinking himself vastly outnumbered by British soldiers, a disillusioned Tate surrendered. According to local legend, Jemima Nicholas, a 47-year-old cobbler, captured 12 Frenchmen single-handedly with her pitchfork. *La gloire*, indeed.

NORTH WALES

Since the 14th century, when Welsh rebel leaders plotted their campaigns against the English from headquarters deep in Snowdonia, the mountains, valleys, and towns of North Wales have rung with cries of a nationalism historically fiercer than the south's. The English King Edward I designed a ring of spectacular fortresses to keep the rebels in the mountains, but Welsh pride never wavered and remains strong despite (or perhaps due to) its centuries of union with England. Straining to distinguish the guttural sounds of the Welsh language, monolinguists will struggle to get their tongues around markedly un-Anglicized town names whose streets appear in Welsh on maps, in English on signs, or vice versa. Even the topography of the region seems to pronounce its distinctiveness: tall, jagged Welsh hills and cliffs contrast sharply with the placid English flatlands to the east.

To escape the crowds that swarm Edward I's coastal castles, head to the mountain footpaths, lakes, and hamlets of Snowdonia National Park, which covers the greater part of northwest Wales. Mount Snowdon, at 3560 ft., is the most precipitous peak in England and Wales. To the west, the unspoiled Llŷn Peninsula invites visitors to its sandy beaches; to the northwest, the Isle of Anglesey is rich in prehistoric remains; and to the east sleep the peaceful villages of the Vale of Conwy.

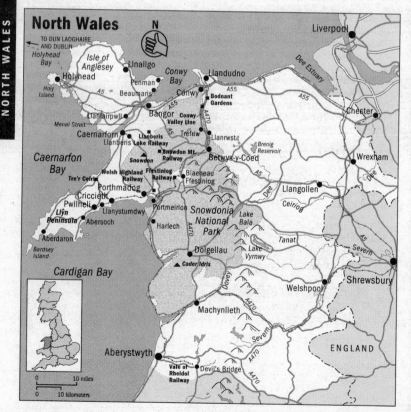

ABERYSTWYTH   ☎01970

Ever since a bevy of academics moved in—the University College of Wales was established here in 1874, and the National Library of Wales in 1909—the crowded streets of Aberystwyth (Abber-RIST-with) have been packed with students. Though salt-stained buildings, a hotel-lined quay, and the inevitable camera-toting tourists betray Aberystwyth's hybrid role as a resort town, it's the would-be scholars who fill seaside flats, raucous pubs, and innumerable veggie cafes. Halfway between St. David's and the Llŷn Peninsula, Aberystwyth is a pleasant stop for travelers heading north toward mountain valleys and craggy peaks.

▐ TRANSPORTATION

A transport hub for all of Wales, Aberystwyth sits at the end of a rail line running from Shrewsbury, England.

Trains: Alexandra Rd. (☎(08457) 484950). Office open M-F 6:20am-5:25pm, Sa 6:20am-3:20pm, Su varies. Trains from **Machynlleth** (30min.; M-Sa 7 per day, Su 4-5 per day; £4) and **Shrewsbury** (2hr.; M-Sa 7 per day, Su 4-5 per day; £11.40-14.50). Machynlleth is the southern terminus of the **Cambrian Coaster** line running up the northern coast to **Pwllheli.** The **Cambrian Coaster Day Ranger** (☎(08457) 484950) covers travel the length of the line (£6.60; after 4:30pm £3.70). The **Vale of Rheidol Railway** (☎625819) runs to sites in the mountains (see p. 464).

Buses: Alexandra Rd., beside the train station. **National Express** (☎(08705) 808080) from **London** via **Birmingham** (#420, 7hr., 1 per day, £19.25). **TrawsCambria** bus #701 from **Cardiff** (4hr., 2 per day, £10.90) and **Holyhead** (4hr., 1 per day, £14.50). **Arriva Cymru** (☎(08706) 082608) from **Machynlleth** (#512/514; 50min.; M-Sa 8 per day, Su 2 per day; £3.80). **Richard Brothers** (☎(01239) 613756) from **Cardigan** via **Synod Inn** (#550/551, 55min., M-Sa 9-11 per day, £4). **Arriva Cymru/Summerdale Coaches** (☎(01348) 840270) runs the same route twice on Su (£4). **Day Rover** tickets (£4.60, children £3.40), valid on most buses in the Ceredigion, Carmarthenshire, and Pembrokeshire area, are available from the driver. The **North and Mid-Wales Rover,** available for 1 day, 3 days, or a week, is valid on all buses and trains north of the imaginary Aberystwyth-Shrewsbury line as well as Arriva Cymru buses south of Aberystwyth.

Taxis: Express (☎612319). 24hr.

▐ PRACTICAL INFORMATION

Tourist Information Centre: Lisburne House, Terrace Rd. (☎612125; fax 626566), corner of Bath St. Chipper, helpful staff doles out B&B photos and rates. Room bookings £1 plus 10% deposit. Open July-Aug. daily 9am-6pm; Sept.-June M-Sa 10am-5pm.

Financial Services: Most banks are along Great Darkgate St. and North Parade. Try **Barclays,** North Parade. Open M and W-F 9am-5pm, Tu 10am-5pm, Sa 10am-12:30pm.

Launderette: Wash 'n' Spin 'n' Dry, 16 Bridge St. (☎625406). Bring change. Wash £2. £1 extra for service wash for students. Open daily 7am-9pm, last wash 8:30pm.

Police: Blvd. St. Brieuc (☎612791), at the end of Park Ave.

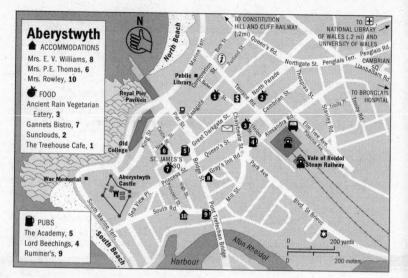

Aberystwyth

▲ ACCOMMODATIONS
Mrs. E. V. Williams, **8**
Mrs. P.E. Thomas, **6**
Mrs. Rowley, **10**

🍎 FOOD
Ancient Rain Vegetarian
Eatery, **3**
Gannets Bistro, **7**
Sunclouds, **2**
The Treehouse Cafe, **1**

🍺 PUBS
The Academy, **5**
Lord Beechings, **4**
Rummer's, **9**

Hospital: Bronglais General Hospital, Caradog Rd. (☎623131).

Internet access: Biognosis, 21 Pier St. (☎636953). £3.50 per hr., minimum 20min. Open M-Th 9:30am-8pm, F 9am-5pm, Sa-Su 11am-6pm.

Post Office: 8 Great Darkgate St. (☎632630). **Bureau de change.** Open M-F 9am-5:30pm, Sa 9am-12:30pm. **Postal Code:** SY23 1DE.

🏛 ACCOMMODATIONS AND CAMPING

Expensive B&Bs (£16-40) snuggle up with student housing on the waterfront. **Bridge St.** has a small B&B community, and a few cheap establishments are scattered on **South Rd.** and **Rheidol Terr.**

Mrs. E. V. Williams, 28 Bridge St. (☎612550). Large rooms with staggeringly comfy beds. Kind proprietress bakes heavenly Welsh cakes and gladly shares the secrets of the mysterious *bara brith.* £15 per person.

Mrs. P. E. Thomas, 8 New St. (☎617329), off Pier St. Mammoth breakfasts served with grace amid Chinese paintings and a giant harp. The spacious rooms all have TVs. £18 per person, £2 off for *Let's Go* users.

YHA Borth (☎871498), 9 mi. north of Aberystwyth in Borth. Beautifully set near beaches, the hostel is often full. Take the train to Borth (10min.; M-Sa 12 per day, Su 8 per day; £1.50) or Crosville bus #511 or 512 (30min., every hr.). From the train station, turn right onto the main road and walk 5min. Kitchen available. Open Apr.-Aug. daily; Sept. M-Sa; Oct. and Mar. Tu-Sa. Dorms £9.80, under 18 £6.75.

Mrs. Rowley, 28 South Rd. (☎612115), off Bridge St. Pleasant bedrooms have TVs and washbasins, the bathrooms ring with wind chimes, and the lounge has a wide assortment of porcine figurines. £15 per person.

Camping: Midfield Caravan Park (☎612542), 1½ mi. from town center on the A4120, 200 yd. uphill from the junction with the A487. From Alexandra Rd., take any bus going to Southgate. One of the loveliest campsites in the area, with a view of town and hills. £5 per person. Electricity £1.50 per night. Showers free.

⬤ FOOD

On **Pier St.**, takeaway spots are cheap and open on Sunday. There's a **market** at Market Hall, St. James Sq. (open M-Sa 8am-5pm), and **Spar**, 32 Terrace Rd. (open daily 24hr.) sells sundries. **The Academy** and **Lord Beechings** serve pub grub to hungry travelers; see **Pubs, Nightlife, and Entertainment,** p. 464.

Gannets Bistro, St. James Sq. (☎617164). Run by the former head of British Airways's catering department—if only airline food were half so good. Main courses stretch the budget (£6.50-11), but a few starters make a satisfying meal (£1-3): the ravioli au gratin (£1.20) and smoked mackerel (£1.50) are first class. Decent selection of vegetarian options. Open M and W-Sa noon-2pm and 6-9:30pm, last orders 1:30pm and 8:30pm.

The Treehouse Cafe, 14 Baker St. (☎615791). Summery tablecloths and wood floors atop the Treehouse Organic Shop. Cool your carnivorous cravings with a beef burger (£3.40) or terrorize chickpeas the world over by ordering hummus with pita (£1.40). The ginger beer and guava juice (both £1.20) are divine. Open M-W 9:30am-5:30pm, Th-Sa 9:30am-5:30pm and 6:30-9:30pm.

Sunclouds, 25 North Parade (☎617750). Watch the world go by as you munch a tasty baguette (£2-2.50) or omelette (£2.50) at the wooden counters of this welcoming cafe. Takeaway available. Open M-Sa 10am-4:30pm.

The Ancient Rain Vegetarian Eatery, 13 Cambrian Pl. (☎612363), on the corner of Union St. Arrayed in bright blue and yellow, serving pancakes (from £2.45), sandwiches (£1.15), and lots of vegan and vegetarian meals from £4. Takeaway available. Open M-Sa 10am-4:30pm.

👁 SIGHTS

⬛**ELECTRIC CLIFF RAILWAY.** At the northern end of the promenade, a small electric railcar creaks up 430 ft. to the top of **Constitution Hill** at an angle normally associated with roller coasters. At the summit waits a spectacular view of the city as well as the wide lens of a camera obscura that allows you to spy on townsfolk below. It's also possible to scale the hill by foot. (☎617642. Open July-Aug. daily 10am-6pm; mid-Mar. to June and Sept.-Oct. 10am-5pm. Trains 6 per hr.; return £2.25, students and seniors £1.75, children £1, under 5 free, families £5.80-6.75. Camera obscura free.)

ABERYSTWYTH CASTLE. South of the Old College on a hilly peninsula, the castle has seen centuries of English oppression and Welsh rebellion. Before Edward I built the present castle in 1277, previous forts had burned down five times, the fifth at the hands of the last Welsh Prince of Gwynedd, Llewelyn ap Gruffydd. When night falls, the crumbling walls are often silhouetted against fiery sunsets over the Atlantic. (Always Open. Free.) Between the castle walls and the back of Old College, **Castle Putting and Crazy Golf** offers the unusual opportunity to make like Tiger Woods (when he's putting) in the shadow of castle ruins and with a view of the sea, all for £1. (Open mid-June to Oct. daily 11am-5pm; Apr.-June Sa-Su 11am-5pm.)

PIER. Aberystwyth's charming fin-de-siecle pier has been battered by the tourist trade. Still, the beachfront and promenade remain much as they were in Victorian times, and pastel townhouses lend the town a tamed, aristocratic air. At the south end of the promenade, the university's **Old College** is a neo-Gothic structure opened in 1877 as a hotel and restored in 1885 as Wales's first university. Prince Charles was drilled in Welsh here before being crowned Prince of Wales in 1969.

NATIONAL LIBRARY OF WALES. An imposing, classical structure overlooking the bay, the National Library of Wales, off Penglais Rd. past the hospital, houses almost every Welsh book or manuscript. The well-designed **Gregynog Gallery** displays the first known Welsh written text (c. 800), the first Welsh printed book

NORTH WALES

(1546), the first Welsh dictionary (1547), the first Welsh map (1573), the first Welsh "Beibl" (1588), and the first Welsh magazine (1735), which managed one issue before it folded. In another corner, scalded toutes and lusty bachelors rise from the pages of the oldest surviving manuscript of the *Canterbury Tales*, dating to the early 15th century. (☎632800. *Open M-F 9:30am-6pm, Sa 9:30am-5pm. Free.*)

🍺🎭 PUBS, NIGHTLIFE, AND ENTERTAINMENT

There are over 50 pubs in Aberystwyth, and the owners all tell tales of the student swarms that keep them buzzing. **The Academy,** St. James Sq., takes the pub scene to school. In this converted chapel, sports are cast on a 16 ft. screen and breakfast is served all day. From Sunday through Thursday, a pint costs as little as 99p. (☎636852. *Open M-Sa noon-11pm, Su noon-10:30pm; food served noon-3pm and 6-8:30pm.*) **Lord Beechings,** Alexandra Rd., is fit for a king and priced for a poor man, serving huge meals for £1.50-6. (☎625069. *Open M-Sa 11am-11pm, Su 11am-10:30pm; food served M-F 11:45am-2:45pm and 6-8:45pm, Sa-Su all day.*) A vine-covered beer garden and reveling students make **Rummer's,** Pont Trefechan Bridge, at the end of Bridge St., a choice stop for a round. (*Open M-W and Sa 7pm-midnight, Th-F 7pm-1am, Su 7-10:30pm.*) Smashed mirrors quake and smashed clubbers shake at **Pier Pressure,** The Royal Pier, Marine Terr. Thursdays rock to 60s, 70s, and 80s, while the weekend's "Cheese Factory" pulls in younger tastes. (☎136100. *Cover £1-4. Open M-W 10:30pm-1am, Th-F 10pm-1am, Sa 9pm-1am.*)

Up Penglais Rd., on the University of Wales campus, the **Aberystwyth Arts Centre** sponsors drama and films in Welsh and English; schedules are available at the TIC. (☎623232. *Prices £3.50-20 depending on event. Box office open daily 10am-8pm.*)

▶ DAYTRIPS FROM ABERYSTWYTH

■ DEVIL'S BRIDGE

Trains from Aberystwyth run mid-July to Aug. M-Th 4 per day 10am-4pm, F-Su 2 per day 10am-2:30pm; Apr. to mid-July and Sept.-Oct. 2 per day 10am-2:30pm. Rides £11, seniors £10, 2 accompanied children £2 each.

Originally built to serve the lead mines, the **Vale of Rheidol Railway** (☎625819) chugs and twists its way on tracks less than 2 ft. apart from Aberystwyth station to the waterfalls and gorges of Devil's Bridge. The **three bridges** (☎890233) were inexplicably built on top of one another; the lower bridge, attributed to the Architect of Evil, was probably built by Cistercian monks from the nearby **Strata Florida Abbey** in the 12th century. (☎(01974) 831261. *Abbey open daily 10am-5pm. Apr.-Sept. £2, concessions £1.50, families £5.50; Oct.-Apr. free.*) The paths to the bridges are turnstile-operated, so take some change—£1 coins are particularly useful. (*Trails to bridges £2.50, students and seniors £2, children £1.25.*) The rungs of **Jacob's Ladder** (£1.20) descend into the **Devil's Punchbowl** gorge, cross the torrent on an arched footbridge, and climb back beside the waterfall to the road.

MACHYNLLETH   ☎01654

And so 'twas to Machynlleth (mach-HUN-hleth) that Owain Glyndŵr, that great 15th-century Welsh rebel and the hero of our story, summoned four men from every commote in the territory to a vast open-air parliament, briefly making the town the capital of Wales. There it was explained that a commote corresponds to 50 hamlets, each containing 9 houses, 1 plow, 1 oven, 1 churn, 1 cat, 1 cock, and 1 herdsman. When the delegates departed, the rebellion unraveled, and the town collapsed into a slumber from which it has yet fully to awaken. Modernity, however, has begun to rouse the tiny mountain town, which combines displays of cutting-edge technology with traditional Welsh character and ancient Celtic history.

TRANSPORTATION. The **train station** (☎702887), on Doll St., receives trains (☎(08457) 484950) from: **Aberystwyth** (30min.; M-Sa 9 per day, Su 7 per day; £3.90); **Shrewsbury** (1½hr.; M-Sa 8 per day, Su 5 per day; £10.50); **Birmingham** (2¼hr.; M-Sa 8 per day, Su 4 per day; £11.70). The **Cambrian Coaster Day Ranger** covers routes from **Aberystwyth** (£6.60, £3.70 after 4:30pm). **Buses** stop by the clock tower. **Arriva Cymru** (☎(08706) 082608) buses #511, 512, and 514 arrive from **Aberystwyth** (40min.; M-Sa 8 per day, Su 2 per day), and buses #512 and 514 from **Dolgellau** (30min.; M-Sa 7-8 per day, Su 2 per day). **TrawsCambria** #701 rolls in once per day from **Aberystwyth** and **Dolgellau** (1hr., £5.10); the bus coming from Dolgellau originates in **Holyhead** (3½hr., £11.70), while the Aberystwyth bus comes through **Cardiff** (5½hr., £14.50). Mountain **bikes**—perfect for exploring the nearby hills—can be rented at **Greenstiles**, 4 Maengwyn St., across from the clock tower. (☎703543. £8 per half-day, £12 per day, £60 per week. 50% discount for ticket-holders to the Centre for Alternative Technology. Open M-Sa 9:30am-5:30pm; Apr.-Oct. also Su 10am-4pm.)

ORIENTATION AND PRACTICAL INFORMATION. The unmistakable heart of town is the **clock tower**, standing Eiffel-like where **Pentrerhedryn St., Penrallt St.,** and **Maengwyn St.** form a T. From the train station, turn left onto Doll St., veer right at the church onto Penrallt St., and continue until you see the clock tower; Maengwyn St. is on the left. The **tourist information centre** (TIC), in the Owain Glyndŵr Centre, Maengwyn St., books rooms for £1 plus a 10% deposit. (☎702401; fax 703675. Open M-Sa 9:30am-5:30pm, Su 10am-5pm.) Other services include: a **Barclays bank** under the tall timepiece (open M-W and F 9am-4:30pm, Th 10am-4:30pm); the **police**, Doll St. (☎702215); **Chest Hospital**, Newton Rd. (☎702266); **Nigel's Launderette**, New St. (wash £2.50, dry 20p, no soap or change machine; open M-Sa 8:30am-8pm, Su 9am-7:30pm; last wash 30min. before close); **Internet access** at the **Machynlleth Public Library**, Maengwyn St., for free (☎702322; open M 5-7pm, Tu-W 10am-1pm and 2-5pm, F 11am-1pm and 2-7pm, Sa 9:30am-1pm) or **Cyberspace**, 6 Penrallt St., for £4 per hr., £1 minimum (☎703953; open M-Sa 10am-5pm); and the **post office**, 51-53 Maengwyn St., inside the **Spar** grocery (☎702323; office open M-F 8:30am-6pm, Sa 8:30am-3pm). **Postal code:** SY20 8AE.

ACCOMMODATIONS AND FOOD. Machynlleth lacks a hostel, but **YHA Corris**, in the old school on Corris Rd. in Corris, is 15min. away by bus #30 or 32. Reminders of nature abound, from the hostel's position on the southern side of the Cader Idris mountain to its conservation motif. (☎/fax 761686. Laundry facilities. Lockout 10am-5pm. Open mid-Feb. to Oct. daily; Jan.-Feb. and Nov. Th-Sa. Dorms £9, under 18 £6.20.) **B&Bs** are numerous, but few are budget-friendly. **Melin-y-Wig,** Aberystwyth Rd., near Celtica, has black-and-white TVs in each room and an ark of a bathtub. (☎703933. From £16 per person.) **Haulfryn,** next door on Aberystwyth Rd., blooms with large, flowery bedrooms and a breakfast room packed with plates from around the world. (☎702206. £15 per person.) **Campers** can seek out the riverside **Llwyngwern Farm,** off the A487 next to the Centre for Alternative Technology. (☎702492. Open Apr.-Sept. £4 per person, £6.50 per 2 people.)

Machynlleth pubs offer nothing spectacular in the way of affordable gluttony, but tasty dishes are served beside a massive stone hearth at the **Skinners Arms,** 14 Penrallt St., near the clock tower. Main courses in the lounge are £5-8; food ordered at the bar is £1.50-4. Come nightfall, it's the liveliest pub in town. (☎702354. Open M noon-11pm, Tu-Sa 11am-11pm, Su noon-10:30pm; food served M-Sa noon-2pm and 6-9pm.) Cheap, healthy feasts are had at the pine tables of the popular **Quarry Shop Cafe and Wholefoods,** 13 Maengwyn St., where the all-vegetarian fare is almost entirely under £4. (☎702624. Open M-Sa 9am-4:30pm, Th 9am-2pm.) Craft your own menu from the groceries at **Spar,** 51-53 Maengwyn St. (open M-Sa 7am-11pm, Su 7am-10:30pm), or at the weekly **market** along Maengwyn St., Pentrerhedryon St., and Penrallt St., dating back to 1291—the CDs and alarm clocks are more recent additions (open W 9am-4pm).

◙ **SIGHTS.** From the gargoyled clock tower, a two-minute downhill walk along Aberystwyth Rd. (the A487) brings you to **Celtica**, in Y Plas. Housed in what used to be the country home of the Marquess of Londonderry, the focus of the museum is a high-tech multimedia experience that traces the millennia-old story of the Celtic peoples. Darkened chambers shrouded in mist feature an impressive replica village, complete with a victorious warrior bearing his enemies' heads. In a bizarre but entertaining denouement, a druid atop a gnarled tree whisks you on a whirlwind video tour of Celtic history, bringing you back to the present. A more traditional and equally engaging exhibit on the Celts occupies the upper floor. (☎702702. Open daily 10am-6pm, last entrance 4:40pm. £5, concessions £3.80, families £13.75. YHA members 30% off.)

High on a hill 3 mi. north of town along the A487, the **Centre for Alternative Technology** is like a giant summer camp whose counselors never leave. A funicular railway, powered by water, draws visitors up a 200 ft. cliff into a village of lily ponds, wind turbines, and energy-efficient homes, including the best-insulated house and largest solar panel roof in Britain. Learn about those living here communally or climb into the Mole Hole to meet Megan the Mole and walk among giant insect replicas. Arriva buses #30 and 34 (5-10min., M-Sa 12 per day) run to the entrance, or ride bus #32 (5min., M-Sa 7 per day) to Pantperthog and walk 200 yd. north and across a bridge. (☎705950. Open Easter-Oct. daily 10am-5:30pm; Nov.-Easter 10am-4pm. Water-powered railway open Easter-Oct. £7, students and seniors £5, children £3.60, families £20, under 5 free. YHA members, cyclists, pedestrians, and those with proof of train or bus travel get a 10% discount.)

Bringing the present into focus, or sometimes strikingly out of focus, the **Museum of Modern Art, Wales,** in Y Tabernacl on Penrallt St., houses rotating exhibits. On summer evenings music floats in from the performance hall next door. (☎703355. Open M-Sa 10am-4pm. Free.) The museum and theater are the center of the annual **Machynlleth Festival,** featuring musical performances and lectures, held over a week in August. (Same number. Tickets £2-10.) For a robustly informative walk through history, visit the **Owain Glyndŵr Interpretive Centre,** Maengwyn St., which occupies a stone building on the site of Glyndŵr's parliament house; placards place the rebel's career in the context of Welsh mythology. (☎702827. Open Easter-Sept. M-Sa 10am-5pm; Su and winter by appointment. Free.)

HARLECH   ☎01766

On the Cambrian coast south of the Llŷn Peninsula and the foothills of Snowdonia, the tiny town of Harlech clings to a steep hillside, commanding panoramic views of sea, sand, and summits. Harlech's castle, its chief attraction, ranks among the most spectacular in Wales, perched 200 ft. above the sea on an utterly impenetrable promontory. The grassy dunes far below its parapets attract those seeking solitude and sea breezes. While fair weather reveals craggy Snowdonia peaks by day and Llŷn town lights sparkling along the bay by night, mist and rolling dark clouds (often the norm) lend an even more haunting texture to the scene.

GAG ME WITH A SPOON Some suitors bring flowers, others serenade with a guitar and ballad, but in old time Wales, wooing often involved a large wooden spoon. Making a lovespoon for one's beloved is a centuries-old Welsh custom. The romantic eating utensils, popular during the 18th and 19th centuries, were often carved to pass the time on long winter evenings. Gentleman wooers translated their love into fancy designs, which made for some ridiculously elaborate ladles. Acceptance of the spoon meant courting could begin, and the term "spooning" has found its way into the English language, implying what might follow. Although the custom has languished, lovespoons can still be found in homes and tourist traps across Wales.

📧 **TRANSPORTATION.** Harlech lies midway on the Cambrian Coaster line. The uphill walk to town from the unstaffed **train station** is a calf-burner; follow signs for the town center and you'll make it eventually. **Trains** arrive from **Machynlleth** (1¼hr.; M-F 6 per day, Sa 7 per day, Su 3 per day; £8.20) and connect to **Pwllheli** and other spots on the **Llŷn Peninsula** (M-F 6 per day, Sa 7 per day, Su 3 per day). The **Cambrian Coaster Day Ranger** (£6.60, after 4:30pm £3.70), which allows unlimited travel on the Coaster line for a day, is cheaper than the single fare from Machynlleth. **Arriva Cymru** (☎(08706) 082608) bus #38 links Harlech to the southern beach town of **Barmouth** (M-Sa 8 per day, £1.80) and northern **Blaenau Ffestiniog** (M-Sa 4 per day, £1.80), stopping at the car park on Stryd Fawr and the train station.

📧📋 **ORIENTATION AND PRACTICAL INFORMATION.** The castle opens out onto **Twtil**; slightly uphill is the town's major street, **Stryd Fawr** (less commonly known as High St.). The **tourist information centre** (TIC), 1 Stryd Fawr, near the castle, doubles as a **Snowdonia National Park Information Centre.** The staff stocks Ordnance Survey maps (£5.25-6.75) and pamphlets on walks up Snowdon and Cader Idris (40p) and books accommodations for £1 plus a 10% deposit. (☎/fax 780658. Open Easter-June and Sept.-Oct. daily 10am-1pm and 2-6pm; July-Aug. 10am-6pm.) Other services include **HSBC bank** (open M, W, F 9:30-11:30am; Tu and Th 12:45-3pm) and the **post office** (☎780231; open M-Tu and Th-F 9am-12:30pm and 1:30-5:30pm, W and Sa 9am-12:30pm), both on Stryd Fawr. **Postal code:** LL46 2YA.

📋📋 **ACCOMMODATIONS AND FOOD.** The closest hostel is **YHA Llanbedr,** 4 mi. south of town; take the train to the Llanbedr stop (10min.) or ride bus #38 and ask to be let off at the hostel. (☎(01341) 241287; fax 241389. Open May-Aug. daily; mid-Feb. to Apr. and Sept.-Oct. Th-M; Jan. to mid-Feb. F-Su. Dorms £8, under 18 £5.35.) Revel in spacious rooms and what may be the best view in Harlech at ⚑**Arundel,** Stryd Fawr. Walk past the TIC on Stryd Fawr and take a right before the Yr Ogof Bistro. Energetic Mrs. Stein (pronounced Steen) will pick you up if the climb from the train station does not appeal. (☎780637. £15 per person.) The **Byrdir Guest House,** on Stryd Fawr near the car park and bus stop, is a former hotel letting comfortable rooms with TVs and washbasins, plus a nearby water trough for your thirsty horse. (☎/fax 780316. Singles £17.50-30; doubles £45.) **Camp** at **Min-y-Don Park,** Beach Rd., between the train station and the beach. (☎780286. Laundry facilities. Open Mar.-Oct. £3 per person, £1 per child. Showers 20p each.)

Spar supermarket greets travelers next to the Plâs Cafe. (Open daily 8am-8pm; in summer until 10pm.) **Yr Ogof Bistro,** left from the castle on Stryd Fawr, offers some of the best cuisine for miles and a large antique organ as the dining room's centerpiece. Vegetarian dishes cost £5-7, and a satisfying three-course Welsh menu goes for £12. (☎780888. Open daily 7-9:30pm.) The sweeping ocean view from the grassy patio of the **Plâs Cafe,** Stryd Fawr, demands a long afternoon tea with dessert (90p-£3.50) or a sunset dinner for £6.25-9.50. (☎780204. Open Mar.-Oct. daily 9:30am-8pm; Nov.-Feb. 9:30am-5:30pm.) The **Lion Hotel's bar,** off Stryd Fawr above the castle, serves simple food (bar snacks 70p-£3.50, main meals £5.50-9.50) and reigns as the top place for an evening pint in this virtually publess town. (☎780731. Open M-Sa noon-11pm, Su noon-10:30pm; food served until 9pm.)

📷📋 **SIGHTS AND ENTERTAINMENT.** ⚑**Harlech Castle,** a World Heritage Site and arguably the most spectacularly located of Edward I's many fortresses, retains much of its former glory, with sweeping views of Snowdonia, brown-sugar sand dunes, and the bay. From the outer bailey, 151 steps descend the cliff to the train station, where the sea once lapped at the boat gate (but has long since receded). Built on legendary King Bendigeidfran's favorite resting spot in the late 13th century, the castle also served as the insurrection headquarters of Welsh rebel Owain Glyndŵr after he captured the castle from Edward I in 1404. (☎780552. Open May and Oct. daily 9:30am-5pm; June-Sept. 9:30am-6pm; Nov.-Mar. M-Sa 9:30am-4pm, Su 11am-4pm. Last admission 30min. before close. £3, concessions £2, families £8.)

NORTH WALES

Public **footpaths** run from Harlech's grassy dunes to the forested hilltops above the town; get recommendations and directions at the TIC. **Theatr Ardudwy,** Coleg Harlech, below the town on the same road as the train station, hosts films, plays, and exhibitions and organizes performances at the castle. Pick up a pamphlet on upcoming shows at the TIC. (☎780667. Movies £3.50, concessions £3; some concerts free; other performances £6.50-16, concessions £1-2 discount.)

LLŶN PENINSULA (PENRHYN LLŶN)

The Llŷn has been a tourist hotspot since the Middle Ages, when religious pilgrims tramped through on their way to Bardsey Island. Now 25 mi. of sandy beaches along the southern coast draw pilgrims of a different faith: sun worshippers coddled by the uncharacteristically fine weather of the towns between Pwllheli and Abersoch. A hilly region of simple beauty, the Llŷn's green fields spread down to the water, bounded by hedges and bright *blodau wylltion* (wildflowers). The farther west you venture, the more unsullied the Llŷn becomes and the scarcer certain conveniences grow—stock up in Porthmadog, Pwllheli, and Criccieth.

▐ TRANSPORTATION

The northern end of the Cambrian Coaster train line reaches through **Porthmadog** and **Criccieth** (KRIK-key-ith) to **Pwllheli** (poohl-HEL-ly), stopping at smaller towns in between. **Trains** begin at **Aberystwyth** and change at **Machynlleth** or **Dyfi Junction** for **Porthmadog** (1½-2hr.; M-F 6 per day, Sa 7 per day, Su 3 per day; return £10.50) and **Pwllheli** (2-2½hr., same frequency, return £12.60). The **Cambrian Coaster Day Ranger** (☎(01766) 512340) offers unlimited travel all along the line (£6.60 per day, evening version £3.70). The line's western end is at **Blaenau Ffestiniog,** inland east of the peninsula, and continues via **Betws-y-Coed** to **Llandudno** on the northern coast; it then connects via **Chester** and **Bangor** (M-Sa 6 per day, Su 3 per day).

National Express (☎(08705) 808080) **bus** #545 arrives in **Pwllheli** from **London** via Birmingham, Bangor, Caernarfon, and Porthmadog (10hr., 1 per day, £21). #380 arrives in **Pwllheli** from **Newcastle-upon-Tyne** via Manchester, Liverpool, and Bangor (11hr., 1 per day). **TrawsCambria** bus #701 connects **Porthmadog** once a day with **Aberystwyth** (2hr.), **Swansea** (6hr.), and **Cardiff** (7hr.). **Express Motors** (☎(01286) 881108) bus #1 stops in **Porthmadog** on its winding route between **Blaenau Ffestiniog** (30min.; M-Sa every hr. until 9:40pm, in summer also Su 5 per day; £1.60-2.20) and **Caernarfon** (1½hr., same frequency, £1.60-2.20). **Berwyn** (☎(01286) 660315) and **Clynnog & Trefor** (☎(01286) 660208) run bus #12 between **Pwllheli** and **Caernarfon** (45min.; M-Sa every hr., Su 4 per day; £2).

A smattering of bus companies, most prominently **Arriva Cymru** (☎(08706) 082608), serves most spots on the peninsula with reassuring haste for £1-2. Check bus schedules in *Gwynedd Public Transport Maps and Timetables,* available free from tourist information centres (TICs). **Arriva** and **Caelloi** (☎(01758) 612719) share responsibility for bus #3, often open-top in the summer, from **Porthmadog** to **Pwllheli** via **Criccieth** (30min.; M-Sa 1-2 per hr., Su 6 per day). Arriva buses #17, the circular 17B, and 18 leave Pwllheli to weave around the western tip of the peninsula. A **Gwynedd Red Rover,** bought from the driver, secures a day of travel throughout the peninsula and Gwynedd and Anglesey counties (£4.80, children £2.40).

PORTHMADOG   ☎01766

Don't get bogged down by Porthmadog's banal town center; this travel hub, minutes from mountain walks and world-class climbing rocks, is ideally situated for touring the Llŷn Peninsula and hiking into Snowdonia. Its principal attraction is the ▐**Ffestiniog Railway,** which departs from Harbour Station on High St. The justly famous but expensive narrow-gauge railway offers spectacular views as it rumbles along the slate-lined hillsides of the Ffestiniog Valley into the hills of Snowdonia. It terminates in Blaenau Ffestiniog, where it connects to the Conwy Valley Line and the Slate Caverns of Llechwedd. (☎516000. 1hr.; mid-Feb. to Nov. 2-10 per day, sporadic departures in Dec. £13.80, seniors £11.10, one child with adult free, additional children half-price, families £27.60, prices lower for shorter journeys. Bikes £2.50.) At the other end of town, across from the train station, the more modest **Welsh Highland Railway** and Russell, their dogged 1906 locomotive, try to recapture the glory days of train travel. Once the longest narrow-gauge railway in Wales, the track runs ¾ mi. to Pen-y-mount, with every effort made to reconstruct the atmosphere of a 1920s steam line. (Information ☎513402, recorded timetables (08703) 212402. July-Sept. daily 6 per day; mid-Apr. to June Sa-Su 6 per day; less service in Oct. £3, children £2, seniors £2.50, families £7.50.)

From Porthmadog's unstaffed **train station,** a right turn onto High St. leads to town; Bank Pl. and Snowdon St. are farther up the street. **Buses** stop at various points along High St., most commonly outside The Australia pub (see below) or in front of the opposite park. Holler for **Dukes Taxis** (☎514799) if you need a lift. **K.K. Cycles** rents **bikes** at 141 High St. (☎512310. £2 per hr., £9 per day. Open daily 8:30am-7:30pm.) The well-stocked **tourist information centre** (TIC) is at the opposite end of High St. from the train station, by the harbor, and books rooms for £1 plus a 10% deposit. (☎512981. Open Easter-Oct. daily 10am-6pm; Nov.-Easter 9:30am-5pm.) Other services include: **Barclays bank,** 79 High St. (open M and W-F 9am-4:30pm, Tu 10am-4:30pm); the **launderette,** 34 Snowdon St. (☎(017740) 124528; wash £2, dry cycle 50p, soap 30p; open M-Sa 8am-5pm, Su 9am-5pm); the **police,** Avenue Rd. (☎512226), opposite the Sportsman Hotel; **Bron y Garth Hospital** (☎770310), in Minffordd; **Internet access** at the **I.T. Centre,** 156 High St. (☎514944; 10p per min., £1.50 minimum; open M-F 9am-5:30pm; some Sa in summer); and the **post office,** at the corner of High St. and Bank Pl., which has a **bureau de change** (☎512010; open M-F 9am-5:30pm, Sa 9am-12:30pm). **Postal code:** LL49 9AD.

The best place to stay in Porthmadog—well, in the Porthmadog area, anyway—is 10min. down Church St. in neighboring Tremadog, a mile from the center of Porthmadog, ½ mi. from the train station. National Express #545 (to London) and #380 (to Manchester) and local buses stop in Tremadog. The birthhome of Lawrence of Arabia is now the hugely comfortable **Snowdon Backpackers Hostel** complete with TV and fireplace lounge, large dining room, and kitchen. The owners impress with boundless local insight and expert advice on area hiking trails. (☎515354; fax 515364; snowdon@backpackers.fsnet.co.uk. Continental breakfast included. Internet access. Laundry facilities. Apr.-Oct. £12.50 per person; Nov.-Mar. £11.50 per person. Doubles, twins, triples £14.50-16.50 per person.) Small signs in windows along **Madoc St.** and **Snowdon St.** mark **B&Bs. Mrs. Skellern,** 35 Madoc St., has basic rooms with TVs. (☎512843. £15-16 per person.)

Not exactly gourmet, Porthmadog's restaurants and cafes congregate on High St. Try the great **Castle Bakery,** 105 High St., where *bara brith* (a type of Welsh bread, £1.65), sandwiches (£1.50-2), and a variety of salads (90p-£1.50) are freshly made. Free samples help make those difficult decisions. (☎514932. Open from 9am.) Scatter crumbs along the stool-lined counter as you wolf down affordable sandwiches (most at £1.35, 50p more for a baguette) at **Jessie's,** 75 High St. (☎512814. Open M-Sa 9am-5pm.) **The Australia,** 31-33 High St., features good grub (£2-6) and a wide-screen TV. (☎510931. Open M-Sa 11am-11pm, Su noon-10:30pm; food served daily noon-2:30pm, M-F also 6-8:30pm; mid-July to Aug. dinner only.)

NEAR PORTHMADOG: PORTMEIRION

Bus #98 from Porthmadog to Croesor arrives in Portmeirion M-Sa 3 per day—once from Porthmadog en route to Croesor (10min.) and twice from Croesor en route to Porthmadog (20min.). #98 also stops in Minffordd 6-7 per day (5min. from Porthmadog, 25min. from Croesor), an easy, scenic 30min. walk from Portmeirion. Minffordd is a stop on the Cambrian Coaster train line (M-Sa 6-7 per day). ☎(01766) 770000. Open daily 9:30am; shops close at 5:30pm, but it's possible to stay later. £5, students and seniors £4, children £2.50, families £12; reduced admission Nov.-Mar. Admission tickets list the times for incoming tides so you know when it is safe to wade in the estuary. Check copies of "Top Ten Attractions: North Wales," a free brochure, for discount vouchers.

NORTH WALES

An eccentric landmark of Italy-fixation, the private village of **Portmeirion,** more of a resort compound than traditional village (the adorable bungalows are rental condos), rises from the woods by a quiet estuary 2 mi. east of Porthmadog. Mediterranean courtyards, pastel buildings, and the occasional palm tree provide an otherworldly contrast to Wales's castles and cottages. The mock-village was built between 1925 and 1972 by Sir Clough Williams-Ellis, whose sole concern was "that strange necessity," beauty, and who wanted to show "how a naturally beautiful place could be developed without defiling it." Though the threat of Disneyfication has been narrowly averted, it still wouldn't seem out of character if a Munchkin or Oompa-Loompa tottered out of a sun-baked building into one of the pooled gardens. As one of Wales's most popular tourist destinations, the village does experience Disney-like crowds. To find some semblance of peace, take one of the four color-coded trails that snakes out from the village.

CRICCIETH   ☎ 01766

Above the coastal town of Criccieth (KRIK-key-ith), 5 mi. west of Porthmadog, the remains of **Criccieth Castle** loom above Tremadog Bay, with lofty views of Snowdonia and across the water to Harlech. Built by Llewelyn the Great in 1230, taken by the Normans in 1283, destroyed by Owain Glyndŵr in 1404 (check out the scorch marks on the walls), and now a World Heritage Site, the castle still puzzles architectural historians, who debate which portion was English and which was Welsh. (☎522227. Open June-Sept. daily 10am-6pm; Apr.-May 10am-5pm. £2.50, concessions £2, families £7. Nov.-Mar. always open. Free.)

Trains (☎(08457) 484950) on the Cambrian Coaster line arrive from **Pwllheli** (15min.; M-F 7 per day, Sa 6 per day, Su 3 per day) and **Machynlleth** (1¾hr.; M-F 6 per day, Sa 7 per day, Su 3 per day). From the station, turn right onto High St. to reach the town center. **Arriva bus** #3 comes from **Porthmadog** and **Pwllheli** (15-25min.; M-Sa 2 per hr., Su 6 per day). The closest **tourist information centre** is in Porthmadog; to buy your way out of trouble, try **HSBC bank,** 51 High St. (Open M-F 10:30am-1pm.) The **post office** is around the corner from the train station. (Open M-Tu and Th-F 9am-5:30pm, W and Sa 9am-12:30pm.) **Postal code:** LL52 OBV.

B&Bs (£15-25) are scattered on **Tan-y-Grisiau Terr.,** across the train tracks from the bus stop, and on **Marine Terr.** and **Marine Cres.,** by the beach near the castle. From **Dan-Y-Castell,** 4 Marine Cres., scaling the edge of the castle hill, the lucky get spacious rooms with sea views, and all can marvel at the collection of figurines (emphasizing cats) that decorates the house. (☎522375. £14 per person.) Dinner-seekers head to **Poachers Restaurant,** 66 High St., down the road from the bus stop; the three-course meal costs £9, and all vegetarian options are £7. (☎522512. Open daily 6-9pm; Su reserve ahead.) Two doors down, **Spar,** High St., stocks groceries in a closet-sized store. (Open daily 8:15am-10pm.) The beer garden of **The Bryn Hir Arms,** along High St. in the opposite direction, provides the ideal setting for a quiet pint. (☎522493. Open M-Th 4-11pm, F-Sa 1-11pm, Su noon-10:30pm.) Branches of **Cadwalader's** ice-cream store dot the Llŷn, but the original lies on Castle St., down the road from the castle's entrance. Grab a tasty cone (85p-£2.20) to complement a beach walk. (Open M 11am-9pm, Tu-F 10:30am-9pm, Sa-Su 10am-9:30pm.)

LLANYSTUMDWY   ☎ 01766

Arriva bus #3 (20min. from Pwllheli, 4min. from Criccieth, 15min. from Porthmadog; 2 per hr.) also stops at **Llanystumdwy,** a tiny town 1½ mi. north of Criccieth. Llanystumdwy was the boyhood home of **David Lloyd George,** British Prime Minister from 1916 to 1922, and the town makes sure you know it. The centerpiece **Lloyd George Museum** chronicles the leader's life with relics from his career, among them his working copy of the Treaty of Versailles and the pen he used to sign it. Exit the museum, turn right, and follow the path behind it to **Highgate,** George's boyhood home. The **Workshop** features the man's tape-recorded uncle, who tells long-winded family anecdotes. A trek through the museum's car park and across the street leads to George's striking grave. (☎522071. Open July-Sept. daily 10:30am-5pm; Apr.-May and Oct. M-F 10:30am-5pm; June M-Sa 9:30am-5pm. £3, concessions £2, families £7.)

PWLLHELI
☎ 01758

The last stop on the Cambrian Coaster rail line, Pwllheli (poohl-HEL-ly), 8 mi. west of Criccieth, is best known for its bus station, which spews buses to every corner of the peninsula and beyond. Its two **beaches**—sandy Abererch Beach to the east, and pebbly South Beach—are hardly spectacular, and both are farther away than the tourist information centre's brochures imply.

The **train station** hugs the corner of Y Maes and Ffordd-y-Cob at Station Sq., with the **bus station** farther down Ffordd-y-Cob and to the right. For **taxis** call 740999. The **tourist information centre** (TIC), Station Sq., books B&Bs for the standard £1 plus a 10% deposit. (☎ 613000. Open Apr.-Oct. daily 10am-6pm; Nov.-Mar. Tu-Sa 10:30am-4:30pm.) Other services include: **HSBC bank,** at the corner of High St. and Penlan St. (☎ 632700; open M-F 9am-5pm); the **police** (☎ 701177); **Internet access** in free 30min. shifts at the **Pwllheli Library,** in Neuadd Dwyfor (the Town Hall), along Stryd Penlan (☎ 612089; open M 2-7pm; Tu, Th, Sa 10am-1pm; W and F 10am-1pm and 2-7pm); and the **post office,** opposite the station at the back of a general store (☎ 612658; open M-F 9am-5:30pm, Sa 9am-12:30pm). **Postal code:** LL53 5HL.

Mrs. Jones, 26 High St., lets out comfortable rooms with TVs and sinks. From the TIC, cross the street and follow Penlan St. until it meets High St., where a right will take you to her door. (☎ 613172. £12 per person.) Across the street, **Bank Place Guest House,** 29 High St., safeguards spacious rooms with TVs and huge breakfasts. (☎ 612103. £13 per person.) **Camping** is good in the area; try **Hendre,** 1½ mi. down the road to Nefyn at Efailnewidd. (☎ 613416. Laundry and showers. Open Mar.-Oct. £8 per tent.) Get Welsh cakes and produce at the open-air **market** in front of the bus station. (Open W 9am-5pm.) The **Spar** supermarket is across from the street on Y Maes Sq. (☎ 612993. Open daily 8am-10pm.) The **Bodawen Cafe,** on Y Maes, serves tasty sandwiches for £1.65-2.25. (Open M-Su 8:30am-4:30pm and later.)

ABERDARON AND TRE'R CEIRI
☎ 01758

Tucked in a sandy cove close to the peninsula's western tip, the peaceful village of **Aberdaron** merges with the mist-blue of sea and sky, where winds brush hillside houses and skittish white sheep. By the beach, enter the **Church of Saint Hywyn** through the oldest doorway in northern Wales for ocean views. (Open in summer daily 10am-6pm; winter 10am-4pm.) Water in the **wishing well,** 1½ mi. west of town, stays fresh even when inundated by the tide. Follow road signs from Aberdaron 2 mi. to what may be the finest sands in the Llŷn, **Porthor.** If conditions are right, the sands live up to their nickname, the "Whistling Sands." Head to the **Bardsey Island Trust Booking Office,** in the center of the village, for information on boats to **Bardsey Island.** Long a religious site—its first monastery was allegedly built in the 6th century—the "Island of Twenty Thousand Saints" was once so holy that three pilgrimages to it equaled one to Rome. Several beautiful walks allow visitors to admire the ruins of the old abbey and hundreds of migratory birds. A National Trust information point lodges in a Coast Guard hut overlooking Bardsey at the Uwchmynydd headland, also known as Wales's Land's End. (☎ 760667. Trust open Easter-Sept. most weekends. Ferries 15-20min., allowing 3½hr. visits; frequency depends on weather and demand. £18.50, children £12.50.)

Bus #17 runs from **Pwllheli** (40min., M-Sa 7 per day, return £2.65); #17B follows a more scenic, coastal route and takes 5min. longer (2 per day). Follow the sign pointing toward Uwchmynydd to the lovely **Bryn Mor,** where elegant rooms have sea views and TVs. (☎ 760344. £18 per person.) Since 1300, when it was a communal kitchen, pilgrims to Bardsey have fended off hunger in the small building occupied by the **Y Gegin Fawr** ("The Big Kitchen") cafe. Tear into the large salads for £4.20-6 or the tasty Welsh rarebit for £3. (☎ 760359. Open July-Aug. daily 10am-6pm; Easter-June and Sept.-Oct. 10am-5:30pm.) **Spar,** around the corner, may be a few years younger, but still provides basic groceries. (☎ 760234. Open Apr.-Oct. daily 8am-9pm; Nov.-Mar. 8am-5:30pm.) The **post office** is inside. (Open M-Tu and Th-F 9am-12:30pm and 1:30-5:30pm, W and Sa 9am-noon.) **Postal code:** LL53 8BE.

NORTH WALES

OH FATHER It may surprise some to know that as recently as 1922, Britain had a Prime Minister whose mother tongue wasn't English. Called by Winston Churchill "the greatest Welshman which that unconquerable race has produced since the age of the Tudors," David Lloyd George, the lad who rose from humble origins on the Llŷn Peninsula to the position of Prime Minister (1916-22), enjoyed a distinguished tenure in office, introducing pensions and universal suffrage, granting (partial) independence to Ireland, and leading Britain to victory in WWI. He became well connected enough during his years in politics to inspire the never-ending song with one line, "Lloyd George knew my father, father knew Lloyd George." But Lloyd George was not known as the "Welsh mountain goat" for his gruff manner alone. So legendary was his philandering that a song with new lyrics soon rang through Welsh valleys, "Lloyd George was my father, father was Lloyd George," and so on forever.

Tre'r Ceiri (trair-KAY-ree: "town of the giants"), on the peninsula's north shore, is Britain's oldest fortress, dating back some 4000 years. Take the Pwllheli-Caernarfon bus #12 to **Llanaelhaearn,** 7 mi. from Pwllheli (15min.; M-Sa every hr., Su 4 per day), then look for the public footpath signposted 1 mi. southwest of town on the B4417. At its upper reaches, keep to the stony track, which is more or less a direct uphill route (elevation 1600 ft.). The remains of 150 circular stone huts are clustered within a double defensive wall, which, however strong, fails to protect against the windy weather. Wear warm clothes.

SNOWDONIA NATIONAL PARK

Rough and handsome, misty purple and mossy green, the highest mountains in Wales dominate horizons across the 840 sq. mi. of Snowdonia National Park (Parc Cenedlaethol Eryri), stretching from forested Machynlleth in the south to sandstrewn Conwy in the north. Known in Welsh as Eryri, "Place of Eagles," Snowdonia's upper reaches are as powerfully graceful as their name suggests. Where sheep don't carpet the landscape, dark pine forests run into gorges and estuaries flow into sun-pierced coves. Though these lands, as in most British National Parks, lie largely in private hands—only 0.3% belongs to the National Park Authority—endless public footpaths easily accommodate its droves of visitors. The second largest of England and Wales's national parks, Snowdonia is also a stronghold of national pride: 65% of its 27,500 inhabitants speak Welsh as their native tongue.

▐ TRANSPORTATION

Trains (☎(08457) 484950) stop at larger towns on the park's outskirts, including **Bangor** and **Conwy.** The **Conwy Valley Line** runs through the park from **Llandudno** through **Betws-y-Coed** to **Blaenau Ffestiniog** (1hr. from Llandudno to Blaenau Ffestiniog; M-Sa 7 per day, Su 2-3 per day; return £14.20). **Buses** service the interior from those towns and others near the edge of the park such as **Caernarfon.** The *Gwynedd Public Transport Maps and Timetables* and *Conwy Public Transport Information* booklets, indispensable for travel in the two counties that comprise the park, are both available for free in the region's tourist information centres (TICs). **Snowdon Sherpa** buses, usually painted blue, maneuver between the park's towns and trailheads with somewhat irregular service, but stop at any safe point in the park on request; a **Day Ticket** secures a day's worth of travel on all Sherpa buses for £2.50 (children £1.25). A Gwynedd **Red Rover ticket** (£4.80, children £2.40) buys unlimited travel for a day on the Sherpa buses and any other bus in Gwynedd and Anglesey counties; a **Snowdon Sherpa Day Ticket** secures a day's worth of rides on Sherpa buses only for £2.50 (children £1.25). Most routes are serviced every 2hr., and Sunday service is sporadic at best. Ask bus drivers for details on how to make a connection.

Narrow-gauge railway lines let you enjoy the countryside in a few select locations without enduring a hike. The **Ffestiniog Railway** (☎(01766) 516000) weaves from Porthmadog (see p. 468) to Blaenau Ffestiniog, where the mountains of discarded slate rival those of Snowdonia. You can travel part of its route to Minffordd, Penrhyndeudraeth, or Tan-y-bwlch. At Porthmadog, the narrow-gauge rail meets the Cambrian Coaster service from Pwllheli to Aberystwyth; at Blaenau Ffestiniog, it connects with the Conwy Valley Line. The **Snowdon Mountain Railway** and the **Llanberis Lake Railway** both make short trips from Llanberis (see p. 475).

ⓘ PRACTICAL INFORMATION

TICs and National Park Information Centres stock leaflets on walks, drives, and accommodations, as well as Ordnance Survey maps. For details, contact the **Snowdonia National Park Information Headquarters,** Penrhyndeudraeth (pen-rin-DAY-dryth), Gwynedd LL48 6LF (☎(01766) 770274). The annual *Snowdonia—Mountains and Coast,* free at TICs across North Wales, contains fistfuls of information on the park and accommodations. If you're cyber-savvy, check out www.gwynedd.gov.uk for bus schedules and tourist info. The following are Snowdonia's **National Park Information Centres:**

Aberdyfi: Wharf Gdns. (☎/fax (01654) 767321). Open Easter-Aug. daily 10am-6pm; Sept.-Oct. closed 1-2pm.

Betws-y-Coed: The busiest and best stocked. See p. 490.

Blaenau Ffestiniog: Isallt Church St. (☎(01776) 830360). In the shadow of the Ffestiniog Railway's steam clouds. Open Easter-Sept. daily 10am-6pm.

Dolgellau: See p. 477.

Harlech: See p. 466.

🏠 ACCOMMODATIONS

This section lists only **YHA Youth Hostels** in Snowdonia; B&Bs are listed under individual towns. The eight hostels in the mountain area are some of the best in Wales and marked on the general Wales transport map. All have kitchens, and meals are available except where noted.

Bryn Gwynant: (☎(01766) 890251; fax 890479), ¾ mi. from the Watkin path, above Llyn Gwynant and along the Penygwryd-Beddgelert road (4 mi. from Beddgelert). Take Sherpa bus #95 from Caernarfon (40min., M-Sa 5 per day) or Llanberis (20min.; M-Sa 5 per day, Su 3 per day). Sherpa summer express #97A comes from Porthmadog or Betws-y-Coed (30min. each way, June-Sept. 3 per day). Lockout noon-5pm. Curfew 11pm. Open Mar.-Oct. daily; Jan.-Feb. F-Sa. Dorms £10, under 18 £6.90.

Capel Curig: (☎(01690) 720225; fax 720270), 5 mi. from Betws-y-Coed on the A5. Sherpa buses #19, 96, 96B, and 97A from Betws and Llanberis stop nearby. At the crossroads of many mountain paths; favored by climbers and school kids. Spectacular view of Mt. Snowdon across a lake. Lockout 10am-5pm. Curfew 11:30pm. Open Easter-Sept. daily; Oct.-Dec. F-Sa. Dorms £10, under 18 £6.90; doubles £28, £21.

Idwal Cottage: (☎(01248) 600225; fax 602952), just off the A5 at the foot of Llyn Ogwen in northern Snowdonia, 4 mi. from Bethesda. Within hiking distance of Pen-y-Pass, Llanberis, and Capel Curig. Bus routes here are scarcer—take Sherpa bus #66 from Bangor (20min., every hr.), changing to #96B at Bethesda (10min.; M-Sa 4-5 per day, Su 3 per day), which goes to the hostel. On Su, #7 from Bangor stops at the hostel (30min., 3 per day). Self-catering. Lockout 10am-5pm. Curfew 11pm. Open mid-Feb. to Aug. daily; Jan. and Sept. to mid-Dec. F-Sa. Dorms £8.50, under 18 £5.75.

Kings (Dolgellau): (☎(01341) 422392; fax 422477), Penmaenpool, 4 mi. from Dolgellau. Take Arriva bus #28 from Dolgellau (5min.; M-F 7 per day, Sa 5 per day, Su 3 per day). Endure the uphill walk to this home in the Vale of Ffestiniog. Open mid-Apr. to Aug. daily; Mar. to mid-Apr. M-Sa. Dorms £9.50, under 18 £6.75.

Llanberis: (☎(01286) 870280; fax 870936), ½ mi. up Capel Goch Rd., with views of Llyn Peris, Llyn Padarn, and Mt. Snowdon; follow signs from High St. Curfew 11:30pm. Open Apr.-Aug. daily; Sept.-Oct. Tu-Sa; Nov.-Mar. F-Sa. Dorms £10, under 18 £6.90.

Lledr Valley: (☎(01690) 750202; fax 750410), on a bluff 5 mi. west of Betws-y-Coed, ¾ mi. past Pont-y-Pant train station, 2 mi. from the majestic tower of Dolwyddelan Castle. Take the infrequent Arriva #84, which runs from Llandudno to Betws-y-Coed via Blaenau Ffestiniog, and ask to be dropped at the hostel (2 per day). No laundry facilities. Lockout 10am-5pm. Curfew 11pm. Open Easter-May, July-Aug., Oct. daily; Feb.-Easter, June, Sept. F-Sa. Dorms £9.25, under 18 £6.50.

Pen-y-Pass: (☎(01286) 870428; fax 872434), in Nant Gwynant, 6 mi. from Llanberis and 4 mi. from Nant Peris. Take Sherpa bus #96 from Llanberis or Betws-y-Coed (25min.; late May to Sept. every hr., otherwise M-Sa 6 per day, Su 9 per day) or #19 from Llanberis or Llandudno (May-Sept. 3 per day). Commands an unusual and splendid position: 1170 ft. above sea level at the head of Llanberis Pass between the Snowdon and Glyders peaks. The doors open onto the Pyg track, or the Llyn Llydaw miner's track to the Snowdon summit. An outdoors shop sells supplies and rents hiking boots, waterproofs, and ice axes. Hostel bar open mid-afternoon to 11pm. Open daily. Dorms £11, students £10, under 18 £7.75.

Snowdon Ranger: Llyn Cwellyn (☎(01286) 650391; fax 650093). The base for the Ranger Path, the grandest Snowdon ascent. Take Sherpa bus #95 from Caernarfon (20min.; M-Sa 8 per day, Su 5 per day) directly to the hostel. No washers. Lockout 10am-5pm. Curfew 11pm. Open Easter-Aug. daily; Sept.-Oct. W-Su; mid-Feb. to Easter and Nov.-Dec. F-Su. Dorms £10, under 18 £6.90.

In the high mountains, **camping** is permitted as long as you leave no mess, but the Park Service discourages it because of recent and disastrous erosion. In the valleys, owner's consent is required to camp. Public campsites dot the roads in peak seasons; check listings below and inquire at TICs for sites in specific towns.

◩ OUTDOOR ACTIVITIES

Weather on Snowdonia's exposed mountains shifts quickly, unpredictably, and wrathfully. No matter how beautiful the weather is below, it *will* be cold and wet in the high mountains. Dress as if preparing for an armed confrontation with the Abominable Snowman: bring a waterproof jacket and pants, gloves, hat, and wool sweater and peel off the layers as you descend. The free *Stay Safe in Snowdonia* offers crucial advice and information on hiking and climbing in the area and what to do in emergencies. (See **Wilderness Safety**, p. 54.) Pick up the Ordnance Survey Landranger Map #115: *Snowdon and Surrounding Area* (1:50,000; £5.25) and Outdoor Leisure Map #17: *Snowdonia, Snowdon, and Conwy Valley Areas* (1:25,000; £6.50), as well as individual mountain path guides (40p) at TICs, park information centres, and bookstores. Call **Mountaincall Snowdonia** (☎(0891) 500449; 36-48p per min.) for a local three- to five-day forecast and ground conditions. Weather forecasts are also tacked outside park centers. Park rangers lead day-walks; ask at the centers. The land in Snowdonia is privately owned—stick to public pathways, or ask the owner's consent to hike through.

CLEARING THE SLATE Those purple mountains' majesty tinting horizons across Northern Wales isn't just a trick of light and atmosphere; the closer you get, the clearer it becomes that the rocks are in fact plum purple in some places and bonnie blue in others. These are the slate mountains that fueled the industrial revolution in Northern Wales and, according to some proud Welsh miners, roofed the world. The slate also fueled a few local egos, as miners regularly held slate-splitting competitions with highly publicized results. The London Exhibition of 1862 featured a 10 ft. by 1 ft. slate sheet 1/16 in. thick; in 1872 a 2½ in. block was split into 45 layers; today, less fanfare is made about the 35 sheets per in. regularly split for decorations like fans and wall ornaments.

Snowdonia National Park Study Centre (☎(01766) 590324), Plas Tan-y-Bwlch, Maentwrog, Blaenau Ffestiniog, Gwynedd LL41 3YU, conducts three- to seven-day courses on naturalist favorites such as wildlife painting (£90-350). **YHA Pen-y-Pass,** Nant Gwynant (☎(01286) 870428; see p. 474) puts groups in touch with guides for mountaineering, climbing, and watersports. **Beics Eryri Cycle Tours,** 44 Tyddyn Llwydyn, leads guided trips from Caernarfon for multi-night forays into the park. (☎(01286) 676637. From £42 per night including bike and accommodations; call ahead.) **Snowdonia Riding Stables,** 3 mi. from Caernarfon, off the A4085 near Waunfawr, leads horse treks. Take Sherpa buses #95 or 95A (10min.; M-Sa every hr., Su 7 per day) and ask to be let off at the turn-off road. (☎(01286) 650342. Rides £13 per hr., £28 per half-day, £48 per day.) The brave can paraglide off the peaks of Snowdonia with the help of Llanberis-based **Snowdonia Paragliding School** (☎(01248) 602103. 3 flights with instruction £75. Weather dependent; call ahead.) Myriad adventures are detailed in the *The Snowdon Peninsula: North Wales Activities* brochure, available in TICs and National Park Information Centres.

LLANBERIS ☎01286

One of the few small Welsh villages lively even on Sundays, lovely Llanberis owes its outdoorsy bustle to the popularity of Mt. Snowdon, whose ridges and peaks unfold just south of town, and its idyllic setting upon peaceful Padarn Lake.

🖅🔃 TRANSPORTATION AND PRACTICAL INFORMATION. Situated on the western edge of the park, Llanberis is a short ride from Caernarfon on the A4086. Catch **KMP** (☎870880) **bus #88** from **Caernarfon** (25min.; M-Sa 2 per hr., Su every hr.; £1.60) or **Arriva** bus **#77** from **Bangor** (40min.; M-Sa every hr., Su 8 per day; £1.55). **Sherpa** bus #96, operated by **Arriva,** winds past Pen-y-Pass on its way from **Betws-y-Coed** (late May to Sept. every hr., otherwise M-Sa 6 per day, Su 9 per day). In town, KMP's Sherpa **#96A** does a complete circle around Llanberis, stopping at major sites like the Snowdon Mountain Railway, Parc Padarn, and Electric Mountain (30min. round-trip; M-F 5 times per day, Sa-Su 5-8 times per day; 20p). The **tourist information centre** (TIC), 41a High St., doles out hiking tips and books beds for £1 plus a 10% deposit. (☎870765; fax 871924. Open Easter-Oct. daily 10am-6pm; Nov.-Easter W and F-Su 11am-4pm.) Pick up gear, maps, and expert trail advice at **Joe Brown's Store,** Menai Hall, High St., owned by one of the world's greatest pioneer climbers. (☎870327. Open M-F 9am-1pm and 2-5:30pm, Sa 9am-6pm, Su 9am-5pm.) Other services include: the **HSBC bank** without a cash machine, 29 High St. (open M-F 10am-2pm), or the bankless cash machine of **Barclays,** at the entrance to the Electric Mountain Railway on the A4086, near its fork with High St.; **Internet access** at Pete's Eats (see below); and the **post office,** 36 High St. (open M-Tu and Th-F 9am-5:30pm, W and Sa 9am-7:30pm). **Postal code:** LL55 4EU.

🖅🖸 ACCOMMODATIONS AND FOOD. Plenty of sheep and cows keep hostelers company at the **YHA Llanberis** (see p. 474), while the **Heights Hotel,** 74 High St., has 24 bunk beds packed into three plain dorms, as well as more expensive hotel-style rooms with bath. Half the town crowds into the bar on weekends. (☎871179; fax 872507. June-Aug. dorms £12, with breakfast £15; Sept.-May £10, £13. Singles £30.) Farther from town, **B&Bs** start at around £15. A cozy 19th-century temperance house, **Snowdon Cottage,** Pentre Castell, sits in the shadow of Dolbadarn Castle. Follow High St. and its extension, the A4086, toward the park and past the Victoria Hotel (5min.). Tired climbers can ask the proprietors for relief: one is a sports therapist, the other an aromatherapist. (☎872015. £14-18 per person.) Head 2 mi. north to find camping at the **Snowdon View Caravan Park,** which has excellent facilities, including a heated swimming pool. (☎870349. £5-7 per tent. Electricity £1.50.)

Llanberis's restaurants have adapted their fare to the healthy demands (and appetites) of hikers. At **Pete's Eats,** 40 High St., opposite the TIC, surf the net (£1 per 15min.) while enjoying a vegetarian mixed grill (£5), super-hot chili (£4.75), and tunes from the jukebox. (☎870358. Open Easter-Oct. M-F 9am-8pm, Sa-Su 8am-8pm; Nov.-Easter M-F 9am-6:30pm, Sa-Su 8am-8pm.) **Spar** is on the corner of High St. and Capel Goch Rd. (Open M-Sa 7am-11pm, Su 7am-10:30pm.)

◙ **SIGHTS.** For a small village, Llanberis brims with attractions; most lie near the fork where the A4086 meets High St. Part self-promotion for Edison Energy, part journey to the center of the earth, **The Electric Mountain** takes visitors on a fascinating underground tour of the Dinorwig power station. Located deep in the heart of a mountain, the station occupies the largest manmade cavern in Europe (St. Paul's Cathedral would fit comfortably inside), which required the removal of 12 million tons of slate. The riveting bus tour is unfortunately flanked by two videos promoting the company. (☎870636. Open Easter-Sept. daily 9:30am-5:30pm; Oct.-Dec. 10:30am-4:30pm; Jan.-Easter Th-Su 10:30am-4:30pm. 1hr. tour £5, students and seniors £3.75, children £2.50, families £12.)

The immensely popular but expensive **Snowdon Mountain Railway** whisks visitors to the top of Snowdon's summit from the terminus on the A4086. The 2½hr. round-trip allows only 30min. at the peak, so be prepared to snap those panoramic shots in a hurry. If you miss your return train you aren't guaranteed a seat on another, and may have to hike down to the bottom. Weather conditions and passenger demand dictate the schedule from mid-May to early September; on a clear day the first train leaves Llanberis at 9am, with subsequent trains twice per hr. until 5pm (Sa 3:30pm). Line up early to get a ticket. (☎870223. Runs mid-Mar. to Oct., but not always to summit. Return £16.90, children £11.90; one-way £11.90, children £8.90. Standby for return £8. Students and seniors get £1 off each way.)

Most other attractions lie by the entrance to **Parc Padarn.** The **Llanberis Lake Railway** takes a short, scenic route from Gilfach Ddu station at Llanberis through the woods along the lake. The **Woodland and Wildlife Center,** at the half-way point, is a nice picnic spot. (☎870549. 40min. round-trip. Open M-F, some Sa, most Su 11am-4:30pm; check TIC for a daily schedule. £4.50, children £3.) Nearby, the imposing **Welsh Slate Museum** has live demonstrations and exhibits on the importance of slate to Welsh history, including a 3-D movie complete with singing rock cutters. The working waterwheel in the Power Hall is a marvel. (☎870630. Open Easter-Oct. daily 10am-5pm; Nov.-Easter Su-F 10am-4pm. Free.) Follow the road into the park until a footbridge to the right leads to **Dolbadarn Castle,** where Prince Llewelyn of North Wales imprisoned his brother for 23 years. Only a single tower remains, but the grassy hill offers lovely views of the lake and park. (Always open. Free.) For an eye-level view of **Ceunant Mawr,** a plummeting, angled waterfall, follow the well-marked footpath on Victoria Terr. by the Victoria Hotel (¾ mi.).

MOUNT SNOWDON AND VICINITY

By far the most popular destination in the park, Mt. Snowdon (Yr Wyddfa, "the burial place") is the highest peak in England and Wales, measuring in at 3560 ft. Over half a million hikers tread the mountain each year. Future hikes were nearly scuttled a few years ago when a plot of land including the summit of Mt. Snowdon was put up for sale, but celebrated Welsh actor Sir Anthony Hopkins sprang to the rescue, contributing a vast sum to the National Trust to help save the pristine peak. Much travel by enthusiasts of all abilities has in past years disrupted Snowdon's ecosystem and eroded some of its face; park officers request that all hikers stick to the well-marked trails to avoid further damage. Six principal paths of varying degrees of difficulty wend their way up Snowdon; TICs and National Park Information Centres stock guides on these ascents (40p each).

Though Mt. Snowdon is the main attraction in the northern part of the park, experienced climbers cart pick-axes and ropes to the **Ogwen Valley.** There, climbs to **Devil's Kitchen** (Twll Du), the **Glyders** (Glyder Fawr and Glyder Fach), and **Tryfan** all begin from **Llyn Ogwen.** Those attempting the climbs should pick up the appropriate Ordnance Survey maps and get advice on equipment and supplies from the helpful folks at **Joe Brown's Store** (see p. 475).

DOLGELLAU   ☎ 01341

Deep in the conifers of the Idris mountain range, the stone buildings of Dolgellau (dol-GECTH-lee) are dark and roughly cut, glaring with callous severity at the surrounding wilderness. The town has been populated since Roman times, when three roads met here and legionnaires scoured the hills for gold. Huddled in the shadow of Cader Idris, Dolgellau offers easy access to local and mountain walks.

TRANSPORTATION AND PRACTICAL INFORMATION. Buses stop in Eldon Sq. near the tourist information centre (TIC). **Arriva** (☎ (08706) 082608) bus #94 (M-Sa 9 per day, Su 4 per day) arrives from: **Barmouth** (20min., £1.75); **Llangollen** (1½hr., £3.30); **Wrexham** (2hr., £4.05). Arriva bus #2 follows a winding, scenic route through the mountains from **Caernarfon** via **Porthmadog** (2hr.; M-Sa 6 per day, in summer also Su 4 per day). A lone **TrawsCambria** bus stops daily from **Holyhead** (3hr., £11.70) and **Cardiff** (6hr., £16.20).

The **tourist information centre,** Eldon Sq., in Tŷ Meirion by the bus stop, books rooms for £1 plus a 10% deposit and has an impressive selection of books on Welsh; it also doubles as a **Snowdonia National Park Information Centre,** complete with an exhibit on local mountains and trails. (☎ 422888; fax 422576. Open Apr.-Sept. 10am-1pm and 2-6pm; Oct.-Mar. Th-M 10am-1pm and 1:30-5pm.) Equip yourself with camping and hiking equipment and Ordnance Survey maps (£5.25-6.75) from **Cader Idris Outdoor Gear,** at Eldon Sq. (☎ 422195. Open M-Sa 9am-5:30pm; May-Sept. also Su 10am-4pm.) Other services include: **HSBC bank,** Eldon Sq. (☎ (08457) 404404; open M-F 9am-5pm); **Dolgellau Launderette,** Smithfield St. (wash £2-3, dry £1, no soap; open daily 9am-7pm, last wash 6:30pm); and the **post office,** inside **Spar** at Plas yn Dre St. (open M-F 9am-5:30pm, Sa 9am-12:30pm). **Postal code:** LL40 1AD.

ACCOMMODATIONS AND FOOD. A **YHA Youth Hostel** is 4 mi. away at **Kings** (☎ 422392; see p. 473). In Dolgellau, lodging is scarce and expensive, starting from £18. Two **B&Bs** with spectacular views of the Idris range cling to the hills just north of town. **Arosfyr,** Pen-y-Cefn St., an old farmhouse in a mountain's dimple, has plush furniture and airy rooms. From the bus stop, walk with the HSBC on your right, down over the bridge, turn left, then right at the school, and follow the steep road until a sign on the right directs you past some tractors. (☎ 422355. Singles £17.50; doubles £33.) Comfortable **Dwy Olwyn,** Coed-y-Fronallt, serves big breakfasts. Cross the Bont Fawr bridge, turn right, then left after the Kwik Save; it's 5min. uphill. (☎ 422822. Singles £22; doubles £33-36.) **Camping** is available at the hostel and at the deluxe **Tanyfron Caravan and Camping Park,** a 10min. walk south on Arron Rd. onto the A470. (☎/fax 422638. £6-10. Electricity £2. Showers free.)

Spar, Plas yn Dre St., stocks groceries. (Open daily 8am-10pm.) Duck under the low portal at **Y Sospan,** Queen's Sq., behind the TIC, for sandwiches (£2-6) or roast lamb baguettes (£3). An inconspicuous framed sign on a side wall proclaims the escape of Rowland Lloyd, a "stoutly made" forger of bank notes, from the local jail in 1808—catch him, and you'll have a £100 reward. (☎ 423174. Cafe open daily from 9am; restaurant upstairs open F-Sa 7-9pm.) A heavenly aroma greets those who descend into the **Popty'r Dref** bakery and delicatessen, Smithfield St., just off Eldon Sq., where homemade jams, large filled rolls (85p-£2), and delectable spongy pastries (£1-2) crowd the shelves. (☎ 422507. Open M-Sa 8am-5pm.)

SIGHTS. In town, the free **Quaker Interpretive Centre,** above the TIC and open the same times, details the history of this hotbed of nonconformity and the circumstances that fueled Quaker emigration to the United States. Once you've completed your history lesson, head out for a hike. The famous 3 mi. of **Precipice Walk** reward with views of the Mawddach Estuary and **Cader Idris** (see below), while the 2½ mi. of **Torrent Walk** circle through mossy woodlands and past waterfalls. Pamphlets (40p) and information for treks are available at the TIC, as is the informative *Local Walks Around Dolgellau* (£3.95).

CADER IDRIS

The origin of the name Cader Idris ("Chair of Idris") remains a mystery. One story has it that in AD 630, a national hero named Idris was killed in battle by a host of marauding Saxons, while another maintains that Idris was a giant who kept house here. The Cwn Annwn, "Hounds of the Underworld," are said to fly around the peaks of the Idris range. This portion of Snowdonia National Park offers scenic walks less crowded than those of Mt. Snowdon to the north, catering to all levels of experience (all cross privately owned farm and grazing land). The five-mile pony track from **Llanfihangel y Pennant** is the longest but easiest way to the summit. A rather complicated route, the path climbs steadily after a relatively level first third. The pony track from **Tŷ Nant** begins at Tŷ Nant farm, 3 mi. from Dolgellau. While the trail is eroded in spots, it is also not particularly strenuous, and offers the most striking views of the surrounding countryside. The **Minffordd Path** (about 3 mi.) is the shortest but steepest ascent, not to be taken lightly. On its way to the summit, the path traverses an 8000-year-old oak wood and rises above the lake of **Llyn Cau.** An 18th-century story holds that a young man swimming in the lake was ingested by a monster and never seen again; another legend claims that anyone who sleeps on the mountainside will awaken either a poet or a madman. (*Let's Go* does not recommend sleeping on haunted mountainsides.) Allow 5hr. for any of these three walks. Individual booklets charting each are available at the National Park Information Centre in Dolgellau (40p). For longer treks, the Ordnance Survey Outdoor Leisure #23 (£5.25) or Landranger #124 (£6.50) maps are essential. Check in with the TIC for the latest information on trail changes and weather forecasts.

If you need a base to climb Cader Idris, stay either in **Dolgellau** (see p. 477) or at the **Corris YHA** (see p. 465). The 6000-hectare **Coed-Y-Brenin Forest Park** is laced with fine biking trails along with miles of trails reserved exclusively for hikers. Covering the peaks and valleys around the Mawddach and Eden Rivers, the forest is best entered 7 mi. north of Dolgellau off the A470, near the **Coed-Y-Brenin Visitor Centre.** (☎(01341) 440666. Open Apr.-Oct. daily 10am-5pm; Nov.-Mar. Sa-Su 10am-4pm.)

CAERNARFON ☎01286

Strikingly well preserved and festively majestic, the walled city of Caernarfon (car-NAR-von) faces the Isle of Anglesey with a world-famous castle at its helm and mountains in its wake. Occupied since pre-Roman times and once the center of English government in northern Wales, Caernarfon has been a hotspot of struggle for regional political control. During a tax revolt in 1294 the Welsh managed to break in, sack the town, and massacre the English settlers. Vestiges of English domination remain (a young Prince Charles, resembling a rabbit caught in headlights, was invested as Prince of Wales at the castle in 1969), but Caernarfon is thoroughly Welsh in character—visitors can hear the town's own dialect of Welsh used in its flower-bedecked streets and inviting pubs.

▉ TRANSPORTATION. The nearest **train station** is in Bangor (see p. 480), though Caernarfon is the well-greased pivot for **buses** from mid-Wales swinging north to Bangor and Anglesey, which arrive on **Penllyn** in the city center. **Arriva Cymru** (☎(08706) 082608) buses #5 and 5X come from **Conwy** via Bangor (1¼hr.; M-Sa 2 per hr., Su every hr.; £2.85, return £3.50), while #5A and 5B come from **Bangor** only (25min.; M-Sa 5-6 per hr., Su every hr.; £1.55, return £2.65). **Express Motors** (☎(01286) 881108) bus #1 and **Arriva** #2 drift in from **Porthmadog** (45min.-1hr.; M-Sa every hr., Su 4 per day; £1.80, return £2.40). **Clynnog & Trefor** (☎(01286) 660208) and **Berwyn** (☎(01286) 660315) run bus #12 from **Pwllheli** (45min.; M-Sa every hr., Su 4 per day; £2.60). **KMP** (☎(01286) 870880) bus #88 zooms from **Llanberis** (25min.; M-Sa 2 per hr., Su every hr.; return £1.60), while its **Sherpa** bus #95 passes by **Beddgelert** and many YHA hostels (30min.; M-Sa 9 per day, Su 5 per day; £2). Arriva's **TrawsCambria** bus #701 arrives daily from **Cardiff** (7½hr.) and **Holyhead** (1½hr.). **National Express** (☎(08705) 808080) bus #545 arrives daily from **London** via **Chester** (9hr., 1 per day, £21). A Gwynedd **Red Rover ticket** earns unlimited bus travel for a day in the county (£4.80, children £2.40); the divine *Gwynedd Public Transport Maps and Timetables* gives info on the bus and train routes between major towns in Gwynedd. For a **taxi**, try **Vale Cabs**, Palace St. (☎676161 or 881345).

⚞🛈 ORIENTATION AND PRACTICAL INFORMATION. The heart of Caernarfon lies within and just outside the town walls. **Bridge St.** is perpendicular to **Penllyn**; to the right, Bridge St. becomes **Bangor St.**, while to the left it leads to **Castle Sq.** Turning right from the square's entrance leads to **Castle Ditch** and the tourist information centre (TIC). **Eastgate St.**, perpendicular to the point where Bridge St. meets Bangor St., continues through a gate onto **High St.** inside the city walls.

The **tourist information centre** is on Castle St., inside Oriel Pendeitsh opposite the castle gate. Pick up the illustrated street map in the free *Visitor's Guide to Caernarfon.* (☎672232. Open Apr.-Oct. daily 10am-6pm; Nov.-Mar. Th-Tu 9:30am-4:30pm.) Get **camping supplies** with a 10% student discount at **14th Peak**, 9 Palace St. (☎675124. Open M-W and F-Sa 9am-5:30pm, Th 9am-5pm, Su 1-4pm.) Other services include: **Barclays bank**, 5-7 Bangor St. (☎672900; open M-Tu and Th-F 9am-4:30pm, W 10am-4:30pm); **Pete's Laundrette**, Skinner St., off Bridge St. (☎678395; full- and self-service; open daily 9am-6pm, last wash 5:30pm); the **police**, Maesincla Ln. (☎673333 ext. 5242); the nearest **hospital**, in Bangor (☎(01248) 3843884); **Internet access** at the **public library**, on the corner of Bangor St. and Lon Pafiliwn, in free 30min. shifts (☎671137; open M-Tu and Th-F 10am-7pm, W 10am-1pm, Sa 9am-1pm) and at **Dimensiwn 4**, 4 Bangor St. (☎678777; £1 per 15min.; open M-Tu and Th-F 9:30am-6pm, W and Sa 9:30am-5pm); and the **post office**, Castle Sq. (☎672116; open M-F 9am-5:30pm, Sa 9am-12:30pm). **Postal code:** LL55 2ND.

🛏 ACCOMMODATIONS. In a town nearly devoid of affordable rooms, budget travelers can thank their lucky stars for **Totter's Hostel,** 2 High St. This Plas-Porth-Yr-Aur (Grand House of the Golden Gate), run by friendly owners Bob and Henryette, has huge rooms with comfortable wooden bunks and a living room equipped with sofas and movies. In the downstairs cellar, a medieval stone arch graces a full kitchen, breakfast toasts and cereals, and a banquet table perfect for post-pub gatherings. (☎672963, mobile (07979) 830470; www.applemaps.co.uk/totters. Free lockers and bikes to borrow. Dorms £11.) **B&Bs**, generally from £20, line **Church St.** inside the old town wall; those on **St. David's Rd.,** a 10min. walk from the castle off the Bangor St. roundabout, are sometimes cheaper. The welcoming proprietress of **Bryn Hyfryd**, St. David's Rd., cares for guests in style with well-furnished rooms with bath, TV, and a boundless breakfast. (☎673840. July to mid-Sept. singles £25, doubles £30; mid-Sept. to June singles £18, doubles £28.) **Marianfa**, St. David's Rd., has spacious rooms replete with TVs and bathrooms. (☎674815; fax 674153; marianfa@aol.com. £18-20 per person.) **Camp** ½ mi. from town at **Cadnant Valley**, Llanberis Rd.; expect caravans in summer. (☎673196. £4-8 per person.)

🍴🍺 FOOD AND PUBS. Cafes and pubs crowd within the town walls. A **Safeway** sells its goods on the Promenade. (Open M-Th 8:30am-10pm, F 8am-10pm, Sa 8am-8pm, Su 10am-4pm.) On Saturdays and some Mondays, a **market** takes over Castle Sq. (9am-4pm.) Climb aboard the **Floating Restaurant,** Slate Quay, where views of strait, castle, and mountains complement seafood steaks (£6-9.45), burgers and chipped potatoes (£4.20), and a kids menu from £1.75. (☎672896. Open Easter to mid-Sept. 11am-7:30pm.) **Crempogau**, at the corner of Palace St. and High St., cooks savory, lunch-worthy pancakes: try the chicken supreme (£2.20) or nibble the Bavarian apple (£1.70) for dessert. (☎672552. Open Apr.-Oct. daily 10:30am-5pm.) **Stones Bistro**, 4 Hole-in-the-Wall St., near Eastgate, is candlelit and crowded. The £10.45 Welsh lamb is worth it; vegetarian main courses go for £8-9.25. (☎671152. Open Tu-Sa 6-11pm.) The stout wooden doors of the **Anglesey Arms** open onto the Promenade just below the castle. Relax outdoors with a pint as the sun dips into the shimmering Menai Strait. (Open M-Sa 11am-11pm, Su noon-10:30pm.)

NORTH WALES

◨ **SIGHTS.** In a nod to Caernarfon's Roman past (and, no doubt, to his own ego), Edward I built ◨**Caernarfon Castle** in imitation of Byzantine Constantinople, with eagle-crowned turrets and polygonal towers. Starting in 1283, Edward spent a fortune constructing this grandest in his ring of North Welsh fortresses; one resentful Welshman called it "this magnificent badge of our subjection." Despite its swagger, the fortress was left unfinished thanks to an empty royal pocket and the distraction of unruly Scots. Summer sees a variety of performances, including scenes from the Welsh epic *The Mabinogi* and reenactments of the American War of Independence. Entertaining and cynical tours run hourly for £1.50, and a 20min. video recounts the castle's history twice hourly for free. The **regimental museum** of the Royal Welsh Fusiliers, inside the castle, is worth a walk-through. (☎677617. Open June-Sept. daily 9:30am-6pm; Apr.-May and Oct. 9:30am-5pm; Nov.-Mar. M-Sa 9:30am-4pm, Su 11am-4pm. £4.20, concessions £3.20, families £11.60.)

Most of Caernarfon's 13th-century **town wall** survives, and a short stretch between Church St. and Northgate St. is open for climbing during the same hours as the castle. To see what today's youth hostels will look like in 2000 years, inspect the ruined barracks at **Segontium Roman Fort.** Plundered to its foundations by zealous builders stealing stones for Caernarfon Castle, the fort impresses with thoughtful displays of archaeological excavations. Ignore the misleading road signs and cross under the A487 at the end of Pool St., then follow Ffordd Cwstenin until the fort appears on the left. (☎675625. Open Apr.-Oct. M-Sa 10am-5pm, Su 2-5pm; Nov.-Mar. M-Sa 10am-4pm, Su 2-4pm. £1.25, concessions 75p.)

The remains of a Celtic settlement scatter atop **Twt Hill,** alongside the Bangor St. roundabout; the jutting peak offers sweeping vistas of town and castle. Equally admirable views can be had from the Menai Strait; 40min. **cruises** run from Slate Quay, opposite the castle. (☎672772. £4, students and seniors £3.50, children £2.) A huge nightclub off Castle St. (descend the stairs next to the post office), **Paradox** sponsors Mancunian pole-dancing on Saturdays and 70s nights on the last Thursday of the month. (☎673100. Smart dress. Cover £2-6. Open 9:30pm-1:30am.)

BANGOR ☎01248

Crowded into a valley by the Menai Strait, Bangor (pop. 12,000) lures visitors as a rail and bus hub and provides a cheap and convenient base for exploring the nearby Isle of Anglesey. Students from the University of Wales keep the city's pubs and clubs raucous until the wee hours.

◨ **TRANSPORTATION.** Bangor is the transport depot for the Isle of Anglesey to the west, the Llŷn Peninsula to the southwest, and Snowdonia to the southeast. The **train station** is on Holyhead Rd., up a hill at the end of Deiniol Rd. (☎(01492) 585151. Ticket office open in high season daily 5:30am-6:30pm; low season 11:30am-6:30pm.) **Trains** (☎(08457) 484950) arrive from: **Llandudno Junction** (20min.; M-Sa 1-2 per hr., Su 10 per day; £3.50); **Holyhead** (30min.; M-Sa 1-2 per hr., Su 10 per day; £5.05); **Chester** (1hr.; 1-2 per hr.; £11.90). The **bus station** is on Garth Rd., downhill from the town clock. **Arriva Cymru** (☎(08706) 082608) **bus #4** arrives from **Holyhead** via **Llangefni** and **Llanfair P.G.** (1¼hr., M-Sa 2 per hr., return £3.90), while on Sunday #44 makes the trip; #53, 57, and 58 come from **Beaumaris** (30min.; M-Sa 2-3 per hr., Su 8 per day; £1.65). Arriva bus #5 and its cousins 5A, 5B, and 5X journey from **Caernarfon** (25min.; M-Sa every 10-20min., Su every hr.; return £2.35); #5 and 5X continue east to **Conwy** (40min.; M-Sa 2 per hr., Su every hr.; £2.35). Transfer at **Caernarfon** for the **Llŷn Peninsula,** including **Pwllheli** and **Porthmadog.** A lone **TrawsCambria** bus #701 follows the coast all the way from **Cardiff** (7¾hr., 1 per day, £19.80) and the other way to **Holyhead** (1hr., 1 per day, £7.50). **National Express** (☎(08705) 808080) buses come from **London** (8½hr., 1 per day, £21).

SOMEDAY MY PRINCE WILL COME While there is today a Prince of Wales, not since the slaying of Llewellyn ap Gruffydd has there been a Welsh prince. Fully aware that, no matter how many intimidating castles he constructed along the northern coast, the Welsh would not be settled until they once again had a Welsh prince and English dominion withdrawn, Edward I made them a promise: their very own Prince of Wales, born in Wales, and speaking not a word of English. When his son, later Edward II, was born, Edward I carried the baby to the window of Caernarfon Castle on the Welsh shield, and presented him as the next Prince of Wales: son of an English king, true, but born in Wales, and speaking not a word of English.

■**⊠ ORIENTATION AND PRACTICAL INFORMATION.** An age-old street plan and roads that don't advertise their names might leave you scratching your head. Bangor sprawls over hills, but its two main streets—**Deiniol Rd.** and **High St.**—run parallel to each other, sandwiching the city. **Garth Rd.** starts from the town clock on High St., and winds past the bus station, soon merging with Deiniol Rd. **Holyhead Rd.** begins its ascent at the train station. The **University of Wales at Bangor** sits on both sides of **College Rd.,** a right off Holyhead Rd. as it reaches the summit.

The **tourist information centre** (TIC), in the Town Hall on Deiniol Rd., near the bus station and across the street from the Theatr Gwynedd, provides a free booklet with an essential town map and books rooms for £1 and a 10% deposit. (☎352786. Open Easter-Sept. daily 10am-1pm and 2-6pm; Oct.-Easter F-Sa 10am-1pm and 2-6pm.) Get **camping supplies** at **The Great Arete,** 307 High St. (☎352710. Open M-Sa 9am-5:30pm.) Other services include: **HSBC bank,** 274 High St. (open M-F 9am-5pm, Sa 9:30am-12:30pm); the **police,** across from the bus station (☎(01248) 370333); the **hospital** (☎384384); **Internet access** at the **YHA** and **Java Cafe** (see below) and the **library** across from the TIC (open M and Th-F 10am-7pm, Tu 10am-5pm, W 10am-1pm, Su 9:30am-1pm); and the **post office,** 60 Deiniol Rd., which has a **bureau de change** (☎373329; open M-F 9am-5:30pm, Sa 9am-12:30pm). **Postal code:** LL57 1AA.

⌐⊡ ACCOMMODATIONS AND FOOD. Finding a room in Bangor during University of Wales's graduation (the second week of July) is a nightmarish prospect unless you book many months ahead. The **YHA Youth Hostel,** Tan-y-Bryn, is ½ mi. from the town center. Follow High St. to the water and turn right at the end onto the A5122 (Beach Rd.), turning right again at the youth hostel sign. Bus #5 (2 per hr.) passes the hostel en route to Llandudnol; ask the driver to drop you off. The rich wood paneling of the entrance hall and wide-beam ceilings betray its former role as country estate, though the packed bunks are probably not original furnishings. Vivien Leigh and Sir Laurence Olivier stayed in what is now Room 6. (☎353516; fax 371176. Meals, foosball, and laundry facilities. Internet access £1.50 per 15min. Reception 7am-10:30pm. Open Apr.-Sept. daily; Oct. and Mar. Tu-Sa; Nov. and Jan.-Feb. F-Sa. Dorms £11, under 18 £7.50.) Quality **B&Bs** are scarce in Bangor; the most agreeable occupy the Victorian townhouses on **Garth Rd.** and its extensions. **Mrs. S. Roberts,** 32 Glynne Rd., between Garth Rd. and High St., has TVs and 13 choices for breakfast, including omelettes. (☎352113. £14 per person.) At **Dilfam,** 10min. from the TIC down Garth Rd., most rooms are white and all have TVs. (☎353030. Singles £18.50; doubles £40.) **Dinas Farm** (☎364227), on the banks of the River Ogwan, offers camping. Follow the A5 past Penrhyn Castle and then turn left off the A5122. (Open Easter-Oct. £3 per person. Electricity £2.)

High St. holds an array of fruit shops and cafes, as well as a **Kwik Save** supermarket toward the water. (Open M-Sa 8am-10pm, Su 10am-4pm.) **Java Cafe,** above a clothing store of the same name on High St., has plush couches and an international menu. Try a rare Mexican burrito (£5.25) or delicious pasta (£5) while surfing the web for £1 per 15min. (☎301612. Open M-Tu 10am-6pm, W-Sa 10am-10pm.) At **Penguin Cafe,** 260 High St., munch sandwiches (£1.50-2.25) or the daily special as you people-watch from a sidewalk table. (☎362036. Open M-Sa 7am-5:30pm.)

NORTH WALES

🌐🎵 SIGHTS AND ENTERTAINMENT. 🏰Penrhyn Castle, George Hay Dawkins-Pennant's 19th-century neo-Norman mansion, squats over two acres just outside Bangor. Its ivy-covered towers guard a 40-acre estate, testament to the staggering wealth accumulated by the owners of Gwynedd's slate quarries. Inside, Penrhyn's opulence makes Versailles seem tastefully understated; the intricately carved stone staircase took 10 years to complete, and even the servants' version seems extravagant. To get to Penrhyn, walk up High St. toward the Bay, then turn right onto the A5122 and go north for 1 mi., or catch bus #5 or 5X from the town center to the entrance to the grounds (10min.; M-Sa 2 per hr., Su every hr.); the castle is an additional mile from the gate. (☎353084 or 363200. Audioguide £1; guide to artwork free. Open July-Aug. W-M grounds 10am-5:30pm, castle 11am-4:30pm; late Mar. to June and Sept.-Oct. W-M grounds 11am-5pm, castle noon-4:30pm. Castle and grounds £6, children £3, families £15. Grounds only £3, children £1.50.)

Humble and steepleless, **St. Deiniol's Cathedral,** on Gwynedd Rd. off High St., has been the ecclesiastical center of this corner of Wales for 1400 years; its Bible Garden cultivates plants mentioned in the Good Book. (☎353983 or 370693. Open M-F 8am-6pm, Sa 8am-1pm, Su 7:30am-6pm.) The **Bangor Museum and Art Gallery,** also on Gwynedd Rd., houses an authentic man-trap, used as an anti-poaching device. (☎353368. Open Tu-F 12:30-4:30pm, Sa 10:30am-4:30pm. Free.) Watch tides ebb and flow at the long, onion-domed Victorian **pier** at the end of Garth Rd.; desserts at its tea shop cost as little as 25p. (Open M-F 8:30am-7pm, Sa-Su 10am-7pm.)

The modern **Theatr Gwynedd,** on Deiniol Rd. at the base of the hill, houses a thriving troupe that performs in both Welsh and English. (☎351708. Box office open M-F 9:30am-5pm, Sa 10am-5pm; on performance days M-F 9:30am-8pm, Sa 10am-8pm, Su 6-8pm. Films £4.30, students and seniors £3.30, children £2; plays £6-18.) Bangor's students propel lively clubs, and many pubs along High St. pump up the volume on weekends. Popular **Time-Amsea,** near Theatr Gwynedd behind the student union, packs 'em onto a huge dance-floor; partiers scarf fast food in the in-house "chill-out room." (☎388032. M 60s/70s, Sa funk. Casual. Cover £3-5. Open June-Oct. M, W, Sa 8pm-1am; Nov.-May M and W-Sa 8pm-1am.) Buy your happiness at **Bliss,** on Dean St. off High St., where Wednesday is student night and Friday has cheap drinks. (☎354977. Smart dress. Cover £3-5. Open W-Sa 8pm-1am.) At **Barrels,** farther down High St., enjoy a smaller dance-floor and ample bar without the cover. (☎372040. Casual. Open Th-Sa 8pm-1am, doors close 10:30-11pm.)

ISLE OF ANGLESEY (YNYS MÔN)

Connected to mainland Wales by the Menai and Britannia Bridges, the Isle of Anglesey feels more like a parallel landscape than an island. Once a center of Celtic druidic culture, the flat, arable land has long provided spiritual and physical sustenance for the region. The isle's old name is Mona mam Cymru (Mona the mother of Wales), and, appropriately, Anglesey hosted the last Royal National Eisteddfod of the millennium in August 1999 (see **Ffestivals,** p. 427). While Beaumaris Castle attracts most visitors, the isle's prehistoric sites and gentle coastline also merit attention.

▐ TRANSPORTATION

Bangor, on the mainland, is the best hub for the island. **Trains** (☎(08457) 484950) run on the north Wales train line to **Holyhead** from **Bangor** (45min., 1-2 per hr., £5); some stop at **Llanfair P.G.** The main bus company is **Arriva Cymru** (☎(08706) 082608), which spins a web of buses over most of the island; a handful of smaller bus companies fill the gaps. Arriva bus #4 travels north from **Bangor** to **Holyhead** via **Llanfair P.G.** and **Llangefni** (1¼hr., M-Sa 2 per hr., £2.75); on Sundays Arriva #44 follows a similar route (1¼hr., 8 per day). Buses #53, 57, and 58 hug the southeast coast from **Bangor** to **Beaumaris** (30min.; M-Sa 2 per hr., Su 8 per day; £1.65), and some continue to **Penmon** (30-45min., 12 per day). Bus #62 journeys to **Amlwch,** on the northern coast, from **Bangor** (50min.; M-Sa 1-2 per hr., Su 5 per day; £1.75); bus #42 from **Bangor** curves along the southwest coast up to **Aberffraw** before cutting north to **Llangefni** (1hr., M-Sa 9 per day, £1.75), stopping at **Aberffraw** on Sunday (50min., 2 per day). From **Amlwch, Lewis y Llan** (☎(01407) 832181) bus #61 cruises into **Holyhead** (50min.; M-Sa 8 per day, Su 4 per day; £1.80). **Lewis**'s #32 shuttles north from **Llangefni** to **Amlwch** (40min.; M-Sa 8 per day, Su 4 per day; £1.50). The Gwynedd **Red Rover ticket** (£4.80, children £2.40) covers a day's bus travel in Anglesey, as well as Gwynedd, including Bangor. Pick up the map-filled *Isle of Anglesey Public Transport Guide*, free at tourist information centres (TICs).

👁 SIGHTS

People have fancied the Isle of Anglesey since prehistory. Burial chambers, cairns, and other remains are scattered on Holyhead and both the eastern and western coasts. Most ancient monuments sit quietly in farmers' fields, so a map detailing exactly how to reach them (without walking through a herd of cows) is helpful. TICs sell Ordnance Survey Landranger Map #114 (1:50,000; £5.25) and the more detailed Ordnance Survey Explorer Maps #262 and 263, each of which cover one half of the island (1:25,000; £5.75). The eight brochures comprising the *Circular Walks on the Island of Anglesey* are a useful alternative for walkers, while the pamphlet *Rural Cycling on Anglesey* is a must for bikers (both free at TICs).

▨ BRYN CELLI DDU. Bryn Celli Ddu (bryn kay-HLEE thee), "The Mound in the Dark Grove," is a burial chamber dating from the late Neolithic period and the most famous of Anglesey's remains. From the outside, this 4000-year-old construction looks like any old mound of earth in the middle of a sheep pasture, but a flashlight helps illuminate the etchings on the walls inside. *(Take Bangor-Holyhead bus #4, which sometimes stops at Llandaniel (M-Sa 9 per day), and walk a mile from there. You can also reach the Bryn from Llanfair P.G. past Plas Newydd; ask at the TIC.)*

PLAS NEWYDD. The 19th-century country home of the Marquess of Anglesey, 2 mi. south of Llanfair P.G., is now run by the National Trust. The 58 ft. Rex Whistler painting that covers an inside room is certainly impressive, but admission is expensive. *(Take bus #42 from Bangor to the house (15min., M-Sa 11 per day, Su 2 per day), or catch the more frequent #4 to Llanfair P.G. (15min., M-Sa 2 per hr.) and walk. ☎(01248) 714795. House open Apr.-Oct. Sa-W noon-5pm, last admission 4:30pm. Garden open Sa-W 11am-5:30pm. £4.60, children £2.30, families £11.50. Garden only £2.60, children £1.30.)*

PENMON PRIORY. The late medieval priory of Penmon is the most readily accessible of Anglesey's sights. The simple church dates to the 11th century and possesses two elaborately carved cross stands, as well as Europe's largest dovecot (shoebox-sized nesting holes for the peaceful birds). From the parking lot, a short train leads to 6th-century St. Seiriol's Well, reputed to have healing qualities. *(Some buses run directly to the Priory; check timetables. Otherwise, take Arriva Cymru bus #57 or 58 from Beaumaris to Penmon (10-20min.; M-Sa 11 per day, Su 4 per day; return £1.85) and follow the sign to Penmon Point, after which the priory is an additional 25min. walk on the same road.)*

LLANALLGO. Three sets of remains cluster near the town of Llanallgo, but getting to them requires a bit of effort. Follow the minor road (to the left of the Moelfre road) to the ancient **Ligwy Burial Chamber.** Between 15 and 30 people are entombed in this squat enclosure, covered with a 25-ton capstone. Farther on stand the 12th-century chapel **Hen Capel Ligwy** and the remains of the Roman **Din Ligwy Hut Group.** *(Arriva bus #62 hits Llanallgo on its Bangor-Cemaes route (35min.; M-Sa 1-2 per hr., Su 5 per day). Ask the driver to stop at the roundabout heading to Moelfre.)*

LLANFAIRPWLL. . .

Llanfairpwllgwyngyllgogerychwyrndrobwllllantysiliogogogoch (HLAN-vire-poohl-gwin-gihl—ah, screw it), the longest-named village in the world, is linked to Bangor by the Britannia Bridge. Devised by a 19th-century humorist to attract attention, the name translates roughly as "Saint Mary's Church in the hollow of white hazel near the rapid whirlpool and the Church of Saint Tysillio near the red cave" (or, alternatively, "we-couldn't-find-a-compelling-reason-to-get-you-to-come-here-so-we-just-created-a-ridiculous-name"). Sensibly, the town's war memorial reads "Llanfair P.G." so as not to overwhelm the roll call of the dead. The town (pop. 2472) is also known locally as "Llanfairpwll." **James Pringle Woollens Factory,** beside the train station, is mobbed by tourists taking snapshots of the town's emblazoned name. The store houses one of Anglesey's two **tourist information centres.** (☎(01248) 713177; fax 715711. Open Apr.-Oct. M-Sa 9:30am-5:30pm, Su 10am-5pm; Nov.-Mar. M-F 9:30am-1pm and 1:30-5pm, Su 10am-5pm.) Puts antiecclesiodis-establishmentarianism in the lexicographical dustbin, doesn't it?

BEAUMARIS   ☎01248

Four miles northeast of the Menai Bridge on the A545, the main street of Beaumaris (bew-MAR-is) runs quietly along the yacht-dotted harbor. In town, savor the magnificent (albeit unfinished) symmetry of **Beaumaris Castle,** the last of Edward I's Welsh fortresses and now a World Heritage site. Begun in 1295 and built on a marsh, the castle's concentric design renders it virtually impregnable. (☎810361. Open June-Sept. daily 9:30am-6pm; Apr.-May and Oct. 9:30am-5pm; Nov.-Mar. M-Sa 9:30am-4pm, Su 11am-4pm. £2.50, concessions £2, families £7.)

On Bunkers Hill, off Steeple Ln., the cells of the former **Beaumaris Gaol,** formerly Anglesey's only prison, show what it was like to be a prisoner in Victorian times (answer: not very pleasant). Out-of-line inmates faced time on the treadwheel, which supplied running water for the jail, solitary confinement, or execution at the courtyard gallows. (☎810921. Open Apr.-Sept. daily 10:30am-5pm. £2.75, concessions £1.75, family £7.) A lighter side of Anglesey's past is captured in the **Museum of Childhood Memories,** 1 Castle St., where legions of tin wind-ups, round-eyed dolls, and pea-shooting piggy banks sing the silly song of nostalgia. Bring 10p coins to try your hand at Depression-era arcade games. (☎712498. Open Easter-Oct. M-Sa 10:30am-5:30pm, Su noon-5pm. Last admission 45min. before close. £3.25, students and seniors £2.75, children £2, families £9.50.) A guided catamaran cruise down the Menai Strait to and around **Puffin Island** leaves from the Starida booth on the pier, as do other local trips. (☎810379; before 10:30am or after 5pm 810251. Cruises 1¼hr. £4, seniors £3.50, children £3.) The week-long **Gŵyl Beaumaris Music Festival** at the end of May features opera, theater, and street performances.

Buses stop on Castle St. The **tourist information centre,** Town Hall, on Castle St., provides a free town map and information on scarce accommodations. (☎810040. Open Easter-Oct. daily 10am-5:30pm.) The **HSBC bank** is on Castle St. (Open M-F 11am-2pm.) The **post office** is at 10 Church St. (Open M-Tu and Th-F 9am-12:30pm and 1:30-5:30pm, W and Sa 9am-12:30pm.) **Postal code:** LL58 8AB.

The closest **YHA Youth Hostel** to Beaumaris is in Bangor (☎353516; see p. 480). Beaumaris itself appeals little as a place to stay. None of the few B&Bs in town offer singles, and doubles cost around £30; consider sleeping across the strait in Bangor or Caernarfon. Institutionalized camping is best at **Kingsbridge Caravan Park,** 1½ mi. out of town toward Llangoed. At the end of Beaumaris's main street, follow the coastal road past the castle until reaching the crossroads. Turn left for Llanfaes; Kingsbridge is 400 yd. on the right. Arriva #57 and 58, running from Bangor through Beaumaris to Glanrafon, stops near the site if you ask. (☎490636. £4 per adult, £2 per child. Electricity £2. Showers free.) Gratify gluttony at the stocked shelves of **Spar,** 11 Castle St. (Open M-Sa 8am-11pm, Su 8am-10pm.)

HOLYHEAD (CAERGYBI)   ☎01407

An unattractive town attached to Anglesey by a causeway and a bridge, Holyhead (pop. 12,000) is primarily known for its ferries to Ireland. **Ferries** and **Stena Sealink** operate ferries and catamarans to **Dublin** and its suburb, **Dún Laoghaire.** Foot passengers check in at the terminal adjoining the train station; car-ferry parties proceed along the asphalt beside the terminal. Arrive 30min. early and remember your passport. (See **By Ferry,** p. 45, for more details.)

In town, the **Maritime Museum** occupies the oldest lifeboat house in Wales, and details the history of Holyhead's maritime industry. (☎764374. Open Apr.-Sept. Tu-Su 1-5pm; Oct. Sa-Su 1-5pm. £3, seniors £1.50, children 50p, families £5.) **St. Gybi's Church,** in the center of town between Stanley St. and Victoria Rd., has lovely stained-glass windows by Edward Burne-Jones and William Morris. The **Caer Gybi** that surround the church date to Roman times. (☎753001. Open May-Sept. daily 11am-3pm; call in winter. Free.) If you have time, explore the many paths of **Holyhead Mountain** near town. Its North and South Stacks are good for birdwatching, and the lighthouse looks longingly to sea. **Caer y Tŵr** and **Holyhead Mountain Hut Group** sit at the mountain's base. The former is an Iron Age hillfort, the latter a settlement inhabited from 500 BC until Roman times.

Reach Holyhead every hr. by **train** from: **Bangor** (30min., £5.05); **Chester** (1½hr., £16.15); **London** (4½-6hr., £57.30). **Arriva Cymru** (☎(08706) 082608) **bus** #4 rumbles from **Bangor** via **Llanfair P.G.** and **Llangefni** (1¼hr., M-Sa 2 per hr., return £3.90); on Sundays #44 journeys from **Bangor,** sometimes stopping in **Ysbyty Gwynedd** (1¼hr., 8 times per day). **National Express** (☎(08705) 808080) hits Holyhead from most major cities. **TrawsCambria** bus #701 arrives from and departs for **Cardiff** once per day (9hr.). For a **taxi,** call 765000.

The **tourist information centre** (TIC) in Terminal One of the train and ferry station, helps book rooms and ferries. (☎762622. Open M-Sa 8:30am-6pm.) Other services include: **HSBC bank,** on the corner of William St. and Market St. (open M-F 9am-5pm); free **Internet access** at the **public library,** Newry Fields (☎762917; open M 10am-5pm, Tu and Th-F 10am-7pm, W and Sa 10am-1pm); and the **post office,** 13a Stryd Boston, off Market St., with a **bureau de change** (open M-F 11am-12:30pm and 3-5:30pm, Sa 11am-12:30pm). **Postal code:** LL65 1BP.

Holyhead **B&Bs** are accommodating to passengers at the mercy of boat schedules; if you call ahead, B&B owners may arrange to greet you at unusual times, but avoid knocking on doors unannounced in the wee hours. B&Bs here often become B&PL (beds and packed lunches) for ferry riders. If not included, a packed lunch is usually a few extra pounds. **Roselea,** 26 Holborn Rd., the closest B&B to the station and ferries, packs a lunch for the day after you sleep in their orthopedic beds. (☎/fax 764391. Singles £18; twins £32-34.) To get to **Orotovia,** 66 Walthew Ave., go up Thomas St., which becomes Porth-y-Felin Rd. as it passes the school, and turn right onto Walthew Ave., not to be confused with Walthew St. or Walthew Ln.; if bogged down with bags, call for a ride from the station. Chocolates on the beds, cable TV, and two dozen brands of cereal are unparalleled luxuries. (☎760259. £17.50 per person; mention *Let's Go* for a possible discount.) A little way down the road, the proprietress of **Witchingham,** 20 Walthew Ave., has a Toto named Jody but is hardly the broom-riding type. If arriving at a reasonable hour, call for a ride from the station. (☎762426. Singles £19; doubles with bath £42.)

CONWY   ☎01492

With a 13th-century castle towering over narrow lanes and a pleasant quayside, Conwy bears its wearisome role as modern tourist mecca well. Edward I, who seemed never to tire of constructing the damn things, had the town's solemn castle built as another link in his chain of North Wales fortresses. It now stands guard over a fine city wall, elegant houses, and a gaggle of eclectic attractions.

▐ TRANSPORTATION

Trains (☎(08457) 484950) only stop at Conwy Station, off Rosehill St., by request, even though Conwy lies on the North Wales train line linking Holyhead to Chester. Trains *do* stop at the nearby, fully staffed **Llandudno Junction** station, one of the busiest in Wales, which connects to the scenic Conwy Valley line. (Llandudno Junction booking office open M-Sa 5:30am-6:30pm, Su 11:30am-6:30pm.) Not to be confused with Llandudno proper (a resort town about a mile north; see p. 488), Llandudno Junction is a 20min. walk from Conwy. Turn left onto a little side road after exiting the station, walk past a supermarket on your left, pass under a bridge, and then climb the stairs to another bridge that leads past pretty gardens and across the estuary to Conwy castle and town. If you haven't the energy for such a hike, nearly every bus route into Conwy includes a stop at the Junction; the most frequent are the Arriva #5 and 5X (3min.; M-Sa 2 per hr., Su every hr.).

Buses are the best way to get directly to Conwy, with the two main stops at Lancaster Sq. and Castle St. before the corner of Rosehill St.; check posted schedules. **National Express** (☎(08705) 808080) comes from: **Liverpool** (2¾hr., 1 per day); **Manchester** (4hr., 1 per day, £10.75); **Newcastle** (10hr., 1 per day). **Arriva Cymru** (☎(08706) 082608) buses #5 and 5X stop in Conwy as they climb the northern coast from **Caernarfon** via **Bangor** toward **Llandudno** (1-1½hr.; M-Sa 2 per hr., Su every hr.; return £3). Bus #19 takes in Conwy on its **Llandudno-Llanrwst** journey down the Vale of Conwy (20min.; M-Sa 1-2 per hr., Su 7 per day; £1.10). The comprehensive *Conwy Public Transport Information* booklet has schedules and maps and is available free at the tourist information centre (TIC).

✳❷ ORIENTATION AND PRACTICAL INFORMATION

The town wall squeezes old Conwy into a roughly triangular shape. The castle lies in one corner; **Castle St.**, which becomes **Berry St.**, runs from the foot of the fortress parallel to the Quay. **High St.** stretches from the Quay's edge to **Lancaster Sq.**, from which **Rosehill St.** circles back to the castle. In the opposite direction, **Bangor Rd.** scrunches northward through a small arch in the wall.

The **tourist information centre**, Castle Entrance, has clear street maps and books beds for £1 plus a 10% deposit. (☎592248. Open Easter-Oct. daily 9:30am-6pm; Nov.-Mar. Th-Sa 10am-4pm.) **Conwy Outdoor Shop**, 9 Castle St., has an extensive, if expensive, selection of camping and traveling supplies; they also **rent bikes** for £12 per day and tents from £7. (☎593390. Open daily 9am-6pm.) Other services include: **Barclays bank**, 23 High St. (☎616616; open M-F 10am-4pm); the **police**, Lancaster Sq. (☎511000); **Llandudno Hospital**, Maesdu Rd. (☎860066; take Arriva bus #19); **Internet access** at the **library**, Civic Hall, Castle St. (☎596242; £2.50 per 30min.; open M and Th-F 10am-5:30pm, Tu 10am-7pm, W and Sa 10am-1pm); and the **post office**, Lancaster Sq. at High St., in The Wine Shop (☎573990; open M-Tu 8:30am-5:30pm, W-F 9am-5:30pm, Sa 9am-1:30pm). **Postal code:** LL32 8DA.

▐ ACCOMMODATIONS AND CAMPING

Swan Cottage, 18 Berry St. (☎596840). One of the few B&Bs within the city walls. Cozy rooms with timber ceilings and TVs. Loft room with view of the estuary. £16 per person.

YHA Conwy, Larkhill, Sychnant Pass Rd. (☎593571; fax 593580; conwy@yha.org.uk). From Lancaster Sq., head down Bangor Rd., turn left up Mt. Pleasant, and right at the top of the hill. The hostel is on the left after 150 yd. This sprawling YHA has a huge self-catering kitchen, laundry facilities, TV room, and luggage lockers (£1). Internet access £2.50 per 30min. Bike rental £7 per half-day, children £2.50; £11.50 per day, children £4.50. Reception 24hr. Open mid-Feb. to Dec. Dorms £12.50, under 18 £8.50.

Llwyn Guest House, 15 Cadnant Park (☎592319). Head from the castle down Rosehill St., past Lancaster Sq., through the arch down Bangor Rd., then turn left across the small bridge at the Cadnant Park sign. Lose yourself in downy duvets while vegging in front of your personal TV. £17 per person.

Glan Heulog, Llanrwst Rd., Woodlands (☎593845). Go under the arch near the Visitor Centre on Rosehill St., down the steps, and across the car park. Turn right and walk 5min. down Llanrwst Rd. Huge house on a hill with TVs and "healthy option" breakfast. Proprietors allow use of their computer for Internet access, requesting only a donation to the charity box. Singles £18-23; doubles and twins £36-42; discounts in off season.

Camping: Conwy Touring Park, Llanrwst Rd. (☎592856). Follow Llanrwst Rd. and posted signs a steep mile out of town. No large groups. Open Easter-Oct. 2-person tent £4-7. Electricity £1.65-2.80.

◖ FOOD

Most Conwy restaurants serve ordinary grub, but the name of High St., along which many are found, might well be a reference to the inflated prices. Fear not, thrifty gourmands, for the ever-reliable **Spar** defends its territory next to Barclays. (Open daily 8am-10pm.) A weekly **market** fills the train station parking lot. (Open summer Sa and winter Tu 8:30am-5pm.) Fine vegetarian and vegan fare (£3-8) awaits at **The Wall Place,** on Chapel St. off Berry St., where traditional Welsh music wafts across the light wood floor; on winter afternoons, the cafe hosts creative workshops. (☎596326. Open Easter-Sept. daily noon-3pm and 6-10pm; mid-Sept. to Easter varies. Music and buffets some Sa; call for info.) For light meals (£3.25-5) and sandwich snacks (from £2), try popular **Pantri Conwy,** Lancaster Sq. (☎592436. Open daily 9am-5pm.) Burgers (£3.20-4) and a nightly vegetarian option (£5) are served alongside other pub grub at the bright and homey **Ye Olde Mail Coach** on High St. (Open M-Sa 11am-11pm, Su 11am-10:30pm; food served daily 11am-7pm.)

◉ SIGHTS

▨**CONWY CASTLE.** More compact than Edward I's colossal fortresses at Caernarfon and Beaumaris, Conwy Castle's menacing design was still challenge enough for would-be attackers. Invaders would need to scale the slippery rock promontory, shielded by water on three sides, before somehow breaching one of two massive barbicans amid a shower of crossbow bolts. And that's just to get to the grim walls and turreted towers of the inner curtain. The prison tower saw many prominent Normans rot beneath its false bottom, and the castle chapel witnessed Henry "Hotspur" Percy's betrayal of Richard II in 1399. Two years later, Welsh rebel Owain Glyndŵr and his band of armed nationalists seized the ramparts. (☎592358. *Open June-Sept. daily 9:30am-6pm; Apr.-May and Oct. 9:30am-5pm; Nov.-Mar. M-Sa 9:30am-4pm, Su 11am-4pm. Tours £1. £3.60, concessions £2.60, families £9.80.)*

PLAS MAWR. Perhaps the best-preserved Elizabethan house in Britain, this 16th-century mansion has been lovingly restored to recall its days as home of merchant Robert Wynn. Climb the watchtower and open one of the small windows for terrific views over the city or stroll the courtyard below. The entrance price includes a free audio tour (1hr.). (☎580167. *Open June-Aug. daily 9:30am-6pm; Apr.-May and Sept. Tu-Su 9:30am-6pm; Oct. 9:30am-4pm. £4.10, concessions £3.10, families £11.30.)*

THE SMALLEST HOUSE. Bang your head into what's billed as Britain's smallest house, another of Conwy's oddities. With a frontage of 6 ft., the 380-year-old two-floor edifice housed an elderly couple and then one 6 ft. 3 in. fisherman before it was condemned in 1900. (*Head down High St. and onto the quay. ☎593484. Open July-Aug. daily 10am-9pm; Easter-June and Sept.-Oct. 10am-6pm. 50p, concessions 30p.)*

TELFORD SUSPENSION BRIDGE. Next to an unsightly rail bridge, Telford's elegant 1826 suspension bridge stretches across the Conwy River from the foot of the castle's grassy east barbican; at the opposite end stands the tollmaster's house, restored to a mini-museum. Both bridge and castle can be seen by boat; vigorous bellowing heralds the departure of the **Queen Victoria** from the quay at the end of High St. (☎573282. *Bridge and house open July-Aug. daily 10am-5pm; Apr.-June and Sept.-Oct. W-M 10am-5pm. Last admission 4:30pm. £1, children 50p. Cruises 30min.; £3, children £2.)*

TOWN WALL. Almost a mile long, the wall was built at the same time as the castle and shielded burghers with its 22 towers and 480 arrow slits—the 12 latrine chutes may have been useful, too. Climb the Mt. Pleasant side for magnificent views.

TEAPOT MUSEUM. "You'd have to be potty to miss it," proclaims the sign under which two grand British traditions—tea and eccentricity—meet. The one-room museum displays 300 years of teapots—some short, some stout, and some shaped like a craggy Lloyd George, a dour Thatcher, and a roomy Pavarotti. Don't knock over the Humpty Dumpty pot; the nearest savior is not a King's horse or a King's man, but the King of Rock and Roll himself, who warns that only fools rush in this packed little room. Glimpses of *risqué* teapots reward the diligent museum-goer. *(Castle St. ☎593429. Open Easter-Oct. M-Sa 10am-5:30pm, Su 11am-5:30pm. £1.50, concessions £1, families £3.50. YHA members 10% off.)*

OTHER SIGHTS AND ENTERTAINMENT. 14th-century **Aberconwy House,** the oldest house in Conwy, has served as a sea captain's home, a temperance center, and now a National Trust sight. *(Castle St. ☎592246. Open Apr.-Oct. W-M 1-5pm, last admission 4:30pm. £2, children £1, families £5.)* Most of the tranquility in Conwy has migrated to **St. Mary's Church,** where the grave that inspired Wordsworth's poem "We are Seven" lies just outside the South Porch. In July, the **North Wales Bluegrass Festival** brings Appalachian dance to Conwy.

LLANDUDNO ☎01492

Until 1849, the flatlands between the Great Orme and the Little Orme bore only indigenous wildflowers and whatever crops farmers could grow in the shadow of the two rock heads. The Mostyn family, however, had grander schemes in mind for the sheltered, beachy strip, and they planted the seeds of a resort town that now blooms with rows of Victorian and Edwardian buildings. The streets just outside the city center are crammed with tourist housing, and the town seems perpetually on holiday, with escapes to nature as easy as a trip to the theater.

▐ TRANSPORTATION. Llandudno (chlan-DOOD-no) is the northern terminus of several lines of transport. The **train station** is at the end of Augusta Rd. (Ticket office open M-Sa 8:40am-3:30pm; July-Aug. also Su 10:15am-5:45pm.) Trains (☎(08457) 484950) arrive on the single-track Conwy Valley line from **Blaenau Ffestiniog** via **Betws-y-Coed** (1hr.; M-Sa 5 per day, Su 2 per day). On the north Wales line, trains enter **Llandudno Junction,** a mile south of town, from **Holyhead** (50min., 18 per day); **Bangor** (20min., 1-3 per hr.); **Chester** (1hr., 1-4 per hr.). **National Express** (☎(08705) 808080) **buses** hit Mostyn Broadway from: **London** (8hr., 1 per day, £21); **Chester** (1¾hr., 1 per day, £7.50); **Manchester** (4hr., 1 per day, £10). **Arriva Cymru** (☎(08706) 082608) buses #5, 5A, and 5X come from **Conwy** (20min.; M-Sa 3 per hr., Su every hr.; £1.35); **Bangor** (1hr., £2.70); **Caernarfon** (1½hr., £3.25). Bus #19 arrives from **Llanrwst** in the Vale of Conwy (1hr.; M-Sa 1-2 per hr., Su 7 per day; £1.20). Bus #96, the Snowdon Sherpa, travels from **Betws-y-Coed** (50min., M-Sa 4 per day, £3); bus #70 makes the same trip less frequently (1½hr., M-Sa 2 per day). Call **Kings Cabs** (☎878156) for **taxis.** Rent **bikes** from **West End Cycles,** 22 Augusta St., near the train station. (☎876891. £10 per day. £25 deposit. Open M-Sa 9am-5:30pm.)

▐▌ ORIENTATION AND PRACTICAL INFORMATION. Llandudno is flanked by two pleasant beaches; the West Shore is less built up than the North, which is decorated with Victorian promenades and tipped by a long pier. A left on Augusta St. as you exit the train station leads to the **tourist information centre** (TIC), Chapel St., which houses a library of free pamphlets and books rooms for £1 and a 10% deposit. (☎876413. Open Easter-Oct. daily 9:30am-5:30pm; Nov.-Easter 10am-4pm.) Other services include: **Barclays bank,** on the corner of Mostyn St. and Market St. (open M-Tu and Th-F 9:30am-4:30pm, W 10am-4:30pm, Sa 10am-12:30pm);

the **police,** Oxford Rd. (☎517171); the **General Hospital** (☎860066); **Internet access** at **CyberSkills,** 50 Madoc St. (☎874627; £2.50 per 30min.; open M-Th 9am-5pm, F 9am-4:30pm, Sa 10am-3pm); and the **post office,** 14 Vaughn St., with a **bureau de change** (☎(0345) 223344; open M-F 9am-5:30pm, Sa 9am-12:30pm). **Postal code:** LL30 1AA.

⬛️ ACCOMMODATIONS AND FOOD. Designed for visitors, Llandudno overflows with B&Bs, guest houses, and cheap hotels. Budget travelers should seek out B&Bs (£12-15) on **Chapel St., Deganwy Ave.,** and **St. David's Rd.** Try **Walsall House,** 4 Chapel St., conveniently located next to the TIC, for rooms with TVs. (☎875279. £15.50-17 per person, £12.50-14 without breakfast.) The popular **YHA Conwy** (see p. 486) is only 20min. away by bus (#5, 5A, and 5X; M-Sa 3 per hr., Su every hr.). Eateries accommodate all appetites. **The Fat Cat Cafe-Bar,** 149 Mostyn St., has a varied menu in an academic atmosphere, including Mexican nachos (£3.55), veggie burritos with wild rice (£5.85), and steak wraps for under £5. (☎871844. Open M-Sa 10am-11pm, Su 10am-10:30pm.) Busy **Ham Bone,** Clonmel St. off Mostyn St., makes baguette sandwiches to order with loads of fixings (£1.40-2), baps with hot pork stuffing and apple sauce (£2), and meat or cheese pies (80p-£1.10) for takeaway. (Open M-Sa 8:30am-5pm.) **Habit,** 12 Mostyn St., has a large, well-priced menu, with main courses from £4 to £6. (☎875043. Open daily 9:30am-5:30pm.) **The Cottage Loaf,** down Market St., off Mostyn St. next to Barclays, maintains a village pub atmosphere with its blooming beer garden, and serves up really good grub, too. (☎870762. Open M-Sa 11am-11pm, Su noon-10:30pm; food served all day.)

◖ SIGHTS. Llandudno's pleasant beaches, Victorian North Shore and quieter West Shore, are both outdone by the looming **Great Orme.** At the 679 ft. summit, wildflowers run amok amid prehistoric remains and a modern visitors center, accessible by foot; the **Great Orme Tramway** departs from Church Walks. (☎876749. 15min. to summit, around 3 per hr. Runs Apr.-Oct. 10am-6pm. Return £3.80, children £2.60; single £2.60, children £1.80. Ticket gets 10% off at Copper Mines.) The two counter-balanced cable cars also stop halfway up at the fantastic **Bronze Age Copper Mines.** Strap on a helmet and bang it against low ceilings as you step through tunnels dug by copper miners 3500 years ago. The silence of the inner cavern is broken only by dripping water (and the occasional hyperactive child). Claustrophobic travelers may want to avoid the narrow tunnels. (☎870447. Open Feb.-Oct. 10am-5pm. £4.40, children £2.80, family £12. Joint tram ticket £7.25, children £5, family £20.) Winter or summer, don't miss the chance to speed down a Welsh mountain in your own luge-like toboggan at **Ski Llandudno.** (☎874707. Open daily 10am-10pm, depending on weather. 2 runs £3.) While vacationing in Llandudno, Lewis Carroll met his muse in Alice Liddell, who spent her childhood summers there. Kids will get a kick out of the **The Rabbit Hole** at the Alice in Wonderland Centre, 3-4 Trinity Sq., a campy recreation of Wonderland. (☎/fax 860062. Open M-Sa 10am-5pm; Easter-Oct. also Su 10am-4pm. £2.95, seniors £2.75, children £2.50.)

◖◗ NIGHTLIFE AND ENTERTAINMENT. Llandudno's two clubs are both a 10min. walk from the town center. **Broadway Boulevard,** Mostyn Broadway, is a versatile venue down Mostyn St. (☎879614. Smart casual; no trainers. Cover £2-5. W open 9pm-2am, Th-Sa 9:30pm-2am. Sometimes closed Th. Last admission midnight.) A bit farther down Mostyn Broadway and left on Clarence Rd. is **Washington,** a complex with two venues, **Capital** on the first floor and **Buzz Club** on the second; a cover often gains admission to both. Capital is lined with portraits of U.S. presidents and caters to an older set; Buzz is a more traditional dance club. (☎877974. No trainers. No cover before 10pm, £2 10-11pm, £3 11-11:30pm. Capital open W-Sa 7pm-midnight. Buzz open F-Sa 7pm-1am.) Try the **North Wales Theatre,** sandwiched between Mostyn Blvd. and the Promenade, for a play or concert. Glossy pamphlets with schedules are at the TIC. (☎872000. Box office open M-Sa 10am-8pm, Su 3 hr. before performance. Tickets £6-26, concessions available.)

PLANE AND SIMPLE Close inspection of Betws-y-Coed book-shelves reveals the oddest of Welsh obsessions: plane crashes. Enter any bookshop to peruse the pages of Roy Sloan's *Aircraft Crashes: Flying Accidents in Gwynedd 1910-1990* (£5.50), or the author's rival work, *Anglesey Air Accidents During the Twentieth Century* (£5.50)—not to be confused, apparently, with a similar tome on all those 19th-century crashes. For more hands-on material, *Down in Wales: Visits to Some Wartime Air Crash Sites* (£6.50), by Terence R. Hill, should satisfy the curious. Then move on to its heart-pounding sequel, *Down in Wales 2: Visits to More Wartime Crash Sites* (£6.95). Tired of aviation disasters? Have no fear, dear reader: the all-knowing TIC has forestalled such a pickle. For £3, they stock Dilys Gater's *Historic Shipwrecks of Wales*.

VALE OF CONWY

Well watered by river and rain, the lush Vale of Conwy hosts walkers, cyclists, and innumerable waterfowl. Hills slope from the foot of Snowdonia's mountains to the tidal Conwy River. In the thick woods around Betws-y-Coed, tripping tributaries converge to meander lazily north to Llandudno. Cyclists take advantage of the scenic terrain: views are glorious and gear-changes infrequent. Pick up the excellent brochure *Walks from the Conwy Valley Line* at local tourist information centres and train stations for details on the area's splendid hiking opportunities.

▛ TRANSPORTATION

The single-track, 27 mi. **Conwy Valley** line (☎(08457) 484950) offers unparalleled views as **trains** hug the river banks between the seaside resort of **Llandudno** and the mountain town of **Blaenau Ffestiniog**, stopping at **Llandudno Junction** (near Conwy) and **Betws-y-Coed** (1hr.; M-Sa 6 per day, Su 3 per day). The **North and Mid Wales Rover ticket** gives virtually unlimited bus and train travel as far south as **Aberystwyth** (1-day £18, 3-day £28, 7-day £42). Most **buses** stop at Betws-y-Coed and Llanrwst; the rest of the valley is relatively untouched. The main bus along the Conwy River is **Arriva Cymru** (☎(08706) 082608) #19, which winds from **Llandudno** and **Conwy** to **Llanrwst** (M-Sa 1-2 per hr., Su 7 per day). From Llanrwst, **Sherpa** bus #96 continues to **Pen-y-Pas** via Betws-y-Coed (8 per day), while #96A runs from **Betws-y-Coed** to **Llanberis** (50min.; M-Sa 4 per day, Su 7 per day). Bus #97A connects Betws-y-Coed with **Porthmadog** (1hr., 3 per day). Arriva sells a one-day **Explorer** pass good for unlimited travel on any of its buses (£5, children £3.50; longer options available).

BETWS-Y-COED   ☎01690

At the southern tip of the Vale of Conwy and the eastern edge of the Snowdonia mountains, the crowded but picturesque village of Betws-y-Coed (BET-oos uh COYD), often called just Betws, reeks of adventurism; *everyone* seems to be communing with the great outdoors. Coursing through town, the Conwy and Llugwy rivers crash over rocks and foamy rapids, while brooding pines darken the hills and lend to the scene a distinctly Alpine air.

▛ **TRANSPORTATION. Trains** (☎(08457) 484950) stop in Betws-y-Coed on the Conwy Valley line (see above). **Sherpa** bus #96, operated by Arriva Cymru, connects Betws-y-Coed with **Llanrwst** and **Llandudno,** stopping at most area hostels (M-Sa 4 per day); #96A arrives from **Llanberis** (40min.; direct 4 per day, others require transfer to bus #96 in Snowdon). Arriva bus #70 runs twice a day from **Corwen** (£2.15). Rent **bikes** from the laid-back cyclists at **Beics Betws**, beside the tourist information centre. (☎710829. £12 per half-day, £16 per day. Open daily 9am-5pm.)

▟ **PRACTICAL INFORMATION.** The main (and only real) street is **Holyhead Rd.**, which is also the A5. It runs northwest from the River Conwy, past the park at the town center, and makes a sharp turn to run west out of town toward Swallow

Falls. The self-proclaimed busiest **tourist information centre** (TIC) in north Wales, also a **National Park Information Centre,** is at the Old Stables, next to a park between the train station and Holyhead Rd. The spirited staff provides information on sights and timetables. (☎710426; fax 710665; www.betws-y-coed.co.uk. Open Easter-Oct. daily 10am-6pm; Nov.-Easter 9:30am-12:30pm and 1:30-4:30pm.) Between April and September, **guided walks** around Betws leave from the TIC. (All walks 6-8 mi., 5-6hr., Th-Su 9:55am. £3.50, children 50p.) A number of outdoor stores line Holyhead Rd., among them two **Cotswold** outlets, one next to the Royal Oak Hotel (☎710710), with a huge selection of gear, the other south of town focusing on specific activities such as cycling and climbing. (☎710234. Both open mid-July to Aug. M-F 9am-6pm, Sa-Su 9am-6:30pm; Sept. to mid-July M-Th 9am-5:30pm, F-Su 9am-6:30pm.) An **HSBC bank** hides at the southern edge of Holyhead Rd. (Open M 9:15am-2:30pm, Tu-F 9:15am-1pm.) The friendly folk at the **post office,** at the T-junction of Holyhead Rd. and Station Rd., **exchange currencies** and pleasantries. (Open M-F 9am-1pm and 2-5:30pm, Sa 9am-7:30pm.) **Postal code:** LL24 0AA.

⌐⌐ ACCOMMODATIONS AND FOOD. Two hostels rest conveniently near town: **YHA Lledr Valley** and **YHA Capel Curig** (see p. 473). Most **B&Bs** charge £17.50 or more and cluster along **Holyhead Rd.** For a comfy lounge and rooms with fine views of riverside lambs, head for **Glan Llugwy,** on the western edge of town. Make the brief walk along Holyhead Rd. toward Swallow Falls, or call kind owners Jean and Graham Brayne for a lift. (☎710592. £17.50-18.50 per person.) **Riverside,** also on Holyhead Rd., offers comfortable beds, TVs, and old-fashioned flavor above the pricey family restaurant. (☎/fax 710650; riverside4u@talk21.com. Singles £20; doubles £34, with bath £40. Discounts in off season.) **Riverside Caravan Park** suns itself by a cemetery behind the train station. (☎710310. Open Mar.-Oct. Tents or caravans £5 per adult, £2.50 per child. Electricity £2. Showers free. No large groups.)

For a supermarket experience, head to **Spar** at the northern bend of Holyhead Rd. (Open daily 8am-10pm.) Most restaurants in Betws-y-Coed cater to tourists and are priced accordingly. At **Three Gables,** Holyhead Rd., homemade pizza runs from £4.60-6.80, and dinnertime brings plenty o' seafood from £8.75-10.50. (☎710328. Open Easter-Oct. M-Su noon-9:30pm; Nov.-Easter F-Su noon-9:30pm.)

◪ SIGHTS. Betws is known for its eight **bridges,** especially Telford's 1815 cast-iron **Waterloo Bridge** at the village's southern end, built the year the battle ensured Napoleon's political demise. Near St. Michael's Church, the miniature **suspension footbridge,** which sways when trod upon, crosses the Conwy. **Pont-y-Pair Bridge,** "the bridge of the cauldron," crosses the Llugwy to the north. The first bridge was built in 1475; Inigo Jones may have contributed to building the second, which consists of 11 stone arches hopping from rock to rock. Behind the train station, weathered gravestones surround humble 14th-century **St. Michael's Church.**

Two miles west of town, signposted off the A5, the swift waters of the Llugwy crash over descending plateaus of rock at **Swallow Falls,** whose original Welsh name, Rhaeadr Ewynnol, means "foaming falls." (Open July-Aug. daily 9am-8pm; Easter-June and Sept. 9am-6pm; Oct.-Easter 24hr. turnstile-operated. £1.) Sherpa bus #96 between Betws and Snowdon stops at the falls, as do most #96A buses to Llanberis and #97A buses to Porthmadog (4min., 1-3 per hr.). Farther along the A5, "the Ugly House," **Tŷ Hyll,** is so named for its unfinished stone facade. According to local legend, a house once constructed in a day and a night (with smoke wafting out the chimney by morning) earned the builder the right to live there. (☎720287. Open Apr.-Sept. daily 9:30am-5:30pm; call for winter hours. £1, children free.)

VALLEY VILLAGES   ☎01492

The Vale of Conwy is still largely untouched by coach-bound tourists, leaving walkers, cyclists, and *Let's Go* loyalists to explore its gorgeous scenery.

BODNANT GARDENS. At the 80-acre Bodnant Gardens, 8 mi. south of Llandudno off the A470, Chilean Fire Bush flirts shamelessly with eucrypheas and hydrangea. The gardens often host summer evening events, including plays. To get there, take

Arriva bus #25 from Llandudno (40min., M-Sa 10 per day) to the garden gates or the Conwy Valley train (M-Sa 6 per day, Su 3 per day) to the Tal-y-Cafn stop 2 mi. away. (☎650460. Open mid-Mar. to Oct. daily 10am-5pm. £5.20, children £2.60.)

TREFRIW. To the south, the town of Trefriw sleeps along the River Crafnant. Lake Crafnant, 3 mi. uphill from town (along the road opposite the Fairy Hotel), is surrounded by some of the highest peaks in Snowdonia. North of town, 1½ mi. along the main road, a rust grotto spews the world's only fully licensed spa-water medicine at the **Trefriw Wells Spa.** Originally used to treat rheumatism and skin diseases, today the spa water eases iron deficiency. A month's supply goes for £6.50. (☎640057. Open Easter-Oct. daily 9:30am-5:30pm; Nov.-Easter M-Sa 10am-dusk, Su noon-dusk. £2.65, seniors £2.50, children £1.50, under 10 free.)

To reach Trefriw, take **Arriva bus** #19 from Conwy, Llandudno, or Llandudno Junction (M-Sa 1-2 per hr., Su 7 per day). B&Bs (£15-18) line Trefriw's long main street. The rustic **YHA Rowen,** halfway between Trefriw and Conwy, is a superb place to rest your weary bones after the treacherous mile hike uphill from the road; the ascent begins ¼ mi. down from the bus stop, which is served by #70 (M-Sa 3-4 times per day) and sometimes #19. (☎650089. Lockout 10am-5pm. Open May-Aug. Dorms £8.50, under 18 £5.75.)

LLANRWST. A useful transit town, Llanrwst has banks and a Tuesday **market.** Along the Conwy River, across the 1636 Old Bridge built by Inigo Jones, the 15th-century stone **Tu-Hwnt-i'r-Bont** hides a tearoom; check the timbers for multilingual graffiti. (Open Easter-Oct. Tu-Su 10:30am-5pm.) A 10min. walk past the tea house reaches **Gwydir Castle,** the 16th-century manor of Sir John Wynne. When the home was auctioned off in 1921, American newspaper giant William Randolph Hearst acquired Lot 88: the wall panels, doorframe, fireplace, and leather frieze of Gwydir's dining room. In 1994, the castle's new owners traced the room to a storage box in a New York museum, repurchased it, and unpacked Lot 88 to its former glory. Outside, the grounds shelter peacocks and a selflessly named yew tree. (☎641687. Open daily 10am-4:30pm. £3, children £1.50.)

LLANGOLLEN ☎01978

Set in a hollow in the hills near the English border, Llangollen (hlan-GO-hlen) hosts the annual International Musical Eisteddfod, which draws thousands every summer. Apart from this cultural extravaganza, all town attractions are natural. Walkers gently tread the surrounding hills on their way to Horseshoe Pass, and weekends bring whitewater canoeists slashing through neighboring streams and into the River Dee, which tumbles through town under a 14th-century bridge.

◪❷ TRANSPORTATION AND PRACTICAL INFORMATION. For a booming tourist town, Llangollen can be difficult to reach for the carless. Most public transport from outside Wales only gets as far as **Wrexham,** 30min. away; **Bryn Melyn** (☎860701) bus #X5 connects Wrexham and Llangollen (30min., M-Sa 2 per hr., £2.20). On Sundays, **Arriva Midland** (☎(01543) 466124) runs a winding version of bus #5 (40min., 4 per day). From Wrexham, **trains** (☎(08457) 484950) connect with **Chester, Shrewsbury,** and **London.** A closer train station to Llangollen, though less well served, is **Ruabon,** from which B&B owners may fetch weary backpackers. **National Express** (☎(08705) 808080) **bus** #420 comes into Wrexham from **London** (5½hr., 1 per day, £19.75). **Arriva Cymru** (☎(08706) 082608) bus #94 connects Llangollen to **Dolgellau** (2hr.; M-Sa 8 per day, Su 4 per day; £3.30) and **Barmouth** (2½hr.; M-Sa 7 per day, Su 4 per day; £4.90). Arriva Cymru's bus #70 runs twice a day from **Llanrwst** and **Betws-y-Coed** via **Corwen;** sometimes you have to change in Corwen, where various buses such as the #94 connect to Llangollen (1hr., £2.20).

The **tourist information centre** (TIC), Town Hall, Castle St., and the Eisteddfod office (see below) all list accommodations; the TIC books rooms for £1 and a 10% deposit. (☎860828; fax 861563; www.llangollen.org.uk. Open Easter-Oct. daily 10am-6pm; Nov.-Easter 9:30am-5pm.) Other services include: **Barclays bank,** opposite the TIC (open M-Tu and Th-F 10am-4pm, W 10:30am-4pm); **Blue Bay Launderette,** 3 Regent St. (wash £2, dry 20p per 5min.; open daily 9am-noon, 12:15-7pm); **Internet access** at **The Gallery Computer World,** 22 Chapel St., opposite the restaurant of the same name (☎ 869384; £3 per 30min.; open M-F 9am-5pm, Sa-Su 9am-noon; ask at the restaurant if no one's around); and the **post office,** 41 Castle St., with a **bureau de change** (open M-F 9am-5:30pm, Sa 9am-12:30pm). **Postal code:** LL20 8RW.

🛏🍴 ACCOMMODATIONS AND FOOD.

The Victorian manse that is the **YHA Llangollen,** Tyndwr Hall, Tyndwr Rd., lies 1½ mi. out of town. Follow the A5 toward Shrewsbury, bear right up Birch Hill, and after ½ mi. take a right at the Y-junction. (☎ 860330; fax 861709. Internet access from £1.50 for first 15min. Open mid-Feb. to Oct. Dorms £10.25, under 18 £7.) **B&Bs** (£15-20) are numerous in Llangollen, especially along Regent St. Just before Regent St., head up Hill St. to **Danika Guest House** for pleasant rooms with TVs, bath, and a tasty breakfast. (☎ (07931) 855646. £20 per person.) Expect a warm greeting from the proprietress of **Bryant Rose,** 31 Regent St., where TVs glow in comfortable, large rooms. (☎ 860389. Singles £20; twins £35; doubles £36.) **Campsites** abound; pick up fliers at the TIC to peruse your options, or try **Eirianfa Riverside Holiday Park,** a mile from town. Follow the A5 toward Corwen until you see the signs. (☎ 860919. 1- or 2-person tent £6, family tent £10. Electricity £2. Laundry and shower facilities.)

Come mealtime, splurge at **The Corn Mill,** Dee Ln., where the patio hangs low over the river. If the main courses (£7-12.25) are too hefty, spend a few pounds on a pint and watch the waterwheel that still spins frantically outside. (☎ 869555. Open M-Sa noon-11pm, Su noon-9pm; food served noon-9:30pm.) At **Cafe and Books,** 17 Castle St., thumb hundreds of used volumes upstairs and savor meals downstairs; the all-day breakfast is £3.85. (☎ 861963. Open Apr.-Sept. daily 9am-6pm; Oct.-May 9am-5pm.) Just up Castle St., **Spar** sells fruits, vegetables, and refreshments. (Open M-Sa 8am-11pm, Su 8am-10:30pm.)

📷 SIGHTS.

Up Hill St. from the town center, **Plas Newydd** is the former home of two noblewomen who fled Ireland in 1778. Charmed by the area, the "Ladies of Llangollen" settled into village life, dividing their time between self-improvement and the elaborate decoration of the house, evident in the beautiful carved-oak walls. As "two of the most celebrated virgins in Europe," their still-undefined relationship—idealized as a "romantic friendship"—appealed to many intellectuals of their time. Wellington and Sir Walter Scott visited, as did Wordsworth, who was moved to pen a poem in their honor. (☎ 861314. Open Easter-Oct. daily 10am-5pm. £2.50, children £1.25, families £6.) Perched on a steep mount high above town are the lyrical ruins of ⬛**Castell Dinas Brân** (Crow Castle), perfect for picnickers. The panoramic drop-away view spans from the peaks of Snowdonia to the flat English midlands. Two main paths access the castle; a 40min. gravel path zig-zags directly up the side, while an hour-long walk runs along a pastoral road and up the grassy hillside. Both are well marked, steep, scoff at weak shoes, and begin just over the canal bridge, next to Dinbryn Rd. A 30min. amble from Llangollen along Abbey Rd., the ruins of 13th-century **Valle Crucis Abbey** grace a leafy valley. Its empty arches frame trees and sky, along with an unfortunate cluster of caravans in the park next door. (☎ 860326. Open Apr.-Sept. daily 10am-5pm; Oct.-Mar. always open. £2, concessions £1.50, families £5.50. Free in winter.)

🎵 THE EISTEDDFOD.

Every summer, the town's population of 3,000 swells to 80,000 for the **International Musical Eisteddfod** (ice-TETH-vod), not to be confused with the roaming Royal National Eisteddfod (see **Ffestivals,** p. 427). From July 8-14 in 2002, the hills will be alive with the singing and dancing of competitors from 50 countries—much to the chagrin of groggy livestock. Book tickets and rooms far in advance through the **Eisteddfod Box Office** or by email at tickets@international-eisteddfod.co.uk. (☎ 862000; fax 862002; www.international-eisteddfod.co.uk. Phone bookings M-F 9am-5pm. Box office open from Feb. 2001 M-Th 9am-4pm, F 9am-3pm. Unreserved seat and admission to grounds on day of show £5, seniors £4, children £3, families £12; concert tickets £7-13.)

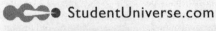

SCOTLAND

A distinct nation within the United Kingdom, Scotland at its best is a world apart. Its cities revel in a culture all their own, from the fevered nightlife of Glasgow to the festival energies of Edinburgh. A little over half the size of England but with a tenth of its population, Scotland possesses open spaces and natural splendor its southern neighbor cannot rival. The craggy, heathered mountains and silver beaches of the west coast and the luminescent mists of the Hebrides solicit any traveler's awe, while farmlands to the south and peaceful fishing villages on the east coast harbor a gentler beauty.

Most Scots will welcome you with geniality and pride; as in the other few unharried corners of the world, hospitality and conversation are highly valued. That is, unless you call them English. British, fine, but *never* English. Before reluctantly joining with England in 1707, the Scots defended their independence for hundreds of years. Since the union, they have nurtured a separate identity, retaining control over schools, churches, and the judicial system. In 1999, Scots finally regained a separate parliament, which gave them more power over domestic tax laws and strengthened their national identity. While the kilts, bagpipes, and find-your-own-clan kits of Glasgow, Edinburgh, and Aberdeen grow swiftly tiresome, a visit to the less touristed regions of Scotland will allow you to encounter the inheritors of ancient traditions: a B&B proprietor speaking Gaelic to her grandchildren, a crofter cutting peat, or a fisherman setting out in his skiff at dawn.

GETTING THERE

Reaching Scotland from outside Britain is usually easiest and cheapest through London, where the **Scottish Tourist Board,** 19 Cockspur St., SW1 Y5BL, stocks gads of brochures and books train, bus, and plane tickets. (☎(020) 7321 5752. Tube: Charing Cross or Piccadilly Circus. Open M-F 9am-6pm, Sa 10am-5pm.)

BY PLANE. Flights are predictably expensive. British Airways (☎(0845) 722 2111) sells a limited number of APEX return tickets starting at £70. British Midland (☎(08706) 070555) offers a Saver fare from London to Glasgow (from £70 return). Book as far in advance as you can (2 weeks if possible) for the cheapest fare. Scotland is linked by ferry (see **By Ferry,** p. 35) to Northern Ireland and the Isle of Man.

BY TRAIN. From London, trains (☎(08547) 484950) to **Edinburgh** and **Glasgow** take only 6hr., but fares are steep—trains can cost up to £95. Overnight trains offer sleeper berths for an extra £30. Book cheaper APEX fares early.

BY BUS. Although the bus trip from **London** takes more than 7hr., it is significantly cheaper than train travel. **National Express** (☎(08705) 808080) services connect England and Scotland via **Glasgow** and **Edinburgh;** see those cities' **Transportation** listings for journey times, frequencies, and prices.

LOCAL TRANSPORTATION

The *Touring Map of Scotland* (£3.50) and the *Touring Guide of Scotland* (£5), available at tourist information centres, provide fodder for sojourn planners.

BY BUS AND TRAIN

In the Lowlands (south of Stirling and north of the Borders), train and bus connections are frequent. In the Highlands, trains snake slowly on a few restricted routes, bypassing the northwest almost entirely, and many stations are unstaffed or non-existent—purchase tickets on board. In general, buses are the best way to travel. They're usually more frequent and far-reaching than trains and always cheaper,

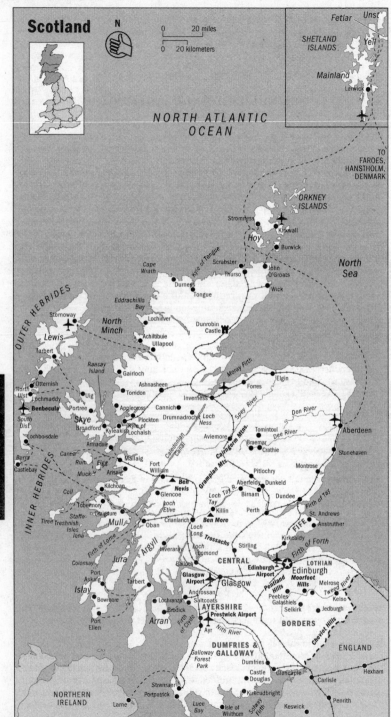

Scotland

N

0   20 miles
0   20 kilometers

SHETLAND ISLANDS

Fetlar
Unst
Yell
Mainland
Lerwick

NORTH ATLANTIC OCEAN

TO FAROES, HANSTHOLM, DENMARK

North Sea

ORKNEY ISLANDS

Stromness
Kirkwall
Hoy
Burwick

Scrabster
Thurso
John O'Groats
Wick

Cape Wrath
Kyle of Tongue
Durness
Tongue
Dunrobin Castle

Eddrachillis Bay
Lochinver
Achiltibuie
Ullapool

OUTER HEBRIDES
North Minch

Stornoway
Lewis
Tarbert
Otternish
North Uist
Lochmaddy
Benbecula
South Uist
Lochboisdale
Barra
Castlebay

Gairloch
Ashnasheen
Torridon
Cannich
Inverness
Drumnadrochit
Loch Ness

Moray Firth
Forres
Elgin

Spey River
Don River
Dee River
Aberdeen
Stonehaven

Raasay Island
Uig
Portree
Skye
Broadford
Plockton
Kyle of Lochalsh
Applecross
Kyleakin
Armadale

Aviemore
Cairngorm Mtns.
Tomintoul
Braemar
Crathie

INNER HEBRIDES
Canna
Rum
Eigg
Muck
Coll
Tiree
Treshnish Isles
Iona
Staffa
Mull
Colonsay
Jura
Islay
Port Askaig
Bowmore
Port Ellen

Mallaig
Arisaig
Ben Nevis
Glencoe
Loch Etive
Kilchoan
Tobermory
Craignure
Oban
Firth of Lorne
Argyll
Inveraray
Loch Awe

Fort William
Caledonian Canal

Grampian Mtns.
Pitlochry
Aberfeldy
Dunkeld
Loch Tay R.
Loch Tay
Killin
Birnam
Ben More
Crianlarich
Trossachs
Loch Lomond
Balloch
Stirling
CENTRAL

Perth
Dundee
Firth of Tay
St. Andrews
Anstruther
FIFE
Kirkcaldy
Firth of Forth
LOTHIAN
Edinburgh Airport
Edinburgh
Pentland Hills
Moorfoot Hills
Melrose
Tweed River
Kelso

Glasgow Airport
Glasgow
Androssan
Saltcoats
AYERSHIRE
Prestwick Airport
Lochranza
Brodick
Arran
Firth of Clyde
Ayr
Nith River

Peebles
Galashiels
Selkirk
Jedburgh
BORDERS
Cheviot Hills
ENGLAND

DUMFRIES & GALLOWAY
Galloway Forest Park
Dumfries
Castle Douglas
Glencaple
Carlisle
Hexham

NORTHERN IRELAND
Larne
Stranraer
Portpatrick
Luce Bay
Isle of Whithorn
Kirkcudbright
Solway Firth
Keswick
Penrith

SCOTLAND

although nonsmokers may find smoggy buses less hospitable than nonsmoking train cars. **Scottish Citylink** (☎ (08705) 505050) provides most intercity service. Bus service declines in the northwest Highlands and grinds to a halt on Sundays.

A great money-saver is the **Freedom of Scotland Travelpass.** It allows unlimited train travel and transportation on most Caledonian MacBrayne ferries, with discounts on some other ferry lines. Purchase the pass *before* traveling to Britain at any Eurail office or by calling (888) 667-9734 (see **By Train,** p. 37; 4 days in 8 US$125; 8 days in 15 US$180; 12 days in 15 US$215; children half-price).

BUS TOURS

If you have limited time in Scotland, or if you want to be thrown together with a group of backpackers, a thriving industry of backpacker tour companies is eagerly poised to whisk you into the Highlands. The two main companies are **MacBackpackers** (☎ (0131) 558 9900; www.macbackpackers.com) and **HAGGiS** (☎ (0131) 557 9393; www.radicaltravel.com), whose offices stare each other down across Edinburgh's High Street (at 105 and 60, respectively). Both cater to the young and adventurous with a number of one- to seven-day tours of the Highlands departing from Edinburgh, and both run hop-on/hop-off tours that let you travel Scotland at your own pace (usually within three months), picking you up anywhere along a tour route and returning you to your original destination. MacBackpackers, specializing in tours of the hop-on/hop-off variety, guarantees accommodation at any of the super-social **Scotland's Top Hostels** chain associated with the company in Edinburgh, Ft. William, Skye, Oban, and Inverness. HAGGiS is geared more toward set tours with specific itineraries (some in England and Ireland), which are slightly more expensive but run by witty and knowledgeable local guides. Although they do not operate their own hostels, HAGGiS does guarantee accommodation at a few favorite stopping points. See **Bus Tours,** p. 42, for prices. **Celtic Connection** (☎ 225 3330; www.thecelticconnection.co.uk) covers Scotland in a variety of three- to seven-day tours, with one-way, return, or hop-on/hop-off options. Book ahead for all companies. Other, less youth-oriented companies provide day and half-day bus tours. **Scotline Tours,** 87 High St. in Edinburgh (☎ 557 0162), charges £10-20, with student and child concessions.

DRIVING

Though Southern and Central Scotland are well served by public transportation, travel in the Highlands and Islands may be greatly restricted without a car. Driving gives you the freedom to explore Scotland at your own pace and to access some of its most remote quarters without fear of being stranded by complicated bus services. As in the rest of Britain, driving in Scotland is on the left, the minimum age to drive with a valid foreign license is 17, and the minimum age to rent is 21, often higher. (For information on driving in the UK, see **By Car,** p. 43.) In rural areas, particularly the Highlands, roads are often **single-track:** both directions of traffic share one lane, and drivers must be prepared to slow to a crawl to negotiate oncoming traffic. The right lane usually has priority; left-hand traffic must reverse to **passing places** (short-term shoulders) to enable opposing traffic to pass, as well as to allow same-way traffic to overtake. Many rural roads are also liberally sprinkled with livestock. Drive slowly and be prepared to wait until the flocks move on.

BIKING

Scotland's biking terrain is scenic and challenging. You can usually rent bikes even in very small towns and transport them by ferry for little or no charge. Fife and regions south of Edinburgh and Glasgow offer gentle country pedaling, and both the northern and western isles are negotiable by bicycle. In the Highlands, touring is more difficult. Most major roads have only one lane, and locals drive at high speeds—keep your eye out for passing places. Bringing a bike to the Highlands by public transportation can be as difficult as pedaling there, as many trains can carry only four or fewer bikes; reservations (£3) are essential. Harry Henniker's *101 Bike Routes in Scotland* (£10) is worth a look before you set out.

MUNRO BAGGING Scottish mountaineering is dominated by the frequently obsessive practice of Munro Bagging. Hugh T. Munro compiled the original list of Scottish peaks over 3000 ft. in 1891; today about 280 are recorded. Any addition sends thousands of hikers scrambling up previously unnoticed peaks to maintain their distinction of having "bagged every Munro." Some people accomplish this feat over a lifetime of hiking; others do it in a frenetic six months. Thankfully, only one Munro, the Inaccessible Pinnacle on Skye, requires technical rock-climbing skills. *The Munros* (£17), produced by the Scottish Mountaineering Club, presents a list of the peaks along with climbing information. In *The First Fifty: Munro Bagging Without a Beard* (£9), the irreverent Muriel Gray presents a humorous account of this compulsive sport.

HITCHHIKING

Many hitchhike in Scotland, except in areas such as the northwest and Inverness, where cars packed with families of tourists make up much of the traffic. Hitchhikers report that drivers tend to be most receptive in the least-traveled areas. Far to the northwest and in the Western Isles, the sabbath is strictly observed, making it difficult or impossible to get a ride on Sundays. Hitchhiking in Scotland, as in many places, is accompanied by many risks; *Let's Go* does not recommend it as a safe mode of transport.

HIKING

Two long-distance footpaths were planned and marked by the Countryside Commission under the Countryside Act of 1967. The **West Highland Way** begins just north of Glasgow in Milngavie and snakes 95 mi. north along Loch Lomond, through Glen Coe to Fort William and Ben Nevis ("from Scotland's largest city to its highest mountain"). The **Southern Upland Way** runs 212 mi. from Portpatrick on the southwest coast to Cockburnspath on the east coast, passing through Galloway Forest Park and the Borders. Most tourist information centres distribute simple maps of the Ways as well as a list of accommodations along the routes. For information on these paths, write or call the **Scottish Tourist Board**, 23 Ravelston Terr., Edinburgh EH4 3EU (☎(0131) 332 2433). Detailed guidebooks for both are available at most bookstores.

Mountain areas like the Cuillins, the Torridons, Glen Nevis, and Glen Coe all have hostels situated in the midst of the ranges, providing bases for spectacular round-trip hikes or bike rides. You can also walk along mainland Britain's highest cliffs at Cape Wrath or ramble across the eerie moors of the Outer Hebrides.

One of the most attractive aspects of hiking in Scotland is that you can often pick your own route across the heather (you should check first with the local ranger or landowner). The wilds do pose certain dangers. Stone markers can be unreliable, and expanses of open heather will often disorient. Heavy mists are always a possibility, and blizzards can surprise you even in July. Never go up into the mountains without proper equipment (see **Wilderness Safety,** p. 54, for details). Leave a copy of your planned route and timetable at the hostel or nearest mountain rescue station, and, from mid-August to mid-October, always ask the hostel warden about areas in which deer hunters might be at work. For information on walking and mountaineering in Scotland, consult Poucher's *The Scottish Peaks* (£13) or the introductory Tourist Board booklet, *Walk Scotland*.

LIFE AND TIMES

The beginnings of Scottish history are shrouded in mist. Little is known of the early people who inhabited Scotland, save that their strength allowed them to repel Roman incursions in their land. **Emperor Hadrian** built a wall across the north of England to protect against attacks from the north (see **An Island to Call Their Own,** p. 67). Other invading tribes were more successful, and by AD 600 the Scottish mainland was inhabited by four groups. The **Picts,** originally the most powerful of the bunch, are also the most mysterious—nothing remains of their language, and only a collection of carved stones and references to them in Latin histories provide information. The Celtic **Scots** arrived from Ireland in the 4th century, bringing their Gaelic language and Christian religion. The Germanic **Angles** invaded Scotland from northern England in the 6th century. In AD 843, the Scots, under **King Kenneth MacAlpin** (Kenneth I), decisively defeated the Picts and formed a joint kingdom. United by the threat of encroaching **Vikings,** various groups were led by the first king of all Scotland, **Duncan,** who was killed by a certain Macbeth in 1040.

The House of Canmore (literally "big-headed" after Duncan's son Malcolm, who was cranially well-endowed) reigned over Scotland until the close of the 13th century. Allied through marriages with the Norman lords who had come to dominate England, the Scottish monarchs found their independence considerably threatened by the increasingly powerful nation to the south. The 13th-century reigns of **Alexander II** and **Alexander III** were characterized by an uneasy peace punctuated with periodic skirmishes, while the Scottish kings successfully contained both civil revolts and Scandinavian attacks.

SQUABBLES WITH ENGLAND

Alexander III died without an heir, and the ensuing contest over the Scottish crown fueled the territorial ambitions of **Edward I** of England. **John Balliol** took the kingship, only to be subjugated by Edward and lose control over most of Scotland to the English monarch. The **Wars of Independence** bred heroic figures like William Wallace (yes, the *Braveheart* guy), who bravely, and for a time successfully, led a company of Scots against the English. But it was the patient and cunning **Robert the Bruce** who emerged as Scotland's leader; against all odds, he led the Scots to victory over Edward II's forces at the **Battle of Bannockburn** in 1314, which won Scotland her independence from the English crown.

In the next centuries the monarchy set rebellious nobles against each other in an attempt to preserve its own waning position. The Scottish kings frequently capitalized on the "Auld Alliance" with France and prevented the English crown from exploiting the monarchy's difficulties with dissatisfied barons. The reigns of **James IV** (1488-1513) and **James V** (1513-42) witnessed the Renaissance's arrival in Scotland just as the effects of the **Reformation** began to appear throughout the country.

The death of James V left the infant **Mary, Queen of Scots** (1542-67), on the throne. The Queen was promptly sent to France, where she later married the future François II. Scottish nobles and commoners were drawn to the appeal of Protestantism, embodied in the form of iconoclastic preacher **John Knox.** Lacking a strong ruler during Mary's absence, Scotland was vulnerable to passionate Protestant revolts, as much political as they were religious. In 1560, the monarchy capitulated. The Protestant **Scottish Parliament** denied the Pope's authority in Scotland and established the Presbyterian Church as Scotland's new official church.

In 1561, after the death of her husband, staunchly Catholic Mary returned to Scotland. Never accepted by Scottish nobles or Protestants, Mary's rule fanned the flames of discontent, and civil war resulted in her forced abdication and imprisonment in 1567. She escaped her Scottish captors only to find another set of shackles across the border; as the Queen languished in an English prison, her son **James VI** was made King. Nine years later, with Catholic Spain a rising threat, Queen Elizabeth of England made a tentative alliance with the nominally Protestant James while executing his mother Mary in 1587.

UNION WITH ENGLAND

Elizabeth's death without an heir in 1603 left James VI to be crowned **James I** of England, uniting both countries under a single crown. James ruled from London, while his half-hearted attempts to reconcile the Scots to British rule were tartly resisted. Scottish Presbyterians supported Cromwellian forces against James's successor **Charles I** during the **English Civil Wars.** Nonetheless, when the English Parliament executed Charles in 1649, the Scots again switched allegiance and declared the headless king's heir to be King Charles II. **Oliver Cromwell** handily defeated him as well, but in a conciliatory gesture gave Scotland representation in the English Parliament. Though Cromwell's governing body eventually dissolved, the political precedent of Scottish representation in Parliament endured.

Two more Stuart monarchs, Charles II and James II, reigned in London after the Civil War. Wide discontent with James's rule led to the Glorious Revolution of 1688, which put the Dutchman **William of Orange** on the English throne. The **War of the Spanish Succession** (1701-1714) convinced Scotland's leaders that its Presbyterian interests were safer with the Anglicans than with long-standing ally Catholic France, and in 1707 the Scottish and English Parliaments were officially united, formally joining the two countries politically, while allowing Scotland to retain significant control over its own ecclesiastical, legal, and judicial affairs.

THE JACOBITE REBELLION

The Scottish supporters of **James II** never accepted the 1707 Union, and after a series of unsuccessful uprisings, they launched the "Forty-Five," the events of 1745 that have captured the imagination of Scots and romantics alike ever since. James's grandson **Bonnie Prince Charlie** landed in Scotland, where he succeeded in mustering unseasoned troops from various Scottish clans. From Glenfinnan, Bonnie Prince Charlie rallied his troops, marching to Edinburgh, where he kept court and prepared for full rebellion. On the march to London, however, the venture was hampered by desertions and the uncertainty of French support, prompting a return to Scotland. Modest French support did materialize, and with new troops under the Scottish standard, Charles led his troops to victory at Stirling and Falkirk in 1746. After that, the rebellion once again collapsed; although Charles eventually escaped to France, his Highland army fell on the battlefield of Culloden.

ENLIGHTENMENT AND THE CLEARANCES

Aside from Jacobite political turmoil, the 18th century proved to be the most economically and culturally prosperous in Scotland's history. As agriculture, industry, and trading all boomed, a vibrant intellectual environment produced such luminaries as **Adam Smith** and **David Hume.** In the 19th century, although political reforms did much to improve social conditions, economic problems proved disastrous. The Highlands in particular were affected by a rapidly growing population combined with lack of available land and food, archaic farming methods, and the demands of rapacious landlords. The resulting poverty resulted in mass emigration, mostly to North America, and the infamous **Clearances.** Between 1811 and 1820, the Sutherland Clearances, undertaken by the Marquis of Stafford, forcibly relocated poor farmers from their lands to the coasts, where farming could be supplemented by fishing. Resistance to the relocations was met with violence—homes were burned and countless people killed. Other Clearances occurred throughout the Highlands; in 1853, the Clearances at Glengarry evicted entire families from their homes and land, whereupon they were not just relocated to another area in Scotland, but forcibly packed on boats and shipped overseas. Meanwhile, the **Industrial Revolution** led to urban growth in southern Scotland and increasingly poor working and living conditions for new industrial laborers.

THE 20TH CENTURY

Scotland, like the rest of Britain, lost a generation of young men in **World War I,** after which the economic depression of the 1930s only exacerbated economic difficulties. Organized labor gained clout in factories and in politics, leading to strong Scottish support for the Labour Party and, later, the **Scottish National Party (SNP),** founded in 1934. Surprisingly, a 1979 referendum on devolution from England was unsuccessful due to an insufficient number of favorable Scottish votes.

Today, Scotland has 72 seats in the United Kingdom's **House of Commons** and is largely integrated into the British economy. The May 1997 elections swept the Conservatives in Scotland out of power and accrued support for the SNP, which bases its platform on devolution for the Scottish nation. September of 1997 brought a victory for the proponents of home rule; Scottish voters supported devolution by an overwhelming 3:1 margin, and the first elections for the new Assembly occurred in 1999. Though the Assembly is able to levy taxes and legislate in other areas, Westminster still controls foreign affairs and fiscal policy. With many Scottish politicians more closely tied to London than to their own constituents, only time will tell whether Scotland is truly on the road to greater independence.

LANGUAGE

Although the early Picts left no record of their language (aside from some influence in place names), settlers in southern Scotland well into the 7th century heard a **Celtic** language related to Welsh. These settlers also brought their native tongues—Celtic Gaelic from Ireland, Norse from Scandinavia, and an early form of English (Inglis) brought by the Angles from northern England. By the 11th century, **Scottish Gaelic** (pronounced GAYL-ick), subsuming Norse and the earlier Celtic and Pictish languages, had become the official language of Scottish law. As the political power of southern Scotland began to rise in the late 11th and early 12th centuries, Gaelic speakers migrated primarily to the Highlands and Islands in northwest Scotland, and Inglis became the language of the Lowlands and, eventually, of the Scottish monarchy. Beginning as a dialectical variation of the English developing in England, Inglis, or **Scots** as it is known, was influenced by Flemish, French, and Latin, and developed into a distinctive linguistic unit.

While a number of post-1700 Scottish literati, most notably Robert Burns and the contemporary Hugh MacDiarmid, have composed in Scots, union with Britain and the political and cultural power of England in the 18th and 19th centuries led to the rise of England's language in Scotland. Today, though **standard English** is spoken throughout Scotland, Scots influences the English of many Scottish men and women. You may not understand a word or two in a sentence. In the Highlands, for example, the "ch" becomes a soft "h," as in the German "ch" sound. Modern Scottish Gaelic, a linguistic cousin of Modern Irish, is spoken by at least 65,000 people in Scotland today, particularly in the western islands. Recent attempts to revive Gaelic have led to its introduction in the classroom, ensuring that some form of the language will continue to exist in Scotland for years to come. For a glossary of Scottish Gaelic and Scots words and phrases, see p. 753.

LITERATURE

Spanning the centuries and including composition in three languages—Scottish Gaelic, Scots, and English—Scottish literature embodies a complexity of experience. In a nation where stories and myths have long been recounted by the fireside, **oral literature** is as much a part of Scotland's literary tradition as novels. Most traces of medieval Scottish manuscripts have unfortunately been lost—not surprising, since raids on monastic centers of learning during this period were fierce and frequent, effectively erasing pre-14th-century literary records. **John Barbour** is the best-known writer in Early Scots—his *The Bruce* (c. 1375) preceded Chaucer and favorably chronicled the life of King Robert I in an attempt to strengthen national unity. **William Dunbar** (1460-1521) composed Middle Scots verse under James IV and is today considered representative of Scots poetry.

In 1760, **James Macpherson** published versions of **"Ossian,"** supposedly an ancient Scottish bard to rival Homer; Macpherson was widely discredited when he refused to produce the manuscripts that he claimed to be translating. **James Boswell** (1740-95), the biographer of Samuel Johnson, composed Scots verse as well as voluminous journals detailing his travels through Great Britain and the Continent. "Scotland's National Bard," **Robert Burns** (1759-96), was acutely aware of his heritage as he bucked pressure from the south that urged him to write in English, instead composing in his native Scots. **Sir Walter Scott** (1771-1832) was among the first Scottish authors to achieve international accolades for his work. *Ivanhoe*, a chivalrous tale of knights and damsels, is one of the best-known, if sappy, novels of all time. **Robert Louis Stevenson** (1850-94) is most famous for his tales of high adven-

---

HAGGIS: WHAT'S IN THERE? Restaurants throughout Scotland produce steamin' plates o' haggis for eager tourists, but we at *Let's Go* believe all should know what's inside that strange-looking bundle before taking the plunge. An age-old recipe calls for the following ingredients: the large stomach bag of a sheep, the small (knight's hood) bag, the pluck (including lights (lungs), liver, and heart), beef, suet, oatmeal, onions, pepper, and salt. Today's haggis is available conveniently canned and includes: lamb, lamb offal, oatmeal, wheat flour (healthy, no?), beef, suet, onions, salt, spices, stock, and liquor (1%).

---

ture, including *Treasure Island* and *Kidnapped*, which still fuel children's imaginations. His *Strange Case of Dr. Jekyll and Mr. Hyde* is nominally set in London, but any Scot would recognize the familiar setting as Edinburgh. Another of Edinburgh's authorial sons include **Sir Arthur Conan Doyle** (1859-1930), whose *Sherlock Holmes* series is beloved by mystery fans the world over.

Scotland's literary present is as vibrant as its past. In the twentieth century, poets **Hugh MacDiarmid** and **Edwin Morgan** have attracted the most attention, while novelists **Lewis Grassic Gibbon** and **Nell Gunn** used their pens to develop the nation's prose tradition. More recent novelists include **Alasdair Gray, Tom Leonard, Janice Galloway,** and **James Kelman,** who won 1995's Booker Prize for his controversial, sharp-edged novel *How Late It Was, How Late. Trainspotting*, the 1993 novel about Edinburgh drug-addicts by **Irvine Welsh,** and its 1996 film adaptation have been both condemned as amoral and hailed as chronicles of a new generation.

MUSIC

The Gaelic music of the West has its roots in the traditional music of Scotland's Irish settlers; as in Ireland, **ceilidhs,** spirited gatherings of music and dance, bring jigs, reels, and Gaelic songs to halls and pubs. Although there are no extant scores of Gaelic music prior to the 17th century, evidence suggests the *clarsach*, a Celtic harp, was the primary medium for musical expression until the 16th century, when the Highlander's **bagpipes** and the violin introduced new creative possibilities. Scots musical heritage centers around **ballads,** dramatic narrative songs. Scotland today possesses a quality national symphony orchestra and opera company.

In the 1970s and 80s, Scotland played a significant role in the development of popular music, launching **The Rezillos, The Skids, Average White Band,** Glasgow's **Orange Juice,** Edinburgh's **Josef K,** and the record label Postcard, which favored Byrdsy guitar chimes and winsome, coy-boy singers. Although mainstream rock was popular during the early 1990s, with groups such as **The Wake, The Proclaimers,** and Aberdeen's **Kitchen Cynics,** Scottish punk rages once again. Slampt and Vesuvius record labels promote Scottish punk bands, including the suggestively named **Yummy Fur** and **Lung Leg.** The quiet folk-rock of **Belle and Sebastian** wails throughout Edinburgh and Glasgow, and Scotland has also mastered the ubiquitous Britpop genre with **Texas** and **Travis,** bands popular on both sides of the border and abroad.

FOOD AND DRINK

The frequenter of B&Bs will encounter a glorious **Scottish breakfast,** including oat cakes, porridge, and marmalade. In general, however, Scottish cuisine greatly resembles English food. Aside from delicious, buttery **shortbread,** visitors are unlikely to take a shine to traditional Scottish dishes, most notably the infamous **haggis,** made from a sheep's stomach. The food might be a let-down, but Scotland's **whisky** (spelled without the "e") certainly is not. Scotch whisky is either "single malt" (from a single distillery), or "blended" (a mixture of several different brands). The malts are excellent and distinctive, the blends the same as those available abroad. Due to heavy taxes on alcohol sold in Britain, Scotch may be cheaper at home or from duty-free stores than it is in Scotland. The Scots know how to party: more generous licensing laws than those in England and Wales mean drinks are served later and pubs open longer.

FESTIVALS

Weekend clan gatherings, bagpipe competitions, and Highland games occur frequently in Scotland, especially in summer. Check for events at tourist information centres and in the local newspapers for the area in which you end up. In addition, the Scottish Tourist Board publishes the annual *Scotland Events*, which details happenings across Scotland. Traditional **Scottish games** originated from competitions in which participants could use only common objects, such as hammers, rounded stones, and tree trunks. Although "tossing the caber" (a pine trunk) may look simple, it actually requires a good deal of talent and practice. *Let's Go* does not recommend participating in caber-tossing for the uninitiated tourist.

Each year a slew of events and festivals celebrates Scotland's distinctive history and culture. June and July's **Common Ridings** in the Borders (p. 523) and the raucous **Up-Helly-A'** in Shetland on the last Tuesday in January (p. 630) are among the best known. Above all events towers the **Edinburgh International Festival** (Aug. 11-31 in 2002; ☎(0131) 473 2001), the largest international festival in the world. The concentration of musical and theatrical events in the space of three weeks is dizzying; Edinburgh's cafes and shops open to all hours and pipers roam the streets. Be sure to catch the **Fringe Festival** (Aug. 4-26 in 2002; ☎(0131) 226 5257), the much less costly sibling of the International Festival. There are literally hundreds of performances every day, including drama, comedy acts, jazz, and a bit of the bizarre. For more information, see p. 521.

YOU OUGHTA BE IN PICTURES

If Scotland looks familiar, it's probably because you've seen parts of it in a dozen movies. Go figure: grand, sweeping landscapes make a nice cinematic backdrop. But the obsessive among us insist on knowing exactly where Mel Gibson, Ewan McGregor, and that dude from Highlander slew Englishmen, shot heroin, and in general screamed until they were blue in the face. For those who must view life through a movie screen, *Let's Go* provides a handy how-to and where-to on reenacting your favorite big-screen Scotlands:

Highlander: So there can be only one castle, and it's **Eilean Donan Castle** (p. 603) at the heads of Loch Long, Loch Alsh, and Loch Duich, near Kyle of Lochalsh. If you haven't seen the movie, you've seen the castle on just about every calendar, tourist brochure, and shortbread tin related to Scotland. Prance around on the photogenic stone bridge and try not to behead any tourists.

Trainspotting: Grab three buddies and a bottle of vodka and head out to **Rannoch Moor**, east of Glen Coe (p. 595). After stepping off the train, walk about 100 ft. toward Buchuaille Etive Mor and come to the realization that Scotland has been "colonized by wankers." Or run frantically down Princes St. in **Edinburgh** (p. 505) after breaking into cars and stealing their radios. *Let's Go* does not recommend shooting heroin after selling stolen goods, and wouldn't know where to get either, anyway.

Braveheart: Hike out to **Glen Nevis**, east of **Fort William** (p. 595), and run up to the summit of one of the mountains while a rotating helicopter films a 360° panorama of your striking image against the horizon. Pretend that the English have killed your father and brother and recently slit your wife's throat, but comfort yourself with the knowledge that you'll get to sleep with the really hot French princess.

Monty Python and the Holy Grail: Rent a boat and row out to the Castle of the Holy Grail, which is actually **Castle Stalker** (p. 570), on Loch Linnhe, by Appin. You might need to ask the family that owns the castle for permission; otherwise, like King Arthur, you could end up getting arrested by the police.

Hamlet: To follow in Mel Gibson's footsteps as the famous Dane, climb the dramatic cliffs by **Dunnottar Castle** (p. 583), in Stonehaven south of Aberdeen, and recite the "To be or not to be" soliloquy. Bring a human skull for effect.

SCOTLAND

SOUTHERN SCOTLAND

Stark contrasts distinguish southern Scotland: just west of burgeoning cities, the beautiful Isle of Arran is an isolated refuge with subtropical climates and Highland tranquility. Until the 17th century, southern Scotland was characterized by skirmishes with its southern neighbors, from the Romans who battled the Picts to the interminable wars with England. The Borders region to the southeast contains monuments and ruins to mark these struggles, and Dumfries and Galloway in the southwest are rich in tales of local-born Robert the Bruce, who led Scotland to independence at Bannockburn in 1314. Both areas have long since calmed, and now walkers and cyclists enjoy their serenity while literary buffs visit the various sites dedicated to national literary icon Robert Burns. Southern Scotland's true draws, though, are the great cities of Edinburgh and Glasgow; nearly 80% of Scotland's population lives in the cities' greater metropolitan areas by the rivers Forth and Clyde. A fountainhead of the Enlightenment and Scotland's capital, Edinburgh preserves its classical beauty and draws enormous crowds each summer during its famous festival. Not to be outdone, Glasgow offers formidable art collections and architecture by day and a kinetic club and pub scene by night.

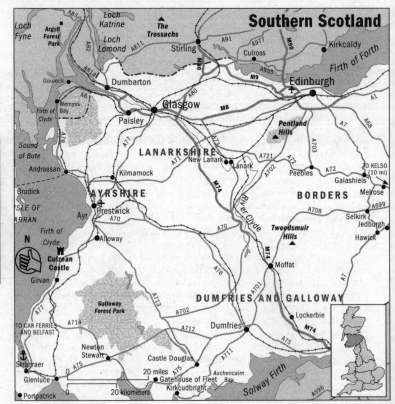

EDINBURGH ☎ 0131

This profusion of eccentricities, this dream in masonry and living rock is not a drop-scene in a theatre, but a city in the world of reality.
  —Robert Louis Stevenson

A city of elegant stone amid rolling hills and ancient volcanoes, Edinburgh (ED-din-bur-ra; pop. 500,000) is the jewel of Scotland. It's next to impossible to have a poor time here, where friendliness thrives, festivals reign, and rollicking pubs pack beneath the regal shadow of Edinburgh Castle. Since David I granted it burgh (town) status in 1130, Edinburgh has been a site of cultural significance. It was the poetic and musical center of the court of the medieval Stuarts, and the seeds of the Scottish Reformation were later sown here when John Knox became minister of St. Giles Cathedral. In the 18th century, the city's dim alleys welcomed first Bonnie Prince Charlie's premature victory celebration, then, more permanently, the leaders of the Scottish Enlightenment; brilliant intellectuals David Hume and Adam Smith joined writers and artists in a heady, forward-thinking atmosphere.

The modern city continues as a cultural beacon, and today its crusted medieval spires rise above streets infused with cosmopolitan verve. During the August festival, the city becomes a theatrical, musical, and literary magnet, drawing international talent and enthusiastic crowds. Motivated largely by tourism, new youth hostels, museums, and government buildings are springing up city-wide. A controversial new Parliament Building grows at a snail's pace at the foot of the Royal Mile, while the reinstated Scottish Parliament, operating since July 1999, reclaims some of the sovereignty Scotland lost in 1707. Such paradox has always been an essential part of Edinburgh. Here, the Old Town's twisting tenements, closes, and wynds, immortalized in Robert Louis Stevenson's *Dr. Jekyll and Mr. Hyde*, contrast starkly with the graceful symmetry and orderly grid of the Georgian New Town. These are exciting times for Edinburgh. You, too, will want to join in.

✈ INTERCITY TRANSPORTATION

Edinburgh lies 45 mi. east of Glasgow and 405 mi. northwest of London on Scotland's east coast, on the southern bank of the Firth of Forth.

Airport: Edinburgh International Airport (☎ 333 1000), 7 mi. west of the city. Buses to the airport depart from Waverly Station. **Edinburgh Airbus Express** (☎ 556 2244; £3.60) and LRT's **Airlink 100** (☎ 555 6363; 25min.; every 10min. until 11:35pm; £3.30, children £2) both make the trip. **Airsaver** gives you 1 trip on Airlink plus 1 day of unlimited travel on local Lothian Buses (£4.20, children £2.50).

Trains: Waverley Station, in the center of town, straddles Princes St., Market St., and Waverley Bridge. Free **bike storage** at the back of the main travel center. Office open M-Sa 8am-8pm, Su 9am-8pm; Su-F until 11pm only for same-night travel reservations. Trains (☎ (08457) 484950) from: **Stirling** (45min., 2 per hr., £5.10); **Glasgow** (1hr., 2 per hr., £7.30); **Aberdeen** (2½hr., every hr., £28); **Inverness** (4hr., every 2hr., £29.90-50.60); **Oban** via Glasgow (4½hr., 3 per day, £24.40); **London King's Cross** (5hr., 2 per hr. 9am-3pm, £81.80-91); **Thurso** (7½hr., 2 per day, £38.20-50.80).

Buses: While the St. Andrew Bus Station (☎663 9233) gets a face-lift, the south side of **St. Andrew Square** is being used by Scottish Citylink, National Express, and all buses from Fife, while buses from West Lothian, the Borders, and Dumfries and Galloway leave from **Waterloo Pl.**, at the east end of Princes St. Call the **Traveline** (☎(0800) 232323) for information. Edinburgh is a major hub of Scotland's bus network. **National Express** (☎(08705) 808080) runs from **London** (10hr., 5 per day, £28), **Scottish Citylink** (☎(08705) 505050) from: **Glasgow** (1hr.; M-Sa 4 per hr., Su 2 per hr.; £3); **Aberdeen** (4hr., at least every hr., £14.50); **Inverness** (4½hr., 8-10 per day, £14); **Thurso** via Inverness (8hr., 4-6 per day, £19); **Belfast** via Stranraer (by bus/ferry, 2 per day, £29-33); **Dublin** via Stranraer (by bus/ferry/bus, 1 per day, £41).

⊏ LOCAL TRANSPORTATION

Public Transportation: Though your feet will suffice, and are often faster, Edinburgh has an efficient, comprehensive bus system. The maroon double-deckers of **Lothian Regional Transport** or **LRT** (☎555 6363) provide the best service. Carry coins, as drivers don't have much change for the 80p-£1 fares. You can buy a one-day **Day-Saver Ticket** (£2.40, children £1.50; off season as low as £1.50 for adults; includes discounts at some tourist attractions) and longer-term passes from any driver or from the **main office**, 1-4 Shrub Pl., on the Old Town side of Waverley Bridge. LRT also sells the **Family Saver Ticket** (£6 for 2 adults and up to 4 children) and the **AirSaver Ticket** (£4.20, children £2.65, 1 day of unlimited travel in the city and 1 trip to or from the airport). After midnight, **Night Buses** make a loop through the city every hr. (£1.50).

Taxis: Taxi stands are at both stations and on almost every corner on Princes St. Call **City Cabs** (☎228 1211) or **Central Radio Taxis** (☎229 2468).

Car Rental: The tourist information centre (TIC) has a list of rental agencies. Most have a minimum age of 21 or 23. Rates from £19 per day. Try **Carnie's Car Hire** (☎346 4155) which rents for minimum 3 days (£64) to customers 21+. The **Radical Travel Centre,** 60 High St. (☎557 9393; see below), will help you get the best rates around.

Bike Rental: Edinburgh Rent-a-Bike, 29 Blackfriars St. (☎556 5560), off High St. One of the grooviest bike rental shops on the planet, owned by a funky former music promoter. 10-speed city bikes £5-10 per day, and 21-speed mountain bikes from £10-15 per day. Cheaper rates after 3 days. Arranges city tours (£15) and Highland "Scottish Cycle Safaris" from £40 per day. Open July-Sept. daily 9am-9pm; Oct.-June 10am-6pm.

Hitching: Hitchers often take public transit to the city's outskirts. For points south (except Newcastle and northeast England), most hitchers ride bus #4 or 15 to Fairmilehead and then catch a ride on the A702 to Biggar. For Newcastle, York, and Durham, many take bus #15, 26, or 43 to Musselburgh and then the A1. Hitchers seeking to go north catch bus #18 or 40 to Barnton for the Forth Rd. Bridge and beyond. *Let's Go* never recommends hitchhiking.

⚜ ORIENTATION

Edinburgh is a glorious city for walking. **Princes St.** is the main thoroughfare in **New Town,** the northern section of Edinburgh. From here you can view the impressive stone facade of the towering Old Town, the southern half of the city across the valley. **The Royal Mile** (Castlehill, Lawnmarket, High St., and Canongate) is the major road in the Old Town and connects **Edinburgh Castle** to the **Palace of Holyroodhouse. North Bridge, Waverley Bridge,** and **The Mound** connect Old and New Town.

🛈 PRACTICAL INFORMATION

TOURIST AND FINANCIAL SERVICES

Tourist Information Centre: Edinburgh and Scotland Information Centre, Waverley Market, 3 Princes St. (☎473 3800), on the north side of the Waverley Station complex (look for the blue triangular sign). Slickly helpful, but mobbed. Books rooms for a £3 fee and 10% deposit. Sells bus, museum, tour, and theater tickets, and hands out excellent free maps and pamphlets. **Bureau de change.** Glitzy souvenir shop. In summer, look out for the **City Centre Representatives** around the city—yellow-slicker-wearing folk who can answer questions (about Edinburgh only) in several languages. Open July-Aug. M-Sa 9am-8pm, Su 10am-8pm; May-June and Sept. closes 7pm; Oct.-Apr. closes 6pm.

Tours: Edinburgh offers a vast number of tours, both by foot and by vehicle; see **Tours** in the **Sights** section (p. 513).

Budget Travel: Edinburgh Travel Centre, Potterow Union, Bristo Sq. (☎668 2221). For flight information call the **branch** at 92 South Clerk St. (☎667 9488). Both open M-W and F 9am-5:30pm, Th 10am-5:30pm, Sa 10am-1pm. **usit Campus Travel,** 53 Forrest Rd. (☎225 6111), issues ISIC cards. Open M-Tu and Th-F 9am-5:30pm, W 10am-5:30pm, Sa 10am-5pm. The **Radical Travel Centre,** 60 High St. (☎557 9393), affiliated with Haggis Tours, books hostels for free, arranges tours and car hire, and advises young independent travelers. Open daily 8am-7pm, later in summer.

Financial Services: Barclays, 18 South St. Andrews St. Open M-Tu and Th-F 9:30am-4:30pm, W 10am-4:30pm. **American Express,** 139 Princes St. (☎718 2503 or (08706) 001600), at the street's west end. Open M-F 9am-5:30pm, Sa 9am-4pm.

LOCAL SERVICES

Camping Supplies: Camping and Outdoor Centre, 77 South Bridge (☎225 3339). All the essentials, but no rentals. Open M-Sa 9am-5:30pm.

Bisexual, Gay, and Lesbian Services: Edinburgh has many gay-oriented establishments and events—pick up the *Gay Information* pamphlet at the TIC, or drop by **Nexus Cafe-Bar,** 60 Broughton St. (☎478 7069), also the site of the **Centre for Lesbians, Gays, and Bisexuals** and the **Atomix** gay and lesbian shop. Open daily 11am-11pm. **Blue Moon Cafe** (☎557 0911), on the corner of Broughton St. and Barony St., dispenses pastries, coffee, and friendly advice. Open M-F 11am-11pm, Sa-Su 9am-11pm. The women-only cafe **Dolls** is next door. For more information, see **Gay and Lesbian Nightlife,** p. 521.

Disabled Services: The TIC has info on disabled access to restaurants and sights, as well as *The Access Guide* and *Transport in Edinburgh*. **Shopmobility** (☎225 9559), at The Mound by the National Gallery, lends free motored wheelchairs. Open M-Sa from 10am.

Public Showers: In the "Superloo" at the train station. Super clean, for a train station. Shower £2, toilet 20p, free towel with £1 deposit. Open daily 4:15am-1am.

EMERGENCY AND COMMUNICATIONS

Emergency: Dial 999 or 112. No coins required.

Police: 5 Fettes Ave. (☎311 3131).

Hospital: Royal Infirmary of Edinburgh, 1 Lauriston Pl. (emergencies ☎536 4000, otherwise call 536 1000). From The Mound take bus #23 or 27, or from Hanover St. take bus #23, 27, 28, or 45.

Internet Access: No place is cheaper than the ultra-convenient, corporate **easyEverything,** 58 Rose St. (☎220 3577). Prices fluctuate; £1 gives 30min. to 3hr. of access. You can come and go as you please and use your £1's worth over the course of 28 days. Open 24hr. For much less value, but much more panache, try **Cafe Cyberia,** 88 Hanover St. (☎220 4403). Open M-Sa 10am-10pm, Su noon-7pm. £2.50 per 30min., students and seniors £2. The no-frills **International Telecom Centre,** 52 High St. (☎558 7114), has 20 coin-operated computers, £1 per 15-20min. It also offers cheap **international phone calls,** prepaid international phone cards, fax services, and free coffee. Open daily 9am-10pm. At the TIC, use the **connect@edinburgh** terminals for £1 per 20min.

Post Office: Edinburgh's main post office is at 8-10 St. James Centre (☎556 9546). Open M 9am-5:30pm, Tu-F 8:30am-5:30pm, Sa 8:30am-6pm. **Postal Code:** EH1.

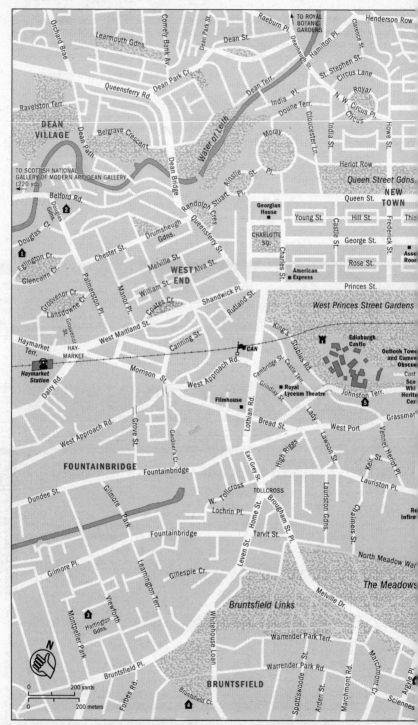

Henderson Row

Raeburn Pl.

TO ROYAL
BOTANIC
GARDENS

Clarence St.

Comely Bank Av.

Dean Park St.

Learmouth Gdns.

Dean St.

Dean Terr.

Hamilton Pl.

St. Stephen St.

Circus Lane

Royal

Queensferry Rd.

Dean Park Cr.

Dean Terr.

India Pl.

N. W. Circus Pl.
Circus

Howe St.

Ravelston Terr.

Water of Leith

Doune Terr.

Gloucester Ln.

India St.

DEAN
VILLAGE

Dean path

Belgrave Crescent

Moray
Pl.

Ainslie

Heriot Row

Queen Street Gdns.

TO SCOTTISH NATIONAL
GALLERY OF MODERN ART/DEAN GALLERY
(220 yds)

Belford Rd.

Dean Bridge

Randolph Cres.

Stuart
Pl.

St.

Georgian
House

Queen St.

NEW
TOWN

Young St.

Hill St.

This

Douglas
Gdns.

2

Drumsheugh
Gdns.

Queensferry St.

CHARLOTTE
SQ.

Castle St.

George St.

Frederick St.

Asse
Roor

Douglas

Eglinton Cr.

1

Chester St.

Melville St.

WEST
END

Alva St.

Charles St.

Rose St.

Glencairn Cr.

Grosvenor Cr.

Palmerston Pl.

Manor Pl.

William St.

Coates Cr.

Shandwick Pl.

American
Express

Princes St.

Lansdowne Cr.

Grosvenor
St.

Rutland St.

West Princes Street Gardens

Haymarket
Terr.

HAY-
MARKET

West Maitland St.

Canning St.

King's Stables Rd.

Edinburgh
Castle

Outlook Towe
and Camer
Obscu

Haymarket
Station

Daly Rd.

Morrison St.

West Approach Rd.

CAN

Cambridge St.
Castle Terr.

Johnston Terr.

Cast
Sco
Whi
Herit
Cer

West Approach Rd.

Grove St.

Gardner's Cr.

Filmhouse

Lothian Rd.

Grindlay St.

Royal
Lyceum Theatre

5

Grassmar

FOUNTAINBRIDGE

Fountainbridge

Bread St.

Lady

West Port

Vennel

Heriot Pl.

Dundee St.

Gilmore Park

Earl Grey St.

High Riggs

Lawson St.

Lauriston Gdns.

Keir St.

Lauriston Pl.

Fountainbridge

W. Tollcross

TOLLCROSS

Brougham St. Pl.

Chalmers St.

Re
Infirm

Gilmore Pl.

Learmington Terr.

Gillespie Cr.

Lochrin Pl.

Home St.

Tarvit St.

Leven St.

North Meadow Wa

Viewforth

Hartington
Gdns.

3

Montpelier Park

Bruntsfield Links

Melville Dr.

The Meadows

N

Warrender Park Terr.

0   200 yards

0   200 meters

Bruntsfield Pl.

Forbes Rd.

Whitehouse Loan

Bruntsfield Cr.

BRUNTSFIELD

Warrender Park Rd.

Spottiswoode St.

Arden St.

Marchmont Rd.

Marchmont Cr.

Argyle Pl.

Sciennes

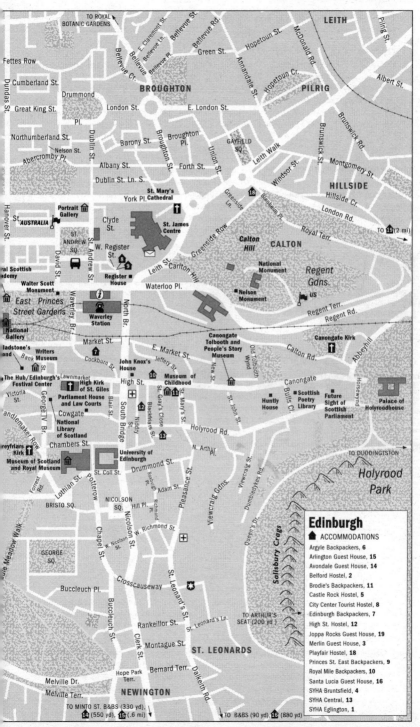

Edinburgh

ACCOMMODATIONS

Argyle Backpackers, 6
Arlington Guest House, 15
Avondale Guest House, 14
Belford Hostel, 2
Brodie's Backpackers, 11
Castle Rock Hostel, 5
City Center Tourist Hostel, 8
Edinburgh Backpackers, 7
High St. Hostel, 12
Joppa Rocks Guest House, 19
Merlin Guest House, 3
Playfair Hostel, 18
Princes St. East Backpackers, 9
Royal Mile Backpackers, 10
Santa Lucia Guest House, 16
SYHA Bruntsfield, 4
SYHA Central, 13
SYHA Eglington, 1

▐ ACCOMMODATIONS

HOSTELS AND CAMPING

Edinburgh is a backpacker's paradise, offering a bevy of cheap and convenient youth hostels, many of them smack-dab in the middle of town, and ranging from the small and cozy to the huge and party-oriented. In some of the larger, more central hostels, security can be an issue, so watch your stuff. Also expect cliques of long-term residents who may swallow you into their midst. The TIC can book you into a hostel for a nominal fee; the more backpacker-oriented **Radical Travel Centre** (see **Tourist and Financial Services,** above) will do it for less. Still, you should call early in summer if you're coming during the Festival (late July to early Sept.).

▨ **Brodies Backpackers,** 12 High St. (☎/fax 556 6770; www.brodieshostels.co.uk), next to The World's End pub on the corner of High St. and St. Mark's St. A relaxed, good-times environment, with a rustic interior. Engaging staff and cozy common room ensure that you'll soon have 56 new best friends. In themed rooms, bunk beds are named after characters in *Trainspotting,* Scottish islands, brands of whisky, and famous patriots. Laundry service. Internet access. Reception open 7am-midnight. Dorms £11.90 M-Th, £13.50 F-Su. Book in advance for £80 per week (laundry included). Prices rise in Aug.

Edinburgh Backpackers, 65 Cockburn St. (☎220 1717, reservations 221 0022; www.hoppo.com). From North Bridge, turn right onto High St. and right again onto Cockburn St. (er, that's pronounced CO-burn). Good location, just off the Royal Mile. Great showers. 110 comfy beds in 6-person, coed rooms. 10% discount at the trendy cafe downstairs. "Legendary" guided pub crawls Tu in summer. Pool table, ping pong, TV, and Internet (£1.50 per 15min.). Reception 24hr. Check-out 10am. Dorms £12, £15 during the festival. Doubles and twins with kitchen access at 34a Cockburn St. £38.50.

Scotland's Top Hostels (hostels@scotlands-top-hostels.com; www.scotlands-top-hostels.com). This chain has a triple presence in Edinburgh with the following 3 well-located hostels. Great sense of community, with social events such as movie screenings, city walking tours, and even techno-*ceilidhs* (traditional Scottish dance). The hostels also form the base for the MacBackpackers Tours which snake into the Highlands (see **Tours,** p. 513). For all, dorms are single-sex, and range in price from £10.50-12. 30p credit card surcharge. 7th night free in the off season. Reception 24hr.

Castle Rock Hostel, 15 Johnston Terr. (☎225 9666). Walking toward the castle on the Royal Mile, turn left onto Johnston Terr. A marvelous example of Old Edinburgh architecture with regal views of the castle. 220 beds in spacious single-sex rooms of 8-12. If you're a fan of big hostels, this is the place you will one day tell your kids about. Laundry service. Ping pong, jukebox, fireplace, Internet access (£1.80 per 30min.). Breakfast £1.60. Book ahead (*months* ahead for Aug.).

Royal Mile Backpackers, 105 High St. (☎557 6120). Walk down High St. from Cockburn St.; the hostel is directly opposite the red Telecom Centre. Head up the stairs and veer left. This spiffy 38-bed facility is smaller and calmer, fostering a great communal feeling. Laundry £2.50.

High St. Hostel, 8 Blackfriars St. (☎557 3984). One of Europe's most atmospheric hostels, with 140 beds and tons of youthful energy. Excellent proximity to High St. Pool table, TV, movies, continental breakfast (£1.60).

Belford Hostel, 6-8 Douglas Gdns. (☎225 6209, reservations 221 0022; fax 476 7139). Self-proclaimed "Scotland's Craziest Church." Take bus #2, 26, 31, 36, 85, or 86 from Princes St. Get off at Haymarket Station, cross the road, and head back toward Princes St. Take the second left onto Palmerston Pl., and follow to the end. Belford is the church on the corner, converted into a bizarre clash of sacred and profane. Gothic stone ceilings soar over pastel bunk beds. A bit far from most things, but has a great bar area and TV room. Dorms £11-13.50; doubles and twins £37.50-42.50.

Argyle Backpackers, 14 Argyle Pl. (☎667 9991; fax 662 0002; argylr@aol.co.uk), south of the Meadows and the Royal Mile. Take bus #40 or 41 from The Mound to Melville Dr. Two renovated townhouses with a relaxing back patio. An alternative to louder city hostels with B&B-style private rooms, some with TV. Check-out 10:30am. Dorms £10; doubles and twins £15 per person. Aug. £5 more.

Playfair Hostel, 8 Blenheim Pl. (☎478 0007), near Royal Terr. At the intersection of Princes St. and North Bridge, turn onto Leith Walk. Bear right at the first roundabout. At the second roundabout, turn right onto Blenheim. Hostel is ahead on your right. Located in a beautiful stone building just below Calton Hill, this hostel boasts the biggest TV screen in Edinburgh. Grab a movie from the incredible selection and kick back with a nice, cold IRN-BRU. Kitchen and laundry facilities. Check-out 10:30am. Dorms £10-15.

Princes St. East Backpackers, 5 West Register St. (☎556 6894). 1 floor above City Centre Tourist Hostel, but an entirely different world. Up lots of steps, with lots of long-term, party-prone guests. Rooms with 4-6 beds, and a couple of doubles. Laundry service and a well-stocked movie room. Internet access £3 per 30min. Breakfast £2. Dorms £9-10, £7.50 for long-termers, £13 in Aug. Doubles £26.

City Centre Tourist Hostel, 5 West Register St. (☎/fax 556 8070; www.touristhostel.freeserve.co.uk). Close to Waverley Station, in the same building as the Princes St. East Hostel. Small, new, and super-clean without an overpowering party atmosphere. Full kitchen. Reception 24hr. Dorms Oct.-Feb. £10, 7th night free; Mar.-Sept. from £12.

SYHA Youth Hostels (www.syha.org.uk). They may not be as fun as some other hostels, but they're certainly clean.

    SYHA Eglinton, 18 Eglinton Cres. (☎337 1120). A mile west of the town center, near Haymarket train station. Walk on Princes St. away from Calton Hill as it becomes Shandwick Pl. Turn right onto Palmerston Pl. and take the second left onto Eglinton Crescent; buzz in at the front gate. Or take bus #3, 4, 28, 33, or 44 from Princes St. to Palmerston Pl. (look for the Scottish flag). 160 beds in 3- to 14-bed dorms. Continental breakfast included, dinner £4.20. Reception 7am-midnight. Check-out 9:30am. Curfew 2am. Pre-paid reservations urged Easter-Sept. Open Jan.-Nov. Dorms July-Aug. £13.75, under 18 £12.25; Sept.-June £12.75, under 18 £11.25.

    SYHA Bruntsfield, 7 Bruntsfield Cres. (☎447 2994). Tidy dorms, quads, and cubicle-like spaces in larger rooms. Sony PlayStation access £1. Dorms July-Aug. £12.75, under 18 £11.50; Sept.-June £11.75, under 18 £10.50.

    SYHA Central, 4 Robertson Close, Cowgate (beds £14), and **SYHA Pleasance,** on New Arthur Pl. near the university (beds £16.50). Reservations ☎337 1120 for both. Open July-Aug.

Camping: Edinburgh Caravans, Marine Dr. (☎312 6874), by the Forth. Take bus #28A from Frederick St. off Princes St. (90p). Electricity, showers, hot water, laundry facilities, and shop. Arrive before 8pm. Open Apr.-Oct. £4 per person, £3 per tent, £1.50 per car.

BED AND BREAKFASTS

During festival season (late July to early Sept.), there are few free rooms anywhere in the city; singles are especially rare. Try to reserve months in advance. B&Bs (£20-30 per person) cluster in three well-stocked colonies. Try Gilmore Pl., Viewforth Terr., or Huntington Gdns. in the **Bruntsfield** district south of the west end of Princes St.; Dalkeith Rd. and Minto St. in **Newington,** south of the east end of Princes St.; or Pilrig St. in **Leith,** northeast of the east end of Princes St. All three areas are fairly easy to walk to, and numerous buses run from Princes St. Some B&Bs open only between May and September. The TIC's £3 booking service can be extremely helpful if you fail to book in advance.

▩ **Joppa Rocks Guest House,** 99 Joppa Rd. (☎/fax 669 8695; www.freepages.co.uk/joppa_rocks). About 3 mi. from the city center on the coast, 50 yd. from the beach; take frequent buses #26 or 26A from the Marks and Spencer on Princes St. (20min., 85p); tell the bus driver where you're going. The sounds of gentle rolling waves replace the noise of the city in this fully stocked B&B. An amazing bargain. All rooms with bath, bathrobes, TV, and slippers. Singles £20; twins £37; doubles £46.

▩ **Merlin Guest House,** 14 Hartington Pl. (☎229 3864). Just under a mile southwest of the Royal Mile, directly off Viewforth, which intersects with Bruntsfield Pl.; take Morningside-bound bus #11, 15, 16, or 17 from Princes St. and tell the bus driver where you're headed. Comfortable rooms in an elegant house. Leafy-green neighborhood close to the city center. All rooms with TV. £16-22.50 per person. Student discounts in winter.

Avondale Guest House, 10 South Gray St. (☎667 6779; isabel.fraser@breathemail.net). From Waverley Station, turn right onto Princes St. and again onto North Bridge St., or catch bus #69, or any Newington-bound bus, to the corner of Minto St. and West Mayfield. Turn right onto West Mayfield and again onto South Gray St. Friendly proprietors welcome you to their small, smartly decorated house. Free Internet access. All rooms with TV. Singles £20-23; doubles £40-46; £5 extra with bath.

Arlington Guest House, 23a Minto St. (☎667 3967; fax 662 9605; www.the-arlington.co.uk). Straight down North Bridge a little over a mi. south of the city center; take buses #8, 8A, 9, 9A, 80, 80A, or 80B. A stately but warm house on a major thoroughfare. Singles £17-23; doubles £30-40.

Santa Lucia Guest House, 14 Kilmaurs Terr. (☎667 8694). Off Dalkeith Rd., 1½mi. south of the city center; take buses #14, 21, 33, or 82. A relaxed atmosphere in a calm neighborhood, all rooms with TV. Singles £18 per person; £2 cheaper without breakfast. Prices vary by season, and are negotiable for *Let's Go* readers.

◨ FOOD

The capital of Scottish tourism, Edinburgh serves traditional fare with great ceremony. You can get cheap haggis at most pubs, and many places offer student and hosteler discounts in the early evening. Sandwich shops abound near the Royal Mile, while takeaway shops on South Clerk St., Leith St., and Lothian Rd. have well-priced Chinese and Indian fare. For groceries, try **Sainsbury's Central** on South St. David St., north of the Scott monument. (Open M-Sa 7am-9pm, Su 9am-8pm.)

▨**The Basement,** 10a-12a Broughton St. (☎557 0097). The menu of this cheap, high-quality restaurant changes daily, with plenty of vegetarian courses. Well-known for Mexican fare weekends and Thai cuisine on W nights. Draws a lively mix of students, musicians, and members of the gay and lesbian community to its candlelit cavern. Try to make reservations F-Sa. Food served daily noon-10pm; drinks served until 1am.

▨**The City Cafe,** 19 Blair St. (☎220 0125). Right off the Royal Mile behind the Tron Kirk, this Edinburgh institution is popular with the young and tightly-clad. Pool tables in the back and a blinking Smirnoff bottle display behind the bar accompany venison burgers (£4-6) and nachos. Incredible shakes, immortalized in the movie *Trainspotting*. Dance club downstairs (see p. 521). Food served until 10pm. Open daily 11am-1am.

The Black Medicine Coffee Co., 2 Nicolson St. (☎622 7209). Proximity to the university and nifty Native American interior design pack this place with sophisticated students most afternoons. Lots of sandwiches (£1-3) and smoothies. Live music (mainly acoustic guitar) Th and Su afternoons. Open daily 8am-8pm.

The Last Drop, 72-74 Grassmarket (☎225 4851). Outside the old gallows (hence the name), this tourist-friendly pub serves good "haggis, tatties, and neeps" (haggis, potatoes, and turnips) in carnivorous and vegetarian versions. Nearly everything on the menu is £3 for students and hostelers before 7:30pm. Open daily 10am-2am.

Lost Sock Diner, 11 East London St. (☎557 6097). One step beyond *My Beautiful Launderette*. Order a delicious meal for £4 while your clothes finish drying. Open M 9am-4pm, Tu-F 9am-10pm, Sa 10am-10:30pm, Su 11am-5pm.

Ndebele, 57 Home St. (☎221 1141). Named for a tribe from Swaziland in southern Africa, this atmospheric restaurant serves generous portions for under £5. Try an avocado, mushroom, and cucumber sandwich (£3), or sample the daily African special. Mind-numbing array of African and South American coffees and fresh juices. African art gallery downstairs; look for the secret drawer. Open daily 10am-10pm.

Kebab Mahal, 7 Nicolson Sq. (☎667 5214). This unglamorous, student-filled hole-in-the-wall will stuff you with great Indian food such as tandoori, curries, chicken tikka, and biryani, all for under £5. Worth the wait. Open Su-Th noon-midnight, F-Sa until 2am.

Blue Moon Cafe (☎557 0911), on the corner of Broughton St. and Barony St. This gay-friendly place is extremely friendly to everyone. Cushy booths, tasteful decor, and charming staff make this coffee shop hard to leave. Breakfast served until 5pm for hungover late risers. Open M-F 11am-11pm, Sa-Su 9am-11:30pm.

The Elephant House, 21 George IV Bridge (☎220 5355). The perfect place to chill, chat, smoke, or pore over the stack of available newspapers. Take in exotic teas and coffees, munch on the best shortbread in the universe, or turn to more filling fare (quiche, nachos, or baked potatoes for under £5) while 600 elephants look on from the wall. Great views of the Castle and Old Town from the back room. Happy hour drink specials M-Sa 9-10pm. Live music Th 7pm. Open M-F 8am-11pm, Sa-Su 10am-11pm.

The Clamshell, 148 High St, (☎225 4338). This Old Town chippy is your best bet for a cheap, late-night meal. For under £2, be daring and try the deep fried pizza, cheeseburger, king rib, or M&Ms. After all, "It's not what *do* we deep fry, it's what *can* we deep fry." Open Su-Th 11am-12:30am, F-Sa 11am-2:30am.

◉ SIGHTS

TOURS. A boggling array of tour companies tout themselves as "the original" or "the scariest"; the most worthwhile is ◪**McEwan's 80/- Edinburgh Literary Pub Tour** (that's "McEwan's eighty shilling," in case you thought you'd found a glaring typo). Led by professional actors, this 2hr., alcohol-friendly crash course in Scottish literature meets outside the Beehive Inn in the Grassmarket. (☎226 6665. June-Sept. daily 7:30pm; Apr.-May and Oct.-Nov. Th-Su 7:30pm; Dec.-Mar. F only. £7, students and children £5.) Or consider a one-on-one encounter with the MacKenzie Poltergeist of Greyfriars Cemetary on the **City of the Dead Tour,** recently featured in the American FoxTV special "The 10 Scariest Places on Earth." (☎447 2230. Daily 8:30 and 10pm. £5, children £4.) The older **Mercat Tours,** leaving from Mercat Cross in front of St. Giles Cathedral, enters Edinburgh's spooky underground vaults. (☎557 6464. Groups depart hourly 11am-9pm. £4-6.)

Edinburgh is best explored by foot, but if you get lazy, **Guide Friday** has an open-top bus tour that lets you jump on and off as you please. Tours leave Waverley Bridge every 10-15min.; tickets get you discounts at many sights and may be used all day. (☎556 2244. £8.50, concessions £7.) Similar bus tours with similar prices include the **Edinburgh Classic Tour,** which offers multilingual narration. (☎555 6363. £7.50, students and seniors £6, children £2.50, after 5pm £4.)

THE OLD TOWN AND THE ROYAL MILE

The Royal Mile (Castlehill, Lawnmarket, High St., and Canongate) defines the length of Old Town—the medieval center of Edinburgh—and passes many of Edinburgh's classic houses and attractions. Defended by Edinburgh Castle at the top of the hill and by Holyrood Palace at the bottom, the Old Town once packed thousands of inhabitants into a scant few square miles, with narrow shopfronts and slum buildings towering to 13 stories (Europe's first skyscrapers, some might argue). However, that history isn't as apparent in the now-fashionable Royal Mile—today, the walk from the castle to the palace is more tourist trap than tenement.

CASTLEHILL AND LAWNMARKET

EDINBURGH CASTLE. Overlooking the city atop an extinct volcano, the castle holds the 15th-century Scottish Crown Jewels and has a view north all the way to Fife, but you have to pay royally at the gate. The intricacies of the structure are the result of centuries of rebuilding. Tour guides revel in recounting how many Englishmen fell in various attempts to take the stronghold; a comprehensive audioguide of the castle's history is also provided. Inside the castle, St. Margaret's Chapel, a Norman church that dates to the 12th century, is believed to be the oldest building in Edinburgh. Also on display are the royal scepter, sword, and crown, as well as the storied but unimpressive Stone of Scone (see Scone Palace, p. 558). The state apartments include Queen Mary's bedroom. One massive cannon (called Mons Meg) and the Scottish National War Memorial await further contemplation, while working cannons deafen at 1pm daily. If you're low on funds, a city view is available at other spots, such as the Nelson

Monument (see p. 517), without the high admission fee and hour-long wait common on summer afternoons. *(At the top of the Royal Mile. ☎ 225 9846. Open Apr.-Oct. daily 9:30am-6pm; Nov.-Mar. 9:30am-5pm. Last admission 45min. before close. Tours every 15min. £7, seniors £5, children £2, under 5 free.)*

THE SCOTTISH PARLIAMENT. While civic controversy rages over the incomplete new building for the Scottish Parliament (Pàrlamaid na h-Alba), the Members rage over various other domestic issues in a temporary Debating Chamber near the Castle. To see the Scottish Parliament in action, go to the former **Church of Scotland Assembly Hall,** accessible through Milne's Close, off the Royal Mile and across from Johnston Terr. The fiery Thursday afternoon questioning session is always packed; reserve tickets ahead and pick them up at the Information Desk in the nearby **Visitor Centre** (Ionad Tadhail), at the corner of the Royal Mile and the George IV Bridge. To observe the Parliament's **Committee Rooms** (Seomraichean Comataidh), in the same building, consult the Information Desk. *(Parliament meets in Debating Chamber Sept.-June W 2:30-5:30pm, Th 9:30am-12:30pm and 2:30-5:30pm. Free. ☎ 348 5000. Bookings 348 5411. Visitor Centre open Sept.-June M and F 10am-5pm, Tu-Th 9am-5pm; July-Aug. M-F 10am-5pm; Aug. to early Sept. also Sa 10am-5pm. Free.)*

THE WRITER'S MUSEUM. This excellent tribute to literary personae, established in Lady Stair's House, contains memorabilia and manuscripts belonging to three of Scotland's greatest literary figures—Robert Burns, Sir Walter Scott, and Robert Louis Stevenson. Nearby is the Makar's Court, where stone tables carved with quotations from Scottish writers lead down to Market St. *(Through the passage at 477 Lawnmarket. ☎ 529 4901. Open M-Sa 10am-5pm; during Festival also Su 2-5pm. Free.)*

OTHER SIGHTS IN THE AREA. The magnetic power of the castle is undeniable, and tourist attractions cluster around it the way midges do a sweaty backpacker. Their target: the eager tourist. Most are relatively expensive, though entertaining if you have money to burn. **The Edinburgh Dungeon,** 31 Market St., next to Waverly Bridge, is a 1½hr. melodramatic reenactment of the city's darker moments. *(Open daily 10am-6pm. £5.50, students and seniors £4.50, children £3.50.)* **The Scotch Whisky Experience** at the Scotch Whisky Heritage Centre, 334 Castle Hill, provides a Disneyworldish tour through the "history and mystery" of Scotland's most famous export. *(Open daily 10am-5:30pm. Adults £6.50, students and seniors £5, children free.)* The **Outlook Tower,** Castle Hill, affords incredible city views from a rooftop terrace in Old Edinburgh. Its 150-year-old **camera obscura** captures a moving image of the streets below. *(Open daily 10am-6pm. Entry to both exhibits £4.25.)* **Gladstone's Land** is the oldest surviving house (c. 1617) on the Royal Mile, which has been carefully preserved and staffed with knowledgeable guides. This remarkable home boasts hand-painted ceilings and a fine collection of 17th-century Dutch paintings. *(483 Lawnmarket. ☎ 226 5856. Open Apr.-Oct. M-Sa 10am-5pm, Su 2-5pm. £3.50, students £2.50.)*

THE HIGH STREET

HIGH KIRK OF ST. GILES. The kirk is Scotland's principal church, sometimes known as **St. Giles Cathedral.** From its pulpit, John Knox delivered the fiery Presbyterian sermons that drove the Catholic Mary, Queen of Scots into exile. Spectacular stained-glass windows illuminate the structure; its crown spire is one of Edinburgh's hallmarks. The **Thistle Chapel** is home to the Order of the Thistle and a wooden angel playing the bagpipes. The cathedral is flanked on the east side by the stone **Mercat Cross,** marking the site of the medieval market (hence, "mercat"), and on the other by the **Heart of Midlothian** inlaid in the pavement. According to city law, spitting on the Heart of Midlothian protects you from being hanged in the square. The cathedral hosts a number of free organ and choral concerts throughout the year; the schedule varies. *(Where Lawnmarket becomes High St., across from Parliament. ☎ 225 4363. Open Easter to mid-Sept. M-F 9am-7pm, Sa 9am-5pm, Su 1-5pm; mid-Sept. to Easter M-Sa 9am-5pm, Su 1-5pm. Requested donation in the Thistle Chapel £1.)*

TRON KIRK. A block downhill from St. Giles, another church pops up on the south side of the High St.: the high-steepled Tron Kirk, built to deal with the overflow of 16th-century religious zealots from St. Giles. Today, it functions as a valuable **information centre** for tourists who are baffled by the myriad sights and tourist traps of the Royal Mile. There's also an interesting archaeology exhibit on the Old Town. *(Open July-Aug. daily 10am-7pm; June and Sept.-Oct. 10am-5pm. Free.)*

MUSEUMS ON THE HIGH STREET. The **Museum of Childhood** has an insightful display of old-school toys and dolls, such as the "creeping baby automata." *(42 High St. ☎529 4142. Open M-Sa 10am-5pm; during Festival also Su 2-5pm. Free.)* At the **Brass Rubbing Centre,** across the street and down Chalmer's Close, you can replicate some fascinating medieval, Celtic, and Gothic patterns. Entrance is free, but rubbing the brass costs anywhere from £1.20-16 depending on the design. *(☎556 4364. Open M-Sa 10am-4:45pm. Last rubbing 3:45pm.)* Nearby, the picturesque **John Knox House,** 43 High St., offers an engaging look at its former inhabitants, John Knox and James Mossman, and the heated Protestant-Catholic conflicts which engulfed them. *(☎556 9579. Open M-Sa 10am-4:30pm. £1.95, students and seniors £1.50, children less.)*

CANONGATE

Canongate, the steep hill that constitutes the last segment of the Royal Mile, was once a separate burgh and part of the Augustinian abbey that gave the royal palace its ecclesiastical name. Here, the Royal Mile's furious tourism begins to dwindle.

■ SCOTTISH POETRY LIBRARY. Located to your right as you descend the hill, this fantastic new building houses an equally fantastic collection of Scotland's poetry in Scots, Gaelic, and English, as well as international poetry, a children's section, and audio and video recordings. It's a relaxing refuge from the main tourist drag in an award-winning piece of expansive modern architecture. The library loans materials out to anyone for a month, free of charge. *(5 Crichton's Close. ☎557 2876. Open M-F noon-6pm, Sa noon-4pm; longer during festival. Free.)*

CANONGATE KIRK. Yet another church on the Royal Mile, this 17th-century chapel is where royals worship when in residence. Adam Smith, founder of modern economics, lies in its sloping graveyard. Nearby, find the famous joint effort of three literary Roberts: Robert Louis Stevenson commemorated a monument erected by Robert Burns in memory of Robert Fergusson. *(Open Easter to mid-Sept. M-F 9am-7pm, Sa 9am-5pm, Su 1-5pm; mid-Sept. to Easter M-Sa 9am-5pm, Su 1-5pm. Free.)*

MUSEUMS ON THE CANONGATE. **Canongate Tolbooth** (c. 1591), with its beautiful clock face and hangman's hook projecting over the Royal Mile, once served as a prison and gallows for "elite" criminals. Now it houses **The People's Story Museum,** an eye-opening, vaguely Marxist look at "the ordinary people of Edinburgh" across the centuries. *(163 Canongate. ☎529 4057. Open M-Sa 10am-5pm; during Festival also Su 2-5pm. Free.)* Across the street, 16th-century **Huntly House,** a nobleman's mansion, contains a hodgepodge of Edinburgh artifacts, including the key to the Canongate Tolbooth. *(142 Canongate. ☎529 4143. Same hours as The People's Story Museum. Free.)*

FUTURE SITE OF THE NEW SCOTTISH PARLIAMENT. There's not much to see right now, as it's all behind the walls at the bottom of the Canongate. But at least the walls are interesting: covered with the drawings of Scottish schoolchildren, they represent the progress of 21st-century Scotland in striking juxtaposition to the ancient, monarchial Palace of Holyroodhouse across the street.

THE PALACE OF HOLYROODHOUSE. This Stewart palace abuts Holyrood Park and the peak of Arthur's Seat (see **Gardens and Parks,** p. 517), and dates from the 16th century. It was home to Mary, Queen of Scots, whose antechamber bears the "bloodstain" of her murdered secretary. Behind the palace lies the 12th-century abbey ransacked during the Reformation. The palace remains Queen Elizabeth II's official Scotland residence. *(At the east end of the Royal Mile. ☎556 7371. Open Apr.-Oct. daily 9:30am-5:15pm; Nov.-Mar. M-Sa 9:30am-3:45pm; closed during official residences in late May and late June to early July. £6.50, seniors £5, children £3.30, families £16.30.)*

SOUTHERN SCOTLAND

DEAD MAN'S BEST FRIEND Greyfriars Cemetery's most famous resident may be one John Gray. According to local legend, Gray once lived on the Cowgate with his faithful mutt, Bobby. After Gray's death, Bobby breached the cemetery every night for 14 years to sleep on his master's tombstone. Touted as Scotland's most photographed monument, a statue of "Greyfriars Bobby" was erected by the city to commemorate the dog's loyalty. Now to debunk the sweet story: the tombstone of John Gray belongs to a policeman of the same name who died well after Bobby's actual master. Records show that Bobby was probably attracted to the spot for the pie shop that occupied a storefront across the street. However, such sobering details didn't stop the Greyfriars Bobby pub from cashing in. One night, pub workers stole out with a screwdriver and reversed the statue's position on its pedestal. Thanks to their maneuver, their pub is now Scotland's most photographed watering hole.

ELSEWHERE IN THE OLD TOWN

GREYFRIARS KIRK. Off George IV Bridge, the kirk, built in 1620, rests in a beautiful, quiet churchyard that, while lovely, is estimated to contain 250,000 bodies and has long been considered haunted. A few centuries ago, body-snatchers like the infamous Burke and Hare dug up their precious corpses here. Linguistics mavens can listen to Gaelic services inside. Look for the grave of loyal pooch Greyfriars Bobby in front of the Church, as well as the famous statue at the corner. *(Beyond the gates atop Candlemakers Row. ☎ 225 1900. Gaelic services Su 12:30pm, English services 11am. Open Easter-Oct. M-F 10:30am-4:30pm, Sa until 2:30pm. Free.)*

NATIONAL LIBRARY OF SCOTLAND. The library has rotating exhibitions from its vast archives, which include a Gutenberg Bible, the last letter of Mary, Queen of Scots, and the only surviving copy of "The Wallace," a wildly popular epic poem which inspired a certain wildly popular Hollywood movie. Alas, these items are not always on display, but the exhibits are excellent. *(George IV Bridge. ☎ 226 4531. Exhibition open M-Sa 10am-5pm, Su 2-5pm; during Festival M-F until 8pm. Free.)*

THE NEW TOWN

Edinburgh's New Town is a masterpiece of Georgian planning. James Craig, a 23-year-old architect, won the city-planning contest in 1767, and his rectangular grid of three parallel streets (Queen, George, and Princes) linking two large squares (Charlotte and St. Andrew) reflects the Scottish Enlightenment's belief in order. Queen St. and Princes St., the outer streets, were built up on only one side to allow views of the Firth of Forth and the Old Town, respectively. On your way in or out, wander through **Charlotte Square,** Edinburgh's most elegant 18th-century square.

THE WALTER SCOTT MONUMENT. Statues of Scott and his dog preside inside the spire of this Gothic "steeple without a church." Climb the winding 287 steps for an eagle's-eye view of the Princes St. Gardens, the castle, and Old Town's Market St. *(On Princes St. between The Mound and Waverley Bridge. Open June-Aug. M-Sa 9am-8pm and Su 10am-6pm; Mar.-May and Sept. daily 9am-6pm; Nov.-Feb. 9am-4pm. £2.50.)*

CALTON HILL. This hill at the eastern end of New Town provides as fine a view of the city and the Firth of Forth as Edinburgh Castle. Get 143 steps higher inside the castellated **Nelson Monument,** built in 1807 in memory of the Battle of Trafalgar. *(☎ 556 2716. Open Apr.-Sept. M 1-6pm, Tu-Sa 10am-6pm; Oct.-Mar. M-Sa 10am-3pm. £2.)* The hilltop grounds are also home to the Old Observatory (1776), the New Observatory (1818), Dugald Stewart's Monument (1837), and the National Monument (1822), affectionately known as "Edinburgh's Disgrace." The structure, an ersatz Parthenon designed by the city to commemorate those killed in the Napoleonic Wars, was scrapped when civic coffers ran dry after a mere 12 columns were erected.

OTHER SIGHTS. Guides staff each room of the elegantly restored **Georgian House**—ask one of them about the speaking tubes that connect the upstairs hall to the kitchen. *(7 Charlotte Sq. From Princes St., take a right onto Charlotte St. and then your second left; the discreetly labeled house is in the middle of the block. ☎ 226 3318. Open Apr.-Oct. M-Sa 10am-5pm, Su 2-5pm; last admission 4:30pm. £5, students and seniors £3.50, children free.)* For still posher architecture, try the **Assembly Rooms**, which embody Neoclassical Edinburgh. They are busy hosting all manner of performances during the Festival, but the Duty Manager may let you can peek at the lavish chandeliers. *(Near the corner of Frederick St. and George St. Box office ☎ 220 4349. Box office open M-Sa 10am-5pm.)*

GARDENS AND PARKS

Just off the eastern end of the Royal Mile, a stroll through **Holyrood Park** or manageable 45min. climb up ⬛**Arthur's Seat** (823 ft.) affords stunning views of both city and countryside, extending as far as the Highlands. Once considered a holy place by the Picts because it appeared and disappeared in the frequent fogs, Arthur's Seat is probably a debasement of the Gaelic "Ard-na-Saigheid," meaning "the height of the flight of arrows," or possibly "Archer's Seat." Traces of forts and Bronze Age terraces dot the surrounding hillside. **Radical Rd.,** named for the politically extreme, unemployed weavers who built it, allows a shorter walk up to the steep Salisbury Crags on the city-facing side of Arthur's Seat. Time your hike so you catch the sunset; during summer, the sun can dip as late as 10pm, so begin climbing around 9pm. The best access to the park is from Holyrood Rd., by the Palace, where a small TIC displays information on the history, geology, and wildlife of the park. The **Scottish Wildlife Trust** (☎ 312 7765) has info on guided tours.

Hidden from the city, the sleepy village of **Duddingston** lies at the foot of Arthur's Seat; from there, take bus #42 from The Mound to visit nearby **Craigmillar Castle,** where Mary, Queen of Scots, sought refuge after the murder of Rizzio and plotted the murder of her husband, Lord Darnley. The surrounding gardens were featured in the BBC production of *Ivanhoe.* *(Craigmillar Castle Rd. ☎ 661 4445. Open Apr.-Sept. M-Su 9:30am-6:30pm; Oct.-Mar. M-Su 9:30am-4:30pm. £2, seniors £1.50, children 75p.)* The **Princes St. Gardens,** located directly in the city center, is a lush park on the site of now-drained Nor' Loch, where Edinburghers used to drown their accused witches. The Loch has been replaced with an impeccably manicured lawn, stone fountains, and enough shady trees to provide shelter from the Scottish "sun." Public football fields and tennis courts carpet the tranquil **Meadows,** an enormous grassy stretch south of the Old Town. In the northern part of town, you can follow the winding way of the **Water of Leith** to the historic **Port of Leith.** Try starting in the picturesque **Dean Village,** accessible by Queensferry St. from the west end of Princes St. The **Royal Botanic Gardens,** Inverleith Row, are Edinburgh's requisite romantic oasis. Take bus #23 or 27 from Hanover St., and don't leave without seeing the **Pringle Chinese Collection,** a miniature Chinese hillside complete with wild water ravine. *(☎ 552 7171. Open Apr.-Aug. daily 9:30am-7pm; Mar. and Sept. 9:30am-6pm; Feb. and Oct. 9:30am-5pm; Nov.-Jan. 9:30am-4pm.)*

🏛 GALLERIES AND MAJOR MUSEUMS

The *Edinburgh Gallery Guide* at the TIC will lead you through the marble halls of Edinburgh's vast and varied collections, most of which are free.

NATIONAL GALLERIES OF SCOTLAND

Free shuttle bus on the hour between the galleries. All open M-Sa 10am-5pm, Su noon-5pm, with longer hours during the festival. All free.

There are four such galleries in Edinburgh, and they form an elite group, all excellent collections housed in stately buildings. There may be fees for special exhibits.

⬛**NATIONAL GALLERY OF SCOTLAND.** The prize gallery stashes a superb collection of works by Renaissance, Romantic, and Impressionist masters including Raphael, Titian, Gauguin, Degas, and Monet, as well as a remarkable collection of Italian and French icons. The basement houses a fine selection of Scottish art. *(On The Mound between the two halves of the Princes St. Gardens. ☎ 624 6516.)*

SCOTTISH NATIONAL PORTRAIT GALLERY. Past the lavishly gilded entrance hall, the gallery mounts the faces of famous Scots, including the definitive portraits of Robert Burns, Bonnie Prince Charlie, and Mary, Queen of Scots. *(1 Queen St., north of St. Andrew Sq. ☎624 6200.)*

SCOTTISH NATIONAL GALLERY OF MODERN ART. In the west end of town, the gallery has an excellent rotating collection that includes works by Braque, Matisse, Kokoschka, and Picasso. If you won't wait for the free Galleries shuttle, take bus #13 from George St., or walk—several picturesque paths take you along the Water of Leith to Belford Rd. *(75 Belford Rd. ☎556 8921.)*

DEAN GALLERY. The newest addition to the National Galleries and dedicated to Surrealist and Dadaist art, the gallery also has a massive collection of work by landmark sculptor Eduardo Paolozzi, best known for his machine-like human figures. A towering, three-story Paolozzi statue dominates the museum. *(73 Belford Rd., across from the National Gallery of Modern Art. ☎624 6200.)*

OTHER MUSEUMS

■**MUSEUM OF SCOTLAND AND ROYAL MUSEUM.** These two connected museums and their stunning architecture are not to be missed. The new **Museum of Scotland** houses a large collection of decorative art and exhibits devoted to Scottish history. The building's design is impressive, though the collection is something of a hodgepodge. Objects include the Monymusk Reliquary (said to have once contained St. Columba's bones and been present at the Battle of Bannockburn) and the Maiden (Edinburgh's pre-French Revolution guillotine, used on the High St. around 1565). Gallery tours and audioguides in various languages are free. Less modern and more motley is the **Royal Museum,** with exhibits on natural history and international art dating back to the Roman era. The rooftop terrace provides a 360° view of the city. Watch the **Millennium Clock** chime every hour—it's a towering, nightmarish display of mechanized Gothic figures. *(Chambers St. ☎225 7534. Open M and W-Sa 10am-5pm, Tu 10am-8pm, Su noon-5pm. Admission for both museums £3, seniors and students £1.50, children free. Year-long pass £5.50. Free Tu 4:30-8pm.)*

OUR DYNAMIC EARTH. Edinburgh is proud of its newest museum, a glitzy, high-tech, high-priced educational lesson in geology, natural history, and ecology: part amusement park, part science experiment, it's billed as an "experience." Computerized time machines take you back to various simulated environments, including a prehistoric volcano and an elaborate rainforest. Kids and science buffs should have a blast. Look for the huge white tent-like structure next to the Palace of Holyroodhouse. *(Holyrood Rd. ☎550 7800. Open Easter-Oct. daily 10am-6pm; Nov.-Easter W-Su 10am-5pm. £6.95, students and disabled £4.95, seniors and children £3.95, families £8.50.)*

MODERN ART GALLERIES. Beneath The Mound down Market St., the **Fruitmarket Gallery** flaunts cheeky modern artwork, emphasizing style over substance. *(☎225 2383. Open M-Sa 11am-6pm, Su noon-5pm. Free.)* Explore new materials at **The City Art Centre,** where exhibits of Scottish modern art slip away faster than Dalí's clocks. *(2 Market St. ☎529 3993. Open M-Sa 10am-5pm. Admission from £0-5, depending on exhibit.)* Don't miss **i2 art and design,** a New Town venue whose shows have included works by Picasso, Miró, and David Hockney. *(66 Cumberland St. ☎557 1020. Open M-F 10am-6pm, Sa 10am-4pm. Free.)* Meanwhile, the wonderful **Royal Scottish Academy** is undergoing long-term reconstruction at its permanent location on The Mound. At time of publication, the gallery was still in search of a temporary home. *(Call 556 8921.)*

◢ ENTERTAINMENT

The summer season sees an especially joyful round of events—music in the gardens, plays and films, and *ceilidhs*—and that's all before the festival comes to town. In winter, shorter days and the crush of students promote a flourishing nightlife. No one knows it better than *The List* ($2), a biweekly comprehensive guide to events in Edinburgh and Glasgow, available at any local newsagent.

THEATER AND FILM

Festival Theatre, 13-29 Nicholson St. (☎ 529 6000). Stages ballet and opera. Box office open daily 10am-6pm. Sometimes drastically reduced tickets (£5.50) on sale at 10am for that evening's show. The affiliated **King's Theatre,** 2 Leven St., promotes serious and comedic fare, musicals, opera, and pantomime. Box office open daily 1-6pm.

Royal Lyceum Theatre, 30 Grindlay St. (☎ 248 4848). Scottish, other British, and international theater. Box office open M-Sa 10am-6pm. £7-16; students half-price.

Bedlam Theatre, 11b Bristo Pl. (☎ 225 9893). The Edinburgh University theater presents excellent student productions of traditional and experimental drama in a converted church with a bedlam-red door. Box office open M-Sa 10am-6pm. £4-5.

Traverse Theatre, 10 Cambridge St. (☎ 228 1404). Performs innovative, sometimes controversial drama. Box office open daily 11am-6pm. £1-2.

The Stand Comedy Club, 5 York Pl. (☎ 558 7272). Presents acts every night, from accomplished headliners and improvisationalists to comedic singers and musical performers. Special 15-shows-per-day program for the Fringe Festival. £1-7.

The Filmhouse, 88 Lothian Rd. (☎ 228 2688). European and arthouse films, though quality Hollywood fare appears as well. £3.20-5.20; F bargain matinee £1.20-2.20.

LIVE MUSIC

Thanks to an abundance of university students who never let books get in the way of a good night out, Edinburgh's live music scene is alive and well. Excellent impromptu and professional folk sessions take place at pubs (see p. 519), and many of the university houses also sponsor live shows; look for flyers near Bristol Sq. Free live jazz can be found at the **Jazz Joint,** 8 Morrison St. (☎ 538 7385; W-Sa 9:30pm-1am), and at the **Cellar Bar,** 1a Chambers St. (☎ 220 4298; Tu-Su 10am-1am). For a complete run-down of Edinburgh's live music scene, pick up *The Gig Guide,* a monthly publication that lists venues and performers for a variety of musical genres. Find it at newsagents and bookstores or ask at the TIC.

For rock and progressive shows, try **The Venue** (☎ 557 3073). **Ripping Records,** 91 South Bridge (☎ 226 7010), lists and sells tickets to rock, reggae, and pop performances. **Negociant's,** 45-47 Lothian St. (not Lothian Rd.), is a pub with frequent live shows downstairs. (☎ 225 6313. Open daily 9am-3am.) Quality Scottish music has to be weeded out from the bad: "Scottish Evenings," sponsored by many of the larger hotels, are about as authentic as vegan haggis. You can find Scottish bands at most local pubs, and country dancing at the **Ross Open-Air Theatre.** Edinburgh occasionally has a **Folk Festival** in the spring; contact the TIC.

⬛ SHOPPING

If you're looking for souvenirs, shops along the **Royal Mile** and **Princes St.** will provide a lifetime's worth of tartans, shortbread, and sheep. For mainstream duds, the stores in **Princes Street Mall** (underground, connected to Waverley Station) and in the massive **St. James Shopping Centre** (on the east end of Princes St.) will look pleasingly familiar. For the funky, vintage, and secondhand, the try the eccentric shops along **Victoria St.,** the **Grassmarket,** and **Cockburn St.** The venerable **Jenner's,** the dignified department store on Princes St., is the Harrod's of Scotland.

⬛ NIGHTLIFE

PUBS

If you can't find a pub in Edinburgh, well, then, we won't say what you are. Edinburgh claims to have the highest density of pubs in Europe, and *Let's Go* doesn't doubt it. *The List* (£2), available from newsagents, catalogues the most authentic pubs, the best live bands, the hippest clubs, and the centers of student nightlife. Scottish licensing laws are more liberal than England's, so you can sample a pint any time of day. Most pubs open at 11am and close between 11pm and 1am.

Pubs directly on the **Royal Mile** usually attract an older crowd, while students and backpackers tend to loiter in the **Old Town** pubs just south. Casual pub-goers gallivant to live music on **Grassmarket, Candlemaker Row,** and **Victoria St.** The New Town also has its worthy share of pubs, some historical, and most strung along **Rose St.,** parallel to Princes St. Gay-friendly **Broughton St.** is increasingly popular for nightlife, though its pubs are more trendy and less traditional.

▓ **The Globe,** 3a Merchant St. (☎220 3833), across from Greyfriars Cemetery. This subterranean, wood-beamed pub bills itself as Edinburgh's true backpackers' destination, and with 2-for-1 drink specials every night, vodka and Red Bull mixers for £1.50, and non-stop musical entertainment, they're not half-wrong. Absinthe shots direct from the Czech Republic £4. Open daily 10am-1am.

▓ **The Tron,** 9 Hunter Sq. (☎226 0931), behind the Tron Kirk. Wildly popular for its incredible deals and location. Students and hostelers get £1 drinks on W nights in term (£1 cover), burgers and a pint for £4 year-round (3-7pm), and all pints are always under £2. 3 floors of carousing. Frequent live music. Open daily 11:30am to at least 1am.

The Three Sisters, 139 Cowgate (☎622 6800). This popular pub offers copious space for dancing, drinking, and socializing—a bit of a meat-market, so the young crowd tends to be slickly dressed. The beer garden provides a delightful outdoor setting. Check out the wooden love booths across from the bar. Open daily 9am-1am.

The Brass Monkey, 14 Drummond St. (☎556 1961). Head down South Bridge and turn right after the university. Take your pint, choose a DVD, and kick back in the cinema lounge. As you're watching *Braveheart* on the big screen with a McEwan's in your hand, you'll realize just how good life can be. Open daily 10am-1am.

Finnegan's Wake, 9b Victoria St. (☎226 3816), promotes the Irish way of life with several stouts on tap and live Irish music every weekend. During the summer months, the pub broadcasts live Gaelic football and hurling on the big screen—and you thought rugby was violent. Open M-Sa noon-1am, Su 1pm-1am.

Biddy Mulligans, 96 Grassmarket (☎220 1246). Located in the middle of Grassmarket, Biddy Mulligans is one of the essential stops on any pub crawler's trail. Although this Irish-themed pub is heavy on the Guinness memorabilia, Biddy's turns into a dance club F-Sa when local DJs blast your favorite classic rock and pop music.

The World's End, 4 High St. (☎556 3628), on the corner of St. Mary's St. A traditional pub which hosts an open-mic Su (10pm-midnight) with free pints for the extroverts willing to take the stage. Great pub food available in 3 sizes: wee, not so wee, and friggin' huge. Open M-F 11am-1am, Sa-Su 10am-1am.

Bannermans Bar, 59 Niddry St., near the Royal Mile. Situated in a series of old cellars, this intimate bar features soft lighting and a relaxed atmosphere. Often has live music on weekends. Try the excellent fruit-flavored beer. Open daily noon-1am.

Whistle Binkie's, 4 Niddry St. (☎557 5114), off High St. A windowless, vaulted interior packs 'em in for live music. Head down into this subterranean pub for a wide variety of entertainment ranging from DJs to acoustic jam sessions. Open daily until 3am.

Peartree House, 38 West Nicolson St. (☎667 7796). With its enormous beer garden, this is a perfect place to savor a pint during the warmer months. Sit back and chat with local university students, or grab some of your mates and challenge them to one of the classic boardgames behind the bar. Open daily noon-midnight.

Pop Rokit, (☎556 4272), corner of Broughton St. and Picardy Pl. More London-chic than Edinburgh-cozy, this trendy bar is a favorite pre-club hangout. Black-clad clientele dine on Mediterranean food amid the smoked glass and concrete interior. DJs spin house and soft funk Th-Su from 9pm. Open daily 11am-1am. Food served until 9:30pm.

CLUBS

Edinburgh may be best known for its pubs, but the club scene is none too shabby, either. It is, however, in constant flux, with clubs continuously closing down and reopening under new management. You're best off consulting the weekly magazine *The List* (£2). Clubs tend to cluster around Edinburgh's historically sleazy and disreputable Cowgate, just downhill from and parallel to the Royal Mile.

Espionage Bar and Club Complex, Victoria St. (☎477 7007). A new, throbbing mecca for the young and fashionable. 5 underground floors recreate different brands of the exotic; among them the Lizard Lounge goes for Native American chic and Pravda for Eastern European (over 100 vodkas available). No cover, but arrive before 10:30pm F-Sa, or you may wait in line for an hour. Open daily 5pm-3am, until 4am weekends.

Subway, Cowgate, (☎225 6766). Liberal door policies and grim concrete furnishings mean Subway's a rowdy place, but bring a large group and indulge in the cheap booze for a fantastic night you probably won't remember. Su-Th all drinks are only a quid. Cover £1, free with student ID. Open daily 7pm-3am.

Eros/Elite, Fountainpark, Dundee St. (☎228 1661). Part of a multi-million pound complex, Eros/Elite is Scotland's largest club. On any given night, there's a continuous stream of buses and taxis carting twentysomethings from neighboring towns. Nonstop chart music and party anthems. Cover £3, with student ID £2. Open daily 5pm-3am.

Po Na Na, 43B Frederick St. (☎226 2224). This Moroccan-themed nightclub oozes glam. Parachute ceilings, red velvet couches, and an eclectic blend of disco, funk, and lounge music ensure a lush night. No cover Su-Th, £3 F-Sa. Open daily 7pm-3am.

La Belle Angele, 11 Hasties Close (☎225 7536). Although the exterior is uninspiring, this laid-back venue showcases the best hip-hop, trance, and progressive house in the city. One F per month, La Belle hosts the blowout "Manga," known for its penetrating drum-and-bass vibes. Cover £2-10. Open daily 7pm-3am.

Peppermint Lounge, Blair St. (☎662 6811), near the Cowgate. Around the corner from the Three Sisters and Subway, Peppermint Lounge is popular with dedicated partiers not quite ready to go home. Colorful lighting, cozy furnishings, and an impressive selection of cocktails make this a hot stop-off for students and backpackers. Cover £1, free with student ID. Open daily 7pm-3am.

GAY AND LESBIAN NIGHTLIFE

In 1995, Edinburgh hosted Scotland's first Gay Pride March, a testament to its growing role as a center of lesbian, gay, and bisexual life. The Broughton St. area of the New Town (better known as the **Broughton Triangle**) is the center of the city's gay community. **Planet Out,** 6 Baxter's Pl., is a mellow gay bar where you can prepare for a wild night. (☎524 0061. Open M-F 4pm-1am, Sa-Su 2pm-1am.) **C.C. Bloom's,** 23-24 Greenside Pl. on Leith St., is a super-friendly, super-fun gay club with no cover. Sunday nights are for karaoke, while the rest of the week is for the dance-floor. (☎556 9331. Open daily 6pm-3am; until 5am during the Festival.) The **Nexus Bar and Cafe,** also in Broughton Triangle, is another local favorite, attracting a range of ages. (Open daily 10am-11pm.) For a drastic change of setting, check out **Queer Sunday** at **Ego,** 14 Picardy Place, a former casino that has an exclusive gay night every Sunday. (☎478 7434. No cover M-Sa, £4 Su. Open daily 7pm-3am.)

▓ FESTIVALS

EDINBURGH INTERNATIONAL FESTIVAL

For a few weeks in August, Edinburgh is *the* place to be in Europe. Prices rise, pubs and restaurants stay open later than late, and street performers have the run of the place. During "Festival Season," a flurry of cultural events and programs take place in the city (see below), but the Edinburgh International Festival proper (Aug. 11-31 in 2002) encompasses higher-brow events such as classical music, ballet, opera, and drama. Tickets for the International Festival (£5-50) are sold by phone and at The HUB (see below) starting the third week of April, and by post or fax beginning in the second week of April. You can purchase tickets at the door for most events. Ask about half-price tickets after 1pm on the performance day and student discounts at most theater productions. For International Festival tickets and a full schedule of events for all festivals, head for the Gothic church just below the Castle on the Royal Mile, now dubbed **The HUB, Edinburgh's Festival Centre,** Castlehill, Edinburgh EH1 2NE. (Inquiries ☎473 2001, bookings 473 2000; fax 473 2003; www.eif.co.uk; www.edinburghfestivals.co.uk.)

SOUTHERN SCOTLAND

▨ FRINGE FESTIVAL

Around the established festival has grown a less formal **Fringe Festival** (Aug. 4-26 in 2002), which now includes over 500 amateur and professional companies presenting theater, comedy, children's shows, folk and classical music, poetry, dance, mime, opera, revue, and various exhibitions. Budget travelers may find the Fringe better suited to their wallets than official offerings; most tickets hover in the £0-5 range. Get the scoop on the best shows at some main haunts, including the Fringe Club at the Teviot Row Union, the Pleasance Theatre on Pleasance St., the Gilded Balloon on Cowgate, the Assembly Rooms, the Theatre Workshop, and the Traverse Theatre. The *Fringe Programme* (available from mid-June) and the *Daily Diary* list performances; get brochures and tickets by mail from the **Fringe Festival Office**, 180 High St., Edinburgh EH1 1QS (☎226 5257; bookings 226 5138; www.edfringe.com). For programs, check out the Festival Office web site or call (0906) 557 5577 (£1 per min.). Bookings can be made online, by post starting in mid-June, by phone (with a credit card) from late June, and in person from July 28. (Box office open 10am-6pm July M-Sa; Aug. daily; Sept.-May M-F.)

MORE FESTIVITIES

The following festivals are just a few of the other events that take place during the five-week period surrounding the Edinburgh International Festival:

Military Tattoo: Tattoo Ticket Sale Office, 32 Market St. (☎225 1188; fax 225 8627). A spectacle of military bands, bagpipes, and drums performed M-Sa nights in the Esplanade. Sa performances followed by fireworks. £9-21. Phone and mail bookings from early Jan. Open M-F 10am-4:30pm; on performance days, open until showtime.

Edinburgh International Film Festival: Film Festival, The Filmhouse, 88 Lothian Rd. EH3 9BZ (☎228 4051, bookings 623 8030). Runs Aug. 11-25 in 2002. Box office sells tickets starting at the end of July.

Edinburgh International Jazz and Blues Festival: (☎467 5200; www.jazzmusic.co.uk). Runs the last week in July and the first week in Aug. in 2002. Opens with a day of free jazz at the Princes St. Gardens. Tickets (£3-9) go on sale in May, and can be purchased over the phone (☎668 2019) or from The HUB.

Edinburgh Book Festival: Scottish Book Centre, 137 Dundee St. EH11 1BG (☎228 5444; www.edbookfest.co.uk). The largest book celebration in Europe. In Charlotte Square Gardens. Runs Aug. 9-25 in 2002. Tickets £3-9; some free events.

Months before the August madness of full-on festival fever hits, May Day sparks the **Beltane Fires.** This pagan event begins with coal jumping around Calton Hill and then moves to Arthur's Seat at sunrise where, legend has it, those who wash their face with the morning dew will receive eternal youth.

HOGWILD ON HOGMANAY

There's always the insanity of **Hogmanay,** Edinburgh's traditional New Year's Eve festival (☎473 3800; www.edinburghshogmanay.org), a serious annual street party that depends heavily on booze. This year, tickets will be available to 180,000 lucky revellers; to reserve, call the Hogmanay Information Hotline. (☎(09069) 150150; 2 ticket limit per person.) Or you could join the **First Foot Club** (☎473 2056), which guarantees a pass (£15) to the street party section of the festival.

▨ DAYTRIPS FROM EDINBURGH

BRAID HERMITAGE NATURE TRAIL. South of the city, enjoy the Lowland countryside at **The Braids,** where a trail cuts through the woods around Braid Burn. Pass through the red archway and up **Blackford Hill** for a perch over the city (15min.). Here you'll find telescope viewing Friday nights from October to March at 7:30pm (£1), and various summer exhibits on astronomy and ecology. *(Bus #40 or 41 from The Mound. Alight at Blackford Ave. and walk away from the city.* ☎668 8405. *Open M-Sa 10am-5pm, Su noon-5pm. £3.50, children £2.50, families £8.)*

LAURISTON CASTLE. The placid fishing village of **Cramond** holds Lauriston Castle, a mansion whose 16th-century tower house and 19th-century additions exude privilege. Its gardens overlook the Firth of Forth. *(Bus #41 from Frederick St. to 2a Cramond Rd. South. ☎336 2060. By guided tour only, 5 per day, 11:20am-4:20pm. Open Apr.-Oct. Sa-Th 11am-5pm; Nov.-Mar. Sa-Su 2-4pm. £4.50, concessions £3.)*

HOPETOUN HOUSE. Hopetoun House, about 10 mi. west of the city center in **South Queensferry,** is considered Scotland's stateliest "Adam" mansion, designed by 18th-century Scottish architect William Adam and his sons Robert and John. The house has a rooftop platform which provides a panoramic vista of the Firth of Forth and its bridges. *(Bus #43 from town to South Queensferry or the train to Dalmeny Station; take a taxi (☎331 5050) the remaining distance. ☎331 2451. Open Apr.-Sept. daily 10am-5pm, last admission 4:30pm. £5.30, students and seniors £4.70, children and disabled £2.70, families £15. Grounds only £2.90, children £1.70.)*

DALMENY HOUSE. The first Tudor Gothic building in Scotland, Dalmeny includes the **Napoleon Room,** which has furniture that supported the emperor at the height of his glory and in the depths of his exile. The **Rothschild Collection** includes remarkable 18th-century French furniture, tapestries, and porcelain. *(Take a bus from St. Andrew Sq. to Chapel Gate in Dalmeny, then walk a mile up the drive. ☎331 1888. Open July-Aug. Su-Tu 2-5:30pm. £4, students £3, seniors £3.50, children £2, under 10 free.)*

ROSSLYN CHAPEL. The exotic stone carvings of Rosslyn Chapel, in the village of Roslin, raised eyebrows in late medieval Scotland. Filled with occult symbols, the chapel became important to the Knights Templar, and the Holy Grail is rumored to lie beneath it. The most famous visible part of the church is the pier known as the Apprentice Pillar, supposedly the work of an apprentice later killed by the jealous master mason. Outside the chapel, footpaths lead to the ruined Roslin Castle in peaceful Roslin Glen. Roslin lies by the **Pentland Hills,** a superb hiking area and haunt of Robert Louis Stevenson. *(Take Penicuik-bound bus, #64 or 87, among others, from Waverley Bridge. Get off at Bilston and head left, following road signs to Roslin. ☎440 2159. Chapel open M-Sa 10am-5pm, Su noon-4:45pm. £4, students and seniors £3.50, children £1.)*

THE BORDERS

From the time Hadrian and his legions were repelled in the 2nd century until just 200 years ago, this 1800 sq. mi. region was caught in a tug-of-war between Scotland and England. Relics of past strife remain: fortified houses and castles dot the landscape, and spectacular abbeys at Dryburgh, Jedburgh, Kelso, and Melrose lie in ruins. These grim reminders of war stand in contrast to a countryside where winding roads and fantastic hill paths reward walkers and cyclists, and where gentle rivers such as the Tweed provided the setting for the works of Sir Walter Scott. Still, the tradition of conflict remains strong, if only in the rugby matches for which the Borders are famous, and to which the locals are fanatically devoted.

▐▌ TRANSPORTATION

The essential *Scottish Borders Travel Guide* (free), which summarizes all bus information, is available at local tourist information centres (TICs). The seven "areas" of the Borders each has a more detailed *Travel Guide* of its own. There are no **trains** in the Borders, but **buses** are frequent. From **Edinburgh,** take an hourly **Lowland** bus #62 to **Peebles** (1hr., £1.35), **Galashiels** (1¾hr., £3.25), or **Melrose** (2¼hr., £3.50); #95 to **Galashiels** or **Hawick** (2hr., every hr., £4.20); or #29 and 30 to **Jedburgh** and **Kelso** (2hr., 8 per day, £4.20). **National Express** (☎(08705) 808080) #383 travels once a day between **Newcastle** and **Edinburgh** via **Jedburgh** and **Melrose;** #394 also hits **Galashiels** and **Glasgow.** McEwan's bus #195 runs from the train station in **Carlisle** to **Galashiels** (2hr.; M-Th 8 per day, F-Sa 9 per day, Su 4 per day; £6.45). No routes lead directly from **Dumfries and Galloway** in the west; come through Carlisle or change at **Biggar** or **Lanark.**

Within the Borders, buses run frequently, if not always promptly. Several **taxi services** operate in the Borders. Try **Campbell's Private Hire** (☎(01721) 720664; mobile (07714) 766997) for transportation or personal guided tours through the region. Three or four people can share a cab for the same price as bus fare.

Hitchhikers report that the lethargy of Border hitching is least painful along the main roads; the A699 runs east-west between Selkirk and Kelso, the A68 connects Edinburgh to Newcastle via Jedburgh, and the A7 runs south through Galashiels and Hawick. The labyrinth of B roads—smaller highways—is less traveled. As always, *Let's Go* does not recommend hitchhiking as a safe mode of travel.

❧ HIKING AND BIKING

The Borders welcome hikers of all levels; take a late afternoon stroll in the hills or wander the wilds for days at a time. Be sure to pick up the superb *Walking in the Scottish Borders*, free at TICs, which details many scenic half-day walks based from towns. The same series includes booklets on cycling, golf, and fishing. Trails weave through the **Tweedsmuirs** (all over 2500 ft. high) to the west along the A708 toward Moffat, as well as the **Cheviot Hills** to the southeast. Closer to Edinburgh, the **Moorfoots** and **Lammermuirs** offer gentler day walks. Eighty-two miles of the **Southern Upland Way**, Scotland's longest footpath (212 mi. total), wind through the Borders. The Way is clearly marked (with a thistle in a hexagon), and the Countryside Commission for Scotland publishes a free pamphlet with route and accommodations info. **St. Cuthbert's Way** rambles for 62 mi. from Melrose to Lindisfarne on the English coast. Retrace ancient footsteps along **Dere St.** (an old Roman road), **Girthgate** (a pilgrimage from Edinburgh to Melrose Abbey), or **Minchmoore;** for info on the trails, pick up the helpful *Scottish Hill Tracks—Southern Scotland*.

For information on the annual regional **Walking Festival,** held in early September, contact Roger Smith, Walking Development Officer (☎(01896) 758991). Local TICs provide plenty of trail guides, leaflets on walks (45p), and Ordnance Survey 1:50,000 Maps (£5). For more info, consult the **Scottish Borders Tourist Board** office in Jedburgh at Murrays Green (see p. 528).

For on- and off-trail **bikers,** the essential *Cycling in the Scottish Borders* includes routes, accommodations, cycle shops, and contact numbers. The *Tweed Cycleway* pamphlet, free from any TIC, describes an 89 mi. route that hugs the Tweed River from Biggar to Berwick. Another free pamphlet outlines the new **Four Abbeys Cycle Route** connecting the abbeys at Melrose, Dryburgh, Jedburgh, and Kelso. *Let's Go* lists bike rental shops in Galashiels and Peebles. **Hawick Cycle Centre,** 45 North Bridge St., Hawick, also rents bikes. (☎(01450) 373352. £5 per 8hr., £10 per day, £50 per week. £20 deposit. ID required. Open M-Sa 9am-5pm.)

🏠 ACCOMMODATIONS AND CAMPING

The *Scottish Borders Holiday Guide*, free at TICs, lists a wide range of Borders accommodations, including campsites. All TICs can help you find a bed, usually for a 10% deposit on the first night's stay. To book rooms in advance, call the Jedburgh TIC with a credit card (☎(01835) 863435). The following **SYHA Youth Hostels** in the Borders are strategically dispersed—a fourth is in **Melrose** (see below).

SYHA Broadmeadows (☎/fax (01750) 76262), 5 mi. west of Selkirk off the A708, and 1¼ mi. south of the Southern Upland Way. Opened in 1931 as the first SYHA hostel, close to the Tweedsmuir Hills. Reception closed 10:30am-5pm. Curfew 10:45pm. Open late Mar. to Sept. Dorms £7.50, under 18 £6.25.

SYHA Coldingham (☎/fax (01890) 771298), outside Coldingham at St. Abbs Head, near the ocean. Surveys the eastern Southern Upland Way and coast. Reception closed 10:30am-5pm. Curfew 11:30pm. Open late Mar. to Oct. Dorms £8.25, under 18 £7.

SYHA Kirk Yetholm (☎(01573) 420631), at the junction of the B6352 and B6401. Watch hikers collapse at the northern terminus of the Pennine Way. Buses run from Kelso (1hr.; M-Sa 5-7 per day, Su 3 per day; £2.65). Reception closed 10:30am-5pm. Curfew 11:30pm. Open late Mar. to Oct. Dorms £8.25, under 18 £7.

MELROSE   ☎01896

Among the loveliest of the region's towns, Melrose (pop. 2400) draws many visitors to its abbey, and is also within convenient reach of Dryburgh Abbey and Sir Walter Scott's country home of Abbotsford.

🛂 PRACTICAL INFORMATION. Buses stop at Market Sq. The **tourist information centre** (TIC), next to a small park and across from the abbey on Abbey St., gives quirky insights into the area's colorful history. (☎822555. Open July-Aug. M-Sa 9am-6pm, Su 10am-5pm; June and Sept. M-Sa 10am-5:30pm, Su 10am-2pm; Oct. M-Sa 10am-4pm, Su 10am-1pm; Apr.-May M-Sa 10am-5pm, Su 10am-1pm.) A **Bank of Scotland** is at Market Sq. (Open M-Tu and Th-F 9am-12:30pm and 1:30-5pm, W 10:30am-12:30pm and 1:30-5pm.) The **post office** is on Buccleuch St. (☎822040. Open M-F 9am-1pm and 2-5:30pm, Sa 9am-12:30pm.) **Postal code:** TD6 9LE.

🏠🍴 ACCOMMODATIONS AND FOOD. A minute from the town center and the abbey ruins, the **SYHA Melrose,** off High Rd., is a superb base for exploring the Borders. The hostel resembles a stately manor more than a backpackers' abode, with 86 beds, an excellent kitchen, laundry facilities, and garden. (☎822521; fax 823505; melrose@syha.org.uk. Continental breakfast included. Reception 7am-11pm. Curfew 11:45pm. Dorms £11.25, under 18 £8.) Or try **Birch House,** down High St.—the only B&B in town—for homey, pine-furnished rooms. (☎822391. Singles £27; doubles £46.) **Camp** at the deluxe **Gibson Park Caravan Club Park,** St. Dunstan's Park, off High St., which claims the cleanest campsite bathrooms ever and great facilities for the disabled. (☎822969. Tent and car £3.50, plus £4 per adult, under 17 £1.20.)

Though not particularly budget, the gourmet cheeses and wholefoods at **The Country Kitchen,** Market Sq., at Palma Pl., are farm-fresh. (☎822586. Open M-F 9am-5pm, Sa 9am-1pm and 2-5pm.) The award-winning **Melrose Station Restaurant,** Palma Pl., in a renovated train station, serves meal-sized sandwiches (£3-5) and exquisite main courses for excruciating prices. (☎822546. Lunch £7, 3-course dinner £17.75. Lunch served W-Su noon-2pm; dinner served Th-Sa from 6:45pm.)

👁🥾 SIGHTS AND HIKING. The town's centerpiece, Cistercian **Melrose Abbey** was begun in 1136, destroyed by the English, rebuilt in an ornate Gothic style, then destroyed again by the English in 1549. Some walls remain remarkably intact, while others provide good ventilation. Search the extensive grounds for the tombstone of Robert the Bruce's embalmed heart (see p. 455). On the lighter side, the monastery's amusing gargoyles include a bagpipe-playing pig and winged cow on the south wall. (☎822562. Open Apr.-Sept. daily 9:30am-6:30pm; Oct.-Mar. M-Sa 9:30am-4:30pm, Su 2-4:30pm. Audio tour included. £3, seniors £2.30, children £1.) Admission to the abbey includes the **Abbey Museum,** which displays objects unearthed from the abbey and regional Roman forts and details Sir Walter Scott's life, death, and poetic dishonesty. Come, see, and briskly conquer the **Trimontium Exhibition,** in Market Sq., which jams information about the Roman fort spanning three Eildon Hills into one small room. Straddle the replica Roman saddle—you know you want to. (☎822651. Open Apr.-Oct. daily 10:30am-4:30pm, Sa-Su closed for lunch. Audio tour included. Museum £1.50, concessions £1, families £4.)

The three volcanic summits of the **Eildon Hills** are an easy, five-mile hike from town. Legend has it that King Arthur and his knights lie in an enchanted sleep (fully armed, of course) in a cavern beneath the hills and will wake when the country needs saving. To reach the hills, walk 200 yd. south of Market Sq. on the Dingleton Rd.; after passing Newlyn Rd. on the right, look for the footpath on the left.

THE PLAID FAD The tourist's desperate quest for his or her ancestral tartan has brought much business—and much amusement—to modern Scots. Originally tartans had no clan affiliation, indicating only the geographic base of the weaver. It wasn't until 19th-century romanticization of the Scottish medieval past that the kilt craze truly began. Overweight King George IV kicked it off by buying a generous £1354 worth of the Regal Stuart tartan to wear during his 1822 visit to Edinburgh. As for the many clans that as yet had no defining plaid, match-ups were confirmed by the serendipitous 1842 publication of *Vestiarium Scotium* (a "discovered" ancient manuscript). Today, tartans are used mostly for ceremonial occasions—and for milking tourists.

NEAR MELROSE

■**DRYBURGH ABBEY.** For those with time and the willingness to walk, the real treasure of the area is Dryburgh Abbey, whose serene grounds host extensive ruins and the graves of Sir Walter Scott and WWI commander Earl Haig. The abbey was built in 1150 and inhabited by Praemonstratensian monks for nearly two centuries. When Edward II began to remove his English troops from Scotland in 1322, the monks prematurely rang their bells in celebration. Angered, the troops retraced their steps and set the abbey afire. A 22 ft. statue of William Wallace and the spectacular **Scott's View** are nearby. *(5 mi. southeast of Melrose. Buses #29 and 30 (15min., every hr., return £2.20) go through St. Boswell's; ask the driver to drop you off. Follow the marked road, cross the footbridge, then turn right (about a 20min. walk). ☎ (01835) 822381. Open Apr.-Sept. 9:30am-6:30pm; Oct.-Mar. 9:30am-4:30pm. £2.50, seniors £1.90, children £1.)*

ABBOTSFORD. Sir Walter Scott wrote most of his Waverly novels in this mock-Gothic estate 3 mi. west of Melrose and died here in 1832. The gaudy house, stuffed with Scott's books, armor, and knickknacks, includes a lock of Bonnie Prince Charlie's hair and a piece of the gown worn by Mary, Queen of Scots at her execution. *(Buses between Galashiels and Melrose via Tweedbank stop nearby. Ask the driver to drop you on the east side of the River Tweed bridge; from the Galashiels side of the road, a dirt path dips down, then climbs uphill to the entrance. ☎ (01896) 752043. Open June-Sept. daily 10am-5pm; mid-Mar. to May and Oct. M-Sa 10am-5pm, Su 2-5pm. £3.80, children £1.90.)*

THIRLESTANE CASTLE. The ancient seat of the Earls and Duke of Lauderdale, Thirlestane Castle stands 10 mi. north of Melrose on the A68 near Lauder. The defensive walls in the Panelled Room and Library are 13 ft. thick, but their beautiful restoration can't hide the castle's bloody history—jealous nobles hanged a host of King James III's low-born supporters here in 1482. *(Various buses to Edinburgh stop nearby; ask the driver to drop you off at the castle entrance. ☎ (01578) 722430. Open Apr.-Oct. M-F and Su 10:30am-5pm. £5.20, children £3, families £13.)*

GALASHIELS ☎01896

Birthplace of tartan and center of the wool-weaving industry since the 13th century, welcoming "Gala" is to be thanked for clothing tweed-clad professors everywhere. Start (and end) your local visit at **Lochcarron's Scottish Cashmere and Wool Centre,** Huddersfield St. The museum informs, but the tour of the 19th-century water-powered loom and modern working wool factory enthralls. (☎752091. Open June-Sept. M-Sa 9am-5pm, Su noon-5pm; Oct.-May M-Sa 9am-5pm. £2.50, children free. Free 40min. tours M-Th every hr. 10:30am-2:30pm, F 10:30 and 11:30am.)

The **bus station,** across Gala Water, sells National Express tickets and **stores luggage** during office hours for 50p. (☎752237. Open M-F 9am-12:30pm and 1:30-5pm, Sa 9am-noon.) Gala Cycles, 38 Island St., **rents bikes** for £5 per half-day and £10 per day. (☎757587. Open M-Tu and Th-F 10am-5pm, W 10am-noon, Sa 10am-5pm.) The **tourist information centre** (TIC), 3 St. John's St., off Bank St., assists with beds and buses. (☎755551. Open July-Aug. M-Sa 10am-6pm, Su 11am-1pm; Apr.-June and Sept.-Oct. M-Sa 10am-5pm.) **Banks** abound on Bank St. The **post office** is at 1 Channel St. (☎754731. Open M-F 9am-5:30pm, Sa 9am-12:30pm.) **Postal code:** TD1 1AA.

Morven Guest House, 12 Sine Pl., around the corner from Poundstretcher on High St., has spacious rooms with bath at a bargain. (☎756255. ₤17 per adult, ₤8.50 per child.) Tasty sandwiches (brie-and-apple ₤1.50) await at the **Supa-Fresh** grocery-deli, 7 Overhaugh St. (☎757307. Open M-Sa 9am-4:30pm.)

12th-century **Traquair House,** the oldest inhabited house in Scotland, stands 12 mi. west of Galashiels off the A72. Take bus #62 and ask the driver to drop you at the entrance. The treasures of the Stewarts of Traquair are displayed upstairs, though the main gates are permanently closed: after Prince Charlie's defeat in 1745, the Earl of Stair swore that they would not be reopened until another Stewart took the throne. Catherine Stewart, the present resident, brews ale in the 200-year-old brewery and has tastings on summer Fridays—when more visitors than usual find themselves entangled in the intricate hedge-maze on the grounds. (☎(01896) 830323. Open June-Aug. daily 10:30am-5:30pm; Apr.-May and Sept. 12:30-5:30pm; Oct. F-Su 12:30-5pm. ₤5, seniors ₤4.50, children ₤2.75, families ₤13.)

PEEBLES   ☎01721

Eighteen miles west of Galashiels, Peebles overlooks the River Tweed, with grassy stretches and restful benches along its banks. A 20min. sally upstream yields **Neidpath Castle,** a small but sturdy fortress with something for everyone—crumbling rooms, river views (one of the best from the bathroom), batik art depicting the life of Mary, Queen of Scots, and a tartan display. The castle inspired many a 19th-century bard, including Sir Walter Scott. (☎720333. Open Easter-Sept. M-Sa 11am-5pm, Su 1-5pm. ₤3, students and seniors ₤2.50, children ₤1, families ₤7.50.) The **Tweeddale Museum and Gallery,** in the Chambers Institute on High St., houses constantly changing exhibitions and the well-marked Chamber's Room, containing Greek friezes placed here in 1859 to "ennoble and enlighten" the viewer. (☎724820. Open M-F 10am-noon and 2-5pm; Easter-Oct. also Sa 10am-1pm and 2-4pm.) On Cross Rd. in a small wooded park, the ruins of **Cross Kirk**—supposedly founded in 1262 when Alexander III and his pals discovered a 4th-century cross here—represent one of the two remaining Trinitarian monasteries in Scotland. The **Beltane Festival** takes place on the third Saturday in June. Formerly a pagan holiday of random sexual encounters, the ceremonies now celebrate not fertility, but the work of elementary school children. Near Peebles, the forests of the Tweed Valley, such as **Glentross** and **Cardrona,** have hiking and cycling paths. *Forests of the River Tweed*, free from the tourist information centre (TIC), has the details.

Said **tourist information centre,** 23 High St., sells local maps; their town walk (25p) is a great way to make the most of your visit. (☎720138; fax 724401. Open July-Aug. M-F 9am-8pm, Sa 9am-7pm, Su 10am-6pm; off-season hours vary slightly, but often closed Su.) Other services include: **banks** along High St.; **bike rental** at **Crossburn Caravan Park,** Edinburgh Rd. (☎720501; open M-Sa 8:30am-6pm; ₤7 per half-day, ₤14 per day, helmets ₤1, deposit ₤60); **Internet access** at the **library,** in the Chambers Institute on High St. (☎720123; open M, W, F 9:30am-5pm; Tu and Th 9:30am-7pm; Sa 9am-12:30pm; ₤2.50 per 30min., concessions ₤1.25); and the **post office,** 14 Eastgate. (☎720119; open M-F 9am-5:30pm, Sa 9am-12:30pm). **Postal code:** EH45 8AA.

Stay with **Mrs. Mitchell,** Viewfield, 1 Rosetta Rd., for refreshing rooms above a wonderful garden. (☎721232. Singles ₤18.50; twins ₤35.) Campers find comfort at the **Rosetta Camping and Caravan Park,** Rosetta Rd., 15min. from the town center on the wooded grounds of Rosetta House, with laundry facilities and an amenity complex with bar. (☎720770; fax 720623. Open Apr.-Oct. ₤4.50 per adult, 50p per child. Weekly: ₤27 and ₤3.) At **Big Eg's,** just outside the center at 14-16 Northgate, tasty fish and chips go for ₤3 takeaway or ₤4.10 sit-down, tea and bread included. The owner's travel advice is free. (☎721497. Open M-Sa 11:45am-11pm, Su 1-8pm.)

JEDBURGH   ☎ 01835

Smack in the heart of Jedburgh (JED-burra; known to locals as "Jethart"), 13 mi. south of Melrose, King David I founded **Jedburgh Abbey** to show both Englishman and Scot that the monarch was not afraid to place magnificent monuments on the fringes of his realm. The abbey was derisively dismantled in the 1540s by the English Earl of Hertford. Among the remarkable surviving relics is a small yet intricately decorated ivory comb that lies at the heart of a 12th-century murder mystery. For the best free view of the abbey, try Abbey Close St. off Castlegate. (☎ 863925. Open Apr.-Sept. daily 9:30am-6:30pm; Oct.-Mar. M-Sa 9:30am-4:30pm, Su 2-4:30pm. £3, seniors and students £2.30, children £1.)

Now a fascinating museum chronicling the monarch, the **Home of Mary, Queen of Scots,** down Smiths Wynd on Queen St., is one of the few remaining examples of a 16th-century fortified house. While in Jedburgh, Mary became so ill due to a compound of childbirth, tough marriages, and riding accidents that her doctor thought she had died. Later, facing death after years of imprisonment, she is said to have wished aloud, "Would that I had died at Jedburgh." The most beautiful gardens in Jedburgh surround the house. (☎ 863331. Open June-Aug. M-Sa 10am-4:30pm, Su 10am-4:30pm; Apr.-May and Oct. M-Sa 10am-4:45pm, Su noon-4:30pm; Mar. and Nov. M-Sa 10:30am-3:30pm, Su 1-4pm. £2, concessions £1, disabled free but access limited.) The 18th-century **Jedburgh Castle Gaol** stands atop a hill on Castlegate over the original Jethart Castle, which was destroyed in 1409 to prevent the English from taking it. Enter between two cannons to learn about prison history. (☎ 863254. Open Apr.-Oct. M-Sa 10am-4:45pm, Su 1-4pm. £1.25, concessions 75p.)

The **bus stand** on Canongate does not have an office, but is located behind that shrine to Borders info, the Jedburgh **tourist information centre** (TIC), Murrays Green, opposite the abbey. The TIC books National Express tickets, reserves rooms for a 10% deposit, and **exchanges currency** for free. Pick up the free publications *Jedburgh Town Trail, Jedburgh Mini-guide,* or *What's On: Scottish Borders.* (☎ 863435; fax 864099; info@scot-borders.co.uk. Open July-Aug. M-F 9am-8pm, Sa 9am-7pm, Su 10am-7pm; June-Sept. M-Sa 9:30am-6pm, Su 10am-6pm; off-season hours reduced.) The **Royal Bank of Scotland** stands on the corner of Jewel-ler's Wynd and High St. (☎ 862563. Open M-Tu and Th-F 9:15am-4:45pm, W 10am-4:45pm; closed 12:30-1:30pm for lunch.) The **post office** is at 37 High St. (☎ 862268. Open M-F 9am-5:30pm, Sa 9am-12:30pm.) **Postal code:** TD8 6DG.

B&Bs pepper the town. At 39 Doune Hill, Mrs. Lowe's **Windyridge** offers modest rooms with panoramic views of castle and abbey. (☎ 864404. Singles £18; doubles £36-40.) Stargazers can camp at the **Jedwater Caravan Park,** 4 mi. south of the town center off the A68; watch for the signs and a side road. (☎/fax 840219. Open Easter-Oct. Tent and two people £8, extra adult £1, children 50p.) For groceries, visit the **Co-op Superstore,** on the corner of Jeweller's Wynd and High St. (☎ 862944. Open M-Sa 8am-8pm, Su 9am-6pm.) For quick snacks, try the sweet **Brown Sugar Coffee Shop and Bakery,** 12 Canongate, including burgers (£2-3.50), teacakes (£1), and toasted sandwiches for £1.50-2.50. (☎ 863399. Open M-Sa 8am-5pm.)

KELSO   ☎ 01573

In the busy hub of Kelso, one of the larger towns in the Borders, palatial **Floors Castle** endures tourist masses. This home is still used as a residence, as the Duke of Roxburgh will attest, and Prince Andrew is known to drop by for the annual charity golf tournament. The castle has scores of turrets, vast grounds, and nearly 400 windows that afford spectacular views of the Tweed. A holly in the gardens marks the site where James II was killed while inspecting a cannon. Try not to make the same mistake. (☎ 223333. Open Easter-Oct. daily 10am-4:30pm. House and gardens £5, seniors and students £4.50, children £3, families £14. Grounds only £3, students and seniors £1.50, children free.) Like Jedburgh's abbey, Kelso's **abbey,** near the Market Sq., is King David-raised, Earl of Hertford-razed. (Open Apr.-Sept. M-Sa 9:30am-6pm, Su 2-6pm; Oct.-Mar. M-Sa 9:30am-4pm, Su 2-4pm. Free.)

MARY, MARY, QUITE CONTRARY Mary, Queen of Scots (1542-87), survived a storm of spicy rumors during her lifetime. Her first husband, King François II of France, reportedly had a shriveled male organ. Wits at the French court speculated on the king's ability to have intercourse and remarked that if the Queen were to become pregnant, the child could not be her husband's. In any case, Mary experienced a "hysterical" (false) pregnancy during her year as Queen of France before François died. Mary's later marriage to the wicked Lord Darnley *did* bear fruit. During the agonizing birth, Mary's companion, Lady Reres, moaned and thrashed in empathy beside Mary while a lady-in-waiting supposedly drew Mary's pains into her friend through witchcraft. Legend has it that Mary's son was stillborn, and that the future King James VI of Scotland (also James I of England) was actually another infant smuggled in to replace the dead child—a story made more tantalizing by the discovery years later of an infant's skeleton hidden between the walls of Mary's apartments.

The **bus station,** off Roxburgh St., near Market Sq., **stores luggage** for 50p per bag. (☎224141. Open M-F 8:45am-5pm, Sa 8:45-11am.) Kelso's **tourist information centre** (TIC), in the old town hall in Market Sq., books rooms for a 10% deposit. (☎223464. Open July-Aug. M-Sa 9am-6pm, Su 10am-5pm; June and Sept. M-Sa 9:30am-5pm, Su 10am-5pm; Oct. M-Sa 10am-4:30pm, Su 10am-1pm; Apr.-May M-Sa 10am-5pm, Su 10am-1pm.) There's free **Internet access** at the **library,** Bowmont St.(Open M-F 10am-1pm and 2-5pm, Sa 9:30am-12:30pm.) The **post office** is at 13 Woodmarket. (Open M-F 9am-5:30pm, Sa 9am-12:30pm.) **Postal code:** TD5 7AT.

🖾Mr. Watson, Clashdale, 26 Inchmead Dr., will treat you like long-lost family, though his fee only commits you to B&B. Join him for a post-dinner drink and try his homemade raspberry jam at breakfast. (☎223405. £15 per person.) **The Home Bakery,** 50 The Square, near Hosemarket, sells pies and sandwiches for around £1.50. (☎226782. Open daily 7:30am-5pm.) Restock at **Safeway,** Roxburgh St. (☎225641. Open M-W and F 8am-8pm, Th 8am-9pm, Sa 8am-6pm, Su 9am-6pm.)

Mellerstain House, one of Scotland's finest Georgian homes, is a few miles from Kelso on the A6089. Begun in 1725 by William Adam and completed by his son Robert, the house is less impressive than its symmetrical gardens and picturesque view of the distant Cheviot Hills. Take buses #68 or 89 (10min.; M-F every hr., Su 8 per day; return £1.20) toward Gordon, and ask the driver to drop you near the house. (☎(01573) 410225. Open Easter-Sept. M-F and Su 12:30-5pm. House and gardens £4.50, seniors and students £3.50, children £2. Gardens only £2.)

DUMFRIES AND GALLOWAY

Galloway, the southernmost region of Scotland, derives its name from medieval Welsh neighbors who dubbed the area *Galwyddel* ("Land of the stranger Gaels"). Today there are few strangers here, since sleepy Galloway sees little of the tourism enjoyed by its north and south. Over the centuries, Dumfries, name of both the neighboring county and the largest town in the area, has passed through the hands of Romans, Vikings, and English feudal lords, each of whom has left behind a sight or two to visit. Castles, gardens, and local heroes (among them Robert the Bruce, Robert Burns, and Mary, Queen of Scots) are plentiful; frustratingly, good public transportation is not. The region is considered Scotland's "quiet country," but locals do know how to celebrate. Every year, on the 25th of January, folks gather to eat, drink, and honor the birth of their favorite poet-son, Robert Burns.

▐▀ TRANSPORTATION

Buses run with relative frequency, but it's difficult to know when and from where they leave. The Dumfries and Galloway Council publishes six free and essential Public Transport Guides, all available from tourist information centres (TICs). The free *Dumfries and Galloway Visitor Guide* also provides useful info on transport services. Several bus companies criss-cross the area; call **Western Buses** (☎ (01387) 253496), **MacEwan's Service** (☎ (01387) 710357), **McCulloch's Coaches** (☎ (01776) 830236), or the **Travel Information Line** (☎ (0345) 090510; open M-F 9am-5pm) for schedule information. A **Day Discoverer Ticket,** available on buses, allows unlimited travel in Dumfries and Galloway, and on Stagecoach buses in Cumbria (£5, children £2; see **Lake District: Local Transportation,** p. 361).

▐▚ HIKING AND BIKING

Dumfries and Galloway enjoy a magnificent stretch of coastline, with a reserve supply of fields, forests, and hills. Two peninsulas, the **Machars** and the **Rhins of Galloway,** jut southward; hikers can follow the 30 mi. **Pilgrim's Way** down the Machars from Glenluce Abbey in the north to the Isle of Whithorn at the southern tip, where St. Ninian founded a chapel in the 4th century. For those with leisure and ambition, the **Southern Upland Way,** Britain's only coast-to-coast long distance footpath, begins at Portpatrick and snakes 212 mi. in a northeasterly direction, passing SYHA hostels in **Kendoon, Wanlockhead, Broadmeadows,** and **Melrose.** For shorter walks, ask a TIC for the free guide *Walking in Dumfries and Galloway,* which details over 30 possible paths. Also pick up the free *Ranger Led Walks and Events.* Before hiking, check the weather (☎ (0891) 500420; premium rate call) and bring the necessary supplies, maps, and compass (see **Wilderness Safety,** p. 54).

Cyclists will find *Cycling in Dumfries and Galloway* (free at TICs) equally useful. The Forest Enterprise also puts out smaller leaflets describing on- and off-trail routes in some of the area's forests—ask at the TIC.

DUMFRIES ☎ 01387

Dumfries (pop. 37,000) hangs its tam on little but the tales of two famous Roberts. In 1306, Robert the Bruce proclaimed himself King of Scotland in Dumfries after stabbing throne-contender Red Comyn at Greyfriars. Robert Burns lived and wrote in Dumfries from 1791 until his death in 1796. Lest its auld acquaintance be forgot, the town has devoted many (many) a site to Burns. Along with these historical claims, the town's central location and transportation connections make it the unofficial capital of southwest Scotland. Even so, Dumfries fails to catch—let alone hold—one's interest; pass through to reach the charm of the countryside.

▐▀▐ TRANSPORTATION AND PRACTICAL INFORMATION

Trains (☎ (08457) 484950) come from: **Carlisle** (35min.; M-Sa every 2hr., Su 4 per day; £6.40); **Glasgow Central** (1¾hr.; M-Sa 8 per day, Su 2 per day; £9.40); **London Euston** (change in Carlisle, 5hr., 9 per day, £68). **Stagecoach Western Scottish** (☎ 253496) **buses** run from **Glasgow Buchanan St.** (#X74; 2hr.; M-Sa 5 per day, Su 2 per day; £6.40, return £8.70) and **Edinburgh St. Andrew Sq.** (#100 or X73; 2hr.; M-Sa 5 per day, Su 1 in the evening; £6.40, return £8.70).

The Dumfries **tourist information centre** (TIC), 64 Whitesands Rd., books accommodations for £1 plus a 10% deposit and sells National Express tickets. Pick up the free *Dumfries and Galloway Visitor Guide.* (☎ 253862; fax 245555. Open June-Sept. M-Sa 10am-5:30pm, Su noon-5pm; Oct.-May M-Sa 10am-5pm, Su 10am-4pm.) Other services include: the **Royal Bank of Scotland,** Queensberry Sq. off High St. (open M-Tu and Th-F 9:15am-4:45pm, W 10am-4:45pm); **Internet access** at **Dumfries IT Centre,** 26-28 Brewery St. (☎ 259400; £4 per hr.; open M-F 9am-6pm, Sa 10am-5pm); and the **post office,** 7 Great King St. (☎ 256690; open M-F 9am-5:30pm, Sa 9am-12:30pm). **Postal code:** DG1 1AA.

🛏🍴 ACCOMMODATIONS AND FOOD

The closest **hostels** are miles away in Newton Stewart (Minigaaff) and Castle Douglas (Kendoon; see p. 532). The TIC can help locate **B&Bs;** a number of reasonably priced abodes lie along **Lockerbie Rd.,** to the north of the city across the tracks. **The Haven,** 1 Kenmore Terr., is a riverfront Victorian home with laundry service and a do-it-yourself kitchen—breakfast is still cooked for you, though. (☎251281. Singles £15; doubles £18-20.) **Selmar House,** 41 Cardoness St., off Lockerbie Rd., has simple rooms near the train and bus stations. (☎250126. £17 per person.)

Cafes, bakeries, and fish-and-chip shops line **High St.,** and **Whitesands Rd.** has other cheap dining options. **Loreborn Fruit and Vegetables** is on Loreborn Rd. (Open M-Sa 9am-5pm.) Choices grow scarce after dark; at **The Queensberry Hotel,** 16 English St., listen to the boastings of the local football team as you gulp down a bowl of excellent soup for £2. (☎253526. Open M-Sa 9am-9pm, Su noon-8pm; food served noon-3pm and 5-9pm.) If you're out for the night, grab a pint at the **Flesher's Arms,** Newell Terr. off Loreborn Rd. (Open M-W 10am-midnight, Th-Sa 10pm-1am.) You can dance off the calories across the street at **Chancers Night Club,** Munches St. (☎263170. Cover F-Sa £1-2. Open Th-Su 10pm-3am.)

👁 SIGHTS AND FESTIVALS

It's all Robbie Burns. Pick up a free copy of *Dumfries: A Burns Trail* in the TIC for an easy-to-follow walking tour that covers all the major sights. Across the river, the **Robert Burns Centre,** Mill Rd., contains an uninspiring scale model of 18th-century Dumfries Town, and, of course, Robert Burns memorabilia, including a cast of his skull. A 20min. film runs through a sentimental version of the poet's life; the 10 million Burns songs make it worth the small fee. (☎264808. Open May-Sept. M-Sa 10am-8pm, Su 2-5pm; Oct.-Mar. Tu-Sa 10am-1pm and 2-5pm. Free. Film £1.50, concessions 75p.) In an ornate mausoleum in **St. Michael's Kirkyard,** St. Michael St., a white marble Burns leans on a plow and seems to gaze in surprise at the attractive muse hovering overhead. The mausoleum was built in 1815 after admirers decided Burns's former grave was too ordinary. (☎255297. Open M-Sa 9am-8pm, Su noon-6pm. Free.) The wee Burns House on Burns St. contains many of the poet's original manuscripts and editions. Burns died here after aggravating an illness by bathing—on a doctor's advice—in a nearby well. (☎255297. Open Apr.-Sept. M-Sa 10am-5pm, Su 2-5pm; Oct.-Mar. Tu-Sa 10am-1pm and 2-5pm. Free.)

The **Dumfries Museum,** Church St., is yet another local museum with worn tools, stuffed birds, and images of Dumfries through the ages. The top floor has panoramic views from Britain's oldest camera obscura, weather permitting. (☎253374. Open Apr.-Sept. M-Sa 10am-5pm, Su 2-5pm; Oct.-Mar. Tu-Sa 10am-1pm and 2-5pm. Free. Camera obscura £1.50, concessions 75p.) The **Old Bridge House Museum,** Mill Rd., packs eclectic paraphernalia into four tiny rooms. The only thing less appealing than the dentures in the dentistry collection is the nightmarish dental equipment. (☎256904. Open Apr.-Sept. M-Sa 10am-5pm, Su 2-5pm. Free.)

Dumfries's **Guid Nychburris Festival** (pronounced "good neighbors"), starting on the third Saturday in June, is a week-long celebration with performances and riding reenactments.

🗺 DAYTRIPS FROM DUMFRIES

CAERLAVEROCK CASTLE. Eight miles south of Dumfries, on the B725 just beyond Glencaple, moated, triangular Caerlaverock Castle (car-LAV-rick) is one of Scotland's finest medieval ruins. No one is sure whether this strategic marvel was built for Scottish defense or English offense; it was seized by England's Edward I in 1300 and passed around like a hot kipper thereafter. *(Western Bus #371 runs to the castle from the Loreburn Shopping Centre, off Irish St. in Dumfries (30min.; M-Sa 12 per day, Su 2 per day; £1, return £1.80).* ☎(01387) 770244. *Open Apr.-Sept. daily 9:30am-6:30pm; Oct.-Mar. M-Sa 9:30am-4:30pm, Su 2-4:30pm. £2.80, seniors £2, children £1.)*

SWEETHEART ABBEY. Also within easy reach is **Sweetheart Abbey,** 7 mi. southwest along the A710. The abbey was founded by Lady Devorguilla Balliol in memory of her husband John. She was later buried in the abbey with her husband's embalmed heart clutched to her breast. The splendid ruins are remarkably preserved. Unfortunately, John Balliol is not. *(Take MacEwan's bus #372 (45min.; M-Sa 15 per day, Su 5 per day; £1.40, return £2.40) to New Abbey from Dumfries's Whitesands depot stand 5. ☎(0131) 668 8800. Open Apr.-Sept. daily 9:30am-6:30pm; Oct.-Mar. M-W and Sa 9:30am-4:30pm, Th 9:30am-1pm, Su 2-4:30pm. £1.50, seniors £1.10, children 50p.)*

RUTHWELL CHURCH. Nine miles southeast of Dumfries, the **Ruthwell Church** contains the magnificent 7th-century **Ruthwell Cross,** which bears dense carvings of vine scrolls and beasts of Celtic art, plus everyone's favorite Anglo-Saxon poem, *The Dream of the Rood,* in the margins—it's the oldest surviving fragment of written English in Scotland. Call Mrs. Coulthard *(☎(01387) 870249)* to get the key to the church. *(Take a Western Buses bus to Annan via Clarencefield and get off at Ruthwell (30min.; M-Sa every hr., Su every 2hr.; £1.40, return £2.55). Church free.)*

DRUMLANRIG CASTLE. Eighteen miles north of Dumfries off the A76 is the home of the Duke of Buccleuch. After taking in the rich collection of paintings, enjoy the castle's fantastic grounds and country park. *(Take Western Bus #246 toward Thornhill (45min., Su 2 per day, £2.45) and ask the driver let you off near the castle. ☎(01848) 330248. Castle open by guided tour Apr.-Sept. daily 11am-5pm. Grounds open Apr.-Sept. 11am-5pm. £6, students and seniors £4, children £2, families £14. Grounds only £3, students and seniors, £2.)*

WANLOCKHEAD. One of Scotland's highest villages comes complete with nosebleeds and a 28-bed **SYHA Youth Hostel.** *(☎/fax (01659) 74252. Reception closed 10:30am-5pm. Open Apr.-Sept. daily; Mar. and Oct. F-Sa. Dorms £8.25, under 18 £7.)* You can reach Wanlockhead by walking along the Southern Upland Way; there is an **Information Shelter** here. Some opt to hitch the B797, which branches off the A76 2 mi. south of Sanquhar, miles downhill from Wanlockhead.

CASTLE DOUGLAS   ☎01556

Halfway between Dumfries and Kirkcudbright, Castle Douglas resembles every town in Scotland's southwest, with marvelous gardens and a castle nearby, but nothing in the town itself. One mile west, the 60-acre **Threave Garden** bursts with blooms gingerly pruned by students of the School of Gardening. *(☎502575. Garden open daily 9:30am-sunset. Walled garden and greenhouses open daily 9:30am-5pm. £4.50, children £3.)* Buses #500 and 501 between Kirkcudbright and Castle Douglas pass the garden turnoff; ask the driver to stop, and walk for 10min. A mile or two farther west, the ruins of ▧**Threave Castle** command an island on the River Dee. Threave was the last stronghold of the Earls of Douglas to surrender to James II in 1453. It was taken again and ravaged in 1640 by Covenanters. The Kirkcudbright-Castle Douglas bus can drop you off at the roundabout on the A75; follow signs for Threave Castle on the road that ends at Kelton Mains Farm. Look for the roofless keep: when you ring the ship's bell nearby, a boatman should arrive to ferry you across the river. (Open Apr.-Sept. daily 9:30am-6:30pm; last boat 6pm. £2, seniors £1.50, children 75p; ferry included.) Southeast from Castle Douglas, through the town of Dalbeattie, lie chilly **beaches** at **Sandyhill** and **Rockcliffe.**

MacEwan's buses #500 and 501 zip to Castle Douglas from Kirkcudbright (45min., 12 per day, £1.50); check the return schedule before heading out. For local lodgings, ask the staff at the **tourist information centre,** Market Hill, to help find a room. (☎502611. Open June-Aug. M-Sa 10am-5:30pm, Su 11am-5pm; Apr.-May and Sept.-Oct. M-Sa 10am-5pm.) A **Royal Bank of Scotland** rules on King St. (Open M-F 9:30am-5:30pm, Sa 10am-5pm.) **SYHA Kendoon**'s proximity to Loch Doon and the Corbetts makes it an ideal base for outdoor types. Take the A713 north to Dalry, turn off and follow the A702 toward Moniaive for less than ¼ mi., then make a left onto the B700 north toward Carsphairn; the hostel is 3 mi. ahead on your left. (☎(01644) 460680. Self-catering. Open mid-Mar. to Sept. Dorms £6.75, under 18 £6.) **Mrs. Laidlaw,** 33 Abercromby Rd., a five-minute walk from town, runs a B&B close to bird watching, fishing, and walking trails. (TV lounge. Doubles £36.)

KIRKCUDBRIGHT   ☎ 01557

Attractive and dignified, Kirkcudbright (car-COO-bree) occupies its coastal spot in the center of Dumfries and Galloway with grace. Old Scottish buildings and Georgian homes line the angular High St. of this small town. Artists and dreamers have burrowed here for centuries, and, if you're in the region, you should too.

☐☑ TRANSPORTATION AND PRACTICAL INFORMATION. Buses #500, 501, and 505 travel from **Dumfries** (every hr.), and bus #431 comes from **Newton Stewart** (1hr.; M-Sa 7-8 per day, Su 2 per day; £2.85), sometimes beginning in **Stranraer.** The **tourist information centre** (TIC), Harbour Sq., books rooms for £1. (☎ 330494; fax 332416. Open mid-June to mid-Sept. daily 9:30am-5:30pm; mid-Sept. to Oct. 10am-4:30pm; Apr.-June 10am-5pm.) Other services include: **The Royal Bank of Scotland,** 37 St. Mary St., at the corner of St. Cuthbert St. (☎ 330492; open M-Tu and Th-F 9:15am-4:45pm, W 10am-4:45pm); **Shirley's Launderette,** 20 St. Cuthbert St. (☎ 332047; wash £2, dry £2); **Internet access** at the **library,** Sheriff Court House, High St. (☎ 31240; £3 per 30min., £5 per hr.; open M and W 2:30-7:30pm, Tu and F 10am-12:30pm and 2:30-7:30pm, Th 10am-12:30pm and 2:30-5:30pm, Sa 10am-12:30pm and 2-5pm); and the **post office,** 5 St. Cuthbert's Pl. (☎ 330578; open M-F 9am-12:30pm and 1:30-5:30pm, Sa 9am-12:30pm). **Postal code:** DG6 4DH.

☐☐ ACCOMMODATIONS AND FOOD. The bright blue house with fountained garden run by fabulous **Mrs. McIlwraith,** 22 Millburn St., captures the character of the town. From the bus stop, turn left onto St. Cuthbert St., walk past the Safeway, and make a left onto Millburn St. at the school sign. (☎ 330056. Singles £17; twins £34.) In a house ringed with roses, **Mrs. McGeough,** 109 St. Mary St., has a common room with TV. If traveling by bus, ask the driver to stop at the garage on St. Mary St. and walk four houses to the left. (☎/fax 331885. Singles £18; doubles £32.) Get groceries at the **Safeway supermarket,** 52 St. Cuthbert St., at Millburn St. (☎ 330516. Open M-W and Sa 8:30am-6pm, Th-F 8:30am-8pm, Su 10am-4pm.) **The Royal Hotel,** St. Cuthbert St., has an all-you-can-eat lunch buffet for £5 and a multi-course dinner of fresh seafood for £6.50, with live music on Sunday nights. (Lunch buffet M-Sa noon-2:30pm. Dinner F-Sa 6:30-9pm, Su noon-3pm. Open M-Sa 11am-11pm, Su noon-10:30pm.) Top off your meal with a pint at the **Selkirk Arms,** High St., the inn where Robert Burns wrote the *Selkirk Grace* in 1794. (☎ 330402. Open M-Sa 11am-11pm, Su noon-10:30pm; food served M-Sa noon-2:30pm and 6:30-9pm.)

☐ SIGHTS. Kirkcudbright's colorful harbor and idyllic countryside prompted a circle of prominent Scottish artists to take up residence in the 1890s. Aspiring and established artists still frequent the town. An excellent gallery at the ▓Tolbooth Art Centre, High St., housed in the oldest surviving tollbooth in Scotland and one-time prison of navy man John Paul Jones, details local history. In the upper studio, visitors can peek over the shoulders of local artists at work. (☎ 331556. Open July-Aug. M-Sa 10am-6pm, Su 2-5pm; Mar.-Apr. and Sept.-Oct. M-Sa 11am-4pm; May-June M-Sa 11am-5pm; Nov.-Feb. Sa 11am-4pm. £1.50, students and children 75p.)

Broughton House, 12 High St., displays the artwork (mostly carefree girls cavorting amid wildflowers) of E.A. Hornel, who drew inspiration for his later paintings from the years he spent in Japan. The backyard is everything a garden could hope to be, with emerald lawns, lily ponds, sundials, and greenhouses. (☎ 330437. Open July-Aug. daily 11am-5:30pm; Apr.-June and Sept.-Oct. from 1pm. £2.50, concessions £1.70, families £6.70.) **MacLellan's Castle,** a 16th-century tower house, dominates the town from Castle St. near Harbour Sq. Sneak into the "Laird's Lug," a secret chamber behind a fireplace from which the Laird could eavesdrop on conversations in the Great Hall. It's not a bad ruin, but you'll spend 20min. here at most. (☎ 331856. Open Apr.-Sept. daily 9:30am-12:30pm and 1:30-6:30pm; Oct.-Nov. M-Sa 9:30am-4:30pm, Su 2-4:30pm. £1.80, seniors and children £1.30.)

About a mile west of town on the A75, **Cardoness Castle** was a rocky stronghold of the McCullochs for five centuries. This is the only castle in Scotland with a two-seat toilet; if you ask nicely, the castle curator may let you try it out with a close friend. (☎(0131) 668 8800. Open Apr.-Sept. daily 9:30am-6:30pm; Oct.-Mar. Sa 9:30am-4:30pm and Su 2-4:30pm. £2, seniors £1.50, children 75p. Toilet free.)

STRANRAER   ☎01776

On the westernmost peninsula of Dumfries and Galloway, Stranraer (stran-RAHR) provides ferry access to Northern Ireland. Locals have a unique accent, as most early residents came from Ireland; they are often referred to as the Galloway Irish.

▣ GETTING THERE AND SAILING AWAY. Trains (☎(08457) 484950) come from **Glasgow** (2½hr.; M-Sa 4-7 per day, Su 2 per day; £16) and **Ayr** (M-Sa 7 per day, Su 2 per day; £10.90). **Scottish Citylink** (☎(08705) 505050) **buses** arrive from: **Ayr** (1½hr., 2 per day, £4.50); **Glasgow** (#923, 2½hr., 2 per day, £8.50); **Dumfries** (#500; 3hr.; M-Sa 4-5 per day, Su 3 per day; £4.50). **National Express** (☎(08705) 808080) runs from: **Carlisle** (2½hr.; £15); **Manchester** (5½hr.; 1 per day; £27); **London** (9hr.; 2 per day; £33). **Ferries** travel to Northern Ireland across the North Channel. **Stena Line** (☎(0990) 707070; www.stenaline.co.uk) sails to **Belfast** (1¾hr.; 5 per day; £18-24, students and seniors £14-17, children £9-12). Five miles up the coast at **Cairnyan, P&O Ferries** (☎(0870) 242 4777) depart for **Larne** (1-2¼hr., 8 per day, £18-25). Sea passage is sometimes discounted with a rail ticket. See **By Ferry**, p. 35, for more info.

▨ PRACTICAL INFORMATION. The **tourist information centre** (TIC), Harbour St., posts a list of B&Bs and books rooms for a deposit. Pick up the handy *What's On* guide. (☎702595; fax 889156. Open June-Sept. M-Sa 9:30am-5:30pm, Su 10am-4:30pm; Apr.-May and Oct. M-Sa 10am-5pm; Nov.-Mar. M-Sa 11am-4pm.) **Banks** are everywhere. **Internet access** is available at the **Stranraer Public Library,** North Strand St., for £3 per 25min. or £5 per 55min. (☎707400. Open M-W and F 9:30am-7:30pm, Th 9:30am-5pm, Sa 9:30am-1pm and 2-4:30pm.) The **Tesco** on Charlotte St. houses Stranraer's **post office.** (☎702587. Open M-W 8:30am-6pm, Th-F 8:30am-8pm, Sa 8am-6pm, Su 11am-2pm.) **Postal code:** DG9 74F.

▛▟ ACCOMMODATIONS AND FOOD. If you're marooned, check B&Bs on the A75 (London Rd.) toward the castles or try the ▨**Jan Da Mar Guest House,** 1 Ivy Pl., on London Rd., whose owners supply nicely furnished rooms and lively conversation, conveniently located between the town center and the ferry terminal. (☎/fax 706194. Singles £18; twins £32). **The Old Manse,** Lewis St., is also near the ferries. (☎702135. Singles £14; doubles £28.) The **Tesco** supermarket, on Charlotte St. at Port Rodie near the ferry terminal, bursts with goods. (Open M-F 8:30am-8pm, Sa 8am-6pm, Su 10am-5pm.) When the sun starts to fade, head to that astonishingly named establishment, **The Pub,** 3 Hanover St. (☎705518. Open M-W 4pm-midnight, Th 4-10pm, Sa noon-1am, Su 12:30pm-midnight.)

◪ SIGHTS. In town, the only sight is the **Castle of St. John,** George St., a 1510 edifice which looks more ill-designed than regal. (☎705544. Open Apr.-Sept. M-Sa 10am-1pm and 2-5pm. £1.20, children 60p.) Four miles east of Stranraer on the A75 the ivy-clad ruins of **Castle Kennedy** are all that remain from 1726 fire. Bring a picnic and walk through splendid gardens to **Lochinlch Castle,** present-day home of the Earl of Stair. You can't enter his mansion, but you can tramp through his flower beds. The nearby lochs and peaceful grounds are a haven for ducks, geese, and grebes. Frequent buses run from Stranraer pass the castle; it's about a mile off the main road. (☎702024. Open Apr.-Oct. daily 10am-5pm. £3, students and seniors £2, children £1.) The **Glenwahn Gardens,** 6 mi. from Stranraer on the A75, are replete with foreign and domestic flora, a man-made pond, and a pagoda with a view of the peninsula. (Open daily 10am-5pm. £2.50, students and seniors £2, children £1.)

WESTERN GALLOWAY

The two peninsulas of Western Galloway are fringed with cliffs, beaches, and great views. The western peninsula, a north-south hammerhead, lies just 25 mi. from Ireland across the North Channel, but land-based transport is tricky without a car.

PORTPATRICK. Eight miles southwest of Stranraer on the A77, the quiet vacation village of Portpatrick opens the **Southern Upland Way** (see p. 524). On weekends, wealthy yacht owners sail here from Northern Ireland for Sunday lunch (but a range of cheap pub food is available for the rest of us). Sixteenth-century **Dunskey Castle** lies secluded on a spectacular cliff overlooking the ocean, a 20min. walk from Portpatrick harbor. On the left side of the harbor as you face the water, a long flight of steps leads to the castle path. Dunskey might be the most secluded, romantic castle you'll visit; beautiful wildflowers and stunning sea views await, though access to the interior has been restricted by the castle's new owner.

    Bus #367 runs to Portpatrick from **Stranraer** (Tu and Th also #411; 20min.; M-F 5-8 per day, Sa 7 per day; return £2.30). Several **caravan parks** back onto the castle and cliffs; to reach them, turn left after the war memorial on the A77 from Stranraer. The **Castle Bay Caravan Park,** the farthest down the road, has a breathtaking stretch of lawn and excellent facilities. (☎ (01776) 810462. £5 per tent.)

SANDHEAD, PORT LOGAN, AND DRUMMORE. At **Sandhead,** south of Stranraer on the eastern shore of the peninsula, the eerie **Kirkmadrine Stones,** three of the earliest Christian monuments in Britain, grace a windswept hill. The *chi-rho* symbol (the first two Greek letters of Christ's name) and other inscriptions date from the 5th or 6th century. Bus #407 on the Stranraer-Stoneykirk-Drummore line stops at Sandhead (4 per day, return £2.40); from Sandhead follow the signposts for 2 mi. off the A716. **Logan Botanic Garden** spreads prettily in **Port Logan,** between Sandhead and Drummore. Audio tours guide visitors through the famous Walled Garden and tranquil Woodland Garden. (Open Mar.-Oct. daily 9:30am-6pm. £3, students and seniors £2.50, children £1, families £7.) Scotland's southernmost point is 4 mi. from **Drummore.** Follow the footpath beyond the lighthouse to a grassy cliff.

GLENLUCE AND GALLOWAY FOREST PARK. The **Pilgrim's Way** (see p. 530) begins at **Glenluce Abbey,** northwest of the peninsula. The abbey has deteriorated since its founding in 1192 by Roland, Earl of Galloway, but still retains some killer acoustics. Legend has it that a wizard lured the Black Plague into the abbey's cellar and starved it to death. Take bus #500 from Stranraer to Glenluce and walk 1½ mi. north along the road to New Luce. (☎ (0131) 668 8800. Open Apr.-Sept. daily 9:30am-6:30pm; Oct.-Mar. Sa 9:30am-4:30pm, Su 2-4:30pm. £1.80, seniors £1.30, children 75p.) Northeast of Stranraer, the **Galloway Forest Park** surrounds **Glen Trool.** The 240 sq. mi. inland reserve with peaks over 2000 ft. offers superb day-long hikes and camping. Call the Newton Stewart Forest District (☎ (01671) 402420).

AYRSHIRE

AYR   ☎ 01292

The city of Ayr (as in fresh AIR; pop. 50,000) makes a good base from which to explore the rolling hills and seaside cliffs of Ayrshire. Scottish weather often dampens the marvelous sandy beaches that line the coast, but no rain can dim local enthusiasm for Robert Burns, the city's hero. His birthplace, the lovely—if unexciting—countryside of Ayrshire is full of first- to third-degree Burns sights.

⚏⏸ TRANSPORTATION AND PRACTICAL INFORMATION. The **train station** is at the crossroads of Station Rd., Holmston Rd., and Castle Hill Rd. **Trains** (☎(08457) 484950) run from **Glasgow** (1hr., about 2 per hr., £6) and **Stranraer** (M-Sa 7 per day, Su 3 per day; £10.20). **Stagecoach** (☎613500) **buses** arrive from **Stranraer** (£5.70) and **Glasgow** (£3.15). For local transport info, call the **bus station,** 73 Sandgate, near Wellington Sq. (☎613500. Open M-Sa 8am-5pm.) The **tourist information centre** (TIC), 22 Sandgate, near the bus station, **changes currency.** Pick up their version of *Let's Go,* a guide to events in Ayrshire and Arran. (☎288688. Open July-Aug. M-Sa 9am-6pm, Su 10am-5pm; Sept.-June M-Sa 9am-5pm.) Other services include: **banks** on High St.; **Internet access** at **Carnegie Library,** 12 Main St. (☎618492; £3 per hr.; open M-Tu and Th-F 10am-7:30pm, W and Sa 10am-5pm); and the **post office,** 65 Sandgate (☎287264; open M-Sa 9am-5:30pm). **Postal code:** KA7 1AB.

⚏⏹ ACCOMMODATIONS AND FOOD. The ▨**SYHA Ayr,** Cragweil House, 15min. from the town center, offers breathtaking views and a barbecue grill. Take a right off Racecourse Rd. onto Blackburn Rd., then a right onto Cragweil Rd. (☎262322; fax 289061. Self-catering. Wash £1, dry £1. Curfew 11:45pm. Open Feb.-Dec. Dorms £9.25, under 18 £8.) If the hostel is full, try **Tramore Guesthouse,** 17 Eglinton Terr., which has a Moroccan decor a few hundred meters from the beach. (☎/fax 266019. £17 per person.) The **Safeway** is across from the train station on Castlehill Rd. (☎283906. Open M-Th 8am-8pm, F 8am-9pm, Sa 8am-6pm, Su 9am-5pm.) For cheap sandwiches (£2.70-3.30) and other baked delights, head for **Cafe Ginger,** 57 Fort St., near the bus station. (☎264108. Open M-Sa 7:30am-5:30pm.) Drink at the most popular pub in town, the tartan-filled, proud-to-be-Scottish ▨**Chapman Billie's,** on Dallair Rd. at Barnes St. (☎618161. Open daily 1pm-12:30am.)

⚏⏵ FESTIVALS. The **Ayr Racecourse** hosts the **Scottish Grand National** in April and the **Ayr Gold Cup** in September. (☎264179. Tickets £10-25; call for race dates.)

NEAR AYR

ALLOWAY

From Ayr's bus station, take Strathclyde Passenger Transport (SPT) bus #E1 to Alloway (10min., every hr., return £2.35) or the hop-on/hop-off Burns Country Open-Top Bus Tour, which reaches Alloway after a scenic 30min. (every hr. 10am-5pm; £3, children £1.50).

Two miles south of Ayr, the village of Alloway blazes with Burns sites. Visit the **Burns Cottage and Museum,** built by you-know-who's dad, where guess-who was born. The museum's excellent collection of Burns memorabilia redeems the saccharine tableaux of family life and realistic barnyard smells. (☎(01292) 441215. Open Apr.-Oct. daily 9am-6pm; Nov.-Mar. M-Sa 10am-5pm, Su noon-4pm. £1.70, seniors and children 80p, families £4.) The **Tam o' Shanter Experience** presents the life of the poet and a lyrical multimedia reading. (☎(01292) 443700. Open Apr.-Oct. daily 9am-6pm; Nov.-Mar. 9am-5pm. £2.80, seniors and children £1.40, families £8. Joint ticket with Cottage and Museum £4.50, seniors and children £2.20, families £12.) The nearby **Burns Monument and Gardens** are free, and divine on a sunny day. A view of the **Brig o' Doon,** a bridge featured in the "Tam o' Shanter" poem, can be had if you climb for it. Stop by the ruined **Alloway Kirk,** where, according to Burns, the devil played the bagpipes; or, for a further taste of historic, haunted Alloway, let **Scruffy Dog Tours** lead you through the Kirk's graveyard with tales of cannibalism and witchcraft. (☎(0775) 494 1801. Tours M-F 8-10:30pm. £6, children £4.)

▨CULZEAN CASTLE

From Ayr take bus A719 to Culzean (30min., M-Sa 6 per day, day return £4.15); tell the driver where you're going, and follow the signs from the main road for about a mile. ☎(01655) 760274. Castle open Apr.-Oct. daily 10:30am-5:30pm. Park open year-round. Free tours July-Aug. daily 11am and 3:30pm. £7, seniors and children £5, families £18. Park only £3.50, seniors and children £2.50, families £9.

Twelve miles south of Ayr, Culzean Castle (cul-LANE) perches imposingly on a coastal cliff. According to legend, one of the cliff's caves shelters the Phantom Piper who plays to his lost flock when the moon is full. The castle's famed oval staircase was designed by Robert Adam; although he drafted nearly 40 blueprints for estate homes and constructed over 20 full-scale castles, his efforts at Culzean are considered his finest. The building's top floor was given to Dwight Eisenhower for use during his lifetime—lesser persons are still not allowed up. In crafty revenge, access the grounds for free by walking north along the beach from the nearby town of Maidens and climbing an unguarded stairway.

ISLE OF ARRAN   ☎01770

The glorious Isle of Arran (AH-ren; pop. 4750) justifiably bills itself as "Scotland in Miniature." Gentle lowland hills and majestic Highland peaks coexist on an island less than 20 mi. long. In the north, the crags of Goatfell and the Caisteal range overshadow pine-filled foothills. Near the western coast, prehistoric stone circles rise suddenly out of the boggy grass. The eastern coastline winds south from Brodick Castle past Holy Island into meadows and white beaches. On sunny days, the waters turn crystalline, providing an enchanting view of the marine life below.

▐▀ TRANSPORTATION

To reach Arran, take a **train** (☎(08457) 484950) to **Ardrossan** from **Glasgow Central** (45min.; M-Sa 5 per day, Su 4 per day; £4.50) or **bus** #580 to **Ardrossan** from **Ayr** (1hr.; M-Sa 2 per hr., Su 5 per day; £2.75). From Ardrossan the **Caledonian-MacBrayne ferry** (☎302166) makes the crossing to **Brodick** on Arran in sync with the train schedule (1hr.; M-Sa 5 per day, Su 4 per day; £4.40). There's also ferry service to **Lochranza** on Arran from **Claonaig** on the Kintyre Peninsula (30min.; usually mid-Apr. to mid-Oct. 8 per day; £4, bikes £1). When returning to Claonaig, be sure of your connection. Pick up a timetable at the tourist information centre (TIC).

  Island **buses** run frequently, and for every ferry there is a connection to and from every part of the island; pick up timetables at a TIC or on board. There are bus stops, but drivers will pick you up anywhere if you flag them down. The **Rural Day Card** (available on the bus; £3, children £1.50) grants a full day of travel. The **Stagecoach Western** office is at Brodick pier. (☎302000. Open daily 8am-5pm.) Stagecoach's **full-day tour** from Brodick Pier travels the perimeter of the island, stopping in Lochranza, Blackwaterfoot, and Whiting Bay. (Departs daily June-Sept. 11am, returns 4:20pm; £7, children £5.) Buses #323 and 324 also circle the island.

▟▌ HIKING AND BIKING

Despite Arran's proximity and excellent connections to Glasgow, swaths of wilderness in the northwest and southeast remain untouched, and some of the villages in these areas are quiet and untouristed. The best walks on the island are well marked, but more demanding hikes are detailed in *Seventy Walks in Arran* (£2.50) and *My Walks of Arran* (£2.25), both available at the TIC. The Forestry Commission arranges various **guided walks** (2-5hr.; £2-4, children free) as does the National Trust for Scotland (☎302462); schedules are at the Brodick TIC. The sign-posted path up popular **Goatfell** (2866 ft.), Arran's highest peak, begins on the road between the Arran Heritage Museum and Brodick Castle. The hike averages 4-5hr., but the view from the cold and windy peak is worth it; on a clear day, it includes the jagged Caisteal range to the north and Holy Island to the southeast. If you don't want to go back down the same way you came up, try descending through the village of **Corrie**. As always when climbing, be sure to wear warm, waterproofed gear.

  Biking on the hilly island is a rewarding challenge; the full circuit along Arran's solitary but well-maintained road takes about 9hr. Pick up a free copy of the SYHA's *Cycling on Arran. Let's Go* lists bike rental stores in Brodick and Blackwaterfoot, or rent from **Whiting Bay Cycle Hires,** located on the jetty in Whiting Bay and operated out of a van on sunny days. (☎(0585) 28779. £9 per day.) **Hitchhikers** report that getting rides out of Brodick isn't hard, though *Let's Go* never recommends hitching; elsewhere, locals are friendly, but pass infrequently.

BRODICK

Be sure to stay in Brodick for longer than the walk from the ferry pier to the bus stop. In addition to its transportation connections, Arran's main town (pop. 2000) holds a gorgeous castle and some tasty restaurants—all against a backdrop of rugged mountains and a peaceful bay.

█▐ TRANSPORTATION AND PRACTICAL INFORMATION Mini-Golf Cycles, behind the miniature golf course on Shore Rd., rents bikes. (☎302272. Bikes £8-9 per day, children's bikes £4 per day. Helmets included. Deposit £10 plus ID. Open daily 9am-7pm.) Or try **Brodick Cycles,** farther down Shore Rd., opposite the village hall. (☎302460. £3-5.50 per 2hr., £5-9.50 per day, £17-36 per week. Deposit £5-50. Open Easter-Sept. M-Sa 9am-1pm and 2-6pm, Su 10am-1pm and 2-6pm.)

The center of Brodick is along Shore Rd., to the right as you disembark from the ferry. A **CalMac** office is at Brodick Pier. (☎302166. Open M-Sa 7:40am-5pm and 6:30-7:20pm, Su 10am-5pm and 6:30-7:20pm.) Arran's only **tourist information centre** distributes free maps, updates a handy "What's On" bulletin board, and books local B&Bs for £1.50 plus a 10% deposit. (☎302140; fax 302395. Open June-Sept. M-Sa 9am-7:30pm, Su 10am-5pm; Oct.-May roughly M-F 9am-5pm, Sa 10am-5pm.) Other services include: the **Royal Bank of Scotland,** Shore Rd. (☎302222; open M-Tu and Th-F 9am-5pm, W 10am-5pm); a **launderette** at the western end of Shore Rd. (☎302427; wash £2.40, dry 90p-£2; open Th-Tu 9am-5pm, W 9am-4pm; last wash 45min. before close); and the **post office,** set back from Shore Rd. on Mayish Rd. (☎302245; open M-F 9am-5:30pm, Sa 9am-12:45pm). **Postal code: KA27 8AA.**

▐▐ ACCOMMODATIONS AND FOOD Brodick B&Bs fill quickly, so call ahead. For only £20 per night, the ▉**Arran Hotel** (☎302265), on Shore Rd. across from the ferry terminal, has enormous rooms complete with color TV, bath, and deluxe breakfast. If the Arran Hotel fills, stay at **Glenard House,** Manse Rd., a red sandstone house run by Mrs. Macmillan. Head away from the pier on Shore Rd. and turn left just after the Heathfield Hotel; it's the fourth house on the left. (☎302318. Open Apr.-Oct. Singles £18; doubles £36.) The seafront **Glenfloral B&B,** Shore Rd., has spacious rooms with TVs and a great vegetarian breakfast. (☎302707. £17 per person.) Mrs. Rayburn's **Crovie** promises a great view if you take the pleasant (and challenging) hike. Take a left from the pier, and walk away from town on the main road; turn onto Crovie Rd. after a mile, and follow it for ½ mi.; Crovie is on your right. (☎302193. £13-16 per person.) The **Glen Rosa Farm,** 2 mi. north of Brodick on the coastal road to Corrie (the B880), lets campers pitch tents. (☎302380. Toilets and cold water. £2.50 per person.) You can also look for grassy spots by the beach, but the golf course is off-limits.

At the **Co-op,** across from the ferry terminal, stock up on groceries. (☎302515. Open M-Sa 8am-10pm, Su 9am-7pm.) **Collins' Good Food Shop,** at the western end of Shore Rd., just past the bridge on your left, has outdoor seating next to a stream. Try the mouthwatering quiche (£1.25) and vegetarian haggis-filled rolls (£1.75); the shop also vends fruits and veggies. (☎302427. Open W 9am-4pm, Th-Tu 9am-5pm.) For lightening-fast Chinese and Thai takeaway, feast at **Shanghai,** at the corner of Kames Rd. and Shore Rd. (☎303777).

▤ SIGHTS AND FESTIVALS Shore Rd. becomes Low Glencloy Rd., which reaches the splendor of ▉**Brodick Castle,** surveying the harbor above fantastic wild and walled gardens. Built on the site of an old Viking fort and the ancient seat of the Dukes of Hamilton, the castle contains a fine porcelain collection, paintings, and scores of dead beasties. The Dukes supposedly shot everything that ran or flew, including 89 stags' heads that all ended up in the entrance hall.

SOUTHERN SCOTLAND

That's 178 baleful eyes waiting to greet you. If you can't visit the castle, look on the back of a Royal Bank of Scotland £20 note. Stagecoach runs a Vintage Coach service (June-Sept. 9 per day; return £2, children £1) to the castle from Brodick Pier. (☎302202. Castle open Apr.-June and Oct. daily 11am-4:30pm; July-Aug. 11am-5pm. Gardens open daily 9:30am-dusk. Castle and gardens £6, concessions £4. Gardens only £2.50, concessions £1.70.) The wooded **country park** around the castle has marked walking trails. The rangers run **guided walks** three times per week from April to September. (☎302462. 1½-7hr.; £2.50-10, children £1.25-5. Call to book ahead.)

Also on Low Glencloy Rd., closer to town, the **Arran Heritage Museum** features a working forge (the beloved "Smiddy") and a cottage stuffed with 19th-century household implements (if you can get up the wee stairs). On some summer Sundays, the museum explodes into a flurry of activity as blacksmiths fire up the forge for horseshoeing demonstrations and woolly sheep are shorn. (☎302636. Open Apr.-Oct. daily 10:30am-4:30pm. £2.25, seniors £1.50, children £1, families £6.) The **Arran Highland Games,** replete with bagpipe parades, arrive in Brodick in early August. The **Isle of Arran Folk Festival** spreads merriment in early June.

NEAR BRODICK: WHITING BAY. Eight miles south of Brodick, the shores of Whiting Bay harbor a stone **SYHA Youth Hostel** amid rolling hills. (☎/fax 700339. Lockout 10:30am-5pm. Curfew 11:45pm. Dorms £8.25, under 18 £7.) Down the road from the hostel sits **The Coffee Pot,** Golf Course Rd., a terrific place for afternoon teas (£1-3) or a bowl of scrumptious homemade soup (£1.50) with a view of Holy Island. (☎700382. Open daily 10am-5pm; July-Aug. 10am-6pm.) The Coffee Pot is also the trailhead for the easy one-mile path to **Glenashdale Falls,** a secluded spot worth savoring. **Lamlash,** Arran's most populated town and one of the best natural harbors in Europe, lies between Brodick and Whiting Bay. The bay is protected by the steep form of Holy Island, to which ferries run frequently.

LOCHRANZA

Idyllic Lochranza, 14 mi. from Brodick at the island's northern tip, shelters a serene harbor ringed with high hills and guarded by the ruins of a 13th-century **castle.** Pick up the key to the castle from the post office and unlock the iron gate to explore the solitary ruins. (Open Apr.-Sept. Free.) Lochranza is also a popular base for ramblers. An excellent half-day walk is the seven-mile **Cock of Arran** route, which circles the northern tip of the island, accessed from opposite Lochranza's tiny church. The beach section takes you past **Fairy Dell,** a lushly ferned sandstone ravine; the bard **Ossian's Cave,** a hole-in-the-cliff with no historical importance; and the now-headless **Cock of Arran,** whose features are hard to spot unless you bring along a magic spyglass, a local, or your own stone rooster. Alternatively, head south up **Glen Catacol** to **Loch Tanna,** passing several waterfalls and several drearier mud pools (4 mi. each way). Before setting out, buy the waterproof *Walker's Map: Arran North* (£6.95) or the Ordnance Survey *Isle of Arran* (£5.25), both available at the Brodick TIC. The third weekend in July brings the **Lochranza Gala Weekend,** when boats with silly themes compete in a down-and-dirty race.

One mile down the coast from Lochranza, the fishing village of **Catacol Bay** harbors the **Twelve Apostles,** 12 connected white houses that differ only in the shapes of their windows. The **Machrie Stones,** various Bronze Age arrangements of upright stones and boulders, are 10 mi. down the road. Ask the bus driver on the Lochranza-Blackwaterfoot bus to drop you off. A mile down the main road brings you to a footpath signposted to **King's Cave,** where Robert the Bruce allegedly passed time watching the spiders while still in hiding. Now fenced off, the cave holds ancient carvings and modern graffiti. It's open for tours on some summer days. Either contact the Brodick TIC (see p. 538) to arrange for a group tour, or call the Kinloch Hotel in Blackwaterfoot (☎860444) for the key

Lochranza Golf Caravan Camping Site (see below) provides **bike rentals** for £4.50 per day. (☎830273; fax 830600. Open daily 8am-8pm.) The **post office** is located in Primrose's, the local grocery store, overlooking castle ruins. (☎830641. Open M-Tu and Th-Sa 8:30am-1:30pm and 2:30-5:30pm, W 8:30am-1:30pm and 5-6pm; supermarket only Su 10am-2pm and 5-6pm.) **Postal code:** KA27 8EU.

In the former town church across from the castle, the ⊠**Castlekirk B&B** has high, arched ceilings, a lounge with stained-glass windows, and enchanting quietude. The talented proprietress fills the ground floor with her own artwork and that of other local artists, forming a gallery that's open W-Su noon-6:30pm. (☎830202. £18-20 per person.) Minutes inland of the castle, the **SYHA Lochranza** graces the town on the main road. This peaceful white mansion has 68 beds, five showers, two friendly and helpful wardens, and one strict curfew. (☎/fax 830631. Laundry wash £1, dry £1. Kitchen lockout 10:30am-5pm. Curfew 11:30pm. Open Mar.-Oct. Dorms £8.50, under 18 £5.) Campers can pitch at the **Lochranza Golf Caravan Camping Site,** ½ mi. inland of town on the main road, with laundry, hot water, and facilities for the disabled. (☎830273; fax 830600. Open Apr.-Oct. £3 per person, £2-4 per tent.) The veggie pasta (£5.80) or the lunch baguettes (£3) at waterfront **Lochranza Hotel** will surely hit the spot. (☎830223. Open daily 11am-9:45pm.)

GLASGOW   ☎0141

Glasgow (pop. 680,000) is like a canvas painted over many times—but in this post-industrial city, each layer is simultaneously visible, a polyglot portrait unmatched by the capital in Edinburgh. Scotland's largest city, Glasgow rose to prominence during the reign of Queen Victoria, exploiting heavy industry to become the world's leading center of shipbuilding and steel production. Outstripping its reputation for dreariness (and the cranes that litter the river Clyde), today's Glasgow showcases some of Europe's most striking architecture, from the Art Nouveau elegance of Charles Rennie Mackintosh's School of Art to the daring curves of the brand new multi-million pound Science Centre. Named UK City of Architecture and Design in 1999, Glasgow has also become a British cultural hub, with dozens of free museums, excellent international cuisine (including the highest concentration of Indian restaurants outside the subcontinent), and shopping second only to London. Perhaps most difficult to replicate, however, are the denizens who energize the city late into the night. Scotland's largest student population and football-mad locals offer a hospitality and humor unusual for a modern metropolis.

⌐ TRANSPORTATION

Glasgow lies on the Firth of Clyde, 45min. west of Edinburgh. The M8 motorway links the two cities.

INTERCITY TRANSPORTATION

Flights: Glasgow Airport (☎887 1111), 10 mi. west in Abbotsinch. Scotland's major airport, served by **Aer Lingus, British Airways,** and others. Scottish Citylink buses run from Buchanan Station (25min., every 10min., £3.30).

Trains: Bus #398 runs between Glasgow's two main stations (4 per hr.; 50p, children 30p), but it's only a 10min. walk.

Central Station, Gordon St. U: St. Enoch. Serves trains from southern Scotland, England, and Wales. Open daily 5:30am-midnight. Travel center open M-Sa 5:30am-10pm, Su 8am-10pm. Bathrooms 20p; shower with soap and towel £2; open M-Sa 5am-midnight, Su 6am-midnight. Lockers £2-4, for up to a day; all luggage is searched; open daily 6am-midnight. Trains (☎(08457) 484950) to: **Ardrossan,** connecting to ferries to Brodick on the Isle of Arran (1hr., 10-12 per day, £4.40); **Dumfries** (1¾hr.; M-Sa 7 per day, Su 2 per day; £9.20); **Stranraer** (2½hr.; M-Sa 8 per day, Su 3 per day; £15.30); **Liverpool** (4hr.; every hr.; £51, return £39.90); **Manchester** (4hr.; every hr.; £51, return £39.90); **London King's Cross** (5-6hr.; M-F 16 per day, Sa 20 per day, Su 5 per day; £50).

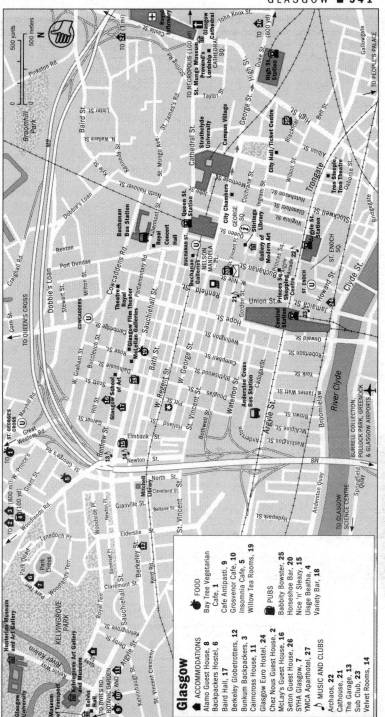

SOUTHERN SCOTLAND

Glasgow

ACCOMMODATIONS
Alamo Guest House, **8**
Backpackers Hostel, **6**
Baird Hall, **17**
Berkeley Globetrotters, **12**
Bunkum Backpackers, **3**
Cairncross House, **11**
Chez Nous Guest House, **2**
Glasgow Euro Hostel, **24**
McLay's Guest House, **16**
Seton Guest House, **26**
SYHA Glasgow, **7**
YMCA Aparthotel, **27**

♪ **MUSIC AND CLUBS**
Archaos, **22**
Cathouse, **21**
The Garage, **13**
Sub Club, **23**
Velvet Rooms, **14**

🍴 **FOOD**
Bay Tree Vegetarian
  Cafe, **1**
Cafe Antipasti, **9**
Grosvenor Cafe, **10**
Insomnia Cafe, **5**
Willow Tea Rooms, **19**

🍺 **PUBS**
Babbity Bowster, **25**
Horseshoe Bar, **20**
Nice 'n' Sleazy, **15**
Uisge Beatha, **4**
Variety Bar, **18**

Queen St. Station, beside Copthorne Hotel, George Sq. U: Buchanan St. Serves trains from the north and east. Open M-Sa 5-12:30am, Su 7-12:30am. Travel center open M-Sa 5:15am-11:15pm, Su 7am-11pm. Bathrooms 20p. Lockers £2-4; all luggage is scanned; open M-Sa 7:30am-9:15pm, Su 11:15am-7pm. Trains (☎(08457) 484950) to: **Edinburgh** (50min., 2 per hr., £7.30); **Aberdeen** (2½hr.; M-Sa every hr., Su 11 per day; £36); **Inverness** (3¼hr., 5 per day, £30); **Fort William** (3¾hr.; M-Sa 3 per day, Su 2 per day; £20).

Buses: Buchanan Station (☎(0870) 608 2608), Hanover St., 2 blocks north of Queen St. Station, houses National Express and Scottish Citylink buses. Ticket office open M-Sa 6:30am-10:30pm, Su 7am-10:30pm. Bathrooms 20p. Luggage storage £2-4 per item. Lockers open daily 6:30am-10:30pm. **Scottish Citylink** (☎(08705) 505050) to: **Edinburgh** (1hr.; M-Sa 4 per hr., Su 2 per hr.; £3); **Perth** (1½hr., every hr., £7.50); **Oban** (3hr.; M-Sa 3 per day, Su 2 per day; £10.70); **Inverness** (3½-4½hr., every hr., £12.80); and **Aberdeen** (4hr., every hr., £14.50). **National Express** (☎(08705) 808080) arrives daily from **London** (8-18hr.; every hr.; £22, return £31).

LOCAL TRANSPORTATION

Travel Center: Strathclyde Transport Authority, St. Enoch's Sq., 2 blocks from Central Station. U: St. Enoch. Immensely useful transport advice, passes, and Underground maps. (☎332 7133. Open M-Sa 8:30am-5:30pm.)

Public Transportation: Glasgow's transportation system includes suburban rail, private local bus services, and the circular **Underground (U)** subway line, a.k.a. the "Clockwork Orange." U trains run M-Sa 6:30am-10:45pm, Su 11am-6pm. 80p, children 40p. **Underground Season Tickets** are a good deal at £6 for 7 days (children £3), or £20 for 28 days (children £10); bring a photo and ID to the office at St. Enoch station. The **Day Discovery Pass** is valid on the Underground after 9:30am (£2.50). For a whirlwind tour, travel fast and far enough to get your money's worth from a **Roundabout Glasgow Ticket,** which covers one day of unlimited Underground and train travel (£3.50, children £1.75). The **Daytripper Ticket** gives families unlimited travel throughout the Strathclyde region by rail, Underground, most buses, and some ferries (1 adult and 2 children £7.50, 2 adults and 4 children £13). Wave your hand to ensure that **buses** stop for you, and carry exact change (fares usually 45-95p, depending on destination).

Taxis: Wide TOA Taxis (☎429 7070). **Albany Cars** (☎556 3111 or 554 4469). Both 24hr.

Bike Rental: Compact and crisscrossed by bike lanes, Glasgow is great for cycling. **West End Cycles,** 16 Chancellor St. (☎357 1344), rents for £12 per day, £50 per week.

✦ ORIENTATION

George Sq. is the center of town; the stations, tourist information centre (TIC), and cathedral are within a few blocks. Sections of **Sauchiehall St.** (SAW-kee-hall), **Argyle St.,** and **Buchanan St.** are pedestrianized, forming busy shopping districts in the city center. As an old Glasgow saying has it, "if you go up Sauchie and down Bucky, you will have shopped your heart out." **Charing Cross,** in the northwest where Bath St. crosses the M8 Motorway, is used as a locator. The vibrant **West End** revolves around **Byres Rd.** and **Glasgow University,** a mile northwest of George Sq.

▌ PRACTICAL INFORMATION

TOURIST, FINANCIAL, AND LOCAL SERVICES

Tourist Information Centre: 11 George Sq. (☎204 4400; fax 221 3524), off George Sq. south of Buchanan and Queen St. Stations, northeast of Central Station. U: Buchanan St. Travel bookshop, accommodations bookings £2 (local) or £3 (national) plus 10% deposit, car rental, CalMac ferry tickets, Western Union money transfers, and a **bureau de change.** Pick up the free *Essential Guide to Glasgow* and *Where to Stay.* Open July-Aug. M-Sa 9am-8pm, Su 10am-6pm; June and Sept. M-Sa 9am-7pm, Su 10am-6pm; Oct.-May M-Sa 9am-6pm.

Tours: Glasgow City Walk (☎579 7976) sets off from the TIC M-Sa 6pm, Su 10:30am. Historic 1½hr. tours leave at 2pm and ghost tours at 7pm and 9pm. £5, concessions £4. **Discovering Glasgow** (☎204 0444) buses leave from George Sq., 2 per hr. 9:30am-4pm. £7, students and seniors £5.50, under 14 £2, families £15. Also from George Sq., the green-and-cream **Guide Friday** (☎248 7644) buses run 2 per hr. 9:30am-5pm. £7, students and seniors £5.50, under 12 £2, families £15.

Financial Services: Banks are plentiful. **Thomas Cook,** 15-17 Gordon St. (☎204 4484), inside Central Station. Open M-W and F-Sa 8:30am-6:30pm, Th 8:30am-7:30pm, Su 10am-4pm. **American Express,** 115 Hope St. (☎(08706) 001060). Open July-Aug. M-F 8:30am-5:30pm, Sa 9am-5pm; Sept.-June M-F 8:30am-5:30pm, Sa 9am-noon.

Launderette: Coin-Op Laundromat, 39-41 Bank St. (☎339 8953). U: Kelvin Bridge. Open M-F 9am-7:30pm, Sa-Su 9am-5pm.

EMERGENCY AND COMMUNICATIONS

Emergency: ☎999.

Police: Stewart St. (☎532 3000).

Hospital: Glasgow Royal Infirmary, 84-106 Castle St. (☎211 4000).

Internet Access: easyEverything Internet Cafe, 57-61 St. Vincent St. (☎222 2365), has 400 computers and the best rates. £1 buys 40-75min. Open daily 24hr. **The Internet Cafe,** 569 Sauchiehall St. (☎564 1052). £3 per 30min., £5 per hr. Concessions £2.50 per 30min. Open M-Th 9am-11pm, F 9am-7pm, Sa-Su noon-7pm.

Post Office: Post offices are sprinkled about the city center on Bothwell St., Sauchiehall St., Hope St., and Renfrew St. near George Sq. The main one is at 47 St. Vincent St. (☎204 3688). Open M-F 8:30am-5:45pm, Sa 9am-5:30pm. **Postal Code:** G2 5QX.

🏠 ACCOMMODATIONS

Book guest houses, B&Bs, and hostels at least a month in advance, especially in August. Last-minute planners may want to try the **SYHA Loch Lomond** (see p. 566) or the **SYHA New Lanark** (see p. 549). The TIC can usually find you a room in the £16-20 range. Otherwise, most of Glasgow's B&Bs scatter to either side of **Great Western Rd.** in the university area or east of the Necropolis near **Westercraigs Rd.** The universities offer summer housing, but available dorms change from year to year; check at the offices listed below.

HOSTELS

🏠 **Bunkum Backpackers,** 26 Hillhead St. (☎/fax 581 4481). A minute from Glasgow University and the West End. Friendly proprietors Jim and Jean provide a social atmosphere and advice about the city, suggesting alternate lodgings when their own beds are full. Dorm rooms have more space than you can imagine and comfy beds. Common room with TV, large selection of movies, and pianola. Free lockers (deposit required), laundry facilities (£1.50 wash), and kitchen. Some parking. Dorms £9. Weekly £45.

SYHA Glasgow, 7-8 Park Terr. (☎332 3004; fax 331 5007). U: St. George's Cross. From Central Station, take bus #44 from Hope St. and ask for the first stop on Woodlands Rd. (at Lynedoch St.), then follow the sign. From Queen St. Station or Buchanan Station, catch bus #11 on Bath St. Once the residence of an English nobleman and later an upscale hotel, this hostel maintains an air of luxury. Prime location 5min. from Glasgow University and overlooking Kelvingrove Park. All rooms with shower. TV and game rooms, bike shed, laundry facilities, and kitchen. Dorms July-Aug. £11.50, under 18 £9.50; Sept.-Oct. £11/£9.50; Nov.-Feb. £10/£8.50; Apr.-June £11/£9.50.

Glasgow Backpackers Hostel, 17 Park Terr. (☎332 9099; Oct.-June ☎(0131) 220 1869). U: St. George's Cross or Charing Cross. Near the SYHA Glasgow (see directions above). Extremely social hostel steps from the lively party scene. Internet access, self-catering kitchen, and no bunks! Laundry £2.50. Open July-Sept. Dorms £11; twins £25.

Glasgow Euro Hostel (☎222 2828; info@euro-hostels.com), corner of Clyde St. and Jamaica St. opposite Central Station. Convenient location in the city center; if you haven't booked in advance, this is your best chance. Impersonal rooms not the first choice for the social traveler, but facilities are clean and complete. Breakfast included. Internet access, laundry, and kitchen. Dorms £13.75.

Berkeley Globetrotters Hostel, 63 Berkeley St. (☎221 7880), about 2 blocks south of Charing Cross, just below Sauchiehall St. Take bus #57 from the city center to Berkeley St. Within walking distance of the city center and the West End, but especially convenient to neither. Rooms are basic, with shared bathrooms. Rock bottom prices make it a good option for the tight budget. Several affiliated hostels down the road have reception at Globetrotters. Dorms £9.50, £8.50 for longer stays; twins £11.

UNIVERSITY DORMS

University of Strathclyde, Office of Sales and Marketing, 50 Richmond St. (☎553 4148). B&B in summer at a number of campus dorms. **Baird Hall,** 460 Sauchiehall St. (☎332 6415). Nicely furnished rooms in a grand location. Small kitchen per floor, laundry facilities, and towels. Open mid-June to Sept. Singles £19; twins £33. Also 11 year-round **guest rooms** often filled by visiting professors. Singles £21; twins £35.

University of Glasgow, 52 Hillhead St. (☎330 5385; fax 334 5465). Summer housing at several dorms. Office open M-F 9am-5pm. **Cairncross House,** 20 Kelvinhaugh Pl. (☎221 9334), offers housing off Argyle St., near Kelvingrove Park. Tea and coffee, soap, towels, and linen provided. Self-catering. Student dorms £13.50.

B&BS

McLay's Guest House, 268 Renfrew St. (☎332 4796; fax 353 0422). Central location near the Glasgow School of Art and Sauchiehall St. With 3 dining rooms and satellite TV and phones in each of the 62 rooms, this posh B&B looks and feels more like a hotel. Singles £22, with bath £27; doubles £38/£46; family room (sleeps 4) £51/£60.

Alamo Guest House, 46 Gray St. (☎339 2395), across from Kelvingrove Museum. Beautiful location, gracious owners, and quiet rooms. Singles £20-22; doubles from £34.

Seton Guest House, 6 Seton Terr. (☎556 7654; fax 402 3655; passway@seton.prestelco.uk). A 20min. walk east of George Sq., or take bus #6, 6A, or 41A. Kindly hosts keep immaculate rooms with ornate chandeliers. Out of the way, but all the quieter for it. Singles £17; twins £32.

Chez Nous Guest House, 33 Hillhead St. (☎334 2977), just above Glasgow University. U: Hillhead. Convenient access to West End. Attractive rooms are small but well kept. Singles £18.50-27.50; doubles £20.50-25 per person.

YMCA ApartHotel, David Naismith Court, 33 Petershill Rd. (☎558 6166; fax 558 2036). Take bus #12A or 16 from Queen St. Station or #12 from Central Station. A 15min. ride from the city center, this 30-floor monstrosity makes up for an uninspiring location with amenities: game room, TV room, restaurant, and bar in addition to small but pleasant rooms. Reception open 24hr. Kitchen flats available. B&B singles £20; doubles £30.

🖸 FOOD

Glasgow is often called "the curry capital of Britain," and for good reason. The area bordered by **Otago St.** in the west, **St. George's Rd.** in the east, and along **Great Western Rd., Woodlands Rd.,** and **Eldon St.** brims with cheap kebab 'n' curry joints. The presence of university students has bred a number of cheap hole-in-the-wall restaurants with excellent food. **Byres Rd.** and **Ashton Ln.,** a tiny hard-to-find cobblestone alley parallel to Byres Rd., thrive with cheap, trendy cafes and bistros. Bakeries along **High St.** below the cathedral serve scones for as little as 20p. For self-caterers, **Woodlands Grocers,** 110 Woodlands Rd. (☎353 3820), is open 24hr.

🖸 Cafe Antipasti, 337 Byres Rd. (☎337 2737) and 305 Sauchiehall St. (☎332 9002). High-quality Italian fare at bargain rates. Intimate but bustling—expect waits for dinner.

Start with the spectacular bruschetta (from £2) and follow with pizza, pasta, or a fancy meal-sized salad (all £5.45-7.45). Open M-Th 9am-11pm, F-Su 9am-midnight.

Grosvenor Cafe, 31-35 Ashton Ln. (☎339 1848). Amazing value and endless menu, but beware of the long lines. Desserts and stuffed rolls 95p-£1.20, bigger dishes £3-4. A more elaborate dinner menu (main courses £5.25-8.45) is available Tu-Sa 7-11pm. Open M 9am-7pm, Tu-Sa 9am-11pm, Su 10:30am-5:30pm.

Insomnia Cafe, 38-40 Woodlands Rd. (☎564 1530), in the West End. The place to gorge, day or night, with eclectic dishes and a hip atmosphere. Dine on pasta with Italian sausage (£5) or satisfy a 4:30am craving for stuffed red peppers and leek risotto (£4.75). Awake daily 24hr. Two doors down, **Crispins** serves top-notch sandwich platters (try their smoked salmon) for £3-4.50. Open Su-Th 7am-midnight, F-Sa 24hr.

The Willow Tea Rooms, 217 Sauchiehall St. (☎332 0521), upstairs from Henderson the Jewellers. A Glasgow landmark, entirely designed by famed local architect Charles Rennie Mackintosh: everything in the building matches, down to the antiquated bathroom. Sip one of 28 kinds of tea (£1.20-1.45 per pot) in the restored Mackintosh room, or snack on meringues with strawberries and cream for £2.10. 3-course afternoon tea £7.75. Open M-Sa 9:30am-4:30pm, Su noon-4:15pm.

The Bay Tree Vegetarian Cafe, 403 Great Western Rd. (☎334 5898), at Park Rd. in the West End (cut through Kelvingrove Park). This popular, cramped cafe serves delicious vegan dishes in mid-sized portions. Pita bread with hummus and salad (£3.50-4.50) starts off a Mid-Eastern-style meal. Wide variety of cakes 75p-£2. 10% student discount, 15% senior discount. Open M-Sa 9am-9pm, Su 9am-8pm.

👁 SIGHTS

Glasgow is a budget sightseer's paradise, with grand museums, chic galleries, and splendid period architecture. Many of the best sights are part of the **Glasgow Museums** group, whose museums, scattered across the city, are free. *The List*, available from newsagents for £1.95, reviews current exhibitions and lists galleries.

THE CITY CENTER

GEORGE SQUARE. This red-paved respite, with small patches of grass, lies in the busiest part of the city. Named for George III, the square's 80 ft. column was originally designed to support a statue of His Royal Highness; in the ultimate snub, Glaswegians replaced George with a statue of Sir Walter Scott. The author wears his plaid, as he always did, over the wrong shoulder (the right). The square is guarded on every side by several statues (12 in total), one of which usually has an orange traffic cone placed on its head by a student from Glasgow's School of Art. The **City Chambers,** on the east side of George Sq., epitomize Victorian confidence: an elaborate marble interior in Italian Renaissance style hides behind its dignified stone facade. Pop into the lobby for 30 seconds, or take a free tour starting at the main entrance. (☎287 4017. Tours M-F 10:30am and 2:30pm.) **The Gallery of Modern Art,** south of George Sq. on Queens St., is housed in a beautiful classical building, once the Royal Exchange. Its eclectic selection of contemporary art is arrayed imaginatively on four levels: Earth, Water, Fire, and Air. (☎229 1996. Open M-Th and Sa 10am-5pm, F and Su 11am-5pm. Free.)

THE ST. MUNGO MUSEUM OF RELIGIOUS LIFE AND ART. The museum surveys every religion you can think of, from Hindu to Native American faiths to Yoruba. It features a fascinating exhibit on the intersection of sex, marriage, gender roles, and religion, though its prized possession is Dalí's painting *Christ of St. John's Cross*. (2 Castle St. ☎553 2557. Open M-Sa 10am-5pm, Su 11am-5pm. Free.)

GLASGOW CATHEDRAL. This Gothic cathedral was the only full-scale cathedral spared the fury of the mid-16th-century Scottish Reformation. The cathedral's lime-green slanted roof and blackened exterior, recalling Glasgow's industrial past, contrast sharply with the ornate carvings and marvelous stained glass of the interior. The stained glass is mostly post-war: look for the purple Adam and Eve in the western window, rendered in graphic detail. The Victorians would not have been amused. (Castle St. Walk to the eastern end of Cathedral St. behind Queen St. Station. ☎ 552 6891. Open Apr.-Sept. M-Sa 9:30am-6pm, Su 2-5pm; Oct.-Mar. M-Sa 9:30am-4pm, Su 2-4pm. Organ recitals held some Tu in July and Aug. 7:30pm. Free.)

NECROPOLIS. In this chilling hilltop cemetery, inspired by Paris's Père Lachaise, tombstones, statues, and obelisks lie aslant, broken and flat on the ground. A 50 ft. statue of John Knox, leader of the Scottish Reformation, tops the hill where amazing views of the city await, laced by silhouettes of crosses and markers. Wander amid the 20 ft. tombs, most of 19th-century industrialists, and remember where all paths of glory lead. At night, visit at your own risk, and watch out for wandering spirits. (Behind the cathedral. Free. And very cool.)

SHOPPING. Glasgow, quite simply, is a first-rate place to shop, second only to London in purchasing verve. **Sauchiehall St.** and **Buchanan St.** are both pedestrianized and lined with interesting stores, as well as pubs, cafes, and art galleries; **Princes Square** is a high-end shopping mall as classy as Kensington. The Mackintosh-designed interior makes it well worth the visit, even if you're out of cash. (48 Buchanan St. ☎ 221 0324.) A new shopping center, the **Buchanan Galleries,** at the end of Buchanan St., opened to protests in 1999 because of its every-mall appearance, but it remains hugely popular among capitalists.

OTHER CENTRAL SIGHTS. Built in 1471 and the oldest house in Glasgow, **Provand's Lordship,** near the St. Mungo Museum, now preserves a collection of antique furniture in musky air. The Renaissance-style garden grows some of Glasgow's finest healing herbs. (3-7 Castle St. ☎ 553 2557. Open M-Th and Sa 10am-5pm, F and Su 11am-5pm. Free.) In their enthusiasm for the Industrial Revolution, Glaswegians destroyed most of their medieval past, only to recreate it later on the ground floor of the **People's Palace** museum, which now recounts the city's history. (On Glasgow Green by the river. ☎ 554 0223. Open M-Th and Sa 10am-5pm, F and Su 11am-5pm. Free.)

THE WEST END

■ **KELVINGROVE PARK AND ART GALLERY.** Starting one block west of Park Circus, Kelvingrove Park is a genteel, wooded expanse on the banks of the River Kelvin, favored by tanning locals and students absorbed in books. Rumored to have been built back to front (the true entrance faces the park, not the street), the spired **Kelvingrove Art Gallery and Museum** occupies the park's southwest corner. The unusual brick building's extensive art collection includes works by Rembrandt, Monet, van Gogh, Renoir, and Cezanne. The museum contains a display on arms and armor (from medieval knights to imperial stormtroopers), as well as silver, costume, and natural history exhibits. (On the corner of Argyle St. and Sauchiehall St. U: Kelvin Hall. ☎ 287 2699. Tours of art collection at regular intervals. Open M-Th and Sa 10am-5pm, F and Su 11am-5pm. Free.)

UNIVERSITY OF GLASGOW. The central spire of the university, a Gothic revival structure devised by Gilbert Scott, is visible from afar. The main building is on University Ave., which runs into Byres Rd., a busy thoroughfare in the West End. The best overall view of the university buildings is from Sauchiehall St. by Kelvingrove Park, but the structures are worth a zoomed-in look as well. (U: Hillhead.) While you're walking the campus that has churned out 57 Nobel laureates, stop by the **Hunterian Museum.** The oldest museum in Scotland includes a death mask of Bonnie Prince Charlie. The huge coin collection upstairs was second only to the King of France's when it was established. (☎ 330 4221. Open M-Sa 9:30am-5pm. Free.) The **Hunterian Art Gallery,** across the street, displays 19th-century Scottish art, the world's second-largest Whistler collection, and reconstructed rooms from the house of Charles Rennie Mackintosh. (☎ 330 5431. Open M-Sa 9:30am-5pm. Free.)

CHARLES RENNIE MACKINTOSH BUILDINGS. Several buildings designed by Charles Rennie Mackintosh, Scotland's most famous architect, are open to the public. Pick up the free *Charles Rennie Mackintosh: Buildings & Tours Guide* at the TIC or any Mackintosh sight and plan your route. The best place to start is the **Glasgow School of Art**, 167 Renfrew St., completed in 1898. Here, Mackintosh fused wrought iron, sweeping bay windows, Scottish Baronial styles, and Art Nouveau influences to create a uniquely modern Glaswegian style. (☎ 353 4526. *Tours M-F 11am and 2pm, Sa 10:30am; July-Aug. also Sa-Su 10:30, 11:30am, and 1pm. £5, students £3.*) The Charles Rennie Mackintosh Society is based at the stark **Willow Tea Rooms;** stop by to imbibe both tea and the surroundings (see **Food,** p. 545).

BOTANIC GARDENS. Serene gardens grace the end of Byres Rd. Humid rooms in the **Main Range** hothouse contain an impressive collection of orchids, ferns, palms, and cacti. Though little more than a glorified greenhouse, **Kibble Palace** has an elegant fishpond surrounded by Neoclassical statues. (*Great Western Rd.* ☎ 334 2422. *Gardens open daily 7am-10pm. Kibble Palace and Main Range open Apr. to late Oct. 10am-4:45pm; late Oct. to Mar. 10am-4:15pm; Main Range opens Sa 1pm, Su noon. All free.*)

MUSEUM OF TRANSPORT. Housing old cars, trains, horse-drawn carriages, fire engines, ambulances, and bicycles, the Museum of Transport appeals to the 10-year-old boy in all of us. This psychological darkside is more prevalent in some than others; your own will tell you whether the Museum of Transport is worth your time. (*On Argyle St., near the Kelvingrove Museum.* ☎ 221 9600. *Open M-Th and Sa 10am-5pm, F and Su 11am-5pm. Free.*)

SOUTH OF THE CLYDE

▨ **POLLOK COUNTRY PARK AND THE BURRELL COLLECTION.** The main attraction of Pollok Country Park, a huge wooded area of shady forest paths and colorful flora, is the famous **Burrell Collection,** which rivals Kelvingrove in variety and quality. The collection was once the private stash of ship magnate William Burrell, reflecting his diverse (but always discriminating) tastes: exquisite pieces from Ancient Greece and Rome, paintings by Cezanne, Degas, and Boudin, and plenty of needlework, from tapestry to textile. Together, the park and collection are well worth the 15min. bus ride from city center. (☎ 287 2550. *Open M-Th and Sa 10am-5pm, F and Su 11am-5pm. Free.*) Also in the park is the less spectacular, more domestic **Pollok House,** a nondescript mansion with a lovely collection of Spanish paintings. (☎ 616 6410. *Take bus #45, 48, or 57 (£1.20) from Jamaica St. Open M-Th and Sa 10am-5pm, F and Su 11am-5pm. Free.*)

▨ **GLASGOW SCIENCE CENTRE.** Opened in June 2001, the Science Centre is the latest addition to Glasgow's striking architectural tradition, and worthy of the city's high standard. Nicknamed the "Armadillo," the Centre gleams in the sunlight as the only titanium-clad complex in the UK, Europe's second example after the Guggenheim Museum in Bilbao, Spain. The Centre is divided into three buildings. The first houses Scotland's largest screen and only IMAX theater, which attracted over 100,000 visitors in its first six months of operation. (*Open Su-W 10am-5pm, Th-Sa 10am-9pm. Tickets £5.50.*) The second, shaped like an orange slice turned on its side, houses hundreds of interactive exhibits. (*Open Tu-Su 10am-5pm. Tickets £6.50.*) Perhaps of greatest interest is the 100m Glasgow Tower, the only building in the world that rotates 360° from the ground up. Scotland's tallest freestanding structure, the tower chronicles the city's history and offers views 20 mi. in every direction. (*Open Su-W 10am-5pm, Th-Sa 10am-9pm. Tickets £5.50.*) The entire complex cost £75 million, 10 times less expensive than London's Millennium Dome but 10 times more successful. (*50 Pacific Quay. U: Cessnock, accessible by Bells Bridge.* ☎ 420 5010.)

▨▨ PUBS AND NIGHTLIFE

Glaswegians have a reputation for partying hard. Three universities and the highest student-to-resident ratio in Britain guarantee a kinetic nightlife scene. *The List*, available from newsagents for £1.95, has detailed nightlife and entertainment listings for both Glasgow and Edinburgh.

SEEING RED After the defeat of Bonnie Prince Charlie's Highland Army at Culloden in 1746, Parliament passed the Proscription Acts, making it illegal to wear tartan, in order to end the constant, acrimonious feuds spawned by Scotland's clan system. The Scots, however, can be a canny, stubborn people, and Glaswegians have since found new ways of channeling their antagonistic energy. Together, Glasgow's "Old Firm" of Celtic and Rangers Football Clubs dominate Scotland's Premier League, but far be it from this city to watch idly as its two favorite teams battle for the Cup each year. The opponents are bitter foes, drawing on religious differences to fuel their passionate enmity (Celtic's supporters are mainly Catholic; Ranger's—surprise!—are Protestant), and it can be dangerous to be caught wearing the Celtic green-and-white or the Ranger blue in enemy territory. Plagued by violent brawls, pubs have had to institute a "No Football Colours at the Bar" rule. Ubiquitous in Glasgow's watering holes, it may be their only trait in common with England's Parliament.

PUBS

There are hundreds of pubs in the city, and you'll never find yourself much more than half a block from a frothy pint. The infamous **Byres Rd.** pub crawl slithers past the Glasgow University area, beginning at Tennant's Bar and proceeding toward the River Clyde. Drinks are cheap to start with, but watch for happy hours, when many pubs reduce prices to a joyous £1.

■ **Uisge Beatha,** 232 Woodlands Rd. (☎564 1596). A Scottish bar with blackened wood furnishings, red velvet seats, and kilt-clad bartenders. "Uisge Beatha" (oos-ga BAY-uh) is Gaelic for "water of life" (read: whisky). With over 100 malt whiskies (£1.85-35), you'll want to make sure you order the right one. Sip the national drink as you listen to Gaelic tunes. Open M-Th 11am-11pm, F-Sa 11am-midnight, Su 12:30-11pm.

■ **Babbity Bowster,** 16-18 Blackfriar St. (☎552 5055). The perfect place to come for the Scottish experience, pure and simple: fewer kilts and less Gaelic music, more friendliness, good drink, and football talk. Just remember that you become a Glasgow Celtic fan immediately upon entrance. Tasty pub grub offers good value, and the (mercifully) vegetarian haggis isn't half bad (£3.50). Open daily 8am-midnight.

The Ark, 42-46 North Frederick St. (☎559 4331), near George Sq. File in two-by-two, and drink amid the bright colors, funky signs, and other animals (human crowds included). 4-pint pitcher £6. Cover some weekend nights. Open daily noon-midnight.

Horseshoe Bar, 17-21 Drury St. (☎204 4056), 1 block north of Gordon St., off Reinfield St. This Victorian, horseshoe-shaped pub, with etched mirrors and carved wooden walls, is a Glasgow institution. It boasts the longest continuous bar in the UK; up to 15 bartenders staff it when the mostly older male crowd swells mid-afternoon. Head upstairs for a hearty 3-course lunch (£2.80; served M-Sa noon-2:30pm). Open M-Sa 8am-midnight, Su 12:30pm-midnight.

Variety Bar, 401 Sauchiehall St. (☎332 4449). Older men's pub by day, art students' hangout by night, and popular with backpackers for its cheap drinks. No frills, just a quality pub. Tu and Su reggae, Th New Orleans soul, F-Sa techno. Happy hour M-Sa 11am-8pm, Su 12:30-8pm: pints of lager £1.50; Guinness £1.60; vodka, rum, whisky dashes £1.35. Open daily 11am-11:45pm.

Nice 'n' Sleazy, 421 Sauchiehall St. (☎333 0900). Eclectic live music downstairs Sa-W, £2.50-3. Upstairs, it almost gets too loud for a bar, believe it or not. Happy hour Su-Th 5-10pm, F 5-8pm; £6 gets you a 4-pint pitcher. Occasional cover Th-Sa. Open daily 11:30am-midnight.

CLUBS

Most clubs are open 11pm-3am, but the bacchanalia reaches its fevered pitch after the pubs close. Many clubs open nightly, but you can count on a wild, wild party Thursday through Saturday.

Archaos, 25 Queen St. (☎204 3189). Look for 2 skeletons just outside the 2nd-floor windows. Frequent student discounts and musical variety pack in the punters. Th is the busiest student night in Glasgow; on Sa put on your best, blackest, tightest duds to dance on the domed floor. Cover £3-9. Open W-Su until 3am.

The Garage, 490 Sauchiehall St. (☎332 1120). Beckons with Mad Hatter decor; look for the yellow truck hanging over the door. Dance club classics blast downstairs. The Attic, upstairs, is indie. Cover £4-6; student discounts usually available. Open Sa 10:30pm-4am, Su-F 11pm-3am.

Sub Club, 22 Jamaica St. (☎248 4600). All types grind to house and techno in the purple basement. Their "sub-culture Saturdays" have been running strong for over a decade. Cover £3-6, Sa £8. Open Th-F and Su 11pm-3am, Sa 11pm-3:30am.

Velvet Rooms, 520 Sauchiehall St. (☎332 0755). Where young 'uns get down. When you get tired of the funky hip-hop in one room, enjoy house music in the other. Smart casual is usually OK, but most dress up a bit. Cover £6, students £4. Open F-Sa 10pm-3am, Tu-Th and Su 11pm-3am.

Cathouse, 15 Union St. (☎248 6606) Grunge and indie please mostly student crowds in this popular 3-floor club. Cover £3-5; student £1-2 less. Open W-Su 10:30pm-3am.

▌♪▐ ENTERTAINMENT AND FESTIVALS

The dynamic student population of Glasgow ensures constant film, theater, and music events. The **Ticket Centre,** City Hall, Candleriggs, will tell you what's playing at the city's dozen-odd theaters. Get the free *City Live* guide, which has great tips. (☎287 5511. Phones answered M-Sa 9am-9pm, Su noon-5pm; office open M-Sa 9:30am-6:30pm, Su 10am-5pm.) Theaters include the **Theatre Royal,** Hope St. (☎332 9000) and the **Tron Theatre,** 63 Trongate (☎552 4267). The **Cottier Theatre,** 935 Hyndland St. (☎357 3868) hosts a wide variety of musical and theatrical events, from avant-garde plays to opera (£4-25). The **Royal Concert Hall,** Sauchiehall St., is a frequent venue for concerts by the Royal Scottish National Orchestra. (☎353 8000. Box office open M-Sa 10am-6pm.) The **Glasgow Film Theatre,** 12 Rose St., screens sleeper hits and cult classics, while art exhibitions and a bar with food occupy the main space. (☎332 8128. Box office open M-Sa noon-9pm, Su 30min. before first film. £4.75, matinees £3.75; concessions £3.25/£2.25.)

Among Glasgow's constant flow of musical shows, temporary art exhibitions, and festivals is the annual **Glasgow International Jazz Festival** (☎552 3552), in the first week in July, which draws jazz greats from all over the world. During mid-August, over 100 of the top kilt-clad bagpipe bands compete for glory and honor on the Glasgow Green at the **World Pipe Championships** (☎221 5414).

NEAR GLASGOW: LANARK ☎01555

Thirty miles southwest of Glasgow, in the peaceful Clyde valley, the recreated village of **New Lanark** allows tourists to experience 19th-century utopian dreams of the Industrial Revolution. Founded in 1785, it was the most productive manufacturing site in Scotland for much of the 19th century, partly due to the somewhat socialist tendencies of the cotton-mill owner. Instead of sending 8-year-olds to work 12-hour days, Robert Owen sent them to school. He also paid living wages, founded an Institute for the Formulation of Character, and started the first semi-cooperative village store and infant school. Visitors can walk through the restored store, a millworker's house, and Owen's own residence, which is surprisingly posh. The visitor center also lets you try cloth production for yourself. Admission to New Lanark includes the *New Millennium Experience,* a ride through scenes in the settlement's colorful history. (☎661345. Open daily 11am-5pm. £4.75, concessions £3.25, families £13-15.) The river valley has lovely hikes. Walk a mile upstream past the hydro-power plant to the **Falls of Clyde,** whose waters turn a furious white as they rocket down vertical drops. Continue on the trail for another ½ mi. to the **Peregrine Falcon Observation Point,** where a local ranger will help you spot the nesting pair.

SOUTHERN SCOTLAND

To reach New Lanark, you'll need to go through Lanark. **Trains** (☎(08457) 484950) from **Glasgow Central** (45min., every hr., return £5.15) run to Lanark's station. (Ticket office open M-Sa 6:10am-10:10pm.) **Irvine's Coaches** (☎(01698) 372452) pass from **Glasgow Buchanan St.** to **Lanark Interchange** (1hr., 5 per day, £3.80). From Lanark, **Stuart's Coaches** (☎773533) run to New Lanark from the tourist information centre (5min., every hr., 55p); otherwise, it's a 20min. walk. The **tourist information centre** is next to the train station. (☎661661; fax 666143. Open Apr.-Sept. M-Sa 10am-6pm, Su noon-5pm; Oct.-Mar. M-Sa 10am-5pm.) Pick up the free *Lanark Heritage Trail* guide, which details **Old St. Kentigern's Church,** where William Wallace married Marion Braidfute. The **post office** is at 28 St. Leonard St. (☎662230. Open M-F 9am-5:30pm, Sa 9am-12:30pm.) **Postal code:** ML11 9AB.

Stay at the ▨**New Lanark Youth Hostel,** Wee Row, Rosedale St., a restored mill workers' dwelling with river views and modern luxuries only dreamed of by earlier occupants: laundry facilities and attached baths in all rooms. (☎666710; fax 666719. Continental breakfast included. Reception closed 10:30am-5pm. Curfew 11:45pm. Dorms £8.50, under 18 £7.25.) **Bankhead Farm,** near the corner of Braxfield Rd. and Lanark Rd., tenders spacious rooms with thick carpets, TVs, desks, and comfortable beds in a converted farmhouse. Take Braxfield Rd. out of the town center. (☎/fax 666560. £16-18 per person.)

CENTRAL
SCOTLAND

Less lofty than the Highlands and more subdued than the cities to the south, central Scotland has its draws. The eastern shoulder, curving from Fife to the Highland Boundary Fault along the North Sea, is plated with historical fishing villages and centuries-old communities scattered amid untouched wilderness. To the east, the countryside flattens from snow-covered mountains into the plains of the Central Lowlands, giving the A82 road from Loch Lomond to Glen Coe some of Scotland's best views. Castles of all vintages and sizes, such as proud, ancient Stirling, testify to the region's strategic importance, while the remote Inner Hebrides, separated by mountains and a strip of sea, offer their own enchanting beauty.

HIGHLIGHTS OF CENTRAL SCOTLAND

STIRRING STIRLING Admire the 5½ ft. sword of William Wallace and one of Britain's grandest castles in the historic royal capital of Scotland (p. 564).

THE BONNY BONNY BANKS Hike the shores of beautiful **Loch Lomond,** the inspiration for the ballad of the same name (p. 566).

ISLE HOPPING Pass through the Isle of Mull's pastel, palm-treed Tobermory (p. 574) on your way to the melodious caves of the stunning Isle of Staffa (p. 577).

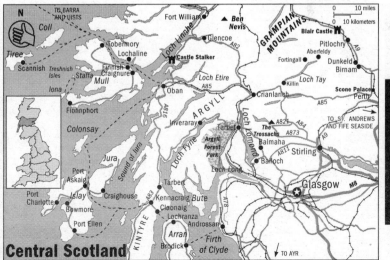

Central Scotland

ST. ANDREWS

☎ **01334**

> Would you like to see a city given over,
> Soul and body to a tyrannising game?
> If you would, there's little need to be a rover,
> For St. Andrews is the abject city's name.
> —Robert F. Murray

The "tyrannising game" of golf overruns the small city of St. Andrews. It was here, at the Royal and Ancient Golf Club (the R&A), that the rules of the game were formally established, and the club's windows overlook the Old Course, the sport's world headquarters. But beyond the tradition that attracts millions of pom-pom clad putt-putt enthusiasts, and the prices they've driven sky-high, there is the beauty of St. Andrews's other glories: the gray stone buildings of Scotland's oldest university, the cathedral ruins of the seat of pre-Reformation Christianity, and restored medieval streets that lead to the North Sea.

▐▀ TRANSPORTATION

Trains (☎ (08457) 484590) from **Edinburgh** stop 5 mi. away in **Leuchars** (LU-cars) on the London-Edinburgh-Aberdeen line (1hr., every hr., ₤8.10); from Leuchars, buses #93-96 run to St. Andrews (5 per hr. 7am-8pm, ₤1.45). **St. Andrews Bus Station** is on City Rd. (☎474238). **Stagecoach Express Fife Buses** (☎(01383) 621249 or 474238) #X59 and X60 come from **Edinburgh** (2hr.; M-Sa 2 per hr. until 6:45pm, fewer on Su; ₤5.70); the #X24 leaves **Glasgow** and changes at Glenrothes to #X59 before arriving in St. Andrews (2½hr.; M-Sa every hr., fewer on Su; ₤5.50). From **Aberdeen, Perth,** and **Inverness,** first take **Scottish Citylink** to Dundee (2 per hr.) and then **Stagecoach Fife** #95, 96, or 96A to St. Andrews (₤2.40, students ₤1.60 on #95 only).

✴ ▐ ORIENTATION AND PRACTICAL INFORMATION

The three main streets in St. Andrews—**North St., Market St.,** and **South St.**—run nearly parallel east to west, terminating near the cathedral at the town's east end.

Tourist Information Centre: 70 Market St. (☎472021; fax 478422). Provides the free *Kingdom of Fife* guide and books accommodations in Fife for a 10% deposit (plus a ₤3 fee elsewhere). Open July-Aug. M-Sa 9:30am-7pm, Su 11am-6pm; May-June and Sept. M-Sa 9:30am-6pm, Su 11am-5pm; Oct.-Apr. M-Sa 9:30am-5pm.

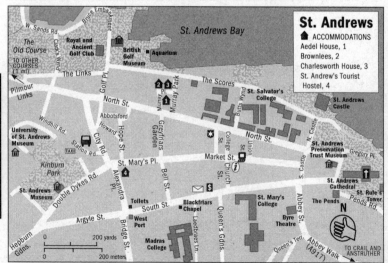

St. Andrews

⌂ ACCOMMODATIONS
Aedel House, 1
Brownlees, 2
Charlesworth House, 3
St. Andrew's Tourist
Hostel, 4

Financial Services: Royal Bank of Scotland, 119 South St. (☎472181). **Bureau de change.** Open M-Tu and Th-F 9:15am-4:45pm, W 10am-4:45pm.

Launderette: 14b Woodburn Terr. (☎475150). Open M-Sa 9am-7pm, Su 9am-5pm; last wash 1½hr. before close.

Internet Access: Costa Coffee, 83 Market St., across from the tourist information centre (TIC). £1 per 20min., £10 per 5hr. Open M-Sa 8am-8pm, Su 10am-8pm.

Hospital: St. Andrew's Memorial, Abbey Walk (☎472327), southeast of town.

Post Office: 127 South St. (☎472321). Open M-Sa 10am-5:30pm. **Postal code:** KY16 9UL.

ACCOMMODATIONS

The new hostel down **Market St.** is the only reliable budget option. Otherwise, **Murray Park** and **Murray Place,** near the Golf links, have some expensive B&Bs (£17-24 per person). Summer housing at the university may provide cheap lodging; inquire at the TIC. St. Andrews also makes an easy daytrip from Edinburgh.

St. Andrews Tourist Hostel, St. Mary's Pl. (☎479911), above Las Posada restaurant. 5min. from the bus station: turn right on City Rd. and left on St. Mary's Pl. This friendly backpacker haven has good facilities in a great part of town. Sparkling bathrooms; the upstairs shower has unparalleled water pressure. Room key £5, hostel key £5 (for post-11pm returns), linens £1 (so don't wet the bed). Kitchen and laundry. Reception 7am-11pm. May-Sept. £12 per person; Oct.-Apr. £10; 4-bed family room £40-48.

Charlesworth House, 9 Murray Pl. (☎/fax 476528; charlesworth@talk21.com). Spacious rooms with TV and bath in a professional atmosphere. £22-27 per person.

Brownlees, 7 Murray Pl. (☎473868; www.brownlees.co.uk). Elegant housing only a few blocks from the Old Course. A calm, traditional feel. All with TV. £22-27 per person.

Aedel House, 12 Murray Pl. (☎472315). Attractive doubles and one single with bath. Book ahead. Open Feb.-Nov. Singles £18; doubles £26.

FOOD

Housing may be pricey, but at least the university has prompted cheap, greasy takeaways. The **Tesco** supermarket sits at 130 Market St. (☎413600. Open M-W 8:30am-7:30pm, Th-F 8:30am-8pm, Sa 8am-7pm, Su 10am-6pm.)

The North Point Cafe, North St. (☎473997). Light snacks like tea steeped in bone china (£1 per pot) and gingerbread (£1.20) in view of the castle ruins. Open daily Easter-Oct. 10am-5pm, Nov.-Easter 10am-4:30pm.

Brambles, 5 College St. (☎475380). Anything but prickly. Vegetarian-friendly menus await, as do long lines of locals. Open M-Sa 9am-10pm, Su 11am-10pm.

The Eating Place, 177-9 South St. Tasty breakfasts all day (under £5) in a friendly diner environment. The fruit-covered Scottish drop pancakes—smaller and less sweet than your average flapjack—are delicious. Open M-Sa 9:30am-5pm, Su 11:30am-5pm.

B. Jannetta, 31 South St. (☎473285). 52 flavors of award-winning ice cream, including Nutella, prove these "Ice Cream Specialists" mean business. Overrun with sticky children when school lets out. 70p per scoop. Open daily 9am-5:30pm.

PUBS

Though they close rather early, St. Andrews's pubs are worth a 19th-hole stop. **The Central,** stereotyped as a Yah hangout ("yes" to the commoner; "yah" mocks the English and Scottish public school accent), attracts a student clientele to its digs on Market St. and College St. Excellent pub meals like chilli and nachos go for £2-4. (☎478296. Open M-Sa 11am-11:45pm, Su 12:30-11:45pm.) **The Victoria,** 1 St. Mary's Pl., resembles the love child of a Scottish pub and a Western saloon. Sip whisky at the two adjoining bars. (☎476964. Happy hour 8-10pm. Open Sa-W 11am-midnight, Th-F 11am-1am.) Don't miss the "Malt of the Day" at **Drouthy Neebors,** 209

South St.—they'll sell you a distinctive single malt (around £1.25) for the price of a blend. (Open Su-Th until 11pm, F-Sa until midnight.) **The Lizard Lounge,** 127 North St., in the basement of the Inn at North St., offers a more self-consciously stylish atmosphere and drink specials (£1 shots, £1.30 lager pints) from 8:30-9:30pm. (☎ 473387. Open M-W 11am-midnight, Th-Sa 11am-1am, Su noon-midnight.)

👁 🔔 SIGHTS AND ACTIVITIES

GOLF, OF COURSE. If you love golf, play golf, or think that you might ever want to play golf, this is your town. The game was so avidly practiced here that Scotland's rulers outlawed the sport three times, fearing for the national defense ("the men neglected their archery for golf!"). At the edge of town, the **Old Course,** a golf pilgrim's Canterbury, stretches regally to a beach as manicured as the greens. According to the 1568 *Book of Articles,* Mary, Queen of Scots, played here just days after her husband was murdered. Nonmembers must present a handicap certificate or letter of introduction from a golf club. If you weren't old when you made your reservation, you will be when it comes to fruition: book a year in advance. You can also enter your name into a near-impossible lottery by 2pm the day before you hope to play. (☎ 466666; fax 477036. Apr.-Oct. £80 per round; Nov.-Mar. £56.) Call the same line to reserve a time at the **New, Jubilee, Eden,** or **Strathtyrum** courses. Booking ahead is preferable, though walk-ins are possible. The budget option is nine-hole **Balgove Course** for £7. (Info line ☎ 466666; fax 477036. Courses Apr.-Oct. £17-40; Nov.-Mar. £15-28.) July 2000 saw the opening of the newest R&A-associated course, the **Kingsbarns Golf Links** (☎ 880222; www.kingsbarns.com.), farther east along the coast.

BRITISH GOLF MUSEUM. Learn about golf's origins as papier-maché mannequins putt and stitch into eternity. Enthusiasts will find the exhibits fascinating; others, less so. (Bruce Embankment. ☎ 478880. Open Easter-Oct. daily 9:30am-5:30pm; Nov.-Easter Th-M 11am-3pm. £3.75, students and seniors £2.75, children £1.50.)

ST. ANDREWS CATHEDRAL. An important site of pilgrimage in the Middle Ages, this 12th-century church was defaced by iconoclastic Protestants during the Reformation and later pillaged by locals; according to legend, the cathedral's stones make up the foundations of the city's homes. For stunning views, climb **St. Rule's Tower,** once part of the original church. (☎ 472563. Open Apr.-Sept. daily 9:30am-6:30pm; Oct.-Mar. 9:30am-4:30pm. Cathedral free. Tower £1.80, seniors £1.30, children 75p.)

ST. ANDREWS CASTLE. Once the local bishop's residence, the castle garners explorable secret tunnels, bottle-shaped dungeons, and high stone walls to keep out (or in) rebellious heretics. For stellar views, descend the stairs on the right of the Castle fence, where seagulls make their nests in the crags. (The end of North Castle St. ☎ 477196. Open Apr.-Sept. daily 9:30am-6:30pm; Oct.-Mar. 9:30am-4:30pm. £2.50, seniors £1.90, children £1; joint ticket with cathedral £3.75, seniors £2.80, children £1.25.)

UNIVERSITY OF ST. ANDREWS. Founded in the 15th century, Scotland's oldest university maintains a well-heeled student body and strong performing arts program. Following in the footsteps of many Scottish kings who studied here, Prince William began his undergraduate course in art history in the fall of 2001. While it's possible to meander into placid quads through the parking entrances on North St., only the one-hour **official tour** grants access to building interiors. Buy a ticket from the Admissions Reception, Butts Wynd, beside St. Salvator's Chapel Tower on North St. (Between North St. and The Scores. ☎ 462245. Tours mid-June to Aug. M-F 11am and 2:30pm. £4.50, concessions £3.50, under 6 free.) Newly opened in conjunction with the 2000 Open Championship, the high-tech **University of St. Andrews Museum and Information Centre** details the university's history. (The Gateway, on your way into town. ☎ 470070. Open June-Sept. daily 10am-6pm; Oct.-May 10am-5pm. £4, concessions £2.)

OTHER SIGHTS AND ACTIVITIES. The baronial **St. Andrews Museum** harks back to the time of St. Regulus, pointing out that golf is but "a small dot" (a tee, perhaps?) in the town's history. (Kinburn Park, down Doubledykes Rd. ☎ 412690. Open Apr.-Sept. daily

10am-5pm; Oct.-Mar. M-F 10:30am-4pm, Sa-Su 12:30-5pm. Free.) A wax chemist distills elixirs among reproductions of early 20th-century shops at the tiny **St. Andrews Preservation Trust Museum.** *(North St. ☎ 412690. Open early June to Sept. daily 2-5pm. Donations welcome.)* The **St. Andrews Aquarium** displays massive eels and orphaned seals a putt away from the golf museum. *(The Scores. ☎ 474786. Open daily 10am-5pm. £4.50, students £3.35, seniors £3.85, children £3.50. Seal feeding daily 11am and 3pm.)* The **Byre Theatre** recently reopened. *(Abbey St. ☎ 474 6101. Student tickets £3-7.50.)*

FIFE SEASIDE   ☎01333

South of St. Andrews, a series of sun-warmed fishing villages cling to the coast of Fife like barnacles to the hull of a fishing boat, making up The East Neuk. With minimal train service and a lack of budget accommodations, two or three of Fife's villages may be best seen as a daytrip from Edinburgh or St. Andrews. The scenic Fife Coastal Walk strings the villages together, while those with a car can take the A917, which stretches from St. Andrews to Elie. Bus service #95 (St. Andrews-Leven) cruises every hour along the A917 with frequent stops, including Crail, Anstruther, Elie, and Pittenween. For the most up-to-date info, call the Fife Council's Public Transport Information Line. (☎ (01592) 416060. Open M-F 9am-4pm.)

CRAIL. Considered the bonniest of Fife's villages, Crail and its harbor offer snap-happy tourists the perfect Kodak moment. Lined with white cottages with orange-tile roofs, the town has one of central's Scotland's most beautiful stretches of beach—a fitting place to gnaw on freshly caught crab claws sold at harbor stalls. In the last week of July, the **Crail Festival** features concerts, parades, and craft shows. Crail's **tourist information centre,** 62-64 Marketgate, adjoins a lackluster local history museum. (☎ 450869. Open June-Sept. M and F-Sa 10am-1pm and 2-5pm, Tu-Th 10am-5pm, Su noon-5pm; Apr.-May Sa-Su 2-5pm. Free.) **Guided walks** of town leave the museum every Sunday at 2:30pm in July and August (1½-2hr., £3).

ANSTRUTHER. The busiest of the seaside towns, Anstruther lies about 5 mi. west of Crail along the A917 (or 9 mi. southeast of St. Andrews along the B9131). The **Scottish Fisheries Museum** is worth a visit for an interesting look at the occupation that brought Fife to prominence. (☎ 310628. Open Apr.-Oct. M-Sa 10am-5:30pm, Su 11am-5pm; Nov.-Mar. M-Sa 10am-4:30pm, Su noon-4:30pm. Last entry 45min. before close. £3.20, students and seniors £2.20.) Off the coast, the **Isle of May** is a nature reserve home to puffins, gray seals, and Scotland's first lighthouse (built in 1636). In summer, **The May Princess** sails from Anstruther to the Isle. (☎ 310103. July-Aug. 1 per day; May-June and Sept. W-M 1 per day. £12.50, children £5.50.) Times depend on weather and tides; call ahead or check with Anstruther's **tourist information centre,** beside the museum. (☎ 311073. Open Easter-Oct. M and F-Sa 10am-5pm, Tu-Th 10am-1pm and 2-5pm, Su 11am-4pm.) Rent bikes at **East Neuk Cycles,** 63 James St. (☎ 312179. £4 per day. Open M-Sa 9:30am-5pm.) On your way to the bay and lighthouse, don't stop—no matter how hungry you are—until reaching **Anstruther Fishbar and Restaurant,** 44-46 Shore St., known for serving Scotland's best fish and chips. The only inhabitants of Fife who have their fish fresher are the seals, and they aren't always keen on sharing. (Open daily 11:30am-10pm.)

SECRET BUNKER. Halfway between Anstruther and St. Andrews, the Secret Bunker crouches beneath a farmhouse. The subterranean shelter was prepared as a home for British leaders during a nuclear war and contains strategy rooms and even a cinema. Locals claim they knew what it was all along. By car, head down A917 or A915 and savor the irony of conspicuous signs reading "THIS WAY TO THE SECRET BUNKER." Those without a car may be less amused: the Bunker is more trouble to get to than it's worth. War buffs only should take bus #61 (Anstruther-St. Andrews) and ask to get off at Strathclyde intersection; walk a mile down B940, and then follow the ½ mi. winding path to the Bunker. (☎ 310301. Open Apr.-Oct. 10am-5pm. £6, students and seniors £5, children £3.25.)

ELIE. The village of **Elie** (EEL-y), 5 mi. west of Anstruther, has become a posh resort and retirement community, perhaps because of beautiful **Ruby Bay,** named for the garnets occasionally found on its sands. In Elie, the sea washes right up onto the streets, and its crystal waters, among the purest in Britain, are excellent for swimming. **Elie Watersports** (☎330962), above the beach and bay, rents windsurfer and sailing dinghies, with lessons for the inexperienced. For a better view of sporting seals and tidal-pool life, walk to the headland by the lighthouse. Down the coast lies **Lady's Tower,** built in the 18th century as a bathing box for Lady Jane Anstruther, who sent a bell-ringing servant through the streets to warn the village of her presence to prevent (or promote?) anyone seeing her scantily clad.

FALKLAND. Farther inland in the Kingdom of Fife, **Falkland Palace and Gardens,** once the hunting lodge of the Stewarts, epitomizes early Renaissance architecture. Its tennis court, built in 1539, is still in use. (☎(01337) 857397. Open Apr.-Oct. M-Sa 10am-5:30pm, Su 1:30-5:30pm; last entry 4:30pm. £5, concessions £4. Grounds only £2.50, concessions £1.70.) The surrounding town shows off some well-preserved 17th-century facades. By car, follow the M90, A92, or A912 from the south. Public transportation is trickier: reach **Glenrothes** by a **Stagecoach Fife bus** (from St. Andrews or Edinburgh £3.50-4) and then transfer to a Falkland-bound bus.

PERTH
☎01738

Frequently referred to as "The Fair City," Perth is exactly that: fair. Pretty, yes. Peaceful, too. But this placid city of 43,000 is not particularly extraordinary either, catering primarily to residents and mild-mannered guests. Perth served as Scotland's capital until 1452, and there are a few solid reasons to visit—beautiful walks, the Black Watch Museum, and the historical significance of nearby Scone Palace—but travelers pressed for time could easily move on.

▐ TRANSPORTATION

The **train station** is on Leonard St. (Ticket office open M-Sa 6:45am-8:45pm, Su 8:15am-8:25pm.) **Trains** (☎(08457) 484950) arrive from: **Glasgow** (1hr., every hr., £9.40); **Aberdeen** (1½hr., 2 per hr., £20.70); **Edinburgh** (1½hr., 2 per hr., £9.40); **Inverness** (2½hr., 8-9 per day, £15.80). The **bus station** is a block away on Leonard St. (Ticket office open M-F 7:45am-5pm, Sa 8am-4:30pm.) **Scottish Citylink** (☎(08705) 505050) buses run journey from: **Dundee** (35min., 2 per hr., £3.60); **Pitlochry** (40min., every hr., £5); **Edinburgh** (1½hr., 2 per hr., £5.50); **Glasgow** (1½hr., every hr., £7.50); **Aberdeen** (2hr., every hr., £11.50); **Inverness** (2½hr., every hr., £10.30).

▐ PRACTICAL INFORMATION

The **tourist information centre** (TIC), Lower City Mills, books rooms for £1 plus a 10% deposit. From the bus station, turn right on Leonard St., continue along South Methven St., then take a left onto Old High St., following the signposts. (☎450600; fax 444863; www.perthshire.co.uk. Open Apr. 9-July 8 M-Sa 9:30am-5:30pm, Su 11am-4pm; July 10-Aug. M-Sa 9:30am-6:30pm, Su 11am-5pm; Sept.-Oct. M-Sa 9:30am-5:30pm, Su 11am-4pm; Nov.-Mar. M-Sa 10am-4pm.) **Guide Friday** runs opentop **bus tours** in summer, making transport easy to far-away places like Scone Palace and Kinnoull Hill. Buy tickets at the TIC or on the bus at the Mill St. stop. (☎(0131) 556 2244. June-Aug. daily every hr. 10am-4pm. £5.50, seniors and students £4, children £2.) Other services include: the **Royal Bank of Scotland,** South St., next to the post office (open M-Tu and Th-F 9:15am-4:45pm, W 10am-4:45pm, Sa 10am-2pm); **Internet access** at **A.K. Bell Library,** Glasgow Rd., either upstairs (book ahead) or in the **A.K. Bell Incredible Cafe** at the front entrance (☎477061; library £2.50 per 30min.; open M, W, F 9:30am-5pm; Tu and Th 9:30am-8pm; Sa 9:30am-4pm; cafe £1 per 15min.; open M-F 9:30am-4:30pm, Sa 9:30am-3:30pm); and the **post office,** 109 South St. (☎624413; open M-Sa 9am-5:30pm). **Postal code:** PH2 8AF.

🏠📖 ACCOMMODATIONS AND FOOD

The **SYHA Perth**, off Glasgow Rd., is the area's only hostel. Take Hillend bus #7 from the post office to Rosebank Rd. (5min.), or walk 15min. up South St. as it becomes County Pl., York Pl., then Glasgow Rd. Near the crest of the hill, turn right on Rosebank. Find utilitarian dorms behind a pleasing exterior in the tradition of SYHA hostels. (☎623658. Lockers available. Laundry. Reception 7-11am and 5-11:30pm. Check-out 9:30am. Lockout 9:30am-1:30pm. Curfew 11:30pm. Open Mar.-Oct. Dorms £9.25, under 18 £8.) Affordable **B&Bs** line Glasgow Rd. below the hostel. Friendly **Mrs. Glennie,** 54 Glasgow Rd., lets rooms that are spare but livable. (☎626723. £16 per person.) For a more upscale experience, **Abercrombie B&B,** 85 Glasgow Rd., has more space and private bathrooms. (☎444728. £25 per person.)

An enormous **Safeway** supermarket resides on Caledonian Rd. (Open M-Tu and Sa 8am-8pm, W-Th 8am-9pm, F 8am-10pm, Su 9am-6pm.) **The Lemon Tree,** 29-41 Skinner Gate, serves up aubergine bake (£4.75), as well as other savory wholefoods. (☎442689. Open M-Sa 9:30am-5pm.) A spicy three-course Indian lunch costs £4 (M-Sa) at **Cafe Amran,** 21 Princes St. (☎620415. Open M-Th noon-2pm and 5pm-midnight, F-Sa noon-2pm and 5pm-1am, Su 4pm-midnight.)

👁️📷 SIGHTS AND ACTIVITIES

Balhousie Castle, off Hay St., once the 16th-century home of the Earls of Kinnoull, now accommodates the **Black Watch Regimental Museum.** It includes weapons, medals, the key to the back door of Spandau prison in Berlin, and the occasional real-life member of the Watch. (☎621281. Open May-Sept. M-Sa 10am-4:30pm; Oct.-Apr. M-F 10am-3:30pm. Free.) In 1559, John Knox delivered an incendiary sermon from the pulpit of **St. John's Kirk,** on St. John's Pl., prompting the destruction of churches and monasteries during the Reformation. Unfortunately, nothing interesting has happened here since. (Open M-F 10am-noon and 2-4pm.)

The **Perth Museum and Art Gallery,** at the intersection of Tay St. and Perth Bridge, provides an idiosyncratic examination of the city. Visitors are invited to sample the medieval toilet seat. (Open M-Sa 10am-5pm. Tours M-F in summer. Free.) The **Fergusson Gallery,** in the Old Perth Water Works on Marshall Pl., holds an excellent series of watercolors by J.D. Fergusson, a local lad influenced by his companion, dancer Margaret Morris. (☎441944. Open M-Sa 10am-5pm. Free.)

A 20min. walk across the **Perth Bridge** leads to ▓**Kinnoull Hill Woodland Park** and its four well-signposted nature walks, all of which finish at a magnificent summit with panoramic views of the river and countryside. Beginners with children can try the **Tower Walk,** while more experienced hikers might choose the **Nature Walk,** which winds through the thick of the forest; none of the walks, however, should prove a challenge. Across the **Queen's Bridge,** near the Fergusson Gallery, the mile-long **Perth Sculpture Trail** begins in the Rodney Gardens. Survey 24 pieces of modern art while weaving through Perth's bankside greenery. The new **Bell's Cherrybank Centre** is known for its gardens' 900-plus types of heather, but also provides a glossy look at Perth and a certain native, Arthur Bell, who took up the whisky business. Visitors receive a free dram and free admission to Pitlochry's Blair Athol Distillery (see p. 561) Catch bus #7 from South St. (every 20min.) or walk 20min. uphill from the hostel along Glasgow Rd. (☎627330. Open Easter-Oct. M-Sa 9am-5pm, Su noon-4pm; Oct.-Easter M-F 10am-4pm. £3, children free.)

🍺🎵 NIGHTLIFE AND ENTERTAINMENT

Snack till the wee hours at **Istanbul Kebab,** 1 County Pl., on South St. (☎449911. Open daily 5pm-1am.) **Mucky Mulligans,** 97 Canal Crescent, hosts live music on Wednesday and Saturday nights. (☎636705. Open W-Th noon-12:30am, F noon-1:30am, Sa noon-1am, Su-Tu 12:30-11:30pm. Cover £1-2 W-Sa after 10:30pm.) **Scaramouche,** 103 South St., next to the post office, serves food by day and has a live DJ

Thursday through Sunday nights. (☎637479. Open M-Th 11am-11pm, F-Sa 11am-11:45pm, Su 12:30-11pm.) Skate or watch a game of curling at the **Dewar's Rink** (☎624188), Glasgow Rd., which is open all summer and on alternate winter weekends. (Open M 11:30am-4pm; Tu-Th 11am-4pm; F 11am-1pm, 2:15-6pm, 6:30-9pm; Sa 3:30-5:30pm and 6:30-8:30pm; Su 2:30-4:30pm.)

◪ DAYTRIPS FROM PERTH

SCONE PALACE. Scone (pronounced SKOON) Palace, less than 3 mi. northeast of Perth on the A93, is considered a regional jewel. Each of Scotland's kings was coronated here at the famous Stone of Scone (see **Stoned**, p. 109). Though the sumptuous grounds are paced by impertinent peacocks, the interiors they guard fall short of dazzling. Scone is still the home of the Earl of Mansfield, and only an undistinguished fraction is open for public viewing. Canny travelers may want to invest in a grounds pass and leave the rest to the Earl. *(Take bus #3 from South St. and tell the driver where you're going (every hr.) or a Guide Friday bus tour (see **Practical Information,** above). ☎(01738) 552300. Open Apr.-Oct. daily 9:30am-4:45pm. £5.60, seniors and students £4.80, under 16 £3.30. Grounds only £2.80, seniors and students £2.40, under 16 £1.70.)*

GLAMIS CASTLE. Macbeth's purported home (pronounced GLOMZ), this childhood playground of the Queen Mum noses its dozen handsome turrets into the sky 35 mi. northeast of Perth on the A94. The collections of armor, paintings, and furniture are significant, but the trek is inconvenient without a car. *(Take Scottish Citylink from Perth to Dundee, then catch Strathtay bus #22 or 22A to Glamis (35min., 5 per day). Call the Perth & Kinross Public Transport Traveline, (0845) 301 1130, for updated info. Castle ☎(01307) 840393. Open July-Aug. daily 10am-5:30pm; Apr.-June and Sept.-Oct. from 10:30am. Last admission 4:45pm. £6.20, students and seniors £4.70, children £3.10. Grounds only halfprice. Free tours every 15min. in summer.)*

DUNKELD AND BIRNAM   ☎01350

Huddled amid the forested hills of Perthshire on either side of the River Tay, the twin medieval towns of Dunkeld and Birnam (a 15min. walk apart) provide easy access to one of Scotland's most isolated regions. The area has long welcomed walkers and hikers to its snow-capped mountains and hilltop forts, while artists and musicians contribute to a unique cultural community.

◪◪ TRANSPORTATION AND PRACTICAL INFORMATION

Birnam's unstaffed **train station** is on the Edinburgh-Inverness line. **Trains** run from: **Perth** (15min., 5 per day, £4.40); **Inverness** (1½hr., 8 per day, £15.40); **Edinburgh** (2hr., 3 per day, £9.30); **Glasgow** (1½hr., 3 per day, £19.30). **Scottish Citylink** (☎(08705) 505050) **buses** stop by the Birnam train station car park from: **Pitlochry** (20min., 6 per day, £5); **Perth** (22min., 3 per day, £4.10); **Edinburgh** (1½hr., 3 per day, £7); **Glasgow** (2hr., 3 per day, £7.50); **Inverness** (2hr., 3 per day, £8.80). If you're coming from Perth or Pitlochry, **local buses**, which stop at the Birnam House Hotel, are cheaper and may get you closer to your destination. Grab the essential and free *Public Transport Guide (Highland Perthshire and Stanley Area)* from any tourist information centre (TIC) or call the Public Transport Traveline (☎(0845) 301 1130). **Rent bikes**, along with canoes and kayaks, at **Dunkeld Cycles**, below the Tay Bridge. (☎728744. Bikes £13 per day. Open daily 9am-5:30pm.)

Nearly all public transport arrives in Birnam (a popular Victorian vacation spot), but most amenities are in quainter Dunkeld. The Dunkeld **tourist information centre**, by the fountain in the town center, 1 mi. from the train station, books accommodations for £1 and a 10% deposit. (☎727688. Open July-Aug. M-Sa 9am-6:30pm, Su 11am-5pm; Apr.-June and Sept.-Oct. M-Sa 9:30am-5:30pm, Su 11am-4pm; Nov.-Dec. W-Su 10am-4pm.) Other services include: Dunkeld's **Bank of Scotland**, High St. (open M-Tu and Th-F 9am-12:30pm and 1:30-5pm, W 10am-12:30pm and 1:30-5pm);

Internet access at the Public Bar of the **Royal Dunkeld Hotel,** Atholl St. (£1 per 10min.); and the Dunkeld **post office,** Bridge St. (open M-W and F 9am-1pm and 2-5:30pm, Th 9am-1pm, Sa 9am-12:30pm). **Postal code:** PH8 0AH.

ACCOMMODATIONS AND FOOD

The masterpiece of three former hostelers and musicians, the ⧫**Wester Caputh Independent Hostel**—frequent site of impromptu jam sessions—splits into cozy B&B-type rooms and intimate hostel dorms with some of Britain's best showers. A stay at the hostel guarantees the fullest appreciation of the area. It's out of town on the A984 and then right on the road to Caputh, but if call ahead they'll pick you up from the train or bus station. (☎/fax (01738) 710617. Breakfast £1.50. Laundry £2-4 per load. Internet access £1 per 15min. Bike rental £6-10. Dorms £8; B&B £10.) Birnam and Dunkeld have dozens of **B&Bs;** the TIC keeps a complete list on its door. The happening **Taybank Hotel** (owned by the legendary folk musician Dougie Maclean of "Caledonia" fame) is by the Dunkeld Bridge and offers simple rooms themed around Scottish musicians. (☎727340; fax 728606; www.taybank.com. £17.50 per person; singles £5 extra.) **Campers** should head for the **Inver Mill Caravan Park,** on the riverside across from Dunkeld and to the north. (☎727477. Open Apr.-Oct. £8-10 for 2 people, tent, and car; £1 each additional person. Laundry £3.)

The **Co-op** supermarket, Bridge St., is in Dunkeld. (Open M-Sa 8am-8pm, Su 9am-6pm.) ⧫**Maclean's Real Music Bar,** in the Taybank Hotel, Dunkeld (see above), serves "famous" stovies (£3.25) and hosts casual gatherings of local and visiting musicians—sometimes even Dougie himself. Spare instruments on the walls let you join in. Thursday and Friday are the best nights for music, with surprise guests and open mic sessions. (☎727340. Open Su-Th noon-11pm, F-Sa noon-11:45pm. Cover F £4, open mic £2.) For great fruit cakes (80p), head to the **Tappit Hen,** 7 Atholl St., Dunkeld. (☎727472. Open summer M-Sa 10:30am-5pm; July-Aug. also Su. 11:30am-4:30pm; winter M-Sa 10:30am-4:30pm.)

SIGHTS AND ACTIVITIES

Painstakingly restored 18th-century houses line the way to the partially charred **Dunkeld Cathedral,** High St., whose restored choir is now a parish church. Alexander Stewart, the "Wolf of Badenoch" and illegitimate son of English king Robert II, sought revenge for his excommunication by razing several Tayside villages and pilfering the cathedral's gold chalices. (Open Apr.-Sept. M-Sa 9:30am-6:30pm, Su 2-6:30pm; Oct.-Mar. M-Sa 9:30am-4pm, Su 2-4pm. Free.) In summer, be sure to stroll through the tranquil meadows of **Stanley Hill** just behind Duchess Anne Hall.

Over the arched Telford Bridge in Birnam, find a flimsy claim to literary fame: Beatrix Potter spent most of her childhood holidays in the area, drawing on her experiences for *The Tale of Peter Rabbit.* The **Beatrix Potter Garden,** across from the Birnam Hotel, recreates the settings of the bunny's escapades, including Mrs. Tiggywinkle's house and Peter's burrow. Next door, the **Birnam Institute** also celebrates the author. (Open M-Sa 10am-4pm, Su 2-4pm. Free.)

The TIC's *Dunkeld & Birnam Walks* (50p) provides maps of area rambles. Paths lead north from Birnam to the great **Birnam Oak,** the remnant of Shakespeare's fabled Birnam Wood, while the brisk and savage waterfalls of the **Hermitage** tumble 1½ mi. away, with a well-marked ¾ mi. path that passes through all designated photo-ops. (Free walking tours from the Dunkeld TIC July to mid-Sept.) Birdwatchers will enjoy the **Loch of the Lowes,** a wildlife reserve 2 mi. east of Dunkeld off the A923 (20min. on a path from the TIC and detailed in *Dunkeld Walks*). For the past eight years, the reserve has served as the summer retreat for some travel-happy ospreys who fly all the way from Gambia. (☎727337. Visitor center open daily mid-July to mid-Aug. 10am-6pm; Apr. to mid-July and mid-Aug. to Sept. 10am-5pm.) Trout season lasts from mid-March to mid-October. Obtain a fishing license (£3-4) for the River Tay from **Kettles,** 15 Atholl St. (☎727556.)

NEAR DUNKELD AND BIRNAM: THE CATERAN TRAIL

Highland Perthshire, northeast of Dunkeld and Birnam, is home to the **Cateran Trail,** a terrific 60 mi. hike "in the heart of Scotland." Cairns and ruins line the loop between the Bridge of Cally, Alyth, Blairgowrie, and the Spittal of Glenshee. The well-marked route approximates that of the "Cateran Bands," medieval cattle-rustlers sent to loot and pillage on behalf of their clans. The trail splits into five easy sections, each a day's hike with B&Bs at the finish. Call the **Cateran Trail Company** (☎ (08000) 277200) to book accommodations; they'll even cart your pack.

LOCH TAY

The most beautiful part of Perthshire is also the most remote. **Aberfeldy,** a low-key base for enjoying the Loch, is accessible by various Perthshire local buses from Pitlochry, Perth, and Dunkeld and Birnam. Schedules vary monthly, but the **Perthshire Public Transport Traveline** (☎ (0845) 301 1130) has the most up-to-date information. Towns around Loch Tay may be reached from Aberfeldy by postbus; however, many only run once per day, making a return trip impossible. The folks at the **Postbus Helpline** (☎ (01246) 546329) can help you sort out the confusion.

The tiny village of **Fortingall,** 4 mi. northwest of Kenmore (beyond Aberfeldy on the A827), is remarkable on two counts: it's home to a 3000-year-old yew tree, the oldest living organism in Europe, and is the supposed birthplace of Pontius Pilate, whose father was a Roman soldier stationed here. **Postbuses** arrive from **Aberfeldy** (#211, 50min., M-Sa 9am). At the opposite end of Loch Tay, the village of **Killin** is a good base for hiking, with reasonably priced B&Bs and a **SHYA Youth Hostel,** which, despite spartan amenities, is the perfect lodge for ramblers: the staff are experienced mountaineers. (☎ (01567) 820546. Open Mar.-Oct. F-Sa. Dorms £8.50, under 18 £7.50.) In Killin, the **Breadalbane Folklore Centre** shares a building with the **tourist information centre,** by the Falls of Douchart on Main St. Learn about Gaelic mythology while gathering information on countless walks and watersports. (☎ (01567) 820254. Open July-Aug. daily 9:30am-6:30pm; May-June and Sept. 10am-6pm; Mar-Apr. and Oct. 10am-5pm; Feb. Sa-Su 10am-4pm. £1.55, concessions £1.05.) An excellent hike starts from behind the schoolyard on Main St. and leads to a marvelous sheep's-eye view of the loch. **Postbuses** arrive from: **Aberfeldy** (#212; 3hr., M-Sa 1 per day); **Crianlarich** (#025; M-Sa 1 per day); **Tyndrum** (#025; M-Sa 1 per day).

Midway between Kenmore and Killin on the west shore of Loch Tay, 7 mi. northeast of town, the **Ben Lawers Visitor's Centre** rests in the shadow of Ben Lawers, one of Britain's most commanding mountains. (☎ (01567) 820397. Open Easter-Sept. daily 10am-1pm and 2-5pm.) Those with a car enjoy direct access to the peak, but beware the flocks of sheep who call the mountain home. Unlucky pedestrians can brave the approximately 7hr. hike to the top. Postbus #212 stops at the bottom of the road that leads to the visitor's center on its way from **Aberfeldy** to **Killin.** A schoolbus also runs to the foot of the hill in the early morning.

PITLOCHRY   ☎01796

Emerging from the mists of the Grampian Mountains, Pitlochry began as a Victorian vacation spot, and summer theater, a dam and salmon ladder, two fine distilleries, famous knitwear, and a web of hill walks continue to make Pitlochry a sweet stop for travelers. The nearby town of Moulin takes care of tourist overflow.

⌐ TRANSPORTATION

Trains (☎ (08457) 484950) stop near the town center from: **Perth** (30min., 9 per day, £8.20); **Glasgow** (1¾hr., 7 per day, £19); **Inverness** (1¾hr., 9 per day, £13.40); **Edinburgh** (2hr., 7 per day, £19). The yellow phone on the platform connects to the info office at Inverness Station. **Scottish Citylink** (☎ (08705) 505050) buses stop outside the Fishers Hotel on Atholl Rd. from: **Perth** (40min., every hr., £5); **Inverness** (2hr., every hr., £8.10); **Edinburgh** (2hr., 10 per day, £8); **Glasgow** (2½hr., 8 per day, £8).

From Perth, Pitlochry is accessible by various local buses; call the **Public Transportation Traveline** (☎(0845) 301 1130) for up-to-date info. Rent **bikes** at **Escape Route,** 8 West Moulin Rd., for £14 per day (☎473859; open Su-F 10am-5pm, Sa 9:30am-5pm) or **The Well House,** 11 Toberargan Rd., for £5 per day (☎472239; opens 7am).

🛈 PRACTICAL INFORMATION

Plenty of postcards await at the **tourist information centre** (TIC), 22 Atholl Rd., as does the 50p *Pitlochry Walks.* (☎472215; fax 474046. Open late May to early Sept. M-Sa 9am-7pm, Su 9am-6pm; mid-Sept. to Nov. M-Sa 9am-6pm, Su 11am-5pm; Nov. to late May M-F 9am-5pm, Sa 10am-2pm.) Other services include: the **Royal Bank of Scotland,** 76 Atholl St. (open M-Tu and Th-F 9am-5pm, W 10am-5pm); the **Pitlochry Launderette,** 3 West Moulin Rd. (☎474044; wash £2.60, dry £1.50; open M-W and F 7:30am-5pm, Th and Sa 9am-5pm; June-Sept. also Tu until 8pm); **Internet access** at the **Computer Services Centre,** 67 Atholl Rd. (☎473711; 10p per min.; open M-F 9am-5:30pm, Sa 9am-noon); and the **post office,** 92 Atholl Rd. (open M-F 9am-5:30pm, Sa 9am-12:30pm). **Postal code:** PH16 5AH.

🛏 🍴 ACCOMMODATIONS AND FOOD

The **SYHA Pitlochry,** Knockard Rd. and Well Brae Rd., 15min. from town, is more notable for its magnificent views than its standard dorms and poor water pressure. From the train and bus stations, turn right on Atholl Rd. and then left uphill onto Bonnethill Rd., where the hostel is signposted. (☎472308; fax 473729. Breakfast £2.20. Laundry £2. Internet access £5 per hr. Reception 7am-11pm. Check-out 10:30am. Curfew 11:45pm. Dorms £9.25, under 18 £8.) **Pitlochry Backpackers,** 134 Atholl St., converted from a former hotel, has singles, twins, and doubles, all with bath. (☎470044. £11 per person.) At the west end of town, **Bowmore Cottage,** 145 Atholl Rd., is a cheery B&B with a backyard patio. Turn left from the train and bus stations onto Atholl Rd. (☎473314; dougie@bowmore.oik.co.uk. £15 per person.) One mile up West Moulin Rd., the wee village of **Moulin** is a perfect base for hillside escapes. Guests at **Mrs. Currie's B&B,** Baringa, Craiglunie Gdns., get good conversation and an insider's glimpse of town history. (☎472868. Open June-Sept. £16 per person; discount if you flash your *Let's Go.*) Two miles past town on Atholl Rd., **camp** at picturesque **Faskally Home Farm.** (☎472007; fax 473896. Open mid-Mar. to Oct. £6 per person and tent. Electricity, sauna, pool, and jacuzzi cost extra.)

Five minutes from Mrs. Currie's, the 300-year-old **Moulin Inn,** Moulin Sq., brews its own "Braveheart ale" and serves affordable grub until 9:30pm. (☎472196. Open Su-Th noon-11pm, F-Sa noon-11:45pm.) On West Moulin Rd., in Pitlochry, the **Pitlochry Co-op** provides groceries. (Open daily 8am-10pm.) Not only does **Ardchoille Fish & Chip Cafe,** 140 Atholl Rd., serve the cheapest eats in town, it does so with atmosphere and quality. (☎472170. Open M-F 10am-9pm, Sa 10am-10pm, Su noon-9pm.)

👁 🎵 SIGHTS AND ENTERTAINMENT

Seeing as the word **"whisky"** comes from an old Gaelic term for "the water of life," Pitlochry may live forever. ◪**The Edradour,** Scotland's tiniest distillery, may not emit enough fumes to satisfy locals, but there *are* enough to feed a distinct Scottish fungus that lives off evaporated alcohol. The delightful tour and sample dram are free. The Edradour's a 2½ mi. walk from Pitlochry (past Moulin along the A924); get there before 3pm, when distilling finishes. (☎472095. Open Mar.-Oct. M-Sa 9:30am-5pm, Su noon-5pm; Nov. to mid-Dec. M-Sa 10am-4pm.) At the **Blair Athol Distillery,** a ½ mi. from the TIC down the main road, enough alcohol evaporates daily to intoxicate the entire town. Kilted guides take you from flowing water to mashing malt to a free dram. (☎472234. Open Easter-Sept. M-Sa 9am-5pm, Su noon-5pm; Oct.-Easter M-F 9am-4pm. Last full tour 1hr. before close. £3.)

Walkers should arm themselves with a copy of *Pitlochry Walks,* available at the TIC for 50p. Footpaths connect the Edradour Distillery with the 15th-century **Black**

Castle ruins, burned way back for fear of the plague. For a quick jaunt, take the path over the suspension footbridge in Moulin to the **Pitlochry Dam** and **salmon ladder.** From the observation chamber, watch as spawning future fillets struggle ceaselessly against the current. The unromantic can get a fishing permit and head 100 yd. upstream. An electronic fish counter keeps tally. (☎473152. Open Apr.-Oct. daily 10am-5:30pm. Observation chamber and dam free; visitor center £2, students £1.20, children £1.) Observe other unusual processes at the **HeatherGems Factory and Visitor Centre,** behind the TIC, where craftsmen cut and polish vacuum-packed heather stems into tourist-pleasing jewelry. (☎474391. Open June-Sept. M-F 9am-5:30pm, Sa 9am-5pm, Su 9:30am-5pm; Oct.-May M-F 9am-5pm, Sa 9:30am-5pm.)

The glitzy **Pitlochry Festival Theatre,** over the Aldour Bridge, boasts a cinema and international performers. The new season opens May 2002. (☎484626. Tickets £13-18, students and hostelers half-price.) In the field down Tummel Cres., **Highland Nights** feature excellent local pipe bands and traditional dancing. (May-Sept. M nights. Tickets available at the gate; £4, students and seniors £3, children £1.) Pick up the free *What's On in Perthshire* at the TIC for further entertainment ideas.

█ DAYTRIPS FROM PITLOCHRY

▓ **BLAIR CASTLE.** Seven miles north of Pitlochry on the A9, the soaring turrets of Blair Castle make a formidable impression, complete with peacocks patrolling the well-groomed lawns. The interior does not disappoint, with instruments of war arrayed in intricate wall patterns and a well-preserved Victorian bathroom. The castle grounds are used to train the Duke of Atholl's army, the only private army in Western Europe. Prepared to fight in both the American Revolution and WWI, the farthest the troops have ever gone is Ireland. *(Take the train to Blair Athol (about £3) and walk 10min., or hop on bus #26 or 87 from the West End Car Park.* ☎481207. *Open Apr.-Oct. daily 10am-6pm, last admission 5pm. £6, seniors and students £5, children £4, families £18.)*

HIKING. After a 4hr. hike, visitors can charge up the 2757 ft. **Ben-y-Vrackie,** which gives views of Edinburgh on a clear day. From Moulin, turn left onto the road directly behind the Moulin Inn and follow the curve until you reach a fork (note the standing stones in the field nearby). Taking the right-hand road brings you to Ben-y-Vrackie; continue along the left-hand road about 2hr. to explore **Craigower Hill,** which has a view to the west along Loch Tommel and Loch Rannoch to the Glencoe Mountains. A 2½ mi. walk from the Pitlochry dam leads to the Pass of Killiecrankie (signposted, and included in *Pitlochry Walks*).

PASS OF KILLIECRANKIE. A few miles north of Pitlochry, the valley of the River Garry narrows into a stunning pass. In 1689, a Jacobite army slaughtered William III's troops here in an attempt to reinstall James VII of Scotland on the English throne. One stranded soldier by the name of Donald MacBean vaulted 18 ft. across **Soldier's Leap,** preferring to risk the steep fall than surrender. Along with spectacular views, the area is home to an intriguing array of wildlife and wild flowers, from the Buzzard and the Great Tit (birds) to the primrose and the Devil's Bit (flowers). For information or a guided walk, stop in at the **National Trust Visitors Centre,** down the path from the pass. *(Elizabeth Yule bus #87 runs from the West End Car Park to the pass in summer (4 per day, £1).* ☎473233. *Centre open Apr.-Oct. daily 10am-5:30pm.)*

STIRLING   ☎01786

Sitting atop a triangle completed by Glasgow and Edinburgh, Stirling has historically presided over passage through the region; it's been said that he who controlled Stirling controlled Scotland. At the 1297 Battle of Stirling Bridge, William Wallace outwitted and overpowered the English army, enabling Robert the Bruce to lead Scotland to independence 17 years later. When James VI took the English throne, he declared Edinburgh the new capital, leaving Stirling to itself. Despite recent bustling development, Scotland's former capital has not forgotten its heroes. The city's moving history and architecture have been rediscovered, and it now swarms with *Braveheart* fans set on capturing the glorious Scotland of old.

▐ TRANSPORTATION

The **train station** is on Goosecroft Rd. (Travel center open M-F 6am-9pm, Sa 6am-8pm, Su 8:30am-10pm. Luggage storage £2-4; open M-Sa 10am-6pm.) **Trains** (☎(08457) 484950) arrive from: **Glasgow** (30min.; M-Sa 2-3 per hr., Su every hr.; £4.30); **Edinburgh** (50min., 2 per hr., £5.10); **Aberdeen** (2hr.; M-Sa every hr., Su 6 per day; £28); **Inverness** (3hr., 4 per day, £32); **London King's Cross** (5½hr., every hr., £44-84). The **bus station** is also on Goosecroft Rd. (☎446474. Ticket office open M-F 8:30am-6pm, Sa 8:30am-5pm. Luggage storage £1; open M-Sa 7am-9pm, Su 12:30-7:30pm.) **National Express** (☎(08705) 808080) buses run from **Glasgow** (2-3 per hr., £3.60) and **Inverness** (every hr., £11.40).

▐ PRACTICAL INFORMATION

Tourist Information Centre: 41 Dumbarton Rd. (☎475019). Open July-Aug. M-Sa 9am-7:30pm, Su 9:30am-6:30pm; June and Sept. M-Sa 9am-6pm, Su 10am-4pm; Oct.-May roughly M-Sa 10am-5pm. Also, the **Stirling Visitor Centre** (☎462517), next to the castle. High-altitude and high-tech with exhibits and 12min. movie. Exchanges currency (£3 commission) and books accommodations for £1. Open July-Aug. daily 9am-6:30pm; Apr.-June and Sept.-Oct. 9:30am-6pm; Nov.-Mar. 9:30am-5pm. Both offices provide free *What's On* and *Royal Stirling Events* calendars and bus timetables.

Tours: If you balk at Stirling's hills, **Guide Friday** (☎(0131) 556 2244) operates 70min. open-top bus tours that begin at the castle esplanade and offer hop-on/hop-off service throughout town and to the Wallace Monument. Tours daily 10am-5pm. £6.50, students and seniors £5, children £2, families £15.

Internet Access: Library, Corn Exchange Rd. (☎432107). £2.50 per 30min., concessions £1.25.

Post Office: 84-86 Murray Pl. (☎465392). **Bureau de change.** Open M-F 9am-5:30pm, Sa 9am-12:30pm. **Postal Code:** FK8 2BP.

▐▐ ACCOMMODATIONS AND FOOD

B&Bs abound near the train station and the university. The **Willy Wallace Hostel,** 77 Murray Pl., a short walk from the bus or train station, has a kitchen and a full laundry services for only £3.50. A delightfully witty staff fosters a good-times atmosphere. (☎446773. Dorms £10; twins £24; doubles £26.) **SYHA Stirling,** on St. John St., halfway up the hill to the castle, occupies the shell of the first Separatist Church in Stirling. Each of the 2- to 5-bed rooms has a shower and toilet. In July and August, overflow singles are used in the **Union St. Annex,** known in cooler months as University of Stirling housing. (☎473442; fax 445715. Reception 7am-11:30pm. Bedroom lockout 10am-2pm. Curfew 2am. Dorms £10, under 18 £8.) **Mrs. Helen Miller's,** 16 Riverside Dr., offers two spotless singles—one with a view of the Wallace Monument—and a breakfast that will hold you until dinner. Turn right from the train station, cross the bridge, go down Seaforth Pl. and Abbey Rd. until the road ends, and turn left onto Riverside Dr. (☎461105. £11 per person.)

Tucked down an alley, **The Greengrocer,** 81 Port St., offers some of the freshest fruits and veggies in town. (☎479159. Open M-F 9am-5:30pm, Sa 8:30am-3:30pm.) Head to **Iceland,** 5 Pitt Terr., for the rest of your grocery needs. (☎464300. Open M-F 8:30am-8pm, Sa 8:30am-6pm, Su 10am-5pm.) **Paco's Restaurant,** 21 Dumbarton Rd., has a dish for every tastebud and a price for every budget, with main courses ranging £4.45-11.45. (☎446414. Open M-Sa from noon, Su from 5pm.) For burgers under £2.50, or for a pleasant tea, try **Sarah Jane's,** 2 Pitt Terr. (☎470139).

CENTRAL SCOTLAND

👁 SIGHTS

▨ STIRLING CASTLE. Planted on a defunct volcano and embraced on all sides by the scenic Ochil Hills, Stirling Castle has prim gardens and superb views of the Forth Valley that belie its militant history. In an effort to erase the violent memory of English attempts to seize the stronghold, Robert the Bruce ordered the castle's destruction after the Battle of Bannockburn. It was rebuilt nonetheless in the 1380s, and Robert's statue ironically stands guard in front of the present structure. The castle's hideous gargoyles glowered over the 14th-century Wars of Independence, a 15th-century royal murder, and the 16th-century coronation of the infant Mary, Queen of Scots; its final military engagement came in 1746, when Bonnie Prince Charlie besieged it while retreating from England (and then gave up and kept retreating). Beneath the cannons pointed at Stirling Bridge lie the 16th-century **great kitchens;** visitors can walk among the recreated chaos of cooks, dogs, bakers, and vast slabs of meat. Free 30min. **guided tours,** leaving twice per hr., give background for further exploration. (☎450000. Open Apr.-Oct. 9:30am-6pm; Nov.-Mar. 9:30am-5pm; last admission 45min. before close. £6.50, seniors £5, children £2.)

The castle also contains the **Regimental Museum of the Argyll and Sutherland Highlanders,** a fascinating military museum including men in kilts, of course. (Open Easter-Sept. M-Sa 10am-5:45pm, Su 11am-4:45pm; Oct.-Easter daily 10am-4:15pm. Free.) The highlight of **Argyll's Lodging,** a 17th-century townhouse on the castle's esplanade, is the purple and gold toilet box in the main bedroom. (Open Apr.-Sept. 9:30am-6pm; Nov.-Mar. 9:30am-5pm. £3, seniors £2.20, children £1.40; free with castle admission.)

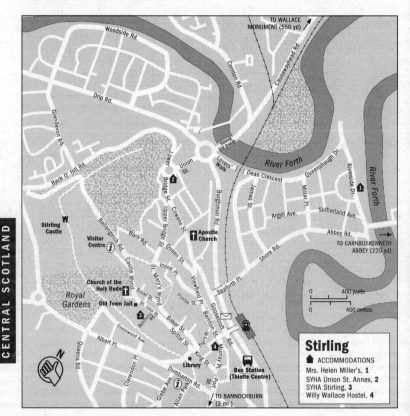

Stirling

⌂ ACCOMMODATIONS

Mrs. Helen Miller's, **1**
SYHA Union St. Annex, **2**
SYHA Stirling, **3**
Willy Wallace Hostel, **4**

HOLLYWOOD'S WHITE LIE(S)
In 1297, a small band of Scottish clansmen, led by William Wallace and hopelessly outnumbered, defeated a legion of well-trained English troops at Stirling. We can all thank *Braveheart*'s blue-faced battle scene for bringing the bare bones of this story to the masses. But allow *Let's Go* to give you the meat: although Hollywood depicts the Scots brandishing poles and charging the English heavy cavalry, in reality the clansmen waited quietly for the English to reach Stirling Bridge. Each time the bridge teemed with soldiers—who were forced to break regiment in order to cross it—the Scots attacked and slaughtered the lot, repeating as necessary until the entire army was dead or hostage. While the big-screen version is known as the Battle of Stirling, the real deal is more appropriately called the Battle of Stirling Bridge. If you *still* think Hollywood cannot tell a lie, ask yourself how a 5 ft. 9 in. Aussie could ever wield Wallace's infamous 5½ ft. sword.

WALLACE MONUMENT. This 19th-century tower offers incredible views to those bravehearted enough to climb its 246-step, wind-whipped spiral staircase. It houses the 5½ ft. sword William Wallace wielded against King Edward I of England and has exhibits on Wallace's capture: Wallace was hanged until semi-conscious, then disemboweled, castrated, beheaded, and quartered, his entrails burnt, and parts of his body dispersed to the corners of Scotland. *(Hillfouts Rd., 1½ mi. from the town center; buses run from train and bus stations to the base. ☎472140. Open July-Aug. daily 9:30am-6:30pm; June and Sept. 10am-6pm; Mar.-May and Oct. 10am-5pm; Nov.-Feb. 10am-4pm. £3.95, students £3, seniors and children £2.75, families £10.75.)*

OTHER SIGHTS. On the east side of town, cross the Abbey Rd. footbridge over the River Forth to find the ruins of 12th-century **Cambuskenneth Abbey,** where an occasional black-faced sheep may eyeball you across the graves of James III and his wife Margaret. *(Open Apr.-Sept. M-Sa 9:30am-6pm, Su 2-6pm. Grounds open year-round. Free.)* Down Castle Hill Wynd, the high walls and timbered roof of the **Church of the Holy Rude** witnessed the coronation of James VI and shook under the fire and brimstone of John Knox; bullet holes can still be seen in the church walls. It's the only church in Scotland once the site of a coronation and still used for regular worship. *(Open May-Sept. daily 10am-5pm; Su service July-Dec. 10am, Jan.-June 11:30am. Frequent organ recitals. Donations requested.)* **Ladies Rock,** a lookout point where women used to watch military action at a distance, is located in **Valley Cemetery** behind the church. Next to the church lies 17th-century **Cowane's Hospital,** built as an almshouse for poor members of the merchant guild. Legend has it that at the stroke of midnight each New Year, the statue of founder John Cowane descends from its niche over the front door and dances a jig in the courtyard. *(Open M-Sa 9am-5pm, Su 1-5pm. Free.)*

Two miles south of Stirling at **Bannockburn,** a statue of a battle-ready Robert the Bruce overlooks the field where his men decisively defeated the English in 1314, after which Scotland was independent for 393 years. *(☎812664. Heritage Centre open Apr.-Oct. daily 10am-5:30pm; Mar. and Nov.-Dec. 11am-4:30pm. Grounds open year-round.)*

THE TROSSACHS   ☎01877

The gentle mountains and lochs of the Trossachs (which means "bristly country") form the northern boundary of central Scotland. Sir Walter Scott and Queen Victoria praised the region, the only easily accessible Scottish wilderness before the 20th century. The Trossachs today are less accessible; only a few buses each day link Glasgow and Stirling to **Aberfoyle** and **Callander,** the two main towns. The A821 winds through the heart of the Trossachs between Aberfoyle and Callander, passing near majestic **Loch Katrine,** the Trossachs' original lure and the setting for Scott's "The Lady of the Lake." A road for walkers and cyclists traces the Loch's shoreline. The **Steamship Sir Walter Scott** moves between Loch Katrine's Trossachs Pier and Stronachlachar. However arresting the scenery, in July and August the crush of passengers may make the trip a hassle. *(☎376316. Cruises Apr.-Oct. Su-F 11am, 1:45, 3:15pm; Sa 1:45 and 3:15pm. $4.60-6, seniors and children $3.20-4.20.)*

Nearby, **Ben A'an'** (1207 ft.) hulks over the Trossachs; the rocky one-hour hike up begins a mile from the pier, along the A821. Before heading to the summit, stop at the nearby Visitor Centre for weather information and trail maps. In Callander, stay at **Abbotsford Lodge,** Stirling Rd., a private country cottage; there's a conservatory restaurant on the grounds. (☎330066. From £19.50 per person.) In Aberfoyle, Ann and John Epps open their secluded home and stunning views to visitors at **Crannaig House,** Trossachs Rd. (☎382276. £21 per person.) Camping is available at the **Trossachs Holiday Park,** off Aberfoyle's town center, voted the best campsite in Scotland for 2001. (☎382614. Open Mar.-Oct. £9 per night.)

Getting to this area is tough: **Scottish Citylink** bus #974, from **Edinburgh** and **Stirling** to **Fort William,** stops in **Callander** (2hr., 2 per day in each direction, £7). **The Trossachs Trundler,** a 1950s-style bus, creaks to **Callander, Aberfoyle,** and **Trossachs Pier** in time for the sailing of the *Sir Walter Scott* (July-Sept. Su-F 4 per day; Day Rover £5.50, seniors and children £3.50). Bus #59 from Stirling connects with the Trundler in **Callander** (Stirling-Trossachs Rover £8, seniors and children £5.50). Or try **postbuses,** which wind their way through selected towns. Find timetables at TICs or call the **Stirling Council Public Transport Helpline** (☎(01786) 442707). **Trossachs Cycle Hire,** on the pier in Callander, rents quality bikes. (☎382614. £3 per hr., £7.50 per half-day, £12 per day. Open Apr.-Oct. daily 8:30am-5:30pm.)

LOCH LOMOND AND BALLOCH   ☎01389

With Scotland's largest lake as its base, the landscape of Loch Lomond is filled with the lush bays, wooded islands, and bare hills immortalized in the famous ballad. Even the lochside towns that shamelessly commercialize "The Bonnie Bonnie Banks" are mostly unpolluted by tourists. Visitors who undertake challenging hikes in such roadless areas as the northeastern edge of Loch Lomond or most of Loch Katrine are rewarded by stunning views and quiet, untrammeled swaths of space. Hikers adore the West Highland Way, which snakes along the entire eastern side of the Loch and stretches 95 mi. from Milngavie north to Fort William.

At the southern tip of Loch Lomond, Balloch is the area's major town, though "major" is loosely meant: with the exception of the youth hostel, everything you need is within a casual walk of the tourist information centre (TIC).

🖸🄷 TRANSPORTATION AND PRACTICAL INFORMATION. The train station is on Balloch Rd., across the street from the TIC. **Trains** (☎(08457) 484950) arrive from **Glasgow Queen St.** (45min., at least 2 per hr., £3.20). The **bus stop** is a few minutes down Balloch Rd., across the bridge to the left of the TIC, but buses bypassing the town center pick up passengers on the A82 near the roundabout. **Scottish Citylink** (☎(08705) 505050) buses #926, 975, and 976 arrive from **Glasgow** (M-Sa 5 per day, Su 3 per day; £3.60). **First Midland** (☎(01324) 613777) travels from **Stirling** (1½hr.; M-F 3 per day, Sa 3 per day, Su 1 per day; £4.60). To reach the eastern side of the loch, take bus #309 or 9 from Balloch to **Balmaha** (40min., 6 per day, £1.50). Buses #305 and 307 head for the village of **Luss** (15min., 7 per day, £1.90).

The **tourist information centre,** Old Station Building, Balloch Rd., books rooms for a £1 fee, stocks bus schedules, hands out the useful *Loch Lomond Official Visitor Guide,* and shows a short film on the loch. (☎753533. Open July-Aug. daily 9:30am-7pm; Sept. 9:30am-7pm; Apr.-May and Oct. 10am-5pm; June 9:30am-6pm.)

🄵 ACCOMMODATIONS. B&Bs congregate on Balloch Rd., conveniently close to the TIC. The **🄼SYHA Loch Lomond** is one of Scotland's largest hostels, with 9 entrances, 53 chimneys, and 180 beds in a stunning 19th-century castle-like building 2 mi. north of Balloch. From the train station, follow the main road for ½ mi. until the roundabout. Turn right, follow the road for 1½ mi., turn left at the sign for the hostel, and it's a short jog up the hill. The high-ceilinged common room is astounding; other amenities include the ghost of Veronica, who, pregnant with the child of a stable boy, took a steep dive from the window of the tower in which her family had locked her. The hostel employees report that the ghost seems only to appear to male guests. Book ahead in summer. (☎850226. Dorms £11.75, under 18 £10.50.) The **SYHA Rowardennan** is the first hostel along the West Highland Way. Huge windows put the loch in your lap. (☎(01360) 870259. Curfew 11:30pm. Open Mar.-Oct. Dorms £9, under 18 £6.) To reach it, take the Inverberg **ferry** to Rowardennan. (☎(01301) 702356. May-Sept. daily; leaves Rowardennan at 10am, 2, 6pm; leaves Inverberg 30min. later. £4, children £1.50.)

The **Tullichewan Caravan and Camping Site** is on Old Luss Rd., up Balloch Rd. from the TIC. Soak in a spa bath or rent **mountain bikes** at this Club Med of campsites. (☎(01389) 759475; fax 755563. Reception open 8:30am-10pm. Bikes £7.50 per 4hr., £10 per 8hr. Deposit £100. Tent and 2 people £6.50-9, with car £8.50-12.50; children £1; additional guests free in winter, otherwise £2.)

◩ SIGHTS. Across the River Leven, **Balloch Castle Country Park** provides 200 acres of gorgeous beach lawn, woods, and gardens, as well as a 19th-century castle that houses a **Visitor's Centre.** If the weather is good, don't miss the opportunity to look for pixies in **Fairy Glen.** (Park open daily dawn-dusk. Visitor's Centre, doubling as a Loch Lomond Park Ranger Station, open Easter-Oct. daily 10am-6pm. Free.) One of the best introductions to the area is **Sweeney's Cruises** boat tours, from the TIC's side of the River Leven. (☎752376. Cruises 1hr., every hr. 10am-4pm. £4.80, children £2.50.) Cruises also sail to Luss, with 30min. ashore (2½hr.; departs 2:30pm; £7.50, children £3.50), and there's also an evening cruise with onboard bar (1½hr.; departs 7:30pm; £6.50, children £3). Avert your eyes (or don't) from the nudist colony on one of the islands in the lake's center (brrr!). Ruins of the **Lomond Castle Hotel** are also visible; the owner burnt it down in an insurance scam. The **Glasgow-Loch Lomond Cycleway,** which covers 21 mi. between the two areas, was the first long distance cycleway in Scotland. The route now forms part of the Inverness-Dover route. Starting at **Bell's Bridge** ½ mi. west of Glasgow's center, the cycleway runs parallel to the River Clyde and follows old rail lines, tow paths, and off-road trails; get info at any TIC.

LOCH LONG

Loch Long stretches like a salty finger northeast toward Loch Lomond. The **Ardgartan Forest Park,** on the northern side of Loch Long, has excellent cycling potential. The park lies beneath the "Arrochar Alps," a series of rugged mountains including five Munro peaks and the 2890 ft. **Cuckolded Cobbler.** Also known as Ben Arthur, The Cobbler is unmistakable—the jagged peak appears to have sprouted the horns befitting a cuckold. A leisurely trail with some rocky segments near the tip begins in the town of Arrochar, halfway between Tarbet and Ardgartan (inquire in town or at the hostel about the trailhead's exact location). To tackle the hike knowledgeably, pick up Ordnance Survey Pathfinder Map #368 (£4.50) or Landranger Map #56 (£5) from a TIC.

The easiest way to enter the area is via the **Arrochar-Tarbet** train station. **Trains** (☎(08457) 484950) run from **Glasgow** (1¼hr.; M-Sa 5 per day, Su 3 per day; £7.40) and **Fort William** (2½hr.; M-Sa 4 per day, Su 3 per day; £12.60). Pick up the *Cycling In The Forest* pamphlet (30p) in the Ardgartan **tourist information centre,** off the A83 at the north end of the loch. (☎(01301) 702432. Open July-Aug. daily 10am-6pm; Apr.-June and Sept.-Oct. 10am-5pm.) Half a mile away, the **SYHA (Loch Long) Ardgartan** has glorious views and a free continental breakfast. Citylink bus #976 passes the hostel. (☎/fax (01301) 702362. Lockout 11am-5pm. Curfew 11:45pm. Open Apr.-Dec. £7.50, under 18 £6.25.)

INVERARAY ☎01499

The most obvious reason for visiting comely and unpretentious Inveraray is its splendid lochside setting, as its tourist attractions are less than captivating. As good as it gets, the **Inveraray Jail** welcomes with a "Torture, Death, and Damnation" exhibit, while the Old Prison (1820) and New Prison (1849) are stuffed with interactive displays such as the "Crank Machine," which prisoners were

CENTRAL SCOTLAND

required to turn 14,400 times daily as a form of useless labor. Guests are invited to "please try" the Whipping Table. (☎302381. Open Apr.-Oct. daily 9:30am-6pm; Nov.-Mar. 10am-5pm. £4.75, students and seniors £3, children £2.30, families £12.95.)

Home to the Duke and Duchess of Argyll, cultivated **Inveraray Castle** contrasts with the rugged mountains that surround it. The present building was erected between 1745-1785 to replace an earlier fortified keep as a sign of a more settled era in British history, but the castle still seems to hold enough weapons to defend all Scotland. (☎302203. Open July-Aug. M-Sa 10am-5:45pm, Su 1-5:45pm; Apr.-June and Sept.-Oct. M-Sa 10am-1pm and 2-5:45pm, Su 1-5:45pm. £4.50, students and seniors £3.50, children £2.50, families £12. Grounds free.) The 126 ft. **Bell Tower** has the second heaviest bells in the world at nearly 8 tons. A free bell-ringing show does not include the rooftop view. (Open May-Sept. daily 10am-1pm and 2-5pm. Tower £2, concessions 75p.) The **Fortnight Festival** occurs in July and August.

Buses #926 and 976 run to Inveraray from **Glasgow** (1¾hr.; M-Sa 3 per day, Su 2 per day; £6.90). The town has a small **tourist information centre** (TIC) on Front St. that books accommodations for a £1 fee. (☎302063. Open July to mid-Sept. daily 9am-6pm; Apr. and mid-Sept. to late Oct. M-Sa 9am-5pm, Su noon-5pm; Nov.-Mar. M-F 10am-4pm, Sa-Su noon-4pm; May-June M-Sa 9am-5pm, Su 11am-5pm.) The **Bank of Scotland** is at Church Sq. (☎302068. Open M-Tu and Th-F 9:15am-12:30pm and 1:30-4:45pm, W 10:30am-12:30pm and 1:30-4:45pm.) The **post office** is on Black's Land. (☎302062. Open M-Tu and Th-F 9am-1pm and 2-5:30pm, W 9am-1pm, Sa 9am-12:30pm.) **Postal code:** PA32 8UD.

The small, no-frills **SYHA Inveraray** is just north of town on Dalmally Rd.; take a left through the arch next to the Inveraray Woollen Mill onto Oban Rd. and walk past the gas station. (☎/fax 302454. Self-catering. 38 beds, 2 showers. Lockout 10:30am-5pm. Curfew 11pm. Open mid-Mar. to Sept. Dorms £8.25, under 18 £7.) Inveraray hides a stash of **B&Bs** up the road past the post office. The **Old Rectory**, Main St. South, has plush beds and a beautiful glass-ceilinged breakfast room. (☎302280. £17.50 per person.) **Lorona Guest House,** on the same street, by the gas station, has soothing rooms and a lounge with a great loch view. (☎302258. Open Easter-Oct. £17 per person.)

OBAN   ☎01631

Oban (OH-ben; pop. 8500), the busiest ferry port on Scotland's west coast, has managed an unabashed embrace of tourism without a Faustian sale of its soul. Lacking notable attractions, the town endears itself with sporadic outbursts of small-town warmth; it's also an excellent base from which to explore the nearby islands and the Argyll countryside. As the sun sets over the blue hills of Mull and the port workers turn in for the day, the streets of Oban fill with folks strolling along the harbor, chatting with neighbors, or heading to the pub for a dram.

⌕ GETTING THERE AND GETTING TO THE HEBRIDES. The **train station** is on Railway Pier. (☎563083. Ticket office open M-Sa 7am-6:10pm, Su 11am-6:10pm.) **Trains** (☎(08457) 484950) run from **Glasgow Queen St.** (3hr., 3 per day, £15) and **Fort William** via **Crianlarich** (4hr., 3 per day, £16). The **bus stop** is near the train station. The **Oban District Bus Office,** 1 Queens Park Pl., provides timetables, sells tickets, and stores luggage for £1.50. (☎562856. Open June-Aug. M-Sa 8:30am-5pm; Sept.-May daily 8:30am-1pm and 2-5pm.) **Scottish Citylink** (☎(08705) 505050) arrives from: **Fort William** (1¾hr., 5 per day, £6.70); **Glasgow** (3hr.; M-Sa 3 per day, Su 2 per day; £10.10); **Inverness** via Fort William (4hr., 4 per day, £11).

Caledonian MacBrayne Ferries (☎566688, reservations (0990) 650000) sail from Railway Pier to the southern Hebrides. Pick up a copy of the *CalMac 2002 Timetable* at the ferry station or tourist information centre. Ferries head to: **Craignure,** Mull (45min.; M-Sa 6 per day, Su 5 per day; £3.55); **Lismore** (50min., M-Sa 3-5 per day, £2.45); **Colonsay** (2½hr.; M, W, F 1 per day; £10.10); **Coll** and **Tiree** (2¾hr. to Coll,

3¾hr. to Tiree; 5 per week; £11.40); **Barra** and **South Uist** (5hr. to Barra, 7hr. to South Uist; M and W-Sa 1 per day; £18.75). If you have a car, book ahead and be prepared to pay exorbitant sums. Foot passengers rarely need to book, but you should call to confirm times. In winter, ferry travel is very limited.

⚏🔢 ORIENTATION AND PRACTICAL INFORMATION. Fronting the harbor, **George St.** is the heart of Oban. **Argyll Sq.**, actually a roundabout, is a block inland, northeast of the pier. **Corran Esplanade** runs along the coast north of town, **Gallanach Rd.** along the coast to the south. A vaulted **tourist information centre** (TIC) inhabits an old church on Argyle Sq. Browse books or the extensive display board, reserve a bed for £1 and a 10% deposit, and find travel timetables. (☎563122. Open July-Aug. M-Sa 9am-9pm, Su 9am-7pm; Sept. M-Sa 9am-6:30pm, Su 10am-5pm; Oct. M-Sa 9am-5:30pm, Su 10am-4pm; Nov.-Mar. M-F 9:30am-5pm, Sa-Su noon-4pm; Apr. M-F 9am-5pm, Sa-Su noon-5pm; May-June M-Sa 9am-6:30pm, Su 10am-5pm.) **Internet access** is available at the TIC for £1 per 12min. The **post office** is in the **Tesco** supermarket, Lochside St. off Argyll Sq. (☎565676. Store open M-Th and Sa 8am-8pm, F 8am-9pm, Su 9am-6pm.) **Postal code:** PA34 4AA.

🏠 ACCOMMODATIONS AND CAMPING. The spacious **Oban Waterfront Lodge,** Corran Esplanade, about ½ mi. from the train station, has the biggest beds around. The friendly staff and placement next to Markie Dan's Pub make for a social atmosphere. (☎566040. Breakfast £1.85, 10% discount vouchers for all-you-can-eat dinner at Markie Dan's. Dorms £10.) To reach the glorious peach bunks and super-pressure showers of **Oban Backpacker's Lodge,** 21 Breadalbane St., take George St. from Railway Pier until it forks; it's on the right prong. Shoot pool, browse through *Cosmo,* and surf the web in the all-purpose lounge. (☎562107. Continental breakfast £1.60. Internet access £5 per hr. Check-out 10:30am. Curfew 2:30am. Dorms £11.) A more intimate lodge, the **Jeremy Inglis Hostel,** 21 Airds Cres., has singles. From the railway station, walk past the TIC and head through Argyll Sq. Aird's Crescent is your first right, just before George St. (☎565065 or 563064. £6.50-12 per person.) The **SYHA Oban,** Rassay Lodge, Corran Esplanade, hugs the waterfront ¾ mi. north of the train station, past St. Columba's Cathedral. Rooms in the annex all come with bath but are a bit more expensive. (☎562025. Lockout 10:30am-1pm. Reception until 11:30pm. Check-out 10:30am. Curfew 2am. Open Mar.-Dec. Dorms £10.25-12.75, under 18 £9.25-10.25.)

B&Bs (£16-20) line **Ardonnel Rd.** and **Dunollie Rd.** Eight rooms, all with bath and TV, welcome you to bright blue **Maridon House,** Dunuaran Rd. Guests have full use of the kitchen. From Argyle Sq., walk to the end of Albany St. and look up. (☎562670; maridonhse@aol.com. July-Aug. £19 per person; Sept.-June £16.) Rough it for the night at the **Camping & Caravanning Club,** situated in a walled garden off the A828 coast road. Amenities include showers, electrical plugs, laundry facilities, and a bar. The #918 bus passes the campground. Ask the driver to drop you off. (Open Apr.-Oct. Tent and 2 people £6-8.50.)

🍴🍺 FOOD AND PUBS. Harborside **George St.,** beginning near the train station, is Oban's food center and nightlife strip. Seafood shops cluster around the ferry terminal. Mussels are atypically cheap in Oban; grab some delicious steamed ones. **Cafe Forty-One,** 41 Combie St., provides inexpensive meals with nary a tourist in sight. (All-day breakfast £3.95, sandwiches 80p-£1.30. Open daily 10am-2:30pm and 6:30-9:30pm.) For fresh fish and chips, stop by **Hungry Macs,** 116 George St. (☎562426; open daily 10am-9:30pm), or try **McTavish's Kitchens,** 34 George St., with tourist-oriented shows of traditional Scottish singing and dancing. A downstairs cafeteria serves good, cheap food. (☎563064. Shows May-Sept. 8:30 and 10:30pm. £4, children £2. Open in summer daily 9am-10pm; winter 9am-6pm.)

Pints go for about £2 in Oban. **O'Donnell's Irish Pub,** Breadalbane St., draws the young with live music Thursday through Monday nights. (☎566159. Open daily

CENTRAL SCOTLAND

noon-1am.) Also competing for local drinkers and cheery hostelers is **Markie Dan's**, next to the Oban Waterfront Lodge on the Esplanade. Frequent live music, drink specials, and a friendly bar staff equal a great atmosphere. Step outside for a marvelous view of the water. (Open daily 11am-1am.)

◖◗ SIGHTS AND ENTERTAINMENT The structure that awkwardly dominates the Oban skyline is **McCaig's Tower.** A free climb leads to a great view overlooking the harbor. To reach the tower, take the steep Jacob's Ladder stairway at the end of Argyll St., then walk left along Ardconnel Rd. and right up Laurel St. to the tower's grassy entrance. Past the north end of town, the ivy-eaten remains of 7th-century **Dunollie Castle**—Oban's oldest building—loom atop a cliff. Dunollie is the seat of the MacDougall family, who once owned a third of Scotland. From town, walk 20min. north along the water until you've curved around the castle; then take the path to the right. Look out or the stinging nettles that line the path. (Always open. Free.) Just 2½ mi. outside town on Glencruitten Rd., **Achnilarig Farms** offers guided horse rides to people of all levels of experience. (☎562745. Open year-round, usually Su-F; hours vary. ₤12 per hr., children ₤10.)

▣ DAYTRIPS FROM OBAN

KERRERA. Five minutes across the bay from Oban is the beautiful, nearly deserted island of **Kerrera** (CARE-er-uh). The island is naturally rich, providing a variety of habitats for local seal colonies and puffins. A ferry comes to Kerrera from **Ganlochhead**, 2 mi. south of Oban. Turn the board to the black side to signal the ferryman; call for winter sailings. (☎563665. Daily 2 per hr. 10:30am-noon and 2-6pm, also M-Sa 8:45am. Return £3, children £1.50, bike 50p.) Wander for a day or stay the night at the **Gylen Bothy** on the island's south tip, 2 mi. from the pier. (☎570223. Kitchen. Bedding provided. Bunkhouse space £7.50.)

LOCH ETIVE AND TAYNUILT. To the north gapes the mouth of Loch Etive, where the **Falls of Lora** change direction with the shifting of the tides. From **Taynuilt**, off the A85, 7 mi. east of the loch mouth, the family-run **Loch Etive Cruises** runs 3hr. tours up the loch into beautiful and otherwise inaccessible countryside. Call the night before you arrive to arrange a free shuttle from your bus to the pier. (☎(01866) 822430. May-Sept. M-F 10:30am and 2pm, Sa-Su 2pm; Apr. and early to mid-Oct. daily 2pm only. £8, children £4, families £20.) **Scottish Citylink** buses stop at Taynuilt on their **Oban-Glasgow** and **Oban-Edinburgh** routes; **Strathclyde Transport** bus #976 also stops at Taynuilt from Oban (₤2.70).

CASTLE STALKER. To reach **Appin**, cross Connel Bridge over the mouth of Loch Etive. The hauntingly beautiful **Castle Stalker** is 10 mi. down the A828 in Portnacroish. This 16th-century Stewart stronghold sits on an islet in Loch Linnhe. Perhaps best known as "Castle Aaaaaaaaa" in *Monty Python and the Holy Grail*, it can only be visited by arrangement during the last three weeks of August. (Take bus #918 to Appin from Oban (M-Sa 4 per day, Su 2 per day; £3.70). ☎730234. £6, children £3. 1½hr. tours Tu and W 9:30am.)

ISLE OF ISLAY ☎ 01496

Much like the whisky for which it's famous, the Isle of Islay (EYE-luh) demands subtle and mature appreciation. A barely inhabited outpost, the real beauty of this walker's paradise lies in the nuances of its residents' daily lives. A brief stroll is flavored by the mellow tones of Scottish Gaelic and images of peat crofters practicing their craft, not to mention the intoxicating aroma of some of the world's finest single-malt whiskies wafting from the island's numerous distilleries.

▣ TRANSPORTATION. Ferries leave from **Kennacraig Ferry Terminal,** 7 mi. south of **Tarbert** on the Kintyre Peninsula, running either to Port Askaig or to Port Ellen (M-Tu and Th-Sa 7:15am, 12:50, 6pm; W 8:15am; Su 12:50pm; either route

THE WHISKY TRAIL
Islay is famed for its fine malt whiskies and boasts seven distilleries; Jura has another for good measure. The malts are known for their peaty flavor—not surprising, considering half of Islay is peat bog. Islay's sparse population, clean and fertile environment (very little farming results in very little pollution), and fresh water supply (numerous lochs and rivers), are all ideal for a flourishing whisky trail. So what gives each malt a distinctive flavor? A plethora of determinants: the water supply, the type and quality of the barley, the temperature, the air quality, the type of wood in which the whisky is stored—even the shape of the pot-still (the large kettle-like structure in which whisky is distilled) matters. Pick up *The Islay and Jura Whisky Trail* leaflet, free from tourist information centres, to aid you in your quest for that perfect dram. Better yet, use our condensed guide:

Ardbeg: (☎302244). On the southeast coast, 4 mi. from Port Ellen. Tours by appointment. £2.

Bowmore: (☎810441), right in town. The oldest distillery on Islay, brewing since 1779. Tours year-round M-F 10:30am and 2pm; in summer also 11:30am and 3pm and Sa 10:30am. £2.

Bunnahabhainn (Bunna-HAV-en): (☎840646). The northernmost distillery. Tours year-round M-Th 10:30am, 1:30, 2:45pm; F 10:30am. Free.

Caol Ila (Cool-EE-la): (☎840207), 1 mi. from Port Askaig. Tours year-round M-Tu and Th-F 10, 11:15am, 1:30, 2:45pm; W 10 and 11:15am. £3.

Jura: (☎820240), near Craighouse village. Tours by appointment only.

Lagavulin: (☎302400), 3 mi. from Port Ellen. A classic. Tours in summer M-F by appointment only. £3.

Laphroaig (La-FROYG): (☎302418), beside Port Ellen, the peatiest of peaty malts. Tours M-F 10:15am and 2:15pm. Free.

£7.05). Travelers from **Arran** can catch bus #448 at the **Claonaig** ferry landing to Kennacraig (☎(01880) 730253; M-Sa 3 per day, £2.45). A combination bus-ferry ticket for travel between **Glasgow** and **Islay** is £20 from **Scottish Citylink** or **CalMac** offices. Every Wednesday in summer, a boat leaves **Oban,** stops on **Colonsay,** and continues to Port Askaig (4hr., £10.10). Check times in the *Strathclyde Transport Area Transport Guide* (to Arran or the Kintyre Peninsula), available at any tourist information centre or from bus drivers. Most bus schedules follow ferry times quite closely, but call to verify your connection or risk being stranded.

Islay Coaches (☎840273) bounce frequently around the island. Bus #451 connects **Port Ellen** and **Port Askaig** via **Bowmore** (M-Sa about 4 per day, Su 1 per day; £1-3); #450 runs from **Bowmore** to **Port Charlotte** (M-Sa 3 per day, £1.30). **Postbuses** also travel between the towns a few times per day. It is easiest to get to and around the island on a Wednesday, and many of the bus times apply to one day only, so read bus schedules carefully. Purchase single tickets, as returns aren't cheaper, and tickets on different buses are not interchangeable. For immediate transportation around the island, contact Carol MacDonald at **Minibus & Taxi Service Island Tours** (☎302155, mobile (0777) 5782155).

PORT ELLEN

Publess Port Ellen is useful only as a base for savoring the solitude of the nearby coastline. To the west, the windswept **Mull of Oa** drops dramatically to the sea. For a taste of its beauty, walk along the Mull of Oa Rd. toward the solar-powered Carraig Fhada lighthouse 1½ mi. away. To the east along the A846, a more substantial journey passes the distilleries, standing stones, ruins of the 16th-century **Dunyveg (Dun-Naomhaig) Castle,** and **Loch an t-Sailein,** otherwise known as "Seal Bay" for its breeding colonies. Seven miles east along the A846, **Kildalton Chapel** holds the miraculously preserved **Kildalton High Cross,** a piece of blue stone thought to date from the 9th century.

Port Ellen's tiny **Kildalton and Oa Information Centre,** next to the post office, is not an official tourist information centre, but stocks bus schedules and leaflets on the area's attractions. (Open Mar.-Dec. M-Sa 9am-noon.) The **post office** is at 54 Frederick Cres. near the ferry terminal, on the corner of Charlotte St. (☎302382. Open M-F 9am-1pm and 2-5:30pm, Sa 9am-12:30pm.) **Postal code:** PA42 7BD.

In town, Mrs. Hedley's **Trout Fly Guest House,** 8 Charlotte St., has decent rooms. If you're hungry, you may have to pay for their delicious £12.50 three-course meal, since there are no restaurants in town. (☎302204; fax 300076. Singles £18.50; doubles £41.) Three miles away in Kintra, the **Kintra Independent Hostel** stands in solitary coastal splendor on a full-fledged working farm. (☎302051. Self-catering. Open Apr.-Sept. Dorms £6.50.) Kintra welcomes **campers** as well, who perch at the southern end of a seven-mile white-sand beach. From Port Ellen, take the Mull of Oa Rd. 1 mi., then follow the right fork marked "To Kintra." (Showers and toilets. £2 per person, £2.50 per tent.) In Port Ellen, Frederick Cres. rings the harbor and holds a **Co-op Foodstore.** (☎302446. Open M-Sa 8am-8pm, Su 12:30-6pm.)

NEAR PORT ELLEN: PORT CHARLOTTE. In West Islay, simple Port Charlotte holds a couple of small museums dedicated to island life. The **Port Charlotte Field Centre,** in a former distillery warehouse on the beach, describes the island's famed wildlife, which includes several rare bird species. (☎850288. Open Apr.-Oct. M-Tu and Th-Sa 10am-3pm, Su 2-5pm. £2, students and seniors £1.20, children £1.) Across the road, the **Museum of Islay Life** reveals Islay's history of Viking raids, clans, and—of course—whisky. (☎850358. Open June-Sept. M-Sa 10am-5pm, Su 2-5pm. £2, students and seniors £1.20, children £1, families £5.) The beyond spartan **SYHA Islay** youth hostel is above the Field Centre. (☎/fax 850385. Curfew 11:45pm. Open Mar.-Oct. Dorms £9, under 18 £7.75.)

BOWMORE

Bowmore, Islay's largest town, is 10 mi. from both Port Ellen and Port Askaig. Arranged in a grid-like, practical design, Bowmore is not exactly laden with architectural splendors but has an undeniable, tiny-town charm. The 18th-century **Bowmore Round Church** on Main St. (also called Kilarrow Parish Church) was built perfectly round to keep Satan from hiding in the corners. (Open daily 10am-5pm. Free.) Behind the town square, **Morrison's Bowmore Distillery,** School St., is the oldest distillery in full-time operation. Drain your complimentary dram after the £2 tour. The coast between Bowmore and Port Ellen is graced by the **Big Strand,** 7 mi. of sandy beach.

Islay's only **tourist information centre** (TIC) calls Bowmore home, and books accommodations for £1. If you plan to explore, pick up *The Isles of Islay, Jura & Coloonday Walks* for 50p. (☎810254. Open July to mid-Sept. M-Sa 9:30am-5:30pm, Su 2-5pm; mid-Sept. to Oct. M-Sa 10am-4:30pm; Nov.-Mar. M-F noon-4pm; Apr. M-Sa 10am-5pm; June M-Sa 9:30am-5pm, Su 2-5pm.) Other services include: a **cash machine** at the **Royal Bank of Scotland,** next to the TIC (☎810555; open M-Tu and Th-F 9:15am-4:45pm, W 10am-4:45pm); the only **launderette** on the island, in the **Mactaggart Leisure Centre,** School St., where you can go for a swim (£2.10) while your clothes take a spin (☎810767; wash £2.80, dry £2.80; open Tu-F 12:30-9pm, Sa 10:30am-4pm, Su 10:30am-5:30pm); and the **post office,** just up the hill on Main St., next to the Round Church (☎810366; open M-W and F 9am-1pm and 2-5:30pm, Th 9am-1pm, Sa 9am-12:30pm). The post office also **rents bicycles** for £10 per day; there are discounts for longer rentals. **Postal code:** PA43 7JH.

Scottish hospitality and rustic rooms await at **Mrs. Omand's B&B,** Tiree House, on Jamieson St. (☎810633. £16 per person.) On the other side of the Jamieson St. gas pump, the proprietors of the **Lambeth Guest House** offer homey lodgings and good conversation. (☎810597. £17 per person.) **Camp** at **Craigens Farm,** a few miles outside town at Gruinart by Bridgend. (☎850256. No facilities. £2 per tent.) A **Co-op Foodstore** is on Main St. (☎810201. Open M-Sa 8am-8pm, Su 12:30-7pm.) On the expensive side, the **Lochside Hotel,** Shore St., serves varied, large main courses for

£6-10. (☎810244. Food served daily noon-2:30pm and 5:30-8:45pm.) Cavort with locals at the only pub in town, the **Bowmore Hotel Pub,** Jamieson St., a.k.a. "Lucci's"—ask for an explanation. (☎810416. Open daily 11am-1am.)

ISLE OF JURA   ☎01496

Near Islay, the tiny Isle of Jura ("Deer Island"; pop. 50) is isolated and unspoiled, full of rugged hills, one wee road, and a Red Deer herd that outnumbers people 10 to one. Jura was remote enough to satisfy even conspiracy-theorist-cum-novelist George Orwell, who penned *1984* here in a cottage free from watchful eyes.

Western Ferries (☎840681) sends a car ferry to Jura from **Port Askaig** across the Sound of Islay (5min.; summer M-Sa 14 per day, Su 6 per day; winter M-Sa 12 per day, Su 2 per day; 90p). Local shuttle buses occasionally meet ferries and drop passengers anywhere on the island for £1-2. Though Islay and Jura are separated by a small distance, think twice before swimming the sound. In addition to strong rip currents, the **Corryvreckan Whirlpool,** the third largest in the world and classified as unnavigable by the Royal Navy, churns violently at Jura's northern tip. Its relentless thrashing can be heard from over a mile away.

CRAIGHOUSE. Jura's only village is a tiny, one-road settlement 10 mi. north of the ferry landing. The 200-year-old **Jura Church** has an exhibition of photographs detailing the history of the island and town. Nearby, the island's only distillery brews **Isle of Jura** whisky. (Call 820240 for tours.) A short walk from Craighouse leads to the abandoned village of **Keils,** one of the island's oldest settlements. Start from the Craighouse distillery and follow the road along the shore for a mile, then follow the signs for the village left and uphill. From Keils, the path continues past a large barn to a fence gate that leads directly to **Cill Earnadail,** an ancient burial site guarded by a bull. (Total distance 2 mi.; round-trip 1hr.)

The only restaurant in Craighouse is the **Antlers Tea Room,** where a warm scone and cuppa cost £1 and Cadbury bars are 33p. (☎820366. Open M-F 10:30am-3:30pm, Sa 10:30am-1pm.) A miniscule **post office** resides at the center of the village, sharing its building with a **grocery store.** (Open M-F 9am-1pm and 2-5:30pm, Sa 9am-12:30pm.) **Postal code:** PA60 7XP.

ISLE OF MULL

Even on the brightest days, mist lingers among Mull's blue hills. Perhaps that's why the island's population clings to the shoreline. Tiny isles fortify Mull to the west and south, including captivating Erraid, the focus of Robert Louis Stevenson's *Kidnapped.* Scenic in its own right, Mull is also a stepping-stone to the popular isles of Iona and Staffa. Though Mull's Gaelic heritage has largely given way to the pressure of English settlers, who now comprise over two-thirds of the population, local craftsmen and itinerant fishermen keep tradition and culture alive.

▐ TRANSPORTATION

Ferries: Caledonian MacBrayne (☎(01631) 566688) runs a ferry from **Oban,** east of Mull, to **Craignure** (45min.; M-Sa 6 per day, Su 5 per day; £3.55). A smaller car and passenger ferry runs from **Lochaline** on the Morvern Peninsula, north of Mull, to **Fishnish** (15min.; M-Sa 14-15 per day, Su 9 per day; £2.15). Note that these ferry times are for summer; winter sailings are few and far between.

Buses: R.N. Carmichael (☎(01688) 302220), **Bowman Coaches** (☎(01680) 812313), and **Highland and Islands Coaches** (☎(01680) 812510) share tour duties and regular routes. Bus #496 meets the Oban ferry at **Craignure** and goes to **Fionnphort** (1¼hr.; M-F 6 per day, Sa 3 per day, Su 1 per day; return £6.90). #495 runs between **Craignure** and **Tobermory** (1hr.; M-F 7 per day, Sa 4 per day, Su 1 per day; return £6.10). Ask tourist information centres (TICs) for timetables. R.N. Carmichael #494 links **Tobermory** and the western village of **Calgary** (45min.; M-F 4 per day, Sa 2 per day; £3.50). You can also jump on friendly **postbuses** (schedules at TICs).

Tours: Daytrip tickets for the **Mull Experience** can be purchased at the CalMac office (☎(0990) 650000) in Oban. The price includes return ferry, coach transport, Mull Railway, and entry to Duart and Torosay Castles. Tour leaves May-Sept. Su-F 10am and noon, also M-Th 2pm. £17.50, children £9.

Bike Rental: A good way to see the island is by bike; rent wheels from **Mull Travel and Crafts** (☎(01680) 812487) in Craignure, 2 doors from the TIC. £7 per half-day, £12 per day. They also **rent cars,** 23+. £26.50-29.50 per day. £100 deposit.

◪ ORIENTATION

Mull's three main hubs, **Tobermory** (northwest tip), **Craignure** (east tip), and **Fionnphort** (southwest tip), form a triangle bounded on two sides by the A849 and the A848. A left turn off the **Craignure Pier** takes you 35 mi. down Mull's main road along the southern arm of the island to **Fionnphort** (FINN-a-furt), where the ferry leaves for **Iona,** a tiny island off Mull's southwest corner. A right turn leads 21 mi. along Mull's northwestern arm to **Tobermory,** Mull's pocket metropolis.

CRAIGNURE   ☎01680

Craignure, Mull's main ferry port, is a wee town with one nameless street. Make like its 10¼ in. gauge miniature **steam train** and toot out of town. (☎812494. Leaves near the campsite. Late Apr. to early Oct. 5-12 per day 11am-5pm. Return £3.50, children £2.50, families £9.50.) The little trooper rolls 1 mi. south through woodlands to the inhabited ⚑**Torosay Castle,** a Victorian mansion filled with Edwardian artifacts, which has stunning views of the ocean and 12 splendid acres of gardens. It's one of the few castles around where you can actually sit on the furniture. (☎812421. Open Apr. to mid-Oct. daily 10:30am-5:30pm. Gardens open year-round 9am-dusk. £4.50, students and seniors £3.50, children £1.50, families £10. Gardens only £3.50, students and seniors £2.75, children £1.) Also worthwhile is the spectacular 700-year-old stronghold of the clan MacLean, **Duart Castle,** 3 mi. west of Torosay. Guide yourself through the state bedroom, the dungeon, and the cell where Spanish sailors were kept for ransom after the Armada's destruction. Take the bus to the end of Duart Rd. and walk the remaining 1½ mi. (☎812309. Open May to mid-Oct. daily 10:30am-6pm. £3.50, students and seniors £3, children £1.75, families £8.75.) **Boat tours** from Oban to the castles leave in summer twice daily. (☎(01866) 822280. £6, students and seniors £5, children £3, families £11.)

The **tourist information centre,** by the ferry terminal, books accommodations for £1 and exchanges money for a £3 commission. (☎812377. Open May-Sept. M-Th and Sa 9am-7pm, F 9am-5pm, Su 10:30am-7pm; Oct.-Apr. M-Sa 9am-5pm, Su 10:30am-5pm.) The **post office** is in the **Spar** store. (Open M-W and F 9am-1pm and 2-5pm, Th and Sa 9am-1pm.) **Postal code:** PA65 6AY.

To get to **The Shielings Holidays Campsite** from the ferry terminal, turn left, then left again at the sign opposite the church. It's past the dilapidated town hall. Enjoy showers, laundry, and a mattress in a carpeted, well-lit PVC tent. (☎/fax 812496. Open Apr.-Oct. 2 people and tent £10, with car £11.50.) Laden with groceries, a **Spar** waits across from the ferry terminal. (☎812301. Open M 7:30am-7pm, Tu-F 8:15am-7pm, Sa 8:30am-7pm, Su 10:30am-1pm and 2:30-6:30pm.)

TOBERMORY   ☎01688

Colorful cafes and pastel houses line an attractive, Mediterranean-style harbor in Tobermory (pop. 1000), Mull's main town. The tiny **Mull Museum** chronicles the island's history with local artifacts and folklore. (Open Easter-Oct. M-F 10:30am-4pm, Sa 10:30am-1:30pm. £1, children 10p.) Local artists display pieces at the **An Tobar Arts Centre,** Argyll Terr., which also hosts musical performances. (☎302211. Open Mar.-Dec. M-Sa 10am-6pm; in summer also Su 1pm; pick up a schedule at the Centre or the TIC.) The **Tobermory Distillery,** on the opposite side of the harbor from the TIC, conducts 30min. tours and offers a generous swig of the final product. All malt-making is still done by hand. (☎302645. Tours Easter-Sept. M-F 10:30am-4pm

THE TOBERMORY GALLEON The "San Juan de Sicilia," a member of the not-so-invincible Spanish Armada, mysteriously sank in Tobermory's harbor in 1588. Soon after the disaster, a legend emerged: the daughter of the Spanish king Philip II came to Tobermory in search of the perfect man. When she found him on board the San Juan de Sicilia, Perfect Man's jealous wife blew the ship sky-high (and then sea-deep). Divers expert and crackpot have long been captivated with the wreck and continually explore it for treasure—perplexing, since there's no reason to expect treasure on a warship. Still, they beat on against the current: in the 1910s and 20s, explorers found some guns, and in 1950 the Royal Navy made a valiant effort, bringing up a cannonball, oak timber, and some coins from the reign of Philip II. The latest search, in 1982, unearthed lead.

2 per hr. Visitor center open Easter-Oct. M-F 10am-4pm. £2.50, seniors £1, children free.) For the freshest in Scottish seafood, rent your own fly rod (£3) from **Tackle and Books,** 10 Main St., a combination angling center and bookstore. They also arrange three-hour **fishing trips** in season. (☎302336. 2-3 trips per week. £15, children £12. Store open July-Aug. M-Sa 9am-5:30pm, Su 11am-4pm; Sept. and June M-Sa 9am-5:30pm.) In the third weekend of April, Tobermory hosts the **Mull Music Festival,** with lively Scottish music. Early July brings the **Mendelssohn Festival.** The **Mull Highland Games** offer caber-tossing and *ceilidhs* on the third Thursday of July.

The **tourist information centre,** on a pier across the harbor from the bus stop, books rooms for £1 (£3 off-island), and sells boat-tour tickets. (☎302182. Open July to mid-Sept. M-Sa 9am-6pm, Su 10am-5pm; Apr. and mid-Sept. to Oct. M-Sa 9am-5pm, Su 10am-5pm; May-June daily 9am-5pm.) Other services include: a **CalMac** ferry office next to the TIC (☎302017; open M-F 9am-6pm; Mar.-Oct. also Sa 9am-4pm); **bike rental** at **Archibald Brown & Son,** 21 Main St. (☎302020, ask for Bryan; £8 per half-day, £13 per day); **Clydesdale Bank,** Main St., the only bank and **cash machine** on the island (bank open M-W and F 9:15am-4pm, Th 9:15am-5:30pm); a full-service **launderette,** by the youth hostel (☎302669; £6; open daily 9am-1pm and 2-5pm, closed some winter Su); **Internet access** at the An Tobar Arts Centre (£1.50 per 15min.; see above); and the **post office,** 36 Main St., on the harbor strip next to the supermarket (open M-Tu and Th-F 9am-5:30pm, W and Sa 9am-1pm). **Postal code:** PA75 6NT.

The small **SYHA Tobermory** hostel, on the far end of Main St. from the bus stop, has a homey kitchen and lounge. (☎/fax 302481. Lockout 10:30am-5pm. Curfew 11:45pm. Open Mar.-Oct. Dorms £8.75, under 18 £7.50.) Beautiful **B&Bs** line the bay. The **Harbour Guest House,** 59 Main St., conveniently opposite the bus stop, cloaks its harborview rooms in green tartan. (☎302209. £19.50 per person, with bath £22.) **Ach-na-Craoibh,** on Erray Rd., has a wide range of accommodations, both B&B and self-catering. Walk up the footpath by the post office, then follow the road as it curves to the right. (☎302301. B&B from £20-25 per night. Self-catering rooms from £90 per week.)

The **Co-op Supermarket** stands by the harbor between the hostel and the post office. (☎302004. Open M-W and Sa 8:30am-6pm, Th-F 8:30am-8pm, Su 12:30-6pm.) Most local restaurants cater to wealthy yacht owners; one exception is the **Tobermory Fish Company,** Main St., which serves delicious smoked trout sandwiches for £1.45 and has attention-grabbing seashells in every shape and size. (☎302120. Open M-F 9am-5pm, Sa 9am-1pm and 2-5pm.) Fishermen, tourists, and locals crowd the spacious pub at the **Mishnish Hotel,** near the TIC. (☎302009. Lunch £3-6, dinner £5-12. Live folk music from 9:30pm most summer nights. Open daily 11am-1am. Lunch served noon-2pm, dinner 6-8:30pm.)

IONA, STAFFA, AND TRESHNISH ISLES

The geologic marvels and contemplative isolation offered by these tiny islands off Mull's west coast make them worth the effort to see. **Iona,** a historic cradle of Christianity, emanates a devout serenity that touches even the most seasoned of travelers. **Staffa,** which translates to "Island of Pillars" in Norse, possesses Fingal's

Cave, magnificent basalt columns immortalized in the music of Mendelssohn. Remote and uninhabited, the **Treshnish Isles** teem with thousands of seabirds and colonies of Common and Atlantic Grey seals.

E TRANSPORTATION. CalMac Ferries (☎(01631) 566688) run to Iona from **Fionnphort** (2 per hr.; return £3.30, children £1.70). As there are no other direct ferries between the islands, it's easiest to see them by **tour**. From Fionnphort, **The Kirkpatricks** run tours to Staffa. (☎(01681) 700358. £12.50, children £5.) Book directly in Fionnphort or at the Oban tourist information centre. The friendly captain at **Turus Mara** leaves from the town **Ulva Ferry** on Mull to Iona, Staffa, and the Treshnish Isles. (☎(01688) 400242, mobile (0831) 638179. Full-day tours £24-40, children £12.50-20.) Other tour companies offer similar services from different ports. From Oban, **Bowman's Tours** (☎(01681) 563221) chugs to Mull, Staffa, and the Treshnish Isles (tours mid.-Apr. to July; £19-35, children £10-17.50), as does **Gordon Grant Marine** (☎(01681) 700338, reservations (0800) 783 8470; tours mid-Apr. to July; £21-35, children £10-17.50).

IONA   ☎01861

The sacred isle of Iona (pop. 150) quivers with purity of color—rocks the hue of Mars, waters the color of the Caribbean, all draped with a very Scottish mist. For nearly two centuries after Irish-bred St. Columba landed his coracle on the island in AD 563, Iona was one of the most celebrated centers of religious life in Europe. Georgian and Victorian followers included James Boswell, Samuel Johnson, Sir Walter Scott, the poet Keats, and Mendelssohn. Today, more than 140,000 visitors pay homage to this tiny outcropping, the sights of which may be seen in a few hours and the peacefulness savored for days.

⚠ PRACTICAL INFORMATION. To the left of the pier, **Ross Finlay** rents all kinds of **bicycles.** (☎700357. £4.50 per half-day, £8 per day. £10 deposit. Open in summer M-Sa 9:15am-6pm, Su 10:15am-6pm; winter daily 11am-1pm and 2-4pm.) In summer, Iona fills with daytrippers from Mull and Oban, making an overnight stay attractive. The small village of **Baile Mor** holds a few shops and B&Bs and a score of well-manicured gardens. To the right of the ferry landing, the **post office** has **Internet access** for £2 per 30min. (☎700515. Open M-Tu and Th-F 9am-1pm and 2-5pm, W 9am-1pm, Sa 9am-12:30pm.) **Postal code:** PA76 6SJ.

🏠🍴 ACCOMMODATIONS AND FOOD. The **Iona Community** has unique accommodations that allow visitors to experience Iona more as St. Columba did, without worldly vanities such as TVs and electricity. Regular six-day retreats on themes of religion and community take place from June to mid-September in the abbey or the more modern MacLeod Centre, combining work and activities. Outside of summer, the retreats are often replaced with open weeks when guests can stay with no theological requirements. (☎(01681) 700404. Vegetarian cuisine. Abbey £185 per week, students £108, youths £98, children £87, under 5 £24; MacLeod Centre £175 per week, students £98, youths £88, children £78, under 5 £21.50. 3-day minimum stay for both.) If the Scottish Episcopal Church is more your style, stay in their **Bishop's House,** a shoreside building with a chapel and decorative windows at the end of the village street. (☎700800. B&B £18; 10% student discount, 15% for religious affiliates.) Through some miracle, groceries bless the island at **Spar,** uphill from the ferry landing. (☎700321. Open Easter-Oct. M-Sa 9am-6pm, Su 10:30am-6pm; Nov.-Easter M-Sa 11am-1pm and 2-4pm.)

🔆 SIGHTS. The ecumenical **Iona Community** lies outside the village, where it cleaves to the massive **Benedictine Abbey,** built on the site of St. Columba's original monastery. Walk up through the village and bear right to reach the abbey, the centerpiece of most views from the ferry. As you enter, be prepared to forfeit £2 at the behest of threatening signs. Visitors are welcome to attend one of the 10min. services. (Open Apr.-Sept. daily 9:30am-6:30pm; Oct.-Mar. 9:30am-4:30pm. Services M-

Th and Sa 9am and 9pm, F 8:15am and 9pm, Su 10:30am and 9pm; in summer daily 2pm.) Adjacent to the abbey, gravestones crowd the entrance to a 10th-century chapel. Inside, **St. Columba's Shrine** once contained a relic of St. Columba and his possessions, making it a popular burial place for local chiefs. Backtrack to find the ruins of a 13th-century **nunnery,** derelict for over 300 years and one of the better-preserved medieval convents in Britain. Signs will get thee from the nunnery to the **Iona Heritage Centre,** located in the "old manse." Here you can learn intriguing snippets about Iona's history, such as what happened "the year the potato went away." (☎700576. Open Easter-Oct. M-Sa 10:30am-4:30pm. £1.50, students and seniors £1, children free.) To visit the tiny 12th-century **St. Oran's Chapel,** turn right just before the abbey. The surrounding burial ground allegedly contains the remnants of more than 60 kings of Scotland, Ireland, and Norway, including the pious Macbeth. Of course, given that the gravestones are over a millennium old, they're a trifle hard to read. On Wednesdays, guides lead an open **pilgrimage** around the island, leaving at 10:15am from St. Martin's Cross. Tuesday nights bring rousing *ceilidhs* to the Village Hall at 10:15pm. On the far side of the island (a 10min. walk), the **Spouting Cave** blasts salt water when the waves are high enough.

If you're coming through Fionnphort, visit the **Columba Centre,** which charts St. Columba's story and the spread of Christianity and monastic life. The sleek exhibition is uphill from the ferry port. (☎700660. Open Easter-Oct. M-Sa 10am-6pm, Su 11am-6pm. £2, students and seniors £1.50, children £1, families £5.)

STAFFA

The incredible island of Staffa, composed of hexagonal basalt columns and rimmed with tidal caves, rises 8 mi. north of Iona. At a weak point in the earth's crust, liquid rock spewed upward and was cooled by ocean water to form columns. Surrounded by treacherous cliffs (particularly slippery in the rain; use of guardrails is essential), Staffa is ruled by an imperial council of six sheep and four cows. Puffins nest on the cliff edge and allow the curious to examine their personal space. When the tide is low, you can walk far inside the infamous ◪**Fingal's Cave** to be surrounded by water and basalt. Wait for the rest of your tour group to go through the cave first so that you can take your time alone. When rough seas roar into the cave, the sound reverberates around the island; the pounding of wave against rock inspired the surging strings in Mendelssohn's *Hebrides Overture.*

TRESHNISH ISLES

The **Treshnish Isles** offer sanctuary for large colonies of seals and ferrets, as well as thousands of species of seabirds. Unthreatened by humans, the animals tolerate up-close examination on these most isolated of isles. Wander along the cliffs as guillemots, razorbills, shags, and other ornithologist favorites land on **Lunga**'s only remnant of human inhabitance—a 13th-century chapel. Legend holds that monks from the Iona Abbey buried their library on one of the isles to save it from the pillages of the Reformation. Many have tried digging under the third ferret from the left, as yet without luck.

HIGHLANDS AND ISLANDS

Long live the weeds and the wilderness yet.
   —Gerard Manley Hopkins, S.J.

Misty and remote, the Scottish Highlands have long been the stuff of fantasy. Yet a trip on the West Highland Railway quickly confirms that these long-romanticized landscapes—often stereotyped as heather-clad outposts doused with the rebellious Scottish spirit—are one of the last stretches of genuine wilderness in Europe. Sheep-dotted moors and towering granite mountains are sliced by the narrow lochs of the Great Glen and imposing mountain ranges like the Cairngorms. Off the coast, the pristine Hebrides arch to the west, while the Norse-influenced Orkney and Shetland Islands stretch off Scotland's horn at John O'Groats. The mainland towns of Inverness, Fort William, and Ullapool are access points for further exploration: trains, buses, and ferries stretch outward from bonny fishing villages and castle-topped cliffsides to rugged islands with seal-strewn shores.

The Highlands have not always been so vacant. Three centuries ago, almost one in three Scots lived north of the Great Glen in fierce, clan-based societies. The defeat of the 1745 Jacobite rising, supported by the clans in opposition to the English king, dealt a heavy blow to Highland society. Later, profit-seeking landlords turned from tenant farming to sheep farming and evicted entire communities in the infamous Highland Clearances of the 18th and 19th centuries. Many Scots, forcibly turned out of their homes, emigrated to Canada, Australia, New Zealand, and the United States. Today, the events of the past continue to haunt the nostalgia-steeped Highlands, and the once-universal Gaelic language (rhymes with "Alec," unlike the Irish "GALE-ick") is spoken only in the Hebrides. Ironically, tourism, the industry that cleared the Highlands to make way for the rich and pleasure-seeking, is now the region's economic fuel. Highlanders themselves typically make ends meet through self-employment, whether by crofting (small, independent farming; a croft is a tenant farmer's plot of land), fishing, or running B&Bs.

HIGHLIGHTS OF THE HIGHLANDS AND ISLANDS

BEN NEVIS Dash up the highest peak in the British Isles, which at 4406 ft. hides its height in a layer of clouds. On a clear day, you can see all the way to Ireland (p. 597).

ORKNEY ISLANDS Seek an unparalleled wealth of ancient ruins with the company of sheep, sky, and ocean (p. 624).

SKYE Explore the mighty Cuillin Hills and sparkling waters of the most accessible and admired of the Hebrides (p. 602).

NORTHWEST HIGHLANDS Trek far from the reaches of the rails to find remote fingers of sea-lochs venturing deep within rugged mountains (p. 618).

◼ TRANSPORTATION IN THE HIGHLANDS AND ISLANDS

Traveling in the Highlands requires a great deal of planning. Transport services are, as a rule, drastically reduced on Sundays and during winter, and making more than one or two journeys per day on any form of transportation is difficult, even in high season. The *Public Transport Travel Guide* (£1), available from tourist information centres, is absolutely essential for whatever region you plan to travel in. The **train** (☎ (08457) 484950), while offering the best views, will only get you so

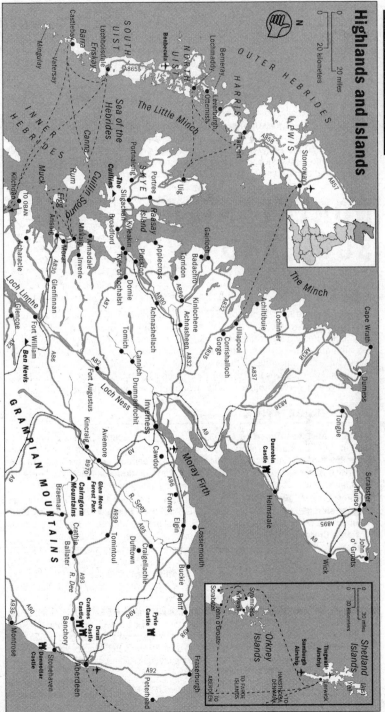

Highlands and Islands

far in the Highlands, and **Scottish Citylink** (☎ (08705) 505050) **buses** do not travel much beyond the main rail routes. Scottish Citylink's unlimited **Explorer Pass** (from £30) is somewhat pricey and not too helpful, though it does provide a 50% discount on Caledonian MacBrayne ferry fares. Access to more remote and possibly rewarding areas depends on small, local bus companies, which are listed in the *Public Transport Travel Guide*. Driving in the Highlands is infinitely more convenient but potentially treacherous; see **Driving,** p. 497, for more information.

Most **ferries** are operated by **Caledonian MacBrayne** (☎(01475) 650100; www.calmac.co.uk), known as "CalMac"; their free timetable is widely available. Special 8- to 15-day **Island Rover** tickets provide discounts on ferry trips, but require substantial travel on consecutive days and are not valid on some sailings during peak times. **Island Hopscotch** tickets may provide modest savings for well-planned routes. Bikes can cross without reservations (usually for a £2 fee), but advance booking for cars, which cost significantly more, is highly recommended.

NORTHEASTERN SCOTLAND

ABERDEEN ☎01224

Whoever dubbed Aberdeen (pop. 210,000) "The Granite City" wasn't off the mark: on a standard day, the gray hues of the city's buildings flow seamlessly into the ashy skies. Perpetually haunted by seagulls, this melancholy mecca of the North Sea oil industry nevertheless shelters the din of partying students and an array of pubs, clubs, and museums. Some visitors use Aberdeen solely as a base for exploring the splendid castles nearby, but those who stay longer realize that Scotland's third-largest city—cosmopolitan and melodramatic—should not be ignored.

▐▀ TRANSPORTATION

Flights: Aberdeen Airport (☎722331). Stagecoach Bluebird #10 runs to the airport from the bus station (every hr., last bus 8:40pm; £1.25) and First Aberdeen (☎650065) #27 runs from the Guild St. stop (13 per day, last bus 5:20pm; £1.35). **British Airways** (☎(08457) 733377) flies from **Heathrow** and **Gatwick** (2 per hr.; standard return £112 plus tax, advance purchase return from £47).

Trains: Guild St. Ticket office open M-Sa 6:15am-8pm, Su 8:45am-7:15pm. 24hr. **luggage storage** £2-4. Trains (☎(08457) 484950) from: **Glasgow** (2hr., every hr., £28); **Inverness** (2¼hr., every 1½hr., £18.20); **Edinburgh** (2½hr., every hr., £21); **London King's Cross** (7½hr.; 3 direct per day, 1 overnight sleeper; £27, £90 respectively).

Buses: Guild St. (☎212266), next to the train station. Ticket office open M-F 7am-5:45pm, Sa 7am-4:30pm, Su 9:30am-3:30pm. **National Express** (☎(08705) 808080) from **London** (5 per day, £34). **Scottish Citylink** (☎(08705) 505050) from **Edinburgh** (4hr., every hr., £17) and **Glasgow** (4hr., every hr., £15). **Stagecoach Bluebird** (☎212266) #10 from **Inverness** (4hr., every hr., £9).

Ferries: The Aberdeen Ferry Terminal, Jamieson's Quay (☎572615). Turn left at the traffic light off Market St., past the P&O Scottish Ferries building. Office open M-F 9am-6pm, Sa 9am-noon. **P&O Scottish Ferries** run to **Stromness, Orkney** (see p. 625) and **Lerwick, Shetlands** (summer M and W-F at 6pm, Tu and Sa at 6pm via Stromness; winter M-F direct trip). Fares are cheap, but bring motion-sickness pills.

Taxis: Mairs City Taxis (☎724040). 24hr.

Car Rental: Nearly all major car rental companies have offices at the airport and in town. **Budget** is one of the cheapest at £40 per day, £160 per week.

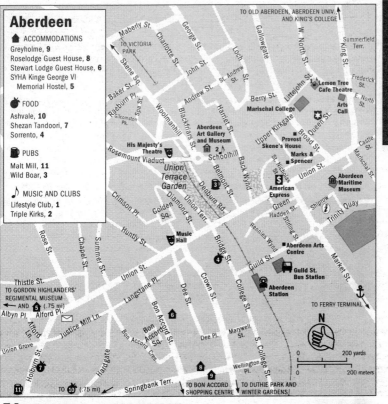

Aberdeen

🏠 ACCOMMODATIONS
Greyholme, **9**
Roselodge Guest House, **8**
Stewart Lodge Guest House, **6**
SYHA Kinge George VI
  Memorial Hostel, **5**

🍴 FOOD
Ashvale, **10**
Shezan Tandoori, **7**
Sorrento, **4**

🍺 PUBS
Malt Mill, **11**
Wild Boar, **3**

🎵 MUSIC AND CLUBS
Lifestyle Club, **1**
Triple Kirks, **2**

PRACTICAL INFORMATION

Tourist Information Centre: Provost Ross's House, Shiprow (☎288828; fax 581367; www.agtb.org). From the bus station, turn right on Guild St., left up Market St., and take the first right onto Shiprow. Books rooms for £1.50 plus a 10% deposit. Open July-Aug. M-Sa 9:30am-7pm, Su 10am-4pm; Sept.-June M-Sa 9:30am-5pm.

Tours: Grampian Coaches (☎650024) runs various day tours to nearby castles, Royal Deeside, the Whisky Trail, and beyond. July-Sept. £8-12, seniors and children £6-10.

Financial Services: The **Royal Bank of Scotland,** 201 Union St. (☎804100). Open M-Tu and Th-F 9am-5pm, W 9:30am-5:30pm, Su 9am-noon. **ChequeCentre** (☎(0800) 243028) has a **bureau de change** at the train station. Open M-F 9am-5:30pm. **Thomas Cook,** Bon Accord Shopping Centre. Open M, W, F-Sa 9am-5:30pm; Tu 10am-5:30pm; Th 9am-8pm; Su noon-5pm. **American Express,** 3-5 St. Nicholas St., 2nd fl. (☎633119), in Lunn Poly Shop. Open M-F 9am-5:30pm, Sa 9am-5pm.

Launderette: A1, 555 George St. (☎621211). Open daily 10am-5pm.

Police: Queen St. (☎386000).

Hospital: Aberdeen Royal Infirmary, Foresterhill Rd. (☎681818).

Internet Access: Costa Coffee, 31-33 Loch St. (☎626468), opposite the Bon Accord Shopping Centre's George St. entrance. 5p per min. Open M-W and F-Sa 8am-6pm, Th 8am-7:30pm, Su 10am-5pm.

Post Office: St. Nicholas Centre, Upperkirkgate (☎633065). Open M-Sa 9am-5:30pm. **Postal Code:** AB10 1HW.

♠ ACCOMMODATIONS

Reasonable B&Bs are near the train station between **Crown St., Springbank Terr.,** and **Bon Accord St.** From the bus and train stations, head left up Guild St., turn right on Bridge St., left on Union St., and look for Crown St. on your left. To get to Springbank Terr. more directly, turn left from Guild St. onto College St., then right onto Wellington Pl. which melds into Springbank Terr.

SYHA King George VI Memorial Hostel, 8 Queen's Rd. (☎646988). Reachable by a long walk on Union St. and Albyn Pl. or a short ride on bus #14, 15, or 27 from Union St. to Queen's Rd. Friendly atmosphere and plush mattresses. Continental breakfast included. Kitchen and laundry facilities. Reception 7am-11pm. Check-out 9:30am. Lockout 9:30am-1pm. Lights out 11:30pm. Curfew 2am. Dorms June-Sept. £13.25, under 18 £11.75; Oct.-May £11.75, £10.25.

Greyholme, 35 Springbank Terr. (☎587081; fax 212287). Hotel-style lodgings in this well-run B&B are tastefully furnished, all with TV. Singles £19-22; doubles £32-34.

Stewart Lodge Guest House, 89 Bon Accord St. (☎573823; fax 592624). More snug than cramped, with a gregarious lobby and staff. Singles £19-22; doubles £30-36.

Roselodge Guest House, 3 Springbank Terr. (☎/fax 586794). Comfortable quarters in a lovely converted home. All rooms with TV. Singles £18-22; doubles £30-34.

♦♥ FOOD AND PUBS

Tins and boxes lure the thrifty to **Safeway,** 215 King St. (☎624404. Open M-W 8am-10pm, Th-F 8am-11pm, Sa 8am-8pm, Su 9am-8pm.)

▨ **The Wild Boar,** 19 Belmont St. (☎625 5357), off Union St. The hippest place for food, drink, and fun. All desserts are homemade, the specials change daily, and come sunset DJs show up and drink specials start. Th nights Latin, F-Sa more up-tempo. Open M-Sa 10am-midnight, Su noon-11pm; food served until 8:45pm, F-Sa until 7:45pm.

▨ **The Ashvale,** 42-48 Great Western Rd. (☎596981). An Aberdeen institution and three-time winner of Scotland's Fish-and-Chip Shop of the Year award. The haddock supper (£3.50) can't be beat. Takeaway around back. Open daily 11:45am-1am.

Sorrento Restaurant, 20 Bridge St. (☎210580). Mercifully uncrowded at night with inventive dishes in a family-run ambience. Open M-Sa 11am-11pm, Su noon-9:30pm.

Shezan Tandoori, 53 Holburn St. (☎590810). Friendly staff whip up a mean *korma* and lamb curry specialties. Chips, dinner, and salad £3.70. Open daily 5pm-3am.

The Malt Mill, 82 Holburn St. (☎573830). Local live music downstairs with bigger names on weekends. An older crowd drinks up top. Student drink specials daily 7-9pm. Last entry 11:45pm. Open M-Th 11am-midnight, F-Sa 11am-1am, Su 12:30-11pm.

⊙ SIGHTS

Aberdeen's must-see architecture is best viewed against a gray sky. For the gloomiest in turrets, **Old Aberdeen** and **Aberdeen University** are a short bus ride (#1-4 or 15) from the city center or a long walk along King St. Once there, the **King's College Visitor Centre,** off High St., has an interesting exhibit on the lives of students past. It hasn't always been pints and discos, you know. (☎273702. Open M-Sa 10am-5pm, Su noon-5pm. Free.) **King's College Chapel** dates from the 16th century and features intricately carved "misery seats," so called because students sat in these un-orthopedic chairs for hours before attending class. (☎272137. Open daily 9am-4:30pm. Guided tours July-Aug. Su 2-5pm. Free.) The twin-spired **St. Machar's Cathedral,** with heraldic ceiling and stained glass, was built in the 14th century. (Open daily 9am-5pm. Services Su 11am and 6pm.) After your visit, take a walk through **Seaton Park** to the Brig O' Balgownie—a gift from Robert the Bruce.

The **Aberdeen Art Gallery,** on Schoolhill, houses a notable collection of 20th-century British art alongside a range of European paintings. (☎523700. Open M-Sa

10am-5pm, Su 2-5pm. Free.) The **Maritime Museum,** in Shiprow next to the TIC, provides a comprehensive look at Aberdeen's oil industry; the exhibits and models on sea life are fascinating. (☎337700. Open M-Sa 10am-5pm, Su noon-3pm. Free.) Just up Broad St., the **Provost Skene's House** is one of few 16th-century Aberdonian mansions to escape demolition. Its Painted Gallery boasts grand depictions of religious scenes. (☎641086. Open M-Sa 10am-5pm, Su 1-4pm. Free.) Across the street, the imposing Gothic hulk of **Marischal College** houses the anthropological **Marischal Museum,** which provides an interesting glimpse into Northeast Scotland's prehistoric past. (☎274301. Open M-F 10am-5pm, Su 2-5pm. Free.) The **Gordon Highlanders Museum,** St. Lukes, Viewfield Rd., displays the pomp, circumstance, and bloody heroism of the kilted fighting regiment. Walk farther down Queens Rd. from the hostel or take bus #14 or 15 from Union St. (☎311200. Open Apr.-Oct. Tu-Sa 10:30am-4:30pm, Su 1:30-4:30pm. £2.50, students and seniors £1.50, children £1.)

Defying the gray conspiracy, Aberdeen is also famous for its greenery, cinching the Britain in Bloom award 10 times since 1963. **Duthie Park** (DA-thee), by the River Dee at Polmuir Rd. and Riverside Dr., has an extensive rose garden, birds and reptiles, and the **Winter Gardens Hothouse.** (Hothouse open daily 9:30am-dusk. Free.) The aviary and extensive woodlands of **Hazlehead Park,** off Queen's Rd., are worth the short bus ride to the western edge of the city (#14 or 15). A garden for the visually impaired with Braille plaques blooms in the nearer **Victoria Park,** west of the city center on Westburn Rd. Aberdeen's beautiful **beach** stretches north for about 2 mi. from the old fishing community of Footdee (fi-TEE, foot of the River Dee) to the Don estuary. Two **amusement parks** rear over the southern end, while the northern sands are cleaner and often quieter. Take bus #14 from the bus station.

ENTERTAINMENT AND NIGHTLIFE

Seagulls aren't the only things to listen to in Aberdeen—five main entertainment venues and other assorted hangouts ensure a steady stream of live music and theater. **The Lemon Tree Cafe Theatre,** 5 West North St., near Queen St., presents folk, jazz, rock, and drama on its two stages. (☎642230. Tickets £5-9, students and seniors £2-3.) The **Music Hall,** on Union St., is your best bet for info on current performances. The hall itself hosts pop bands and orchestra recitals. (☎641122. Box office open daily 9am-5pm.) **His Majesty's Theatre,** Rosemount Viaduct, hosts opera, ballet, and theater; book tickets through the Music Hall. The **Aberdeen Arts Centre,** 33 King St., stages avant-garde and traditional plays. (Book through Music Hall. Tickets £3-6, students and seniors £1-2.) Pubs like **The Wild Boar** and **The Malt Mill** frequently host hip live bands in an alcohol-friendly atmosphere (see p. 582). For info on all venues, snag *What's On in Aberdeen* from the TIC or art gallery.

Aberdeen also has pumping nightlife, courtesy of student throngs forced indoors by the cold weather. On the last Saturday night of the month, the **Lifestyle Club** takes over the **Lemon Tree** (see above) and brings down the house with top-notch funk, jazz, soul, and hip-hop blends. (Cover £4. Open 5pm-3am.) **Langstane Place,** south of Union St., is the place to prowl for **dance clubs** on remaining weekend nights. **The Triple Kirks,** 12 Schoolhill, just below the Aberdeen Art Gallery, is a ruined church that rivals any club in Glasgow. Groove to everything from jazz to disco to techno in its **Exodus Nightclub,** or listen to stand-up at its monthly **Comedy Cafe.** £1 drink promotions are frequent at the bar. (☎619921. Cover £2-4. Club open Th-Su 10:30pm-2am, bar open M-Sa 11am-midnight, Su noon-11pm.)

DAYTRIPS FROM ABERDEEN: THE GRAMPIAN COAST

The East Grampian coast is dotted with some of the most dramatic castles in Scotland, from well-preserved residences to crumbling ruins.

■ DUNNOTTAR CASTLE. Splendidly decrepit Dunnottar Castle stands a romantic 30min. walk from seaside **Stonehaven,** 15 mi. south of Aberdeen. Built in the 12th century by Earl Marischal's family, the castle was the backdrop for Franco Zeffirelli's *Hamlet* (starring Mel Gibson), and has witnessed several gruesome historical events (like the burning of an entire English garrison by William Wallace in 1297). The castle commands gut-wrenching sea views; if you crawl through the tunnel at the base of the cliff, you'll find a pebbly beach that rattles with the receding waves. *(Trains (20min., 17-25 per day, £2.90) and Bluebird Northern bus #101 (30min., 2 per hr., return £3.65) connect Aberdeen to Stonehaven.* ☎*(01569) 762173. Open Easter-Oct. M-Sa 9am-6pm, Su 2-5pm; Nov.-Mar. M-F 9am-dusk. £3.50, children £1.)*

FYVIE CASTLE. Northwest on the inland A947, 25 mi. from Aberdeen, the amazingly intact 13th-century Fyvie Castle endures a brace of curses: in one of the towers, there's a sealed chamber that, if opened, causes the laird to die and his wife to go blind. It's happened . . . twice! For those still in possession of their eyesight, the exterior is striking, adorned with five lofty turrets—one added by each family that has owned the castle since the 14th century. *(Stagecoach Bluebird (*☎*(01224) 212266) runs from Aberdeen (#305, 1hr., every hr.).* ☎*(01651) 891266. Open June-Aug. daily 11am-5:30pm; May and Sept. 1:30-5:30pm; Oct. Sa-Su 1:30-5:30pm; last admission 4:45pm. Grounds open daily 9:30am-dusk. £6, seniors and children £4.)*

ROYAL DEESIDE

Tourist industry wizards have dubbed the area between Aberdeen and Braemar "Royal Deeside," and the name is apt. It's royal since Queen Victoria established her Highland retreat here in 1852, and it's Deeside because it runs along the River Dee. This favorite getaway for British monarchs is threaded by a multitude of tourist trails that shepherd motorists past the regal residences, including the Castle Trail and the Victorian Heritage Trail. If you don't have a car, the efficient **Bluebird "Heather-hopper" bus** #201 runs every hr. between Aberdeen and Braemar (day-long rover pass £7, children £3.50), whisking passengers from Aberdeenshire, traditionally a stronghold of "Lowland" culture, to the edge of the Highlands, where Gaelic no longer thrives, but hill-walking, fishing, and skiing opportunities do.

The first stop on the Bluebird bus route (30min. from Aberdeen), modest **Drum Castle** is pleasantly undertouristed. The Scots ballad "The Laird of Drum" immortalizes a former castle-master who, at over 70 years of age, wooed and married a 16-year-old milkmaid on his estate. (He insisted she was legal.) Hop off the bus at Drumoak and walk a mile to the castle and its Garden of Historic Roses. (☎ (01330) 811204. Open June-Aug. daily 11am-5:30pm; late Apr. to May and Sept. 1:30-5:30pm; Oct. Sa-Su 1:30-5:30pm. Grounds open daily 9:30am-dusk. £5, students and seniors £3.50, children free. Joint ticket with Crathes Castle available; see below.)

Crathes Castle, a few miles down the #201 route, is considerably more crowded. Grand without being extravagant, the interior contains curiosities like the Horn to Leys, a 1323 gift from Robert the Bruce, and a "trip stair" designed to bungle burglars. A "Green Lady" allegedly haunts the castle, perhaps contributing her thumb to the superlative gardens, whose blooms decorate ingenious alcoves and hedge-lined passages. (☎ (01330) 844525. Castle open Apr.-Sept. daily 11am-5:30pm; Oct. 10:30am-4:30pm. Last admission 45min. before close. Garden open daily 9:30am-sunset. £7, concessions £5. Garden or castle only £4.50, concessions £3. Joint ticket with Drum Castle purchasable only at Crathes; £10, concessions £7.25.)

An hour farther along, the turrets of **Balmoral Castle** overlook the little town of Crathie. The Queen's holiday palace, Balmoral was a gift from Prince Albert, who helped design its present form. The exterior is fittingly majestic, but being a royal hideaway, most of the interior is closed to the public. (☎ (013397) 42334. Open mid-Apr. to July M-Sa 10am-5pm. £4.50, seniors £3.50, under 16 £1.) **Horseback riding** (pony trekking) lends an antiquated air to the Balmoral Estates. Call ahead for two-hour treks starting at 9:30am and 1:30pm (£20 per person).

BRAEMAR ☎ 013397

Situated on the River Dee, Braemar is the southern gateway to the Cairngorm Mountains and a hiker's paradise. The fully furnished 17th-century **Braemar Castle** was once a stronghold of the Farquharson clan. (☎41219. Open Apr.-Oct. Sa-Th

10am-6pm, last entry 5:30pm. £3, students and seniors £2.50, children £1.) The first Saturday in September, Braemar's population swells from 410 to 20,000 during the one-day **Braemar Gathering**, a famous Highland Games always attended by the Prime Minister and Queen. Advanced booking is essential for a seat; uncovered stand tickets cost about £12, providing no more than damp grass for a chair. (Information ☎55377, bookings (01330) 825917.) The second week of July is **Braemar's Gala Week**, featuring such random events as battle reenactments, a mountain rescue display, and "children's activities with bouncy castle."

The only way into (and out of) Braemar by public transportation is on the **Bluebird "Heather-hopper" bus** #201, which originates in Aberdeen (from Crathie and Balmoral 15min., from Aberdeen 2¼hr.; 1-2 per hr.; day-long rover pass £7, children £3.50). In town, rent **bikes** from the **Mountain Sports Shop,** around the bend on Invercauld Rd. (☎41242. £15 per day.) The **tourist information centre** (TIC), Mar Rd., at the Mews, supplies a comprehensive list of places to stay. (☎41600. Open July-Aug. daily 9am-7pm; Sept. 10am-6pm; Oct. and Apr. to late May M-Sa 10:30am-1:30pm and 2-5:30pm, Su noon-5pm; Nov.-Mar. M-Sa 10:30am-1:30pm and 2-5pm; late May to June M-Su 10am-7pm.) Stock up on hiking grub at the **Alldays** across the street (open M-Sa 7:30am-9pm, Su 9am-9pm), which is also home to the **post office** (open M-F 9am-noon and 1-5:30pm, Sa 9am-1pm). **Postal code**: AB35 5YL.

The 64-bed **SYHA Braemar** occupies a stone house 5min. from town on Glenshee Rd., surrounded by Scotland's oldest pines. Fear not the 11:45pm lockout—most of Braemar is closed by then anyway. (☎41659. Reception 7-10:30am and 5-11pm. July-Aug. dorms £9.25, under 18 £8; Sept.-June £8, £5.) The **Rucksacks Bunkhouse**, 15 Mar Rd., behind the TIC, has room for 26, 10 of whom sleep in said bunkhouse and use their own sleeping bags. (☎41517. Dorms £8.50; bunkhouse £7.) Three doors from the SYHA, the **Campbell Guest House** has spacious rooms with bath. (☎41675. Singles and doubles £18-20 per person.) The **Invercauld Caravan Club Site,** 5min. past the hostel on Glenshee Rd., welcomes tents to its crowded premises. (☎41373. Open Dec.-Sept. £5 per person.)

▓ **HIKING NEAR BRAEMAR** The area around Braemar bristles with signposted hikes for all skill levels, centering around the hypnotic **Linn of Dee,** Gaelic for "rocky gorge." Along the river, the leisurely **Derry Lodge Walk** is popular for sightings of red deer, red squirrels, and grouse. The more challenging **Lairig Ghru trail,** which stretches 20 mi. north to Aviemore, also starts at the Linn. The name means "gloomy pass," which isn't off the mark: the path is heartbreakingly desolate as it winds between steep mountainsides and past Ben Macdui. It's also difficult, so don't overestimate your ability or underestimate your need for an Ordnance Survey map (Outdoor Leisure #3). To get to the Linn, drive 20min. from Braemar on the Linn of Dee Rd., or catch the daily **postbus** from the Braemar post office at 1:30pm (no return). Otherwise, walk or bike the scenic 7 mi.

Hikers will want to start early to finish the whole Lairig Ghru; consider spending the night before at the **SYHA Inverey,** where there are usually more deer than guests. The daily postbus stops at the hostel before swinging by the Linn. (☎(013397) 41969. No showers. Open mid.-May to Sept. Dorms £6.75, under 18 £6.) The **SYHA Glendoll** is a difficult 13 mi. hike from Braemar. Follow the A93 2 mi. south to the Glen Callater turn-off, then take the Jock's Rd. footpath (for athletes only, apparently). Take an Ordnance Survey map and compass and notify the Braemar police of your plans. (☎(01575) 550236. Open Apr.-Sept. Dorms £8.25, under 18 £7.25.)

CAIRNGORM MOUNTAINS ☎01479

The towering Cairngorms, 120 mi. north of Edinburgh, are real Scottish wilderness: misty, mighty, and arctic even in summer. These mountains have also suffered the deforestation that nearly stripped Scotland of its native pine and birch forests. While the peaks are bare, covered only with heather, reindeer, and, for much of the year, the snow that attracts skiers and dogsledders, the region does contain Britain's largest expanse of nature preserves. With reforestation and wildlife on the rise, the Cairngorms may soon become Scotland's first National Park.

▢ TRANSPORTATION

The largest town in the Cairngorms, **Aviemore** is conveniently located on the main Inverness-Edinburgh rail and bus lines. **Trains** (☎ (08457) 484950) arrive at the station on Grampian Rd., just north of the tourist information centre (TIC), from **Inverness** (45min., 7-8 per day, £7.50) and **Edinburgh** and **Glasgow** (2¼hr., 7 per day, £28.70). Southbound **buses** stop at the shopping center north of the train station; northbound buses brake before the Cairngorm Hotel. **Scottish Citylink** (☎ (08705) 505050) runs nearly every hr. from: **Inverness** (40min., 15 per day, £4.70); **Glasgow** (3½hr., 15 per day, £12.50); **Edinburgh** (3hr., 12 per day, £12.50). **Kincraig,** 6 mi. south of Aviemore on the A9, is accessible by Scottish Citylink #957 from Perth.

The principal path into **Glen More Forest Park** and the area's prettiest road trip, the **Ski Rd.** begins just south of Aviemore (on the B970) and jogs eastward, merging with the A951. The road passes the sandy beaches of **Loch Morlich** before carrying on to **Glenmore** and ending at the Cairngorm base. From Aviemore's train station, **Highland Country** "Munro Bagger" **buses** #37 and 337 travel the same route, taking in **Kincraig** (summer, 10 per day). A similar winter service carries all-too-eager skiers.

The **Cairngorm Service Station,** on Aviemore's Main St., rents **cars.** (☎810596. £34-42 per day, £185-235 per week.) **Bike rental** (half-day £10, full-day £14) is available from **Bothy Bikes,** Grampian Rd. (☎810111), next to the train station, and **Inverdruie Bikes,** Ski Rd. (☎810787), in Aviemore. **The Glenmore Shop and Cafe,** near the Loch Morlich hostel, rents bikes, skis, and mountain boards. (☎861253. Bikes £3 per hr., £8 per half-day, £13 per day. Open daily 8:30am-5:30pm.)

◪◪ ORIENTATION AND PRACTICAL INFORMATION

While the Cairngorms themselves are quiet, their largest town, **Aviemore,** is not. This concrete roadside strip caters to tourists with its clutter of pricey hotels; once you've used its urban amenities, escape to the mountains. **Glenmore** offers the most intimate access, and **Kincraig,** though farther away, sustains visitors with a welcome breath of non-touristed air on the tranquil shores of Loch Insh.

The **Aviemore and Spey Valley tourist information centre,** on Grampian Rd., Aviemore's main artery, books local B&Bs for a £3 fee, sells bus tickets, and exchanges currency for a commission during peak season. (☎810363. Open July to mid-Sept. M-F 9am-5:30pm, Sa 10am-5pm, Su 10am-4pm; mid-Sept. to June M-F 9am-5pm, Sa 10am-4pm.) The **Rothiemurchus Estate Visitors Centre** lies nearly a mile down the Ski Rd. from Aviemore toward the Cairngorms. (☎812345. Open daily 9am-5:30pm.) **Kincraig Stores** serves as the Kincraig **post office** and unofficial info center. (☎(01540) 651331. Post office open M-Tu and Th-F 9am-1pm. Store open M-Sa 8am-6pm, Su 8:30am-1pm.) Other services include: **Bank of Scotland,** Grampian Rd., across from Tesco (open M-Tu and Th-F 8am-5pm, W 10am-5pm); **Internet access** at **SYHA Aviemore** (£5 per hr.; see below); and the **post office,** Grampian Rd. (open M-F 9am-5:30pm, Sa 9am-12:30pm). **Postal code:** PH22 1RH.

▤ ACCOMMODATIONS

Check the tourist board's *Aviemore and Spey Valley* publication for a complete list of seasonal hostels and year-round B&Bs (£15-25).

▨ **Lazy Duck Hostel** (☎821642; www.lazyduck.co.uk), Badanfhuarain, in nearby Nethy Bridge. Catch Highland Country bus #334 from Aviemore (20min., 8 per day). One of Scotland's smallest hostels—bedding 8 at most—is also one of its best. A snug cottage with magical loft and covered garden, congenial ducks and geese, excellent kitchen, and 2 family guest houses. Dorms £8.50 per person.

Carrbridge Bunkhouse Hostel (☎(01479) 841250), Dalrachny House, Carrbridge. A 10min. walk along a marked footpath from Carrbridge train station. Sparely done, but a perfect haunt for the serious hiker, nature lover, or bargain hunter. Kitchen, hot showers, and sauna, plus hardcore personality. All this for £7 a night.

SYHA Aviemore (☎810345). 100 yd. south of the TIC. All the amenities, but about as much genuine soul as the latest boy band. 114 beds with 4-8 beds to a room. Breakfast included. Curfew 2am. Dorms £12.25, under 18 £10.75; July-Aug. £1 extra.

Glen Feshie Hostel (☎(01540) 651323), 11 mi. south of Aviemore, 5 mi. from Kincraig. Call ahead for a lift from the station; otherwise it's a 9 mi. walk along Loch-an-Eilein to Balachroik House. Comfortable atmosphere and living quarters close to numerous hikes. Linen and porridge breakfast included. Showers, kitchen. Dorms £8.

Insh Hall Lodge (☎(01540) 651272), 1 mi. downhill from Kincraig on Loch Insh; Scottish Citylink #957 runs to the hostel from Kincraig. Year-round accommodations with bath for skiers and hikers. Sauna and gym. Stay at least 2 nights for free use of watersports equipment. Basic rooms of good size. Rooms from £17.50; full board £35.50.

SYHA Loch Morlich (☎861238), Glenmore. A tyrannical lights-out policy keeps guests from reading, writing, or chatting past 11:30pm. Lovely setting but impersonal atmosphere. The Highland Country Bus departs from Aviemore train station and stops in front of the hostel, summer and winter. Curfew 11:30pm. Dorms £9.25, under 18 £8.

Camping: Glenmore Forest Camping and Caravan Park (☎861271), opposite the SYHA Loch Morlich. Ample space and good facilities, though crowded in summer. Open Dec.-Oct. £3.70-5 per person. **Rothiemurchus Camp and Caravan Park** (☎812800), 1½ mi. south of Aviemore on Ski Rd. A close runner-up. £3.50 per person.

⚡ FOOD

The local **Tesco** supermarket is north of the Aviemore train station. (Open M-W and Sa 8:30am-8pm, Th-F 8:30am-9pm, Su 9am-6pm.) At the Aviemore station, take in high tea ($5.85 for 3 courses) at the modestly titled **Number One Restaurant.** For a chicer spot, **Cafe Mambo,** 12-13 Grampian Rd., serves burgers ($5-7), "fetish" cocktail pitchers ($11.50), and sinful hot chocolate ($1.50). Stay to dance it off if you've had one too many fetish cocktails. (☎811670. Restaurant and bar open Su-W 11am-11pm, Th-Sa noon-1am; food served until 9pm. Club open F-Sa 10pm-1am.)

⚡ HIKING, SKIING, AND OTHER REINDEER GAMES

The Cairngorm region has Scotland's highest concentration of ski resorts. In winter, alpine skiers converge at the **Cairngorm Ski Place,** set to unveil its brand new (and highly controversial) funicular railway in December 2001. The railway will be the highest in the UK and provide access to the spectacular peaks in all weather conditions. From May 2002, the observation deck will also have a Mountain Exhibition with details on one of the UK's most marvelous natural regions. (Round-trip $7.50, students and seniors $6.50, children $5. Take Highland County Bus #37 from Aviemore, whose final stop is at the foot of the railway in the Ski Place car park.)

Unfortunately, the funicular railway does not provide access to the popular peak of **Ben MacDui,** Britain's second highest at 4296 ft. To get there, take the **Northern Corries Path** from the car park to its terminus, and then navigate an unmarked route to Ben MacDui's peak—a seven-hour undertaking suggested only for mountaineers with some experience, but definitely worth the exertion. Be prepared for all weather, at any time of year, and bring a stock of food. Consult the **Cairngorm Rangers** (☎(01479) 861703); office next to the car park) before setting out.

Other hikes for all skill levels abound. In the ski area, many signposted trails, all of which leave from the car park, scour Mt. Cairngorm. The Cairngorm Rangers also host free guided hikes, usually on Thursdays and Sundays. For forest walks, **Glenmore Forest Park Visitors Centre** has a few good options, the most popular of which is the easy-going **Pass of Ryovan** walk through woods and along Green Lochen, signposted from the Centre. (☎861220. Open daily 9am-5pm.) Closer to Aviemore, the daunting but renowned **Lairig Ghru** path heads south through 20 mi. of gloomy valleys to Braemar. This one's only for the bravest of souls, so make sure you have your Ordnance Survey Outdoor Leisure map (#3) and your stamina.

For skiers, a day ticket at Cairngorm with rail passes costs $20 (students $16, children $10). Several companies run ski schools and rent equipment; pick up a copy of *Skiing Information* at the Aviemore TIC for details. Down the hill 3 mi. from the funicular, the **Cairngorm Reindeer Centre** is home to 150 velvet-horned sled-pullers. For a fee, visitors get a 1½hr. frolic amid the herd. (☎861228. Open daily 10am-5pm. Visits at 11am; May-Oct. also at 2:30pm. Call ahead to confirm afternoon visit. £5, seniors and children £3. Paddock £1.50.) In summer, the **Highland Country** bus service runs from Aviemore to the funicular and Reindeer Centre (see **Transportation,** p. 586). Otherwise, you can bike the 10 mi. The **Highland Wildlife Park** in Kincraig is dedicated to preserving local beasts. Scottish Citylink #957 stops there from Aviemore en route to Edinburgh, Perth, and Pitlochry. (☎(01540) 651270. Open June-Aug. daily 10am-7pm, last admission 5pm; Apr.-May and Sept.-Oct. 10am-6pm, last admission 4pm; Nov.-Mar. 10am-4pm, last admission 2pm.)

> ⚠ **SAFETY PRECAUTIONS.** Although the Cairngorms rise only 4000 ft., the weather patterns of the **Arctic tundra** characterize the region. Explorers may be at the mercy of bitter winds and unpredictable mists *any day of the year.* Furthermore, many trails are not posted and trekkers must be able to rely on their own proficiency with a map and compass. Make sure to use an Ordnance Survey map (Landranger #35 and 36), or preferably, yellow Outdoor Leisure map #3. Both are available at the tourist information centre. Be prepared to spend a night in **sub-freezing temperatures** no matter what the temperature is when you set out. Leave a description of your intended route with the police or at the mountain station, and learn the locations of the shelters (known as bothies*)* along your trail. See **Wilderness Safety,** p. 54.

ELGIN   ☎01343

Elgin (whose "g" is pronounced as in Guinness, not gin; pop. 20,000) is a relatively urban town halfway between Aberdeen and Inverness whose spectacular **cathedral** warrants a stopover between the two cities. Once regarded as the most beautiful of Scottish churches, the cathedral was looted and burned by the Wolf of Badenoch at the end of the 14th century, then further tormented by fire, Edward III, the Reformation, and Cromwell's bullets. Thanks to careful restoration, the church remains a breathtaking sight. (☎547171. Open Apr.-Sept. daily 9:30am-6pm; Oct.-Mar. M-Sa 9:30am-4pm, Su 2-4pm. £2.50, seniors £1.90, children £1.) Next door, all 110 plants mentioned in the Good Book thrive in the **Biblical Garden.** (Open May-Sept. daily 10am-7:30pm. Free.) The **Elgin Museum** displays spoils collected by local notables in the Age of Empire, including a shrunken head from Ecuador and a mummy from Peru. (☎543675. Open Easter-Oct. M-F 10am-5pm, Sa 11am-4pm, Su 2-5pm; winter groups only. £2, students and seniors £1, children 50p.)

The **train station,** 5min. from town along South Guildry St., greets trains (☎(08457) 484950) from **Inverness** (45min., 11 per day, £7.50) and **Aberdeen** (1½hr., 10 per day, £11.50). **Buses** stop behind High St. and the St. Giles Centre. **Stagecoach Bluebird** (☎(01343) 544222) #10 arrives from **Inverness** (1¼hr., 2 per hr., £7) and **Aberdeen** (2¼hr., every hr., £7). The **tourist information centre** (TIC), 17 High St., books accommodations. (☎542666; fax 552982. Open Apr.-Oct. M-Sa 10am-5:30pm; June-Sept. also Su 10am-2pm; Nov.-Mar. M-F 10am-4pm, Sa 10am-2pm.) Other services include: **Internet access** at **Elgin Library** (☎562600; £2 per 30min.; open M-F 10am-8pm, Sa 10am-4pm); and the **post office,** in the **Tesco** supermarket on Batchen Ln. (open M-F 8:30am-8pm, Sa 8am-6pm, Su 10am-5pm). **Postal code:** IV30 1LY.

Elgin is full of **B&Bs.** The Rosses let rooms with TV in their colorful **Bungalow,** 7 New Elgin Rd. From the train station, turn right and head straight until reaching the rotary, then take the first right over the railway bridge. After the next rotary, it's the third house on the left (5min.). Otherwise, walk 15min. along New Elgin Rd. from the town center. (☎542035. £15 per person.) Eat a two-course lunch for only £3 (noon-2:30pm) at the **Thunderton House** pub, Thunderton Pl. off the High St. (☎554921. Open Su-W until 11pm, Th until 11:45pm, F-Sa until 12:30am.)

NEAR ELGIN

FORRES. Quieter than Elgin and a perennial winner in the cutthroat Britain in Bloom competition, Forres boasts the magnificent **Sueno's Stone,** a richly carved Pictish cross-slab (Scotland's tallest) viewable day and night for free in a locked glass house. **Stagecoach Bluebird** #10 makes the 30min. trip (2 per hr., £2.40).

LOSSIEMOUTH. An alternative to Elgin for an overnight stay, secluded Lossiemouth, 6 mi. north of Elgin on the A941, has two sandy, windswept beaches: **East Beach,** connected to the mainland by a footbridge, and **West Beach,** which is cleaner, less crowded, and leads to a lighthouse. Bus #329 connects "Lossie" to Elgin (20min., 3 per hr.). Halfway to Lossie, stop off at **Spynie Palace,** once the digs of the Bishops of Moray, which has the largest tower house in Scotland. (☎ (01343) 546358. Open Apr.-Sept. daily 9:30am-6pm; Oct.-Mar. Sa 9:30am-4pm and Su 2-4pm. £1.80, seniors £1.30, children 75p. Joint ticket with Elgin Cathedral £3, seniors £2.25, children £1.20.) In Lossiemouth, the spacious rooms of **Mrs. Stephen's,** 54 Queen St., offer good value. (☎ (01343) 813482. £16 per person.) Campers pitch tents at **Silver Sands Leisure Park.** (☎ (01343) 813262. Open Mar.-Oct. £11 per tent.)

THE MALT WHISKY TRAIL. The world-famous Speyside area has 57 working distilleries, making it prime territory for dram-drinking. The 62 mi. Malt Whisky Trail staggers past seven of them, all of which dispense free booze. **Stagecoach Bluebird** #10 covers Keith, Elgin, and Forres (all key Speyside stopovers) twice per hr. on its way from Aberdeen to Inverness and back. Always tell the driver where you want to go. The **Stagecoach** (☎ (01343) 544222) **Bluebird Day Rover** ticket gives unlimited one-day travel (£9.50, children £4.50), and the **Off Peak Day Rover** gets unlimited travel M-F after 9am or all day on weekends (£7, children £3).

The best (and only free) tour is at **Glenfiddich Distillery** in Dufftown, 17 mi. south of Elgin, where whisky is bottled on the premises. When brewing was illegal, the black fungus on the trees was a dead giveaway to police. Take Bluebird bus #336 from Elgin (40min., 6 per day) to the distillery. (☎ (01340) 820373. Open Jan. to mid-Dec. M-F 9:30am-4:30pm; Easter to mid-Oct. also Sa 9:30am-4:30pm and Su noon-4:30pm.) If you ask the driver, the #336 bus to Glenfiddich will stop at **The Speyside Cooperage,** ¼ mi. south of Craigellachie on the A941, where casks are still handmade. (☎ (01340) 871108. Open Jan. to mid-Dec. M-F 9:30am-4:30pm; June-Sept. also Sa 9:30am-4pm. Tours £2.95, seniors £2.45, children £1.75.) A self-guided tour takes you to **Strathisla Distillery,** the "home and heart" of Chivas Regal, and the oldest working distillery in the Highlands (est. 1786). It's a 10min. crawl from the Keith bus or train station. (☎ (01542) 783044. Open Feb. to mid-March M-F 9:30am-4pm; mid-March to Nov. M-Sa 9:30am-4pm, Su 12:30-4pm. £4.)

TOMINTOUL AND THE SPEYSIDE WAY. Rather than nurse a malt, ramblers traipse the **Speyside Way,** an 84 mi. trail along the river from Buckie at Spey Bay to Aviemore in the Cairngorms. Grab a trail map at the Elgin TIC. The trail traverses Scotland's highest village, **Tomintoul,** surrounded by the Highland hills of the **Glenlivet Estate.** Here you can hike 7 mi. to the famous **Glenlivet Distillery,** Ballindalloch. (☎ (0154) 278322. Open July-Aug. M-Sa 10am-6pm, Su 12:30-6pm; mid-March to June and Sept.-Oct. M-Sa 10am-4pm, Su 12:30-4pm. £2.50, under 18 free.)

If you're not driving, biking, or long-distance hiking, Tomintoul is difficult to reach. **Roberts Buses** (☎ (01343) 544222) runs from Keith and Dufftown (#362, Tu and Sa 1 per day) and Elgin (#363, Th 1 per day, £4). The **tourist information centre,** The Square, dispenses info on various trails around town. (☎ (01807) 580285. Open July-Aug. M-Sa 9:30am-6:30pm; Apr.-June and Sept.-Oct. 9:30am-1pm and 2-5pm.) Cheap accommodations abound in Tomintoul, starting with the basic **Gordon Hotel Bunkhouse,** The Square. See the hotel reception to check in, and bring your own sleeping bag. (☎ (01807) 580206. Overnight stay £7.)

THE GREAT GLEN

INVERNESS   ☎ 01463

To reach just about anything in the Highlands, you'll have to pass through the transport hub of Inverness (pop. 42,000), which has shops, pubs, and amenities, but not much else. Luckily, you don't have to be a Nessie nut to appreciate Britain's largest inland body of water, the Loch Ness, only 5 mi. away. And hey, even if you don't see the real monster, vendors are all too happy to sell you a stuffed one.

▣ TRANSPORTATION

Trains: Academy St., in Station Sq. Travel center open M-Sa 6:25am-8:30pm, Su 9:15am-8:30pm. 24hr. **luggage storage** £2-4. Trains (☎ (08457) 484950) from: **Aberdeen** (2¼hr., 7-10 per day, £18.20); **Kyle of Lochalsh** (2½hr., 2-4 per day, £14); **Thurso** (3½hr., 2-3 per day, £12.50); **Edinburgh** (3½-4hr., 5-7 per day, £30.60); **Glasgow** (3½hr., 5-7 per day, £30.60); **London** (8hr., 1 per day, £27-98).

Buses: Farraline Park (☎ 233371), off Academy St. **Highland Bus and Coach** sells tickets for most companies and stores luggage (£1). Office open M-Sa 8:30am-6:30pm, Su 10am-6:30pm. **Scottish Citylink** (☎ (08705) 505050) from: **Kyle of Lochalsh** (2½hr., 2 per day, £10.10); **Aberdeen** (3½hr., 1-2 per hr., £9.50); **Thurso** (3½hr., 4-5 per day, £10); **Edinburgh** (4½hr., 8-10 per day, £14); **Glasgow** (4½hr., 10-12 per day, £14); **London** (10hr., 1 per day, £34). Both Citylink and **Rapsons Coaches** (☎ (01463) 222244) from **Ullapool** (1½hr., M-Sa 2-6 per day, £6).

Taxis: Rank Radio Taxis (☎ 220222).

Car Rental: Arnold Clark Car Hire, Harbour Rd. (☎ 713322). From £16-18 per day, £80-90 per week. Minimum age 23.

Bike Rental: Barney's convenience store, 35 Castle St. (☎ 232249). £12 per day. Open daily 7:30am-10:30pm.

✦❓ ORIENTATION AND PRACTICAL INFORMATION

The River Ness divides Inverness; most of what you need is on the east bank.

Tourist Information Centre: Castle Wynd (☎ 234353; fax 710609). Appropriately monstrous, so try not to get lost. The staff helps track Nessie by bus, boat, or brochure, and books non-hostel beds (£3) and Calmac ferries. **Bureau de change,** and the cheapest **Internet access** in town (£1 per 20min., £2.50 per hr.). Open mid-June to Aug. M-Sa 9am-7pm, Su 9:30am-5pm; Sept. to mid-June M-Sa 9am-5pm, Su 10am-4pm.

Tours: Guide Friday (☎ 224000) hop-on/hop-off open-top bus tours leave every 45min. daily May-Sept. from the tourist information centre (TIC). Inverness and Culloden tour £7.50, seniors and students £6, children £2.50. Inverness city tour £5.50, £4, £2.50. Numerous tours service **Loch Ness** (see p. 594). **Puffin Express** (☎ 717181) runs daily summer minibus tours to John O'Groats and the North (£20, children £12) and Cawdor Castle, Clava Cairns, and Culloden battlefield (£7.50). Pick up *Highland Journeys: Tours With A Difference* from the TIC to find out how to get virtually anywhere.

Financial Services: Royal Bank of Scotland, 38 Academy St. Open M-Tu and Th-F 9:15am-4:45pm, W 10am-4:45pm. **Branch,** 60 Union St. Open same hours plus Sa 10am-2pm. **Thomas Cook,** across from the train station, exchanges money. Open M and W-Sa 9am-5:30pm, Tu 10am-5:30pm. **American Express,** 43 Church St. (☎ 718008). Open M-F 9am-5:30pm, Sa 9am-1pm.

Launderette: 17 Young St. (☎ 242507). Open M-F 8am-8pm, Sa 8am-6pm, Su 10am-4pm; last wash 1hr. before close. £3 per wash, £1.40 per dry.

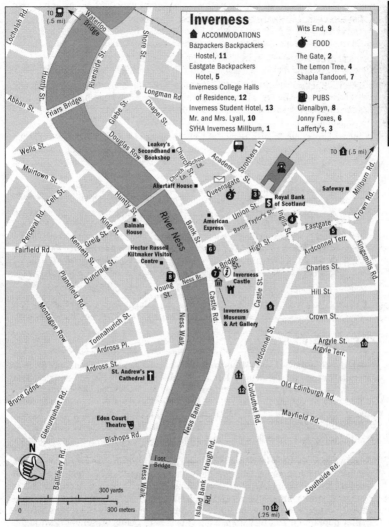

Inverness

ACCOMMODATIONS
Bazpackers Backpackers
  Hostel, **11**
Eastgate Backpackers
  Hotel, **5**
Inverness College Halls
  of Residence, **12**
Inverness Student Hotel, **13**
Mr. and Mrs. Lyall, **10**
SYHA Inverness Millburn, **1**
Wits End, **9**

FOOD
The Gate, **2**
The Lemon Tree, **4**
Shapla Tandoori, **7**

PUBS
Glenalbyn, **8**
Jonny Foxes, **6**
Lafferty's, **3**

Police: Old Perth Rd. (☎ 715555).

Hospital: Raigmore Hospital, Old Perth Rd. (☎ 704000).

Internet Access: MTC, 2 Grant St. (☎ 715450), on the west side of Waterloo Bridge. £5 per hr. Open M-Th 9am-5pm, F 9am-4:30pm. Also **The Gate** cafe (see **Food and Pubs,** below) and the **TIC** (see above).

Post Office: 14-16 Queensgate (☎ 243574). Open M-F 9am-5:30pm, Sa 9am-6pm. Send Post Restante to **Royal Mail Enquiry Office,** Inverness, 7 Strothers Ln., IV1 1AA (☎ 256240). Open M-F 7am-5:30pm, Sa 7am-12:30pm. **Postal Code:** IV1 1AA.

ACCOMMODATIONS

■ **Mr. and Mrs. Lyall,** 20 Argyll St. (☎ 710267). Handsome rooms with TV, tea and coffee, and a warm welcome. Continental breakfast included. An eye-popping £10 per person.

Inverness Student Hotel, 8 Culduthel Rd. (☎236556). 57 beds in rooms of 6-10, free hot chocolate, and great views. Pub crawl with the friendly staff. Breakfast £1.60. Laundry £2.50. Bikes £6.50 per half-day. Internet £5 per hr. Reception 6:30am-2:30am. Check-out 10:30am. Credit card reservations 30p. July-Sept. £11; Oct.-June £10.

Wits End, 32 Ardconnell St. (☎239909). The owners love backpackers. Soak your cares away in the skylit bathroom, complete with tub. No smoking. Dorms £11; twins £24.

Eastgate Backpackers Hostel, 38 Eastgate (☎718756), above a Chinese restaurant. 38 beds in rooms of 6-8. Bike hire, free tea, coffee, and breakfast. Dorms £8.90; twins £11 per person; less in winter. The **Church Hall annex** has basic dorm beds for £7.

Bazpackers Backpackers Hotel, 4 Culduthel Rd. (☎717663). A down-home atmosphere next to the Student Hotel. 36 beds in rooms of 4-8; also 2 doubles. Kitchen, cozy fireplace, coed rooms and bathrooms. No smoking. Reception 7:30am-midnight. Check-out 10:30am. Credit card reservations 50p. Mid-June to Sept. dorms £10, doubles £14; Oct. to mid-June £8.50, £12.

SYHA Inverness Millburn, Victoria Dr. (☎231771). From the train station, turn left on Academy St., go up Millburn Rd., and turn right on Victoria Dr. (10-15min.). With card-swipe checkpoints and 9:30am hostel-wide announcements, this state-of-the-art SYHA has an Orwellian feel. 166 beds in rooms of 2-6. Continental breakfast included. Lockers, laundry (£1), kitchen, and TV room. Internet access £5 per hr. Check-out 10:30am. Curfew 2am. Dorms July-Aug. £13.75, under 18 £12; Sept.-June £12.75, £11.75.

Inverness College Halls of Residence, 23 Culduthel Rd. (☎713430). 10min. past the Castle and Student Hotel (it's on the left) or take bus #5 or 7 from the city center. Quiet singles and doubles. Breakfast £1.50. Open July-Aug. £11 per person; singles £16.

Camping: Most grounds fill with caravans in summer. **Bught Caravan and Camping Park** (☎236920) is closest to town, near the Ness Islands. £4.10 per tent, £5.90 per car.

🍴🍺 FOOD AND PUBS

Reach the colossal **Safeway,** Millburn Rd., by turning right onto Academy St. from the train station and following it left. (Open M-F 8am-10pm, Sa 8am-8pm, Su 9am-6pm.) Inverness's restaurants are unexceptional. **Shapla Tandoori Restaurant,** 2 Castle Rd., may be pricier than usual, but the sizzling curries (£5-9) and river views make it worthwhile. (☎241919. Open daily noon-11:30pm.) For home-baked goods and fabulous soups (£1.75), try the folksy **Lemon Tree,** on Inglis St., off High St. (☎241114. Open M-Sa 8:30am-5:45pm.) **The Gate,** 21 Queensgate, is a yuppified haunt with frothy mochas and Internet for £3 per 30min. (☎711700. Open M-F 10am-12:45am, Sa 10am-11:45pm, Su noon-11:30pm.) For live music, **Johnny Foxes,** 26 Bank St., is a happening bar near the main bridge. (☎236577. Open M-Sa 11am-1am, Su 12:30pm-midnight.) Purists will appreciate **Lafferty's,** 96 Academy St., for its suitably stodgy atmosphere and loud Irish music. (☎712270. Open M-W noon-11pm, Th-F noon-1am, Sa noon-midnight, Su 2-11pm.) Across the river on Young St., play pool or darts at **Glenalbyn,** which hosts R&B bands on some Friday nights and Sunday afternoons. Don't miss the Sunday night *ceilidh*. (☎231637. Open Tu-W and F 11am-1am, M and Th 11am-11pm, Sa 11am-11:45pm, Su 12:30-11pm.)

🔦 SIGHTS

Disillusion awaits those who remember Inverness as home to Shakespeare's Macbeth: nothing of the "Auld Castlehill" remains. Gullible travelers are lured into "joining the government army," a 40min. tour of the reconstructed **Inverness Castle** peppered with verbal abuse from your commanding officer. (Tours Easter-Nov. M-Sa 10:30am-5:30pm. £3, students and seniors £2.70, children £2.) Down the hill, the **Inverness Museum and Art Gallery,** in Castle Wynd, is of interest only for its introduction to Highland birdlife: study the collection of stuffed birds and search for their counterparts in the wild. (☎237114. Open M-Sa 9am-5pm. Free.) If you have an ear for Highland music, visit the fascinating

▣**Balnain House,** 40 Huntley St., a museum, store, cafe, and bar all in one. Try your hand at the bagpipe, fiddle, or *clarsach*, then show off your skills at summer Wednesday *ceilidhs* and jam sessions Monday through Thursday nights. (☎715757. Open July-Aug. M-F 10am-10pm, Sa-Su 10am-6pm; Sept.-June daily 10am-5pm. Cellar Bar open M-Th until 1am, F-Sa until 1:30am. Exhibit £2.50, students and seniors £2, children £1.) Up the road, the **Hector Russell Kiltmaker Visitor Centre,** 4-9 Huntly St., demonstrates plaid production. (☎222781. Open mid-May to Sept. M-Sa 9am-9pm, Su 10am-5pm; Oct. to mid-May M-Sa 9am-5pm. £2, concessions £1.) **Leakey's Secondhand Bookshop,** at the end of Church St. in atmospheric Greyfriar's Hall, claims to be Scotland's largest secondhand bookshop. Don't look for anything specific—the books aren't organized. (☎239947. Open M-Sa 10am-5:30pm.)

Upstream from the city center, over the Ness Bridge and 10min. along **Ness Walk,** the swift River Ness forks and forks again, forming the **Ness Islands**—narrow islets connected to both banks by small footbridges and blanketed with virgin forest.

♫ ENTERTAINMENT AND FESTIVALS

The **Eden Court Theatre,** Bishop's Rd., stages surprisingly urbane productions, hosts dance and music shows, and screens films. (☎234234. Tickets £5-9.) Dolphins are sometimes spotted on **Moray Firth Cruises,** especially 3hr. before high tide. Boats leave from the quay on Shore St., downstream from the city center. (☎717900. 1½hr.; Mar.-Oct. 5-6 cruises per day; £10, students and seniors £8, children £7.50.)

In late July, strongmen hurl cabers during the **Inverness Highland Games.** (☎724262; tickets £3.50, concessions £2), while pipe-and-drum bands dominate the **Inverness Tattoo Festival** (☎235571; tickets £3-5). In mid-August, the **Marymas Fair** recreates 19th-century street life with craft stalls, concerts, and proletarian strife. (☎715760.) The **Northern Meeting,** the world's premier piping competition, comes to Eden Court Theatre in early September. (☎234234. Tickets £16.)

▨ DAYTRIPS FROM INVERNESS

Those planning to visit numerous spots in a day should invest in either Stagecoach Inverness **Off Peak Rover** or Highland Country **Tourist Trail Day Rover** tickets. These allow unlimited bus travel to and from Inverness and sights like Culloden Battlefield, Cawdor Castle, Nairn, Fort George, and Castle Stuart. Buses leave from the Inverness bus station or Queensgate. (Both summer only. £6, concessions £4.)

CULLODEN BATTLEFIELD. Though barren, these fields are rich with history. In 1746, Bonnie Prince Charlie, charismatic but no genius in battle, lost 1200 men to the King's army in a 40min. bloodbath, ending the Jacobite cause. A pretty 1½ mi. south, the stone circles and chambered cairns (mounds of rough stones) of the **Cairns of Clava** recall the Bronze Age. *(Highland Country bus #12 (return £2) leaves from the post office at Queensgate. Visitor center ☎(01463) 790607. Open Apr.-Oct. daily 9am-6pm; Feb.-Mar. and Nov.-Dec. 10am-4pm. Battlefield free. Center £3.50, concessions £2.50.)*

CAWDOR CASTLE. The castle has been the residence of the Thane of Cawdor's descendants since the 15th century and is still inhabited for much of the year. The late Lord Cawdor IV detailed its priceless items in a series of humorous and witty signs. Don't miss the garden maze and nature walks. *(Highland Country bus #12 (return £4.50) leaves from the post office at Queensgate. ☎(01667) 404615. Open May-Sept. daily 10am-5:30pm. £5.50, students and seniors £4.50, children £2.80.)*

MONIACK CASTLE. Built in 1580 as the home of the Frasers, Moniack Castle, 7 mi. west of Inverness, still houses the family and their wine-making business. Guided tours of the winery run every 20min. *(☎(01463) 831283. Open Mar.-Oct. M-Sa 10am-5pm; Nov.-Feb. M-Sa 11am-4pm. £2.50, children free.)*

NEAR INVERNESS: DUNROBIN CASTLE

The castle is 300 yd. from Dunrobin station, 1½ mi. from Golspie. Trains from Inverness run once per day (2hr., £11.40). You must request the stop. Stagecoach Inverness (☎(01463) 239292) sends bus #25X twice per day (2hr., £6.50). Castle ☎(01408) 633177. Open Apr. to mid-Oct. daily 10:30am-5:30pm, last entry 5pm. £5.50, students £4.50, seniors and children £4, families £16.

There is little of note in the stretch of moors between Inverness and the northern ferry ports save for **Dunrobin Castle,** the spectacular seat of the Dukes of Sutherland and the largest house in the Highlands. Though sections of the mansion date to the 14th century, most of the architecture is ecstatically Victorian, redesigned in the Scottish Baronial style by Charles Berry, fresh from finishing London's Houses of Parliament. Many of the castle's finest rooms are on display, and the grounds, modeled after Versailles, are dramatically situated against an ocean backdrop. The castle **museum** assembles a variety of aristocratic trophies, from animal heads to opium pipes. Outdoors, the **Falconry Display** allows visitors the opportunity to handle various birds of prey and see whether they really hear the falconer.

LOCH NESS ☎01456

Unfathomably mysterious, Loch Ness guards its secrets 5 mi. south of Inverness. In AD 565, St. Columba repelled a savage sea monster as it attacked a monk; whether a prehistoric leftover, giant seasnake, or cosmic wanderer, the Loch Ness monster has captivated the world ever since. Shaped like a wedge, the loch is 700 ft. deep just 70 ft. from its edge. Its bottom caverns extend down so far that no one has definitively determined how vast it really is, or what life exists at its bottom.

The easiest way to see the loch is with one of a dime-a-dozen tour groups, three of which depart from the Inverness TIC. **Jacobite Cruises,** Tomnahurich Bridge, Glenurquhart Rd., whisks you around any number of ways, to Urquhart Castle or on coach and boat trips. (☎(01463) 233999. £10-14.50, students £8-11, including castle admission.) **Kenny's Tours** circles the loch on a minibus. (☎(01463) 252411. Tours 10:30am-2:20pm and 2:30-5pm. £12.50, concessions £9.50.) **Guide Friday** offers its own three-hour bus and boat tour. (☎(01463) 224000. May-Sept. daily 10:30am and 2:30pm. £13.50, students and seniors £11.50, children £6.50.) A slew of boat trips leave from touristy Drumnadrochit, on the loch's northwest shore; most last 1hr. and cost £8-10 per adult, with concessions available.

Sixteen miles down the western shore road (the A82), a lone bagpiper drones from unforgettable ⛰Urquhart Castle (URK-hart), one of the largest in Scotland before it was blown up in 1692 to prevent Jacobite occupation. Most tours from Inverness stop at the ruins and a number of photos of Nessie have been fabricated there. (☎450551. Open June-Aug. M-Sa 9:30am-7:45pm, Su 9:30am-5:45pm; Apr.-May and Sept. daily 9:30am-5:45pm; Oct.-Mar. M-Sa 9:30am-3:45pm. £3.80, seniors £2.80, children £1.20.) In nearby **Drumnadrochit,** not one but two visitor centers expound on the Nessie legend. The **Official Loch Ness Exhibition Centre** wins the competition with its 40min. audiovisual display. (☎450573. Open July-Aug. daily 9am-8pm; June and Sept. 9am-6pm; Oct. 9:30am-5:30pm; Nov.-Easter 10am-5:30pm; Easter-May 9:30am-5pm. £5.95, students and seniors £4.50, children £3.50.) The **Great Glen Cycle Route** careens past the loch on its way to Fort William. You can also **bike** along the eastern shore on the narrow B582. Eighteen miles down, the River Foyers empties into the loch in a series of idyllic waterfalls.

Near Drumnadrochit, the hip **Loch Ness Backpackers Lodge,** Coiltie Farm House, East Lewiston, within walking distance of Loch Ness, is served by several buses from Inverness (ask for Lewiston). It has cozy cabin-like rooms and runs boat trips for £4.50. (☎450807; hostel@lochness-backpackers.com. Continental breakfast £1.50. Dorms £9.50; doubles £24.) The somewhat less comfortable **SYHA Loch Ness** stands alone on the loch's western shore, 7½ mi. south of the castle. (☎(01320) 351274. Open mid-Mar. to Oct. Reserve in advance July-Aug. Dorms £8.25, under 18 £7.25; July-Aug. 25p more.) Both hostels lie on the Scottish Citylink bus routes between Inverness and Fort William (#919, every 2hr., £4.50 from Inverness).

GLEN AFFRIC AND GLEN CANNICH ☎01456

West of Loch Ness, Glen Affric and Glen Cannich stretch toward the mountains amid one of Scotland's largest indigenous pine forests. Full of hiking opportunities, this remote area has been spared the throngs of tourists attracted by Nessie's tall tales, making it one of the best places to experience Scotland as it used to be.

The main access points for the glens are the villages of **Cannich,** at a turn in the A831, and **Tomich,** farther on. In summer, **Highland Country** (☎(01463) 233371) **buses** run from **Inverness** to **Cannich** (1hr.; M-F 4 per day, Sa 1 per day), some extending to **Tomich** (M-F 2 per day). **Ross Minibuses** (☎(01463) 761250) also run to Cannich and Tomich from **Inverness** and **Beauly** a few times a week. Cannich's two **hostels** stand side by side in nearly identical brown buildings. From the Glen Affric Hotel, head down the road lined with pine trees, away from the Spar. **Glen Affric Backpackers** sleeps 70 in rooms for four or fewer—no bunks. The easy-going wardens are knowledgeable about the area. (☎(01456) 415263. £6 per person.) With more rules and more expense, the **SYHA Cannich** is a second choice. (☎415244. Reception 7-10:30am and 5-11:30pm. Curfew 11:30pm. Open Apr.-Oct. Dorms £8.25, under 18 £7; July-Aug. £8.50, £7.25.) Next door, at the **Cannich Caravan & Camping Park,** you can **rent bikes.** (☎415364. Open Apr.-Oct. Bikes £7.50 per day. Tent pitch £3.50-6.50.) **Slater's Arms,** down the road toward Glen Affric, serves standard meals for £2-7. (☎415215. Open daily 9am-11pm.) The **Spar** next door is the only shop for miles, and contains the Cannich **post office.** (Open M-Sa 9am-8pm, Su 10am-6pm.)

Various walks into Glen Cannich depart from behind the Glen Affric Hotel, beside the bus stop. A four-mile walk or bike ride west down the forest road leading out of Cannich takes you to the trailhead for the popular **Dog Falls Forest Walk** on the eastern edge of the Glen Affric Caledonian Forest Reserve. Passing by the waterfall, you'll get a good look at the heart of the 400-year-old pine forest, home to red deer, fox, adder, and otter. For more walks in Glen Affric, pick up *A Guide to Forest Walks and Trails: Glen Affric* (50p), or *Fifty Walks Near Tomich and Cannich* (£2), both available at Glen Affric Backpackers.

Tomich offers easier access to the more spectacular Glen Affric, including the breathtaking **Plodda Falls Walk.** Walk or bike 6 mi. down the forest road out of Tomich to reach the trailhead. Your efforts won't go unrewarded, as you watch the narrow cascades of Plodda Falls crash into the foaming water of the gorge below—all from your viewpoint on a restored bridge spanning the gorge. In Tomich, budget accommodation is hard to come by; the hardy should continue another 3 mi. west to the (extremely) basic **Cougie Lodge.** (☎415459. Open Apr.-Sept. Dorms £8.) Farther in the same direction, the remote but ever-popular **SYHA Glen Affric,** Alltbeithe, is little more than a wood cabin buried in the mountains, located at a crossroad of trails to Tomich, Ratagan, and Clunie. (No phone. Open Apr.-Oct. Dorms £7.75, under 18 £7.) Bring a sleeping bag when staying at either of these hostels, and call the SYHA central reservations line (☎(08701) 553255) or ask the warden at SYHA Cannich for exact directions. To navigate the Glen Affric area successfully, don't go without Ordnance Survey map Landranger #25.

FORT WILLIAM AND BEN NEVIS ☎01397

In 1654, General Monck built the town of Fort William among Britain's highest peaks to keep out "savage clans and roving barbarians." These days, the largest town in the Highlands has let down its guard, and the surrounding mountains induce seasonal tidal waves of skiers and hikers. Packed with outdoor-equipment outfitters, Fort William makes an excellent base camp for excursions to Ben Nevis, Britain's tallest mountain, and other outdoor activities.

▐ TRANSPORTATION

The **train station** is just beyond the north end of High St. Trains (☎(08457) 484950) arrive from **Glasgow Queen St.** (3¾hr.; M-Sa 3 per day, Su 2 per day; £18) and **London Euston** (12hr., 1 per day, £70-96.50) on the magnificent ▧**West Highland Railway.**

Built at the turn of the last century, the railway is a triumph of Victorian engineering, crossing glens, moors, and rivers while skirting some of Scotland's best scenery. **Buses** arrive at High St. or at the stand opposite the Safeway by the train station. **Scottish Citylink** (☎(08705) 505050) arrives from: **Mallaig** (1½hr., M-Sa 2 per day, £5.70); **Oban** (1½hr., 2-4 per day, £6.90); **Kyle of Lochalsh** (1¾hr., 1 per day, £10.20); **Inverness** (2hr., 5-6 per day, £7.20); **Glasgow** (3hr., 4 per day, £11.90); **Edinburgh** (6hr., 2 per day, £15.20). Get schedules at the tourist information centre. **Alba Taxi** (☎701112) is open 24hr. Rent cycles at **Offbeat Bikes,** 117 High St. (☎704008. £10 per half-day, £15 per day, including helmet, map, and tool kit; child seat £7.)

🚩 PRACTICAL INFORMATION

Reach the north end of **High St.,** Fort William's main street, through the underpass at the train station. The friendly **tourist information centre** (TIC) **exchanges currency.** (☎703781. Open mid-June to mid-July M-Sa 9am-7pm, Su 10am-6pm; mid-July to Aug. M-Sa 9am-8:30pm, Su 9am-6pm; Sept.-Oct. M-Sa 9am-6pm, Su 10am-5:30pm; Nov.-Mar. M-Sa 9am-5pm, Su 10am-4pm; Mar.-June M-Sa 9am-6pm, Su 10am-4pm.) **Lloyds TSB** is on North High St. (☎702029. Open M-Tu 9:30am-4pm, W 10am-4pm, Th 9:30am-5:30pm, F 9:30am-5pm.) For equipment, maps, and weather reports from the summits, head to **Nevisport,** a cathedral of the outdoors at the north end of High St. (☎704921. Hiking and climbing boots £3.50-7.50 per day. Deposit required. Open June-Sept. daily 9am-7pm; Oct.-May M-Sa 9am-5:30pm, Su 9:30am-5pm.) The **mountain rescue post** (☎702361), in the **police station** at the south end of High St., has forms that must be filled out before you climb Ben Nevis. Get **Internet access** at funky and borderline absurd **ThingKING,** 76 High St. (Open M-Sa 9:30am-5:30pm, Su noon-4pm. £1.50 per 15min., 40p each additional 5min.) The **post office** is at 5 High St. (☎702827. Open M-F 9am-5:30pm, Sa 9am-12:30pm.) **Postal code:** PH33 6AR.

🏠 ACCOMMODATIONS

Fort William teems with budget bunkhouses around Fassifern Rd., behind the Alexandra Hotel. Other B&Bs roost farther up the hill on **Alma Rd.** and **Argyll Rd.**

📷 Farr Cottage Accommodation and Activity Centre (☎772315; fax 772247), in Corpach. The best place to stay within reach of Ben Nevis. Corpach is 2 train stops north of Fort William or a 10min. bus ride from the car park on Middle St. behind the post office (M-Sa 3 per hr., Su every hr.; 80p). Comfortable rooms with 4-10 beds and TVs. Stuart Nicol and his hilarious staff will keep you entertained at the in-house bar. Stuart dons his kilt almost every night to give Scottish history lessons and whisky talks. For a small fee, staff will drive guests to outdoor activities, including canyoning, whitewater rafting, and horse trekking. Continental breakfast £2. Homemade pizzas £3. Internet access. Mountain bikes £10 per day. Laundry and kitchen. Dorms £11; less for longer stays.

Fort William Backpackers Guest House, Alma Rd. (☎700711), From the train station (5min.), bear right onto Belford Rd. and head away from the town center. Turn right onto Alma Rd. after the hospital and go left at the split; the hostel is uphill on your right. This snug 30-bed hostel welcomes with a hot cup of tea. Luminous windows offer excellent mountain views. Continental breakfast £1.60. Curfew 2am. Dorms £11, in winter £10.

SYHA Glen Nevis (☎702336), 3 mi. east of town on the Glen Nevis Rd., across from the trail up Ben Nevis. Highland Bus and Coach and West Highland Motor Service bus #42 run from Fort William to the hostel and back in summer (M-Sa 14 per day, Su 7 per day; £1.05). Book well in advance in July and Aug. Continental breakfast included. Reception 24hr. Bedroom lockout 9:30am-12:30pm. Dorms £9, under 18 £16.

Ben Nevis Bunkhouse (☎702240), at Achintee Farm, a 2 mi. walk along Achintee Rd. Sleeps 24 in a 200-year-old barn with full kitchen and bathing facilities. Book ahead July-Aug. Lockout 10:30am-4pm. Dorms £9; twins £22.

Rhu Mhor Guest House, Alma Rd. (☎ 702213). This B&B, on a quiet street, offers a variety of single, double, and triple rooms, all with fantastic views of the sun setting over the Nevis Range. Open April-Oct. Book ahead July-Aug. From £17 per person.

Glen Nevis Caravan & Camping Park (☎ 702191), on the Glen Nevis Rd., ½ mi. before the SYHA hostel. Open mid-Mar. to Oct. 2-person tent £7.10, with car £12; less in off season. Showers free.

FOOD AND PUBS

Stock up at the **Tesco** supermarket at the north end of High St. (Open M-W 8:30am-6:30pm, Th-F 8:30am-7pm, Sa 8:30am-6pm, Su 10am-5pm.) Those eschewing the wilderness can make for the **Garrison,** near Tesco, where sandwiches start at £2.50 and cooked dishes are £4-5. (Open daily 9am-8pm.) Before striking for the hills, get a packed lunch of juice, two filled rolls, cake, fruit, and a candy bar (£3) at the **Nevis Bakery,** 49 High St. (☎ 704101). Follow the crowd to one of Fort William's few hot nightspots, the justifiably popular **Ben Nevis Bar,** 103-109 High St. You'll find beer drinkers every night and live music at least once a week, and the bar is *the* place to celebrate after you've tackled the summit of the same name. (☎ 702295. Open M-Sa 11am-12:15am, Su 12:30pm-12:15am; food served noon-10pm.)

SIGHTS AND ENTERTAINMENT

The best sights around Fort William are all natural, all the time. Rock jocks should visit **Treasures of the Earth,** in Corpach, with its fine collection of minerals, gemstones, crystals, and fossils. (☎ 772283. Open July-Sept. daily 9:30am-7pm; Feb.-June and Oct.-Dec. 10am-5pm. £3, seniors £2.75, children £1.50.) Slickly tourist-oriented as Fort William is, its **West Highland Museum,** next to the TIC, is a rustic treasure, with a room full of taxidermy, displays on the mountaineering of yore, and a stirring Bonnie Prince Charlie exhibit. (☎ 702169. Open M-Sa 10am-5pm; July-Aug. also Su 2-5pm; shorter off-season hours. £2, students and seniors £1.50, children 50p.) Past Smiddy Alpine Lodge in Corpach, **Kilmallie Hall** hosts dancing, folk-singing, and other traditional entertainment regularly. (Open June-Sept. From 8pm.)

OUTDOOR ACTIVITIES

BEN NEVIS. On the 65 days per year that the highest peak in Britain (4406 ft.) deigns to lift its veil of cloud, the unobstructed view spans from Scotland's western coast all the way to Ireland. The interminable switchbacks of the tourist trail ascend from the Fort William town park to Ben Nevis's summit; go north ½ mi. along the A82 and follow signs. The hike up takes about 3hr. and the descent 2-3hr. You will be cold, so dress accordingly. A much more arduous **ridge walk** deviates from the tourist trail. When the tourist trail makes a sharp turn to the right near Lochan Meall an t-Suidhe, the experienced can walk parallel to the loch instead, following a small path by the stream. Leave the path where it descends to Coire Leis and clamber up the steep grass slopes to Carn Dearg Meadhonach; continue to the summit of Carn Mór Dearg. Along the ridge, a trail veers right toward the southeastern slopes of Ben Nevis by a lovely mountain lake; scramble the final 1000 ft. up steep terrain and claim the top of the world. Leave a full 8½hr. of daylight for the 9½ mi. round-trip, and don't set foot on the trail without weather information, an Ordnance Survey map, a hat, gloves, warm clothes, a windbreaker, proper footwear, a tank, and plenty of food and drink. Okay, maybe not the tank. You must register with the **mountain rescue post** (☎ 702361), in the **police station** at the south end of High St. in Fort William, before you head out. See **Wilderness Safety,** p. 54, for more precautions.

INCHREE FALLS. For more than just great views, canyon down the 500 ft. **Inchree Falls** with the guides at **Vertical Descents.** The adrenaline buzz is worth the expense. Set aside the tales of Scottish museums and castles and tell your friends about the flumes, rocks, and 20 ft. jumps you braved with a wetsuit, helmet, and other protective gear (well, leave out the part about the protective gear). The trip takes 2hr. (☎ (01855) 821593. Canyoning May 15-Sept., bookings flexible. £30 includes all equipment.) For another wet and thrilling experience, call **Free Spirits,** which takes groups along whitewater trails (grades II-V) of varying difficulty. Between shouts of "paddle left," the guides' jokes will have you in stitches. (☎ (01887) 830633. Flexible scheduling. Most trips £25.) Don't let the temperature or crying skies keep you away—in both canyoning and rafting, wetsuits keep you surprisingly warm.

SKIING. Speaking of warmth (or lack thereof), Fort William offers some of Scotland's best skiing and snowboarding. Four miles north of Fort William on the A82, the slopes of **Aonach Mor** (4006 ft.) cushion the **Nevis Range** ski area. Though smaller than the Cairngorm facility, the range features Scotland's longest ski runs and a state-of-the-art cable car that lifts you 2150 ft. to a trailside restaurant. (☎ 705825. Ski range open May-June daily 10am-5pm; July-Aug. Th-F 9:30am-9pm, Sa-W 9:30am-6pm. Cable car and marked hiking trails open year-round. Return £6.75, children £4.15.) **Buses** run from Fort William to the slopes (5 per day, return £3.25). Aonach Mor (10min. drive from Fort William) is also open for snow-sports December through April. (Day tickets £19.75, children £11, families £17.75.)

GAMES AND RACES. A few miles up the road past the SYHA hostel splash the falls where, on the first Saturday in August, hundreds of businessmen who base their virility on daredevilry rocket down the rapids on homemade rafts during the **Glen Nevis River Race.** On the first Saturday in September, the area hosts the **Ben Nevis Race,** a punishing event in which runners sprint up and down the mountain (you, too, can pick up an entry form at the TIC). The record time for the grueling 5 mi. up, 5 mi. down is an incredible 82min. Fort William dons kilts and tosses cabers at the **Lochaber Highland Games** on the last Saturday in July.

GLEN COE   ☎ 01855

Stunning in any weather, Glen Coe is best seen in the rain, when a web of mist laces the valley's innumerable rifts and silvery waterfalls spill into the River Coe. Only on rare days is the view marred by shining sun; the glen records over 100 inches of rain a year. Glen Coe is infamous as the site of a 1692 massacre, when the Clan MacDonald welcomed a company of Campbell soldiers, henchmen of William III, into their chieftain's home. After enjoying the MacDonalds' hospitality for over a week, the soldiers proceeded to slaughter their hosts, violating the age-old tradition of Highland Hospitality. Neither rain nor dramatic history deters hikers and skiers from passing time in this beautiful valley.

ꗧꗄ TRANSPORTATION AND PRACTICAL INFORMATION. Scottish Citylink (☎ (08705) 505050) **buses** arrive in Glencoe village from **Glasgow** (3hr., 4 per day, £10) and **Edinburgh** (5hr., 2 per day, £14). The **Oban-Fort William** bus #918 stops at nearby **Ballachulish** (M-Sa 4 per day, Su 1 per day; £6.50). **Postbuses** putter daily in the area but at irregular times; get a schedule from the tourist information centre (TIC) or hostel. For bike rental, try **Mountain Bike Hire,** at the Clachaig Inn, across the river from the Visitor Centre (☎ 811252; £8.50 per half-day, £12 per day), or the **Strathassynt Guest House,** next to the TIC (☎ 811261; £8 per half-day, £12 per day).

  Glencoe village, essentially a single street, rests at the edge of Loch Leven, at the mouth of the River Coe and the western end of the Glen Coe valley. The A82 runs the length of the valley. **Glen Coe Visitor Centre,** 3 mi. southeast of Glencoe village on the A82, gives hiking advice, sells maps, and shows a film on the Massacre of Glencoe. (☎ 811307. Open mid-May to Aug. daily 9:30am-5:30pm; Apr. to mid-May and Sept.-Oct. 10am-5pm. Film 50p, concessions 30p.) The **tourist information centre** in Ballachulish, 1 mi. west of the village, books accommodations for a £1.50 fee.

(☎811296. Open July-Aug. M-Sa 9am-6:30pm, Su 10am-5pm; Apr.-June M-Sa 10am-5pm, Su 10am-5pm; Sept.-Oct. M-Sa 9am-5pm.) There are no **cash machines** in Glencoe village or Ballachulish, and the **Royal Bank of Scotland** is only open Tuesday and Friday 9:30am-4:30pm. The **Spar** supermarket (see below) offers a cash-back service with a £5 purchase. The **post office** in Glencoe village is in the Spar. (☎811367. Open M-F 9am-12:30pm and 1:30-5:30pm, W 9am-12:30pm, Sa 9am-12:30pm.)

ACCOMMODATIONS AND FOOD The agreeable clapboard **SYHA Glencoe** rests 2 mi. southeast of Glencoe village on the river's east side. The 62 beds fill up fast. (☎811219; fax 811284. Laundry facilities. Internet access. Reception 7am-midnight. Curfew midnight. Dorms £8.50, under 18 £5.) If you hike to the hostel and find it full, backtrack 500 yd. to the white-walled **Leacantium Farm Bunkhouse.** The farm keeps three bunkhouses, from the basic Alpine barn to the super-cozy Ben End suite. (☎811256. £6.50-7.50. Weekly £45.) Follow the painted white rocks to the farm's riverside **Red Squirrel Camp Site** next door. (£4.50 per person, under 12 50p. Hot showers 50p.) **Clachaig Inn,** Glencoe, is a family-run B&B with views of nearby summits and an attached restaurant. (☎811679. From £22 per person.)

Small but sufficient supermarkets in the area include **Spar,** in Glencoe village (☎811367; open M-Sa 8am-9pm, Su 9am-5pm), and **The Co-op,** in Ballachulish (☎811253; open M-W and Sa 8:30am-6pm, Th-F 8:30am-7pm). The **Clachaig Inn** (see above), 5min. across a footbridge from the Visitor Centre, serves the area's best food for £6-10, including some vegetarian dishes. The public bar is a lively gathering point, and the traditional trail's-end pub for hikers. A sign outside proclaims that no Campbells are allowed within. (☎811252. Open F 11am-midnight, Sa 11am-11:30pm, Su-Th 11am-11pm; food served noon-9pm.)

SIGHTS AND HIKING Glen Coe provides a range of challenges. Walkers stroll the floor of the magnificent cup-shaped valley, climbers head for the cliffs, and winter ice-climbers hack their way up frozen waterfalls. Trailheads, usually 2-3 mi. beyond the Glen Coe Visitor Centre, are difficult to access without a car. However, for a small fee most area hostels will shuttle hikers to the trails and arrange a time for pickup. Low-impact camping is also permitted near trails.

The **Coire Nan Lochan** will take you to the summits of the **Three Sisters,** Glen Coe's most distinctive peaks. Well-equipped, sure-footed hikers prepared to use hands, knees, and hindquarters can scramble up the 3766 ft. **Bidean nam Bian** or try the 4 mi. traverse of the **Aonach Eagach** ridge on the north side of the glen. Saner walkers can find the **Lost Valley,** once called the Coire Gubhail—Corrie of Plunder—because the MacDonalds hid pilfered goods there. The trail follows the stream on the south side of the glen, just west of the Coe Gorge (3hr. round-trip). You can avoid the 1000 ft. climb by taking the **Glen Coe Ski Centre Chairlift,** off the A82 in the middle of Glen Coe. (☎851226. Open June-Aug. daily 9:30am-4:30pm, weather permitting. £4, seniors £3, children £2.50, families £11.) For a cruise around the loch, perhaps to see some seals, **Boat Trips and Fishing Trips** leave from Ballachulish West Pier (☎811658). Call for details; sailing times are subject to demand and weather.

ROAD TO THE ISLES

The lochside Road to the Isles (Rathad Iarainn nan Eilean, now the A830), originally traveled by crofters to sell their wares in the larger towns, traverses breathtaking mountain valleys on its journey westward from Fort William to Mallaig.

The ride on the **West Highland Railway** offers sublime panoramas at a fast clip (June-Sept. M-Sa 4 per day, Su 3-4 per day; Oct.-May M-Sa 2 per day, Su 1 per day; £12). In summer, "The Jacobite" steam train chugs from **Fort William** in the morning to **Mallaig** (stopping at Glenfinnan) and back in the afternoon; on a rainy day, you won't miss much by taking the cheaper, modern version. (☎(01524) 732100. June-Sept. 1 per day in either direction. £16, day return £21. BritRail passes not valid.) **Buses** make the same trip once per day (1½hr.; M-F; July-Sept. also Sa; £5.50).

GLENFINNAN. The road sets off westward from Fort William along Loch Eil, arriving after 12 mi. at spectacular Glenfinnan, on the head of Loch Shiel. A **monument** recalls August 19, 1745, the day Bonnie Prince Charlie rowed up Loch Shiel and rallied the clans around the Stewart standard to signal the rebellion of '45 (see **The Jacobite Rebellion,** p. 500). Trains often stop atop the famously photogenic **Glenfinnan Viaduct** to give passengers a sentimental gaze. After you climb the narrow spiral staircase and squeeze through the hatch at the top, a knee-high railing is all that lies between you and the end of your trip—be careful! A worthy **visitor centre** provides the accompanying history lesson and postcards. (☎(01397) 722250. Centre and monument open mid-May to Aug. daily 9:30am-6pm; Sept.-Oct. and Apr. to mid-May 10am-5pm. £1.50, concessions £1.) If you're feeling lazy, drift on **Loch Shiel Cruises** as far as Acharacle, at the far end of the loch. Trips depart from the Glenfinnan House Hotel, up the road from the visitor centre. (☎(01397) 722235. 1-3½hr. cruises June-Sept. Su-F; Apr.-May and Oct. Su-M, W, F. £5-12.)

Glenfinnan is 30min. from Fort William (£3.90) and 50min. from Mallaig (£5) by train; by bus the trips are roughly the same (£2.50 and £4). **◪Glenfinnan Sleeping Car,** a vintage railway-car-turned-hostel at the train station, provides a unique bed. (☎722295 or 701292. Bunk £8, with bedding £10.) For a twilight loch view, eat at the **Glenfinnan House Hotel** pub. (Open Su-W 11am-midnight, Th-Sa 11am-1am.)

ARISAIG AND LOCH MORAR. The road finally meets the west coast at the sandy beaches of Arisaig. **Murdo Grant** (☎(01687) 450224) operates ferries and day cruises from Arisaig to Rum, Eigg, and Muck and goes to Skye, Mull, and Canna by charter (May-Sept. daily 11am, return £13-17). The trips allow for a few hours on the island of your choice. Arisaig is 30min. from Mallaig by rail (£2). A 3 mi. walk along the A830 from Arisaig or Morar Station leads to the placid **Camusdarach campsite** near the beach. (☎(01687) 450221. £5 per tent, £1 per person.) **Dr. Ian Pragnell** (☎(01687) 450272) rents **bikes** (£10 per day) and willingly shares his knowledge of local cycling routes. Across the road and down a short footpath from the campsite, brilliant white beaches afford views of the Inner Hebrides. Rocky outcrops cut across the sand, creating secluded beach coves accessible only by foot. Another fine walk follows the banks of **Loch Morar,** Britain's deepest freshwater loch (1017 ft.), complete with its own monster, Morag, cousin to Nessie.

MALLAIG ☎01687

Past Morar looms the relative megalopolis of Mallaig (MAL-ig), a fishing village where cruises and ferries leave for the Inner Hebrides. Fill time in town with a visit to **Mallaig Marine World.** A tankful of ballan wrasse fish change sex and color every now and then. Kinky. (☎462292. Open July-Aug. M-Sa 9am-9pm, Su 10am-6pm; Apr.-June and Sept.-Oct. M-Sa 9am-7pm, Su noon-5:30pm; Nov.-Mar. and mid-Jan. to mid-Feb. M-Sa 9am-5:30pm. £3, students and seniors £2.25, children £1.75, families £7.50.)

Bruce Watt (☎462320) runs ferries and day cruises from Mallaig along lovely Loch Nevis to **Tarbet** and **Inverie** (M, W, F; June to mid-Sept. also Tu and Th; £7-12). The one village in Great Britain reachable by water only, Inverie (pop. 60) sits on the wild and roadless **Knoydart peninsula,** emptied by the Highland Clearances. **CalMac** (☎462403) skips from Mallaig to Armadale on **Skye** (M-Sa 6-7 per day; June-Aug. also Su; £2.80, 5-day return £4.75) and to the **Small Isles.** Rent cars for area explorations from **Morar Motors.** (☎462118. 21+. £32-38 per day.) The **tourist information centre** is around the block from the train station. (☎462170. Open July-Aug. M-Sa 9am-8pm, Su 10am-5pm; Apr.-June and Sept.-Oct. daily 10am-6:30pm; Nov.-Mar. M, W, F 9am-2pm.) Other services include: **Bank of Scotland,** near the station (open M-Tu and Th-F 9:15am-1pm and 2-4:45pm; W 10am-1pm and 2-4:45pm); **Internet access** across the street in the **Lochaber College Library;** and the **post office,** in the **Spar** shop up the road from Sheena's (☎462419; open M-F 9am-5:30pm, Sa 9am-1pm). **Postal code:** PH41 4PU.

Sheena's Backpackers Lodge, with beds roomy enough to sleep two, fills fast after early train and ferry arrivals in summer, so book ahead. Turn right from the train station, and the lodge is past the bank, above the restaurant. (☎462764. Dorms

£9.50.) For more private luxury, continue down the street to the newly renovated **Old Bank House B&B,** Main St. (☎462988. £16 per person.) The **Spar** and **Nevis Stores,** Station Rd. across from the hostel, sell groceries. (Nevis ☎462240. Open M-F 9am-9pm, Sa 9am-5:30pm.) The **Fisherman's Mission Cafe,** across from the train station, serves filling grub, including a £4 lasagna with chips and peas. (☎462086. Open M-F 8:30am-10pm, Sa 8:30am-noon; food served M-F 8:30am-1:45pm and 5:30-10pm.)

THE INNER HEBRIDES

THE SMALL ISLES ☎01687

From the water, they form silent gray-green silhouettes—remote, rugged, and seemingly uninhabited. Lacking vehicle-landing facilities and almost untouched by tourism, **Rum, Eigg, Muck,** and **Canna** often require visitors to jump from their ferry to a small dinghy before setting foot on solid land. Those who make the trip are rewarded with a true taste of island life—jalopies cruise the roads instead of tourist caravans, electricity is provided by generators, and coastline stretches everywhere the eye can see.

Caledonian MacBrayne (☎462403) ferries sail from **Mallaig** to Rum, Eigg, Muck, Canna, and back. There are both non-landing trips (M 10:30am and Sa 12:30pm, £12.65) and trips that allow time on the isles. (Eigg M, T, Th 10:30am; F 9am; Sa 6:30am and 1:40pm; 5-day return £8.30. Muck Tu and Th 10:30am; F 12:50pm; Sa 6:30am and 1:40pm; 5-day return £12.85. Rum and Canna M and W 10:30am; F 12:50pm; Sa 6:30am and 1:40pm; 5-day return £12.35 and £13.80, respectively.) For daytrips, look into the more cruise-oriented **Murdo Grant** (☎450224), sailing from **Arisaig** (2 train stops from Mallaig) May to September at 11am to: **Rum** (Tu and Th; June-Aug. also Sa-Su; return £18); **Eigg** (F-W, return £14); **Muck** (M, W, F; return £14). Murdo Grant can run summer cruises from Arisaig to **Canna** by request.

RUM. Rum (often spelled Rhum) is the most astounding of the Small Isles, with a mountainous majesty that rivals even its famous neighbor, Skye. Also the largest of the Small Isles, Rum is owned by the National Trust of Scotland and carefully managed by Scottish Natural Heritage. Deer, highland cattle, golden eagles, and rarer creatures are the main inhabitants; the entire human population emigrated in 1826 during the Highland Clearances. The grand total of today's full-time residents has risen to 25. Because ferry daytrips leave very little time, only an overnight stay can do the island justice. The locals are infectiously friendly, and the island is covered with informative hiking trails; the **Loch Scresort Trail** is most popular. A wealthy Lancashire mill owner built lavish **Kinloch Castle** in 1901. (☎462037. Excellent tours daily in summer, £4.) Behind the castle, **Kinloch Castle Hostel** requires advance booking. (☎462037. Dorms £12; singles and doubles also available.) To **camp** on Rum (tent pitch £5), obtain prior permission from the Chief Warden, Scottish Natural Heritage, Isle of Rum, Scotland PH43 4RR (☎462026).

EIGG. The isle of Eigg (pop. 78) shelters the largest community of the Small Isles amid vertical cliffs, sandy beaches, and green hills. In **Massacre Cave,** the island's entire population (all 395 MacDonalds) were slaughtered by rival MacLeods in the 16th century. St. Donnan and 52 companions were martyred by the warrior women of the pagan Queen of Moidart at **Kildonnan** in 617. In summer, ranger John Chester offers weekly **guided walks** from the pier that reveal the island's bloody history. (☎482477. £2.) A minibus also meets each ferry for a trip across the island to the **Singing Sands,** a perfect beach that sounds out at visitors' footsteps (M-Sa, some Su; return £3). For **bike hire** inquire at the craft shop by the pier. (☎482417. £7 per day.) If you call ahead, you can stay at the remarkably modern **Glebe Barn.** (☎482417. £9.50; twins £22.) For B&B, the best value is beautiful **Laig Farm Guest House.** (☎482412. Full board with packed lunch £30.) Both are 2 mi. away along the main road; if it's raining, you can call ahead for a taxi (☎482494; return £3.50).

MUCK AND CANNA. Muck, the tiny (1½ mi. by 5 mi.) southernmost isle, is an experiment in communal living. The entire island is a single farm owned by the MacEwens, who handle farming, transport along the Muck 1 road, and shopping on the mainland. Stay with **Mrs. Harper,** who may pick you up from the pier (☎462371; B&B £16, with dinner £27), or at **Port Mor Guest House** (☎462365; dinner and B&B £30). If you intend to muck about outside, bring food, as places to eat or shop are open sporadically. The miniature isle of Canna ("porpoise" in Gaelic) offers a few miles of trails for hikers and seabird enthusiasts, but no shops or budget accommodations.

ISLE OF SKYE

Skye is often raining, but also fine: hardly embodied; semi-transparent; like living in a jellyfish lit up with green light. Remote as Samoa; deserted, prehistoric. No room for more.
—postcard from Virginia Woolf

Often described as the shining jewel in the Hebridean crown, Skye, from the serrated peaks of the Cuillin Hills to the rugged tip of the Trotternish Peninsula, possesses unparalleled natural beauty. The island's charms are by no means a secret, as the endless procession of vehicles on the Skye Bridge attests. But most visitors keep to the main roads, and vast swaths of terrain remain unscarred. As elsewhere in the Highlands, the 19th-century Clearances saw entire glens emptied of their ancient settlements, and today, northern migration pushes the English population of the island toward 40%. Nonetheless, the island resists pandering to tourists. Skye has no fast food chains, only three cash machines (in Kyle of Lochalsh, Portree, and Broadford), and Gaelic culture persists in genealogy centers and local music events. Though spotty public transportation may force you to concentrate your travels, Skye's uninhibited wilderness ensures you won't be disappointed.

◼ GETTING THERE

The tradition of ferries carrying passengers "over the sea to Skye" ended with the **Skye Bridge,** which links the island to the mainland's **Kyle of Lochalsh. Trains** (☎(08457) 484950) arrive at Kyle of Lochalsh from **Inverness** (2½hr.; M-Sa 4 per day, Su 2 per day; £15). **Skye-Ways** (☎(01599) 534328), in conjunction with **Scottish Citylink,** runs **buses** daily from: **Fort William** (2hr., 3 per day, £11); **Inverness** (2½hr., 2 per day, £10); **Glasgow** (5½hr., 3 per day, £18). **Pedestrians** can traverse the Skye Bridge's 1½ mi. footpath or take the **shuttle bus** (2 per hr., 70p). **Cars** no longer wait in ferry lines, but the one-way bridge toll is a weighty £7.

From the Outer Hebrides, **Caledonian MacBrayne** ferries sail to **Uig** from **Tarbert** on Harris or **Lochmaddy** on North Uist (1¾hr.; M-Sa 1-2 per day; £8.50, 5-day return £14.55). Ferries also run to **Armadale** in southwestern Skye from **Mallaig** on the mainland (30min.; M-Sa 7 per day, June-Aug. also Su; £2.80, 5-day return £4.75). For reservations and schedules, call the offices in Tarbert (☎(01859) 502444) or Mallaig (☎(01687) 462403).

◼ LOCAL TRANSPORTATION

Touring Skye without a car takes either effort or cash. To avoid headaches and long unplanned hikes along the highway, pick up the handy *Public Transport Guide to Skye and the Western Isles* (£1) at any tourist information centre (TIC).

Buses: Buses on Skye are run by different operators; cherish your transport guide, and be careful not to pay twice when making connections, which are infrequent and somewhat pricey (Kyleakin-Uig £7.50; Kyleakin-Armadale £4). The only reliable service hugs the coast from Kyleakin to Broadford to Portree on the A87. On **Sundays,** nothing runs except **Skye Ways/Scottish Citylink** and the buses that meet the Armadale ferry.

Biking: Cycling is possible, but be prepared for steep hills, nonexistent shoulders, and rain. Most buses will not carry bikes. To **rent** bikes in Kyleakin, try the **Dun Caan Hostel** (☎(01599) 534087; £10 per day); in Broadford, **Fairwinds Cycle Hire** (☎(01471) 822270; £7 per day, £5 deposit); in Portree, **Island Cycles** (☎(01478) 613121; £10-12 per day); and in Uig, **Uig Cycle Hire** (☎(01470) 542311; £8-10 per day).

Car Rental: Sutherland's Garage (☎(01471) 822225), Broadford. 21+. Free collection at Kyleakin. From £35 per day; £250 deposit. **MacRaes Car Hire** (☎(01478) 612554), Portree. 21+ with an international driver's license. From £30 per day.

Tours: Nick's Tour, out of the Dun Caan Hostel (☎(01599) 534087; 8hr., daily, £15), and **MacBackpackers** (☎(01599) 534510; 9hr., daily, £15) visit island highlights. **Peter MacDonald,** a descendent of the Lord of the Isles, runs excellent day-tours for 4 or more from Kyle or Armadale. (☎(01471) 534510; 7hr., daily, £96-108 per group.) Scottish National Heritage and the Highland Council Ranger Service offer free **walking tours** (☎(01599) 524270). For the eager and adventurous, the fantastic ■ **MacBackpackers Skye Trekker Tour,** departing from Kyleakin, is a 2-day, eco-conscious hike into the Cuillin Hills, with all necessary gear provided plus a free dinner and £5 toward camping grub. (☎(01599) 534510. Weekly departures Tu 7:30am. Call ahead.)

Hitchhiking: Fairly easy and efficient, although *Let's Go* does not recommend hitching.

♫ ENTERTAINMENT AND FESTIVALS

Skye's nightlife is vigorous. Snag a copy of the weekly *What, Where, and When* leaflet or *The Visitor* newspaper for a list of special events and check out postings in TICs. Traditional music in English and Gaelic is abundant, and dances—half folk, half rock—take place frequently in village halls, usually after 11pm. The **Highland Games,** a day of bagpipes and boozing in Portree on the first Wednesday of August, and the **Skye Folk Festival,** featuring *ceilidhs* in Portree, Broadford, and Dunvegan during the second week of August, further liven things. Contact the TICs in Kyle of Lochalsh, Portree, Broadford, Dunvegan, or Uig for information.

KYLE OF LOCHALSH AND KYLEAKIN   ☎01599

Almost as an afterthought, Kyle of Lochalsh ("Kyle" for short) and Kyleakin (Ky-LAACK-in) hug the Skye Bridge like bookends. The latter is young and boisterous, a backpackers' hub with three hostels and countless tours. Kyle has done less to capitalize on its fortuitous position, but its cash machine, tourist information centre, and train station make it of practical value to travelers.

☑ PRACTICAL INFORMATION. The Kyle **train station** (☎534205) is near the pier, with the **bus station** a minute to the left. Highland Country **buses** meet incoming trains to head for Kyleakin across the bridge. The Kyle **tourist information centre** (TIC), overlooking the pier from the hill, books beds on either side of the channel for £3. (☎534276. Open Apr.-Oct. M-Sa 9am-5:30pm, July-Sept. also Su 10am-4pm.) Other services include: the last **cash machine** for miles at the **Bank of Scotland,** Main St., in Kyle (open M-Tu and Th-F 9am-12:30pm and 1:30-5pm, W 10am-12:30pm and 1:30-5pm); **Internet access** at the chip shop in Kyleakin (£1.50 per 20min.; open Tu-Sa 5-9:30pm, Su 5-8pm); and the **post office** next door, which sells Citylink bus tickets (open M-F 9am-5:30pm, Sa 9am-12:30pm). **Postal code:** IV40 8AA.

☞ ACCOMMODATIONS. In Kyle of Lochalsh, **Cu'chulainn's Backpackers Hostel,** above a popular pub, has the usual amenities and especially cozy beds. (☎534492. Sheets 50p plus £5 key deposit. Dorms £9.) Over the bridge in Kyleakin, a slew of hostels huddle near the pier. The friendly owners of ■**Dun Caan Hostel** have recently renovated; enjoy a movie in the lounge or relax in your hand-made bunk. (☎534087; fax 534795. Book ahead. Dorms £10.) The easygoing warden of the **SYHA Kyleakin,** on the village green, is a top-notch source for outdoors information and a

Scrabble master to boot. The vibe is young and friendly. (☎534585. Laundry facilities. Internet access £5 per hr. Dorms July-Aug. £11, under 18 £9.50; Sept.-June £10, £8.50.) At the ultra-social **Skye Backpackers** next door, somewhat cramped quarters only add to the communal flavor. (☎534510. Breakfast £1.60. Laundry £2.50. Internet access £5 per hr. Curfew 2am. Dorms July-Aug. £11, Sept.-June £10; doubles and twins £23. Credit card reservations 30p.) For **B&B**, no one beats **Mrs. Chiffer's**, Olaf Rd., three blocks from Skye Backpackers. (☎534440. £13 per person.)

🍴🍽 **FOOD AND PUBS** Grab groceries at the **Co-op**, beside the Kyle bus station. (Open M-Sa 8am-10pm.) Cooked food is available at the **Pier Coffee Shop** in Kyleakin, which serves toasties for £2, fried haggis for £3, and a reputedly "orgasmic" chocolate cake for £1.25. (☎534641. Open M-Tu and Th-Su 9am-8pm.) Kyleakin boasts great nightlife, thanks to a steady stream of backpackers and tourists. The **King Haakon Bar**, at the end of the village green, has a free jukebox and frequent live music on weekend nights. (☎534164. Open M-Th noon-midnight, F noon-1am, Sa noon-11:30pm, Su 12:30-11pm.) Live music is also common at **Saucy Mary's**. (Open M-Th 5pm-midnight, F 5pm-1am, Sa 5-11:30pm, Su 5-11pm.)

◩ **SIGHTS** The **Bright Water Visitor Centre** on the pier offers a kids-oriented look at local history and folklore. (☎530040. Open Apr.-Oct. M-Sa 9am-6pm. Free.) The center also runs boat trips to **Eilean Ban**, the island under the Skye Bridge, which has an old lighthouse and frequent seal and otter sightings. Sailing times depend on tides, so call ahead. (M-Sa 3-4 trips per day. £8, children £5.) Quiet **Kyleakin** harbor alights in oranges, pinks, and purples during clear sunsets—for the best views, climb to the memorial on the hill behind Castle Moil Restaurant. A slippery scramble takes you to the small ruins of **Castle Moil** itself. Cross the little bridge behind the SYHA hostel, turn left, follow the road to the pier, and take the gravel path. Legend relates that the original castle on this site was built by "Saucy Mary," a Norwegian princess who stretched a stout chain across the Kyle and charged ships a fee to come through the narrows. She also used to flash ships who paid the toll— hence the name Saucy Mary and not Entrepreneurial Mary. (Always open. Free.)

SOUTHERN SKYE   ☎01471

BROADFORD. Situated on a rocky bay 8 mi. west of Kyleakin, Broadford is remarkable only for its 24hr. convenience store and bus links to the southern half of Skye. The **tourist information centre** (TIC) sits in a car park along the bay south of the bus stop. (☎822361; fax 822141. Open M-Sa 9am-5:30pm; Apr.-Aug. also Su 10am-4pm.) Five minutes up the road is a blessed **cash machine** at the **Bank of Scotland**. (Open M-Tu and Th-F 9:30am-12:30pm and 1:30-5pm, W 10am-12:30pm and 1:30-5pm.) A second cash machine is by **Skye Surprises**, the 24hr. convenience store/petrol station/car rental/launderette by the TIC. It's open daily; look for the hairy Highland cow model out front. (Laundry £3.50.) The **post office** is open M-Tu and Th-F 9am-1pm and 2-5:30pm, W and Sa 9am-1pm. **Postal code:** IV49 9AB.

Two hostels grace the Broadford area. The **SYHA Broadford** has soothing views ½ mi. from Broadford's main bus stop, on a signposted side road. (☎822442. Reception from 5pm. Check-out 9:30am. Curfew midnight. Open Feb.-Oct. Dorms £9.25, under 18 £8.) Three miles east of town, the **Fossil Bothy Hostel**, 13 Lower Breakish, is a renovated bunkhouse with room for eight on a tranquil coast (the hostel is the larger of the two buildings numbered "13"). Any Broadford-Kyleakin bus can drop you off at the Lower Breakish turnoff on the A87; it's a poorly signposted, 15min. walk from there. A taxi from Broadford costs about £3. (☎822644. Self-cleaning. Dorms £8.) For food in Broadford, stock up at the **Co-op**. (Open M-Sa 8am-10pm.) **The Fig Tree**, near the post office, is cheap. (☎822616. Open M-Sa 10:30am-8pm.)

SLEAT PENINSULA AND ARMADALE. Two miles south of Broadford, the single-lane A851 veers southwest through the foliage of the Sleat Peninsula (SLATE), dubbed "The Garden of Skye." Both **Skye-Ways** and **Highland Country** buses run between Armadale and Broadford (4-6 per day, about £3). Past 17 mi. of south-ward hills, Armadale sends ferries to Mallaig. In town, the **Armadale Castle Gardens** and **Museum of the Isles** unite a disintegrating MacDonald castle, expansive gardens, and an excellent if somewhat pro-MacDonald exhibit on the Hebrides. Formerly the Clan Donald Centre, its Study Centre is one of the best places for genealogical research. They even give free consultations. (☎844305. Open Apr.-Oct. daily 9:30am-5pm. Research from £5 per half-day. Gardens and museum £4, concessions £2.60.) One such MacDonald, Peter, runs the ◪**Flora MacDonald Hostel,** known for incredible views of the Sound of Sleat. He'll pick you up from the Armadale ferry and eagerly tell you about his ancestor, the hostel's famous namesake. (☎844272. Kitchen and TV. Dorms £8.) The **SYHA Armadale** has less appealing digs but a more convenient location, overlooking the water 10min. around the bay from the pier. (☎844260. Lockout 10:30am-5pm. Curfew 11:45pm. Open Apr.-Sept. Dorms £8.50, under 18 £7.25.) North of Armadale at Ostaig, the famous Gaelic college, **Sabhal Mor Ostaig,** runs one-week summer courses in piping, Gaelic, and fiddling. Sample their dorm-room style **B&B** while pretending to be Scottish for a week. (☎844373. Courses £110-125. Singles £20; twins £16 per person.)

⚑ HIKING IN SOUTHERN SKYE Though southern Skye is sometimes abandoned for the more dramatic Cuillins to the north, the graceful landscape here is many an islander's favorite scene. The **Sleat Peninsula** has some of Skye's most verdant greenery, including the **Kinloch Forest** on the Broadford-Armadale bus route. From the Forestry Commission car park, a footpath traces a lovely circular route past a deserted settlement called **Letir Fura,** from which **Loch na Dal** is visible (round-trip 2hr.). A popular, longer hike takes in Skye's southernmost tip, **The Point of Sleat.** The trailhead begins at the end of the A851, south of **Ardvasar** at the **Aird of Sleat.** After an hour's walk, you'll be rewarded with awesome views of the western island **Rum** from the watery inlet of **Acairseid an Rubha.** Continue another 40min. to the **Point of Sleat,** with its lighthouse and panorama of the Cuillins. As the path is obscure, the Ordnance Survey Landranger Map #32 is essential (round-trip 3hr.).

THE CUILLINS AND CENTRAL SKYE   ☎01478

Renowned for its hiking and formations of cloud and mist, the Cuillin Hills, the highest peaks in the Hebrides, dominate central Skye from Broadford to Portree. Legend says the warrior Cúchulainn was the lover of the Amazon ruler of Skye, who named the hills for him when the hero returned to Ireland to die. The Kyleakin-Portree road wends its way through the Red Cuillins, which rise at dramatic angles from the road and present a foreboding face to the aspiring hill walker until meeting the toothed Black Cuillins in **Sligachan** (SLIG-a-han).

⚑⌂ ACCOMMODATIONS AND FOOD If you plan to scale some peaks, expert mountaineers give tips on exploring the area at the **SYHA Glenbrittle,** near the southwest coast. A jocular atmosphere compensates for spartan quarters. (☎640278. Open Apr.-Sept. Dorms £8.25, under 18 £7; June-Aug. 25p more.) Campers should head to **Glenbrittle Campsite,** in a grand setting at the foot of the Cuillins. (☎640404. Open Mar.-Oct. Shop open 8:30am-8:30pm. £3.50 per person.) **Glenbrittle** can be reached by Highland Country bus #360 from Portree and Sligachan (M-Sa 2 per day, last bus from Portree at noon). Below the mountains at the junction of the A863 to Portree and the A850 to Dunvegan, the village of **Sligachan** is little more than a hotel, pub, and campsite in a jaw-dropping setting. Even more than Glenbrittle, Sligachan is a true hiker's hub; the famous trail through Glen Sligachan departs south from here (see **Hiking and Climbing,** below), though there are few budget lodgings in town. Your best bet is the **Sligachan Hotel,** a classic hillwalker's and climber's haunt. (☎650204. Breakfast included. £22-30 per person.) Save money and become one with the outdoors at the **Sligachan Campsite,** across the road. (☎650333. Open Easter-Oct. £4 per person.) In society and refreshment, **Seumas' Bar,** next to the hotel, lacks, well, nothing. A broad selection of beers (try their own ale, Slig 80 Shilling, for £2.20), grub (salmon steak £7) and nearly every malt in existence awaits. (Open daily 10:30am-11:30pm; food served noon-9pm.)

⚡ HIKING AND CLIMBING. The Cuillin Hills are good for both rock climbing and hiking. The booklet *Walks from Sligachan and Glen Brittle* (£2), available at tourist information centres, suggests routes. Warm, waterproof clothing and Ordnance Survey Outdoor Leisure Map #8 (1:25,000; £6.50) are essential; consult **Wilderness Safety,** p. 54, for more advice. The treacherously pitted peat is always drenched, so expect sopping wet feet. If you don't want to go it alone, **MacBack-packers Skye Trekker Tour** hikes the gorgeous coastal path from Elgol, camping overnight at Camasunary and moving north through Glen Sligachan the next day. A guide, fellow backpackers, and transport to and from trailheads are all part of the deal. (☎(01599) 534510. £45. See **Local Transportation,** p. 603.)

A short but scenic path follows the stream from Sligachan near the campsite to the head of **Loch Sligachan.** After crossing the old bridge, fork right off the main path through the gate and walk upstream along the right-hand bank. The narrow, often boggy path leads past pools and miniature waterfalls (3 mi. round-trip). In 1899, a fit (and barefoot!) Gurkha soldier ascended and descended **Glamaig,** the 775 yd. oversized anthill to the left, in just 55min. Give yourself 3½hr., and even then do so only if you feel at ease on steep slopes with unsure footing. The smaller trail, which branches off the main trail after about 15min., leads up the ridge between the higher peaks, granting views of the ocean and offshore isles.

Experienced climbers might try the ascent into the **Sgurr nan Gillean Corrie,** to the southwest of Glamaig, which rises 3167 ft. above a tiny mountain lake. For more level terrain, take the eight-mile walk down **Glen Sligachan** through the heart of the Cuillins to the beach of **Camasunary,** with views of the isles of Rum and Muck. From Camasunary, you can hike 5 mi. along the coast to Elgol.

A less intimate view of the Cuillins unfolds at **Elgol,** 14 mi. southwest on the A881 from Broadford. From Elgol, a sailing trip to **Loch Coruisk** with **Bella Jane Boat Trips** reveals extraordinary panoramas. (☎(01471) 866244. Apr.-Oct. M-Sa; call in off season. Reservations recommended. Return £13; Maxi Return with 4½hr. onshore £19.) From Camasunary beach, you can also hike to Loch Coriusk (1½hr.) along a coastal trail that traverses steep rocks at the intimidating "Bad Step." **Postbuses** (service 106) rumble into Elgol from Broadford (M-F 2 per day, Sa 1 per day).

THE MINGINISH PENINSULA   ☎01478

Ten miles west of the Cuillins, arresting but less rugged views continue to surround the B8009. This is the Minginish Peninsula, a peaceful realm largely devoid of tourists but packed with flesh-eating midges. **Nicolson buses** run here from Portree and Sligachan (M-F 3 per day, Sa 1 per day), stopping at **Carbost,** where some descend to visit the **Talisker Distillery** along serene Loch Harport. The tour is bland, but the whisky isn't: Skye's only malt packs a fiery finish. (Open Apr.-Oct. M-F 9:30am-4:30pm; July-Aug. also Sa; Nov.-Mar. 2-4:30pm. £3.50.) Buses continue to **Portnalong,** where there are two hostels. The **Skyewalker Independent Hostel,** on Fiskavaig Rd., is a recently renovated schoolhouse with 34 beds, a cafe, campsites, a post office, and free pickup from Sligachan. (☎640250. Dorms £7. Tent pitch £2.50.) The **Croft Bunkhouse,** in a converted cowshed, sleeps 14 in a gigantic two-tiered platform-style bed—bring a sleeping bag—and sports a ping-pong table and dart board. (☎640254. Dorms £6.50.) Up the road, the **Taigh Ailean Hotel** offers both bed and breakfast with style and comfort. (☎640271. From £20 per person.)

PORTREE   ☎01478

Skye's capital, Portree (pop. 2500), with its busy shops and attractive harbor, is a welcome cosmopolitan respite (relatively speaking) from the surrounding wilderness. Bonnie Prince Charlie took shelter with Flora MacDonald here in 1746, Samuel Johnson and James Boswell visited the divine Miss M. several years later, and tourists have kept Portree in motion ever since, enjoying similar hospitality.

⚠ PRACTICAL INFORMATION. Buses stop at Somerled Sq. To reach the **tourist information centre** (TIC), Bayfield Rd., from the Square, face the Portree Hotel, then turn right down the narrow lane, and left onto Bridge Rd. The staff elucidates bus routes and books accommodations for £1.50 and a 10% deposit. (☎612137. Open July-Aug. M-Sa 9am-8pm; Su 10am-6pm; Sept.-Oct. and Apr.-June M-F 9am-5:30pm, Su 10am-5pm; Nov.-Apr. M-F 9am-5pm, Sa 10am-4pm.) Other services include: the **Bank of Scotland,** Somerled Sq. (open M-Tu and Th-F 9am-12:30pm and 1:30-5pm, W 10am-12:30pm and 1:30-5pm); a **launderette,** next to the Independent Hostel (open M-Sa 9am-9pm; £3 per load); and the **post office,** Gladstone Buildings, on Quay Brae by the harbor (☎612533; open M-Sa 9am-5:30pm). **Postal code:** IV51 9DB.

⚠ ACCOMMODATIONS. The **Portree Independent Hostel,** The Green, has a prime location, spacious kitchen, and gregarious guests. (☎613737. Dorms £9.50; twins £21.) An enthusiastic staff and comfy beds await at **Portree Backpackers Hostel,** 6 Woodpark, Dunvegan Rd., across from the Co-op. Walk along Bridge Rd. and then Dunvegan Rd. for 10min. (☎613641. Laundry facilities. Dorms July-Aug. £9, Sept.-June £8.50; doubles and twins £18.) One mile north of town along the A855 to Staffin, find the lovely **Torvaig campsite.** (☎691 1209. Open Apr. to mid-Oct. £3.)

⚠⚠ FOOD AND PUBS. The **Safeway** on Bank St. (open M-Sa 8:30am-8pm) and super-cheap **The Bakery** on Somerled Sq. (open M-F 9am-5pm, Sa 9am-4:45pm) feed budget travelers. Near the Portree Backpackers Hostel, 15min. from town, the funky cafe at the **An Tuireann Arts Centre** uses organic local produce; there's also a free contemporary gallery. Walk up Bridge Rd., then Dunvegan Rd., and turn left past the Co-op. (☎613306. Open M-Sa 10am-5pm. 10% student discount.) Seafood restaurants line the **harbor.** The town's uninspiring pubs include the **Royal Hotel Lounge Bar,** on Bank St. near the harbor (☎612525; open M-Sa 11am-midnight, Su 12:30-11pm; live music W-Sa in summer), and the upstairs pub at the **Caledonian Hotel** (☎612641; open Su-F 11am-1am, Sa 11am-12:30am; live music F-Sa).

NORTHERN SKYE ☎01470

Thanks to two scenic roads and miles of untouched shoreline, you can travel the northern part of Skye in blissful ignorance of the thousands of other tourists running amok on the island. The northwestern circuit follows the A850 from Portree to Dunvegan Castle, then down the A863 along the scenic west coast; the northeastern circuit hugs the A855 and A856 around the Trotternish Peninsula through Uig and Staffin and back to Portree. From Portree, **Nicolson buses** (M-Sa 4 per day) and **postbuses** (M-Sa 9:45am) leave for the northwest route; the northeast is covered by **Scottish Citylink** and **Highland Country** buses on the Portree-Flodigarry Circular route (M-Sa 4-8 per day, June-Sept. also Su 3 per day).

⚠TROTTERNISH PENINSULA. Northeast of Portree, the A855 snakes along the east coast of the Trotternish Peninsula past the **Old Man of Storr,** a finger of black rock visible for miles, and the **Quirang** rock pinnacles. The spectacular formations were created when Skye's ancient volcanoes spewed lava too heavy for the weaker sedimentary rock below; as the lava hardened, the lower-lying rock gave way, and these protrusions remain. Close inspection of the Old Man of Storr reveals tiny white crystals—the result of air bubbles trapped in the basalt. The Old Man is accessible by a steep and soggy hike that begins in the nearby car park (round-trip 1hr.); ask the bus driver to let you off there. The footpath to the Quirang begins in a car park along the road from Staffin to Uig. It ascends first to the **Prison,** loops upward to the **Needle,** and finally arrives at the **Table,** a flat grassy promontory with some of Skye's best views (round-trip 3hr.).

Nearby **Staffin Bay** offers bountiful fossils and remarkable views of Skye and the mainland, while **Kilt Rock** bears lava columns similar to those on the Isle of Staffa. Strong, well-shod walkers can try the challenging but magnificent 12 mi. hike along the **Trotternish Ridge,** which runs the length of the peninsula from the Old Man of Storr to Staffin. The less mighty can take the buses from Portree to Staffin.

DUNVEGAN CASTLE. Buses run from Portree to Dunvegan Castle, the seat of the clan MacLeod and an interesting dose of clan history. The castle, unusual as one of the few ancient strongholds still owned by a clan chief, contains a variety of relics, notably the **Fairy Flag,** a 1500-year-old silk, and **Rory Mor's Horn,** capable of holding two liters of claret. Traditionally, the ascending MacLeod chief must drain the horn in one draught "without setting or falling down" to prove his manhood. Present chief John MacLeod emptied the horn in just under 2min. (☎521206. Open late Mar. to Oct. daily 10am-5:30pm; Nov.-Mar. 11am-4pm. £5.50, students and seniors £5, children £3. Gardens only £3.80, children £2.)

DUNTULM CASTLE. At the tip of the peninsula, Duntulm Castle was the MacDonalds' formidable stronghold until a nurse dropped the chief's baby boy from a window, thereby cursing the house. The one remaining room is sealed off, perhaps to deflect bad karma. (Always open. Free, but watch for falling babies.)

Near Duntulm at Kilmuir, the **Skye Museum of Island Life** recreates old crofter life in a village of tiny, 200-year-old black houses. (☎552206. Open Easter-Oct. M-Sa 9:30am-5:30pm. £1.75, students £1.50, seniors £1.25, children 75p.) Nearby along the same turn-off from the highway, **Flora MacDonald's Monument** pays tribute to the Scottish folk hero who sheltered Bonnie Prince Charlie. On a bluff 5 mi. north of Staffin, the **Dun Flodigarry Backpackers Hostel** has a small shop, kitchen, and common area, and is the starting point for many hikes. Take the bus bound for Staffin from Portree and ask to be let off at the hostel. (☎/fax 552212. Dorms £8-9.)

UIG   ☎01470

The town of Uig (OO-ig) flanks a windswept bay on the peninsula's west coast, the terminus for ferries to the Outer Hebrides and the final resting place for most long-distance buses from Glasgow and Inverness. The small but helpful **tourist information center** is found in the **SYHA Uig,** 30min. from the pier; facing the sea, turn left on the A586, and the large white house will be on your left. (☎542211. Lockout 9:30am-5pm. Curfew 10:40pm. Lights out 11pm. Open mid-Mar. to Oct. Dorms £8.25, under 18 £7.25.) More convenient for ferry connections, **Oronsay B&B** is by the pier; all rooms are with bath and there's **bike rental** around back. (☎542316. £15-18 per person. Bikes £2 per hr., £11 per day.) **The Pub at The Pier** gives discounts to hostelers on standard pub grub. (☎542212. Open M-Sa 11am-11pm.)

THE OUTER HEBRIDES

The landscape of the Outer Hebrides is extraordinarily beautiful and astoundingly ancient. Much of its exposed rock has been around for more than half as long as the planet itself, and distant inhabitants have left behind a rich sediment of tombs, standing stones, and antiquities. The culture and customs of the Hebridean people are rooted in religion and a love of tradition, and scattered family crofts remain the norm on many islands. While television and tourism have diluted traditional ways of life, you are still most likely to hear Gaelic spoken here; on the strongly Calvinist islands of Lewis, Harris, and North Uist, most establishments close and even public transportation ceases on Sundays (though one or two places may assist lost souls with an afternoon pint); and to the south, on the islands of Benbecula, South Uist, and Barra, tight-shuttered sabbatarianism gives way to Catholic chapels and plates of the Pope on living-room walls. While many young Hebrideans seek to escape the isolation of these islands, just as many city-sick "Inlanders" are beginning to migrate westward for seclusion and quiet. Together, the Western Isles remain one of Scotland's most undisturbed and unforgettable realms.

⌐ TRANSPORTATION

Three major **Caledonian MacBrayne** (☎(01475) 650100) **ferries** serve the Western Isles—from Oban and, less frequently, Mallaig to Barra and South Uist, from Skye to Harris, and from Ullapool to Lewis. Once in the archipelago, ferries and infrequent buses connect the islands. If you know ahead of time which islands you will visit, consider buying an **Island Hopscotch ticket** from CalMac; it will save you money on a month's worth of ferry rides, plus you can bring your bike along for free. **Cycling** is excellent provided you like the challenge of windy hills and don't melt in the rain. Though traffic is light, **hitchhikers** report frequent rides. (*Let's Go* does not recommend hitchhiking.) Inexpensive car rental (from ₤20 per day) is possible at several places throughout the isles, but they'll probably prohibit you from taking vehicles on ferries. Except in bilingual Stornoway and Benbecula, all road signs are in Gaelic only. Tourist information centres (TICs) often carry translation keys, and *Let's Go* lists Gaelic equivalents after English place names where necessary. For up-to-date transport information, consult the *Skye and Western Isles Public Transport Travel Guide* (₤1 at TICs).

⌐ ACCOMMODATIONS AND CAMPING

Since ferries arrive at odd hours, try to book a bed ahead. An area TIC will book B&Bs for ₤1.50. Camping is allowed on public land in the Hebrides, but freezing winds and sodden ground often make it miserable. Lewis has one SYHA Youth Hostel, in the remote South Lochs area: the **SYHA Kershader,** Ravenspoint, Kershader, South Lochs. It's your standard SYHA, with laundry and even a shop next door. (☎(01851) 880236. Dorms ₤8.25, under 18 ₤7.25.) A. Macdonald (☎(01851) 830224) runs the W9 **bus** service from Stornoway, but you must call ahead.

The Outer Hebrides are home to the unique ☒**Gatliff Hebridean Trust Hostels,** four 19th-century thatched croft houses turned into simple year-round hostels. The atmosphere and authenticity of these hostels make them an ideal way to experience the Western Isles. They accept no advance bookings, but it is very unusual that travelers are turned away. Despite basic facilities, all provide cooking equipment, gas stoves, cutlery, crockery, and hot water. The hostels have coal fires and are not centrally heated, so you'll want a good sleeping bag. All hostels are ₤6 per person, under 18 ₤5, and offer camping with use of hostel facilities for ₤3.

Berneray (Bhearnaraigh), off North Uist. Beautifully thatched and whitewashed affair near an amazing beach. Frequent buses on the W19 and W17 routes shuttle between the hostel, the Otternish pier (where ferries arrive from Harris), the Lochmaddy pier on North Uist, and the Sollas Co-op food store (30min., M-Sa 6-9 per day, ₤1).

Garenin (Na Gearranan), Lewis, 1½ mi. from Carloway. Unsurpassed surroundings: a trail leads along cliff tops to the sandy beaches of Dalmore and Dalberg. Buses on the W2 "West Side Circular" route from Stornoway (M-Sa 10-11 per day) go to Carloway, if not Garenin village itself. Free taxi service meets some buses at Carloway.

Howmore (Tobha Mòr), South Uist, about 1hr. from Lochboisdale. Coin-operated electricity! Overlooks a ruined chapel, within striking distance of the remains of Ormiclate Castle. W17 buses from Lochboisdale to Lochmaddy will stop at the Howmore Garage (M-Sa 5-8 per day, ₤1); from there, follow the sign 1 mi. west from the A865.

Rhenigidale (Reinigeadal), a substantial hike from Tarbert in North Harris. Free minibuses run to the hostel from the car park next to the Tarbert TIC (M-Sa 2 per day); you must call ahead. (☎(01859) 502221; by 8pm the night before for the morning bus or 3pm for the afternoon.) The bus will take your pack if you want to venture the tough 6 mi. hike. From Tarbert, take the road toward Kyles Scalpay for 2 mi. and follow the signposted path left to Rhenigidale. The path ascends 850 ft. for stunning views before zigzagging down steeply (3hr. total). To get to the hostel by road, follow the turn-off to Maaruig (Maraig) from the A859 (13 mi. from Tarbert).

LEWIS (LEODHAS)   ☎01851

Photographs fail time and again to convey Lewis's strange aura. Relentlessly desolate, the landscape is flat, treeless, and speckled with quiet lochs. Drifting mists shroud untouched miles of moorland and half-cut fields of peat, complementing exploration of Lewis's many archaeological sites, most notably the Callanish Stones. Somewhat incongruously, the island is also home to "the most consistent surf in Europe" and hosted an international surfing competition in 1999. Lewis's passive roads are good for biking—Pentland Rd., starting in Stornoway, earns raves. However, check weather forecasts, as a gusty day may require you to pedal hard even downhill. Make sure to rent your bike on a Saturday—otherwise, you'll have nothing to do on Sunday, when virtually everything grinds to a halt. See **The Outer Hebrides: Transportation,** p. 609, for information on how to reach Lewis.

STORNOWAY   ☎01851

Stornoway (Steornobhaigh), Lewis's main town, is unlike anything else in the Outer Hebrides. Its artificially forested bay, well-kept castle, and industrial and fishing centers contrast vividly with the countryside around it. The largest town in the northwest (pop. 8000), Stornoway hosts the Hebridean festival in mid-July.

▉▊ TRANSPORTATION AND PRACTICAL INFORMATION. CalMac ferries sail from **Ullapool** (M-Sa 2-3 per day; £13, 5-day return £22.35). **Buses** from Stornoway make rounds on Lewis; the bus station has schedules. Destinations include **Tarbert** (An Tairbeart) on Harris (M-Sa 3-4 per day, £2.65) and **Ness** (Nis), **Callanish** (Calanais), and **Carloway** (Carlabhaigh) on Lewis. Car hire companies are cheaper than on the mainland. Try **Lochs Motors,** across from the bus station (☎705857; 21+; from £20 per day), or **Mackinnon Self Drive,** 18 Inaclete Rd. (☎702984; 21+; from £24 per day). Rent bikes at **Alex Dan's Cycle Centre,** 67 Kenneth St. (☎704025. £2 per hr., £8 per day, £29 per week. Open M-Sa 9am-6pm.) To get to the Stornoway **tourist information centre** (TIC), 26 Cromwell St., turn left from the ferry terminal, then right onto Cromwell St. The TIC books **coach tours** of Lewis. (☎703088. Open Mar.-Sept. M-Sa 9am-6pm and to meet late ferries; Oct.-Feb. M-Sa 9am-5pm.) **Stornoway Trust** organizes free **walks** of Stornoway and the countryside, as well as private vehicle tours. (☎704733. Apr.-Oct.) Other services include: **Bank of Scotland,** across from the TIC (open M-Tu and Th-F 9am-5pm, W 10am-5pm); **Erica's Launderette,** 46 Macaulay Rd., the only one in Harris and Lewis and a bit of a walk (☎704508; open M-Tu and Th-Sa 9am-3pm); **Internet access** at the **Stornoway Library** (☎703064; £2 per 30min., £3.50 per hr.; open M-Th and Sa 10am-5pm, F 10am-7pm); and the **post office,** 16 Francis St. (open M-F 9am-5:30pm, Sa 9am-12:30pm). Send **poste restante** to the Royal Mail Delivery Office, Sandwick Rd. **Postal code:** HS1 2AA.

▉ ACCOMMODATIONS. The best place to lay your head and wax your board is the new ▇**Fair Haven Hostel,** a comfortable mecca for wayward surfers, over the surf shop at the intersection of Francis St. and Keith St. From the pier, turn left onto Shell St., which becomes South Beach, then turn right on Kenneth St. and right again onto Francis St. The fresh cooked meals are better than anything of a comparable price in town; they catch the wild salmon themselves. Hostel guests can also get surfing discounts. (☎705862. Dinners £7.50. Dorms £10, with breakfast £12.50, with full board £20.) The **Stornoway Backpackers Hostel,** 47 Keith St., 2min. farther up Keith St., has free tea, coffee, and cereal, and is always open. (☎703628. Dorms £9.) Many **B&Bs** oblige early ferries with a crack-of-dawn breakfast. To get to **Mr. and Mrs. Hill,** Robertson Rd., from the TIC, head up Church St. and turn left onto Matheson Rd.; Robertson Rd. is on the right. (☎706553. £17-19 per person.)

▉▊ FOOD AND NIGHTLIFE. Cheap food is easy to come by in Stornoway, including groceries at the **Co-op** on Cromwell St. (Open M-Sa 8am-7pm.) For an unexpectedly good taste of Asia, head to ▇**Thai Cafe,** 27 Church St., where mouthwatering main dishes (£4-6) are served in a lovely, candlelit setting. (☎701811.

CHECK, MATE In 1831, a man was walking along the dunes of West Lewis, bracing himself against a heavy wind. Suddenly a hard gale tripped him up and, as he regained balance, he witnessed a tribe of small, grim figures rising menacingly from the sand at his feet. Dashing off in fright, he returned to tell his family and friends about his perilous encounter in the Kingdom of Fairies. The "tribe" was actually a set of 78 walrus-tooth gamepieces left behind by ancient Vikings, who apparently were avid chess players when not sacking the country. Today the **"Lewis Chessmen"** can be seen at the British Museum (see p. 131). A native exhibit on the subject is found in Stornoway, on Francis St. at the Museum nan Eilean. (☎ 703773. Open Apr.-Sept. M-Sa 10am-5:30pm; Oct.-Mar. Tu-F 10am-5pm, Sa 10am-1pm.)

Open M-Sa noon-2:30pm and 5-11pm.) The **Bank Street Deli** has everything from curries (£4) to pizza (£3.50) for takeaway; most of the menu is under £2. (☎ 706419. Open M-W 9am-6pm, Th-F 9am-2pm, Sa 9am-11:30pm.) The **An Lanntair Gallery** (see below) also houses the town's best cafe (smoked salmon roll £2; closes 30min. before gallery). Don't miss out on Stornoway's vibrant **nightlife.** Pubs and nightclubs crowd the area between Point St., Castle St., and the two waterfronts. There's no better place to watch a big-time sporting event than the **Crown Inn** on North Beach St. (Open M-W until 11pm, Th-F until midnight, Sa until 11:30pm.) The **Caley Bar,** South Beach St., offers an upbeat local scene (Th and Sa "Karaoke-Disco" nights). **The Heb,** a hip club/bar/cafe, is nothing you'd ever expect in the Outer Hebrides. (Th-Sa disco from 10pm. 18+. Cover £2. Open M-W 11am-8pm, Th 11am-1am, F 11am-2am, Sa 11am-11:30pm.)

◪ **SIGHTS** The **An Lanntair Gallery,** in the Town Hall on South Beach St., hosts art exhibits and events including musical and historical evenings. (☎ 703307. Open M-Sa 10am-5:30pm. Free.) The free **Museum nan Eilean** on Francis St. (see **Check, Mate,** below) has fascinating Hebridean exhibitions. Meander the grounds of majestic **Lewis Castle,** northwest of town. Built in the 19th century by a merchant and opium smuggler, the castle now shelters a college. The entrance is on Cromwell St., but you can admire it from across the water at the end of North Beach St. or from a clearing reached by turning left after the footbridge from New St.

LEWIS SIGHTS AND SURF

Most of Lewis's biggest attractions, including the Callanish Stones, Dùn Carloway Broch, and the Arnol Black House, are ranged along the west coast and can be reached with the **W2 bus service,** which operates on a circuit beginning at the Stornoway bus station (M-Sa 5 per day in either direction). Maclennan Coaches offers a £5 day-rover pass for this route, or a return ticket to see one, two, or three of the sights from May to October (£3.50, £4, and £4.50 respectively). Alternatively, travel with a minibus tour company, such as **Out and About Tours** (☎ 612288; half-day from £7) or **Albannach Guided Tours** (☎ 830433; from £8), both departing from the TIC.

▨ **CALLANISH STONES (CALANAIS).** The impressive Callanish Stones, 14 mi. west of Stornoway on the A858, are second only to Stonehenge in grandeur and a thousand times less overrun. The speckled, greenish-white stones were hewn from Lewisian gneiss, the three-billion-year-old rock hidden beneath the island's peat bogs. Local archaeologists believe that prehistoric peoples used the stones to track the movements of the moon, employing complex trigonometry and a level of technical knowledge unavailable to the Greeks 2000 years later. Others are skeptical, but admit that the circle may have been designed by primitive astronomers. The Visitor Centre has a comprehensive exhibit. (☎ 621422. Visitor Centre open Apr.-Sept. M-Sa 10am-6pm; Oct.-Mar. 10am-4pm. Exhibit £1, students and seniors 75p, children 40p. Stones themselves always open and free.)

Local writer Gerald Ponting has published guides to Callanish and 20 neighboring sites with explicit directions (40p-£4); get them from the Stornoway TIC. A mile before Callanish, postbuses follow the B8011 across the bridge to **Great Bernera** (Bearnaraigh), where the **Bostadh Iron Age House** marks an Iron Age village. (Open Tu-Sa noon-4pm. £1-2.) Perhaps more spectacular are the idyllic **white beaches** nearby. Twenty miles farther west stand the surprisingly lush **Glen Valtos** and the expansive sands at **Timsgarry,** flanked by dozens of deserted islets.

CARLOWAY BROCH (DÙN CHARLABHAIGH). On the A858 5 mi. north of Callanish, the crofting town of **Carloway** (Carlabhaigh) is dominated by the Carloway Broch, an Iron Age tower with a partially intact staircase and breathtaking view of hills and lochs. Once it would have protected farmers and their cattle from Viking raiders, now it shelters tourists from high winds. Still, watch your footing: a sudden gust of wind may bring you closer to the landscape than you'd like. (Visitor Centre open Apr.-Oct. M-Sa 10am-6pm. Broch always open and free.) The **Garenin Hebridean Trust Hostel,** 1½ mi. from Carloway (see p. 609), stands within the restored **Gearrannan Blackhouse Village,** a wonderful visit if you haven't seen many traditional croft houses, though there won't be much new here if you have. (☎643416. Open M-Sa 10am-4pm. Guided tours £1.50. £1, concessions 50p.)

ARNOL BLACK HOUSE. On the A858, beyond Shawbost, a small town north of Carloway, stands this restored thatched-roof crofter's cottage. A chimney was intentionally left out, as smoke from the peat fire was supposed to conserve heat and improve the thatch by seeping through the roof—hence the name. Inhale a hearty lungful of peat smoke and get a watery-eyed glimpse of the dim interior. (☎710395. Open Apr.-Sept. M-Sa 9:30am-1pm and 2-6:30pm; Oct.-Mar. M-Th and Sa 9:30am-1pm and 2-4:30pm. £2.50, seniors £1.90, children 75p.)

SURF'S UP. Beyond scattered villages and grassy moors, the **Butt of Lewis** (Rubha Robhanais) is the island's northernmost point. A lighthouse on the disintegrating cliffs overlooks beaches below; at night you can hear the growl of the corncrake, a rare and elusive bird. Just around the corner from the Butt is the **Port of Ness,** home to a popular surf beach. Another occasional option for wave-seekers is Uig, the central western area of Lewis. **Kneep Reef** doesn't have much to offer in terms of surf, but the endless deserted beach will cheer even the most eager sports enthusiast. Here, or for better results at **Valtos** or **Europie** beaches, search the sands for Neolithic artifacts and the pink shells fabled to be mermaid fingernails. The most frequented surf on the island is at **Dalmor** beach, near the town of Dalbeg, site of an international surf competition in 1999. Head to **Hebridean Surf Holidays** (☎705862), on the corner of Keith St. and Francis St. in Stornoway by the hostel, and ask for Derek—he'll tell you where the swells are. His all-inclusive surfing lessons are £35 per day, or he can simply rent you the equipment and transport you to the beach (from £3). The best swells frequent different beaches depending on wind and tidal cycles, so it is essential to have a guide familiar with such patterns.

If you don't ride with Derek, the handy **W2 bus route** runs past Dalbeg and Dalmor beach, while buses operating the **W4 route** (2-4 per day) from Stornoway and Garynahine pass Kneep Reef and other spectacular surf spots in the Uig district. The Galson Motors bus on the **W1 route** can whisk you from Stornoway along the northwest coast to the Butt and the Port of Ness (M-F 9-10 per day, Sa 6 per day).

HARRIS (NA HEARADH)

Harris technically shares an island with Lewis, but in all other respects it's an entirely different world. Here, Lewis's deserted flatlands give way to another kind of desolation, more rugged and spectacular, with steely gray mountains ranged one against the other. Toward the west coast, the Forest of Harris (ironically enough, a treeless mountain range splotched with heather) descends to brilliant crescents of yellow beaches bordered by indigo waters and *machair*—sea meadows of soft grass and summertime flowers. In the 19th century, these idyllic shores were cleared for sheep grazing and the islanders moved to the boulder-strewn east coast. They responded to the east's complete lack of arable land by developing still-visible "lazybeds," furrowed masses of seaweed and peat compost laid on bare rock. The island's main road, the A859, bumps through the mountains from Tarbert to Stornoway. The Golden Road (so named because of the king's ransom spent in blasting it from the rock) twists from Tarbert to Harris's southern tip via the desolate east coast, making a harrowing bus trip or grueling bike ride. Small roads branch from Tarbert west to the small fishing community on the island of Scalpay (Scalpaigh), now connected to Harris by a new causeway. See **The Outer Hebrides: Transportation,** p. 609, for information on how to reach Harris.

HIKING. Encompassing rocky stretches and heathered slopes, Harris's hiking is near-orgasmic. The largest peaks lie within the Forest of Harris, whose main entrances are off the B887 to Huisinish Point, at **Glen Meavaig,** and farther west at **Amhuinnsuidhe Castle** (about 15 mi. from Tarbert), erected in 1863 and still a private residence. The **W12 bus** from Tarbert services all of these points, though it is infrequent in summer (Tu and F 3 per day). An excellent 4hr. hike runs down to Glen Meavaig from **Ardvourlie** in the north and past Loch Bhoisimid; to get to Ardvourlie, take the **W10 bus** from Tarbert or Stornoway (Harris Coaches, M-Sa 3-4 per day). If you don't have time for exhaustive exploration, hop any fence near Tarbert and hike up **Gillaval** (1554 ft.), which overlooks the town and harbor islands. The view from the top is stupendous; allow yourself at least an hour for the trip up. For the most comprehensive walk, try the new **Harris Walkway,** from Clisham in the south to Scaladal in the north, via Tarbert. The hike is long but not difficult. Always be sure to carry the proper Ordnance Survey map in these remote parts.

TARBERT   ☎ 01859

Tarbert (An Tairbeart) straddles the narrow isthmus that divides Harris into North and South. As the island's center (pop. 500), it has the most amenities, including B&Bs. **Ferries** serve Tarbert from **Uig, Skye** (M-Sa 1-2 per day; £8.50, 5-day return £14.55). Check with **CalMac** (☎502444), in Tarbert at the pier, for timetables. **Buses** (☎502441) run from **Stornoway** and **Leverburgh** (45min. in either direction, M-Sa 3-5 per day, £2.65) and stop in the car park behind the tourist information centre (TIC). Prices at **Gaeltech Car Hire** (☎520460) average £25 per day. The island's beguiling nothingness is seen well by **bike;** rent from **Paula Williams.** (☎520319. £10 per day.) When **hiking** in Harris's treeless landscape, there's little risk of getting lost. Still, marked trails are scarce, so bring a compass, sturdy boots, and a map.

The **tourist information centre,** Pier Rd. (☎502011; open early Apr. to mid-Oct. M-Sa 9am-5pm and for late ferry arrivals) can give you the hours for **Internet access** at **Sir E. Scott School library,** 10min. on the A859 to Stornoway. The **Bank of Scotland** is uphill from the pier. (Open M-Tu and Th-F 9am-12:30pm and 1:30-5pm, W 10am-12:30pm and 1:30-5pm.) The **post office,** Main St., is to the right. (Open M-Tu and Th-F 9am-1pm and 2-5:30pm, W 9am-1pm, Sa 9am-12:30pm.) **Postal code:** HS3 3BL.

The well-located **Rockview Bunkhouse,** Main St., is stuffed with beds less than 5min. from the pier. Walk uphill past the TIC and hang left at the grocer's. It's run by two postal clerks, so you can also check in at the post office. (☎502211. Dorms £9.) Effie MacKinnon keeps a spacious B&B at **Waterstein House,** across from the TIC. (☎502358. £15 per person.) **A.D. Munro,** Main St., up from the TIC, serves Tarbert as grocer, butcher, and baker. (☎502016. Open M-Sa 7:30am-6pm.) The **First-fruits Tearoom,** next to the TIC, ladles out tasty soups. (☎502439. Open Apr.-Sept. 10:30am-4:30pm.) The **Harris Hotel** serves lunches (£5-9) and pints (£2) in its bar across from the main hotel building. The food is average, but come Sunday, it's all you've got. (☎502154. Meals served daily noon-2:15pm and 7-8:45pm.) Bill Lawson presents **Evenings of Song, Story, and Slides** at the hotel, for those interested in local history and culture. (☎520258. May-Sept. W at 8:30pm. £3.)

RODEL AND LEVERBURGH. After exploring Tarbert and the mountains, head to Rodel (Roghadal), at Harris's southern tip, site of **St. Clement's Church.** Peek at the three MacLeod tombs; the principal one, built in 1528, is hewn from local black gneiss (volcanic rock). Up the road is Leverburgh, where a **CalMac** (☎(01876) 500337) **ferry** sails to Otternish on North Uist (M-Sa 3-4 per day; $4.75, 5-day return $8). **Buses** (☎502441) run from **Tarbert** (45min., M-Sa 3-5 per day, $2.65). The upscale, funky **Am Bothan Bunkhouse,** is conveniently located near the ferry—the bus passes it about ¼ mi. up the road. (☎(01859) 520251. Dorms $12.)

THE UISTS (UIBHIST)

Coming from anywhere in the peak-strewn Highlands, the extreme flatness of the Uists (YOO-ists) will be a shock. Save for a thin strip of land along the east coast, these islands are completely level, packed with so many lochs that it's difficult to distinguish where the islands end and the water begins. A rare shard of sunlight reveals a world of thin-lipped beaches, crumbling black houses, wild jonquils, and quiet streams hiding some of Europe's best salmon-fishing spots.

The population is tiny and decentralized, scattered across small crofts. The main villages of **Lochmaddy** (Loch nam Madadh) on North Uist (Uibhist a Tuath) and **Lochboisdale** (Loch Baghasdail) on South Uist (Uibhist a Deas) are but glorified ferry hubs. Small **Benbecula** (Beinn na Faoghla) lies between its two larger neighbors and possesses the Uists' sole airport. If you think this spread-out arrangement will make backpacking difficult, you're absolutely right. There are only five hostels in the Uists, and transportation to them is tricky; prepare to walk. Crossing from North Uist to South Uist, Calvinism gives way to Roman Catholicism. Although Sunday remains a day of church-going, secular public activity is much more acceptable here than in the north.

▐ TRANSPORTATION

CalMac ferries float to **Lochmaddy** from **Uig, Skye** (1¾hr.; 1-2 per day; $8.50, 5-day return $14.55); the ferry also connects with **Tarbert, Harris** (see p. 613). Ferries drift to **Otternish** from **Leverburgh, Harris** (M-Sa 3-4 per day; $4.75, 5-day return $8) and to **Lochboisdale** from **Oban** (7hr.; M and W-Sa 1 per day; $18.75, 5-day return $3) and **Mallaig** (3½hr., W 1 per day, $13.85).

All modes of transportation are scarce. **Bus** #W17 runs along the main road from Lochmaddy to the airport in **Balivanich** and **Lochboisdale** (2hr., M-Sa 4-6 per day, $3.10). Buses also connect to meet at least one ferry per day in **Otternish** for departures to Harris, and **Ludag** in the south for connections to Barra (5-9 per day, $1). If you are arriving on a late ferry, there may not be a bus until the next day. Call ahead to book with a B&B that will pick you up or prepare to camp. Get a schedule in the Lochmaddy or Lochboisdale tourist information centre (TIC). For **car rental,** call **Maclennan's Self Drive Hire,** Balivanich, Benbecula. (☎(01870) 602191. From $22.50 plus tax and gas.) The Uists' few drivers are often friendly to **hitchhikers,** but it's rude to ask on Sundays; *Let's Go* never recommends hitchhiking.

▐ PRACTICAL INFORMATION

Tourist information centres on the piers at **Lochmaddy** (☎(01876) 500321) and **Lochboisdale** (☎(01878) 700286) book accommodations for $1 within the Western Isles, $3 elsewhere. (Both open Apr. to mid-Oct. M-Sa about 9am-5pm and to meet late ferries.) Lochboisdale has a **Royal Bank of Scotland** (open M and Th-F 9:15am-4:45pm, W 10am-4:45pm) and Lochmaddy a **Bank of Scotland** (open M and Th-F 9:30am-12:30pm and 1:30-4:30pm, W 10:30am-12:30pm and 1:30-4:30pm); both have **cash machines.** Benbecula also boasts a cash machine-blessed bank (☎(01870) 602044), along with the Uists' sole launderette, **Uist Laundry,** by Balivanich Airport (☎(01870) 602876; open M-F 8:30am-5pm, Sa 9am-1pm). **Internet access** is available at **Cafe Taigh Chearsabhagh,** Lochmaddy (currently free, prices to be determined), and **Past and Present Cafe,** Lochboisdale ($1 per 15min.; see **Food** below for both).

ACCOMMODATIONS

The only **hostel** near Lochmaddy is the **Uist Outdoor Centre,** which also offers courses in rock climbing, canoeing, and water sports during the day. Bring a sleeping bag and book ahead. Follow signposts up from the pier for a mile and turn right. (☎(01876) 500480. Linen £2. Dorms £8.) The other hostels are far from town and reachable only by clever navigation. For the excellent **Taigh Mo Sheanair,** near Clachan, ride any of the buses that travel the main stretch from Lochmaddy to Lochboisdale. The bus driver can let you off at the Clachan shop on Balishare Rd., from where it's a mile's signposted walk. (☎(01876) 580246. Dorms £9; **camping** £4 per person.) Easier to reach but more primitive is the **Gatliff Hebridean Trust Hostel** on **Berneray** (see p. 616), serviced directly by bus from Lochmaddy (30min., M-Sa 6-9 per day, £1). Another basic **Gatliff Hebridean Trust Hostel** is on South Uist at **Howmore** (Tobha Mòr), a mile from the Lochmaddy-Lochboisdale bus route (see p. 609). The bus also passes through **Balivanich,** Benbecula, where the **Taigh-na-Cille Bunkhouse,** 22 Balivanich, sleeps 10. (☎(01870) 602522. Dorms £10-11.)

B&Bs are scarce and difficult to reach. In Lochmaddy, Mrs. Morrison greets guests at the ◙**Old Bank House.** (☎(01876) 500275. £18-20 per person.) In Lochboisdale, **Mrs. MacLellan's,** Bay View, is above the ferry terminal. (☎(01878) 700329. £16-18 per person.) **Mrs. MacDonald's,** Kilchoan Bay, a mile along the main bus route, is a bit nicer if you're willing to sacrifice some convenience. (☎(01878) 700517. £15 per person.) You can **camp** almost anywhere, but ask the crofters first.

FOOD

The cheapest food stores on the islands are the **Co-ops** in Sollas (Solas) on North Uist, Creagorry (Creag Ghoraidh) on Benbecula, and Daliburgh (Dalabrog) on South Uist. For supper in either ferry hub, your only option is somewhat pricey but tasty pub grub (£4-10) at the **Lochmaddy Hotel** (☎(01876) 500331) or the **Lochboisdale Hotel.** (Food served in both noon-2pm and 6-9pm.) Across the street from the Lochmaddy Hotel, the small **Cafe Taigh Chearsabhagh** sells baked goods and sandwiches for £2-3. (☎(01876) 500293. Open M-Sa 10am-5pm.) In Lochboisdale, the ◙**Past and Present Cafe** has a varied menu, great cappuccino, and long hours. (Open daily 10am-10pm.) If you're going out to Bharpa Langass, follow the signs to **Langass Lodge** (☎(01876) 580282) for a post-Cairn pint. Halfway between Lochmaddy and Clachan, this classy hunting lodge holds some down-and-dirty drinking sessions. Mention *Let's Go* and get Niall to make you his special Pimms.

SIGHTS

The vibrant ◙**Taigh Chearsabhagh Museum and Arts Centre** in Lochmaddy has a rotating gallery of contemporary Scottish artists and an extensive photo exhibit in its museum on North Uist life. The Centre also offers two- to three-day art courses from £10 per day. (☎(01876) 500293. Open daily 10am-5pm. Gallery free. Museum £1, students and seniors 50p.) Elsewhere on North Uist, the A865 runs past wide beaches at **Sollas,** sea-carved arches and Victorian folly at **Scolpaig,** and the site of Sloc a'Choire, a spouting cave and hollow arch, at **Tigharry.** It is said that a young lass once hid in the arch rather than marry the man to whom her parents had betrothed her; listen carefully and you might still hear her echoing cries. Two miles past Locheport Rd. on the A867 is the chambered cairn **Barpa Langass,** which dates back 3000 years, and the nearby standing stone circle **Pobull Fhinn.** On North Uist's southern tip at **Carinish** lie the ruins of 13th-century **Trinity Temple,** probably the islands' most noteworthy building. Bus #W17 from Lochmaddy swings near Langass and Carinish. Birdwatchers enjoy the **Balranald Reserve** on western North Uist, north of Bayhead (signposted "RSPB"). May and June are the best months for observation, but you'll almost always see lapwings, oyster-catchers, and rare red-necked phalaropes. Bus #W18 passes by from Lochmaddy (M-Sa 3-4 per day).

The A865 (and #W17 bus) continues its run southward into Benbecula, past historical sites visually indistinguishable from the surrounding landscape. In north Benbecula, the B892 forks off, passing splendid beaches to the west, and arriving at **Nunton,** former spiritual home to nuns massacred during the Reformation. In Culla Bay, where the nuns were tied and left to drown, the seaweed seems to grow like hands on the rocks. The newly restored **Nunton Steadings** (☎ (01870) 602039) provides information on crofting and natural and local history. Farther south crumble the scanty remains of the 14th-century **Borve Castle.**

South Uist has paltry attractions, centered around the birthplace of Flora MacDonald in Milton, where a commemorative cairn stands by the A865. The nearby **Kildonan Museum** houses some local artifacts and a showcase for Uist Craft Producers. (☎ (01878) 710343. Open M-Sa 10am-5pm, Su 2-5pm.) Access to the **moorland** in the Uists is free, but there are few well-marked footpaths. For vistas of loch and moor, hop over the roadside fence and climb **Blashaval Hill,** a short walk west of Lochmaddy on the A865. TICs offer handy *Western Isles Walks* leaflets (50p), as well as a summertime *Out and About* schedule of **guided walks** led by the Southern Isles Amenity Trust. (☎ (01870) 602039. £0-2.)

NEAR THE UISTS

BERNERAY. The tiny island of Berneray (Beàrnaraigh), connected to North Uist's north coast by a causeway, is a rare gem. A favorite retreat of Prince Charles and home to the best-equipped **Gatliff Hebridean Trust Hostel** (see p. 609), it boasts a gorgeous west coast of white beach and *machair* (sea meadow), a thriving seal population, and a friendly human population of 140 that first saw electricity in 1969. You can easily walk the island's 8 mi. circumference, passing a standing stone or two along the way. Berneray is a brief walk from the Otternish pier (where Harris ferries arrive); frequent **buses** run from Lochmaddy (30min., M-Sa 6-9 per day, £1).

ERISKAY. On February 4, 1941, with strict wartime alcohol rationing in effect, the *S.S. Politician* foundered on a reef off the isle of Eriskay (Eiriosgaigh), between South Uist and Barra while carrying 207,000 cases of whisky to America. The concerned islanders mounted a prompt salvage operation, and Eriskay hasn't been the same since. The local pub, named after the ship, displays some of the original bottles. The island is perhaps even more notable as the place where Bonnie Prince Charlie first set foot on Scottish soil, at **Prince Charles's Bay.** The unique pink flower that grows on the island is said to have been brought by seedlings stuck to the Prince's shoe. Eriskay is connected to South Uist by a free causeway; contact the TIC for information on the new bus service.

BARRA (BARRAIGH) ☎ 01871

Little Barra, the southern outpost of the Outer Isles, is unspeakably beautiful, a composite of moor, *machair*, and beach. On sunny days, the island's colors are unforgettable; sand dunes crown waters flecked with shades of light-dazzled blue, wreathed below by dimly visible red, brown, and green kelp. The best times to visit are May and early June, when the primroses bloom. Believed to be named after St. Findbar, the island is also the ancient stronghold of descendants of the Irish O'Neils. As late as the 16th century, islanders returned to Ireland for religious festivals. Though the primroses and beaches beckon, be warned that Barra is not the most easily accessible, or budget-friendly, of the Outer Hebrides.

◪ **TRANSPORTATION. CalMac** (☎ (01878) 700288) **ferries** stop at **Castlebay** (Bagh A Chaisteil), Barra's main town, from **Oban** (5hr.; M, W-Th, Sa 1 per day; £18.75) and **Lochboisdale, South Uist** (1¾hr.; Tu, Th-F, Su 1 per day; £5.30). A 60-passenger ferry (☎ (01878) 720265) runs to **Eoligarry** (Eolaigearraidh) on Barra from **Ludag, South Uist** (M-Sa 2 per day; £5, children and bicycles £2.50). Times change daily, and the monthly schedule is difficult to read, so call the tourist information centre

(TIC) for help (☎(01878) 720233). **Hebridean Coaches** (☎(01870) 620345) runs to **Ludag** from the **airport** on Benbecula and Lochboisdale (M-Sa 4-9 per day).

You can see almost all of Barra in a day. Those without cars can take the **postbus** around the island (☎810312; departs Castlebay for Eoligarry M-Sa, £2) or **H. Mac-Neil's minibus** (☎810262; 4 per day, £2.75). **Barra Car Hire** (☎810243) rents from £18 per half-day. By far the best way to see Barra is by **bike**. To rent from **Castlebay Cycle Hire**, drop by the long wooden shed on the main road. (☎810284. From £11 per day, less for 2 or more days. Open daily 10am-1pm.) If you're tired of dry land, try a guided sea-kayaking tour with **Chris Denehy,** and take in the surrounding deserted islands, populated with seals, otter, eagles, and the occasional basking shark. (☎810443. £12 per half-day, £20 per day.)

🛈 PRACTICAL INFORMATION. Castlebay is Barra's primary town, and holds a helpful **tourist information centre,** around the bend and to the right from the pier. They'll find you a B&B for a £3 fee, but book ahead—a wedding, festival, or even positive weather forecast can fill every bed for miles. (☎810336. Open mid-Mar. to mid-Oct. M-Sa 9am-5pm, Su 10-11am; also 1hr. after late ferry arrivals.) Be forewarned: Barra has **no cash machine,** and the only **bank** is across from the TIC. (Open M-Tu and Th-F 9:15am-12:30pm and 1:30-4:45pm, W from 10am.) You can get up to £50 cash back on a credit card if you buy something at the **Co-op** (see below). **Internet access** is available at the **Castlebay School library,** 10min. past the Castlebay Hotel. Book its one terminal ahead. (☎810471. £2 per 30min., £3.50 per hr. Open M-F 9am-1pm and 2-4:30pm, Tu and Th also 6-8pm, Sa 10am-12:30pm.)

Barra is home to the excellent **Dunard Hostel,** a short walk uphill from the pier and around the bend. Run by one of the few young couples who've remained on the island past childhood, the hostel is a wonderfully social, truly Hebridean experience. (☎810443. Dorms £10. **Camping** £7.) Or try **Mrs. Clelland's,** 47 Glen—she runs the cheapest B&B around Castlebay. (☎810438. £18 per person.) Next is Mrs. MacKechnie's **Ravenscroft,** in Nask: spare digs with lots of space. (☎810574. Open May-Sept. £20 per person.) For a drink and solid eats, hit the **Castlebay Bar** uphill from the harbor. (☎810223. Live music Sa-Su. Open M-Sa 11:30am-11:30pm, Su 12:30pm-midnight.) Just below is the **Co-op** food store. (Open M-Sa 8:30am-6pm.)

◨ SIGHTS. Kisimul Castle, bastion of the old Clan MacNeil, floats in stately solitude in the middle of Castlebay Harbor. It lay in ruins for two centuries, and last year was given to Historic Scotland for reconstruction (see graybox, below). It is now open to the public via a rowboat that ferries from the pier to the castle gate. (Call 810313 to be picked up at the pier. £3, students and seniors £2.30, children £1.) For a terrific sampling of island life and Gaelic culture, the local exhibits at the **"Dualchas" Barra Heritage and Cultural Centre,** near the school, are well worth a visit. (☎810413. Open Apr.-Sept. M-F 11am-4pm. £1, children 50p.) The road west from Castlebay passes the brooding, cloud-topped mass of **Ben Tangasdale** before reaching an amazing white beach at **Halaman Bay.** From there the road extends northward past turquoise waters and more white sand. Near the village of **Borve** (Borgh), one squat standing stone remains visible on the left. While an excavation near here did reveal a skeleton and Nordic armor, the stone itself has become a favorite spot for cattle defecation. Opposite Allasdale, **Seal Bay** makes an excellent picnic spot, so bring some herring and make a friend. A detailed map of Barra can reveal numerous standing stones and cairns dotting the hills east of the road.

On the north coast, the huge beach of **Traigh Mhor** provides a spectacular landing spot for daily Loganair flights to Glasgow; planes land only at low tide. Farther north in **Eoligarry** is **Cille Bharra Cemetery.** Still in use, it contains "crusader" headstones thought to have served as ballast in the warship of a clan chief. Inside the neighboring **St. Barr's Church,** step through shrines, Celtic crosses, and Norman stones, as pilgrim candles flicker through the dust. To see the whole island, follow the single-lane **A888,** which makes a 14 mi. circle around the rather steep slopes of Ben Heavel. An excellent road for biking, it follows the coast past stunning beaches and mountains; a detour north to **Eoligarry** winds by ponds and dunes.

> ## WILL THE REAL MACNEIL PLEASE STAND UP?
> On Barra, ancient stronghold of the MacNeil Clan, more than half of the island's 1300 inhabitants still bear the surname MacNeil. In fact, there's so much overlap that the local phonebook listings are sorted by nickname. Yet all MacNeils are not equal: one, known simply as The MacNeil of Barra, owns almost the entire island. Every year, The MacNeil visits Barra to collect £5 in feudal dues from the island's crofters, whose farms he owns. The MacNeil's tyranny has also kept Barra bereft of a cash machine, as he owns the bank but refuses to install one. The MacNeil does have a generous side, however: he recently sold gorgeous Kisimul Castle to the National Trust for Scotland for £1 and a bottle of whisky.

NEAR BARRA: VATERSAY AND MINGULAY

A causeway connects Barra to **Vatersay** (Bhatarsaigh), the small, southernmost inhabited island in the Outer Hebrides. Check out its scenic beaches and the monument to the *Annie Jane*, a ship that sunk off Vatersay in 1853 while carrying 400 would-be emigrants to Canada. Buses run to Vatersay from the Castlebay post office, by the pier (M-Sa 3-4 per day). Bird watchers should visit the deserted island of **Mingulay,** still farther south. Call Mr. Campbell to inquire about boat trips from Castlebay in summer. (☎810223. 2 per week in good weather, £20.)

THE NORTHWEST HIGHLANDS

If you don't mind comically limited public transportation, the pristine beauty of Scotland's northwest is irresistible. Spectacularly isolated, the region is punctuated by small hamlets, dominated by jagged mountains and heather-covered hills, threaded with lochs and waterfalls, and lapped by ocean waves. Grand expanses of mountain and moor stretch along the coast, from the imposing Torridon Hills to the eerie volcanic formations of Inverpolly near Ullapool and finally to Cape Wrath, where waves crash against the highest cliffs in mainland Britain.

▐ TRANSPORTATION

Without a car, tramping the northwestern coast is tricky in summer and nearly impossible the rest of the year. Inverness is the area's main transport hub. **Trains** (☎(08457) 484950) from Inverness run to **Kyle of Lochalsh** (2½hr., 4 per day, £14) and **Thurso** (3¼hr., 3 per day, £12.50). **Scottish Citylink** (☎(08705) 505050) and **Rapson Buses** serve the same routes and also go to **Ullapool,** from where ferries leave for the Outer Hebrides, midway up the northwest coast (1½hr.; in summer M-Sa 4-6 per day, Apr.-May and Sept. to mid-Oct. 4 per day; £5). From April to October, the **Northern Explorer Ticket** provides decent bus transportation, looping from Inverness to Ullapool, Durness, Tongue, and Thurso—if you're lucky, you'll even get a bit of a tour guide. The ticket covers a week of unlimited travel (£25), but you can also ride and pay somewhat pricey single fares (1 bus per day; Ullapool-Durness £10, Durness-Thurso £7; 10% SYHA discount). **Postbuses** are another convenient option—as always, consult the public transport guide, or call a local hostel warden for specific routes in outlying regions. Those who **hitchhike** dance with fate. The few locals drive like devils on the area's narrow, winding roads, but pick up hikers if they don't run them over first. *Let's Go* never recommends hitchhiking.

NEAR KYLE OF LOCHALSH ☎01599

Though the tourist masses rush onward to Skye, the region just east of Kyle of Lochalsh is breathtaking in its own right. The made-for-postcard must-see of the area is **Eilean Donan Castle** (EL-len DOE-nin or "that KA-sil in HI-lan-der"), the restored 13th-century seat of the MacKenzie family and the most photographed monument in Scotland. For the best photographs—those that leave out the unattractive motorway and parking lot—station yourself on the bridge 200 yd. west on the A87. Your photos will be infinitely more impressive than the castle's interior. The castle stands beside the A87 between Inverness and Kyle; take a Scottish Citylink bus and get off at Dornie. (☎555202. Open Apr.-Oct. daily 10am-5:30pm; Mar. and Nov. 10am-3pm. £3.95, concessions £3.20, families £9.50.) If you miss the bus back, **Dornie,** stretched along Loch Long, makes a peaceful place to stay. The small **Silver Fir Dornie Bunkhouse,** Carndubh, sleeps four. Walk 10min. along the loch, 200 yd. past the Catholic chapel, and look for the blue fence. (☎555264. Free tea and coffee. Self-cleaning. Linen £1. £10 per person.)

Six miles off the A87 at Camushunie, Killilan, the ☒**Tigh Iseaball Bunkhouse** is the region's friendliest hostel. With a lovely setting at a mountain's base, the hostel has ping-pong, pool, and a basketball hoop. There's no public transportation, but the owner is happy to pick up those who call ahead from Kyle or Dornie. (☎588205. Tasty free-range eggs included. Dorms £7.50.) The bunkhouse is near the 370 ft. **Falls of Glomach,** an amazing but otherwise tough 1½hr. hike from Glen Elchig. Farther east, the 3505 ft. **Five Sisters of Kintail** tower above the A87, and on the other side of the highway, the spectacular **Mam Ratagan pass** leads to secluded Glenelg.

PLOCKTON ☎01599

Six miles north of Kyle of Lochalsh, the tiny village of Plockton—with palm trees, a rocky beach, and green mountains surrounding a tranquil harbor—certainly deserves the starry-eyed tourists who gasp at its perfection. The **Leisure Marine Office,** on the waterfront, rents canoes, rowboats, and motorboats ($5-12 per hr.). As you relax on the bay's clear waters, keep your eyes peeled for seals, otter, and the occasional porpoise. **Callum's Seal Trips,** at the Main Pier or the Pontoon next to the car park, are free if no seals surface. Signs at either location indicate the departure point for the next trip. (☎544306. 1hr. tours Apr.-Oct. daily at 10am, noon, 2, 4pm, and sometimes evenings. £5, children £3.)

Plockton sits on the main **Inverness-Kyle of Lochalsh rail line,** which runs 5-6 trains per day in each direction. It's also served by the **Kyle-Plockton-Ardnarff postbus service** (#119), departing from Kyle of Lochalsh at 9:45am, arriving in Plockton at 10:35am, then departing from Plockton at 2pm and arriving back in Kyle at 2:55pm. Opposite the train station, the **Station Bunkhouse,** 5min. from the water, has comfortable bedrooms in a two-story cabin. (☎544235. Dorms Apr.-Oct. £10; Nov.-Mar. £8.50.) The owners run a small B&B, **Nessun Dorma,** next door. (£15 per person; singles £20.) For the best meal in town, pricey **Plockton Inn,** opposite the church, specializes in local seafood and cheeses. (Lunch daily noon-2:30pm, dinner 6-9pm.)

APPLECROSS ☎01520

If pleasure is measured in stunning views and dangerous thrills, then the trip to the remote village of Applecross alone merits the visit. The direct route, across the harrowing **Bealach-na-Ba ("Cattle") Pass,** is for the iron-hearted only. At 2054 ft., the steep, single-track Pass is Britain's highest road, punctuated by hairpin turns and various breeds of livestock with little regard for their own lives and even less for yours. On a clear day, drivers are rewarded with expansive views of Skye and the Small Isles; the rest of the time, vehicles are surrounded by mist, and the cliff drop just 5 ft. away is practically invisible. The circuitous **coastal route** is a safer option, offering a much improved beauty-to-risk ratio.

Applecross itself is a lively town whose fantastic local pub tops off a day of outdoor adventure. After recuperating from your journey on the pleasant beach, check out **Mountain & Sea Guides** for half- and full-day kayaking and trekking trips

(£22-35) or longer sea kayaking and mountaineering courses. (☎744393. 3-day to 1-week trips from £145.) From the head of Applecross Bay, a rugged, signposted **hike** rounds the northern peninsula 8 mi. to Kenmore. While still in town, don't miss a meal and pint at the ⧉**Applecross Inn** on the waterfront. The menu rotates but the award-winning food is always delicious, local, and well priced, especially the Ploughman's Lunch of rich cheeses, pickled toppings, red grapes, and breads (£6). On Friday nights from 9:45pm, local musicians play traditional Highland music; join in if you've got talent. (☎744262. Open daily 10am-midnight.)

Pretty **Applecross Campground** is uncrowded. (☎744268. £9 per tent and 2 adults; 1 day free for weekly bookings.) For more solid shelter, **Applecross Inn** has both **B&B** and **hotel** lodgings (£25-35 a night per person). The faraway village is serviced by **postbus** #92 (M-Sa) from **Torridon** (M-Sa 10:30am) and **Shieldaig** (M-Sa 11:30am).

TORRIDON   ☎01445

Just north of the Applecross Peninsula (entire pop. 230), the tiny village of Torridon lies enclosed by Loch Torridon and the Torridon Hills, second in cragginess only to the Cuillins of Skye. This small, beautiful locale draws visitors with its multitude of hiking and climbing opportunities. The highest and closest peak is **Liathach** (3456 ft.), considered by some the biggest bully in Britain. A small climbing community has developed in its shadow.

From Inverness, **trains** (☎(08457) 484950) run to **Achnasheen** (1¼hr.; M-Sa 4 per day, Su 2 per day); there, **postbus** #91 (12:10pm) connects to Torridon. Buses do not meet every train; call ahead (☎(01463) 234111) to confirm times. **Duncan Maclennan** (☎(01520) 755239) shuttle buses connect with the Inverness train at **Strathcarron** station (1hr.; June-Sept. M-Sa 12:30pm, Oct.-May M, W, F only). The staff at the **Ranger Station and Countryside Centre**, at the crossroads into Torridon, 200 yd. from the Torridon hostel, possesses an encyclopedic knowledge of the surrounding region and stocks maps detailing area walks. (Open M-Sa 10am-5pm, Su 1-5pm.) At the base of the daunting Liathach, the large **SYHA Torridon** offers spartan rooms and a friendly staff—not to mention rowdy hill walkers trumpeting their latest exploits. (☎791284. Open Mar.-Oct. Dorms £9.25, under 18 £8.) If you're game for some exploring, the remote coastal **SYHA Craig** is 13 mi. west of Torridon along the B8021. It's a one-hour hike from the end of the road at **Diabaig**, which **postbus** #91 reaches after Torridon. (Open mid-May to Sept. No phone or bedding; bring a sleeping bag. Dorms £6.50, under 18 £5.75.) Between the Torridon hostel and the ranger office, the **Torridon Campsite** has an exquisite location, though it would be difficult to choose an unimpressive one in this region. (☎791313. £3 per tent.) The small **general store** 15min. down the road is your only bet for supplies. (Open M-Sa 9:30am-6pm, Su 10am-noon and 4-6pm.)

GAIRLOCH   ☎01445

Flanked by beautiful coastal scenery and inland mountains, the village of **Gairloch** is 20 winding mi. north of Torridon. Though somewhat less spectacular than Applecross or Plockton, a trip to Gairloch still rewards with a wide, sandy beach—where an occasional seal appears—and the cluttered but impressive **Gairloch Heritage Museum**. (☎712287. Open Apr.-Sept. M-Sa 10am-5pm; Oct. M-F 10am-1:30pm; winter months by arrangement. £2.50, seniors £2, children 50p.) Horseback riders can hire an animal from the **Gairloch Trekking Centre**, ¼ mi. off the main road at Flowerdale. (☎712652. £5 per 30min.) Six miles north along the coast road from Gairloch, the **Inverewe Gardens** are a glorious profusion of flowers and shrubs from all over the world. **Westerbus** (☎712255) runs from Gairloch to the gardens at least once per day Monday through Saturday, but it's best to check the timetable at the tourist information centre (see below) before setting out. (☎781229. Garden open mid-Mar. to Oct. daily 9:30am-9pm; Nov. to mid-Mar. 9:30am-5pm. Visitor center open Apr.-Oct. daily 9:30am-5:30pm. £5, concessions and SYHA hostelers £4. Guided garden walks mid-Apr. to mid-Sept. M-F 1:30pm.)

Westerbuses runs to Gairloch from **Inverness** (2¼-2¾hr., M-Sa 5:05pm, £7). For a £3 fee, the **tourist information centre** books **B&Bs** in Gairloch and Dundonnell, just east of the Ardessie Gorge. (☎712130. Open mid-July to Aug. daily 9am-6pm; mid-Apr. to mid-July 9am-5:30pm; Sept.-Oct. 9am-5:30pm; Nov. to mid-Apr. M-Sa 9am-5:30pm.) Find a quiet, lochside bed at the **SYHA Carn Dearg,** 2 mi. northwest of town in a grand setting. Get off the Gairloch bus at the village of **Strath** and walk toward the sea from there. (☎712219. Reception 7am-10:30am and 5-11:30pm. Curfew 11:30pm. Open mid-May to Sept. Dorms £8.75, under 18 £7.50.) Just beyond the hostel, campers can pitch at the beachside **Sands Holiday Centre** (☎712152; £8-10 per tent) or right in Strath at the **Gairloch Caravan & Camping Holiday Park** (☎712373; £8.50 per tent).

ULLAPOOL   ☎01854

Compared to its northwest neighbors, buzzing Ullapool feels downright cosmopolitan. But while tourists are drawn by amenities, pub life, and transport links to the Outer Hebrides, no amount of company can mar Ullapool's mountain views and narrow bay. The area is rife with **hikes** long and short, including an excellent local ramble through the woodlands of **Ullapool Hill,** where the summit offers impressive views of Glenn Achall. Footpaths begin behind the swinging gates 200 yd. past the school on North Rd. and behind the Royal Hotel on Shore St. (round-trip 2hr.). The **SYHA Youth Hostel** (see below) provides a free leaflet detailing a longer walk that traverses **Scots Pine** and the **Inverpolly Nature Reserve.** They can also suggest how to **cycle** to nearby hostels in **Carbisdale** and **Achiniver.** In town, the award-winning **Ullapool Museum,** housed in an old church on West Argyle St., uses audiovisual displays to recount the history of Ullapool and the surrounding region. (☎612987. Open M-Sa 9:30am-5:30pm. £2, students and seniors £1.50, children free.)

Except for 1am arrivals, **ferries** from **Stornoway, Lewis** (M-Sa 2-3 per day; £13, 5-day return £22.35) are met by **Scottish Citylink** and **Rapsons Buses** to and from **Inverness** (1½hr., £5.30). Ullapool's **tourist information centre,** Argyle St., books rooms for a £3 fee. (☎612135; fax 613031. Open Apr.-Oct. M-Sa 9am-5:30pm, Su noon-4:30pm; Nov.-Mar. M-Sa 2-5:30pm.) **Caledonian MacBrayne** (☎612358) runs a variety of day-long summer **cruise tours** to Lewis (from £15.20). Smaller boats conduct wildlife-watching **tours** (☎612472; £8-15) to the nearby **Summer Isles** (see p. 621); inquire at the booths by the pier. **Scotpackers West House** (see below) runs half- and full-day minibus **tours** of the area (£10-15, for guests £9-13.50). The **post office** sits at West Argyle St. (☎612228. Open M-Tu and Th-F 9am-1pm and 2-5:30pm, W and Sa 9am-1pm.) **Postal code:** IV26 2TY.

🖪**Scotpackers West House,** West Argyle St., answers all backpacker needs with towering bunks and easy chairs. Internet access is free for guests (£1 per 20min. for non-guests) and bike rental is £10 per day. (☎613126. Dorms £9.25.) The affiliated **Crofton House** has double rooms, but phone the hostel first. (☎612683. £25 per room.) The well-situated **SYHA Youth Hostel,** Shore St., 100 yd. right of the pier, compensates for smallish bunks with outstanding harbor views and amenities. Book ahead. (☎612254. Laundry facilities. Internet access 50p per 12min. Bike hire £6-12 per day. Dorms £9.25, under 18 £8.) At the west end of town, pitch your tent for £5 at the **Broomfield Holiday Park** (☎612026). **All-Days,** West Argyle St., has groceries galore (open M-Sa 7am-10pm, Su 8am-10pm). 🖪**The Seaforth,** by the pier, is the place to be seen, with frequent live music and a mouth-watering selection of whiskies. After a high-quality meal (£6-9), sample a hard-to-find Laphroaig 15 Year Old, a startlingly distinctive malt. (Open daily 10am-midnight.) **The Ceilidh Place,** 14 West Argyle St. (☎612103), is a hotel, cafe, bar, bookstore, and gallery; the cafe is open until 9pm and stomps to Celtic music several nights a week in summer.

NEAR ULLAPOOL   ☎01854

CORRIESHALLOCH GORGE. . ACHILTIBUIE. Northwest of Ullapool, a gentler beauty awaits at **Achiltibuie,** a small village flanked by two alluring nature reserves and a trio of sandy beaches. **Spa Coaches** leave from Ullapool (M-F 2 per day, Sa 1 per day; £2.50). If driving, take the A835 north 10 mi., then turn left at the well-marked one-lane road and follow it west 15 mi. The idyllic 🖪**SYHA Achiniver** occupies an old cottage ¼ mi. from a sandy beach and 3 mi. from Achiltibuie. Ask the bus driver to let you off at the roadside sign for the hostel; the sign claims it's ½ mi. from there, though it's actually less. (☎622254. Open mid-May to Sept. Dorms £7.50, under 18 £6.25.) It's worth walking into Achiltibuie proper for the ◼Lily Pond Cafe, which serves a delicious three-course roast lunch for £7 (12:30-5pm) using only the freshest ingredients. (Open mid-Apr. to Sept. daily 10am-6pm; June-Aug. also Th-Su 7-9pm.) The Cafe is part of the odd Hydroponi-cum, a self-proclaimed "garden of the future," where produce is grown without soil because cultivating fruits outdoors is impossible. (☎622202. Tours Easter-Sept. 10am-5pm. £4.75, students and seniors £3.50, children £2.75.) At the Achilti-buie Smokehouse, patrons can watch as salmon and other foods are sliced and smoked. Buy your culinary souvenirs here: 200g of smoked Highland eel is only £16. (☎622353. Open M-Sa 9:30am-5:00pm. Free.)

Off the coast of Achiltibuie, the lovely **Summer Isles** are so named because local crofters graze their sheep here during high season. The Isles are home to rugged rock formations, radiant beaches, and a seal colony. Tour them from **Ullapool** (see p. 621) or, more thoroughly, on the passenger vessel **Hectoria** from **Badentarbet Pier** in Achiltibuie. The Hectoria passes by the seal colony and allows an hour ashore for exploring. (3½hr. tours M-Sa at 10:30am and 2:15pm. £15, children £7.50.)

LOCHINVER
☎01571

Thirty miles up the northwest coast, the unremarkable town of Lochinver is a nec-essary outpost for the wild region of **Assynt,** breathtakingly desolate but nearly impossible to penetrate without a car. The **Assynt Visitor Centre** on the waterfront in Lochinver has an informative exhibit on the area, and serves as a **tourist information centre** with a £3 booking service. (☎844330. Open Easter-Oct. daily 10am-5pm.) The **Ranger Service** (☎844654) based here offers free **guided walks** during summer.

Assynt is known for its long-distance treks up the imposing mountains of **Suilven** and **Canisp** (8-10hr.); though lengthy, these trails are well cleared and accessible to walkers of all levels. Get advice from the Visitor Centre and supplies from **Assynt Adventures,** up the road in Lochinver. Another good hike stays closer to town. Turn left from the Visitor Centre; the signposted second left leads to **Glencanisp Lodge,** where a footpath famed for sightings of deer, otter, and golden eagles proceeds to skirt the River Inver. At the path's end, retrace your steps to return home (round-trip 2hr.). The **Culaig Wood Walk,** starting beyond the field near the pier, is shorter. From the Achmelvich hostel (see below), a **nature trail** crosses the town of **Alt-na-Bradhan** before reaching the striking rock formation at **Clachtoll** (round-trip 5hr.).

The only public transport to enter this forbidding country are the **Northern Explorer** buses, **Rapsons Coaches,** and **Spa Coaches** from Ullapool (1hr., 2-3 per day, £3-4), as well as **postbus** #123 from the Lairg train station (M-Sa 1pm). The **Spar** supermarket at the town's entrance (open M-Sa 8am-6:30pm, Su 9am-5:30pm) is across from the Esso **petrol station.** At the other end of town, before the pier and behind the stone wall, the **Royal Bank of Scotland** has a **cash machine.** (Bank open M-Tu and Th-F 9:15am-12:30pm and 1:30-4:45pm, W from 10am.)

The **Ardglas Guest House,** across the stone bridge, is Lochinver's cheapest **B&B,** with fine views and spacious rooms. (☎844257. Singles and doubles £16.) **Hostels** are far away, but in dramatic locations with great access to hiking and cycling trails. The rugged (read: bare) **SYHA Achmelvich,** Recharn, is 3 mi. down a stunning footpath or 20min. by the 11:15am postbus. (☎844480. Reception 7-10:30am and 5-11pm. Curfew 11pm. Open Apr.-Oct. Dorms £6.75, under 18 £6.) Mr. MacLeod runs the nearby **Achmelvich campsite,** beside a Caribbean-style beach—until you sample the icy waters. (☎844393. Tent pitch £7.) Farther inland, the heart-rending ruins of **Ardvreck Castle** on Loch Assynt sit opposite the social **Inchnadamph Lodge,** Assynt Field Centre, which has endless amenities and a boisterous atmosphere. (☎822218. Breakfast included. Internet access £2 per first 30min., £1 per each additional 30min. Dorms £9.95; doubles and twins £13.50-15.) Ullapool-Lochinver buses, including the Northern Explorer, stop here on request.

DURNESS
☎01971

A quiet village on Scotland's north coast, Durness combines outstanding natural beauty with plenty of activities, making it a popular stop on a northwest tour. Ten minutes west of town, the secluded **Balnakeil Beach** would seem tropical if it weren't for the puffin colony farther out on **Faraid Head.** A mile up the road from the town center, the **Smoo Caves** take their name from *smuga*, the Viking word for hiding place—legend has it that centuries ago the bastard son of a McKay chieftain hid the bodies of 18 men here. When the eerie caverns aren't flooded, you can float via rubber dinghy past the interior waterfall. (☎511704; ask for Colin. 15min. tours depart from cave entrance Apr.-Sept. daily 10am-5pm. £2.50, children £1.) At the Smoo cave inlet, **Cape Sea Tours** runs wildlife boat-watches at noon and 7pm, taking in Faraid Head and the Cliffs of Moine Schist, with frequent sightings of gray seals, white-beaked dolphins, minke whales, and the ubiquitous puffin. (☎511284 or 511259. £6.50, children £3.50.) Britain's highest cliffs tower at **Cape Wrath,** 12 mi. west of Durness. From the Cape Wrath Hotel (1½ mi. west down the road from the town center), a ferry crosses to **Kyle of Durness** (☎511376; return £3.80), where it's met by a **minibus** that completes the trip to Cape Wrath (☎511287 or 511343; return £6.50). Together, the ferry and bus operate on demand May through September starting at 9:30am. (Incidentally, the Cape closes every now and then so the Royal Air Force can practice blowing stuff up—the ferry operator will tell you when you call.)

To reach Durness, hop on **postbus** #104 or 105 from the **Lairg** train station. **Highland Country** bus #387 arrives from **Thurso** (2½hr., June to mid-Sept. M-Sa 1 per day, £7) and **Tim Dearman** coaches from **Inverness** and **Ullapool** (same frequency, at least £10). The **tourist information centre** books local B&Bs for £3. (☎511259. Open mid-July to mid-Aug. M-Sa 9am-6pm, Su 10am-6pm; Mar. to mid-July and mid-Aug. to Oct. daily 10am-5pm.) The **post office** is down the road. (Open M-Tu and Th-F 9am-5:30pm, W and Sa 9am-12:30pm.) The best budget lodgings are provided by the amiable **Lazycrofter Bunkhouse,** whose dull exterior does little justice to its luxurious bunks and nifty showers. (Daytime ☎511209 or evening 511366. £9.) The simple **SYHA Durness,** 1 mi. from town along the A838, has only one shower for its 40 guests. (☎511244. Reception 7-10:30am and 5-11pm. Curfew 11pm. Open Apr.-Sept. Dorms £6.75, under 18 £6.) **Sango Sands Camping Site** overlooks the sea next to the visitor center. To the left find a sandy beach, to the right the site's own pub. (Tent pitch £4. Showers 50p.) Mrs. Sutherland provides a less communal respite at her **Smoo Falls B&B,** 15min. toward the caves from the town center. (☎511228. £17 per person, with bath £19; singles £21-24.) **Mace supermarket** stocks essentials in town. (☎511209. Open M-F 8am-5:30pm, Sa 9am-12:30pm and 1:30-5:30pm.)

TONGUE
☎01847

The town of Tongue twists east of Durness on the kyle (strait) bearing the same name. To the north, long, empty beaches ring turquoise waters, while imposing ridges and mountains rise from the loch's south end. The 14th-century ruins of **Castle Varrick** stand precariously above the water. The **Northern Explorer** hits Tongue (June-Sept. M-Sa) on its way between Thurso and Durness, as do **school buses** (M-F). A **postbus** reaches town from the Lairg train station (M-Sa). Knowledgeable wardens and surprisingly comfortable digs await at **SYHA Tongue,** perching at Tongue's tip, ¾ mi. toward the causeway of Loch Eriboll. The postbus will drop you outside the door. (☎611301. Open Apr.-Sept. Dorms £8.25, under 18 £7.)

THURSO AND SCRABSTER
☎01847

A big fish in a very, very small pond, Thurso, bursting at the seams with a population of 9000, is considered a veritable Tokyo by the crofters and fishermen of Scotland's desolate north coast. The city has no museums, and doesn't seem to care; even the refreshingly frank **tourist information centre** (TIC), Riverside Rd., treats the obligatory **castle ruins** east of town with indifference. (TIC open June-Sept. daily 10am-6pm; May and Oct. M-Sa 9am-5pm, Su 11am-5pm; Apr. M-Sa 10am-5pm.)

Thurso's distinct urban character is complemented by one of the best **surfing beaches** in Europe, just below the castle. Scrabster, 2½ mi. east, is no more than a ferry port to the Orkney Islands.

Infectiously friendly, ◙**Sandra's Backpackers Hostel,** 24-26 Princes St., sports the spirit of Thurso in miniature. Dorms each have TV, kitchenette, and bath, and the owners provide lifts to Scrabster for ferry connections. (☎894575. Breakfast included. Internet access 75p per 15min. Bike rental £8 per day. Dorms £8.50, £7.50 with your own linen.) The **Thurso Youth Club Hostel,** stashed in a converted mill, is open only in July and August. From the train station, walk down Lover's Ln., turn left on Janet St., cross the footbridge over the river, and follow the footpath to the right. (☎892964. Breakfast and linen included. Dorms £8.) Heather Shone runs the amazing **Kramada B&B,** 30 Sinclair St., in the center of town; her ornate wooden rooms are obscenely luxurious. (☎893592. £22 per person.)

For good eats, **Sandra's Snack Bar and Takeaway,** underneath the hostel, is a happening backpacker hangout with rock-bottom prices and tasty pizzas, curries, and fried fish. Hostel guests get a 10% discount. (☎894595. Open M-F 7:30am-11:30pm, Sa 10am-2am, Su 12:30-10:30pm.) On Wednesdays, young and old alike come for traditional live music at **Commercial ("Comm") Bar,** 1 Princes St., Thurso's most popular gathering. (☎893366. Open M-Th 11am-midnight, F-Sa 11am-1am, Su noon-11pm. W music starts 9:45pm.) **Newmarket Bar,** Traill St., also serves up a lively pint. (☎895803. Open M-Sa 11am-midnight, Su 11am-11pm.)

JOHN O'GROATS   ☎01955

While you may have heard of the town—it's the Isle of Great Britain's northern-most—John O'Groats is hardly pretty, having been systematically robbed of native charm and stormed by touristy shops. If stuck on the mainland for a night, head for Thurso (see p. 623). Fortunately, the seas around John O'Groats have been spared uglification. **Wildlife Cruises,** run by **John O'Groats Ferries,** leave the docks daily at 2:30pm to explore the rugged waters of Pentland Firth, home to razorbills, gray seals, kittiwakes, great black backs, and other animals you've never heard of. (1½hr. £12, children £6, under 5 free. No booking required.) **Dunnet Head,** halfway between Thurso and John O'Groats, is the true northernmost point of mainland Britain, but **Duncansby Head,** about 2 mi. outside John O'Groats, has a more impressive view overlooking the Pentland Firth. The **tourist information centre** (TIC), by the pier, helps plan escapes to the more attractive surrounding areas. (☎611373. Open June-Sept. daily 10am-6pm; Apr.-May and Oct. 10am-5pm.)

To reach town from **Wick** train station, take **Highland Country** bus #77 (40min.; M-Sa 4-7 per day, Su 4 per day). From May to August, **Orkney Bus** (run by John O'Groats Ferries) rides from **Inverness** (daily 2:20pm, June-Aug. also 7:30am; £12). **Harrold Coaches** run from **Thurso** (1hr., M-Sa 2-4 per day). Both routes ignore the train schedules but do pass by the simple **SYHA John O'Groats,** somewhat removed 3 mi. away at Canisbay. (☎611424. Open Mar.-Sept. Dorms £8.25, under 18 £7.)

ORKNEY ISLANDS   ☎01856

Bjørn was here.
   —ancient rune carved into Orcadian standing stone

Across the broad and occasionally rough Pentland Firth, the emerald villages, red sandstone cliffs, and iris-studded farmlands of the Orkneys (pop. 19,500) are remote treasures reserved for the perseverant traveler. Removed from the tourist trail, Orkney's timeless assemblage of paddocks, beaches, and gardens—trod by Orcadians for millennia—are relatively challenging to reach, and even more diffi-cult to travel between once you get there. Still, though public transportation is minimal, and samplings of Orkney's Stone Age sights are visible elsewhere in Scot-land, the 70-island archipelago retains some of the best-preserved Pictish and Viking villages, monuments, and burial chambers in Europe. The Pentlend Skerries and the islands of Westray, Papa Westray, and Copinsay (all pronounced to rhyme with "see") are also sacred to ornithology pilgrims—337 species of birds alight on or inhabit Orkney, and the feathered outnumber people 100 to 1.

Mainland (sometimes called Pomona) is Orkney's main island, with its two largest towns. The small capital city of Kirkwall encases a dramatic 12th-century cathedral, still in use, and a fine medieval and Renaissance palace. Quieter still, Stromness invites visitors to wander down small wynds to the waterside, where the cliffs shelter elderducks, fulmar petrels, and the occasional puffin in summer. The southeastern seaside holds more modern secrets as well—at low tide, broken prows and sterns of sunken blockships rear up from the sea foam along the Churchill Barriers, causeways built by POWs during WWII.

✖ GETTING THERE

Ferries connect Orkney to mainland Scotland. The new **Pentland Ferries** (☎ 831226) run the most budget-friendly service to Orkney, from **Gills Bay,** just west of John O'Groats on the A836, to **St. Margaret's Hope,** on Orkney. From there, a free bus meets the ferry to bring passengers to **Kirkwall.** The bus servicing the late ferry is unreliable; call ahead to make sure one is planned. (1hr.; 9:45am, 1:45pm, 6:45pm; £10, children £5, under 5 free; reservations recommended in off season.)

John O'Groats Ferries (☎ (01955) 611353) travels from **John O'Groats** to **Burwick, Orkney,** where a free bus takes passengers to Kirkwall. (Ferry 45min., bus 35min.; June-Aug. 9, 10:30am, 4, 6pm; May 9am and 6pm; Sept. 9am and 4:30pm; return £28, off-peak afternoon departure and morning return £25.) The **Orkney Bus,** run by John O'Groats Ferries from **Inverness** (Bus Platform #1), connects with the ferry in John O'Groats. A single ticket purchased in Inverness covers all transportation from Inverness to **Kirkwall.** (From Inverness to Kirkwall 5hr.; May 2:20pm; June-Aug. also 7:30am; £28, return £40.) The 7:30am bus must be booked in advance; once in Burwick, travelers have the option of joining a whirlwind guided tour of the archipelago back in time for the 6pm ferry, ending in Inverness at 9pm. (Transport and day-tour £44, children £22, under 5 free. Reservations ☎ (01955) 611353.) A free bus also runs from **Thurso** train station to John O'Groats.

P&O Scottish Ferries (☎/fax (01224) 572615) depart from **Scrabster** (near Thurso) for **Stromness, Orkney.** The longer ride takes you past the famous Old Man of Hoy (see p. 629); these ferries are a bit cozier than their John O'Groats counterparts (2hr.; Apr.-Oct. daily at noon, M-F also 6am, M and F-Sa also 5:45pm; Nov.-Mar. M-Sa at noon, M and F also 6am; return £33, low-season £31, 5-day return £24; 10% student and senior discount). A bus departs from **Thurso** train station for Scrabster before each crossing (85p). P&O also sails from **Aberdeen** to **Stromness** every Saturday at noon (8hr.; June-Aug. also Tu at noon; single from £43.50, return from £87).

◩ LOCAL TRANSPORTATION

Orkney Coaches (☎ 870555) run between **Kirkwall** bus station and **Stromness Pier Head** (30min., M-Sa 1-2 per hr., £2.20). **Orkney Ferries** (☎ 872044) service the outer islands. Ferries leave from **Kirkwall** to: **Shapinsay** (45min., 5-6 per day, £2.50); **Sanday** (1½hr., 2 per day, £5); **Westray/Papa Westray** (1½hr., 2-3 per day, £5); **Eday** (2hr., 2 per day, £5); **Stronsay** (1½-2hr., 1-2 per day, £5); **North Ronaldsay** (2¾hr., weekly on F in summer only, £5). Ferries leave from **Houton Pier,** accessible from Kirkwall by bus (30min., 5 per day, £1.40) to **Hoy** (45min.; Tu-Th 3 per day, M and F 6 per day, Sa-Su 2 per day; £2.50) and **Flotta** (M-Sa 3 per day, occasional Su service in summer; £2.50). Ferries leave from **Tingwall** (catch a bus from Kirkwall bus station, 35min., 5 per day) to **Rousay/Egilsay/Wyre** (30min., M-Sa 6 per day, £2.50). For exact times, get the *Islands of Orkney* from the Stromness or Kirkwall tourist information centres. Winter ferries are far less frequent. It's also possible to fly to many of the islands from Kirkwall Airport; call **British Airways** (☎ 872494).

Car rental, if you can afford it, is by far the most convenient way of getting around Orkney; for rental agencies, see **W.R. Tullock** and **Peace's Car Hire** in Kirkwall (below), and **Stromness Car Hire** (p. 627). The less profligate should consider **biking**, though the rain and wind can be problematic. Bikes can be rented in Kirkwall from **Bobby Cycle Centre** (below) or in Stromness at **Orkney Cycle Hire** (p. 627). Rates are slightly cheaper in Kirkwall, and the town has better access to the good Mainland sights; consider taking the bus from Stromness.

KIRKWALL   ☎ 01856

Friendly and self-confident, Kirkwall (pop. 7000) exists primarily for those who live and work there. Unaccustomed to tourists, the historic town—whose ancient structures testify to its significance—is the administrative and social center of the Islands, and provides the most appealing base for exploring their mysteries.

⚐ PRACTICAL INFORMATION. Rent cars from **Peace's Car Hire** (☎872866) and **W.R. Tullock** (☎876262), both of which will meet you at the airport or ferry port (21+; £34-43 per day). **Bobby Cycle Centre**, Tankerness Ln., off Broad St., rents **bikes.** (☎875777. £8-10 per day. Open M-Sa 9am-5:30pm.) The **tourist information centre** (TIC), 6 Broad St., books B&Bs for £1.50 and is the only place in Orkney with **Internet access.** (☎872856. Open Apr.-Sept. daily 8:30am-8pm; Oct.-Apr. M-Sa 9:30am-5pm.) Other services include: **Bank of Scotland,** 56 Albert St. (open M-Tu and Th-F 9am-5pm, W 10am-5pm); **Kelvinator Launderama,** Albert St. (open M-F 8:30am-5:30pm, Sa 9am-5pm); and the **post office,** 15 Junction Rd. (☎874249; open M-Tu and Th-F 9am-5pm, W 9am-4pm, Sa 9:30am-12:30pm). **Postal code:** KW15 1AA.

⚏☐ ACCOMMODATIONS AND FOOD. Kirkwall's **SYHA Youth Hostel** is on Old Skapa Rd. Turn left and follow the main road from the TIC for ½ mi. as it evolves from Broad St. into Victoria St. Cross over Union St., Main St., and then High St., where SYHA signs will carry you home (15min). Lodgings are unluxurious, but the warm atmosphere more than compensates. (☎872243. Reception 7:30-10:30am and 5-11:30pm. Lockout 10:30am-5pm. Curfew midnight. Open Apr.-Oct. Dorms £9, under 18 £7.75.) If you're catching an early ferry out of Kirkwall, **Peedie Hostel,** 1 Ayre Rd., near the pier, has tiny bunk beds and an equally tiny bathroom. (☎875477. Dorms £9.50.) At **Vangee B&B,** Weyland Park off Cromwell Rd., Mrs. Hume rents tasteful, harbor-view rooms that seem targeted by the cannons across the street. (☎873013. £14 per person.) **Camp** at **Pickaquoy Centre Caravan & Camping Site,** on Pickaquoy Rd. off the A965. (☎879900. £3.50-4.65 per person.) You can pitch a tent almost anywhere on the islands, but ask landowners first.

    Safeway dominates the corner of Broad St. and Great Western Rd. (☎228876. Open M-F 8am-9pm, Sa 8am-8pm, Su 9am-6pm.) **Buster's Diner,** 1 Mounthoolie Ln., is draped in tacky Americana and cooks up tasty pizza for under £5—but what's with the Statue of Liberty? (☎876717. Open M-F noon-2pm and 5-10pm, Sa noon-2am, Su noon-10pm.) **Trenabies Cafe,** 16 Albert St., encourages caffeine addictions and tooth decay with sweet pastries and cappuccino. (☎874336. Open M-F 8am-6pm, Sa 9:30am-6pm.) Whether you're downing a Dark Island Ale while watching football or sipping a Highland Park whisky and arguing religion with the locals, **The Bothy Bar** is the place to be in Kirkwall. (☎876000. Open M-W 11am-midnight, Th-Sa 11am-1am, Su noon-midnight; food until 9:30pm.)

◨ SIGHTS. South of the TIC on Broad St., **St. Magnus Cathedral,** begun in 1137, houses the bones of its founder's uncle, St. Magnus himself. Grave markers dating from the 16th and 17th centuries line the aisles; their grim *memento mori* ("Remember Death") and halting poetry are poignant reminders of the past. (Open Apr.-Sept. M-Sa 9am-6pm, Su 2-6pm; Oct.-Mar. M-Sa 9am-1pm and 2-5pm. Free.) Across Palace Rd. from the cathedral, the **Bishop's and Earl's Palaces** once housed the Bishop of Orkney and his enemy, the wicked Earl Patrick Stewart, who was later executed for treason. Now roofless, the Earl's Palace's illustrated plaques give a good impression of a 17th-century earl and his domestic affairs. (☎871918. Both buildings open Apr.-Sept. daily 9:30am-6pm; Oct.-Nov. M-Sa 9:30am-4pm, Su

> **BA'. . .NOT JUST FOR SHEEP** Amid all the puffin sightings and archaeological digs lurks a more lively Orkney tradition—the Ba'. Best described as a large rugby game with no rules and no limit on time or team size, the Ba' takes place on New Year's Day. Two teams—whose ranks have been known to swell to 400—take to the streets of Kirkwall, the Uppies (from the upper part of town) and the Doonies (you figure it out). The action begins in front of St. Magnus Cathedral, when a specially crafted Ba' ball is thrown to the waiting throngs. The massive scrum can continue for hours, ending at nightfall. There are no time-outs or penalties, although the once-tried practice of smuggling the Ba' ball in a car is frowned upon. The Uppies quest to chuck the ball into the harbor, while the Doonies labor to hit the side of the town hall: the hardy soul deemed most valuable player gets to keep it.

2-4pm. £2, seniors £1.50, children 75p. £7.50 combination ticket allows entry into both palaces plus Skara Brae, Maes Howe, and the Broch of Gurness.)

It's worth your while to visit the **Orkney Museum,** Tankerness House, opposite St. Magnus Cathedral, where fun exhibits help contextualize the islands' sights. Ancient artifacts, early photographs, and paintings by native son Stanley Cursiter share space in the house and garden of an Orkney Laird (absentee landowner). (☎873191. Open May-Sept. M-Sa 10:30am-5pm, Su 2-5pm; Oct.-Apr. M-Sa 10:30am-5pm. Free.) Twenty minutes south of town lies the **Highland Park Distillery Visitor Centre,** Holm Rd., the world's northernmost whisky distillery and purveyors of acclaimed single malts. Walk to the end of Broad St./Victoria St., turn left on Clay Loan, right on Bignold Park Rd., and take the right fork onto Holm Rd. (☎874619. Open Apr.-Oct. M-F 10am-5pm; July-Sept. also Sa-Su noon-5pm, last tour 4pm; Nov.-Mar. M-F 1-5pm, tours at 2pm. £3, students and seniors £2, children £1.50.)

STROMNESS   ☎01856

Founded in the 16th century as a fishing and whaling port, Stromness (pop. 2000) is a town of narrow cobblestone streets and beautiful open vistas. The **P&O Ferry** floats here from Scrabster (see p. 625); almost everything is along the harbor on Victoria St. The **Pier Arts Centre** heads Victoria St. and is worth a walk-through to view the work of contemporary Scottish artists. (☎850209. Open Tu-Sa 10:30am-12:30pm and 1:30-5pm; July-Aug. also Su 2-5pm. Free.) The **Stromness Museum,** 52 Alfred St., tackles the history of the sea with artifacts from the whaling and fishing industries. (☎850025. Open May-Sept. daily 10am-5pm; Oct.-Apr. M-Sa 10:30am-12:30pm and 1:30-5pm. £2.50, students and seniors £2, children 50p.)

Stromness Car Hire, 75 Johns St., **rents cars** from £25 per day, less after two days. (☎850973 or 851777. £12.50 deposit. 21+.) **Rent bikes** at **Orkney Cycle Hire,** 54 Dundas St. (☎850255. £5.50-6.50 per day. Open daily 8:30am-9pm.) The **tourist information centre** (TIC), in an 18th-century warehouse on the pier, provides the free *Stromness Heritage Guide.* (☎850716. Open Apr.-Oct. M-W and F-Sa 8am-8pm, Th 8am-6pm, Su 9am-4pm; Nov.-Mar. M-F 9am-5pm; also open to meet late ferry arrivals.) The **Bank of Scotland** is on Victoria St. (open M-F 9:45am-12:30pm and 1:30-4:45pm, W from 10:45am), as is the **post office,** 37 Victoria St. (☎850225; open M-F 9am-1pm and 2-5:15pm, Sa 9am-12:30pm). **Postal code:** KY16 3BS.

A ½ mi. from the TIC (turn left onto Victoria St., then right onto Hellihold Rd.), the **SYHA Stromness** is not as infernal as its address suggests. Perched above the pier, it offers comforting sea views, a relaxing dining area, and a friendly warden. (☎850589. Lockout 10:30am-5pm. Open mid-Mar. to Oct. Dorms £8.25, under 18 £7.) The rooms at **Brown's Hostel,** 45-47 Victoria St., 5min. down the same route, have better beds but less space in a B&B atmosphere. (☎850661. £2 key deposit. Dorms £9.) The **Point of Ness Caravan and Camping Site** is a mile from the pierhead. (☎875353, ext. 2404 851235. Open May to mid-Sept. £3-5.25.) On the pier, **Julia's Coffee Shop,** 20 Ferry Rd., has delicious baked goods and sandwiches for £2-5. Down a creamy hot chocolate as sunlight pours through bay windows. (☎850904. Open M-Sa 9am-5pm; Easter-Sept. also Su 10am-4pm.)

OTHER MAINLAND SIGHTS

Mainland is endowed with an astonishing wealth of Stone Age and Viking remains, particularly around Stromness and Kirkwall—not to mention the billowing mist, rocky promontories, and primrose expanses that cover the islands. Excellent walks abound, but getting to many sights without a car or superhuman stamina can be tricky, since public transport is either scant or absent. In the summer, **bus** #8A runs twice per day in either direction from Kirkwall to Stromness, hitting the three main archaeological sites: the Standing Stones of Stenness, the Ring of Brodgar, and Skara Brae. Despite endless uphills and winds that make downhills laborious, **cycling** may be the best and cheapest way to do Orkney justice.

If you want guidance, ranger-naturalist Michael Hartley of **Wildabout Tours** squires visitors around Mainland and Hoy in his minibus on half- and full-day tours. With a vigorous imagination and encyclopedic knowledge of Orkney, Michael helps visitors envision the Islands of over 5000 years ago. (☎851011. Tours March-Oct. daily. From £10; student and hosteler discounts.) Orkney native John Grieve leads **Discover Orkney Tours** (☎872865), which crafts trips to meet your interests (from £10). John will also take you to the other islands—a great way to see the smaller landmasses if you lack time or transport (from £29). Both guides leave from the TICs in Kirkwall and Stromness. If arranged ahead of time, John Grieve will also pick you up from your ferry, plane, or accommodation.

■ **SKARA BRAE.** Dating back 4000 years, Skara Brae was once a bustling Stone Age village. As the ocean crept farther in, waves gradually consumed the village houses; after approximately 600 years of continuous habitation, the villagers abandoned the settlement. Preserved in sand, the village slept quietly until 1850, when a violent storm ripped out the side of the cliff and revealed nine houses, a workshop, and covered town roads, all in perfect condition. While the visitor center is open only during the day, the site remains accessible until nightfall—a trip at dusk avoids tourists and the admission fee. The **Skaill House** is the 17th-century home of the lairds of Breckness, the family who rediscovered the island. *(By the Bay of Skaill.* ☎841501. *Open Apr.-Sept. daily 9:30am-6:30pm; Oct.-Mar. M-Sa 9:30am-4:30pm, Su 2-4:30pm. Skara Brae and Skaill House £4.50, seniors £3.30, children £1.30.)*

RING OF BRODGAR. Five miles from Skara Brae on the A965, the sedimentary sandstones of the Ring of Brodgar once witnessed gatherings about which no two archaeologists agree. Some believe the upright ring, which now counts 36 stones but used to number 60, marked a meeting place for local chieftains; others propose that dead bodies were left here to the elements and the birds. Now filled in for the safety of visitors, a deep ditch around the circle would have warded off dogs and wild predators. The Ring has stayed true to its heritage as a venue for unusual assemblies. Drawn by deep amber sunsets that silhouette the stones against a blazing sun, a motley crew congregates annually for the summer solstice.

STANDING STONES OF STENNESS. Only a mile from the Ring on the A965, the Standing Stones of Stenness are somewhat less impressive. The stones once numbered 12, but by 1760 only four remained—no one knows what became of the other eight, but some suggest that they were knocked down by locals angered by the monument's pagan origins. Recently, evidence of a possible priests' settlement has been found near the site.

MAES HOWE TOMB. Accessible from the A965, the tomb may have held the bones of the earliest settlers in the area from approximately 2700 BC. According to runic graffiti, Viking raiders broke through the roof and spent three glorious days hauling treasure out of the chamber. The runes are almost more of an attraction than the tomb itself—the largest collection of runic inscriptions in the world, they enabled linguists to crack the runic alphabet and translate profound statements such as "This was carved by the greatest rune carver" and "Ingigerth is the most exquisite of women." (☎761606. *Open Apr.-Sept. daily 9:30am-6:30pm; Oct.-Mar. M-Sa 9:30am-4:30pm, Su 2-4:30pm. £2.50, seniors £1.90, children £1.)*

THE BROUGH OF BIRSAY. An island showing evidence of early Christian and Viking habitation, the Brough is just off the northwest coast of Mainland. Once the administrative and religious center of Orkney, the island's kirkyard holds a Pictish stone engraving of a royal figure with a crown, suggesting that Orcadian kings once ruled from here. The Brough is accessible by foot only in the hour before and after low tide. Bird-watching is absorbing, but linger too long and the puffins may become your bedfellows. *(Open mid-June to Sept. £1.50, seniors £1.10, children 50p.)*

CHURCHILL BARRIERS. In 1940, Prime Minister Churchill erected these massive barriers to seal four straights that once led to the naval anchorage at **Scapa Flow.** The previous year, German U-boats had entered the straights during an exceptionally high tide, killing 800 seamen and escaping unscathed. Over ¼ million tons of rock were exhausted in the undertaking, and the barrier's **causeways** now provide access from Mainland to the smaller southeast islands of **Lamb Holm, Glimps Holm, Burray,** and **South Ronaldsay.** If you cross the barriers at dusk, look closely for one of the sinister oil tankers that patrols the distant North Sea, shrouded in mist.

Scapa Flow witnessed another infamous WWII event: the scuttling of 74 German warships by Admiral Ludwig von Reuter, which earned him the world record for most ships sunk at one time. To the delight of scuba divers, seven of the wrecks remain. **Scapa Scuba** offers a lesson to the non-certified, equipment, and dive to the wrecks for £55. (**☎**851218.) If you don't want to get wet, Roving Eye Enterprises does the marine work for you via a roaming underwater camera. (**☎**811360. *Tours leave Houton Pier daily 1:20pm.)*

SMALLER ISLANDS

BEYOND THE BARRIERS. On **Lamb Holm,** the **Italian Chapel** is all that remains of Camp 60, a prison that held several hundred Italian POWs during WWII. When not put to work on the Churchill Barriers (see above), the Italians—using only cement, corrugated iron, and shipwrecked wood—transformed their bare cement hut into a beautiful house of worship. (Open Apr.-Sept. daily 9am-10pm; Oct.-Mar. 9am-4:30pm; occasionally closed F afternoon, the traditional time for Orkney weddings. Services first Su of the month. Free.) During summer, **Orkney Coaches** chug daily over the Churchill Barriers from Kirkwall to the Burwick Ferry (#10, 2-4 per day); **Rosie Coaches** go nearly as far, to St. Margaret's Hope on the north coast of South Ronaldsay (year-round M-Sa 3-5 per day). A tiny 8-bed hostel and organic farm, **Wheems,** stands on South Ronaldsay. Call ahead and they might pick you up. (**☎**831537. Open Apr.-Oct. Dorms £6.50.)

HOY. The landscape of Hoy ("High Island"), the second-largest island in Orkney, is surprisingly rocky and mountainous. All visitors to Orkney should glimpse its most famous landmark, the **Old Man of Hoy,** a majestic 450 ft. sea stack off the West Coast of the island. On a clear day, the P&O ferry from Scrabster to Stromness gives an excellent view of the tower. Hikers can take the steep marked footpath from Rackwick, 2 mi. away (3hr. round-trip). The hefty **North Hoy Bird Reserve** offers respite for guillemots and a host of other species. Dedicated puffin-scouts should see several here during breeding season, from late June to early July—the rest of the year the pudgy birds rough it on the seas. The **SYHA Hoy** near the pier and the eight-bed **SYHA Rackwick** farther south, 2 mi. from the Old Man of Hoy, offer accommodations and share a telephone number. These hostels do not provide linen, and there are no sleeping bags available on the island. (**☎**873535. Hoy open May to mid-Sept.; Rackwick open mid-Mar. to mid-Sept. Dorms £7.50, under 18 £6.25.) Food and supplies are also difficult to procure, especially on Sundays.

SHAPINSAY. A mere 45min. from Kirkwall, with frequent ferry service, Shapinsay is the most accessible of the outer isles. Mostly a wide-open space, Shapinsay's landscape is defined by **Ward Hill,** the island's highest point at 210 ft., from where you can see almost all the Orkney Islands on a clear day, as well as the **Storm beaches.** Formerly home to the lairds of Balfour, **Balfour Castle,** an excellent example of the Victorian Baronial style, was completed in 1848 and is now a posh B&B. The big house opens its doors to the public weekly from May to September. Romantics can rent the castle and its chapel for weddings. For those who don't want to see inside, the castle is perfectly visible from the ferry. (☎711282, tours 872856. Tours leave Kirkwall pier W 2:15pm. £15.) **Burroughston Broch,** an Iron Age fortified shelter, lies 5 mi. from the ferry pier. Archaeology buffs will be thrilled by the round home, which was excavated in the 1860s. For bird fans, the **Bird Hide,** about a mile from the ferry, looks out over Royal Society for the Protection of Birds wetland reserve. (Open daily dawn-dusk. Free.) There are no youth hostels on Shapinsay, but the Kirkwall TIC (☎872856) can provide information on B&Bs.

PAPA WESTRAY. The "isle of the priests" once supported an early Christian Pictish settlement. Most pilgrims to the island now content themselves with bird-watching or archaeology. The rare Scottish primrose, thought to grow only in Orkney and isolated spots in the Highlands, can be found in fields. On the south coast, the **Knap of Howar** is the location of the earliest standing houses in northern Europe (c. 3500 BC). The **Bird Sanctuary** at North Hill sports the largest colony of Arctic terns in Europe. Two miles from the pier, **SYHA Papa Westray,** Beltane House, is open year-round. (☎(01857) 644267. Dorms £8, under 18 £7.)

WESTRAY. The largest of Orkney's northern isles sits just next to Papa Westray, and boasts ruined **Noltland Castle** and the **Knowe O'Burristae Broch,** along with other ancient ruins and magnificent cliffs. Legend holds that the castle is linked underground to the Gentlemens' Cave, where Jacobite supporters of Bonnie Prince Charlie hid. Bird-watchers rejoice on **Noup Head Reserve,** while budget travelers celebrate the island's two hostels. **The Barn,** Chalmersquoy, is practically a B&B, minus the second B. (☎(01857) 677214. £11.75, children £8.80.) **Bis Geos Hostel,** near Pierowall, is brand new. (☎(01857) 677420. Dorms £10.)

EDAY. The peat-covered hills of Eday hide Stone Age field walls, chambered tombs like **Vinquoy and Huntersquoy Cairns,** the towering **Stone of Setter,** and on the Calf of Eday, the remnants of an Iron Age roundhouse. **SYHA Eday Hostel,** London Bay, on the main north-south road 4 mi. from the pier, also welcomes campers. (☎(01857) 622206. Open Mar.-Oct. Dorms £6.75, under 18 £6. Camping £2.)

ROUSAY. Some will argue that Orkney's finest archaeological sights lie not on Mainland, but on the isle of Rousay. Here the **Midhowe Broch and Cairn** sports not only a Bronze and Iron Age dwelling, but also the largest known Stone Age cairn of its kind. The **Knowe of Yarso Cairn** stands on a high cliff overlooking Eynhallow Sound, and the **Westness Walk** winds past archaeological sights from the Neolithic, Pictish, Viking, medieval, and crofting eras. Stay at the **Rousay Hostel** on Trumland Farm near the pier; turn left from the ferry port and walk 5min. down the main road. (☎821252. Bedding £2 for those without sleeping bags. Dorms £6.)

NORTH RONALDSAY. The most remote of Orkney's islands is not lacking in archaeological sights of its own, with the **Broch of Burrian,** the **Brae of Stennabreck,** and an unusual standing stone with a hole through it. Better yet, the island's famous seaweed-eating sheep graze on the beaches. Nesting birds are all over the place—you can even stay at the **North Ronaldsay Bird Observatory Hostel.** An unreal £10 return flight to and from the island is available if you spend the night here. (☎(01857) 633200. No kitchen. Dorms £8; full board and lodging £17.)

SHETLAND ISLANDS   ☎01595

The Shetlands and Orkneys only became part of Scotland in the 15th century when King Christian I of Denmark and Norway mortgaged them to pay for his daughter's dowry, and in many ways Shetland, closer to Norway than to Great Britain, is still a country unto itself. Shetlanders look proudly to their Viking heritage, rather than to Scotland or Britain, an influence that lingers in their Nordic craftsmanship,

Scandinavian architecture, and festivals such as the longship-burning Up-Helly-A'. Most Shetlanders will look askance if you imply that their homeland is part of the UK—"Scotland," they will tell you, "is down there." Local poet Hugh MacDiarmid aptly describes the difference between Orkney and Shetland: "The Orcadian is a farmer with a boat, the Shetlander is a fisherman with a croft." Besides fish, the hardy crops and animals that can survive here—peat, ponies, and sheep, sheep, sheep—support agriculture, while North Sea oil drilling has brought prosperity. The Shetlands are an alluring destination, but unless you're an oil tycoon, watch your cash—after London, Shetland is the priciest place in Britain.

GETTING THERE AND CROSSING THE NORTH SEA

The fastest way to Shetland is by **plane,** assuming the weather cooperates. **Sumburgh Airport** lies on the southern tip of Mainland right near the town of Sumburgh. **Leasks** buses run from the airport to **Lerwick** (1hr.; M-F 6 per day, Sa 4 per day, Su 2 per day; £2), arriving at the **Viking Bus Station** (☎694100), 5min. from the city center on Commercial Rd. Flights arrive from **Orkney,** but you must stay over Saturday night—otherwise prices rise to the hundreds (35min.; M-Sa 1 per day; £83, £65 if booked 1 week ahead). **Ridgeway Travel** (☎(01856) 873359), by the Kirkwall tourist information centre (TIC) in Orkney, can get you tickets. **British Airways** (☎(08457) 773 3377) also flies from: **Aberdeen** (£99); **Edinburgh** (£168); **Glasgow** (£168).

Ferries arrive at **Holmsgarth Terminal,** a 20min. walk northwest of Lerwick town center, and the smaller **Victoria Pier,** across from the TIC downtown. **P&O Scottish Ferries** (☎(01224) 572615) arrive from **Aberdeen** (14hr.; M-F 6pm; June-Aug. also Tu noon, 20hr.; £58, berth from £85, return from £104) and **Stromness, Orkney** (8hr.; Apr.-Dec. Su noon; June-Aug. also Tu 10pm; Jan.-Mar. variable; £39, return £78). **P&O Smyril Line** runs mid-May to mid-Sept. from Lerwick to **Bergen, Norway** (13½hr.; M 11:30pm; £68, berth from £77), and to **Iceland** (W 2am, 31hr., £150) via the **Faroe Islands** (13hr., £68), with a 10% student discount outside summer.

LOCAL TRANSPORTATION

Infrequent public transport makes getting around the Shetlands difficult. **Ferries** within the archipelago are heavily subsidized; the longest trips cost about £2. All except those to Fair Isle transport bikes for free. Shetland's main **bus** lines are **John Leask & Son** (☎693162) and **Shalder Coaches** (☎880217). The TIC stocks the vital *Shetland Transport Timetable* (80p) with bus, ferry, and plane schedules. To reach remote areas on the decent road system, try **Bolts Car Hire** (☎693636; 21+) or **Grantfield Garage** (☎692709; 23+), both on North Rd. and both from £25 per day. Bolts also has a branch at Sumburgh Airport (☎(01950) 460777). **Eric Brown's Cycle Hire,** at Lerwick's Grantfield Garage, North Rd., 500 yd. past the ferry terminal, rents fully equipped touring bikes. (☎692709. £7.50 per day, £45 per week. Open daily 8am-9pm.) Remember that the strong winds can make biking difficult.

Various **tour** companies offer painfully pricey ways of seeing more of the Shetlands. The most affordable are the **Leasks Coach Tours,** on the Esplanade in Lerwick, which cost £8.50-12 for Mainland tours and £20 for tours to Yell and Unst. (☎693162. Open M-Sa 7:30am-5pm, Su 9:30am-2pm.) More expensive options are the folklore-oriented **Island Trails** (☎(01950) 422408), the **Shetland Wildlife Tours** (☎(01950) 422483), and the artsy **See Shetland** (☎693434; £30 for a day tour).

ORIENTATION AND PRACTICAL INFORMATION

Lerwick is on the eastern coast of the main island (called Mainland) and is served by the A970, which runs the island's length. The **Shetland Islands Tourism information centre,** Market Cross, books beds anywhere in the islands for £3. (☎693434; fax 695775. Open May-Sept. M-F 8am-6pm, Sa 8am-4pm, Su 10am-1pm; Oct.-Apr. M-F 9am-5pm.) Other services include: the **Royal Bank of Scotland,** 81 Commercial St. (☎694520; open M-F 9:15am-4:45pm, W 10am-4:45pm); **Lerwick Laundry and Dry**

Cleaners, 36 Market St. (☎693043; $4; open M-F 8:30am-1pm and 2-5:30pm, Sa 9am-1pm); free **Internet access** at the **Shetland Library,** in the church on Lower Hillhead (☎694430; open M, W, F 10am-7pm; Tu, Th, Sa 10am-5pm), and the **youth hostel** (see below); and the **post office,** 46-50 Commercial St. (☎693372; open M-F 6:30-8am and 8:45am-5:30pm; Sa 6:30-8am, 8:45-11am, 1-3pm). **Postal code:** ZE1 0AA.

ACCOMMODATIONS AND CAMPING

The **SYHA Youth Hostel,** Islesburgh House at King Harald St. and Union St., has excellent facilities, elegant curtains, and a cafe, but rules are inflexible and the environment somewhat cold. (☎692114. Reception open 9-9:30am, 4-4:30pm, and 9:45-10:15pm; at other times try the neighborly Community Centre. Lights out 11:30pm. Open Apr.-Sept. Dorms $9.25, under 18 $8.) Harbor views are yours at **Mrs. Nicholson's** B&B, 133 North Rd., where puppy-dog looks garner singles. (☎693362. $16-20 per person.) There are three **campgrounds** on Mainland, but you can camp almost anywhere with the landowner's permission. **Clickimin Caravan and Camp Site** is closest to the Lerwick ferry terminal; turn left on Holmsgarth Rd. (the A970), then through the roundabout and right on North Lochside. If you're arriving by bus, ask the driver to drop you off. (☎741000. Open May-Sept. Pitches $6-7.)

Camping **böds** (Old Norse for barns) are a *very* basic accommodations alternative. Mainland's four böds are available April to September: **Betty Mouat's** near the airport, **The Sail Loft** next to the pier in Voe, the **Voe House** in Walls, and **Johnnie Notions** (no electricity) at Hamnavoe, Eshaness, in the far northeast. The **Windhouse Lodge,** on Yell, is the best equipped. All böds cost $5 per night and must be booked in advance through the Lerwick TIC. Bring sleeping bags, a camping stove, and 50p coins for electricity (when available); the grass and roof are already there.

FOOD AND PUBS

Inexpensive eats cluster in the center of **Lerwick.** Head to **D.G. Leslie's,** on the Esplanade, for groceries. (☎693073. Open M-Th 8am-8pm, F-Sa 8am-7pm, Su 10am-7pm.) **Osla's Cafe,** on the Esplanade, specializes in pancakes that are worth the trip, no matter what time of day. (☎696005. Open May-Aug. M-Sa 9am-7pm; Sept.-Apr. M-Sa 10am-5pm.) Also on the Esplanade, the **Peerie Shop Cafe** serves massive sandwiches, baked goods, and organic cider in a bright, lively setting. The Special Hot Chocolate ($1.60) is a treat. (☎692817. Open July-Aug. M-Sa 9am-9pm; Sept.-June M-Sa 10am-6pm.) Lerwick's cheapest food (everything under $2!) awaits at the **Islesburgh Community Centre Cafe,** King Harald St., next to the hostel. (☎692114. Open M-Sa 9am-5pm.) **The Lounge,** 4 Mounthooly St., is the town's busiest pub; a more subdued lounge bar is upstairs. (☎692231. Live music Sa afternoons and some W nights. Open M-Sa 11am-1am.) A friendly, eccentric crowd fills **Thule Bar** on the Esplanade. (☎692508. Open M-Sa 8am-1am, Su 12:30pm-1am.)

WOOL

Shetland is one of the best places in the world to buy woollens (you may have noticed a few sheep here and there). To avoid paying relatively high prices in Lerwick's tourist shops, get bargains upstairs at the **Shetland Woollen Company,** 68 Commercial St., where leftover sweaters can be found for as low as $5. (☎693610. Open May-Sept. M-Sa 9am-5pm; Oct.-Apr. M-F 9am-5pm.) There are also branches in Sandwick, Yell, and Scalloway, on Castle Rd. (☎880243). Huge piles of cheap sweaters ($11-22) collect at the **Judane Shetland Limited Knitwear Factory,** Blackhill Mills, Gremista Industrial Estate (☎693724), 1½ mi. north of Lerwick town center on the A970, opposite the factory stack. **The Spider's Web,** 41 Commercial St., showcases high-quality knitwork done by individuals from their homes. (☎693299. Open M-Sa 9am-5pm, and Su if there is a cruise ship in port.) On northerly **Unst,** you can simultaneously shop for knitwear and enjoy apple pie at **NorNova Knitwear** in Muness. (☎(01957) 755373. Open daily 10am-4pm, often later.)

◉ MAINLAND SIGHTS

LERWICK SIGHTS. Weather permitting, cruise around the bay on the **Dim Riv,** a full-scale replica of a Viking longship that launches every summer Monday at 7pm. Riders may be asked to row. (☎ 693471. Advance booking at the TIC is a must. Cruises £5, children £2.) Not much of a sight in itself, the giant, pentagonal **Fort Charlotte,** a relic of the Cromwellian era just off Commercial Rd. at the north end of town, supplies the best views of Lerwick and its harbor. (Open daily 9am-10pm. Free.) Only a mile west of the city center on Clickimin Rd., the ruins of **Clickimin Broch,** a stronghold from the 4th century BC, still look tough enough to repel invaders. (Always open. Free.) For a taste of Shetland's Norse heritage, check out the Up-Helly-A' Exhibition in the **Galley Shed,** Saint Sunniva St., Lerwick. (Open mid-May to Sept. Tu 2-4pm and 7-9pm, F 7-9pm, Sa 2-4pm. £2.50, concessions £1.) **The Shetland Museum,** in the library building on Lower Hillhead, gives a paltry look at local archaeology and marine history. (☎ 695057. Open M, W, F 10am-7pm; Tu, Th, Sa 10am-5pm. Free.)

SCALLOWAY. There's not much to see in Shetland's ancient capital, 7 mi. west of Lerwick, except 17th-century **Scalloway Castle.** Once home to the villainous Earl Patrick Stewart, the crumbling edifice can now be yours. Get the key from the Shetland Woolen Company (next door) or the Scalloway Hotel. (Open M-Sa 9:30am-5pm, Su by appointment only. Free.) **Shalder Coaches** leave from the Viking Bus Station in Lerwick (M-Sa 5-6 per day, £2 return).

JARLSHOF AND SOUTH MAINLAND. At the southern tip of Mainland, next to Sumburgh Airport, Jarlshof is one of the most remarkable archaeological sites in Europe. Layers of human settlement have accumulated here from Neolithic times to the Renaissance, discovered in 1896 when a storm uncovered the site. (☎ 460112. Open Apr.-Sept. daily 9:30am-6:30pm. £2.50, seniors £1.90, children £1.20.) A mile up the road, the **Old Scatness Broch** is the fascinating scene of an ongoing excavation. Archaeological remains were discovered in 1975 during airport construction; since then an entire Iron Age village and over 20,000 artifacts have been found. (☎ 694688. Open M-Th 10:30am-5pm, Sa-Su 10:30am-5:30pm. Free.) On nearby **Sumburgh Head,** thousands of gulls, guillemots, and puffins rear their young each year. All South Mainland sights can be reached by the **Leasks bus** that runs to Sumburgh Airport from Lerwick (1hr., 2-6 per day, return £3.50).

NORTH MAINLAND. The northern part of Mainland has the wildest and most deserted coastal scenery, much of which is accessible only by car. At **Mavis Grind,** northwest of Brae, Mainland is almost bisected; this 100-yard-wide isthmus is flanked by the Atlantic Ocean and the North Sea. Farther northwest stand the jagged volcanic sea-cliffs on **Eshaness,** where you can view nesting birds, ocean-sprayed stacks, and the standing arch of **Dore Holm.** On Sundays, when buses and ferries are rare, **Leask Coach Tours** runs three different tours of north Mainland. (☎ 693162. Tours leave at 2:15pm. £8.)

⟡ SMALLER ISLANDS

BRESSAY AND NOSS. Hourly ferries (5min., £1.25) sail from Lerwick to the west coast of the island of Bressay. Hike to the summit of conical **Ward of Bressay** (743 ft.) for a sweeping view of the sea. From Bressay's east coast, 3 mi. from the Lerwick ferry port (follow the "To Noss" signs), dinghies go to the tiny isle of Noss; just stand at the "Wait Here" sign and wave (mid-May to Aug. Tu-W and F-Su 10am-4pm; return £2.50, seniors and children £1). Great skuas (a.k.a. bonxies), large primeval birds, will dive-bomb you at this spectacular bird sanctuary; wave a hat over your head to ward them off. (Noss is open to visitors Tu-W and F-Su 10am-5pm; overnight stays are forbidden.)

MOUSA. The tiny, uninhabited island of Mousa, just off the east coast of Mainland, holds the world's best preserved Iron Age broch, a 50 ft. drystone fortress that has endured 1000 years of Arctic storms. Available flashlights help you climb the intact staircase onto the broch's roof. Catch a Sumburgh-bound Leask bus at the Viking Bus Station in Lerwick and ask the driver to let you off at the Setter Junction for Sandsayre (£2.80 return); it's a 15min. walk from there to the ferry. (☎(01950) 431367. Ferry departs mid-Apr. to mid-Sept. M-Th and Sa noon, F and Su 12:30pm and 2pm. £7, children £3.50.) During the week in the summer, **Leask Coach Tours** leads tours of Mousa, leaving from the Esplanade in Lerwick. (☎693162. £10, including ferry.)

■ **ST. NINIAN'S ISLE.** 6 mi. away on the west side of Mainland, an unusual **tombolo**—a beach surrounded on both sides by the sea—links St. Ninian's Isle, site of an early monastery, to Mainland's west coast. Inhabited from the Iron Age to the late 18th century, the isle is now home to a ruined church and plenty of rabbits and sheep. A bus bound for Sumburgh departs Lerwick twice a day (at noon and 5:05pm) to meet a shuttle that goes to Bigton, which is connected to St. Ninian's by the tombolo. The Lewis-bound bus also returns via Bigton twice daily (depart Bigton 8:05 and 1:50pm). In order to visit St. Ninian's within a day—necessary, since there are no accommodations at Bigton—you have to take the noon bus from Lerwick to Bigton, and the 1:50pm bus from Bigton to Lerwick, which allows about 1¼ hr. to explore the beach and island: not enough, but still worthwhile.

YELL. If you tire of bird- and seal-watching on starkly remote Yell, head for the north end of the main road at Gloup; a three-mile hike from here takes you to the desolate eastern coast. The remains of an Iron Age fort on the Burgi Geos promontory have held tenaciously to a perfect defensive position—jagged outcroppings face the sea and a 3 ft. ridge leads between cliffs to the mainland. Killer whales are occasionally spotted in Bluemull Sound between Yell and Unst. **Ferries** run from Toft on Mainland to Ulsta on Yell (20min., 2 per hr., £1.25).

UNST. Unst is home to the northernmost everything in Britain. **Muness Castle** (Britain's northernmost) was built in the late 16th century; the key-keeper at the white cottage will give you a flashlight to pierce its spooky darkness. At **Haroldswick Beach,** gannets crash the ocean near crumbling, abandoned air-raid shelters. The celebrated northernmost bird reserve at **Hermaness** is graced by a pair of black-browed albatrosses and countless puffins. Ferries from Belmont on Unst and Gutcher on Yell divert routinely to Oddsta on the island of **Fetlar,** where birdwatchers view the crimson-tailed finch. **Ferries** run from **Gutcher** on northern Yell to **Belmont** on Unst (10min., 1-2 per hr., £1.25). A daily **Leask** bus leaves Lerwick at 8am and connects with ferries to Haroldswick on Unst, stopping by Unst's Gardiesfauld Hostel along the way (bus and ferry £10).

Find a gorgeous coastal view and a sunny indoor patio at the **Gardiesfauld Hostel,** in Uyeasound in the south of Unst—the northernmost hostel in Britain. (☎(01957) 755259. Dorms £8, under 18 £6.50. Tent pitch for 2 people £6.) Because only **one bus** runs by the hostel daily (8am departure from Lerwick), it's easy to get stranded here for the day. Those without some private means of transport should consider riding the bus to Unst's main town, **Baltasound,** which has better access to the island and a few **B&Bs.** The Baltasound **post office** (open M-Tu and F 9am-1pm and 2-5:30pm, W 9am-1pm and 2-4:30pm, Th and Sa 9am-1pm) lets you experience Britain's northernmost **postal code:** ZE2 9DP.

OTHER ISLANDS. Shetland's outermost islands are the most isolated in Britain. **Planes** depart for the outer islands from **Tingwall** on Mainland, but ferries, at an unbelievable £2.15 per single journey (except for Whalsay, which is only £1.25), are a cheaper choice. Rooms and transport are hard to come by, and booking several weeks in advance is a must. Bring supplies to last at least a week, as the ferries often do not operate in inclement weather. Many ferries run from **Walls, Vidlin,** or **Laxo** on Mainland, all of which can be reached by bus from Lerwick (bus generally under 1hr. and £2; consult the *Shetland Transport Timetable*).

Whalsay, a relatively large fishing community (pop. 1000), is accessible by bus and ferry from Lerwick. Talk to the Lerwick TIC for bookings of the primitive **Grieve House** böd (roof under which to sleep £5). The **Out Skerries** support 85 hardy fishermen. Planes (5 per week, £20) swoop down from Tingwall, while ferries converge from Lerwick (2½hr., 2 per week) and Vidlin (1½hr., 10 per week). **Papa Stour** (pop. 35) has a frothy coastline with abundant bird life and sea-flooded cliff arches. The only place to stay is **Mrs. Holt-Brook's.** (☎873238. £18 per person; singles available.) To get to Papa Stour, take a plane (Tu only, £16) from Tingwall, or a boat (call 810460 to book in advance; 7 per week, £2.15).

Far to the west, rugged **Foula** is home to 40 humans, 2000 sheep, and the highest sheer cliff in Britain at 1220 ft. Barely Scottish, the inhabitants of Foula had their own monarch until the late 17th century, and spoke the now-extinct Nordic language of Norn until 1926. From April to October, ferries (☎753226) drift from Walls (Tu, Sa, and every other Th) and Scalloway (every other Th), while planes fly from Tingwall (15min., 7 per week, £21.30).

Fair Isle, midway between Shetland and Orkney and home of the famous Fair Isle knit patterns, is billed as the most remote island in Britain. In summer, a **ferry** (☎760222) runs every other Thursday from Lerwick and two to three times per week from Sumburgh (Apr.-Sept., £2.15). Planes (☎840246) depart from Tingwall (25min.; Apr.-Oct. M, W, F 2 per day; May to mid-Oct. also Sa 1 per day; £37.20) and Sumburgh (May-Oct. Sa, £37.20). Beds are available at the **Fair Isle Bird Observatory Lodge.** (☎760258. Open Apr.-Oct. Room and full board £25-40.)

🎵 FESTIVALS

The **Shetland Folk Festival** in early May lures fiddlers from around the world, while the **Shetland Fiddle and Accordion Festival** takes place in Lerwick in mid-October; call the TIC for details. The famous **Up-Helly-A' Festival,** on the last Tuesday in January, is a Viking extravaganza with outlandish costumes, a torch-lit procession through the streets, and a ship-burning in the town park. Shetlanders plan months in advance for this impressive light-bearing event—after the bonfire dies out blackness settles in again (with only short reprieves of daylight) until late spring.

NORTHERN IRELAND

The predominantly calm tenor in Northern Ireland has been overshadowed overseas by media headlines concerning politics and bombs that, while disturbing and accurate, fail to reflect that the North is a society of mostly peaceful citizens, however divided they might be. There is much to savor: Northern Ireland's natural beauty includes the green Glens of Antrim and gotta-see-it-to-believe-it geology of the Giant's Causeway, while the cease-fires of recent years have allowed Belfast and Derry to develop into hip pub-loving cities. The deeper problem than the violent fringe groups on both sides is the huge division in civil society that sends Protestants and Catholics to separate neighborhoods, separate stores, separate pubs, and often separate schools, with separate, though similar, traditional songs and slang. The 1998 Good Friday Agreement, granting Home Rule and hoping to lead the North out of its struggles, has been struggling itself. Home Rule was suspended and reinstated in February 2000, and by the summer of 2001 a lack of progress on paramilitary promises to "put weapons beyond use" brought the Good Friday government to a halt. London took the reins again, if only briefly, and both sides have renewed their efforts to make their country as peaceful as it is beautiful.

HIGHLIGHTS OF NORTHERN IRELAND

BELFAST Decode the compelling political murals on a black cab tour (p. 642).

GLENS OF ANTRIM Stroll through tiny villages flecked among mountains, forests, and lush valleys, then hike along the nearby coast (p. 655).

GIANT'S CAUSEWAY Marvel at these 60-million-year-old volcanic rock formations, the stuff of Irish myth and legend (p. 658).

MONEY. Legal tender in Northern Ireland is the British pound. Northern Ireland issues its own bank notes, which are equal in value to their English and Scottish counterparts, but are not accepted outside Northern Ireland. All British notes, including Scottish bills, are accepted in the North. The Republic of Ireland's pounds are generally not accepted in the North, with the exception of some border towns which will calculate the exchange rate and add an additional surcharge.

SAFETY AND SECURITY. Northern Ireland has one of the lowest tourist-related crime rates in the world. Although sectarian violence is now dramatically less common than during the Troubles (see p. 638), some neighborhoods and towns still experience turmoil during sensitive political times. It's best to remain alert and cautious while traveling during **marching season,** July 4-12 (see **Orange Day,** p. 667). August 12, when the **Apprentice Boys** march in Derry, is also a testy period. In general, be prepared for transport delays and for shops and services to be closed. Vacation areas such as the Glens and the Causeway Coast are less affected. Use common sense in conversation, and, as always in dealing with a culture not your own, be respectful of local religious and political perspectives.

Border checkpoints have been removed, and armed soldiers and vehicles are now less visible in Belfast and Derry. **Do not take photographs** of soldiers, military installations, or vehicles; your film will be confiscated and you may be detained for questioning. Taking pictures of political murals is not a crime, although many feel uncomfortable doing so in residential neighborhoods. Unattended luggage is always considered suspicious and worthy of confiscation. It is generally unsafe to hitch in Northern Ireland. *Let's Go* never recommends hitchhiking.

The phone code for all of Northern Ireland is 028.

LIFE AND TIMES

Throughout its turbulent history, Northern Ireland has been steadfast in its resolve to remain divided. The frustrations of the recent peace talks only prove how important it is to Northerners to retain their individual cultural identities even at the cost of lasting peace. The 950,000 Protestants are generally **Unionists,** who want the six counties of Northern Ireland to remain in the UK. The 650,000 Catholics tend to identify with the Republic of Ireland, not Britain, and many are **Nationalists,** who want the six counties to be part of the Republic. The extremist problem-children on either side are known as **Loyalists** and **Republicans,** respectively, groups who tend to prefer defending their stance with rocks and petrol bombs. In December 1999, the world felt a stirring of optimism after the reinstatement of Home Rule (i.e., self-government) in the North, but continued tensions over disarmament of the extremist factions ("You put your guns down." "You put 'em down first.") and recent political victories for hardliners have kept peace a sweet but distant dream. For more background on the history of Northern Ireland, see the **Life and Times** of the Republic of Ireland, p. 637.

A DIVIDED ISLAND: IT STARTS

The 17th century's **Ulster Plantation** scattered English and Scottish settlers on what had been Gaelic-Irish land in the island's northeast (see p. 666). French Protestants sought refuge in Ulster, as did merchants and working-class immigrants from nearby Scotland. Institutionalized religious discrimination limited Catholic access to land ownership and other basic rights, but made it an attractive destination for

Scots Protestants, who lost no time buying beachfront property for condos. By the end of the 19th century, Belfast was a booming industrial center with thriving textile mills and shipbuilding factories, most of which refused to hire Catholic workers. During its 300 years, the Ulster Plantation created a working- and middle-class population in Ulster that identified with the British Empire and did not support Home Rule. The **Orange Order**—named for William of Orange, who had outwarred arch-nemesis Catholic James II in the 1690s—organized Protestants in local lodges. They ordained July 12th as a holiday—**Orange Day**—on which to hold parades celebrating William's victory at the **Battle of the Boyne.** The Order's constituency and radicalism continued to grow despite legislative opprobrium, culminating in its explosive opposition to the first Home Rule Bill in 1886 (see p. 667).

Lawyer-politician **Edward Carson,** with sidekick **James Craig,** attempted to translate Ulster Unionism into terms the British elite could understand. In 1912, when Home Rule seemed possible, Carson held a mass meeting, and Unionists signed the Ulster Covenant of Resistance to Home Rule. In 1914, Home Rule appeared even more likely, so the Unionist **Ulster Volunteer Force** (**UVF;** see p. 667) armed itself. **WWI** gave Unionists more time to organize and showed British leaders that the imposition of Home Rule on all of Ulster would mean havoc: the UVF intended to fight the **Irish Republican Army** (**IRA;** see p. 668), who in turn would fight the police. The **1920 Government of Ireland Act** created two parliaments for North and South. In the south, it was quickly superseded by the **Anglo-Irish Treaty** and **Civil War** (see p. 668). In the north, however, the "temporary" measure became the basis government until 1973. The Parliament met at **Stormont,** near Belfast.

The new statelet included only six of the nine counties of Ulster, excluding Catholic Donegal, Monaghan, and Cavan. This arrangement suited the one million Protestants in the six counties but threatened the several hundred thousand Protestant Unionists living elsewhere on the island and the half-million Catholic Nationalists living within the new Ulster. Orange Lodges and other strongly Protestant groups continued to control politics, and the Catholic minority boycotted elections. Anti-Catholic discrimination was widespread. The IRA continued sporadic campaigns in the North through the 20s and 30s with little result. In the Irish State, the IRA was gradually suppressed. **WWII** gave Unionists a chance to show their loyalty—the Republic (then the Irish Free State; see p. 668) stayed neutral and stayed out while the North welcomed Allied troops, ships, and airforce bases. The need to build and repair warships raised employment in Belfast and allowed Catholics to enter the industrial workforce for the first time. Over the following two decades, a grateful British Parliament poured money into loyal little Ulster, yet discrimination persisted. The government at Stormont neglected to institute social reform, and parliamentary districts were unequally drawn to favor Protestants. After a brief, unsuccessful try at school desegregation, Stormont ended up granting subsidies to Catholic schools. As the Republic gained a surer footing, violence (barring the occasional border skirmish) receded on the island.

THE TROUBLES

The economy grew, but bigotry and resentment festered. The American civil rights movement inspired the 1967 founding of the **Northern Ireland Civil Rights Association** (**NICRA**), which worked to end anti-Catholic discrimination in public housing. Protestant extremists included the acerbic **Reverend Ian Paisley,** whose **Ulster Protestant Volunteers** (**UPV**) overlapped in membership with the now-illegal paramilitary UVF. The first NICRA march was raucous but nonviolent. The second, in Derry in 1968, was a bloody mess disrupted by Unionists and then by the water cannons of the **Royal Ulster Constabulary** (**RUC**), the north's Protestant police force.

John Hume and Protestant **Ivan Cooper** formed a new civil rights committee in Derry but were overshadowed by Bernadette Devlin's radical, student-led **People's Democracy** (**PD**). The PD encouraged, and NICRA opposed, a four-day peaceful march from Belfast to Derry starting on New Year's Day, 1969. The RUC's physical assault on Derry's Catholic Bogside once the marchers arrived led Derry authorities to rule RUC out of the Bogside; the area became **Free Derry.** On August 12,

1969, Catholics threw rocks at the annual Apprentice Boys parade along the city walls. The RUC attacked Bogside residents, and a two-day siege ensued. Free Derry remained independent, but the violence showed that the RUC alone could not maintain order. The British Army arrived—and hasn't left yet.

Between 1970 and 1972, leaders alternated concessions and crackdowns to little effect. The rejuvenated IRA split: while the "Official" faction faded into insignificance, the **Provisional IRA,** or **Provos** (today's IRA), faltered ideologically but gained guns. British troops became their main target. In 1970, John Hume founded the **Social Democratic and Labor Party (SDLP),** with the intention of bringing about social change through the support of both Catholics and Protestants; by 1973, it had become the moderate political voice of Northern Catholics. British policies of **internment without trial** outraged Catholics and led the SDLP to withdraw from government. The pattern was clear: no concessions could be made to one side without inspiring reprisal from the other. On January 30, 1972, British troops fired into a crowd of nonviolent protesters in Derry. Fourteen Catholics were killed—the soldiers claimed they hadn't fired the first shot, while Catholics said the soldiers shot at unarmed, fleeing marchers. The British government's reluctance to investigate this **Bloody Sunday** increased Catholic outrage. Only in 1999 did official reexamination of the event begin; the inquiry will likely take years.

In early 1972, the British embassy in Dublin was torched, and the IRA bombed a British army barracks. After further bombings in 1973, Stormont was replaced by the **Sunningdale Executive,** which split power between Catholics and Protestants. This move was immediately crippled by a massive Unionist work stoppage, and **direct British rule** began. A referendum asking if voters wanted Northern Ireland to remain part of the UK was boycotted by Catholics, and the violence continued, causing an average of 275 deaths per year between 1970 and 1976. In 1978, 300 Nationalist prisoners in Maze Prison in Northern Ireland began a campaign to have their special category as political prisoners restored. The movement's climax was the 10-man H-Block **hunger strike** of 1981. Leader **Bobby Sands** was elected to Parliament from a Catholic district in Tyrone and Fermanagh while he starved. Sands died after 66 days and became a martyr; his face is still seen on murals in the Falls section of Belfast (see p. 649). The remaining prisoners officially ended the strike seven months and two days after it began.

Sands's election was no anomaly. The hunger strikes galvanized Nationalists, and support for **Sinn Féin,** the political arm of the IRA, surged in the early 80s. In 1985, British Prime Minister Margaret Thatcher and Taoiseach Garret FitzGerald signed the **Anglo-Irish Agreement,** granting the Republic of Ireland (officially declared in 1948; see p. 668) a "consultative role" but no legal authority in the governance of Northern Ireland. Relations between London and Dublin improved, but extremists on both sides were infuriated. Protestant paramilitaries attacked "their own" RUC, while the IRA continued bombing England. In 1991 and 1992, the Brooke Initiative led to the first multi-party talks in the North in over a decade, but they managed, conveniently, to forget to invite Sinn Féin. The **Downing Street Declaration,** issued at the end of 1993 by Prime Minister John Major and Taoiseach Albert Reynolds, invited the IRA to participate in talks if they refrained from violence for three months.

THE 1994 CEASE-FIRE: FAT LADY?

On August 31, 1994, the IRA announced a complete cessation of violence, while Loyalist guerillas cooperated by announcing their own cease-fire. **Gerry Adams,** Sinn Féin's leader, called for direct talks with the British government. The peace held for over a year. In February 1995, John Major and Irish Prime Minister John Bruton issued the **joint framework** proposal, which suggested a Northern Ireland Assembly that would include the "harmonizing powers" of the Irish and British governments and the right of the people of Northern Ireland to choose their own destiny. Subsequently, the British government began talks with Loyalists and, for the first time, Sinn Féin. Disarmament was the most prominent problem in the 1995 talks—both sides refused to put down their guns.

The IRA ended their cease-fire on February 9, 1996 with the bombing of an office building in London. Despite this, the peace talks went on, albeit sluggishly and precariously. Sinn Féin refused to participate because it did not agree to totally disarm. Sinn Féin's popularity had been growing in Northern Ireland—in the May elections, it gathered 15% of the vote—but their credibility was seriously jeopardized on June 15, 1996, when a blast in a Manchester shopping district injured more than 200 people.

As the peace process chugged along, the Orangemen's annual marches grew more contentious and more violent. The government created a **Parades Commission** to oversee the rerouting of parades and encourage the participation of both sides in negotiations. Protestants believe the Commission's decisions infringe on their right to practice their culture; Catholics argue that the marches are a form of harassment and intimidation from which they deserve protection. **Orange Day 1996** saw another burst of violence after the Parades Commission banned an Orange march on a Catholic street in Protestant Portadown. Unionists clashed with police, and after four days of violence they were allowed through. This time, Catholics responded with a hail of debris. The turmoil spread to Belfast and Derry.

In October 1996, the IRA bombed British army headquarters in Belfast, killing one soldier and injuring 30. In early 1997, the IRA tried to influence upcoming British elections by making bomb threats. Thoroughly angered, John Major condemned Sinn Féin. In May 1997, the Labour party swept the British elections and **Tony Blair** became Prime Minister. Sinn Féin made its most impressive showing yet: Gerry Adams and Martin McGuinness won seats in Parliament but refused to swear allegiance to the Queen and were barred from taking their places. The government ended its ban on talks with a still uncooperative Sinn Féin, but hopes for a renewed cease-fire were dashed when the car of a prominent Republican was bombed; in retaliation, the IRA shot two members of the RUC.

THE GOOD FRIDAY AGREEMENT

The 1997 marching season gave Mo Mowlam, the British government's Northern Ireland Secretary, a rough introduction to her new job: the Orange Order started marching a week early in Portadown and more than 80 people were hurt in the ensuing riots. On July 19, the IRA announced an "unequivocal" cease-fire to start the following day. In September 1997, Sinn Féin joined the peace talks. The **Ulster Unionist Party (UUP),** the voice of moderate Protestants, joined shortly thereafter; UUP leader **David Trimble** assured Protestants that he would not negotiate directly with Sinn Féin. The peace process continued, but without universal support. In January 1998, another dozen lives were lost to sectarian extremism. After two Protestants were killed in early February, Unionist leaders charged Sinn Féin with breaking its pledge to support only peaceful actions and tried to oust party leaders from the talks. Foreign facilitators continued to push for progress, holding the group to a strict April deadline.

The delegates approved a draft of the **1998 Northern Ireland Peace Agreement** (or **Good Friday Agreement**) in the wee hours of Saturday, April 11. The pact emphasized that change in the North could come only with the consent of its people and declared that the people must determine individually whether to identify as Irish, British, or both. On Friday, May 22, in the first island-wide vote since 1918, the Agreement was voted into law. A resounding majority (71% of the North and 94% of the Republic) approved of the Agreement, which divided governing responsibilities of Northern Ireland three ways. The main body, a 108-member **Northern Ireland Assembly,** assigns committee posts and chairs proportionately to the parties' representation. Catholics see this as an opportunity for reclaiming the political power they were long denied. (On June 25, the UUP and the SDLP won the most seats, while Sinn Féin garnered more support than ever before.) The second strand of the new government, a **North-South Ministerial Council,** serves as the cross-border authority. The final strand, the **British-Irish Council,** approaches similar issues but on a broader scale, concerning itself with the entirety of the British Isles.

While many felt that a lasting peace was finally within reach, several issues remained unresolved. Sinn Féin called for the disbanding of the RUC, which had been cited by the UN for intimidation and harassment. Blair declared that the RUC could continue to exist, but appointed a small, one-year commission to review the RUC's recruiting, hiring, training practices, culture, and symbols. In the end of May 1998, a march by the Junior Orange Order provoked violence in Portadown. In light of this disturbance, the Parades Commission hesitated to grant Orange Day marching permits. On June 15, the Parades Commission rerouted the Tour of the North, banning it from Catholic areas in Belfast. Aside from two short stand-offs with the RUC, the parade proceeded without conflict. But the day after the assembly elections, Nationalists and police officers at a parade in West Belfast recommenced their violence: early July saw hundreds of bombings and assaults on security forces as well as a slew of arson attacks on Catholic churches.

Other parades passed peacefully, but a standoff began over the fate of the July 4 **Drumcree** parade, which had been banned from war-torn Garvaghy Rd. Angered by the decision, thousands participated in a week-long standoff with the RUC. Wide-spread rioting ensued, and Protestant marchers were angered by what they saw as the disloyalty of their own police force. Neither side would budge, and the country looked with anxiety toward July 12. On the night of July 11, however, a Catholic home in almost entirely Protestant Ballymoney was firebombed by local hooli-gans, and three young boys were killed. Marches still took place the following day; but instead of rioting against the Orangemen, Catholics looked on in silent reproach. The Drumcree standoff gradually lost numbers, and the Church of Ire-land publicly called for its end. Although some tried to distance the boys' deaths from the events at Drumcree, the murders led to a reassessment of the Orange Order and a new sobriety about the peace process.

Then, on August 15, a bombing in religiously mixed **Omagh** killed 29 people and injured 382. A splinter group calling itself the **"Real IRA"** claimed responsibility; their obvious motive was to undermine the Good Friday Agreement. Sinn Féin's Gerry Adams unreservedly condemned the bombing. The US has now outlawed the Real IRA and inducted them into the Terrorist Hall of Infamy, despite Sinn Féin's concern that criminalization will only attract more fanatics.

In October 1998, Catholic John Hume and Protestant David Trimble received the Nobel Peace Prize for their participation in the peace process. The coming year, however, was full of disappointments. The formation of the Northern Ireland Assembly, a fundamental premise of Good Friday, was a failure. Two major provi-sions of the Agreement highlighted serious rifts between partisan politicians: the gradual decommissioning of all paramilitary groups' arms and the early release of political prisoners. Disagreement over the **Northern Ireland (Sentences) Bill,** which required the release of all political prisoners, split the UK Parliament for the first time during the talks. Dissenters feared the bill did not sufficiently link the release of prisoners to full disarmament. During summer 1999, the deadline for the Assem-bly's inauguration was pushed back. Unionists refused to take seats with Sinn Féin; yet another round of negotiations ensued. In July, First Minister Trimble failed to appear on the day that he was due to appoint the newly elected Assembly. Many interpreted Trimble's behavior as responsive to his own Unionist political party rather than to the voters who had approved the Peace Agreement. National-ist Deputy PM Seamus Mallon resigned the following day.

Orange Day 1999 came and went with little fanfare. The messy stuff didn't start until August 12, when the Apprentice Boys marched through Derry and Belfast. Catholics in Belfast staged a sit-down protest in the path of the marchers, only to be forcefully removed by the RUC. On the streets of Derry, petrol bombs and riot gear were once again in fashion.

CURRENT EVENTS

December 1999—London returns Home Rule to Northern Ireland after 27 years of British domination. A power-sharing government was formed under the leadership of Trimble and Mallon, but the IRA's hidden weapon caches remained a central problem and threatened the collapse of the new assembly, whose four parties included the Democratic Unionist Party, the UUP, the Labour Party, and, to the tune of much controversy, Sinn Féin.

In late January 2000, Trimble demanded the IRA put its weapons "beyond use" and predicted a return to British rule if his demands were not met. The IRA's unwillingness to comply hamstrung the February peace talks, and just to make things a little more interesting, the dissident IRA Continuity Group (still peeved at the "Official" IRA's compromises) bombed a rural hotel in Irvinestown. Every Irish political group, including Sinn Féin, condemned the attack. Though the blast injured no one, it was an unwelcome reminder of the past in the midst of a stalled peace process. Britain suspended the power-sharing experiment just 11 weeks after its implementation and reintroduced direct British rule.

On May 29, 2000, Britain restored the power-sharing scheme after the IRA promised to begin disarming. In June, they allowed two ambassadors to inspect their secret weapon caches. These advances did little to dispel conflict through the rest of summer. In the Republic, "Teflon" **Bertie Ahern** of the Fianna Fail Party scraped out a "no confidence" victory against the opposition Labour Party. Marching season was again a nasty affair, although Blair and Ahern expressed satisfaction over its containment. The Orange Order, reacting to a Parades Commission decision, barricaded streets and rioted again police in Belfast and Portadown.

On July 28, the last political prisoners in **Maze Prison** walked free under the highly criticized Good Friday provisions, and by September 29 the Maze was completely empty of all prisoners. Supporters gave them heroes' welcomes, but other civilians and relatives of the deceased found the early release of convicted murderers, some carrying life sentences, appalling. Many of the released men expressed remorse and stated that their war was over, but others refused to apologize. Her Majesty has not yet declared what is to be done with Her Prison.

The story remains the same in the North—political squabbling at the negotiation tables and on the floors of various Parliaments continues, punctuated now and then by bombs or plastic bullets out in the streets. Both sides are making efforts to repair the past—the Bloody Sunday inquiry continues with testimony from British military as well as IRA figures, and the European Court of Human Rights has recently awarded compensation to the families of 10 IRA fighters lost to the British government's "shoot to kill" policy. Meanwhile, the slow path to disarmament points to a safer future—in the spring of 2001, the IRA was still dragging its heels but allowed international diplomats a third visit to their secret arms dumps. The inspectors confirmed that the weapons (rumored to be enough to keep a small country in the war-making business for a decade) are unused.

On the other hand, the British national elections in June were huge victories for Protestant extremists. The DUP took several seats from the more moderate UUP, and Ian Paisley came in calling for an end to the 1998 Agreement his party opposes. On July 1, 2001, David Trimble made good on his threat to resign if the IRA didn't begin serious decommissioning. Anglo-Irish negotiations were renewed in England, while Belfast dealt with some of the worst rioting seen since the Good Friday pact was implemented. A new deadline was set: the Unionist and Nationalist parties had to agree to a new peace plan by early August. Orange Day passed in its yearly orbit, and eyes were turned more toward the negotiation tables than the streets. On August 10, London took the reins for 24hr., then reinstated Home Rule, opening up a Good Friday loophole and giving the North six more weeks to reach an agreement, put their weapons on the shelf, and salvage the peace.

BELFAST

Despite the violent associations summoned by the name Belfast, the North's capital feels more neighborly than most international and even Irish visitors expect. The second-largest city on the island, Belfast (pop. 330,000) is Northern Ireland's cultural, commercial, and political center; in stark contrast to the rest of the island, the city has been a booming site of mercantile activity for centuries. Today, Belfast's reputation as a thriving artistic center is maintained by renowned writers and an annual arts festival. Such luminaries as Nobel Prize-winner Seamus Heaney and fellow poet Paul Muldoon have given birth to a modern, distinctively Northern Irish literary renaissance that grapples with—and transcends—the difficult politics of the area. The Belfast bar scene, a mix of Irish-British pub culture with international trends, entertains locals, foreigners, and a lively student population.

✈ INTERCITY TRANSPORTATION

Airports: Belfast International Airport (☎9442 2888), in Aldergrove, services **Aer Lingus** (☎(0845) 973 7747), **British Airways** (☎(0845) 722 2111), **Jersey European** (☎9045 7200), **British Midland** (☎9024 1188), and **Sabena** (☎9448 4823). **Airbus** (☎9033 3000) runs to Belfast's Europa and Laganside bus stations in the city center (M-Sa 2 per hr. 5:45am-10:30pm, Su about every hr. 7:10am-8:45pm; £5, return £8). **Belfast City Airport** (☎9045 7745), at the harbor, is the destination of **Manx Airlines** (☎(0845) 7256 256) and **Jersey European. Trains** run from the City Airport **(Sydenham Halt)** to Central Station (M-Sa 25-33 per day, Su 12 per day; £1).

Trains: ☎ **Infoline** 9033 3000. Trains arrive at Belfast's **Central Station,** East Bridge St. (☎9089 9400; inquiries M-Sa 7:30am-6pm, Su 9:30am-6:30pm). Some also stop at **Botanic Station** on Botanic Ave. in the University area, or **Great Victoria Station,** next to the Europa Hotel. To: **Derry** (2½hr.; M-F 7 per day, Sa 6 per day, Su 3 per day; £6.70); **Dublin** (2hr.; M-Sa 8 per day, Su 5 per day; £17); **Bangor** (35min.; M-F 39 per day, Sa 25 per day, Su 9 per day; £3); **Larne** (M-F 21 per day, Sa 16 per day, Su 6 per day; £3). To get to Donegall Sq. from Central Station, turn left and walk down East Bridge St. Turn right on Oxford St., then take your first left onto May St., which runs into Donegall Sq. A better option for the luggage-encumbered is the **Centrelink** bus service, free with rail tickets (see **Local Transportation,** below).

Buses: There are 2 main stations in Belfast. Buses traveling to and from the west, the north coast, and the Republic operate out of **Europa Station** off Great Victoria St., behind the Europa Hotel (☎9032 0011; inquiries M-Sa 7:30am-6:30pm, Su 12:30-5:30pm). Buses to **Dublin** (3hr.; M-Sa 7 per day, Su 4 per day; £10.50) and **Derry** (1¾hr.; M-Sa 19 per day, Su 6 per day; £6.50). Buses to and from Northern Ireland's east coast operate out of **Laganside Station** off Donegall Quay (☎9033 3000; inquiries M-Sa 8:30am-5:45pm). If you're on foot, take a left when you exit the terminal onto Queen's Sq. and walk past the clock tower. Queen's Sq. becomes High St. and runs into Donegall Pl.; a left here will get you to City Hall and Donegall Sq. (at the end of the street). The **Centrelink** bus connects both stations with the city center and the hostels and B&Bs near Queen's University (see **Local Transportation,** below). For all bus information, you'd be hard-pressed to stump Translink's web site, www.translink.co.uk.

Ferries: From the ferry terminal, off Donegall Quay, **SeaCat** (☎(08705) 523 523; www.seacat.co.uk) departs for: **Troon,** Scotland (2½hr., 2-3 per day); **Heysham,** England (4hr., Apr.-Nov. 1-2 per day); the **Isle of Man** (2¾hr., Apr.-Nov. 1-2 per day). Fares £10-30 without car, cheapest if booked 4 weeks in advance. **Norse Merchant Ferries** (☎9077 9090; www.norsemerchant.com) run to **Liverpool,** England. **P&O Ferries** in **Larne** (☎(0870) 2424 777) run to **Cairnryan,** Scotland, and to **Fleetwood,** England. For info on ferries and hovercraft to Belfast from **England** and **Scotland,** see **By Ferry,** p. 35. To reach the city center from the ferry terminal, exit left onto Donegall Quay. Turn right onto Albert Sq. at the Customs House (a large Victorian stone building). After 2 short blocks, turn left on Victoria St. (not Great Victoria St.). Turn right again at the clock tower onto High St., which runs into Donegall Pl. Here, a left will lead you to Donegall Sq., where you can catch a **Centrelink** bus (see **Local Transportation,** below). Late at night and early in the morning, the docks can be somewhat unsafe; take a **taxi.**

Car Rental: Avis, 69-71 Great Victoria St. (☎9024 0404; fax 9024 9054). 23+. £38 per day, £172 per week, discounted rates for longer rentals. Open M-F 8am-6pm, Sa 8am-1pm. Other offices at **Belfast International Airport** (☎9442 2333; open M-F 7:15am-

11:30pm, Sa-Su 7:30am-11:30pm) and **Belfast City Airport** (☎9045 2017; open M-F 7:30am-9:30pm, Sa 9am-5pm, Su noon-9:30pm). **Budget,** 96-102 Great Victoria St. (☎9023 0700). Ages 23-70. Open M-F 9am-5pm, Sa 9am-12:30pm. Other offices at **Belfast International Airport** (☎9442 3332; open daily 7:30am-11:30pm) and **Belfast City Airport** (☎9045 1111; open M-Sa 8am-9:30pm, Su 10am-9:30pm).

▣ LOCAL TRANSPORTATION

Local Transportation: The red **Citybus Network** (☎9024 6485) is supplemented by **Ulsterbus**'s suburban "blue buses." Travel within the city center 60p, concessions 30p. Citybuses going south and west leave from Donegall Sq. East; those going north and east leave from Donegall Sq. West (£1). 4-journey tickets £3.40, concessions £1.70. 7-day **"gold cards"** allow unlimited travel in the city (£12.60). 7-day **"silver cards"** permit unlimited travel in either North Belfast, West/South Belfast, or East Belfast (£8.30). All transport cards and tickets can be bought from the kiosks in Donegall Sq. West (open M-Sa 8am-6pm) and around the city. The **Centrelink** bus connects all major areas of Belfast in the course of its cloverleaf-shaped route: Donegall Sq., Castlecourt Shopping Centre, Europa and Laganside Bus Stations, Central Train Station, and Shaftesbury Sq. The buses can be caught at any of 24 designated stops (every 12min.; M-F 7:25am-9:15pm, Sa 8:30am-9:15pm; 60p, free with bus or rail ticket). Late **Nightlink** buses shuttle the tipsy from Donegall Sq. West to various small towns outside of Belfast F-Sa 1 and 2am; £3, payable on board or at the Donegall Sq. West kiosk.

Taxis: 24hr. metered cabs abound: **Value Cabs** (☎9023 0000); **City Cab** (☎9024 2000; wheelchair accessible); **Fon a Cab** (☎9023 3333); **Abjet Cabs** (☎9032 0000). Residents of West and North Belfast utilize the huge **black cabs** you'll see in the city center; some are metered, but others follow set routes (under £1).

Bike Rental: McConvey Cycles, 183 Ormeau Rd. (☎9033 0322). £10 per day, £40 per week. Deposit £50. Locks supplied. Panniers £1 per week. Open M-Sa 8:30am-6pm.

✴ ORIENTATION

Europa Station on **Great Victoria St.** is near several landmarks: the Europa hotel, the Crown Liquor Saloon, and the Opera House. To the northeast is the **City Hall** in **Donegall Sq.** A busy shopping district extends north for four blocks between City Hall and the enormous Castlecourt Shopping Centre. Donegall Pl. becomes **Royal Ave.** and runs from Donegall Sq. through the shopping area. In the eastern part of the shopping district, the **Cornmarket** area shows off characteristically Belfastian architecture and pubs in its narrow **entries** (small alleyways). The stretch of Great Victoria St. between the Europe Station and **Shaftesbury Sq.** is known as the **Golden Mile** for its highbrow establishments and Victorian architecture. **Botanic Ave.** and **Bradbury Pl.** (which becomes **University Rd.**) extend south from Shaftesbury Sq. into **Queen's University**'s turf, where student pubs, and budget accommodations await. In this southern area, the busiest neighborhoods center around **Stranmillis Rd., Malone Rd.,** and **Lisburn Rd.** The city center, Golden Mile, and university are quite safe; Belfast is generally safer for tourists than most American or European cities.

Divided from the rest of Belfast by the Westlink Motorway, working class **West Belfast** is more politically volatile than the city center. There remains a sharp division between sectarian neighborhoods: the Protestant neighborhood stretches along **Shankill Rd.,** just north of the Catholic neighborhood, which is centered on **Falls Rd.** The two are separated by the **peace line.** The **River Lagan** splits industrial **East Belfast** from Belfast proper. The shipyards and docks that brought the city fame and fortune extend north on both sides of the river as it grows into **Belfast Lough.** During the week, the area north of City Hall is deserted after 6pm. Although muggings are infrequent in Belfast, use taxis after dark, particularly near the clubs and pubs of the northeast area. West Belfast's murals are best seen by day.

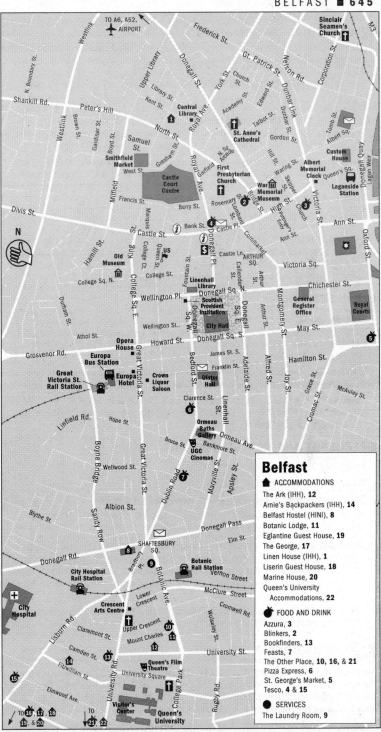

NORTHERN IRELAND

Belfast

🏠 ACCOMMODATIONS

The Ark (IHH), **12**
Arnie's Backpackers (IHH), **14**
Belfast Hostel (HINI), **8**
Botanic Lodge, **11**
Eglantine Guest House, **19**
The George, **17**
Linen House (IHH), **1**
Liserin Guest House, **18**
Marine House, **20**
Queen's University
  Accommodations, **22**

🍎 FOOD AND DRINK

Azzura, **3**
Blinkers, **2**
Bookfinders, **13**
Feasts, **7**
The Other Place, **10, 16,** & **21**
Pizza Express, **6**
St. George's Market, **5**
Tesco, **4** & **15**

⬤ SERVICES

The Laundry Room, **9**

⚡ PRACTICAL INFORMATION

TOURIST AND FINANCIAL SERVICES

Tourist Information Centre: The Belfast Welcome Centre, 47 Donegall Pl. (☎9024 6609), has a great booklet on Belfast and info on surrounding areas. The harried staff likes specific questions. Open June-Sept. M-Sa 9am-7pm, Su noon-5pm; Oct.-May M-Sa 9am-5:30pm. **Irish Tourist Board (Bord Fáilte),** 53 Castle St. (☎9032 7888), provides info on the Republic and makes reservations for accommodations "south of the border." Open June-Aug. M-F 9am-5pm, Sa 9am-12:30pm; Sept.-May M-F 9am-5pm.

Banks: Banks are easily found. The major players are: **Ulster Bank,** 47 Donegall Pl. (☎9027 6000); **First Trust,** 1-15 Donegall Sq. North (☎9031 0909); **Bank of Ireland,** 54 Donegal Pl. (☎9023 4334); **Northern Bank,** 14 Donegall Sq. West (☎9024 5277). Most banks open M-F 9am-4:30pm.

Currency Exchange: Thomas Cook, 22-24 Lombard St. (☎9088 3800). Cashes Thomas Cook traveler's checks with no commission, others 2%. Open May-Oct. M-Tu and Th 5:30am-10pm, W 5:30am-11pm, F-Su 5:30am-midnight; Nov.-Apr. daily 5:45am-8pm. Branch at **Belfast International Airport** (☎9444 7500). Open May-Oct. daily 5:30am-midnight; Nov.-Apr. Sa-Th 5:30am-9pm. Most banks, the HINI hostel, and post offices change currency and cash traveler's checks for a small fee.

LOCAL SERVICES

Luggage Storage: For security reasons there is no luggage storage at airports, bus stations, or train stations. The **Belfast Welcome Centre** (see above) will store luggage for £2. All 4 **hostels** will hold bags during the day for guests, and **The Ark** will hold bags during extended trips if you've stayed there (see **Accommodations,** below).

Bisexual, Gay, and Lesbian Information: Rainbow Project N.I., 33 Church Ln. (☎9031 9030). Open M-F 10am-5:30pm. **Lesbian Line** (☎9023 8668). Open Th 7:30-10pm.

Launderette: The Laundry Room (Duds 'n' Suds), Botanic Ave. (☎9024 3956). TV for the wait. About £3-4 per load. Open M-F 8am-9pm, Sa 8am-6pm, Su noon-6pm. **HINI,** 22 Donegall Rd. (see **Hostels,** p. 647).

EMERGENCY AND COMMUNICATIONS

Emergency: ☎999. No coins required.

Police: 65 Knock Rd. (☎9065 0222).

Crisis Lines: Samaritans (☎9066 4422). 24hr. line for depression.

Hospitals: Belfast City Hospital, 9 Lisburn Rd. (☎9032 9241). From Shaftesbury Sq. follow Bradbury Pl. and take a right at the fork.

Internet Access: The **Belfast Central Library,** 122 Royal Ave. (☎9050 9150). 30min. free email; £2 per hr. for web surfing. Open M and Th 9:30am-8pm, Tu-W and F 9:30am-5:30pm, Sa 9:30am-1pm. **Revelations Internet Cafe,** 27 Shaftesbury Sq. (☎9032 3337). £4 per hr., students and hostelers £3 per hr. Open M-F 10am-10pm, Sa 10am-6pm, Su 11am-7pm.

Post Office: Central Post Office, 25 Castle Pl. (☎9032 3740). Open M-Sa 9am-5:30pm. **Postal code:** BT1 1NB.

🏠 ACCOMMODATIONS

Nearly all Belfast's budget accommodations are near Queen's University, south of the city center. Walk 10-20min. from the bus or train station, or catch a **Centrelink** bus to Shaftesbury Sq. or **Citybus** #59, 69-71, or 84-85 from Donegall Sq. East. Reservations are recommended in summer.

HOSTELS AND DORMS

■ **Arnie's Backpackers (IHH),** 63 Fitzwilliam St. (☎9024 2867). 10min. from Europa Station on Great Victoria St. Take a right and head away from the Europa Hotel; at Shaftesbury Sq., take the right fork on Bradbury Pl., then fork left onto University Rd.; Fitzwilliam St. is the 4th left off University. Relaxed, friendly atmosphere. Key deposit £2 or ID. Luggage storage during the day. 8-bed dorms £7; 4-bed £8.50.

■ **The Ark (IHH),** 18 University St. (☎9032 9626). 10min. from Europa Station on Great Victoria St. Take a right; at Shaftesbury Sq., fork right on Bradbury Pl., then left onto University Rd. University St. is left off University Rd. Great sense of community: perfect strangers gather for meals and the occasional Tarantino video. Internet access. Laundry. Curfew 2am. 6-bed dorms £6.50; 4-bed dorms £7.50; doubles £28.

Belfast Hostel (HINI), 22 Donegall Rd. (☎9031 5435; www.hini.org.uk), off Shaftesbury Sq. Foreboding concrete facade belies the inviting interior. Internet access. Laundry. Reception 24hr. Dorms £8-10.

The Linen House Youth Hostel (IHH), 18-20 Kent St. (☎9058 6400), in West Belfast. Opposite the entrance to City Hall, turn left onto Donegall Pl. (Royal Ave.), then left onto Kent St. before the library. A somewhat impersonal, converted 19th-century linen factory. Internet access. Laundry. 18-bed dorms £6.50; 6- to 10-bed dorms £7.50; 8-bed dorms with bath £8.50; singles £12; doubles £28.

Queen's University Accommodations, 78 Malone Rd. (☎9038 1608). Take bus #71 from Donegall Sq. East; a 25min. walk from Europa. University Rd. runs into Malone Rd.; halls are on your left. Typical college dorms available late July to Aug. and Christmas and Easter vacations. Singles and doubles £12 per person, £9.70 international students, £8.20 UK students.

B&BS

The B&B universe, just south of Queen's University between Malone Rd. and Lisburn Rd., is one of healthy competition and camaraderie.

■ **Marine House,** 30 Eglantine Ave. (☎9066 2828). A mansion that feels warmer than its size might suggest. Singles £22; doubles £40, with bath £45; triples £57.

The George, 9 Eglantine Ave. (☎9068 3212). Renowned for its spotlessness and stained glass. All rooms with bath. Singles £22; doubles £44.

Botanic Lodge, 87 Botanic Ave. (☎9032 7682), on the corner of Mt. Charles Ave. Comfortable B&B close to the center. All rooms with sink and TV. Singles £22; doubles £40.

Liserin Guest House, 17 Eglantine Ave. (☎9066 0769). Comfy beds and huge lounge. All rooms with shower and TV. Coffee, tea, and biscuits available all day. Singles £22; doubles £40; triples £60.

Eglantine Guest House, 21 Eglantine Ave. (☎9066 7585). Sister to the Liserin and treats its guests with equal hospitality. Singles £22; doubles £38; triples £57.

◧ FOOD

Dublin Rd., Botanic Rd., and the Golden Mile have the most restaurants. Bakeries and cafes dot the shopping areas; nearly all close by 5:30pm, though on Thursdays most of the city center stays open until 8:45pm. **Tesco Supermarket** at 2 Royal Ave. (☎9032 3270) and 369 Lisburn Rd. (☎9066 3531) sells slightly cheaper food. (Open M-W and Sa 8am-7pm, Th 8am-9pm, F 8am-8pm, Su 1-5pm.) For fruits and vegetables, plunder the lively **St. George's Market,** East Bridge St., in the big warehouse between May and Oxford St. (Open Tu and F 6am-3pm.)

■ **Bookfinders,** 47 University Rd. (☎9032 8269). Atmospheric bookstore-cafe with mismatched dishes and counterculture paraphernalia. If you push the right door, you may end up in Narnia. Art gallery upstairs features student work. Soup and bread £1.75, sandwiches £2.20-2.50; extensive vegetarian options. Open M-Sa 10am-5:30pm.

Blinkers, 1-5 Bridge St. (☎9024 3330). An authentic diner—cluttered ashtrays and all—with prices to match. One of the few late-night spots north of City Hall. Quarter-pound burger £2.30. Open M-Th 9am-10pm, F-Sa 9am-10:30pm.

The Other Place, 79 Botanic Ave. (☎9020 7200), 133 Stranmillis Rd. (☎9020 7100), and 537 Lisburn Rd. (☎9029 7300). Reasonably priced all-day breakfast menu with chalkboard-listed specials. An array of ethnic foods, from Thai to Cajun, accompanied by an eclectic soundtrack. Open daily 8am-11pm.

Azzura, 8 Church Ln. (☎9024 2444). This tiny cafe dishes out pizzas and gourmet sandwiches for £2.50 and mountains of pasta for about £4. Open M-Sa 9am-5pm.

Pizza Express, 25-27 Bedford St. (☎9032 9050). Sounds like your typical franchise, but the grandeur of a spiral staircase and Tuscan decor suggests otherwise. 1- to 2-person pies £4-6. Open M-Sa noon-11:30pm.

Feasts, 39 Dublin Rd. (☎9033 2787). Pleasant street-side cafe serving Irish and international farmhouse cheeses in sandwiches (£3.50) and other dishes. Makes pasta on the premises (£5-6.50). Open M-F 9am-6:30pm, Sa 10am-6pm.

⊙ SIGHTS

If you do one thing in this city, take a ▓**black cab tour** of the murals and sights of West Belfast, bookable at most hostels. Quality varies; two guaranteed winners are **Original Black Taxi Tours** (passionate; ☎ (0800) 032 2003; £7.50 per person) and **Black Taxi Tours** (witty; ☎9064 2264; £7.50 per person). **Citybus** offers several tours of the city's sights. (☎9045 9484. Depart from Castle Pl., in front of the post office.)

DONEGALL SQUARE, CORNMARKET, AND EAST BELFAST

BELFAST CITY HALL. The administrative and geographic center of Belfast is distanced from downtown streets by a grassy square. Its 173 ft. green copper dome is visible from any point in the city. Inside A. Brunwell Thomas's Neoclassical 1906 structure, portraits of the city's Lord Mayors somberly line the halls. The **City Council's** oak-paneled chambers are deceptively austere, considering the council's reputation for rowdy meetings that sometimes devolve into fist fights. In front of the main entrance, an enormous marble **Queen Victoria statue** grimaces formidably. The interior of City Hall is accessible only by tour. (☎9032 0202, ext. 2346. 1hr. tours June-Sept. M-F 10:30, 11:30am, 2:30pm; Sa 2:30pm only; Oct.-May M-Sa 2:30pm. Free.)

LINEN HALL LIBRARY. Originally located across the street in the Linen Hall that became present-day City Hall, this library moved to its current location in 1894. It contains a famous collection of political documents relating to Northern Ireland. (17 Donegall Sq. North. ☎9032 1707. Open M-F 9:30am-5:30pm, Sa 9:30am-4:30pm.)

CORNMARKET ENTRIES. Cornmarket has been a marketplace for centuries. Though the area is dominated by modern buildings, relics of old Belfast remain in the tiny alleys, or **entries,** that connect some of the major streets. Between Ann St. and High St. runs **Pottinger's Entry.** Off Lombard St. and Bridge St., **Winecellar Entry** hosts Belfast's oldest pub, **White's Tavern** (see **Pubs and Clubs,** p. 651).

ODYSSEY. Belfast's newest and biggest attraction is opening its doors little by little. The Odyssey will eventually include a huge indoor arena, a multiplex cinema and IMAX, and a pavilion of shops, bars, and restaurants—including a Hard Rock Cafe. (2 Queen's Quay. ☎9045 1055.) Also inside is the new **W5 Discovery Centre,** a science center that beckons geeks of all ages. (☎9046 7700. Open M-F 10am-6pm, Sa-Su noon-6pm; last admission 5pm. £5, students and seniors £3.50, children £3, families £14.)

THE GOLDEN MILE

"The Golden Mile" refers to a strip along Great Victoria St. encrusted with many of Belfast's crown sites.

GRAND OPERA HOUSE. The city's pride and joy was bombed by the IRA, restored to its original splendor, and then bombed again. Come by for a Saturday tour. (☎9024 0411. Tours Sa 11am. £3, seniors and children £2. Office open M-W 8:30am-8pm, Th 8:30am-9pm, F 8:30am-6:30pm, Sa 8:30am-5:30pm.) See **Arts and Entertainment, p. 650**.

THE CROWN LIQUOR SALOON. The National Trust transformed this popular pub into a showcase of the carved (wood), the gilded (ceilings), and the stained (glass). Box-like snugs fit groups of two to 10. See **Pubs and Clubs,** p. 651.

QUEEN'S UNIVERSITY AREA

BOTANIC GARDENS. Behind the university, meticulously groomed gardens offer a welcome respite from city streets. Inside the gardens lie two 19th-century greenhouses, the toasty **Tropical Ravine House,** and the more temperate Lanyon-designed **Palm House.** Don't forget to stop and smell the rose gardens. (☎9032 4902. Gardens open daily 8am-dusk. Tropical House and Palm House open Apr.-Sept. M-F 10am-noon and 1-5pm, Sa-Su 2-5pm; Oct.-Mar. M-F 10am-noon and 1-4pm, Sa-Su 2-4pm. Free.)

ULSTER MUSEUM. This first-class museum fills its huge display halls with Irish and modern art, local history, antiquities, and the Mummy of Takabuti. The treasure from a Spanish Armada ship that sank off the Causeway Coast in 1588 is also on display. (In the Botanic Gardens, off Stranmillis Rd. ☎9038 3000 or 9038 1251. Open M-F 10am-5pm, Sa 1-5pm, Su 2-5pm. Free, except for some traveling exhibitions.)

WEST BELFAST AND THE MURALS

Separated from the rest of the city by the Westlink motorway, the neighborhoods of West Belfast have historically been at the heart of the political tensions in the North. The Catholic area (centered on **Falls Rd.**) and the Protestant neighborhood (centered on **Shankill**) are grimly separated by the **peace line,** a gray and seemingly impenetrable wall. The most dominant feature of the neighborhoods is their family community. West Belfast is not a center of consumer tourism or a "sight" in the traditional sense. The streets display political murals, which you will soon come across as you wander among the houses. It is best to visit the Falls and Shankill during the day, when the murals can be seen. Visit one and then return to the city center before heading to the other, as the area around the peace line is desolate.

THE FALLS. This Catholic neighborhood is much larger than Shankill and houses a younger, growing population. On Divis St., the **Divis Tower,** a high-rise apartment building, is an ill-fated housing development built by optimistic social planners in the 1960s that soon became an IRA stronghold. The British army still occupies the top three floors, and Shankill residents refer to it as "Little Beirut." Continuing west, Divis St. turns into **Falls Rd.** The **Sinn Féin** office is easily spotted: one side plastered with an enormous portrait of Bobby Sands (see **The Troubles,** p. 638) and an advertisement for the Sinn Féin newspaper, *An Phoblacht.* Continuing down the Falls, several murals feature Celtic art and the Irish language, displaying scenes of traditional music and dance or portraits of Famine victims. Murals in the Falls, unlike those of Shankill, are becoming less militant in nature, though a few remain in the Lower Falls that refer to specific acts of violence.

SHANKILL. North St., to the left of the tourist information centre (TIC), turns into Shankill Rd. as it crosses the **Westlink** and then arrives in Protestant Shankill, once a thriving shopping district. Turning left (coming from the direction of North St.) onto most side roads leads to the peace line. Some murals in Shankill seem to glorify the UVF and UFF rather than celebrate aspects of Orange culture. The densely decorated **Orange Hall** sits on the left at Brookmount St. The side streets on the

A PRIMER OF SYMBOLS IN THE MURALS OF WEST BELFAST

PROTESTANT MURALS

Red, White, and Blue: The colors of the British flag; often painted on curbs, signposts, etc., to demarcate Unionist murals and neighborhoods.

The Red Hand: The symbol of Ulster (found on Ulster's crest), usually used by Unionists to emphasize the separation of Ulster from the rest of Ireland. Symbolizes the hand of the first Viking king, which he supposedly cut off and threw on a Northern beach to establish his primacy.

King Billy/William of Orange: Sometimes depicted on a white horse, crossing the Boyne to defeat the Catholic King James II at the 1690 Battle of the Boyne. The Orange Order was later founded in his honor.

The Apprentice Boys: A group of young men who shut the gates of Derry to keep out the troops of James II, beginning the great siege of 1689. They have become Protestant folk heroes, inspiring a sect of the Orange Order in their name. The slogan **"No Surrender,"** also from the siege, has been appropriated by radical Unionists, most notably Rev. Ian Paisley.

Lundy: The Derry leader who advocated surrender during the siege; now a term for anyone who wants to give in to Catholic demands.

Taig: Phonetic spelling of the Irish given name Teague; Protestant slang for a Catholic.

Scottish Flag: Blue with a white cross; recalls the Scottish-Presbyterian roots of many Protestants whose ancestors were part of the Ulster Plantation.

CATHOLIC MURALS

Orange and Green: Colors of the Irish Republic's flag; often painted on curbs and signposts in Republican neighborhoods.

Landscapes: Usually imply Republican territorial claims to the North.

The Irish Volunteers: Republican tie to the earlier (nonsectarian) Nationalists.

Saiorsche: "Freedom"; the most common Irish term found on murals.

Éireann go bráth: "Ireland forever"; a popular IRA slogan.

Tiocfaidh ár lá: (CHOCK-ee-ar-LA) "Our day will come."

Slan Abnaile: (slang NA-fail) "Leave our streets"; directed at the primarily Protestant RUC police force.

Phoenix: Symbolizes united Ireland rising from the ashes of British persecution.

Lug: Celtic god, seen as the protector of the "native Irish" (Catholics).

Green ribbon: IRA symbol for "free POWs."

Bulldog: Britain.

Bowler Hats: A symbol for Orangemen.

right guide you to the **Shankill Estate** and more murals. Through the estate, Crumlin Rd. heads back to the city center past an army base, the courthouse, and the jail, which are linked by a tunnel. The oldest Loyalist murals are found here. The Shankill area is shrinking as middle-class Protestants leave, but a growing Protestant population lives on Sandy Row, a turn off of Donegall Rd. at Shaftesbury Sq. An orange arch topped with King William marks its start.

🎵 ENTERTAINMENT

Belfast's cultural events are covered by the monthly *Arts Council Artslink*, free at the TIC. More listings appear in the daily *Belfast Telegraph* (and its Friday arts supplement) and Thursday's *Irish News*. The **Crescent Arts Centre,** 2 University Rd., supplies general arts info and specific news about its own exhibits and concerts, which take place September through May. The Centre also hosts eight-week courses in yoga, trapeze, writing, trad (traditional music), and drawing. (☎9024 2338. Open M-Sa 9:30am-5pm.) **Fenderesky Gallery,** 2 University Rd., in the Crescent Arts building, hosts contemporary shows year-round. (☎9023 5245. Open Tu-Sa 11:30am-5pm.) The **Old Museum,** 7 College Sq. North, is Belfast's largest venue for new artwork. (☎9023 5053, for tickets 9023 3332. Open M-Sa 9am-5:30pm. Free.)

Belfast's theater season runs from September to June. The **Grand Opera House,** 2-4 Great Victoria St. (☎9024 1999), hosts opera, ballet, musicals, and plays. (☎9024 1919, 24hr. info 9024 9129. Box office open M-W 8:30am-8pm, Th 8:30am-9pm, F 8:30am-6:30pm, Sa 8:30am-5:30pm. Tickets from £8. 50% off student rush available M-Th after noon.) **The Lyric Theatre** plays at 55 Ridgeway St. (☎9038 1081. Box office open M-Sa 9:30am-7pm. Tickets M-Th around £8.50., F-Su £12.50; students £6, except Sa.) **The Group Theatre,** Bedford St., brings comedy to Ulster Hall. (☎9032 9685. Box office open Sept.-May M-F noon-3pm. Tickets £2-6.)

Music-wise, **Ulster Hall,** Bedford St. (☎9032 3900), brings Belfast everything from classical to pop. Try independent box offices for tickets: **Our Price** (☎9031 3131) or the **Ticket Shop** at Virgin (☎9032 3744). **The Grand Opera House** (see above) resounds with classical vocal music. **Waterfront Hall,** 2 Lanyon Pl., is Belfast's newest concert center, hosting performances throughout the year. (☎9033 4400. Tickets £10-35, usually £12; student discounts available.)

🍺🎭 PUBS AND CLUBS

Get current nightlife info from *The List*, available at the TIC, hostels, and restaurants. The city center closes early and is deserted late at night; we suggest starting in Cornmarket, visiting old downtown, and finishing near the university.

- 🏛 **Lavery's,** 12 Bradbury Pl. (☎9087 1106). 3 unpretentious floors. W live music, DJs weekends, free; disco on 2nd floor £1; 3rd-floor dance club £5. Open until 1am.
- 🏛 **Oneil's,** Joys Entry (☎9032 6711), off High St. Spacious pub by week, crazy club by weekend. Th live rock. Open M-F noon-10pm, Sa 9:30pm-3am, Su 9:30pm-2:30am.
- 🏛 **The John Hewitt,** 51 Lower Donegall St. (☎9023 3768). Newish, named after a poet, and suited for business lunches. Run by and for charity. Th trivia, F jazz, much trad.

Morning Star Pub, 17-19 Pottinger's Entry (☎9032 3976), between Ann St. and High St. Look for the Victorian wrought-iron bracket hanging above the entry. Award-winning bar food awaits upstairs. Open M-Sa 11:30am-11pm, Su 11:30am-7pm.

White's Tavern, 2-4 Winecellar Entry (☎9024 3080), off Lombard St. and Bridge St.; look for a left turn off High St. Belfast's oldest tavern (since 1630). W gay night. Open M-Tu 11:30am-11pm, W 11:30am-1:30am, Th-Su 11:30am-1am.

Queen's Cafe-Bar, 4 Queen's Arcade (☎9032 1347), off Fountain St. Friendly, low-pressure atmosphere in a glitzy shopping arcade off Donegall Pl. Mixed, gay-friendly crowd. DJs on Sa nights. Call in advance for private parties.

Hercules Bar, 61-63 Castle St. (☎9032 4587). Working man's pub with fab local music. Trad F-Sa, blues and jazz other nights. Open M-Th 11:30am-11pm, F-Sa 11:30am-1am.

Kelly's Cellars, 30 Bank St. (☎9032 4835), off Royal Ave. after the Fountain St. pedestrian area. The oldest (mercifully) unrenovated pub in Belfast. Trad F and Sa afternoons and Sa nights; occasional bands. Open M-W 11:30am-8pm, Th-Sa 11:30am-1am.

Robinson's, 38-40 Great Victoria St. (☎9024 7447). 4 floors of theme bars. Most renowned for **Fibber McGee's** (in the back; incredible trad Tu-Sa twice daily). Non-trad usually F night and Sa afternoons. Decent nightclub upstairs Th-Sa (cover F £5, Sa £8).

Morrisons, 21 Bedford St. (☎9024 8458). Painstakingly reconstructed "traditional" atmosphere. F-Sa live bands, cover £5-7.

Crown Liquor Saloon, 46 Great Victoria St. (☎9024 9476). This National Trust-owned pub had its windows blown in by a bombing, but the inside feels original. Tourist crowd.

The Fly, 5-6 Lower Cres. (☎9050 9750). Look for big torches. Very popular; buggy decor. 1st floor for pints, 2nd for mingling, and an Absolut lounge on the 3rd. No cover.

The Botanic Inn ("The Bot"), 23 Malone Rd. (☎9066 0460). Huge and popular student bar. Pub grub £4-5. Tu trad, Th-Sa 60s-80s music. 21+. Cover £2. Open until 1am.

The Empire, 42 Botanic Ave. (☎9024 9276). Once a church; now resembles a Victorian music hall. Sept.-June Tu comedy, Th-Su live bands. Cover M-Th and Su £3; F-Sa £4.

The Corner Cafe and Bar, 11a Strawmills Rd. (☎9066 3266). Former studio of artist William Conor—airy, white, and high-ceilinged. Crowded on weekends.

GAY AND LESBIAN NIGHTLIFE

On Wednesday nights Belfast's oldest pub, **White's Tavern,** becomes one of its most progressive. **Queen's Cafe-Bar** always attracts a diverse crowd (see above).

The Kremlin, 96 Donegall St. (☎9080 9700). Look for the imposing statue of Stalin. Hot gay nightspot with countless venues and events. Tight security. Cover varies; free Su-M, W, and before 9pm. Open M and W until 1:30am; Tu, Th, F 3am; Sa 4am.

Parliament Bar, 2-6 Dunbar St. (☎9023 4520), at Talbot St. Th-F and Su disco, cover £5-10. Su drag karaoke. Tu drag bingo. Open Th and Su until 1am, F 3am, Sa 4am.

◤ DAYTRIP FROM BELFAST

ULSTER FOLK AND TRANSPORT MUSEUMS

Take the Bangor road (A27) east from Belfast. Buses and trains stop here on the way to Bangor. ☎9042 8428. Open July-Sept. M-Sa 10am-6pm, Su 11am-6pm; Oct.-Feb. M-F 10am-4pm, Sa 10am-5pm, Su 11am-5pm; Mar.-June M-F 10am-5pm, Sa 10am-6pm, Su 11am-6pm. Folk Museum £4, concessions £2.50. Transport Museum same. Combined admission £5, £3

The Ulster Folk and Transport Museums stretch over 176 acres in Holywood. Established by an Act of Parliament in the 1950s, the ▨**Folk Museum** contains over 30 buildings from the past three centuries and all nine Ulster counties. Most of the buildings are transplanted originals, reconstructed stone by stone in the museum's landscape. The Transport Museum and the Railway Museum are across the road from the Folk Museum. Inside the **Transport Museum,** horse-drawn coaches, cars, bicycles, and trains display the history of moving vehicles. The hangar-shaped **Railway Museum** stuffs in 25 old railway engines.

DOWN AND ARMAGH

NEWCASTLE AND THE MOURNES

The 15 rounded peaks of the Mourne Mountains sprawl across the southeastern corner of Northern Ireland. Volcanic activity pushed up five different kinds of granite beneath a shale crust 50 million years ago. No road penetrates the center of the mountains, leaving hikers in welcome solitude. Outdoorsy types often spend the night in Newcastle, where arcades and waterslide parks line the waterfront.

◧ **TRANSPORTATION.** Newcastle's **bus station** is at 5-7 Railway St. (☎4372 2296), at the end of Main St. away from the mountains. Buses run to: **Downpatrick** (40min.; M-F 12 per day, Sa 11 per day, Su 6 per day; £2.30); **Newry** (1hr.; M-F 12 per day, Sa 10 per day, Su 3 per day; £3.60); **Belfast** (1¼hr.; M-F 24 per day, Sa 18 per day, Su 10 per day; £4.80); **Dublin** (3hr.; M-Sa 4 per day, Su 2 per day; £10). **Rent bikes** at **Wiki Wiki Wheels,** 10b Donard St., beside the Xtra-Vision building left of the bus station. (☎4372 3973. £6.50 per day, £30 per week; children £5 per day. ID deposit. Open M-Sa 9am-6pm, Su 2-6pm.) For a **taxi,** call **Donard Cabs** (☎4372 4100 or 4372 2823).

⊞♞ ORIENTATION AND PRACTICAL INFORMATION. Newcastle's main road stretches along the waterfront; initially called **Main St.** (where it intersects **Railway St.**), its name subsequently changes to **Central Promenade** and then to **South Promenade.** The **tourist information centre** (TIC), 10-14 Central Promenade, is in a blue-and-white building 10min. down the main street from the bus station. Get a free map and visitor guide. (☎4372 2222. Open July-Aug. M-Sa 9:30am-7pm, Su 1-7pm; Sept. and June M-Sa 10am-5pm, Su 2-6pm.) Rent **camping equipment** at **Hill Trekker,** 115 Central Promenade. (☎4372 3842. Open Tu-W and Sa-Su 10am-5:30pm, Th 10am-4:45pm, F 10am-6:15pm.) Other services include: **First Trust Bank,** 28-32 Main St. (☎4372 3476; open M-F 9:30am-4:30pm); **Internet access** at **Anchor Bar** (see below), free if you buy a pint; and the **post office,** 33-35 Central Promenade (☎4372 2418; open M-W and F 9am-5:30pm, Th and Sa 9am-12:30pm). **Postal code:** BT33 0AA.

♠♖⌂ ACCOMMODATIONS, FOOD, AND PUBS B&Bs in this summer resort town are plentiful but pricey; fortunately, there is also a hostel. The Mournes are a free and legal camping alternative. Follow Railway St. toward the water and take a right onto Downs Rd. at the Newcastle Arms to reach **Newcastle Youth Hostel (HINI),** 30 Downs Rd. Quarters are tight, but such discomforts are appeased by the prime location. (☎4372 2133. Dorms £9.50, under 18 £8.50.) **Drumrawn House,** 139 Central Promenade, a 15min. walk from the bus station, is Georgian townhouse with marvellous sea views. (☎4372 6847. £21.50 per person.) The **camping** is fine at **Tollymore Forest Park,** 176 Tullybrannigan Rd., 2 mi. down the A2 or a quick ride on the "Busybus" (10min.; 10am and noon; summer also 4:30pm; 75p) from the Newcastle Ulsterbus station. (☎4372 2428. £9 per tent, £11 per caravan. Electricity £1.50.)

The fruitcake-like density of junk food (sweet *and* savory) on the waterfront impresses. **⍟Seasalt,** 51 Central Promenade, is a stylish deli-cafe with Mediterranean edge. It becomes a delicious, reservations-only, three-course bistro weekend nights. (☎4372 5027. Bistro meal £15. Open M-Tu 9am-6pm, W-Su 9am-9pm.) **Cafe Maud's,** 106 Main St., offers hipness with a view. (☎4372 6184. Open M-Su 9am-9:30pm.) **The Cookie Jar,** 112 Main St. or in the Newcastle Shopping Centre, serves sandwiches (under £2) and pastries. (Open M-Sa 9am-5:30pm.) **Anchor Bar,** 9 Bryansford Rd. (☎4372 3344), is a traditional-feeling pub, with food and web access.

▨ HIKING Before heading for the hills, stop at the **Mourne Countryside Centre,** 91 Central Promenade. A friendly and knowledgeable staff leads hikes and offers a broad selection of guides and maps of the mountains. Those planning short excursions can purchase *Mourne Mountain Walks* (£6), which describes 10 one-day hikes. If you're staying in the Mournes overnight, buy the topographical *Mourne Country Outdoor Pursuits Map* for £6. (☎4372 4059. Centre open year-round M-F 9am-5pm.) The **Mourne Heritage Trust** two doors down is also worth a stop.

The **Mourne Wall,** built between 1904 and 1923, encircles 12 of the mountains just below their peaks. Walking the 22 mi. wall takes a strenuous 8hr. The Mournes' highest peak, **Slieve Donard** (2788 ft.), towers above Newcastle. The trail up is wide and well maintained (5hr. round-trip). **Donard Park** provides the most direct access to the Mournes from Newcastle; it's convenient to both Slieve Donard and nearby **Slieve Commedagh.** The park lies on the corner of Central Promenade and Bryansford Rd. To hike, follow the dirt path at the back of the car park as it crosses two bridges and eventually joins the Glen River Path for about 1½ mi. to reach the Mourne Wall. At the wall, turn left for Slieve Donard or right for Slieve Commedagh. Those seeking a more remote trek might try **Slieve Bernagh** (2423 ft.) or **Slieve Binnian** (2450 ft.), most easily accessed from **Hare's Gap** and **Silent Valley,** respectively. The two craggy peaks, both with tremendous views, can be combined into a 12 mi. half-day hike.

Wilderness **camping** is popular. Common spots include the **Annalong Valley,** the shores of **Lough Shannagh,** and near the **Trassey River.** While camping around the Mourne Wall is allowed, camping in the forest itself is strictly prohibited because of potential forest fires. Weather conditions can change suddenly. Remember to bring warm clothing since the mountains get cold and windy at night.

NORTHERN IRELAND

ARMAGH

Religious zealotry and violent conflict have long been associated with Armagh. The hilltop fort *Ard Macha* ("Macha's Height") was built in pagan times but converted in the 5th century, supposedly as St. Patrick's base of operations. The city has sought to transcend the sectarian scars of its troubled past by emphasizing its role as the ecclesiastical capital of both the Republic and Northern Ireland.

🖪🖬 TRANSPORTATION AND PRACTICAL INFORMATION. Buses (☎3752 2266) go from Lonsdale Rd. to **Belfast** (1hr.; M-F 22 per day, Sa 15 per day, Su 7 per day; £5) and **Enniskillen** (2hr., M-Sa 1-2 per day, £5.50). **Brown's Bikes,** 21A Scotch St., **rents bikes** for £7 per day, £30 per week. (☎3752 2782. Open M-Sa 9am-5:30pm.)

English St., Thomas St., and **Scotch St.** comprise Armagh's city center. To the east lies the **Mall.** West of the city center, two cathedrals sit on neighboring hills. The **tourist information centre** (TIC) is at 40 English St. (☎3752 1800. Open M-Sa 9am-5pm, Su 1-5pm.) Other services include: banks **First Trust,** English St. (☎3752 2025) and Ulster, Market St. (☎3752 2053); **Internet access** at **Armagh Computer World,** 43 Scotch St. (☎3751 0002; £3 per hr.; open M-Sa 9am-6pm); and the **post office,** 31 Upper English St. (☎3751 0313; open M-F 9am-5:30pm, Sa 9am-12:30pm). Poste Restante goes to 46 Upper English St. (☎3752 2856). **Postal code:** BT61 7AA.

🏠 ACCOMMODATIONS. Armagh Youth Hostel (YHANI), behind Queen's University campus, is huge and clean. From the TIC, turn left twice, follow Abbey St. for two blocks, and traverse the parking lot; the hostel entrance is in a small abbey. (☎3751 1800. Laundry £3. Reception 8-11am and 5-11pm. Lock-up at 9pm; security code for later access. 6- and 4-bed dorms £11.50; doubles £13.) Make a right on Desart Ln., then turn left to reach **Desart Guest House,** 99 Cathedral Rd., the second left off Desart Ln., a formidable mansion with rooms sunny, clean, and plush. (☎3752 2387. Singles £20; doubles £35.) The **Padua Guest House,** 63 Cathedral Rd., is just past the Catholic Cathedral. (☎3752 2039. Doubles £32.)

🍴🍷 FOOD AND PUBS. Finding an eatery in the city center or near the Shambles Market is easy; affording the food is more difficult. Your best bet is to get groceries at **Sainsbury's** in the Mall Shopping Centre, Mall West. (☎3751 1050. Open M-W and Sa 8:30am-8pm, Th-F 8:30am-9pm.) The **Basement Cafe,** under the Armagh Film House on English St., is cheap and chic. (☎3752 4311. Open M-Sa 9am-5:30pm.) **Elichi** promises Italo-Indo-European takeaway, or at least a respectable pizza. (☎3751 8800. Open daily 5pm-midnight.) **Turner's,** on English St. across from the Shambles, is the newest twentysomething hotspot. (☎3752 2028. F live band, Sa DJ.) **The Shambles Lounge,** English St., hosts an older crowd for after-work pints and weekend dinners. (☎3752 4107. Cover £5. Food served 6-9:30pm.)

🖾 SIGHTS. Armagh's cathedrals lord it over the city from two opposing hills. To the north on Cathedral Rd. sits the 1873 Roman Catholic **Cathedral of St. Patrick,** whose imposing exterior contrasts mightily with the ultra-modern sanctuary, which seems to have been designed by a federation of pagans and Martians. (☎3752 4177. Open daily until dusk. Free.) To the south is the **Cathedral of St. Patrick,** or rather, "the Protestant one." Authorities claim that this 13th-century church rests on the site where The Pat founded his main house of worship in AD 445. (☎3752 3142. Open Apr.-Oct. daily 9:30am-5pm; Nov.-Mar. 9:30am-4pm. Tours June-Aug. M-Sa 11:30am and 2:30pm. Free.)

Up College Hill, north of the Mall, the **Armagh Observatory** (☎3752 2928) was founded in 1790 by Archbishop Robinson. Star-struck tourists can observe a modern weather station and 1885 refractory telescope. More celestial wonders await in the nearby **Planetarium.** (☎3752 3689. 45min. shows July-Aug. 3-5 per day; Apr.-June M-F 1 per day. Open M-F 10am-4:45pm, Sa-Su 1:15-4:45pm. Seating limited; book ahead. £3.50, students £2.50.) The **Palace Demesne** (dah-MAIN), south of the town center, is not open to visitors, but the **Palace Stables Heritage Centre** its slick multimedia show are. A **Franciscan Friary** occupies a peaceful corner of the grounds. (☎3752 9629. Open Apr.-Sept. M-Sa 10am-7pm, Su 1-7pm; Oct.-Mar. M-Sa 10am-5pm, Su 2-5pm. £2.80, students £2.20.)

Two miles west of Armagh on Killylea Rd. (A28), mysterious **Navan Fort** was the capital of the Kings of Ulster for 800 years. This may look like a grassy mound of dirt, but with imagination, historical knowledge, and many pints, you might see extensive fortifications and elaborate religious paraphernalia strewn across the site. Queen Macha is said to have founded the fort, although it is also associated with St. Patrick, who probably chose Armagh as a Christian center because of its proximity to this pagan stronghold. (Always open. Free.)

NORTHERN IRELAND

ANTRIM AND DERRY

The A2 coastal road skitters along the edge of Antrim and Derry, connecting the scenic attractions of both counties. West of Belfast, stodgy and industrial Larne gives way to lovely seaside villages. The nine Glens of Antrim stimulate scenery fiends. Near the midpoint of the island's northern coast, the Giant's Causeway spills its geologic weirdness into the ocean. The industrial landscape reappears past the Causeway, with the carnival lights of Portrush and Portstewart. The road terminates at turbulent, fascinating Derry, the North's second-largest city.

LARNE

Larne is a working town whose significance to tourists lies in is its ferries to and from Scotland. **P&O Ferries** (☎(0990) 980777) operates boats from Larne to **Cairnryan**, Scotland, and **Fleetwood**, England. The **train station** rests adjacent to a roundabout, down the street from the tourist information centre (TIC) on Narrow Gauge Rd. (☎2826 0604. Open daily 7:45am-5:45pm.) The **bus station** is just south of town, on the other side of the A8 overpass. (☎2827 2345. Open M-Sa 9am-5:30pm.)

To reach town from the harbor, take a right outside of the ferry port. It's a good idea to cab it in the evening, as this route passes through a rough neighborhood. The **tourist information centre,** Narrow Gauge Rd., books rooms. (☎2826 0088. Open July-Sept. M-F 9am-6pm, Sa 9am-5pm; Oct.-Easter M-F 9am-5pm; Easter-June M-Sa 9am-5pm. 24hr. computerized info kiosk outside.) **Northern Bank** is at 19 Main St. (☎2827 6311. Open M 9:30am-5pm, Tu-F 10am-3:30pm, Sa 9:30am-12:30pm.)

Rather than lingering near the ferry port, seek beds down the Glenarm Rd., in the more affluent area closer to town. **Inverbann** has spacious, TV- and bath-endowed rooms. (☎2827 2524. £15 per person.) The **Co-op Superstore** stocks up on Station Rd., next to the bus station. (☎2826 0737. Open M-W 9am-9pm, Th-F 9am-10pm, Sa 9am-8pm, Su 1-6pm.) Larne's main street is littered with sandwich shops.

GLENS OF ANTRIM

Cosmetic surgery, glacier-style, left nine deep scars in the mountainous coastline of northeastern Co. Antrim. The water that collected in these "glens," spurred the growth of trees, ferns, and other lush flora not usually seen in Ireland. The A2 coastal road connects the mouths of the glens, while roads leading inland grant access to packs of marauding weekenders.

⬛ TRANSPORTATION

Two **Ulsterbus** (Belfast ☎9032 0011, Larne 2827 2345) routes serve the glens year-round: #156 from **Belfast** stops in Larne, Ballygally, Glenarm, and Carnlough (summer M-Sa 6-7 per day, Su 3 per day; off season M-Sa 5-7 per day, Su 1 per day; £2.80-5.20) and sometimes continues to Waterfoot, Cushendall, and Cushendun (summer M-F 4 per day, Sa-Su 2 per day; off season M-F 2 per day); #150 runs between **Ballymena** and **Glenariff** (M-Sa 5 per day, £2.60), then to Waterfoot, Cushendall, and Cushendun (M-F 5 per day, Sa 3 per day; £4.30). The **Antrim Coaster** (a.k.a. "#252") goes coastal from **Belfast** to **Coleraine** and stops at every town along the way (2 per day, £7.50). **Cycling** the glens is fabulous from Ballygally to Cushendun; beyond Cushendun, the hilly road makes even motorists groan. The **Ardclinis Adventure Centre** in Cushendall rents bikes (see below).

GLENARIFF

Beautiful, broad Glenariff is guarded from any would-be wicked stepmothers by the village of **Waterfoot**, 9 mi. up the coast from Glenarm. Thackeray dubbed the area "Switzerland in miniature" because of the steep and rugged landscape. The glen lies inside the large **Glenariff Forest Park**, 4 mi. south of Waterfoot on the Glenariff road (A43). The **bus** between Cushendun and Ballymena (#150) stops at the official park entrance (M-F 5 per day, Sa 3 per day). If you're walking from Waterfoot, enter 1½ mi. downhill by taking the road that branches left toward the Manor Lodge Restaurant. The park's many trails range from half- to five-mile round-trips. The three-mile ⬛**Waterfall Trail**, marked by blue triangles, follows the fern-lined Glenariff River from the park entrance to the Manor Lodge. The entrance to the **Moyle Way**, a 17 mi. hike from Glenariff to Ballycastle, is directly across from the park entrance. All of the walks begin and end at the car park, where you will also find the **Glenariff Tea House**, which has food *and* free trail maps. (☎2565 8769. Open Easter-Sept. daily 11am-6pm.) **Glenariff Forest Park Camping**, 98 Glenariff Rd., is self-explanatory. (☎2175 8232. Tents £10, off season £7.)

CUSHENDALL

Cushendall is nicknamed the capital of the Glens, most likely because its village center consists of *four* shop-lined streets instead of just one. In addition to its commercial significance, Cushendall is also well situated less than 5 mi. from Glenaan, Glenariff Glenballyeamon, Glencorp, and Glendun.

🖪🛂 TRANSPORTATION AND PRACTICAL INFORMATION. Ulsterbus (☎9033 3000) #162 runs from Belfast (£6.20) via Larne (£5.20), then north to Cushendun (July-Aug. M-F 4 per day, Sa-Su 2 per day; Sept.-June M-F 2 per day). #252 (Antrim Coaster) stops everywhere, including Cushendall; #150 stops in Glenariff (see **Transportation**, p. 655). **Ardclinis Activity Centre**, 11 High St. (☎2177 1340), **rents bikes** (£10 per day; deposit £50) and gives tips on hill- and gorge-walking and canoeing.

   The **tourist information centre** (TIC), 25 Mill St., is near the bus stop at the Cushendun end of town. (☎2177 1180. Open July-Sept. M-F 10am-1pm and 2:30-5pm, Sa 10am-1pm; Oct. to mid-Dec. and Feb.-June Tu-Sa 10am-1pm.) **Northern Bank** is at 5 Shore St. (☎2177 1243. Open M 9:30am-12:30pm and 1:30-5pm, Tu-F 10am-12:30pm and 1:30-3:30pm.) The **post office** is on Mill St. (☎2177 1201. Open M and W-F 9am-1pm and 2-5:30pm, Tu and Sa 9am-12:30pm.) **Postal code:** BT44.

🖪🗖🛒 ACCOMMODATIONS, FOOD, AND PUBS. ⬛Glendale, 46 Coast Rd., is friendly and spacious. (☎2177 1495. All rooms with bath. £17 per person.) **Ballyeamon Camping Barn (ACB)**, 6 mi. south of Cushendall on B14, is far from town but close to Glenariff Forest Park and the Moyle Way. (☎2175 8451 or (077) 0344 0558. Book ahead and call for pickup. Blankets £2. Dorms £7.) **Spar Market**, 2 Coast Rd., past Bridge Rd., has plentiful fruits and veggies. (☎2177 1763. Open daily 7:30am-10pm.) **Arthur's**, Shore St., serves fresh sandwiches. (☎2177 1627. Open daily 10am-5pm.) **Joe McCollam's (Johnny Joe's)**, 23 Mill St. (☎2177 1876), features impromptu ballads, jigs, and limericks. Most nights see music, but it's guaranteed weekends.

🖪 SIGHTS. Sights concentrate in the miniscule, picturesque seaside village of **Cushendun**, 5 mi. north of Cushendall on the A2. Buses head to Cushendun from Cushendall. In 1954, the National Trust bought the entire village, a whitewashed and black-shuttered set of buildings lying by a vast beach and perforated by wonderful, murky **caves** carved into red sea cliffs. **Mary McBride's**, 2 Main St. (☎2176 1511), used to be the *Guinness Book of World Records*'s "smallest bar in Europe." The original bar is still there, but it has been expanded to create a lounge.

CAUSEWAY COAST

Past Cushendun, the northern coast shifts from lyrical to dramatic mode. Sea-battered cliffs tower 600 ft. above white beaches, then give way to the spectacular Giant's Causeway. The A2, the major route along the coast, gives good **cycling.**

Ulsterbus (☎ 7043 3334 or 7032 5400) #172 buses between Ballycastle and Portrush along the coast (1hr.; M-F 6 per day, Sa 4 per day, Su 5 per day; £3.70) with frequent connections to Portstewart. The "Triangle" service (#140) connects Portrush, Portstewart, and Coleraine (9am-5pm every 10min., less frequent service 6:55-9am and 5-10:30pm). The #252 "Antrim Coaster" runs up the coast from Belfast to Portstewart via most towns. (☎ 9033 3000. 2 per day, £13.30 from Belfast.) Ulsterbus also runs tours from Belfast, Portrush, and Portstewart (£3-9). The **Bushmills Bus** coasts between Coleraine, 5 mi. south of Portrush, and the Causeway. (☎ 7043 3334. July-Aug. 7 per day.)

BALLYCASTLE

The Causeway Coast leaves the sleepy Glens behind when it hits Ballycastle, a bubbly seaside town that shelters Causeway-bound tourists. Friendly Ballycastle makes a nice base for budget travelers exploring the coast. Summer weekends bring carloads of locals to the town's beaches, pubs, and discos.

■▰ ORIENTATION AND PRACTICAL INFORMATION Ballycastle's main street runs perpendicular to the waterfront, starting at the ocean as **Quay Rd.,** becoming **Ann St.,** and then turning into **Castle St.** as it passes the **Diamond.** Most restaurants and shops are along Ann St. and Castle St. As Quay Rd. meets the water, the road lefts sharply onto **North St.,** where more stores and food await.

Ulsterbus stops at the end of Quay Rd., coming from: **Cushendall** (50min., M-F 1 per day) and **Belfast** (3hr., 6 per day). The **Antrim Coaster** stops here. **Cushleake B&B,** Quay Rd., **rents bikes.** (☎ 2076 3798. £6 per day.) The **tourist office,** 7 Mary St., has 24hr. computerized information outside. (☎ 2076 2024. Open July-Aug. M-F 9:30am-7pm, Sa 10am-6pm, Su 2-6pm; Sept.-June M-F 9:30am-5pm.) Other services include **First Trust Bank,** Ann St. (☎ 2076 3326; open M-Tu and Th-F 9:30am-4:30pm, W 10am-4:30pm) and the **post office,** 3 Ann St. (☎ 2076 2519; open M-Tu and Th-F 9am-1pm and 2-5:30pm, W 9am-1pm, Sa 9am-12:30pm). **Postal Code:** BT54 6AA.

▰◪▨ ACCOMMODATIONS, FOOD, AND PUBS Watch out for the Ould Lammas Fair, held the last Monday and Tuesday in August—B&Bs and hostels fill long in advance. The **Castle Hostel (IHH),** 62 Quay Rd., slightly out of town next to the Marine Hotel, is relaxed. (☎ 2076 2337. Laundry £4. Dorms £7; private rooms £8.50 per person.) **Ballycastle Backpackers (IHO)** is on North Rd. next to the Marine Hotel. (☎ 2076 3612 or (077) 7323 7890. Dorms £7.50.) **Fragrens,** 34 Quay Rd., is one of Ballycastle's oldest houses. (☎ 2076 2168. £15 per person, with bath £17.)

SuperValu, 54 Castle St., is a 10min. walk from the hostels. (☎ 2076 2268. Open M-Sa 8am-10pm, Su 9am-10pm.) ▨**Flash-in-the-Pan,** 74 Castle St., prepares disorientingly delicious chipper fare. (☎ 2076 2251. Open Su-Th 11am-midnight, F-Sa 11am-1am.) **Herald's,** 22 Ann St., serves big-yet-cheap portions. (☎ 2076 9064. Internet access. Open daily 8am-9pm.) Tourists head for tiny, fire-warmed **House of McDonnell,** 71 Castle St. (☎ 2076 2975. F trad, Sa folk.) **Central Bar,** 12 Ann St., rollicks. (☎ 2076 3877. Su piano sing-alongs, W trad, Th and Sa karaoke.)

◪ NEAR BALLYCASTLE: RATHLIN ISLAND Just off the coast at Ballycastle, bumpy, boomerang-shaped **Rathlin Island** ("Fort of the Sea") is the ultimate in escapism for 20,000 puffins, the odd golden eagle, 100 human inhabitants, and four daily ferry loads of tourists. Its windy surface supports few trees, but it's a paradise of orchids and purple heather. For a more complete presentation of the island's intertwined history and myths, visit the island's own **Boat House Heritage Centre** at the opposite end of the harbor from the ferry. (☎ 2076 3951. Open May-Aug. daily 10am-4pm; other months by arrangement. Free.) The **lighthouse** is the best place from which to view birds, but it's accessible only with the warden's supervision (call 2076 3948 in advance). **Caledonian MacBrayne** ("CalMac") runs a ferry service from Ballycastle to the island. The small office at the Ballycastle pier, open before each departure, sells tickets (☎2076 2024). The **Soerneog View Hostel** (SIR-nock; ☎2076 3954; 2-bed dorms £8) is less secluded than the **Kinramer Camping Barn (ACB)**, which is 4½ mi. from the harbor (☎2073 3948; sheets £1; dorms or camping beds £5). **McCuaig's Bar** is the single entertainment center and food source for the entire island. (☎2076 3974. Food served 9am-9pm.)

GIANT'S CAUSEWAY

Advertised as the eighth natural wonder of the world, the Giant's Causeway is Northern Ireland's most famous sight. Be warned that 2000 visitors arrive each day in July and August. A spillage of 40,000 hexagonal columns of basalt form a 60-million-year-old honeycomb path from the foot of the cliffs far into the sea. Geologists have decided that the Causeway resulted from an unusually steady cooling of lava that stimulated crystallization. **Giant's Causeway Visitor Centre** sits at the pedestrian entranceway to the Causeway from the car park. Besides offering the usual tourist information, a bureau de change, and a post office, it sells an excellent leaflet of walks that will guide you the 8 mi. back to Whitepark Bay or along several shorter circular routes. (☎2073 1855. Centre open July-Aug. 10am-7pm; June daily 10am-6pm; Mar.-May and Sept. 10am-5pm; Nov.-Feb. 10am-4:30pm.) Every 15min., it runs Causeway Coaster minibuses the ½ mi. to the columns (£1 return). Many paths loop to and from the Causeway. Two begin at the Visitor Centre, one passing along the high cliffs and another along the low coast close to the Causeway. The paths meet after 1 mi.

DERRY (LONDONDERRY)

Only Dublin rivals Derry for the most long-lasting contributions to Irish political history. The past is remarkably present in the city's landmarks and districts, from the administrative centers within its city walls to the murals of the Bogside neighborhood without. Once a Celtic holy place, the arrival of Christianity converted Derry into a monastic center in the 6th century. The city became a major commercial port under the 17th-century Ulster Plantation (see p. 637), and then, under the English feudal system, an outpost of London's authority, which took the liberty of renaming it Londonderry. (Phone books use this title, but most Northerners call the city Derry.) The city's troubled history spans from the siege of Derry in 1689, when the now-legendary **Apprentice Boys** closed the city gates on the Catholic King James II, to the civil rights turmoil of the 1960s, when protests against anti-Catholic discrimination exploded into violence. Modern Derry is in the middle of a determined and largely successful effort to cast off its legacy. Despite occasional unrest in sectarian areas of the city, many residents still believe consensus is possible, and some come together in the city's brilliant music scene and irrepressible pubs.

▐ TRANSPORTATION

Trains: Duke St., Waterside (☎7134 2228), on the east bank. Trains go to **Belfast** via **Antrim** (2hr.; M-F 9 per day, Sa 7 per day, Su 3 per day; £7.90). Connections may be made from Coleraine to **Portrush.**

Buses: Most stop on Foyle St. between the walled city and the river. Ulsterbus (☎7126 2261): #212 to **Belfast** (1¾hr.; M-F 15 per day, Sa 13 per day, Su 6 per day; £8); #234 to **Coleraine** and **Portrush** (M-F 5 per day, Su 1 per day; £11); #274 to **Dublin** via **Omagh** (4¼hr.; M-Th and Sa 5 per day, F 6 per day, Su 4 per day; £11); #273 to **Omagh** (1hr.; M-F 12 per day, Sa 9 per day, Su 6 per day; £5.20). Lough Swilly (☎7126 2017) heads to: **Buncrana** (35min.; M-F 10 per day, Sa 12 per day, Su 4 per day; £3); **Letterkenny** (1hr.; M-Sa 10-13 per day; £4.20); **Malin Head** (1½hr.; M-Sa 2-3 per day; £7). Northwest Busways (☎(077) 82619 in the Republic) runs to **Malin Town** via **Carndonagh** (M-Sa 7 per day) and to **Buncrana** (M-Sa 9 per day).

Taxi: Derry Taxi Association (☎7126 0247). Also offers tours for around £20.

Bike Rental: Happy Days, 245 Lone Moor Rd. (☎7128 7128). £9 per day, £35 per week. ID deposit.

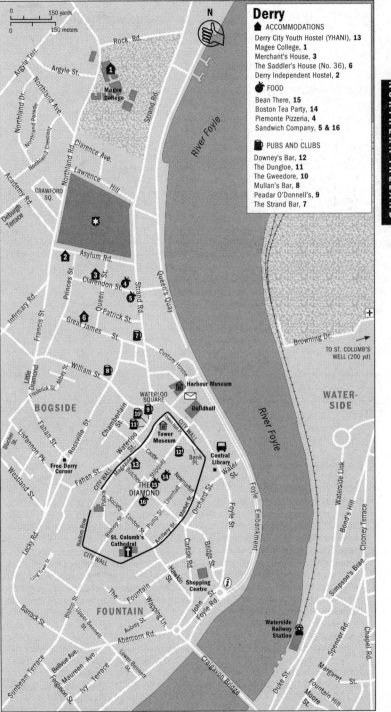

NORTHERN IRELAND

Derry

ACCOMMODATIONS

Derry City Youth Hostel (YHANI), **13**
Magee College, **1**
Merchant's House, **3**
The Saddler's House (No. 36), **6**
Derry Independent Hostel, **2**

FOOD

Bean There, **15**
Boston Tea Party, **14**
Piemonte Pizzeria, **4**
Sandwich Company, **5 & 16**

PUBS AND CLUBS

Downey's Bar, **12**
The Dungloe, **11**
The Gweedore, **10**
Mullan's Bar, **8**
Peadar O'Donnell's, **9**
The Strand Bar, **7**

◼◼ ORIENTATION AND PRACTICAL INFORMATION

Derry straddles the **River Foyle** just east of the border with Republican Co. Donegal. The **city center** and the **university area** both lie on the Foyle's western banks. The medieval **walled city**, now Derry's downtown, has a pedestrianized shopping district around **Waterloo St.** In the center of the old city lies the **Diamond,** from which radiate four main streets: **Shipquay St., Butcher St., Bishop St.,** and **Ferryquay. Magee University** is north on **Strand Rd.** The Catholic **Bogside** neighborhood that became Free Derry in the 70s is west of the city walls. Most of the Protestant population lives on the Foyle's eastern bank, where the housing estates known as the **Waterside** are located. The train station, on the east side of the river, can be reached from the center by way of the **Craigavon Bridge** or a free shuttle at the bus station.

Tourist Information Centre: 44 Foyle St. (☎ 7126 7284), in the Derry Visitor and Convention Bureau. Ask for the *Derry Tourist Guide, Visitor's Guide,* and free city maps. 24hr. computerized info kiosk. Books accommodations throughout the North.

Financial Services: First Trust, 15-17 Shipquay St. (☎ 7136 3921). Open M and F 9:30am-4:30pm, Tu-Th 11:30am-4:30pm.

Launderette: Ringers, 141 Strand Rd. (☎ 7126 6006). Pool table and TV. Wash £1.80, dry £2; £1.25 each for students. Open M-Th 8am-8pm, F-Sa 8am-6pm. Last wash 1½hr. before close.

Police: Strand Rd. (☎ 7136 7337).

Hospital: Altnagelvin Hospital, Glenshane Rd. (☎ 7134 5171).

Internet Access: Central Library, Foyle St. (☎ 7127 2300). Free until 1pm, then £2.50 per hr. Open M and Th 9:15am-5:30pm, Tu-W and F 9:15am-8pm, Sa 9:15am-5pm.

Post Office: 3 Custom House St. (☎ 7136 2563). Open M-Th 8:30am-5:30pm, F 9am-5:30pm, Sa 9:30am-12:30pm. Unless addressed to 3 Custom House St., Poste Restante letters will go to the Postal Sorting Office, 15-31 Great James St. (☎ 7131 8466), on the corner of Little James St. **Postal code:** BT48.

◼ ACCOMMODATIONS

▨ **Derry Independent Hostel (Steve's Backpackers),** 4 Asylum Rd. (☎ 7137 7989 or 7137 0011). 7min. from the city center down Strand Rd.; Asylum Rd. is the left just before the RUC station. This relaxed hostel offers maps and advice. Internet free for residents, £3 per hr. for others. Laundry £3. Key deposit £2. Dorms £7.50.

▨ **The Saddler's House (No. 36),** 36 Great James St. (☎ 7126 9691). Friendly, knowledgeable owners make their Victorian house your ultimate comfort zone. They also run **The Merchant's House,** 16 Queen St. Both £20 per person, with bath £25.

Derry City Youth Hostel (YHANI), Magazine St. (☎ 7128 4100), off Butcher St. outside the Diamond but within the city walls. Large. Continental brekkie £1.50, Irish £2.50. Laundry £3.50. Check-out 10am. 8- to 10-bed dorms £7; 4-bed with bath £8-9.50. Doubles and twins with breakfast and bath £13 per person.

Magee College (☎ 7137 5255; fax 7137 5629; accommodations@ulst.ac.uk), on the corner of Rock Rd. and Northland Rd. Walk ¼ mi. up Strand Rd. and turn left onto Rock Rd.; Magee is at the top of the hill on the left. The housing office is on the ground floor of Woodburn House, a red-brick building just after the main building. Laundry free. Mandatory reservations M-F 9am-5pm. Available mid-June to Sept. Singles in 5-bedroom flats £14.10, students £11.75.

◖ FOOD

Excellent takeaways and cafes abound in Derry, but restaurants are pricey. **Tesco** supermarket, in the Quayside Shopping Centre, is a few minutes' walk from the walls along Strand Rd. (Open M-Th 9am-9pm, F 8:30am-9pm, Sa 8:30am-8pm, Su 1-6pm.) Stores with later hours are scattered around Strand Rd. and Williams St.

Boston Tea Party, 13-15 Derry Craft Village (☎ 7135 3711), off Shipquay St. Delicious and incredibly inexpensive. Outside seating is a relief. Open M-Sa 9:30am-5:30pm.

Piemonte Pizzeria, 2a Clarendon St. (☎ 7126 6828), at Strand Rd. Pizza to please all palates. Individual pizzas £4-7. The takeaway next door is cheaper and is open 30min. later. Restaurant open Su-Th 5-11:30pm, F-Sa 5pm-1:30am.

Bean There, 20 the Diamond (☎ 7128 1303). Cakes, coffee, and Internet access.

Sandwich Company, the Diamond (☎ 7137 2500), at Bishop's St. Tasty sandwiches. 61 Strand Rd. location (☎ 7126 6771) less crowded. Both open M-F 8:30am-5pm.

SIGHTS

THE WALLS. Derry's city walls, 18 ft. high and 20 ft. thick, were erected between 1614 and 1619. They have never been breached, hence Derry's nickname "the Maiden City." A walk along the top of this mile-long perimeter takes about 20min. The stone tower topping the southeast wall past New Gate was built to protect **St. Columb's Cathedral,** the symbolic focus of the city's Protestant defenders. Stuck in the center of the southwest wall, **Bishop's Gate** was remodeled in 1789 into an ornate triumphal gate in honor of William of Orange.

ST. COLUMB'S CATHEDRAL. Built between 1628 and 1633, this was the first purpose-built Protestant cathedral in Britain or Ireland (all the older ones were confiscated Catholic cathedrals). The original lead-coated wood spire was in disrepair at the time of the Great Siege, so the city's defenders removed its lead and smelted it into bullets and cannonballs. Like many Protestant churches in the North, St. Columb's is bedecked with war banners, including flags from the Crimean War, the World Wars, and the two yellow flags captured from the French at the Great Siege. A tiny, museum-like **chapter house** at the back of the church displays the original locks and keys of the four main city gates and relics from the 1689 siege. *(Located on London St. off Bishop St. in the southwestern corner of the city. ☎ 7126 7313. Open Easter-Oct. M-Sa 9am-5pm; Nov.-Mar. M-Sa 9am-1pm and 2-4pm. Suggested donation £1.)*

TOWER MUSEUM. Engaging walk-through dioramas and audiovisual displays relay Derry's history. A series of short videos illustrate Derry's economic, political, and cultural past. The whole museum deserves at least 2hr. *(Union Hall Pl., just inside Magazine Gate. ☎ 7137 2411. Open July-Aug. M-Sa 10am-5pm, Su 2-5pm; Sept.-June Tu-Sa 10am-5pm. Last entrance 4:30pm. £4.20, students and seniors £1.60, families £8.50.)*

THE FOUNTAIN ESTATE. The Protestant Fountain Estate is reached from the walled city by exiting through the left side of Bishop's Gate; it is contained by Bishop St., Upper Bennett St., Abercorn St., and Hawkin St. This small area of only 600 residents holds the more interesting Protestant murals.

THE BOGSIDE. This famous Catholic neighborhood is easily recognizable. A huge sign west of the city walls at the junction of Fahan St. and Rossville Sq. declares "You Are Now Entering Free Derry." It was originally painted in 1969 on the end of a row house; the houses of the block have since been knocked down, but this endwall remains with a frequently repainted but never reworded message. The powerful mural is surrounded by other striking Nationalist artistic creations, and the spot is referred to as **Free Derry Corner.** Nearby, a stone monument commemorates the 14 protesters shot dead on Bloody Sunday.

PUBS AND ENTERTAINMENT

Peadar O'Donnell's, 53 Waterloo St. (☎ 7137 2318). Named for the famous Donegal Socialist who organized the Irish Transport and General Workers Union and took an active role in the 1921 Irish Civil War. Banners and sashes of all nationalities and orders cover the ceiling; the floor is littered ankle-deep with *craic*. Live bands nightly.

▩ **Mullan's Bar,** 13 Little James St. (☎ 7126 5300), on the corner of William St. and Rossville St. An incredible pub with idiosyncratically lavish decor, from stained-glass ceilings and bronze lion statues to plasma flat-screen TVs. Hosts frequent and excellent jazz.

The Gweedore, 59-61 Waterloo St. (☎ 7126 3513). The back door has been connected to Peadar's since Famine times. Rock, bluegrass, and funk nightly.

Downey's Bar, 33 Shipquay St. (☎ 7126 0820). A surreal decorative scheme attracts a young and colorful crowd. 20 purple pool tables and an open ceiling over the bar. Live bands nightly. The attached club, formerly known as **Vibe,** is undergoing renovation and is expected to reopen around Halloween 2002. Call for more info.

The Strand Bar, 35-38 Strand Rd. (☎ 7126 0494). 4 decadent floors. W-Sa trad downstairs; nightly 70s-80s DJs on 2nd floor; M-Sa nightclub on 3rd floor (cover £2-5).

The Dungloe (dun-LO), 41-43 Waterloo St. (☎ 7126 7716). 2 floors of 1950s appeal. Tu trad, W bands in back, Th trad in back, F disco upstairs, Sa bands up- and downstairs.

The Playhouse, 5-7 Artillery St., specializes in the work of young playwrights and performers. (☎ 7126 8027. Tickets £6, students and seniors £4.) Each year in early June, the **Walled City Festival** turns Derry into "Carnival City." (For more information call 7136 5151.) In early August, the city puts on her woman's weeds for the **Maiden City Festival** (☎ 7134 6677).

REPUBLIC OF IRELAND (ÉIRE)

Literary imaginations have immortalized Ireland's natural scenery from the ancient times of Celtic bards to Yeats and Joyce. The largely agricultural and sparsely populated island has experienced little physical change over thousands of centuries, yet amid stunning seascapes and misty mountains lie pockets of civilization, ranging in size from one-street villages to small market towns to Dublin and a handful of cities, all inspiration for some of the finest writing ever to grace the English language. While some fear that the cosmopolitan flowering of Ireland's larger centers means the end of folkways, the survival of traditional music, dance, storytelling, and pub culture proves otherwise. For today's visitors, Ireland promises an old-world welcome alongside an incipient urban edge.

It's useful to know that Ireland is traditionally divided into four provinces: **Leinster,** the east and southeast; **Munster,** the southwest; **Connacht,** the province west of the river Shannon; and **Ulster,** the north. Six of Ulster's nine counties make up Northern Ireland, part of the United Kingdom. "Ireland" can mean the whole island or the Republic, depending on who's listening. It's best to refer to "Northern Ireland" or "the North" and "the Republic." "Southern Ireland" is not a viable term.

For even more detailed coverage of the Emerald Isle, run—don't walk—to your nearest book emporium for a copy of the lovely *Let's Go: Ireland 2002.*

HIGHLIGHTS OF THE REPUBLIC OF IRELAND

DUBLIN Admire the grounds of **Trinity College** (p. 682), windowshop on **Grafton St.** (p. 688), then head around the corner to **Temple Bar** for a night of tomfoolery (p. 690).

RING OF KERRY Run the peninsula's circuit (p. 715), taking in exquisite mountains, lakes, and forests in **Killarney National Park** (p. 719).

GALWAY Down pints of Guinness while you enjoy the musical vigor and copious *craic* of the city's myriad pubs (p. 730).

CO. DONEGAL Brush up on your Gaelic in Ireland's largest *gaeltacht* (p. 746), and hike past Europe's highest sea cliffs at **Slieve League** (p. 745).

LIFE AND TIMES

ANCIENT HISTORY

Our fragmented knowledge of ancient Irish culture comes from the scant remains of its stone structures, landscaping, and metalware. Among these remains are **dolmens,** table-like arrangements of huge stones; **passage tombs** (see **Newgrange,** p. 699), and pint-sized **stone circles.** Bronze poured in circa 2000 BC, and Ireland's agrarian society was retooled into a warrior aristocracy. By 900 BC, it was bronze, schmonze—the **Irish Golden Age** brought about impressive projects like **ring forts** (ooh; see **Dún Aengus,** p. 728). Although some **Celts** may have arrived as unfashionably early as 2000 BC, their real migration started in 600 BC and lasted about 600 years. The Celts prospered on their peaceful isle, living in small farming communities with regional chieftains and provincial kings ruling territories called *tuatha.* The pagan life was good—or so epics like the *Táin* would have us believe.

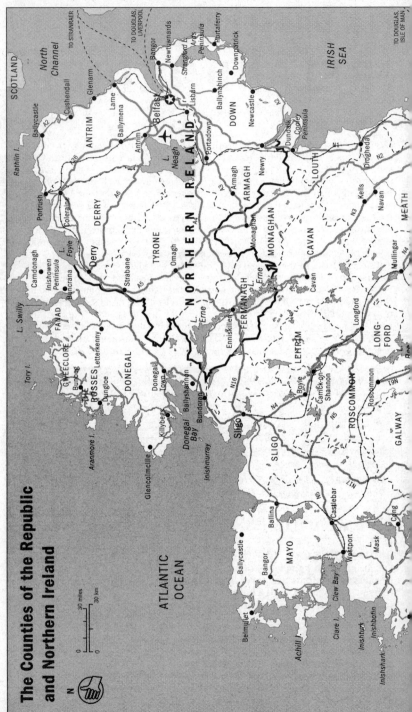

The Counties of the Republic and Northern Ireland

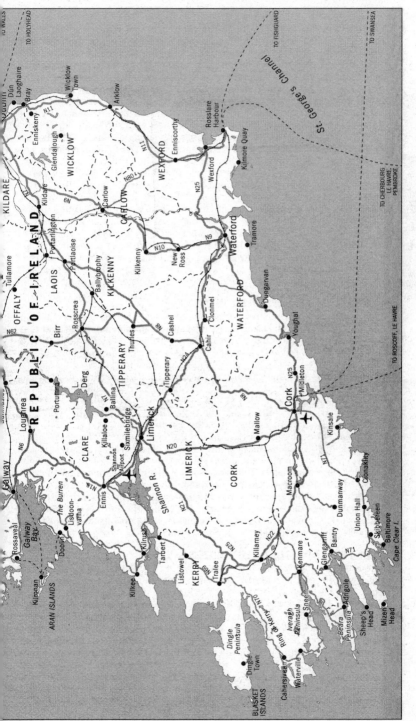

PIRATES AND VIKINGS AND CHRISTIANS, OH MY!

Starting in the 5th century with **St. Patrick,** Ireland was shown the light, Christian-style. St. Pat was born in Scotland and kidnapped by Irish pirates (*arr*). Enslaved and forced to tend Irish pirate sheep (*baa...arr*), he quickly found Jesus. He escaped back home, but at the command of a prophetic vision he performed an about-face and returned to Ireland. Other monks entering Ireland after the 5th century recorded the indigenous system of writing they found on **ogham stones** and introduced the Viking-inspired **round tower** to the architectural lexicon. Then the Continental barbarians took their pillaging a bit too far, and during the 6th to 8th centuries hordes of asylum-seeking monks came to Ireland. They built **monastic cities,** illuminated manuscripts like the **Book of Kells,** and earned Ireland its reputation as the "land of saints and scholars." Rather than scraping and bowing to Rome, monastic cities allied themselves with wily Irish chieftains like the **Uí Néills** (O'Neills) of Ulster. This monkish prosperity was interrupted by **Viking** invasions in the 9th and 10th centuries. The hornéd ones raided most frequently along the southern coast, where they founded settlements at Limerick, Waterford, and Dublin. Then in 1002, High King **Brian Ború** set off a period of inter-*tuath* strife; after his death on the battlefield, chieftain **Dermot MacMurrough** sought the assistance of English Norman nobles. Richard de Clare (a.k.a. **Strongbow**) arrived in 1169 and cut a bloody, Anglo-Norman swath through south Leinster. Strongbow married Dermot's daughter, **Aoife,** in 1171, affirmed his loyalty to King Henry II, and with characteristic generosity offered to govern Leinster on England's behalf.

FEUDALISM AND ITS DISCONTENTS

Thus the English came to Ireland and settled down for a nice, long occupation. There was constant bickering between Gaelic, who dominated agrarian Connacht and Ulster, and English lords, whose strongholds included the **Pale,** a fortified domain around Dublin. The two sides were culturally similar, though the Crown fretted up a storm over potential cross-pollination; the 1366 **Statutes of Kilkenny** banned English colonists from speaking, dressing, or marrying Irish. Feudal skirmishes and economic decline plagued the island until the rise of Leinster's charismatic **Earls of Kildare,** who ruled from 1470 to 1534; they were so charismatic, in fact, that the fussy Crown passed more oppressive laws. Then Henry VIII created the Church of England, and the 1537 **Irish Supremacy Act** declared him head of the Protestant **Church of Ireland**—effectively making the island property of the Crown. **Thomas FitzGerald,** at odds with Henry, sponsored an uprising in Munster in 1579. Not to be outdone by Leinster, the Ulster Earl **Hugh O'Neill** led his own rebellion. The King of Spain promised naval assistance; his Armada arrived in Kinsale in 1601, but sat around polishing its blunderbusses while English armies demolished Irish forces. O'Neill and the other major Gaelic lords left Ireland in 1607 in the **Flight of the Earls.** While the world looked on in feigned astonishment, the English took control of the land and parceled it out to Protestants.

PLANTED AND ASCENDED PROTESTANTS

The English project of dispossessing Catholics of their land and replacing them with Protestants (mostly Scottish tenants and laborers, themselves displaced by the English but too polite to mention it) was known as the **Ulster Plantation.** In 1642, **Owen Roe O'Neill** returned from the Continent to lead the now-landless Irish in insurrection and formed the **Confederation of Kilkenny,** an uneasy alliance between the Church and Irish and English lords. The concurrent English Civil Wars made a *really* big mess of things; **Oliver Cromwell**'s victory rendered negotiations between King and Confederation something of a moot point. And then Dear Ollie turned to Ireland. Following standard procedure, the Lord Protector destroyed anything he did not occupy. Catholics were massacred and whole towns razed as entire tracts of land were confiscated and doled out to soldiers and Protestant vagabonds. Native Irish could go "to

Hell or to Connacht," both desolate and infertile, one with a more tropical climate. By 1660, most Irish land was owned by Protestant immigrants. The Restoration settled things down a bit; Charles II passed the 1665 **Act of Explanation,** requiring Protestants to relinquish one-third of their land to the "innocent papists." We all know how well that must have worked.

In 1688, Catholic **James II,** driven from England by Protestant **William of Orange** and his Glorious Revolution, came to Ireland to gather military support. James tried to take Derry in 1689, but a rascally and heroic band of **Apprentice Boys** closed the gates on him and started the 105-day **Siege of Derry.** William ended the war and sent his rival into exile on July 12, 1690, at the **Battle of the Boyne.** Many Northern Protestants still celebrate the victory on July 12 (called **Orange Day** in honor of King Billy). At the turn of the 18th century a set of **Penal Laws** brought further Irish oppression, banning (among other things) the practice of Catholicism. In Dublin and the Pale, the Anglo-Irish garden-partied, gossiped, and architectured their way toward a second London. The term **"Ascendancy"** was coined for them; it described a social class whose elitehood depended upon Anglicanism. **Trinity College** was their quintessential institution. Away from the Ascended nonsense, the Catholic merchant class grew in cities like Galway and Tralee; they learned in secret **hedge schools** and practiced their religion furtively, using large, flat **Mass rocks** when they couldn't get their hands on altars.

REBELLION AND UNION

The *liberté*-fever inspired by the American and French revolutions was particularly strong among a secret group called the **United Irishmen.** The bloody **Rebellion of 1798** erupted with a furious band of peasants and priests and ended with their last stand at **Vinegar Hill** in Co. Wexford. Any hopes England held of making Irish society less volatile by relaxing anti-Catholic laws were canceled by such misbehavior. With the 1801 **Act of Union,** the Crown abolished Irish "self-government" altogether. The Dublin Parliament died, and "The United Kingdom of Great Britain and Ireland" was born. The Church of Ireland entered into an unequal arranged marriage, changing her name to the "United Church of England and Ireland." Dublin's mad gaiety vanished, the Anglo-Irish gentry collapsed, and agrarian violence and poverty escalated. Union, however, meant Irish representatives now held seats in the British Parliament. Irish Catholic farmers with newfound suffrage elected **Daniel O'Connell** in 1829, forcing Westminster to repeal the anti-Catholic laws that would have barred him from taking his seat. "The Liberator" promptly forced Parliament to allot money for improving Irish living conditions. Unfortunately, O'Connell's crusade for the welfare of his people wasn't enough to protect them from a malicious little fungus.

THE FAMINE AND SOCIAL REFORM

The potato was the wundercrop of the rapidly growing Irish population, and their reliance on it had devastating effects when the heroic spud fell victim to fungal disease. During the years of the **Great Famine** (1847-51), an estimated two to three million people died and another million emigrated. After the Famine, the societal structure of surviving Irish peasants completely reorganized itself. The bottom layer of truly penniless farmers had been eliminated altogether. Depopulation continued, and **emigration** became an Irish way of life. English injustice fueled the formation of more angry young Nationalist groups—in 1858, crusaders for a violent removal of their oppressors founded a secret society known as the **Fenians,** while the 1870s saw the creation of the **Land League,** which pushed for further reforms.

In 1870, MP **Isaac Butt** founded the **Irish Home Rule Party.** Home Ruler **Charles Stewart Parnell** was a charismatic Protestant aristocrat with a hatred for everything English. Despite surviving implication in the **Phoenix Park murders,** Parnell couldn't beat an 1890 adultery rap. The scandal split all of Ireland into Parnellites and anti-Parnellites. While squabbling politicians let their ideals fall to the wayside, civil society waxed ambitious. The fairer sex established

REPUBLIC OF IRELAND

the **Irish Women's Suffrage Federation** in 1911. Marxist **James Connolly** led strikes in Belfast and Dublin. Meanwhile, various groups (like the **Gaelic Athletic Association** and the **Gaelic League**) tried to revive an essential, unpolluted "Gaelic" culture. Arthur Griffith began a tiny movement and little-read newspaper, both of which went by the name **Sinn Féin** (SHIN FAYN, "Ourselves Alone"). Thousands of Northern Protestants opposing Home Rule organized a quasi-militia called the **Ulster Volunteer Force (UVF).** Nationalists led by **Eoin MacNeill** responded by creating the **Irish Volunteers.**

THE EASTER RISING, INDEPENDENCE, AND CIVIL WAR

Summer 1914: Irish Home Rule seemed imminent, and Ulster was ready to go up in flames. Instead, someone shot an archduke, and the world went up in flames. British PM Henry Asquith passed a **Home Rule Bill** in return for Irish bodies to fill out the British army. 670,000 Irishmen signed up to fight the Kaiser. Meanwhile, the Fenians and **Padraig Pearse** planned a nation-wide revolt for **Easter Sunday, 1916.** A crucial shipment of arms went astray, however, and the uprising fell through. The Pearse group rescheduled their uprising for the following Monday, April 24; they seized Dublin's **General Post Office** and hunkered down for five days of brawling in the streets. The Crown retaliated—15 "ringleaders" were publicly executed. The Irish grew sympathetic to the rebels and increasingly anti-British. The Volunteers reorganized under Fenian bigwig **Michael Collins,** who brought them to Sinn Féin, and **Éamon de Valera** became the party president. In 1918, the British tried to introduce a draft in Ireland, and the Irish lost what little complacency they had left.

Extremist Irish Volunteers started calling themselves the **Irish Republican Army (IRA)** and became Sinn Féin's military might. Thus the British saw another, and not their last, **War for Independence.** In 1920, British PM **David Lloyd George** passed the **Government of Ireland Act,** which divided the island into Northern Ireland and Southern Ireland. Hurried negotiations then produced the **Anglo-Irish Treaty,** creating a 26-county Irish Free State but recognizing British rule over the northern counties. Everyone split on whether to accept the treaty. A nay-saying portion of the IRA occupied the Four Courts in Dublin and sparked two years of **civil war.** To skip over all the ugly details: the pro-treaty government won. Sinn Féin denied the legitimacy of the Free State government and expressed their disapproval by refusing to refer to the country by the official name of "Éire."

THE ERA DE VALERA AND RECENT HISTORY

Under the guidance of **Éamon de Valera,** the government ended armed resistance by Republican insurgents. In 1927, he founded his own political party, **Fianna Fáil,** won the 1932 election, and held power for much of the next 20 years. In 1937 de Valera and the voters approved the permanent Irish Constitution. It establishes the country's legislative structure, consisting of two chambers: the **Dáil** (DAHL) and the **Seanad** (SHA-nud). The Prime Minister is the **Taoiseach** (TEE-shuch), and the **President** is the ceremonial head of state. Ireland stayed officially neutral during WWII (known as **The Emergency**), though many Irish citizens identified with the Allies, and around 50,000 served in the British army. Then, in 1948, "the Republic of Ireland" was officially announced, ending British Commonwealth membership altogether. Britain, which didn't quite catch all that, recognized the Republic a year later. The government declared (harumph) that the UK would maintain control over Ulster until the North consented to join the Republic.

In the 1960s, increased contact with the rest of the world accelerated economic growth, put the brakes on emigration, and fueled national confidence. Ireland entered the European Economic Community, now the **European Union (EU),** in 1973. In 1985, FitzGerald signed the **Anglo-Irish agreement,** which let Éire stick an official, though not a legal, nose in Northern negotiations. The Irish broke progressive social and political ground in 1990 by choosing **Mary Robinson,** who happened to be of the female persuasion, to be their President.

The small, leftist **Labour Party** also enjoyed enormous, unexpected success, paving the way for further social reform. In 1993, Taoiseach **Albert Reynolds** declared his top priority was to stop violence in Northern Ireland. A year later he announced a cease-fire agreement between Sinn Féin and the IRA. Fianna Fáil won the June 1997 general election, making **Bertie Ahern,** at a spring-chick-enish 45, the youngest Taoiseach in Irish history. Ahern joined the peace talks that produced the **Good Friday Peace Agreement** in April of 1998. (For the recent status of the Good Friday Agreement, see p. 640.) In the summer of 2001, the Irish populace defeated the **Nice Treaty,** which was the first step in the addition of 12 new nations to the EU. The referendum shocked Ireland's pro-Treaty government and caused quite a little stir on the Continent. However, most people blamed a low voter turnout and an insidious but vocal "Say No" campaign; politicians remain confident that the Irish will come 'round in the end.

LITERATURE AND LANGUAGE

HISTORY OF THE IRISH LANGUAGE
The oldest vernacular literature and the largest collection of folklore in Europe are both Irish. The constitution declares Irish the national language of the Republic, yet there are only 60,000 individuals in the exclusively Irish-speaking communities, or **gaeltacht** (GAYL-tacht). The most prominent *gaeltacht* are in Connemara, Co. Donegal, the Dingle Peninsula, and the Aran Islands, and these geographically disparate communities are further divided by three almost mutually incomprehensible dialects: **Connemara** Irish, **Donegal** Irish, and the southern **Munster** Irish. The language reentered the lives of the privileged classes with the advent of the **Gaelic Revival.** In 1893, **Douglas Hyde** (who later became the first president of Éire) founded the **Gaelic League** in order to inspire enthusiasm for Irish. Today, Irish has grown in popularity among native English speakers. The modern Irish-literature community produces dozens of works in Gaelic every year.

LEGENDS AND FOLKTALES
In early Irish society, what the bard sang about battles, valor, and lineage was the only record a chieftain had by which to make decisions. Poetry and politics of the Druidic tradition were so intertwined that the *fili*, trained poets, and *breitheamh* (BREH-huv), judges of the Brehon Laws, were often the same people. Poets living in the chieftains' households invented the art of verse satire and composed "cycles" of tales narrating the life stories of a set of heroes and villains. The most extensive is the **Ulster Cycle,** which includes the adventures of King Conchobar (Conor) of Ulster, his arch-enemy (and ex-wife) Queen Medbh of Connacht, and his nephew and champion **Cúchulainn** (KOO-hu-lin). Literati have periodically compiled Ireland's **folktales.** These tales include otherworldly creatures such as **banshees** and the **faeries. Leprechauns,** a degenerate conflagration of Ireland's mythic creatures, are embraced mainly by foreign cultures.

SWIFT, WILDE, AND SHAW
In long-colonized Dublin, **Jonathan Swift** (1667-1745) wrote some of the most marvelous satire in the English language. While defending the Protestant Church of Ireland, Swift felt compelled to write about the sad condition of starving Irish peasants. In the mid-19th century, cosmopolitan Dublin's talented young writers often moved on to London to make their names. **Oscar Wilde** (1856-1900) produced many sparklingly witty works, including *The Importance of Being Earnest* (1895). Playwright **George Bernard Shaw** (1856-1950) was also born in Dublin but moved to London in 1876. Shaw won the Nobel Prize for Literature in 1925.

YEATS AND THE REVIVAL
Toward the end of the 19th century, a vigorous and enduring effort known today as the **Irish Literary Revival** took over. Members of this movement turned to Irish culture for inspiration, overturning the assumption that the English were more

sophisticated. The early poems of **William Butler Yeats** (1865-1939) create a dreamily rural Ireland of loss and legend. Yeats's vision changed remarkably after he realized how the Gaelic Revival had promoted the nationalism that led to the violence of the Civil War. In 1923, he became the first Irishman to win the Nobel Prize for Literature. In 1904, Yeats and Lady Gregory founded the **Abbey Theatre** in Dublin (see p. 688), but conflict arose almost immediately: how exactly was this new body of "Irish" drama to be written? A sort of compromise was found in the work of **John Millington Synge,** whose experiences on the Aran Islands led him to write *The Playboy of the Western World* (1907), destroying the pastoral myths of "classless" Irish peasantry. **Sean O'Casey**'s plays (such as 1924's *Juno and the Paycock*) were well received by Dublin's middle class, as they were the first portrayals of gritty urban life in their fair city.

JOYCE, BECKETT AND RECENT AUTHORS

Ireland's most famous expatriate is **James Joyce** (1882-1941), godfather and patron saint of modernism. Joyce's writing, however, never left Ireland; his novels and stories exclusively describe the lives of Dublin denizens. Joyce's most accessible writing is the collection of short stories titled *Dubliners* (1914), while his masterwork is generally agreed to be the ground-breaking mock-epic *Ulysses* (1922). Like Joyce, **Samuel Beckett** (1906-89) fled to Paris to pursue his writing career; unlike Joyce, he left most of vernacular Ireland behind. His novels, plays (*Waiting for Godot*), and bleak prose poems convey a stark pessimism about language, society, and life. Beckett won the Nobel Prize in 1969, but did not accept it on the grounds that Joyce had never received it.

After the 1940s, Irish poetry once again commanded widespread appreciation. **Patrick Kavanaugh** (1906-67) debunked a mythical Ireland, while **Paul Muldoon** adds quirk and confusion to humdrum existence. Notorious wit, playwright, poet, and terrorist **Brendan Behan** created semi-autobiographical works about delinquent life in plays like *The Quare Fellow* (1954). Mild-mannered schoolteacher **Roddy Doyle** won the 1994 Booker Prize for *Paddy Clarke Ha Ha Ha.* Ireland's most famous living poet is **Seamus Heaney,** who won the Nobel Prize for Literature in 1995.

MUSIC

Irish traditional music, or **trad,** is the centuries-old array of dances, melodies, and embellishments that has been passed down through generations of musicians. The tunes can be written down, but trad more often consists in improvisation. Irish traditional music may be heard either recorded or in impromptu pub sessions. Bestselling studio artists include **Altan** and the **Chieftains.** Most traditional musicians play before smaller, more intimate audiences of locals at a pub. *Let's Go* lists many pubs with regular sessions, but you'll find the best music by asking local enthusiasts. Sessions typically alternate between fast-paced instrumental music and folk songs.

In Ireland there is surprisingly little distinction between music types—a fine musician uses a variety of sources. The London-based **Pogues** fused rock and trad, and whipped out reels and jigs of drunken, punk-damaged revelry. **My Bloody Valentine** wove shimmering distortions to land themselves on the outskirts of grunge. Ireland's rock musicians have also set their sights on mainstream super-stardom; **U2** is Ireland's biggest rock export, and **Sinéad O'Connor** stood her own as an independent female star with attitude long before becoming an international phenom. In recent years, **The Cranberries** and **Boyzone** have achieved great success abroad.

SPORTS

The Irish take enormous pride in their two native sports: hurling and Gaelic football. In 1884, the **Gaelic Athletic Association (GAA)** was founded to establish official rules and regulations for these and other ancient Irish recreations. **Gaelic football** is like a cross between football and rugby, though older than both. As fans like to say, if football is a game, then **hurling** is an art. This fast and dangerous-looking game was first played in the 13th century, and is perhaps best imagined as a blend of lacrosse and field hockey. The women's version of the game is called **camogie.** **Football** (or soccer) enjoys nearly as fanatical a following, and the Irish are also fiercely devoted to the football clubs of England. Co. Kildare is well appreciated as a breeding ground for champion **racehorses.** On the byways of Ulster and in certain places in Cork, the strange, quasi-golf game of **road bowling** sees enthusiastic fans lining the twisty playing fields ("roads," that is).

FOOD AND DRINK

The basics of Irish cuisine are simple: specialties include *colcannon* (a potato dish), Guinness stew, and Irish stew. Loud and long will the Irish bards sing the praises of the man who first concocted **black pudding;** as one local butcher put it, it's "some pork, a good deal of blood, and grains and things—all wrapped up in a tube." **White pudding** uses milk instead of blood. Regional specialties include Cork's **crubeen** (tasty pigs' feet), Dublin's **coddle** (boiled sausages and bacon with potatoes), and Waterford's **blaa** (sausage rolls). Best of all culinary delights is **soda bread,** a heavy white loaf especially tasty when fried. Another indigenous bread is **barm brack,** a spicy mixture of dried fruits and molasses mixed to a lead-like density. **Seafood** can be a real bargain in smaller towns' **chippers;** Guinness-marinated mussels and oysters are splendid.

People of all ages and every social milieu head to pubs for conversation, food, drink, music, and *craic* (pronounced crack; "a good time"). Most pubs host evening trad sessions, and in rural pubs there's a chance that a *seanachaí* (SHAN-ukh-ee; travelling storyteller) might drop in. Pubs are generally open Monday through Saturday from 10:30am to 11:30pm (11pm in winter) and Sunday from 12:30 to 2pm and 4 to 11pm (closed 2-4pm). Many pubs, especially in Dublin, are now able to obtain late licenses. Other pubs have been granted special "early" licenses allowing them to open at 7:30am (yee-haw!).

Beer wins a landslide victory as the drink of choice. **Guinness** inspires a reverence otherwise reserved for the Holy Trinity. Known variously as "the dark stuff," "the blonde in the black skirt," or simply "I'll have a pint, please," it's a rich, dark brew with a head thick enough to stand a match in. **Murphy's** is a similar, slightly creamier Cork-brewed stout. **Irish whiskey,** invented by clever monks, is sweeter than its Scottish counterpart (spelled "whisky"); **Jameson** is popular everywhere. In the west, you may hear locals praise "mountain dew," a euphemism for **poitín** (put-CHEEN), an illegal methanol-based distillation sometimes given to cows in labor that ranges in strength from 115 to 140 proof.

MEDIA

The largest **newspapers** in the Republic are *The Irish Times* and *The Irish Independent. The Times* takes a liberal stance and is renowned for its excellent coverage of international affairs. *The Independent* is more internally focused and often maintains a chatty writing style. Many regional papers offer in-depth local news; the largest is *The Cork Examiner*. **British papers** are sold throughout Ireland. In 1961, the Republic's national radio service made its first television broadcast, naming itself **Radio Telefís Éireann (RTE).** The government's most recent developments include the start of Irish-language radio and TV stations, called Telifís na Gaelige, aimed at promoting the use of Irish in modern media forms.

> **THE EURO.** The Republic of Ireland is switching over to the euro on January 1, 2002. The punt will remain legal tender through July 1, 2002, after which it's all euros all the time. *Let's Go* lists prices in both euros (€) and the Irish pound (£) based on actual figures or fixed conversion rates.

COUNTY DUBLIN

Dublin and its suburbs form a single economic and commercial unit, linked by a web of mass transit: the electric DART, suburban rail, and Dublin buses. The city teems with weekending suburbanites, tourists, and international hipsters on the prowl, while the suburbs offer a less polluted (though hardly pastoral) alternative.

DUBLIN   ☎01

In a country known for a relaxed lifestyle and rural sanctity, the international flavor and boundless energy of Dublin are all the more visible. But while Dublin may seem gritty by Irish standards, it's still as friendly a major city as you'll find. Not quite as cosmopolitan but just as eclectic as New York or London, Ireland's capital is home to vibrant theater, music, and literary communities, and multiple generations of pubs learning to coexist peacefully. Today's Dublin faces the challenge of retaining its identity as a city with a devotion to history, an appreciation of culture, and a sense of irony that takes the tourist trade in stride. The city may hardly look like the rustic "Emerald Isle" promoted on tourist brochures, but its people still embody the charm and warmth that have made their country famous.

◼ INTERCITY TRANSPORTATION

Rail lines, bus lines (both state-run and private), and the national highway system radiate from Dublin. Major highways **N5** and **N6** lead to **N4**, while **N8**, **N9**, and **N10** all feed into **N7**, dumping buses and cars into Dublin's vehicular sphere. Because intercity transport is so Dublin-centric, you may find it more convenient to arrange your travel in other parts of the Republic while you're in the capital.

Airport: Dublin Airport (☎844 4900). **Dublin buses** #41, 41B, and 41C run to Eden Quay in the city center with stops along the way (every 20min., £1.15/€1.45). The **Airlink shuttle** (☎844 4265) runs nonstop to Busáras Central Bus Station and O'Connell St. (20-25min., every 10min. 5:15am-11:30pm, £3/€3.80) and on to Heuston Station (50min., £3.50/€4.50), but is hardly worth the markup from #41. **Taxis** to the city center cost £10-12/€12.70-15.50. Wheelchair-accessible cabs may be available; see **Taxis.** Note: slow-moving Dublin traffic doesn't distinguish express from local buses.

Trains: Irish Rail, Iarnród Éireann (EER-ann-road AIR-ann) travel center, at 35 Lower Abbey St. (☎836 6222). Info desks and booking windows at all 3 of the city's major stations may have long lines. Purchase a ticket in advance at the center, or buy one at a station 20min. before departure. The travel center also spews data on DART, suburban rail, international train tickets, and ferries. Open M-F 9am-5pm, Sa 9am-1pm. For specific routes, call the 24hr. talking timetables, with schedules of trains to: **Belfast** (☎805 4277); **Cork** (☎805 4200); **Galway/Westport** (☎805 4222 or 805 4244); **Killarney/Tralee** (☎805 4266); **Limerick** (☎805 4211); **Sligo** (☎805 4255); **Waterford** (☎805 4233); **Wexford/Rosslare** (☎805 4288). Bus #90 circuits Connolly, Heuston, and Pearse Stations and Busáras (every 10min., 65p/€0.85). Connolly and Pearse are also **DART** stations serving the north and south coasts.

Connolly Station, Amiens St. (☎703 2358 or 703 2359), north of the Liffey and close to Busáras Bus Station. Buses #20, 20A, and 90 head south of the river, and the DART runs to Tara on the south quay. Open M-Sa 7am-10pm, Su noon-9pm. Trains to: **Belfast** (2hr.; M-Sa 8 per day, Su 5 per day; £21/€26.70); **Wexford** via **Rosslare** (3hr., 3 per day, £11/€14); **Sligo** (3½hr.; M-Th and Sa-Su 3 per day, F 4 per day; £14.50/€18.50).

Heuston Station (☎703 2132, night 703 2131), south of Victoria Quay and west of the city center, a 25min. walk from Trinity College. Buses #26, 51, 90, and 79 run from Heuston to the city center. Open daily 6:30am-10:20pm. Trains to: **Galway** (2½hr.; M-Sa 5 per day, Su 4 per day; £16/€20.30, F and Su £22/€28); **Limerick** (2½hr., 9 per day, £26.50/€33.65); **Waterford** (2½hr.; M-Sa 4 per day, Su 3 per day; £13/€16.50); **Cork** (3½hr.; M-Th and Sa 8 per day, F 11 per day, Su 6 per day; £33.50/€42.50); **Tralee** (4hr.; M-Th and Sa 5 per day, F 7 per day, Su 4 per day; £34/€43.20).

Pearse Station (☎ 703 3634), just east of Trinity College on Pearse St. and Westland Row. Open daily 6:30am-11:30pm. Receives southbound trains from Connolly Station.

Buses: Info available at the **Dublin Bus Office,** 59 O'Connell St. (☎873 4222); the **Bus Éireann** window is open M-F 9am-5:30pm and Sa 9am-1pm. Intercity buses to Dublin arrive at **Busáras Central Bus Station,** Store St. (☎836 6111), directly behind the Customs House and next to Connolly Station. Take Bus Éireann to: **Waterford** (2¾hr.; M-Sa 7 per day, Su 5 per day; £7/€8.90); **Wexford** (2¾hr.; M-Sa 10 per day, Su 7 per day; £8/€10.15); **Belfast** (3hr., 6-7 per day, £11/€14); **Rosslare** (3hr.; M-Sa 10 per day, Su 7 per day; £10/€12.70); **Galway** (3½hr., 13 per day, £9/€11.50); **Limerick** (3½hr.; M-Sa 13 per day, Su 7 per day; £10.50/€13.50); **Sligo** (4hr., 4-5 per day, £9.60/€12.20); **Derry** (4¼hr.; 4-5 per day; £11/€14); **Donegal** (4¼hr., 5-6 per day, £10.50/€13.50). **Shannon Airport** via shuttle connection twice per hr. from: **Cork** (4½hr., 6 per day, £13.50/€17); **Limerick** (4½hr., 13 per day, £10.50/€13.50); **Westport** (5hr., 2-3 per day, £10/€12.70); **Killarney** (6hr., 5 per day, £15/€19); **Tralee** (6hr., 7 per day, £15/€19).

Ferries: Bookings in **Irish Rail** office. **Irish Ferries** also has an office off St. Stephen's Green at 2-4 Merrion Row (☎855 2222 or (1890) 313 131; www.irishferries.com). Open M-F 9am-5pm, Sa 9:15am-12:45pm. **Stena Line** ferries arrive from Holyhead at **Dún Laoghaire** (☎204 7777); from there the **DART** shuttles passengers into central Dublin (£1.30/€1.70). **Buses** #7, 7A, and 8 go from Georges St. in Dún Laoghaire to Eden Quay (£1.30/€1.70), though the DART is easier. Irish Ferries arrive from Holyhead at the **Dublin Port** (☎607 5665), from which buses #53 and 53A run every hr. to Busáras (80p/€1); **Dublin Bus** also runs ferry port connection buses tailored to ferry schedules (£2-2.50/€2.50-3.20). **Merchant Ferries** docks at the Dublin port, and goes to **Liverpool** (7½hr.; 1-2 per day; from £50/€63.50, car from £170/€215); booking available only from **Gerry Feeney,** 19 Eden Quay (☎819 2999). The **Isle of Man Steam Packet Company** (UK ☎(1800) 551 743) docks at Dublin Port and sends 1 boat per day to its own country; rates depend on dates and term of stay.

▣ LOCAL TRANSPORTATION

Travel passes were designed for people intending to move around a *lot;* each pass has a time limit that requires several trips a day to validate its price. Travel Wide passes offer unlimited rides for a day or a week (1 day £3.50/€4.45, 1 week £13/€16.50). A Dublin Bus week runs from Sunday to Saturday inclusive; a weekly pass bought Friday night will expire after only one day. Dublin Bus months, similarly, are calendar months. Other tickets allow for both bus and suburban rail/DART travel. (One-day short hop £5.20/€6.60, week £17/€12.60, month £63/€80.)

Buses: Dublin Bus, 59 O'Connell St. (☎873 4222). Open M 8:30am-5:30pm, Tu-F 9am-5:30pm, Sa 9am-1pm. Buses are cheap (£0.60-1.15/€0.76-1.46; prices rise according to distance). They run 5am-11:30pm, but are most frequent 8am-6pm (generally every 8-20min., off-peak hours every 30-45min.) North to: **Howth, Balbriggan,** and **Malahide.** West to: **Rathcoole, Maynooth,** and **Celbridge.** South to: **Blessington, Enniskerry, Dún Laoghaire,** and **Bray.** Dublin Bus runs the **NiteLink** service to the suburbs (Th-Sa every hr. 12:30-3:30am, £3/€3.80.) The **Airlink** service (#747 and 748) connects Dublin airport to the Central Bus Station (£3/€3.80) and Heuston Station (£3.50/€4.45), with stops including O'Connell St. (every 10-15min. 6:30am-11:45pm). **Wheelchair-accessible** buses are limited: the only options are the **OmniLink** service (#300), which cruises around Clontarf (60p/€0.75) and the #3 bus from Whitehall to Sandymount (via O'Connell St.).

DART: From **Connolly, Pearse,** and **Tara St.** Stations in the city center, the electric DART trains shoot south past **Bray** and north to **Howth.** Tickets are sold in the station and must be presented at the end of the trip. Trains every 10-15min. from about 6:30am to 11:30pm; £0.55-1.10/€0.75-1.40.

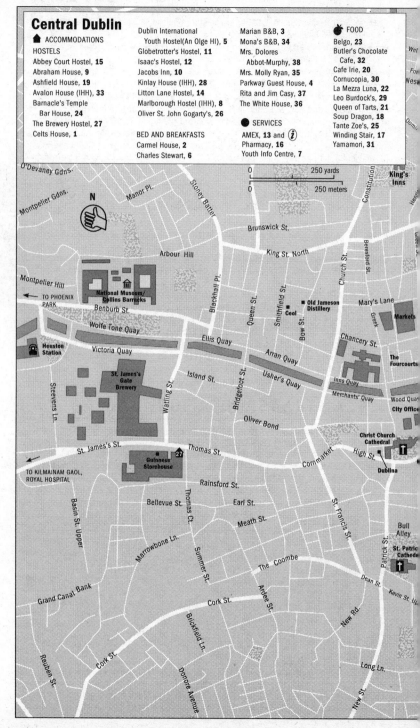

Central Dublin

ACCOMMODATIONS

HOSTELS
Abbey Court Hostel, **15**
Abraham House, **9**
Ashfield House, **19**
Avalon House (IHH) **33**
Barnacle's Temple
  Bar House, **24**
The Brewery Hostel, **27**
Celts House, **1**

Dublin International
  Youth Hostel(An Olge HI), **5**
Globetrotter's Hostel, **11**
Isaac's Hostel, **12**
Jacobs Inn, **10**
Kinlay House (IHH) **28**
Litton Lane Hostel, **14**
Marlborough Hostel (IHH), **8**
Oliver St. John Gogarty's, **26**

BED AND BREAKFASTS
Carmel House, **2**
Charles Stewart, **6**

Marian B&B, **3**
Mona's B&B, **34**
Mrs. Dolores
  Abbot-Murphy, **38**
Mrs. Molly Ryan, **35**
Parkway Guest House, **4**
Rita and Jim Casy, **37**
The White House, **36**

● **SERVICES**
AMEX, **13** and ⓘ
Pharmacy, **16**
Youth Info Centre, **7**

🍎 **FOOD**
Belgo, **23**
Butler's Chocolate
  Cafe, **32**
Cafe Irie, **20**
Cornucopia, **30**
La Mezza Luna, **22**
Leo Burdock's, **29**
Queen of Tarts, **21**
Soup Dragon, **18**
Tante Zoe's, **25**
Winding Stair, **17**
Yamamori, **31**

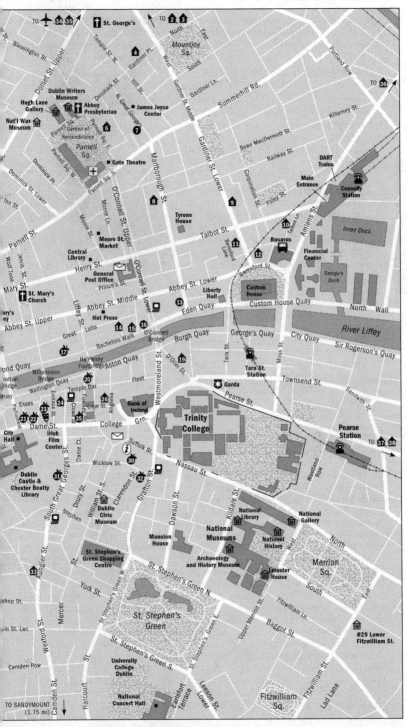

Suburban Rail: From **Connolly Station** north to **Malahide, Donabate,** and **Drogheda;** south to **Wicklow** and **Arklow;** west to **Maynooth** and **Mullingar.** The north- and south-bound lines stop at **Tara St.** and **Pearse Stations** as well. From **Heuston Station** to **Kildare.** Trains are frequent (roughly 30 per day) every day except Su.

Taxis: Blue Cabs (☎676 1111), **ABC** (☎285 5444), and **City Group Taxi** (☎872 7272) have wheelchair-accessible taxis (call in advance). All 24hr. £2.20/€2.75 plus 90p/ €1.15 per mi.; 80p/€1 call-in charge. It's easiest to pick up cabs at taxi stands around the city, including in front of Trinity, Lower Abbey St. at the bus station, and Parnell St.

Car Rental: Budget, 151 Lower Drumcondra Rd. (☎837 9611) and at the airport. Summer from £35/€44.50 per day, £165/€210 per week; winter £30/€38, £140/€178. Ages 23-75. **Alamo,** at the airport (☎844 4162). Summer from £35/€44.50 per day, £195/€248 per week; winter £30/€38, £175/€222. Ages 25-74. Be warned that Dublin traffic is heavy; parking spaces are scarce and expensive.

Bike Rental: Raleigh Rent-A-Bike, Kylemore Rd. (☎626 1333). Limited one-way rental system (£15/€19 surcharge). £10/€12.70 per day, £40/€50.80 per week. Deposit £50/€63.50. Open M-Sa 8:30am-6pm. Dealers closer to city center include **Cycle Ways,** 185-6 Parnell St. (☎873 4748). Open M-W and F-Sa 10am-6pm, Th 10am-8pm. **Dublin Bike Tours** (☎679 0899), behind the Kinlay House hostel on Lord Edward St., rents and provides advice on route planning. £10/€12.70 per day, £40/€50.80 per week; students £8/€10.20, £35/€44.50. ID deposit. Open daily 9:30am-5:30pm.

Hitchhiking: Since Co. Dublin is well served by bus and rail, there is no good reason to thumb it. Hitchers coming to Dublin generally ask drivers to drop them off at the bus or DART stops outside the city. Those leaving Dublin take buses to the outskirts where the motorways begin. Buses #25, 25A, 66, 66A, 67, and 67A from Wellington Quay go to Lucan Rd., which turns into N4 (to Galway and the West). For a ride to Cork, Limerick, and Waterford (N7), hitchers usually take bus #51, 51B, 68, or 69 from Fleet St. to Aston Quay to Naas ("nace") Rd. N11 (to Wicklow, Wexford, and Rosslare) can be reached by bus #84 from Eden Quay or #46A from Fleet St. toward Stillorgan Rd. Bus #38 from George Quay or #39 from Burgh Quay to Navan Rd. goes to N3 (to Donegal and Sligo). Buses #33, 41, and 41A from Eden Quay toward Swords send hitchers on their way to N1 (Belfast and Dundalk). *Let's Go* does not recommend hitchhiking.

✷ ORIENTATION

In general, Dublin is refreshingly compact, though navigation is complicated by the ridiculous number of names a street adopts along its way. The **River Liffey** divides Dublin's **North** and **South Sides.** The streets running alongside the Liffey are called **quays** (KEYS); their names change each block. Bridges also have their own names. Buying a map with a street index is a fabulous idea. The core of Dublin is ringed by **North** and **South Circular Rd;** most of the city's major sights are located within this area. **O'Connell St.** is the primary link between north and south Dublin. South of the Liffey, O'Connell St. becomes **Westmoreland St.,** passes **Fleet St.** on the right, curves around Trinity College on the left, and then becomes **Grafton St.** One block south of the river, **Fleet St.** becomes **Temple Bar.** While Temple Bar is the name of a street, it usually applies to the area as a whole. **Dame St.,** which runs parallel to Temple Bar and terminates at Trinity College, defines the southern edge of the district. **Trinity College** is the nerve center of Dublin's cultural activity. The college touches the northern end of **Grafton St.** Grafton's southern end opens onto **St. Stephen's Green.** North Side merchants hawk merchandise for cheaper prices than those in the more touristed South. **Henry St.** and **Mary St.** comprise a pedestrian shopping zone that intersects with O'Connell just after the **General Post Office (GPO),** two blocks from the Liffey. The North Side has the reputation of being a rougher area, especially after dark. This reputation may not be wholly deserved, but tourists should avoid walking in unfamiliar areas on either side of the Liffey at night, especially when alone. It is wise to steer clear of Phoenix Park after dark.

7 PRACTICAL INFORMATION

TOURIST AND FINANCIAL SERVICES

Bord Fáilte Visitors Centre: Suffolk St. (☎605 7700; www.visitdublin.com), in a converted church. Accommodations service £1/€1.30 and 10% non-refundable deposit; credit card bookings by phone or email (☎(0800) 6686 6866; reservations@dublin-tourism.ie). **American Express** (☎605 7709; open M-Sa 9am-5pm), **Bus Éireann**, and **Argus Rent-a-Car** (☎605 7701 or 490 4444; fax 490 6328; open M-Sa 9am-5pm). You can also book tours, concerts, plays, and most anything else in Dublin that requires a ticket (through TicketMaster); booking fee is £1.50/€1.90. Centre open July-Aug. M-Sa 9am-8:30pm, Su 11am-5:30pm; Sept.-June M-Sa 9am-5:30pm. Reservation desks close 30min. early.

Northern Ireland Tourist Board: 16 Nassau St. (☎679 1977 or (1850) 230 230). Books accommodations in the North. Open M-F 9:15am-5:30pm, Sa 10am-5pm.

Community and Youth Information Centre: Sackville Pl. (☎878 6844), Marlborough St. Library of resources on youth and special-needs groups, careers, outings, travel, hostels (no bookings), camping, sports, counseling, and referrals. Open M-W 9:30am-1pm and 2-6pm, Th-F 9:30am-1pm and 2-5pm, Sa 9:30am-1:30pm and 2:30-5pm.

Budget Travel: usit NOW, 19-21 Aston Quay (☎679 8833), near O'Connell Bridge. The place for Irish travel discounts. Photo booths £4/€5.10. Internet access with ISIC card £1/€1.30 per 15min., £2.50/€3.20 per 45min. Open M-W and F 8:30am-6:30pm, Th 8:30am-8:30pm, Sa 10am-5:45pm.

Hosteling Organization: An Óige Head Office (Irish Youth Hostel Association/HI), 61 Mountjoy St. (☎830 4555; www.irelandyha.org), at Wellington St. Follow O'Connell St. north, ignoring its name changes. Mountjoy St. is on the left, about 20min. from O'Connell Bridge. Book and pay for HI hostels here. Also sells package bike and rail tours. The *An Óige Handbook* lists all HI hostels in Ireland and Northern Ireland. Membership £12/€15.25, under 18 £6/€7.60. Open M-F 9:30am-5:30pm.

Financial Services: Bank of Ireland, AIB, and **TSB** branches with **bureaux de change** cluster on Lower O'Connell St., Grafton St., and in the Suffolk St. and Dame St. areas. Most banks are open M-F 10am-4pm. Bureaux de change also found in the General Post Office and in the tourist office main branch. **American Express,** 41 Nassau St. (☎679 9000). Traveler's check refunds. Currency exchange; no commission for AmEx Traveler's Cheques. Client mail held. Open M-F 9am-5pm. Smaller branch inside the Suffolk St. tourist office.

LOCAL SERVICES

Luggage Storage: Connolly Station. £2/€2.50 per item per day. Open M-Sa 7:40am-9:20pm, Su 9:10am-9:45pm. **Heuston Station.** £1.50-4/€1.90-5.10 per item, depending on size. Open daily 6:30am-10:30pm. **Busáras.** £2.50/€3.20 per item, lockers £3-7/€3.80-8.90. Open M-Sa 8am-7:45pm, Su 10am-5:45pm.

Women's Resources: Women's Aid helpline (☎(1800) 341 900) staffed 10am-10pm. **Dublin Well Woman Centre,** 35 Lower Liffey St. (☎872 8051) is a private health center for women. It also runs a **clinic** (☎668 3714) at 67 Pembroke Rd.

Gay and Lesbian Resources: Gay Switchboard Dublin is a good resource for events and updates and sponsors a hotline (☎872 1055; Su-F 8-10pm, Sa 3:30-6pm). **National Gay and Lesbian Federation,** Hirschfield Centre, 10 Fownes St. (☎671 0939), in Temple Bar, offers counseling on legal concerns. **Lesbians Organizing Together (LOT),** 5 Capel St. (☎872 7770). Drop-in resource center and library open Tu-Th 10am-5pm. **Outhouse,** 65 William St. (☎670 6377). Queer community resource center.

Launderette: Laundry Shop, 191 Parnell St. (☎872 3541), near Busáras. Wash and dry £6-8/€7.60-10.20. Open M-F 8am-7pm, Sa 9am-6pm, Su 11am-5pm. **All-American Launderette,** 40 S. Great Georges St. (☎677 2779). Wash and dry £5/€6.35; full service £5.50/€7. Open M-Sa 8:30am-7pm, Su 10am-6pm.

EMERGENCY AND COMMUNICATIONS

Emergency: ☎999 or 112. No coins required.

Police (*Garda*): Dublin Metro Headquarters, Harcourt Terr. (☎666 9500); Store St. Station (☎666 8000); Fitzgibbon St. Station (☎666 8400); Pearse St. (☎666 9000). **Garda Confidential Report Line:** ☎(1800) 666 111.

Counseling and Support: Tourist Victim Support, Harcourt Sq. (☎478 5295, 24hr. helpline (1800) 661 771). Open M-Sa 10am-6pm, Su noon-6pm. **Samaritans,** 112 Marlborough St. (☎(1850) 609 090 or 872 7700). **Cura,** 30 S. Anne St. (☎708 4689). Catholic-funded support for women with unplanned pregnancies. Open M and W 10:30am-6:30pm, T and Th 10:30am-8:30pm, F-Sa 10:30am-2:30pm.

Hospital: St. James's Hospital, James St. (☎453 7941). Take bus #123. **Mater Misericordiae Hospital,** Eccles St. (☎830 1122), off Lower Dorset St. Buses #10, 11, 13, 16, 121, and 122. **Beaumont Hospital,** Beaumont Rd. (☎837 7755 or 809 3000). Buses #27B, 51A, 101, 103, and 300. **Tallaght Hospital** (☎414 2000), farther south Buses #49, 49A, 50, 54A, 65, 65B, 75-77, 77A, 201, and 202.

Internet Access: Free Internet is available at the **central library,** Henry St. and Moore St. (☎873 4333). Open M-Th 10am-8pm, F-Sa 10am-5pm. You can pay for access at many hostels and some shops. The best deals are £2/€2.50 per hr. Reliable cyber cafes operate on a use first, pay later basis. Several chains abound, the best being **The Internet Exchange,** with branches at 146 Parnell St. (☎670 3000) and Fownes St. in Temple Bar (☎635 1680). Membership rate £2/€2.50 per hr. Open daily 9am-10:30pm. **Global Internet Cafe,** 8 Lower O'Connell St. (☎878 0295), a block north of the Liffey and on the right. Wide array of services, excellent coffee and smoothies, fully trained staff. £5/€6.35 per hr., members £2.40/€3. Open M-F 8am-11pm, Sa 9am-11pm, Su 10am-11pm.

Post Office: General Post Office (GPO), O'Connell St. (☎705 7000). Poste Restante pickup at the **bureau de change** window. Open M-Sa 8am-8pm, Su 10am-6:30pm. **Postal code:** Dublin 1. (Dublin is the only place in the Republic with postal codes. Even-numbered codes are for areas south of the Liffey, odd-numbered are for the north.) Smaller post offices around the city open M-F 8:45am-6pm.

◪ ACCOMMODATIONS AND CAMPING

Dublin has a handful of marvelous accommodations, but high demand for lodging keeps less-than-marvelous places open too. Reserve at least a week in advance. Bord Fáilte-approved B&Bs and hostels aren't necessarily better than unapproved ones. Phoenix Park may tempt the desperate, but camping there is a terrible idea, not to mention big-time illegal. If the accommodations below are full, consult Dublin Tourism's annually updated *Dublin Accommodation Guide* (£3/€3.80), or ask hostel and B&B staff for referrals.

HOSTELS

The Brewery Hostel, 22-23 Thomas St. (☎453 8600; fax 453 8616; breweryh@indigo.ie). Follow Dame St. past Christ Church through its name changes or take bus #123. Next to the Guinness brewery and a 20min. walk from Temple Bar. One of the best hostels in Dublin, with excellent facilities and a personable atmosphere. Rooms are a bit snug but the beds are good. Cheerful kitchen and small dining area open 23hr. (closed 11pm-midnight for cleaning). All rooms with bath. Free parking. Continental breakfast included. Free luggage storage. Laundry across the street. 10-bed dorms £10.50-12.50/€13.50-16; 8-bed £12-13.50/€15.25-17; 4-bed £15-16.50/€19-21; doubles £44-46/€56-58.50.

Globetrotter's Tourist Hostel (IHH), 46-7 Lower Gardiner St. (☎873 5893; fax 878 8787; www.iol.ie/globetrotters). A dose of luxury for the weary. Beds are small, but there's plenty of room to stow your travel flotsam. Internet access. Breakfast included. Free luggage storage. Towels 50p/€0.65. Dorms £13-17/€16.50-21.60; singles £47.50-52.50/€60.30-66.70; doubles £70-80/€89-100.

Litton Lane Hostel, 2-4 Litton Ln. (☎872 8389; fax 872 0039), off Bachelor's Quay. A former studio for the likes of U2, Van Morrison, and Sinéad O'Connor. Staff is professional yet quirky and laid back. Parking available. Internet access. Continental breakfast included. Luggage storage opened every hr. Key deposit £2/€2.50. Check-in 3pm, check-out 10:30am. Dorms £10.50-16/€13.50-20.30; doubles £44-52/€56-66.

Abraham House, 82-3 Lower Gardiner St. (☎855 0600; fax 855 0598). Respectable, tidy rooms with calming color schemes and an accommodating receptionist. Bureau de change. Internet access. Free luggage and bike storage. Kitchen open until 10pm. Light breakfast and towels included. Laundry £4/€5.10. 12-bed dorms £10-11/€12.70-14; 8-bed £11-13/€14-16.50; 6-bed £12-14.50/€15.25-18.50, with bath £13-16/€16.50-20.50; 4-bed £12.50-16/€16-20.50, with bath £14-18/€18-23; private rooms £14-15/€18-19 per person, with bath £17-20/€21.50-25.50.

Barnacle's Temple Bar House, 19 Temple Ln. (☎671 6277; fax 453 8616). "The burning hot center of everything." A well-kept if rather impersonal hostel in the hopping heart of Dublin—expect noise. Lounge with open fire and TV. Skylights in some rooms. All rooms with bath and water pressure that will make you sing. Continental breakfast included. Laundry, luggage room, and safe deposit box. Massive dorms £10.50-13/€13-16.50; 10-bed £12-15/€15.50-19; 6-bed £14-17/€18-21.50; 4-bed £17-18/€20.50-23; singles £44-58/€56-74; twins and doubles £50-58/€62-74.

Kinlay House (IHH), 2-12 Lord Edward St. (☎679 6644; fax 679 7437). Slide down the oak banisters in the lofty entrance hall and gaze at Christ Church Cathedral across the street from the soft couches in the TV room. Bureau de change. Internet access. Wake-up calls. Breakfast included. Lockers 50p/€0.65; free luggage storage. Laundry £5/€6.35. 15- to 24-bed dorms £11/€14; 20-bed partitioned into 4-bed nooks £13/€16.50; 4- to 6-bed £15.50/€19.75, with bath £17.50/€22; singles £25/€31.75; doubles £38/€48, with bath £43/€54.50. Nov.-May prices £1-2.50/€1.30-3.20 less.

Avalon House (IHH), 55 Aungier St. (☎475 0001; fax 475 0303; www.avalon-house.ie). Turn off Dame St. onto Great Georges St.; the hostel is a 10min. walk down on your right. A stumble away from Temple Bar—this is your best bet near the city center. Top-notch security, Internet access, and an adequate kitchen. Coed showers, toilets, and dorms. Dorms provide privacy with a split-level setup. Smoking in designated areas only. Bike rack. Small continental breakfast included. Free luggage storage opened every 2hr., or get a large personal luggage cage (£1/€1.30). Towels £1/€1.30 with £5/€6.35 deposit. Dorms £13.50-15.75/€17-19.50; singles £25-30/€31.75-38; twins £24-27.50/€30.50-35.

Abbey Court Hostel, 29 Bachelor's Walk, O'Connell Bridge (☎878 0700; fax 878 0719). From O'Connell Bridge, turn left to face this emphatic blue and orange addition to Dublin's hostel scene. A little pricey, but clean, comfy, and well kept. Great location. **Internet access** £1/€1.30 for 15min. Continental breakfast included. Free luggage storage; security box 50p/€0.65. 12-bed dorms £13.50-16/€17-20; 6-bed £17.50-19.50/€22-25; 4-bed £20-22/€25-28; doubles £60-70/€76-88.

Jacobs Inn, 21-28 Talbot Pl. (☎855 5660; fax 855 5664). 2 blocks north of the Custom House, Talbot Pl. stretches from the back of the bus station up to Talbot St. Rooms, all with bath, are spacious, and cheery. Kitchen and TV room are sterile without the cheer. Bureau de change. Breakfast £2.75-4.50/€3.50-5.70. Lockers £1/€1.30 nightly rate plus £5/€6.35 deposit. Towels £1/€1.30. Laundry £5/€6.35. Bike storage at Isaac's (see below). Room lockout 11am-3pm. Dorms £10-13/€12.70-16.50; doubles £44-48/€56-61; triples £19.50-21.50/€25-27 per person. Weekends £1/€1.30 higher.

Ashfield House, 19-20 D'Olier St. (☎679 7734; fax 679 0852). Smack in the center of Dublin, offers a variety of bedrooms and big yellow common areas. Good security. Light breakfast included. Kitchen open until 10pm. **Bureau de change. Internet access.** Luggage storage; lockers £1/€1.30 plus £10/€12.70 deposit. Laundry £4/€5. May-Oct. dorms £11.50-18/€14-23; private rooms £13-14/€16.50-18 per person. Weekend prices £1-2/€1.30-2.50 higher. Nov.-Apr. all prices £1-2/€1.30-2.50 lower.

Dublin International Youth Hostel (An Óige/HI), 61 Mountjoy St. (☎830 4555; fax 830 1600; www.irelandyha.org). O'Connell St. changes names 3 times before the left turn onto Mountjoy St. Welcome to the mothership. This convent-turned-hostel has made giant improvements: a keycard system and lockers beef up security; beds are decent; rooms and bathrooms are clean. Car park and shuttles to Temple Bar. Wheelchair-accessible. Cafe has cheap meals (£3.50/€4.45) and packed lunches (£2/€2.50). Breakfast included. Luggage storage £1/€1.30. Towels £1/€1.30. Laundry £4/€5.10. High season dorms £7.50/€9.53, under 18 £10/€13.50.

Celts House, 32 Blessington St. (☎830 0657), a 15min. walk from the city center. 38 comfy, solid wooden bunks in a brightly painted setting. Key deposit £5/€6.35. Reception 9am-11pm. May-Sept. 8-bed dorms £11.50/€14.50; 6-bed £14.50/€18.50; 4-bed £13.50/€17; doubles £40/€51. Sept.-May 8-bed dorms £10/€12.70.

Marlborough Hostel (IHH), 81-82 Marlborough St. (☎874 7629; fax 874 5172). Look for the red door between O'Connell and Gardiner St. Large rooms and a barbecue patio. Bike shed. **Internet access.** Small continental breakfast included. £5/€6.35 linen deposit. Check-out 10:30am. June-Oct. 4- to 10-bed dorms £11.50-13/€14.50-16.50; doubles £40/€50.80. Nov.-May £9-10/€11.50-12.70; £30/€38.

Isaac's Hostel, 2-5 Frenchman's Ln. (☎855 6215; fax 855 6574), off the lower end of Gardiner St. behind the Custom House. Especially attractive to the young and energetic. Cafe. **Internet access.** Towels £1/€1.30. Laundry £5/€6.35. Bed lockout 11am-2:30pm. Apr.-Oct. big dorms £9-10/€11.50-12.70; 4-bed £15/€19; singles £24/€30.50; doubles £40/€51. Nov.-Mar. £1/€1.30 less.

Oliver St. John Gogarty's Temple Bar Hostel, 18-21 Anglesea St. (☎671 1822; fax 671 7637). Joyce once roomed here with Gogarty. Although legend holds that Gogarty ran Joyce off with a gun, perhaps James just found it a tad pricey. The location is unbeatable for frolicking in Temple Bar. **Internet access.** Laundry £2/€2.50. Key deposit £5/€6.35. June-Sept. dorms £18/€23; twins £44/€56; triples £57/€72. Mar.-May and Oct. £16/€20, £40/€51, £54/€68.50. Nov.-Feb. £14/€18, £36/€46, £48/€61.

BED AND BREAKFASTS

B&Bs with a green shamrock sign out front are approved by Bord Fáilte; those without haven't been inspected but may be cheaper and better located—establishments with good locations often find that Bord Fáilte's advertising is unnecessary. On the North Side, B&Bs cluster along **Upper** and **Lower Gardiner St.,** on **Sheriff St.,** and near **Parnell Sq.** Exercise caution when walking through the inner-city area at night. The B&Bs listed below are warm and welcoming standouts in this neighborhood. Dublin Tourism's annually updated *Dublin Accommodation Guide* ($3/€3.80) lists the locations and rates of all approved B&Bs.

▨ **Rita and Jim Casey,** Villa Jude, 2 Church Ave. (☎668 4982), off Beach Rd. Bus #3 to the first stop on Tritonville Rd.; Church Ave. is back a few yards. Call for directions from the Lansdowne Rd. DART stop. Mr. Casey is the former mayor of Sandymount, and he and lovely Rita specialize in the royal treatment. Clean rooms and big breakfasts for the best B&B price in Dublin. Singles £17.50/€22; doubles £35/€44.45.

Parkway Guest House, 5 Gardiner Pl. (☎874 0469). Rooms are plain but high-ceilinged and tidy; the location (just off Gardiner St.) is excellent. Run by a mother-and-son team. Full Irish breakfast. Singles £25/€30.50; doubles £36-40/€46-51, with shower £44-50/€56-63.50.

Charles Stewart Budget Accommodation, 5-6 Parnell Sq. (☎878 0350 or 878 1767; fax 878 1387; www.iol.ie/~cstuart). Continue up O'Connell St. past Parnell St. and look to your right. Full Irish breakfast. Singles £25/€31.75; twins/doubles £60/€76, with bath £70; triples with bath £94/€120.

Carmel House, 16 Upper Gardiner St. (☎874 1639; fax 878 6903). Elegant breakfast room and lounge replete with fresh cut flowers and fairly priced, considering the area's skyrocketing rates. Singles £30-45/€38-57; doubles £50-60/€63.50-76.

Marian B&B, 21 Upper Gardiner St. (☎874 4129). Brendan and Catherine McElroy provide lovely rooms at a better price than comparable neighborhood accommodations. Singles £22/€28; doubles £40/€50.80.

Mona's B&B, 148 Clonliffe Rd. (☎837 6723). Firm beds in rooms kept tidy by a charming proprietress who offers homemade bread with her full Irish breakfast. Open May-Oct. Singles £20/€25.40; doubles £40/€50.80.

Mrs. Molly Ryan, 10 Distillery Rd. (☎837 4147), off Clonliffe Rd.; on your left if you're coming from the city center. In a yellow house attached to #11. The unsinkable Molly Ryan, in her countless years, has never marked the B&B with a sign. Small rooms, small prices, no breakfast. As honest as they come. Singles £15/€19; doubles £22/€28.

Mrs. Dolores Abbot-Murphy, 14 Castle Park (☎269 8413). Ask the #3 bus driver to drop you off at Sandymount Green. Continue past Browne's Deli and take the first left; at the end of the road look right. A 5min. walk from Sandymount DART stop. Cheerful rooms in a charming cul-de-sac. Breakfast included. Singles £25/€31.75; doubles £44/€56.50, with bath £46/€59.

The White House, 125 Clontarf Rd. (☎833 3196). Sink into your bed and gaze out at pristine rose gardens. Singles £25/€31.75, off season £24/€30.50; doubles £44/€56.50, with bath £48/€61.

CAMPING

Most campsites are far from the city center, but camping equipment is available in the heart of the city. It is illegal and unsafe to camp in Phoenix Park.

Camac Valley Tourist Caravan and Camping Park, Naas Rd., Clondalkin (☎464 0644; fax 464 0643; camacmorriscastle@tinet.ie), near Corkagh Park. Take bus #69 (35min. from city center, £1.15/€1.50). Food shop and kitchen. Laundry £3.50/€4.45. Open June-Aug. Hikers/cyclists £4.50/€5.70; 2 people with car £10/€12.70; 2 people with caravan £12/€15.25; 2 people with camper £11/€14. Showers 50p/€0.65.

Shankill Caravan and Camping Park (☎282 0011; fax 282 0108). The DART and buses #45 and 84 from Eden Quay run to Shankill, as does bus #45A from the Dún Laoghaire ferry port. £4.50-5/€5.70-6.35 per tent plus £1/€1.30 per adult, 50p/€0.65 per child. Showers 50p/€0.65.

🚺 FOOD

Dublin's many **open-air markets** sell fixings fresh and cheap. Vendors hawk fruit, fresh strawberries, flowers, and fish from their pushcarts. The later in the week, the livelier the market. The cheapest **supermarkets** around Dublin are in the **Dunnes Stores** chain, with a full branch at St. Stephen's Green. (☎478 0188. Open M-W and F-Sa 8:30am-7pm, Th 8:30am-9pm, Su noon-6pm.) The **Runner Bean,** 4 Nassau St., vends whole foods, homemade breads, veggies, fruits, and nuts for the squirrel in you. (☎679 4833. Open M-F 7:30am-6pm, Sa 7:30am-3pm.)

🔳 **Cafe Irie,** 11 Fownes St. (☎672 5090), above the clothing store Sé Sí Progressive. Probably the best value in Temple Bar. A small eatery with an impressive selection of lip-smackingly good sandwiches under £3/€3.80. Vegan-friendly. Great coffee. A little crunchy, a little jazzy, a whole lotta good. Open M-Sa 9am-8pm, Su noon-5:30pm.

🔳 **Cornucopia,** 19 Wicklow St. (☎677 7583). This vegetarian horn o' plenty spills huge portions onto your plate. Servers are more than happy to translate organic ingredients. If you can find the space, sit down for a rich meal (about £5/€6.35) or snack (£1.50/€1.90). Open M-W and F-Sa 9am-8pm, Th 9am-9pm.

La Mezza Luna, 1 Temple Ln. (☎671 2840), on the corner of Dame St. Refined but not pretentious. Celestial food. Try the wok-fried chicken for £8/€10. Daily lunch specials around £5/€6.35; served noon-5pm. Delicious desserts £4/€5. Open M-Th 12:30-11pm, F-Sa 12:30-11:30pm, Su 4-10:30pm.

Tante Zoe's, 1 Crowe St. (☎679 4407), across from the back entrance of the Foggy Dew pub. Creole food in an elegantly casual setting. The staff will help you get just the right spiciness. Entrees £10-12/€13-15.25. Open daily noon-4pm and 6pm-midnight.

Queen of Tarts, 3 Cork Hill (☎670 7499). This little red gem of a cafe offers homemade pastries, scones, cakes, and coffee. Limited seating in the courtyard. Open M-F 7:30am-6pm, Sa 9am-6pm, Su 10am-6pm.

Belgo, Sycamore St. (☎672 7555). An authentic and upbeat Belgian restaurant with many Belgian beers. Benefit from the early bird menu: £5/€6.35 at 5:30, £6/€7.60 at 6, and £7/€8.90 at 7pm. Open M-Th and Su until 11pm, F-Sa until midnight.

Yamamori Noodles, 71-72 S. Great Georges St. (☎475 5001 or 475 5002). Exceptional Japanese cuisine, reasonably priced. Cleaner than a hospital. Traditional black, red, and white decor. Entrees for under £10/€12.70; tofu steak £6/€7.60. Open M-W and Su 12:30-11pm, Th-Sa 12:30-11:30pm.

Butler's Chocolate Cafe, 24 Wicklow St. (☎671 0591). Sinning never felt so good. In this luxury sweet shop lattes start at £1.25/€1.60 and a Bailey's milkshake is £2.25/€2.75. Open M-W and F-Su 8am-5 or 6pm, later on Th.

Leo Burdock's, 2 Werburgh St. (☎454 0306), up from Christ Church Cathedral. The real-deal fish and chips. A holy ritual for many Dubliners. Takeaway only. Fish £3/€3.80, chips £1.20/€1.50. Open M-Sa noon-midnight, Su 4pm-midnight.

The Winding Stair Bookshop and Cafe, 40 Lower Ormond Quay (☎873 3292), near the Ha'penny Bridge. A relaxed cafe overlooking the river shares its lower level with a bookshop. Contemporary Irish writing, periodicals, and soothing music wind you down. Salads around £4/€5.10, sandwiches £2/€2.50. Open M-W 9:30am-6pm, Th-F 9:30am-8pm, Sa 9:30am-6pm, Su 1-6pm.

Soup Dragon, 168 Capel St. (☎872-3277). A dozen different soups by kitchen wizards (£3/€3.80-£9/€11.50), as well as healthy juices, fruits, and breads. Roar. Open M-F 8am-5:30pm and Sa 1-5pm.

Dail Bia, 46 Kildare St. (☎670 6079). Dublin's bilingual, all-Irish restaurant. Irish food, fresh and free from the turgid trappings of a carvery lunch. Between the high-traffic lunch and dinner hours, read a paper and enjoy the remarkable brightness of this basement establishment. Delicious scones, cakes, and sandwiches. Many sandwiches under £3.50/€4.45. Open M-F 8am-7pm, Sa 9:30am-5pm.

Bewley's Cafes. A Dublin institution, though some locals claim it ain't what it used to be. Dark wood paneling and marble table tops gesture to an "oriental" look. Meals are plain but affordable. Decadent pastries £1/€1.30. Many branches, including 78 Grafton St., with a room honoring its most famous patron, James Joyce (☎635 5470; open daily 7:30am-11pm, later on weekends).

◎ SIGHTS

TRINITY COLLEGE. Behind ancient walls sprawls Trinity's expanse of stone buildings, cobblestone walks, and green grounds. The British built Trinity in 1592 as a Protestant religious seminary that would "civilize the Irish and cure them of Popery." The college became part of the path members of the Anglo-Irish elite trod on their way to high positions, both governmental and social. Until the 1960s, the Catholic church deemed it a cardinal sin to attend Trinity; once the church lifted the ban, the size of the student body more than tripled. *(Between Westmoreland and Grafton St. in the center of Dublin; the main entrance fronts the block-long traffic circle now called College Green. Pearse St. runs along the north edge of the college, Nassau St. to the south. ☎608 1000. Grounds always open. Free.)* Trinity's **Old Library** holds an invaluable collection of ancient manuscripts, including the duly renowned **Book of Kells.** Upstairs, the **Long Room** contains Ireland's oldest harp—called the **Brian Ború Harp** and seen on Irish coins—and one of the few remaining 1916 proclamations of the Republic of Ireland. *(From the main gate, go straight; the library is on the south side of Library Sq. Open June-Sept. M-Sa 9:30am-5pm, Su noon-4:30pm; Oct.-May M-Sa 9:30am-4:30pm, Su noon-4:30pm. £4.50/€5.70, students and seniors £4/€5.10.)*

GRAFTON STREET. The few blocks south of College Green are off-limits to cars and ground zero for shopping tourists and residents alike. Grafton's **street performers** range from string octets to jive limboists. Upstairs at the Grafton St. branch of Bewley's and inside the coffee chain's former chocolate factory is the **Bewley's Museum.** Tea-tasting machines, corporate history, and a display on Bewley's Quaker heritage number among the marvels. *(Open daily 7:30am-11pm. Free.)*

LEINSTER HOUSE. The Duke of Leinster chose to make his home on Kildare St. back in 1745, when most of the urban upper-crust lived north of the Liffey. By building his house so far south, where land was cheaper, he was able to afford an enormous front lawn. Now Leinster House provides chambers for the **Irish parliament,** or **An tOireachtas** (on tir-OCH-tas). When the Dáil is in session, visitors can view the proceedings by contacting the Captain of the Guard, who conducts **tours** of the galleries. *(☎ 678 9911. Passport necessary for identification. Tours meet Sa every hr. in the adjacent National Gallery.)*

THE NATIONAL LIBRARY. Its entrance room chronicles Irish history and exhibits many literary goodies. A genealogical research room can help visitors trace even the thinnest twiglets of their Irish family trees. The reading room is stunning, with an airy, domed ceiling. *(Kildare St., adjacent to Leinster House. ☎ 661 2523. Open M-W 10am-9pm, Th-F 10am-5pm, Sa 10am-1pm. Free. Academic reason required to obtain a library card and entrance to the reading room; just "being a student" is usually enough.)*

ST. STEPHEN'S GREEN. This 22-acre park was a private estate until the Guinness clan bequeathed it to the city. Today, the grounds are teeming with public life: punks, couples, gardens, fountains, gazebos, strollers, swans, an artificial lake, a waterfall, a statue of Henry Moore, and a partridge in a pear tree. During the summer musical and theatrical productions are given near the old bandstand. *(Kildare, Dawson, and Grafton St. all lead to it. Open M-Sa 8am-dusk, Su 10am-dusk.)*

MERRION SQUARE. The Georgian buildings and elaborate doorways off Merrion Sq. and adjacent **Fitzwilliam St.** feed your architectural longings. After leaving 18 Fitzwilliam St., Yeats took up residence at 82 Merrion Sq. Farther south on **Harcourt St.,** playwright George Bernard Shaw and Dracula's creator, Bram Stoker, were neighbors at #61 and #16, respectively. At one point the Electricity Supply Board tore down a row of the townhouses. Irate Dubliners had a row of a different sort, and to compensate, the ESB now funds **#29 Lower Fitzwilliam St.,** a townhouse-turned-museum demonstrating the lifestyle of the 18th-century Anglo-Irish elite. *(☎ 702 6165. Open Tu-Sa 10am-5pm, Su 2-5pm. A short audiovisual show leads to a 25min. tour of the house. £2.50/€3.20, students and seniors £1/€1.30.)*

NEWMAN HOUSE. This fully restored building was once the seat of **University College Dublin,** the Catholic answer to Trinity. *A Portrait of the Artist as a Young Man* chronicles Joyce's time here. The poet Gerard Manley Hopkins spent the last years of his life teaching classics at the college. The cursory tour is geared to the architectural and the literary. *(85-86 St. Stephen's Green South. ☎ 706 7422. Admission by guided tour. Open to individuals June-Aug. Tu-F noon-5pm and Sa 2-5pm. Groups admitted year-round with advance booking. Adults £3/€3.80, concessions £2/€2.50.)*

THE SHAW BIRTHPLACE. This museum serves as both period piece and glimpse into the childhood of G.B. Shaw. Mrs. Shaw held recitals here, sparking little George's interest in music; her Victorian garden inspired his fascination with landscape painting. *(33 Synge St. ☎ 475 0854 or 872 2077. Down Camden, turn right on Harrington, and turn left onto Synge St. Take buses #16, 19, or 122 from O'Connell St. Open Easter-Oct. M-Sa 10am-5pm, Su 11am-5pm; no tours 1-2pm. Open for groups outside hours by request. £4/€5.10, students and seniors £3/€3.80, children £2/€2.50. Joint ticket with Dublin Writers Museum £4.60/€5.85; with Writers Museum and Joyce Museum £6.50/€8.50.)*

TEMPLE BAR. West of Trinity, between Dame St. and the Liffey, the Temple Bar neighborhood writhes with activity. Narrow neo-cobblestone streets link cheap cafes, hole-in-the-wall theaters, rock venues, and used clothing and record stores.

In the early 1980s, the Irish transport authority intended to replace the neighborhood with a seven-acre transportation center. The artists and nomads who lived there started a typical artist-and-nomad brouhaha about being forced into homelessness. Temple Bar immediately grew into one of Europe's hottest spots for nightlife, forcing the artists and nomads into homelessness. To steer the growth to ends more cultural than alcoholic, the government-sponsored Temple Bar Properties has spent over £30 million to build a whole flock of arts-related tourist attractions, with independent coattail-riders springing up as well.

DUBLIN CASTLE. Norman King John built the castle in 1204 on top of the Viking settlement; more recently, a series of structures from various eras has covered the site, culminating in an uninspired 20th-century office complex. Since 1938, every Irish president has been inaugurated here. The **State Apartments,** once home to English viceroys, now entertain EU representatives and foreign heads of state. Next door, the intricate inner dome of **Dublin City Hall** (designed as the Royal Exchange in 1779) shelters statues of national heroes. *(Dame St. at Parliament St. and Castle St. ☎ 677 7129. State Apartments open M-F 10am-5pm, Sa–Su and holidays 2-5pm; closed during official functions. £3/€3.80, students and seniors £2/€2.50. Grounds free.)*

CHRIST CHURCH CATHEDRAL. Originally built in the name of Catholicism, Irish cathedrals were forced to convert to the Church of Ireland in the 16th century. Sitric Silkenbeard built a wooden church on this site around 1038; Strongbow rebuilt it in stone in 1169. Further additions were made in the following centuries. Stained glass sparkles above the raised crypts, one of which supposedly belongs to Mr. Strongbow and his favorite lutefisk. *(At the end of Dame St., across from the Castle. Take bus #50 from Eden Quay or 78A from Aston Quay. ☎ 677 8099. Open daily 9:45am-5:30pm except during services. Donation strongly encouraged.)*

ST. PATRICK'S CATHEDRAL. The body of this, Ireland's largest cathedral, dates to the 12th century, although much was remodeled in 1864. St. Patrick allegedly baptized converts in the park next door. Artifacts and relics from the Order of St. Patrick lie inside. Jonathan Swift spent his last years as Dean of St. Patrick's, and his crypt is above the south nave. *(From Christ Church, Nicholas St. runs south and downhill, eventually becoming Patrick St. Take bus #49, 49A, 50, 54A, 56A, 65, 65B, 77, or 77A from Eden Quay. ☎ 475 4817. Open Mar.-Oct. daily 9am-6pm; Nov.-Feb. Sa 9am-5pm and Su 9am-3pm. £2.70/€3.50; concessions free.)*

DUBLIN'S VIKING ADVENTURE. Converse with Dubliners of the 9th and 10th centuries. If that gets old, try to make the actors to break character. *(Essex St. West. ☎ 679 6040. Take bus #51, 51B, 78A, or 79; or the DART to Tara Street Station and bus #90 to Essex Quay. £5.50/€7, students and seniors £4.25/€5.40, children £3/€3.80.)*

■ **GUINNESS STOREHOUSE.** Come to the sparkling new Storehouse and find out how Guinness brews its black magic and perpetuates the myth of the world's best stout. The Storehouse offers a self-guided tour with multimedia eye and ear candy. As your great reward, ye shall conclude your pilgrimage on the top floor, overlooking 64 acres of Guinness and imbibing a free pint of dark, creamy goodness. *Sláinte.* *(St. James's Gate. From Christ Church Cathedral, follow High St. west through its name changes—Cornmarket, Thomas, and James. Take bus #51B or 78A from Aston Quay or #123 from O'Connell St. ☎ 408 4800. Open Oct.-Mar. 9:30am-5pm; Apr.-Sept. 9:30am-7pm. £9/€11.50, students £6/€7.60, seniors and children £4/€5.10.)*

KILMAINHAM GAOL. A place of bondage and a symbol of freedom—almost all the rebels who fought in Ireland's struggle for independence between 1792 and 1921 spent time here. The jail's last occupant was **Éamon de Valera,** the future leader of Éire. Today, Kilmainham is a museum that traces the history of penal practices over the last two centuries. *(Inchicore Rd. Take bus #51 from Aston Quay, #51A from Lower Abbey St., or #79 from Aston Quay. ☎ 453 5984. Open Apr.-Sept. daily 9:30am-4:45pm; Oct.-Mar. M-F 9:30am-4pm and Su 10am-4:45pm. Tours every 35min. £3.50/€4.45, seniors £2.50/€3.20, students and children £1.50/€1.90.)*

DUBLINESE Mastering the Dublin dialect has posed a persistent challenge for writers and thespians of the 20th century. The following is a short introduction to Dubliners' favorite phrases.

Names for Outsiders: The rivalry between Dubliners and their country cousins is fierce. For Dubliners, all counties outside their own blur into one indiscriminate wasteland populated with "culchies," "plonkers," "turf-gobblers," and "muck-savages."

In Times of Difficulty: Dublinese is expeditious in keeping others in line. Idiots are rebuked as "eejits"; in dire situations, they are called "head-the-ball." Total exasperation calls for "shite and onions." When all is restored to order, it's said that "the job's oxo and the ship's name is murphy."

Affectionate Nicknames for Civic Landmarks: Over the past couple of decades, the government has graced the city with several public artworks that personify the Irish spirit in the female form. Dubliners have responded with poetic rhetoric. Off Grafton St., the statue of the fetching fishmongress Molly Malone is commonly referred to as "the dish with the fish" and "the tart with the cart." The goddess of the River Liffey sits in a fountain on O'Connell St. and is popularly heralded as the "floozy in the jacuzzi," "Anna Rexia," and even "the whore in the sewer" (pronounced HEW-er).

REPUBLIC OF IRELAND

O'CONNELL STREET. Dublin's biggest shopping thoroughfare starts at the Liffey and leads to **Parnell Square.** At 150 ft., it was once the widest street in Europe. The central traffic islands contain monuments to Irish leaders: **O'Connell's statue** faces the Liffey and O'Connell Bridge; at the other end of the street, **Parnell's statue** points toward nearby Mooney's pub. A block up O'Connell street, where Cathedral St. intersects it on the right, the 1988 statue of a woman lounging in water is officially named the Spirit of the Liffey or **"Anna Livia,"** but has many pseudonyms. On Grafton St., a newer statue of **Molly Malone** has her own aliases (see **Dublinese,** above). One monument you won't see is **Nelson's Pillar,** which stood outside the General Post Office for 150 years. In 1966 the IRA commemorated the 50th anniversary of the Easter Rising by blowing the Admiral out of the water.

THE GENERAL POST OFFICE. Not just a fine place to send a letter, the Post Office was the nerve center of the 1916 Easter Rising. Padraig Pearse read the Proclamation of Irish Independence from its steps. When British troops closed in, mailbags became barricades. Outside, a number of bullet nicks are visible. (O'Connell St. ☎ 705 7000. Open M-Sa 8am-8pm, Su 10am-6:30pm.)

THE CUSTOM HOUSE. Dublin's greatest architectural triumph, the Custom House was designed and built in the 1780s by James Gandon, who gave up the chance to be St. Petersburg's state architect and settled in Dublin. Carved heads along the frieze represent the rivers of Ireland; Liffey is the only lady. (East of O'Connell St. at Custom House Quay. ☎878 7660. Visitors center open mid-Mar. to Nov. M-F 10am-12:30pm and Sa-Su 12:30-2pm; Nov. to mid-Mar. W-F 10am-5pm and Su 2-5pm. £1/€1.30.)

FOUR COURTS. Another of Gandon's works. On April 14, 1922, General Rory O'Connor seized the Four Courts on behalf of the anti-Treaty IRA; two months later, the Free State government of Griffith and Collins attacked the Four Courts garrison, starting the Irish Civil War (see p. 668). The building now houses Ireland's highest court. (Inn's Quay is several quays to the west of the Custom House. ☎872 5555. Open M-F 9am-4:30pm. Free.)

OLD JAMESON DISTILLERY. Learn how science, grain, and tradition come together to form liquid gold—whiskey, that is. A film recounts Ireland's spirit-ual rise, fall, and renaissance; the subsequent tour walks you through the actual creation of the drink. Finish with a glass of Irish firewater; be quick to volunteer in the beginning, and you'll get to sample a whole tray of different whiskeys. Feel the burn. (Bow St. From O'Connell St., turn onto Henry St. and continue straight as the street dwindles to Mary St., then Mary Ln., then May Ln.; the warehouse is on a cobblestone street on the left. ☎807 2355. Tours daily 9:30am-5:30pm. £5/€6.50, students and seniors £3/€3.80.)

PHOENIX PARK. Europe's largest enclosed public park is most famous for the "Phoenix Park murders" of 1882. The Invincibles, a Republican splinter group, stabbed Lord Cavendish, Chief Secretary of Ireland, and his trusty Under-Secretary 200 yd. from the **Phoenix Column.** A Unionist journalist forged a series of letters linking Parnell to the murderers (see p. 667). The Column, capped with a phoenix rising from flames, is something of a pun—the park's name actually comes from the Irish *Fionn Uísce*, "clean water." The 1760 acres incorporate the **President's residence** (*Áras an Uachtaraín*), the US Ambassador's residence, cricket pitches, polo grounds, and red deer. The park is peaceful during daylight hours but unsafe at night. *(Take bus #10 from O'Connell St. or #25 or 26 from Middle Abbey St. west along the river.)* **Dublin Zoo,** one of the world's oldest and Europe's largest, is in the park. It contains 700 critters and the **world's biggest egg.** The habitats are large and the animals tend to move around a bit, except the lions, who feel it is their royal prerogative to sleep over 20 hours a day. *(Bus #10 from O'Connell St. ☎ 677 1425. June-Aug. open M-Sa 9:30am-6pm, Su 10:30am-6pm. Closes at sunset in winter. £6.30/€8, students £4.80/€6, seniors £3.70/€4.75, families £18.50-22/€23.50-28.)*

⬛ MUSEUMS AND GALLERIES

THE NATIONAL MUSEUMS

General Information for all 3 museums ☎ 677 7444. All open Tu-Sa 10am-5pm and Su 2-5pm. All free. The Museum Link bus runs from the adjacent Natural History and Archaeology museums to Collins Barracks every hr. All-day pass £2/€2.50; one-way 85p/€1.

A museum within a museum, ⬛**The Natural History Museum**'s creepily fascinating collection of world wildlife displays not so much the natural world as how museums used to interpret their role in it. A skeleton of the ancient Irish Elk, glass cases of classic taxidermy, and jars of native tapeworms are mysteriously compelling. *(Upper Merrion St.)* **The National Museum of Archaeology and History,** the largest of Dublin's museums, has extraordinary artifacts spanning the last two millennia. One room gleams with the **Tara Brooch** and other Celtic gold work. Another section is devoted to the Republic's founding years. *(Kildare St., adjacent to Leinster House. Guided tours £1/€1.30; call for times.)* **The Collins Barracks** are home to the **National Museum of Decorative Arts and History.** The most sophisticated of the three, the prodigal son of the National Museum family gleams with exhibits that range from the deeply traditional to the subversively multi-disciplinary. *(Benburb St., off Wolfe Tone Quay. Take the Museum Link or bus #10 from O'Connell. #90 to Heuston Station stops across the street. 1-2 guided tours per day. £1/€1.30.)*

OTHER MUSEUMS AND GALLERIES

THE NATIONAL GALLERY. This collection of over 2400 canvases includes paintings by Vermeer, Rembrandt, and El Greco. Works by 19th-century Irish artists comprise a major part of the collection. The new Millennium Wing, housing a Centre for the Study of Irish Art and new gallery space, will be open for 2002. *(Merrion Sq. West. ☎ 661 5133. Open M-Sa 9:30am-5:30pm, Th 10am-8:30pm, Su noon-5pm. Free tours Sept.-June Sa 3pm; Su 2, 3, 4pm; July-Aug. daily 3pm. Admission free.)*

THE IRISH JEWISH MUSEUM. The museum is a restored former synagogue that houses a large collection of artifacts, documents, and photographs chronicling the history of the Jewish community in Ireland since 1079 (when five arrived and were sent packing). The most famous Dublin Jew covered is, predictably, Leopold Bloom of *Ulysses* fame. *(3-4 Walworth Rd., off Victoria St. S. Circular Rd. runs to Victoria St.; from there the museum is signposted. Any bus to S. Circular Rd., including #16 and 20, will get you there. ☎ 490 1857. Open May-Sept. Tu, Th, Su 11am-3:30pm; Oct.-Apr. Su 10:30am-2:30pm. Groups may call to arrange an alternate visiting time.)*

THE DUBLIN WRITERS MUSEUM. Read your way through placard after placard describing the city's rich literary heritage, or listen to it all on an audio tour. Manuscripts, rare editions, and memorabilia blend with caricatures, paintings, a great bookstore, and an incongruous Zen Garden. *(18 Parnell Sq. North. ☎872 2077. Open June-Aug. M-F 10am-6pm, Sa 10am-5pm, Su 11am-5pm; Sept.-May M-Sa 10am-5pm. £3.10/€4, students and seniors £2.89/€3.75. Combined ticket with either Shaw Birthplace or James Joyce Centre £4.60/€5.85.)*

JAMES JOYCE CULTURAL CENTRE. This museum features Joyceana ranging from portraits of individuals who inspired his characters to the more arcane fancies of the writer's nephew, who runs the place. Call for info on lectures, walking tours, and Bloomsday events. *(35 N. Great Georges St. Up Marlborough St. and past Parnell St. ☎878 8547. Open M-Sa 9:30am-5pm, Su 12:30-5pm; July-Aug. Su 11am-5pm. £3/€3.80, students and seniors £2/€2.50.)*

HOT PRESS IRISH MUSIC HALL OF FAME. Dublin's anthem to its musical wonders takes you through memorabilia-laden displays on the history of Irish music from bards to the studio, heaping lavish praise on stars like Van Morrison, U2, and, uh, Boyzone. *(57 Middle Abbey St. ☎878 3345. Open daily 10am-6pm. £6/€7.60; concessions £4/€5.10.)*

GAELIC ATHLETIC ASSOCIATION MUSEUM. Those intrigued and/or mystified by the world of Irish athletics will appreciate this establishment at **Croke Park.** The GAA presents the rules, history, and heroes of its national sports, with the help of touchscreens and audiovisual displays. *(☎855 8176. Open May-Sept. daily 9:30am-5pm; Oct.-Apr. Tu-Sa 10am-5pm, Su noon-5pm. Last admission 4:30pm; admission on game days to ticket-holders only. £3/€3.80, students and seniors £2/€2.50, children £1.50/€1.90.)*

🎵 ENTERTAINMENT

Whether you fancy poetry or punk, Dublin is equipped to entertain you. The free weekly *Event Guide* is available at the tourist office, Temple Bar restaurants, and the Temple Bar Info Centre. The glossier *In Dublin* (£2/€2.50) comes out every two weeks with feature articles and listings for music, theater, art exhibitions, comedy shows, clubs, museums, gay venues, and movie theaters. Click to www.visitdublin.com for hot spots updated daily.

MUSIC

Dublin's music scene attracts performers from all over the world. Pubs see a lot of musical action, since they provide musicians with free beer and a venue. There is often a cover charge (£3-4/€3.80-5.10) for better-known acts. *Hot Press* (£1.50/€1.90) has the most up-to-date listings, particularly for rock.

Traditional music (trad) is not only a tourist gimmick, but a vibrant and important element of Dublin's music world. Some pubs in the city center have trad sessions nightly, others nearly so: **Hughes, Oliver St. John Gogarty,** and **McDaid's** are all good choices (see **Publin,** p. 688). The best pub for trad in the entire city is 🏚**Cobblestones,** King St. North (☎872 1799), in Smithfield. No rock here, but live shows every night, a trad session in the basement, and real live spontaneity. Big-deal bands frequent the **Baggot Inn,** 143 Baggot St. (☎676 1430). U2 played here in the early 80s; some people are still talking about it. **The Temple Bar Music Centre,** Curved St. (☎670 9202), has events and concerts virtually every night. The **National Concert Hall,** Earlsfort Terrace, provides a venue for classical concerts and performances. They have nightly shows in July and August, and their summer lunchtime series makes a nice break on occasional Tuesdays and Fridays. (☎671 1533. Tickets £6-12/€7.60-15.25, students half-price; summer lunchtime tickets £3-6/€3.80-7.60.) Programs for the **National Symphony** and smaller local groups are available at classical music stores and the tourist office. The new **HQ** (☎878 3345), in the Irish Music Hall of Fame on Middle Abbey St., considers itself one of the nicest venues in Europe. Big acts play **Olympia,** 72 Dame St. (☎677 7744), and **Vicar St.,** 99 Vicar St., (☎454 6656), off Thomas St. The stars perform for huge crowds at the **Tivoli Theatre,** 135-138 Francis St. (☎454 4472), and the musical monsters come to **Croke Park,** Clonliffe Rd. (☎836 3152), and the **R.D.S.** (☎668 0866) in Ballsbridge.

THEATER

There is no true "Theatre District" in Dublin—but smaller theater companies thrive off Dame St. and Temple Bar. Box office hours are usually for phone reservations; box offices stay open until curtain on performance nights. Showtime is generally 8pm. Dublin's most famous stage is the ◪**Abbey Theatre,** founded by Yeats and his collaborator Lady Gregory in 1904 to promote the Irish cultural revival and modernist theater (a bit like promoting both corned beef and soy burgers). Today, the Abbey is Ireland's National Theatre. *(26 Lower Abbey St. ☎878 7222. Box office open M-Sa 10:30am-7pm. Tickets £10-17.50/€12.70-22; Sa matinees 2:30pm, £8/€10.20; M-Th student rate £8/€10.20.)* The **Peacock Theatre** is the Abbey's experimental downstairs studio theater. *(☎878 7222. Box office open M-Sa at 7:30pm. Lunch events £8/€10.20, students £5/€6.35; theater tickets £8-10/€10.20-12.70, Sa 2:45pm matinees £6/€7.60.)*

CINEMA

Ireland's well-subsidized film industry reeled with the arrival of the **Irish Film Centre,** 6 Eustace St., in Temple Bar. The IFC mounts tributes and festivals, including a French film festival in October and a **gay and lesbian film festival** in early August. A variety of classic and European art house films appear throughout the year. You have to be a "member" to buy tickets. (☎679 3477. Weekly membership £1/€1.30; yearly membership £10/€12.70, students £7.50/€9.50. Membership must be purchased at least 15min. before start of show; each member can buy only 4 tickets per screening. Matinees £2/€2.50; 5pm showing £2.50/€3.20; after 7pm £4/€5.10, students £3/€3.80. 18+.) **The Screen,** D'Olier St. (☎672 5500), also rolls artsy reels. First-run movie houses cluster on O'Connell St., the quays, and Middle Abbey St. The **Savoy,** O'Connell St. (☎874 6000), and **Virgin,** Parnell St. (☎872 8400), offer a wide selection of major releases. Generic movie tickets cost about £5.50/€7 per person. If those screens aren't big enough for you, head to the **Sheridan IMAX,** Parnell Centre, Parnell St. (☎817 4200).

SPORTS AND RECREATION

Dubliners aren't as sports-crazed as their country cousins, but that's not saying much. Games are still a serious business, especially since most tournament finals take place here. The season for **Gaelic football** and **hurling** (see **Sports,** p. 670) runs from mid-February to November. Action-packed and often brutal, these contests are entertaining for any sports-lover. Games are played in **Croke Park** and on **Phibsborough Rd.** Tickets are theoretically available at the turnstiles, but they tend to sell out quickly. For more sports information, check the Friday papers or contact the **Gaelic Athletic Association** (☎836 3232). **Horseracing** and its attendant gambling are at Leopardstown Racetrack, in Foxrock (☎289 2888).

◪ PUBLIN

Dublin's pubs come in every shape, size, specialty, and subculture. Ask around or check *In Dublin, Hot Press,* or *Event Guide* for music listings. ID-checking almost always takes place at the door rather than at the bar and is more enforced in Dublin than in most of Ireland. A growing number of places are blurring the distinction between pubs and clubs, with rooms or dance-floors opening after certain hours or after live music; pay attention and hit two birds with one pint.

The *Let's Go* **Dublin Pub Crawl** aids you in discovering the city while researching the perfect pint. We recommend you begin your expedition at Trinity gates, stroll up Grafton St., teeter to Camden St., stumble to S. Great Georges St., then triumphantly drag your soused and sorry self to Temple Bar. Start early—say, noon.

GRAFTON STREET, TRINITY, AND VICINITY

◪ **The Long Stone,** 10-11 Townend St. (☎671 8102). Old books and hand-carved banisters lend a rustic-medieval feel. Lots of interesting rooms; the largest has a huge carving of a bearded man whose mouth serves as a fireplace. Carvery lunches 12:30-2:30pm. Open M-W noon-11:30pm, Th-F 10am-12:30am, Sa 3pm-12:30am, Su 4-11pm.

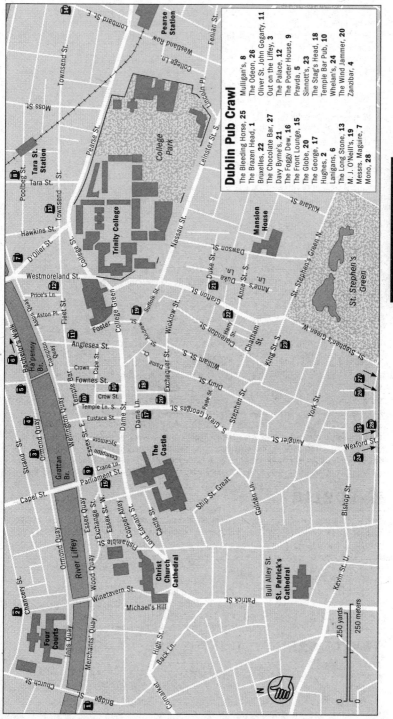

Dublin Pub Crawl

The Bleeding Horse, 25
The Brazen Head, 1
Bruxelles, 22
The Chocolate Bar, 27
Davy Byrne's, 21
The Foggy Dew, 16
The Front Lounge, 15
The Globe, 20
The George, 17
Hughes, 2
Lanigans, 6
The Long Stone, 13
M. J. O'Neill's, 19
Messrs. Maguire, 7
Mono, 28

Mulligan's, 8
The Odeon, 26
Oliver St. John Gogarty, 11
The Palace, 12
The Porter House, 9
Pravda, 5
Sinnott's, 23
The Stag's Head, 18
Temple Bar Pub, 10
Whelan's, 24
The Wind Jammer, 20
Zanzibar, 4

REPUBLIC OF IRELAND

Sinnott's, S. King St. (☎478 4698). A classy crowd of twentysomethings gathers in this spacious, wood-raftered basement pub. Fancies itself a spot for readers and writers, but let's be honest: it's for drinkers. Chart music packs the dance-floor until 2am. Open M-Sa 10:30am-2am, Su until 12:30am.

McDaid's, 3 Harry St. (☎679 4395), off Grafton St. across from Anne St. The center of Ireland's literary scene in the 50s. Book-covered walls and a gregarious crowd downstairs; during peak hours it's hotter than the devil's behind. You can try a more sedate set up above. Open M-W 11am-11:30pm, Th-Sa 11am-12:30am, Su 11am-11pm.

M.J. O'Neill's, Suffolk St. (☎679 3614), across from the tourist office. The enormous yet intimate maze of rooms is fairly quiet by day, but by night a fun, young crowd has it pulsing. Sports screen. Late closing Th-F 12:30am, Sa midnight.

Bruxelles (☎677 5362), across from McDaid's. Dark, comfortable pub, with international flags hanging from the ceiling. Blues funk that will draw you in off the street to shake your soul. Open M-W and Su until 1:30am, Th-Sa 2:30am.

Davy Byrne's, 21 Duke St. (☎677 5217), off Grafton St. A lively, middle-aged crowd fills the pub in which Joyce set the "Cyclops" chapter of *Ulysses*. The images of the writer himself on the walls hint at more recent redecorating. Open M-W 11am-11:30pm, Th-Sa 11am-12:30am, Su 11am-11pm.

HARCOURT AND CAMDEN STREETS

The Bleeding Horse, 24 Upper Camden St. (☎475 2705). You can't beat it, 'cause it ain't dead yet. All sorts of little nooks for private affairs. Late bar with DJ Th-Sa. Open M-W until 11:30pm, Th 2:30am, F-Sa 2am, Su 11pm.

The Odeon, Old Harcourt Train Station (☎478 2088). The Odeon has a columned facade, and the 2nd-longest bar in Ireland (after the one at the Galway races). Everything here is gargantuan. The upstairs is cozier (but still huge). Come to see and be seen. DJ on Sa, as well as casino, lounge, and dance (cover around £6/€7.60). Open Su-W until 12:30am, Th-F 2:30am, Sa 3am.

The Chocolate Bar, Harcourt St. (☎478 0225), in the Old Harcourt Train Station. Young clubbers drink here every night. Dress sharp. Be there early on Th-Sa and you've got the golden ticket to escape the £6-10/€7.60-12.70 cover at **The PoD** (see **Clublin,** below).

WEXFORD AND SOUTH GREAT GEORGES STREETS

▨**The Stag's Head,** 1 Dame Ct. (☎679 3701). This beautiful Victorian pub has stained glass, mirrors, and yes, you guessed it, evidence of deer decapitation. The largely student crowd dons everything from t-shirts to tuxes and spills out into the alleys. Excellent grub. Entrees £7/€9. Food served M-F 12:30-3:30pm and 5-7pm, Sa 12:30-2:30pm. Late bar Th-F until 12:30am. Closed Su.

▨**Whelan's,** 25 Wexford St. (☎478 0766), continue down S. Great Georges St. People in the know know Whelan's. The stage venue in back hosts big-name trad and rock, with live music every night starting at 9:30pm (doors open at 8:30pm). Cover £5-8/€6.35-10.20. Open 12:30-3:30pm for lunch (£5-6/€6.35-7.65). Open late W-Sa.

Mono, 26 Wexford St. (☎475 8555), next door to Whelan's. A neon club scene; varying DJs with occasional theme nights. Cover from £3/€3.80. Open Tu-Su 10:30am-2am, M 4pm-2am. Upstairs club closed Tu.

The Globe, 11 S. Great Georges St. (☎671 1220). Attracts those who like to get a little freaky, but nothing to get nervous and dye your hair over. A fine spot to relax with a Guinness or a frothy cappuccino. Open M-W noon-11:30pm, Th-Sa noon-midnight, Su 2-11pm. **Rí Rá** nightclub attached (see **Clublin,** below).

TEMPLE BAR

▨**The Porter House,** 16-18 Parliament St. (☎679 8847). The largest selection of world beers in the country and 8 self-brewed kinds of porter, stout, and ale. Excellent sampler tray includes a sip of stout made with oysters and other oddities (£6/€7.60). Occasional trad, blues, and rock. Open late F-Sa.

▨ **The Front Lounge,** Parliament St. (☎670-4112). The velvet seats of this gay-friendly bar are popular with a very mixed, very trendy crowd. Open M and W noon-11:30pm, Tu and Sa noon-12:30am, F noon-1:30am, Su 4-11:30pm.

▨ **The Palace,** 21 Fleet St. (☎677 9290), behind Aston Quay. This classic, neighborly pub has old-fashioned wood paneling and close quarters; head for the comfy seats in the skylit back room. The favorite of many a Dubliner.

The Foggy Dew, Fownes St. (☎677 9328). Like a friendly, mellow village pub but twice as big. The Foggy Dew makes a great spot for a pint or two without the artsy flash of other Temple Bar pubs. Live rock Su nights. Late bar Th-Sa until 2am.

Oliver St. John Gogarty (☎671 1822), at Fleet St. and Anglesea St. Lively and convivial atmosphere in a traditional but touristed pub. Named for Joyce's nemesis and one-time roommate, who appears in *Ulysses* as Buck Mulligan (see p. 694). Stately, plump trad sessions daily from 2:30pm. Open daily 10:30-2am. (Also see **Hostels,** p. 678.)

Messrs. Maguire, Burgh Quay (☎670 5777). Hours of enjoyment for those who explore this classy watering hole under the spell of homemade microbrews. The Weiss stout is a spicy delight. Late bar W-Sa. Trad Su-Tu 9:30-11:30pm. Open Su-Tu 10:30am-midnight, W-Th 10:30am-1:30am, F 10:30am-2am, Sa 12:30pm-2am.

Temple Bar Pub, Temple Ln. South. (☎672 5286). This sprawling bar is a worthwhile stop—tourists certainly think so—and one of the very few wheelchair-accessible pubs. Outdoor and indoor space. Music M-Sa 4-6pm and 8pm-close, Su all day.

THE BEST OF THE REST

▨ **Zanzibar** (☎878 7212), at the Ha'Penny Bridge. Mix of orientalist decor and pop culture. Quite the hotspot. Get your heart in rhythm as you make your way through the fabulous high-ceilinged bar to the dance-floor in back. DJ M-Th from 10pm, F-Sa from 9pm. Open M-Th 5pm-2:30am, F-Sa 4pm-2:30am, Su 4pm-1am.

The Brazen Head, 20 North Bridge St. (☎679 5186), off Merchant's Quay. Dublin's oldest and one of its liveliest pubs, established in 1198 as the first stop after the bridge on the way into the city. The courtyard, with its beer barrel tables, is quite the pickup scene on summer nights. The United Irishmen met here (see p. 667). Nightly Irish music. F-Sa late bar until 12:30am.

Mulligan's, 8 Poolbeg St. (☎677 5582), behind Burgh Quay off Tara St. Upholds its reputation as one of the best pint-pourers in Dublin. The crowd consists mainly of middle-aged men. A taste of the typical Irish pub: low-key and nothing fancy. Really.

Lanigans, Clifton Court Hotel, Eden Quay (☎874 3535). Imagine a pub with Irish singers that actually attracts more Dubliners than tourists. Stop imagining and head to Lanigans. Half of it is quiet and dark throughout the day, lit by solitary candles in Bailey's bottles. The other half has live music nightly at 9pm. Patches the generational gap with Irish dancing M-Th. Open M-W 10:30am-11:30pm, Th-Sa until 1am, Su until 11:30pm.

The Wind Jammer, Townsend St. (☎677 2576), at East Lombard St. Cheerful yellow pub with pictures of vessels will make you want to take that pint out on the Liffey. Also good for mornings when you need a pint with your mueslix, this "early house" opens at 7:30am every day and closes Su-W at 11:30pm, Th-Sa at 12:30am.

Pravda (☎874 0090), on the north side of the Ha'penny Bridge. The Russian late bar and Russian DJ action goes Russian Th-Sa. Actually, there's nothing Russian about the place other than Cyrillic wall murals. Trendy, popular, and gay-friendly. Probably Russian-friendly, too. Late bar F-Sa until 2:30am.

▧ CLUBLIN

In Dublin's nightlife war, clubs currently have a slight edge over pub rock venues, though the pubs are fighting back with later hours. To get home after 11:30pm, when Dublin Bus stops running, dancing queens take the **NiteLink bus** (every hr., Th-Sa 12:30-3:30am, £2.50/€3.20), which runs designated routes from the corner of Westmoreland and College St. to Dublin's suburbs. **Taxi** stands are located in front of Trinity, at the top of Grafton St. by St. Stephen's Green, and on Abbey St. Lower. Be prepared to wait 30-45min. on Friday and Saturday nights.

▓ **The Kitchen,** The Clarence Hotel, Wellington Quay (☎ 677 6635), in Temple Bar, through an understated entrance behind the hotel on Essex St. With 2 bars and a dance-floor, this U2-owned club is exceptionally well designed and the hottest spot in town. Impossible to get into on many nights. Dress as a rocker or a model. Cover £5-10/€6.35-12.70, students £1/€1.30 less on W-Th. Cookin' Th-Sa until 2:45am.

Rí-Rá, 1 Exchequer St. (☎ 677 4835), in the back of the Globe (see **Publin,** p. 690). Generally good music that steers clear of pop and house extremes. 2 floors, several bars, more nooks and crannies than a crumpet, and quite womb-like downstairs. Cover £6-7/€7.60-8.90. Open daily 11pm-2:30am.

The PoD, 35 Harcourt St. (☎ 478 0225). Spanish-style decor meets hardcore dance music. As trendy as The Kitchen. The truly brave venture upstairs to **The Red Box** (☎ 478 0225), a separate, more intense club with a warehouse atmosphere, brain-crushing music, and an 8-deep crowd at the bar designed to winnow out the weak. Often hosts big-name DJs—cover charges skyrocket. Cover £8-10/€10.20-12.70; Th ladies free before midnight; Th and Sa £5/€6.35 with ISIC card. Open until 3am. Start the evening at the Chocolate Bar or the Odeon, which share the building (see **Pubs,** p. 690).

The Shelter (Velur), at the Vicar St. theater (☎ 454 6656). Funk, soul, and a little bit of Austin Powers sound mixed with people who wear multiple shades of gray, black, and brown. Live bands and DJs. Cover £6/€7.60. Open Th-Sa.

Gaiety, S. King St. (☎ 677 1717), just off Grafton St. This elegant theater shows its late-night wild side every F and Sa midnight-4am. Numerous rooms and 4 bar areas. Enjoy the best of all worlds with DJs and live music, salsa, jazz, swing, latin, and soul. Cover around £8/€10.20.

Club M, Blooms Hotel, Anglesea St. (☎ 671 5622), in Temple Bar. Look for the big orange building. One of Dublin's largest clubs, attracting a crowd of all ages and styles, with multiple stairways and a few bars in the back. If at first you don't succeed, grind, grind again. Cover Su-Th £5/€6.35 (ladies free before midnight), F-Sa £10/€12.70.

Tomato, 60 Harcourt St. (☎ 476 4900). A smaller venue, usually blasting house and glam-girly sounds. We'd better call the calling off off. Open nightly. Cover Th £6/€7.60, F-Sa £8/€10.20, W student night £3/€3.80 or free.

The Funnel, 24 City Quay (☎ 677 5304). A smoky, mixed crowd grooves under military netting to psychedelic techno, funk, house, and garage. Occasional live acts. Cover before 11pm £5/€6.35; otherwise hovers around £7/€8.90.

Klub ZaZu (Switch), 21-25 Eustace St. (☎ 670 7655). The only 18+ club in Temple Bar, so a younger crowd here. M gay night, F drum and bass, Sa techno, Su funky groove, otherwise a lot of deep house. Cover Su-Th £5/€6.35, F £8/€10.20, Sa £9/€11.50.

GAY AND LESBIAN NIGHTLIFE

▓ **The George,** 89 S. Great Georges St. (☎ 478 2983). This throbbing, purple man o' war is Dublin's first and most prominent gay bar. A mixed-age crowd gathers throughout the day to chat and sip. The attached nightclub opens W-Su until 2am. Frequent theme nights. Su night bingo is accompanied by so much entertainment that sometimes the bingo never happens. Look spiffy—no effort, no entry. Cover £6-8 after 10pm.

▓ **The Front Lounge,** Parliament St. (☎ 670-4112). See **Publin,** above.

Out on the Liffey, 27 Upper Ormond Quay (☎ 872 2480). Ireland's 2nd gay bar; its name plays on the more traditional Inn on the Liffey a few doors down. Comfortably small. The short hike from the city center ensures a local crowd most nights. Tu drag, W karaoke, F-Sa DJ. No cover. Late bar W and Th until 12:30am, F and Sa until 1:30am.

♫ FESTIVALS

BLOOMSDAY. Dublin returns to 1904 each year on June 16, the day of Leopold Bloom's 18hr. journey, which frames the narrative (or lack thereof) of Joyce's Ulysses. Festivities are held all week long, starting before the big day and (to a lesser extent) continuing after it. The James Joyce Cultural Centre (see p. 687) sponsors a reenactments and a Guinness breakfast. (☎ 873 1984.)

MUSIC FESTIVALS. The **Festival of Music in Great Irish Houses** (☎278 1528), held during mid-June, organizes concerts of period music in 18th-century homes across the country. The **Feis Ceoil** music festival (☎676 7365) goes trad in mid-March. The **Guinness Blues Festival** (☎497 0381), a three-day extravaganza in mid-July, gets bigger and broader each year. Ask at the tourist office about fleadhs (FLAHS), daylong trad festivals that pop up periodically.

ST. PATRICK'S DAY. The half-week leading up to March 17 occasions a city-wide carnival of concerts, fireworks, street theater, and intoxicated madness, celebrating one of Ireland's lesser-known saints (☎676 3205).

THE DUBLIN THEATRE FESTIVAL. This premier cultural event, held the first two weeks of October, screens about 20 works from Ireland and around the world. Tickets may be purchased all year at participating theaters, and, as the festival draws near, at the Festival Booking Office. (47 Nassau St. ☎677 8439. Tickets £10-16/€12.70-20.30, student discounts vary by venue.)

THE DUBLIN FILM FESTIVAL. Nearly two weeks of Irish and international movies with a panoply of seminars in tow. (Early to mid-March. ☎679 2937.)

DUBLIN SUBURBS

Strung along the Irish Sea, Dublin's suburbs (reachable by DART, suburban rail, or Dublin buses) offer a calm alternative to the voracious human tide on the Liffey but host far too many crowds to fit the bill of Ireland's romanticized rural villages. Two regions that stand out from the uniform suburban sprawl are the tranquil Howth Peninsula to the north and the area around Dún Laoghaire, south of Dublin Bay. Both can be seen in an afternoon.

HOWTH   ☎01

The secret is out. Howth (rhymes with "both"), an affluent Eden dangling from the mainland, is becoming an increasingly popular destination. If the sun is shining on a weekend, expect the place to be full of madding crowds. And who could blame them? Less than 10 mi. from Dublin, Howth plays like a highlight reel of Ireland: rolling hills, pubs, a literary landscape, fantastic sailing, and a castle.

The best way to experience Howth's heather and seabird nests is the three-hour **cliff walk,** well trod but narrow, which rings the peninsula. At the harbor's end, **Puck's Rock** marks the spot where the devil fell when St. Nessan shook a Bible at him. (It was just that easy.) The nearby **lighthouse,** surrounded by tremendous cliffs, housed Salman Rushdie for a night during the height of the *fatwa* against him. To get to the trailhead from town, turn left at the DART and bus station and follow Harbour Rd. around the coast for about 20min. Several sights are clustered in the middle of the peninsula; go right as you exit the DART station and then left after a ¼ mi. at the entrance to the Deer Park Hostel. Up this road lies the private **Howth Castle,** a charmingly awkward patchwork of materials, styles, and degrees of upkeep. Just offshore, **Ireland's Eye** once provided both religious sanctuary and strategic advantage for monks, whose former presence is visible in the ruins of **St. Nessan's Church,** and one of the coast's many **Martello towers,** which opened for visitors in summer of 2001. **Ireland's Eye Boat Trips** jet passengers across the water. (☎831 4200, mobile (087) 267 8211. 15min.; 2 per hr. 11am-6pm, weather permitting; £5/€6.35 return, students £3/€3.80, children £2.50/€3.20.) Find them on the East Pier, toward the lighthouse.

To get to Howth, take a northbound **DART** to the end of the line (30min., 6 per hr., £1.15/€1.46), but pay attention at the Howth Junction as the line splits to serve Malahide as well. **Buses** #31 and 31B leave from Dublin's Lower Abbey St. Turn left out of the DART station and walk toward the harbor on the aptly named Harbour Rd.; the **tourist office** is on the right in the Old Courthouse. (☎832 0405. Open May-Aug. M 11am-1pm, T-F 11am-1pm and 1:30-5pm.) There is a cash machine at the **Bank of Ireland** on Main St., but no human tellers inside. The **post office** (☎831 8210) leads a tenuous existence at 27 Abbey St.

Gleann na Smól ("The Valley of the Thrush"), on the left at the end of Nashville Rd. off Thormanby Rd., is the affordable B&B option closest to the harbor. They have firm beds for the weary, MTV and CNN for the post-literate, and a generous supply of reading matter. (☎832 2936. Singles £30/€38.10; doubles £42/€53.50. 10% discount with ISIC card.) The top-notch beds of **Hazelwood** are 1 mi. up Thormanby Rd., at the end of the cul-de-sac in the Thormanby Woods estate. Bus #31B runs up Thormanby Rd., or call from the DART station for a lift. (☎839 1391; www.hazelwood.net. All rooms with bath. Doubles £60/€76.)

Spar supermarket is on St. Laurence Rd. off Abbey St. (☎832 6496. Open M-Sa 8am-10pm, Su 8am-9pm.) **P.D. Reflections,** on Harbour Rd. just before the golf shop, offers hearty, veggie-friendly portions for meager prices. (☎839 7826. Meals under £6.75/€8.50. Open daily 8am-8:30pm.) Hey now, no frauds at **Maud's,** Harbour Rd., a spunky cafe with sandwiches and ice cream. Try their signature "Pooh Bear Delight." (☎839 5450. Ice cream £0.80-2.45/€1-3.10. Open daily 10am-8pm.) Climb Thormanby Rd. to drinks and an incredible view at **The Summit** and its adjoining nightclub **K2.** (☎832 4615. Club open F-Su; cover £5-7/€6.35-9.) Join the fishermen at the **Lighthouse,** Church St., and relax with a pint and frequent trad. (☎832 2827. Sessions M and F from about 9pm, Su afternoons.)

DÚN LAOGHAIRE ☎01

As one of Co. Dublin's major ferry ports, Dún Laoghaire (dun-LEER-ee) is many tourists' first peek at Ireland. Fortunately, this is as good a place as any to begin your rambles along the coast.

■☑ **ORIENTATION AND PRACTICAL INFORMATION.** You can reach Dún Laoghaire in a snap with a **DART** from Dublin (£1.10/€1.40), or on southbound **buses** #7, 7A, 8, or (on a longer, inland route) #46A from Eden Quay. From the ferry port, **Marine Rd.** climbs up to the center of town. **George's St.,** at the top of Marine Rd., holds most of Dún Laoghaire's shops. **Patrick St.,** the continuation of Marine Rd., is the place for cheap eateries.

The **tourist office** hums at the ferry terminal and will outfit you with maps and pamphlets. (Open M-Sa 10am-6pm.) The terminal also has a **bureau de change.** (Open M-Sa 9am-4pm, Su 10am-4pm.) Other services include: the **Bank of Ireland,** 101 Upper George's St. (☎280 0273; open M-W and F 10am-4pm, Th 10am-5pm); **bike rental** at Mike's Bikes on Patrick St. (☎280 0417; £12/€15.25 per day, £8-9/€10.20-11.50 per week; open M-W and F-Sa 9am-6pm, Th 9am-9pm, Su 9am-1pm); and free **Internet access** at the **Dún Laoghaire Youth Info Centre,** in the church on Marine Rd. (☎280 9363; Open M-F 9:30am-5pm, Sa 10am-4pm).

■ **ACCOMMODATIONS.** Dún Laoghaire is prime ground for B&Bs, only some of which are modestly priced. Three hostels are also within walking distance, the best being ■**Belgrave Hall** at 34 Belgrave Sq. From the Seapoint DART station, head left down the coast, then zigzag through the intersections: right, left, right, and left again. This top-tier hostel feels old but not run-down. Frolic with lovable Irish wolfhounds in a family-friendly setting. (☎284 2106; www.dublinhostel.com. Bike rental £10/€12.70 per day. Internet access. Free parking. Small continental breakfast included. Laundry £5/€6.35. Summer F-Su 10-bed dorm £15/€19, M-Th £13/€16.50.) **Marina House,** at 7 Old Dunleary Rd., is rough and ready, with raw wood and solid, comfy beds in slightly cramped rooms. The owners might join you at night for drinks out back. (☎284 1524 or (086) 233 9283; www.marinahouse.com. Internet access. Nonsmoking bedrooms. May-Sept. big dorms £12/€15.25; 4-bed £15/€19; doubles £40/€50.80. Oct.-Apr. dorms £10/€12.70; doubles £35/€44.45.)

■☑ **FOOD AND PUBS.** Tesco vends downstairs in the Dún Laoghaire Shopping Centre. (☎280 0668. Open M-W and Sa 8:30am-7pm, Th-F 8:30am-9pm, Su 11am-6pm.) Fast-food restaurants and inexpensive coffee shops line George's St. **The Red Onion,** 60 Upper George's St., is the place to be seen for chic coffee and glitzy brunches. (☎230 0275. Most entrees £6/€7.60. Spinach and goat cheese wrap £5.90/€7.50. Fancy lunch served noon-3pm.) **Purty Kitchen** pub opens its loft for a purty little nightclub with pop and jazz, Thursday through Sunday until 2:30am. (☎284 3576. Happy hour M-F 5:30-6:30pm, pints £2/€2.50. Cover £7.) The other good pubs are up north in **Monkstown**, but if you insist on staying south, try **Farrell's,** upstairs in the Dún Laoghaire Shopping Centre; the panoramic coastal view looks just fine through a pint glass. (☎284 6595. Sandwiches under £2/€2.50. Open M-W 10:30am-11:30pm, Th-Sa 10:30am-12:30am, Su 12:30-11pm.)

◉♫ SIGHTS AND ENTERTAINMENT. Attention lit geeks: *He* was here. The young writer stayed in the **James Joyce Tower** in 1904 as a guest of Oliver St. John Gogarty, the surgeon, poetic wit, man-about-town, and first civilian tenant of the tower. The museum is a motherload of Joycenalia: his death mask, some love letters to Nora Barnacle, a page from the original manuscript of *Finnegan's Wake*, and many editions of *Ulysses*, including one illustrated by Henri Matisse. Upstairs, the Round Room reconstructs the author's bedroom; the Joyce novice can at least enjoy views from the gun platform of "many crests, every ninth, breaking, plashing, from far, from farther out, waves and waves." *(From the Sandycove DART station, go down to the coast, turn right, and continue to the Martello tower in Sandycove; or take bus #8 from Burgh Quay in Dublin to Sandycove Ave. ☎280 9265. Open Apr.-Oct. M-Sa 10am-1pm and 2-5pm, Su 2-6pm; Nov.-Mar. by appointment. £4/€5.10, students and seniors £3/€3.80, university students £3.60/€4.60.)*

At the base of the tower lies the **Forty Foot Men's Bathing Place,** another, more infamous, Joyce-blessed spot. A wholesome crowd with a bevy of toddlers splashes in the shallow pool facing the road, but behind a wall, on the rocks below the battery and adjacent to the tower, men skinny-dip year-round; apparently, it doesn't concern them that they're a tourist attraction. The Dún Laoghaire harbor itself is a sight; head down to the **piers**—the setting for Samuel Beckett's *Krapp's Last Tape*—to soak up the sun or brood with extended alienated pauses. Farther south from Dún Laoghaire, posh **Killiney** (kill-EYE-nee) has the most gorgeous beach around. Pick up the heritage map of Dún Laoghaire for details on seven Killiney-area walks. From the top of **Killiney Hill Park,** the views are breathtaking—that dark smudge on the horizon is called Wales. *(To reach the park from Castle St., turn left on Dalkey Ave. and climb Dalkey Hill, then take Burmah Rd. into the park. Free.)*

Dún Laoghaire's best *craic* can be had at the **Comhaltas Ceoltoiri Éireann** (COLE-tus KEE-ole-tori AIR-run), next door to the Belgrave Hall hostel. This is the national headquarters of the huge international organization for Irish traditional music, and it houses bona fide, non-tourist-oriented trad sessions *(seisiuns)*, as well as *céilí* dancing. *(☎280 0295. From July to mid-Aug. sessions M-Th at 9pm. £6/€7.60, with informal jam session after. Year-round F night céilí £5/€6.35.)*

EASTERN IRELAND

WICKLOW TOWN ☎0404

Touted both for its seaside pleasures and as a base camp for aspiring Wicklow mountaineers, Wicklow Town has a wide selection of restaurants and plenty of accommodations within walking-distance of its pubs.

▣▨ TRANSPORTATION AND PRACTICAL INFORMATION. Trains run to Dublin's Connolly Station (1¼hr., 3-4 per day, £7.50/€9.50) and to Rosslare Harbour via Wexford (2hr., 3 per day, £15/€19). The station is a 15min. walk east of town on Church St. **Bus Éireann** goes to Dublin (1½hr.; M-Sa 9 per day, Su 6 per day; £4.50/€5.70). **Wicklow Hiring,** Abbey St., **rents bikes.** (☎68149. £10/€12.70 per day, £30/€38.10 per week. Deposit £30/€38.10 per day. Open M-Sa 8:30am-1pm and 2-

ULYSSES **PUB PRIMER** So you meant to read *Ulysses* but were intimidated by its 700-odd pages, thousands of cryptic allusions, and general screwyness. Despite ranking in the estimations of many as the greatest book of the 20th century, very few people have read the modernist masterwork in its entirety. *Let's Go*, however, is here to help you:

The letter "s" both begins and ends the book. "S" stands for "Stephen" (Dedalus, one of the two main characters); "P" is for "Poldy" (nickname of Leopold Bloom, the other); and "M" for "Molly" (Poldy's wife, and the coolest of the three). Taken together, S-M-P stands for subject-middle-predicate, or logical sentence structure.

By calling him "Poldy," Molly takes the "Leo," or lion, out of her husband, suggesting a theme of female domination, and yet the final words of the book, from her stream-of-consciousness monologue—"yes I said yes I will Yes"—have drawn much critical attention as a moment of submission and affirmation. Who's to say?

Ulysses uses 33,000 different words, 16,000 of which are used only once. William Shakespeare, in all his plays, only used 25,000.

Joyce once said that he expected readers to devote nothing less than their entire lives to untangling his epic. For the less ambitious, this Primer should suffice.

5:30pm.) The **tourist office** in Fitzwilliam Sq. has free maps and can tell you all about the Wicklow Way. (☎69117. Open June-Sept. M-F 9am-6pm, Sa 9:30am-5:30pm; Oct.-May M-F 9:30am-5:30pm; always closed 1-2pm.) Other services include: **AIB** bank on your left as you approach the busiest section of Main St. (open M 10am-5pm, Tu-F 10am-4pm); **Internet access** at **Wicklow IT Access Centre** on Main St. (before 3pm £3.50/€4.45 per hr.; after 3pm £5/€6.35, students £2.50/€3.20; open M-F 10am-1pm, 2-6pm, 7-10pm; Sa 10am-1pm and 2-6pm); and the **post office,** Main St. (☎67474; open M-F 9am-5:30pm, Sa 9:30am-12:50pm and 2:10-5:30pm).

ACCOMMODATIONS AND CAMPING. The lovely ◪**Wicklow Bay Hostel** garners *Let's Go's* most enthusiastic recommendation. From Fitzwilliam Sq., walk to the river, cross the bridge, and head left to the yellow building called "Marine House." (☎69213; fax 66456; www.wicklowbayhostel.com. Closed Jan. Dorms £8.50-9/€10.85-11.50; private rooms £11/€14 per person.) Travelers will be content in almost any of the B&Bs on Patrick Rd., uphill from Main St. and past the church. **Camp** at **Webster's Caravan and Camping Park** at Silver Strand, 2½ mi. south of town on the coastal road. (☎67615. Open June-Aug. 1-person tent £4.50/€5.70; 2-person £8/€10.20. Showers 70p/€0.90.)

FOOD AND PUBS. Greasy takeaways and fresh produce shops glare at each other across Main St. The **SuperValu,** on Wentworth Pl. just off Church St., offers a grand selection. (☎61888. Open M-W and Sa 8am-8pm, Th-F 8am-9pm, Su 10am-7pm.) Expect fine dining at ◪**The Bakery Cafe.** Come before 7:30pm on weekdays and spoil yourself with three delectable courses for £15/€19. (☎66770. Su brunch £7/€8.80. Open M-Sa 6-10pm, Su noon-4pm and 6-10pm.) **Philip Healy's,** Fitzwilliam Sq. (☎67380), serves food all day but doubles as a lively nocturnal hotspot on weekends. The **Bridge Tavern,** Bridge St. (☎67718), reverberates with the sweet sounds of trad, local chatter, and clinking pints. (Tunes nightly at 10pm. Open M-W 10:30am-midnight, Th-Sa 10:30am-12:30am, Su 10:30am-11:30pm.)

SIGHTS. Wicklow's premier attraction is ◪**Wicklow's Historic Gaol,** and now you don't have to steal a loaf or lead a rebellion to get in. The newly opened museum fills nearly 40 cells with displays relating to the gaol, its history, and the messy business of shipping convicts off to Australia. (☎61599. Tours every 10min. Open Apr.-Oct. daily 10am-6pm, last admission 5pm. £4.20/€5.35, students and seniors £3.30/€3.25, children £2.60/€3.30.) The first left past Market Sq. leads to what remains of the **Black Castle.** Many assaults and changes in ownership have left only a few wind-worn stones, but the promontory is a great vantage point over meadows and waves. A cliff trail provides smashing views en route to ▨**St. Bride's Head** (a.k.a. Wicklow Head), where St. Patrick landed in AD 432. Either cut through the golf course from the Black Castle or head out the coastal road past the clubhouse and find the trailhead in the parking lot on the left (1hr.). On some days, sea lions frolic at the grassy rocks. Adventurous walkers can continue for 1½hr. to reach the isolated **lighthouse.** The closest strips of sun and sand are **Silver Strand** and **Jack's Hole,** though most head to the larger ▨**Brittas Bay,** halfway to **Arklow.**

WICKLOW MOUNTAINS

Over 2000 ft. high, carpeted in fragrant heather and rushing with sparkling water, the Wicklow summits provide a happy home to grazing sheep and scattered villages alike. This region epitomizes the romantic image of pristine rural Ireland.

GLENDALOUGH   ☎ 0404

In the 6th century St. Kevin gave up his life of ascetic isolation and set up one humdinger of a monastery in a spectacular valley. Little **Glendalough** (GLEN-da-lock, "glen of two lakes") sits on a tributary of R756, just where the **Glenealo River** pools into its **Upper** and **Lower Lakes.** The **Glendalough Visitors Centre** presents ample information on the valley's intriguing past. (☎ 45325. Open June-Aug. daily 9am-6:30pm; Sept. to mid-Oct. 9:30am-6pm; mid-Oct. to mid-Mar. 9:30am-5pm; mid-Mar. to May 9:30am-6:30pm. Tours every 30min. during high season. £2/€2.50, students and children £1/1.27.) The monastic ruins themselves are free and always open. The 100ft. **round tower** is one of the best preserved in all of Ireland. The **cathedral** was once the largest in the country; in its shadow stands **St. Kevin's Cross,** which was carved before the monks had tools to cut holes clean through the stone. (We're talking *old.*) The 11th-century **St. Kevin's Church** acquired the misnomer "St. Kevin's Kitchen" because of its chimney-like tower. The **Upper** and **Lower Lakes** are a rewarding digression from monasticism. Cross the bridge at the far side of the monastery and head right on the paved path to reach the serene Lower Lake (5min.) and the magnificent Upper Lake (25min.).

Pilgrims arrive by **car** on R756, on **foot** along the Wicklow Way, or in **buses** run by **Wicklow Tours** (☎ 67671) or **St. Kevin's Bus Service.** (☎ (01) 281 8119. From St. Stephen's Green in Dublin; M-Sa 11:30am and 6pm, Su 11:30am and 7pm; £10/€12.70 return.) Road signs point you to the **tourist office,** located in a small trailer across from the Glendalough Hotel. (☎ 45688. Open mid-June to Sept. M-Sa 10am-1pm and 2-6pm.) The **National Park Information Office,** between the lakes, is the best source for hiking information on the region. (☎ 45425. Open May-Aug. daily 10am-6pm; Apr. and Sept. Sa-Su 10am-6pm.) When the park office is closed, call the **ranger office** (☎ 45800), located in nearby Trooperstown Wood.

▨**The Glendaloch Hostel (An Óige/HI)** lies on the left, a five-minute walk up the road past the Glendalough Visitors Center. An Óige reopened this beauty several seasons ago after a substantial £1.3/€1.65-million face-lift. (☎ 45342. Bike rental. Internet access. Light breakfast £2.50/€3.20, full Irish £4.50/€5.70; dinners £6.50/€8.30; vegetarian options. Towels 50p/€0.65. Laundry £4/€5.10. Dorms £13/€16.50; doubles £32/€40.65. Off season £1-2/€1.27-2.50 less.) B&Bs abound in neighboring **Laragh,** where you'll find the **Wicklow Heather,** 75 yd. up the road back toward Glendalough, a family- and vegetarian-friendly restaurant. (☎ 45157. Most entrees £7-13/€8.90-16.50. Su 3-course lunch £13/€16.50. Open daily 8:30am-10pm.) **Lynham's Pub** lures travelers with siren-like cover bands and rock sessions. (☎ 45345. Open daily until 11:30pm.)

▧ HIKING THE WICKLOW WAY

Founded in 1981, Ireland's oldest marked hiking trail is also its most spectacular. Stretching from Marlay Park at the border of Dublin to Clonegal, Co. Carlow, the 76 mi. **Wicklow Way** meanders south through Ireland's largest highland expanse. Yellow arrows and signs keep the trail well marked as it weaves over heathered summits and through steep glacial valleys. Civilization is rarely more than several mi. away, but wilderness precautions should still be taken. Bring warm, windproof layers and raingear, and while the terrain never gets frighteningly rugged, sturdy footwear is still a must. Water is best taken from farmhouses (with permission), not streams. Open fires are illegal within a mile of the forest. Most Wicklow tourist offices sell the invaluable *Wicklow Way Map Guide* (£4.50/€5.70).

Six days of hiking for 7-8hr. will carry you from one end to the other, though many side trails around the Way make excellent day-hikes; *Wicklow Way Walks* (£6/€7.60) outlines a number of these loops. The northern 44 mi. of the Way, from Dublin to Aghavannagh, attract the most people with the best scenery and all of the hostels; An Óige publishes a pamphlet detailing four- to five-hour hostel-to-hostel walks. (Available at An Óige hostels in Co. Wicklow and Dublin.)

In order to avoid trail erosion, bikes are only allowed on forest tracks and paved sections of the Way, but plenty of off-Way roads provide for equal beauty. A highlights trek would run the 20 mi. from Powerscourt Waterfall near Enniskerry to Glendalough, passing the stupendous **Lough Dan** and the even-more-stupendous **Lough Tay,** offering views as far as Wales. For information, contact the **National Park Information Office** (☎ 45425), located between Glendalough's lakes (see p. 697).

▐ ACCOMMODATIONS AND CAMPING

The splendor of the Wicklow Way isn't exactly a well-kept secret—many accommodations take advantage of the endless stream of bodies tired after a day's hiking. **Camping** is feasible but generally requires planning ahead. Many local farmhouses will let you set up your tent on their land if you ask. National Park lands are fine for short-term, low-impact camping, but pitching a tent in state forest plantations is prohibited. Approved accommodations along the Way can be booked through the All-Ireland Room Reservation service. (Freephone ☎ (00) 800 668 668 66; www.ireland.travel.ie.) A number of B&Bs offer **camping** and pickup if you call ahead; the *Wicklow Way Map Guide* comes with a sheet that lists about 20. An Óige runs a cluster of hostels that lie close to the Way; except for the Glendaloch Hostel, all bookings are handled through the head office (☎ 01 830 4555; anoige@iol.ie). Hostels run from north to south in the following order:

Glencree (An Óige/HI), Stone House, Enniskerry (☎ (01) 286 4037). 7½ mi. out the Glencree road from Enniskerry or 2 mi. off the Way. A bit remote. June-Sept. dorms £7/ €8.90; Oct.-May £6.50/€8.30.

Knockree (An Óige/HI), Lacken House, Enniskerry (☎ (01) 286 4036), right on the Way. A reconstructed farmhouse 4 mi. from the village and 2 mi. from Powerscourt Waterfall. From Enniskerry, take the right fork of the road leading uphill from the village green, turn left at Buttercups Newsagent, and follow signs for Glencree Dr. Sheets £1/€1.27. Lockout 10am-5pm. June-Sept. dorms £7/€8.90; Oct.-May £6.50/€8.30.

Tiglin (An Óige/HI), a.k.a. **Devil's Glen,** Ashford (☎ (0404) 40259), by the Tiglin Adventure Centre, 5 mi. from the main trail. From Ashford, take the Roundwood road for 3 mi., then follow the signs for the Tiglin turnoff and R763 on the right. Basic, single-sex dorms. Towels 50p/€0.65. Curfew 11pm. June-Sept. £7/€8.90; Oct.-May £6/€7.60.

▧ **Glendaloch (An Óige/HI).** See **Glendalough,** p. 697.

Glenmalure (An Óige/HI), Glenmalure. At the end of a dead-end road 7½ mi. along the Way south from Glendalough. By road, head from Glendalough to Laragh and take every major right turn. Back-to-nature lodging; doesn't even have a telephone. June-Sept. dorms £6.50/€8.30; Oct.-May £5.50/€7.

BOYNE VALLEY   ☎ 041

The thinly populated Boyne Valley hides Ireland's greatest archaeological treasures, and is about a one-hour bus ride from Dublin. Massive passage tombs like **Newgrange** create subtle bumps in the landscape that belie their cavernous underground chambers. These wonders are older than the pyramids and at least as puzzling. The Celtic High Kings once ruled from atop the **Hill of Tara,** leaving a healthy dose of mysterious folklore in their wake. Every so often, farmers plow up artifacts from the 1690 Battle of the Boyne (see p. 666).

BRÚ NA BÓINNE: NEWGRANGE, KNOWTH, DOWTH

Along the curves of the river between Slane and Drogheda sprawls Brú na Bóinne (broo na BO-in-yeh, "homestead of the Boyne"). The Boyne Valley may not have all the passage tombs in the world, just the biggest and best—in this 2500-acre region there are no fewer than 40 passage tombs, all with more than five millennia of history behind them. Neolithic engineers (no doubt looking to attract lazy future travelers) constructed Newgrange, Dowth, and Knowth within walking distance of each other. One explanation for these projects proposes that people had extra time on their hands thanks to improvements in farming, and so naturally decided to build mega-structures that would remain intact and waterproof for some 5000 years. (Apparently Tetris had not yet been discovered.) The larger mounds took a good half-century to build, back when a decent lifespan was 30 years.

The most impressive of the three main sites, for archaeologists if not for visitors, is **Knowth** (rhymes with "mouth"). Apparently there was a hunter-gatherer settlement here in 4000 BC, followed by an extraordinary number of subsequent dwellers. The enormous passage tomb houses an unusual two burial chambers, and carvings that are well preserved, as prehistoric art goes. Long-term excavations and the demands of preservation prevent the general public from entering, but the Visitors Center **tour** (see below) offers a peek. **Newgrange** regained a fraction of its ancient prominence in the 1960s when a roof box was discovered over the passage entrance. At dawn on the shortest day of the year (Dec. 21), 17 gilded minutes of sunlight reach straight to the back of the 60 ft. passageway and irradiate the burial chamber. Such alignment with the solstice, while impressive, is quite common in passage tombs—but Newgrange is unique in having a separate entrance exclusively for the worshipped golden orb. In the cool depths of the one-acre mound lie two-thirds of all the Neolithic art in Western Europe. Amid the intricately carved patterns you can read graffiti from 18th-century visitors who clearly didn't have the brains of their distant ancestors. Excavations keep **Dowth** (rhymes with "Knowth") closed to the public. To gain admission, get a Ph.D. in archaeology.

To access Knowth and Newgrange, you have to book at tour at the ◪**Brú na Bóinne Visitors Centre,** on the south side of the River Boyne, across from the tombs themselves. The place is mobbed every day of the summer, and Sundays are especially manic. A nifty film about the winter solstice runs every 15min. Remember to dress appropriately to visit the passage tombs—most of the tour takes place outside, and many Neolithic tombs lack central heating. (☎(041) 988 0300. *Open June to mid-Sept. daily 9am-7pm; late Sept. 9am-6:30pm, Nov.-Feb. 9:30am-5pm; Mar.-Apr. and Oct. 9:30am-5:30pm; May 9am-6:30pm. Last admission to center 45min. before close. Admission to center only £2/€2.50, seniors £1.50/€1.90, students and children £1/€1.27, families £5/ €6.35. Center and Newgrange tour £4/€5.10, £3/€3.80, £2/€2.50, £10/€12.70. Center and Knowth £3/€3.80, £2/€2.50, £1.25/€1.50, £7.50/€9.50. Center, Newgrange, and Knowth £7/€8.90, £5/€6.35, £3.25/4.10, £17.50/€22.30. Last tour 1½hr. before close.*)

Bus Éireann (☎836 6111) shuttles to the Centre from **Dublin** (1½hr.; M-Sa every 15min., Su every hr.; return £10/€12.70). Several **bus tours** from Dublin include admission to the sights. Bus Éireann covers Newgrange and either Tara/Trim or Mellifont/Monasterboice (Sa-Th, £19/€24.20).

HILL OF TARA

From prehistoric times until at least the 10th century, Tara was the socio-politico-cultural heart of Ireland. Three of the 70 sites strewn about the hill have been excavated, leaving archaeologists and scholars with a mountain of questions. They do know that ancient peoples built a Stone Age tomb and an Iron Age fort here. Later, control of the hill entitled a warlord to be High King and it was the seat of the powerful Uí Néill family. When St. Patrick and Christian fever descended on Ireland, pagan Tara was a religious hotspot no more. Nevertheless, the hill's aura persists.

The site is about 5 mi. east of **Navan** on the N3. Take any **local bus** from Dublin to Navan (1hr.; M-Sa 37 per day, Su 15 per day; £5.50/€7) and ask the driver to let you off at the turnoff, which is on the left and marked by a small brown sign. Then you've got about a mile of uphill legwork to enjoy. The actual buildings have long been buried or destroyed; what you'll see are concentric rings of grassy, windswept dunes. They are always open for exploration, but to make any sense of them you have to hit the **Visitors Center,** in the old church, for a slideshow and an excellent guided tour. The tour covers the sites at the top of the hill, although Tara actually encompasses 100 acres of many smaller mounds and ring forts. *(☎(046) 25903. Open mid-June to mid-Sept. daily 9:30am-6:30pm; early May to mid-June and mid-Sept. to Oct. 10am-5pm; £1.50/€1.90, seniors £1/€1.30, students and children 60p/€0.76.)*

SOUTHEAST IRELAND

A power base for the Vikings and then for the Normans, the Southeast feels the Celtic influence much more faintly than the rest of Ireland. The Southeast's most fruitful tourist attractions are its beaches, which draw native admirers to the coastline stretching from Kilmore Quay to tidy Ardmore. Wexford is a charismatic town, packed with historic sites and convenient to many of the region's finest attractions, while Waterford has resources, nightlife, and the grit of a real city.

KILKENNY ☎056

While the Celtic Tiger launches itself into the 21st century, the best-maintained medieval city in Ireland has launched an historical preservation campaign. Kilkenny's handsome streets, nine churches, and 80 pubs are all graced by the architecture of distant eras.

E TRANSPORTATION Trains come into **MacDonagh Station,** Dublin Rd. (☎22024. Open M-Sa 7am-8:15pm, Su 9am-1pm and 2:45-9pm; ticket window open only around departure times.) Kilkenny is on the main **Dublin-Waterford** rail line (M-Sa 4-5 per day, Su 3-4 per day). **Buses** (☎64933 or (051) 879 000) stop at the station and at the tea shop on Patrick St.; buy tickets at either place. Buses go to: **Cork** (3hr., 2-3 per day, £10/€12.70); **Dublin** (2hr., 5-6 per day, £7/€8.90); **Galway** (5hr.; M-Sa 5 per day, Su 3 per day; £17/€21.60); and **Waterford** (1½hr., 1-2 per day, £5/€6.35). **J.J. Kavanagh's Rapid Express** (☎31106) has routes in the area with prices that beat Bus Éireann's (**Dublin:** M-Sa 4 per day, Su 2 per day; £4.50/€5.70). **Rent bikes** at **J.J. Wall Cycle,** 88 Maudlin St.: £7/€8.90 per sentimental day, £40/€50.80 per melancholic week, and a tear-jerking ID deposit. They also rent lawnmowers and chainsaws. (☎21236. Open M-Sa 9am-6pm.) Hitchers take N10 south to Waterford and N10 past the train station to Dublin. *Let's Go* does not recommend hitchhiking.

■ ORIENTATION AND PRACTICAL INFORMATION From **MacDonagh Station,** turn left on **John St.** and go downhill to the large intersection with **High St.** and **the Parade,** dominated by the castle on your left. Most activity takes place in the triangle formed by High St., **Rose Inn St.,** and **Kieran St.** The **tourist office,** Rose Inn St., has free maps. (☎51500; fax 63955. Open July-Aug. M-Sa 9am-7pm, Su 11am-1pm and 2-5pm; Apr.-June and Sept. M-Sa 9am-6pm, Su 11am-1pm and 2-5pm; Oct.-Mar. M-Sa 9am-5pm.) Other services include: the **Bank of Ireland,** on Parliament St. (☎21155; open M 10am-5pm, Tu-F 10am-4pm); **Internet access** at **Celtel,** Rose Inn St., two shops toward the Parade from the tourist office (☎20303; £4/€5.10 per hr., students 20% off, members 50% during select hours; open M-Sa 9am-8pm, Su noon-8pm); and the **post office,** High St. (☎21891; open M-Tu and Th-Sa 9am-5:30pm, W 9:30am-5:30pm).

⌨ ACCOMMODATIONS AND CAMPING The average Kilkenny B&B will set you back ₤20/€25.40, but some places hike prices up to ₤30/€38.10 on weekends. A call ahead in the summer or on weekends will save you a passel o' headaches. The Waterford road and more remote Castlecomer Rd. have the highest concentration of sleeps-and-eats. ▣**Foulksrath Castle (An Óige/HI)**, in Jenkinstown 8 mi. north of town on N77 (Durrow Rd.), is in fact a 15th-century castle—also one of the nicest hostels in Ireland and certainly the cheapest rate going for royal quarters. Turn right at signs for Connahy; the hostel is ¼ mi. down on the left. (☎67674; call ahead, leave a message 10am-5pm. Continental breakfast ₤2.50/€3.20, full Irish ₤3.50/€4.45. Sheets ₤1.50/€1.90. Dorms ₤6.50-7.50/€8.25-9.50; children ₤1/€1.30 less.) That little old house by the Superquinn is **Demsey's B&B**, 26 James's St. The delightful proprietors rent out spacious, well-decorated, TV-blessed rooms. (☎21954. Parking ₤1/€1.30 per night. Singles ₤23.50-25/€30-32; doubles with bath ₤40-44/€50-56.) Camp at **Nore Valley Park**, 7 mi. south of Kilkenny between Bennetsbridge and Stonyford, marked from town. This is a class act, with hot showers, TV room, play-area for the kiddies, crazy golf course, go-carts, and picnic and barbecue areas. (☎27229 or 27748. Laundry ₤4.50/€5.70. Open Mar.-Oct. Backpackers ₤5/€6.35; 2-person tent ₤7.50/€9.50.)

⬛ FOOD. Dunnes Supermarket, Kieran St., sells housewares and food. (☎61655. Open M-Tu and Sa 8:30am-7pm, W-F 8:30am-10pm, Su 10am-6pm.) ▣**Pordylo's,** Butterslip Ln., between Kieran St. and High St., is one of the best eateries on the island. They serve zesty dinners from across the globe (₤8-15/€10.20-19), many of which love vegetarians. (☎70660. Reservations recommended. Open daily 6-11pm.) The eccentric owner of **Langton's,** 69 John St., has earned a gaggle of awards for his ever-changing highbrow restaurant. (☎65123. Full lunch menu with an Irish twist served daily 11:30am-3:30pm; sophisticated dinner menu in the double digits served daily 6-10:30pm.) The entrance to **Ml. Dore** is on High St. and Kieran St. It's not impossible to find sandwiches for ₤3/€3.80 and light entrees for ₤8/€10.20 in this clean, fresh cafe. (☎63374. Open M-Sa 8am-10pm, Su 9am-9pm; summer Su until 10pm.)

⬛ PUBS. "The Marble City" is also known as the "Oasis of Ireland"—Kilkenny's watering holes have a range of live music on most nights, especially in the summer. **The Pump House,** 26 Parliament St., remains a favorite among locals and hostelers. The ultra-hip upstairs enclave will make you wish you packed some Prada. (☎63924. M-Th summer trad, Su rock and blues.) Thespians from the Watergate Theatre converge at **Cleere's,** also on Parliament St. A black box theater in back hosts vivacious music and theater several times a month. (☎62573. W open mic night; cover ₤2/€2.50.) **Anna Conda,** near Cleere's, has outstanding trad. (☎71657. M and F-Sa music. No cover.) Cool Parisians are crowded as cattle at **Paris, Texas,** High St. (☎61822), where hipster cowpokes shimmy, smoke, and lasso themselves a good time. **Matt the Miller's,** 1 John St. at the bridge, is huge, thronged, and magnetic. Pilgrims are sucked in and forced to dance to silly Europop. (☎61696. M rock music and late bar until 1:30am; cover ₤2-4/€2.50-5.10.) **Kyteler's Inn,** Kieran St., is the 1324 house of Alice Kyteler, Kilkenny's witch, whose husbands (all 4) had a knack for getting poisoned on their first anniversaries. The food and drink have since become safer, and trad fills the air twice a week. (☎21064; www.kytelers.com. Check the web site for updated listings.)

◼◪ SIGHTS AND ENTERTAINMENT. Although Kilkenny is a sight in itself—the government has either preserved or recreated most of the buildings' medieval good looks—13th-century **Kilkenny Castle,** on the Parade, is the bee's knees. It housed the Earls of Ormonde from the 1300s up through 1935, and many rooms have been restored to their former opulence. The basement houses the **Butler Gallery** and its modern art exhibitions. You'll find a cafe on this level in the castle's kitchen, home of the castle's ghost. (☎ 21450. Castle and gallery open June-Sept. daily 10am-7pm; Oct.-Mar. Tu-Sa 10:30am-12:45pm and 2-5pm, Su 11am-12:45pm and 2-5pm; Apr.-May daily 10:30am-5pm. Castle access by guided tour only. £3.50/€4.45, students £1.50/€1.90.) The 52-acre landscaped **park** adjoining the castle provides excellent scenery for an afternoon jaunt. (Open daily 10am-8:30pm. Free.) If you're interested in Killkennalia, including the down-and-dirty on folkloric tradition, take a **Tynan Walking Tour.** Besides spinning some animated yarns, the tour is the only way to see the old city gaol. Tours depart from the tourist office on Rose Inn St. (☎ 65929, mobile (087) 265 1745. 1hr. tours Mar.-Oct. M-Sa 6 per day, Su 4 per day; Nov.-Feb. Tu-Sa 3 per day. £3.50/€4.45, students and seniors £3/€3.80.)

Rumor has it that crafty 14th-century monks brewed a light ale in the **St. Francis Abbey** on Parliament St.; the abbey is in ruins but its industry survives in the yard, at the **Smithwicks Brewery.** Commercial use started in 1710, making it the oldest brewery in Ireland—the black-skirted bombshell didn't get a-brewin' for another half-century. Unfortunately, the company now profanes the holy site by brewing Budweiser as well (boo, hiss). Every day 50 tickets are given out at the main gate security guard station. First, make sure you're over 18 years old. Next, collect your ticket and show up at 3pm outside the green doors on Parliament St. for an audiovisual tour and ale tasting. (☎ 21014. Tours July-Aug. M-F.) Thirteenth-century **St. Canice's Cathedral** sits uphill off Dean St. The 100 ft. tower next to the cathedral was built in pre-Norman, pre-scaffolding times. With £1.50/€1.90 and a bit of faith, you can climb the six steep ladders to a panoramic view of the town and its surroundings. (☎ 64971. Open Easter-Sept. M-Sa 9am-1pm and 2-6pm, Su 2-6pm; Oct.-Easter M-Sa 10am-1pm and 2-4pm, Su 2-4pm. Donation requested.)

Each August, Kilkenny holds its **Arts Festival,** which has a daily program of theater, concerts, recitals, and readings by famous European and Irish artists. (☎ 52175. Event tickets £0-12/€15.25; student and senior discounts vary by venue. Sold at the Eircom shop on Parliament St. or by phone.) The city's population increases by more than 10,000 when the **Cat Laughs** (☎ 63837), which features international comedy acts during the first weekend of June.

CASHEL   ☎ 062

The town of Cashel lies tucked between a series of mountain ranges on N8, 12 mi. east of Tipperary Town. Legend has it that the devil furiously hurled a rock from high above the Tipperary plains when he discovered a church being built in Cashel. The assault failed to thwart the plucky citizens, and today the town sprawls defiantly at the base of the 300 ft. **Rock of Cashel.**

Take **Bus Éireann** (☎ 62121) to: **Cork** (1½hr., 6 per day, £9.60/€12.20), **Dublin** (3hr., 6 per day, £12/€15.25), and **Limerick** (1hr., 5 per day, £9.20/€11.75). Hitching to Cork or Dublin along N8 is common; thumbing west to Tipperary and Limerick on N74 is also feasible. Let's Go does not recommend hitchhiking. The **tourist office** splits rent with the heritage center in the City Hall on Main St. (☎ 61333. Open July-Aug. M-Sa 9:15am-6pm, Su 11am-5pm; Apr.-June and Sept. M-Sa 9:15am-6pm.) **McInerney's,** next to SuperValu, **rents bikes.** (☎ 61225. £7/€8.90 per day, £30/€38.10 per week. Open M-Tu and Th-Sa 9:30am-6pm.) **AIB** has a **bureau de change.** (Open M-W and F 10am-12:30pm and 1:30-4pm, Th 10am-12:30pm and 1:30-5pm.) The **post office** rocks the Cashel on Main St. (☎ 61418. Open M and W-F 9am-1pm and 2-5:30pm, Tu 9:30am-1pm and 2-5:30pm, Sa 9am-1pm.)

A five-minute walk from Cashel on Dundrum Rd., and just a few hundred yards from the ruins of Hore Abbey, is the stunning **☒O'Brien's Farm House Hostel.** O'Brien's deserved gold stars for its incredible view of the Rock, cheerful rooms, and extremely courteous hosts. (☎ 61003. Full-service laundry £6/€7.60. 6-bed dorms £9-10/€11.50-12.70; doubles £30/€38.10. Camping £4.50-5/€5.70-6.35.) Just steps from the Rock, in a quiet residential neighborhood on Dominic St., you'll find a bargain at the quaint **Rockville House.** (☎ 61760. Singles £25/€31.75; doubles £38/€48.25; triples £57/€72.40.) **SuperValu,** Main St., has the bigger selection of groceries (☎ 61555; open M-Sa 8am-9pm, Su 8am-6pm), but **Centra,** Friar St., is open later

(☎61421; open daily 7am-11pm). **The Bake House,** on Main St. across from the tourist office, is the town's top spot for decadent sweets—it's especially popular with families and golden-agers. (☎61680. Open M-Sa 8am-7pm, Su 9am-6pm.) Impale yourself on fresh fish at the eye-catching **Spearman.** (☎61143. Lunch £6-7/€7.60-9, dinner around £15/€19. Open daily 12:30-2:30pm and 6-9pm.) Cashel's pub crawl is a straight shot down Main St. The *craic* is nightly and the atmosphere timeless at **Feehan's** (☎61929). Bartenders at **Dowling's** make it their one and only business to pour the best pint in town. Innocuous-looking **Mikey Ryan's** (☎61431) hides a mighty multilevel beer garden.

The small **heritage center,** in the same building as the tourist office on Main St., features temporary exhibitions and permanent installations including "The Rock: From 4th to 11th Century" and its much-anticipated sequel, "The Rock: 12th to 18th Century." (☎62511. Open May-Sept. daily 9:30am-5:30pm; Oct.-Apr. M-F 9:30am-5:30pm. Free.) The **Brú Ború Heritage Centre,** at the base of the Rock, performs traditional music and dance. (☎61122. Performances mid-June to mid-Sept. Tu-Sa at 9pm. £9/€11.50, with dinner £27/€34.30.)

◪ **THE ROCK OF CASHEL.** You'll notice it on the horizon from miles away— that huge limestone outcropping topped with medieval buildings is the ▧**Rock of Cashel,** sometimes called **St. Patrick's Rock.** The Rock is attached to a number of legends, some historically substantiated, others more dubious. Periodic guided tours are informative if a bit dry; exploring the buildings yourself is a less erudite if equally awe-inspiring option. The 1495 burning of the **Cashel Cathedral** by the Earl of Kildare was a highlight for Cashel's illustrious history. When Henry VII demanded an explanation, Kildare replied, "I thought the Archbishop was in it." As any Brit worth his blue blood would, Hank made him Lord Deputy. However, the 13th-century cathedral survived the Earl, and today's visitors can inspect its vaulted Gothic arches. The **museum** at the entrance to the castle complex preserves the 12th-century **St. Patrick's Cross.** A stirring film on medieval religious structures is shown every hr. or so. *(Rock on mid-June to mid-Sept. daily 9am-7:30pm; mid-Sept. to mid-Mar. 9:30am-4:30pm; mid-Mar. to mid-June 9:30am-5:30pm. Last admission 45min. before close. £3.50/€4.45, students £1.80/€2.30.)*

WEXFORD ☎053

The incessant fights between Gaels, Vikings, and Normans drafted the blueprint for modern Wexford's labyrinth of narrow, snaggling streets. Park the car and pound the pavement to visit Wexford's main attractions—its quality pubs and restaurants. Conquest after bloody conquest has left this huddled harbor town with an interesting tale to tell.

▣ **TRANSPORTATION. Trains** chug into **O'Hanranhan (North) Station,** on Redmond Sq. (☎22522), then hustle to Rosslare (15min., 3 per day, £2/€2.50) and Dublin's Connolly Station (2¾hr.; 3 per day; M-Th and Sa-Su £11.50/€14.50, F £15/€19). **Buses** stop at the train station. If the station office is closed, check the Station Cafe (☎24056) across the street for info. Buses run to Rosslare (20min.; M-Sa 12 per day, Su 9 per day; £2.80/€3.65) and Dublin (2¾hr.; M-Sa 10 per day, Su 8 per day; £9.50/€12). Buses to and from Limerick (4 per day, £12/€15.25) connect with **Irish Ferries** and **Stena Sealink** sailings. A list of **taxi** companies is posted in the train station. **Hayes Cycle Shop,** 108 South Main St., **rents bikes.** (☎22462. £10/€12.70 per day, £40/€50.80 per week. £50/€63.50 or ID deposit. Open M-Sa 9am-6pm; bikes available by arrangement on Su.) Hitchers find that the odds of getting a ride are highest around noon or 5-7pm when the boats come in and traffic is heavier; savvy hitchers make a point of specifying either the Dublin road (N11) or the Waterford road (N25). *Let's Go* does not recommend hitchhiking.

⚠️🛂 ORIENTATION AND PRACTICAL INFORMATION. Most of Wexford's action takes place one block inland, along the twists and turns of **Main St.** A plaza called the **Bullring** is near the center of town, a few blocks from where North Main St. changes to South. Another plaza, **Redmond Square,** sits at the northern end of the quays near the train station. The **tourist office** is on Crescent Quay. Pick up *Discover Wexford* (£2/€2.50), *Front Door to Ireland* (free map), or the free *Welcome to Wexford.* (☎23111. Open July-Aug. M-Sa 9am-6pm, Su 11am-5pm; Apr.-June and Sept.-Oct. M-Sa 9am-6pm; Nov.-Mar. M-F 9:30am-5:30pm.) Banks include **AIB** (☎22444) and **Bank of Ireland** at the Bullring (☎21365). The **library** has free **Internet access;** call ahead to reserve a one-hour slot. (☎21637. Open Tu 1-5:30pm, W 10am-4:30pm and 6-8pm, Th-F 10am-5:30pm, Sa 10am-1pm.) Find the **post office** on Anne St. (☎22587. Open M and W-Sa 9am-5:30pm, Tu 9:30am-5:30pm.)

🏠 ACCOMMODATIONS. If the hostels and B&Bs listed are full, ask the proprietors for recommendations or look along N25 (the Rosslare road or New Town Rd.). During the opera festival, rooms are reserved up to a year ahead of time. **Kirwan House Hostel (IHH),** 3 Mary St., is a refurbished 200-year-old Georgian house right in the heart of town with some slants and creaks in its wooden floors, a bbq-friendly patio out back, and plenty of communal cheer inspired by Eamonn Healy, staffer and resident gentleman. (☎21208; kirwanhostel@tinet.ie. Internet access. Laundry next door. Dorms £7.50-9/€9.50-11.50; doubles £24/€30.50; triples £36/€46.) **The Blue Door,** 18 Lower George St., is the thoroughbred of B&Bs: immaculately clean, with a small garden, views of the castle, and a professional yet personable staff. Look for the crisp white building with flower baskets and yup, you guessed it, a blue door. (☎21047; bluedoor@indigo.ie. Singles £30/€38.10; doubles £50/€63.50.) On the eastern edge of town, **Ferrybank Caravan and Camping Park** has clean sites with striking ocean views. (☎44378. Laundry £1.50/€1.90. Open Easter-Oct. 1-person tent £6/€7.60; 2-person £8/€10.20. Showers £1/€1.30.)

🍴 FOOD. The **Dunnes Store** on Redmond Sq. has everything from food to clothes to lampshades. (☎45688. Open M-Tu 9am-8pm, W 9am-9pm, Th-F 9am-10pm, Sa 9am-7pm, Su 10am-7pm.) Check out all those old Guinness ads at **The Sky and the Ground,** 112 S. Main St. Scaled-down versions of the pricier fare served at the late-night upstairs restaurant is available here until 6pm. Lunch is so good they occasionally sell out the entire menu. (☎21273. Most main courses £5-7/€6.35-8.90. Su-Th live music, typically trad.) **Gusto's,** 106 S. Main St., is to be relished. Its small, cafe-like appearance belies high-quality breakfasts (£2.50-4/€3.20-5.10), sandwiches, soups, and a slightly arty-sophisticate vibe. The panini (£3-4/€3.80-5.10) are a warm treat. (☎24336. Open M-F 8:30am-6pm, Sa 8:30am-5pm.)

🎭 SIGHTS AND ENTERTAINMENT. The remains of the Norman **city walls** run the length of High St. **Westgate Tower,** near the intersection of Abbey St. and Slaney St., is the last of the wall's original six gates. The tower gate now holds the **Westgate Heritage Centre,** where an excellent half-hour audiovisual show recounts the history of the town. You'll walk out thinking Wexford's the most important place in Ireland. (☎46506. Open M-F 10am-4pm. £1.50/€1.90, children 50p/€0.65.) At the **Friary Church,** in the Franciscan Friary on School St. (☎22758), the peaceful fellows gadding about in brown robes are Franciscan monks of an order that has lived in town since 1230. The **historical society** (☎21637) runs evening **walking tours** (free), depending on weather and interest—call 22663 after 5pm for availability. *Welcome to Wexford* (free at the tourist office) details a 45min. self-guided "Magical History" tour.

Many of the pubs in town have music, surprise surprise. For detailed information on events, get *The Wexford People* (£1.10/€1.40) from a newsagent, or leaf through it in a pub. The funky **Wexford Arts Centre,** Cornmarket, presents free visual exhibitions and performances of music, dance, and drama. On Wednesday nights in June and August, join an open trad session or pay £2/€2.50 to watch. (☎23764.

Evening performances generally £5-6/€6.35-7.60. Center open M-Sa 8:30am-6pm.) The **Theatre Royal**, High St., produces performances throughout the year, culminating in the internationally acclaimed **Wexford Festival Opera**, held in late October and early November. (☎22400, box office 22144. Box office open May-Sept. M-F 11am-1pm and 2-5pm; Oct.-Nov. M-F 9:30am-5:30pm.)

🖼🖼 **PUBS AND CLUBS.** The two halves of **Mooney's Lounge**, Commercial Quay by the bridge, each drawing a different crowd, comprise *the* late-night hotspot in Wexford. (☎21128. 18+. All sorts of live music Th-Su. Occasional cover £2-3/€2.50-3.80. Open M-W until 11:30pm, Th-Su until 2:30am.) A classy crowd flocks to **The Centenary Stores**, Charlotte St. off Commercial Quay—a stylish pub and dance club in a former warehouse. Try the patio for those sunny afternoon pints. (☎24424. Excellent trad Su mornings and M and W nights, blues and folk Tu nights, DJ spins on a black-lit dance-floor Th-Su 10:30pm-2:30am. Nightclub cover £5/€6.35.) On the corner of Redmond Pl. facing the water, **The Ferryman**—completely refurbished and under a new name (formerly O'Faolain's)—will guide you over the Guinness, dark river of forgetting. (☎23877. Carvery lunch £6/€7.35, served 12:30-3pm. Open M-W 10:30am-11:30pm, Th-Sa 10:30am-12:30am, Su 10:30am-11pm.)

ROSSLARE HARBOUR   ☎053

Rosslare Harbour is a decidedly pragmatic seaside village whose primary function is welcoming voyagers and bidding them *bon voyage* as they depart for France or Wales. Unlike the seaports of popular imagination, Rosslare isn't host to international intrigue, spies, or casinos; it doesn't even have many pubs and restaurants.

The Rosslare **rail office** (☎33592) is open daily 6am-10pm. Trains run from the ferry port to: **Dublin** (3hr., 3 per day, £11.50/€14.50); **Limerick** (2½hr., 1-2 per day, £10.50/€13.35) via **Waterford** (1¼hr., £6.50/€8.25); **Wexford** (15min., 3 per day, £2/€2.50). **Buses** share an office with the trains (☎33595); they stop at Kilrane Church and the Catholic church before heading to **Dublin** (3hr., 10-12 per day, £10/€12.70); **Galway** via Waterford (4 per day, £17/€21.60); **Killarney** (M-Sa 5 per day, Su 3 per day; £16/€20.30) via **Cork** (£13.50/€17.10) and Waterford (£9.20/€11.70). The **ferry** terminal is open daily 6:30am-9:30pm. **Stena Line** (☎61567, recorded info 61505) and **Irish Ferries** (☎33158; fax 33544; www.irishferries.com) serve the port; boats shove off for Britain (about 1 per day) and France (roughly every other day). Trains and buses often connect with the ferries; **Irish Rail** (☎33114) and **Bus Éireann** (☎(051) 879 000) have desks in the terminal. Hitchers find that rides are hard to come by. *Let's Go* does not recommend hitchhiking.

The Rosslare-Kilrane **tourist office** is 1 mi. from the harbor on the Wexford road in **Kilrane**. (☎33622 or 33232. Open daily 10:15am-8pm.) If you need help in the ferry terminal, head to the **port authority desk** (☎33114). Exchange currency at the **Bank of Ireland**, on St. Martin Rd. past the supermarket. (☎33304. Open M-F 10am-12:30pm and 1:30-4pm.) The **post office**, in the SuperValu, has a **bureau de change**. (☎33201. Open M-F 9am-1pm and 2-5:30pm, Sa 9am-1pm.)

Seaport accommodations are by nature convenient but mercenary. There is a noticeable difference between approved and non-approved B&Bs; here more than anywhere in Ireland, you can take the Bord Fáilte shamrock as a measure of quality. A good choice is 🖼**Mrs. O'Leary's Farmhouse**, off N25 in Kilrane, a 15min. drive from town. Set on a glorious 100-acre farm right by the seaside, Mrs. O'Leary's is a holiday unto itself. (☎33134. Call for pickup from town. £18/€23, with bath £20/€25.50.) Take a right at the top of the cliff, then head left around the far corner of the Hotel Rosslare; the **Rosslare Harbour Youth Hostel (An Óige/HI)** is past the supermarket to the left. Cinder-block bedrooms open onto a courtyard; brand new mattresses are a plus. Try for one of the quads. (☎33399; fax 33626. Internet access 8am-6pm £1.25/€1.60 per 15min., 6pm-8am £1/€1.30 per 15min. Luggage storage £1/€1.30 per day. Check-in 5pm. 4- to 6-bed dorms £8-12/€10.20-15.25.)

REPUBLIC OF IRELAND

The restaurants in Rosslare Harbour tend to be expensive—your best bet is to grab some groceries and get out. The **SuperValu,** to your right on the way to the hostel, has a substantial selection. (☎33107. Open M-F 8am-7pm, Sa 8am-6pm, Su 9am-1pm.) If chippers are your thing, you'll be right at home in Rosslare, land of quick fried fish. You might also try the **Portholes,** which combines meals with a mini-maritime-museum and tables for pool sharks. (☎33110. Entrees £6-9/€7.60-11.50; food served noon-2:30pm and 6-9pm.) Now that you've eaten and rested up in Rosslare, it's time to move on to bigger and better adventures...

WATERFORD   ☎051

A skyline of huge metal silos and harbor cranes greet the first-time visitor to Waterford. Fortunately, behind this industrial facade lies a city with 10 centuries of fascinating history. The Vikings founded Vadrafjord around AD 914, making it the oldest city in Ireland. Scores of pubs and shops demand an indulgent break from touring the small towns dozing across the rest of the county.

⌐ TRANSPORTATION

Airport: ☎875 589. Served by **Euroceltic** (www.euroceltic.com). Follow the Quay, turn right at Reginald's Tower, then left at the sign. 20min. from town. No city buses head that way, so take a car or taxi.

Trains: Plunkett Station, across the bridge from the Quay. (☎317 889, 24hr. recorded timetable 876 243). Staffed M-Sa 9am-6pm, Su at departure times. To: **Dublin** (2½hr.; M-Th 6 per day, F 5 per day; M-Th £13.50/€17.15, F £17/€21.60); **Kilkenny** (40min.; M-Sa 4-5 per day, Su 3 per day; £5.50/€7); **Limerick** (2¼hr., M-Sa 2 per day, £10.50/€13.35); **Rosslare Harbour** (1hr., M-Sa 2 per day, £6.50/€8.25).

Buses: ☎879 000. Station on the Quay, across the street from the tourist office. To: **Dublin** (2¾hr.; M-Sa 10-12 per day, Su 6 per day; £7/€8.90); **Cork** (2½hr.; M-Sa 13 per day, Su 10 per day; £10/€12.70); **Galway** (4¾hr., 5-6 per day, £13.50/€17.15). **City buses** leave from the Clock Tower on the Quay. 75p/€0.95 for most areas around the Cork road. **City Imp** minibuses (75p/€0.95) also cruise the town.

Bike Rental: Altitude, 22 Ballybricken St (☎870 356), past the *Garda* station at the far side of the green. £10/€12.70 per day. Includes helmet, delivery to and pickup from local accommodations. Credit card deposit.

Hitchhiking: Rare Waterford hitchers place themselves on the main routes, away from the tangled city center. To reach N24 (Cahir, Limerick), N10 (Kilkenny, Dublin), or N25 (New Ross, Wexford, Rosslare), they head over the bridge toward the train station. For the N25 to Cork, they continue down Parnell St.; others take city buses out to the Crystal Factory before sticking out a thumb. *Let's Go* does not recommend hitching.

◼✴❷ ORIENTATION AND PRACTICAL INFORMATION

Modern Waterford sits on the ruins of the triangular Viking city. The hornéd ones must have had a knack for urban planning, because the area between the **Quay, Parnell St. (the Mall),** and **Barronstrand St.** is still hopping, even without the sweet music of falsterpipes filling the air.

Tourist Office: On the Quay (☎875 788), across from the bus station. From the train station, cross Rice Bridge and turn left. Open July-Aug. M-Sa 9am-6pm and Su 11am-5pm; Sept.-Oct. M-Sa 9am-6pm; Nov.-Mar. M-Sa 9am-5pm; Apr.-June M-Sa 9am-6pm.

Financial Services: AIB (☎874 824), by the clock tower, and **Bank of Ireland** (☎872 074), both on the Quay and open M 10am-5pm, Tu-F 10am-4pm.

Launderette: Duds 'n Suds, 6 Parnell St. (☎841 168 or 858 790). Full-service only. 5lbs. £5/€6.35. Open M-Sa 8:30am-8pm.

Emergency: Dial 999 or 112. No coins required.

Police (*Garda*): Patrick St. (☎874 888).

Hospital: Waterford Regional Hospital (☎873 321). Follow the Quay east to the Tower Hotel. Turn left, then follow signs straight ahead to the hospital.

Internet Access: Voyager Internet Cafe, Parnell Court, Parnell St. (☎843 843). At the intersection of Parnell St. and John St. in a dreary shopping center. £1.50/€1.90 per 15min., 10p/€0.13 per min. thereafter. Open M-Sa 10am-7pm.

Post Office: the Quay (☎874 321). The largest of several letter-dispensaries. Open M and W-F 9am-5:30pm, Tu 9:30am-5:30pm, Sa 9am-1pm.

ACCOMMODATIONS

Most B&Bs in the city center are nothing to write home about; those outside town on the Cork road are better. All Waterford's hostels have gone the way of the dodo.

Beechwood, 7 Cathedral Sq. (☎876 677). From the Quay, go up Henrietta St. Mrs. Ryan invites you into her charming home, located on a silent pedestrian street. Look out the window at Christ Church Cathedral. Doubles £32/€40.60.

Derrynane House, 12 the Mall (☎875 179). Watch the noisy street through fantastic floor-to-ceiling windows. Clean but not sparkling, Derrynane is showing its age. Singles £18/€23; doubles £35-36/€44.45-46.

Mayor's Walk House, 12 Mayor's Walk (☎855 427). A 15min. walk from the train station. Quiet, subdued rooms at a simple price. The Ryders offer advice, biscuits, and a bottomless pot of tea. Open Feb.-Nov. Singles £18/€23; doubles £30/€38.10.

FOOD

Despite the overwhelming presence of fast-food chains, Waterford does have some budget-friendly restaurants. Pick up cheap groceries at **Dunnes Stores** in the City Square Mall. (☎853 100. Open M-W 9am-7pm, Th-F 9am-9pm, Sa 9am-6pm, Su noon-6pm.) **Treacy's,** on the Quay between the Granville Hotel and the tourist office, has a small deli and an uncharacteristically large selection for a late-night grocery. (Open daily 8am-11pm.)

Cafe Luna, 53 John St. (☎834 539). A late-night cafe serving pasta, salads, and sandwiches with a creative twist. Homemade soup and half a sandwich for £3.15/€4. Most entrees £3-5/€3.80-6.35. Open M-Tu until 12:15am, W-Su until 3:30am.

Haricot's Wholefood Restaurant, 11 O'Connell St. (☎841 299). Vegetarians and carnivores live in harmony with Haricot's tasty, innovative dishes. Most entrees £5-7/€6.35-8.90. Open M-F 9:30am-8pm, Sa 10 am-6pm.

Gino's, John St. (☎879 513), at the Apple Market. A busy, bright, family restaurant that serves pizza prepared right before your eyes. Call in for takeaway orders. Individual pizza £2.95/€3.75 plus 70p/€0.90 per topping. Homemade ice cream. Open daily until 10:45pm (sit-down) or 11pm (takeaway).

PUBS AND CLUBS

The Quays are flooded with pubs, and the corner of John and Parnell St. has its share as well. The good times continue past pub closings at 12:30am, when late bars and weekend discos kick it into high gear.

T&H Doolan's, George's St. (☎841 504). Serving for 300 years, in an awe-inspiring building that has been standing for over 800. Ask the likeable barkeep about Sinéad O'Connor, who crooned here during her college days. Trad nightly at 9:30pm.

The Gingerman, Arundel Lane (☎875 041). Trad sessions jam at the front tables, and the good times spill into the dramatic dark-wood-and-mirrors rear. Fortify yourself with *calcannon* (deluxe mashed potatoes) and ribs (£5/€6.35). Food served until 8pm.

The Woodman (☎858 130), at Parnell St. and John St. A small traditional pub. Shuts down at 12:30am on weekends, so click those heels and head to the adjoining **Ruby's Nightclub,** which throbs with chart hits until 2:30am. Get your pre-boogie buzz in the pub's front lounge before 10pm to evade the £5-7/€6.35-8.90 cover.

◎ SIGHTS

You can cover all of Waterford's sights in a day, but only if you are as swift as a Viking raider and as organized as a Norman invader. Buying the **City Pass** from **Waterford Tourism,** 1 Arundel St. (☎852 550), will get you a 33% discount at the Waterford Crystal Factory, Waterford Treasures, and Reginald's Tower.

▨ **THE WATERFORD CRYSTAL FACTORY.** Two miles from the city center on N25 (the Cork road), Waterford proves why its dining room set asks such a pretty penny. To get there, catch the City Imp outside Dunnes on Michael St. and request a stop at the factory (10-15min., every 15-20min., 80p/€1) or take city bus #1 (Kilbarry-Ballybeg; 85p/€1.10), leaving across from the Clock Tower twice per hr. and passing the factory on a slightly more circuitous route. (☎373 311 or 332 500. 1hr. tours every 15min.; audiovisual shows on demand. Tours Mar.-Oct. daily; Nov.-Dec. M-F 9am-5:15pm; Jan.-Feb. M-F 9am-3:15pm; £4.50/€5.70. Gallery open Mar.-Dec. daily 8:30am-6pm; Jan. M-F 9am-5pm; Feb. daily 9am-5pm.)

▨ **WATERFORD TREASURES.** This £4.5 million exhibition (huzzah for the EU!) was named the **1999-2000 Ireland Museum of the Year,** letting you experience a sleek presentation of the city's history at your own pace. (At the Granary. ☎304 500. Open June-Aug. daily 9am-9pm; May and Sept. 9:30am-6pm; Oct.-Apr. 10am-5pm. £4/€5.10, students and seniors £3/€3.80.)

REGINALD'S TOWER. Hulking at the end of the Quay, Reginald's Tower has guarded the city's entrance since the 12th century. Its virtually impenetrable 10 ft. thick Viking walls have housed the wedding reception of Strongbow and Aoife (see p. 666), a prison, and a mint. (☎873 501. Tours on demand. Open June-Sept. daily 9:30am-6:30pm; Oct.-May 10am-5pm. £1.50/€1.90, seniors £1/€1.30, students 60p/€0.75.)

♫ ENTERTAINMENT

The tourist office can provide an annual list of major events in town, and any local newspaper, including the free *Waterford Today*, should have more specific entertainment listings. Keep your eyes peeled for posters as well. The seasonal **Waterford Show** at City Hall is an entertaining performance of Irish music, stories, and dance. A ticket costs £8/€10.20, but gets you a glass of Bailey's or wine. (☎358 397 or 875 788; after 5pm try 381 020 or (087) 681 7191. May-June and Sept. Tu, Th, Sa 9pm. July-Aug. Tu-Th and Sa 9pm.) Waterford's largest festival is the **Spraoi** ("spree"), on the August bank holiday weekend. A celebration of life, the universe, and everything, the Spraoi attracts bands from around the globe (☎841 808).

SOUTHWEST IRELAND

With an inconsistent and dramatic landscape ranging from lush lakes and mountains to stark, ocean-battered cliffs, Southwest Ireland is a land rich in storytellers and history-makers. The urban activity of Cork City and the area's frantic pace of rebuilding and growth contrast with the ancient rhythm of nearby rural villages.

CORK CITY   ☎021

In its capacity as Ireland's second-largest city, Cork (pop. 150,000) orchestrates many of the athletic, musical, and artistic activities for the Irish southwest. The river quays and pub-lined streets reveal architecture both grimy and grand, evidence of Cork's history of ruin and reconstruction.

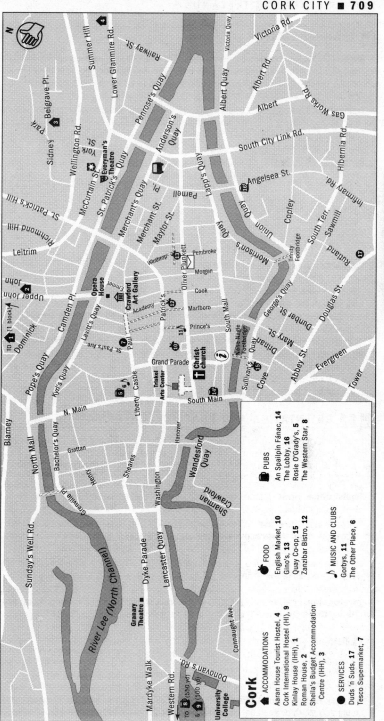

Cork

▲ ACCOMMODATIONS
Aaran House Tourist Hostel, **4**
Cork International Hostel (HI), **9**
Kinlay House (IHH), **1**
Roman House, **2**
Sheila's Budget Accommodation
Centre (IHH), **3**

● SERVICES
Duds 'n Suds, **17**
Tesco Supermarket, **7**

☻ FOOD
English Market, **10**
Gino's, **13**
Quay Co-op, **15**
Zanzibar Bistro, **12**

♪ MUSIC AND CLUBS
Gorbys, **11**
The Other Place, **6**

⊞ PUBS
An Spailpín Fánac, **14**
The Lobby, **16**
Rosie O'Grady's, **5**
The Western Star, **8**

▆ TRANSPORTATION

Airport: Cork Airport (☎431 3131), 5 mi. south of Cork on the Kinsale road. **Aer Lingus** (☎432 7155), **British Airways** (☎(800) 626 747), and **Ryanair** (☎(01) 609 7800). A taxi (£7-8/€9-10) or bus (16-18 per day, £2.50/€3.17) will deliver you from the airport to the bus station on Parnell Pl.

Trains: Kent Station, Lower Glanmire Rd. (☎450 6766; www.irishrail.ie). Open M-Sa 6:35am-8:30pm, Su 7:50am-8pm. Train connections to: **Dublin** (3hr.; M-Sa 7 per day, Su 5 per day; £33.50/€42.54); **Killarney** (2hr.; M-Sa 7 per day, Su 4 per day; £14/€17.78); **Limerick** (1½hr.; M-Sa 7 per day, Su 4 per day; £14/€17.78).

Buses: Parnell Pl. (☎450 8188), Merchants' Quay. Inquiries desk open daily 9am-6pm. Bus Éireann goes to major cities, including: **Dublin** (4½hr., 5-6 per day, £13.50/€17); **Galway** (4hr.; M-Sa 7 per day, Su 4 per day; £13/€16.50); **Killarney** (2hr.; M-Sa 13 per day, Su 10 per day; £10/€12.70); **Limerick** (2hr., 14 per day, £10.10/€12.85); **Waterford** (2¼hr., M-Sa 13 per day, £10.50/€13.40). **City buses** run M-Sa every 10-30min. 7:30am-11:15pm; reduced service Su 10am-11:15pm. Fares from 70p/€0.89.

Ferries: Ringaskiddy Terminal (☎427 5061), 8 mi. south of the city. Call **Brittany Ferries** (☎437 8401) or **Swansea-Cork Ferries** (☎427 1166.)

Car Rental: Great Island Car Rentals, 47 McCurtain St. (☎481 1609). £40/€50.79 per day, £160/€203 per week. 23+. **Budget Rent-a-Car,** Tourist Office, Grand Parade (☎427 4755). £33/€41.90 per day, £195/€247.60 per week. 23+.

Bike Rental: The Bike Shop, 68 Shandon St. (☎430 4144). Rents bikes for £7/€8.89 per day, £30/€38.10 per week. The Raleigh Rent-a-Bike program at **Cycle Scene,** 396 Blarney St. (☎430 1183), allows you to return their bikes at the other Raleigh locations across Ireland. £10/€12.70 per day, £40/€50.79 per week. £50/€63.49 deposit.

Hitchhiking: Hitchhikers headed for West Cork and Co. Kerry walk down Western Rd. to the Crow's Nest Pub, or they take bus #8. Those hoping to hitch to Dublin or Waterford may want to stand on the hill next to the train station on the Lower Glanmire Rd. *Let's Go's* does not recommend hitchhiking.

▆ ORIENTATION AND PRACTICAL INFORMATION

Downtown Cork is the tip of an arrow-shaped island in the **River Lee.** The southern side is filled with quiet avenues, and the sight-saturated **Shandon** district dominates the north side. Downtown action concentrates on streets **Oliver Plunkett, Patrick,** and **Paul.** Cork is pedestrian-friendly.

Tourist Office: Grand Parade (☎427 3251), near the corner of South Mall. Open June-Aug. M-F 9am-6pm, Sa 9am-5:30pm; Sept.-May M-Sa 9:15am-5:30pm.

Budget Travel Office: usit, Oliver Plunkett St. (☎427 0900), around the corner from the tourist office. **Internet access** with usit card £3.50/€4.45 per hr. Open M-F 9:30am-5:30pm, Sa 10am-2pm.

Financial Services: TSB, 4-5 Princes St. (☎427 5221). Open M-W and F 9:30am-5pm, Th 9:30am-7pm. **Bank of Ireland,** 70 Patrick St. (☎427 7177). Open M 10am-5pm, Tu-F 10am-4pm.

Luggage Storage: Lockers £1/€1.30 at the **train station.** Storage at the **bus station** £1.50/€1.90 per item, £1/€1.30 each additional day. Open M-F 8:35am-6:15pm, Sa 9:30am-6:15pm; June-Aug. also Su 9am-6pm.

Launderette: Duds 'n' Suds, Douglas St. (☎431 4799), around the corner from Kelly's Hostel. Wash £2/€2.50, dry £2.50/€3.20. Open 8am-9pm, last load 7pm.

Emergency: Dial 999. No coins required.

Police (*Garda*): Anglesea St. (☎452 2000).

Hospital: Mercy Hospital, Grenville Pl. (☎427 1971). £20/€25.40 fee for emergency room access. **Cork Regional Hospital,** Wilton St. (☎454 6400), on the #8 bus route.

Internet Access: Cork City Library (☎427 7110), across from the tourist office. £1/ €1.30 for 30min. Open Tu-Sa 10am-1pm and 2-5:30pm; computers turn off at 5pm.

Post Office: Oliver Plunkett St. (☎427 2000), at Pembroke. Open M-Sa 9am-5:30pm.

ACCOMMODATIONS

Western Rd. near University College is knee-deep in B&Bs. The other concentration of accommodations is in the slightly more central area along McCurtain St. and Lower Glanmire Rd., near the bus and train stations.

Sheila's Budget Accommodation Centre (IHH), 4 Belgrave Pl. (☎450 5562), near the intersection of Wellington Rd. and York St. Centrally located; big kitchen and summertime barbecues. All rooms nonsmoking. Bike rental £6/€7.62. Internet access £1/ €1.30 for 10min. Free luggage storage. Key deposit £5/€6.35. The 24hr. reception desk doubles as a general store and offers breakfast (£1.50/€1.90). Check-out 10:30am. 6-bed dorms £9/€11.50, 4-bed £10/€12.70; doubles £24/€30.50.

Cork International Hostel (An Óige/HI), 1-2 Redclyffe, Western Rd. (☎454 3289), a 15min. walk from the Grand Parade. Bus #8 stops across the street. Immaculate and spacious rooms, all with bath. Continental breakfast £2/€2.50. Reception 8am-midnight. 10-bed dorms £8-9/€10-11.50; 6-bed £9-10/€11.50-12.70; 4-bed £10.50-11.50/€13.30-14.60; doubles £28/€35.55. Reduced prices for those under 18.

Kinlay House (IHH), Bob and Joan Walk (☎450 8966; www.kinlayhouse.ie), down the alley to the right of Shandon Church. Kinlay House's bright colors and warm atmosphere offset its large, motel-like layout. Each room has a locker and wash basin. Video library and game room. Internet access £1.50/€1.90 for 15min., £5/€6.35 per hr. Continental breakfast included. Laundry £4/€5.08. Free parking. 10- to 14-bed dorms £9/ €11.43; singles £18/€22.86; doubles £30/€38.10. 10% ISIC discount.

Aaran House Tourist Hostel, Lower Glanmire Rd. (☎455 1566). From the train station, turn right and walk 75 yd.; a bright sign marks the hostel on the left. 8-bed dorms £7.50/€9.50; 4-bed £8/€10.20, with bath £8.50/€10.80; 2-bed £9.50/€12.10.

Roman House, St. John's Terrace, Upper John St. (☎450 3606). Cross the North Channel by the Opera House, make a left on John Redmond St., then bear right onto Upper John St. Cork's only B&B catering specifically to gay and lesbian travelers. Washbasins, TVs, armchairs, and tea- and coffee-making facilities in every room. Vegetarian breakfast option. Singles from £28/€35.55; doubles £40/€50.79.

FOOD

The **English Market,** accessible from Grand Parade, Patrick St., and Princes St., displays a wide variety of meats, fish, cheeses, and fruits.

The Gingerbread House, Paul St. (☎429 6411), in the Huguenot Quarter. Huge windows and cool jazz; scrumptious breads, pastries, and quiche all made fresh on the premises. Open M-W and Sa 8:15am-7pm, Th-F 8:15am-9pm, Su 8:15am-6pm.

Quay Co-op, 24 Sullivan's Quay (☎431 7660). A vegetarian's delight, and no chore for carnivores. Excellent soups and desserts. Daily specials around £5/€6.35. Open M-Sa 9am-9pm. Store open M-Sa 9am-6:15pm.

Gino's, 7 Winthrop St. (☎427 4485), between Patrick St. and Oliver Plunkett St. Primo pizzas. Lunch special includes pizza and homemade ice cream for £5.60/€7.10. Beware the throngs of noontime schoolkids. Open M-Sa noon-11pm, Su 1-11pm.

Zanzibaar Bistro, 34 Patrick St. (☎427 2895), just down Cook St. Pan-Zanzibaarbaric menu covers several continents. Open M-Sa noon-10pm, Su 5-10pm.

SIGHTS

All Corkonian sights can be reached on foot; pick up *The Cork Area City Guide* at the tourist office (£1.50/€1.90).

■**UNIVERSITY COLLEGE CORK (UCC).** Built in 1845, UCC's campus is a collection of brooding Gothic buildings, manicured lawns, and sculpture-studded grounds—all of which make for a fine afternoon walk or a picnic along the Lee. One of the newer buildings, **Boole Library,** celebrates number-wizard George Boole, mastermind of Boolean logic and model for Sherlock Holmes's arch-nemesis Prof. James Moriarty. *(Main gate on Western Rd. ☎ 490 3000. Always open. Free.)*

CORK CITY GAOL. If your time in Cork is tight, make sure to see the Cork City Gaol. The museum is a reconstruction of the gaol as it appeared in the 1800s. Descriptions of Cork's social history accompany tidbits about miserable punishments, such as the "human treadmill" that was used to grind grain. *(Sunday's Well Rd. From Fitzgerald Park, cross the white footbridge at the western end of the park, turn right onto Sunday's Well Rd., and follow the signs. ☎ 430 5022. Open Mar.-Oct. daily 9:30am-6pm; Nov.-Feb. 10am-5pm; last admission 1hr. before close. £4/€5, students and seniors £3.25/€4, families £11/€14. Admission includes audio tour.)*

ST. ANNE'S CHURCH. Commonly called Shandon Church, St. Anne's sandstone- and limestone-striped steeple inspired the red and white "rebel" flag, still flying throughout the county. Like most of Cork, the original church was ravaged by 17th-century pyromaniacal English armies; construction of the current church began in 1722. Notoriously out of sync with each other 59 minutes out of 60, the four clocks have earned the church its endearing nickname, "the four-faced liar." *(Walk up Shandon St., take a right on unmarked Church St., and continue straight. ☎ 450 5906. Open June-Sept. M-Sa 9:30am-5:30pm. £3.50/€4.45, students and seniors £3/€3.80, families£10/€12.70. Group rates available.)*

■ ■ PUBS AND NIGHTLIFE

An Spailpín Fánac (uhn spal-PEEN FAW-nuhk), 28 South Main St. (☎ 427 7949), across from the Beamish brewery. One of Cork's more popular pubs as well as one of its oldest (est. 1779). Live trad most nights; unaccompanied singing and storytelling every Su. Pub grub served M-F noon-3pm.

The Lobby, 1 Union Quay (☎ 431 9307), has given some of Ireland's biggest folk acts their start. 2 floors overlook the river. Live music nightly, from trad to acid jazz. Occasional cover £2-5/€2.50-6.35.

Rosie O'Grady's, N. Main St. (☎ 427 8253). Brace yourself. A wild, swelling crowd and pulsing trad render the Rosie's experience one of Cork's liveliest. Big student scene in the winter. Live trad Su-M and W. Lunch served M-F noon-2:30pm.

The Western Star, Western Rd. (☎ 454 3047). About a 25min. walk from the town center, this largely student bar rocks with the chart-toppers nightly. Summer guests can enjoy the outdoors bar on the patio by the Lee River. Free barbecue F-Sa.

Gorbys, Oliver Plunkett St. (☎ 427 0074), near the fountain. Track lighting illuminates young groovers. Lower dance-floor and the retro-flavored upstairs. Cover £4-5/€5.10-6.35, concessions available at local pubs; Tu £1/€1.30 before 11:45pm. Closed W.

Sir Henry's, South Main St. (☎ 427 4391). Arguably the most popular dance club in Cork, and also the most intense. Prepare to wedge yourself between sweaty, semi-conscious bodies on the 3 dance-floors.

The Other Place, in a lane off South Main St. (☎ 427 8470). Cork's gay and lesbian disco rocks F and Sa 11:30pm-2am. Dance-floor and cafe-bar upstairs (opens earlier). Highly appreciated by Cork's gay population, especially the younger set, on weekend nights. Cover £4/€5, free before 10pm.

♫ ENTERTAINMENT

Everyman's Theatre (a.k.a. "the Palace"), MacCurtain St., stages big-name musicals, plays, operas, and concerts. (☎ 450 1673. Tickets $8-18/€10.50-23. Box office open M-F 9am-6pm, Sa 10am-5:30pm, until 8pm on show nights.) **Hurling** and **Gaelic foot-**

ball take place every Sunday afternoon at 3pm from June to September; for additional details, call the GAA (☎ 439 5368) or consult *The Cork Examiner*. Be cautious when venturing into the streets on game days—screaming, jubilant fans have been known to mow tourists down, or, even more dangerous, force them to take part in the revelry. You can buy tickets to local games at the **Pairc Uí Chaoimh** (park EE KWEEV) stadium; take bus #2 to Blackrock.

⚡ DAYTRIPS FROM CORK

BLARNEY CASTLE. Ireland's tourism epicenter and resting place of the celebrated **Blarney Stone.** You might just find yourself bending over backwards to kiss the stone in hopes of acquiring the legendary eloquence bestowed on the smoocher. The Irish consider the whole thing a bunch of blarney; they're more concerned with the sanitary implications of so many people kissing the same hunk 'o rock. (*Bus Éireann runs buses from Cork to Blarney M-F 15 per day; Sa 16 per day; Su 10 per day; £3/ €3.81 return. Blarney Castle info ☎ 438 5252. Open June-Aug. M-Sa 9am-7pm, Su 9:30am-5:30pm; Sept. M-Sa 9am-6:30pm, Su 9:30am-dusk; Oct.-Apr. M-Sa 9am-6pm or dusk, Su 9:30am-5pm or dusk; May M-Sa 9am-6:30pm, Su 9:30am-5:30pm; last admission 30min. before close. Come early in the morning to avoid the crowds. £3.50/€4.45, seniors and students £2.50/€3.17, children £1/€1.30.*)

MIDLETON. Sweet, sweet Jameson is distilled in Midleton. Those in search of the "water of life" (a translation of the Irish word for "whiskey") come to Midleton for the **Jameson Heritage Centre.** The center rolls visitors through a one-hour tour that includes a glass of the potent stuff at the end—for demonstrative purposes only, of course. (*Located on the N25; buses run frequently from Cork. ☎ 461 3594. Open Mar.-Oct. daily 10am-6pm; tours every 30-45min., last tour 4:30pm. Open Nov.-Feb. by tour only, M-F noon and 3pm, Sa-Su 2 and 4pm. £4.50/€5.70; students and seniors £4/€5; children £2/€2.50.*)

WEST FROM CORK CITY

From Cork City, you have two choices for your westward rambles—either an inland or coastal route. A coastal **bus** runs from Cork to **Skibbereen,** stopping in **Bandon, Clonakilty,** and **Rosscarbery** (M-Sa 8 per day, Su 6 per day). An inland bus travels from Cork to **Bantry,** via Bandon and **Dunmanway** (M-Sa 7 per day, Su 4 per day). Located in relative isolation at the intersection of R586, R587, and R599, **Dunmanway** is a hidden treasure; the village lets its scenic setting speak for itself. Of course, it doesn't hurt to have a fabulous hostel like the ▧**Shiplake Mountain Hostel (IHH),** located in the hills 3 mi. from town. Shiplake's luckiest guests stay in three colorful gypsy caravans, equipped with heat, electricity, and breathtaking views. (☎ 45750. Dorms £8/€10.16; caravans £9/€11.43 per person; singles £15/€19. **Camping** £4/€5 per person.) Over the mountains to the northwest, quiet **Ballingeary** is the failing heart of one of West Cork's declining *gaeltachts*.

Every summer the population of upscale **Kinsale** temporarily quintuples with the flood of tourists and tourist money. Visitors come to swim, fish, and eat at any of Kinsale's 12 famed and expensive restaurants. **Clonakilty** ("Clon"), home to real Irish hero **Michael Collins,** lies between Bandon and Skibbereen on N71. The fishing village of **Union Hall** is home to the legendary ▧**Maria's Schoolhouse Hostel** (IHH; ☎ 33002; dorms £8/€10; doubles £25-40/€32-51) and the zany ▧**Ceim Hill Museum,** 3 mi. outside town (☎ 36280; open daily 10am-7pm; £3/€3.80, children £1/€1.30). The biggest town in Western Cork, **Skibbereen** ("Skib") is a convenient stop for travelers roaming the coastal wilds. The tiny fishing village of **Baltimore** has traded its pirates for tourists, who come to explore its aquatic offerings and stay in ▧**Rolf's Hostel (IHH),** a 300-year-old complex of stone farmhouses a 10min. walk up the signposted turnoff immediately before the village on the Skibbereen Rd. (☎ 20289. Dorms £9/€11.50; 4-bed dorms £10/€12.70; doubles £26/€33.)

CAPE CLEAR ISLAND ☎028

The islands in the stretch of ocean between Baltimore and Schull may be the fiercest, most outlandish places in all of southern Ireland. High cliffs plunge into the sea, earning the islands a legacy of shipwrecks. The landscape of wild, beautiful Cape Clear Island (*Oileán Chléire*) hasn't changed much over the centuries. Along with windmills, a castle, and bird observatory, Cape Clear has **Cléire Goats** (☎39126), the best-bred goats in Ireland, if not the world. For 80p/€1 you can test the owner's claim that his goat's milk ice cream is richer and more scrumptious than the generic bovine stuff. Swallow a hefty dose of island lore in early September at the annual **International Storytelling Festival,** which features puppet workshops, music sessions, and a weekend's worth of memorable tales. (☎39157. £6/€7.60 per event, £24/€30.50 for the festival.)

Capt. Conchúr O'Driscoll (☎39135) runs Cape Clear's **ferries** to and from Baltimore. Contact Capt. Kieran Molloy (☎28138) about ferries to and from Schull. Life here is leisurely and hours are approximate—B&Bs rise and fall according to residents' willingness to host guests. For current opening hours and general island information, head to the **information office** in the **Pottery Shop** at the end of the pier. (☎39100. Open June and Sept. 3-6pm; July-Aug. 11am-1pm and 3-6pm.)

Cléire Lasmuigh (An Óige/HI), the Cape Clear Island Adventure Centre and Hostel, is a 10min. walk from the pier; follow the main road and keep left. The hostel is in a picturesque stone building with killer views of the harbor. (☎39198. June-Sept. £8/€10.20; Oct.-May £7/€9.) The island has no resident *Garda* to regulate after-hours drinking, so the fun often lasts until 4am or later. Music fills **Cotter's Bar** on weekends, and the neighboring **Club Chléire** contributes comparable *craic* with trad on Fridays and bands Saturdays. (Open June F-Sa; July-Aug. F-Su.)

MIZEN HEAD ☎028

Fifteen miles past **Schull,** Ireland comes to an abrupt end at spectacular **Mizen Head,** whose cliffs rise 700 ft. from the waves. To get to the **Mizen Vision** museum and **lighthouse,** you'll have to cross a harrowing suspension bridge. The small, windy viewing platform is the most southwesterly point in Ireland. Return to the **Visitor Centre** to peruse more exhibits or munch pricey treats in the cafe. (☎35115. Open June-Sept. daily 10am-6pm; mid-Mar. to May and Oct. 10:30am-5pm; Nov. to mid-Mar. Sa-Su 11am-4pm. £3.50/€4.45, students £2.75/€3.50.)

BANTRY ☎027

According to the big *Book of Invasions*, Ireland's first human inhabitants landed just 1 mi. from Bantry. Today's invaders take the form of tourists eager to enjoy Bantry's elegance or to trek to the more remote points further west. Bantry's biggest tourist attraction is **Bantry House,** a Georgian manor with an imposing garden overlooking Bantry Bay. The long and shaded driveway to the house is a 10min. walk from town on Cork Rd. (☎50047. Open from mid-Mar. to Oct. daily 9am-6pm. £7/€8.90, students and seniors £5.50/€7, accompanied children free.)

Buses stop outside Julie's Takeaway in Wolfe Tone Sq. **Bus Éireann** heads to **Glengarriff** (M-Sa 3-4 per day, Su 2 per day; £2.35/€3) and to **Cork** via **Bandon** (M-Sa 3-4 per day, Su 2 per day; £8.80/€10). From June to September, buses go to **Skibbereen** (2 per day), **Killarney** via **Kenmare** (2 per day), and **Schull** (1 per day). The **tourist office,** Wolfe Tone Sq., has a **bureau de change** and maps of Bantry and Sheep's Head Peninsula. (☎50229. Open July-Aug. daily 9am-6pm; Apr.-June and Sept.-Nov. M-Sa 9:30am-5:30pm.) **Bantry Independent Hostel (IHH),** on Bishop Lucey Pl. in Newtown, has decent bunks, formidable security, and a secluded setting. (☎51050. Laundry £4/€5.10. Open from mid-Mar. to Oct. 6-bed dorms £8/€10.20; doubles £20/€25.40.) Four miles from town, on the Glengarriff road in Ballylickey, the **Eagle Point Camping and Caravan Park** sits on a private beach. (☎50630. Laundry £4/€5.10. Open May-Sept. £5/€6.35 per person. Showers free.)

Bantry is a good place to access **Sheep's Head** (*Muintir Bhaire*), an alternative for anyone eager to evade the company of camera-toters and the exhaust of tour buses. Walkers and cyclists take advantage of the peaceful roads and the well-plotted **Sheep's Head Way** (info available at the Bantry tourist office).

BEARA PENINSULA

The wild and majestic landscape of the Beara does nothing to disrupt the region's profound sense of tranquility. Spectacular mountains march down the center of the peninsula, separating the rocky south from the lush northern shore. Cycling the **Beara Way** is a joy. The **Healy Pass,** running between **Adrigole** in the south and **Lauragh** in the north, offers stunning views of counties Cork and Kerry.

CASTLETOWNBERE   ☎027

One of Ireland's largest fishing ports (and smelling the part), this commercial hub goes about its business as long-distance cyclists speed through en route to the coastal villages farther west and north. Castletownbere's seat at the foot of hefty **Hungry Hill** (2245 ft.) makes it a fine launch pad for daytrips up the mountain. The best scenery on the Beara is on **Dursey Island,** reached by Ireland's only cable car. The cables begin 5 mi. out from Allihies, off the Castletownbere road. (Car runs M-Sa 9-10:30am, 2:30-4:30pm, 7-7:30pm; Su hours vary. Return £2.50/€3.20.) Castletownbere also sends ferries to **Bere Island:** Murphy's Ferry Service (☎75014; 30min.; June-Aug. 8 per day; Sept.-May 4-5 per day; return £4/€5.10) and Bere Island Ferry (☎75009; June 21-Sept. M-Sa 7 per day, Su 5 per day; return £4/€5.10.)

  Bus Éireann offers a year-round service to **Cork** (3hr., 1-2 per day, £14/€17.80) and a summer route between Castletownbere and **Killarney** via **Kenmare** (M-Sa 1 per day, £8.80/€11.20). The molehill-sized **tourist office** is behind O'Donoghue's by the harbor (☎70054; open June-Sept. M-F 10am-5pm), and the **AIB** has the peninsula's **only cash machine.** (☎70015. Open M 10am-5pm, Tu-F 10am-4pm.) **Hire bikes** year-round at **SuperValu.** (☎70020. £7/€9 per day. Open M-Sa 8am-9pm, Su 9am-9pm.) Six miles west on the Allihies road is ⬛**Garranes Farmhouse Hostel (IHH).** The sea views from this intimate clifftop cottage are worth the trek, or the £7/€9 cab, from Castletownbere. Sometimes the attached **Dzogchen Buddhist Centre** (☎73032) absorbs all the rooms, so phone ahead. (☎73147. Laundry £8/€10.20. Dorms £8/€10.20; singles £15/€19; doubles £20/€25.40.) Seafood lovers should head to **The Lobster Bar.** (☎70031. Main menu served June-Aug. only.)

RING OF KERRY

The term "Ring of Kerry" is generally used to describe the entire **Iveragh Peninsula,** but it more correctly refers to a particular set of roads: N71 from Kenmare to Killarney, R562 from Killarney to Killorglin, and the long loop of N70 west and back to Kenmare. If you don't like the prepackaged private bus tours based out of Killarney, **Bus Éireann** runs a summer circuit through all the major Ring towns (2 per day). Buses travel around the Ring counterclockwise. In summer, other buses also travel clockwise from Waterville back to Killarney (2 per day). **Bikers** may find themselves jammed between buses and cliffs on the narrow roads, though traffic can often be avoided by doing the Ring clockwise. Additionally, cycling clockwise lets you face the eye candy rather than leaving it behind.

KILLORGLIN TO VALENTIA ISLAND   ☎066

Killorglin sits placidly on the banks of the River Larne, 13 mi. west of Killarney and in the shadow of Iveragh's mountainous spine. Tourists tend to pass through on their merry way west to the showier scenery, but what the town lacks in day-to-day sights it more than makes up for with an annual mid-August festival—the riotous **Puck Fair** celebrates the crowning of a particularly virile specimen as King Puck. Pubs stay open until 3am, then close for about an hour so publicans can rest their pint-pulling arms. Be aware that the town's hostel and B&Bs often book up as early as a year in advance of the revelry. The bright, bucolic **Laune Valley Farm Hostel (IHH),** 1¼ mi. from town off the Tralee road, harbors a population of cows, chickens, dogs, and ducks—don't forget to save your table scraps. Fresh milk and eggs from the farm are for sale. (☎976 1488; launehostel@ireland.com. 8-bed dorms $8/€10.20; doubles $20/€25.40, with bath $25/€31.75. **Camping** $3.50/€4.45 per person.) Tent up at **West's Caravan and Camping Park,** 1 mi. east of town on the Killarney road in the shadow of **Carrantoohill,** Ireland's tallest peak. (☎976 1240. Fishing, pool, table tennis, and tennis courts. Laundry $4/€5.10. Open Easter to mid-Oct. $3.25/€4. Showers 50p/€0.65.)

Although best known as the birthplace of patriot Daniel O'Connell, **Cahersiveen's** (CARS-veen) upbeat attitude and excellent location will impress even those immune to history lessons. This little Ringside hamlet has no shortage of night-life—though a far cry from its all-time high of 52, Cahersiveen's 30 pubs keep the shelves well stocked with *craic*. The **Sive Hostel (IHH),** 15 East End, Main St., has a welcoming and well-informed staff, comfortable beds, and a third-floor balcony. (☎947 2717. Sheets 50p/€0.65. Laundry $4/€5.10. 4- to 8-bed dorms $8/€10.20; doubles $20-25/€25.40-31.75. **Camping** $4/€5.10 per person.) Campers revel in **Mannix Point Caravan and Camping Park,** at the west end of town. The site adjoins a nature reserve and faces the romantic ruins of Ballycarbery Castle across the water. The common area is complete with turf fire and antique piano. (☎947 2806. Kitchen. Open mid-Mar. to Oct. $4/€5.10 per person. Showers 50p/€0.65. Laundry $2/2.50 wash, $2/€2.50 dry.) You'll find the juiciest steaks, the freshest fish, and Ireland's first indoor barbecue at ◙QC's **Chargrill Bar & Restaurant,** Main St. (☎947 2244. Entrees $7-13/€9-16.50. Food served noon-3pm and 6-9:30pm.)

Shady country roads thread across **Valentia Island,** linking beehive huts, ogham stones, and small ruins—the views of the mountainous mainland will more than make your trip worthwhile. Bridge and ferry connections to the mainland are at opposite ends of the island. A **car ferry** departs from **Reenard Point,** 3 mi. west of Cahersiveen, and drops passengers at **Knightstown,** the island's population center. (☎947 6141. Cars return $5/€6.35, pedestrians $1.50/€1.90, cyclists $3/€3.20.) The bridge connecting Valentia to the mainland starts at **Portmagee,** 10 mi. west of Cahersiveen. Should you choose to spend the night on the island, you'll have an array of budget accommodations at your fingertips. Follow the main road and turn right just after the Pitch & Putt to get to **Coombe Bank House.** (☎947 6111. Continental breakfast $2/€2.50. Free laundry. Dorms $10/€12.70; B&B $20/€25.40.)

WATERVILLE TO CAHERDANIEL   ☎066

Wedged between the quiet Lough Cussane and crashing Atlantic waves, **Waterville** sees most tourists only briefly before they rumble on to more sensational destinations. The meditative traveler is left to amble along the shore, which was once treasured by Charlie Chaplin for the liberating anonymity it granted him. Expect the unexpected at ◙**Peter's Place,** on the southern end of town facing the water. Cozy quarters foster camaraderie rather than claustrophobia. (4-bed dorms June-Aug. $8/€10.20; Sept.-May $7.50/€9.50; doubles $16/€20.30. **Camping** $4/€5.10.)

About 8 mi. off the shore of the Iveragh Peninsula, the stunning **Skellig Rocks** rise abruptly from the sea. While the multitudes rush around the Ring of Kerry, those who detour to the Skelligs are rewarded with an encounter unforgettable for bird-lovers and the ornithologically indifferent alike. As your boat bounces by **Little Skellig,** the rock pinnacles appear to be snow-capped; increased proximity reveals that the peaks are actually covered with 24,000 pairs of crooning, nest-wetting gannets—the largest such community in Europe. Boats dock at the larger **Skellig Michael.** Climb the vertigo-inducing 630 steps to reach a not-anticlimactic **monastery.** There is no toilet or shelter on the rock, but you're welcome to picnic on its steep faces. The **ferry voyage** takes 45min.-1½hr. (depending on conditions, point of departure, and boat) and costs $25/€31.75. Joe Roddy and Sons (☎947 4268 or (087) 284 4460) and Sean Feehan (☎947 9182) depart from **Ballinskelligs;** Michael O'Sullivan (☎947 4255) and Mr. Casey (☎947 2437 or (087) 239 5470) leave from **Portmagee.** Seanie Murphy picks up passengers in **Reenard** and Portmagee (☎947 6214 or (087) 236 2344). Ferries run from April to October depending on the weather; they usually leave between 10 and 11am and land for at least 2hr. on the island. Phone ahead for reservations and to confirm departures.

There's mercifully little to attract the Ring's droves of travel coaches to **Caherdaniel**. However, the hamlet does lie near **Derrynane National Park** and miles of beaches ringed by sparkling dunes. Guests have the run of the house at **The Travelers' Rest Hostel**. A relaxed sitting room and small dorms make this hostel look and feel more like a B&B. Breakfast in the garden with Snowy the goat. (☎947 5175. Continental breakfast £3/€3.80. 4- to 6-bed dorms £8.50/€10.80; singles £10.50-13/€13.35-16.50; doubles £21/€26.70.) Campers perch over the beach 1 mi. east of town on the Ring of Kerry Rd. at **Wave Crest Camping Park**. (☎947 5188. Laundry £4/€5.10 per load. Shop open 8am-10pm. Site open mid-Mar. to Oct. and off season by arrangement. £3.50/€4.45 per person including tent. Showers 50p/€0.65.)

KENMARE ☎064

A bridge between the Ring of Kerry and Beara, Kenmare has adapted to a continuous stream of visitors. Everything you'd expect of a classic Irish town is here (yes, we're talking about colorful houses and misty mountain views and the like). Tourists fresh off the bus may dilute Kenmare's appeal, but pleasant surroundings overshadow the sweater stalls and postcard stands.

⚏ TRANSPORTATION AND PRACTICAL INFORMATION. Buses leave from Brennan's Pub on Main St. to **Sneem** (35min., June-Sept. M-Sa 2 per day) and **Killarney** (1hr.; 2-3 per day). **Rent bikes** at **Finnegan's**, on the corner of Henry and Shelbourne St. (☎41083. £8/€10.20 per day, £40/€50.80 per week. Open June-Aug. M-Sa 9:30am-9pm; Sept.-May M-Sa 9:30am-6:30pm.) The **tourist office** is on the Square. (☎41233. Open July-Oct. M-Sa 9am-6pm, Su 10am-5pm.; May-June M-Sa 9am-1pm and 2-5:30pm.) **AIB** is at 9 Main St. (☎41010. Open M-Th 10am-4pm, F 10am-5pm.) The **post office** has **Internet access** on the corner of Henry and Shelbourne St. (☎41490. £1/€1.30 per 10min.; £5/€6.35 per hr., students £4/€5.10. Cheaper 7-9pm. Open June-Sept. M-F 9am-5:30pm, Sa 9am-1pm; Oct.-May M-F 9am-1pm and 2-5:30pm, Sa 9am-1pm. Computers available 9am-9pm.)

⚐ ACCOMMODATIONS AND CAMPING. Fáilte Hostel (IHH), on the corner of Henry and Shelbourne St., is clean and perfectly located. (☎42333. Curfew 1am. Dorms £8.50/€10.80; private rooms £9.50/€12 per person; doubles £22-28/€28-35.55.) **Keal Na Gower House B&B,** the Square, is a small B&B within earshot of a brook. One room has a bathtub; the other 2 have brook views. (☎41202. £20/€25.40 per person.) Three miles west of town on the Sneem road, the **Ring of Kerry Caravan and Camping Park** overlooks mountains and a bay. (☎41648. Open Apr.-Sept. 1-person tent £8.50/€10.80, 2-person tent and car £11.50/€14.60.)

⚏ FOOD AND PUBS. The Pantry, Henry St., has a limited selection of healthy organic stuff. (☎42233. Open M-Sa 9:30am-6pm.) Italian award-winners (from £9/€11.50) are served in an old stone townhouse at **An Leath Phingin,** 35 Main St. (☎41559. Open M-Tu and Th-Su 6-10pm.) **The New Delight,** Henry St., offers you every veggie. (☎42350. Entrees £5.50-6/€7-7.60. Open June-Aug. daily 10am-8pm; Feb.-May and Sept.-Christmas M-Sa 10am-5pm.) Kenmare's pubs attract tourists, but native Guinness-guzzlers hear too much good music to quibble over "Kiss me, I'm a leprechaun" hats. **O'Donnabháin's,** Henry St., is a favorite among all ages. (☎42106. Su disco.) **The Square Pint** has a looooong bar and live music. (☎42357. Food served noon-5pm.) Wise visitors follow locals to **Moeran's Bar,** at the top of Main St. (☎41368. Trad mid-May to Oct. nightly; Nov.-Apr. 2-3 nights per week.)

⚐ SIGHTS. There are plenty of good hikes in the country around Kenmare but few sights in the town itself. The ancient **stone circle**, a two-minute walk down Market St. from the Square, is the largest of its kind in southwest Ireland, but it ain't no Stonehenge. (Always open. £1/1.30.) The stone circle is one stop on Kenmare's **tourist trail** (maps at the tourist office). **The Kenmare Lace and Design Centre,** upstairs next to the heritage center, has demonstrations of the famous Kenmare lace-making technique. (Open Mar.-Sept. M-Sa 10am-1pm and 2-5:30pm. Free.)

KILLARNEY ☎064

Only a short walk away from some of Ireland's most extraordinary scenery, Killarney manages to celebrate its tourist-based economy without offending the leprechaun-loathing visitors out there.

▐ TRANSPORTATION. Kerry Airport (☎976 4350) is in Farranfore, halfway to Tralee on the N22. **Ryanair** (☎(01) 609 7800) flies to London Stansted; **Aer Arann Express** (☎(1890) 462 726) goes to Dublin. **Trains** come into **Killarney Station** (☎31067, recorded info (1890) 200 493, enquiries (1850) 366 222), off East Avenue Rd. near the intersection with Park Rd. 4 trains per day run to: **Cork** (2hr., £14/€17.80), **Dublin** (3½hr., £35.50/€45), **Limerick** (3hr., £15.50/€19.70). The **bus station** is on Park Rd. (☎30011), connected to the outlet mall. **Buses** go to: **Cork** (2hr., 10-14 per day, £9.40/€12); **Dingle** (2hr.; M-Sa 9 per day, Su 3 per day; £9.20/€11.75); **Dublin** (6hr., 5-6 per day, £15/€19); **Galway** (7-9 per day, £13.50/€17.15; via Tarbert ferry £14.50/€18.45). Many buses leave from here on the **Ring of Kerry Circuit.** There is also a summer **Dingle/Slea Head** tour (June to mid-Sept. M-Sa 2 per day, £9.70/€12.40). You'll find several places to **rent bikes** in Killarney, including **O'Sullivans**, Bishop's Ln., next to Neptune's Hostel. (☎31282. Free panniers, locks, and park maps. £7/€8.90 per day, £35/€44.45 per week. Open daily 8:30am-6:30pm.)

◪▌ ORIENTATION AND PRACTICAL INFORMATION. Most of Killarney is packed into three crowded streets. **Main St.**, in the center of town, begins at the **Town Hall**, then becomes **High St. New St.** and **Plunkett St.** both head in opposite directions from Main St. **East Avenue Rd.** connects the train station back to town hall, meeting the **Muckross road**, which leads to the Muckross Estate and Kenmare.

The **tourist office** on Beech St. is deservedly popular. (☎31633. Open July-Aug. M-Sa 9am-8pm, Su 10am-1pm and 2:15-6pm; June and Sept. M-Sa 9am-6pm, Su 10am-1pm and 2:15-6pm; Oct.-May M-Sa 9:15am-5:30pm.) Other services include: **TSB**, next to Town Hall; **Internet access** at **Cafe Internet**, 18 New St. (☎36741; open June-Aug. M-Sa 9:30am-11pm, Su 10am-11pm; Sept.-May M-Sa 9:30am-9pm, Su 10am-9pm); and the **post office** on New St. (☎31288 or 31051; open M and W-Sa 9am-5:30pm, Tu 9:30am-5:30pm).

▛ ACCOMMODATIONS AND CAMPING. With every other house a B&B, it's easy enough to find cushy digs in Killarney. Cheap digs may require more work. Camping is not allowed in the National Park, but there are excellent campgrounds nearby. Hostels in town include **The Súgán (IHH)**, Lewis Rd., only 2min. from the bus or train station. Small, ship-like bunk rooms blur the distinction between intimacy and claustrophobia; exuberant staff and impromptu storytelling and music in the firelit common room provide a happy escape. (☎33104. 4- to 8-bed dorms £9/€11.50.) The first walkway off New St. on the right is Bishop's Ln., where you'll find immense and immaculate **Neptune's (IHH)**. (☎35255; www.neptunes-hostel.com. Tour booking. Internet access £1/€1.30 per 10min. Breakfast £1.70-4/€2.15-5.10. Laundry £5/€6.35. Curfew 3am. 8-bed dorms £7.50-8.50/€9.50-10.80; 6-bed £8-9/€10.20-11.50; 3- to 4-bed £9-10/€11.50-12.70. Doubles £26/€33. 10% ISIC discount.) **The Railway Hostel (IHH)**, Park Rd., is the first right toward town from the bus station, a modern building with sunny rooms and a pool table. Friendly staffers prowl hardwood floors. (☎35299. Internet access £1/€1.30 per 12min. Curfew 3am. Dorms £8.50-9/€10.80-11.50; singles £15/€19; doubles £25/€31.75.)

Outside town, you'll find **⬛Peacock Farms Hostel (IHH)**, overlooking Lough Guitane and surrounded by wooded slopes. Take the Muckross road out of town, turn left just before the Muckross post office, then go 2 mi. and follow the signposts up a steep hill; or call for a ride from the bus station. (☎33557. Organic continental breakfast £2/€2.50. Open Apr.-Oct. 8-bed dorms £8/€10; 4-bed £9.50/€12. Twins £22/€28.) **Fossa Caravan and Camping Park and Hostel** is 3½ mi. west of town on the Killorglin road. (☎31497. Open Apr.-Oct. Hostel July-Aug. dorms £7.50/€9.50; Apr.-June and Sept.-Oct. £7/€9. **Camping** July-Aug. £4.25/€5.50 per person; Apr.-June and Sept.-Oct. £3.50/€4.50. Showers 80p/€1.)

☐ FOOD. Food in Killarney is affordable at lunchtime, but prices skyrocket when the sun goes down. **◼The Stonechat,** Fleming Ln., is a small stone cottage just far enough from High St. for quiet meals. Specializes in veggies; chicken and fish dishes are also available. (☎34295. Open M-Sa 11am-5pm and 6pm-10pm.) **Cyrano's,** on the lower level of Innisfallen Centre, knows variety. Sate that silver tongue with dessert and a cappuccino. (☎35853. Lunch specials £5.75/€7.40. Open M-Sa 9:30am-6pm.) **Teo's,** 13 New St., offers a taste of the Mediterranean in the heart of shamrock country. (☎36344. Open Mar.-Sept. daily noon-10:30pm; Oct.-Feb. noon-9pm.) Find glorious baked goods, sandwiches, and hot evening meals at **The Country Kitchen,** 17 New St.; close enough to the park for perfect takeaway and worth a visit just for dessert. (☎33778. Lunch served until 5pm; dinner £6-9/€7.60-11.50. Open July-Aug. M-F 8am-8pm, Sa 9am-6pm; Sept.-June M-Sa 9am-6pm.)

◼◼ PUBS AND CLUBS. Trad is a staple in Killarney's pubs on summer nights, but herds of tourists looking for the next great jig have made for a crowded, noisy drinking experience. Several nightclubs simmer from 10:30pm until 2:30 or 3am; most charge £3-5/€3.80-6.35 cover but often offer discounts before 11pm. Patrons both foreign and domestic mingle in the upbeat, comfortable atmosphere of **◼O'Connor's Traditional Pub,** 7 High St. (☎31115. Free "Pub Theatre" show every night at 9pm. M and Th trad 9:30-11:30pm.) **◼The Grand,** High St., is an extremely popular club. (☎31159. Arrive before 10:45pm to dodge the £4-5/€5.10-6.35 cover.)

KILLARNEY NATIONAL PARK

Glaciers sliced up the Killarney region, scooping out a series of lakes and glens and scattering silk-smooth rocks and precarious boulders across the terrain before continuing their march toward the next defenseless landscape. As a result, Killarney National Park makes for preternaturally dazzling hiking, biking, and climbing. The park, stretched across 37 sq. mi. of prime Kerry real estate between Killarney to the northeast and Kenmare to the southwest, incorporates a string of forested mountains and the famous **Lakes of Killarney.** An indigenous but elusive herd of 850 red deer is reported to be at large in the glens that surround the lakes. The park's size demands a map; as luck would have it, maps and other printed materials are available at the Killarney tourist office or the Park's **Information Centre,** behind Muckross House. (☎31440. Open July-Sept. daily 9am-7pm.) The park's most popular destinations are **Ross Castle** and **Lough Leane, Muckross House** on **Middle Lake,** and the **Gap of Dunloe** just west of the park area and bordered in the southwest by **Macgillycuddy's Reeks,** Ireland's highest mountain range.

THE KERRY WAY

Killarney National Park is a perfect starting point for those rugged few who plan to walk the spectacular 134 mi. **Kerry Way,** which offers Ring of Kerry vistas without Ring of Kerry tour buses. An especially inspiring stretch of the Way runs between Waterville and Caherdaniel, filled with views that have been known to elicit a tear or two from even the gruffest pint-puller. The Killarney tourist office sells a *Kerry Way* guide, which has topographic maps. The *Ordnance Survey* includes minor roads, trails, and archaeological points of interest. (The entire Way passes through maps #78, 84, and 83; £5.20/€6.50 each, waterproof £14/€17.80.) Look for the unobtrusive wooden posts marked with a yellow walking man and you won't be far off. Those hoping to log serious mileage can bring along a tent or rely on the hostels and B&Bs along the Way. A free listing of accommodations is available through Cork/Kerry Tourism (☎(064) 31633) and in some tourist offices. Rains can make the Way unsafe from October to March, and trekkers should always embark equipped with sturdy boots, waterproof clothing, and a good map.

DINGLE PENINSULA

For decades, the Dingle Peninsula was the Ring of Kerry's under-touristed second banana. Word has finally gotten out, and the tourist blitz encroaches on the spectacular cliffs and sweeping beaches. A *gaeltacht* to the west of Dingle Town preserves the centuries-old heritage of storytellers and Irish-speakers. The peninsula is best explored by bike—the entire western circuit, from Dingle Town to Slea Head, up to Ballydavid, and back, is only a daytrip, while the mountainous northern regions make for more arduous excursions. Maps available in area tourist offices describe the **Dingle Way,** a 95 mi. walking trail that circles the peninsula.

Glorious **Slea Head** presents to the world a face of jagged cliffs and a hemline of frothy waves; the most rewarding and unforgettable way to see the area is to **bike** along the predominantly flat **Slea Head Drive** (R559). **Ventry** is home to the ■**Ballybeag Hostel** (☎915 9876; ballybeag@iol.ie. July-Aug. 4-bed dorms $11/€14; doubles $26/€33; Sept.-June $10/€12.70; $22/€28), as well as the ■**Celtic and Prehistoric Museum** (☎915 9941. Open Mar. to mid-Nov. daily 10am-5pm; other months call ahead. $3/€3.80, children $2/€2.50.)

Appearing like a mirage off the westernmost tip of Ireland, the ghostly ■**Blasket Islands** occupy a special place in Irish cultural history and in the hearts of all who visit. The islands' beauty and aching sense of eternity explain the prolific literary output of the final generation to reside there. **Blasket Island Ferries** sail from Dunquin. (☎066 915 6422. Apr.-Oct. daily 2 per hr. 10am-6pm, weather permitting; $14/€17.80 return, students $12/€15.25.) You can also check out ■**Great Blasket Centre,** just outside Dunquin on the road to Ballyferriter. (☎915 6444. Open July-Aug. daily 10am-7pm; Easter-June and Sept.-Nov. 10am-6pm; last admission 45min. before close. $2.50/€3.18, seniors $1.75/€2.23, students $1/€1.27.)

While Dingle Town is well connected to Killarney and Tralee, public transport within the peninsula is scarce. There is no direct bus service to the villages north of Dingle Town. For detailed bus information, call the Tralee station (☎23566).

DINGLE TOWN   ☎066

Although the *craic* is still home-grown, ever-expanding hordes of tourists smother the docks and pubs of this bayside town. To be fair, Dingle does have fantastic hostels, a swingin' music scene, easy access to its namesake peninsula's more isolated hideaways, and one helluva dolphin.

▐ TRANSPORTATION

Buses: Information available from the Tralee bus station (☎712 3566). **Bus Éireann** runs to: **Ballydavid** (Tu and F 3 per day, £3.15/€4 return); **Ballyferriter** (M and Th 3 per day, £2.50/€3.20); **Dunquin** (M and Th 4-5 per day, Tu-W and F-Sa 1-2 per day; £2.45/€3.15); **Tralee** (1¼hr.; M-Sa 6 per day, Su 3 per day; £6.20/€7.90). June-Sept. additional buses tour the south of the peninsula from Dingle (M-Sa 2 per day).

Bike Rental: Paddy's Bike Shop, Dykegate St. (☎915 2311), rents quality bikes. £6/€7.60 per day, £30/€38.10 per week. Aluminium frames £8/€10.20 per day. Panniers £1/€1.30 per day, £5/€6.35 per week. Open daily 9am-7pm.

◤▐ ORIENTATION AND PRACTICAL INFORMATION

The streets of downtown Dingle resemble a grid pattern just enough to confuse Manhattanites. **Strand St.** runs next to the harbor along the marina; **Main St.** is its parallel counterpart farther uphill. **The Mall, Dykegate St.,** and **Green St.** connect the two, running perpendicular to the water. On the eastern edge of town, a roundabout splits Strand St. into **The Tracks,** which continue along the water, **The Holy Ground,** which curves up to converge with the Mall, and the **Tralee road.**

Tourist Office: Strand St. (☎915 1188). Open July-Aug. M-Sa 9am-7pm, Su 10am-5pm; Sept.-Oct. and mid-Mar. to June M-Sa 9am-6pm, Su 10am-5pm.

Financial Services: AIB, Main St. (☎915 1400). Open M 10am-5pm, Tu-F 10am-4pm. **Bank of Ireland,** Main St. (☎915 1100). Same hours.

Launderette: Níolann an Daingin, Green St. (☎ 915 1837), behind El Toro. Wash and dry from £6. Open M-Sa 9am-1pm and 2-5:30pm.

Internet Access: At the **library** (☎51499). 30min. free each day. Open Tu-Sa 10:30am-1:30pm and 2:30-5pm. **Dingle Internet Cafe,** Main St. (☎915 2478). £2/€2.50 per 20min., £5/€6.35 per hr. Cheaper before noon. Open Apr.-Sept. M-Sa 9am-10pm, Su 2-7pm; Oct.-Mar. daily 10am-6pm.

Post Office: Upper Main St. (☎915 1661). Just the place for mailing Fungi postcards. Open M-F 9am-5:30pm, Sa 9am-1pm.

ACCOMMODATIONS AND CAMPING

Ballintaggart Hostel (IHH; ☎915 1454; www.dingle-accommodation.com). A 25min. walk east of town on the Tralee road. Mrs. Earl of Cork's ghost supposedly haunts the enormous bedchambers, cobblestone courtyard, and elegant common rooms. Free shuttle to town 3-5 times per day. Laundry £4.50. Peak season 8- to 12-bed dorms £9/€11.50; 4-bed £10-11/€12.70-14. Doubles £30/€38.10; triples £45/€57.15. Off season £1-2/€1.30-2.50 cheaper. **Camping** £8/€10.20 per small tent.

Rainbow Hostel (☎915 1044; www.net-rainbow.com). Take Strand St. west out of town and continue straight through the roundabout for ¼ mile. Jackson Pollock-style interior decor and fierce camaraderie in the cavernous kitchen. Free lifts to and from town all day in the Rainbow-Mobile. Bike rental £7/€8.90 per day. Internet access £1/€1.30 per 10min. Laundry £5/€6.35. 5- to 12-bed dorms £9/€11.50; doubles and twins £22/€28; triples £33/€42. **Camping** £5/€6.35.

Grapevine Hostel, Dykegate St. (☎915 1434), off Main St. Smack in the middle of town and just a brief stagger from Dingle's finest pubs. Friendly folks guide you through the musical, cushy-chaired common room to close but comfy bunk rooms. 4-bed dorms £9.50-10.50/€12-13.35; 8-bed £8.50-9.50/€10.80-12.

O'Coileain B&B, Dykegate St. (☎915 1937; archeo@eircom.net), where it meets the Holy Ground. At this ideal retreat right in the center of town, the young proprietors and their wee helpers show guests to handsome rooms with bath. Tea and coffee in the modern sitting room. Bike rental £6/€7.60 per day. £20/€25.40 per person.

FOOD AND PUBS

SuperValu, The Holy Ground, stocks a SuperSelection of groceries and juicy tabloids. (☎915 1397. Open July-Aug. M-Sa 8am-10pm, Su 8am-9pm; Sept.-June M-Sa 8am-9pm, Su 8am-7pm.) **An Grianán,** on Dykegate St., near the Grapevine Hostel, vends crunchy wholefoods and organic vegetables. (☎915 1910. Open M-F 9:30am-1pm and 2-6pm, Sa 10am-6pm.) Dingle has 52 pubs for 1500 people, and, not surprisingly, many of them cater to tourists. Don't fret—there's still plenty of smack to be had. We mean crack. *Craic.*

The Oven Doors, The Holy Ground (☎915 1056), across from SuperValu. Crispy pizzas (£4.60-7/€5.85), spectacular sundaes (£3.65/€4.65), and incredible cakes draw mobs to this art-bedecked cafe. Try the seed-topped apple crumble (£2.30/€3). Open May-Sept. daily 9:30am-10pm; mid-March to Apr. and Oct.-Jan. 10am-7pm.

The Forge, The Holy Ground (☎915 2590). This large, festive family restaurant serves hot lunches from £5/€6.35 and pricier but delightful dinners (£7-15/€9-19). Open Mar.-Oct. M and W-Su noon-2:30pm and 6-9:30pm.

The Global Village, Main St. (☎915 2325). Fantastic variety of meals from around the world, several of them veggie-oriented. Swap travel stories with the owner, who collected many of the recipes himself. Lunch £4-7/€5.10-9, dinner £8-15/€10.20-19. Open mid-Mar. to Oct. daily noon-3pm and 6-10pm.

🌊**An Droichead Beag (The Small Bridge),** Lower Main St. (☎915 1723). The most popular pub in town unleashes 401 sessions of trad a year—9:30pm every night and the odd afternoon as well. Numerous nooks nurture conversation, and the **disco** upstairs opens M, W, and Sa nights. No cover.

An Conair, Spa Rd. (☎915 2011), off Main St. The mixed crowd enjoys exceptional trad and lusty ballads, but not enough to prevent beer-gardenward migration on fair evenings. M set dancing. W-Sa trad from 9:30pm; July-Aug. also Su 5-7pm.

🔦 SIGHTS AND ENTERTAINMENT

Fungi the Dolphin and his dear, sweet mum swam into Dingle Bay one day in 1983, and within weeks the two became local celebrities. Mom has gone on to the great tuna can in the sky, but Fungi-the-Egomaniacal continues to enjoy near-incessant assaults by wetsuited tourists. **Boat trips** to see him leave from the pier between 10am and 7pm in summer. (About 1hr.; £7/€8.90, children £3/€3.80, free if Fungi gets the jitters and can't find his understudy.) Watching the antics from the shore east of town is a cheaper, squintier alternative. The Mountain Man camping store in town sells *The Easy Guide to the Dingle Peninsula* (£5/€6.35), which includes walks, cycling tours, history, and a map. **Sciúird Archaeology Tours** takes you on a whirlwind bus tour of the area's ancient spots. (☎915 1606 or 915 1937. 3hr. tours depart from the pier or your accommodation. 2 per day, £9/€11.50. Book ahead.) There are several **Slea Head Tours,** two-hour minibus trips highlighting the peninsula's scenery and historic sites: try **Moran's** (☎915 1155 or (086) 275 3333) or **O'Connor's** (☎(087) 248 0008; both leave from the pier; £8/€10.20; book ahead).

TRALEE   ☎066

While tourists tend to identify Killarney as the core of Kerry, Tralee (pop. 20,000) is the county's residential and economic capital. Multimillion-pound projects have added splashy attractions to the cosmopolitan city center, but no tourist development could possibly top the city's famed gardens. The annual **Rose of Tralee** is a centuries-old pageant that has Irish eyes glued to their tellys every August.

🚆 **TRANSPORTATION. Trains** (☎712 3522) tie Tralee to: **Cork** (2½hr.; M-Sa 4 per day, Su 3 per day; £18/€22.90); **Dublin** (4hr.; M-Sa 4 per day, Su 3 per day; £35.50/€45.10); **Galway** (5-6hr., 3 per day, £35.50/€45.10); **Killarney** (40min., 4 per day, £5.50/€7.50); **Waterford** (4hr., M-Sa 1 per day, £13/€16.50). **Buses** (☎712 3566) go to: **Cork** (2½hr., 10-14 per day, £10/€12.70); **Dingle** (1¼hr.; July-Aug. M-Sa 8 per day, Su 5 per day; Sept.-June 2-4 per day; £6.20/€7.90); **Galway** (9-11 per day, £13.50/€17.10); **Killarney** (40min.; June-Sept. 12-14 per day, Oct.-May 5-6 per day; £4.60/€5.85); **Limerick** (2¼hr., 7-8 per day, £9.60/€12.20). **Rent bikes** from **O'Halloran,** 83 Boherboy. (☎712 2820. £6/€7.60 per day, £30/€38.10 per week. Helmet £1/€1.30 per day. Open M-Sa 9:30am-6pm.)

➕🔢 **ORIENTATION AND PRACTICAL INFORMATION.** Tralee's streets are hopelessly knotted; in-the-know travelers arm themselves with free maps from the tourist office. The main avenue is variously called the **Mall** (as it passes by the **Square**), **Castle St.,** and **Boherboy. Edward St.** connects this main thoroughfare to the train and bus stations. **Denny St.** runs south to the **tourist office,** in Ashe Memorial Hall. (☎712 1288. Open July-Aug. M-Sa 9am-7pm, Su 9am-6pm; May-June and Oct. M-Sa 9am-6pm; Nov.-Apr. M-F 9am-5pm.) **AIB,** Denny St. (☎712 1100), at Castle St., and **Bank of Ireland** (☎712 1177), a few doors down, are both open M 10am-5pm and Tu-F 10am-4pm. You can get two 50min. **Internet** sessions per week at the **library,** Moyderwell St. (☎712 1200. Book by phone or in person in the morning. Open M, W, F-Sa 10am-5pm; Tu and Th 10am-8pm.) The **post office** is on Edward St. (☎712 1013. Open M and W-Sa 9am-5:30pm, Tu 9:30am-5:30pm.)

⚑ ACCOMMODATIONS AND CAMPING. Tralee's hostels can barely contain the rosy festival-goers in late August. Rows of pleasant B&Bs line Edward St. as it becomes Oakpark Rd.; others can be found along Princes Quay, close to the Park. **Courthouse Lodge (IHH)**, 5 Church St., is centrally located but buffered by a quiet street. (☎712 7199. All rooms with bath. Internet access £1/€1.30 per 10min. Linens £1/€1.30. Laundry £5/€6.35. Dorms £10/€12.70; singles £17/€21.60; doubles £25-30/€31.75-38.10.) **Collis-Sandes House (IHH)** is near-perfect, but far from town and sometimes booked up by groups. Follow Oakpark Rd. (N69) 1 mi. from town, take the first left after Spar Market, and follow signs another ½ mi. to the right; or call for pickup. (☎712 8658; www.colsands.com. Continental breakfast £2/€2.50. Laundry £3.50/€4.50 wash, £3.50/€4.50 dry. 14-bed dorms £9/€11.50; 8-bed with bath £10.25/€13; 6-bed £9.50-11.80/€12-15; 4-bed £10.25-11.80/13-15; singles £19.50/€25; doubles and twins £30/€38. **Camping** £5.10/€6.50 per person.) Pamper yourself at **Dowling's Leeside,** Oakpark Rd. (☎712 6475; DowlingsBandB@hotmail.com. Singles £20/€25.40; doubles and twins £38/€48.25.) **Woodlands Park Campground,** Dan Spring Rd. is a national award-winner. (☎712 1235; wdlands@eircom.net. Open Apr.-Sept. £4-4.75/€5-6 per tent. Showers 80p/€1. Laundry £5/€6.35.)

▥▤ FOOD AND PUBS. If they don't sell it at the massive **Tesco** in the Square, you probably shouldn't be eating it. (☎712 2788. Open M-W and Sa 8:30am-8pm, Th-F 8:30am-10pm, Su 10am-6pm.) Get quality homemade Irish food, fast, fresh, and cheap at ▧**Pocott's,** 3 Ashe St. (☎712 9500. Open July-Sept. M-Sa 9am-9:30pm, Su noon-7pm; Oct.-June M-Sa 9am-7pm, Su noon-7pm.) Head to **Mozart's,** 4 Ashe St., for a medley of well-prepared delights—bagel sandwiches (£2.50/€3.20) in the morning, stuffed baguettes (£3-4/€3.80-5.10) in the afternoon, stir-fries and steaks (£6.50-13/€8.25-16.50) in the evening. (☎712 7977. Open M-Th 9:30am-7pm, F-Sa 9:30am-9:30pm.) **Brat's Place,** Milk Market Ln., is a veg-head's dream. (Open M-Sa 12:30-2:30pm, later if the food lasts.) **Seán Óg's,** 41 Bridge St., has a hand-built fireplace and "Drinking Consultants" practicing their trade at the long bar. (☎712 8822. Trad M-Th.) Across the street, **Abbey Inn** draws an edgy crowd with live rock most weekends. When U2 played here in the late 70s, the manager made them sweep the floors to pay for their drinks because he thought they were so bad. (☎712 3390. Th live music, DJ other nights. Open M-Sa until 2:30am, Su until 1am.) **Willie Darcy's Corner** (☎712 4343), on the Square, is pure class—all ages meet over candlelit tables, and genial conversation takes the place of music.

◨ SIGHTS. Tralee is home to Ireland's second-largest museum, ▧**Kerry the Kingdom,** in Ashe Memorial Hall on Denny St. (☎712 7777. Free audio tours in French and German. Open mid-Mar. to Oct. daily 10am-6pm; Nov.-Dec. noon-4:30pm. £6/€7.60, students £4.75/€6.) Across the way, another from the ranks of Ireland's second largest (**town park,** in this case) blooms each summer with the **Roses of Tralee.** Just down the Dingle road, true superlativity occurs at the **Blenneville Windmill and Visitors Centre,** the largest operating windmill in the British Isles. (☎712 1064. Open Apr.-Oct. daily 10am-6pm. £2.75/€3.50, students £2.25/€2.85.)

WESTERN IRELAND

Ask the gentleman sitting next to you at the pub—he will probably agree that the west is the "most Irish" part of Ireland. Yeats once said (and he could have been on a barstool at the time), "For me, Ireland is Connacht." Western Ireland's gorgeous desolation and enclaves of traditional culture are now its biggest attractions. Though wretched for farming, the land from Connemara north to Ballina is a boon for hikers and cyclists. Galway, long a successful port, is currently a haven for young ramblers. The Cliffs of Moher, the barren moonscape of the Burren, and a reputation as the center of the trad music scene attract travelers to Co. Clare.

LIMERICK CITY ☎061

Despite a thriving trade in off-color poems, Limerick has long endured a bad reputation. Although its Georgian streets and parks remain elegant, industrial developments gave the city a featureless urban feel. However, today's Limerick is renewed and thriving. A large student population fosters an intense arts scene, adding to a wealth of cultural treasures that have long gone unnoticed.

▐ TRANSPORTATION

Trains: ☎315 555. To: **Cork** (2½hr., 5-6 per day, £14/€17.80); **Dublin** (2hr., 9-10 per day, £27/€34.30); **Waterford** (2hr.; 1-2 per day; £13.50/€17).

Buses: Colbert Station, off Parnell St. (☎313 333, 24hr. talking timetable 319 911). Buses to: **Cork** (2hr., 14 per day, £9.60/€12.20); **Dublin** (3½hr., 13 per day, £10.50/€13.40); **Galway** (2hr., 14 per day, £9.60/€12.20); **Killarney** (2½hr.; M-Sa 6 per day, Su 3 per day; £9.80/€11.20); **Waterford** (2½hr., 6-7 per day, £10.50/€13.30). A **local bus** network runs from city center to suburbs (1-2 per hr., 75p/€0.95).

Bike Rental: Emerald Alpine, Patrick St. (☎416 983). £12/€15.25 per day, £50/€63.50 per week. Deposit £40/€50.80. Open M-Sa 9:15am-5:30pm.

▐ ORIENTATION AND PRACTICAL INFORMATION

Limerick's streets form a grid pattern, bounded by the **Shannon River** to the west and the **Abbey River** to the north.

Tourist Office: Arthurs Quay (☎317 522; www.shannon-dev.ie). Open July-Aug. M-F 9am-6:30pm, Sa-Su 9am-6pm; May-June and Sept.-Oct. M-Sa 9:30am-5:30pm; Nov.-Apr. M-F 9:30am-5:30pm, Sa 9:30am-1pm.

Financial Services: Bank of Ireland (☎415 055) and **AIB** (☎414 388) are among the many banks on O'Connell St. Both are open 10am-4pm.

Emergency: ☎999. No coins required.

Police (*Garda*): Henry St. (☎414 222).

Internet Access: Webster's, Thomas St. (☎312 066). £1.50/€1.90 for 15min., £2.50/€3.20 for 30min., £20/€25.40 all day. Open M-Sa 9am-9pm, Su 1-9pm.

Post Office: Main office on Lower Cecil St. (☎315 777), just off O'Connell St. Open M and W-Sa 9am-5:30pm, Tu 9:30am-5:30pm.

▐ ACCOMMODATIONS

B&Bs are throughout the city, but getting a bed under £25/€31.75 might entail an expedition out along the Ennis road.

An Óige Hostel (HI), 1 Pery Sq. (☎314 672). Around the corner from Finnegan's. Heavy stair workout between the dorms, TV room, kitchen, and backyard garden. Sheets £1. Continental breakfast £2.25/€2.90, packed lunches £2.65-3.60/€3.40-4.60. Lockout 10am-2pm. Reception until 10pm. £5/€6.35 key deposit allows later access. June-Sept. 14-bed dorms £9.50/€12; Oct.-May £8.50; £1/€1.30 discount for HI members.

Broad St. Hostel, Broad St. (☎317 222; broadstreethostel@tinet.ie). Vigilant security and cleaning staff compensate for the impersonal feel. Internet access 50p/€0.65 per 6min. Continental breakfast included. Laundry £2/€2.50. Dorms £10.50/€13.30; singles £15/€19; doubles and twins £34/€43.

Alexandra House, O'Connell St. (☎318 472), south of the Crescent. Victorian, comfy, and nicely decorated. Singles £20/€25.40; doubles and twins £44-50/€56-63.50.

FOOD

The Glen Tavern, Lower Glentworth St. (☎411 380). Quick and great value for breakfast, lunch, or dinner. Most meals £3-5/€3.80. Food served M-F 8am-9pm. Doubles as a pub in the evening. Ballad and trad sessions W, Th, Su.

The Green Onion, Rutland St. (☎400 710). Extensive menu and artsy decor. Lunch £5-7/€6.50-9. After 6pm, dinner prices fly high (£10-15/€12.70-19); the "all-day" menu has simpler (and cheaper) options. Open M-Sa noon-10pm.

O'Grady's Cellar Restaurant, O'Connell St. (☎418 286). Look for the little green awning. This subterranean spot serves as a midday refuge from the bustling streets. Irish cuisine anchors the menu. Meals £5-7/€6.50-9. Open daily 9:15am-10:30pm.

PUBS AND CLUBS

Trad-seekers can certainly get their nightly fix at Limerick's pubs, though the chase may be a bit more challenging than in other Irish cities. Limerick's insatiable army of students keeps dozens of nightclubs thumping.

Dolan's, Dock Rd. (☎314 483). Worth a Shannon-side walk from the city center to hear nightly trad played for rambunctious local patrons.

Locke Bar and Restaurant, Georges Quay (☎413 733). Join the classy crowd on the quay-side patio, or head inside where owner Richard Costello, a former member of Ireland's national rugby team, joins in trad sessions several nights a week.

The Globe, Cecil St. (☎313 533). 2 floors of manic clubbery, with suggestive artwork and flashing video screens. Cover £5/€6.35.

The Warehouse (☎314 483), behind Dolan's on Dock Rd. Authentic reggae on Th, ABBA tribute periodically. Cover £5-9/€6.35-11.50, higher for well-known acts.

SIGHTS

Although massive **King John's Castle** was built to protect the conquered city of Limerick, John himself never actually visited his fortress. In fact, he made only one trip to Ireland, during which he supposedly pulled the beards of his subjects for kicks. Ah, the English. (☎411 201. Open Mar.-Dec. daily 9:30am-5:30pm. Last admission 4:30pm. £5/€6.35, students and seniors £3.75/€5, families £12.50/€16.) The fascinating **Hunt Museum,** in the Custom House, keeps Ireland's largest collection of art and artifacts outside the National Museum in Dublin. (☎312 833. Open M-Sa 10am-5pm, Su 2-5pm. £4.20/€5.35, seniors and students £3.20/€4.) **Walking tours** cover either the northern, sight-filled King's Island region or the more downtrodden locations of Frank McCourt's *Angela's Ashes.* (☎318 106. King's Island tour daily 11am and 2:30pm; Angela's Ashes tour daily 2:30pm. Both depart from St. Mary's Action Centre, 44 Nicholas St. £4/€5.10.)

SHANNON AIRPORT   ☎061

Fifteen miles west of Limerick off the Ennis road (N18), Shannon Airport (☎471 444, **Aer Lingus** info 471 666) sends jets to North America and Europe. There's a small **tourist office** (☎471 664) in the arrival hall. At the **Bus Éireann** ticket office (☎474 311) you can get tickets to: **Dublin** (4½hr., 5 per day, £10.50); **Ennis** (45min.; M-Sa 22 per day, Su 13 per day; £3.70/€4.70); **Limerick** (40min.; M-Sa 9 per day, Su 7 per day; £3.70/€4.70); **Waterford** (£12/€15.25). **Alamo** (☎75061) and **Thrifty** (☎472 649) **rent cars** to those over 23. **Dan Dooley Rent-a-Car** will rent to 21- and 22-year-olds. (☎062 53103. Rates vary; as low as £32/€40.65 for 2-5 days.)

DOOLIN   ☎065

Something of a shrine to Irish traditional music, Doolin draws thousands of visitors every year to its pubs for *craic* that you'll feel from your tappin' toes to your Guinness-soaked head. Crashing waves and rolling hills crisscrossed by stone walls are just a few minutes out of town. Most of Doolin's 200-odd residents run its accommodations and pubs; others split their time between farming and wondering how so many backpackers end up in their little corner of the world.

■◪ **ORIENTATION AND PRACTICAL INFORMATION.** Doolin is shaped like a barbell, made up of two villages about a mile apart. Close to the shore is the **Lower Village,** connected to the **Upper Village** by **Fisher St.,** where it turns into **Roadford.** The nearest **cash machine** is in Ennistymon, 5 mi. southeast. A traveling **bank** comes to the Doolin Hostel every Thursday at 10:30am; there's a **bureau de change** at the **post office** in the Upper Village. (☎707 4209. Open M-F 9am-1pm and 2-5:30pm, Sa 9am-1pm.) **Buses** stop at the Doolin Hostel and the campsite (see **Accommodations,** below), and advance tickets can be purchased at the hostel. Route #15 runs from **Kilkee** and from **Dublin** via **Ennis** and **Limerick** (M-Sa 1-2 per day, Su 1 per day). Bus #50 runs from **Galway** (1½hr.) via multiple other **Burren** destinations on its way to the **Cliffs of Moher** 15min. away (summer M-Sa 5 per day, Su 2 per day; off season M-Sa 1 per day). The **Doolin Bike Store,** outside Aille River Hostel, **rents bikes.** (☎707 4282. £7/€9 per day. Open M-Su 9am-8pm.)

◪ **ACCOMMODATIONS AND CAMPING.** Tourists pack Doolin in the summer, so book ahead. ◪**Aille River Hostel** has clean, well-maintained rooms. (☎707 4260. Internet access. Free laundry. July-Aug. dorms £8.50/€10.80; Sept.-May £8/€10.15. Doubles and triples £8/€10.15 per person. Camping £4/€5.) ◪**Westwind B&B,** behind McGann's in the Upper Village, has rooms both sunny and immaculate. The owners advise spelunkers and other Burren explorers. (☎707 4227. £13-15/€16.50-19 per person.) The spotless ◪**Doolin Cottage B&B** is next to the Aille. (☎707 4762. Open Mar.-Nov. £14/€17.80 per person sharing, with bath £16/€20.30.) **Flanaghan's Village Hostel,** ½ mi. up the road from the Upper Village, has spacious rooms and a back garden with farm creatures. (☎707 4564. Laundry £5/€6.35. Dorms £7.50/€9.60; doubles £17-20/€21.60-25.40.) The small **Rainbow Hostel (IHH),** Upper Village, has pastel rooms and a casual atmosphere. The owners give free 1½hr. walking tours of the Burren for hostelers. (☎707 4415. Laundry £3/€3.80. Dorms £7.50/€9.60; doubles £17/€21.60.) **Nagle's Doolin Camping Ground,** near the harbor, has a kitchen, laundry facilities, and a view of the Cliffs of Moher. (☎707 4458. Laundry £3/€3.80. £4/€5.10 per tent plus £1.50/€2 per person. Showers 50p/€0.65.)

◨▤ **FOOD AND PUBS.** The **Doolin Deli,** near O'Connor's in the Lower Village, stuffs sandwiches (£1.70/€2.15) and groceries. (☎707 4633. Open June-Sept. M-Sa 8:30am-9pm, Su 9:30am-9pm.) **The Lazy Lobster,** Upper Village, serves classic and orientalist seafood dishes. (3 courses £20/€25.40. Open daily 6:30-10pm.) If Doolin looks like a ghost town, fear not: everyone is in the pubs, which serve good, cheap food. **McDermott's** (☎707 4328), Upper Village, is a favorite of locals and tourists. Packed sessions nightly at 9:30pm in summer, weekend nights in winter. **O'Connor's** (☎707 4168), Lower Village, is the most touristed pub, with drink and song nightly at 9:30pm (plus Su afternoons). **McGann's** (☎707 4133), Upper Village, has music at 9:30pm in summer nightly, in winter Thursday through Sunday only.

◪ **DAYTRIP FROM DOOLIN: CLIFFS OF MOHER.** The Cliffs of Moher are among Ireland's justifiably über-touristy attractions. The stunning view from the edge plunges 700 ft. straight down to the open sea. The majestic headland affords views of Loop Head, the Kerry Mountains, the Twelve Pins, and the Aran Islands. Adventurous visitors climb over the stone walls and trek along an officially closed clifftop path for more spectacular views and a greater intimacy with the possibility of falling. The **tourist office** houses a **bureau de change** and a **tea shop.** (☎065 708

1171. Open daily 9:30am-5:30pm.) To reach the cliffs, head 3 mi. south of Doolin on R478 or grab the Bus Éireann summer-only Galway-Cork bus (M-Sa 3 per day). **Liscannor Ferries** operates a fantastic cruise from Liscannor that sails directly under the cliffs. (☎ (065) 708 6060. 55min; 1 per day, weather permitting; £10/€12.70.)

NEAR DOOLIN: THE BURREN ☎ 065

Entering the Burren's disorienting and magical 100 sq. mi. landscape is like entering a skewed fairyland. Lunar limestone stretches end in secluded coves, where dolphins rest after a long day fishing or cavorting with the locals. Mediterranean, Alpine, and Arctic wildflowers announce their bright contours from cracks in mile-long rock planes, while 28 species of butterfly flutter by. Geologists can't explain why such a variety of animalian and botanic species coexists in the area, except that it has something to do with the end of the Ice Age. (Excellent work, "geology.") The best way to see the Burren is to **walk** or **cycle** it, but be prepared for exhausting climbs. Tim Robinson's maps (£5/€6.35) detail the **Burren Way,** a 26 mi. hiking trail from Liscannor to Ballyvaughan; *Burren Rambler* maps (£2/€2.55) are also detailed. All of the nearby tourist offices (Kilfenora, Ennis, Corofin, Cliffs of Moher) stock these maps and other Burren info. **Bus** service in the Burren is some of the worst in the Republic. Bus Éireann (☎ 682 4177) connects Galway to Burren towns a few times per day during the summer, infrequently during the winter. Buses stop at: the Doolin Hostel in Doolin, Burke's Garage in **Lisdoonvarna,** Linnane's in **Ballyvaughan,** and Winkie's in **Kinvara.** Other buses run year-round from Burren towns to **Ennis.** Bus tours from **Galway** are another popular way to see the Burren. Gerard Hartigan of Lahinch gives a more thorough **minibus tour.** (☎ 708 1737. 4-4½hr. £15/€19 per person.)

ARAN ISLANDS ☎ 099

On the westernmost edge of Co. Galway, 15 mi. from the mainland, the Aran Islands (*Oileán Árann*)—Inishmore, Inishmaan, and Inisheer—feel like the edge of the world. Their green fields are hatched with a maze of limestone walls, the result of centuries of labor. The landscape is as moody as the Irish weather and tends to adopt its disposition. These majestic, mythical islands have continually sparked the imaginations of Irish people and foreigners alike. We know little of the earliest islanders, who left behind only mysterious cliff-peering forts. Early Christians flocked here seeking seclusion; the ruins of their churches and monasteries also litter the islands. Clans fought for control of the Arans in medieval times, and Elizabeth I later set up an island garrison. The Islands' cultural isolation began drawing artistic attention at the end of the 19th century. In 1894, Dublin-born writer John M. Synge asked W.B. Yeats for creative criticism; he was told to go the Arans, learn Irish, and write plays about the islanders. Synge followed the advice and was rewarded with international acclaim. The groundbreaking 1934 film *Man of Aran* added to the islands' fame. Tourism is the biggest local industry on today's Islands, and the Arans maintain a strange balance—minibuses wait at the pier to show tourists (in 2hr.) the beauty of centuries of daily labor.

▐▀ TRANSPORTATION

Four ferry companies (all with booths in the Galway tourist office) serve the islands from four points of departure. Ferries to Inishmore are reliable and leave daily, barring extreme weather conditions; other routes are less certain—if your ferry cancels for weather, check with the others. All of the companies provide shuttle buses from the Galway tourist office for Rossaveal departures.

   Island Ferries: (☎(091) 561 767, after hours 72273) serves all 3 islands from **Rossaveal** (4 per day, £15/€19 return); Galway bus departs 1½hr. before boat. They also offer a package: the Galway bus, return ferry to Inishmore, and a night at the Mainistir House Hostel with breakfast for £21/€26.70.

Queen of Aran II: (☎566 535 or 534 553) runs to **Inishmore** from **Rossaveal.** Galway bus departs 1¼hr. before boat. 4 per day. Return £15/€19, students £10/€12.70.

O'Brien Shipping/Doolin Ferries: (Doolin ☎(065) 707 4455, after hours (065) 707 1710; Galway (091) 567 283). **Galway** to any island return £12/€15.25. **Doolin** to **Inishmore** (return £20/€25.40), **Inishmaan** (return £18/€23), **Inisheer** (return £15/€19). Doolin fares include inter-island travel; other inter-island trips return £5/€7.60.

Liscannor Aran Ferries: (☎065 81368). 2 daily ferries from **Liscannor** to **Inishmaan** and **Inisheer.** Return £17/€21.60.

INISHMORE

The archaeological sites of the largest and most touristed Aran island, include dozens of ruins and churches and the amazing Dún Aengus ring fort. Crowds spread from Kilronan Pier, at the island's center, and lose themselves amid stone walls and cliffs, coalescing at major sights. Minivans traverse the island looking for customers. Countless species of wildflower grow between 7000 mi. of stone walls.

🖩🚊 TRANSPORTATION AND PRACTICAL INFORMATION. Roving **minibuses** cost about $5/€6.35 per person. **Aran Bicycle Hire** rents bikes. (☎61132. $6/€7.60 per day, $21/€26.70 per week. Deposit $9/€11.45. Open Mar.-Nov. daily 9am-5pm.) The Kilronan **tourist office** changes money, holds bags (75p/€0.95), and sells the *Inis Món Way* ($1.50/€1.90) and other maps. (☎61263. Open July-Sept. daily 10am-6:45pm; Oct. 10am-5pm; Nov.-Mar. 10am-4pm.) The **post office** is uphill from the pier. (☎61101. Open M-F 9am-5pm, Sa 9am-1pm.)

🏠 ACCOMMODATIONS. Buses to the hostels may meet the ferry; call ahead for more info. The huge, sunny ▓**Kilronan Hostel,** above the pub, is clean and close to the pier. (☎61255. Dorms $10/€12.70, all with bath.) **Mainistir House (IHH)** is a haven for writers, musicians, and yuppies. Joël cooks up legendary dinners (book before 6pm; $8.50/€10.80) and morning muffins. (☎61169. Bike rental $6/€7.60 per day. Laundry $5/€6.35. Dorms $8.50/€10.80; singles $15/€19; doubles $24/€30.50.) **The Artist's Lodge** is cozy and inviting, with an impressive video collection and a crackling fire. Take the turnoff across from Joe Watty's pub on the main road, walk a bit, and look right. (☎61457. Dorms $7/€9.) **An Aharla** is a slightly worn family home-turned-hostel with a laid-back feel and a quiet location. Take the turnoff across from Joe Watt's; it's the first building on the left. (☎61305. Dorms $7/€9.)

🍴🍺 FOOD AND PUBS. The **Spar Market,** past the hostel, is an unofficial community center for Inishmorons. (☎61203. Open in summer M-Sa 9am-8pm, Su 10am-6pm; winter M-Sa 9am-8pm, Su 10am-5pm.) The flavorful buffets at ▓**Mainistir House** are the best deal around (see above). ▓**Tigh Nan Phaid,** in a thatched building at the Dún Aengus turnoff, bakes bread and smokes fish. (☎61330. Open July-Aug. daily 10am-9pm; Mar.-June and Sept.-Dec. 10am-5pm.) Uphill from the town center, **The Ould Pier** serves tasty fish-and-chip configurations. (☎61228. Open July-Aug.) **Tí Joe Mac** (☎61248) is a pub overlooking the pier. West of the harbor on the main road, **Joe Watty's** offers food and lively trad. **The American Bar** (☎61303) attracts younger islanders and tourists with midsummer-night music.

🅖 SIGHTS. The sights themselves are crowded, but popular minibuses render paths between them pleasantly desolate. Cycling or walking makes for a rewarding day-long excursion. The TIC sells $1.50/€2 maps of the **Inis Mór Ways** that outline the yellow trail arrows system; the arrows can vanish in the fog, so invest in a good map. The island's most famous monument is magnificent first-century-BC **Dún Aengus,** 4 mi. west of the pier at Kilronan. The fort's walls are 18 ft. thick and form a semicircle around the sheer drop of Inishmore's northwest corner. **Be very careful:** strong winds have blown tourists off the edge and to their deaths. Left off the main road a ½ mi. past Kilmurvey is **Dún Eoghanachta,** a huge circular fort with 16 ft. walls; to the right past Eoghanachta are the **Seven Churches.** Both sites are evidence of the island's earliest inhabitants. The island's best beach is at **Kilmurvey.** The **Black Fort** (Dún Dúchathair), a mile south of Kilronan over eerie terrain, is larger than Dún Aengus, a millennium older, and an unappreciated beauty. Uphill from the pier in Kilronan, the new, expertly designed **Aran Islands Heritage Centre** (Ionad Árann) beckons the inquisitive. Soil and wildlife exhibits, old Aran clothes, a cliff rescue cart, and *curraghs* combine for a fascinating introduction to the island's natural and human life. (☎ 61355. Open June-Aug. 10am-7pm; Apr.-May and Sept.-Oct. 11am-5pm. £4/€5, students £2/€2.50.)

INISHMAAN

Seagulls circle the cliffs and goats chew their cud, but there's little human activity to observe in the limestone fields of Inishmaan. Despite recent dramatic changes on the other two islands, Inishmaan remains a fortress, quietly avoiding the hordes of barbarians invading from Doolin and Galway—this is a place for feasting your eyes and contemplating. The *Inishmaan Way* brochure (£1.50/€2) describes a five-mile clifftop walk past all of the island's sights. The thatched cottage where John Synge wrote is a mile down the main road. A bit farther down is 7th-century **Dún Chonchúir** (Connor Fort). At the western end of the road is **Synge's Chair**, where the writer came to reflect. An even more dramatic landscape awaits farther down the path where the coastline comes into view. To the left of the pier, the ruins of 8th-century **Cill Cheannannach** church was an islander burial ground until the mid-20th century. A mile north of the pier, **Trá Leitreach** is Inishmaan's most sheltered beach. Entering the **Knitwear Factory,** near the island's center, is uncannily like stepping into a Madison Ave. boutique. (☎ 73009. Open M-Sa 10am-5pm, Su 10am-4pm.) For **tourist information,** try the **Inishmaan Co-op** (☎ 73010); take the turnoff for the knitwear factory, continue straight, and then turn right after the factory. **Mrs. Faherty's B&B** is signposted from the pier and serves dinner. (☎ 73012. Open mid-Mar. to Nov. Singles £27/€34.25; doubles £47/€60.) **Tigh Congaile B&B** is on the right side of the first steep hill from the pier. (☎ 73085. £16/€20.25.) Its **restaurant** perfects seafood. (Open June-Sept. daily 9am-9pm.) The **An Dún Shop** (☎ 73067) sells food at the entrance to Dún Chonchúir. **Padraic Faherty's** thatched pub is the center of life on the island and serves a bit of grub until 6:30pm.

INISHEER

The Arans have been described as "quietness without loneliness," but Inishmaan can get damn lonely, and Inishmore isn't always quiet. Inisheer, the smallest Aran, is the perfect compromise. On clear days of otherworldly peacefulness, daytripping visitors will wonder if these few square miles hold the key to the pleasures of a simpler life. The **Inis Oírr Way** covers the island's major attractions on a four-mile path. The first stop is in town at **Cnoc Raithní,** a burial mound that is 2000 years older than Christianity. Walking along the shore leads to the overgrown graveyard of **St. Kevin's Church** (Teampall Chaomhain). Below the church, a pristine beach stretches back to the edge of town. Farther east along the water, a grassy track leads to majestic **An Loch Mór,** a 16-acre inland lake brimming with wildfowl. The ring fort **Dún Formna** is above the lake. Past the lake you'll find the **Plassy wreck,** a sunken ship that washed up on Inisheer in 1960. The walk back to town leads past the remains of 14th-century **O'Brien Castle,** razed by Cromwell in 1652. On the west side of the island, **Tobar Einne,** St. Enda's Holy Well, cures. ✂**Ara's Eanna,** ("House O'Culture") screens films, organizes art exhibits, and runs workshops and a cafe. (☎ 75150. Open May-Sept. 10am-5pm.)

Rothair Inis Oírr rents bikes. (☎ 75033. £6/€7.60 per day, £33/€42 per week.) **Internet access** is the **library** (☎ 75008), a beige building up the road from the pier and past the beach. The **Brú Hostel (IHH),** visible from the pier, is spacious and popular. (☎ 75024. Laundry £4/€5. Dorms £8.50/€10.80; private rooms £11.50/€14.60 per person.) **Bríd Póil's B&B** is often booked six months in advance, but it's worth calling for last-minute cancellations. (☎ 75019. Meals £12/€15.25. £16/€20.30 per person, with bath £17/€26.60.) The **Ionad Campála Campground** stretches its tarps near the beach. (☎75008. Open May-Sept. ₤2/€2.50 per tent, ₤10/€12.70 per week. Showers 50p/€0.65.) **Tigh Ruairí,** an unmarked white pub-shop on the main road, has Inisheerie groceries. (☎75002. Open July-Aug. daily 9am-8:30pm; Sept.-June M-Sa 9am-7:30pm, Su 10:45am-12:30pm.) ▨**Fisherman's Cottage** serves organic, island-grown meals, and has **'net access.** (☎75053. Open daily 11am-4pm and 7-9:30pm.) **Tigh Ned's** pub, next to the hostel, caters to a young set; the **Ostan Hotel**'s pub, just up from the pier, is dim and crowded. (☎75020. Easter-Oct. nightly trad.)

GALWAY CITY ☎091

In the past few years, Co. Galway's reputation as Ireland's cultural capital has brought flocks of young Celtophiles to Galway City. Mix over 13,000 local university students, a large population of twentysomething Europeans, and waves of international backpackers, and you get a college town on *craic*. Galway is the fastest-growing city in Europe, and it has the youth and energy to prove it.

▐ TRANSPORTATION

Flights: 3 small **Aer Lingus** planes fly to **Dublin** daily.

Trains: Eyre Sq. (☎561 444). Open M-Sa 7:40am-6pm. Trains to **Dublin** (3hr.; M-F 5 per day, Sa-Su 3-4 per day; M-Th and Sa ₤15/€19, F and Su ₤21/€27) via **Athlone** (M-Th and Sa ₤7.50/€9.50, F and Su ₤13.50/€17); transfer at Athlone for all other lines.

Buses: Eyre Sq. (☎562 000). Open July-Aug. M-Sa 8am-7pm, Su 8:30am-7pm; Sept.-June M-Sa 8:30am-6pm, Su 8:30am-noon and 1:40-6pm. **Bus Éireann** to: **Belfast** (1-3 per day); **Cork** (5 per day); **Dublin** (7-9 per day); **Cliffs of Moher** (summer 1-4 per day). Private coaches provide Dublin-bound bussery: **P. Nestor** (☎797 144) leaves from Imperial Hotel, Eyre Sq.; **Citylink** (☎564 163) from Supermac's, Eyre Sq.; **Michael Nee** (☎51082) from Forester St. through Clifden to Cleggan, meeting the Inishbofin ferry.

Local Transportation: City buses (☎562 000) leave Eyre Sq. and head to every neighborhood. Service M-Sa 8am-9pm, Su 11am-9pm.

Taxis: Big O Taxis, 21 Upper Dominick St. (☎585 858).

Bike Rental: Europa Cycles, Hunter Buildings, Earls Island (☎563 355), opposite the cathedral. ₤5/€6.35 per day. Deposit ₤30/€38. Open M-F 9am-6pm.

Hitchhiking: Dozens wait on the Dublin road (N6) scouting rides to Dublin, Limerick, or Kinvara. Most catch bus #2, 5, or 6 from Eyre Sq. to this main thumb-stop. University Rd. leads drivers to Connemara via N59. *Let's Go* doesn't recommend hitching.

✦❷ ORIENTATION AND PRACTICAL INFORMATION

Bus or rail to Galway will deposit you at **Eyre Sq.,** a central block of lawn and monuments with the train and bus station uphill on its southeastern side. B&Bs huddle northeast of the square along **Prospect Hill;** commerceland spreads out in the other direction. West of the square, **Woodquay** has quiet(er) commercial and residential activity. **Station Rd.,** a block east of **Williamsgate St.,** leads into Galway's heart, where cafes and pubs crackle with activity. Fewer tourists venture over the bridges into the more bohemian left bank of the **Corrib,** where great music and some of Galway's best pubs await untapped. The pubs along the docks in the southeast of the city are largely fishermen hangouts. When weather permits, guitar players and lusty paramours lie by the river along the **Long Walk.**

Tourist Office: Forster St. (☎563 081). Aran info. Open July-Aug. daily 9am-7:45pm; May-June and Sept. daily 9am-5:45pm; Oct.-Apr. Su-F 9am-5:45pm, Sa 9am-12:45pm.

Budget Travel: usit now, Mary St. (☎565 177). Open May-Sept. M-F 9:30am-5:30pm, Sa 10am-3pm; Oct.-Apr. M-F 9:30am-5:30pm, Sa 10am-1pm.

Financial Services: Bank of Ireland, 19 Eyre Sq. (☎563 181). Open M-W and F 10am-4pm, Th 10am-5pm.

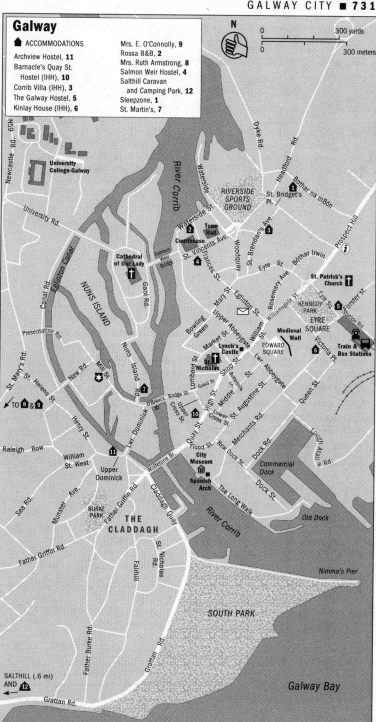

Galway

♠ ACCOMMODATIONS

Archview Hostel, **11**
Barnacle's Quay St.
  Hostel (IHH), **10**
Corrib Villa (IHH), **3**
The Galway Hostel, **5**
Kinlay House (IHH), **6**

Mrs. E. O'Connolly, **9**
Rossa B&B, **2**
Mrs. Ruth Armstrong, **8**
Salmon Weir Hostel, **4**
Salthill Caravan
  and Camping Park, **12**
Sleepzone, **1**
St. Martin's, **7**

REPUBLIC OF IRELAND

Emergency: ☎ 999. No coins required.

Police (*Garda*): Mill St. (☎ 538 000).

Hospital: University College Hospital, Newcastle Rd. (☎ 524 222).

Internet Access: Net Access, the Old Malte Arcade, High St. (☎ 569 772). £5/€6.35 per hr., students with ID £4/€5.10. Free coffee when you log in.

Post Office: Eglinton St. (☎ 562 051). Open M-Sa 9am-5:30pm, Tu from 9:30am.

ACCOMMODATIONS AND CAMPING

In the last few years, the number of hostel beds in Galway has tripled, but you'll still need to call at least a day ahead in July and August and on weekends.

HOSTELS AND CAMPING

Barnacle's Quay Street Hostel (IHH), Quay St. (☎ 568 644). Shop St. becomes Quay. Spacious rooms and peerless location. Excellent security. Laundry £5/€6.35. All rooms with bath. Dorms £8.50-15/€11-19; doubles and twins £16-18/€20-23 per person.

Sleepzone, Bóthar na mBán (☎ 566 999), northwest of Eyre Sq. Takes the "s" out of "hostel"—car park, Internet access (£5/€6.35 per hr.), and a peaceful terrace. All rooms with bath. Laundry £5/€6.35. Mar.-Oct. Dorms £11-13/€14-16.50; doubles £14.50/€18.40 per person; twins £16/€20.30. Nov.-Apr. all rooms £1/€1.30 less.

Salmon Weir Hostel, 3 St. Vincent's Ave. (☎ 561 133). Extremely friendly and down-to-earth. Laundry £5/€6.35. Curfew 3am. Dorms £11/€14; twins and doubles £28/€36.

The Galway Hostel, Eyre Sq. (☎ 566 959), across from the station. Busy and hospitable. June-Sept. Dorms £8-15/€10-19; doubles £32/€40.60. Sept.-May cheaper.

Kinlay House (IHH), Merchants Rd. (☎ 565 244). Frikkin' huge. Internet access. Small breakfast included. Laundry £4/€5. Mar.-Sept. Dorms £11-12.50/€14-16; singles £20/€25.40; doubles £29-33/€37-42. Cheaper in winter.

Archview Hostel, Dominick St. (☎ 586 661). Worn but very well located in the heart of Galway's Bohemia. Dorms £8/€10.15; off season £7/€8.90. Weekly: £35/€44.50.

Corrib Villa (IHH), 4 Waterside (☎ 562 892), past the courthouse. Clean rooms; beds of varying comfort. Laundry £5/€6.35. Dorms £9/€11.40.

Salthill Caravan and Camping Park (☎ 523 972 or 522 479). Beautiful location on the bay, about ½ mi. west of Salthill. A good hr. walk along the shore from Galway. Open Apr.-Oct. £3/€3.80 per hiker or cyclist.

B&BS

St. Martin's, 2 Nuns Island Rd. (☎ 568 286), at the end of Dominick St. Gorgeous setting. All rooms with bath. Singles £25/€32; £22.50/€29 per person sharing.

Mrs. E. O'Connolly, 24 Glenard Ave. (☎ 522 147), Salthill, off Dr. Mannix Rd. Take bus #1 from Eyre Sq. £12/€15.25 with continental breakfast, £15/€19 with full Irish.

Mrs. Ruth Armstrong, 14 Glenard Ave. (☎ 522 069), close to Salthill. Full Irish breakfast, with a side of friendly chatter. £17/€21.60 per person.

Rossa B&B, 21 St. Brendan's Ave. (☎ 562 803). £17.50/€22.25 per person.

FOOD

The east bank has the greatest concentration of restaurants. **SuperValu,** in the Eyre Sq. mall, is a chef's playground. (☎ 567 833. Open M-W and Sa 9am-6:30pm, Th-F 9am-9pm.) **Evergreen Health Food,** 1 Mainguard St., has the healthy stuff. (☎ 564 215. Open M-Sa 8:45am-6:30pm). On Saturday mornings, a market sets seafood, pastries, and fruit in front of St. Nicholas Church on Market St. (Open 8am-1pm.)

Anton's (☎582 067). Over the bridge near the Spanish Arch and a 3min. walk up Father Griffin Rd. Self-consciously hip eateries on the other side of the river could learn a lot from this cheap treasure. Open M-F 8am-6pm.

Java's, Abbeygate St. (☎567 400). Hip, dimly lit cafe. The craving and the raving flock here at all hours to satisfy hunger and various other pangs. Open daily 10:30am-4am.

Bananaphoblacht, Dominick St. (☎561 478). All Irish-speaking staff and a vibrant after-hours scene. Open daily 10:30am-2am; summer Th-Sa until 3am.

Da Tang, Middle St. (☎561 443). Businessmen and hipsters crowd together in this busy Chinese noodle house. Takeaway available. Open M-W and F 12:30-3pm and 5:30-11pm, Th 12:30-3pm and 6-10:30pm, Sa 12:30-11pm, Su 6-10:30pm.

McDonagh's, 22 Quay St. (☎565 809). Fish-and-chips madness; very popular. Restaurant open daily noon-midnight; takeaway M-Sa noon-midnight, Su 5-11pm.

Couch Potato, Abbeygate St. (☎561 664). No idiot boxes, but plenty of spuds the size of them. Sandwiches £4-6.25/€5-8. Open M-Sa noon-10pm, Su 1-10pm.

👁 SIGHTS AND FESTIVALS

Rededicated as John F. Kennedy Park, **Eyre Square** has a small collection of monuments around its grassy common stand. Across the river to the south of Dominick St., **Claddagh** was an Irish-speaking, thatched-cottage fishing village until the 1950s. Stone bungalows replaced the cottages, but a bit of the small-town appeal and atmosphere still persist. The famous Claddagh rings, traditionally used as wedding bands, are mass-produced today. The **Nora Barnacle House,** 8 Bowling Greed, is the home of James Joyce's life-long companion. The table where he composed a few lines to Nora draws the admiration of Joyce addicts. (☎564 743. Open mid-May to mid-Sept. W-Sa 10am-1pm and 2-5pm. Opening times may vary; call ahead. £1/€1.30.) By the river, the **Long Walk** makes a pleasant stroll, bringing you to the **Spanish Arch.** Built in 1584 as a defensive bastion for the port, this worn, one-story stone curve is revered by townspeople despite its unimpressive stature.

Festivals rotate through Galway all year long, with the greatest concentration during the summer months. Reservations for accommodations during these weeks are of the utmost importance. For two crazed weeks in mid-July, the largest arts festival in Ireland reels in famous trad musicians, rock groups, theater troupes, and filmmakers. (☎583 800; www.galwayartsfestival.ie).

🎭 PUBS AND CLUBS

Galway's pubs come in all flavors. Trad blazes across town nightly, but Dominick St. is the best place to hear it. Only big gigs have cover charges. For schedules check *The List,* free and available at most pubs and newsagents. Between midnight and 12:30am, the pubs drain out and the tireless go dancing. Unfortunately, Galway's clubs lag slightly behind its pubs in the fun factor. On the other hand, those who arrive between 11:30pm and 12:15am are legally assured a free meal with their entrance fee. The place-to-be often rotates at disco-ball speed; a good way to find out what's hot is simply to follow the herd after last call.

Roisín Dubh ("The Black Rose"), Dominick St. (☎586 540). Bookshelved front hides Galway's hottest live music scene. Largely rock and singer-songwriters. Music enthusiasts of all ages turn out in droves. Cover £6-13/€7.60.

The Crane, 2 Sea Rd. (☎587 419), a bit beyond the Blue Note. The place to hear trad in Galway. Enter through the side door and hop up to the 2nd floor. Trad "whenever."

The King's Head, High St. (☎566 630). Easy to love. 3 floors and a huge stage devoted to nightly rock. Upstairs music varies.

The Hole in the Wall, Eyre Sq. An ideal meat-market with huge booths for groups, 3 bars for mingling, and tables to dance on. Flirtation spills into the small beer garden.

Monroe's, Dominick St. (☎583 397). Trad in a veritable *craic* warehouse. Nightly sessions weekdays from 9:30pm, weekends 10:30pm. Tu and Th Irish dancing.

La Graal, 38 Lower Dominick St. (☎567 614). Wine (only) bar and restaurant, La Graal is the center for Galway's Latin community. Gay-friendly. Th salsa dancing.

The Blue Note, William St. West (☎589 116). Hipsters lounge on lush couches and listen to guest DJs. Galway's best destination for turntable music. Indie films in winter.

The Quays, Quay St. (☎568 347). Beer-sticky, cathedral-like, and popular with the younger crowd and scamming yuppies. Open nightly 10pm-1:30am. £5/€6.35 cover.

Seaghan Ua Neachtain (a.k.a. **Knockton's**), Quay St. (☎568 820). The oldest pub in Galway. Study streams of pedestrians from streetcorner tables. Nightly trad.

Busker Browne's/The Slate House (☎563 377), between Cross St. and Kirwin's Ln. in an old nunnery. Get thee to this upscale bar with wall-to-wall couches. 3rd-floor "Hall of the Tribes" is the most spectacular lounge in Galway. Su live jazz.

McSwiggin's, Eyre St. (☎568 917), near Eglinton St. A sprawling mess of small rooms and stairwells spanning 3 stories, McSwiggin's holds hundreds of tourists at a time.

Skeffington Arms (☎563 173), across from Kennedy Park. "The Skiff" is a well-decorated, multi-storied hotel with 6 different bars. A pub crawl unto itself.

Cuba, Prospect Hill. Located under the club and live music venue, this colorful bar liberates itself on weekends and becomes an independent rogue club. Decorations recreate Havana so convincingly, you'll fear Castro. Sa salsa, Su stand-up comedy.

CONNEMARA

Connemara, a thinly populated region of northwest County Galway, extends a net of inlets and islands into the Atlantic Ocean. The rough gang of inland mountains, desolate stretches of bog, and rocky offshore islands are among Ireland's most arresting and peculiar scenery. Driving west from Galway City, the relatively tame and developed coastal strip stretching to Rossaveal suddenly gives way to the pretty fishing villages of Roundstone and Kilkieran. Farther west, Clifden, Connemara's largest town, draws Connemara's largest crowds. Ancient bogs spread between the coast and the rock-studded green slopes of the two major mountain ranges, the **Twelve Bens** and the **Maamturks.** Northeast of the Maamturks is Joyce Country, named for a long-settled Connemara clan. Tom Joyce, the original Welsh settler of the region, was said to be 7 ft. tall, and many of his descendents still tower over more diminutive bog creatures. Ireland's largest *gaeltacht* is also located along the Connemara coastline, and Irish-language radio (Radio na Gaeltachta) broadcasts from Costelloe. **Cycling** is a particularly rewarding way to absorb the region. The 60 mi. routes from Galway to Clifden (via Cong) and Galway to Letterfrack are popular despite fairly challenging dips and curves toward their ends. The seaside route through Inverin and Roundstone to Galway is another option. In general, the dozens of backroads in north Connemara make for beautiful and worthwhile riding. **Hiking** through the boglands and along the coastal routes is also popular—the **Western Way** footpath offers dazzling views as it winds 31 mi. from Oughterard to Leenane through the Maamturks. **Buses** serve the main road from Galway to Westport, stopping in Clifden, Oughterard, Cong, and Leenane. N59 from Galway to Clifden is the main thoroughfare; R336, R340, and R341 make more elaborate coastal loops. **Hitchhikers** report that locals are likely to stop; *Let's Go* does not recommend taking advantage of locals' generosity.

CLIFDEN ☎091

Clifden (An Clochán) is called the capital of Connemara because of its size, not because of any membership in the *gaeltacht*. The town is a clump of tourist-directed buildings resting between a cliff and a pair of modest peaks. Clifden is a convenient if tacky place to stock up before heading into the great wide yonder.

TRANSPORTATION. Bus Éireann pulls into the library on Market St. from **Westport** via **Leenane** (1½hr., late June to Aug. 3 per day) and **Galway** via **Oughterard** (2hr.; June-Aug. M-Sa 3 per day, Su 2 per day; Sept.-May 1 per day; £6.50/€9.15). **Michael Nee** (☎51082) buses from courthouse to **Cleggan** (June-Sept. 1 per day, Oct.-May 2 per week; £6/€7.60) and **Galway** (June-Sept. 2 per day; £6/€7.60). **Rent bikes** from **Mannion's**, Bridge St. (☎21160, after hours 21155. £7/€8.90 per day, £40/€50.80 per week. Deposit £10/€12.70. Open M-Sa 9:30am-6:30pm, Su 10am-1pm and 5-7pm.) **C&A Cabs** (☎21309) cost 70p/€0.90 per mi.

ORIENTATION AND PRACTICAL INFORMATION. Market St. meets **Main St.** and **Church Hill** at **The Square.** The **tourist office**, Galway Rd., has info on all of Connemara. (☎21163. Open July-Aug. M-Sa 9:45am-5:45pm and Su noon-4pm; May-June and Sept. M-Sa 9:30am-5:30pm.) An **AIB bank** (☎21129) is in The Square. The **post office** (☎21156) is on Main St.

ACCOMMODATIONS. B&Bs litter Clifden's streets and charge around £18-20 per person. Reservations are necessary in July and August. **The Clifden Town Hostel (IHH)**, Market St., has great facilities, spotless rooms, and a quiet atmosphere close to the pubs. Despite the modern decor, stone walls remind you that the house is 180 years old. (☎21076. Dorms £8/€10.15; doubles £24/€30.50; triples £30-33/€38.10-41.90; quads £36/€45.60.) The roomy dorms of **Brookside Hostel,** Hulk St., overlook fat sheep in the backyard. Head straight at the bottom of Market St. (☎21812. Dorms £8/€10.15; doubles £18/€22.85.)

FOOD AND PUBS. O'Connor's SuperValu, Market St., stocks cheap eats. (Open M-F 9am-7pm, Su 10am-6pm.) **Cranmeer,** Church Hill (☎21174) has stunning pizzas that stretch the waistline without stretching the budget. (Takeaway or dine-in. Open daily 5-10:30pm.) **Walsh's,** the Square, is a busy bakery with a large seating area and food for less than £2/€2.50. (☎21283. Open June-Sept. M-Sa 8am-9pm; Oct.-May 8:30am-5:20pm.) Join in the music at **Mannion's,** Market St. (☎21780. Music in summer nightly; winter F-Sa.) The town's best pint by consensus is at **King's,** the Square (☎21800), while **Malarkey's,** Church Hill, is packed and jammin'.

SIGHTS. Clifden's cliffs are less than impressive, but the 10 mi. **Sky Rd.** loops around the head of land to the west of town, paving the way to some legitimately dizzying heights. It's a beautiful route for bicycling, although it involves quite a few strenuous climbs. A mile down Sky Rd. stands what's left of **Clifden Castle,** once home to Clifden's founder, John D'Arcy. Farther out, a peek at the bay reveals the spot on a bog near Ballyconneely where US pilots John Alcock and Arthur Brown landed the first nonstop transatlantic flight in 1919. One of the nicer ways to acquaint yourself with Connemara is to hike south to their monument, situated just off the Ballyconneely road 3 mi. past Salt Lake and Lough Fadda.

INISHBOFIN   ☎095

Inishbofin, the "island of the white cow," has gently sloping hills (flat enough for pleasant cycling) scattered with rugged rocks, an excellent hostel, and near-deserted sandy beaches. Living as they do 7 mi. from the western tip of Connemara, the 200 rough-and-tumble islanders keep time according to the ferry, the tides, and the sun; visitors can easily adapt to their system. Days on Inishbofin are best spent meandering through the rocks and wildflowers of the island's four peninsulas. Paths are scarce, but the hills are rewarding. (Locals do not usually object to hikers wandering the peninsulas, but consult the community center before setting out.) Most items of historical interest are on the southeast peninsula. **Knock Hill** affords spectacular views of the island. **Bishop's Rock,** a short distance off the mainland, becomes visible at low tide. Cromwell supposedly once tied a recalcitrant priest to the rock and forced his comrades to watch as the tide drowned him.

The ragged northeast peninsula is fantastic for bird watchers: gulls, cornets, shags, and a pair of peregrine falcons fish among the cliffs and coves. Inishbofin provides a perfect climate for vegetation hospitable to the corncrake, a bird that's near extinction everywhere except in Seamus Heaney's poems.

Ferries leave for Inishbofin from **Cleggan,** a tiny village with stunning beaches 10 mi. northwest of Clifden. Two **ferry companies** serve the island. Malachy King operates the *Island Discovery* and the *Galway Bay,* which comprise the larger, steadier, and faster of the two fleets. (☎44642. 45min.; July-Aug. 3 per day; Apr.-June and Sept.-Oct. 2 per day; return £10/€12.70, children £5/€6.35. Tickets available at the pier, in Clifden, or on the boat.) The *M.V. Dún Aengus/Queen of Aran* runs year-round. (Contact Paddy O'Halloran, ☎45806. 45min.; July-Aug. 3 per day; Apr.-June and Sept.-Oct. 2 per day; Nov.-Apr. 1 per day; return £10/€12.70. Tickets purchased most conveniently on the ferry.) Both ferries carry bikes for free. Free parking is available at the Cleggan Pier. Stock up at the **Spar** before you go, especially if you're taking a later ferry. (☎44750. Open daily 9am-10pm.) **Bike rental** is available at the Inishbofin pier (☎45833) for £6-7.50 per day. To sort out your stay, call ahead or visit the **Community Resource Centre** (☎45909, fax 45889) to the left of the pier on the main road. The pleasant staff provides maps (£1.50-3.50/€1.90-4.45), updated information on services, and **Internet access** (M-F 9:30am-12:30pm).

Kieran Day's excellent ◪**Inishbofin Island Hostel (IHH)** is a 15min. walk from the ferry landing; take a right at the pier and head up the hill. The hostel is the unmistakably yellow building. Visitors are blessed with a large conservatory, swell views, and bits of poetry from disparate sources. (☎45855. Sheets 50p/€0.65. Laundry £4/€5.10. Dorms £7.50/€9.55. **Camping** £4/€5.10 per person.) The **Emerald Cottage,** a 10min. walk west from the pier, welcomes guests with home-baked goodies. (☎45865. Singles and doubles £16/€20.30 per person.) Close to the pier, **Day's Pub** (☎45829) serves food from noon to 5pm. **Day's Shop** is behind the pub and sells picnic-applicable items. (☎45829. Open M-Sa 11am-1pm and 3-5pm, Su noon-3pm.) The smaller and more sedate **Murray's Pub,** a hotel-bar 15min. west of the pier, is the perfect place for conversation, slurred or otherwise. The island's nightlife is surprisingly vibrant, with frequent trad performances in the summer.

CONNEMARA NATIONAL PARK ☎095

Connemara National Park occupies 7¾ sq. mi. of mountainous countryside and is home to thousands of birds. The far-from-solid terrain of the park is composed of bogs thinly covered by a screen of grass and flowers. Be prepared to muddy your legs and raise your pulse. Guides lead free two- to three-hour walks over hills and through bogs (July-Aug. M, W, F 10:30am), tell about the history, breeding, and feeding of the Connemara ponies (M, W, F 2pm), and offer several children's programs on Tuesdays and Thursdays. The ◪**Visitors Centre** and its adjoining museum team up with perversely funny anthropomorphic peat and moss creatures to teach visitors the differences between hollows, hummocks, and tussocks. Follow this with the dramatic 25min. slide show about the park, which elevates the battle against opportunistic rhododendrons to epic scope. (☎41054. Open June daily 10am-6:30pm; July-Aug. 9:30am-6:30pm; May and Sept. 10am-5:30pm. £2/€2.55, students £1/€1.25.) The **Snuffaunboy Nature** and **Ellis Wood Trails** are easy 20min. hikes. The Snuffaunboy features alpine views while the Ellis Wood submerges walkers in an ancient forest; both teem with wildflowers. A guidebook mapping out 30min. walks (50p/€0.65) is available at the Visitors Centre, where staff helps plan longer hikes. For the more adventurous, trails lead from the back of the **Ellis Wood Trail** and 10min. along the **Bog Road** onto ◪**Diamond Hill,** a two-hour hike that rewards climbers with views of bog, harbor, and forest, or, depending on the weather, lots of mist. (Diamond Hill was closed in 2001 for erosion control; call ahead to confirm opening.) Park visitors often base themselves in nearby Letterfrack at the ◪**Old Monastery Hostel** (a sharp right and up the hill from the crossroads), one of Ireland's finest. The owner cooks buffet dinners in the vegetarian and (mostly) organic style during the summer (call by 5pm); he also provides fresh scones and porridge for breakfast. (☎41132. Bike rental £7/€8.90 per day. Internet access £3/€3.80 per hr. Laundry £5/€6.35. Dorms £8-10/€10-13; doubles £12/€15.25. **Camping** £5/€6.35.)

WESTPORT ☎098

One of the only planned towns in Ireland, Westport still looks marvelous in her original Georgian-period costumes. Visitors would be well advised to follow the Carrowbeg River's lead and head to the Quay, have a pint outside, and watch the wide, blue water become red, then blue again, as the sun sets. Hustle back to Bridge St. for pure, unadulterated *craic*. Sounds like somewhere you'd want to go, no? Book your accommodations in advance or you might have some trouble; tourists flock to Westport like hungry seagulls to harbor feed.

▐ TRANSPORTATION. Trains puff into **Altamont St. Station** (☎25253) from **Dublin** via **Athlone** (2-3 per day; £15/€19). **Buses** leave Mill St. on the Octagon for **Ballina, Castlebar, Galway,** and **Knock.** For a **taxi,** call **Brendan McGing** at ☎25529. **Rent bikes** from **Old Mill Holiday Hostel,** James St., past the tourist office from the Octagon and through an archway. (☎27045. £7/€8.90 per day.) The N60 passes through **Clifden, Galway,** and **Sligo** on its way to Westport, and **hitchhikers** report it to be an easy route; *Let's Go* as easily states that hitchhiking is not safe.

▟▞ ORIENTATION AND PRACTICAL INFORMATION. The tiny **Carrowbeg River** trickles through **Westport's Mall. Bridge St.** and **James St.,** the town's main drags, extend south. **Shop St.** connects the **Octagon,** at the end of James St., to the **Town Clock** at the end of Bridge St. **High St.** and **Mill St.** lead out from the town clock, the latter into **Altamont St.,** where the train station lies beyond a long stretch of B&Bs. The **tourist office** is on James St. (☎25711. Open July-Aug. M-Sa 9am-6:45pm, Su 10am-6pm; Apr.-June and Sept.-Oct. M-Sa 9am-5:45pm.) The **Bank of Ireland** is at North Mall. (☎25522. Open M-W and F 10am-4pm, Th 10am-5pm.) **Internet access?** Try **Dunning's Cyberpub,** the Octagon. (☎25161. Open daily 9am-11:30pm.)

▛▟▞ ACCOMMODATIONS, FOOD, AND PUBS. The ▧**Granary Hostel,** a mile from town on Louisburgh Rd., near the main entrance to Westport House, is flanked by a peaceful garden and conservatory. (☎25903. Open Apr.-Oct. £7.50/€9.55.) The **Old Mill Holiday Hostel (IHH),** James St., between the Octagon and the tourist office, has character and comfort. (☎27045. Kitchen and common-room lockout 11pm-8am. Dorms £9/€11.45.) Peruse local art while waiting for a table at ▧**McCormack's,** Bridge St. Locals praise the exemplary teas and pastries. (☎25619. Open M-Tu and Th-Sa 10am-6pm.) ▧**Matt Molloy's,** Bridge St. (☎26655), officially runs trad sessions nightly at 9:30pm, but really any time of the day is deemed appropriate. **Cosy Joe's,** Bridge St. (☎28004) remains cozy despite its four floors and two bars. (M-Tu live music, Th-Sa DJ. Open M-W and Su 10:30am-11:30pm, Th-Sa 10:30am-12:30am; food served M-Sa 11:30am-6pm.) A run-down exterior hides **Henehan's Bar,** Bridge St. (☎25561), and its beer garden. It has music in summer nightly and on winter weekends.

▣▟ SIGHTS AND HIKING. Westport House's current state of commercial exploitation must be a bitter pill to swallow for Lord Altamont, its elite inhabitant, but the **grounds** there are beautiful, free, and a 45min. stroll from town—take James St. above the Octagon, bear right, and follow the signs to the Quay. interesting is the **Clew Bay Heritage Centre** at the end of the Quay. The exhibit is a veritable garage sale of history, and this charmingly crammed center brims with knickknacks and scraps of the past. (☎26852. Open July-Sept. M-F 10am-5pm, Su 2:30-5pm; Oct.-June M-F 10am-2pm. £2/€2.55, students £1/€1.30.)

Conical **Croagh Patrick** rises 2510 ft. over Clew Bay. The summit has been revered as a holy site for thousands of years; perhaps because of its height, it was sacred to Lug, sun god, god of arts and crafts, and one-time ruler of the Túatha de Danann. After arriving here in AD 441, St. Patrick engaged in praying and fasting for the standard 40 days and 40 nights, argued with angels, and then banished snakes from Ireland. The barefoot pilgrimage to the summit originally ended on St. Patrick's feast day, March 17, but the death-by-thunderstorm of 30 pilgrims in AD 1113 moved the holy trek to Lughnasa—**Lug's holy night** is on the last Sunday in

July, when the weather is more forgiving. Others climb the mountain just for the exhilaration and the view; it takes about 4hr. to complete the climb and descent. Be warned: the terrain can be quite steep, and the footing unsure. Well-shod climbers start their excursion from the 15th-century **Murrisk Abbey;** pilgrims and hikers also set out for Croagh Patrick along the Tóchar Phádraig, a path from **Ballintubber Abbey.** Founded in 1216 by King O'Connacht Cathal O'Connor, the abbey is still a religious center. The new and useful **Croagh Patrick Information Centre** offers tours, showers, luggage storage, and enough info to drive the snakes out of any country.

ACHILL ISLAND   ☎ 098

Two decades ago, Achill (AK-ill) Island was Co. Mayo's most popular holiday destination. Its popularity has inexplicably dwindled, but Ireland's biggest little island remains one of its most beautiful and personable. Ringed by glorious beaches and cliffs, Achill's interior consists of a few mountains and more than a few bogs. The town of Achill Sound, the gateway to the island, has the most amenities of any nearby settlement, but Keel has more promising nightlife. Dugort, north of Keel, is less busy, but its hostel, pub, and restaurant provide services enough for any weary backpacker. To the West of Keel, the seaside resorts of Pollagh and Dooagh form a flat strip along Achill's longest beaches and serve as brief stopovers on the way to Achill's more westerly (and more potent) vistas at Keem Bay and Croaghaun Mountain. **Cycling** the Atlantic drive is another great way to see the island. The **Achill Seafood Festival** goes down the second week in July, and during the first two weeks of August, Achill hosts the **Scoil Acla** (☎ 45284), a festival of trad and art.

   Buses run infrequently over the bridge linking Achill Sound, Dugort, Keel, and Dooagh to Westport, Galway, and Cork (summer M-Sa 5 per day; off season M-Sa 2 per day), and to Sligo, Enniskillen, and Belfast (summer 3 per day; off season 2 per day). Hitchers report relative success during July and August, but cycling is more reliable and is preferred by *Let's Go* (which would *never* recommend hitchhiking, even if given the choice). The island's **tourist office** is next to the Esso station in Cashel, on the main road from Achill Sound to Keel. (☎ 47353. Open M-F 10am-5pm.) There is a **cash machine** in Achill Sound but no bank anywhere on the island; don't forget to change your money on the mainland.

   Achill Sound's strategic location at the island's entrance accounts for the high concentration of shops and services in its center, but practicality isn't the only reason to stop here; come for the cash machine and stay for the internationally famous stigmatic and faith healer who holds services at **Our Lady's House of Prayer.** The OLHOP is about 200m up the hill from the town's main church and is open for services daily 9:30am-6pm. She (the healer, not Our Lady) draws thousands to the attention-starved town each year, but local opinions remain polarized. About 6 mi. south of Achill Sound (turn left at the first crossroads), two ruined buildings stand—or rather, lie—in close proximity. The ancient **Church of Kildavnet** was founded by St. Dympna after she fled to Achill to escape her father's incestuous intentions. Nearby, a lonely and crumbling 16th-century tower house with memories of better days calls itself the remains of **Kildavnet Castle.** Swaggerin' Grace O'Malley, Ireland's favorite medieval pirate lass, once owned the castle. Achill Sound has a **post office** with a **bureau de change** (☎ 45141; open M-F 9:30am-12:30pm and 1:30-5:30pm), a **SuperValu** supermarket (open daily 9am-7pm), a **Bank of Ireland cash machine,** and a **pharmacy** (☎ 45248; open July-Aug. M-Sa 9:30am-6pm; Sept.-June Tu-Sa 9:30am-6pm). **Cycle rental** is available at the **Achill Sound Hotel.** (☎ 45245. $7/€8.90 per day, $30/€38.10 per week. Deposit $40/€50.80. Open daily 9am-9pm.) The **Wild Haven Hostel,** a block past the church on the left, positively glows with polished wood floors and antique furniture. The sunny conservatory doubles as a swank ivy-walled dining room. (☎ 45392. Sheets $1/€1.30. Laundry $4.50/€5.75. Lockout 11am-3:30pm, except on rainy days. Dorms $9.50/€12.10; private rooms $12/€15.25 per person. **Camping** $4/€5.10.) If that doesn't work out, choo-choo-

choose the **Railway Hostel,** just before the bridge to town. The hostel is a simple affair in a former station—the last train pulled out about 70 years ago—and it is bursting with dorm-style rooms packed for maximum occupancy. The proprietors can be found at the Mace Supermarket in town. (☎45187. Sheets £1/ €1.30. Laundry £1.50/€1.90. Dorms £7/€8.90; doubles £16/€20.30.) Opposite the Railway Hostel, **Alice's Harbour Bar** flaunts gorgeous views, a stonework homage to the deserted village, and a boat-shaped bar, as well as a brand-new disco that spins top-40 hits on summer weekends and attracts the young rural hipster set of Upper Achill. (☎45138. Bar food £4-6/€5-8; served noon-9pm. Cover for disco £5/€6.35.)

BALLINA   ☎096

Fisher armies in olive-green waders invade Ballina each year during the salmon season, at which time the town seems the center of a weird cult. Ballina has at least one non-ichthyological attraction, though: every Saturday night, almost everyone in a 50 mi. radius, from sheep farmers to students, descends on the town like a stampeding herd of lemmings. These weekly influxes ruffle the feathers of the humble hub, but leave it slightly hipper for the wear.

⌗⁊ TRANSPORTATION AND PRACTICAL INFORMATION. The **train station** is on Station Rd. (☎71818). **Trains** arrive from **Dublin** (M-Sa 3 per day, £15/€19). The nearby **bus station** (☎71800; open M-Sa 9:30am-6pm) hosts **buses** from: **Sligo** (2hr., M-Sa 3-4 per day, £7.30/€9.30); **Galway** via **Westport** (2hr.; M-Sa 18 per day, Su 5 per day; £9.70/€12.30); **Dublin** via **Mullingar** (4hr., 6 per day, £8/€10.15). The city center is a short walk from the bus station; turn left exiting the car park, take a right at the first intersection, and hang left at the post office. **Michael Hopkins,** Lower Pearse St. (☎21609), **rents bikes.** (£7/€8.90 per day, £30/€38.10 per week. Deposit £30/€38.10. Open Apr.-Sept. M-Sa 9am-6pm.) The **tourist office** is on Cathedral Rd., on the river by St. Muredach's Cathedral, with **Internet access.** (☎70848. Open June-Aug. daily 10am-5:30pm; Mar.-May and Sept. 10am-1pm and 2-5:30pm.) A **Bank of Ireland** is on Pearse St. (☎21144).

⌗⌗ ACCOMMODATIONS AND FOOD. Much to the budget traveler's chagrin, there are no hostels in Ballina, but dozens of **B&Bs** line the main approach roads into town. **Lismoyne House,** Kevin Barry St., next to the bus station, has stately rooms with high ceilings and long bathtubs. (☎70582. £20/€25.40 per person.) **Belleek Camping and Caravan Park** is 2 mi. from Ballina toward Killala on the R314, behind the Belleek Woods. (☎71533. Laundry and kitchen. Open Mar.-Oct. £4/ €5.10 per person with tent, families £9/€11.45.)

Aspiring gourmets prepare to feast at the **Quinnsworth** supermarket on Market Rd. (☎21056. Open M-W and Sa 8:30am-7pm, Th-F 8:30am-9pm, Su noon-6pm.) Lard-soaked takeaway may be cheap, but it's not always welcome. Fortunately, most Ballinalian restaurants are attached to pubs and serve identical menus in the pub for cheaper. The money you save may even be enough for some pints.

⌗⌗ PUBS AND CLUBS. Gaughan's has been pulling the best pint in town since 1936. No music or TV here—just great grub, homemade snuff, and a welcome conversation with Pints O'Guinness. Jolly, musical drinkers raise **The Parting Glass,** Tolan St. over and over again. (☎72714. Trad sessions weekly; call ahead for schedule.) **Murphy Bros.,** Clare St. (☎22702), across the river, pours pints for twentysomethings amid dark wood furnishings. **Longnecks,** Clare St. (☎22702), attached to Murphy Bros., is where Ballina's more mature pubbers party like it's 1979. (Cover £5-6/€6.35-7.60. Open Th-Su midnight-2:30am.) Top 40-lovin' folks arrive in herds when **The Pulse,** Ballina's most popular nightclub, opens its doors. (Open W and F-Su 11:30pm-2am. Cover £4-5/€5.10-6.35.) At **The Loft,** Pearse St., young and old mix like oil and water. (☎21881. Live music Tu-F and Su.)

REPUBLIC OF IRELAND

NORTHWEST IRELAND

The farmland of the upper Shannon spans northward into Co. Sligo's mountains, lakes, and ancient monuments. A mere sliver of land connects Co. Sligo to Co. Donegal, the second-largest and remotest of the Republic's counties, with its most marvelous scenery. Donegal's *gaeltacht* is a storehouse of genuine, unadulterated Irish tradition.

SLIGO

☎ 071

A cozy town with the sophistication of a large city, present-day Sligo often gets lost in a haze of Yeats nostalgia. At night, the town's thriving pub scene is as diverse as any in Ireland. The Yeats Memorial Building and countless other landmarks remember the bygone days of the wordsmith, but Sligo Town, with its pub sing-alongs and watercolor skies, is very much for the living.

⊏ TRANSPORTATION

Trains: McDiarmada Station, Lord Edward St. (☎ 69888). Open M-Sa 7am-6:30pm, Su 20min. before each departure. Trains to **Dublin** via **Carrick-on-Shannon** and **Mullingar** (3 per day, £13.50/€17.15).

Buses: McDiarmada Station, Lord Edward St. (☎ 60066). Open M-F 9:15am-6pm, Sa 9:30am-5pm. **Luggage storage** M-F 9:30am-1:30pm and 2:45-6pm (£1.50/€2). Buses to: **Belfast** (4hr., 1-3 per day, £12.40/€15.75); **Dublin** (4hr., 4 per day, £9/ €11.45); **Galway** (2½hr., 3-4 per day, £11/€14).

Taxis: Cab 55 (☎ 42333). At least £3/€3.80 in town, 50p/€0.65 per mi. outside.

Bike Rental: Flanagan's Cycles, Market Sq. (☎ 44477, after hours 62633). £7/€8.90 per day, £30/€38.10 per week. Deposit £35/€44.45. Open M-Sa 9am-6pm.

◼✴🛈 ORIENTATION AND PRACTICAL INFORMATION

To reach the main drag from the station, take a left on **Lord Edward St.** and follow him straight onto **Wine St.,** then turn right onto **O'Connell St.** at the post office. More shops, pubs, and eateries beckon from **Grattan St.,** a left turn off O'Connell St. To get to the river, continue down Wine St. and turn right just after the Yeats building onto idyllic **Rockwood Parade,** where plenty of swans and locals take their feed.

Tourist Office: Northwest Regional Office, Temple St. (☎ 61201), at Charles St. From the station, turn left along Lord Edward St., then follow the signs right onto Adelaid St. and around the corner to Temple St. Open June-Aug. M-Sa 9am-8pm, Su 10am-6pm; Oct.-May M-F 9am-5pm.

Financial Services: AIB, 49 O'Connell St. (☎ 41085). Open M-W and F 10am-4pm, Th 10am-5pm.

Launderette: Pam's Laundrette, 9 Johnston Ct. (☎ 44861), off O'Connell St. Wash and dry from £6/€7.60. Open M-Sa 9am-7pm.

Emergency: ☎ 999. No coins required.

Police (*Garda*): Pearse Rd. (☎ 42031).

Internet Access: Cygo Internet Cafe, 19 O'Connell St. (☎ 40082). £5/€6.35 per hr., students £4/€5.10. Open M-Sa 10am-7pm.

Post Office: Wine St. (☎ 42646). Open M and W-Sa 9am-5:30pm, Tu 9:30am-5:30pm.

◤ ACCOMMODATIONS

There are plenty of high-quality hostels in Sligo, but they fill up quickly, particularly in mid-August, when the Yeats International Summer School is in session. B&Bs cluster along Pearse Rd. on the south side of town and near the station.

☒ **Harbour House,** Finisklin Rd. (☎71547). A 10min. walk from the bus station. A plain stone front hides a luxurious hostel. Continental breakfast £2/€2.55. Dorms £11/€14; private rooms £13/€16.50 per person; singles £17/€21.60.

☒ **Railway Hostel,** 1 Union Place (☎44530). From the main entrance of the train station, take 3 lefts and you're there. Homey, with generous extras: the kitchen has TV, stereo, and free tea and coffee. Dorms £7.50/€9.55; twins £9/€11.45 per person.

The White House Hostel (IHH), Markievicz Rd. (☎45160). Take the first left off Wine St. after the bridge; reception is in the brown house. A little run down, but retro carpeting and a laid-back staff will bring you back to that 70s-era commune you never joined. Sheets 50p/€0.65. Key deposit £2/€2.55. Dorms £7/€8.90.

Yeats County Hostel, 12 Lord Edward St. (☎46876), across from the bus station. Spacious rooms, private backyard, and location recommend this comfortable roost. Key deposit £5/€6.35. Dorms and triples £7/€8.90; doubles £21/€27.

Renaté House, Upper John St. (☎62014). From the station, go straight for 1 block and left for a half-block. Business-like and spotless, with elegant leather furnishings. Singles £23.50/€30, with bath £25.50/€32.40; doubles £34/€43, with bath £38/€48.25.

◖ FOOD

Little-known Yeats lyric: "For fresh fruits you can fondle / for not too much dough / head to O'Connell / and go to Tesco." **Tesco Supermarket,** O'Connell St., has aisles-worth of cheap food. (☎62788. Open M-Tu and Sa 8:30am-7pm, W-F 8:30am-9pm, Su 10am-6pm.) ☒**Kate's Kitchen,** Castle St. (☎43022), offers sophisticated pâtés and other delicacies.

Hy-Breasil, Bridge St. (☎61180), just over the river. Utopia of coffee and fresh-squeezed juice (£1.60/€2). Local art on the walls. Open M-F 8:45am-6pm, Sa 10am-6pm.

Ho Wong, Market St. (☎45718). Cantonese and Szechuan takeaway with an Irish-Asian flair. Entrees £4-7/€5-9. Open M-Th 5pm-12:30am, F-Sa 5pm-1:30am, Su 5pm-1am.

Pepper Alley (☎70720), along the river on the town side of the footbridge. Huge selection of cheap sandwiches for lunch. Open M-W 8am-6pm, Th-Sa 8am-10pm.

Java Sandwich Express, Rockwood Parade (☎49845). Sink in and savor extravagant lattes. Everything from Kombucas to smoothies. Sandwiches £2/€2.55.

◧◖ PUBS AND CLUBS

Over 70 pubs crowd Sligo's main streets, filling the town with live music during the summer. Events and venues are listed in *The Sligo Champion* (75p/€0.95). Many pubs post signs restricting their clientele to 21+, but such age discrimination is illegal in Ireland and is rarely enforced, particularly against attractive young thangs.

☒ **Shoot the Crows,** Grattan St. Owner Ronin holds court at this hippest destination for Sligo pint-seekers. Dark faery-folk dangle from the ceiling as weird skulls and crazy murals look on in amusement. No phone, so unnecessary ringing can't interrupt weekend revelry. Music Tu and Th 9:30pm.

☒ **McLynn's,** Old Market St. (☎60743). 3 generations in the making, Mclynn's was ranked best pub for music in Sligo by *The International Pub Guide*. Enter quietly in case you're interrupting an impromptu trad session. Lord of the Dance Michael Flatley's favorite pub, but don't hold that against them. Music most nights.

Hargadon Bros., O'Connell St. (☎70933). A pub worth spending your day in. Open fires, old Guinness bottles, and *poitín* jugs in a maze of dark and intimate nooks. Pints unfettered by modern audiovisual distractions; no music but for muffled sips and the clinking of glasses. Open M-W 10:30am-11:30pm, Th-Sa 10:30am-12:30am, Su 5-11pm.

The Belfry, Thomas St. (☎62150), just off the bridge. Modern-medieval decor, with big bell and bigger chandelier. 2 floors, 3 bars, 30 Irish whiskeys—you do the math. DJ Sa.

REPUBLIC OF IRELAND

Toff's (☎62150), on the river behind the Belfry pub. A well-lit, crowded dance-floor reveals that local club-goers drink better than they dance. Th-Sa Disco. 21+. Cover £5/€6.35; £1/€1.30 discount with card from the Belfry.

Equinox, up Teeling St. Darker, with a younger crowd. Newfangled neon lights, zebra-patterned stools, and dance music. Cover £5/€6.35. Open W-Su.

👁 SIGHTS

One of Sligo's more Yeats-free sights is the 13th-century **Sligo Abbey,** on Abbey St. (☎46406. Open Apr.-Oct. daily 10am-6pm; Nov.-Mar. call for weekend openings; last admission 45min. before close. £1.50/€1.90, students 60p/€0.75.) The **Dominican Friary** is old but hardly ruined. ◪**The Model Arts Centre and Niland Gallery,** on the Mall, holds an impressive collection of modern Irish art in an elegant and airy space. (☎41405. Open Tu-Sa 10am-5:30pm. Free.) The **Sligo County Museum** preserves small reminders of Yeats, including pictures of his funeral. (Open June-Sept. Tu-Sa 10:30am-12:30pm and 2:30-4:50pm; Oct.-May 10:30am-12:30pm. Free.) The **Sligo Art Gallery,** in the Yeats Memorial Building on Hyde Bridge, rotates exhibitions of contemporary Irish art with an annual exhibit on northwest Ireland in October. (☎45847. Open M-Sa 10am-5:30pm, except bank holidays.) The Yeats Society displays an exhibit on their main man, in the **Yeats Memorial Building** (☎42693 for more information).

🏃 NEAR SLIGO: YEATS!

DRUMCLIFF. Yeats composed His grave's epitaph a year before His 1939 death in France. His wife didn't get around to carrying out His dying wish (to be buried in France, disinterred a year later, and buried next to Benbulben; see below) until nine years later, which is sort of creepy. The grave is in **Drumcliff**'s churchyard, 4 mi. northwest of Sligo, just to the left of the church door. On Sunday evenings in the summer, the church sponsors concerts (☎56629). In response to yet another of Yeats's dying requests—My final resting station / should be near film animation—the church also projects an informative and artful animated feature on Drumcliff's pre-Yeatsian significance as a 6th-century Christian site.

BENBULBEN. Farther north of Drumcliff, the eerie **Benbulben,** rich in mythical associations, protrudes from the landscape like the keel of a foundered boat. St. Colmcille founded a monastery on the peak in AD 547, and it continued to be a major religious center until the 16th century. The climb up the 1729 ft. mountain (ben) is inevitably windy; the summit can be gusty. If you can keep from being blown away, though, standing at the 5000 ft. drop at the mountain's edge can be a humbling and beautiful experience. Signs on the Drumcliff road guide travelers to Benbulben; for detailed directions to the trails, ask at the Drumcliff gas station.

LISSADELL HOUSE. Eva Gore-Booth and her sister Constance Markievicz entertained that Yeats guy and his circle 4 mi. northwest of Drumcliff at **Lissadell House.** The house's current restoration reflects an attempt to return to the grandeur of those heady times. Former man o' the house Henry Gore-Booth was an avid hunter, but the real trophy on display—a formerly ferocious and now quite dead brown bear—was actually shot by the butler. To reach the house from the Drumcliff road, take the first left after Yeats Tavern Hostel and follow signs.

DONEGAL TOWN   ☎073

The sign outside Donegal Town reads: "Gateway to North and Northwest Donegal." This is a fitting title for this sleepy town, which does indeed act as a clearinghouse for travelers heading to more isolated destinations to the north and west. Somehow, though, this "fort of the foreigner" (the translation of Dún na nGall) keeps invasion at bay while still providing beautiful scenery and a smile.

TRANSPORTATION

Buses: Bus Éireann (☎21101). To: **Derry** (M-Th and Sa 6 per day, F 7 per day, Su 3 per day; £8.10/€10.30); **Dublin** (M-Sa 5 per day, F 6 per day, Su 4 per day; £10.50/€13.35); **Galway** (M-Sa 4-5 per day, Su 3 per day; £10.50/€13.35) via **Sligo** (£7.70/€9.80). **McGeehan's Coaches** (☎(075) 46150) go to **Dublin;** they also bus to **Killybegs, Ardara, Glenties, Glencolmcille,** and **Dungloe** (2 per day). Both stop outside the Abbey Hotel on the Diamond; timetables are posted in the lobby.

Taxis: McCallister (☎(087) 277 1777). **McBrearty** (☎(087) 413 6832).

Bike Rental: The Bike Shop, Waterloo Pl. (☎22515), the first left off the Killybegs road from the Diamond. £7/€8.90 per day, £45/€57.15 per week. Deposit £30/€38.10. Open M-Sa 10am-6pm.

ORIENTATION AND PRACTICAL INFORMATION

The center of town is the **Diamond,** a triangle bordered by Donegal's main shopping streets. Three roads extend from the Diamond: the **Killybegs road, Main St.,** and **Quay St.** (the **Ballyshannon road**).

Tourist Office: Quay St. (☎21148; www.donegaltown.ie). Just outside of the Diamond on the Ballyshannon/Sligo road, next to the quay. There are few tourist offices in the county; it's wise to stop here before heading north. Open July-Aug. M-Sa 9am-8pm, Su 10am-4pm; Sept.-Oct. and Easter-June M-F 9am-5pm, Sa 10am-2pm.

Financial Services: AIB (☎21016), the Diamond. Open M-W and F 10am-4pm, Th 10am-5pm.

Launderette: Derma's, the Diamond (☎22255). Load £9/€11.45. Open M-Sa 9am-7pm.

Emergency: ☎999. No coins required.

Police (*Garda*): ☎21021.

Internet Access: The Blueberry Tea Room has a cyber cafe. £5/€6.35 per hr., £3/€3.80 per 15-30min. Open summer M-Sa 9am-7pm.

Post Office: Tirconaill St. (☎21007), past Donegal Castle and over the bridge. Open M-F 9am-1pm and 2-5:30pm, Sa 9am-1pm.

ACCOMMODATIONS AND CAMPING

Calling ahead for hostels is imperative, especially during the high season. The tourist office will provide you with a list of Donegal Town B&B options.

Donegal Town Independent Hostel (IHH/IHO; ☎22805), ½ mi. out on the Killybegs road. Bright rooms, some with murals. Call ahead for a possible pickup. Dorms £7-7.50/€9-9.50; doubles £18/€22.85. **Camping** £4/€5.10 per person.

Ball Hill Youth Hostel (An Óige/HI; ☎/fax 21174), 3 mi. from town. Go 1½ mi. out of town on the Killybegs road, turn left at the sign, and continue toward the sea. Horseride, swim, hike, boat, and bonfire. £5-6.50/€6.35-8.30; youth discounts.

Atlantic Guest House, Main St. (☎21187). On a busy street, but has the privacy of a fancy hotel. Singles £20/€25.40, with bath £22/€28.

FOOD

A good selection of cafes and takeaways occupy the Diamond and nearby streets. For groceries, head to the **SuperValu,** minutes from the Diamond down the Sligo road. (☎22977. Open M-W and Sa 9am-7pm, Th-F 9am-9pm.) **Simple Simon's,** the Diamond, sells fresh baked goods, local cheeses, and homeopathic remedies for the hippie in you. (☎22687. Open M-Sa 9am-6pm.)

REPUBLIC OF IRELAND

The Blueberry Tea Room, Castle St. (☎22933), on the corner of the Diamond that leads to the Killybegs road. Justifiably popular, with food that could be described as home-cooked if your mother actually knew how to cook. Open M-Sa 9am-7pm.

The Harbour Restaurant, Quay St. (☎21702), across from the tourist office. A family place with range: pizza, lasagna, steak. Open M-Th 4-10:30pm, F-Su noon-10:30pm.

The Coffee House and Deli Bar, the Diamond (☎21014), attached to the Abbey Hotel. Try the "Plate of the Day." Open June-Aug. 9am-7pm; Sept.-May 9am-6pm.

PUBS AND CLUBS

Weekends during the summer are busy and full of music, particularly in early July during the Summer Festival, when many pubs host touring acts.

The Schooner Bar and B&B, Upper Main St. (☎21671). A mix of hostelers and locals, and the best trad and rock sessions in town on weekends. Sa drum and bass DJs.

Baby Joe's, Main St. (☎22322). Recently changed hands, name, and style. Lots of wrought iron and electric blue and an equally funky crowd. Live bands most weekends.

The Olde Castle Bar and Restaurant, Castle St. (☎21062). Renovated medieval feel. A low-key crowd and great Guinness. Open summer until 11:30pm, winter until 11pm.

Charlie's Star Bar, Main St. (☎21158). Well-lit, spacious, and sparkling with restrained good times. Folks gather here for GAA games and for ballads (summer W-Su evenings).

McGroarty's, the Diamond (☎21049). The biggest bar in town packs in a well-mannered crew of locals and tourists for live blues and ballads on the weekend. No cover.

The Voyage Bar, the Diamond (☎21201). Ask the owner about its name and a tear glints: "Everyone has a voyage to make in life." Younger crowd. Rock weekends.

The Coach House, Upper Main St. (☎22855). Spontaneous sing-alongs are known to break out at any time of day in this wood-beamed local hangout. Downstairs, the **Cellar Bar** opens its doors nightly at 9:30pm for trad and ballads. Confident musicians and singers are encouraged to join in. Cover £1/€1.30.

SIGHTS

DONEGAL CRAFT VILLAGE. Six craftspeople open their workshops to the public in Donegal's craft village. The innovative work of a potter, a jeweler, a painter, an ironsmith, and two sculptors make great gift alternatives to the legions of mass-produced leprechauns sold elsewhere. *(About a mile south of town on the Sligo road. ☎22225. Open July-Aug. M-Sa 10am-6pm, Su noon-6pm; Sept.-June call ahead.)*

DONEGAL CASTLE. Originally the seat of several chieftains, Donegal was torn apart by Irish-English conflict during the 17th century. *(Castle St. ☎22405. Open Mar.-Sept. daily 10am-5:15pm; Oct.-Feb. weekends 10am-5:15pm. Guided tours on the hour. £3/€3.80, students and children £1.25/€1.60, seniors £2/€2.55, families £7.50/€9.55.)*

WATERBUS. A new addition to Donegal Town's tourism machine, the Waterbus shuttle provides aquatic tours of Donegal Bay. The tour is at once scenic and morbid, as it encompasses many sights associated with the Famine-era "coffin ship" industry. *(Leaves from the quay next to the tourist office. ☎23666. Departures depend on tides; call ahead. £7/€8.90, concessions £5/€6.35.)*

LOUGH ESKE. The most worthwhile of Donegal Town's sights actually lies a few miles outside of town at Lough Eske ("fish lake"), an idyllic pond set among a fringe of trees and ruins. The crumbling but majestic **Lough Eske Castle,** built in 1861, lies lough-side, its slightly overgrown grounds and the seriously decrepit buildings providing a gorgeous site for picnics and afternoon rambles. Continue following the path around front to find a **Celtic high cross** surrounded by breathtaking gardens that contain the burial site of the castle's former master. The easy hike to the lough and back takes about 2hr. Follow signs for "Harvey's Point" (marked from the Killybegs road). After about 3 mi., you'll come to half of a metal gate supported by a single stone pillar. Turn right at the gate and follow the path to reach the remains of Lough Eske Castle.

SLIEVE LEAGUE PENINSULA ☎073

Just west of Donegal Town, the Slieve League Peninsula's rocky cliffs jut imposingly out of the Atlantic. The cliffs and mountains of this sparsely populated area harbor coastal hamlets, untouched beaches, and some of the best scenery in all of Ireland. R263 extends along the peninsula's southern coast, linking each charming village to the next. Backpackers and cyclists navigating the hilly terrain are advised to work their way westward, then northward, toward Glencolmcille.

THE SLIEVE LEAGUE WAY

■Slieve League Mountain claims the hotly contested title (in Ireland—other countries seem to espouse entirely different ideas) of "highest sea cliffs in Europe." The face of its sheer, 2000 ft. drop really is spectacular—on a clear day, a hike over the cliffs will move you to marvel at the infinite expanse of the Atlantic and the compact hamlets along the inland portion of the peninsula. To reach the mountain, turn left halfway down Carrick's Main St. and follow the signs for Teelin. A right turn at the Cúl A' Dúin pub will put you on the inland route to Slieve League. The more popular route involves hanging a left at the pub and following the coastal route to **Bunglass** (a 1½hr. walk from Carrick), where there is a car park at the head of the cliff path. From here, the trail heads north and then west along the coast. One hour along the path from the car park, the mountaintop narrows to 2 ft., becoming the infamous **One Man's Pass.** On one side of this pass, the cliffs drop 1800 ft. to the ocean below. No worries, though—the rocky floor on the other side is only 1000 ft. down. There are no railings here, and those prone to vertigo generally opt to lower their centers of gravity by slithering across the 33 yd. platform. The path continues along the cliffs all the way to **Rossarrell Point,** 6 mi. southeast of Glencolmcille. The entire hike from the Teelin car park to Rossarrell Point takes about 4-6hr., depending on frequency of stops; length of legs; and sudden, life-threatening, and totally random weather conditions. Other, shorter routes involving loop-like figures can also be plotted. (For advice and in the interest of safety, discuss your plans with a hostel owner and carry the Ordnance Survey Discovery Series #10, which covers this region.) **Never go to Slieve League in poor weather;** it's always a good idea to ask a local expert for advice and to tell someone when you expect to return.

GLENCOLMCILLE ☎073

Wedged between two sea-cliffs at the northwestern tip of the Slieve League peninsula, ■Glencolmcille (Gleann Cholm Cille; glen-kaul-um-KEEL) is actually a parish, a collection of several tiny, Irish-speaking villages that have come to be regarded as a single entity. This sometime-pilgrimage site centers around the street-long village of **Cashel,** which lies just off R236 along the aptly-named Cashel St. Buses of tourists roll in for the Folk Village (see **Sights,** below), but few venture to the desolate, wind-battered cliffs that lie just beyond.

■■ **TRANSPORTATION AND PRACTICAL INFORMATION.** The **Bus Éireann** (☎21101) funmobile leaves from the village corner to **Donegal Town,** stopping in **Killybegs** and **Kilcar** (1-3 per day). **McGeehan's** leaves from Biddy's Bar for **Carrick, Kilcar, Killybegs, Ardara, Glenties, Fintown,** and **Letterkenny** (1-2 per day). Glencolmcille's tiny **tourist office** is on Cashel St. (☎30116. Open July-Aug. M-Sa 10am-7:30pm, Su 11am-6pm; Apr. to mid-Nov. M-Sa 10am-6pm, Su 11am-1:30pm.) A **bureau de change** can be found at the **post office,** which is east of the village center (☎30001; open M-F 9am-1pm and 2-5:30pm, Sa 9am-1pm), but the nearest **banks** (read: **cash machines**) are in Killybegs and Ardara.

■■■ **ACCOMMODATIONS, FOOD, AND PUBS.** It's not a trip to Co. Donegal without a visit to old Mary at ■Dooey Hostel (IHO). To get there, turn left at the end of the village and follow the signs uphill for almost a mile. The hostel is built into the hillside overlooking the sea; a garden's worth of flowers grows from the rocky face that is the hostel's corridor. (☎30130; fax 30339. Dorms £7/€8.90; doubles £14/ €17.80. **Camping** £4/€5.10.) Five miles southwest of Cashel lies Malinbeg, and in it you'll find the welcoming **Malinbeg Hostel,** which combines more bells and whistles with superlative views. Call in advance for a pickup from the Glen. (☎30006 or 30965. 4-bed dorms £7/€8.90; doubles £18-20/€23-25; family rooms £44-48/€56-61.)

The **Lace House Restaurant,** above the tourist office on Cashel St., is a chipper with small windows to admire the sea cliffs and a large menu of fried foods. (☎30444. Open daily 10am-9pm.) **An Chistan** (AHN KEESHT-ahn; "the kitchen"), at the Foras Cultúir Uladh, is affordable for lunch. (☎30213. Open May-Sept. daily 9am-9pm; Apr. and Oct. noon-9pm.) **Byrne and Sons Food Store,** Cashel St., supplies basic nutritive and printed matter. (☎30019. Open M-Sa 9am-10pm, Su 9am-1pm and 6-9pm.) The town's three pubs have a dark, dusty, 1950s feel to them: imagine spare rooms with plastic-covered snugs and, for once, a minimal amount of wood paneling. The pubs are primarily a haven for locals, but they develop an affinity for visitors during July and August, when they each host several nights a week of trad. Most famous is the unassuming 120-year-old **Biddy's,** at the mouth of Carrick Rd., a favorite of the older crowd. (☎30016. Trad in summer 3ish times per week.) **Roarty's** (☎30273) is the next pub down Cashel St. Last is **Glen Head Tavern** (☎30008), the largest and youngest of the trio. Practically the whole village could fit into its lounge, which hosts legendary sessions.

◪ SIGHTS. Glen is renowned for its handmade products—particularly its sweaters, which are on sale at numerous "jumper shops" on the roads surrounding the town. A bit past the village center is craft-pioneer Father McDyer's **Folk Village Museum and Heritage Centre,** the town's main attraction for most tourists. The museum is housed in three thatch-roofed stone cottages; the 1850s schoolhouse is open to the general public. Guided tours describe the furniture and tools from each of these eras in Irish history. The **sheeben** sells homemade heather, fuchsia, and seaweed wines and whiskey marmalade. (☎30017. Open Easter-Sept. M-Sa 10am-6pm, Su noon-6pm. Tours July-Aug. 2 per hr.; Apr.-June and Sept. every hr. £2/€2.55, concessions £1.25/€1.60.) Fine beaches and cliffs make for excellent hiking in all directions. A five-mile walk southwest from Cashel leads to **Malinbeg,** a winsome hamlet at the edge of a sandy cove that now has its own hostel. When a sunny day happens to grace Donegal, a trip to the **Silver Strand** will be rewarded with stunning views of the gorgeous beach and surrounding rocky cliffs. An hour's walk north of town through land dotted with prehistoric ruins (including St. Colmcille's stations of the cross), **Glen Head** is easily identified by the Martello tower at its peak. The tourist office and the hostel both have maps. A third, three-hour walk from town begins at the Protestant church and climbs over a hill to the ruins of the ghostly "Famine village" of ▧Port, in the valley on the other side. This eerie village has been empty since its last, hunger-stricken inhabitants emigrated. The road east from Glencolmcille to Ardara proceeds through the stunning **Glengesh Pass.** Nine hundred feet above sea level, the road scales the surrounding mountains using such secret weapons as hairpin turns.

THE DONEGAL GAELTACHT ☎075

The four parishes in Co. Donegal's northwest corner comprise the largest *gaeltacht* in the Republic. Though the Rosses, Gweedore, Gartan, and Cloghaneely all maintain distinct identities, they are united by their intensely traditional culture, which has flourished in geographic isolation. There are few visitors to the area, and locals often feign incredulity about its appeal. Do not let them fool you— there will always be plenty to discover in the isolated north. **Fintown,** near **Glenties,** is one nice option for a base as you explore the *gaeltacht.*

DUNLEWY, MOUNT ERRIGAL, AND GLENVEAGH

R251 leads east through the village of **Dunlewy,** past the conical **Errigal Mountain,** and on to **Glenveagh National Park.** Dunlewy, which straddles the border of Gweedore and Cloghaneely parishes, rivals Crolly as a base camp for exploring the **Derryveagh Mountains.** Its hostels offer proximity to a pub and store and their own set of scenic trails, including the ascent to Errigal, a ramble through the **Poison Glen,** and the numerous paths in Glenveagh National Park. Dunlewy's hostels are just off R251. The **Errigal Youth Hostel (An Óige/HI),** only a mile from the foot of Errigal, is clean but basic—perfect for backpackers with their minds on the trail. (☎31180. Lockout 10am-5pm. Curfew 1am. £6.50-9.50/€8.25-12.) The **Backpackers Ireland Lakeside Hostel,** a few hundred yards down the road, is another decent option for hikers. (☎32133. £8-10/€10-13.)

A few minutes up the road is a turnoff to **Dunlewy Lake** and the **Poison Glen.** Within the glen is the former manor of an English aristocrat and his abandoned church. If you continue along the paved road around a few curves, you'll reach an unmarked car park that signals the beginning of the trail up the side of **Errigal Mountain** (at 2466 ft./€3232, Ireland's second-highest peak). This trail is the only feasible way of reaching the summit; expect your scramble through loose scree and over a narrow ridge to take 2-3hr. Be sure to keep an eye on the clouds—if visibility drops, your trip down could be shortened by several hours.

East of Dunlewy on the R251, you'll find **Glenveagh National Park'**s 37 sq. mi. of forest glens, bogs, mountains, and red deer. The park is often pretty deserted, so make sure to hold on to that map as you explore. Rangers lead **guided nature walks** and more strenuous **hill walks.** The **visitors center** has information about these as well as self-guided routes and a cafeteria-style **restaurant.** (☎37090. Park and center open Mar. to early Nov. daily 10am-5pm. Call ahead for information or to schedule a walk. Park admission £2/€2.55, students and children £1.50/€1.90, seniors £1/€1.30, families £5/€6.35. Park guide £5/€6.35.)

BUNBEG, DERRYBEG, AND BLOODY FORELAND

Bunbeg Harbour, the smallest enclosed harbor in Ireland, lies on the R257 in an area great for cycling. Relics of British occupation line the harbor. Boats (☎32487 or (087) 293 4895) sail from Bunbeg to **Tory Island** and **Gola Island,** a nearer-but-not-larger land mass that has deserted beaches and beautiful views. The mile of R257 between Bunbeg and **Derrybeg** has not escaped the roaming hand of tourism. Those who have grown tired of beautiful hikes and remote wilderness are sure to find relief in Derrybeg's suburban splendor. North of Derrybeg on R257, the **Bloody Foreland,** a short length of scarlet rock, juts out into the sea. At sunset on clear evenings, the foreland composes one of Ireland's most famous views. Farther west, the headland at **Meenlaragh (Magheraroarty)** offers much unspoiled beach.

To reach Derrybeg by **bus,** try **Swilly's** (☎(074) 22863), whose Donegal-Derry service hits the town daily. Derrybeg's **AIB** has a **bureau de change.** (☎31193. Open M-W and F 10am-12:30pm and 1:30-4pm, Th 10am-12:30pm and 1:30-5pm.) The **post office** (☎31165) is open weekdays 9am-1pm and 2-5:30pm.

There are no budget accommodations in Bunbeg or Derrybeg; the best places in the area to seek out beds are Crolly, Dunlewey, and—for the truly adventurous—Tory Island. The **Bunbeg House** (☎31305), on the waterfront, serves sandwiches and seafood as well as an expensive dinner menu. At the west end of Derrybeg is **Teach Niocain,** which is not only a **grocery** with fantastic hot bar and sandwich shop but also a **launderette.** (☎31065. Chicken wings 8 for £1/€1.30. Wash and dry £5/€6.35. Open daily 7:30am-10pm.) The irresistible ▧**Hudi Beag's** pub, at the west end of town, grounds Derrybeg's musical tradition. (☎31016. M trad.)

REPUBLIC OF IRELAND

LETTERKENNY
☎ 074

Letterkenny (Leitir Ceannan) may be Donegal's commercial center, transportation hub, and civil engineering nightmare, but it's also surprisingly cosmopolitan. Most tourists still arrive in town to make bus connections, but the appeal of a short stay here should not be overlooked.

⊟ TRANSPORTATION

Buses: The almighty **Bus Depot** occupies the eastern side of the roundabout at the junction of the Port (Derry) road and Pearse Rd., in front of the shopping center.

Bus Éireann (☎21309) runs a "Hills of Donegal" tour, including **Dungloe, Glenveigh National Park,** and **Gweedore** (M-Sa 1 per day, £13/€16.50). Regular service to: **Derry** (30min.; M-Sa 6 per day, Su 3 per day; £5/€6.35); **Dublin** (4½hr.; M-Th and Sa-Su 5 per day, F 6 per day; £10/€12.70); **Galway** (4¾hr., 4 per day, £12/€15.25) via **Donegal Town** (50min., £5/€6.35); **Sligo** (2hr.; M-Sa 5 per day, Su 4 per day; £9/€11.50).

Doherty's Travel (☎(075) 21105). Buses for **Dungloe** and **Burtonport** depart from Dunnes daily at 5pm (£5/€6.35).

Feda O'Donnell Coaches (☎(075) 48114 or (091) 761 656). To **Galway** (2-3 per day, £10/€12.70) via **Donegal Town** (£5/€6.35) and to **Crolly** (2 per day, £5/€6.35) via **Dunfanaghy.**

McGinley Coaches (☎35201). 2 per day to **Gweedore** via **Dunfanaghy** and to **Dublin** (£11/€14).

Lough Swilly Buses (☎22863). To **Derry** (M-Sa 9 per day, £4.40/€5.60); south to **Dungloe** (M-Sa 4 per day, £8/€10.20); north toward the **Fanad Peninsula** (M-Sa 2 per day, £7/€8.90); north toward the **Inishowen Peninsula** (M-F 4 per day, Sa 3 per day) via **Buncrana** (£4.50/€5.70), **Cardonagh** (£5/€6.35), and **Moville** (£5.50/€7).

McGeehan's (☎(075) 46150) goes once a day to **Killybegs** (£7/€8.90) and once a day to **Glencolmcille** (£9/€11.50; driver may stop in Killybegs upon request).

Northwest Busways (☎(077) 82619) sends buses around Inishowen (M-F 4 per day, Sa 3 per day), stopping in **Buncrana** (£4.50/€5.70), **Carndonagh** (£5/€6.35), and **Moville** (£5.50/€7).

Bike Rental: Church St. Cycles (☎26204), by the cathedral. £40/€50.80 per week. Deposit £40/€50.80. Open M-Sa 10am-6pm.

🛈 PRACTICAL INFORMATION

Tourist Office: Bord Fáilte (☎21160), off the rotary at the of Port Rd. and Blaney Rd. Open July-Aug. M-Sa 9am-8pm, Su 10am-2pm; Sept.-June M-F 9am-5pm.

Financial Services: AIB, 61 Main St. (☎22877 or 22807). Open M-F 10am-4pm.

Launderette: Duds 'n' Suds, Pearse Rd. (☎28303). Open June-Sept. M-Sa 8am-7pm, Oct.-May M-Sa 8am-9pm. Wash and dry about £6.50/€8.25.

Internet Access: Cyberworld, Main St. (☎20440), in the basement of Four Lanterns. £5/€6.35 per hr. Open M-Sa 11:30am-9:30pm, Su 1-7:30pm.

Post Office: Halfway down Main St. (☎22287). Open M and W-F 9am-5:30pm, Tu 9:30am-5pm, Sa 9am-5:30pm.

🏠 ACCOMMODATIONS

The Port Hostel (IHO), Orchard Crest (☎25315). In a sheltered glade up the hill from the An Grianán Theatre close to the city center. A variety of directed fun, including barbecues, pub crawls, and roadtrips to the beach and Glenveagh. Laundry £3.50/€4.45. Dorms £7.50/€9.50; private rooms £8.50-9.50/€10.80-12.

The Arch Hostel (IHO), Upper Corkey (☎57255), 6 mi. out of town in Pluck. Take the Derry (Port) road from the roundabout near the bus station and continue straight. Turn right at the sign for Pluck and fork right at Seamus Doherty Auto Parts; the hostel is the unmarked farm to the right after the stone arch. Better yet, call from town for pickup. 6 beds in a converted stable loft—a spartan dream. £7.50/€9.50 per person.

REPUBLIC OF IRELAND

White Gables, Mrs. McConnellogue, Lower Dromore (☎22583). Head 3 mi. out the Derry road and take the Lower Dromore turnoff from the N13/N14 roundabout; the house is ½ mi. down. Call for pickup from town. Thoroughly pastoral, with clean, cheery rooms and a balcony overlooking flocks of sheep. £16/€20.30, with bath £17/€21.60.

FOOD AND PUBS

Tesco, in the Letterkenny Shopping Centre behind the bus station, has all you could ask for in a grocery store. (Open M-Tu and Sa 8:30am-7pm, W 8:30am-8pm, Th-F 8:30am-9pm, Su noon-6pm.) **Simple Simon Living Food,** Oliver Plunkett Rd., has an admirable selection of organic and vegetarian foods, as well as supplements and herbal remedies. (☎22382. Open M-Sa 9am-5:30pm.)

Cafe Rico, 3-4 Oliver Plunkett Rd. (☎29808), at the end of Main St. across from the library. Full breakfasts, desserts, and sandwiches in an often-frantic and always-funky coffee shop. Takeaway too. Open M-F 8:30am-5:30pm, Sa until 6pm, Su 11am-4pm.

Galfees, with 2 locations: the nicer is at 63 Main St. (☎28535), near the High Rd. fork. Most evening entrees £4-5/€5.10-6.35. Cheaper evening menu served from 5pm. Bistro upstairs 6-9:30pm. Open M-Sa 9am-10pm, Su noon-7pm. The other branch is in the basement of the Courtyard Shopping Centre (☎27173), where Irish illustrations and wooden walls transcend the mall ambience.

India House, Port Rd. (☎20470), across from the Theatre. Though this sit-in restaurant is expensive, takeaway promises vegsters and meat-eaters alike a variety of flavor at moderate prices. Meat dishes £7/€9, vegetarian £4/€5. Open Tu-Su 5:30-11pm.

McGinley's, 25 Main St. (☎21106). Hugely popular student bar in the chapel-like upstairs; older-but-still-hip crowd on the Victorian ground floor. W-Su rock and blues.

Globe Bar, Main St. (☎22977). Fuscia facade; gaggles of hipsters within. Drink promotions (M-Th) lure the kids, and nightly DJs keep them there. M and W rock, other days it's DanceDanceDance.

Cottage Bar, 42 Main St. (☎21338). A kettle on the hearth, animated conversation around the bar, and nuns drinking Guinness in the corner. Tu and Th trad.

APPENDIX

CLIMATE

Avg Temp (lo/hi), Precipitation	January			April			July			October		
	°C	°F	mm	°C	°F	mm	°C	°F	mm	°C	°F	mm
London	2/6	36/43	77	6/13	43/55	56	14/22	57/72	59	8/14	46/57	70
Cardiff	2/7	36/45	108	5/13	41/55	65	12/20	54/68	89	8/14	46/57	109
Edinburgh	1/6	34/43	57	4/11	39/52	39	11/18	52/64	83	7/12	45/54	65
Dublin	1/8	34/46	67	4/13	39/55	45	11/20	52/68	70	6/14	43/57	70

BANK HOLIDAYS IN 2002

Government agencies, post offices, and banks are closed on the following days (hence the term "Bank Holiday"), and businesses—if not closed—may have shorter hours. Transportation in rural areas grinds to a halt, while traffic congestion can reach ridiculous levels. Sights, on the other hand, are more likely to be open, but can get crowded with holidaymakers.

DATE	HOLIDAY	AREAS
January 1	New Year's Day	UK and Republic of Ireland
January 2	New Year's Holiday	Scotland
March 18	St. Patrick's Day	Republic of Ireland and Northern Ireland
March 29	Good Friday	UK and Republic of Ireland
April 1	Easter Monday	UK and Republic of Ireland
May 6	May Day Bank Holiday (first Monday in May)	UK and Republic of Ireland
June 3	Golden Jubilee Bank Holiday	UK
June 3	First Monday in June	Republic of Ireland
June 4	Spring Bank Holiday	UK
July 5	Tynwald Fair Day	Isle of Man
July 12	Battle of the Boyne (Orangeman's Day)	Northern Ireland
August 5	Summer Bank Holiday (first Monday in August)	Republic of Ireland and Scotland
August 26	Summer Bank Holiday (last Monday in August)	UK except Scotland
October 28	Halloween Weekend (last Monday in October)	Republic of Ireland
December 25	Christmas Day	UK and Republic of Ireland
December 26	Boxing Day/St. Stephen's Day	UK and Republic of Ireland

TELEPHONE CODES

CITY CODES		COUNTRY CODES	
London	020	**United Kingdom**	44
Manchester	0161	**Ireland**	353
Cardiff	029	**Australia**	61
Edinburgh	0131	**Canada**	1
Glasgow	0141	**New Zealand**	64
Belfast	028	**South Africa**	27
Dublin	01	**United States**	1

Northern Ireland can also be reached from the Republic of Ireland by dialing 048.

TIME ZONES

From late March to late October, Britain and Ireland use British Summer Time, one hour ahead of **Greenwich Mean Time (GMT);** in winter, both countries revert to GMT. This means that, most of the time, Britain and Ireland are one hour earlier than (most of) continental Europe; five hours later than New York City (EST); six hours later than Chicago (CST); eight hours later than Seattle (PST); ten hours later than Nanakuli, Hawaii; eight hours earlier than Perth, Australia; ten hours earlier than Sydney; and twelve hours earlier than Auckland, New Zealand.

MEASUREMENTS

Britain and Ireland operate on the metric system, though Britain's conversion is as yet incomplete: while the weather report will give the temperature in Celsius, road signs still indicate distances in miles. It should be noted that gallons in the US are not identical to those across the Atlantic; one US gallon equals 0.83 Imperial gallons. Pub aficionados will want to note that a US pint (16 ounces) likewise equals 0.83 Imperial pints (which are 20 ounces each). The following is a list of Imperial units and their metric equivalents.

MEASUREMENT CONVERSIONS

1 inch (in.) = 25.4mm	1 millimetre (mm) = 0.039 in.
1 foot (ft.) = 0.30m	1 metre (m) = 3.28 ft. = 1.09 yd.
1 yard (yd.) = 0.914m	1 kilometre (km) = 0.62 mi.
1 mile (mi.) = 1.61km	1 gram (g) = 0.035 oz.
1 ounce (oz.) = 28.35g	1 kilogram (kg) = 2.202 lb.
1 pound (lb.) = 0.454kg	1 millilitre (ml) = 0.034 fl. oz.
1 fluid ounce (fl. oz.) = 29.57ml	1 litre (L) = 0.264 gal.
1 UK gallon (gal.) = 4.546L	1 square mile (sq. mi.) = 2.59km²
1 acre (ac.) = 0.405ha	1 square kilometre (km²) = 0.386 sq. mi.

In Britain and Ireland, **electricity** is 240 volts AC, enough to melt your favorite 110V American curling iron, although probably compatible with your 220V European toaster. 240V appliances won't function on 120V, either. See **Packing**, p. 29, for specific information.

LANGUAGE

The varieties of world English can sometimes lead to bewilderment. The vocabulary of American English, in particular, diverges from British English to a considerable extent. Here's a list of British words travelers are most likely to encounter.

BRITISH ENGLISH	AMERICAN ENGLISH	BRITISH ENGLISH	AMERICAN ENGLISH
all over the shop	in disarray	boot	car trunk
aubergine	eggplant	boozer	pub
bap	a soft bun	braces	suspenders
barmy	insane, erratic	brilliant	awesome, cool
bathroom	room with a bathtub	busker	street musician
bed-sit, or bed sitter	studio apartment	cashpoint	ATM or cash machine
biro	ballpoint pen	caravan	trailer, mobile home
biscuit	a cookie or cracker	car park	parking lot
bobby	police officer	cheeky	mischievous
give a bollocking to	shout at	cheers, cheerio	thank you, goodbye
bonnet	car hood	chemist, chemist's	pharmacist, pharmacy

APPENDIX

BRITISH ENGLISH	AMERICAN ENGLISH
chips	french fries
chuffed	happy
circle	theater balcony
coach	intercity bus
concession	discount on admission
courgette	zucchini
crisps	potato chips
dear	expensive
dicey, dodgy	problematic, sketchy
the dog's bollocks	the best
dosh	money
dual carriageway	divided highway
dustbin	trash can
ensuite	with attached bathroom
fag	cigarette
fanny	vagina
first floor	second floor
geezer	man
fortnight	two weeks
full stop	period (punctuation)
gob	mouth
grotty	grungy
half-six in the morning	6:30am
high street	main street
hire	rental, to rent
holiday	vacation
hoover	vacuum cleaner
ice-lolly	popsicle
interval	intermission
"in" a street	"on" a street
jam	jelly
jelly	Jell-O
jumble sale	yard sale
jumper	sweater
kip	sleep
kit	sports team uniform
knackered	tired, worn out
lavatory, "lav"	restroom
lay-by	roadside turnout
leader (in newspaper)	editorial
wanker	masturbator; see prat
way out	exit
W.C. (water closet)	toilet, restroom
legless	intoxicated
to let	to rent
lift	elevator
loo	restroom
lorry	truck

BRITISH ENGLISH	AMERICAN ENGLISH
mate	pal
mobile phone	cellphone
motorway	highway
naff	cheap, in poor taste
petrol	gasoline
phone box, call box	telephone booth
take the piss	make fun
pissed	drunk
plaster	Band-Aid
prat	stupid person
prawn	large shrimp
props	pub regulars
pudding	dessert
pull	to seduce
public school	private school
punter	average person
quay	river bank
queue up, queue	line up
quid	pound (in money)
return ticket	round-trip ticket
ring up	to phone
roundabout	rotary road interchange
rubber	eraser
sack	to fire someone
self-catering	with kitchen facilities
self-drive	car rental
serviette	napkin
a shag, to shag	sex, to have sex
single carriageway	non-divided highway
single ticket	one-way ticket
snogging	making out
sod it	forget it
stalls	orchestra seats
sultana	a type of raisin
sweet(s)	candy
swish	swanky
ta-ta	goodbye
tariff	cost
toilet	restroom
torch	flashlight
tosser	term of abuse; see prat
trainers	sneakers
trunk call	long-distance phone call
vest	undershirt
waistcoat (weskit)	men's vest
wellies	waterproof rubber boots
yob	prole
"zed"	the letter Z

BRITISH PRONUNCIATION

Berkeley	BARK-lee	Maryleborn	MAR-lee-bun
Berkshire	BARK-sher	Magdalen	MAUD-lin
Birmingham	BIRM-ing-um, not "ham"	Norwich	NOR-ich
Derby	DAR-bee	Salisbury	SAULS-bree
Dulwich	DULL-idge	Shrewsbury	SHROWS-bree
Edinburgh	ED-in-bur-ra	Southwark	SUTH-uk
Ely	EEL-ee	Thames	TEMS
Gloucester	GLOS-ter	Warwick	WAR-rick
Greenwich	GREN-ich	Woolwich	WOOL-ich
Hertfordshire	HART-ford-sher	Worcester	WOO-ster
Grosvernor	grovnor	gaol	JAIL
Holborn	HO-bun	quay	KEY
Leicester	LES-ter	scones	SKONS

WELSH WORDS AND PHRASES

Consult **Llanguage,** p. 426, for the basic rules of Welsh pronunciation. Listed below are a number of words and phrases you may encounter on the road.

WORD/PHRASE	PRONUNCIATION	MEANING
allan	ahl-LAN	exit
ar agor	ahr AG-or	open
ar gau	ahr GUY	closed
bore da	boh-RA DAH	good morning, hello
cyhoeddus	cuh-HOY-this	public
diolch yn fawr	dee-OLCH uhn VOWR	thank you
dydd da	DEETH dah	good day
dynion	dihnion	men
Ga i peint o cwrw?	gah-EE pint oh coo-roo?	Can I have a pint of beer?
hwyl	huh-will	cheers
ia	eeah	yes (sort of—it's tricky)
iawn	eeown	well, fine
llwybr cyhoeddus	hlooee-BIR cuh-HOY-this	public footpath
merched	mehrch-ED	women
nage	nahgah	no (sort of—it's tricky)
nos da	nos dah	good night
noswaith dda	nos-WAYTHE tha	good evening
os gwelwch yn dda	ohs gwell–OOCH uhn tha	please
perygl	pehr-UHGL	danger
preifat	"private"	private
safle'r Bus	savlehr boos	bus stop
stryd Fawr	strihd vahor	High Street
Sut mae?	sit my? or shoo my?	How are you?

SCOTTISH GAELIC WORDS AND PHRASES

Consult **Language,** p. 501, for information on Scottish Gaelic. Listed below are a number of words and phrases you may encounter on the road.

WORD/PHRASE	PRONUNCIATION	MEANING
Ciamar a tha sibh?	KI-mer a HA shiv?	How are you?
Tha gu math	HA gu MA	I'm fine

WORD/PHRASE	PRONUNCIATION	MEANING
Gle mhath	GLAY va	very well
Gabh mo leisgeul	GAV mo LESH-kul	excuse me
Tapadh leibh	TA-pa LEEV	thank you
De an t-ainm a th'oirbh?	JAY an TEN-im a HO-riv?	What's your name?
Tha mi ag iarraidh uisge-beatha.	HA mee ag EAR-ee OOSH-ka BAY-ha.	Give me whisky.
Slainte mhath	SLAN-che VA	cheers, good health
Is mise...	ISH MISH-uh	My name is...
Seo	SHAW	This is... (to introduce someone)
Madainn mhath	MA-ting VA	good morning
Latha ma	LA-huh MA	good day
Oidhche mhath	a-HOY-chuh VA	good night
Failte gu...	FAL-chuh goo	Welcome to...
taigh	TAI	house
ionad	EE-nud	place, visitor center
sraid	SRAHJ	street
rathad	RAH-hud	road
beinn	BEN	mountain
gleann	GLAY-ahn (smushed together)	valley
coire	COH-ruh	corry
baile	BAL-eh	town
dubh	DOOV	black
ruadh	ROO-ah	red
buidhe	BOO-ye	yellow
allt	ALT	stream

SCOTS WORDS AND PHRASES

Consult **Language**, p. 501, for more info on Scots, a distinct dialect of English. Listed below are some of the many Scots words and phrases used in standard Scottish English:

WORD/PHRASE	PRONUNCIATION	MEANING
ben		mountain
the bonny		awesome, cool (Glasgow only)
brane	BRAY	slope, hill
braw		bright, strong, great
burn		stream
craic	CRACK	great fun, "it's a craic"
glen		valley
Haud yer weesht		shut up, be quiet
ken		to know
kirk		church
lad		boy
lass		girl
Sassenach	SAS-uh-nach	Lowlander
strath		broad valley
Teuchter	TYOOCH-ter	someone from north Scotland
tipple		a drink
wee		little
Weegie	WEE-gee	Glaswegian
Yer gleachit!	YER GLEEch-it	You're falling apart!

APPENDIX

IRISH WORDS AND PHRASES

The following bits of the Irish language are either used often in Irish English or are common in Irish place names. Spelling conventions almost never match English pronunciations: for example, "mh" sounds like "v," and "dh" sounds like "g."

WORD/PHRASE	PRONUNCIATION	MEANING
aisling	ASH-ling	vision or dream, or a poem or story thereof
An Lár	on lahr	city center
Baile Átha Cliath	BAL-yah AW-hah CLE-ah	Dublin
bodhrán	BOUR-ohn	traditional drum
Bord Fáilte	bored FAHL-tshuh	Irish Tourist Board
Conas tá tú?	CUNN-us thaw too?	How are you?
céilí	KAY-lee	Irish dance
craic	krak	good cheer, good pub conversation
Dáil	DOY-il	House of Representatives
Dia dhuit	JEE-a dich	good day, hello
Dia's Muire dhuit	JEE-as MWUR-a dich	reply to "good day"
dún	doon	fort
Éire	AIR-uh	Ireland; official name of the Republic of Ireland
fáilte	FAWLT-cha	welcome
feis	fesh	an assembly, Irish festival
fir	fear	men
fleadh	flah	a musical festival
gaeltacht	GAYL-tokt	a district where Irish is the everyday language
garda, Garda Síochána	GAR-da SHE-och-ANA	police
go raibh maith agat	guh roh moh UG-ut	thank you
inch, innis, ennis	inch, innis, ennis	island, river meadow
kil	kill	church, cell
knock	nok	hill
lei thras	LEH-hrass	toilets
lough	lohk	lake
mná	min-AW	women
mór	more	big, great
ní hea	nee hah	no (sort of—it's tricky)
oíche mhaith dhuit	EE-ha woh ditch	good night
Oifig an Phoist	UFF-ig un fwisht	Post Office
poitín	po-CHEEN	moonshine (semi-toxic homemade liquor)
rath	rath or rah	earthen fort
sea	shah	yes (sort of—it's tricky)
seanachaí	SHAN-ukh-ee	storyteller
Seanad	SHAN-ud	Senate
Sinn Féin	shin fayn	"Ourselves Alone"; the political wing of the IRA
sláinte	SLAWN-che	cheers, to your health
slán agat	slawn UG-ut	goodbye
sraid	shrawd	street
Tá mé i mo idirgalacht-ach bhithiúnach.	ta-MAY imah va-HOO-nock idder gah-lachtach	I am an inter-galactic space criminal.
Taoiseach	TEE-shukh	Prime Minister
teachta dála (TD)	TAKH-ta DAH-lah	member of Irish parliament
trá	thraw	beach
uilleann	ILL-in	"elbow"; bagpipes played with the elbow

INDEX

INDEX

Will you have enough stories to tell your grandchildren?

Yahoo! Travel

Do You
Yahoo!
?

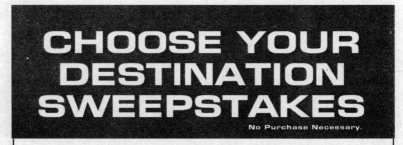

CHOOSE YOUR DESTINATION SWEEPSTAKES

No Purchase Necessary.

Explore the world with Let's Go® and StudentUniverse!
Enter for a chance to win a trip for two to a Let's Go destination!

Separate Drawings! May & October 2002.

GRAND PRIZES:

Roundtrip StudentUniverse Tickets

✓ Select one destination and mail your entry to:

☐ Costa Rica
☐ London
☐ Hong Kong
☐ San Francisco
☐ New York
☐ Amsterdam
☐ Prague
☐ Sydney

* Plus Additional Prizes!!

Choose Your Destination Sweepstakes
St. Martin's Press
Suite 1600, Department MF
175 Fifth Avenue
New York, NY 10010-7848

Restrictions apply; see offical rules for
details by visiting Let'sGo.com or sending SASE
(VT residents may omit return postage) to the address above.

Name: _____

Address: _____

City/State/Zip: _____

Phone: _____

Email: _____

Grand prizes provided by:

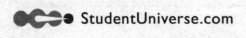 StudentUniverse.com   Real Travel Deals

---

Drawings will be held in May and October 2002. NO PURCHASE NECESSARY. These are not the full official rules, and other
restrictions apply. See Official Rules for full details.
To enter without purchase, go to www.letsgo.com or mail a 3"x5" postcard with
required information to the above address. Limit one entry per person and per household.

Void in Florida, Puerto Rico, Quebec and wherever else prohibited by law. Open to legal U.S. and Canadian residents
(excluding residents of Florida, Puerto Rico and Quebec) 18 or older at time of entry. Round-trip tickets are
economy class and depart from any major continental U.S. international airport that the winner chooses.
All mailed entries must be postmarked by September 16, 2002 and received by September 27, 2002.
All online entries must be received by 11:59 pm EDT September 16, 2002.

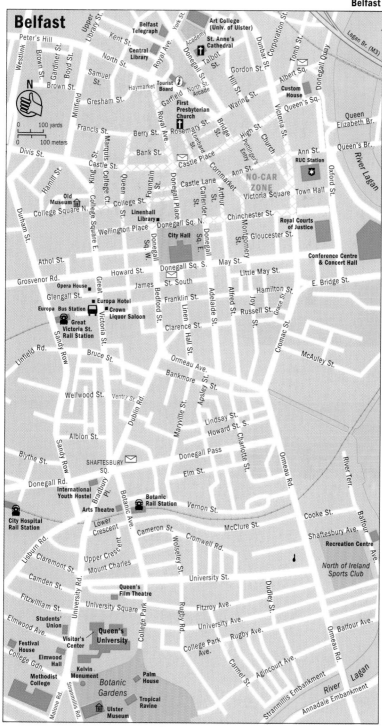

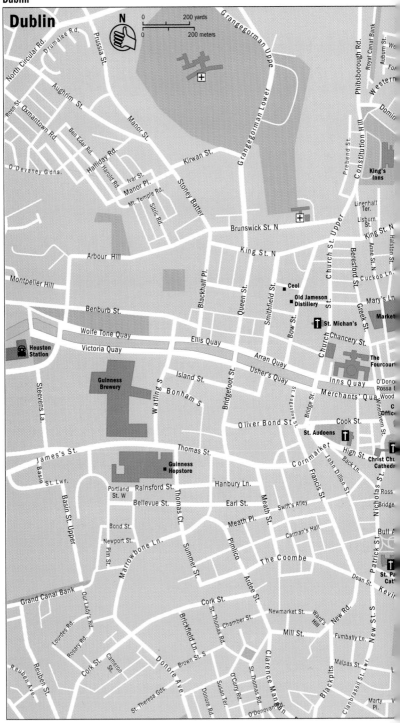

Cork and Galway

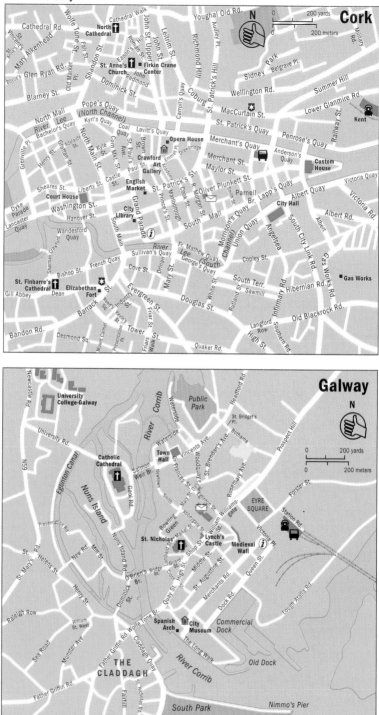

Cork

0   200 yards
0   200 meters

Cathedral Walk · Youghal Old Rd.
Cathedral Rd.
North Cathedral
Wolfe Tone St.
John St. Upper · John St.
Leitrim St.
Richmond Hill
St. Patrick's Hill
Audley Pl.
Sidney Park · Belgrave Pl.
St. Vincent's
St. Anne's
Mary Aikenhead
Fair Hill
St. Anne's Church · Firkin Crane Center
John Redmond
Roman St.
Wellington Rd.
Summer Hill
Glen Ryan Rd.
Old Market Pl.
Shandon St.
Dominick St.
Coburg St.
MacCurtain St.
Lower Glanmire Rd.
Blarney St.
Kent
Railway St.
Pope's Quay (North Channel)
North Mall
Lee River
Bachelor's Quay
Kyrl's Quay · Coal Quay
Lavitt's Quay
Carroll's Quay
St. Patrick's Quay
Penrose's Quay
Anderson's Quay
North Main St.
Adelaide
Henry St.
Grattan St.
Kyle St. · Corn Mkt. St.
St. Paul's Ave.
Brown St.
Opera House
Merchant's Quay
Custom House
Victoria Quay
Grenville Pl.
Crawford Art Gallery
Emmet Pl.
Drawbridge
Merchant St.
Maylor St.
Maylor St.
Sheares St.
Liberty St.
Castle St.
English Market
St. Patrick's St.
Cook St.
Oliver Plunkett St.
R. Morgan St.
Parnell Br. · Lapp's Quay
Albert Quay
Court House
Washington St.
City Library
Grand Parade
Prince's St.
Marlborough St.
South Mall
Morrison's Quay
Union Quay
City Hall
Albert Quay
Albert Rd.
Dyke Parade
Lancaster Quay
Hanover St.
Wandesford Quay
Sharman Crawford St.
South Main
River Lee (South)
Sullivan's Quay
Fr. Mathew Quay
George's Quay
Angelsea
Copley St.
Victoria Rd.
French Quay
Cove St.
Diman
Mary St.
White St.
South Terr.
Rutland St.
South City Link Rd.
Gas Works Rd.
Gas Works
St. Finbarre's Cathedral
Elizabethan Fort
Gill Abbey
Bishop St.
Dean St.
Reed's St.
Kingston
Evergreen St.
Friar St.
Douglas St.
Sawmill
Hibernian Rd.
Old Blackrock Rd.
Barrack St.
Mount Carmel
Klein's St.
Presentation Rd.
Tower St.
Friars Walk
High St.
Langford Row
Southern Rd.
Bandon Rd.
Desmond Sq.
Quaker Rd.

Galway

0   200 yards
0   200 meters

Newcastle Rd.
University College-Galway
River Corrib
Public Park
St. Bridget's Pl.
Headford Rd.
Prospect Hill
University Rd.
Waterside
Bothama
N59
Eglinton Canal
Catholic Cathedral
Town Hall
St. Vincents Ave.
Woodquay
St. Brendan's Ave.
Rosemary Ave.
Forster St.
Nuns Island
Salmon Weir Br.
Newtown
St. Francis St.
Smith
St. Mary's
Eyre St.
Eglinton St.
EYRE SQUARE
Station Rd.
Gaol Rd.
Bowling Green
Abbeygate St.
William St.
Williamsgate
Victoria Pl.
Presentation Rd.
St. Nicholas
Market St.
Shop St.
Lynch's Castle
Medieval Wall
St. Helens St.
New Rd.
Mill St.
Nuns Island Rd.
Lombard St.
Cross St.
Middle St.
St. Augustine St.
Queen St.
St. Mary's Rd.
Henry St.
O'Brien's Bridge Br.
Quay St.
High St.
Merchants Rd.
Dock Rd.
Raleigh Row
William St. West
Dominick St.
Spanish Arch
City Museum
Commercial Dock
Sea Road
Munster Ave.
Father Griffin Rd.
Wolfe Tone Br.
The Long Walk
River Corrib
Old Dock
THE CLADDAGH
Claddagh Quay
Father Griffin Rd.
St. Nicholas Rd.
Fairhill
South Park
Nimmo's Pier
Lough Atalia Rd.

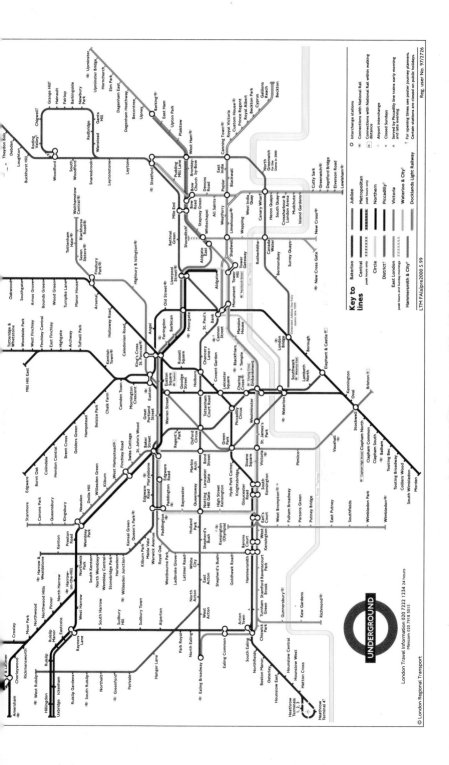

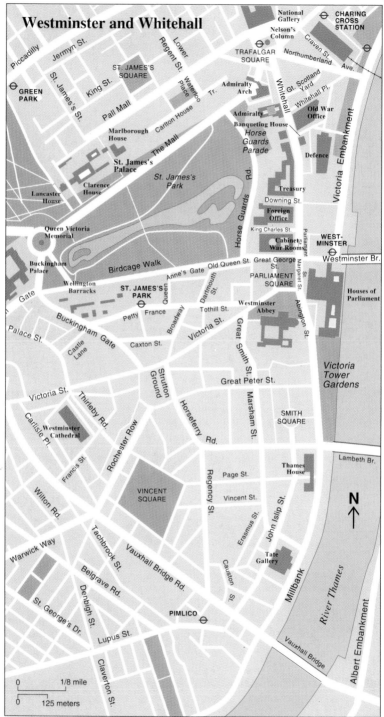

Westminster and Whitehall

National Gallery

CHARING CROSS STATION

Nelson's Column

Craven St.

TRAFALGAR SQUARE

Northumberland Ave.

Piccadilly

Jermyn St.

ST. JAMES'S SQUARE

Regent St.

Lower Regent St.

Waterloo Place

Whitehall

Gt. Scotland Yard

St. James's St.

King St.

Admiralty Arch

Whitehall Pl.

GREEN PARK

Pall Mall

Carlton House Tr.

Admiralty

Old War Office

Marlborough House

Banqueting House

Horse Guards Parade

St. James's Palace

The Mall

Defence

Clarence House

St. James's Park

Treasury

Horse Guards Rd.

Downing St.

Lancaster House

Foreign Office

Victoria Embankment

King Charles St.

Queen Victoria Memorial

WEST-MINSTER

Parliament St.

Cabinet War Rooms

Westminster Br.

Buckingham Palace

Birdcage Walk

Anne's Gate

Old Queen St.

Great George St.

Margaret St.

PARLIAMENT SQUARE

Gate

Wellington Barracks

ST. JAMES'S PARK

Dartmouth St.

Broadway

Westminster Abbey

Abingdon St.

Houses of Parliament

Palace St.

Buckingham Gate

Petty France

Tothill St.

Great Smith St.

Queen's

Victoria St.

Victoria Tower Gardens

Castle Lane

Caxton St.

Victoria St.

Thirleby Rd.

Strutton Ground

Great Peter St.

Marsham St.

Carlisle Pl.

Westminster Cathedral

Rochester Row

Great Peter St.

SMITH SQUARE

Francis St.

Horseferry Rd.

Lambeth Br.

Thames House

N

↑

Wilton Rd.

VINCENT SQUARE

Page St.

Vincent St.

John Islip St.

Regency St.

Erasmus St.

Tate Gallery

Warwick Way

Tachbrook St.

Vauxhall Bridge Rd.

River Thames

Belgrave Rd.

Causton St.

Millbank

Albert Embankment

St. George's Dr.

Denbigh St.

PIMLICO

Lupus St.

Vauxhall Bridge

Claverton St.

0   1/8 mile

0   125 meters

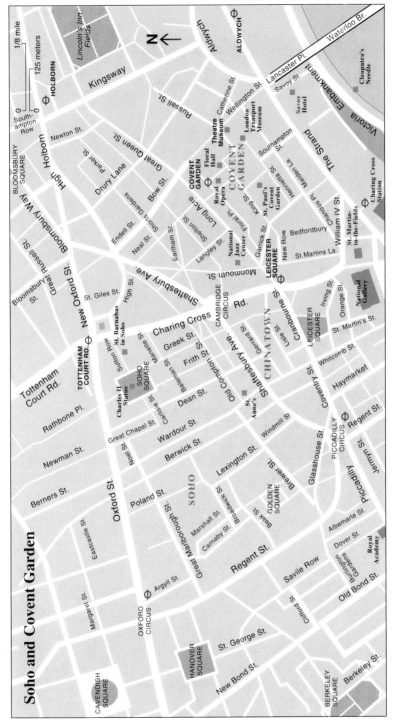

London: Soho and Covent Garden

Soho and Covent Garden

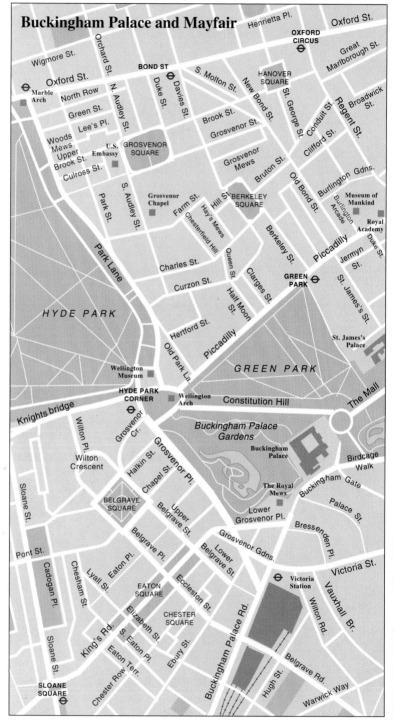

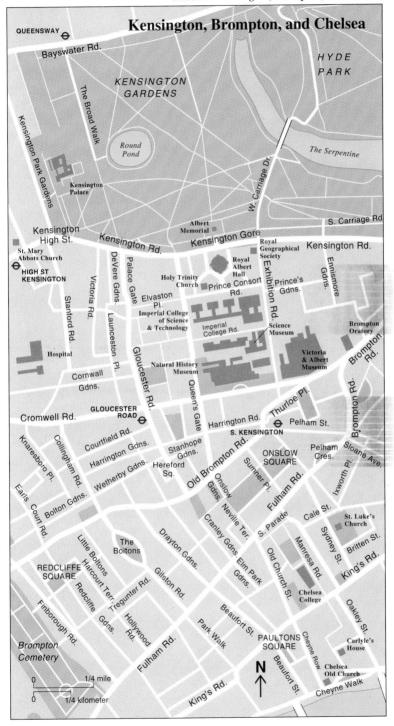

Kensington, Brompton, and Chelsea

London: City of London

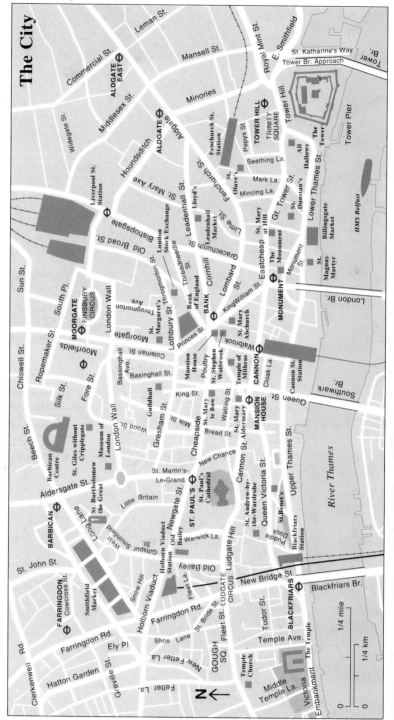